Handbook of Social Indicators and Quality of Life Research

Kenneth C. Land • Alex C. Michalos
M. Joseph Sirgy
Editors

Handbook of Social Indicators and Quality of Life Research

Editors
Kenneth C. Land
Duke University
Hudson Hall 130
Durham, NC 27708
USA

M. Joseph Sirgy
Department of Marketing
Pamlin College of Business
Virginia Polytechnic Institute
Pamplin Hall 2025
Blacksburg, VA 24061-0236
USA
sirgy@vt.edu

Alex C. Michalos
Faculty of Arts
Brandon University
18th Street 270
Brandon, MB R7A 6A9
Canada
michalos@brandonu.ca

ISBN 978-94-007-2420-4   e-ISBN 978-94-007-2421-1
DOI 10.1007/978-94-007-2421-1
Springer Dordrecht Heidelberg London New York

Library of Congress Control Number: 2011942486

© Springer Science+Business Media B.V. 2012
No part of this work may be reproduced, stored in a retrieval system, or transmitted in any form or by any means, electronic, mechanical, photocopying, microfilming, recording or otherwise, without written permission from the Publisher, with the exception of any material supplied specifically for the purpose of being entered and executed on a computer system, for exclusive use by the purchaser of the work.

Printed on acid-free paper

Springer is part of Springer Science+Business Media (www.springer.com)

Editorial Advisory Board

Robert Cummins, Deakin University, Australia
Ed Diener, University of Illinois, USA
Richard A. Easterlin, University of Southern California, USA
Liz Eckermann, Deakin University, Australia
Richard Estes, University of Pennsylvania, USA
Abbott L. Ferriss, Emory University, USA
Wolfgang Glatzer, Goethe University, Germany
Anna L. D. Lau, Hong Kong Polytechnic University, China
Filomena Maggino, Universita degli Studi di Firenze, Italy
Valerie Moller, Rhodes University, South Africa
Torbjorn Moum, University of Oslo, Norway
Heinz-Herbert Noll, ZUMA, Germany
Don Rahtz, College of William and Mary, USA
Ruut Veenhoven, Erasmus University, Netherlands
Josh Samli, University of North Florida, USA
Bruno D. Zumbo, University of British Columbia, Canada

Acknowledgments

The idea for a Handbook of Social Indicators and Quality of Life Research arose among members of the International Society for Quality of Life Studies (ISQOLS) a few years ago. The aim of the handbook is to create an overview of the field of quality of life studies in the early years of the twenty-first century that can be updated and improved upon as the field evolves and the century unfolds. The editors would like to thank the authors, Editorial Advisory Board and all the referees who volunteered their time to help us deliver this fine collection. We are also grateful to Myriam Poort, editorial director and Esther Otten and Welmoed Spahr, publishing editors from Springer Science and Business Media B.V., Dordrecht for their initial enthusiasm and continued support of the project.

Contents

1 Prologue: The Development and Evolution of Research on Social Indicators and Quality of Life (QOL) 1
Kenneth C. Land, Alex C. Michalos, and M. Joseph Sirgy

2 The Good Life: Eighth Century to Third Century BCE 23
Alex C. Michalos and Steven R. Robinson

3 Happiness, Also Known as "Life Satisfaction" and "Subjective Well-Being" 63
Ruut Veenhoven

4 Subjective Wellbeing Homeostasis 79
Robert A. Cummins, Anna L.D. Lau, and Melanie T. Davern

5 Positive Psychology and the Quality of Life 99
Corey L.M. Keyes, Barbara L. Fredrickson, and Nansook Park

6 Modern Economic Growth and Quality of Life: Cross-Sectional and Time Series Evidence 113
Richard A. Easterlin and Laura Angelescu

7 National Accounts of Well-Being 137
Ed Diener, and William Tov

8 Time Use as a Social Indicator 159
John P. Robinson and Steven Martin

9 Issues in Composite Index Construction: The Measurement of Overall Quality of Life 181
Michael R. Hagerty and Kenneth C. Land

10 Measuring the Quality of Life and the Construction of Social Indicators 201
Filomena Maggino and Bruno D. Zumbo

11 Quality of Life Well-Being in General Medicine, Mental Health and Coaching 239
Michael B. Frisch

12 Education and Quality of Life 265
Jason D. Edgerton, Lance W. Roberts, and Susanne von Below

13 Review of Research Related to Quality of Work Life (QWL) Programs 297
M. Joseph Sirgy, Nora P. Reilly, Jiyun Wu, and David Efraty

14 Spirituality, Religiosity, and Subjective Quality of Life 313
Ralph L. Piedmont and Philip H. Friedman

15 Consumer Well-Being (CWB): Various Conceptualizations and Measures 331
Dong-Jin Lee and M. Joseph Sirgy

16 Perceived Quality of Life of Children and Youth 355
E. Scott Huebner, Rich Gilman, and Claudia Ma

17 The Quality of Life of Adults 373
Elizabeth Eckermann

18 Cross-National Comparisons of Quality of Life in Developed Nations, Including the Impact of Globalization 381
Wolfgang Glatzer

19 Quality of Life in Developing Countries 399
Laura Camfield

20 Economies in Transition: Revisiting Challenges to Quality of Life 433
Richard J. Estes

21 Quality of Life in Australia 459
Robert A. Cummins, Jacqueline Woerner, Adrian Tomyn, and Adele Gibson-Prosser

22 Quality of Life in East Asia: The Case of Hong Kong 473
Daniel T.L. Shek

23 The Quality of Life of Muslim Populations: The Case of Algeria 499
Habib Tiliouine and Mohamed Meziane

24 Quality of Life in Latin America and the Caribbean 529
Mariano Rojas

25 Quality of Life in Argentina 547
Graciela Tonon

26 "Failed" and "Failing" States: Is Quality of Life Possible? 555
Richard J. Estes

Index 581

Prologue: The Development and Evolution of Research on Social Indicators and Quality of Life (QOL)

Kenneth C. Land, Alex C. Michalos, and M. Joseph Sirgy

Social indicators are statistical time series "…used to monitor the social system, helping to identify changes and to guide intervention to alter the course of social change" (Ferriss 1988:601). Examples include unemployment rates, crime rates, estimates of life expectancy, health status indices, school enrollment rates, average achievement scores, election voting rates, and measures of subjective well-being such as satisfaction with life as a whole and with specific domains or aspects of life. This chapter reviews the historical development of the field and describes the uses of social indicators and the concept of quality of life (QOL). A concluding section addresses prospects for future developments in social indicators and interdisciplinary research guided by the QOL concept.

The Historical Development of the Field of Social Indicators and QOL Studies

We commence with a review of the development of the field of social indicators and QOL studies starting from 1960s, the period of 1970s and 1980s, and lastly the 1990s and 2000s.

Social Indicators and QOL Research in the 1960s and Pre-1960s

The concepts of social indicators and QOL have evolved over the past several decades more or less autonomously in several scholarly disciplines. It is convenient, therefore, to organize this review in terms of these disciplinary origins.

Social Indicators and QOL Research in Sociology, Economics, and Political Science

The term *social indicators* was given its initial meaning in an attempt, undertaken in the early 1960s by the American Academy of Arts, to detect and anticipate the nature and magnitude of the second-order consequences of the space program for American society (Land 1983:2; Noll and Zapf 1994:1). Frustrated by the lack of sufficient data to detect such effects and the absence of a systematic conceptual framework and methodology for analysis, some members of the Academy project attempted to develop a system of social indicators – statistics, statistical series, and other forms of evidence – to detect and anticipate social change as well as to evaluate specific programs and

K.C. Land
Department of Sociology, Duke University, Hudson Hall 130, 27708 Durham, NC, USA

A.C. Michalos (✉)
Brandon University, 18th Street 270, R7A 6A9 Brandon, MB, Canada
e-mail: michalos@brandonu.ca

M.J. Sirgy
Department of Marketing, Pamplin College of Business, Virginia Polytechnic Institute, Pamplin Hall 2025, 24061-0236 Blacksburg, VA, USA
e-mail: sirgy@vt.edu

K.C. Land et al. (eds.), *Handbook of Social Indicators and Quality of Life Research*,
DOI 10.1007/978-94-007-2421-1_1, © Springer Science+Business Media B.V. 2012

their impact. The results of this part of the Academy project were published in a volume (Bauer 1966) bearing the name *Social Indicators.*

Generally, the sharp impulse of interest in social indicators in the 1960s grew out of the movement toward collection and organization of national social, economic, and demographic data that began in Western societies during the seventeenth and eighteenth centuries and accelerated in the twentieth century (Carley 1981:14–15). The work of sociologist William F. Ogburn and his collaborators at the University of Chicago in the 1930s and 1940s on the theory and measurement of social change is more proximate and sociologically germane (Land 1975). As chairman of President Herbert Hoover's Research Committee on Social Trends, Ogburn supervised production of the two-volume *Recent Social Trends* (President's Committee on Social Trends 1933), a path-breaking contribution to social reporting. Ogburn's ideas about the measurement of social change influenced several of his students – notably Albert D. Biderman, Otis Dudley Duncan, Albert J. Reiss, Jr., and Eleanor Bernert Sheldon, who played major roles in the emergence and development of the field of social indicators in the 1960s and 1970s.

Another historical origin in sociology is the work of Howard W. Odum at the University of North Carolina, who published *Southern Regions of the United States* (1936). This volume brought together indicators under an institutional framework, revealing regional disparities in welfare and demonstrating the need for more definitive data. Involved in the study was Margaret Jarman Hagood, who developed one of the first indices of well-being, a level of living index of farm families (Ferriss 2004).

The appearances of these studies were not isolated events. Several other influential analysts commented on the lack of a system for charting social change. They advocated that the US government establish a "system of social accounts" that would facilitate a cost–benefit analysis of more than the market-related aspects of society already indexed by the National Income and Product Accounts (see, e.g., National Commission on Technology, Automation and Economic Progress 1966; Sheldon and Moore 1968). The need for social indicators also was emphasized by the publication of the 101-page *Toward a Social Report* (US Department of Health, Education, and Welfare 1969) on the last day of the Johnson administration in 1969. Conceived

of as a prototypical counterpart to the annual economic report of the president, each of its seven chapters addressed major issues of social concern, namely health and illness, social mobility, the physical environment, income and poverty, public order and safety, learning, science, and art, and participation and alienation, and each assessed prevalent conditions. The *Report* established the linkage of social indicators to the systematic reporting on social issues for the purpose of public enlightenment, but did not elaborate upon policy implications of the findings, as some scholars had advocated.

Social Indicators and QOL Research in Health and Medicine

Turning to the concept of *Quality of Life and health,* the history of QOL in medical sciences and public health can be traced back to the 1940s. A link between QOL and health policy became visible in the USA during World War II. Social scientists who were involved in the World War II effort drew attention to social and psychological forces driving health and well-being (Ogburn 1943; Stouffer 1949).

The World Health Organization (WHO 1948) recognized the importance of the concept of QOL from the onset. The organization's constitution stated that health is "physical, mental, and social well-being and not merely the absence of disease or infirmity." This definition is essentially a QOL definition of health – illness is not only physiological well-being but also psychological, social, and economic aspects of well-being. To this day, the demand for a more "holistic" view of medical problems invokes quality of life.

The concept of "wellness" became vogue in the 1950s when Dr. Halbert Dunn, the first director of the National Office for Health Statistics, introduced the idea of high-level wellness (Dunn 1959). He defined it as "an integrated method of functioning which is oriented toward maximizing the potential of which the individual is capable, within the environment where s/he is functioning."

Talcott Parsons, the father of modern sociology, defined health as "the state of optimum capacity for the effective performance of valued tasks" (Parsons 1958:168). He viewed illness as a deviation from the social expectation that a person should be able to perform the functions associated with his or her social role. This perspective has been the basis for health and

QOL indicators and perhaps the bedrock of health status assessment to date.

Examples of early work in health-related QOL in 1950s and 1960s include the needs-based approach to health (e.g., Neugarten et al. 1961; Wylie 1970). QOL measures were developed focusing on how a specific disease interferes with meeting the needs of the patient.

Social Indicators and QOL Research in Management

Research and writing on *quality of work life (QWL)* has been the turf of organizational behavior scientists and management scholars. QWL sprung from the humanistic theories of Argyris (1957), McGregor (1960), Maslow (1954), all of which emerged following the Hawthorne studies and the Human Relations Movement (see Schermerhorn et al. 1994).

In some sense, the Relay Assembly Test Room experiment of the Hawthorne studies (see Schermerhorn et al. 1994) is the first study to account for increased productivity in terms of quality of life in the work setting. The experiment was conducted in 1927 by a group of researchers from Harvard University, led by Elton Mayo, whose objective was to establish the effects of worker fatigue on productivity. In this study, six operators who assembled relays were isolated for intensive study in a special test room. The operators were subjected to various rest pauses, length of workday, and length of workweek, while their productivity was regularly measured. The outcome was that overall, the productivity of the relay assemblers increased overtime, regardless of the specific changes made in the work setting by the researchers. Mayo and his colleagues concluded that the new "social setting" created in the test room accounted for the increased productivity. Two factors in particular were singled out. First, there was positive group development. That is, the operators shared both good social relations with one another and a common desire to do a good job. Second, supervision was more participative than that otherwise experienced by the operators. In the test room, the operators were made to feel important, given much information, and frequently consulted for their opinions on what was taking place, which was not the case in their normal work situation. In other words, one might say that the increased productivity of the relay assemblers in the test room was possibly a function of the higher level of QWL (being consulted by their supervisor and having meaningful interactions with their colleagues), which they enjoyed in the test room but not in their regular work setting.

The Human Relations Movement emerged following the Hawthorne studies underscoring the creation of good human relationships between managers and subordinates. Argyris (1957) further focused on the relationship between individuals and organizations. He argued that the formal organization is based on specific concepts of rationality and division of labor and specialization to the extreme, and thus does not provide the individual with channels for self-fulfillment. The individual adapts to this in various ways, including apathy and noninvolvement. Management realizing the apathy reacts by increasing the amount of control on the individual. But this of course only makes the problem worse. The way out of this vicious circle is to try to provide the satisfaction of people's need for self-actualization in their work. This is a prime concern for the workers' quality of work life. Argyris advocated specific steps that should be taken to achieve it.

1. *Decreasing the conflict between the individual and the organization*: This may be achieved if the formal structure of the organization is changed to allow the worker/employee to experience more activity than passivity, greater relative independence than dependence, a longer rather than a shorter time perspective, and finally be in an equal if not higher position than his/her peers.

2. *Job enlargement*: This is understood in either or both of two ways: (a) increasing the number of tasks that the individual has to perform and (b) giving the individual more control over his/her environment.

3. *Participative or employee-centered leadership*: Individual employees, who make up and keep the organization alive, must enjoy self-expression in the organization. The present organizational structure will have to be modified if group-centered leadership is to exist. No longer would a few individuals be responsible for defining the group's goals, evaluating its behavior, and providing direction, rewards, and punishments. The activities would be handed over to the group. Argyris quotes instances where these changes have been instituted into organizations with a resultant increase in productivity and individual growth and self-involvement.

McGregor (1960) was among the first management scholars to underscore the concept of QWL. McGregor described two styles of management he termed Theories X and Y. Theory X managers believe that workers in general are lazy, dislike responsibility, are self-centered, and are motivated strictly by extrinsic rewards (e.g., money). Hence, managers should allocate a lot of energy toward directing and controlling people, and organizing the elements of productive enterprise. Theory Y managers, on the other hand, believe that workers are inherently *not* lazy. Rather, they are responsible and industrious. They enjoy mastery of creativity and achievement. They are motivated mostly by intrinsic rewards (e.g., a sense of self-esteem, a sense of belongingness, a sense of social recognition, and a sense of self-actualization). Managers who believe in the central tenets of Theory Y focus their efforts to allow workers to achieve their individual goals while working toward organizational goals. This attention to the satisfaction of workers' needs through organizational means has been the impetus behind the QOL movement in management thought and practice (Blake and Mouton 1964, 1969).

Social Indicators and QOL in the 1970s and 1980s

Social Indicators and QOL Research in Sociology, Psychology, Economics, and Political Science

At the end of the 1960s, the enthusiasm for social indicators was sufficiently strong and broad-based for Duncan (1969:1) to write of the existence of a *Social Indicators Movement*. In 1972, the US National Science Foundation began to provide support for the Social Science Research Council Center for Coordination of Research on Social Indicators in Washington, D.C. The Russell Sage Foundation initiated support for research that led to the publication of several major efforts to define and develop a methodology for the measurement of indicators of subjective well-being as measures of the quality of life (Campbell and Converse 1972; Andrews and Withey 1976; Campbell et al. 1976). The Federal Government initiated a series of comprehensive social indicator chart books showing trends in a variety of social forces with limited analyses and few policy implications (US Office of Management and Budget 1974, 1978; US Bureau of the Census 1981).

Policy implications, however, were outlined in a series of issues of *The Annals* (Gross 1967; Taeuber 1978, 1981).

Social scientists recognized the need for more comprehensive data, especially in time series. This led to establishing several important surveys in the USA that provide important indicators today: the National Opinion Research Center's (NORC) General Social Survey, begun in 1972, the Bureau of Justice Statistics' annual National Crime Victimization Survey and, later, the Survey of Income and Program Participation.

Under editorship of Alex Michalos, the first volume of the international journal *Social Indicators Research* appeared in 1974, providing a medium for exchange of research findings. At the same time, the Organization for Economic Cooperation and Development (OECD) stimulated the issuance of national social reports based upon social indicators. This led to the initiation of social surveys and the improvement of other data-gathering efforts in several member nations in the OECD. This also was promoted by the Statistical Commission of the United Nations and United Nations Educational, Scientific, and Cultural Organization (UNESCO). Many nations continue to issue annual or biennial social reports, such as *Donnes Sociales* (France), *Datenreport* (Germany), *Inequality in Sweden*, and *Social Trends* (UK).

Michalos (2005) celebrated the first 30 years of publication of *Social Indicators Research* with a collection of its most cited papers from the 1974–2003 period. Citation rates are objective indicators of a variety of important features of scientific articles. For example, Narin (1976) reviewed 24 studies published between 1957 and 1975 that generally confirmed the hypothesis that citation counts are positively correlated with peer rankings of the quality of scientific articles, eminence of scientists, graduate schools, graduate departments, editor evaluations, Nobel prizes and other awards, authors' incomes, access to resources, initial appointments, and mobility. Eight of 12 studies that provided correlation coefficients had values of at least 0.6, with 5 of those above 0.7. The lowest value was 0.2. Lawani and Bayer (1983) undertook a very thorough study comparing peer assessments of cancer research papers with the papers' citation rates and concluded that "Highly rated papers are more highly cited than average papers." Granting all this, there are good reasons for using citation counts with caution (Michalos 2005:4–7).

In the period from March 1974 to December 2003, there were a total of 1,392 titles published in *Social Indicators Research*. Since the journal seldom published book reviews, editorials, or letters, most of those titles represented articles. Eight hundred and twenty articles (58.9%) were not cited at all, which is a bit higher than the 55–57% general average for the whole *Science Citation Index* database, lower than the 74.7% for all social sciences material, and higher than the 48% for social science articles alone. The 572 (41.1%) cited articles generated 4,979 citations, with a classic hyperbolic distribution curve in which relatively few articles attract many citations and relatively many articles attract few citations. The mean number of citations per published article was 3.6, with a mode and median value of zero, and a standard deviation of 11.8. There were 34 articles with 35 or more citations each, and those 34 (2.4%) articles attracted 2,208/4,979=44.4% of all citations. The top 68 (4.9%) articles attracted 2,997/4,979=60.2% of all citations. Given their extraordinary contribution to the journal's total citation count, and the fact that articles with 35 or more citations were nearly three standard deviations above the mean, those articles form a fairly distinguished lot.

Among the 34 most cited articles, there are 10 articles (29.4%) each from 1974–1979 and 1990–1999, and 14 (41.1%) from 1980 to 1989. By authors' countries of origin, there are 16 (47.1%) from the USA, 5 (14.7%) each from Canada and Australia, 3 (8.8%) from the Netherlands, 2 (5.9%) from the UK, and 1 (2.9%) from Israel. Collectively, 37 authors produced the 34 papers, and there are 16 single-authored papers.

Examining the content of the articles, one might be shocked to discover that all but one of them (McCall 1975) focused on some aspect of subjective indicators. In view of the historical facts that the field was originally dominated by researchers interested in objective indicators and that today practically all researchers agree that objective and subjective indicators are equally important, the near total dominance of subjective indicators research in the classics is both surprising and disturbing. Presumably, one if not the main reason for the dominance of subjective indicators research is that there are relatively more psychologists and people interested in personal reports about a good quality of life than there are others. While "Others" would include a wide variety of people, e.g., sociologists, demographers, gerontologists, geographers, environmentalists, economists, political scientists, and population health researchers, each group would have a relatively narrow range of interests compared to those interested in the psychological structure of perceived well-being. Whether or not there is anything to that explanation, it would be a pity if objective indicators research came to be relatively neglected in the future.

The first and last articles in Michalos (2005) were published 22 years apart, but they addressed the same basic problem, with some different additional hypotheses and methodologies. The basic problem was to empirically determine the total number of domains required for a full assessment of the perceived quality of life of individuals and communities. The paper by Andrews and Withey (1974) was the lead article in the first issue of *Social Indicators Research* and it was followed by several articles and by their fine book, Andrews and Withey (1976). Cummins (1996) tackled the problem by scanning 1,500 articles providing data on life satisfaction, looking for "different terms that had been used to describe domains of life satisfaction." His primary aim was to determine how many domain names could be categorized under one of the seven domain headings of his Comprehensive Quality of Life Scale (ComQol). The latter's domains include material well-being, health, productivity, intimacy, safety, community, and emotional well-being. He found that 83% of the 351 domain names could be reasonably classified into one or another of ComQol's seven domains. For example, ComQol's category of "intimacy" includes things like family life, family relations, friendships, marriage, living partner, and spouse.

Since the procedures and criteria for success used by Andrews and Withey, and Cummins were different, one would not have expected both approaches to yield identical results. Anyone reading the philosophic literature since *The Republic* of Plato would have expected to see fairly similar results. A good overview may be found in Tatarkiewicz (1976). Around the world and across time, people regard good health, family and friends, beautiful things, financial, and other forms of security as important features of a good life. Andrews and Withey, and Cummins showed us that the core of important life domains is not as broad as the great numbers of possible domain names or items might suggest.

The relative insignificance to life satisfaction of half a dozen "standard classification variables," including income, in the presence of a dozen domain satisfaction variables was already documented by Andrews and

Withey (1974, 1976), and similar results were reported by Inglehart and Rabier (1986) for eight west European countries. Duncan (1975) put the question bluntly when he asked: Does money buy satisfaction? Diener and Biswas-Diener (2002) published an excellent review of a substantial chunk of the literature around this question and reported that "...more money may enhance SWB when it means avoiding poverty and living in a developed nation, but income appears to increase SWB little over the long-term when more of it is gained by well-off individuals whose material desires rise with their incomes" (p. 119).

Kammann et al. (1984) developed an affect-balance scale that was similar to Bradburn's (1969) in having separate items for positive and negative affect, and in using a "balance or net scoring formula to obtain the overall well-being score." While Bradburn's scale has 10 items, Kammann's has a 96-item version called Affectometer 1 and a 40-item version called Affectometer 2. With Bradburn's scale, respondents are asked *whether or not* they have had a particular feeling "during the past few weeks," while with the affectometers, they are asked *how often* they have had a feeling in that period, with five options: not at all, occasionally, some of the time, often, all the time. Many researchers, using many different samples, found that Bradburn's Negative Affect (NA) and Positive Affect (PA) scales were relatively independent, while the affectometers' NA and PA scales had an average association of $r = -0.66$.

Atkinson (1982) presented results from a longitudinal (panel) study involving "a representative sample of 2,162 Canadians interviewed in 1977 and again in 1979." Apart from some results dealing with a subset ($N = 285$) of the national sample used in Campbell et al. (1976), this was the first published report "on the stability of QOL measures over time." In order to assess levels of change in people's lives from the first to the second survey, respondents were asked in the second wave if their current status was the same, better, or worse, for life in general and for specific domains. They were also asked which of 16 significant life events they had experienced in that period, e.g., divorce/separation, serious injury, new job, or house. His most important conclusions were expressed thus: "Our findings...[show] that significant numbers of respondents perceive changes in their lives and those changes were reflected, for better or worse, in their satisfaction levels. The fact that these changes took

place over a 2 year period indicates that, while adaptation probably does occur, it is not instantaneous and will be detected by an indicator series which utilizes fairly frequent measurements" (pp. 128–129).

While Atkinson only had a panel study with two waves involving a few hundred people, the German Socio-Economic Panel Study allows researchers to examine survey results from over two dozen waves involving over 25,000 people. Detailed studies by Lucas et al. (2004), Lucas (2005), and Lucas and Donnellan (2007) have shown that normally stable life satisfaction and happiness scores can be destabilized by events like a loss of employment or the loss of a loved one. Following such catastrophic events, many people's scores might not only drop considerably, but might never return to their precatastrophic levels. In the light of such evidence, researchers who posit that individuals have a set-point of subjective well-being from which little permanent change would be possible have had to alter their positions (Headey 2008, Diener and Biswas-Diener 2008).

Campbell et al. (1976) recognized that they did not have a "very elaborate theory" and that it was "quite conceivable" that standards of comparison and aspiration levels might be different for different domains of life and for life as a whole. The plain fact is that social indicators research has never had an abundance of theories or theoreticians. On the contrary, a lot of the work has been done in the positivistic tradition that generally underemphasized the importance of theories and overemphasized the importance of good measurement (Michalos 1971). Although many of the positivist views about what science is and ought to be are not tenable (Michalos 1980a, b, c), with regard to the structure of scientific theories, the positivist idea of constructing them in the form axiomatic systems is worthwhile. Among other things, such systems have the virtues of making the basic concepts, postulates, and immediate implications of theories relatively transparent. That is why Michalos (1985) gave Multiple Discrepancies Theory (MDT) a form suggesting such systems.

In the 1985 paper, evidence was reviewed revealing the influence of seven comparison standards (yielding seven potential discrepancies or gaps) on people's reported satisfaction and happiness. Briefly, these were the gaps between what people have and want, relevant others have, the best one has had in the past, expected to have 3 years ago, expects to have after 5 years, deserves, and needs. It was assumed that by rolling these seven standards into one theory, the latter would enjoy the explanatory power of the lot. Since there was also evidence that satisfaction and happiness were determined to some extent by people's age, sex, education, ethnicity, income, self-esteem, and social support, the latter variables were added as "conditioners."

In Michalos (2008), it was remarked that temperament, the natural environment, communities of various kinds, and life events and/or issues should also be added to the list of conditioners. The most important feature of the theory is the assumption that six of the gap variables and all of the conditioners would have *both direct and indirect effects* on satisfaction and happiness. The primitive models regarded as competitors in Michalos (1980a) were really parts of a bigger integrated model, which became *Multiple Discrepancies Theory (MDT)*. Complicated as MDT is, it is still far from sophisticated enough to capture the complex web of variables involved in the determination and composition of satisfaction, happiness, or subjective well-being.

MDT was supposed to provide a new foundation for all kinds of utility theories. While utility theories generally and philosophical utilitarianism in particular typically begin with revealed preferences or some sort of a *given* affect-laden attitude or interest, MDT was "designed to break through and explain" those preferences, attitudes, or interests. Insofar as MDT explained satisfaction and happiness as the *effects* of other things (perceived discrepancies and conditioners), satisfaction and happiness were not just *incorrigible givens* but could be altered by altering those other things. What is more, as indicated in the paper, MDT's explanatory power was considerable. For the convenience sample of 682 undergraduates described in the 1985 paper, MDT explained 49% of the variation in scores for reported happiness, 53% for life satisfaction, and, on average, 57% for satisfaction in the 12 domains. The theory explained as much as 79% of the variance in reported satisfaction with family relations and as little as 35% of the variance in satisfaction with education.

The most extensive testing of MDT was based on a sample of over 18,000 undergraduates in 39 countries (Michalos 1991a, b, 1993a, b). In broad strokes, the theory explained on average 52% of the variance in scores for the 14 dependent variables used in the 1985 paper, including 51% for males and 53% for females.

The theory worked best on samples of undergraduates from Austria and Finland (64% variance explained on average) and worst on the sample from Mexico (36% variance explained). Samples from Bangladesh, Sweden, and Switzerland also had average explanatory figures in the 60s, while the average figures for Egypt and Thailand were in the 30s. For the group as a whole, on average, the goal-achievement gap was exactly as influential as the social-comparison gap, while for males, the social-comparison gap and for females, the goal-achievement gap, respectively, were most influential. Of the six gaps influencing the goal-achievement gap, the social-comparison gap was by far the most influential.[1]

Diener (1994) provided a fine summary of the field of subjective well-being studies as late as the summer of 1993, although the material it reviewed and the agenda for research that it recommended is much more contemporary than its date of origin would suggest. The aim of the paper was to alert social indicators researchers to relevant recent research from the field of psychology, especially research related to the affective aspects of subjective well-being, including the pleasantness and unpleasantness experienced in feelings, emotions, and moods. He was particularly interested in reminding us of the variety of emotions that people experience (e.g., sadness, fear, anger, guilt, affection, joy) and showing us the variety of methods available to measure them. "It is now widely agreed," he said, "that emotion is composed of behavioral, nonverbal, motivational, physiological, experimental, and cognitive components." Emotions may be revealed through facial expressions (e.g., smiling), action readiness, coping activities, and self-reports. Self-reports are the standard instruments used by survey researchers, but such reports lack precision because (1) different people identify and name different experiences in different ways, (2) some people deny or ignore some kinds of emotions, (3) some are reluctant to report what they

---

[1] Related to MDT was the research by Sirgy and his colleagues on *judgment theory* (Meadow et al. 1992). A life satisfaction measure was developed and validated based on the notion that life satisfaction is a function of a comparison between perceived life accomplishments and a set of evoked standards. These standards involve derivative sources (e.g., the life accomplishments of relatives, friends, associates, past experience, self-concept of strengths and weaknesses, and average person in similar position) and different forms (e.g., standards based on ideal, expected, deserved, minimum tolerable, and predicted outcomes).

feel, and (4) people experience and remember diverse emotions with different levels of intensity, different frequencies, and durations. In short, "Contributions in other areas of psychology lead us to conceive of subjective well-being in a more differentiated, less monolithic way. The goal will then be, not to discover *the* cause of subjective well-being, but rather to understand the antecedents of various types of subjective well-being parameters. Subjective well-being cannot be considered to be a brute, incontrovertible fact, but will, like all scientific phenomena, depend on the types of measures used to assess it" (p. 140).

Among other things, researchers' methods might include a variety of assessments of nonverbal behaviors (e.g., sleeping and eating habits, alcohol consumption), reports from significant others, electromyographic facial recording, diverse priming protocols, experience sampling of moods, video and audio records, self-reports of goals, self-worth and helplessness, and in-depth interviews. In the future, subjective well-being research is likely to be characterized by multiple measures of the multiple components of the construct.

Reflecting on the array of more or less subtle techniques that are currently available for measuring perceived well-being, one must be concerned about the political and moral implications of expanding research opportunities. Among the "uses and abuses of social indicators and reports" reviewed in Michalos (1980b), the possibility was mentioned that our efforts might lead to a technocratic and elitist society that would be subversive for democracy. As our understanding of the complex roots of human judgments and evaluations of their lives become more sophisticated, there is a danger of paralysis. In the presence of great uncertainty about exactly what personal reports about people's own lives are worth, people may become reluctant to engage in social and political activities, even those that appear progressive. While that is certainly possible, it is reasonable to believe that a better world is possible, and that our best weapons against imperfect democracies driven by imperfect understanding and appreciation are improved understanding and appreciation, leading to improved personal and public decision-making and action, in short, to more perfect democracies.

In contrast to the 1970s, government-sponsored social indicators activities slowed in the 1980s, as reductions in funding or nonrenewals led, for example, to the closing of the Center for Coordination of Research on Social Indicators; the discontinuation of related work at several international agencies; the termination of government-sponsored social indicators reports in some countries, including the USA; and the reduction of statistical efforts to monitor various aspects of society. Several explanations have been given for this turnabout (Andrews 1989; Bulmer 1989; Ferriss 1989; Innes 1989; Johnston 1989; Rockwell 1987; Rose 1989). Certainly, politics and the state of national economies in the early 1980s are among the most identifiable proximate causes. Owing to faltering economies and budget deficits, governments reduced spending. In addition, many perceived that social indicators were not fulfilling their initial promise of contributing to public policy-making. This was due, in part, to an overly simplistic view of how and under what conditions knowledge influences policy.

Social Indicators and QOL Research in Health and Medicine

With respect to *QOL and health*, much research in the 1970s started to address the trade-off between QOL and quantity of life. The work of Barbara McNeil and these questions of trading off treatment alternatives have put QOL squarely into medical decision-making, and QOL became a major topic at meetings of the Society for Medical Decision-Making (McNeil et al. 1975). In that vein, the concept of *Quality-Adjusted Life Years (QALY)* was first introduced.

One of the early health-related QOL survey research instruments that was developed in the 1970s and is still used today is self-rated health question ("During the past month, would you consider your health in general to be excellent, very good, good, fair, or poor?"). This measure was first used by the US National Center for Health Statistics.

Social Indicators and QOL Research in Management

With respect to *management*, research on QOL surged in 1970s and 1980s. For example, Andrews and Withey's (1976) measure of QWL (the Efficacy Index) was found to be significant and a very strong predictor of life satisfaction. The study controlled for the effects of family, money, amount of fun one is having, house/apartment, things done with family, time to do things, spare-time activities, recreation, national government, and consumer. Campbell et al. (1976) showed that satisfaction with work contributes approximately 18% variance accounted for in life satisfaction, controlling for the effects of nonworking activities, family life, standard of living, savings and investments, marriage, friendships, and housing. In most QOL studies, attitude toward work closely linked to life satisfaction (e.g., Schmitt and Bedian 1982; Shaver and Freedman 1976). Furthermore, early research on self-esteem and job satisfaction among salespeople established the link between them (e.g., Bagozzi 1978, 1980a, b, c).

Research in management in the 1970s and 1980s also addressed the question: How does QWL contribute to overall QOL? During this period, a number of psychological strategies were uncovered documenting the means by which employees maximize satisfaction (and minimize dissatisfaction) across a variety of life domains. These are spillover, segmentation, and compensation (e.g., Rain et al. 1991; Staines 1980). The *spillover effect* refers to the process and outcome by which affective experiences in the work life domain influence the affect experienced in other life domains and overall life, and conversely one's overall life satisfaction/dissatisfaction spills over to the job domain. Studies (e.g., Champoux 1976; Dreher 1982; Martin and Schermerhorn 1983; Near et al. 1980; Staines 1980; Rice et al. 1980; Rousseau 1978) indicate that the positive relationship predicted by the spillover model is generally supported. The *segmentation effect* refers to the method by which people isolate experiences and affect in one life domain, thus preventing affect transfer between life domains. Empirically speaking, such a phenomenon is evidenced through a lack of correlation between satisfaction in one life domain (e.g., job satisfaction) and other life domains (e.g., leisure satisfaction, family satisfaction, life satisfaction). The *compensation effect* refers to the method by which people attempt to balance their affect across life domains.

Social Indicators and QOL Research in Marketing

The QOL concept in *marketing* can be traced back to 1970s. Marketing scholars first took notice in the early 1970s. H. Naylor Fitzhugh of Pepsi-Cola Company became the first vice president of the Public Policy and Social Issues Division of the American Marketing Association (AMA). Under his leadership, the AMA sponsored a workshop entitled "Social Indicators for

Marketing – New Tools for Marketing Management" during the 1971 AMA International Conference in San Francisco (Clewett and Olson 1974). A second AMA-sponsored "social indicators" conference was held in February 1972 in Washington under the leadership of Irving Crespi of the Gallup Organization and Salvatore Divita of George Washington University (Clewett and Olson 1974). The third AMA-sponsored "social indicators" conference was held in February 1973 in Washington, DC, under the leadership of James R. Butts of American University and Allen Clayton of Lever Brothers Company (Clewett and Olson 1974). Fifteen papers from the 1972 and 1973 conferences were selected and published as a conference proceedings type of publication by the AMA in 1974, and Robert L. Clewett and Jerry C. Olson edited the proceedings (Clewett and Olson 1974).[2]

The fourth "Marketing and Quality of Life" conference was held in 1978, which was also sponsored by the AMA (Reynolds and Barksdale 1978). The fifth conference of marketing and quality of life was sponsored by the Academy of Marketing Science and was held in 1985 at Florida Atlantic University (Samli 1987). The sixth conference was held at Virginia Polytechnic Institute and State University (Virginia Tech) in 1989 and was sponsored by a host of professional societies such as the AMA, the Academy of Marketing Science (AMS), the Association for Consumer Research, the Society for Consumer Psychology (Division 23 of the American Psychological Association), and the International Society for System Sciences (Meadow and Sirgy 1989). From the seventh conference, two special issues were published, one in the *Journal of Business Research* (Sirgy 1991a), and the other in the *Journal of Business and Psychology* (Sirgy 1991b). After the seventh conference, the AMS established the Quality of Life-and-Marketing conference as one of its regular specialty conferences and sponsored the eighth conference in 1992 (Sirgy 1991).

---

[2] Clewett and Olson (1974) mentioned in the preface section of their proceedings publication that another conference was scheduled to be held in June 1974 in Oxford, England. The conference organizers were named as Arthur Cullman of Ohio State University and Elizabeth Richards of WARNACO. The sponsor of that conference was named as the British Market Research Society. An attempt was made to locate the proceedings of that conference with no success. At this time, the authors do not know whether such a conference actually took place and whether the proceedings of that conference were published.

From this conference, best papers were selected and published in a book (Sirgy and Samli 1995). The ninth conference was held in Williamsburg, Virginia, USA (local university host was the College of William and Mary), in 1995 and again was sponsored by AMS (Meadow et al. 1995). From this conference, two special issues in the *Journal of Business Research* (Chon 1999) and the *Journal of Macromarketing* (Fisk and Dickinson 1997) were developed. In 1996, the *Journal of Macromarketing*, under the editorship of Robert Nason, made QOL studies in marketing a regular section in the journal, with Joe Sirgy the section editor.

In 1995, Joe Sirgy together with a number of his marketing colleagues decided to expand the network by forming the International Society for Quality of Life Studies (www.isqols.org). Joe Sirgy became the executive director of the society with Josh Samli as its first president.

Social Indicators and QOL Research in the 1990s and 2000s

Social Indicators and QOL Research in Sociology, Psychology, Economics, and Political Science

The 1980s ended with the question of "What Ever Happened to Social Indicators?" (Rose 1989) and the mistaken conclusion that the field had faded away. Shortly afterward, however, interest in social indicators revived, and since the mid-1990s, the field has been expanding. Again, under the editorship of Michalos, the *Social Indicators Research Book Series* began in 1997 with a volume on the *Quality of Life in South Africa*, edited by Valerie Møller. By 2011, the series contained 44 volumes.

The revival of interest became vividly apparent in the 1990s (Land 1996) owing to *the widespread political, popular, and theoretical appeal of the Quality Of Life concept*. This concept emerged and became part of the Social Indicators Movement in the late 1960s and early 1970s as social scientists in highly developed Western industrial societies raised doubts about economic growth as the major goal of societal progress (Noll and Zapf 1994:1–2). They cited the "social costs" of economic growth and raised doubts about whether "more" should be equated with "better." Their discussion posed QOL as an alternative to the more and more

questionable concept of the affluent society, and they incorporated QOL in discussions of social policy and politics as a new, but more complex, multidimensional goal. As a goal of social and economic policy, QOL encompasses many or all domains of life and subsumes, in addition to individual material and immaterial well-being, such collective values as freedom, justice, and the guarantee of natural conditions of life for present and future generations (Cummins 1996; Diener and Suth 1997; Ferriss 2001). The political use of the QOL notion is paralleled in the private sector by the widespread use and popularity of numerous rankings – based on weighted scales of multiple domains of well-being – of the "best" places to live, work, do business, and play be they cities, states, regions, or nations.

The theoretical appeal of the QOL concept as an integrating notion across the social sciences and related disciplines is, in part, due to the perceived importance of measuring individuals' subjective assessments of their satisfaction with various life domains and with life as a whole. For instance, QOL has become a concept that bridges the discipline of marketing research and strategic business policy with social indicators. Marketing is an important social force – with far-reaching direct and indirect impacts on the prevailing QOL in a society – through consumer satisfaction (Samli 1987; Sirgy and Samli 1995) and its impact on satisfaction with life as a whole. The intersection of marketing research with social indicators through the QOL concept led to the organization in the mid-1990s of the multi-disciplinary International Society for Quality of Life Studies (ISQOLS) (http://www.isqols.org).

In addition to the widespread appeal of the QOL concept, another key development in the field of social indicators in the 1990s and early 2000s is evident: *The field has entered a new era of the construction of composite or summary social indicators*. Often these indices are used to summarize indicators (objective and/or subjective) of a number of domains of life into a single index of the quality of life for the population or society as a whole or for some significant segment thereof (e.g., children and youth, the elderly, racial and minority groups, cities and states or regions within the nation). Many of the pioneers of the Social Indicators Movement in the 1960s and 1970s backed away from the development of summary indices, instead concentrating on basic research on social indicators, measuring of the quality of life, and developing a richer social data base. Today, however, researchers attempt to answer one of the original questions motivating the Social Indicators Movement: How are we doing overall in terms of the quality of life? With respect to our past? With respect to other comparable units (e.g., cities, states, regions, nations)? Responses to these questions are encouraging and include the following examples: (1) at the level of the broadest possible comparisons of nations with respect to the overall quality of life, the *Human Development Index* (United Nations Development Programme 2004), Diener's (1995) *Value-Based Index of National Quality of Life*, and Estes' (1988, 1998) *Index of Social Progress*; (2) at the level of comparisons at the national level over time in the USA, the *Fordham Index of Social Health* (Miringoff and Miringoff 1999) and the *Genuine Progress Indicator* (Redefining Progress 1995), and, for a specific subpopulation, the *Child Well-being Index* developed by Land et al. (2001, 2004; Land 2004).

Møller et al. (2009) edited a collection of papers called *Barometers of Quality of Life around the Globe* in which several examples of comprehensive collections of indicators are presented. In their contribution to the volume, Mangahas and Guerrero (2008) remarked that they called their social monitoring system in 1981 the Social Weather Stations Project "on the idea that surveys can serve like observation posts to monitor social conditions, much as meteorological stations monitor weather conditions" (p. 24). In Noll's (2008) contribution to that volume, one reads about the development of the Eurobarometer since its first survey in 1974, perhaps the first usage of the "barometer" metaphor.

In over 30 years of publication of *Social Indicators Research*, many authors have illustrated a great variety of ways to represent the multidimensional space of diverse concepts of quality of life with some kind of unidimensional scale. Such reductions are designed to simplify complicated collections of statistical time series and are practically bound to oversimplification. Nevertheless, as Saltelli (2007) and others have explained, for purposes of communication in the popular press, simplicity is very important, even simplicity at the risk of oversimplification (Michalos et al. 2007).

ISQOLS formed a Committee for Societal QOL Indexes in 2000, under the chairmanship of Michael Hagerty, with the aim of evaluating 22 well-known indexes against a set of 14 generally accepted adequacy criteria. The report of the committee was published in Hagerty et al. (2001). Of the 22 indexes examined in that report, only two are discussed in the Møller, Huschka, and Michalos volume, namely, the Eurobarometer and the UNDP's Human Development Index. So, that report provides a good supplement to the papers in the Møller, Huschka, and Michalos volume.

A more substantial supplement to the Hagerty et al. paper was published by Sirgy et al. (Sirgy et al. 2006a, b, c, d) with the somewhat grand title of "The quality of life (QOL) research movement: past, present and future." While the authors of that overview intended to provide a worldwide perspective, close examination of its contents revealed an Anglo-Saxon–North American bias. The bias can be adjusted to some extent with the help of reviews by Noll (2002), Berger-Schmitt and Jankowitsch (1999), several papers in Glatzer et al. (2004), and the Møller, Huschka, and Michalos volume.

Noll's (2008) contribution to the Møller, Huschka, and Michalos volume is properly subtitled "Rich sources for quality of life research" because the diverse cultures, regions, and great number of research centers and research instruments available in Europe have combined to produce a magnificent mine of social indicators research. In the concluding section of his paper, granting that there are problems with "cross-country comparability," Noll celebrates the diversity of approaches used in the European surveys as providing "an experimental setting, enhancing the research potential by providing additional opportunities to study the implications of using the one or the other measurement approach" (p. 17).

Beginning after the Eurobarometer that included nine nations, the first European Values Study (EVS) survey occurred in 1981 covering ten Western European countries. In 1990, more European countries, Canada, and the USA were added, and by 1999–2000, there were 33 countries. While the EVS is run relatively infrequently, the Eurobarometer surveys occur in the spring and fall of every year, giving a database covering over 30 years. The European Community Household Panel Study (ECHP) was a longitudinal annual survey running for 8 years, 1994–2001. The European Social Survey began in 2002/2003, and the European Quality of Life Survey (EQLS) in 2003. One of the most attractive features of the European Social Survey, in Noll's view, is that it is based on a eudaimonic rather than a hedonic concept of well-being. While hedonists emphasize "positive feelings" following the historic tradition of Protagoras, eudaimonists emphasize "being well and doing well" in Aristotle's phrase or "positive doings and functionings" in Amartya Sen's phrase. Concluding his contribution, Noll wrote that "if one expects that quality of life research faces a bright future in Europe it is not only due to the richness of data, but also due to the fact that enhancing quality of life in all member states is among the major policy goals of the European Union" (p. 19). Good supplements to this paper may be found in Hagerty et al. (2002) and Vogel (2003).

The contribution by Shin (2008) in the Møller, Huschka, and Michalos volume is a fine follow-up to the comprehensive collection published in *Social Indicators Research* (i.e., *The Quality of Life in Korea: Comparative and Dynamic Perspective*) by Shin et al. (2003). The Korea Barometer Surveys described by Shin (2008) began in 1988 "with the installation of the democratic Sixth Republic." With 10 national surveys running from October 1988 to July 2004, the Korea Barometer provides an extraordinary record of changes in the quality of life of a country in transition "from a low-income country into an economic powerhouse…from a repressive military dictatorship into a maturing democracy…from a nation of mostly rural people into one of urbanites… [and] from a nation with a predominately traditional Confucian culture into a multi-cultural nation…" (p. 60). Summarizing his findings, Shin remarked that "Koreans neither interpret nor value democracy in the same way as Westerners do," and that, unfortunately, "democratization, globalization, industrialization, urbanization, and many other changes that have taken place in Korea during the past two decades have not contributed to the building of a nation of greater well-being. Instead, those changes have transformed the country into a nation of lesser well-being" (p. 62).

Graham's (2008) contribution to the Møller, Huschka, and Michalos volume compared results from the 2001 Latinobarometro with pooled data from the US General Social Survey from 1973 to 1998 and the Russian Longitudinal Monitoring Survey of 2000. She provided a fine illustration of how attitudinal surveys from diverse parts of the globe could reveal new insights and provoke new research questions and problems for policy makers. Among her most interesting findings from the Latin American data, she discovered that "…the non-linear relationship between income and happiness holds for countries that are at very low

levels of GDP per capita, like Honduras and Guatemala. Earlier literature on the developed economies posited that non-linearities set in well after basic needs were met, at roughly $10,000 per capita. The Latin America results suggest that the level is much lower… [and as others have found] Average country income levels had no significant effects on happiness in any of the countries we studied, even the very poor ones, while relative income differences dominated" (pp. 98–99).

The Survey of Living Conditions in the Arctic (SLiCA) reported by Kruse et al. (2008) represents another collaborative initiative involving eight countries and many more indigenous people and communities. It took the researchers about 3 years and eleven workshops to craft their questionnaire, which included "950 variables per respondent" and "7,200 observations," and it took about 6 years (2001–2006) to collect data. Respondents were divided into approximately 76% Inuit from Canada, Greenland, and Alaska, and 24% Chukchi, Evan, Chuvan, and Yukagir from Chukotka in Russia. As reported in other regions of the world concerning other people, in this collection and elsewhere, "Inuit adults who receive a poverty level personal income (60% or less of the median income in their indigenous settlement region) are less likely to be very satisfied with their life as a whole than adults who receive higher personal incomes (32 versus 43%). But at higher levels of personal income, the level of income is not always associated with a higher likelihood of being very satisfied with life as a whole" (p. 123). Results from the SLiCA will be essential building blocks for an "Arctic Social Indicators system."

The contribution of Cummins et al. (2008) to the Møller, Huschka, and Michalos volume describes the construction and application of the Australian Unity Well-being Index (AUWI), which is composed of a Personal Well-being Index (PWI) and a National Well-being Index (NWI). The PWI is based on an average of respondents' reported levels of personal satisfaction with seven domains of their own lives (e.g., health, personal relationships), and the NWI is based on an average of respondents' reported levels of personal satisfaction with six domains of national life (e.g., the economy, the environment). The PWI and NWI are not aggregated. The first application of the AUWI occurred in a national survey in April 2001, and the report in the Møller, Huschka, and Michalos volume covers results of 17 such surveys.

In his contribution to the Møller, Huschka, and Michalos volume, Mattes (2008) described the Afrobarometer as "a systematic, cross-national survey of public attitudes in sub-Saharan Africa" (p. 162). The main scale used in the survey is called the Lived Poverty Index (LPI), and it is constructed by averaging five possible responses to five items formatted in the same way, i.e., "Over the past year, how often, if ever have you or your family gone without...? (e.g., enough food to eat, enough clean water for home use)." The possible responses are "never" (=0), "just once or twice" (=1), "several times" (=2), "many times" (=3) and "always" (=4). Results of three rounds of national surveys are discussed, including 12 countries in 1999–2001, 16 countries in 2002–2003 and 18 countries in 2005–2006 (with 25,359 responses in the third round). One of the most interesting findings related to the LPI is that "while lived poverty has weak if not perverse linkages with GDP growth, it has moderately strong and predictable linkages with democratization... the more a country expanded political liberties and political rights between 2003 and 2005, the lower its level of lived poverty in 2005 $(r = -.625^{**})$" (p. 178). Møller (1997) would be a good supplement to this paper.

In the last paper of the Møller, Huschka, and Michalos collection, Inoguchi and Fujii (2008) described the AsiaBarometer as "a regional opinion survey project regularly conducted in a broader East Asia encompassing East, Southeast, South and Central Asia with a focus on daily lives of ordinary people" (p. 187). The project included national surveys in 10 countries of Asia in 2003, 13 countries in East and Southeast Asia in 2004, 14 countries in South and Central Asia in 2005, 7 countries in East Asia in 2006 and 6 countries in Southeast Asia in 2007. Two of the countries surveyed in 2005 (Turkmenistan and Bhutan) had never had any opinion surveys before. Sensitivity to local cultures, issues, aspirations, and languages is emphasized at every step of the development of the surveys, from questionnaire construction to analysis and dissemination of results. As reported by others in the Møller, Huschka, and Michalos collection, Inoguchi and Fujii remark that "Economic development brings about the improvement of income level, but it does not enhance social stability and sense of security" (p. 202). Good supplements to this paper may be found in Bowles and Woods (2000), Tang (2000), Shin et al. (2003), and Shek et al. (2005).

Social Indicators and QOL Research in Planning

The period of 1990s and 2000s experienced a surge of *community indicators projects*. Many towns, cities, counties, cantons, and regions initiated their own community indicator projects, in essence social indicator projects at a local level. These community indicator projects involve the use of both objective and subjective indicators related to social, economic, and environmental well-being of community residents. The interest in community indicator projects prompted the International Society for Quality of Life Studies (ISQOLS) to organize its first conference on community QOL indicators in 2002. This was followed by another major conference on community QOL indicators in 2004. ISQOLS, in collaboration with other professional associations such as the National Planning Council Association and the American Planning Association, spawned another organization called the Community Indicators Consortium (www.communityindicators.net) and organized annual conferences that have been held since 2004. In this vein, Sirgy and colleagues developed a book series related to best practices in community indicator projects (Sirgy 1991, 2006a, b, c, d, 2007a, b, c, 2009). Related to this activity, ISQOLS initiated a certification program to train QOL researchers to become professionally proficient in the science of community indicators research (Sirgy 2007).

Social Indicators and QOL Research in Health and Medicine

With respect to *QOL and health*, the World Health Organization Quality of Life (WHOQOL) group defined QOL as "individuals' perceptions of their position in life in the context of the culture and value systems in which they live, and in relation to their goals, expectations, standards, and concerns" (The WHOQOL Group 1996). The QOL concept in health has been broadened to include environmental aspects. Much research in health-related QOL has been based on this definition. Examples of a most commonly used health-related QOL instrument, based on this definition of health, is the Short-Form 36-item Health Survey (SF-36) capturing functional status and well-being (Stewart and Ware 1992). Also, the 1990s and 2000s witnessed much research activity in the development of disease-specific health-related QOL instruments. Hundreds of such measures were developed cutting across medical conditions, illness domains, and patient populations (Patrick and Chiang 2000).

With respect to the rise of institutions related to health-related QOL, the 1990s and 2000s witnessed a surge of institutional activity. New journals were established devoted to health-related QOL such as *Quality of Life Research* and *Health and Quality of Life Outcomes*. Many health-related QOL publications appeared in the traditional medical journals such as *Medical Care, Journal of Clinical Epidemiology, American Journal of Public Health, British Medical Journal, Journal of the American Medical Association, New England Journal of Medicine*, and the *Lancet*, as well as the myriad of specialty journals. The International Society for Quality of Life Research, a professional association dedicated to health-related QOL, was established in 1995. Health-related QOL groups were also established within many professional societies, including those that focus on a particular condition and others that cut across many different health conditions such as the Cochrane Collaboration.

Social Indicators and QOL Research in Management

With respect to *management*, the 1990s and 2000s saw much research on the effectiveness of specific QWL programs such as alternative work arrangements, employee involvement, and job design (e.g., Schermerhorn et al. 2003); employee involvement programs (Cummings and Worley 2001); and job design (Schermerhorn et al. 2003). Much of that research has established that the consequences of QWL programs are not limited to QWL enhancement. QWL programs contribute to employee job motivation and job performance, employee loyalty and commitment to the organization, low turnover rate, lower rates of employee absenteeism, and lower strife between management and labor (Cartwright and Cooper 2009; Korman 1994; Warr 2007).

Social Indicators and QOL Research in Marketing

Marketing research guided by the QOL concept experienced a surge in the 1990s and 2000s (Lee and Sirgy 2005; Sirgy 2001). Much research focused on the development of consumer well-being measures related to specific industry sector. For example, Meadow and Sirgy (2008) developed a measure to capture elderly's satisfaction with local shopping in ways that is directly related to life satisfaction. Sirgy et al. (2008) developed a measure of consumer well-being capturing community residents' satisfaction with local retail institutions and shopping, the retail services available to help consumers assemble consumer goods, the financial services allowing consumers to own high-cost durable goods, consumption of goods and services purchased locally, the servicing and repair of locally purchased durable goods, and the disposal of these goods. This construct of consumer well-being was found to positively influence community well-being and life satisfaction. In the housing sector, Grzeskowiak et al. (2006) developed a housing well-being measure to help builders develop residential real estate that enhance the QOL of homeowners. In the travel and tourism industry, Neal et al. (2007) developed a measure capturing tourist satisfaction with tourism services in relation to leisure well-being and life satisfaction. In the telecommunications industry, Sirgy et al. (2007a) developed a consumer well-being related to the use of cell phones. In higher education, Sirgy et al. (2007b) developed a college campus quality of life measure. In relation to personal transportation and automobiles, Sirgy et al. (2006a, b, c, d) developed a consumer well-being measure capturing the contribution of personal transportation on life satisfaction. In relation to the Internet, Sirgy et al. (2006a, b, c, d) developed a measure of consumer well-being directly related to the use of the Internet and the Internet's impact on the user's QOL.

Uses of Social Indicators and QOL Research

The uses of social indicators can be described in terms of four major functions, namely the enlightenment function, the public policy function, the medical function, and the managerial function.

The Enlightenment Function

The Social Indicators Movement was motivated by the principle that it is important to *monitor changes over time* in a broad range of social phenomena that extend beyond the traditional economic indicators and that include *indicators of quality of life* (Andrews 1986:401; Noll and Zapf 1994:5). Many organized actors in contemporary society – including government agencies, organizations and activists interested in social change programs, scholars, and marketing researchers interested in market development and product innovations – monitor indicators in which they have a vested interest and want to see increase or decline (Ferriss 1988:603).

A second principle that has been part of the Social Indicators Movement from the outset (e.g., Biderman 1970; Land 1996) is that a critically important role of social indicators in contemporary democratic societies is *public enlightenment through social reporting.* In brief, modern democracies require social reporting to describe social trends, explain why an indicator series behaves as it does and how this knowledge affects interpretation, and highlight important relationships among series (Parke and Seidman 1978:15).

It also is important to document the consequences that are reasonably attributable to changes in a series. This includes the systematic use of social indicators to *forecast trends in social conditions and/or turning points therein* (Land 1983:21). To be sure, the projection or forecasting of social conditions is filled with uncertainties. Techniques range from the naïve extrapolation of recent trends to futuristic scenario construction to complex model building with regression, time series, or stochastic process techniques. Moreover, there appears to be intrinsic limits to the accuracy of forecasts in large-scale natural and social systems (Land and Schneider 1987). But demands for the anticipation of the future (at a minimum, for the description of "what will happen if present trends continue"), for foresight and forward thinking in the public and private sectors, and for the assessment of critical trends (Gore 1990) appear to be an intrinsic part of contemporary postindustrial societies. Thus, it is prudent to expect that the "anticipation" task will become an increasingly important part of the enlightenment function of social indicators.

As the decades of the 1990s and 2000s unfolded, the model of a comprehensive national social report in the tradition pioneered by Ogburn and Olson clearly had faltered in the USA, at least in the sense of Federal government sponsorship and/or production. But the key ideas of monitoring, reporting, and forecasting were evident to greater or lesser extents in the production of continuing, periodic subject-matter-specific publications by various Federal agencies, including *Science Indicators* (published by the National Science

Foundation), *The Condition of Education, Youth Indicators,* and *Educational Indicators* (published by the Department of Education), the *Report to the Nation on Crime and Justice* (published by the Department of Justice), *Health USA* (published by the Department of Health and Human Services), and numerous Bureau of the Census publications. Special topics involving groups of Federal agencies also receive attention from time to time. For instance, the Federal Interagency Forum on Child and Family Statistics began in 1997 an annual publication on *America's Children: Key National Indicators of Well-being.* In addition, the USA has numerous private research organizations, policy institutes, and scholars that continue to produce reports, monographs, and books interpreting social trends and developments in various areas of social concern. Caplow et al. (1991) published a privately generated, comprehensive social report on the USA. The report follows a framework that was employed for several other countries (France, Germany, Italy, and others). These social reports provided the basis for a study of the comparative social change in the several Western countries.

In contrast to the situation in the USA, comprehensive social reports/social indicators compendiums continue to be published periodically in several other countries. Examples are the *Social Trends* series published annually since 1970 by the UK's Central Statistical Office, the *Datenreport* series published biennially since 1983 by the Federal Republic of Germany, the *Social and Cultural Report* published biennially by the Social and Cultural Planning Office of the Netherlands, and *Australian Social Trends* published annually by the Australian Bureau of Statistics. Citations and summary reviews of these and other social indicators/social reports publications can be found in the quarterly newsletter and review of social reports, *SINET: Social Indicators Network News* (http://www.soc.duke.edu/dept/sinet/index.html/).

The difference in the organization of social indicators/reporting work in the USA as compared to that in other countries is in part attributable to the lack of central statistical office responsible for the coordination of all Federal statistical activities in the USA. More generally, despite the invention of the ideas of social indictors and comprehensive social reporting in the USA, the sector reports on science, health, education, crime, and housing are all that remain of official Federal reporting systems. While US Federal administrations have issued reports that attempt to review national social conditions (US President's National Goals Research Staff 1970; US President's Commission for a National Agenda for the Eighties 1980), the US Congress has proposed but never finally mandated a social report on the Nation.

Whether a new round of legislative effort will eventually create the necessary institutional base for a national social report remains to be seen. Perhaps marking a turning point and indicative of things to come is Public Law 100–297, enacted April 28, 1988, which requires an annual education indicators report to the President and Congress. Another possibility centers upon an effort by the US General Accounting Office (2003), acting at the behest of a Congressional committee, to develop a system of "key indicators" for the USA (see also www.keyindicators.org).

The Policy Analysis Function

Policy analysts distinguish various ways of guiding or affecting public policy, including *problem definition, policy choice and evaluation of alternatives,* and *program monitoring* (MacRae 1985:20–29). In the formative days of social indicator development, Bertram M. Gross advocated the application of social indicators to policy evaluation and development (Gross and Springer 1967). The social reporting/public enlightenment approach to social indicators centers around the first of these, namely, the use of social indicators in problem definition and the framing of the terms of policy discourse. Indeed, studies of the actual use of social indicators suggest that this is precisely the manner in which they have affected public action (Innes 1989).

But policy analysts always have hoped for more from social indicators, namely, the shaping of public policy and planning through the policy choice process. At a minimum, this requires the identification of key variables that determine criterion indicators and changes therein (i.e., causal knowledge). More generally, it requires the construction of elaborate causal models and forecasting equations (often in the form of a "computer model") that can be used to simulate "what would happen if" under a variety of scenarios about policies and actions. An example of this is the development of the US National Cancer Institute model for the control and reduction of the incidence of cancer in the USA to the year 2000 (Greenwald and Sondik 1986). Various policy and action scenarios and

their implications for cancer mortality were simulated and estimated with this computer model. These simulations led to a decision to allocate funds to a prevention, education, screening, and treatment, and their implications for cancer mortality were simulated and estimated with this computer model. These simulations led to a decision to allocate funds to a prevention program rather than to additional clinical treatment.

The Medical Function

Health-related QOL assessment has had a great deal of utility on medicine and medical interventions. Much of health-related QOL encourages the medical profession to concentrate on "accurate depiction of how health influences and is influenced by the experience of the body and the mind within a social and cultural context" (Sirgy et al. 2004). This research is helping clinicians develop medical interventions that do not only focus on the physical health of the patient but also "social health." In other words, measuring health-related QOL of particular patients or patient populations guide individual interventions as well as the development of medical interventions directed to large-scale diseased populations.

At the international level, health-related QOL research is also guiding public policy regarding disparities in health status within and across the developed world and developing world. International health organizations such as the World Health Organization (WHO) are leading this effort. The goal is to treat disease in a social context. That physical illness is highly intertwined with the social, economic, and environmental conditions of people. That illness cannot be "cured" or prevented by strictly focusing on physical ailments. Public policies are formulated to address the social, economic, and environmental conditions of diseased populations.

The Managerial Function

Two functions of corporate management – working life and marketing – have important QOL components. First, Russell Ackoff, emeritus professor of operations research and systems science at University of Pennsylvania, argued that QWL is the answer to America's corporate world (Ackoff 1994). That is, if corporate management focused its efforts on enhancing QWL, the result would be significantly higher profits. Ackoff conceptualizes the business enterprise as a social system producing and distributing wealth and raising the standard of living. The QWL within a social system is the key to business success. Work can be designed to be challenging and enjoyable. Doing so would increase workers commitment to the organization and the motivation to excel and achieve excellence.

Study after study has shown that a happy employee is a productive employee (Greenhaus et al. 1987). A happy employee is a dedicated and loyal employee. Much research has shown that QWL may have a significant impact on employee behavioral responses such as organizational identification, job satisfaction, job involvement, job effort, job performance, intention to quit, organizational turnover, and personal alienation (e.g., Carter et al. 1990; Efraty and Sirgy 1990; Efraty et al. 1991; Lewellyn and Wibker 1990). Sirgy (1991) summed up the managerial implications of QWL research as follows:

- Provide employees with prompt performance feedback
- Allow employees to participate in important decisions that affect the health and welfare of the entire organization
- Establish role clarity
- Meet employees' informational and motivational needs
- Compensate employees well
- Compensate employees fairly and equitably
- Use alternative work arrangement to balance the demands of work and nonwork domains
- Design jobs that satisfy individual needs
- Match job design with employee needs
- Assign workers low in social and growth needs to routine jobs
- Assign workers high in social but low in growth needs to traditional work groups
- Assign workers who are low in social but high in growth needs to enriched jobs
- Assign workers who are high in social and growth needs to self-managed teams
- Use of information technology to facilitate performance and enhance productivity

In addition, the growth of the marketing discipline and the evolution of the QOL concept in marketing thought are important markers in the history of marketing, administrative, and policy sciences. The growth and acceptance of the QOL concept in marketing and related disciplines is important in that professionals in all kinds of organizations are more likely than ever to adopt the QOL concept as a point of reference. This point of reference or philosophy serves to guide their decision-making in the service of the various organizational stakeholders (e.g., customers, suppliers, distributors, creditors, employees, the local community, and the environment). Doing so would benefit society significantly. In other words, QOL studies in marketing are designed to help marketing managers make develop marketing programs to enhance the QOL of customer groups in ways not to adversely impact other organizational stakeholders such as employees, the local community, and the environment.

Prospects for the Future

We modestly anticipate that social indicators and QOL research will continue to serve the enlightenment function for societies and their citizens and politicians. We expect that decision makers of all kinds will find many applications in the future of social indicators and QOL research to policy choice and evaluation. In particular, such applications probably will occur in three areas. The first is the additional development of evidence-based, theoretically informed, and policy-relevant indicators and models for national- and/or regional-level analyses within particular fields, such as health, education, crime, and science (Bulmer 1989). In such applications, the phenomena to be included are definable and delimited, and the limitations of the data on which the indicators are based are known. The health field, particularly, may be expected to pursue change sequences, as evident in the pages of *Health USA*.

We also expect the use of social indicators and QOL research to expand in the field of social impact assessment (Finsterbusch 1980; Land 1982). Social impact assessment has developed as part of environmental impact assessment legislation and attempts to anticipate the social effects of large-scale public projects (e.g., dams, highways, nuclear waste disposal facilities) as well as to assess the damage of both natural and human-made disasters (e.g., earthquakes, oil spills, nuclear plant accidents). The use of QOL measures, now quite reliably measured, could enhance evaluation of public intervention efforts, such as the program of the Appalachian Regional Commission and the Delta Regional Authority, now evaluated by less precise methods (Ferriss 2004). This application of social indicators in impact assessments brings the field back full circle to its point of origination in the American Academy effort of the 1960s.

We also expect the many time series of indicators now available will increasingly be used by social scientists to assess theories, hypotheses, and models of social change, thus bringing social indicators and QOL data to bear on core issues in understanding positive social change in every walk of life. With a tremendous increase in the richness of data available for many societies today as compared to two or three decades ago, a new generation of social indicators and QOL researchers has returned to the task of constructing QOL indices and other performance metrics. Thus, the field of social indicators and QOL research probably will see several decades of development and competition among various indices and measures with a corresponding need for careful assessments to determine which indices and measures have substantive validity for which populations in the assessment of the QOL and its changes over time and social space.

References

Ackoff, R. L. (1994). *The democratic organization: A radical prescription for recreating corporate America and rediscovering success.* New York: Oxford University Press.

Andrews, F. M. (Ed.). (1986). *Research on the quality of life.* Ann Arbor: Institute for Social Research.

Andrews, F. M. (Ed.). (1989). The evolution of a movement. *Journal of Public Policy, 9,* 401–405.

Andrews, F. M., & Withey, S. B. (1974). Measures of perceived life quality: Results from several national surveys. *Social Indicators Research, 1,* 1–26.

Andrews, F. M., & Withey, S. B. (1976). *Social indicators of well-being: Americans' perceptions of life quality.* New York: Plenum.

Argyris, C. (1957). *Personality and organization.* New York: Harper and Row.

Atkinson, T. (1982). The stability and validity of quality of life research. *Social Indicators Research, 10,* 113–132.

Bagozzi, R. P. (1978). Salesforce performance and satisfaction as a function of individual differences: Interpersonal and situational factors. *Journal of Marketing Research, 15,* 517–531.

Bagozzi, R. P. (1980a). Performance and satisfaction in an industrial salesforce: An examination of their antecedents and similarity. *Journal of Marketing, 44,* 65–77.

Bagozzi, R. P. (1980b). Salespeople and their managers: An exploratory study of some similarities and differences. *Sloan Management Review, 21,* 15–25.

Bagozzi, R. P. (1980c). The nature and causes of self-esteem, performance, and satisfaction in the sales force: A structural equation approach. *Journal of Business, 53,* 315–331.

Bauer, R. A. (Ed.). (1966). *Social indicators.* Cambridge: MIT Press.

Berger-Schmitt, R., & Jankowitsch, B. (1999). *Systems of social indicators and social reporting: The state of the art.* Mannheim: Centre for Survey Research and Methodology (ZUMA).

Biderman, A. D. (1970). Information, intelligence, enlightened public policy: Functions and organization of societal feedback. *Policy Sciences, 1,* 217–230.

Blake, R. R., & Mounton, J. S. (1969). *Building a dynamic corporation through grid organizational development.* Reading: Addison-Wesley.

Blake, R. R., & Mouton, J. S. (1964). *The managerial grid.* Houston: Gulf.

Bowles, P., & Woods, L. T. (Eds.). (2000). *Japan after the economic miracle.* Dordrecht: Kluwer.

Bradburn, N. M. (1969). *The structure of psychological well-being.* Chicago: Aldine.

Bulmer, M. (1989). Problems of theory and measurement. *Journal of Public Policy, 9,* 407–412.

Campbell, A., & Converse, P. E. (1972). *The human meaning of social change.* New York: Russell Sage.

Campbell, A., Converse, P. E., & Rodgers, W. L. (1976). *The quality of American life: Perceptions, evaluations, and satisfactions.* New York: Russell Sage.

Caplow, T., Bahr, H. M., Modell, J., & Chadwick, B. A. (1991). *Recent social trends in the United States, 1960–1990.* Montreal/Kingston: McGill-Queens University Press.

Carley, M. (1981). *Social measurement and social indicators: Issues of policy and theory.* London: George Allen and Unwin.

Carter, C. G., Pounder, D. G., Lawrence, F. G., & Wozniak, P. J. (1990). Factors related to organizational turnover intentions of Louisiana extension service agents. In H. Lee Meadow & M. Joseph Sirgy (Eds.), *Quality-of-life studies in marketing and management* (pp. 170–181). Blacksburg: International Society for Quality-of-Life Studies.

Cartwright, S., & Cooper, C. L. (Eds.). (2009). *The oxford handbook of organizational well-being.* Oxford: Oxford University Press.

Champoux, J. E. (1976). *Work and nonwork: A review of theory and research* (Technical Report) (The Roberto O. Anderson Graduate School of Business and Administrative Sciences, Albuquerque: The University of New Mexico).

Chon, K. (1999). Special issue: Travel/tourism and quality of life. *Journal of Business Research.*

Clewett, R. L., & Olson, J. C. (Eds.). (1974). *Social indicators and marketing.* Chicago: American Marketing Association.

Cummings, T. G., & Worley, C. G. (2001). *Essentials of organization development and change.* Cincinnati: South-Western College Publishing.

Cummins, R. A. (1996). The domains of life satisfaction: An attempt to order chaos. *Social Indicators Research, 38,* 303–328.

Cummins, R. A., et al. (2008). Quality of life down-under: The Australian unity well-being index. In V. Møller, D. Huschka, & A. C. Michalos (Eds.), *Barometers of quality of life around the globe: How are we doing?* (pp. 135–160). Dordrecht: Springer.

Diener, E. (1994). Assessing subjective well-being: Progress and opportunities. *Social Indicators Research, 31*, 103–157.

Diener, E. (1995). A value based index for measuring national quality of life. *Social Indicators Research, 36*, 107–127.

Diener, E., & Biswas-Diener, R. (2002). Will money increase subjective well-being? A literature review and guide to needed research. *Social Indicators Research, 57*, 119–169.

Diener, E., & Biswas-Diener, R. (2008). *Happiness: Unlocking the mysteries of psychological wealth.* Malden, Massachusetts: Blackwell Publishing.

Diener, E., & Suth, E. (1997). Measuring the quality of life: Economic, social and subjective indicators. *Social Indicators Research, 40*, 189–216.

Diener, E., Suh, E. M., Lucas, R. E., & Smith, H. L. (1999). Subjective well-being: Three decades of progress. *Psychological Bulletin, 125*, 276–302.

Dreher, G. F. (1982). The impact of extra-work variables on behavior in work environments. *Academy of Management Review, 7*, 300–304.

Duncan, O. D. (1969). *Toward social reporting: Next steps.* New York: Russell Sage.

Duncan, O. D. (1975). Does money buy satisfaction? *Social Indicators Research, 2*, 267–274.

Dunn, H. L. (1959). High-level wellness for man and society. *American Journal of Public Health, 49*(6), 786–792.

Efraty, D., & Sirgy, M. J. (1990). Job satisfaction and life satisfaction among professionals and paraprofessionals. In H. L. Meadow & M. J. Sirgy (Eds.), *Quality-of-life studies in marketing and management* (pp. 157–169). Blacksburg: International Society for Quality-of-Life Studies.

Efraty, D., Sirgy, M. J., & Claiborne, C. B. (1991). The effects of personal alienation on organizational identification: A quality-of-work life model. *Journal of Business and Psychology, 6*, 57–78.

Estes, R. J. (1988). *Trends in world development.* New York: Praeger.

Estes, R. J. (1998). Social development trends in transition economies, 1970–95. In K. R. Hope Sr. (Ed.), *Challenges of transformation and transition from centrally planned to market economies.* Nagoya: United Nations Centre for Regional Development.

Ferriss, A. L. (1988). The uses of social indicators. *Social Forces, 66*, 601–617.

Ferriss, A. L. (1989). Whatever happened, indeed! *Journal of Public Policy, 9*, 413–417.

Ferriss, A. L. (2001). The domains of the quality of life. *Bulletin de Methodologie Sociologique, 72*(October), 5–19.

Ferriss, A. L. (2004). The quality of life concept in sociology. *The American Sociologist, 35*(3 Fall), 37–51.

Finsterbusch, K. (1980). *Understanding social impacts: Assessing the effects of public projects.* Beverly Hills: Sage.

Fisk, G., & Dickinson, R. (1997). Special issue: Quality of life. *Journal of Macromarketing, 17*(Spring), 3–39.

Glatzer, W., von Below, S., & Stoffregen, M. (Eds.). (2004). *Challenges for quality of life in the contemporary world.* Dordrecht: Kluwer.

Gore, A., Jr. (1990). The critical trends assessment act: Futurizing the United States government. *The Futurist, 24*, 22–28.

Graham, C. (2008). Measuring quality of life in Latin America: Some insights from happiness economics and the Latinobarometro. In V. Møller, D. Huschka, & A. C. Michalos (Eds.), *Barometers of quality of life around the globe: How are we doing?* (pp. 71–106). Dordrecht: Springer.

Greenhaus, J. H., Bedian, A. G., & Mossholder, K. W. (1987). Work experiences, job performances, and feelings of personal and family well being. *Journal of Vocational Behavior, 31*, 200–215.

Greenwald, P., & Sondik, E. J. (Eds.). (1986). *Cancer control objectives for the nation: 1985–2000* (National Cancer Institute Monographs, Vol. 2). Washington, DC: U.S. Government Printing Office.

Gross, B. M. (Ed.). (1967, May). *Social goals and indicators for American society* (Vol. I, The Annals 371). Philadelphia: American Academy of Political and Social Science.

Gross, B., & Springer, M. (1967). A new orientation in American government. *The Annals of the American Academy of Political and Social Science, 371*, 1–19.

Grzeskowiak, S., Joseph Sirgy, M., Lee, D.-J., & Claiborne, C. B. (2006). Housing well-being: Developing and validating a measure. *Social Indicators Research, 79*, 503–541.

Hagerty, M. R., Cummins, R. A., Ferriss, A. L., Land, K. C., Alex, C., Michalos, M. P., Sharpe, A., Sirgy, J., & Vogel, J. (2001). Quality of life indexes for national policy: Review and agenda for research. *Social Indicators Research, 55*, 1–96.

Hagerty, Michael. R., Vogel, J., & Møller, V. (Eds.). (2002). *Assessing quality of life and living conditions to guide national policy, social indicators research.* Dordrecht: Kluwer.

Headey, B. (2008). Life goals matter to happiness: A revision of set-point theory. *Social Indicators Research, 86*, 213–231.

Inglehart, R., & Rabier, J.-R. (1986). Aspirations adapt to situations – But why are the Belgians so much happier than the French? A cross-cultural analysis of the subjective quality of life. In F. M. Andrews (Ed.), *Research on the quality of life* (pp. 1–56). Ann Arbor: Institute for Social Research.

Innes, J. E. (1989). Disappointment and legacies of social indicators. *Journal of Public Policy, 9*, 429–432.

Inoguchi, T., & Fujii, S. (2008). The AsiaBarometer: Its aim, its scope and its development. In V. Møller, D. Huschka, & A. C. Michalos (Eds.), *Barometers of quality of life around the globe: How are we doing?* (pp. 187–232). Dordrecht: Springer.

Johnston, D. F. (1989). Some reflections on the united states. *Journal of Public Policy, 9*, 433–436.

Kammann, R., Farry, M., & Herbison, P. (1984). The analysis and measurement of happiness as a sense of well-being. *Social Indicators Research, 15*, 91–115.

Korman, A. K. (Ed.). (1994). *Human dilemmas in work organizations: Strategies for resolution.* New York: The Guilford Press.

Kruse, J., et al. (2008). Survey of living conditions in the Arctic (SLiCA). In V. Møller, D. Huschka, & A. C. Michalos (Eds.), *Barometers of quality of life around the globe: How are we doing?* (pp. 101–134). Dordrecht: Springer.

Land, K. C. (1975). Theories, models and indicators of social change. *International Social Science Journal, 27*, 7–37.

Land, K. C. (1982). Ex ante and ex post assessment of the social consequences of public projects and policies. *Contemporary Sociology, 11*, 512–514.

Land, K. C. (1983). Social indicators. *Annual Review of Sociology, 9*, 1–26.

Land, K. C. (1996). Social indicators and the quality-of-life: Where do we stand in the mid-1990s? *SINET: Social Indicators Network News, 45*, 5–8.

Land, K. C. (2004). An evidence-based approach to the construction of summary quality-of-life indices. In W. Glatzer, S. von Below, & M. Stoffregen (Eds.), *Challenges for quality of life in the contemporary world* (pp. 107–124). New York: Springer.

Land, K. C., & Schneider, S. H. (1987). Forecasting in the social and natural sciences: An overview and statement of isomorphisms. In K. C. Land & S. H. Schneider (Eds.), *Forecasting in the social and natural sciences* (pp. 7–31). Boston: Reidel.

Land, K. C., Lamb, V. L., & Mustillo, S. K. (2001). Child and youth well-being in the United States, 1975–1998: Some findings from a new index. *Social Indicators Research, 56*(December), 241–320.

Land, K. C., Lamb, V. L., & Mustillo, S. K. (2004). The child well-being index. *SINET: Social Indicators Network News, 77*(February), 1–6.

Lawani, S. M., & Bayer, A. E. (1983). Validity of citation criteria for assessing the influence of scientific publications: new evidence with peer assessment. *Journal of the American Society for Information Science, 34*, 59–66.

Lee, D.-J., & Joseph Sirgy, M. (2005). *Well-being marketing: Theory, research, and applications.* Seoul: Pakyoungsa Publishing.

Lewellyn, P. A., & Wibker, E. A. (1990). Significance of quality of life on turnover intentions of certified public accountants. In H. L. Meadow & M. J. Sirgy (Eds.), *Quality-of-life studies in marketing and management* (pp. 182–193). Blacksburg: International Society for Quality-of-Life Studies.

Lucas, R. E. (2005). Time does not heal all wounds: A longitudinal study of reaction and adaptation to divorce. *Psychological Science, 16*, 945–950.

Lucas, R. E., & Donnellan, M. B. (2007). How stable is happiness? Using the STARTS model to estimate the stability of life satisfaction. *Journal of Research in Personality, 41*, 1091–1098.

Lucas, R. E., Clark, A. E., Georgellis, Y., & Diener, E. (2004). Unemployment alters the set point for life satisfaction. *Psychological Science, 15*, 8–13.

MacRae, D., Jr. (1985). *Policy indicators: Links between social science and public policy.* Chapel Hill: University of North Carolina Press.

Mangahas, M., & Guerrero, L. L. B. (2008). Two decades of social weather reporting in the Philippines. In V. Møller, D. Huschka, & A. C. Michalos (Eds.), *Barometers of quality of life around the globe: How are we doing?* (pp. 23–36). Dordrecht: Springer.

Martin, T. N., & Schermerhorn, J. R. (1983). Work and nonwork influences on health. *Academy of Management Review, 8*, 650–659.

Maslow, A. H. (1954). *Motivation and personality.* New York: Harper.

Mattes, R. (2008). The material and political bases of lived poverty in Africa: Insights from the Afrobarometer. In V. Møller, D. Huschka, & A. C. Michalos (Eds.), *Barometers of quality of life around the globe: How are we doing?* (pp. 161–186). Dordrecht: Springer.

McCall, S. (1975). Quality of life. *Social Indicators Research, 2*, 229–248.

McGregor, D. (1960). *The human side of enterprise.* New York: McGraw-Hill.

McNeil, B. J., Keller, E., & Adelstein, S. J. (1975). Primer on certain elements of medical decision making. *New England Journal of Medicine, 293*(5), 211–215.

Meadow, H. L., & Sirgy, M. J. (Eds.). (1989). *Quality-of-life studies in marketing and management.* Blacksburg: International Society for Quality-of-Life Studies.

Meadow, H. L., & Sirgy, M. J. (2008). Developing a measure that captures elderly's well-being in local marketplace transactions. *Applied Research in Quality of Life, 3*(1), 63–80.

Meadow, H. L., Mentzer, J. T., Rahtz, D. R., & Joseph Sirgy, M. (1992). A life satisfaction measure based on judgment theory. *Social Indicators Research, 26*(1), 23–59.

Meadow, H. L., Sirgy, M. J., & Rahtz, D. (Eds.). (1995). *Developments in quality-of-life studies in marketing* (Vol. 5). Blacksburg: International Society for Quality-of-Life Studies.

Michalos, A. C. (1971). *The Popper-Carnap controversy.* The Hague: Nijhoff.

Michalos, A. C. (1980a). Philosophy of science: Historical, social and value aspects. In P. T. Durbin (Ed.), *The culture of science, technology and medicine* (pp. 197–281). New York: The Free Press.

Michalos, A. C. (1980b). Satisfaction and happiness. *Social Indicators Research, 8*, 385–422.

Michalos, A. C. (1980c). *North American social report: Vol. 1. Foundations, population and health.* Dordrecht: Reidel.

Michalos, A. C. (1985). Multiple discrepancies theory (MDT). *Social Indicators Research, 16*, 347–413.

Michalos, A. C. (1991a). *Global report on student well-being: Vol. 1. Life satisfaction and happiness.* New York: Springer.

Michalos, A. C. (1991b). *Global report on student well-being: Vol. 2. Family, friends, living partner and self-esteem.* New York: Springer.

Michalos, A. C. (1993a). *Global report on student well-being: Vol. 3. Employment, finances, housing and transportation.* New York: Springer.

Michalos, A. C. (1993b). *Global report on student well-being: Vol. 4. Religion, education, recreation and health.* New York: Springer.

Michalos, A. C. (Ed.). (2005). *Citation classics from social indicators research.* Dordrecht: Springer.

Michalos, A. C. (2008). Education, happiness and well-being. *Social Indicators Research, 87*, 347–366.

Michalos, A. C., Sharpe A., Arsenault J-F., Muhajarine N., Labonte R., Scott K., & Shookner M. (2007, December). *An approach to the Canadian index of well-being.* Toronto: Atkinson Charitable Foundation Working Paper.

Miringoff, M. L., & Miringoff, M. L. (1999). *The social health of the nation: How America is really doing.* New York: Oxford University Press.

Møller, V. (Ed.). (1997). *Quality of life in South Africa, social indicators research.* Dordrecht: Kluwer.

Møller, V., Huschka, D., & Michalos, A. C. (Eds.). (2009). *Barometers of quality of life around the globe: How are we doing?* Dordrecht: Springer.

Narin, F. (1976). *Evaluative bibliometrics: The use of publication and citation analysis in the evaluation of scientific activity*. Washington, DC: Computer Horizons.

National Commission on Technology, Automation and Economic Progress. (1966). *Technology and the American economy* (Vol. 1). Washington, DC: U.S. Government Printing Office.

Neal, J. D., Uysal, M., & Joseph Sirgy, M. (2007). The effect of tourism services on travelers' quality of life. *Journal of Travel Research, 46*, 154–163.

Near, J. P., Rice, R. W., & Hunt, G. R. (1980). The relationship between work and nonwork domains: A review of empirical research. *Academy of Management Review, 5*, 415–429.

Neugarten, B. L., Havighurst, R. J., & Tobin, S. S. (1961, April). The measurement of life satisfaction. *Journal of Gerontology, 16*, 134–143.

Noll, H.-H. (2002). Social indicators and quality of life research: Background, achievements and current trends. In N. Genov (Ed.), *Advances in sociological knowledge over half a century* (pp. 168–206). Paris: International Social Science Council (ISSC).

Noll, H.-H. (2008). European survey data: Rich sources for quality of life research. In V. Møller, D. Huschka, & A. C. Michalos (Eds.), *Barometers of quality of life around the globe: How are we doing?* (pp. 1–22). Dordrecht: Springer.

Noll, H.-H., & Zapf, W. (1994). Social indicators research: Societal monitoring and social reporting. In I. Borg & P. P. Mohler (Eds.), *Trends and perspectives in empirical social research* (pp. 168–206). New York: Walter de Gruyter.

Odum, H. W. (1936). *Southern regions of the United States*. Chapel Hill: University of North Carolina Press.

Ogburn, W. (Ed.). (1943). *American society in wartime*. Chicago: University of Chicago Press.

Parke, R., & Seidman, D. (1978). Social indicators and social reporting. *Annuals of the American Academy of Political and Social Science, 435*, 1–22.

Parsons, T. (1958). Definition of health and illness in light of American values and social structure. In J. E. Gartly (Ed.), *Patients, physicians, and illness: A sourcebook in behavioral science and health* (pp. 165–187). New York: Free Press.

Patrick, D. L., & Chiang, Y. P. (2000). Measurement of health outcomes in treatment effectiveness evaluations: Conceptual and methodological challenges. *Medical Care, 38*(9 Suppl), II14–II25.

President's Research Committee on Social Trends. (1933). *Recent trends in the United States*. New York: McGraw-Hill.

Progress, R. (1995). *The genuine progress indicator: Summary of data and methodology*. San Francisco: Redefining Progress.

Rain, J. S., Lane, I. M., & Steiner, D. D. (1991). A current look at the job satisfaction/life satisfaction relationship: Review and future considerations. *Human Relations, 44*, 287–307.

Reynolds, F. D., & Barksdale, H. C. (Eds.). (1978). *Marketing and the quality of life*. Chicago: American Marketing Association.

Rice, R. W., Near, J. P., & Hunt, R. G. (1980). The Job-satisfaction/ life-satisfaction relationship: A review of empirical research. *Basic and Applied Social Psychology, 1*, 37–64.

Rockwell, R. C. (1987). Prospect for social reporting in the United States: A receding horizon. In J. R. Pitts & H. Mendras (Eds.), *The Tocqueville review* (Vol. 8). Charlottesville: University Press of Virginia.

Rose, R. (Ed.). (1989). Whatever happened to social indicators: A symposium. *Journal of Public Policy, 9*(4), 399.

Rousseau, D. M. (1978). Relationship of work to nonwork. *Journal of Applied Psychology, 63*, 513–517.

Saltelli, A. (2007). Composite indicators between analysis and advocacy. *Social Indicators Research, 81*, 65–77.

Samli, A. C. (1987). *Marketing and the quality-of-life interface*. Westport: Quorum Books.

Schermerhorn, J. R., Hunt, J. G., & Osborn, R. N. (1994). *Managing organizational behavior*. New York: Wiley.

Schermerhorn, J. R., Hunt, J. G., & Osborn, R. N. (2003). *Organizational behavior*. New York: Wiley.

Schmitt, N., & Bedian, A. G. (1982). A comparison of LISREL and two-stage least squares analysis of a hypothesized life-job satisfaction reciprocal relationship. *Journal of Applied Psychology, 67*, 806–817.

Shaver, P., & Freedman, J. (1976). Your pursuit of happiness. *Psychology Today, 10*, 27–29.

Shek, D. T. L., Chan, Y. K., & Lee, P. S. N. (Eds.). (2005). *Quality-of-life research in Chinese, Western and global contexts*. Dordrecht: Springer.

Sheldon, E. B., & Moore, W. E. (Eds.). (1968). *Indicators of social change: Concepts and measurements*. New York: Russell Sage.

Shin, D. C. (2008). Monitoring democratic politics, a market economy, and citizen well-being: The South Korea barometer. In V. Møller, D. Huschka, & A. C. Michalos (Eds.), *Barometers of quality of life around the globe: How are we doing?* (pp. 37–70). Dordrecht: Springer.

Shin, D. C., Rutkowski, C. P., & Park, C.-M. (Eds.). (2003). *The quality of life in Korea: Comparative and dynamic perspectives*. Dordrecht: Kluwer.

Sirgy, M. J. (1991). Quality-of-life studies in marketing and management: An overview. *Journal of Business and Psychology, 6*, 38–45.

Sirgy, M. J. (Ed.). (1991a). Special issue: Quality-of-life studies in marketing and management. *Journal of Business and Psychology, 6*(Fall).

Sirgy, M. J. (Ed.). (1991b). Special issue: Quality of life. *Journal of Business Research, 23*(August).

Sirgy, M. J. (2001). *Handbook of quality-of-life research: An ethical marketing perspective*. Dordrecht: Kluwer Academic Publishers (translated in 2004 into Japanese by Interwork Publishers).

Sirgy, M. J. (2007). *The science of community quality-of-life research: A certification manual*. Blacksburg: International Society for Quality-of-Life Studies.

Sirgy, M. J., & Coskun Samli, A. (Eds.). (1995). *New dimensions in marketing/quality-of-life research*. Westport: Quorum Books.

Sirgy, M. J., Rahtz, D., & Lee, D.-J. (2004). *Community quality-of-life indicators: Best cases*. Dordrecht: Kluwer Academic Publishers.

Sirgy, M. J., Michalos, A. C., Ferriss, A. L., Easterlin, R., Patrick, P., & Pavot, W. (2006a). The quality-of-life (QOL) research movement: Past, present, and future. *Social Indicators Research, 76*, 343–466.

Sirgy, M. J., Lee, D.-J., & Kressmann, F. (2006b). A need-based measure of consumer well-being (CWB) in relation to personal transportation: Nomological validation. *Social Indicators Research, 79*, 337–367.

Sirgy, M. J., Lee, D.-J., & Bae, J. (2006c). Developing a measure of internet well-being: Nomological (Predictive) validation. *Social Indicators Research, 78*(2), 205–249.

Sirgy, M. J., Rahtz, D., & Swain, D. (2006d). *Community quality-of-life indicators: Best cases II*. Dordrecht: Kluwer Academic Publishers.

Sirgy, M. J., Lee, D.-J., Kamra, K., & Tidwell, J. (2007a). Developing and validating a measure of consumer well-being in relation to cell phone use. *Applied Research in Quality of Life, 2*(2), 95–124.

Sirgy, M. J., Grzeskowiak, S., & Rahtz, D. (2007b). Quality of college life (QCL) of students: Developing and validating a measure. *Social Indicators Research, 80*(2), 343–360.

Sirgy, M. J., Phillips, R., & Rahtz, D. (2007c). *Community quality-of-life indicators: Best practices III*. Blacksburg: International Society for Quality-of-Life Studies.

Sirgy, M. J., Lee, D.-J., Grzeskowiak, S., Chebat, J.-C., Herrmann, A., Hassan, S., Hegazi, I., Ekici, A., Webb, D., Chenting, Su, & Montana, J. (2008). An extension and further validation of a community-based consumer well-being measure. *Journal of Macromarketing, 28*(3), 243–257.

Sirgy, M. J., Phillips, R., & Rahtz, D. (2009). *Community quality-of-life indicators: Best practices IV*. Dordrecht: Springer Publishers.

Staines, G. (1980). Spillover versus compensation: A review of the literature on the relationship between work and nonwork. *Human Relations, 33*, 111–129.

Stewart, A. L., & Ware, J. E. (Eds.). (1992). *Measuring functioning and well-being: The medical outcomes study approach*. Durham: Duke University Press.

Stouffer, S. A. (1949). *The American soldier*. Princeton: Princeton University Press.

Taeuber, C. (Ed.). (1978, January). *American in the seventies: Some social indicators* (The Annals 435). Philadelphia: American Academy of Political and Social Science.

Taeuber, C. (Ed.). (1981, January). *America enters the eighties: Some social indicators* (The Annals 453). Philadelphia: American Academy of Political and Social Science.

Tang, K.-L. (Ed.). (2000). *Social development in Asia*. Dordrecht: Kluwer.

Tatarkiewicz, W. (1976). *Analysis of happiness*. Hague: Nijhoff.

U.S. Bureau of the Census. (1981). *Social indicators, III*. Washington, DC: U.S. Government Printing Office.

U.S. Department of Health, Education, and Welfare. (1969). *Toward a social report*. Washington, DC: U.S. Government Printing Office.

U.S. General Accounting Office. (2003). *Forum on key national indicators: Assessing the nation's position and progress*. Washington, DC: U. S. Government Printing Office.

U.S. Office of Management and Budget. (1974). *Social indicators, 1973*. Washington, DC: U.S. Government Printing Office.

U.S. Office of Management and Budget. (1978). *Social indicators, 1977*. Washington, DC: U.S. Government Printing Office.

U.S. President's Commission for a National Agenda for the Eighties, Panel on the Quality of American Life. (1980). *The quality of American life*. Washington, DC: U.S. Government Printing Office.

U.S. President's National Goals Research Staff. (1970). *Toward balanced growth: Quantity with quality*. Washington, DC: U.S. Government Printing Office.

United Nations Development Programme. (2004). *Human development report 2004*. New York: Oxford University Press.

Vogel, J. (Ed.). (2003). *European welfare production: Institutional configuration and distributional outcome*. Dordrecht: Kluwer.

Warr, P. (2007). *Work, happiness, and unhappiness*. New York: Lawrence Erlbaum Associates.

WHOQOL Group. (1996). *What quality of life?* World Health Organization

World Health Organization. (1948). *Constitution of the World Health Organization. Basic documents*. Geneva: World Health Organization.

Wylie, M. L. (1970). Life satisfaction as a program impact criterion. *Journal of Gerontology, 25*(1), 36–40.

The Good Life: Eighth Century to Third Century BCE*

Alex C. Michalos and Steven R. Robinson

Introduction

In very broad strokes, one may think of the quality of life of an individual or community as a function of the actual conditions of that life and what an individual or community makes of those conditions. What a person or community makes of those conditions is in turn a function of how the conditions are perceived, what is thought and felt about those conditions, what is done, and finally, what consequences follow from what is done. People's perceptions, thoughts, feelings, and actions, then, have an impact on their own and others' living conditions.

Taking the two main variables together (conditions of life and what people make of them), one can construct four scenarios which, with some exaggeration, may be described as different kinds of paradise and hell.

1. If people's living conditions are good, and people accurately perceive and think about them, feel good, and act appropriately, we may describe that as Real Paradise.
2. If people's living conditions are bad, and people accurately perceive and think about them, feel bad, and act appropriately, we may describe that as Real Hell.

3. If people's living conditions are bad, and people inaccurately perceive and think about them, feel good, and act inappropriately, we may describe that as the classical Fool's Paradise.
4. If people's living conditions are good, and people inaccurately perceive and think about them, feel bad, and act inappropriately, we may describe that as a Fool's Hell.

Although some complicated epistemological and evaluative material was smuggled into the four scenarios, it may be neglected for present purposes. The most important point to be made here is that the classical notion of a Fool's Paradise requires at least the sort of two-variable model mentioned in the first paragraph. This notion is based on the common sense view that there is a real world, however roughly apprehended, and that there are good reasons for believing that some perceptions, etc. are more acceptable than others.

As the remnants of the works of ancient authors are examined below, and as one would easily discover by examining the works of contemporary authors, the common sense view of the human condition is not universally appreciated and accepted. While anyone with any democratic sensitivity would grant that each person's assessment of his or her own life should be accorded some privileged status, it is far from obvious that such privilege should override all other considerations. Nevertheless, for some of the ancients and their modern followers, it is apparently supposed that people's personal assessments of the quality of their lives are not only privileged but also ultimately definitive. So, for example, it seems to be supposed that if some people are satisfied living in unsanitary environments, breathing polluted air and drinking polluted

---

*We would like to thank Deborah C. Poff for helping us improve this paper in several respects.

A.C. Michalos (✉)
Brandon University, 270 – 18th Street, Brandon, MB R7A 4P9, Canada
e-mail: michalos@brandonu.ca

S.R. Robinson
Philosophy Department, Brandon University, 270 – 18th Street, Brandon, MB R7A 6A9, Canada
e-mail: Robinsons@brandonu.ca

K.C. Land et al. (eds.), *Handbook of Social Indicators and Quality of Life Research*, DOI 10.1007/978-94-007-2421-1_2, © Springer Science+Business Media B.V. 2012

water, abusing and being abused by family members and strangers, suffering imposed restrictions on opportunities for personal achievement and development, and generally facing an array of life chances promising a life that is relatively nasty, brutish, and short rather than pleasant, elegant, and long, then that is acceptable. It seems to be supposed, wittingly or not, that however constrained the perceptions, beliefs, and so on of the people living in such conditions and assessing them as satisfactory, their assessments are paramount. For people holding such populist and somewhat postmodern views, there can be no Fool's Paradise, because there can be no fools foolish enough to misjudge their own satisfaction. For people holding such views, the quality of life, the good life, is completely internalized and determined by each person's own experiences. Then, since each person has privileged access to his or her own experiences, personal reports of those experiences must be equally privileged.

For the purposes of this essay, it does not matter if one accepts the one or two-variable view of the basic elements required for a proper assessment of the quality of life. In keeping with an old sociological tradition of revealing one's most important assumptions rather than trying to eliminate them, it is worthwhile to present the options and the author's biases up front. Inherent in the notion of a Fool's Paradise is the commitment to a higher, more scientific level of knowledge or awareness from which peoples' everyday, unreflective notions of happiness may be interrogated and evaluated. It is important to remember that the world contains many people living in poverty, lacking adequate food, shelter, and medical care, and facing life chances offering little hope of relief. The good life that we must want and achieve for all people is not just a life in which people feel good, no matter how terrible their real life conditions are, but one in which they feel good with the best of all reasons, because the objectively measurable conditions of their lives merit a positive assessment. In the ancient world, it was those we label "philosophers" who most self-consciously took up the task of working beyond common-sense notions towards an evidential basis for such epistemic claims. That is why this chapter will concentrate mostly on the work of the ancient philosophers.

Veenhoven (2000) provided an excellent review of many classificatory schemes for the idea of quality of life and presented his own preferred schemes. Some of these may be found in his essay on happiness in this volume. The most complete explanation of our general taxonomy of issues concerning the definition of "quality of life" may be found in Michalos (1980, 2008). It would take us too far off our main topic to examine this approach and compare it with Veenhoven's in any reasonable level of detail. Briefly and roughly speaking, we think the word "quality" in the phrase "quality of life" is used to refer to two kinds of things, descriptions and evaluations, which are conceptually distinct but in fact usually more or less blended. Veenhoven believes there are many kinds of qualities, but he prefers a scheme with four main species. In particular, he thinks that there are the qualities of livability, life-ability, utility, and life appreciation. He seems to grant that these four species are neither exhaustive of all possible types nor mutually exclusive in pairs. He recognizes that practically everything can be regarded as useful for something, which implies that everything in the other three categories could be included in the utility category. Sure we agree that no scheme developed so far is powerful enough to capture the great variety of ideas and issues involved in defining and measuring quality of life. For the purposes of this essay, we think the fourfold scheme presented above is particularly useful, although Veenhoven's fourfold scheme would also be workable.

This overview of ideas about the good life from the eighth to the third century BCE is based primarily on the writings of a few outstanding philosophers selected from a remarkably long list of candidates. Specialists in ancient philosophy may wonder why Cynics, Cyrenaics, Stoics, and Skeptics have been neglected, and the answer is simple enough. It seemed more useful to provide more details on the work of a few than fewer details on the work of many. The overview here will provide interested readers with sufficient background information to undertake further explorations on their own and give others enough information to appreciate the main similarities and differences between ideas of the good life then and now. A good overview of some of the ideas of philosophers neglected here may be found in Parry (2004).

Dover (1974) published a fine study of "popular morality" in the fourth century BCE based primarily on the writings of forensic and political orators, dramatists, and poets, and explicitly omitting the views of most philosophers (Dover 1974, p. xii). As Dover understood it, "popular morality" frequently involved assumptions and pronouncements about the good life and the best way to live. Most Greeks were not familiar with the writings of most philosophers, and the writings of the relatively better known orators, dramatists, and poets did not display the highest regard for them. So, Dover thought that it was best to leave the views of the philosophers aside in his attempt to give an accurate account of the views of average folks. Here we will examine the views of some outstanding philosophers of the period, including their views of what average folks thought. While all the philosophers mentioned here were extraordinary people with relatively extraordinary views compared to their contemporaries, some common and fairly conventional themes appear in all the works cited. The persistence and relevance of these same themes today is perhaps the most interesting product of our investigation.

All of the philosophers discussed in this overview lived on the lands near the eastern Mediterranean, Aegean, and Black Seas, including what we now call the Middle East. Readers should be aware that "not a single work of any of the "Presocratic" philosophers has been preserved from antiquity to the present" (McKirahan 1994, p. ix). Thus, for all of the philosophers before and even many of those after Socrates, the literature review that follows is a review of bits and pieces of their thoughts, sayings, and/or writings. For the presocratics especially, there are fragments purported to be actual quotations, but often liable to be paraphrased or rough approximations of the philosophers' actual views. Often enough there is no way to confirm or disconfirm authenticity, and even when authenticity is relatively well established, there is often considerable controversy concerning the most appropriate interpretation of a fragment in its original language and the most appropriate translation of the original text. Add to these problems the number of centuries of reproductions, errors of omission and commission, and commentaries by more or less well-informed, well-intentioned (the main reports we have of the views of some philosophers come from hostile critics), and well-resourced researchers, and the difficulty of producing an accurate overview of the work of our ancestors becomes clear. Were it not for the excellent analyses of McKirahan (1994) and Annas (1993, 1999), this overview would have been greatly impoverished. As the text will reveal, our debt to these two authors is substantial, and it is matched by much admiration for and appreciation of their work.

General Issues

Because a somewhat detailed examination of authors might lead readers to focus only on the trees as it were but fail to see the forest, we supposed that some general comments would be useful. They have been assembled here under the rubrics of Tragedy, Orphism, and Politics.

Tragedy

With the exception of Homer, Hesiod, and Theognis, the authors reviewed here are all philosophers, and yet these same philosophers were oftentimes reacting to expressions of contrary ideas in print or in practice by the non-philosophers around them (sophists, dramatists, orators, poets). It might therefore interest readers to be aware of some of the powerful positions that these philosophers were up against in putting forth their own theories. An example is tragedy. Tragedy was not just a dramatic genre, but tended to project a set of substantive views about the scope and meaning of human life. Plato, for one, saw those substantive tragic views as socially corrosive, and apparently sought to supplant them in his own work. An example of the substantive views to be found in tragedy is that humans are not in control of their destinies and are the playthings of the gods. The tragic plays thus have implications for notions of human agency, success, and happiness, ranging from extreme religious conservatism to outright pessimism. For example, in the play *Oedipus at Colonus*, the playwright Sophocles (1954) has his chorus declare, almost as if it is the moral of the story, that the best thing for humans – the highest human good – is to not even be born in the first place; second best is to die quickly (ll.1224ff). It would not be stretching things too far to suggest that the tragic poets were toying with the idea that all of human life is a Fool's Paradise – and that the notorious cases they dramatize in their plots teach us the lesson that it cannot really be otherwise. The tragedians claimed this privileged insight not on the basis of scientific inquiry but rather by offering a hard look at our collective self-deceptions. By contrast, the philosophers (with the exception of some like Heraclitus, perhaps) tend to reject outright the substantive theses of tragedy, and instead see "critical human reason" as providing a deeper understanding of human nature which can empower us to master ourselves and guarantee our human happiness and success in life.

Orphism

Greek religion divided into two in the crucial period that we are surveying here. There was the standard version that we are all familiar with (Delphic/Homeric religion) which employed public, politically established cults based on well-known myths and traditional practices; and then there was "mystery religion" (Orphic/Bacchic) which operated in private cults based on secret teachings. In the former, there was a clear doctrine of a dismal afterlife (captured effectively in Homer's *Odyssey* Bk XI, as Odysseus visits the underworld to commune with the dead). On Homer's view, our earthly life is brief and is really all we get; it is therefore important that we use it correctly and not throw away our one-and-only chance at happiness. By contrast, in the Orphic "mystery religion," human souls are immortal and travel from life-to-life in a sequence of bodies, some not even human (described in our section below on Pythagoras). It is taken for granted that life here on earth is bad (in fact it is meant to be a kind of punishment), and true happiness comes only to those who have been purified of their bodies through long practice of morally upright behavior; those blessed ones rejoin the gods in the afterlife. It is also taken for granted by the Orphics that "higher" lives here on earth have more opportunity for happiness, and that "lower" lives are correspondingly miserable (including higher and lower human lives), and that souls earn differential placements in the next life through the moral choices they make. It seems to us that whether a philosopher has Orphic or Delphic/Homeric sympathies is going to profoundly affect the way they view happiness in this life. For Orphics, there might once again be a real possibility of sliding into the view that what most humans take for happiness is a Fool's Paradise – but unlike the tragedians, the Orphics believe that there is "a way out" into a Real Paradise (for Orphic philosophers, this "way out" leads through science, mathematics, and philosophy).

Now, of the philosophers we will consider here, Pythagoras, Empedocles, and Plato all have clearly Orphic sympathies. We would therefore expect that their views of human happiness will be conditioned by their belief in an afterlife that rewards morally upright behavior

in this otherwise generally bad and unhappy life of ours. For instance, in Plato's account of Socrates' trial, *Apology*, Socrates declares he is happy with the outcome, despite the fact that he was convicted of a serious crime he did not commit and will promptly be executed – unjustly. This shows how a belief in the afterlife can complicate definitions of happiness in the here and now. Socrates goes on to describe the imagined afterlife as an "extraordinary happiness" [EUDAIMONIA], spending his time there questioning the other dead just as he had questioned the living: "I think it would be not unpleasant;" moreover, "They are happier there than we are here in other respects…if indeed what we are told is true" (Plato 2000, p. 42). If Plato shares the views he attributes to Socrates, then it is at least questionable the extent to which he would authentically commit to any view of happiness that lines up with popular conceptions. Other philosophers considered here, like Heraclitus, Protagoras, Antiphon, Democritus, and Epicurus, emphatically reject Orphic principles and espouse a correspondingly this-worldly conception of happiness.

Politics

There is an inherent aristocratic bias in most Greek views of happiness or success in human life. All of the authors considered here were members of an educated elite in Greece, though not all of them are elitists, strictly speaking. A standard ancient Greek formula was that happiness corresponds to goodness: "living well and doing well," where living well means enjoying the good things in life, and doing well means winning praise and fame for one's moral responsibility and leadership. Only aristocrats really had any opportunity to "do well" (i.e., to engage personally in high-profile activities that could benefit their whole community and thereby draw praise). The "little people" had little scope to perform beneficial acts and therefore little scope to be "good" – and likewise little hope of enjoying "the good things in life." Nonetheless, there was a very definite decline in the prospects of the aristocracy across the period discussed here, and with it a democratizing tendency in conceptions of both goodness and happiness (so for Aristotle, in principle, almost every free man has the potential to be happy – slaves, however, do not). An important part of this story is that some of our authors (like Homer, Theognis, and perhaps Plato) took a staunchly aristocratic line (i.e., some people are inherently better and therefore properly more happy than others), while other authors, like Hesiod, Aristotle, Democritus, and Epicurus, take a much more democratic line (i.e., nothing "heroic" is required in order to achieve happiness). These two ideologies spar with each other throughout our period, and a philosopher's politics sometimes informs what he says about human happiness. In this regard, it is worth mentioning one of the lyric poets, named Simonides. He was employed professionally to write praise poetry celebrating the greatness, and happiness, of his wealthy patrons. What he says in those poems not only conveys his own sense of proper limitations on expectations for happiness but also illustrates the degree to which aristocratic power had declined by his day. For instance, the following lines were written to celebrate the career of a notorious tyrant:

> To become a truly good man is difficult, in hands and feet and mind foursquare, fashioned without reproach.... For this reason I shall never cast away my allotted span of life on an empty, unrealizable hope by searching for something that cannot come into existence: a human being altogether blameless.... I am not prone to fault-finding; I am satisfied with anyone who is not bad nor too shiftless.... All things are honorable in which the shameful is not mingled. (Plato 1992a, b, *Protagoras*, p. 34–44)

And likewise, all people are happy who succeed in not debasing themselves *too much*. For Plato, this was far too democratic a conception of life and happiness.

These background notions and assumptions about human happiness (tragedy, Orphism, and political ideologies) were culturally effective in ancient Greece during this period. But in a sense, perhaps, they are timeless: At any rate, one could find a range of modern expressions from our own time to parallel them. They should be kept in mind as one surveys the following outline of ancient conceptions of happiness.

Homer (Eighth Century BCE)

Among the writers of the Archaic Age (c. 750–480 BCE), questions about the best life for an individual or about the best kind of person to be had paramount importance. The heroes of the epic poems ascribed to Homer, the *Iliad* and the *Odyssey*, were larger than life characters, born to and raised in privileged, noble, and wealthy families, occasionally boasting gods or goddesses in their family trees and displaying physical attractiveness and dexterity, as well as the qualities of practically wise leadership, strength of character, courage, justice, generosity, and piety. The best kind of people were aristocrats, and the best kind of life was aristocratic. Enjoying all the advantages of nobility, such people would have a clear sense of *noblesse oblige* and act accordingly. Still, a notable conflict may be found between Homer's two classic epics, in the characters of Odysseus and Achilles (the main figures of the *Odyssey* and the *Iliad*, respectively). Homer seemingly puts them both forward as role models, but they differ significantly. Achilles is straight and true, noble and honest, but he is weak willed and ruled by his passions, giving rise to tragic action that destroys his friends, and eventually himself. Hence, he is a tragic figure. Odysseus, on the other hand, is wily and clever but morally unprincipled; he thinks nothing of lying, cheating, and manipulating others for his ends. He is always working on schemes to trick people. Nonetheless, he succeeds in all things, including his arrival home from Troy and reunification with his long-suffering wife and son. So in contrast to Achilles, Odysseus has a happy ending. Homer portrays them both in entirely positive terms, leaving us to puzzle out who we think is best, if either, and why. Definitely, Odysseus would seem to be "happiest." The pathetic scene between Achilles and Priam, the father of dead Hector, over Hector's corpse in Bk XXIV of *Iliad* has been called the pattern for subsequent tragic visions in Greek poetry.

According to McKirahan, changes in Greek society from the beginning to the end of the Archaic Age brought changes in people's vision of a good life from that of competitive to cooperative success:

> ...the various strands of the Homeric heroic ideal began to unravel. In particular, good birth, wealth, and fighting ability no longer automatically went together. This sort of situation forced the issue: what are the best qualities we can possess? What constitutes human ARETE [i.e., excellence, virtue or goodness]? The literary sources contain conflicting claims about the best life for a person, the best kind of person to be, and the relative merits of qualities thought to be ingredients of human happiness. (McKirahan 1994, p. 358)

Granting that there was a variety of conflicting claims from a variety of "literary sources," the evidence to be presented here will show that there was also a relatively common central core of ideas about a good life and a good person that persisted from the eighth century BCE to the fourth century BCE, a core that may be discerned even today.

Hesiod of Ascra (Late Eighth/Early Seventh Century BCE)

The poems of Hesiod provide some insight into the lives of people of his generation and their assessments of what is good or bad. They lived in a world that was regarded as intelligibly ordered and fundamentally understandable, although filled with divine influences ranging from the purely mysterious to the fairly anthropomorphic Olympian gods. The connotative range of the concept of divinity for ancient Greeks was significantly different from its range today. Anything imagined as immortal, ageless, and capable of independent motion or power was regarded as divine. Hence, for example, when the sixth century BCE Milesian philosopher Thales posited water or Anaximander posited some indefinite but spatially and temporally unlimited stuff as the ultimate building material of the world, that material would have been regarded as divine. Anaximenes (c. 546 BCE) is reported to have believed that the ultimate building material was air or "dark mist," and "gods and divine things" originated from that material (McKirahan 1994, pp. 31–48). In the *Apology*, an irate Socrates rhetorically challenged his accusers with the question "Do I not even believe that the sun or yet the moon are gods, as the rest of mankind do?" (Plato 1914, p. 99).

The following passages from Hesiod's *Works and Days* indicate his views of some key features of a good life for individuals and communities:

> Those who give straight judgments to foreigners and citizens and do not step at all aside from justice have a flourishing city and the people prosper in it.
>
> There is Peace, the nurse of children, throughout the land, and wide-seeing Zeus never ordains harsh war for them. Famine and Disaster never attend men of straight judgment, but with good cheer they feed on the fruits of their labors. For these the Earth bears the means of life in abundance… But for those who have thoughts of evil violence and cruel deeds, wide-seeing Zeus son of Kronos has ordained justice. Often indeed the entire city of an evil man suffers,… Famine and Disease together, and the people perish.
>
> Women do not give birth, but houses are diminished… (McKirahan 1994, p. 14)

Although these lines contain names of deities long discarded by people today (e.g., Peace, Famine, Disaster, etc.), they also contain familiar themes of the good life, i.e., flourishing and prosperous communities, populated by honest people, living in peace, and enjoying the fruits of their labor, without worries about where the next meal will come from, with an absence of disease, and with justice for all. Later in the same poem, Hesiod describes the antithesis of a good society through a kind of inversion of these themes. The bad life is characterized as one in which

> A father will not be like his children nor will they be at all like him, nor will a guest be friendly to his host or comrade with comrade or brother with brother as before. They will quickly come to dishonor their parents and they grow old,…
>
> There will be no thanks for one who keeps his oath or is just or good, but men will rather praise evildoers and violence… The evil person will harm the better man, addressing him with crooked words… Bitter greed will be left for mortal humans, and there will be no defense from evil (McKirahan 1994, p. 17).

There is a bit of an anomaly with this author because his two surviving poems seem to be at odds. It has been proposed that he was writing in two different registers: one (*Theogony*) for performance competition before elite judges – praising the justice of kings – and the other (*Works & Days*) for general consumption, condemning the rich and promoting the anti-aristocratic ethic of the common farmer – very different. The latter poem's description of the "town" as a dangerous place where "gift-devouring kings" dispense "justice" for a fee looks a lot like the second quotation (above) giving Hesiod's vision of complete decline in the last age of the world. In contemporary terms, one might say that Hesiod's bad society is one in which the institution of morality has been totally undermined, including people's sense of justice, resulting in the total destruction of its social capital.

Pythagoras of Samos (c. 560–480 BCE)

Pythagoras is one of history's most extraordinary people, brilliant, charismatic, and enigmatic. He and his friends created associations that engaged in socioeconomic, political, religious, and academic activities. Although he seems to have written nothing, so remarkable were his talents and character that incredible legends were attached to him, e.g., that he could walk on water and be in two different places at the same time. The man himself was likely not a philosopher, nor a mathematician, but rather an early Orphic religious cult-leader who used number-magic as part of his cult doctrine. Most of what we associate with him has been retrojected back onto him by his followers, who considered any revision in the understanding of his doctrine to be the true meaning of the original prophet (and hence attributed it directly to him as the original intent of his words). Central to this cult was the idea of purification (ultimately, purification of the body from the soul), which in time led his followers to create a genuine school of philosophy (the Pythagoreans) based on the notion that scientific learning and abstract mathematics were the kinds of purification that Pythagoras had had in mind.

Economically and politically, Pythagorean societies were relatively successful aristocracies, religiously they were relatively secretive and ascetic, and academically they came in time to nourish highly original scientists and mathematicians. While the theorem bearing Pythagoras' name was not new, being known to earlier Babylonians, his followers seem to have discovered that musical intervals could be expressed mathematically, i.e., that musical qualities could be expressed quantitatively. Since the essence of social indicators or quality of life research is precisely the measurement (quantification) of qualities, it is fair to regard the Pythagoreans as the first researchers in our field.

As one might have expected, these initial efforts were not uniformly successful. Pythagoras himself is reported to have believed that the ultimate material of the universe was numerical in some sense, but the sense was quite unclear. According to McKirahan (1994, p. 112),

> The Pythagoreans believed that number is fundamental to all things, that the basic features of all things are numerical, that numerical considerations are basic in understanding all things, that all things are generated in a similar way to numbers. These statements are all ways of claiming primacy for numbers, but they are different ways....They were not interested in analyzing different ways numbers are primary, only in establishing that numbers are in fact primary. They formulated their thesis vaguely, to accommodate the different relations they found between things and numbers...to judge by Aristotle's criticisms [in his *Metaphysics*], their vague notion of priority does not stand up to analysis...

For present purposes, the details of the Pythagorean scheme are not as important as the general idea that the universe is not only intelligibly ordered but also constructed out of entities with geometrical shapes that, in principle perhaps, might be measurable. The following fragment by a relatively obscure writer from the first century AD known as Aetius expresses this idea:

> There being five solid figures called the mathematical solids, Pythagoras says that earth is made from the cube, fire from the pyramid, air from the octahedron, water from the icosahedron, and from the dodecahedron is made the sphere of the whole. (McKirahan 1994, p. 102)

With the "mathematical solids" as basic building blocks, Pythagoras imagined that the universe, which he called the KOSMOS, was somehow held together or connected by HARMONIA, i.e., by some sort of principle of harmony, which he had shown was intimately related to numerical analysis. He apparently believed that all living things (plants as well as animals) have immortal souls which at death transmigrate among diverse species, trading up or down as it were, depending partly on individuals' behavior and character. It is unclear if souls were supposed to be discrete, singular entities, aggregations of entities connected by the same principle of harmony holding the universe together, or merely that very same principle under a new name when it is applied to holding the parts of an individual's body together. The first of these alternatives would probably be the easiest to combine with a theory of transmigration. In any event, the aim of the relatively ascetic Pythagorean "way of life" was to bring increased harmony to an individual's soul, thereby improving that individual's chances for trading up rather than down and ultimately being released from the whole process. This notion of a harmonious soul or a soul at peace with itself found a place in the writings of many philosophers in the period reviewed here. To some extent, it is a feature of our contemporary popular psychology revealed in remarks about people having or needing to "get it all together," "pull themselves together," and "getting your heart and head together."

The Pythagorean "way of life" was pretty clearly divided into two main paths, the path of scholarship engaged in a variety of intellectual inquiries versus a path of religious asceticism engaged in following an array of more or less reasonable rules, e.g., eating in moderation and only vegetables, not eating beans, not keeping swallows in the house, and not urinating facing the sun. However one assesses the two distinct paths characterizing the Pythagorean "way of life," this figure's most important contributions to our subject lie elsewhere. These are, first, his discovery of the fact that qualitative features of the world can be quantified and, second, his theory that the observable conditions of an individual's life and the individual's observable behavior have an impact on that individual's unobservable soul. Most importantly, by positing an unobservable immortal soul as the final recipient of any rewards or punishments justly visited upon an individual for his or her own behavior, Pythagoras directed our attention away from overt appearances to covert realities. After all is said and done, according to Pythagoras, the good life we seek is the unobservable harmony of that unobservable entity, the immortal soul.

Heraclitus of Ephesus (c. 540–480 BCE)

Heraclitus was born to an aristocratic family and throughout his life maintained deep doubts about (if not disdain for) the capacities and character of those with less fortunate origins. Of the hundred or so remaining fragments of his works, those positing a world constantly undergoing changes while preserving identities are most frequently associated with his philosophy, e.g., "Upon those who step into the same rivers, different and again different waters flow" (McKirahan 1994, p. 122). He believed that the universe was not made but always existed, and formed a coherent unity displaying great diversity. The ultimate material building blocks were fire, water, and earth, which were distinct but periodically transformed into one another. The fundamental principle of order was referred to as the LOGOS, which is a multipurpose word connoting discourse, word, story, opinion, reason, and cause, to mention a few. As if this variety of usual meanings were not confusing enough, Heraclitus sometimes identified the LOGOS with justice, fire, strife, war, God, soul, and law.

Perhaps because he was so deeply impressed by the diversity of the world around him, he noticed that much of that diversity was constructed (to use a modern term) by observing the world from different perspectives or using different standards of comparison. For any of his contemporaries interested in defining "the" good life, the descriptive and evaluative relativism of some of his fragments would have been deeply disturbing. For example, consider the following:

The sea is the purest and most polluted water: to fishes drinkable and bringing safety, to humans undrinkable and destructive.

Pigs rejoice in mud more than pure water.

We would call oxen happy when they find bitter vetch to eat.

Physicians who cut and burn complain that they receive no worthy pay, although they do these things.

The road up and the road down are one and the same.

To God all things are beautiful and good and just, but humans have supposed some unjust and others just. (McKirahan 1994, pp. 121–125)

Thus, safe drinking water is important to fishes and humans, but the same water is different for each species. It may be appropriate to think of rejoicing pigs and happy oxen, but different things produce these pleasant states in these different species. Pain and those who inflict it upon others are normally regarded as bad, but physicians inflict it upon their patients, believing it to be good and worthy of some valuable payment for services rendered. The gradient of a road may be advantageous or disadvantageous to a traveler depending on the direction of his or her travel, though the gradient is the same for all travelers. Most devastating of all, what appears just or unjust to humans is really uniformly just, beautiful, and good to God. That is to say, everything in the world is really just, beautiful, and good in some objective sense known only to God, although to humans (and presumably all other sentient species according to other fragments), some things appear to be unjust, ugly, and bad.

In the presence of such paradox, one might suppose that Heraclitus would have been unable and unwilling to provide any recommendations for living "the" good life. In fact, since vague and contradictory premises have unlimited implications, confused philosophical foundations provide fertile soil for practically any desired crop. Thus, besides valuing personal safety, justice, happiness, and beauty as suggested above, according to Heraclitus, "Right thinking is the greatest excellence, and wisdom is to speak the truth and act in accordance with nature, while paying attention to it" (McKirahan 1994, p. 120). The "right thinking" or "wisdom" referred to is practical as well as theoretical. It is revealed in one's assertions and actions, which are guided by careful observation of the natural world followed by behavior that is appropriate to the conditions of that world as well as to one's particular species. The good life is one lived in communities in which people willingly follow customs and obey conventional laws that are consistent with an ideal law sometimes referred to as "the divine law." It is a life relatively free of drunkenness, anger, and violence. While there is a place for religion and religious rituals, there is no room for bathing oneself in blood or singing hymns "to the shameful parts [phalli]." Finally, Heraclitus believed that "It is not better for humans to get all that they want" (McKirahan 1994, p. 128). At a minimum, this last fragment implies that the mere maximization of desire satisfaction is neither necessary nor sufficient for the good life. So, Heraclitus probably would have been unimpressed with Lewin et al.'s (1944) aspiration theory or Michalos' (1985) multiple discrepancies theory.

Theognis (Late Sixth and Early Fifth Century BCE)

The poetry of Theognis reveals further erosion of the idea of a good life as the product of a fortunately noble birth and/or ancestry, followed by all the privileges such a life would imply. According to McKirahan, democratic reforms of Solon and Peisistratus led to shifts in economic wealth and political power in Athens going into the fifth century BCE. The following passages attributed to Theognis seem to have been written by an observer who was not only distressed by the social and political transformations occurring around him but also convinced that the aristocratic virtues being lost by poor breeding could not be compensated by the best education money could buy, i.e., that no amount of good nurture could substitute for good nature. Apparently, two of the most evil characteristics of the dreaded Sophists often criticized in the writings of Plato and Aristotle were, first, their claim to do precisely what Theognis believed could not be done and, second, their willingness to accept fees for doing it, i.e., for teaching the nouveau riche and their offspring how to appear to have the virtues of the aristocracy.

> ...a noble man does not mind marrying a lowly (KAKOS) woman of a lowly (KAKOS) father, if her father gives him a lot of money.
> Nor does a woman refuse to be the wife of a lowly (KAKOS) man...
> They honor money...
> Wealth has mixed the race...
> It is easier to beget and raise a child than to instill good thoughts in it... never will he make a bad (KAKOS) man good (AGATHOS) by teaching. (McKirahan 1994, pp. 362–363)

Anaxagoras of Clazomenae (c. 500–428 BCE)

Although Anaxagoras was a teacher, consultant, and/or a friend of the great orator and statesman Pericles, he seems to have had no interest in worldly affairs or speculations on the good life. In the *Phaedo*, Socrates expressed great disappointment in Anaxagoras' naturalistic explanations that "made no use of intelligence, and did not assign any real causes for the ordering of things, but mentioned as causes air and ether and water and many other absurdities" (Plato 1914, p. 339). Among the fragments of his works, the following is particularly revealing: "The Greeks are wrong to accept coming to be and perishing, for no thing comes to be, nor does it perish, but they are mixed together from things that are and they are separated apart" (McKirahan 1994, p. 199). That is, what appears to begin to exist or to pass into nonexistence is really only a reorganization or reconfiguration of some everlasting materials, e.g., he asks "how could hair come to be from not hair or flesh from not flesh?" Presumably, then, the constituent elements of the worst sort of life would be the same as those of the best sort of life, only reconfigured or reorganized somehow.

Another fragment seems to have articulated a common view in the fifth century BCE, i.e., "Appearances are a sight of the unseen" (McKirahan 1994, p. 200). According to Vlastos (1945, p. 590), "This is the general principle of scientific procedure among the historians and the medical men: What can not be known (or seen) directly must be judged from what can."

Empedocles of Acragas (c. 492–432 BCE)

Empedocles was a gifted son of relatively wealthy aristocrats, who displayed enough sympathy for democracy to get himself exiled from his native home in Sicily. In McKirahan's (1994, p. 290) view,

> Empedocles sparkles like a diamond among the Presocratics – many-faceted and appearing different from different directions. A poet and a politician, a physician and a philosopher, a scientist and a seer, a showman and a charlatan, he was a fallen divinity who proclaimed himself already a god, and a visionary who claimed to control nature.

Broadly speaking, his poetic fragments described a universe whose basic material building blocks are the four everlasting elements, earth, air, fire, and water, which are brought together by Love to form compounds, and subsequently divided and subdivided by Strife to form other kinds of compounds. "Love" and "Strife" are names used to describe cosmic forces that are not only physical but psychological and moral as well. Love is sometimes referred to as Friendship, Joy, and Harmony. It is Love that makes the basic elements "yearn for one another," and the harmony produced by Love's activity is morally good. On the contrary, it is Strife and "evil Quarrels" that cause compounds to "split apart," producing war and other kinds of wretchedness.

Human bodies are animated by DAIMONES, which function like souls but have an ontological status which is grander than souls. DAIMONES are not immortal, but they are relatively "long-lasting" compounds subject to the forces of Love and Strife. Empedocles told an elaborate story of the origins of all species, including such memorable fragments as the following:

> By her [Love] many neckless faces sprouted, and arms were wandering naked, bereft of shoulders, and eyes were roaming alone, in need of foreheads…
> Many came into being with faces and chests on both sides, man-faced ox-progeny, and some to the contrary rose up as ox-headed things with the form of men… (McKirahan 1994, p. 246).

At some time, the DAIMONES enjoyed a state of bliss overseen by Love that was eventually shattered as a result of an act of murder provoked by Strife. Human beings are the product of that Fall, with human bodies wrapped around DAIMONES as "an alien garb of flesh." Depending on individuals' own behavior, their DAIMONES might be reincarnated in greater or lesser beings. When Empedocles wrote, "I have already once become a boy and a girl and a bush and a bird and a fish," he was implying that his DAIMON carried the essence of his personal identity and was the ultimate unobservable recipient of any rewards and punishments due to him. Such soul-like essences might be reincarnated as

> …prophets and bards and physicians and chiefs among men on earth, and from there they arise as gods mightiest in honors.
> Sharing the same hearth and table with other immortals relieved of human distress, unwearied (McKirahan 1994, p. 253).

The next step up from being able to dine "with other immortals" would bring some kind of closure to the process of reincarnation, at which point one's individuality would be blended with that of a supreme being conceived of as "only mind, holy and indescribable."

Important features of Empedocles' vision of a good life are clearly discernable in this sketch of his metaphysics, which is fully informed by his ethics. Love, friendship, harmony, peace, social and self-esteem, and joy are all positively valued, while strife, quarrels, murder, war, and "human distress" are all negative. Other fragments add familiar themes. Following the Fall, the "wretched race of mortals" found themselves "quarreling" in a "joyless place, where Murder, Anger… and squalid Diseases and Rottings…wander in darkness." "False oaths" are condemned, along with eating meat and beans (McKirahan 1994, pp. 252–254).

Protagoras of Abdera (c. 490–420 BCE)

Because of his prominence in Plato's dialogue of the same name, Protagoras is perhaps the best known of the so-called Older Sophists. Others included Prodicus and Hippias (both also featured in the *Protagoras*), and Gorgias. Like Anaxagoras, Protagoras was on friendly terms with Pericles. Although Protagoras had an aristocratic background, he made a living as an itinerant teacher of relatively advanced studies of rhetoric. Of the few fragments reliably attributed to him, the most famous is, "A human being is the measure of all things – of things that are, that they are, and of things that are not, that they are not" (McKirahan 1994, p. 379). While we have seen elements of skeptical relativism in fragments attributed to philosophers before Protagoras (e.g., in Heraclitus), this fragment is a particularly bold statement of the relativity of all assertions, including those concerning what is just or unjust, beautiful or ugly, and even true or false. Writing in the third century CE, Diogenes Laertius added that "Protagoras was the first to declare that there are two mutually opposed arguments on any subject" (McKirahan 1994, p. 374). As if all this was not troublesome enough, in another bold fragment Protagoras professed a reasoned agnosticism.

> Concerning the gods I am unable to know either that they are or that they are not, or what their appearance is like. For many are the things that hinder knowledge: the obscurity of the matter and the shortness of human life (McKirahan 1994, p. 364).

The clear implications of such principles, then, are that the best life and the best sort of person to be are entirely dependent on individual preferences, and Protagoras certainly had his own preferences. According to Plato (1924), Protagoras said that he could make people better in the sense of more excellent in managing their personal as well as public affairs. Perhaps more importantly for his commercial interests,

Aristotle (1999) reported that Protagoras claimed the ability to make "the worse case the better" and to teach others how to accomplish the same feat. If he could deliver the product as advertised, his teaching would have been worth plenty to anyone with aspirations for a career in commerce, law, or politics. Apparently, enough people believed that he could deliver the product to make him famous, wealthy, and politically influential. It is unlikely that he would have preferred these features of the aristocratic good life without the universally attractive qualities of good health, loving friends, and family. There is no evidence that he had any concerns about his soul or that anything short of Real Paradise would have satisfied him. According to Poster (2006, p. 5),

> Protagoras himself was a fairly traditional and upright moralist. He may have viewed his form of relativism as essentially democratic – allowing people to revise unjust or obsolete laws, defend themselves in court, free themselves from false certainties – but he may equally well have considered rhetoric a way in which the elite could counter the tendencies towards mass rule in the assemblies. Our evidence on this matter is unfortunately minimal.

Plato's *Protagoras*, one of our main sources, is actually a very interesting document. Strikingly, Protagoras' famous dictum (individual relativism) never arises in it. Instead, Plato attributes to Protagoras a very sophisticated (one might even say, convincing) version of cultural relativism (see the "Great Speech," pp. 15–23). Then, amazingly, Socrates leads Protagoras and the other sophists into a trap by praising their abilities as masters of the *objective* "science of measure" which, with coaxing, they confess to being. Socrates draws this out of them with the bait of a "hedonistic calculus" which they are proud to admit they are experts at using (they are portrayed as if quite flattered that Socrates articulates this position so well and attributes it to them). Socrates, however, then snaps the trap shut by confronting them with the fact that Protagoras' science of measure does not match his professed cultural relativism. The upshot may well be contrary to Poster's assessment above: that the sophists are *pretending to be* cultural relativists in order to protect themselves from social conservatives, while in reality, and behind closed doors, they are convinced hedonists (which would shock and outrage the social conservatives) – and that hedonism is part of the substantive content that they are teaching to their young

proteges. You can perhaps see Plato here redirecting the charges that were actually laid against Socrates onto the sophists instead. This then resonates with the dramatic opening of the dialogue where Protagoras boasts that sophistry is a very dangerous profession, but that he has "taken measures" to protect himself from repercussions.

Antiphon of Rhamnous (c. 480–411 BCE)

Although there are several Antiphons cited by various authors in antiquity, Antiphon of Rhamnous seems to have been a relatively wealthy orator, statesman, philosopher, teacher of rhetoric, and professional speechwriter. For present purposes, it is important to note that McKirahan (1994, p. 396) described him as "possibly the earliest advocate of hedonism in Greek philosophy," i.e., the first recorded philosopher to regard the pursuit of pleasure or a pleasurable life as the final end (TELOS) or good life for humans. The remaining fragments of his work show that he carefully distinguished natural (PHYSIS) from conventional (NOMOS) phenomena, regarding the former as necessary and universal and the latter as unnecessary and variable. Granting that it could be advantageous for people to live in accordance with conventional laws and customs, he argued that nature provided a more reliable guide to human well-being. The following passages capture the core of his position:

> Living and dying are matters of PHYSIS, and living results for them from what is advantageous, dying from what is not advantageous. But the advantages which are established by the NOMOI are bonds on PHYSIS, and those established by PHYSIS are free.
>
> And so, things that cause distress, at least when thought of correctly, do not help PHYSIS more than things that give joy. Therefore, it will not be painful things rather than pleasant things which are advantageous. For things that are truly advantageous must not cause harm but benefit. Now the things that are advantageous by PHYSIS are among these.
>
> <But according to NOMOS, those are correct> who defend themselves after suffering and are not first to do wrong, and those who do good to parents who are bad to them, and who permit others to accuse them on oath but do not themselves accuse on oath. You will find most of these cases hostile to PHYSIS. They permit people to suffer more pain when less is possible and to have less pleasure when more is possible, and to receive injury when it is not necessary (McKirahan 1994, p. 394).

A clearer foundation for attaining a good life without tears could not be constructed. Provided that things are "thought of correctly," what is pleasant is naturally, universally life-enhancing, and what is painful is life-destroying. More precisely, provided that one thinks "correctly," one's experiences of pleasure and pain ought to be regarded as nature's reliable guides to appropriate human action. So, the best sort of person will make careful and accurate observations of nature, think "correctly" about what causes "distress" and "joy," successfully apprehend nature's guides to a long and pleasant life, and scrupulously follow those guides. Consequently, such a person will enjoy the best sort of life. In other words, the best sort of person will be able to distinguish a Fool's Paradise from Real Paradise, and live happily ever after in the latter.

Unfortunately, the good life achievable by Antiphon's prescriptions is not necessarily morally good or just. Another part of the same fragment quoted above clarifies his view of justice and its relation to a good life.

> ...Justice is a matter of not transgressing what the NOMOI prescribe in whatever city you are a citizen of. A person would make most advantage of justice for himself if he treated the NOMOI as important in the presence of witnesses, and treated the decrees of PHYSIS as important when alone and with no witnesses present. For the decrees of NOMOI are extra additions, those of the PHYSIS are necessary; those of the NOMOI are the products of agreement, not of natural growth, whereas those of PHYSIS are the products of natural growth, not of agreement (McKirahan 1994, pp. 393–394).

Since a transgressor of conventional laws may avoid "both disgrace and penalty" if there are no witnesses to the acts, while a transgressor of natural laws (so far as that might be possible) would suffer the consequences even if there are no witnesses, the former is a less serious matter than the latter. Therefore, in the pursuit of the good life, Antiphon advises each person to follow nature's directives favoring personal pleasure over pain. Below we will show some interesting ways in which Democritus and Epicurus offered improvements to the rougher hedonism of Antiphon.

Democritus of Abdera (c. 460–370 BCE)

According to Vlastos (1946, p. 62), "Democritean ethics...[was]...the first rigorously naturalistic ethics in Greek thought." If a system of "naturalistic ethics" is understood as one in which all ethical terms or moral values are definable in non-ethical terms or non-moral values, it is unlikely that any fifth century BCE philosopher would have had the philosophic or scientific conceptual resources required to produce such a system. However, it is fair to say that if anyone could have produced such a system, Democritus would have done it and that the system he did produce was a brilliant attempt to provide a scientific foundation for claims about the best sort of life and the best sort of person.

The ultimate material building blocks of Democritus' universe were atoms, which were too small to be observed by human senses but were theoretically imagined to exist in an unlimited void, to be unlimited in number, shape, and size, and to be constantly in motion. The shapes were imagined to be rough or smooth, concave or convex, and hooked or otherwise irregularly constructed. As they moved, they would collide, and parts of some would fit nicely together with others, while still others simply became randomly and unstably entangled. Besides this random churning and clustering of the atoms, a primitive gravitational principle was supposed to operate such that atoms were attracted to others like themselves. The result of all this unobservable atomic activity in the limitless void was the formation of relatively well-formed, perceptible compounds, i.e., the world as observed by human senses, including all living things.

Human beings were thought to be unique clusters of compounds consisting of body and soul atoms which were equally material, although soul atoms were uniformly spherical like those constituting fire. The shape and smoothness of the atoms clustered together to form soul-compounds were supposed to account for the latter's capacity to initiate change and movement in itself and its body-compound. While the two compounds were supposed to be thoroughly integrated, the body was occasionally described as the "instrument" or "tent" of the soul, and the soul was clearly regarded as "the responsible agent." Since souls and bodies were essentially thoroughly integrated compounds, the death of a human being implied the dispersion of the atoms constituting those compounds. Therefore, there were no immortal souls in Democritus' universe. There were, however, "daemons" (i.e., DAIMONES), as indicated in the fragment "The soul is the dwelling-place of the daemon," which Vlastos (1945, p. 582) interpreted as, "in the soul you will find the only daemon there is to find," Since such beings were not supposed to be immortal, their existence could have been granted by an atomist, provided that the supremacy of natural laws and/or mechanisms were unchallenged.

Human sensation of all kinds was reduced to the sense of touch insofar as seeing, hearing, and so on were supposed to be the result of the atoms of observed objects impacting those of sensory organ-compounds, which in turn impacted the atoms of soul-compounds. Important as sense perception was to one's knowledge of the world, it was notoriously unreliable. A fragment attributed to Democritus by Sextus Empiricus asserted that "We in fact understand nothing exactly [or exact], but what changes according to the disposition both of the body and of the things that enter it and offer resistance to it" (McKirahan 1994, p. 334). Two fragments provided by McKirahan (1994, p. 335) reveal that our hard-headed empiricist, materialist atomist had a significantly rationalist commitment to his theoretical speculations.

> There are two kinds of judgment, one legitimate and the other bastard. All the following belong to the bastard: sight, hearing, smell, taste, touch. The other is legitimate and is separated from this. When the bastard one is unable to see or hear or smell or taste or grasp by touch any further in the direction of smallness, but <we need to go still further> toward what is fine, <then the legitimate one enables us to carry on>... By convention [or, custom], sweet; by convention, bitter; by convention, hot; by convention, cold; by convention, color; but in reality, atoms and void.

By implication and direct assertion, Democritus' metaphysics and epistemology provide a plausible foundation for his views of the good life and the best sort of person to be. It was generally assumed by the medical scientists of his time that mental functioning was partly a function of bodily functioning, and that both were influenced by external physical and social conditions as well as by individuals' internal conditions. For example, it was believed that excessively hot and cold winds, or "violent organic motion is injurious to health in general and mental health in particular" (Vlastos 1945, p. 583). According to Democritus' theory, good health was a function of a kind of "dynamic equilibrium" or harmonious balance among the internal atoms of an individual and the external atoms of his or her environment. Excessively hot winds disorganized the routine movement of bodily atoms. Cooler winds and physical rest contributed to "a tight, stable condition of the bodily atoms," while excessively cold winds produced a kind of atomic paralysis. "A soul unbalanced by too much heat or too much cold would go out of its mind" (Vlastos

1945, p. 585). In short, all observable mental and physical disorders could be explained by unobservable disordered and discordant atomic activity, while observable human well-being could be explained by unobservable orderly and harmonious atomic activity. These views were consistent with Anaxagoras' fragment claiming that appearances provide a clue to the nature of reality and, of course, with the Pythagorean view of the importance of harmony.

Clearly, a good life implied by these principles would be a life free of excesses, guided by intelligent self-control, which were aspects of a good life later warmly endorsed by Socrates, Plato, Aristotle, and Epicurus. A fragment attributed to Democritus by Diogenes Laertius asserted that "The goal of life is cheerfulness, which is not the same as pleasure...but the state in which the soul continues calmly and stably, disturbed by no fear or superstition or any other emotion" (McKirahan 1994, p. 339). Another fragment asserted that

> Cheerfulness arises in people through moderation of enjoyment and due proportion in life. Deficiencies and excesses tend to change suddenly and give rise to large movements in the soul. Souls which undergo motions involving large intervals are neither steady nor cheerful (McKirahan 1994, p. 338).

Some commentators have interpreted Democritus' notion of "cheerfulness" as "tranquility," "unperturbedness," "calm," or "undismay," but Vlastos (1945, p. 583) thought that the state of the soul intended to be captured by "cheerfulness" was not "a passive state but...a dynamic quality, able to withstand external shock without losing its inner balance." He also claimed that fifth century BCE writers commonly assumed that pleasure was necessary for a good life. More precisely, Democritus seems to have provided a relatively more rigorous scientific account of at least some of the common sense of his time. In Vlastos' words, the philosopher found

> ...a hygienic view of pleasure ready to hand. He does not have to enunciate either the doctrine that pleasure is the normal concomitant of well-being and pain or the reverse; nor of the corollary that, therefore, the quest for pleasure should be assimilated to the discipline of the 'measure'. This latter was also implicit in the theory and practice of contemporary medicine. 'To live for pleasure' is the medical term for the haphazard, unregulated life, the negation of medical regimen. The doctor would have to advise – in the very words of Democritus... 'accept no pleasure, unless it agrees with you'. The word ...used here is the key concept of Hippocratean regimen: it denotes

what is in harmony with nature and is thus essential in preserving and restoring health. It is interesting to see that…nearly all the normative terms of Democritean ethics…are also used by the medical writers to express the conduciveness of any process or act (whether of the body itself, or of its natural environment, or of the physician) to the state of health" (Vlastos 1945, p. 587).

As explained in Michalos (2004), there is significant and sometimes troublesome overlap in the World Health Organization's robust definition of health as "complete physical, mental and social well-being" and the idea of a good quality of life or a good life, all things considered. The confounded notion of health-related quality of life and the research tradition based on that notion suffer severely from the overlaps. It is at once extremely interesting and distressing to discover the age of this particular set of problems.

Using the vocabulary introduced at the beginning of this essay, it is particularly interesting to see that Democritus and his contemporaries had the necessary conceptual tools to distinguish Real Paradise from a Fool's Paradise. In the former, cheerfulness included pleasures and these were the products of atomic activity that was sustainably harmonious, while in the latter, experienced pleasures fell short of cheerfulness and were the products of atomic activity that was not sustainably harmonious. The Real Paradise that one aimed for had equally important observable and unobservable aspects.

Democritus said that "Teaching re-forms a man, and by re-forming, makes his nature," and Vlastos (1946, p. 55) commented that "the concept of nature as itself the product of teaching and custom is not unique in Democritus. It is the common property of the age." This common notion implied that individuals were partly responsible for their own lives, and that with proper training and individual initiative, one could increase one's self-sufficiency and decrease one's vulnerability to chance mishaps. Democritus recommended "hard work" partly in the interests of obtaining these latter two goods, but also to obtain the pleasure of achievement. He was opposed to drunkenness, anger, and all kinds of self-indulgence. One of his fragments says that "One must not respect others any more than oneself, and not do evil if no one will know about it any more than if all men will. But respect yourself most of all, and let this be established as a law for your soul, so that you will do nothing unseemly" (Kahn 1998, p. 36). Dedicated scientist and philosopher that he was, he also valued wisdom of the most practical sort. "'Wisdom' is

the understanding of what is possible within the limits of what is necessary. It is, therefore, in the first place a shrewd, sharp-eyed knowledge of affairs which can 'direct most things in life'" (Vlastos 1946, p. 61).

Finally, it must be recorded that Democritus was the first philosopher to recommend downward comparisons as part of a strategy for attaining happiness. In a fragment quoted by Kahn (1998, pp. 34–35), he said,

> …one should keep one's mind on what is possible and be satisfied with what is present and available, taking little heed of people who are envied and admired and not fixing one's attention upon them, but observe the lives of those who suffer and notice what they endure, so that what you presently have will appear great and enviable and you will no longer suffer evil in your soul by desiring more than you have…[One should] compare one's life to those who are less fortunate and count oneself happy by considering what they suffer and how much better your own life is. If you hold fast to this frame of mind, you will live more cheerfully and drive not a few plagues from your life: envy and jealousy and ill-will.

Insofar as he believed that this strategy was based in some aspect of human nature, Democritus should also be regarded as the founder of downward comparison theory as elucidated, for example, in Wills (1981). Since this theory is a species of the more generic social comparison theory (Merton and Kitt 1950), Democritus may be considered the founder of the latter as well.

Plato of Athens (c. 427–347 BCE)

According to Kahn (1998, p. 43), "Plato and Socrates [469–399 BCE] have been described as a double star [by Shorey 1933] which the most powerful telescope will never succeed in resolving." According to Diogenes Laertius (2000a, p. 281), at the age of twenty, Plato attended a lecture by Socrates and thereafter became a student and a scholar in the former's Academy in Athens. Assuming there is some truth in this story, Plato might have been exposed to Socrates for 7 or 8 years, as much as a young student might be exposed to a famous and charismatic old teacher.

Since Socrates did not write anything and Plato did not publish anything in his own name but featured Socrates as the primary speaker-protagonist in most of his dialogues, it is impossible to determine exactly who said what, first and when, and what each man believed that the other did or did not believe. Since the nineteenth century, many scholars have taken a developmental approach to Plato's works, separating them into early, middle, and late dialogues, with the assumption that the early ones reveal more of the views of the historic Socrates while the middle and late ones reveal the mature views of Plato himself, articulated by a wonderfully fictionalized Socrates. In several papers and a couple of excellent books, Annas (1993, 1999) showed that the developmental approach was quite foreign to ancient scholars and that the latter generally treated the philosophical works of Plato and others as comprehensive wholes rather than discrete components produced at different stages of a person's career and subsequently patched together. For our purposes, it is not necessary to decide exactly who said what or when, or to know the biographical history of each man, though it is worthwhile to know that the historical records are far from clear.

Socrates is reported by Diogenes Laertius (2000a, pp. 149–163) to have been the son of a sculptor and a midwife, a pupil of Anaxagoras and Archelaus, a soldier who displayed courage in battle, and a man who made a "regular habit" of dancing because he thought "that such exercise helped to keep the body in good condition." Kahn (1998, p. 48) called him "the founder of classical Greek moral theory" on the grounds that he reconciled "two central themes of the Greek moral tradition," namely, "virtue" (ARETE) and "happiness" (EUDAIMONIA). Much more will be said about these "two central themes" as this review progresses. For now it is enough to notice that ARETE connoted excellence in practically any sense, e.g., a knife, horse, lute, or human being could display ARETE, each in its own relatively unique way. EUDAIMONIA, which literally means "favoured by the DAIMONES (near-gods or gods)" is usually translated as "happiness," but it connotes something closer to what people nowadays would call well-being rather than happiness. Today, in common parlance, "happiness" is very close to a perhaps extended feeling of pleasure. Because the English "happiness" is linguistically more versatile than "well-being," translators typically prefer the former, e.g., we can talk about happy people, happy lives, and happy gardening, but not well-being people, lives, and gardening. Nevertheless, modern readers should remember that our "well-being" is closer to the Greeks' "happiness" than to our "pleasure." As we will show below, the Greek words for pleasure and pain were also central to philosophical discourse about a good life. Moral philosophers working in the eudaemonist

tradition (e.g., Socrates, Plato, and Aristotle) agreed that people should reflect on their lives as a whole, discover what is most important or valuable (i.e., life's final end or TELOS), and plan and live their lives to achieve that end. According to Kahn (1998, p. 37), the notion of TELOS first appeared in Plato's dialogues and was more fully developed by Aristotle. As reported in the *Apology* (Plato 1914), Socrates was, unfortunately, condemned to death by an Athenian court for allegedly corrupting young people by persuading them to reject theological explanations in favor of naturalistic explanations of natural phenomena and by teaching them how "to make the worse case the better" along the lines of Protagoras and other Sophists. He correctly denied the truth of both charges, but that did not change the court's verdict.

Diogenes Laertius (2000a, pp. 277) claimed that Plato was the son of a mere "citizen of Athens" (his father) but was a descendent of Solon and beyond him of the god Poseidon on his mother's side. In fact, this biographer went so far as to assert on the authority of Plato's nephew, Speusippus, that Plato's real father was not Ariston, the Athenian citizen, but Apollo himself. Like the father of Jesus in the Gospel according to Matthew (which was written about 400 years after Plato's death), Ariston left his wife "unmolested" until after Plato was born. Such fantastic legends attest to the fact that Plato was recognized as quite extraordinary by his contemporaries and successors.

There are several passages in Plato's dialogues that reveal the conventional views of his contemporaries about the good life, views which he and Socrates spent their lives analyzing and usually criticizing as shallow at best and counter-productive at worst. For example, in the *Euthydemus* (Plato 1924, pp. 403–409), Socrates began his exploration by asking the purportedly "stupid" question "Do all we human beings wish to prosper?" and proceeded to explain the nature of prosperity as commonly conceived. His young listener, Cleinias, readily assents to Socrates' suggested answers to his questions.

> …since we wish to prosper, how can we prosper? Will it be if we have many good things? …of things that are, what sort do we hold to be really good?…Anyone will tell us that to be rich is good, surely?…Then it is the same with being healthy and handsome, and having other bodily endowments in plenty?…it is surely clear that good birth and talents and distinctions in one's own country are good things… What of being temperate, and just, and brave?… and where in the troupe shall we station wisdom?…[And]

Good fortune, Cleinias: a thing which all men, even the worst fools, refer to as the greatest of goods.

In the *Laws* (Plato 1926a, p. 117), Plato's Athenian Stranger says that

Men say that the chief good is health, beauty the second, wealth the third; and they call countless other things 'goods' – such as sharpness of sight and hearing, and quickness in perceiving all the objects of sense; being a king, too, and doing exactly as you please; and to possess the whole of these goods and become on the spot an immortal, that, as they say, is the crown and top of all felicity.

Plato's most detailed description of conventional views of the good life appear in Book 2 of the *Republic* (Plato 1930), where Socrates gave his account of "the origin of the city" based on meeting individual needs in the most efficient way and was provoked by Glaucon to move beyond that to a description of "the origin of a luxurious city." The following passages give the essential elements:

The origin of the city…is to be found in the fact that we do not severally suffice for our own needs, …As a result of this…we, being in need of many things, gather many into one place of abode as associates and helpers…the first…of our needs is…food…The second is housing and the third is raiment…[So there must be]…a farmer…builder… weaver…cobbler…[And because]…One man is naturally fitted for one task, and another for another…more things are produced, and better and more easily when one man performs one task according to his nature…[So there must be]…Carpenters…and smiths and many similar craftsmen…shepherds and other herders…[importers and exporters and]…others who are expert in maritime business…A market-place…and money as a token for the purpose of exchange…[and a]…class of shopkeepers… [and]…wage-earners…[The residents of such cities will recline]…on rustic beds…feast with their children, drinking of their wine…garlanded and singing hymns to the gods in pleasant fellowship…(Plato 1930, pp. 149–159)

At that point, Glaucon intervened and reminded Socrates that the residents must also have "relishes," and Socrates added,

salt…and olives and cheese; and onions and greens…figs and chickpeas and beans, and they will toast myrtle-berries and acorns…washing them down with moderate potations; and so, living in peace and health, they will probably die in old age and hand on a like life to their offspring (p. 159).

Still dissatisfied, Glaucon insisted that the city and life Socrates described would merely be adequate for "a city of pigs," and that to live well people must be able to "…recline on couches…and dine from tables and have made dishes and sweetmeats." Socrates agreed and said that a "luxurious city" might, after all, be a better place to find "the origin of justice and injustice in states," although the state he just described was "a healthy state, as it were" (p. 161). To move beyond the "healthy state," he asserted that

the requirements we first mentioned, houses and garments and shoes, will no longer be confined to necessities, but we must set painting to work and embroidery, and procure gold and ivory and similar adornments…[requiring a further enlargement of the city-state and]…the entire class of huntsmen, and the imitators, many of them occupied with figures and colours and many with music – the poets and their assistants, rhapsodists, actors, chorus-dancers, contractors – and the manufacturers of all kinds of articles, especially those that have to do with women's adornment…tutors, nurses wet and dry, beauty-shop ladies, barbers…cooks and chefs…Doctors, too,… [and]…our neighbour's land… [as the neighbours will also want our land]…if they too abandon themselves to the unlimited acquisition of wealth, disregarding the limit set by our necessary wants…We shall go to war as the next step…[implying the need for an army of professional soldiers] (pp. 161–165).

Thus, the "healthy state" would satisfy human needs without leading to war, but for a good life as conventionally conceived, a "luxurious state" would be required, which would lead to war. Clearly, Socrates and Plato must have thought, a good life as conventionally conceived left something to be desired. A good life should not imply endless wars with one's neighbors. In the *Phaedo* (Plato 1914, p. 231), Socrates explicitly asserted that

The body and its desires are the only cause of wars and factions and battles; for all wars arise for the sake of gaining money, and we are compelled to gain money for the sake of the body. We are slaves to its service.

The common sense of their contemporaries and the insatiable desires of their own bodies had to be resisted, and they made it their life's work to discover a correct account of not just *a* but *the* good life. Beyond the healthy state and the luxurious state, there must be an ideal state (KALLIPOLIS), whose form and function could serve as a model of an ideal soul and provide a clear path leading to the good life. Indeed, the historical Socrates, if accurately portrayed in the *Apology* (Plato 1914, pp. 107–109), seems to have believed that he was commanded by a god at Delphi to spend his life in philosophy, examining himself and others and making people "ashamed to care for the acquisition of wealth and for reputation and honour, when [they] neither care nor take thought for wisdom and truth and the perfection of [their souls]."

As explained above, Antiphon and Democritus believed that there was a natural connection between human well-being and experienced pleasures and pains. Generally speaking, they believed that whatever was experienced as pleasant was life-enhancing, and whatever was experienced as painful was life-destroying. Thus, a good life could be obtained by following nature's guides to human well-being. Every eudaemonist had to address this widely held and not entirely unreasonable position, and Socrates and Plato certainly provided some penetrating analyses. However, neither man was able to produce a single coherent theory of pleasure. In fact, according to Annas (1999, p. 138), "many scholars hold that...[there are]...five different theories of pleasure" in the five Platonic dialogues in which pleasure is explicitly investigated. On some view of the nature of theories, this might be true. Nevertheless, most of the evidence from all the dialogues indicates that on any theoretical view of pleasure, neither Plato nor Socrates regarded the pursuit of pleasure or a life of pleasure as a human being's final end, i.e., neither man was a hedonist. Since a life of pleasure was and apparently still is regarded by many people as an attractive aim for life as a whole, it is worthwhile to examine Plato's investigations of this option. Our review will follow the lead of the ancients and Annas in treating the Platonic corpus as a whole rather than as a developed sequence of ideas. In the end, it will be clear why "Plato's thoughts about pleasure have always been recognized as various, and as hard to make consistent" (Annas 1999, p. 5). It will also be clear that Plato was a creative genius of the highest order.

Of all Plato's discussions of the relationship of pleasure to our final end, that in the *Protagoras* comes nearest to endorsing hedonism. The relevant passages are notoriously controversial. Taylor (1998, p. 62) listed studies by 11 experts who regarded those passages as providing good evidence that Plato was at least sympathetic to hedonism at some point in his life and by 12 others who regarded them merely as accurate reports of hedonism as he understood it (see above, "Protagoras"). We believe the latter, majority view is accurate, and that in those passages Plato was only doing what any good philosopher would do, namely, presenting a theory for consideration as fully and faithfully as possible, regardless of his or her commitment to it.

Fortunately, however, we do not have to settle this troublesome issue here.

In this dialogue, Socrates began by getting the Sophist Protagoras to admit "that some pleasant things are not good, and also that some painful things are not bad and some are, while a third class of them are indifferent – neither bad nor good" (Plato 1924, pp. 223–225). This in itself is hardly an auspicious beginning for someone aiming to establish the reasonableness of hedonism as a theory of the good life. The two philosophers then agreed that "most people" think that "while a man often has knowledge in him, he is not governed by it, but by something else – now by passion, now by pleasure, now by pain, at times by love, and often by fear" (p. 227). They decided to show that the commonly held idea of "being overcome by pleasure" (AKRASIA) was "erroneous." This would be a strange undertaking for a hedonist, since such people believe that pleasure is precisely the final end that is supposed to triumph over all others.

Pursuing more deeply the idea of "being overcome by pleasure," Socrates claimed that allegedly pleasant but bad things like certain "food or drink or sexual acts" are not regarded as bad in virtue of the pleasure they produce. Pleasure, delight, or enjoyment themselves are uniformly good in themselves. Rather, such things are regarded as bad only if

> ...later on they cause diseases and poverty, and have many more such ills...[and] in causing diseases they cause pains...And in causing poverty they cause pains...[In short,] the only reason why these things are evil is that they end at last in pains, and deprive us of other pleasures...[Similarly, such painful things as] physical training, military service, and medical treatment conducted by cautery, incision, drugs, or starvation...are good...because later on they result in health and good bodily condition, the deliverance of cities, dominion over others, and wealth...[things which] end at last in pleasures and relief and riddance of pains (Plato 1924, pp. 229–233).

Notice, first, that the goods and ills listed in the quotation are the classic, common sense bodily and external ones, e.g., health and wealth versus disease and poverty. There is no mention of the cardinal virtues, justice, courage, temperance, or wisdom. Second, the common sense goods are supposed to be pursued for the equally common sense purposes of getting pleasure and avoiding pain. Most importantly, Socrates has led his listeners to the conclusion that if the pleasurable is good and the painful is bad or evil, then AKRASIA would imply, for example, that "a man does evil, knowing it to be evil and not having to do it, because he is overcome by the good" (p. 237), or what is equally absurd, a man does what is painful, knowing it to be painful and not having to do it, because he is overcome by what is pleasant, i.e., in the interest of or forced by pleasure he knowingly chooses pain. So, the doctrine of AKRASIA had to be rejected.

Among pleasures and pains, at this point in this dialogue, Socrates thought that variations could only be assessed "when the one is greater and the other smaller, or when there are more on one side and fewer on the other" (Plato 1924, p. 237). So, for example, weighing pleasures and pains, one would naturally prefer greater and/or more pleasures to smaller and/or fewer pleasures and the latter to pains of any size or numbers. He did not suggest that people should calculate what we now call "discount rates" according to which the proverbial bird in hand might be worth more than two or more in the bush, but he did observe that regarding "size," "thickness and number," and "sounds," things appear "greater when near and smaller when distant" (p. 239). To address this problem, he recommended precise measurement. In language that would have warmed the hearts of hedonists from Bentham (1789) to Kahneman (1999) (not to mention number-crunching social indicators researchers), he wrote,

> Now if our welfare consisted in doing and choosing things of large dimensions, and avoiding and not doing those of small, what would be our salvation in life? Would it be the art of measurement [METRITIKI TECHNE], or the power of appearance? Is it not the latter that leads us astray…and many a time causes us to take things topsy-turvy…whereas the art of measurement would have made this appearance ineffective, and by showing us the truth would have brought our soul into the repose of abiding by the truth, and so would have saved our life. Would men acknowledge, in view of all this, that the art which saves our life is measurement, …[indeed, not merely measurement but] knowledge [EPISTEME] of measurement, … the salvation of our life depends on making a right choice of pleasure and pain – of the more and the fewer, the greater and the smaller, and the nearer and the remoter – is it not evident…(Plato 1924, pp. 239–241).

Of course, there is nothing here about applying measurement to produce the greatest net pleasure, happiness, or good for the greatest number as in the utilitarians Bentham (1789) and Mill (1863), but a clearer defense of hedonism could not have been made. Granting all of the above, Socrates was able to show that it is not pleasure that leads people astray but

…that it is from defect of knowledge that men err, when they do err, in their choice of pleasures and pains – that is, in the choice of good and evil; and from defect not merely of knowledge but of the knowledge…of measurement. And surely…the erring act committed without knowledge is done through ignorance. Accordingly 'to be overcome by pleasure' means just this – ignorance in the highest degree…Then surely, … no one willingly goes after evil or what he thinks to be evil; it is not in human nature, apparently, to do so – to wish to go after what one thinks to be evil in preference to the good; and when compelled to choose one of two evils, nobody will choose the greater when he may the lesser (Plato 1924, pp. 243–247).

Annas (1999, p. 158) commented on the extraordinary nature of all these passages as follows:

> Nowhere else in Plato is the function of reason, in shaping the happy life, taken to be that of playing a purely instrumental role in enabling us to maximize pleasure as that is ordinarily conceived. Nowhere else is pleasure, as that is ordinarily conceived, taken to be something which can be taken up uncriticized and untransformed into the happy life. In all the other four dialogues [which deal with pleasure at length] pleasure is an element which appears greatly altered in the final product. The *Protagoras* passage, in which the ordinary notion of pleasure becomes our final end and has reason to serve it, is thus exceptional. However, it has chanced to fit in well with post-utilitarian theories of pleasure to such an extent that its eccentricity as a Platonic position tends to escape us.

In Plato's *Gorgias* (Plato 1925a), there are at least four arguments against the view that the good or happy life (i.e., well-being) for a human being is identical to a pleasurable life, or briefly, that pleasure is the final end (TELOS). First, Socrates suggested an analogy between the satisfaction of human needs producing experienced pleasure and filling an empty jar with water. Insofar as one's needs are not met, one experiences pain, which is removed as one's needs are met. We will call this the "needs satisfaction theory of pleasure." It is a primitive ancestor of Maslow's (1954) well-developed theory. Using this theory of the source if not the nature of pleasure, Socrates claimed that aiming at a life of pleasure would be like aiming at a life forever filling a "leaky jar." Since one of his acceptability criteria for a good life was self-sufficiency or near self-sufficiency for individuals and communities, positing a final end that was inherently dependent on continuous replenishment was obviously unacceptable (Plato 1925a, pp. 415–419). Self-sufficiency or near self-sufficiency is a highly regarded trait going all the way back to Homer's heroes. Clearly, the needs satisfaction theory of pleasure and the self-sufficiency criterion of acceptability for a good life were incompatible. As we will see below, alternative theories of pleasure were introduced in other dialogues.

Second, Socrates asserted that because it is possible to experience pleasure and pain at the same time (e.g., as the pain of being thirsty is removed by the pleasure of drinking) but "it is impossible to be badly off, or to fare ill, at the same time as one is faring well," it follows that "enjoyment is not faring well, nor is feeling pain faring ill, so that the pleasant is found to be different from the good" (Plato 1925a, pp. 429–431). Third, he claimed that because "the foolish and the wise, and the cowardly and the brave, feel pain and enjoyment about equally" but only "the wise and brave [are] good, and the cowards and fools bad," there must be a difference between feeling enjoyment and being good as well as feeling pain and being bad, and therefore, a difference between a life of pleasure and a good life (Plato 1925a, pp. 435–439).

A fourth argument in the *Gorgias* began with the assumption that "bodies," "figures," "colors," "music," "laws, and observances" are said to be "fair…either in view of their use for some particular purpose that each may serve, or in respect of some pleasure arising… [from them, i.e., either because they are] beneficial or pleasant or both" (Plato 1925a, pp. 353–355). Next, Socrates asserted that if something is fair, it is good, "For that is either pleasant or beneficial" (p. 363). Finally, then, observing that it is not pleasant "to be medically treated…But it is beneficial" (p. 369), it follows immediately that things in general and life as a whole in particular may be fair, good, and beneficial but not pleasant. So, a good life cannot be identical to a pleasant life.

Plato's *Philebus* (Plato 1925b) contains a rich array of novel classifications and distinctions among pleasures, old and new arguments against the idea that pleasure could be the final end for human beings, old and new suggestions about the role of measurement in the search for a good life, and two direct rejections of hedonism. Beginning with the last item in this list, Socrates summarized several pages of the dialogue with the remark that

> Philebus says that pleasure is the true goal of every living being and that all ought to aim at it, and that therefore this is also the good for all, and the two designations 'good' and 'pleasant' are properly and essentially one; Socrates, however, says that they are not one, but two in fact as in name, that the good and the pleasant differ from one another in nature, and that wisdom's share in the good is greater than pleasure's (Plato 1925b, pp. 373–375).

As we saw above, apparently for the sake of accurately reporting a hedonist's position, in the *Protagoras*, Socrates defended the thesis attributed to Philebus in this passage and rejected the thesis he defended here. So far as anyone knows today, Philebus is an unknown and possibly fictional proponent of hedonism. About twenty pages later, at the very end of the dialogue, Socrates concluded that

> Philebus declared that pleasure was entirely and in all respects the good…[But] I, perceiving the truths which I have now been detailing, and annoyed by the theory held not only by Philebus but by many thousands of others, said that mind [NOUS] was a far better and more excellent thing for human life than pleasure (Plato 1925b, p. 397).

Searching for "the nature of any class," Socrates and the young Protarchus, who was trying to decide whether or not he should be a hedonist, agreed that they should examine "the greatest things" rather than the smallest. Accordingly, they proceeded to investigate those pleasures "which are considered most extreme and intense." Assuming that the greatest pleasures "gratify the greatest desires" and that such desires are often possessed by

> …people who are in a fever, or in similar diseases, feel more intensely thirst and cold and other bodily sufferings which they usually have; and …feel greater want, followed by greater pleasure when their want is satisfied… [it follows that] to discover the greatest pleasures [they] should have to look, not at health, but at disease…[as well] greater pleasures…in intensity and degree [may be found] in riotous living…intense pleasure holds sway over the foolish and dissolute even to the point of madness and makes them notorious…and if that is true, it is clear that the greatest pleasures and the greatest pains originate in some depravity of soul and body, not in virtue (Plato 1925b, pp. 323–325).

The theory implicit in the assumption that the greatest pleasures "gratify the greatest desires" is simply the theory that pleasure is produced by the satisfaction of desires or wants, i.e., pleasurable affect is the effect of people getting what they desire or want. We will call this the "desire satisfaction theory of pleasure." It is an ancestor of Lewin et al.'s (1944) aspiration theory. Since it is unlikely that anyone would imagine that a life of "riotous living" leading to "madness" and "depravity of soul and body" could be the final end, highest good, and best life for a human, it is unlikely that anyone holding this theory would be attracted to hedonism.

Among the assumptions made in the *Philebus* to show that "the good and the pleasant differ," there is the familiar needs satisfaction theory of pleasure and the self-sufficiency criterion of acceptability for a good life. Applying the self-sufficiency criterion, early in the dialogue Socrates considered the question of whether a "life of pleasure" or a "life of wisdom" could be "the good" or the good life, and rapidly concluded that neither option would be acceptable. After all, a life of enjoyment of which one had no knowledge and a totally joyless life of wisdom would each leave something to be desired and would, therefore, not be self-sufficient or choice-worthy (Plato 1925b, pp. 233–239).

Besides the needs and desire satisfaction theories of pleasure, in the *Philebus*, Socrates apparently accepts a slightly different theory (with roots extending at least to Pythagoras) based on harmony, which I will call the "harmony theory of pleasure." Without attempting to unravel all the metaphysical niceties and definitions suggested in the text, the basic ideas are that

> …when, in us living beings, harmony is broken up, a disruption of nature and a generation of pain also take place at the same time…But if harmony is recomposed and returns to its own nature, then I say that pleasure is generated, …[So, for examples, hunger is] a kind of breaking up and a pain…And eating, which is a filling up again, is a pleasure…Then, too, the unnatural dissolution and disintegration we experience through heat are a pain, but the natural restoration and cooling are a pleasure (Plato 1925b, pp. 271–273).

There are clear echoes in these passages of the views of Pythagoras and Democritus regarding ordered, natural harmony and its natural products of experienced pleasure and pains in all "living beings." Although there is a difference between refilling empty vessels whose natural state is supposed to be full and recomposing decomposed parts of naturally whole entities, the two theories about the natural origins of pleasure and pain seem to have fit fairly comfortably together in Plato's mind. In describing the pain of hunger and the pleasure of its termination, he moved from the relatively atomistic language of "breaking up" to the replenishment language of "filling up." Presumably, then, on both of these theories of pleasure, if human beings aimed for and successfully reached their natural state as a final end, they could count on it being pleasurable. However, neither theory would justify the

pursuit of pleasure itself as a final end, i.e., neither theory would justify hedonism.

By a somewhat different path, these two theories of pleasure led to another reason for rejecting hedonism. The argument began with Socrates reminding Protarchus that they had "often heard it said of pleasure that it is always a process or generation and that there is no state or existence of pleasure" (Plato 1925b, p. 351). There is no hint of who said it, but it seems to be a consequence of the processes of producing pleasure according to both theories. Socrates then remarked that

> one part of existences always exists for the sake of something, and the other part is that for the sake of which the former is always coming into being…One is the generation of all things (the process of coming into being), the other is existence or being (Plato 1925b, p. 353).

Of these two sorts of things, "generation for the sake of being" and "being for the sake of generation," Socrates believed that the former made more sense as, for example, "shipbuilding is for the sake of ships" while "ships" do not exist "for the sake of shipbuilding." Quite generally, then, he concluded that

> …every instance of generation is for the sake of some being or other, and generation in general is for the sake of being in general…[Furthermore, and crucially] that for the sake of which anything is generated is in the class of the good, and that which is generated for the sake of something else…must be placed in another class…Then if pleasure is a form of generation, we shall be right in placing it in a class other than that of the good (Plato 1925b, p. 355).

Thus, if pleasure is in some "class other than that of the good," it cannot be a candidate for the "highest end," and the hedonists are wrong in positing pleasure as our final end and a life of pleasure as the best sort of life.

Along the lines of our distinction between a Fool's Paradise and Real Paradise, in the *Philebus*, Plato distinguished "real pleasures" from "false pleasures." Just as some people have opinions "not based upon realities," although the opinions themselves are real enough, Socrates said that "pleasure and pain stand in the same relation to realities." More precisely,

> …he who feels pleasure at all in any way or manner always really feels pleasure, but it is sometimes not based upon realities, whether present or past, and often, perhaps most frequently, upon things which will never even be realities in the future (Plato 1925b, pp. 305–307).

"True pleasures" later turn out to be identical to "pure," "unmixed," and "real pleasures," After asserting that he did "not in the least agree with those who say that all pleasures are merely surcease from pain," Socrates gave several examples of "true pleasures," i.e., pleasures which naturally arise although "the want of which is unfelt and painless, whereas the satisfaction furnished by them is felt by the senses, pleasant, and unmixed with pain" (Plato 1925b, p. 343). The examples include pleasures

> ...arising from what are called beautiful colours, or from forms, ...and sounds...[with] beauty of form...[meaning] the straight line and the circle and the plane and solid figures formed from these...For I assert that the beauty of these is not relative...but they are always absolutely beautiful by nature and have peculiar pleasures in no way subject to comparison with the pleasures of scratching; ...those sounds which are smooth and clear...are beautiful, not relatively, but absolutely, and that there are pleasures which pertain to these by nature and result from them...pleasures of smell are a less divine class; ...And further let us add to these the pleasures of knowledge, if they appear to us not to have hunger for knowledge or pangs of such hunger as their source (Plato 1925b, pp. 343–345).

Clearly, then, we have here a fourth theory of the origin and nature of pleasures, for these "true pleasures" do not involve meeting needs, satisfying desires, or reconstituting harmonies. Rather they are, for example, the direct products of things that are naturally "absolutely" beautiful eliciting natural feelings of pleasure, joy, or delight. We will call this the "true pleasures theory" to distinguish it from the other three. If it was not obvious before, Socrates has made it clear in these passages that "true pleasures" are ontologically distinct from others, since they "are in no way subject to comparison with the pleasures of scratching," i.e., they are not supposed to be comparable to the pleasures arising either from meeting needs, satisfying desires, or reconstituting harmonies.

Unfortunately, almost immediately, Socrates compared the incomparable "true pleasures" to others and found the former to be superior. Arguing from analogy, he claimed that just as the purest, "unadulterated" whiteness "is both the truest and the most beautiful of all whitenesses," it must be the case that "any pleasure, however small or infrequent, if uncontaminated with pain, is pleasanter and more beautiful than a great or often repeated pleasure without purity" (Plato 1925b, pp. 349–351). Nevertheless, he never argued that the pursuit of such pleasure could be or should be one's final end.

Another path leading to the rejection of hedonism proceeds from the observation that there is a neutral state between pleasure and pain. Supposing that pain is generated by some sort of "destruction" of one's natural state and pleasure is generated by some sort of "restoration," Socrates noticed that there is a third condition between these two in which one would "necessarily be devoid of any feeling of pain or pleasure, great or small" (Plato 1925b, p. 277). He reminded Protarchus that they agreed that anyone "who chose the life of mind and wisdom was to have no feeling of pleasure, great or small," though he did not add at this point in the dialogue that earlier they also agreed that a life totally devoid of pleasure would never "appear desirable...to anyone" (Plato 1925b, p. 237). At this point, Socrates apparently found such a life very "desirable," for he asserted that someone choosing "the life of mind and wisdom" would be choosing "the most divine of lives" because, as Protarchus said, "it is not likely that gods feel either joy or its opposite" (Plato 1925b, p. 277). Whatever else one makes of this position, it must be granted that it implies that a life in the neutral state between pleasure and pain would be superior to that of a life of pleasure and that, therefore, the hedonists' view of our final end or best sort of life is mistaken. It also implies that one might live a virtuous life without pleasure, i.e., that pleasure is not a necessary product or supervening property of a virtuous life, contrary to claims made by Socrates elsewhere.

After thoroughly destroying hedonism as a plausible account of our final end or the good life for human beings, and inconsistently making the case for a life of wisdom, Plato tried to construct a positive view that would meet his criterion of self-sufficiency. He avowed, first, that it was absurd "to say that there is nothing good in the body or many other things, but only in the soul, and that in the soul the only good is pleasure, and that courage and self-restraint and understanding and all the other good things of the soul are nothing of the sort" (Plato 1925b, p. 357). That is, he accepted the traditional, common sense view that there are goods of the body (e.g., health), external goods (e.g., wealth) and goods of the soul (e.g., wisdom).

Next, he divided all arts into two kinds, one of which involved relatively exact measurements (e.g., arithmetic, building) and the other not (e.g., music). Within each of these kinds, he made an additional distinction yielding, for example, an arithmetic "of the people" and "of philosophers." The latter was supposed to possess a "higher degree of clearness and purity," e.g., the philosopher's "art of dialectic" was supposed to deal with "the truest kind of knowledge," which is "knowledge which has to do with being, reality, and eternal immutability," Those engaged in this art were engaged in the "contemplation of true being" (Plato 1925b, pp. 361–367), and such investigations were regarded as superior to those of the natural philosophers like Anaxagoras before him and Epicurus after him. The latter dealt with things that had "no fixedness whatsoever" and, therefore, yielded no "certainty."

Finally, then, reminding Protarchus of their agreement that "wisdom's share in the good is greater than pleasure's," that whoever "possesses the good...has no further need of anything, but is perfectly sufficient," that knowledge of immutable reality is superior to all other kinds of knowledge, and that a "mixed life" with pleasure and wisdom would be superior to an "unmixed life" of either pleasure or wisdom, Socrates concluded that the good life they sought, described now as "the most adorable life" (p. 379), must involve some sort of "mixture" or combination of elements. Into the "mixture," he was forced to include not only theoretical knowledge of immutable reality but also practical knowledge (e.g., about "building houses"), "perfect knowledge of our individual selves," "truth," "music" although "it is full of guesswork and imitation and lacked purity," "true and pure pleasures...and also those which are united with health and self-restraint, and...all those which are handmaids of virtue in general...but as for the pleasures which follow after folly and all baseness, it would be very senseless for anyone who desires to discover the most beautiful and the most restful mixture or compound...to mix these with mind" (Plato 1925b, pp. 379–387). Our two philosophers agreed, then, that this "mixture" or "compound" brought them to "the vestibule of the good and of the dwelling of the good" (p. 289).

From "the vestibule," Socrates perceived that a mixture containing all the right elements but lacking an appropriate "measure and proportion" of each one would be "in truth no compound, but an uncompounded jumble" (p. 389). Accordingly, he asserted that

> ...the power of the good has taken refuge in the nature of the beautiful; for measure and proportion are everywhere identified with beauty and virtue...Then if we cannot catch the good with the aid of one idea, let us run it down with three – beauty, proportion and truth, and let us say

> that these, considered as one, may more properly than all other components of the mixture be regarded as the cause, and that through the goodness of these the mixture itself has been made good (Plato 1925b, pp. 389–391).

The sense in which the three elements "beauty, proportion, and truth" could properly "be regarded as the cause" of the total set of elements required for a good life (i.e., the total "mixture" or "compound") is not entirely clear. Plato seems to have assumed that this subset of elements was in some way uniquely constitutive and/or determinant of the whole set. He may also have assumed that the subset was that for the sake of which the total set of good things existed or would be "choiceworthy." In any case, it seems fair to say that the total "mixture" or "compound" of elements of "the good" or of a good life, of which the three-element subset could be "regarded as the cause," is as close to a complete account of "the good" or of a good life as Plato ever produced.

Several themes from the dialogues just reviewed appeared again in Plato's magnum opus, *Republic*, e.g., the four theories of pleasure (need satisfaction, desire satisfaction, harmony, and true pleasures), the insufficiency of pleasure or wisdom alone as the final end, and the idea of a neutral state between pleasure and pain. In Book 9 of the *Republic*, Socrates referred to the neutral state as a state of "calm," and used it to explain the difference between "real" or "true" and "apparent" pleasures. When someone moves from a "state of calm" to a "state of pain," he said, they are likely to misperceive and misdescribe the former state as a "state of pleasure," and similarly, a move from a "state of calm" to a "state of pleasure" would likely produce a judgment that the former state was a "state of pain." However, "there is nothing sound in these appearances," and the "true," "real," or "pure" pleasures are not "preceded by pain" (Plato 1992a, b, pp. 254–255).

The central questions of the *Republic* are concerned with the nature of the best sort of life to live, the good life, "the life that for each of us would make living most worthwhile" (Plato 1930, p. 71) and more precisely, whether "the life of the just man is more profitable" than that of the unjust man (p. 83) or "whether it is also true that the just have a better life than the unjust and are happier" (p. 101). As the central questions are phrased, it is clear that the aim is to discover the most advantageous sort of life for individuals from the point of view of their own self-interest. Insofar as the specific question became that of the relation between living "the life of the just man" and living the life most advantageous from the point of view of one's own self-interest, the problem became profoundly moral and difficult. The problem became moral because "the life of the just man" implied some concern for others, a concern that as conventionally understood might be not only beyond but also directly opposed to one's own self-interest. The problem of reconciling such concerns (for others and self) was undoubtedly at least as difficult in the fourth century BCE as it is now.

To address the basic problem and noticing that "there is the justice [DIKAIOSUNE] of a single man and also the justice of a whole city," Plato's Socrates adopted the strategy of examining "the larger thing" in the interest of understanding "the smaller" (Plato 1992a, b, p. 43). Earlier we reviewed his story of the "origin of the city" in general, as well as the "healthy" and "luxurious" cities. It was suggested that "luxurious" cities might be better places to find "the origin of justice and injustice in states." Plato's ideal cities were populated with relatively unidimensional people, more unidimensional than one might have expected after reading his account of the variety of people populating the cities of the origins stories. Applying the general principle that "one man is naturally fitted for one task," he imagined finally three broad classes of people in the ideal city, namely, a class of "producers" consisting of "money-lovers," a class of "guardians" consisting of "honor-lovers," and a class of "rulers" consisting of "wisdom-lovers" (philosophers), selected from the cream of the "guardians." Reflecting on the virtues of courage, moderation, wisdom, and justice, Socrates concluded that in the ideal city, as they have "heard many people say and have often said" themselves, "justice is doing one's own work and not meddling with what isn't one's own" (Plato 1992a, b, p. 108). Accordingly, if justice in "the larger" city is similar to justice in "the smaller" human soul, one ought to find structures and functions in the latter similar to those in the former, i.e., one ought to find that souls have three parts with three distinct functions, with justice in the soul similar to justice in the city.

Immediately, Socrates asserted that "It would be ridiculous for anyone to think that 'spiritedness,' 'love of learning,' and 'love of money' did not come from 'individuals'" (Plato 1992a, b, p. 111). The deeper question is whether such things come from one or more parts of individuals. Since "the same thing [cannot] be,

do, or undergo opposites, at the same time, in the same respect, and in relation to the same thing," but people often have appetites for things they choose to resist and passions they would rather not have, Socrates thought that such kinds of opposition could not proceed from a soul without distinct parts. Thus, he concluded (for the first time, according to Frede 2003, p. 11) that human souls have three parts and called

> ...the part of the soul with which it calculates the rational part and the part with which it lusts, hungers and thirsts, and gets excited by other appetites the irrational appetitive part...[and] the spirited part [that] by which we get angry...[and which is] by nature the helper of the rational part, provided that it hasn't been corrupted by bad upbringing (Plato 1992a, b, pp. 112–116).

Therefore, on the analogy of the nature of justice in the city given the city's structure and functions, he concluded that justice in the human soul must occur when "each part is doing its own work" and the rational part is allowed to rule, "since it is really wise and exercises foresight on behalf of the whole soul, and for the spirited part to obey and be its ally" (p. 117). Justice in the city and in the human soul is the great harmonizer, bringing disparate parts together so that they become "entirely one, moderate and harmonious," and injustice is "a kind of civil war between the three parts" (p. 119).

Insofar as justice in the city and the soul is supposed to function in the same way to produce harmony and reduce discord, justice in each place and the interests of individuals and communities are mutually supportive. A well-ordered city led by wisdom-loving rulers supported by honor-loving and money-loving citizens who know their place and appropriately play out their roles is the perfect sort of city for individuals with similarly well-ordered souls to flourish. Individuals with well-ordered souls whose spirit and appetites are led by reason will be at peace with themselves and will, therefore, be inclined to contribute to the common good, recognizing it as essential for their own well-being. In Book 6 of the *Republic*, Socrates lamented the fact that because there were no cities with constitutions "suitable for philosophers," anyone with a "philosophic nature" had it "perverted and altered," but if someone with the appropriate nature "were to find the best constitution, as it is itself the best, it would be clear that it is really divine and that other natures and ways of life are merely human" (Plato 1992a, b, p. 171). Thus, such is the interdependent relationship between an ideal city and an ideal individual that it is impossible for the latter to exist apart from the former. This is about as much of a reconciliation between the interests of any individual and the public interest, self and other, as one could hope to have.

Besides imagining that human souls had three distinct parts with distinct functions, Socrates believed that the successful performance of the distinct functions yielded distinct kinds of pleasures. Citizens who know their place and appropriately play out their fairly rigidly prescribed and circumscribed roles are supposed to get distinct kinds of pleasures. We will call this the "class theory of pleasure." Since there was no clear distinction between human characteristics resulting from inheritance versus good upbringing and education, "class" is used here only to reflect the general sense of Plato's idea. In his words,

> ...there are three primary kinds of people: philosophic, victory-loving, and profit-loving...And also three forms of pleasure, one assigned to each of them...if you chose to ask three such people in turn to tell you which of their lives is most pleasant, each would give the highest praise to his own...Then, since there's a dispute between the different forms of pleasure and between the lives themselves, not about which way of living is finer or more shameful or better or worse, but about which is more pleasant and less painful,...[we should apply criteria of] experience, reason and argument [to settle the dispute] (Plato 1992a, b, pp. 251–252).

Supposing that everyone has some experience of having some kinds of victories and making some profits, but "the pleasure of studying the things that are cannot be tasted by anyone except a philosopher," Socrates concluded that

> The praise of a wisdom-lover and argument-lover is necessarily truest. Then, of the three pleasures, the most pleasant is that of the part of the soul with which we learn, and the one in whom that part rules has the most pleasant life (Plato 1992a, b, pp. 252–253).

Since Plato's Socrates would have been as aware as everyone else of the fact that any school child experiences the pleasure of learning, the philosopher's pleasure that he was referring to in these passages was that achievable only by the select few of guardians who had roughly 10 years of training in liberal arts, 5 additional years of training in dialectic, 15 years of public administration, and "Then, at the age of 50, those who've survived the tests and been successful both in practical matters and in the sciences...[and have] seen the good itself, ...must each in turn put the city, its citizens, and

themselves in order, using it as their model" (Plato 1992a, b, pp. 211–212).

As we have seen, the content of this "model," of "the good" itself, was far from clear. In the middle Books of the *Republic*, Plato presented his metaphysical theory of the ideal "forms" which was apparently intended to provide a general context or ontological scheme forming the foundation of his ethical and political theories. Since the general theory and the nature of the "forms," as well as their precise connection to his other theories and views are all relatively unclear, they have been omitted from this discussion.

Summarizing the general case he tried to make in the *Republic* for pursuing justice in one's own soul and city in terms of traditionally accepted good by-products that would have been attractive to any Greek familiar with his work, Plato wrote,

> From every point of view, then, anyone who praises justice speaks truly, and anyone who praises injustice speaks falsely. Whether we look at the matter from the point of view of pleasure, good reputation, or advantage [or profit], a praiser of justice tells the truth, while one who condemns it has nothing sound to say and condemns without knowing what he is condemning...[Furthermore,] this is the original basis for the conventions about what is fine and what is shameful...Fine things are those that subordinate the beastlike parts of our nature to the human – or better, perhaps, to the divine; shameful ones are those that enslave the gentle to the savage (Plato 1992a, b, p. 261).

In brief, in these passages Plato justified the pursuit of justice in terms of self-interest as his contemporaries, and perhaps ours, understood it. If one were unfamiliar with the rest of his work, one might think these passages were written by someone who regarded "pleasure, good reputation, or advantage" as capturing our final end or the best life for a human being, with "justice" as merely a significant means. In the presence of as much of his total corpus as we have seen here, however, one would have to conclude that, like "pleasure," he regarded "good reputation" and "advantage" as mere "handmaids of virtue in general," i.e., things that served the interest of virtue, making it more attractive and easier to embrace. For Plato, our final end or best sort of life included a rich mixture of things hierarchically ordered with virtue in its various forms at the top.

No new theories of pleasure are introduced in Plato's last work, the *Laws* (Plato 1926a, b), and the function of pleasure is mainly that of a "handmaid." Early in Book 1, the Athenian Stranger described "pleasures and pains" as "the two fountains which gush out by nature's impulse" and produce happiness to "whoever draws from them a due supply at the due place and time...but whososever does so without understanding and out of due season will fare contrariwise" (Plato 1926a, pp. 42–43). Thus, the final end is well-being in the fairly robust sense of EUDAIMONIA, and one is enabled to reach that end by following pleasures and pains that are guided by understanding [EPISTEME]. Lest anyone missed his points about the place and role of pleasure in this scenario, the Stranger added the remark that

> ...each of us...possesses within himself two antagonistic and foolish counsellors, whom we call by the names of pleasure and pain...and opinions about the future...and in addition to all these there is 'calculation' [LOGISMOS], pronouncing which of them is good, which bad; and 'calculation', when it has become the public decree of the State, is named 'law' (p. 67).

Thus, an individual's own power of reason supported by a community's reason articulated in its laws guide the naturally "foolish counsellors" "pleasure and pain" to human well-being.

In Book 5 of the *Laws*, the Stranger summarizes his case for living a virtuous and noble life in terms of a package of by-products similar to that offered by Plato's Socrates in the *Republic*. Personal "advantage," which usually implied material wealth, is not mentioned explicitly in the package, but "nobility" would have had the same implication.

> The temperate, brave, wise, and healthy lives are more pleasant than the cowardly, foolish, licentious and diseased. To sum up, the life of bodily and spiritual virtue, as compared with that of vice, is not only more pleasant, but also exceeds greatly in nobility, rectitude, virtue and good fame, so that it causes the man who lives it to live ever so much more happily [EUDAIMONESTERON] than he who lives the opposite life (Plato 1926a, p. 347).

So, for Plato in the *Laws*, the final end or best life as a whole for humans was a happy life, which in his eudemonistic terms was virtuous in all its forms, healthy, noble, experienced as pleasant, and justifiably famous. Although he occasionally described such a life as "dear to God," insofar as "like is dear to like" (Plato 1926a, p. 295) and his philosophy certainly had what Annas (1999, p. 163) called "an unworldly streak," when all the features of the total package of goods constituting the good life are taken into account, it is a life that would still be attractive to people with fairly conventional values.

Anonymous Iamblichi (c. 400 BCE)

Some of the most astute observations about the relations of conventional laws and justice (NOMOI) to the laws of nature (PHYSIS) may be found in fragments attributed to a relatively obscure author known as Iamblichus. Simply put, he claimed, first, that because human beings are naturally disposed to pursue their own interests and pleasures and that the strong would naturally serve themselves at the expense of the weak, the latter have a natural interest in forming political communities and subjecting their activities to a set of laws which, by common consent, were supposed to provide justice for all participants. Secondly, however, he claimed because nobody would be strong enough to guarantee his or her own protection, let alone justice, in the presence of great masses of people, however weak they might be individually, even the very strong have a natural interest in living in communities governed by rules of justice. In short, conventional laws are firmly rooted in human nature, and they are neither unnecessary nor artificial.

Iamblichus believed that the implications of living in communities that have good laws and law-abiding people (i.e., communities characterized by EUNOMIA) are quite different from those characterized by the opposite qualities (i.e., by ANOMIA). The following passages describe the sorts of social capital he envisioned:

> In the first place, trust arises from EUNOMIA, and this benefits all people greatly and is one of the great goods. For as a result of it, money becomes available and so, even if there is little it is sufficient since it is in circulation... Fortunes and misfortunes in money and life are managed most suitably for people as a result of EUNOMIA. For those enjoying good fortune can use it in safety and without danger of plots, while those suffering ill fortune are aided by the fortunate...Through EUNOMIA...the time people devote to PRAGMATA [a word which can mean 'government', 'public business', or 'troubles'] is idle, but that devoted to the activities of life is productive. In EUNOMIA people are free from the most unpleasant concern and engage in the most pleasant, since concern about PRAGMATA is most unpleasant and concern about one's activities is most pleasant. Also, when they go to sleep, which is a rest from troubles for people, they go to it without fear and unworried about painful matters, and when they rise from it they have other similar experiences...Nor...do they expect the day to bring poverty, but they look forward to it without fear directing their concern without grief towards the activities of life, ... And war, which is the source of the greatest evils for

people...comes more to those who practice ANOMIA, less to those practicing EUNOMIA (McKirahan 1994, pp. 406–407).

Social indicators researchers will be struck by the fact that Iamblichus cited trust as the very first benefit to members of societies characterized by EUNOMIA, since measures of trust are probably the most frequently used indicators of social capital today (Van de Walle et al. 2005). Following trust, many familiar observable and unobservable features of a good life appear in the quotation, i.e., money and financial security, personal safety, freedom to pursue and enjoy the pleasures of one's special interests and activities, absence of worries and fears, peaceful and restful sleep, hopefulness for the future, and freedom from war.

In passages following the above quotation, Iamblichus described the implications of living in communities characterized by ANOMIA, which are essentially the opposites of those above. Besides being populated by people living with mistrust, fear, and insecurity, such communities are the seedbeds for tyranny because those people have desperate needs for relief and turn to apparently strong but often unscrupulous leaders. In the end, as he remarked in the beginning, Iamblichus was sure that nobody would ever be strong enough to prevent the great masses of people from casting out tyrants and bringing justice for all.

Aristotle of Stageira (c. 384–322 BCE)

Judged by the impact of his works on scholars across many centuries and continents, it is arguable that Aristotle was the most influential philosopher who ever lived. He was the son of a Macedonian physician named Nicomachus, who served king Philip, father of Alexander the Great, a sometime student of Aristotle. Since Aristotle studied and worked with Plato for 20 years (367–347 BCE) at the latter's Academy in Athens, they shared some views. However, when Plato died in 347 BCE, the leadership of his Academy passed to his nephew, Speusippus, not to Aristotle. The latter moved on and in 334, established his own school in Athens called the Lyceum.

According to Aristotle (1999, p. xiv), "the nearly complete modern English translation of Aristotle's extant works (in [The Revised Oxford Translation]) fills about 2,450 pages," though many works are lost.

Discussions of the good life appear prominently in five treatises, namely, *Eudemian Ethics*, *Nicomachean Ethics*, *Magna Moralia*, *Rhetoric*, and *Politics*. The *Eudemian Ethics* and *Nicomachean Ethics* are the first couple of relatively long and systematic theoretical treatises ever written on ethics. While they are attributed to Aristotle, in both cases the texts were apparently assembled from students' notes and present problems of internal coherence. The *Eudemian Ethics* is generally regarded as the earlier of the two volumes, and three of its Books, 4–6, are identical to Books 5–7 in the *Nicomachean Ethics*. The *Magna Moralia* seems to be genuinely Aristotelian, but of lesser importance and it is not considered here.

Some of the most frequently quoted passages in the history of philosophy come from the *Nicomachean Ethics* and concern our topic directly. For example,

> Every craft and every line of inquiry, and likewise every action and decision, seems to seek some good; that is why some people were right to describe the good as what everything seeks. But the ends [that are sought] appear to differ; some are activities, and others are products apart from the activities. Wherever there are ends apart from the actions, the products are by nature better than the activities...
>
> Suppose, then, that the things achievable by action have some end that we wish for because of itself, and because of which we wish for the other things, and that we do not choose everything because of something else – for if we do, it will go on without limit, so that desire will prove to be empty and futile. Clearly, this end will be the good, that is to say, the best good...
>
> What is the highest of all the goods achievable in action? As far as the name goes, most people virtually agree; for both the many and the cultivated call it happiness [EUDAIMONIA], and they suppose that living well and doing well are the same as being happy. But they disagree about what happiness is, and the many do not give the same answer as the wise (Aristotle 1999, p. 3).

As this essay demonstrates, the situation was even more complicated than Aristotle's remarks suggest, for "the wise" had significantly different views among themselves. However, it is clear from Aristotle's phrase "that living well and doing well are the same as being happy" that he is not talking about a mere extended feeling of pleasure. In fact, shortly after the passages quoted above, he wrote,

> The many, the most vulgar, would seem to conceive the good and happiness as pleasure, and hence they also like the life of gratification. In this they appear completely slavish, since the life they decide on is a life for grazing animals (Aristotle 1999, p. 4).

Regarding views of "the many," Aristotle's best account is given in the *Rhetoric* and runs as follows:

> ...for the sake of illustration, let us ascertain what happiness, generally speaking, is, and what its parts consist in; ...Let us then define happiness [EUDAIMONIA] as well-being combined with virtue, or independence of life, or the life that is most agreeable combined with security, or abundance of possessions and slaves, combined with power to protect and make use of them; for nearly all men admit that one or more of these things constitutes happiness. If, then, such is the nature of happiness, its component parts must necessarily be: noble birth, numerous friends, good friends, wealth, good children, numerous children, a good old age; further bodily excellences, such as health, beauty, strength, stature, fitness for athletic contests, a good reputation, honour, good luck, virtue. For a man would be entirely independent, provided he possessed all internal and external goods; for there are no others. Internal goods are those of mind and body; external goods are noble birth, friends, wealth, honour. To these we think should be added certain capacities and good luck; for on these conditions life will be perfectly secure. Let us now in the same way define each of these in detail. Noble birth... (Aristotle 1926, pp. 47–49).

These passages are merely the beginning of several pages of more detailed definitions of components and/or conditions of a happy life or of a life of someone "living well and doing well." Logically speaking, Aristotle was not as tidy as one would have preferred in constructing his definitions, and he was no more adept than we are at sorting out components or constituents from conditions or determinants of happiness. However, he certainly provided an excellent list of candidates for components and conditions of happiness. What's more, as a report of the common views of his contemporaries (i.e., "the many"), he gave us a gem of sociological and psychological observation. For present purposes, one should notice especially that there are relatively few items in his list that most people today would exclude from our list, e.g., slaves certainly and possibly noble birth and numerous children. In the latter cases, most people today might list some children and perhaps at least a middle class birth. Presumably, only relatively young people would be interested in "fitness for athletic contests." Regarding slaves, although most of us today reject while Aristotle and most of his contemporaries accepted the institution of slavery, "From Homer on, being captured into slavery was a paradigm of human disaster, a brutal form of bad luck" (Williams 1993, pp. 197–198). I suppose this would not be an extraordinary view today and that, therefore, the idea

of being a slave has been universally unattractive across all these years.

After the pages of definitions of components and conditions of happiness, Aristotle proceeded to define "good" and to list things that are good according to his definition. Presumably, in these passages he is still giving us the views of "the many."

> "Let us assume", he wrote, "good to be whatever is desirable for its own sake, or for the sake of which we choose something else; that which is the aim of all things, or of all things that possess sensation or reason;...and that whose presence makes a man fit and also independent; and independence in general; and that which produces or preserves such things...The virtues...must be a good thing; for those who possess them are in a sound condition, and they are also productive of good things and practical...Pleasure also must be a good; for all living creatures naturally desire it. Hence it follows that both agreeable and beautiful things must be good; ...Happiness [EUDAIMONIA], since it is desirable in itself and self-sufficient...justice, courage, self-control, magnanimity, magnificence, and all other similar states of mind, for they are virtues of the soul. Health, beauty, and the like, for they are virtues of the body and produce many advantages;...Wealth...A friend and friendship...honour and good repute...Eloquence and capacity for action... natural cleverness, good memory, readiness to learn, quick-wittedness, and all similar qualities...the sciences, arts, and even life, for even though no other good should result from it, it is desirable in itself. Lastly, justice, since it is expedient in general for the common weal" (Aristotle 1926, pp. 59–63).

Although the list appears here to end with "justice," Aristotle continues for some pages listing things regarded as good by his contemporaries. It seems to us that our contemporaries would regard all the good things in this list as still good. Apparently, then, if Aristotle and we are accurate in our judgments about the conventional wisdom of our contemporaries, there are some great similarities of views across nearly 2,500 years. Of course, there are some fairly well-known differences as well, e.g., most of our contemporaries would not endorse or enjoy denying a variety of human rights to females and foreigners, watching slaves fighting to the death, reading the entrails of dead animals, sacrificing bulls to gods, and so on. A complete list of such items might reveal more differences than similarities, but there is no need to produce such a list now. For present purposes, it is more important to examine the views of one of the most illustrious "wise" men of Aristotle's time, namely, Aristotle himself.

Aristotle was by all accounts one of the most conventional of all ancient philosophers, always respectful of previous and current thinkers and mindful of the need to appropriately contextualize his own contributions. For example, in Book 1 of the *Nicomachean Ethics* he tells his readers that "the facts harmonize with a true account" of any particular subject and that "all the features that people look for in happiness appear to be true of the end described in our account" (Aristotle 1999, p. 10). Nevertheless, his own views were not entirely consistent with conventional wisdom. Indeed, as Annas (1993, p. 331) remarked quite generally,

> ...ancient [ethical] theories are all more or less revisionary, and some of them are highly counter-intuitive. They give an account of happiness which, if baldly presented to a non-philosopher without any supporting arguments, sounds wrong, even absurd. This consequence is frequently evaded because it is assumed that ancient ethical theories are morally conservative, concerned to respect and justify ancient ethical intuitions without criticizing or trying to improve them. But this assumption is false, ... all the ancient theories greatly expand and modify the ordinary non-philosophical understanding of happiness, opening themselves to criticism from non-philosophers on this score.

Regarding Aristotle's revisionism in particular, Annas (1993, p. 431) wrote,

> Ancient debates about virtue and happiness are recognizably debates about the place of morality in happiness;... Aristotle revises the commonsense notion of happiness in insisting that virtue is necessary for happiness: health, wealth and the goods of popular esteem cannot make a person's life satisfactory. Our lives will only achieve a final end which is complete and self-sufficient – the aim that we all inchoately go for, and try to make precise through philosophy – if our aims and actions are subordinated to, and given their roles and priorities by, a life of virtuous activity: a life, that is, lived in a moral way, from a disposition to do the morally right thing for the right reason, and with one's feelings endorsing this. Nonetheless, happiness requires external goods as well.

Let us, then, briefly review Aristotle's post-reflective, philosophical views about the good or happy life. Following conventional wisdom, he seems to have accepted the notion that some sort of independence is necessary for a good life. He introduced two technical terms to capture this idea, "completeness" and "self-sufficiency," using the following definitions:

> We say that an end pursued in its own right is more complete than an end pursued because of something else, and that an end that is never choiceworthy because of something else is more complete than ends that are choiceworthy both in their own right and because of this end. Hence, an end that is always choiceworthy in its own

right, never because of something else, is complete without qualification.

> Now happiness [EUDAIMONIA], more than anything else, seems complete without qualification. For we always choose it because of itself, never because of something else. Honor, pleasure, understanding, and every virtue we certainly choose because of themselves, since we would choose each of them even if it had no further result; but we also choose them for the sake of happiness, supposing that through them we shall be happy. Happiness, by contrast, no one ever chooses for their sake, or for the sake of anything else at all.

> The same conclusion [that happiness is complete] also appears to follow from self-sufficiency. For the complete good seems to be self-sufficient...we regard something as self-sufficient when all by itself it makes a life choiceworthy and lacking nothing; and that is what we think happiness does (Aristotle 1999, pp. 7–8).

In other words, Aristotle apparently believed that, in the first place, one chooses to live a particular way of life because one regards that way as not requiring anything beyond itself. Today, we might say that it is both sustainable and worthy of being sustained, e.g., we choose understanding because it is good in itself but also because it contributes to our general well-being, to "living well and doing well." If someone asked, "But why do you choose to live well and do well?" we might wonder if the questioner understood English, because the question seems to presuppose that the alternative of preferring to live poorly and do poorly is reasonable. It is, after all, a logical truism that living well and doing well is better than living poorly and doing poorly, just as breathing well is better than breathing poorly.

Granting this, Aristotle recognized that the formal conditions of completeness and self-sufficiency lacked content, and that "we still need a clearer statement of what the best good is" for a human being. He provided this content, as Plato did before him, essentially by assuming that just as every part of a human being has some characteristic function which may be performed well or poorly, so human beings themselves may be said to have some function, and their "best good" would be obtained by performing that function excellently.

> What, then, could this [characteristic function] be? For living is apparently shared with plants, but what we are looking for is the special function of a human being; hence we should set aside the life of nutrition and growth. The life next in order is some sort of life of sense perception; but this too is apparently shared with horse, ox, and every animal.

The remaining possibility, then, is some sort of life of action of the [part of the soul] that has reason…We have found, then, that the human function is activity of the soul in accord with reason or requiring reason…Now, each function is completed well by being completed in accord with the virtue proper [to that kind of thing]. And so the human good proves to be activity of the soul in accord with virtue, and indeed with the best and most complete virtue, if there are more virtues than one. Moreover, in a complete life. For one swallow does not make a spring, nor does one day; nor, similarly, does one day or a short time make us blessed and happy. This, then is a sketch of the good; for, presumably, we must draw the outline first, and fill it in later (Aristotle 1999, pp. 8–9).

Unfortunately, both the *Nicomachean Ethics* and the *Eudemian Ethics* do not provide unambiguous guides to filling in that "sketch." Readers are sometimes confused by Aristotle's use of the two terms "blessed" and "happy," but they are practically synonyms in both volumes. However, in both volumes there is a significant discrepancy between the position offered in the last books and all the others. In the last books of each of these volumes, the best sort of life is one of contemplation. In Book 8 of the *Eudemian Ethics*, it is contemplation of God, i.e.,

any mode of choice and acquisition that either through deficiency or excess hinders us from serving and from contemplating God – that is a bad one…Let this, then, be our statement of what is the standard of nobility and what is the aim of things absolutely good (Aristotle 1952, p. 477).

In Book 10 of the *Nicomachean Ethics*, it is intellectual contemplation.

If happiness is activity in accord with virtue, it is reasonable too for it to accord with the supreme virtue, which will be the virtue of the best thing. The best is understanding, or whatever else seems to be the natural ruler and leader, and to understand what is fine and divine, by being itself either divine or the most divine element in us. Hence complete happiness will be its activity in accord with its proper virtue; and we have said that this activity is the activity of study…

For this activity is supreme, since understanding is the supreme element in us, and the objects of understanding are the supreme objects of knowledge.

Further, it is the most continuous activity, since we are more capable of continuous study than any continuous action.

Besides, we think pleasure must be mixed into happiness; and it is agreed that the activity in accord with wisdom is the most pleasant of the activities in accord with virtue…Moreover, the self-sufficiency we spoke of will be found in study more than in anything else. For admittedly the wise person, the just person, and the other virtuous people all need the good things necessary for life. Still, when these are adequately supplied, the just

person needs other people as partners and recipients of his just actions; and the same is true of the temperate person, the brave person, and each of the others. But the wise person is able, and more able the wiser he is, to study even by himself; and though he presumably does it better with colleagues, even so he is more self-sufficient than any other [virtuous person]…

[Besides] the activity of understanding, it seems, is superior in excellence because it is the activity of study, aims at no end apart from itself, and has its own proper pleasure, which increases the activity…Hence, a human being's complete happiness will be this activity, if it receives a complete span of life, since nothing incomplete is proper to happiness…as far as we can, we ought to be pro-immortal, and go to all lengths to live a life in accord with our supreme element…

Moreover, each person seems to be his understanding, if he is his controlling and better element…For what is proper to each thing's nature is supremely best and most pleasant for it; and hence for a human being the life in accord with understanding will be supremely best and most pleasant, if understanding, more than anything else, is the human being. This life, then, will also be happiest (Aristotle 1999, pp. 163–165).

These passages clearly reveal several respects in which some sort of intellectual activity, translated as "the activity of study" and identified with "the activity of understanding" here, satisfies Aristotle's conditions for a good or happy life. Perhaps, it would be even more accurate to say that it is excellence (i.e., virtue or ARETE) in study and/or understanding that gives the happiest life according to these passages. Compared to all other kinds of virtuous activity, "study" and/or "understanding" are relatively more complete, self-sufficient, continuously sustainable, engaged in for their own sake across the whole of one's life, and most closely related to the essential feature of human beings.

The idea that a happy or good life would involve "a complete span of life" was central to most ancients' views. According to Annas, for ancient ethicists,

…the entry point for ethical reflection [was]…the agent's reflection on her life as a whole, and the relative importance of her various ends. This contrasts strongly with modern theories, for which hard cases and ethical conflicts are often taken to be the spur to ethical thinking…Ancient ethics takes its start from what is taken to be the fact that people have, implicitly, a notion of a final end, an overall goal which enables them to unify and clarify their immediate goals. Ethical theory is designed to enable us to reflect on this implicit overall goal and to make it determinate. For, while there is consensus that our final end is happiness (*eudaimonia*), this is trivial, for substantial disagreement remains as to what happiness consists in (Annas 1993, pp. 11–12)

To a social indicators/quality of life researcher, one of the most striking features of Annas' excellent review of ancient ethical theories is the relative frequency with which the phrase "life as a whole" occurs. A rough count indicated that it occurred about 90 times in 455 pages, i.e., on average, once every five pages. Since the most frequently studied and measured aspect of people's lives in the social indicators movement over the past 30 years has been satisfaction or happiness with life as a whole (Michalos 2005), we seem to have been following a very old and distinguished tradition. There is, however, a difference in the connotation of "life as a whole" for the ancients and us. For the ancients, the phrase is used to provoke reflection on the whole of one's life from birth to death, while for us, it is used primarily to provoke reflection on all the salient domains or features of one's life as currently lived. In Michalos (1985) and later publications, for example, the life satisfaction question asked, "How do you feel about your life as a whole right now?" and the assumption of the simple linear, bottom-up explanation of responses to this question was based on the idea that respondents would reflect on the satisfaction currently obtained from the specific domains or features of their lives (e.g., satisfaction obtained from jobs, friends, family relations, and so on) and somehow calculate an answer that appropriately takes all the salient domains or features into account. It is possible that some respondents would mix the ancient with the contemporary connotation of "life as a whole" and craft their responses to our question based on a somewhat different array of things from birth to death, but there was little evidence of this.

Contrary to the somewhat academic, contemplative good lives sketched in the final chapters of the *Nicomachean Ethics* and *Eudemian Ethics*, the preceding chapters of both treatises sketch good lives requiring considerably more variety. In Book 1 of the former, readers are told that "a human being is a naturally political animal" (Aristotle 1999, p. 8). In Book 6, one finds that "Political science and prudence are the same state, but their being is not the same" (p. 92). A few pages earlier, "It seems proper to a prudent person to be able to deliberate finely about things that are good and beneficial for himself, not about some restricted area…but about what sorts of things promote living well in general" (p. 89).

In Book 1 of the *Politics*, Aristotle provided a naturalistic account of the origin of city-states that runs from the natural unions of men and women "for the sake of procreation" and natural rulers and natural slaves "for the sake of survival" to households "to satisfy everyday needs," to villages promising still greater security, and finally, to city-states "for the sake of living well." City-states are characterized as "complete communities" displaying "total self-sufficiency" (Aristotle 1998, pp. 2–3). An ordinary human being cannot flourish outside of a city-state. "Anyone who cannot form a community with others," he says, "or who does not need to because he is self-sufficient, is no part of a city-state – he is either a beast or a god" (p. 5). Clearly, then, Aristotle's requirement for self-sufficiency in a good or happy life is not absolute, but relative to a community which would be absolutely self-sufficient. Being able to live in such a community constitutes an important external good. The similarities between his and Plato's views on community and individual interdependence are striking.

According to Annas (1993, p. 151),

> Aristotle is saying here that our lives…will be lacking in something important if we are not functioning parts of a city-state. Only in this context can we 'live well' rather than just living; for only this form of community demands of us what we would call *political* abilities. If we do not take part in a political community of equals, and live as active citizens, our lives will not develop as they would naturally have done – that is, they will be in some way stunted.

Several times in the *Nicomachean Ethics* Aristotle insisted on the necessity of external goods for a completely happy life. For example, after noting that "happiness is… activity in accord with virtue," he wrote,

> Nonetheless, happiness evidently also needs external goods to be added, as we said, since we cannot, or cannot easily, do fine actions if we lack the resources. For, first of all, in many actions we use friends, wealth, and political power just as we use instruments. Further, deprivation of certain [externals] – for instance, good birth, good children, beauty – mars our blessedness. For we do not altogether have the character of happiness if we look utterly repulsive or are ill-born, solitary, or childless; and we have it even less, presumably, if our children or friends are totally bad, or were good but have died. And so, as we have said, happiness would seem to need this sort of prosperity added also (Aristotle 1999, p. 11).

A few pages later, he asked, "Why not say that the happy person is one whose activities accord with complete virtue, with an adequate supply of external goods, not for just any time but for a complete life?" (Aristotle 1999, p. 14).

Aristotle recognized that people naturally have some virtue, e.g., from birth people may be more or less brave, temperate, and just. But the sort of virtue that concerned him most was that because of which a person's actions might be regarded as praiseworthy or blameworthy, i.e., typically actions for which one is personally responsible or actions voluntarily and freely chosen. He thought that if one adds understanding in the form of prudence to natural virtue, one may obtain "full virtue." For example, one might be naturally bright and admired for that, but if a naturally bright person has sufficient prudence to study hard enough to become wise beyond nature's gift, such a person would be praiseworthy. It is this sort of excellence or virtue (ARETE) realized in and through an agent's deliberately chosen activity that Aristotle regarded as necessary for a good life. The development of such virtue was described as similar to the development of a skill or craft (TECHNE) insofar as one becomes a skilled craftsperson by deliberately engaging in some activities, with one's understanding of them increasing as one's skill improves. Thus, a fully virtuous person would do the right thing fully understanding that and why it is right, all things considered.

He distinguished the "possession" or "state" of virtue from "using" or the "activity" of virtue, and insisted that the former or mere capacities for action could not be sufficient for a good or happy life. After all, he remarked, "someone may be in a state that achieves no good – if, for instance, he is asleep or inactive in some other way" (Aristotle 1999, pp. 10–11). In his view, the good life was a life of "unimpeded" action proceeding from certain appropriate states and appropriately enjoyed.

> For actions in accord with the virtues to be done temperately or justly it does not suffice that they themselves have the right qualities. Rather, the agent must also be in the right state when he does them. First, he must know [that he is doing virtuous actions]; second, he must decide on them, and decide on them for themselves; and, third, he must also do them from a firm and unchanging state (Aristotle 1999, p. 22).

All things considered, Aristotle's characterization of a good or happy life is the clearest example we have from the ancients of the view that the quality of a person's or of a community's life is a function of the actual conditions of that life and what a person or community makes of those conditions. Conceptually, he could clearly distinguish Real Paradise and Hell from a Fool's Paradise and Hell.

Most importantly, he regarded all four cases as essentially and objectively involving human action that would be praiseworthy or blameworthy. A good or happy life is not simply given by nature, God, or gods. It requires internal and external gifts and good luck beyond our control, but it also requires individual and communal initiative. For example, individuals naturally have the capacity to reason and to act bravely and justly more or less. With the right education, training, and hard work, one may come to exercise these capacities excellently. A good or happy life, according to Aristotle, is achieved exactly insofar as one deliberately engages in the unimpeded excellent exercise of one's capacities for the sake of doing what is fine, excellent, or noble (KALON), provided that the deliberation and activities are undertaken from a developed disposition (i.e., a virtuous character) and accompanied by an appropriate amount of external goods and pleasure. In short, a good or happy life consists of a harmonious mixture of internal and external goods in the first place, and regarding the former, an equally harmonious mixture of reason, appetite, and emotion. From his perspective, a discordant or inactive life would not be worth living and the idea of a happy scoundrel would be an oxymoron.

Epicurus of Samos (c. 341–271 BCE)

According to Diogenes Laertius (2000b, p. 529), Epicurus was born on the island of Samos, the son of Athenian citizens and moved to Athens around 306 BCE when he was 18. If the dates of his birth and death are accurate, he was born about 7 years after Plato's death and 19 years before Aristotle's death. The same source reported that "his bodily health was pitiful" (Diogenes 2000a, b, p. 525) and provided a quotation from Epicurus' letter to Idomeneus saying that he had "continual sufferings from strangury and dysentery" (Diogenes (2000b, p. 549).

Dewitt (1967, p. 3) described him as

> …the most revered and the most reviled of all founders of thought in the Graeco-Roman world…The man himself was revered as an ethical father, a savior, and a god. Men wore his image on finger-rings; they displayed painted portraits of him in their living rooms; the more affluent honored him with likenesses in marble. His handbooks of doctrine were carried about like breviaries; his sayings were esteemed as if oracles and committed to memory as

if Articles of Faith. His published letters were cherished as if epistles of an apostle…On the twentieth day of every month his followers assembled to perform solemn rites in honor of his memory, a sort of sacrament.

He and his ideas were "the special targets of abuse" by Platonists, Stoics, Christians, and Jews (DeWitt 1967, p. 3). Critics claimed that Epicurus was a sophist since he aided his itinerant school teacher father for a fee, that he plagiarized his atomic theory from Democritus, that he was an adulterer who also had frequent relations "with many courtesans," "vomited twice a day from over-indulgence," was "a preacher of effeminacy," a sycophant, atheist, name-caller, drug dealer, and critic of other people's work without having any original ideas of his own (Diogenes 2000a, b, pp. 531–537). Still, at the end of his summary of the views of Epicurus' critics, Diogenes Laertius said that all "these people are stark mad" (p. 537).

As evidence against Epicurus' critics, Diogenes Laertius (2000b, pp. 537–541) provided plenty of direct quotations from the philosopher contradicting charges of his critics and claimed that the

> philosopher has abundance of witnesses to attest his unsurpassed goodwill to all men – his native land, which honoured him with statues in bronze; his friends,…his gratitude to his parents, his generosity to his brothers, his gentleness to his servants…and in general, his benevolence to all mankind…Friends…came to him from all parts and lived with him in his garden…a very simple and frugal life…In his correspondence he himself mentions that he was content with plain bread and water…and a little pot of cheese, that, when I like, I may fare sumptuously.

DeWitt (1967, p. 6) reported that the total extant body of Epicurus' works consists of "a booklet of 69 pages," although Diogenes Laertius (2000b, p. 555) claimed that the philosopher "eclipsed all before him in the number of his writings…[which amounted] to about 300 rolls, and contain not a single citation from other authors." While none of his writings is complete, Book X of Diogenes Laertius' text contains substantial parts of four of them. Of these four, three are written to his disciples. The *Letter to Herodotus* is a summary of Epicurus' physics and/or metaphysics, the *Letter to Pythocles* deals with astronomy and meteorology, and the *Letter to Menoeceus* deals with ethics. The fourth treatise contains his 40 "Principal" or "Authorized Doctrines," of which "almost all are contradictions of Plato" (DeWitt 1967, p. 48) . These four works are conveniently collected in a single volume edited by

Inwood et al. (1994), which also includes some of the "so-called 'Vatican Sayings'…[which] is a mixture of sayings from Epicurus and other Epicureans" discovered in the Vatican Library, and Testmonia of other scholars, some of which were hostile to his philosophy, like Cicero and Plutarch.

Epicurus' school in Athens was called "the Garden" and was not very different from Plato's Academy and Aristotle's Lyceum. They contained the residences of the founders and disciples, a library, and some lecture rooms. The emphasis of the curricula at the three schools was different. The island of Samos was politically and culturally very much an Ionian community, making it scientifically and technologically progressive. Besides Epicurus, among the famous names associated with Ionia were Anaximander, Thales, Anaxagoras, Pythagoras, Heraclitus, Hippocrates, and Asclepius.

As we will see in greater detail shortly, Epicurus believed that the chief end or aim of human beings was peace of mind or tranquility (ATARAXIA) and a healthy body (APONIA). Metaphorically speaking, he compared the "turmoils of the soul" with "storms and squalls at sea" (DeWitt 1967, p. 226). For present purposes, what has to be emphasized is that he regarded scientific knowledge and methods as the essential vehicles for the journey to peace of mind and a healthy body. Near the end of his *Letter to Herodotus* he wrote, "Further, we must hold that to arrive at accurate knowledge of the cause of things of most moment is the business of natural science, and that happiness depends on this…(Diogenes 2000a, b, p. 607). In this sentence and many others, "happiness" is used to translate MAKARIOS, which sometimes is closer to "blessed" in English, but is often interchangeable in Greek with EUDAIMONIA (Aristotle 1999, p. 318). At the beginning of his *Letter to Menoeceus* he wrote, "So we must exercise ourselves in the things which bring happiness [EUDAIMONIA], since, if that be present, we have everything, and, if that be absent, all our actions are directed toward attaining it" (Diogenes 2000a, b, p. 649).

At the beginning of his *Letter to Pythocles* he wrote,

> In your letter to me,…you try, not without success, to recall the considerations which make for a happy life… you will do well to take and learn…the short epitome in my letter to Herodotus…remember that, like everything else, knowledge of celestial phenomena…has no other end in view than peace of mind and firm conviction. We do not seek to wrest by force what is impossible, nor

to understand all matters equally well, nor make our treatment always as clear as when we discuss human life or explain the principles of physics in general...: our one need is untroubled existence (Diogenes 2000a, b, pp. 613–615).

Concerning the use of the science of "celestial phenomena," Epicurus was convinced that inattention to facts and diverse possible naturalistic explanations combined with attention to mythology and religion were jointly responsible for troubled minds. The following passages are representative of many more as he worked his way through possible naturalistic explanations of such "celestial phenomena" as the sun, moon, turnings of the sun and moon, regularity of orbits, variations in the lengths of days and nights, stars, clouds, rain, thunderbolts, winds, hail, and so on:

> All things go on uninterruptedly, if all be explained by the method of plurality of causes in conformity with the facts, ...But when we pick and choose among them [explanations], rejecting one equally consistent with the phenomena, we clearly fall away from the study of nature altogether and tumble into myth...Those who adopt only one explanation are in conflict with the facts and are utterly mistaken as to the way in which man can attain knowledge...always keep in mind the method of plural explanation and the several consistent assumptions and causes...[For example,] Clouds may form and gather either because the air is condensed under the pressure of winds, or because atoms which hold together and are suitable to produce this result become mutually entangled, or because currents collect from the earth and the waters; and there are several other ways in which it is not impossible for the aggregations of such bodies into clouds may be brought about (Diogenes 2000a, b, pp. 615–627).

The upside of his adherence to the "method of plurality of causes" was that it freed him and those who followed him from troublesome beliefs such that natural phenomena like "solstices, eclipses, risings and settings, and the like" were the result of "the ministration or command, either now or in the future, of any being who at the same time enjoys perfect bliss along with immortality" (Diogenes 2000a, b, p. 607). Although he believed that "God is a living being immortal and blessed" and that "verily there are gods" (p. 649), he did not appeal to such beings to account for natural phenomena. The downside, of course, was that many contemporary and later theists regarded such views as heresy.

While he did not need an invisible God or gods to create and maintain the regularities perceived everywhere, like Democritus before him, he did need invisible "atoms and the void." Early in his *Letter to Herodotus* he affirms the standard assumption that "nothing comes into being out of what is non-extant." Since there are clearly bodies that move, there must be space for them to move in. Some bodies are "composite," made up of "elements" that have "weight," "vary indefinitely in their shapes," are "indivisible and unchangeable, and necessarily so"...[and]...the sum of things is unlimited both by reason of the multitude of the atoms and the extent of the void." As in Democritus, both human bodies and souls are composites of different sorts of atoms, and when people die their atoms are totally dispersed.

Some atoms are "in continual motion through all eternity" moving linearly "upward *ad infinitum*" or "downward," some moving in a vibratory fashion in composites or compounds, some swerving a bit inexplicably, and others swerving as a result of human beings' free choices (Diogenes 2000a, b, pp. 569–593). While randomly swerving atoms might account for collisions and aggregations or combinations, it is unclear why or how they would account for free choice. In any event, freely chosen activities creating swerving atoms were posited as necessary for people to be accountable and held responsible for their own actions. There was nothing comparable to swerves in Democritus' physics or metaphysics, which made his world thoroughly deterministic and incapable of supporting an institution of morality such that some actions would be morally praiseworthy and others morally blameworthy. Regardless of all Epicurus' condemnations of mythology and "the gods worshipped by the multitude," in the interests of ensuring that people are the free agents of their own future, he was even more critical of a thoroughly deterministic physics. Thus in his *Letter to Menoeceus* he wrote,

> Destiny, which some introduce as sovereign over all things, he [who follows Epicurus' teaching] laughs to scorn, affirming rather that some things happen of necessity, others by chance, others through our own agency. For he sees that necessity destroys responsibility and that chance or fortune is inconstant; whereas our own actions are free, and it is to them that praise and blame naturally attach. It were better, indeed, to accept the legends of the gods than to bow beneath that yoke of destiny which the natural philosophers have imposed...the misfortune of the wise is better than the prosperity of the fool. It is better, in short, that what is well judged in action should not owe its successful issue to the aid of chance (Diogenes 2000a, b, 659).

So, the rabbit of free human agency was pulled out of the apparently thoroughly deterministic hat of his own physics and metaphysics. He may have been the first to perform this trick, but he was certainly not the last. To be clear, atomic swerves were probably not the uncaused causes of free choice as Cicero claimed (Inwood et al. 1994, pp. 47–51). Rather, at least some swerves were the effects of free choice (free human volition) on atoms.

The peace of mind or tranquility that Epicurus insisted as the final aim for humans was in some ways similar to and in others different from all those who came before him. In his introductory material preceding the three letters, Diogenes Laertius (2000b, p. 543) said that "in his correspondence" Epicurus "replaces the usual greeting, 'I wish you joy,' by wishes for welfare and right living, 'May you do well' and 'Live well.'" This is practically the same language we saw Aristotle using earlier, i.e., "for the many and the cultivated...suppose that living well and doing well are the same as being happy." Aristotle's emphasis on "internal goods...of mind and body" and "external goods" like "wealth and honour" is similar to views expressed by Epicurus. For example, to Menoeceus he wrote,

> We must also reflect that of desires some are natural, others are groundless; and that of the natural some are necessary as well as natural, and some natural only. And of the necessary desires some are necessary if we are to be happy [EUDAIMONIA], some if the body is to be rid of uneasiness, some if we are even to live. He who has a clear and certain understanding of these things will direct every preference and aversion toward securing health of body and tranquility of mind, seeing that this is the sum and end of a blessed life (Diogenes 2000a, b, p. 653).

Between Epicurus' letters to Pythocles and Monoeceus, Diogenes Laertius inserted a list of characteristics of "the wise man," providing his readers with an aid "to the conduct of life, what we ought to avoid and what to choose" (p. 643). While some would be affirmed by "the many and the cultivated" Greeks of his day (and by many people today), some would be challenged and rejected.

> There are three motives to injurious acts among men – hatred, envy, and contempt; and these the wise man overcomes by reason...He will be more susceptible of emotion than other men; that will be no hindrance to his wisdom...Even on the rack the wise man is happy...[he will not] punish his servants... fall in love... trouble himself about funeral rites... make fine speeches...[engage in] sexual indulgence...marry and rear a family... drivel,

when drunken... take part in politics... make himself a tyrant...[or commit suicide] when he has lost his sight... [He will] take a suit into court...leave written words behind him...have regard to his property and to the future...never give up a friend...pay just so much regard to his reputation as not to be looked down upon... be able to converse correctly about music and poetry, without however actually writing poems himself...will make money, but only by his wisdom...be grateful to anyone when he is corrected...found a school...give readings in public, but only by request...on occasion die for a friend (Diogenes 2000a, b, pp. 643–647).

Supposing that "the wise man" is better than average at "living well and doing well," it appears that such a person would find the quality of life good if it were free of mental and physical pain, full of like-minded friends, and intellectually stimulating. In fact, this is the sort of life Epicurus and his disciples probably would have had in the privacy of his residence and school, "the Garden." It is worth noting, however, that Epicurus' view represents something of a turning point in ancient views of the political and social dimensions of human happiness. Contrary to Aristotle's recommendation to actively engage life and the world in all its diversity in the pursuit of excellence, Epicurus recommended a relatively passive and contemplative life in pursuit of a healthy body and peace of mind. Plato, Antiphon, and others, like Aristotle, take the "doing well" portion of the formula to mean significant demands for social engagement. Even the trust required by Antiphon to constitute social capital requires an active collective effort to maintain just institutions (EUNOMIA). But for Epicurus, such pursuits are apt to be vexatious and perhaps even painful, frustrating, or futile. How much better to turn away and enter the comfortable enclave of the Garden with one's philosophical friends and colleagues? This could be seen as representing the final defeat of the aristocratic trend in Greek ethics: Now, virtually anybody is capable of "doing well," in principle, regardless of their station in life.

What, then, is the nature and role of pleasure in the good life envisioned by Epicurus? We have seen that Plato, Aristotle, and Epicurus often refer to the final aim or end of life as happiness, although the happiness they are referring to is not exactly the same thing. On the role of pleasure, there appears to be a fundamental difference between the views of Plato and Aristotle on the one hand and Epicurus on the other. For the former, pleasure was at best a "handmaiden to virtue" and never the final goal. However, in his *Letter to Monoeceus* Epicurus claimed that

We call pleasure the alpha and omega of a blessed life. Pleasure is our first and kindred good. It is the starting-point of every choice and of every aversion, and to it we come back, inasmuch as we make feeling the rule by which to judge of every good thing (Diogenes 2000a, b, p. 655).

To this direct quote from Epicurus, Diogenes Laertius (2000b, p. 663) adds this: "And we choose the virtues too on account of pleasure and not for their own sake, as we take medicine for the sake of health."

The trouble is that when Epicurus describes the nature of pleasure, it seems to be inextricably joined to virtue. To Monoeceus he wrote,

When we say, then, that pleasure is the end and aim, we do not mean the pleasures of the prodigal or the pleasures of sensuality, as we are understood to do by some through ignorance, prejudice, or willful misrepresentation. By pleasure we mean the absence of pain in the body and of trouble in the soul…it is sober reasoning, searching out the grounds of every choice and avoidance, and banishing those beliefs through which the greatest tumults take possession of the soul. Of all this the beginning and the greatest good is prudence [PHRONESIS]…from it spring all the other virtues, for it teaches that we cannot lead a life of pleasure which is not also a life of prudence, honour, and justice; nor lead a life of prudence, honour, and justice, which is not also a life of pleasure. For the virtues have grown into one with a pleasant life, and a pleasant life is inseparable from them (Diogenes 2000a, b, p. 657).

Taking these passages literally, the analogy of medicine and health is inaccurate. It would be more accurate to say that the relation between pleasure and the virtues is analogous to that between health and a good life. Health is clearly instrumentally valuable for a good life, but also intrinsically valuable and hence, constitutive of a good life, as Aristotle recognized. Sen (1999, pp. 36–37) makes a similar point about freedom.

Annas noticed that the connection Epicurus made between pleasure and virtues was also made by John Stuart Mill in *Utilitarianism* over 2,000 years later.

Mill …fully realizes that in claiming that pleasure is the agent's *summum bonum* he runs into the problem of completeness. He regards it as comparatively simple to show that happiness (by which he explicitly means pleasure and the absence of pain) is desirable as an end; but he has to show something far harder, namely that happiness thus conceived is the *only* thing desirable as an end. In particular, he recognizes that he has to square this with the recognition that we seek the virtues for their own sake. His solution is to expand the notion of happiness in such a way that seeking the virtues for their own sake counts as seeking happiness, since doing the former counts as part of being happy (Annas 1993, p. 339).

At another point, Annas clearly indicates the importance of these expansions for the morality of the hedonists' position.

So if, as Epicurus holds, pleasure is our complete final end, and we also need real friendships, then…We need, in our lives, real friendships, which may sometimes involve caring about others as much as about ourselves. What gives this its point in our lives is ultimately pleasure. But this does not lead to selfishness, or to viewing friendship instrumentally; for pleasure as our final end has been expanded to include the pleasure from genuine other-concern. The argument is, as the Epicureans saw, exactly the same as with the virtues; the pleasure we seek is expanded so that we achieve it precisely by having non-instrumental concern for virtuous action and the interests of others (Annas 1993, p. 240).

This is certainly ethics without tears. If caring for others gave most people as much pleasure as caring for oneself, the average price of moral virtue for most people would probably be reduced considerably and make morally good behavior much easier to sell to most people. While we appreciate the motivation for the position, we are not convinced by the expansion. Expansion of ordinary concepts in extraordinary ways often creates more problems than it solves. As suggested earlier, the expansion of the idea of good health to the idea of "complete physical, mental and social well-being" confounds health with the broader idea of quality of life, and makes otherwise reasonable questions about the impact of health on the quality of life redundant (Michalos 2004).

Besides the problem of expanding the meaning of "pleasure" to include concern for others as well as oneself, a problem arises because Epicurus distinguished at least two kinds of pleasure, static and kinetic. Peace of mind or tranquility (ATARAXIA) and the absence of physical pain (APONIA) are static pleasures in the sense that they represent ends in themselves, final ends. "Kinetic pleasure is the pleasure of getting to this latter state, static pleasure, the pleasure of being in it" (Annas 1993, p. 336). For example, a thirsty person finds kinetic pleasure in drinking and static pleasure when thirst is thoroughly quenched; a person with physical pain finds kinetic pleasure as the pain is reduced and static pleasure when it is entirely gone.

The clear implication of Epicurus' remark that "By pleasure we mean the absence pain in the body and of trouble in the soul" is that, contrary to the views of Socrates and Plato, there is no neutral point between pleasure and pain. So far as the latter exists, the former does not, and *vice versa*. Since people are not always in pain, they must sometimes experience pleasure. What's more, one of Epicurus' Authorized Doctrines says that "The magnitude of pleasure reaches its limit in the removal of all pain" (Diogenes 2000a, b, p. 665). For example, once one's hunger or thirst are satisfied with food or drink, the pain of wanting both is removed, leaving one in a state of pleasure. If the pain of wanting anything at all, mentally or physically, is removed, then one's life would be "complete and perfect." Armed with these premises, Epicurus was led to one of the most famous and intriguing philosophic arguments ever written. To Monoeceus he wrote,

> Accustom thyself to believe that death is nothing to us, for good and evil imply sentience, and death is the privation of sentience; therefore a right understanding that death is nothing to us makes the mortality of life enjoyable, not by adding to life an illimitable time, but by taking away the yearning after immortality…Whatsoever causes no annoyance when it is present, causes only a groundless pain in the expectation. Death, therefore, the most awful of evils, is nothing to us, seeing that, when we are, death is not come, and, when death is come, we are not. It is nothing, then, either to the living or to the dead, for with the living it is not and the dead exist no longer (Diogenes 2000a, b, p. 651).

This argument probably engages contemporary philosophers nearly as much as it has engaged all philosophers since Epicurus, e.g., see Gordon and Suits (2003). The bottom line is that once one experiences freedom from physical and mental pain, that is as good as it gets. Just as one has no interest in eating more or drinking more when one's hunger and thirst are satisfied, one should have no interest in living more because extending the length of time one is in the state of being free of physical and mental pain will not make it more pleasurable. It can only bring more of the same. If nothing else, this is a very hardy view of death.

This is not the place to examine this notorious argument, but it is worth quoting for readers who have never seen it. For present purposes, the problem arising from the static versus kinetic distinction that merits more attention is that some people believe that Epicurus completely psychologized pleasure and, more generally, the good life by insisting that the final end was the static pleasure described as peace of mind and a healthy body. We have already seen that he claimed that "Even on the rack the wise man is happy." In his letter to Idomeneus, the sentence following the sentence quoted earlier about his "sufferings" is "…over against them all I set gladness of mind at the remembrance of our past conversations." According to Annas, (1993, pp. 349–350),

> …it is not in any way illogical that the good Epicurean should be said to be happy even while screaming in pain on the rack. For he has what matters: the right internal attitude to what happens to him, and this is not removed by present pain…Epicurus' thesis about happiness on the rack appears paradoxical only if taken out of context; it makes perfect sense given his stress on two points. First, happiness is a condition that involves life as a whole, and does not come and go with particular intense episodes of pleasure or pain. But second, happiness is not to be identified with the course of our life as a whole, but with the inner attitude the agent has to that extended course, an attitude that is not dependent on the way that course goes on. Thus, being happy is consistent with the collapse or reversal of the outward course of one's life…Epicurus has produced a bland rather than a shocking hedonism by fitting pleasure into a eudaimonistic framework; the radical and interesting part of his theory lies in his internalizing our final end, so that what we aim at, what we bend our lives towards and monitor our actions to achieve, is something which, once achieved, is altogether indifferent to the temporal shape of a human life.

This seems to us to be perhaps generous, but unfair to Epicurus. After telling us over and over in many contexts that the pleasurable end we seek is peace of mind and a healthy body, it is more than "paradoxical" to say that he does not, after all, regard the state of his bodily health as important. What matters, says Annas, is "attitude." If this were true, we would have to say that he did not believe that the good life required objectively good circumstances plus an appropriate attitude toward them. Only attitude mattered to him. All the talk about the importance of scientific knowledge to a good life would have been pointless. One might have reached a proper attitude with the right drugs or the power of positive thinking. Hence, in our terms, he could not logically distinguish a Fool's Paradise from Real Paradise. His most considered philosophical view about the good life would have been inconsistent with his most frequently used description of it. It is possible, but seems very unlikely. It seems more likely that in those passages about his own suffering and wise men on the rack, he only means to say that regardless of the suffering, he knows that on the whole (not every part) a wise man and he himself have had a good life. It is certainly logically possible, and there is now plenty of evidence that objectively catastrophic events in people's lives (e.g., serious physical injury, death of loved ones) are consistent with people's judgments that on the whole, their lives are good (Michalos 2010, 2005, 2003). It also often happens that objectively measured maladies are found that have been destroying the quality of people's lives, although they have been unaware of it. Such people typically recognize that they have been living in a Fool's Paradise.

Summary

This essay has reviewed ideas about the good life according to some of the most remarkable historic figures writing in the period from the eighth century to the third century BCE. Although many of the beliefs of these men are little more than historical curiosities for us today, many of them are still relevant and shared by many of our contemporaries. As well, a surprising number of embryonic roots of some contemporary controversies and views have been revealed. The following list provides a brief summary of some highlights:

- Writing in the eighth century BCE, the good life of Homer's heroes, included wealth, physical health and attractiveness, strength of character, courage, justice, generosity, and piety.
- For Homer's near contemporary, Hesiod, a good life included flourishing and prosperous communities, populated by honest people, living in peace, and enjoying the fruits of their labor, with an absence of worries and disease.
- About 200 years later, Pythagoras claimed that the good life we seek lies in the unobservable harmony within an unobservable entity, the immortal soul.
- Pythagoras' contemporary, Heraclitus, espoused a confusing mixture of absolutist and relativistic views, but believed that the maximization of desire satisfaction is neither necessary nor sufficient for the good life.
- A later contemporary of Pythagoras, Anaxagoras, issued something close to a scientific credo for his age and many to follow, namely, that "Appearances are a sight of the unseen."
- A close contemporary of Anaxagoras, Empedocles, posited a transmigrating soul-like DAIMON within each individual that ultimately experienced a current good or bad life and accumulated credits or debits toward a following life.
- Another fifth century philosopher, Protagoras, was a clear relativist, holding that the best life and the

best sort of person to be are entirely dependent on individual preferences.

- His contemporary, Antiphon of Rhamnous, claimed that the best sort of life can be led by making careful and accurate observations of nature, thinking "correctly" about what causes "distress" and "joy," and generally following nature's guides to a long and pleasant life.
- A younger contemporary of Antiphon, Democritus, mixed his own atomism with Anaxagoras' credo and Pythagoras' emphasis on harmony, believing that all observable mental and physical disorders could be explained by unobservable disordered and discordant atomic activity, while observable human well-being could be explained by unobservable orderly and harmonious atomic activity.
- Democritus was also the first philosopher to recommend downward comparisons as a strategy for attaining happiness and, by implication, was an early advocate of social comparison theory.
- A young contemporary of Democritus, Plato, recognized the importance of external goods like wealth and goods of the body like health, but regarded goods of the mind like moral virtue as most important for a good life.
- Although Plato clearly rejected the idea that the good life was identical to a life of pleasure, he believed that pleasure had a useful role to play in a good life, and he recognized at least five theories of pleasure's origin, identified here as a desire satisfaction theory, a needs satisfaction theory, a harmony theory, a true pleasures theory, and a class theory of pleasure.
- A relatively obscure contemporary of Plato, known as Iamblichus, was an early advocate of what we now call social capital theory, insofar as he recognized the importance of trust and law-abidingness for good human relations.
- Plato's greatest student, Aristotle, believed that EUDAIMONIA, happiness, "living well and doing well," is achieved insofar as one deliberately engages in the unimpeded excellent exercise of one's capacities for the sake of doing what is fine, excellent, or noble, provided that the deliberation and activities are undertaken from a virtuous character and accompanied by an appropriate amount of external goods and pleasure.
- Finally, Epicurus agreed that "living well and doing well" was required for pleasure and that pleasure

consisted of a healthy body, peace of mind, and moral virtue. Rather than aiming at Aristotle's vigorous active life in the world of affairs, Epicurus aimed for a relatively passive, intellectually stimulating life surrounded by friends in his Garden.

All things considered, these ancient philosophers left quality of life researchers with quite a legacy.

References

Annas, J. (1993). *The morality of happiness*. Oxford: Oxford University Press.

Annas, J. (1999). *Platonic ethics, old and new*. Ithaca: Cornell University Press.

Aristotle. (1926). *The 'Art' of rhetoric* (J. H. Freese, Trans.). Cambridge: Loeb Classical Library, Harvard University Press.

Aristotle. (1952). *The Athenian constitution, the Eudemian ethics, on virtues and vices* (H. Rackham, Rev. Trans.). Cambridge: Loeb Classical Library, Harvard University Press.

Aristotle. (1998). *Politics* (C. D. C. Reeve, Trans.). Indianapolis: Hackett Pub. Co.

Aristotle. (1999). *Nicomachean ethics* (T. Irwin, Second edition trans.). Indianapolis: Hackett Pub. Co.

Bentham, J. (1789). *An introduction to the principles of morals and legislation*. Oxford: Oxford University Press.

DeWitt, N. W. (1967). *Epicurus and his philosophy*. Cleveland: World Publishing Co.

Diogenes, L. (2000a). *Lives of eminent philosophers* (Vol. 1, R. D. Hicks, Trans.). Cambridge: Loeb Classical Library, Harvard University Press.

Diogenes, L. (2000b). *Lives of eminent philosophers* (Vol. 2, R. D. Hicks, Trans.). Cambridge: Loeb Classical Library, Harvard University Press.

Dover, K. J. (1974). *Greek popular morality in the time of Plato and Aristotle*. Indianapolis: Hackett Publishing Co.

Frede, D. (2003). Plato's ethics: An overview. In E. N. Zalta (Ed.), *The Stanford encyclopedia of Philosophy* (Fall 2003 ed.). http://plato.stanford.edu/archives/fall2003/entries/plato-ethics/

Gordon, D. R., & Suits, D. B. (Eds.). (2003). *Epicurus: His continuing influence and contemporary relevance*. Rochester/New York: RIT Cary Graphic Arts Press.

Inwood, B., Gerson, L. P., & Hutchinson, D. S. (Eds.). (1994). *The Epicurus reader: Selected writings and testimonia*. Indianapolis: Hackett Publishing Co.

Kahn, C. H. (1998). Pre-platonic ethics. In S. Everson (Ed.), *Companions to ancient thought: 4, ethics*. Cambridge: Cambridge University Press.

Kahneman, D. (1999). Objective happiness. In D. Kahneman, E. Diener, & N. Schwarz (Eds.), *Well-being: The foundations of hedonic psychology* (pp. 1–25). New York: Russell Sage Foundation.

Lewin, K., et al. (1944). Level of aspiration. In Hunt JMcV (Ed.), *Personality and behaviour disorders* (pp. 333–378). New York: Ronald Press Co.

Maslow, A. H. (1954). *Motivation and personality*. New York: The Free Press.

McKirahan, R. D. (1994). *Philosophy before Socrates: An introduction with texts and commentary*. Indianapolis: Hackett Publishing Co.

Merton, R. K., & Kitt, A. S. (1950). Contributions to the theory of reference group behavior. In R. K. Merton & P. F. Lazarsfeld (Eds.), *Continuities in social research* (pp. 40–105). New York: The Free Press.

Michalos, A. C. (1980). *North American social report: Vol. 1. Foundations, population and health*. Dordrecht: D.Reidel.

Michalos, A. C. (1985). Multiple discrepancies theory (MDT). *Social Indicators Research, 16*(4), 347–413.

Michalos, A. C. (2003). *Essays on the quality of life*. Dordrecht: Kluwer Academic Publishers.

Michalos, A. C. (2004). Social indicators research and health-related quality of life research. *Social Indicators Research, 65*(1), 27–72.

Michalos, A. C. (Ed.). (2005). *Citation classics from social indicators research*. Dordrecht: Springer.

Michalos, A. C. (2008). *Trade barriers to the public good: Free trade and environmental protection*. Montreal: McGill-Queen's University Press.

Michalos, A. C. (2010). Stability and sensitivity in perceived quality of life measures: Some panel results. *Social Indicators Research, 98*(3), 403–434.

Mill, J. S. (1863). *Utilitarianism*. London: Parker, Son and Bourn.

Parry, R. (2004). Ancient ethical theory. In E. N. Zalta (Ed.), *The Stanford encyclopedia of philosophy* (Fall 2004 ed.). http://plato.stanford.edu/archives/fall2004/entries/ethics-ancient/

Plato. (1914). *Euthyphro, Apology, Crito, Phaedo, Phaedrus* (H. N. Fowler, Trans.). Cambridge: Loeb Classical Library, Harvard University Press.

Plato. (1924). *Laches, Protagoras, Meno, Euthydemus* (W. R. M. Lamb, Trans.). Cambridge: Loeb Classical Library, Harvard University Press.

Plato. (1925a). *Lysis, Symposium, Gorgias* (W. R. M. Lamb, Trans.). Cambridge: Loeb Classical Library, Harvard University Press.

Plato. (1925b). *The Statesman, Philebus, Ion,* (H. N. Fowler & W. R. M. Lamb, Trans.). Cambridge: Loeb Classical Library, Harvard University Press.

Plato. (1926a). *Laws, books I–VI* (R. G. Bury, Trans.). Cambridge: Loeb Classical Library, Harvard University Press.

Plato. (1926b). *Laws, books VII–XII* (R. G. Bury, Trans.). Cambridge: Loeb Classical Library, Harvard University Press.

Plato. (1930). *The republic, books I–V* (P. Shorey, Trans.). Cambridge: Loeb Classical Library, Harvard University Press.

Plato. (1992a). *Protagoras* (S. Lombardo & K. Bell, Trans.). Indianapolis: Hackett Publishing Co., Inc.

Plato. (1992b). *Republic* (G. M. A. Grube & C. D. C. Reeve, Trans.). Indianapolis: Hackett Publishing Co., Inc.

Plato. (2000). *The trial and death of Socrates* (3rd ed., G. M. A. Grube & J. M. Cooper, Trans.). Indianapolis: Hackett Publishing Co., Inc.

Poster, C. (2006). Protagoras (c. 490–c. 420 BCE). *The Internet encyclopedia of philosophy*. Accessed April 3, 2006.

Sen, A. (1999). *Development as freedom*. New York: Random House.

Shorey, P. (1933). *What Plato said*. Chicago: University of Chicago Press.

Sophocles. (1954). *Sophocles I, the complete Greek tragedies*. Chicago: University of Chicago Press.

Taylor, C. C. W. (1998). Platonic ethics. In S. Everson (Ed.), *Companions to ancient thought: 4, ethics* (pp. 49–76). Cambridge: Cambridge University Press.

Van de Walle, S., Van Roosbroek, S., & Bouckaert, G. (2005). *Data on trust in the public sector.* OECD, Public Governance and Territorial Development Directorate, Public Governance Committee, November 10, 2005.

Veenhoven, R. (2000). The four qualities of life: Ordering concepts and measures of the good life. *Journal of Happiness Studies, 1*(1), 1–39.

Vlastos, G. (1945). Ethics and physics in Democritus: Part one. *Philosophical Review, 54*, 578–592.

Vlastos, G. (1946). Ethics and physics in Democritus: Part two. *Philosophical Review, 55*, 53–64.

Williams, B. (1993). Pagan justice and christian love. In T. Irwin & M. Nussbaum (Eds.), *Virtue, love and form: Essays in memory of Gregory Vlastos* (pp. 195–208). Edmonton: Academic Printing and Publishing.

Wills, T. A. (1981). Downward comparison principles in social psychology. *Psychological Bulletin, 90*, 245–271.

Happiness, Also Known as "Life Satisfaction" and "Subjective Well-Being"

3

Ruut Veenhoven

What Is "Happiness"?

The word "happiness" is used in various ways. In the widest sense, it is an umbrella term for all that is good. In this meaning, it is often used interchangeably with terms like "well-being" or "quality of life" and denotes both individual and social welfare. This use of words suggests that there is one ultimate good and disguises differences in interest between individuals and society. It further suggests that all merits can be integrated in one final scale of worth, which is not the case. The term is merely an umbrella for different notions of what is good. Below, I will delineate four qualities of life and show that the concept of happiness fits only one of these.

Four Qualities of Life

Quality of life concepts can be sorted using two distinctions, which together provide a fourfold matrix. That classification is discussed in more detail in Veenhoven (2000).

The first distinction is between chances and outcomes, that is, the difference between opportunities for a good life and the good life itself. A second difference is between outer and inner qualities of life, in other words between "external" and "internal" features. In the first case, the quality is in the environment; in the

latter, it is in the individual. Lane (1994) made this distinction clear by distinguishing "quality of society" from "quality of persons." The combination of these two dichotomies yields a fourfold matrix. This classification is presented in Table 3.1.

Livability of the Environment

The left top quadrant denotes the meaning of good living conditions, shortly called "livability."

Ecologists see livability in the natural environment and describe it in terms of pollution, global warming, and degradation of nature. Currently, they associate livability typically with preservation of the environment. City planners see livability in the built environment and associate it with such things as sewer systems, traffic jams, and ghetto formation. Here the good life is seen as a fruit of human intervention.

In the sociological view, society is central. Livability is associated with the quality of society as a whole and also with the position one has in society.

Livability is not what is called happiness here. It is rather a precondition for happiness, and not all environmental conditions are equally conducive to happiness.

Life Ability of the Person

The right top quadrant denotes inner life chances, that is, how well we are equipped to cope with the problems of life. Sen (1992) calls this quality of life variant "capability." I prefer the simple term "life ability," which contrasts elegantly with "livability."

The most common depiction of this quality of life is absence of functional defects. This is "health" in the limited sense, sometimes referred to as "negative health." Next to absence of disease, one can consider excellence

R. Veenhoven (✉)
Erasmus University, Rotterdam, The Netherlands
e-mail: veenhoven@fsw.eur.nl

K.C. Land et al. (eds.), *Handbook of Social Indicators and Quality of Life Research*,
DOI 10.1007/978-94-007-2421-1_3, © Springer Science+Business Media B.V. 2012

Table 3.1 Four qualities of life

	Outer qualities	Inner qualities
Life chances	Livability of environment	Life ability of the person
Life results	Utility of life	Satisfaction with life

of function. This is referred to as "positive health" and associated with energy and resilience. A further step is to evaluate capability in a developmental perspective and to include acquisition of new skills for living. This is commonly denoted by the term "self-actualization." From this point of view, a middle-aged man is not "well" if he behaves like an adolescent, even if he functions without problems at this level. Since abilities do not develop alongside idleness, this quality of life is close to the "activity" in Aristotle's concept of eudaemonia. Lastly, the term "art of living" denotes special life abilities; in most contexts, this quality is distinguished from mental health and sometimes even attributed to slightly disturbed persons. Art of living is associated with refined tastes, an ability to enjoy life, and an original style of life.

Ability to deal with the problems of life will mostly contribute to happiness, as defined here, but is not identical. If one is competent in living, one has a good chance at happiness, but this endowment does not guarantee an enjoyable outcome.

Utility of Life

The left bottom quadrant represents the notion that a good life must be good for something more than itself. This assumes some higher values. There is no current generic for these external outcomes of life. Gerson (1976: 795) refers to these effects as "transcendental" conceptions of quality of life. Another appellation is "meaning of life," which then denotes "true" significance instead of mere subjective sense of meaning. I prefer the simpler "utility of life," while admitting that this label may also give rise to misunderstanding.

When evaluating the external effects of a life, one can consider its functionality for the environment. In this context, doctors stress how essential a patient's life is to its intimates. At a higher level, quality of life is seen in contributions to society. Historians see quality in the addition an individual can make to human culture, and rate, for example, the lives of great inventors higher than those of anonymous peasants. Moralists see quality in the preservation of the moral order and would

deem the life of a saint to be better than that of a sinner. As an individual's life can have many environmental effects, the number of such utilities is almost infinite.

Apart from its functional utility, life is also judged on its moral or esthetic value. For instance, most of us would attribute more quality to the life of Florence Nightingale than to that of a drunk, even if it appeared in the end that her good works had a negative result. In classic moral philosophy, this is called "virtuous living" and is often presented as the essence of "true happiness."

Here the focus is on mere "experiential" happiness, on how much one likes the life one lives. The difference is well expressed in the earlier-mentioned statement of Mill (1863) that he preferred an unhappy Socrates to a happy fool. Moral excellence is clearly not the same as feeling good.

Core Meaning: Subjective Enjoyment of Life

Finally, the bottom right quadrant represents the inner outcomes of life. That is the quality in the eye of the beholder. As we deal with conscious humans, this quality boils down to subjective enjoyment of life. This is commonly referred to by terms such as "subjective well-being," "life-satisfaction," and "happiness" in a limited sense of the word. This is the kind of happiness the utilitarian philosophers had in mind, and it is also the kind of happiness addressed here.

Humans are capable of evaluating their life in different ways. We have in common with all higher animals that we can appraise our situation affectively. We feel good or bad about particular things, and our mood level signals overall adaptation. As in animals, these affective appraisals are automatic, but unlike other animals, humans can reflect on this experience. We have an idea of how we have felt over the last year, while a cat does not. Humans can also judge life cognitively by comparing life as it is with notions of how it should be.

Most human evaluations are based on both sources of information, that is, intuitive affective appraisal and cognitively guided evaluation. The mix depends mainly on the object. Tangible things such as our income are typically evaluated by comparison; intangible matters such as sexual attractiveness are evaluated by how it feels. This dual evaluation system probably makes the human experiential repertoire richer than that of our fellow creatures.

In evaluating our life, we typically summarize this rich experience in overall appraisals. For instance, we

3 Happiness, Also Known as "Life Satisfaction" and "Subjective Well-Being"

appreciate several domains of life. When asked how we feel about our work or our marriage, we will mostly have an opinion. Likewise, most people form ideas about separate qualities of their life, for instance, how challenging their life is and whether there is any meaning in it. Such judgments are made in different time perspectives – in the past, present, and future.

Mostly such judgments are not very salient in our consciousness. Now and then, they pop to mind spontaneously. Though not in the forefront of consciousness all the time, estimates of subjective enjoyment of life can be recalled and refreshed when needed. This makes these appraisals measurable in principle.

Four Kinds of Satisfaction

Even when we focus on subjective satisfaction with life, there are still different meanings associated with the word happiness. These meanings can also be charted in a fourfold matrix. In this case, that classification is based on the following dichotomies: life aspects versus life as a whole and passing delight versus enduring satisfaction.

Above, we have seen that appraisals of life can concern aspects, such as marriage or work-life, and one's life as a whole. The word "happiness" is used in both contexts. Obviously, such appraisals are linked. Enjoyment of aspects of life will typically contribute to the satisfaction with life as a whole (so-called bottom–up effect), and enjoyment of one's life as a whole appears to foster the satisfaction with life aspects (top–down). Still, these are not identical matters. One can have a happy marriage but still be dissatisfied with life as a whole, or be satisfied with life as a whole in spite of an unhappy marriage.

Next, the experience of enjoyment can be short lived or enduring. Again, the word happiness is used for both phenomena. Sometimes it refers to passing moods and on other occasions to stable satisfaction. Once more, these matters are related but not the same.

When combined, these distinctions produce the fourfold matrix presented in Table 3.2. The distinction between part and whole is presented vertically, and the distinction between passing and enduring enjoyment, horizontally.

Instant Satisfaction

The top left quadrant represents passing enjoyments of life aspects. Examples would be delight in a cup of tea

Table 3.2 Four kinds of satisfaction

	Passing	*Enduring*
Part of life	Pleasure	Domain satisfaction
Life as a whole	Top experience	Happiness

at breakfast, the satisfaction of a chore done, or the enjoyment of a piece of art. I refer to this category as "instant-satisfactions." Kahneman (1999:4) calls it "instant utilities." This quadrant represents hedonistic happiness, especially when the focus is on sensory experience. The concept of happiness used here is broader, however. It concerns both overall satisfaction and life as a whole. Though fleeting enjoyment obviously contributes to a positive appreciation of life, it is not the whole of it.

Domain Satisfaction

The top right quadrant denotes enduring appreciation of life aspects, such as marriage satisfaction and job satisfaction. This is currently referred to as domain satisfactions. Though domain satisfactions depend typically on a continuous flow of instant satisfactions, they have some continuity of their own. For instance, one can remain satisfied with one's marriage even if one has not enjoyed the company of the spouse for quite some time. Domain satisfactions are often denoted with the term happiness: a happy marriage, happy with one's job, etc. Yet in this chapter, the term happiness is used in the broader sense of satisfaction with life as a whole. One would not call a person happy who is satisfied with marriage and job but still dissatisfied on the whole because his health is failing. It is even possible that someone is satisfied with all the domains one can think of but feels depressed.

Top Experience

The bottom right quadrant denotes the combination of passing experience and appraisal of life as a whole. That combination occurs typically in top experiences, which involve short-lived but quite intense feelings and the perception of wholeness. This is the kind of happiness poet's write about. Again, this is not the kind of happiness aimed at here. A moment of bliss is not an enduring appreciation of life. In fact, such top experiences even seem detrimental to lasting satisfaction, possibly because of their disorienting effects (Diener et al. 1991).

Core Meaning: Lasting Satisfaction with One's Life as a Whole

Lastly, the bottom right quadrant represents the combination of enduring satisfaction with life as a whole. This is what I mean with the word happiness and is then synonymous with "life satisfaction." This is the meaning the utilitarian philosophers had in mind when talking about happiness as the "sum" of pleasures and pains. In such contexts, they denoted a balance over time and thus a durable matter.

Definition of Happiness

Overall happiness is the *degree to which an individual judges the overall quality of his/her own life as a whole favorably*. In other words, how much one likes the life one leads. This definition is explained in more detail in Veenhoven (1984:22–25).

Components of Happiness

When evaluating the favorableness of life, we tend to use two more or less distinct sources of information: our affects and their thoughts (Veenhoven 2009). One can decide that one feels fine most of the time, and one can also judge that life seems to meet one's (conscious) demands. These appraisals do not necessarily coincide. We may feel fine generally but be aware that we failed to realize our aspirations. Or one may have surpassed one's aspirations but feels miserable. Using the word "happiness" in both these cases would result in three different kinds of happiness, the overall judgment as described above and these two specific appraisals. Therefore, the components are referred to as "hedonic level of affect" and "contentment." To mark the difference with the encompassing judgment, I will refer to happiness (the core concept) as overall happiness. A synonym for overall happiness is "life satisfaction."

Hedonic Level of Affect

Hedonic level of affect is the degree to which various affects that someone experiences are pleasant in character. Hedonic level of affect is not the same as "mood." We experience different kinds of mood: elated moods, calm moods, restless moods, moody moods, etc. Each of these moods is characterized by a special mixture of affective experience, one of which is "hedonic tone" or "pleasantness." The concept of hedonic level concerns only the pleasantness experienced in affects, that is, the pleasantness in feelings, in emotions, as well as in moods. So a high hedonic level may be based on strong but passing emotions of love, as well as on moods of steady calmness.

A person's average hedonic level of affect can be assessed over different periods of time: an hour, a week, a year, as well as over a lifetime. The focus here is on "characteristic" hedonic level, that is o say, the average over a long time span such as a month or a year. The concept does not presume subjective awareness of that average level.

Contentment

Contentment is the degree to which an individual perceives his/her aspirations are met. The concept presupposes that the individual has developed some conscious wants and has formed an idea about their realization. The factual correctness of this idea is not at stake. The concept concerns the individual's subjective perception.

Synonyms

The above-defined concept of "overall happiness" is denoted with different words. In the 1950s, the words *adjustment* and *morale* were sometimes used in this meaning, and since the 1960s, the term *life satisfaction* came into use for this purpose. In 1984, Ed Diener introduced the term *subjective well-being*,[1] abbreviated as SWB, and this term is still dominant in psychology.

The term life satisfaction is mostly used for "overall happiness," but refers in some cases particularly to its cognitive component and is then synonymous with "contentment." In such context, the term happiness is typically used for the affective appraisal of life and then synonymous with "hedonic level of affect."

The term subjective well-being is also used in wider meanings than happiness as defined here. Sometimes the term refers to good mental functioning and then denotes the meaning of life ability in the top right quadrant of Scheme 1. At other occasions, the term is used as a generic for all subjective enjoyment and then covers all the quadrants of Scheme 2.

---

[1] Ed Diener defines subjective well-being as being satisfied with one's life while feeling good, and this conceptualization also involves both cognitive and affective appraisals of life.

3 Happiness, Also Known as "Life Satisfaction" and "Subjective Well-Being"

Table 3.3 Some currently used questions about happiness

Single questions
- Taking all together, how happy would you say you are: very happy, quite happy, not very happy, not at all happy?
  (standard item in the World Value Studies)
- How satisfied are you with the life you lead? Very satisfied, fairly satisfied, not very satisfied, not at all satisfied?
  (standard item in Euro-barometer surveys)
- Here is a picture of a ladder. Suppose the top of the ladder represents the best possible life for you and the bottom of the ladder the worst possible life. Where on the ladder do you feel you personally stand at the present time? (0–10 ladder like rating scale)
  (Cantril's (1965) present life ladder rating)

Multiple questions (summed)
- Same question asked twice: at the beginning and at the end of interview
  How do you feel about your life as a whole? Delighted, pleased, mostly satisfying, mixed, mostly dissatisfying, unhappy, terrible?
  (Andrews and Withey's (1976) Life 3)
- Five questions, rated on a 1–7 scale ranging from strongly agree to strongly disagree.
  (Diener et al. 1985 Satisfaction With Life Scale SWLS)
  - In most ways my life is close to ideal.
  - The conditions of my life are excellent.
  - I am satisfied with my life.
  - So far I have gotten the important things I want in life.
  - If I could live my life over, I would change almost nothing

Can Happiness Be Measured?

Measurement has long been understood as "objective" and "external" assessment, analogous to the measurement of blood pressure by a doctor. By now we know that happiness cannot be measured that way. Steady physiological correlates have not been discovered and probably never will be. Nor have any overt behaviors been found to be consistently linked to inner enjoyment of life. Like most attitudinal phenomena, happiness is only partially reflected in behavior. Suicidal behavior is probably more indicative of happiness. Almost all people who attempt or commit suicide are quite unhappy. However, not all the unhappy seek resort to suicide. In fact, only a fraction does.

Inference from overt behavior being impossible, we must make do with questioning, that is, simply asking people how much they enjoy their life as a whole. Questioning is an appropriate method of measurement in this case since happiness is defined as something we have on our mind.

Questions on happiness can be posed in various contexts – clinical interviews, life-review questionnaires, and common survey interviews. The questions can be posed in different ways – directly or indirectly and by means of single or multiple items.

Common Questions

Some common questions are presented in Table 3.3.

Validity Doubts

Critics have suggested that responses to questions on happiness actually measure other phenomena. Rather than indicating how much the respondent enjoys life, answers would reflect his normative notions and desires.

No Notion

One of the misgivings is that most people have no opinion at all about their happiness. They would be more aware of how happy they are supposed to be, and report that instead. Though this may happen incidentally, it does not appear to be the rule. Most people know quite well whether or not they enjoy life. Eight out of ten Americans think of it every week. Responses on questions about happiness tend to be prompt. Nonresponse on these items is low, both absolutely (±1%) and relatively to other attitudinal questions. "Don't know" responses are infrequent as well.

A related assertion is that respondents mix up how happy they actually are with how happy other people

---

In my view, this last item is not appropriate. One can be quite satisfied with life but still be open for the opportunity to try something else think they are, given their situation. If so, people considered to be well-off would typically report to be very happy, and people regarded as disadvantaged should characterize themselves as unhappy. That pattern is observed sometimes, but it is not general. For instance, in The Netherlands, good education is seen as a prerequisite for a good life, but the highly educated appear slightly less happy in comparison to their less educated counterparts.

Colored Answers

Another objection concerns the presence of systematic bias in responses. It is assumed that questions on happiness are interpreted correctly but that responses are often false. People who are actually dissatisfied with their life would tend to answer that they are quite happy. Both ego defense and social desirability would cause such distortions.

This bias is seen to manifest itself in over-report of happiness; most people claim to be happy, and most perceive themselves as happier than average. Another indication of bias is seen in the finding that psychosomatic complaints are not uncommon among the happy. However, these findings allow other interpretations as well. Firstly, the fact that more people say to be happy than unhappy does not imply over-report of happiness. It is quite possible that most people are truly happy (some reasons will be discussed below). Secondly, there are also good reasons why most people think that they are happier than average. One such reason is that most people are like critical scientists and think that unhappiness is the rule. Thirdly, the occurrence of headaches and worries among the happy does not prove response distortion. Life can be a sore trial sometimes but still be satisfying on a balance.

The proof of the pudding is in demonstrating the response distortion itself. Some clinical studies have tried to do so by comparing responses to single direct questions with ratings based on depth interviews and projective tests. The results are generally not different from responses to single direct questions posed by an anonymous interviewer.

Reliability Doubts

Though single questions on happiness seem to measure what they are supposed to measure, they measure it rather imprecisely.

When the same question is asked twice in an interview, responses are not always identical. Correlations are about +70. Over a period of a week, test–retest reliability drops to circa +60. Though responses seldom change from "happy" to "unhappy," switches from "very" to "fairly" are rather common. The difference between response options is often ambiguous. The respondent's notion about his/her happiness tends to be global. Thus, the choice for one answer category or the next is sometimes haphazard.

Because choice is often arbitrary, subtle differences in interrogation can exert considerable effect. Variations in place where the interview is held, characteristics of the interviewer, sequence of questions, and precise wording of the key item can tip the scale to one response or the other. Such effects can occur in different phases of the response process, in the consideration of the answer as well as in the communication of it.

Bias in Appraisal

Though most people have an idea of how much they enjoy life, responding to questions on this matter involves more than just bringing up an earlier judgment from memory. For the most part, memory only indicates a range of happiness. Typically, the matter is re-assessed in an instant judgment. This re-appraisal may be limited to recent change (Are there any reasons to be more or less happy than I used to be?), but it can also involve quick re-evaluation of life (What are my blessings and frustrations?). In making such instant judgments, people use various heuristics. These mental simplifications are attended with specific errors. For instance, the "availability" heuristic involves orientation on pieces of information that happen to be readily available. If the interviewer is in a wheelchair, the benefit of good health is salient. Respondents in good health will then rate their happiness somewhat higher, and the correlation of happiness ratings with health variables will be more pronounced. Several of these heuristic effects have been demonstrated by Schwarz and Strack (1991).

Bias in Response

Once a respondent has formed a private judgment, the next step is to communicate it. At this stage, reports can be biased in various ways as well. One source of bias is inherent to semantics; respondents interpret words differently and some interpretations may be emphasized by earlier questions. For example, questions on happiness are more likely to be interpreted as referring to "contentment" when preceded by questions on success in work, rather than items on mood. Another source of response bias is found in considerations of self-presentation and social desirability. Self-rating of happiness tends to be slightly higher in personal interviews than on anonymous questionnaires. However, direct contact with an interviewer does not always inflate happiness reports. If the interviewer is in a wheelchair, modest self-presentation is encouraged.

Much of these biases are random and balance out in large samples. So in large samples, random error does not affect the accuracy of happiness averages. Yet it does affect correlations; random error "attenuates" correlations. Random error can be estimated by means of multiple-trait multiple-method (MTMM) studies, and correlations can be corrected (disattenuated) on that basis. A first application on satisfaction measures is reported by Saris et al. (1996).

Some biases may be systematic, especially the bias produced by technique of interrogation and sequence of questions. Bias of that kind does affect the reliability of distributional data. In principle, it does not affect correlations, unless the measure of the correlate is biased in the same way (correlated error). To some extent, systematic error can also be estimated and corrected. See also Saris et al. (1996).

Comparability Across Nations

Average happiness differs markedly across nations. In Scheme 4, we will see that Russians score currently 5.4 on a 0–10 scale, while in Canada, the average is 7.7. Does that mean that Russians really take less pleasure in life? Several claims to the contrary have been advanced. Elsewhere I have checked these doubts Ouweneel and Veenhoven (1991), Veenhoven (1993). The results of that inquiry are summarized below.

The first objection is that differences in *language* hinder comparison. Words like "happiness" and "satisfaction" would not have the same connotations in different tongues. Questions using such terms would therefore measure slightly different matters. I checked that hypothesis by comparing the rank orders produced by three kinds of questions on life satisfaction: a question about "happiness," a question about "satisfaction with life," and a question that invites to a rating between "best and worst possible life." The rank orders appeared to be almost identical. I also compared responses on questions on happiness and satisfaction in two bilingual countries and found no evidence for linguistic bias either.

A second objection is that responses are differentially distorted by *desirability bias*. In countries where happiness ranks high in value, people would be more inclined to overstate their enjoyment of life. I inspected that claim by checking whether reported happiness is indeed higher in countries where hedonic values are most endorsed. This appeared not to be the case. As a second check, I inspected whether reports of general happiness deviate more from feelings in the past few weeks in these countries, the former measure being more vulnerable for desirability distortion than the latter. This appeared not to be the case either.

A third claim is that *response styles* distort the answers dissimilarly in different countries. For instance, collectivistic orientation would discourage "very" happy responses because modest self-presentation is more appropriate within that cultural context. I tested this hypothesis by comparing happiness in countries differing in value collectivism but found no effect in the predicted direction. The hypothesis failed several other tests as well.

A related claim is that happiness is a typical *western concept*. Unfamiliarity with it in non-western nations would lead to lower scores. If so, we can expect more "don't know" and "no answer" responses in non-western nations. However, that appeared not to be the case.

The issue of "cultural bias in the measurement" of happiness must be distinguished from the question of "cultural influence on the appraisal" of life. Russians can be truly less happy than Canadians, but be so because of a gloomier outlook on life, rather than as a result of an inferior quality of life. This latter matter will be discussed in Section 4 of this chapter.

How Happy Are We?

Throughout time, social critics have bemoaned the miseries of life. Man is said to be unhappy, and real happiness is projected in past paradise or future utopia. Optimists, who stressed human adaptability and social progress, have always denounced such bilious claims. By lack of an empirical gauge, the discussion remained inconclusive. During the last few decades, many surveys have been carried out, some drawing on world samples (available in the World Database of Happiness). Together, the data support the optimist view.

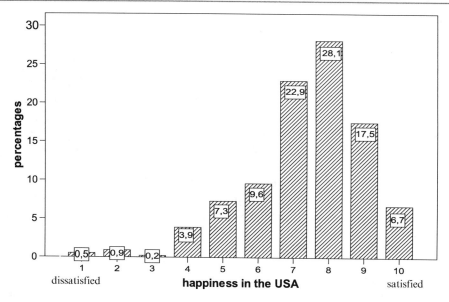

Fig. 3.1 Life-satisfaction in the USA 2007 (Source: World Value Survey 5)

Table 3.4 Life satisfaction in nations around 2005. Average scores on scale 0–10

• Denmark	8.3
• Switzerland	8.0
• Canada	7.6
• USA	7.4
• Israel	7.0
• Japan	6.5
• Korea (South)	6.0
• India	5.5
• Ukraine	5.0
• Afghanistan	4.1
• Zimbabwe	3.0
• Togo	2.6

Source: World Database of Happiness (Veenhoven 2010) Rank Report Average Happiness

Most People Are Happy

Figure 3.1 presents the distribution for responses to the 10-step question on life satisfaction in the USA. The most frequent responses are 7, 8, and 9 and less than 2% scores below neutral. The average is 7.4. This result implies that most people must feel happy most of the time. That view has been corroborated by yearly follow-up studies over many years (Ehrhardt et al. 2000) and by studies that use the technique of experience sampling (Schimmack and Diener 2003).

The high level of happiness is not unique to the USA. Table 3.4 shows similar averages in other western nations. In fact, average happiness tends to be above neutral in most countries of the world. So happiness for a great number is apparently possible.

No Mere Resignation

Nevertheless, some social critics are still reluctant to believe that modern man is happy. Reported happiness is discounted as sullen adjustment. Rather than really enjoying their life, people would just give up hope for a better one and try to adjust to the inevitable (e.g., Ipsen 1978). Various defensive strategies would be used: simple denial of one's misery, downward comparison, and a tendency to see things rosier than they actually are. Depressives would see the world more realistic. In addition to the above discussion on validity, two counter-arguments can be mentioned.

Firstly, such resignation must give itself away in a discrepancy between the "adjusted" judgment of life and "raw" affective experience. Appraisal of affect is probably less vulnerable to cognitive adaptation because it is a direct experience and thus less open to defensive distortion. It is also less threatening to admit that one felt depressed in the last few weeks than to admit disappointment in life. Various surveys have assessed both general happiness and last week's affect balance. The results do not suggest that people claim to be happy but actually feel lousy (research reviewed in Veenhoven 1984: 106/113). Time sampling of mood states also shows that pleasant affect dominates unpleasant affect (see, e.g., Bless and Schwarz 1984 for a meta-analysis of 18 studies).

Secondly, people are typically unhappy when they live in miserable conditions. As we have seen, unhappiness is the rule in poor third world countries. In western nations, happiness is typically lower where adverse conditions accumulate, such as in persons who are poor, lonely, and ill (Glatzer and Zapf 1984:282–397).

Together, these findings suggest that people tend to enjoy their lives once conditions are tolerable. From an adaptive biological point of view, this does not seem strange. Nature is unlikely to have burdened us with chronic unhappiness. Like "health," happiness would seem to be the normal condition.

Why Still So Many Complaints?

The prevalence of happiness does not wash away the multitude of suffering and complaining. Even the happy are not without complaints. The German Welfare Survey found that half of the subjects who say to be satisfied with their life as a whole report frequent worries (Glatzer and Zapf 1984:180). If not due to response distortion, what else can explain this pattern of worried happiness?

Firstly, it is important to note that happiness and complaining do not exclude each other logically. One can be satisfied with life as a whole but still be aware of serious deficits. In fact, both stem from a reflection on life. Secondly, worrying may contribute to happiness in the end. Only through realistic acknowledgement of danger can we cope effectively with the problems of life.

What Causes Us to Be More of Less Happy?

Having established *that* people differ in happiness, the next question is *why*. So far, the determinants of happiness are only dimly understood. Still, it is clear that various levels of human functioning are involved: collective action and individual behavior, simple sensory experiences and higher cognition, stable characteristics of the individual and his environment, as well as freaks of fate. Table 3.5 presents a tentative ordering of factors and processes in a sequence model.

The model presumes that the judgment of life draws on the *flow of life experiences*, particularly on positive and negative experience. This is what the utilitarian philosophers referred to as "pleasures and pains." The flow of experiences is a mental reaction to the *course of life events*.

Table 3.5 Evaluation of life: a sequence model of conditions and processes

Life chances →	Course of events →	Flow of experience →	Evaluation of life
Societal resources			
• Economic welfare			
• Social equality			
• Political freedom	*Confrontation with:*	*Experiences of:*	Appraisal of average affect
• Cultural lush			
• Moral order	• Deficit or affluence	• Yearning or satiation	
• Etc…			Comparison with standards of the good life
Personal resources	• Attack or protection	• Anxiety or safety	
• *Social position*			Striking an overall balance of life
– Material property	• Solitude or company	• Loneliness or love	
– Political influence			
– Social prestige	• Humiliation or honor	• Rejection or respect	
– Family bonds			
– Etc..	• Routine or challenge	• Dullness or excitement	
• *Individual abilities*	• Ugliness or beauty	• Repulsion or rapture	
– Physical fitness			
– Psychic fortitude	• Etc…	• Etc…	
– Social capability			
– Intellectual skill			
– Etc…			
Conditions for happiness			**Appraisal process**

This includes major one-time events, such as marriage or migrations, as well as repetitive mundane events, like getting up in the morning and doing the dishes. The events that happen in life are partly a matter of good or bad luck, such as in the case of accidents. The occurrences of life events also depend on given conditions and capacities. Traffic accidents are less frequent in well-organized societies and among attentive persons. Thus, the chances of "rewarding" and "aversive" events are not the same for everybody. This is commonly referred to as *life chances*. Present life chances root in past events and chance structures, in societal history, as well as individual development.

An example may illustrate this four-step model: A person's life chances may be poor because he/she lives in a lawless society, is in a powerless position in that society, and is personally neither smart nor nice (step 1). That person will run into many adverse events. He/she will be robbed, duped, humiliated, and excluded (step 2). Therefore, that person will frequently feel anxious, angry, and lonely (step 3). Based on this flow of experience, that person will judge life as a whole negatively (step 4). Causality can skip a step. For instance, poor legal protection (step 1) may instigate feelings of anxiety (step 3) directly because the person anticipates on events that are likely to happen but have not occurred. Life chances (step 1) can even enter the evaluation of life (step 4) right away when comparisons enter the judgment. Likewise, not all life events in step 2 follow from life chances at step 1. Some events are a matter of good or bad luck and happen irrespective of social position or psychological capabilities. Nor is the flow of life experiences (step 3) entirely shaped by the course of events (step 2). How pleasant or unpleasant we feel also depends on dispositions and interpretations.

Livability of the Environment

Research on happiness has focused on its relation to life chances. Below is a review of the main findings up to 2010.

Quality of Society

Average happiness differs greatly across nations. We have seen earlier that differences cannot be explained by cultural bias in the measurement of happiness. We

Table 3.6 Happiness and characteristics of nations around 2005

	Correlation with average happiness		
Condition in nation	Zero order	Wealth controlled	N
Wealth			
• Purchasing power per head[a]	+.67	–	137
Freedom			
• Economic[a]	+.57	+.36	128
• Political[a]	+.50	+.31	130
• Personal	+.40	−.03	85
Equality			
• Disparity in incomes	−.10	+.23	119
• Discrimination of women	−.79	−62	99
• Disparity in happiness	−.52	−.16	97
Brotherhood			
• Tolerance	+.48	+.39	77
• Trust in people	+.14	−.38	50
• Voluntary work	−.09	+.17	74
• Social security	+.44	+.15	107
Justice			
• Rule of law[a]	+.64	+.30	146
• Respect of civil rights[a]	+.52	+.28	130
• Corruption[a]	−.65	−.32	146
Explained variance (R)	.70		122

Data: World Database of Happiness (Veenhoven 2010), States of Nations

[a]Included in regression

will see later that they can neither be attributed to cultural variation in outlook on life. On the other hand, there is a strong basis for interpretation of this variation in terms of differential livability of society. Scheme 6 presents many strong correlations between average happiness and societal qualities (Table 3.6).

Much of the above-mentioned correlates of average happiness are part of the "modernity" syndrome. Hence, similar patterns emerge if we consider further indicators of modernity, such as urbanization, industrialization, informatization, and individualization. The more modern the country, the happier its citizens are. This finding will be a surprise to prophets of doom who associate modernity with anomie and alienation. Though modernization may involve problems indeed, its benefits are clearly greater (Veenhoven 2005).

3 Happiness, Also Known as "Life Satisfaction" and "Subjective Well-Being"

Table 3.7 Happiness and position in society

	Correlation *within* western nations	Similarity of correlation *across* all nations
Social rank		
• Income	+	–
• Education	±	–
• Occupational prestige	+	+
Social participation		
• Employment	±	+
• Participation in associations	+	+
Primary network		
• Spouse	++	+
• Children	0	?
Friends	+	+

Source: World Database of Happiness (Veenhoven 2010), Correlational Findings.
++ = Strong positive
+ = Similar correlations
+ = Positive
± = Varying
0 = No relationship
– = Different correlations
– = Negative
? = Not yet investigated
? = No data

Table 3.8 Happiness and life-abilities

	Correlation *within* western nations	Similarity of correlation *across* all nations
Proficiencies		
• Physical health	+	+
• Mental health	++	+
• IQ	0	+
Personality		
• Internal control	+	+
• Extraversion	+	+
• Conscientiousness	+	?
Art of living		
• Lust acceptance	+	+
• Sociability	++	+

Source: World Database of Happiness (Veenhoven 2010), Correlational Findings.
++ = Strong positive
+ = Similar correlations
+ = Positive
± = Varying
0 = No relationship
– = Different correlations
– = Negative
? = Not yet investigated
? = No data

Individual Position in Society

Numerous studies all over the world have considered differences in individual happiness within countries. Because most of these studies are inspired by egalitarian social policy, the emphasis is often on social differences, such as in income, education, and employment. Contrary to expectation, these positional differences bear little relationship to happiness, at least not in modern affluent society. Together, positional variables explain mostly no more than 10% of the variance in happiness. The main findings are summarized in Table 3.7.

Life Ability of the Individual

The strongest correlations observed are at the psychological level; happy people are typically better endowed than the unhappy. The common variance explained by such variables tends to be around 30%. Some main findings are summarized in Table 3.8.

Much of the findings on individual variation in happiness boil down to a difference in *ability to control one's environment*, and this pattern seems to be universal.

Course of Life Events

The effect of life events on happiness has received little attention. One of the few sophisticated studies that considered the matter is the four-wave "Australian Quality of Life Panel Study" by Heady and Wearing (1992).

First, this study showed that the course of life events is not the same for everybody. Some people find troubles repeatedly; they have accidents, are laid off, quarrel with family, fall ill, etc. On the other hand, there are also people who are lucky most of the time; they meet nice people, get promoted, have children who do well, etc. These systematic differences in the course of events depend to some extent on life chances. In the study, favorable events appeared to happen more often to persons who were well educated and psychologically extraverted. Adverse events were more frequent among neurotics but occurred less to people with good intimate attachments. Both favorable and unfavorable events happened more to persons who were young and psychologically open. Together, the life chances considered explained about 35% of the variation in life events over 8 years.

The study also demonstrated that the course of life events affects the appraisal of life. First, it was found that the balance of favorable and adverse events in 1 year predicts reported happiness in the next year. The more positive that balance, the greater the satisfaction with life. Life events explained some 25% of the differences in life satisfaction, of which about 10% were independent of social position and personality.

Next, longitudinal analysis indicated that change in characteristic pattern of events was followed by change in happiness. Respondents who shifted to a more positive balance became happier.

Flow of Experience

As of yet, hedonic experience is not well understood. Though the feelings of disgust and delight are quite tangible, it is not clear how they come about and why.

Function of Hedonic Experience

Much of our likes and dislikes seem to be inborn reactions to situations that are good and bad for human survival. Evolution has probably eliminated our forefathers who did not enjoy food, shelter, and company, or lacked dislikes for danger. As such, certain life events are likely to elicit pleasant experiences, while others invoke unpleasant feelings. Playing tennis with friends is typically more fun than sitting in jail alone.

Though it is quite plausible that hedonic experience reflects the gratification of basic needs, it is not so clear what these needs are precisely. Current theory suggests that there are various "organic needs" (food, shelter, sex), "social needs" (belonging, esteem), and broader "self-actualizing" needs (mastery, control, variety, meaning, etc.). Conceptions differ, however, and it is difficult to establish to what extent these strivings are inborn and how they are linked to hedonic experience.

Cognitive theories suggest that pleasant experience can also be induced by perceived realization of goals. For instance, that we enjoy playing tennis because we successfully execute an intention and dislike the jail because it does not fit our plans. The gratifying effects of perceived reality-want fits may draw on an underlying need for control.

Pleasant and Unpleasant Events

Many adverse events evoke similar reactions in most people, particularly events that exceed human adaptability. Everybody suffers when burned or starved. However, within the limits of human faculties, reactions tend to differ. For instance, not everybody feels equally as bad when his/her house burns down. Reactions vary with earlier exposure to hardship, with meaning attributed to the event, and with psychological resilience. Still, most people get more or less upset by the loss of their property. Variability is probably greater in the pleasurable experiences people derive from life events. Though most of us enjoy feasts, this is not true for everybody. Some people lack the social skills required for feasting, are not accepted by the participants, or have a limited capacity for enjoyment anyway.

The various personal characteristics that mold experiential reactions on life events belong to the same class of "life chances" that also influence the course of events. Low social status may result both in few invitations for feasts and in uneasy feelings at the occasional celebrations one attends. Still, the life events evoke experience and not the life chances. Effects of daily events on daily experiences have been studied by means of time sampling. In this method, respondents note several times during the day how well they feel at that moment and what they are doing. Based on such studies, Csikszentmihalyi and Wong (1991) found that we tend to feel better in company than we do alone and finer in leisure activities than we do at work. Structured leisure activities such as sporting appeared more rewarding than unstructured pastimes, such as television viewing. This pattern is probably universal. Personality explains about 30% of the variance in pleasant affect; situations explain another 10%, and person–situation interaction, 20%.

Inner Manufacturing of Feeling

Though it is clear *that* events evoke experiences, it is not so clear *how* such effects come about. In fact, little is known of how likes and dislikes are processed. We have some idea about the psychophysiology of sensations, but the inner fabrication of affective experience is hardly understood. Psychology has been more successful in grasping thinking than affect.

In the 1960s, the discovery of pleasure centers in the brain seemed to promise a breakthrough (Olds and Milner 1954; Rolls 1979). That promise has become somewhat bleak by now. There is no such thing as a single happiness gland. Pleasurable experience seems to result from different biochemical signals in both the body and the brain, the interactions of which are still largely unknown.

Capacity for Enjoyment

Wherever situated, the human capacity for enjoyment is great. Reward areas in the brain seem to be greater than areas that produce unpleasant experience, and most people tend to feel good most of the time (Bless and Schwarz 1984). Suffering may be more salient than satisfaction, but it is not more frequent.

There is some logic in this phenomenon. Why would nature doom us to be unhappy most of the time? If experiences of like and dislike serve to indicate conditions that are good and bad for the organism, we should expect that happiness is the rule. Evolution tends to produce a good fit of species to its environment, which is reflected in predominance of pleasurable experiences. Dysphoric experience is to keep away from harmful situations; it instigates withdrawal. Therefore, unhappiness can be permanent only in adverse living conditions from which no escape is possible. In such conditions, species tend to die out. In this view, chronic unhappiness can at best be a temporary phenomenon in the declining stage. However, the human species does not seem to be drawing to its end, and if we get extinct, that will be due to ecological disaster rather than to maladaptation to our living environment.

The organic disposition to enjoy things may not be as strong in everybody. There can be temperamental differences in happiness proneness. Twin studies show greater resemblance in happiness between monozygotic twins than dizygotic twins, even when reared apart. However, this does not mark happiness itself as a temperamental trait; the similarity in enjoyment of life can also result from other traits that are instrumental to happiness, such as heritable variation in "energy" or "resilience." The results of a follow-up study from birth on do not suggest that there is a marked temperamental disposition to be happy or unhappy. Babies observed to be cheerful did not appear to be more likely to report high life satisfaction in adulthood (Research reviewed in Veenhoven 1994).

Inner Process of Evaluation

What goes on in people when they evaluate their life? Speculations on these matters were a main issue in antique philosophy of happiness. This issue enjoys a renewed interest nowadays. It is not just curiosity about the inside of the black box that draws the attention, but rather the far-reaching consequences of the different points of view for the possibilities of creating greater happiness (to be discussed in the next section).

Calculus or Inference?

Utilitarian philosophers spoke of happiness as the "sum of pleasures and pains," established in a "mental calculus." This view on the evaluation process is still dominant nowadays. Happiness is seen to be assessed in a similar way as accountants calculate profit. We would count our blessings and blights and then strike a balance. The judgment is then a bottom–up process, in which appraisals of various aspects of life are combined into an overall judgment.

In this line, Andrews and Withey (1976) suggested that satisfaction with life as a whole is calculated from satisfactions with life domains. In this view, we first evaluate domains of life, such as our job and marriage, by means of comparing the reality of life with various standards of success, like "security" and "variation." Next, we would compute an average, weighted by perceived importance of domains. Andrews & Withey demonstrate high correlations between satisfaction with life as a whole and life domain appraisals but found no evidence for the presumed weighing. Michalos' (1985) multiple discrepancy theory also depicts happiness as the sum of various sub-evaluations. In his thinking, sub-evaluations are assessments of discrepancy between perceptions of how one's life "is" with notions of how it "should be." The five main comparison standards are presented as what one "wants," what one "had" earlier in life, what one "expected" to have, what one thinks "other people" have, and what one thinks is "deserved." Michalos provides ample evidence that small discrepancies are accompanied by high satisfaction with life as a whole. Multiple regression analysis showed that happiness is primarily a function of perceived discrepancy between reality and "wants." Though enjoyment of life as a whole is statistically correlated with appraisals of various aspects of life, it has not been established that happiness is causally determined by these sub-evaluations. The correlation can also be due to top–down effects. For instance, when assessing his job satisfaction, a person can reason: "I am generally happy, so apparently I like my job." Panel analysis has demonstrated strong effects of this kind. Actually, the effect of happiness on perception of have–want discrepancies is greater than the effect of gap size on happiness (Heady et al. 1991).

Inference on the Basis of Feeling

A rival theory is that evaluations of life draw on cues that provide indications of the quality of life as a whole. An internal cue of this kind is how well one generally feels; if pleasant affect dominates, life cannot be too bad. An external cue is how happy other people think one is (reflected appraisal).

The available evidence suggests that internal affective cues are far more important than external social ones. Happiness is much more related to matters of mood than to reputation. In assessing how we generally feel, we seem to focus on the relative frequency of positive and negative affects, rather than on the remembered intensity of joy and suffering (Diener et al. 1991). A typical heuristic seems to involve departing from the mood of the moment, which can be read quite vividly, and next considering how representative that mood is for general affective experience (Schwarz 1991).

Schwarz and Strack (1991) showed that evaluations of life as a whole draw on how one generally feels. This facilitates the judgmental task. Most people know well how they generally feel. The alternative of "calculating" happiness is more difficult and time consuming. It requires selection of standards, assessments of success, and integration of the appraisals into an overall judgment. Not only does this involve more mental operations, but it also entails many arbitrary decisions. Still, people sometimes choose to follow this more difficult road. A condition that encourages calculative evaluation is uncertainty about one's typical mood. For instance, in depression, it is hard to estimate how one generally feels. Another factor that invites to the calculative approach may be the availability of salient information for comparison, such as the earlier-mentioned confrontation with a person in a wheelchair.

Evaluations of specific aspects of life can less well be derived from estimates of general affect. One can be satisfied with one's job but still feel generally lousy because of a bad marriage and poor health. On the other hand, calculating is less difficult when specific life domains are concerned. The field is easier to oversee, and the standards are usually more evident.

Possibility of Greater Happiness

Much of the research on happiness is prompted by the hope of finding ways to create greater happiness for a greater number. However, several theories about happiness which imply that improvement of living conditions will not reduce discontent.

One such theory is that happiness is relative. Another is the theory that happiness is a trait. Both theories have been tested and have been rejected (Veenhoven 1995). Another comforting finding is that average happiness can be as high as 8 on a 0–10 scale. Remember Scheme 5 that shown an average of 8.2 in Denmark and 8.1 in Switzerland. What is possible in these countries should also be possible in other nations.

Conclusion

Happiness can be defined as subjective enjoyment of life as a whole. Empirical studies on happiness show considerable difference – both difference in average happiness across countries and differences between citizens within countries. At its present stage, our understanding of happiness already shows that greater happiness for a greater number is possible in principle and indicates some ways for achieving that goal.

References

Andrews, F. M., & Withey, S. B. (1976). *Social indicators of well-being*. New York: Plenum Press.

Bless, H., & Schwarz, N. (1984). *Ist schlechte Simmung die Ausnahme? Eine Meta-analyse von Stimmungsuntersuchungen* [Is bad mood exceptional? A meta analysis]. Paper, University of Heidelberg, Dept. of Psychology, Germany.

Cantril, H. (1965). *The pattern of human concern*. New Brunswick: Rutgers University Press.

Csikszentmihalyi, M., & Wong, M.-H. (1991). The situational and personal correlates of happiness: A cross national comparison. In F. Strack et al. (Eds.), *Subjective wellbeing* (pp. 193–212). London: Pergamon.

Diener, E., Emmons, R. A., Larsen, R. J., & Griffin, S. (1985). The satisfaction with life scale. *Journal of Personality Assessment, 49*, 71–75.

3 Happiness, Also Known as "Life Satisfaction" and "Subjective Well-Being"

Diener, E., Pavot, W., & Sandvik, E. (1991). Happiness is the frequency, not intensity of positive and negative affect. In F. Strack et al. (Eds.), *Subjective wellbeing*. London: Pergamon.

Ehrhardt, J., et al. (2000). Stability of life satisfaction over time analysis of change in ranks in national population. *Journal of Happiness Studies, 1*, 177–205.

Gerson, E. M. (1976). On quality of life. *American Sociological Review, 41*, 793–806.

Glatzer, W., & Zapf, W. (Eds.). (1984). *Lebensqualität in der Bundesrepublik (Quality of life in West-Germany)*. Frankfurt am Main: Campus Verlag.

Headey, B., & Wearing, A. (1992). *Understanding happiness: A theory of subjective well-being*. Melbourne: Longman Cheshire.

Heady, B., Veenhoven, R., & Wearing, A. (1991). Top-down versus bottom-up: Theories of subjective well-being. *Social Indicators Research, 24*, 81–100.

Ipsen, D. (1978). Das Konstrukt Zufriedenheit [The construct of satisfaction]. *Soziale Welt, 29*, 44–53.

Kahneman, D. (1999). Objective happiness. In D. Kahneman, E. Diener, & N. Schwarz (Eds.), *Wellbeing: Foundations of hedonic psychology* (pp. 3–25). New York: Russell Sage Foundations.

Lane, R. E. (1994). Quality of life and quality of persons: A new role for government? *Political theory, 22*, 219–252.

Mill. J. S. (1863). *Utilitarianism*. London: Fontana Press 1990 (20th print).

Olds, J., & Milner, O. (1954). Positive reinforcement produced by electrical stimulation of septal areas and other regions of the rat brain. *Journal of Comparative and Physiological Psychology, 47*, 419–427.

Ouweneel, P., & Veenhoven, R. (1991). Cross-national differences in happiness: Cultural bias or societal quality? In N. Bleichrodt & P. J. Drenth (Eds.), *Contemporary issues in cross-cultural psychology* (pp. 168–184). Lisse: Swets & Zeilinger.

Rolls, E. T. (1979). Effects of electrical stimulation of the brain of behavior. *Psychological Surveys, 2*, 151–169.

Saris, W., Scherpenzeel, A., & Veenhoven, R. (Eds.). (1996). *Satisfaction in Europe*. Budapest: Eötvös University Press.

Schimmack, U., & Diener, E. (Eds.) (2003). Experience sampling method. *Special Issues Journal of happiness Studies, 4*(1)

Schwarz, N., & Strack, N. (1991). Evaluating one's life: A judgment model of subjective well-being. In F. Strack et al. (Eds.), *Subjective wellbeing* (pp. 27–48). London: Pergamon.

Sen, A. (1992). Capability and wellbeing. In A. Sen & M. Nussbaum (Eds.), *The quality of life* (pp. 30–53). Oxford: Clarendon.

Veenhoven, R. (1984). *Conditions of happiness*. Dordrecht: Kluwer (now Springer).

Veenhoven, R. (1988). The utility of happiness. *Social Indicators Research, 20*, 333–354.

Veenhoven, R. (1991). Is happiness relative? *Social Indicators Research, 24*, 1–34.

Veenhoven, R. (1993). *Happiness in nations: Subjective appreciation of life in 56 nations 1946–1992*. Rotterdam: Erasmus University Rotterdam, Risbo, Studies in Social and Cultural Transformation.

Veenhoven, R. (1994). Is happiness a trait? Tests of the theory that a better society does not make people any happier. *Social Indicators Research, 32*, 101–160.

Veenhoven, R. (1995). The cross-cultural pattern of happiness. Test of predictions implied in three theories of happiness. *Social Indicators Research, 34*, 33–68.

Veenhoven, R. (1996). Happy life-expectancy: A comprehensive measure of quality-of-life in nations. *Social Indicators Research, 39*, 1–58.

Veenhoven, R. (1997). Progrés dans la compréhension du bonheur. *Revue Québécoise de Psychologie, 18*, 29–74.

Veenhoven, R. (1998). Vergelijken van geluk in landen [Comparing happiness across nations]. *Sociale Wetenschappen, 42*, 58–84.

Veenhoven, R. (2000). The four qualities of life. *Journal of Happiness Studies, 1*, 1–39.

Veenhoven, R. (2005). Is life getting better? How long and happy do people live in modern society? *European Psychologist, special section on 'Human development and Well-being', 10*, 330–343.

Veenhoven, R. (2008). Healthy happiness: Effects of happiness on physical health and consequences for preventive healthcare. *Journal of Happiness Studies, 9*, 449–464.

Veenhoven, R. (2009). How do we assess how happy we are? In A. K. Dutt & B. Radcliff (Eds.), *Happiness, economics and politics: Towards a multi-disciplinary approach* (pp. 45–69). Cheltenham: Edward Elger Publishers.

Veenhoven, R. (2010) *World database of happiness: Continuous register of research on subjective enjoyment of life*. Rotterdam: Erasmus University Rotterdam. Available at: http://worlddatabaseofhappiness.eur.nl

Subjective Wellbeing Homeostasis

4

Robert A. Cummins, Anna L.D. Lau,
and Melanie T. Davern

An Introduction to Subjective Wellbeing

This chapter explains the concept of Subjective Wellbeing homeostasis. It concerns the proposal that Subjective Wellbeing (SWB) is managed by a system of psychological devices which have evolved for this purpose. The chapter begins by presenting some of the psychometric characteristics of SWB and introduces homeostasis as a theoretical construct that can account for these characteristics. This is followed by a discussion of the relationship between SWB and depression. The chapter ends with recommendations for measurement scales.

Subjective Wellbeing Is Positive

The single most important thing about Subjective Wellbeing (SWB) is that it is positive. It is normal for people to feel good about themselves. The demonstration of this is presented below in the form of data gathered by the Australian Unity Wellbeing Index project (Cummins et al. 2003). This project measures the SWB of the Australian population several times each year. Each survey involves a telephone interview of 2,000 new respondents nationwide. The project commenced in April 2001, and the accumulated data from the 25

surveys conducted to April 2011 have been gathered from 50,000 respondents. Most of the figures presented in this chapter are based on data from these surveys.

The scale used to measure and conceptualize SWB is the Personal Wellbeing Index (International Wellbeing Group 2006) which has a unique construction. It is designed as the first-level deconstruction of the highly abstract question, "How satisfied are you with your life as a whole?" In order to achieve this design aim, each of the seven items has two important characteristics. The first is the semi-abstract nature of each question, such as "How satisfied are you with your relationships?" This format is deliberately non-specific. It allows the response that people give to be dominated by non-specific mood affect (the essence of SWB, see later), slightly flavored with cognitions attached to personal relationships (for the use of affect as information, see Schwarz 1999; Schwarz and Strack 1991). A more specific question, such as "How satisfied are you with your friends?," would elicit a more cognitively driven response.

The second characteristic of the eight items (domains) that comprise the Personal Wellbeing Index is that when they are together regressed against "Satisfaction with life as a whole," each one contributes unique variance. These matters of theoretical construction are elaborated in the test manual.

Each item is rated on an end-defined 0–10 scale (Jones and Thurstone 1955) that is anchored by "completely dissatisfied" and "completely satisfied" (see Cummins and Gullone 2000 for an argument as to why this form of scale is superior to a Likert scale). The data are then averaged across the seven domains for each respondent and the result transformed onto a 0–100 scale. The results below come from Cummins et al. (2008) and show the distribution of SWB in the Australian population:

R.A. Cummins (✉) • A.L.D. Lau
School of Psychology, Deakin University, Burwood, VIC,
Australia
e-mail: robert.cummins@deakin.edu.au

M.T. Davern
McCaughey Centre, Melbourne University, Melbourne, VIC,
Australia

K.C. Land et al. (eds.), *Handbook of Social Indicators and Quality of Life Research*,
DOI 10.1007/978-94-007-2421-1_4, © Springer Science+Business Media B.V. 2012

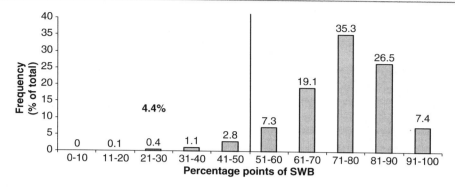

Fig. 4.1 Population distribution of Personal Wellbeing Index

The distribution of SWB is approximately normal within the positive (satisfied) sector of the response scale. Only 4.4% of respondents score in the negative (dissatisfied) sector, and an explanation as to why these values may be considered to represent pathology will be provided later.

Subjective Wellbeing Is Stable

The second intriguing feature of SWB is its stability. This can be demonstrated by two kinds of data. One uses the mean scores from population surveys, and the other are data obtained from individuals.

To take the population data first, two reports (Cummins 1995, 1998) first demonstrated the extraordinary level of SWB stability, and therefore predictability, of population mean scores. The first of these papers combined data from population surveys performed in various Western countries. It included highly diverse studies, each one having been conducted by different researchers, using different scales of measurement, at different times over the decades 1970–1990. The key to combining these disparate results was to convert all scores to the standardized 0–100 range called "percentage of Scale Maximum" (%SM) as shown by Eq. 4.1.

$$x\%SM = \frac{(Score-1)}{Maximum\ possible\ score} \times 100 \quad (4.1)$$

This formula transforms data in a three-step process as: (a) The scale score is reduced by 1. Thus, a group mean score of 4.1 becomes 3.1. (b) The maximum score provided by the response scale is reduced by 1 so that the response scale commences with zero. If the scale is already in this form (eg 0–10), then this step is omitted. Thus, a scale scored 1–5 is recoded 0–4; (c) a percentage is then calculated against the maximum scale score. For example, a score of 4 on a 1–5 scales is calculated as $3/4 \times 100 = 75\%SM$ or percentage "points" as they will now be referred to.

When the values from 16 population surveys were recoded in this manner (Cummins 1995), it was found that all lay quite close to one another. Using the survey mean scores as data, they averaged 75 points, and their standard deviation was 2.5. This grand mean of 75 is within the modal range of Fig. 4.1 (71–80 points) and so shows convergent validity for these Australian data. The standard deviation can be used to show just how close to one another the 16 population sample means really are. When a normative range is created by using the distance of two standard deviations on either side of the mean, there is a 95% probability that any new survey mean will be located within such a range. Thus, these early results indicate a normative population range for SWB mean scores that extends between 75±5 and 70–80 points.

Of course, this estimate is heavily contaminated with error variance resulting from the many methodological differences between the studies. Much greater stability is revealed by the 25 surveys conducted to date through the Australian Unity Wellbeing Index project. Over the 10-year period of these surveys (2001–2011), the mean SWB has varied over a range of 3.1 points (73.2–76.3). In statistical terms, these 25 values produce a mean of 74.93 points, a standard deviation of 0.75, and, therefore, a normative range of 73.43–76.43 points. In other words, the mean score of a random survey of people in Australia can be predicted, with 95% certainty, to lie within a 3.0% point range. There is no precedent in the literature for such extraordinary stability in measures of SWB. Outside Australia, however, there is much greater variation in population mean scores.

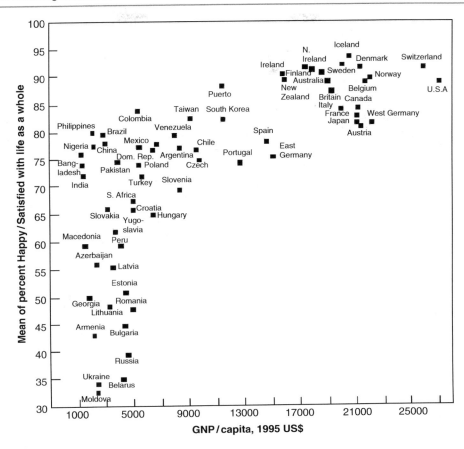

Fig. 4.2 The relationship between SWB and GNP by country

SWB in Non-Western Countries

When the population mean scores from non-Western countries are examined, it is evident that there is considerable variation. Countries differ in wealth and culture, and SWB is sensitive to both types of influence. Figure 4.2 shows the relationship between national wealth and SWB.

This figure (World Bank 1997) shows Subjective Wellbeing plotted against the level of economic development. To measure SWB, these researchers used the 4-point response scale of very happy (100 points), quite happy (66.6 points), not very happy (33.3 points), and not at all happy (0 points). The use of this scale is commonplace, yet its poor validity is evident when matched against the actual SWB distribution shown in Fig. 4.1. Two of the scale categories (not at all happy and not very happy) are allocated to values below the mid-point of the scale, yet only about 4% of the Australian population report SWB below this level. As a consequence, the 96% of people in Western populations who have a positive SWB are effectively faced with a binary response choice when using this 4-category scale. They must select between "quite happy" (66.6 points) and "very happy" (100 points). While these types of scale have enjoyed wide currency in surveys over the past 40 years, their continued use in the light of contemporary understanding about SWB can hardly be justified, as will now be demonstrated.

While the vertical axis in Fig. 4.2 depicts SWB, the statistic it employs is the percentage of people who rated themselves as either very or quite happy. Thus, in the terms of Fig. 4.1, the vertical axis represents the percentage of people who rate themselves at or above 50 points. The following matters are notable:

(a) The true percentage for Australia, assuming that our 2001–2008 data reasonably reflect how the data for 1997 would have been, is about 96%, as taken from Fig. 4.1. However, the score for Australia in Fig. 4.2 is about 88%. This is an indication of either poor sampling or limitations of the measurement instrument. With this in mind, the results shown in Fig. 4.2 should be taken as indicative only.

(b) While there is a strong overall relationship between national wealth and SWB, this relationship is clearly not linear.

(c) There is more going on to change SWB than just income. The countries with incomes <$5,000 vary widely in SWB, and yet there is no simple relationship with wealth. This indicates that population SWB can be heavily influenced by many other factors such as civil disturbance, food shortage, disease, bad governance, etc. Importantly, SWB may also vary according to culture.

People differ in the way they respond to scales of satisfaction. In the face of super-human endeavors, many laconic adventurers express modesty when asked how they rate their own achievement, while others who have achieved minor success puff themselves with self-congratulatory pride. Such response differences are also evident at the level of whole cultures. People are socialized as to the acceptable manner of expressing their feelings. As a consequence, people in some countries have no hesitation in rating high satisfaction as 10/10, while people from other countries who feel the same level of satisfaction express a more modest rating.

Such differences constitute a cultural response bias. This form of bias has been well documented (e.g., Lee et al. 2002; Stening and Everett 1984) and is evidently different between East Asians such as Japanese and Caucasians such as White Americans. Specifically, Asians are less likely to rate themselves at the ends of the scale due to cultural modesty. This tends to yield a lower score in samples of Asians because the process of avoiding scale extremes causes disproportionately fewer high values than low values due to the relative frequency of each (see Fig. 4.1).

Further evidence for cultural response bias has been provided by Lau et al. (2005) who compared the SWB of Hong Kong Chinese and Australians. While the mean SWB was higher for the Australians, there was no difference in the sample standard deviations of the two groups. One explanation is that, within the Chinese sample, the distribution had been extended downward due to the presence of poorer living conditions at the low end of the distribution, but this has been offset by a truncated upper distribution due to cultural modesty. The overall result was to produce no difference in the distribution despite a shift in the mean score. Pretty obviously, cultural response bias has important implications for the interpretation of cross-cultural SWB data.

In summary, it is clear that differences in national wealth and culture are going to affect international comparisons of SWB. This is hardly surprising. What is surprising is the relatively small amount of difference that these factors produce. Cummins (1997) repeated his 1995 analysis using 45 population mean scores derived from both Western and non-Western nations (Cummins 1997). This time, the overall mean score was 70 points with a standard deviation of 5.0. Thus, the effective normal range is double that of the previous analysis, being from 60 to 80 points. Two interesting factors stand out from this analysis. The first is that that the SWB of world populations can be predicted, with 95% certainty, to lie within a 20-point range. However, this range could be extended by deliberately including more countries with low SWB. The second point of interest is that both the Western and world ranges coincided at their upper margin of 80 points. This value is consistent with a ceiling imposed on SWB by a management system, and this system will be discussed shortly. Notable, however, due to the imposition of this upper margin, the difference between these Western and world ranges is caused by the greater downward extension of the world range.

The above analyses have been based on the use of sample means as data. When measures of life satisfaction from individuals are used, the standard deviation is much larger, but is also very consistent. Using the data shown in Fig. 4.1, the mean is 74.92 points, the standard deviation is 12.36, and so, the normal range is 50.21–99.64 points. It can be seen that this range rather neatly fits the positive sector of the response scale distribution; however, it is certainly too large to be regarded as the true normal range. This is because the calculation involves the 4.4% of people who fall below this range, and as will be argued later, this is considered to indicate the presence of pathology. So, a new range can be calculated omitting these values. This produces a mean of 76.45 and a standard deviation of 10.13. Using these new values, the normal range becomes 56.19–96.71. A further slight adjustment can be made on the assumption that the true distribution is normal and that the 4.4% of values that fell below 50 are overly representative of the lower portion of the remaining distribution. This idea is supported by the slightly uneven distribution above and below the median in Fig. 4.1. So, if the above calculation is adjusted downward slightly, it gives a normal range between 55 and 95 and a mean of 75 points. Of course, this is only an approximation and requires verification by other methodologies, but it is a reasonable basis for further theory building.

How Can These Data Patterns Be Explained?

It is apparent from the section above that SWB is exhibiting some determined characteristics which are as follows:

1. It is highly stable.
2. It is normally restricted to the positive sector of the dissatisfied–satisfied continuum.
3. It shows a normal distribution consistent with what Psychologists refer to as an individual difference and is under strong genetic determination (e.g., Lykken and Tellegen 1996). That is, its distribution is consistent with SWB being an innate personal characteristic.
4. In relation to wealth, it shows a curvilinear, asymptotic relationship. This is evident in Fig. 4.2 and will also be demonstrated for Australian data (Fig. 4.4, see later). This is a typical output from a management system that can be saturated. That is, supplying more of some relevant resource (money) may or may not cause an increase in output. The effect of the resource is dependent on the level of deprivation. Thus, for poor countries, all other things being equal, increased wealth will increase SWB. But this will continue only up to some ceiling value (about 80 points for group means), which reflects full and unrestricted functioning of the system in relation to that resource.

So what kind of a system might be responsible for such behavior? There is a substantial literature in which researchers describe the models they imagine responsible for SWB. The earliest of these were the "Physical and Spiritual Model" (Liu 1975), the "Lewinian Lifespace Model" (Campbell et al. 1976), and the "Two-Dimensional Conceptual Model" (Andrews and Withey 1976), but all of these were mainly concerned with the composition of Quality of Life into its objective and subjective components. It took more than a

decade for subsequent researchers to incorporate some of the psychometric characteristics described above into their models.

The first of these pioneers were two Australian researchers, Headey and Wearing (Headey et al. 1984a, b; Headey and Wearing 1986, 1987, 1989). Using data from a panel study, they observed that people appeared to have a "set point" for their SWB. That is, in the absence of significant life events, people tended to maintain a relatively steady level of SWB, and that if an event caused SWB to change then, over time, it tended to regain its previous level. They called this their "Dynamic Equilibrium Model" and considered the management of SWB to be vested in a genetically inbuilt psychological system, based in stable personality characteristics, which had the primary purpose of maintaining self-esteem. They characterized the positive sense of SWB as a "Sense of Relative Superiority" because it had the consequence of making people feel that their subjective life experience is better than average for the population.

The second researchers to take up this challenge were Stones and Kozma (1991) who proposed their "Magical Model of Happiness." Like Headey and Wearing, they depicted SWB as a self-correcting process that maintains stability around set points that differ between individuals. They also regard SWB stability as a function of a dispositional system (Kozma et al. 2000 now referred to this as the "Propensity Model"). However, they also found that the propensity for stability could not be entirely explained through personality variables alone and that the best predictor of future SWB was the level of past SWB.

All of these data are consistent with the idea also proposed by other authors (Hanestad and Albrektsen 1992; Nieboer 1997; Ormel 1983; Ormel and Schaufeli 1991) that SWB is neurologically maintained in a state of dynamic equilibrium. However, these earlier models did not attempt to account for the nature of the relationship between SWB in dynamic equilibrium and other demographic and psychological variables. This feature requires that theoretical attention be given to the processes of SWB management, which we call SWB homeostasis.

In 1998, Cummins first used the term "homeostasis" to describe the basic mechanism underpinning SWB management. The term implies an analogy between the physiological management of internal body states, such as body temperature, and the management of SWB. While the homeostatic management of body temperature lies within the autonomic system, SWB is considered

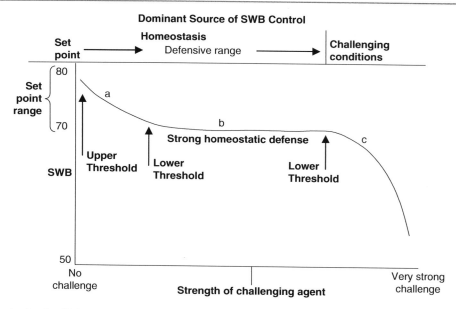

Fig. 4.3 Changing levels of SWB as homeostasis is challenged

to be managed by dispositional, genetically pre-wired, neurological systems.

The term "homeostasis" is charged with meaning. Describing management in these terms makes very clear predictions concerning the relationship between SWB and other variables. The variable being managed, SWB must conform to the standard performance requirements of homeostatic systems, and these include the four characteristics that have been previously listed as 1–4. In addition to these, other characteristics should also be displayed if SWB management may be considered homeostatic. These include the following:

5. There must be a threshold value which is being defended by the homeostatic processes. There must also be evidence that, as this value is approached, the system works harder than normal to retain control. Then, as the threshold value is exceeded, there must be evidence that homeostasis has failed and is no longer controlling the level of SWB.
6. Following homeostatic defeat, over time, the system should act to regain control. If this is successful, the level of SWB should return to a stable approximation of its set point.
7. The aim of homeostasis is to maintain the variable it is managing within a narrow range of values. Thus, SWB must evidence a "set-point range" which reflects the normal moment-to-moment range in which SWB will be found for each individual. The magnitude of this range may also be an individual difference, with some ranges being more tightly controlled than others.
8. SWB should respond to variables that either enhance or challenge the operation of the homeostatic system. But the nature of the relationship with such variables should be consistent with the operation of a homeostatic system. The implications of these requirements are illustrated with the aid of Fig. 4.3. This figure comprises several parts as follows:

(a) The vertical axis shows the 0–100 scale of SWB and includes an illustrative set-point range of 70–80 points.
(b) The lower horizontal axis shows the strength of a negative challenge to SWB, such as might be delivered by poverty or anxiety.
(c) The upper horizontal axis shows the dominant source of control. This source of control can change if the strength of the challenging agent is strong.
(d) The curving "response line" depicts the changes in SWB due to changes in the challenging agent. The upper (80-point) and lower (70-point) margins of the set-point range are identified as "thresholds" and indicated by vertical arrows.
(e) An important limitation in this depiction is that the position of the response line will vary between

people, determined by their set-point range. Thus, for people who have a lower set point, the response line will also be lower.

(f) A second limitation in this depiction is that it shows the theoretical outcome of the combined influences of supportive and challenging agents acting on the homeostatic system at any one time. Due to such multiple influences, any empirical investigation of the relationship between SWB and its sources of influence can only be expected to approximate the pattern that is shown.

The predictions derived from Fig. 4.3 are as follows:

1. Under conditions of zero threat, SWB will average to its set point, which in this case is 75 points.

2. As mild sources of threat are experienced, the level of SWB will vary within its set-point range. Moreover, its position within the range will be a probability statement determined by the balance of good and bad momentary experience and the resilience of the homeostatic system. Thus, a sustained environment where good experience dominates will cause SWB to average higher than the set point, while the reverse chronic experience will cause SWB to average lower than the set point. However, the extent of such fluctuations is predicted to be quite modest. Since the magnitude of the set-point range is calculated to be around 10–12% points (Cummins et al. 2008, Sect. 3.8.1), the total movement of SWB due to such influences will not be more than a few percentage points on either side of the set point. This phase is shown in Fig. 4.3 as (a).

3. As the strength of threat intensifies, the strength of the homeostatic defense also increases in an attempt to maintain stable levels of SWB. The result is phase (b) in which homeostasis manages to hold the line and prevent SWB from decreasing below its lower threshold value of 70 points. The evidence for this lower threshold to be located at about 70 points, on average, is presented in Cummins (2003). Importantly during this phase (b), the value of SWB is insensitive to changing levels of the challenging agent. That is, although the strength of the challenge is increasing, SWB will be held steady at the value approximating the lower threshold. This phase will continue as long as the homeostatic system is effective. However, at some higher strength of challenge, homeostasis will be overwhelmed.

4. Once the strength of the challenging agent becomes too strong for homeostatic management, the value of SWB enters phase (c). In this phase, the dominant source of control has shifted from homeostatic processes to the challenging agent. Now, the value of SWB is sensitive to the strength of the challenging agent, and as the strength of the challenge increases, the value of SWB will sharply fall.

Within this theoretical and predictive background, two kinds of elaboration will now be presented. The first concerns the nature of the homeostatic system itself. The second examines empirical evidence for the proposition that the relationship between SWB and challenging agents conforms to the outcomes predicted by this homeostatic model.

The Mechanisms of Homeostasis

Ever since theorists in the 1970s first pondered the nature of a management system for SWB (see the previous Section), it has been accepted that life quality can be considered in two parts, one objective and the other subjective. The traditional measures of life quality are objective and focus on the circumstances of living, sometimes called the "quality of living." These objective variables are tangible in that they can be simultaneously observed by a number of people, usually as estimates of frequencies or quantities. Examples may be the number of friends a person has or the degree of their physical disability. Certainly, such measures involve degrees of subjective judgment, but when they are carefully performed, such measures can yield a high degree of inter-rater agreement.

The other part of life quality is subjective, and the variables here are quite different. They can only be directly experienced by each individual person, such as their degree of felt happiness or satisfaction. Consequently, they can only be measured by asking the individual concerned how they feel about their life. It is not valid to infer SWB either from ratings made by other people (i.e., proxy responses – see Cummins 2002 for a review) or from objective measures, due to the influence of homeostasis.

Considering first the objective side of life quality, two of the most fundamental variables are wealth and relationships. Each of these has considerable capacity to either support or challenge SWB. Importantly for this discussion, their capacity to protect SWB allows them to be conceptualized as external homeostatic buffers.

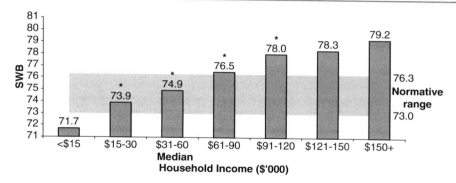

Fig. 4.4 SWB vs. household income

The External Buffers

There are serious misconceptions as to what money can and cannot do in relation to personal wellbeing. Looking first at those who are rich, people experience rapid adaptation to high living standards, so living in a mansion with servants simply feels "normal," not luxurious, with the passage of time. Moreover, high wealth cannot shift the set point to create a perpetually happier person. Set points for SWB are proposed to be under genetic control (Cummins et al. 2003; Lykken and Tellegen 1996), so in this sense, money cannot buy happiness. No matter how rich someone becomes, at a level of income that saturates the wealth-dependent buffering capacity of the homeostatic system, additional wealth will not raise SWB further.

The real power of wealth is to protect wellbeing through its capacity to be used as a flexible resource to assist homeostasis (Cummins 2000). It does this by allowing people to minimize the unwanted challenges they experience in their daily life. Wealthy people pay others to perform tasks they do not wish to do themselves. Poor people, who lack such financial resources, must fend for themselves to a much greater extent. As a consequence, their level of SWB is far more at the mercy of their environment. Because of this influence, SWB rises with income.

The results shown in Fig. 4.4, and those that follow, are generated from cumulative data obtained from the Australian Unity Wellbeing Index. This figure depicts the relationship between SWB and gross household income. It is based on the responses of about 30,000 people and shows the normative range for sample mean scores described earlier. The * at the top of columns indicates that the level of SWB is significantly higher than that for the previous lower income level. As can be seen, SWB rises with income up to $91,000–$120,000, but at higher incomes, there is no further systematic rise in SWB. It is interesting that this optimal income range is about double the median income in Australia. However, this level of income is quite common among dual-income households, and about 20% of the population have a level of household income at or above this level.

The pattern of the relationship between SWB and wealth is similar to the international data shown in Fig. 4.2. The SWB increments, resulting from this wealth resource, are most apparent up to the point where the living environment is under reasonable control. This seems to occur at about US$15,000 GDP/capita and at about AUS$91,000–$120,000 for households in Australia.

These results are convergent evidence that the power of money lies in its usefulness as a flexible resource, which can be used to diminish the probability of encountering chronic negative life events. In terms of Fig. 4.3, this represents a shift in the sample from being dominantly at (c) and (b) to being dominantly at (a) and (b). That is, the resource of money has an effect in two stages. The first is the most obvious. As income rises, fewer people within the sample experience homeostatic defeat due to some factor that can be ameliorated through the resource of money. This represents the significant rise in Fig. 4.4 up to $91,000–$120,000. Above this level of income, there will be a continued but gradual rise in average SWB, as progressively, more of the sample experience a lifestyle that allows their SWB to inhabit the upper portion of their set-point range. However, of course, there will always be some people with a level of SWB that lies below its

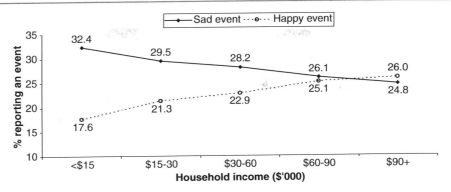

Fig. 4.5 Income vs. happy and sad events

set point irrespective of the financial situation. The cause will be attributable to situations, such as parenting unpleasant children, which are not amenable to resolution through money.

A further observation from Fig. 4.4 is that SWB plateaus at about 80 points. As noted previously, this reflects the limitations to the upward movement of SWB due to set points and the impositions of homeostatic control.

This explanatory idea, that the real power of wealth is to protect wellbeing through its capacity as a flexible resource, can be tested in various ways. One is to examine the way in which rich and poor people experience their lives. Rich people should be more likely than poor people to experience a happy event in their lives and less likely to experience a sad event. To test this proposition, we ask the question, "Has something happened to you recently causing you to feel happier or sadder than normal?" The results are as follows.

From our cumulative data, about 50% of respondents recall that they have recently experienced such an event. The percentages of people reporting either a happy or a sad event are presented in Fig. 4.5. It can be seen that, in accordance with the predicted influence of money as a flexible resource, poor people are more likely to have experienced an event that made them sadder than normal and less likely to have experienced an event that made them feel happier than normal. This differential influence decreases with increasing income, up to a gross household income of about $60,000–$90,000 per year. At this level of income and beyond, people tend to experience about the same probability of positive and negative events. In conclusion, these results support the theory of money as a flexible resource

and the homeostatic relationship with SWB as shown in Fig. 4.3.

A second major external resource is a relationship with another adult that involves mutual sharing of intimacies and support. Almost universally, the research literature attests to the power of such relationships to moderate the influence of potential stressors on SWB (for reviews, see Henderson 1977; Sarason et al. 1990). Our results are shown in Fig. 4.6 (Cummins et al. 2008).

This figure depicts the SWB of people living in households that differ in the nature of relationships between the inhabitants. The pattern of these results is simple. All seven groups where the respondent lives with their partner rate either higher than, or within, the normal-range SWB for sample means. Even the lowest of these groups, living with a partner and other adults, has a level of SWB that lies firmly in the normal range. This is very different for the other six groups shown in this figure.

People living in the absence of a partner show consistently lower SWB. In fact, the only non-partner group to lie within the normal range consists of those living with their parents. All the other five groups lie below the normal range, and one of these, living with other adults and children, lies below 70 points, which is the cutoff for enhanced risk of depression (see later).

Of course, these rankings are going to also be affected by household income. It might be expected that the power of the two external buffers to protect SWB is additive, and this will now be demonstrated in Fig. 4.7 below. This demonstrates the interaction between income and household structure.

The top line shows the effect of income on the SWB of people living only with their partner. It can be seen that this living arrangement makes people very

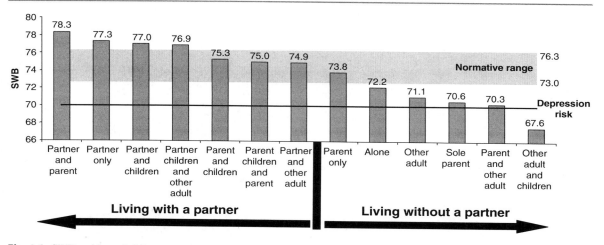

Fig. 4.6 SWB and household structure

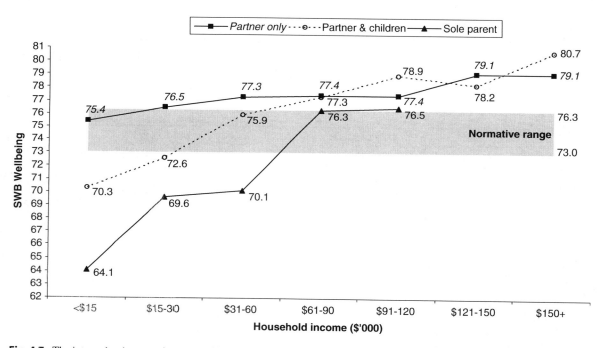

Fig. 4.7 The interaction between income and household composition

resilient. Even at the lowest household income, SWB lies in the middle of the normal range. Notably, it does not change very much as income increases, rising only 3.7 points across the entire income range. This is another example of the ceiling created by set points – that money as a resource cannot be used to increase SWB beyond the set-point range for each individual. Thus, since SWB is already in the normal range at the lowest income level for this group, the only influence of higher income is to increase the probability that SWB lies toward the top of its set-point range.

The second line in this figure shows partners who are living with one or more children. Their resilience is lower because children drain the emotional and financial resources of their parents. Thus, at the lowest income level, SWB lies well below the normal range. This reflects the demands made by children exceeding the resources available to some parents. However, at an

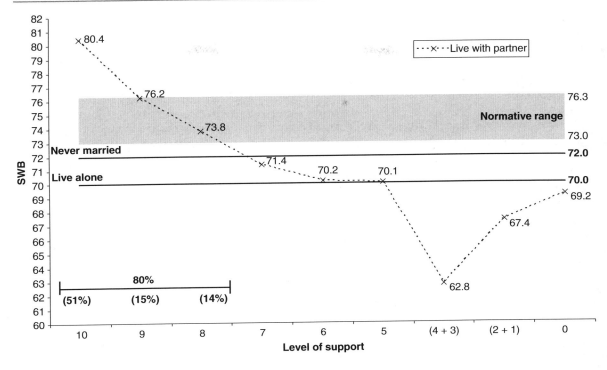

Fig. 4.8 Partner support vs. SWB

income of $30,000–$60,000, the financial and relationship resources become sufficient for homeostatic control to be returned. Thereafter, rises in income do not statistically differ between the couples with and without children.

The situation for single parents is more extreme. Since they lack the resource of an adult partnership, they require an income of $60,000–$90,000 to regain homeostatic control. It is also informative to observe that the three-person household (partners plus child) on low income has higher SWB than the two-person household (one parent plus child). This is quite the reverse of the relative wellbeing normally assumed by Economists (see Trigger 2003). Economists usually calculate household wellbeing as income discounted by the number of people in the household. Clearly, this method is incorrect in relation to SWB. The increased consumption of goods by the additional adult is more than offset by the instrumental and emotional support they are able to provide.

In summary, both income and relationship support are highly effective external buffers for SWB homeostasis, and their combined influence appears to be additive. However, our data also reveal an important caveat in regard to the strength of relationship support. While it is almost universally assumed that the association between support and SWB is linear, our results indicate otherwise. In Survey 14 (Cummins et al. 2005), we asked people how much support they received from their partner. The relationship with SWB is shown below.

As expected, the highest levels of support are associated with the highest wellbeing, and as the level of support decreases, SWB decreases also. This is consistent with relationship support as a homeostatic resource. However, the relationship between support and SWB is clearly non-linear, and Fig. 4.8 shows the following features:

1. Normal-range SWB is only associated with a level of partner support that lies at 8/10 or above.
2. At a level of support from 5 to 7, SWB corresponds to the levels which, on average, are experienced by people without a partner, who have never married or who live alone. Thus, at these levels of support, there is no net advantage to SWB from the partner relationship.
3. At levels of support from 3 to 4, SWB falls very sharply. This fall is probably attributable to the reciprocal nature of relationships. That is, in order

to mutually benefit from a relationship, both partners must give support to one another. When this becomes one-sided, as in low levels of received support, the relationship actually becomes negative for one partner in that it represents a net drain on their resources.

4. At levels of support that are 1–2, the associated SWB rises somewhat and becomes higher still when the strength of support is rated as zero. It seems likely that this represents a disengagement from the relationship, in that support is not being supplied by either partner, and so, it is less draining of personal resources.

It is interesting that the majority of people in a relationship (80%) have a level of support at 8 or above and that this level of support corresponds with normal SWB. This suggests that people who experience a level of support from their partner that is at 7 or less are likely to seek a new partner. In summary, the relationship between SWB and both of the external buffers conforms fairly well to the predictions of homeostasis. But this is only the external aspects of homeostatic control. There is an additional set of buffers to assist homeostasis that are internal to each person

Internal Buffers

When the external buffers are not strong enough to prevent something bad happening, all is not lost. At the heart of homeostasis is a set of genetically programmed internal buffers. These comprise protective devices that are brought into action because SWB is being threatened. At the simplest level, these involve the automatic processes of adaptation and habituation. These act over time to make us less aware of challenging experiences. An example of this phenomenon can be observed in relation to the gradual loss of motor functioning with age. Because people adapt their behavior and expectations to fit the reality of their diminishing motor capacity, the loss of functioning only weakly engages awareness, and so fails to threaten SWB. The extent to which this can happen is amazing. Many people with Multiple Sclerosis, which induces a gradual loss of motor functioning, report normal levels of SWB even when they lose the capacity to independently breathe and require mechanical ventilation (Bach et al. 1991).

We propose that this kind of adaptation is assisted by a set of cognitive buffers. These use cognition to restructure reality and so to minimize the impact of unavoidable negative experiences. The ways that the cognitive buffers do this are highly varied. For example, one can find meaning in the event ("God is testing me"), fail to take responsibility for the failure ("it was not my fault") or regard the failure (dropping a vase) as useful ("I did not like that old vase anyway and now I can buy another"). There are many such devices that essentially involve maintaining a sense of control, collectively called Secondary Control techniques (Rothbaum et al. 1982).

There are other ways of restructuring reality that do not involve the sense of control. One is protection of self-esteem through "splintering." For example, when dropping the vase, one may think "Well, so I am a bit clumsy, but it doesn't matter because I am so good at (making friends, cooking, writing, etc.)." Here, the cause of the bad event has been relegated to some aspect of performance that the person regards as unimportant to their sense of identity. Another method is to restructure an imaginary future, e.g., "Well this has been a bad day, but tomorrow will be better."

The effect of these cognitive devices, when effectively employed, is restoring peace of mind. Some explanation for the experience has been found that allows the person to feel that their sense of self and ability to understand the world is intact. Indeed, they may even benefit from the experience in the long term. Therefore, the sense of threat has been dissipated, and SWB returns to its set-point range. A detailed discussion of these internal buffering systems is provided in Cummins and Nistico (2002) and Cummins et al. (2002).

It is important to note in relation to all this that the homeostatic system, as described, has the role of maintaining a positive sense of wellbeing that is both non-specific and highly personalized. It is concerned only with the abstract core feelings that the individual has about themselves and only in the most general sense. One consequence of this is to imbue people with a "positivity bias" in relation to themselves. So, people generally feel they are "superior" to others or better than average (Diener et al. 1999; Headey and Wearing 1988, 1989). They believe they are luckier, happier, and more moral (Andrews and Withey 1976). This is all part of the general positive bias that is "value added" by the brain to such thought processes and which leads, under the normal circumstances of living, to a generalized positive self-view (Taylor and Brown 1988; Weinstein 1989).

It is these characteristics that allow the personal sense of wellbeing to be so defendable against the slings and arrows of misfortune. Because these self-beliefs are held at such an abstract level, specific instances of personal bad luck or incompetence that might otherwise damage the sense of personal wellbeing can be dismissed by using the internal buffers to maintain the abstract belief. This general idea is not novel. For example, Tesser et al. (1989) provide empirical support for a model of Self-Evaluation Maintenance, in which the self recognizes good performance on a variety of dimensions yet aspires to "be good at" (or personally values) only a few such dimensions. Thus, one's own performance is not threatening to self-evaluation provided that failures are confined to non-valued dimensions in life. Such processes assist people who are deaf, for example, to maintain a positive self-view (Bat-Chava 1994).

So, SWB is heavily defended, and this gives a sense of how important it is to maintain positive feelings about the self. But SWB is generally acknowledged to be a mixture of affect and cognition. So, is this what homeostasis is defending, or is there some deeper state that we are determined to maintain?

What Is Homeostasis Defending?

Most contemporary theorists regard the measurement of SWB, obtained through a considered verbal or written response, to involve both affective and cognitive processes. This was first recognized by Campbell et al. (1976) who suggested that this amalgam should be measured through questions of "satisfaction." This form of question has since become standard for SWB measurement. However, relatively little research has been directed to examining the relative contribution of affect and cognition. Certainly, the two components are separable (Lucas et al. 1996), but whether, as claimed by Diener et al. (2004), SWB represents a dominantly cognitive evaluation is moot. To the contrary, recent research (Davern et al. 2007) points to the essence of SWB as a construct these authors call "Core Affect."

The term Core Affect was coined by Russell (2003) to describe a neurophysiological state that is experienced as a feeling and which may be conceptualized as a deep form of trait affect or mood. He describes it as analogous to felt body temperature in that it is always there, it can be accessed when attention is drawn to it, extremes are most obvious, and it exists without words to describe it. Naturally enough, Russell regarded Core Affect in conformity with the circumplex model of affect, comprising a blend of hedonic (pleasant–unpleasant) and arousal values (activation–deactivation).

The reason Davern et al. were attracted to adopt this term was Russell's determined description of Core Affect as a biologically influenced mood, rather than an emotion. Specifically, he made it clear that while the feeling of Core Affect can be consciously accessed, it is not tied to any specific object in the manner of an emotional response. Instead, it is a mood state, which refers to how the individual senses themselves in an abstract but personal way. If the perception of the Core Affect feeling becomes linked to a cause, then the feeling state makes the transition from mood to emotion.

A more recent account of Core Affect, however, has muddied this distinction. Russell (2009) makes it clear that Core Affect may be involved in either moods or emotions. He proposes that Core Affect may become directed at something and, indeed, that Core Affect may itself be changed by a variety of other influences. Thus, a new term is required that describes the mood affect associated with homeostasis. We propose the term Homeostatically Protected Mood (HPMood) to describe a feeling state with the following characteristics:

1. It is a biologically determined positive mood that comprises the most basic experienced feeling. It is hardwired for each individual, comprising the tonic state of affect that provides the activation energy, or motivation, for behavior.
2. HPMood is not only the dominant affective constituent of SWB, as determined by Davern et al., but also the basic steady-state set point that homeostasis seeks to defend.
3. HPMood perfuses all higher process, including personality (for a review of the neurobiology of personality, see Depue and Collins 1999), memory, and momentary experience. It perfuses all cognitive processes to some degree, but most strongly the rather abstract notions of self (e.g., I am a good person). These self-perceptions are held at strength of positivity that approximates the set-point HPMood.

Consistent with this fundamental role, we hypothesize that the process of evolution has advantaged the survival of individuals who experience a level of

HPMood corresponding to 70–80 points pleasant or positive. Notably, SWB values above and below this range are associated with different forms of cognitive functioning, each of which having its own advantages and disadvantages. For example, higher SWB is associated with enhanced friendliness and problem solving (Lyubomirsky et al. 2005) but has the downside of poor information processing, an exaggerated sense of control, and therefore enhanced risk taking. Lower SWB, on the other hand, leads to more careful information processing (for a review, see Forgas 2008) and greater preparedness for threat (Sweeny et al. 2006) but carries the risk of low motivation and even depression if it becomes chronic. Thus, we propose, 75 points is a trade-off between the advantages and disadvantages of higher and lower values. This level then, on average, constitutes the optimum set-point range for SWB, corresponding to the most adaptive range of mood affect.

As measured by Davern et al. (2007), HPMood can be parsimoniously represented as the combined affects of happiness, contentment, and excitement. These represent the activated and deactivated pleasant quadrants of the affective circumplex (for a review of affect, see Cropanzano et al. 2003). Davern et al. tested the relative strength of HPMood, cognition, and all five factors of personality as predictors of SWB. The cognitive component of SWB was measured using 7 items derived from multiple discrepancies theory (Michalos 1985). These items address the perceived gap between what the respondent currently has and general life aspirations, what age-matched others have, the best one has had in the past, expected to have 3 years ago and expects to have after 5 years, deserves, and needs.

Consistent with previous research, all three components correlated significantly with SWB and with one another. However, when the variances were controlled by structural equation modeling, it was demonstrated that affect and MDT are the dominant components of SWB. Indeed, after accounting for both of these, personality made only a very small contribution to the explanation of SWB variance. The simplified model from this paper is reproduced in Fig. 4.9. The personality factors are designated as: N – Neuroticism, E – Extraversion, O – Openness, A – Agreeableness, and C – Conscientiousness.

This finding has been replicated using independent data (Blore 2008), from which we deduce that mood is the dominant component of SWB. We also propose

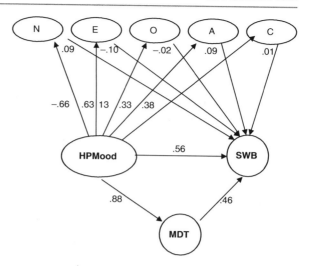

Fig. 4.9 Simplified Affective–Cognitive Model of SWB (Davern et al. 2007)

HPMood as the driving force behind individual set point levels in SWB homeostasis.

Over the past few years, there have been several critics of set-point theory (e.g., Fujita and Diener 2005; Headey 2008; Lucas 2007) based on observed changes in the SWB of individuals over time. The first two of these papers report data from the German Socio-Economic Panel Study from 1984 to 2000. For example, Fujita and Diener showed that, over this 16-year period, about 10% of the sample showed a change in satisfaction of about 30 points. They conclude that SWB "can and does change for some people."

All of these authors interpret changes in SWB over time as indicative that the set point has changed. However, homeostasis theory and HPMood offer an alternative possibility. It is possible that when people report a level of SWB outside their set-point range, they have simply lost contact with their set-point mood affect. That is, at the time of data collection, their level of SWB was being controlled by a powerful emotional state, such as depression, that overwhelmed homeostasis, and so dominated their awareness. Within this alternative conception, each person's HPMood and set point may remain unaltered, and the abnormal level of SWB reflects attention to the dominating emotional state.

This alternative conception also predicts that, over time, external and internal resources will be directed to the restoration of homeostasis, as has been discussed. If these resources are sufficient, they will reduce the perceived level of challenge to the point that that homeostatic control is restored. When this occurs, the person regains contact with their HPMood, and their reported SWB returns to its set-point range.

Another interesting possibility is that set points do, in fact, change over the life span (Land, personal communication). Results from the Framingham Heart Longitudinal Study have found that a number of physiological parameters that must be maintained within homeostatic bounds for survival – such as blood pressure – have "optimal" values that change with age. Such changes are adaptive, in that individuals who deviate far from the optimal values are at higher risk of mortality. Through analogy, it is possible that SWB set points also change over the life span, quite possibly in an upward direction to compensate for functional loss. We certainly find (Cummins et al. 2005) that the highest levels of SWB occur in old age.

SWB and Depression

From all of the above, SWB can be predominantly characterized as a stable positive mood that is normally held within a narrow range of values for each individual. The level of this set-point range is genetically determined, and a homeostatic system acts to defend our perception of Homeostatically Protected Mood as our normal sense of affective self. Importantly, SWB is an approximation of HPMood, which is why, under normal conditions, SWB approximates the set-point range. However, if the level of challenge to SWB becomes too great, homeostasis fails. When this occurs, our affective experience is redirected from HPMood to the dominating emotion, either positive or negative.

Under such conditions, SWB no longer conforms to the set-point range of HPMood. If it is made to be higher, due to the induction of an acute positive emotion, then the processes of adaptation and habituation soon return the dominant affective experience back to HPMood. Whether, as claimed by Positive Psychology, it is possible to maintain a substantially higher level of positive affect than the set-point range on a chronic basis is moot. As of this writing, no reliable empirical evidence is available to support such a view, which is also counter to homeostatic theory.

If SWB is made to be lower, through the induction of a negative emotion, then the same processes of adaptation and habituation will normally allow recovery back to the set-point range of HPMood. However, if the negative challenge is chronic and strong, recovery may not take place. The homeostatic system has a limited capacity to recover normal functioning, and if this capacity is exceeded, adaptation will not occur, homeostasis will be persistently defeated, and the loss of positive affect will remain as the dominating experience. This is the reason that the poor countries in Fig. 4.2 have such low SWB. They contain a high proportion of their population who are living under conditions of chronic homeostatic defeat. We have recently reported the same phenomenon in Australia through a study of 4,000 people providing care for a disabled family member at home (Cummins et al. 2007). Their mean level of SWB was 59 points.

We propose that this loss of positive mood is the essence of depression. The relationship between SWB and the depression sub-scale of the Depression Anxiety Stress Scales (Lovibond and Lovibond 1995) is shown in Fig. 4.10 using cumulative data from our surveys.

This figure is based on DASS increments of 3.0 points. This increment size is the smallest range for our cumulative sample that allows an $N > 20$ per group. The group N's range from 785 for depression group (0.1–3.0) to 23 for depression group (33.1–36.0). The figure reveals a clearly inverse relationship between the falling PWI and rising depression scores. However, the rate at which PWI falls appears to slow at a depression score of 15.1–18 (*moderate*) to 24.1–27.0 (severe), with these depression categories referenced from the scale manual. The amount of change between these four contiguous scores, which differ sequentially by <2 points, can be contrasted with the amount of change in the four immediately higher and lower scores, which all differ sequentially by >2 point, as shown in Table 4.1.

This table shows the changing rate of PWI decrease and the appearance of the homeostatic plateau over the middle grouping. As the level of challenge (depression score) increases from 0 to 18, the value of SWB moves down in a linear fashion to approximate the start of the homeostatic plateau. This is phase (a) in Fig. 4.3. Then, over the depression rating of 18–27, homeostasis "holds the line" and SWB remains relatively unchanged (phase b). However, at a depression score of 27 or greater, homeostasis is overwhelmed; control of SWB passes from the homeostatic system to the challenging agent, and SWB drops markedly (phase c).

A more detailed description of these results in relation to homeostatic theory is as follows:

1. In reference to Fig. 4.10, the fact that the highest PWI value corresponds to a depression score of zero

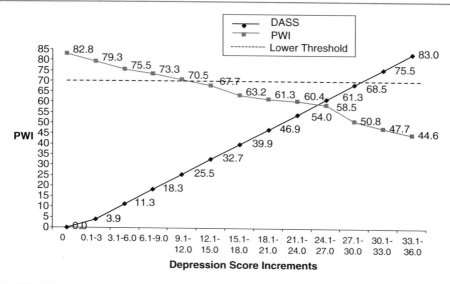

Fig. 4.10 PWI and DASS depression means across increments of depression scores

is logical. Moreover, the value of 82.8 points is consistent with theory, based on two assumptions, both of which have been previously argued. The first is that the normal range for individual set points is 55–95, and the second is that the normal set-point range is 5–6 points on either side of the mean. Then, if zero depression is taken as implying that each SWB value approximates the top of each set-point range, then this SWB distribution extends from $(55+6)=61$ to $(95+6)\approx 100$. The halfway point on this range is 80.5 points, which is a reasonable approximation to the measured value of 82.8 points.

2. The start of the plateau in Fig. 4.10 occurs at a PWI of 63.2, and it ends at 58.5 points. This is also consistent with theoretical prediction. In a previous report using population sample mean scores from 19 different countries as data, the overall mean was found to be 74.4 and the standard deviation 5.1 points (Cummins 2003). It was also calculated that 70 points, corresponding to about one standard deviation below the mean, was the lowest value on the plateau, below which the value SWB fell sharply.

The current data set uses the scores of individuals rather than population mean scores. The overall mean is 73.40, and the standard deviation is much larger as 14.54. One standard deviation below the mean is 58.9 points, which approximates the lower end of the plateau in Fig. 4.10. Thus, the results using either population mean scores as data, or the scores of individuals as data, converge to yield a common finding, that is, that

Table 4.1 The relative degree of change for the PWI and DASS

Depression increments	6.1–9.0 (normal) to 15.1–18.0 (moderate)	15.1–18 (moderate) to 24.1–27.0 (severe)	24.1–27.0 (severe) to 33.1–36.0 (extreme)
DASS range	21.6	21.4	21.7
PWI range	10.1	4.7	13.9
Phases of change related to Fig. 4.3	(a)	(b)	(c)

SWB values that lie one standard deviation below the normative mean approximate the boundary between homeostatic maintenance and homeostatic defeat. Thus, SWB values that lie much further from the normative mean than one standard deviation are likely under the control of the challenging agent rather than homeostasis (refer to Fig. 4.3).

Perhaps the most interesting question raised by these results is why plotting the PWI against the DASS shows this plateau effect. The DASS items measure the extent of negative affect (downhearted and blue), life being meaningless, low personal self-worth, etc. In other words, even quite strong negative feelings about the self can co-exist with normal or even high levels of SWB. There is, thus, a degree of disconnection between negative and positive feelings about the self as long as homeostasis is functional. This is highly adaptive in allowing negative feeling to be acknowledged while also maintaining normal levels of SWB. However, once the level of challenge becomes overwhelming, positive feelings about the self evaporate, and it is possible that true depression sets in.

Recommended Scales

There are three scales that we recommend for use within the framework that has been outlined. The oldest of these is the single question, "How satisfied are you with your life as a whole?" (Andrews and Withey 1976). This question perfectly fulfills the criteria for an item measuring SWB to be both personal and abstract (Cummins et al. 2003). No one can compute the answer to the question in terms of cognition. So, it is answered in reference to the ongoing mood state, which normally approximates the set-point level of Homeostatically Protected Mood. The drawback to using this question, however, is that it is a single item. As such, it is not as reliable as a multi-item scale, so two alternative scales have been devised.

The first is the most widely used index of SWB, the Satisfaction with Life Scale (Diener et al. 1985). This measures satisfaction through five items, each of which involves an overall judgment of life in general. The scores from these items are then summed as a measure of SWB. For a copy of the scale, go to http://s.psych.uiuc.edu/~ediener/hottopic/hottopic.html. The psychometric properties of the scale can be accessed through the publications listed on this web page.

The importance of the SWLS is that it represents an expanded version of "life as a whole." The items are not designed to give individual insights into the structure of SWB. This feature makes it different from the second scale to be recommended. The Personal Wellbeing Index (International Wellbeing Group 2006) has a quite different design, as the "first-level deconstruction" of life as a whole. Until very recently, the PWI contained seven items, referred to as "domains," where each item represents a broad, semi-abstract area of life. The theoretical basis for the PWI is that the domains together describe the experience of overall life satisfaction. The manual is available from International Wellbeing Group (2006).

The PWI is designed to be a "work in progress," with the scale evolving as new data show ways for it to be successfully modified. The International Wellbeing Group oversees this evolution, and in 2006, an eighth domain of Spiritual/Religious satisfaction was added to the scale.

The disadvantage of the PWI over the SWLS is that, because the domains are slightly more specific in their focus, they are further away from HPMood. The advantage of the PWI is that each of the domains carries its own information concerning a broad aspect of life. Because of this, the scale can be analyzed at either the level of individual domains or by combining the domains to form a single SWB score. There are also parallel versions of the PWI for adults who have a cognitive or intellectual disability, school children, and pre-school children (Cummins and Lau 2005a, b, c).

Summary and Conclusions

From the results that have been presented, we propose that SWB has the following characteristics:

(a) It is a remarkably stable indicator of human functioning that is normally maintained as positive by a system of homeostatic controls.

(b) Each person has a set point for their SWB. This is genetically determined for each individual person and may have a value between 55 and 95 points. The average for the Australian population is 75 points.

(c) Each person has a set-point range, which is their normal operating range for SWB on either side of their set point. The magnitude of this range is about 5–6 points around the set point. Thus, the normal range for the SWB of individuals is 5–6 points beyond the range of set points (55–95 points) or approximately 50–100 points.

(d) Because any demographic group will contain a heterogeneous mix of set points, there is a ceiling for group average scores at about 83 points. That is, no matter how good the living environment is, the mean level of SWB for a randomly populated group will not exceed 83 points.

(e) The level of SWB can be made to move to almost any lower level by a strong challenge that defeats homeostasis.

(f) Challenges to homeostasis are resisted by external and internal buffers. The external buffers of money and relationships function to attenuate the potential force of a challenge. The internal buffers act to deflect the experience of homeostatic challenge away from the abstract sense of self.

(g) Homeostasis is defending Homeostatically Protected Mood, which is an abstract and positive feeling about the self. Under normal conditions, SWB, as measured, is dominated by HPMood.

(h) Depression represents the failure of homeostasis. In depression, the positive sense of HPMood is lost, being replaced by negative feelings attributable to the challenging agent.

(i) Whether any intervention is capable of raising SWB will importantly depend on its initial level. If the starting condition is homeostatic defeat, then SWB can be raised by providing relevant resources. However, homeostasis theory predicts that SWB cannot be chronically increased beyond its set-point range. This means that the only SWB increment available to someone who is already under normal homeostatic control lies within the margins of their set-point range. This understanding has important implications for those who seek to increase happiness.

Acknowledgment We thank Ann-Marie James for her assistance in the preparation of this manuscript and Australian Unity for their continued support of this research. We also acknowledge the key role played by Renee Bear, Wendy Kennedy, and Melissa Weinberg in coining the term Homeostatically Protected Mood.

References

Andrews, F. M., & Withey, S. B. (1976). *Social indicators of well-being: American's perceptions of life quality.* New York: Plenum Press.

Bach, J. R., Campagnolo, D. I., & Hoeman, S. (1991). Life satisfaction of individuals with Duchenne muscular dystrophy using long-term mechanical ventilatory support. *American Journal of Physical Medicine and Rehabilitation, 70,* 129–135.

Bat-Chava, Y. (1994). Group identification and self-esteem of deaf adults. *Personality and Social Psychology Behavior, 20,* 494–502.

Blore, J. D. (2008). *Subjective wellbeing: An assessment of competing theories.* Unpublished doctoral thesis, Deakin University, Geelong.

Campbell, A., Converse, P. E., & Rodgers, W. L. (1976). *The quality of American life: Perceptions, evaluations, and satisfactions.* New York: Russell Sage.

Cropanzano, R., Weiss, H. M., Hale, J. M. S., & Reb, J. (2003). The structure of affect: Reconsidering the relationship between negative and positive affectivity. *Journal of Management, 29,* 831–858.

Cummins, R. A. (1995). On the trail of the gold standard for life satisfaction. *Social Indicators Research, 35,* 179–200.

Cummins, R. A. (1997). Quality of life: Its relevance to disability services. In P. O'Brien & R. Murray (Eds.), *Working in human services* (pp. 225–268). Auckland: Dunmore Press.

Cummins, R. A. (1998). The second approximation to an international standard of life satisfaction. *Social Indicators Research, 43,* 307–334.

Cummins, R. A. (2000). Personal income and subjective wellbeing: A review. *Journal of Happiness Studies, 1,* 133–158.

Cummins, R. A. (2002). Proxy responding for subjective wellbeing: A review. *International Review of Research in Mental Retardation, 25,* 183–207.

Cummins, R. A. (2003). Normative life satisfaction: Measurement issues and a homeostatic model. *Social Indicators Research, 64,* 225–256.

Cummins, R. A., & Gullone, E. (2000). *Why we should not use 5-point Likert scales: The case for subjective quality of life measurement.* Paper presented at the second international conference on Quality of Life in Cities, Singapore: National University of Singapore.

Cummins, R. A., & Lau, A. L. D. (2005a). *Personal wellbeing index-pre- school manual* (3rd ed.). Melbourne: School of Psychology, Deakin University and Hong Kong: Department of Rehabilitation Sciences, Hong Kong Polytechnic University. Retrieved June 30, 2009, from http://www.deakin.edu.au/research/acqol/instruments/wellbeing_index.htm

Cummins, R. A., & Lau, A. L. D. (2005b). *Personal wellbeing index – Intellectual disability manual* (3rd ed., pp. 1–37). Melbourne School of Psychology, Deakin University and Hong Kong: Department of Rehabilitation Sciences, Hong Kong Polytechnic University. Retrieved June 30, 2009, from http://www.deakin.edu.au/research/acqol/instruments/wellbeing_index.htm

Cummins, R. A., & Lau, A. L. D. (2005c). *Personal wellbeing index – school children, manual* (3rd ed.). Melbourne: School of Psychology, Deakin University and Hong Kong: Department of Rehabilitation Sciences, Hong Kong Polytechnic University. Retrieved June 30, 2009, from http://www.deakin.edu.au/research/acqol/instruments/wellbeing_index.htm

Cummins, R. A., & Nistico, H. (2002). Maintaining life satisfaction: The role of positive cognitive bias. *Journal of Happiness Studies, 3,* 37–69.

Cummins, R. A., Gullone, E., & Lau, A. L. D. (2002). A model of subjective well being homeostasis: The role of personality. In E. Gullone & R. A. Cummins (Eds.), *The universality of subjective wellbeing indicators: Social indicators research series* (pp. 7–46). Dordrecht: Kluwer.

Cummins, R. A., Eckersley, R., Pallant, J., Van Vugt, J., & Misajon, R. (2003). Developing a national index of subjective wellbeing: The Australian unity wellbeing index. *Social Indicators Research, 64,* 159–190.

Cummins, R. A., Woerner, J., Tomyn, A., Knapp, T., & Gibson, A. (2005). *Australian unity wellbeing index: Report 14.0 – "The wellbeing of Australians – Personal relationships".* Melbourne: Australian Centre on Quality of Life, School of Psychology, Deakin University. Retrieved June 30, 2009, from http://www.deakin.edu.au/research/acqol/index_wellbeing/index.htm

Cummins, R. A., Hughes, J., Tomyn, A., Gibson, A., Woerner, J., & Lai, L. (2007). *Australian unity wellbeing index: Report 17.1 the wellbeing of Australians – Carer health and wellbeing.* Melbourne: Australian Centre on Quality of Life, School of Psychology, Deakin University. Retrieved June 30, 2009, from http://www.deakin.edu.au/research/acqol/index_wellbeing/index.htm

Cummins, R. A., Woerner, J., Gibson, A., Lai, L., Weinberg, M., & Collard, J. (2008). *Australian unity wellbeing index: Report 19.0. The wellbeing of Australians – Links with exercise, nicotine and alcohol.* Melbourne: Australian Centre on Quality of Life, School of Psychology, Deakin University. ISBN 978 1 74156 113 5. Retrieved June 30, 2009, from http://www.deakin.edu.au/research/acqol/index_wellbeing/index.htm

Davern, M., Cummins, R. A., & Stokes, M. (2007). Subjective wellbeing as an affective/cognitive construct. *Journal of Happiness Studies, 8*, 429–449.

Depue, R. A., & Collins, P. F. (1999). Neurobiology of the structure of personality: Dopamine facilitation of incentive motivation and extraversion. *Behavioral and Brain Sciences, 22*, 491–569.

Diener, E. D., Emmons, R. A., Larsen, R. J., & Griffin, S. (1985). The satisfaction with life scale. *Journal of Personality Assessment, 49*, 71–75.

Diener, E. D., Suh, E. M., Lucas, R. E., & Smith, H. L. (1999). Subjective well-being: Three decades of progress. *Psychological Bulletin, 125*, 276–302.

Diener, E. D., Napa Scollon, C. N., & Lucas, R. E. (2004). The evolving concept of subjective well-being: The multifaceted nature of happiness. In P. T. Costa & I. C. Siegler (Eds.), *Recent advances in psychology and aging* (pp. 187–219). Amsterdam: Elsevier Science BV.

Forgas, J. P. (2008). The strange cognitive benefits of mild dysphoria: On the evolutionary advantages of not being too happy. In J. P. Forgas, M. G. Haselton, & W. von Hippel (Eds.), *Evolutionary psychology and social cognition* (pp. 107–121). New York: Psychology Press.

Fujita, F., & Diener, E. (2005). Life satisfaction set point: Stability and change. *Journal of Personality and Social Psychology, 88*, 158–164.

Hanestad, B. R., & Albrektsen, G. (1992). The stability of quality of life experience in people with type 1 diabetes over a period of a year. *Journal of Advanced Nursing, 17*, 777–784.

Headey, B. (2008). The set-point theory of well-being: Negative results and consequent revisions. *Social Indicators Research, 85*, 389–404.

Headey, B., & Wearing, A. (1986). *The sense of relative superiority – Central to well-being.* Melbourne: University of Melbourne.

Headey, B., & Wearing, A. (1987). *A theory of life satisfaction and psychological distress.* Melbourne: University of Melbourne.

Headey, B., & Wearing, A. (1988). The sense of relative superiority – Central to well-being. *Social Indicators Research, 20*, 497–516.

Headey, B., & Wearing, A. (1989). Personality, life events, and subjective well-being: Toward a dynamic equilibrium model. *Journal of Personality and Social Psychology, 57*, 731–739.

Headey, B., Holmstrom, E., & Wearing, A. (1984a). The impact of life events and changes in domain satisfactions on wellbeing. *Social Indicators Research, 15*, 203–227.

Headey, B., Holmstrom, E., & Wearing, A. (1984b). Well-being and ill-being: Different dimensions? *Social Indicators Research, 14*, 115–139.

Henderson, S. (1977). The social network, support and neurosis. The function of attachment in adult life. *British Journal of Psychiatry, 131*, 185–191.

International Wellbeing Group. (2006). *Personal wellbeing index manual.* Melbourne: Australia, Deain University.

Retrieved June 30, 2009, from http://www.deakin.edu.au/research/acqol/instruments/wellbeing_index.htm

Jones, L. V., & Thurstone, L. L. (1955). The psychophysics of semantics: An experimental investigation. *The Journal of Applied Psychology, 39*, 31–36.

Kozma, A., Stone, S., & Stones, M. J. (2000). Stability in components and predictors of subjective well-being (SWB): Implications for SWB structure. In E. Diener & D. R. Rahtz (Eds.), *Advances in quality of life: Theory and research* (pp. 13–30). Dordrecht Kluwer Academic Publishers.

Lau, A. L. D., Cummins, R. A., & McPherson, W. (2005). An investigation into the cross-cultural equivalence of the personal wellbeing index. *Social Indicators Research, 72*, 403–430.

Lee, J. W., Jones, P. S., Mineyama, Y., & Zhang, X. E. (2002). Cultural differences in responses to a Likert scale. *Research in Nursing and Health, 25*, 295–306.

Liu, B. (1975). Quality of life: Concept, measure and results. *American Journal of Economics and Sociology, 34*, 1–13.

Lovibond, S. H., & Lovibond, P. F. (1995). *Manual for the depression anxiety stress scales.* Sydney: Psychology Foundation.

Lucas, R. E. (2007). Adaptation and the set-point model of subjective well-being: Does happiness change after major life events? *Current Directions in Psychological Science, 16*, 75–79.

Lucas, R. E., Diener, E., & Suh, E. (1996). Discriminant validity of well-being measures. *Journal of Personality and Social Psychology, 71*, 616–628.

Lykken, D., & Tellegen, A. (1996). Happiness is a stochastic phenomenon. *Psychological Science, 7*, 186–189.

Lyubomirsky, S., King, L., & Diener, E. (2005). The benefits of frequent positive affect: Does happiness lead to success? *Psychological Bulletin, 131*, 803–855.

Michalos, A. C. (1985). Multiple discrepancies theory (MDT). *Social Indicators Research, 16*, 347–413.

Nieboer, A. P. (1997). *Life events and well-being: A prospective study on changes in well-being of elderly people due to a serious illness event or death of the spouse.* Amsterdam: Thesis Publishers.

Ormel, J. (1983). Neuroticism and well-being inventories. Measuring traits or states? *Psychological Medicine, 13*, 165–176.

Ormel, J., & Schaufeli, W. B. (1991). Stability and change in psychological distress and their relationship with self-esteem and locus of control: A dynamic equilibrium mode. *Journal of Personality and Social Psychology, 60*, 288–299.

Rothbaum, F., Weisz, J. R., & Snyder, S. S. (1982). Changing the world and changing the self: A two-process model of perceived control. *Journal of Personality and Social Psychology, 42*, 5–37.

Russell, J. A. (2003). Core affect and the psychological construction of emotion. *Psychological Review, 110*, 145–172.

Russell, J. A. (2009). Emotion, core affect, and psychological construction. *Cognition & Emotion, 23*, 1259–1283.

Sarason, I. G., Sarason, B. R., & Pierce, G. R. (1990). Social support: The search for theory. *Journal of Social and Clinical Psychology, 9*, 137–147.

Schwarz, N. (1999, February). Self-reports: How the questions shape the answers. *American Psychologist, 54*(2), 93–105.

Schwarz, N., & Strack, F. (1991). Evaluating one's life: A judgement model of subjective well-being. In F. Strack, M.

Argyle, & N. Schwarz (Eds.), *Subjective well-being: An interdisciplinary perspective* (pp. 27–47). New York: Plenum Press.

Stening, B. W., & Everett, J. E. (1984). Response styles in a cross-cultural managerial study. *Journal of Social Psychology, 122*, 151–156.

Stones, M. J., & Kozma, A. (1991). A magical model of happiness. *Social Indicators Research, 25*, 31–50.

Sweeny, K., Carroll, P. J., & Sheppard, J. A. (2006). Is optimism always best? Future outlooks and preparedness. *Current Directions in Psychological Science, 15*, 302–306.

Taylor, S. E., & Brown, J. D. (1988). Illusion and well-being: A social psychological perspective on mental health. *Psychological Bulletin, 103*, 193–210.

Tesser, A., Pilkington, C. J., & McIntosh, W. D. (1989). Self-evaluation maintenance and the mediational role of emotion: The perception of friends and strangers. *Journal of Personality and Social Psychology, 57*, 442–456.

Trigger, D. (2003). *Does the way we measure poverty matter?* Canberra: University of Canberra, National Centre for Social and Economic Modelling.

Weinstein, N. D. (1989). Optimistic biases about personal risks. *Science, 246*, 1232–1233.

World Bank. (1997). *World values surveys; GNP/capita purchasing power estimates from World Bank, world development report, 1997*. Retrieved June 30, 2009, from http://margaux.grandvinum.se/SebTest/wvs/articles/folder_published/article_base_56

Positive Psychology and the Quality of Life

5

Corey L.M. Keyes, Barbara L. Fredrickson, and Nansook Park

Historically, psychological and social sciences have focused on the nature and causes of human well-being. However, until very recently, most research equated well-being with the absence of the "three Ds": disease, disorder, and disability. At least four scientific trends over the past 50 years have helped to change the course of research on human well-being, culminating in *Positive Psychology*, which can been succinctly defined as the scientific field devoted to the study of optimal human functioning (see, e.g., Seligman and Csikszentmihalyi 2000). First, the study of stress and health matured to include models of individuals' perceptions of stress and their coping strategies. Second, the research field of gerontology matured, along with the increasing life expectancy of the population, to include the study of successful aging, which provided conceptions of positive human development in the face of aging. Third, the period of humanism and social welfare that characterized the 1960s and 1970s provided a strong rationale for the study of how individuals view the quality of their lives and how to improve it. Fourth, the study of resilience emerged during the 1970s and has thrived since as the investigation of protective factors and assets that enable usual or exceptional development under conditions of risk and adversity.

Positive psychology shares much in common with the field of social indicators and quality of life research. However, not all quality of research can or should be characterized as positive. Research on the quality of life can be divided into one of four approaches based on whether it employs a subjective or objective approach and whether its foci are negative or positive indicators. While the subjectivist approach relies on self-reports of quality of life, an objectivist approach relies instead on sources of information that exists independent of the participant (e.g., poverty status) or, if reported on by the participant, can be verified (e.g., education attainment). In turn, whereas some quality of life indicators are negative in that researchers seek to understand or remediate the presence of undesirable conditions (e.g., violence) or states (e.g., fear), others are positive in that researchers measure the presence of desirable conditions (e.g., cooperation) or states (e.g., happiness, joy, flourishing). Positive psychology is therefore an important model within the quality of life tradition that emphasizes positive indicators and thereby addresses an imbalance in the historical corpus of research in human well-being as the absence of the negative.

Positive psychology is concerned not just with positive states like emotions but also with more enduring positive characteristics of the individual: talents, abilities, values, and strengths of character (Peterson 2006). Positive traits lead to optimal functioning not only by enabling positive emotions but also in their own right by facilitating lives characterized by engagement, meaning, and fulfilling relationships with others

C.L.M. Keyes (✉)
Department of Sociology, Emory University, Room 225
Tarbutton Hall, 1555 Dickey Drive, Atlanta, GA 30322, USA
e-mail: ckeyes@emory.edu

B.L. Fredrickson
Department of Psychology, University of North Carolina at Chapel Hill, 309 Davie Hall, CB 3270, Chapel Hill, NC 27599, USA

N. Park
Department of Psychology, University of Rhode Island, Kingston, RI 02881-0808, USA

K.C. Land et al. (eds.), *Handbook of Social Indicators and Quality of Life Research*, DOI 10.1007/978-94-007-2421-1_5, © Springer Science+Business Media B.V. 2012

(Park 2004; Park and Peterson 2003; Peterson et al. 2007). Accordingly, positive traits contribute to hedonic and eudaimonic well-being. Although distinguishable, these types of well-being are not incompatible and may even be synergistic in producing a full life (Keyes 1998; Keyes et al. 2002; Keyes 2002, 2005a, b, 2007; Ryff 1989; Peterson et al. 2005b).

In this chapter, we review research from three streams of positive psychology which are particularly relevant to the subjective and positive spectrum of quality of life research. The first is Keyes' research on human flourishing, which is the presence and absence of a positive state of mental health. The second is Fredrickson's research on the role of positive emotional states and their dynamics in broadening and building the necessary resources that sustain flourishing and other desirable outcomes. The third stream of research is on character virtues and strengths by Parks, Peterson, and Seligman. This latter stream of research attempts to measure and associate the presence of durable character traits with desirable outcomes such as flourishing and positive emotions. These three streams of research do not fully describe the diversity of concepts and theories being studied under the rubric of positive psychology (see, e.g., Snyder and Lopez 2002 for a comprehensive listing of positive psychology topics). However, the three streams of research presented here represent, in our opinions, exemplars of quality of life research in themselves, namely, that quality of life increases insofar as more individuals achieve a state of flourishing, experience more positive emotions in life, and have more character strengths that lead to personal and interpersonal conduct that are aligned with virtue.

Flourishing: Mental Health as "Something Positive"

In 1941, the noted medical historian, Henry Sigerist, remarked that health, whether mental or physical, was more than the absence of illness; it was the presence of "something positive" (p. 100). Until recently, however, mental *health* remained undefined, unmeasured, and therefore unrecognized among researchers and at the level of governments and nongovernmental organizations. Rather, mental health was seen throughout the twentieth century and before then as the absence of mental disorder. In 1999, the surgeon general, then Dr. David Satcher, conceived of mental health as "... *a state of successful performance of mental function, resulting in productive activities, fulfilling relationships with people, and the ability to adapt to change and to cope with adversity*" (U.S. Public Health Service 1999, p. 4). In 2004, the World Health Organization published an historic first report on mental health promotion, conceptualizing mental health as not merely the absence of mental illness, but the presence of "... *a state of well-being in which the individual realizes his or her own abilities, can cope with the normal stresses of life, can work productively and fruitfully, and is able to make a contribution to his or her community*" (World Health Organization 2004, p.12).

These definitions affirmed the existing behavioral and social scientific vision of mental health as not merely the absence of mental illness but the presence of something positive (e.g., Jahoda 1958). Social and psychological scientists have been studying "something positive" in the domain of subjective well-being – individuals' evaluations and judgment of their own lives – for about 50 years (Keyes 2006). This research has yielded as many as 13 specific dimensions of well-being in the US population. When factor analyzed, studies show that the manifold scales measuring subjective well-being represent the latent structure of hedonic well-being (i.e., positive emotions toward one's life) or eudaimonic well-being (i.e., positive psychological and social functioning in life) (see, e.g., Keyes, Shmotkin, & Ryff).

Years of subjective well-being research unintentionally yielded clusters of mental health symptoms that mirror the cluster of symptoms used in the DSM-IV-TR (American Psychiatric Association 2000) to diagnose major depressive episode (MDE). In the same way that depression requires symptoms of anhedonia, mental health consists of symptoms of hedonia such as emotional vitality and positive feelings toward one's life. In the same way that major depression consists of symptoms of malfunctioning, mental health consists of symptoms of positive functioning.

Table 5.1 presents the dimensions of subjective well-being, which form the clusters of symptoms of flourishing. The diagnosis of states of flourishing (i.e., mental health) was modeled after the DSM-III-R approach to diagnosing MDE (Keyes 2002). Each measure of subjective well-being is considered a symptom insofar as it represents an outward sign of an unobservable state. In the absence of specific diagnostic tests, underlying conditions must be inferred from symptoms (or items). Mental health as well as mental illnesses

5 Positive Psychology and the Quality of Life

Table 5.1 Descriptions of 13 dimensions of subjective well-being used to measure and diagnose the categories of the mental health continuum in the USA

1. *Positive affect*: cheerful, in good spirits, calm and peaceful, satisfied, and full of life
2. *Avowed personal quality of life:* happiness or life satisfaction
3. *Self-acceptance:* holds positive attitudes toward oneself and past life and concedes and accepts varied aspects of self
4. *Social-acceptance:* has positive attitude toward others while acknowledging and accepting people's differences and complexity
5. *Personal growth:* shows insight into own potential, sense of development, and open to new and challenging experiences
6. *Social actualization:* believes that people, social groups, and society have potential and can evolve or grow positively
7. *Purpose in life:* holds goals and beliefs that affirm sense of direction in life and feels that life has a purpose and meaning.
8. *Social contribution:* feels that one's life is useful to society and the output of own activities is valued by or valuable to others.
9. *Environmental mastery:* exhibits capability to manage complex environment and can choose or manage and mold environs to suit needs.
10. *Social coherence:* interested in society or social life and feels that society and culture are intelligible, somewhat logical, predictable, and meaningful
11. *Autonomy:* exhibits self-direction that is often guided by own, socially accepted and conventional internal standards, and resists unsavory social pressures
12. *Positive relations with others:* has warm, satisfying, trusting personal relationships, and is capable of empathy and intimacy
13. *Social integration:* has a sense of belonging to a community and derives comfort and support from community

lack specific diagnostic tests, and remain identifiable only as collections of symptoms and outward signs (i.e., syndromes) of the underlying state or condition. To be diagnosed as *flourishing* in life, individuals must exhibit high levels on at least one measure of hedonic well-being and high levels on at least six measures of positive functioning. Individuals who exhibit low levels on at least one measure of hedonic well-being and low levels on at least six measures of positive functioning are diagnosed as *languishing* in life. Adults who are *moderately mentally healthy* do not fit the criteria for either flourishing or languishing in life.

A continuous assessment of the mental health continuum sums all measures of mental health that are coded into 10-point ranges after the Global Assessment of Functioning (GAF) approach in the DSM-III-R. For reasons articulated by Kessler (2002) in the domain of psychopathology, I have used, and recommend that others use, both the categorical and continuous

assessment for mental health because each approach provides valuable information and to see whether results and conclusions vary by each approach.

All findings published to date on adults are from the MacArthur Foundation's Midlife in the United States survey (MIDUS). This survey was a random digit dialing sample of noninstitutionalized English-speaking adults between the ages of 25 and 74 living in the 48 contiguous states, whose household included at least one telephone. The telephone survey and mailed questionnaires were conducted in 1995. The MIDUS used DSM-III-R (American Psychiatric Association 1987) criteria to diagnose four mental disorders (i.e., MDE, panic, generalized anxiety, and alcohol dependence), which were operationalized by the Composite International Diagnostic Interview Short Form (CIDI-SF) scales (see Kessler et al. 1998).

The Two Continua Model of Mental Health

Confirmatory factor analysis was used to test the theory that the MIDUS measures of mental health and mental illness belong to two latent continua. Three scales served as indicators of mental health: The summed scale of emotional well-being (i.e., single item of satisfaction + scale of positive affect), the summed scale of psychological well-being (i.e., six scales summed together), and the summed scale of social well-being (i.e., the fives scales summed together). Four summary measures served as indicators of mental illness as operationalized as the number of symptoms of MDE, generalized anxiety, panic disorder, and alcohol dependence. Two competing theories – the single factor and the two factor model – were tested. The single factor model hypothesizes that the measures of mental health and mental illness reflect a single latent factor, support for which would indicate that the absence of mental illness implies the presence of mental health. The two factor model hypothesizes that the measures of mental illness represent the latent factor of mental health that is distinct from, but correlated with, the latent factor of mental illness that is represented by the measures of mental illness. The data strongly supported the two factor model, which was a nearly perfect fitting model to the MIDUS data (Keyes 2005a).

The latent factor of mental illness correlated −53 with the latent factor of mental health. Although there is a tendency for mental health to improve as mental illness symptoms decrease, this connection is relatively modest. Languishing adults report the highest prevalence of any of the four mental disorders as well as the highest prevalence of reporting two or more mental disorders during the past year. In contrast, flourishing individuals report the lowest prevalence of any of the four 12-month mental disorders or their comorbidity. Compared with languishing or flourishing, moderately mentally healthy adults were at intermediate risk of any of the mental disorders or two or more mental disorders during the past year. The modest correlation between the latent continua reflects the tendency for the risk of mental illness to increase as mental health decreases. For example, the 12-month risk of MDE is over five times greater for languishing than flourishing adults.

Support for the two factor model provides the strongest scientific evidence to date in support of the complete health approach to mental health. That is, the evidence indicates that the absence of mental illness does not imply the presence of mental health, and the absence of mental health does not imply the presence of mental illness. Thus, neither the pathogenic nor salutogenic approaches alone accurately describe the mental health of a population. Rather, mental health is a complete state that is best studied though the combined assessments of mental health with mental illness. Using a dichotomous diagnostic assessment of psychopathology that is cross tabulated with the three categories of the mental health continuum yields six categories. There are individuals who are flourishing, who are moderately mentally healthy, or who are languishing and have not had an episode of a mental illness during the past year. However, there are also individuals who are flourishing, who are moderately mentally healthy, or who are languishing and have experienced an episode of a mental illness during the past year. Complete mental health is a state in which individuals are free of mental illness and are flourishing. In papers published to date, individuals with a mental illness who were moderately mentally healthy or flourishing were collapsed into one group, because so few flourishing individuals report an episode of mental illness, and pooling these groups did not affect the results.

Mental Health as Flourishing Is Salutary

Research has supported the hypothesis that anything less than complete mental health results in increased impairment and disability (Keyes 2002, 2004, 2005a, b). Adults who were diagnosed as completely mentally healthy functioned superior to all others in terms of the fewest workdays missed, fewest half-day or less cutbacks of work, lowest level of health limitations of activities of daily living, the fewest chronic physical diseases and conditions, the lowest healthcare utilization, and the highest levels of psychosocial functioning. In terms of psychosocial functioning, this meant that completely mentally healthy adults reported the lowest level of perceived helplessness (e.g., low perceived control in life), the highest level of functional goals (e.g., knowing what they want from life), the highest level of self-reported resilience (e.g., learning from adversities), and the highest level of intimacy (e.g., feeling very close with family and friends). In terms of all of these measures, completely mentally healthy adults functioned better than adults with moderate mental health, who, in turn, functioned better than adults who were languishing.

Adults with a mental illness who also had either moderate mental health or flourishing reported more workdays missed or more work cutbacks than languishing adults. However, languishing adults reported the same level of health limitations of daily living and worse levels of psychosocial functioning than adults with a mental illness who also had moderate mental health or flourishing. Individuals who were completely mentally ill – i.e., languishing and one or more of the mental disorders – functioned worse than all others on every criterion. In general, adults with a mental illness who also had either moderate mental health or flourishing function no worse than adults who were languishing and did not have a mental disorder. Thus, mental illness that is combined with languishing is more dysfunctional than the situation when a mental illness occurs in the context of moderate mental health or flourishing.

The complete mental health diagnostic states have been shown to be independent risk factors for cardiovascular disease (CVD; Keyes 2004). This study focused on the combination of the categorical diagnosis of mental health with major depressive episode because the latter has been shown to be a risk factor for heart and arterial diseases. The unadjusted prevalence of any CVD was 8% among completely mentally healthy adults, compared with 12% of adults with moderate mental health, 12% of adults who were languishing, and 13% of adults with "pure" depression (i.e., had MDE but also fit the criteria for moderate mental health or flourishing). Among adults who were languishing and had an episode of major depression, the prevalence of any CVD was 19%. In multivariate analyses, completely mentally healthy adults had the lowest risk of a CVD. In fact, adults who fit the criteria for anything less than complete mental health had levels of relative risk for CVD that were comparable to the relative risk associated with diabetes, smoking cigarettes, and lack of physical exercise.

A recent paper (Keyes 2005b) investigated the association of the complete mental health diagnoses with chronic physical conditions with age. The MIDUS study included self-reported assessments of 27 chronic physical health conditions adapted from the Medical Outcomes Study. The complete mental health diagnosis was associated with 85% of the chronic physical conditions measured in the MIDUS study (*Note:* this paper focused only on major depressive disorder as the form of mental illness). The prevalence of chronic physical conditions was highest among adults who are languishing and had an episode of major depression and lowest among completely mentally healthy adults. The prevalence of chronic physical conditions was slightly higher among moderately mentally healthy adults than completely mentally healthy adults, while languishing adults reported even more chronic conditions than adults with moderate mental health.

Overall, adults with major depression and languishing had an average of 4.5 chronic conditions. Adults with depression but also had moderate mental health or flourishing had an average of 3.1 chronic conditions, which was the same as adults who were languishing but without any mental illness. Moderately mentally healthy adults without any mental illness had an average of 2.1 chronic conditions, compared with adults with complete mental health who had on average of 1.5 chronic conditions. Multivariate regression analyses confirmed that, when compared against completely mental healthy adults, chronic physical conditions increased as the level of mental health decreased. It is noteworthy that mental health status was a significant predictor of chronic physical conditions even after adjustment for the usual sociodemographic variables as well as body mass index, diabetes status, smoking status, and level of physical exercise.

Multivariate analyses also revealed statistically significant interactions of age with two of the complete mental health diagnostic states. While chronic physical conditions increased with age, there were two interaction effects: pure languishing by age and languishing with an episode of major depression by age. Young languishing adults have an average of one more chronic condition than young flourishing adults; midlife languishing adults report an average of about 1.7 more conditions than flourishing midlife adults; and languishing older adults have an average of 2.6 more chronic conditions than flourishing older adults. Similarly, young languishing adults with MDE report an average of 2.6 more chronic conditions than flourishing young adults; midlife languishing adults with MDE have an average of 3.5 more conditions than flourishing midlife adults; and languishing older adults who also had MDE have an average of 4.2 more chronic conditions than flourishing older adults. In short, languishing with, and languishing without, a mental illness is associated with increasingly larger amounts of chronic physical disease with age.

Results from this study suggest two noteworthy findings. First, adults who were completely mentally healthy had the lowest number of chronic physical conditions at all ages. Second, the youngest adults who were languishing had the same number of chronic physical conditions as older flourishing adults. Younger languishing adults who also had MDE had 1.5 more chronic conditions than older flourishing adults. In other words, the absence of mental health – whether it is pure languishing or languishing combined with a mental illness – appears to compound the risk of chronic physical disease with age. In turn, we (Keyes and Grzywacz 2005) have found healthcare utilization to be lowest among adults who are flourishing. Rates of overnight hospitalizations over the past year, outpatient medical visits over the past year, and number of prescription drugs were lowest among adults who were flourishing and physically healthy, followed by adults who were either flourishing but had physical illness conditions or adults who were not flourishing but were physically healthy. In short, complete mental health – i.e., flourishing and the absence of mental illness – should be central to any national debate about healthcare coverage and costs. Rather than focusing all discussions around healthcare delivery and insurance, our nation must also increase and protect the number of individuals who are healthy, driving down the need for healthcare.

Population Prevalence: Too Little Flourishing

Evidence to date suggests that flourishing, a central component of complete mental health, is a desirable condition that any community, corporation, or government would want to protect or promote in its citizens. The USA aspires to mental health but has not directly promoted it. Our government has redistributed over 50 years of taxpayer's money toward psychopathology research and services through the NIMH, as well as the Substance Abuse and Mental Health Services Administration (SAMHSA). What have we gained from all of this spending? How much of the adult population is mentally healthy?

The current approach to national mental health is not working because approximately, one-half of the adult population is moderately mentally healthy, while only 17% are completely mentally healthy. Because complete mental health should be our goal, the current approach to national mental health is a failure. Worse yet, 10% of adults are mentally unhealthy, as they are languishing and did not fit the criteria for any of the four mental disorders (and they averaged about 1 symptom of mental illness, suggesting that languishers may not be subsyndromal). In addition, 23% of adults fit the criteria for one or more of the four mental disorders measured in the MIDUS. Of that 23%, 7.0% had a mental illness and fit the criteria for languishing, meaning individuals not only had an episode of mental illness along with the absence of mental health (i.e., languishing). Of the 23% with a mental illness, 14.5% had moderate mental health and 1.5% was flourishing.

Keyes (2007) has argued that a mentally healthy population should have at least one-half of its population at the level of flourishing. The point prevalence of 12-month mental disorder at nearly 25% of the adult population provides strong justification for continued national investment in the reduction of mental illness. However, the fact that barely 2 in 10 adults, rather than over 5 in 10, are flourishing suggests the need for new investments in the promotion of mental health as flourishing. The size of the adult population with moderate mental health and its "proximity" to being completely mentally healthy suggest one of the most potentially cost-effective leverage points for increasing national mental health. Evidence reviewed earlier suggests that reducing the size of the moderate mental health group by increasing its mental health could substantially reduce direct (e.g., healthcare usage) and indirect (e.g., workdays missed) costs. How can we increase flourishing?

Positive Emotions and Dynamics

Clearly flourishing mental health is highly desirable. With only about 17% of US adults meeting this criterion of complete mental health, there is much room for improvement. How might we promote flourishing? When the concept of flourishing mental health was first introduced (Keyes 1999) and published in the research literature (Keyes 2002), it inspired an effort to understand the emotional dynamics that might underlie this and other instances of human flourishing, like successful, satisfying marriages and effective, synergistic teamwork.

Positive Emotions and the Broaden-and-Build Theory

This effort extended a relatively new theory on the evolved, adaptive significance of positive emotions, namely, the broaden-and-build theory (Fredrickson 1998, 2001). This theory holds that, unlike negative emotions, which narrow people's ideas about possible actions in ways that aided our ancestor's survival in life-threatening circumstances (e.g., fight, flee), positive emotions broaden people's thought and action repertoires (e.g., play, explore), in ways that spurred our ancestor's development of key assets, including their physical, mental, psychological, and social resources. In time, the resources gained during positive emotional states would have left our ancestors better equipped to survive later threats to life and limb that they would inevitably face. So although positive emotions are transient, the personal resources accrued across repeated pleasant moments are durable. As these resources accumulate, they function as reserves that can be drawn on to manage future threats and increase odds of survival. So experiences of positive emotion, although fleeting, can spark dynamic processes with downstream repercussions for growth and resilience.

Several key aspects of the broaden-and-build theory have been empirically tested and supported. For instance, laboratory experiments have shown that, relative to neutral and negative states, induced positive emotions widen the scope of people's attention (Fredrickson and Branigan 1998; Rowe et al. 2007), broaden people's repertoires of desired actions (Fredrickson and Branigan 1998), dismantle people's physiological preparation for specific actions sparked by negative emotions (Fredrickson et al. 2000), and increase their openness to new experiences (Isen 1970; Kahn and Isen 1993). At the interpersonal level, induced positive emotions, again relative to neutral and negative states, increase people's sense of "oneness" with close others (Waugh et al. 2006), their trust in acquaintances (Dunn and Schweitzer 2005), and their ability to recognize strangers of another race (Johnson and Fredrickson 2005). Prospective correlational studies have further shown that people who, for whatever reasons, experience or express positive emotions more than others cope more effectively with adversity (Fredrickson et al. 2003; Folkman and Moskowitz 2000; Stein et al. 1997; Bonanno and Keltner 1997) and enjoy more successes in their work (Diener et al. 2002) and in their relationships (Harker and Keltner 2001; Waugh and Fredrickson 2006). People with more positive emotions and outlooks have also been shown to live longer (Danner et al. 2001; Levy et al. 2002; Moskowitz 2003; Ostir et al. 2000). Moreover, field experiments have demonstrated that interventions that increase people's daily experiences of positive emotions build people's physical, psychological, social, and mental resources (Fredrickson et al. 2008).

One implication of the broaden-and-build theory is that positive emotions do not merely mark or signal current mental health; they also produce and thereby forecast future gains in mental health. People's current positive emotions, then, may influence their prospects for flourishing down the road. In short, the broaden-and-build theory of positive emotions, together with its growing empirical support, provides an explanation for how and why positive emotions might forecast optimal functioning: By broadening people's mindsets and building consequential resources, positive emotional states over time transform people for the better, enabling them to survive, thrive, and even flourish.

Flourishing and the Dynamics of Positive Emotion

How much positive emotion is needed to flourish? A nonlinear dynamics model developed to describe flourishing business teams suggests an answer. Losada (1999) observed 60 management teams as they crafted their annual strategic plans. Every speech act was rated by a team of coders who viewed the meetings behind one-way mirrors. Utterances were coded as "positive" if speakers showed support, encouragement, or appreciation and as "negative" if they showed disapproval, sarcasm, or cynicism. They were coded as "inquiry" if they offered questions aimed at exploring a position and as "advocacy" if they offered arguments in favor of the speaker's viewpoint. They were coded as "self" if they referred to the person speaking, the group present, or the company and as "other" if they referenced a person or group neither present nor part of the company.

Later, Losada identified which teams were flourishing, defined as showing uniformly high performance across three indicators: profitability, customer satisfaction, and evaluations by superiors, peers, and subordinates. Other teams had mixed or uniformly low performance. Analyses of the time series of the observed data, including their lead-lag relationships, led Losada (1999) to develop a set of coupled differential equations to capture the dynamics of different types of teams.

The model derived for flourishing, high-performance teams followed the classic "butterfly" trajectory of the Lorenz system, first discovered in the 1960s to underlie the complex dynamics of weather patterns (Losada 1999; Losada and Heaphy 2004). For flourishing teams, the dynamic structure reflected the highest positivity ratio and the broadest range of inquiry and advocacy. It was also the most generative and flexible. Mathematically, its trajectory in phase space never duplicates itself, representing maximal degrees of freedom and behavioral flexibility. In the terms of physics and mathematics, this is a chaotic attractor.

The model derived for medium performance teams was different. Although it began with a structure that mirrored the model for flourishing teams, albeit with a lower positivity ratio and narrower range of inquiry and advocacy, its behavioral flexibility was insufficient for resilience. In fact, the dynamic model calcified into a limit cycle after an encounter with extreme negativity. The model suggests that following extreme negativity, these teams lose behavioral flexibility and their ability to question: They languish in an endless loop centered on self-absorbed advocacy.

The model derived from low-performance teams was different still. It reflected the lowest positivity ratio and never showed the complex and generative dynamics of the model derived from high-performance teams, but instead was stuck in self-absorbed advocacy from the start. But worse than being stuck in an endless loop, its dynamics showed the properties of a fixed point attractor, suggesting that low-performance teams eventually lose behavioral flexibility altogether.

The nonlinear dynamic model that emerged from Losada's empirical analysis of business teams translated several tenets of the broaden-and-build theory into mathematics. As predicted by the theory, the mathematical model shows that higher levels of positive emotions are linked with (a) broader behavioral repertoires, (b) greater flexibility and resilience to adversity, (c) more social resources, and (d) optimal functioning (Losada 1999; Losada and Heaphy 2004).

In fact, the most potent single variable within Losada's model is the ratio of positive to negative emotions. If this ratio is known, we can predict whether the complex dynamics of flourishing will be evident. Developing Losada's mathematical model further, Fredrickson and Losada (2005) identified the positivity ratio at which the dynamical structure bifurcates between the limit cycle of medium performance teams and the complex dynamics of flourishing, high-performance teams. This turns out to be a ratio of positive to negative emotions of about 3 to 1. Fredrickson and Losada (2005) hypothesized that only at or above this ratio would positive emotions be in sufficient supply to seed human flourishing.

Fredrickson and Losada (2005) sought to test whether this ratio separates those who flourish from those who do not against observed data on human flourishing at multiple levels of analysis. They first drew from archival data gathered by Fredrickson and colleagues in which college students took Keyes' (2002) survey to diagnose flourishing mental health. Then, each day for a month, these students indicated the extent to which they felt each of several positive and negative emotions over the past 24 h. Fredrickson and Losada (2005) then calculated the ratio of positive to negative emotions experienced over the entire month. For individuals classified as flourishing, the ratio was 3.2 to 1, whereas for those not flourishing, the ratio was 2.3 to 1. As predicted, these ratios fell on either side of the hypothesized ratio of about 3 to 1 (Fredrickson and Losada 2005).

Data from Gottman's (1994) in-depth and longitudinal studies of marriage are also relevant. Gottman and colleagues observed couples discussing an area of conflict in their relationship. Researchers measured positive and negative emotions using two coding schemes: One focused on positive and negative speech acts and another focused on observable positive and negative emotions. Gottman reported that among marriages that last and that both partners find to be satisfying – what might be called flourishing marriages – mean positivity ratios were 4.9 to 1. By contrast, among marriages identified as being on cascades toward dissolution – languishing marriages at best – mean positivity ratios were 0.8 to 1 (Gottman 1994).

At three levels of analysis – for individuals, marriages, and teams – flourishing was associated with positivity ratios above about 3 to 1. Likewise, for individuals, marriages, or business teams that do not function so well – those that might be identified as languishing – positivity ratios fell below about 3 to 1. Coherence is thus emerging among theory, mathematics, and observed data regarding positive emotions and human flourishing. First, Fredrickson's (1998, 2001) broaden-and-build theory describes the psychological mechanisms through which positive emotions might fuel human flourishing. Second, Losada's nonlinear dynamics model (1999), Losada and Heaphy (2004) describes the mathematical relations between certain positivity ratios and the complex dynamics of human flourishing. And third, fine-grained empirical observations at three levels of analysis – within individuals, couples, and teams – support Fredrickson's theory and Losada's mathematics.

The finding that certain ratios of positive to negative emotions can predict whether people can be classified as flourishing represents just the start of deeper inquiry into what constitutes complete mental health. Although the evidence is thus far only predictive, it has already motivated further inquiry into whether certain ratios of positive to negative emotions might also cause flourishing to unfold. If we can identify interventions to selectively elevate people's positive emotions, we may discover how to seed the complex, generative, and resilient dynamics of human flourishing.

Character Strengths and Virtues

Centuries ago, the Athenian philosophers – Socrates, Plato, and especially Aristotle – framed morality in terms of good character and in particular virtues – i.e., traits of character that make someone a good person (Rachels 1999). This tradition is also found in Eastern cultures in the writings of Confucius (1992), who discussed such virtues as *jen* (benevolence), *yi* (duty),

5 Positive Psychology and the Quality of Life

li (etiquette), *zhi* (wisdom), and *xin* (sincerity). Although specific definitions of happiness and good character may vary across different eras and cultures, emphasis on the importance of character and virtues for personal and societal well-being has been a constant.

In recent years, positive psychologists have reclaimed good character and virtue as an important topic of study. For several years, from a positive psychology perspective, a group of researchers have been involved in a project that describes important strengths of character and how to measure them as individual differences. This research program is sometimes identified as the *Values in Action (VIA) Project,* after the nonprofit organization – the VIA Institute – that sponsored the initial work.

The VIA Project approaches good character as a family of widely valued traits, each of which exists in degrees and is manifest in a range of thoughts, feelings, and behaviors. At present, it is not wedded to a given theory. An impetus for the project was the need to know more about good character, and no consensual theory had emerged within psychology or elsewhere. The classification is best described as aspirational, meaning that it attempts to specify mutually exclusive and exhaustive categories of moral traits without claiming finality or a deep theory (Bailey 1994).

The VIA Classification organizes character strengths in terms of a framework that emerged from a literature review of the texts of the world's influential religious and philosophical traditions (e.g., the books of *Exodus* and *Proverbs* in the case of Judaism, the *Analects* in the case of Confucianism, and so on) (Dahlsgaard et al. 2005). A core set of virtues was acknowledged as important in all of these traditions:

1. Wisdom and knowledge – cognitive strengths entailing the acquisition and use of knowledge
2. Courage – emotional strengths involving the exercise of will to accomplish goals in the face of opposition, external or internal
3. Humanity – interpersonal strengths that involve "tending and befriending" others
4. Justice – civic strengths underlying healthy community life
5. Temperance – strengths protecting against excess
6. Transcendence – strengths that forge connections to the larger universe and provide meaning

In its current form, the VIA Classification includes 24 positive traits organized in terms of the six core virtues (Table 5.2). *Virtues* are the core characteristics valued by moral philosophers and religious thinkers. *Character strengths* are the psychological ingredients – processes or mechanisms – that define the virtues. They are distinguishable routes to displaying one or another of the virtues.

The hierarchical organization – strengths under virtues – is a conceptual scheme and not a hypothesis to be tested with data. Indeed, empirical investigations of the structuring of character strengths yield a coherent picture but not exactly the one implied in Table X (Park and Peterson 2006c; Peterson and Seligman 2004). The VIA project is a work in progress. Changes in the classification are to be expected as empirical data accumulate.

Various ways to measure the 24 VIA strengths have been devised, including self-report questionnaires suitable for adults and young people, structured interviews to identify what are called signature strengths, informant reports of how target individuals rise to the occasion (or not) with appropriate strengths of character (e.g., hope when encountering setbacks), a content analysis procedure for assessing character strengths from unstructured descriptions of self and others, and strategies for scoring positive traits from archived material like obituaries (Park and Peterson 2006a, b; Peterson et al. 2005a). Space does not permit a detailed description of what has been learned about the reliability and validity of these different methods. Suffice it to say that the internal consistency of the questionnaire measures has been established as well as test-retest stability over several months. Their validity has been investigated with the known-groups procedure and more generally by mapping out their correlates (Park and Peterson 2006c; Peterson and Seligman 2004).

These measures of the VIA strengths allow a systematic study of character in multidimensional terms (Park et al. 2004). Past research on good character has focused on one component of character at a time, leaving unanswered questions about the underlying structure of character within an individual. Some individuals may be creative and authentic but are neither brave nor kind, or vice versa (Park 2004). Furthermore, measuring a full range of positive traits may reduce concerns about socially desirable responding by allowing most research participants to say something good about themselves. Although some people may be low in most of the strengths in our classification, when compared to others, the data show that virtually everyone has defining

Table 5.2 Values in action (VIA), classification of virtues, and character strengths

Virtues	Strengths
A. Wisdom and knowledge	
	1. Creativity: thinking of novel and productive ways to do things
	2. Curiosity: taking an interest in all of ongoing experience
	3. Open-mindedness: thinking things through and examining them from all sides
	4. Love of learning: mastering new skills, topics, and bodies of knowledge
	5. Perspective: being able to provide wise counsel to others
B. Courage	
	1. Authenticity: speaking the truth and presenting oneself in a genuine way
	2. Bravery: *not* shrinking from threat, challenge, difficulty, or pain
	3. Perseverance: finishing what one starts
	4. Zest: approaching life with excitement and energy
C. Humanity	
	1. Kindness: doing favors and good deeds for others
	2. Love: valuing close relations with others
	3. Social intelligence: being aware of the motives and feelings of self and others
D. Justice	
	1. Fairness: treating all people the same according to notions of fairness and justice
	2. Leadership: organizing group activities and seeing that they happen
	3. Teamwork: working well as member of a group or team
E. Temperance	
	1. Forgiveness: forgiving those who have done wrong
	2. Modesty: letting one's accomplishments speak for themselves
	3. Prudence: being careful about one's choices; *not* saying or doing things that might later be regretted
	4. Self-regulation: regulating what one feels and does
F. Transcendence	
	1. Appreciation of beauty and excellence: noticing and appreciating beauty, excellence, and/or skilled performance in all domains of life
	2. Gratitude: being aware of and thankful for the good things that happen
	3. Hope: expecting the best and working to achieve it
	4. Humor: liking to laugh and joke, bringing smiles to other people
	5. Religiousness: having coherent beliefs about the higher purpose and meaning of life

strengths of character within themselves. One hypothesis is that identifying and exercising these "signature strengths" may lead to psychologically flourishing life.

Evidence concerning the correlates of the VIA strengths is accumulating, and it is clear that certain character strengths are linked to flourishing and their absence to languishing. Among adults, several strengths in particular show a robust relation with life satisfaction, happiness, and psychological well-being measured in different ways: love, gratitude, hope, curiosity, and zest (Park et al. 2004). Among youth, the robust predictors of life satisfaction are love, gratitude, hope, and zest (Park and Peterson 2006c). And among very young children between 3and 9 years of age, those described by their parents as showing love, zest, and hope are also described as happy (Park and Peterson 2006a). Thus, the character strengths of love, hope, and zest are

consistently related to life satisfaction for individuals across all ages. Gratitude is associate with life satisfaction for individuals with 7 years of age and older. Perhaps strength such as gratitude may require cognitive maturation. Although cross-sectional, these data considered together imply a developmental sequence to the most fulfilling character strengths. The strengths that contribute to well-being at younger ages continue to be important, but additional strengths enter the picture with maturation.

In addition, balance among character strengths and its relationship with life satisfaction has been examined by calculating the standard deviation of scores across VIA strengths within individuals. People whose character strengths have lower standard deviations – i.e., whose scores are less discrepant with one another and arguably more balanced – report higher life satisfaction, especially if they are older adults. Perhaps the integration of one's strengths with maturity reflects wisdom (Erikson 1963). Although this finding is intriguing, the effect size is small. Further investigation is needed.

In several retrospective studies, the effects of life events on character strengths and life satisfaction were examined, with sensible patterns resulting. Histories of physical illness or psychological disorder are each associated with across-the-board lower levels of character strengths and life satisfaction, but only among those who have not recovered (Peterson et al. 2006). Physical illness from which one has recovered is linked to high in bravery, kindness, and humor, and severe psychological disorder that has resolved is linked to high in appreciation of beauty and love of learning. Furthermore, higher levels of these strengths are related to greater life satisfaction. These findings suggest that in the wake of negative life events, certain character strengths may work as a buffer and help to maintain or even increase well-being despite challenges.

Other aspects of flourishing life are also related to the character strengths in the VIA Classification. First, academic achievement among school children 1 year later was predicted by strengths such as perseverance, love, and gratitude among others above and beyond their IQ scores. Second, love was the strongest predictor for military performance among West Point cadets evaluated by their commanding officers and peers in 1 year longitudinal study. Third, teaching effectiveness assessed by student performance on standardized tests was longitudinally predicted by teacher's zest, humor, and social intelligence. Fourth, life satisfaction among children was related by self-regulation of their parents, although this strength was not strongly related to parents' own life satisfaction.

Researchers have also investigated some of the problems associated with lower levels of character strengths, with several strengths in particular consistently emerging as important. The strongest predictor of work dissatisfaction is the absence of zest, which is also associated with the stance that work is "just" a job (Peterson et al. 2009). In other words, people with high zest perceive their job as a calling and have higher satisfaction at work. Negative affect and alienation are strongly linked to the absence of zest and the absence of hope. Depression is similarly correlated with decreased zest and decreased hope, and also with the absence of love and the absence of perspective, underscoring the interpersonal deficits that characterize languishing.

Not surprisingly, those low in love report insecure attachment styles also (Peterson and Park 2007).

Given the importance of character to the psychological good life, questions of course arise about how good character might be cultivated. This work is in its infancy, and to date, only a handful of character strengths have been seriously considered, like hope (optimism), gratitude, kindness, social intelligence, leadership, creativity, and fairness (Park and Peterson 2008). The problem with most of these endeavors, at least as seen from the vantage of the VIA Project, is that they focus on one strength of character at a time. Unanswered by these studies is whether other strengths, not on focus and not measured, are changed as well.

A few intervention studies have addressed character in multidimensional terms. In one such study, adults completed a VIA survey and identified their top strengths, which they were then asked to use for a week in novel ways (Seligman et al. 2005). Relative to a comparison group without this instruction, these individuals showed meaningful increases in happiness as well as decreases in depression for up to 6 months of follow-up. Not surprisingly, these changes were evident only if research participants continued to find new ways to use their strengths. Most did this even without the explicit request to do so. It should also be noted that other research participants merely asked to use their signature strengths showed no lasting benefits. Finding *novel* ways to use strengths is therefore critical and reflects the importance of ongoing personal growth in producing a flourishing life.

In two other intervention studies, one with moderately depressed college students and the other with formally diagnosed adults with unipolar depression, Seligman et al. (2006) investigated the effects of what they termed positive psychotherapy. Positive psychotherapy focuses on client strengths and includes a sustained version of the exercise already described to use one's signature strengths in novel ways. Both of these studies found meaningful benefits of positive therapy relative to a no-treatment comparison group. Depression decreased, and life satisfaction increased.

Conclusion

As Aristotle (2000) proposed long ago, happiness is the purpose of life. Also, believing that happiness is the purpose of life, his Holiness the Fourteenth Dalai Lama has said that "... the very motion of our life is towards happiness…" (Dalai Lama and Cutler 1998, p. 13). However, happiness is often misconstrued to refer to the fleeting moments of feeling good or feeling pleasure. The Dalai Lama's and Aristotle's conception of happiness is premised on notion of eudaimonia, which – roughly translated – refers to "good soul or spirit." This notion of happiness is best translated as human flourishing that is the result of a cultivation of a conscious, deliberate, rational application of principles of conduct toward the pursuit of excellence aligned with each individual's unique capabilities. Flourishing in life is believed to be the ultimate aim of life in that it is rewarding in itself; it is, thus, the end toward which all other forms of conduct are aimed, and it constitutes one of the highest goods in life.

To date, research has shown that flourishing is one of the higher goods in life in that flourishing individuals are the most productive, least likely to have chronic physical disease with age, have the lowest level of disability, the highest level of psychosocial assets, and the lowest level of healthcare utilization and costs. Newer research on adolescents who are flourishing (Keyes 2006) also shows that flourishing youth report the lowest level of conduct problems (i.e., skipped school, arrests, smoking, drinking, and drug use) and the highest level of psychosocial assets (e.g., integration into school, intimate relationships with adults, positive self-concept, and self-determination). In turn, positive emotions such as joy, contentment, and love, which are markers of quality of life in themselves, have been shown to be connected with sustaining the dynamics of flourishing. Interestingly, flourishing individuals experience a ratio of more positive than negative emotions in their daily lives. However, flourishing individuals do experience some negative emotions, and they do not experience an excessive amount of positive emotions.

It remains to be seen, however, whether the VIA strengths and virtues support the theory of eudaimonia. That is, does living in accordance with one's virtues lead to flourishing in life? If so, is this connection explained, in part, by the emotional dynamics of virtuous individuals such that they experience both negative and positive emotions in their life pursuits, but the balance of emotions is outweighed by more positive than negative, and not an overabundance of positive emotions? The research done to date with the VIA strengths and virtues has focused on a limited set of outcomes, some negative and some positive (e.g., emotional well-being). These intervention studies of the VIA strengths and virtues are consistent with the positive psychology premise that deliberate attention to what a person does well – signature strengths – is a fruitful avenue to a better life. However, further work is needed to rigorously test the theory of *eudaimonia.*

Positive psychology has been a key framework for the study of flourishing, positive emotional dynamics, and character strengths and virtues. This research seeks to balance out the bulk of theory and research in quality of life studies that focus on the causes and dynamics of pathology, and it supports the premise of positive psychology that attention to "the positive" sheds light on what makes life worth living.

References

American Psychiatric Association. (1987). *Diagnostic and statistical manual of mental disorders* (3rd ed., Rev.). Washington, DC: American Psychiatric Association.

American Psychiatric Association. (2000). *Diagnostic and statistical manual of mental disorders* (4th ed., text revision). Washington, DC: American Psychiatric Association.

Aristotle. (2000). *The Nicomachean ethics* (R. Crisp, Trans.). Cambridge: Cambridge University Press.

Bailey, K. D. (1994). *Typologies and taxonomies: An introduction to classification techniques.* Thousand Oaks: Sage Publications.

Bonanno, G. A., & Keltner, D. (1997). Facial expressions of emotion and the course of conjugal bereavement. *Journal of Abnormal Psychology, 106*, 126–137.

Confucius (1992). *Analects* (D. Hinton, Trans.). Washington, DC: Counterpoint.

Dahlsgaard, K., Peterson, C., & Seligman, M. E. P. (2005). Shared virtue: The convergence of valued human strengths across culture and history. *Review of General Psychology, 9*, 209–213.

Dalai Lama, His Holiness, & Cutler, H. C. (1998). *The art of happiness: A handbook for living.* New York: Riverhead Books.

Danner, D. D., Snowdon, D. A., & Friesen, W. V. (2001). Positive emotions in early life and longevity: Findings from the nun study. *Journal of Personality and Social Psychology, 80*, 804–813.

Diener, E., Nickerson, C., Lucas, R. E., & Sandvik, E. (2002). Dispositional affect and job outcomes. *Social Indicators Research, 59*, 229–259.

Dunn, J. R., & Schweitzer, M. E. (2005). Feeling and believing: The influence of emotion on trust. *Journal of Personality and Social Psychology, 88*, 736–748.

Erikson, E. (1963). *Childhood and society* (2nd ed.). New York: Norton.

Folkman, S., & Moskowitz, J. T. (2000). Positive affect and the other side of coping. *American Psychologist, 55*, 647–654.

Fredrickson, B. L. (1998). What good are positive emotions? *Review of General Psychology, 2*, 300–319.

5 Positive Psychology and the Quality of Life

Fredrickson, B. L. (2001). The role of positive emotions in positive psychology: The broaden-and-build theory of positive emotions. *American Psychologist, 56*, 218–226.

Fredrickson, B. L., & Losada, M. F. (2005). Positive affect and the complex dynamics of human flourishing. *American Psychologist, 60*, 678–686.

Fredrickson, B. L., Mancuso, R. A., Branigan, C., & Tugade, M. M. (2000). The undoing effect of positive emotions. *Motivation and Emotion, 24*, 237–258.

Fredrickson, B. L., & Branigan, C. (2003). Positive emotions broaden the scope of attention and thought-action repertoires. *Cognition & Emotion, 19*, 313–332.

Fredrickson, B. L., Tugade, M. M., Waugh, C. E., & Larkin, G. R. (2003). What good are positive emotions in crisis? A prospective study of resilience and emotions following the terrorist attacks on the United States on September 11th, 2001. *Journal of Personality and Social Psychology, 84*, 365–376.

Fredrickson, B., Cohn, M., Coffey, K. A., Pek, J., & Finkel, S. M. (2008). Open hearts build lives: Positive emotions, induced through loving-kindness meditation, build consequential personal resources. *Journal of Personality and Social Psychology, 95*, 1045–1062.

Gottman, J. M. (1994). *What predicts divorce? The relationship between marital processes and marital outcomes.* Mahwah: Erlbaum.

Harker, L. A., & Keltner, D. (2001). Expressions of positive emotion in women's college yearbook pictures and their relationship to personality and life outcomes across adulthood. *Journal of Personality and Social Psychology, 80*, 112–124.

Isen, A. M. (1970). Success, failure, attention, and reaction to others: The warm glow of success. *Journal of Personality and Social Psychology, 15*, 294–301.

Jahoda, M. (1958). *Current concepts of positive mental health.* New York: Basic Books.

Johnson, K. J., & Fredrickson, B. L. (2005). "We all look the same to me": Positive emotions eliminate the own-race in face recognition. *Psychological Science, 16*, 875–881.

Kahn, B. E., & Isen, A. M. (1993). The influence of positive affect on variety seeking among safe, enjoyable products. *Journal of Consumer Research, 20*, 257–270.

Kessler, R. C., Andrews, G., Mroczek, D., Ustun, B., & Wittchen, H.-U. (1998). The World Health Organization Composite International Diagnostic Interview Short Form (CIDI-SF). *International Journal of Methods in Psychiatric Research, 7*, 171–185.

Keyes, C. L. M. (1998). Social well-being. *Social Psychology Quarterly, 61*, 121–140.

Keyes, C. L. M. (1999). *Languishing and flourishing in life.* Presentation at the First Summit of Positive Psychology. Lincoln: The Gallup Organization.

Keyes, C. L. M. (2002). The mental health continuum: From languishing to flourishing in life. *Journal of Health and Social Behavior, 43*, 207–222.

Kessler, R. C. (2002). The categorical versus dimensional assessment controversy in the sociology of mental illness. *Journal of Health and Social Behavior, 43*, 171–188.

Keyes, C. L. M. (2004). The nexus of cardiovascular disease and depression revisited: The complete mental health perspective and the moderating role of age and gender. *Aging and Mental Health, 8*, 266–274.

Keyes, C. L. M. (2005a). Mental illness and/or mental health? Investigating axioms of the complete state model of health. *Journal of Consulting and Clinical Psychology, 73*, 539–548.

Keyes, C. L. M. (2005b). Chronic physical disease and aging: Is mental health a potential protective factor? *Ageing International, 30*, 88–104.

Keyes, C. L. M. (2006). Mental health in adolescence: Is America's youth flourishing? *American Journal of Orthopsychiatry, 76*, 395–402.

Keyes, C. L. M. (2007). Promoting and protecting mental health as flourishing: A complementary strategy for improving national mental health. *American Psychologist, 62*, 95–108.

Keyes, C. L. M., & Grzywacz, J. G. (2005). Health as a complete state: The added value in work performance and healthcare costs. *Journal of Occupational and Environmental Medicine, 47*, 523–532.

Keyes, C. L. M., Shmotkin, D., & Ryff, C. D. (2002). Optimizing well-being: The empirical encounter of two traditions. *Journal of Personality and Social Psychology, 82*, 1007–1022.

Levy, B. R., Slade, M. D., Kunkel, S. R., & Kasl, S. V. (2002). Longevity increased by positive self-perceptions of aging. *Journal of Personality and Social Psychology, 83*, 261–270.

Losada, M. (1999). The complex dynamics of high performance teams. *Mathematical and Computer Modeling, 30*, 179–192.

Losada, M., & Heaphy, E. (2004). The role of positivity and connectivity in the performance of business teams: A nonlinear dynamics model. *American Behavioral Scientist, 47*, 740–765.

Moskowitz, J. T. (2003). Positive affect predicts lower risk of AIDS mortality. *Psychosomatic Medicine, 65*, 620–626.

Ostir, G. V., Markides, K. S., Black, S. A., & Goodwin, J. S. (2000). Emotional well- being predicts subsequent functional independence and survival. *Journal of the American Geriatrics Society, 48*, 473–478.

Park, N. (2004). Character strengths and positive youth development. *The Annals of the American Academy of Political and Social Science, 591*, 40–54.

Park, N., & Peterson, C. (2003). Virtues and organizations. In K. S. Cameron, J. E. Dutton, & R. E. Quinn (Eds.), *Positive organizational scholarship: Foundations of a new discipline* (pp. 33–47). San Francisco: Berrett-Koehler.

Park, N., & Peterson, C. (2006a). Character strengths and happiness among young children: Content analysis of parental descriptions. *Journal of Happiness Studies, 7*, 323–341.

Park, N., & Peterson, C. (2006b). Methodological issues in positive psychology and the assessment of character strengths. In A. D. Ong & M. van Dulmen (Eds.), *Handbook of methods in positive psychology* (pp. 292–305). New York: Oxford University Press.

Park, N., & Peterson, C. (2006c). Moral competence and character strengths among adolescents: The development and validation of the values in action inventory of strengths for youth. *Journal of Adolescence, 29*, 891–905.

Park, N., & Peterson, C. (2008). The cultivation of character strengths: Teaching the psychological good life. In M. Ferrari & G. Poworowski (Eds.), *Teaching for wisdom: Cross-cultural perspectives on fostering wisdom* (pp. 57–75). Mahwah: Erlbaum.

Park, N., Peterson, C., & Seligman, M. E. P. (2004). Strengths of character and well-being. *Journal of Social and Clinical Psychology, 23*, 603–619.

Peterson, C. (2006). *A primer in positive psychology*. New York: Oxford University Press.

Peterson, C., & Park, N. (2007). Attachment security and its benefits in context. *Psychological Inquiry, 18*, 172–176.

Peterson, C., & Seligman, M. E. P. (2004). *Character strengths and virtues: A handbook and classification*. New York/Washington, DC: Oxford University Press/American Psychological Association.

Peterson, C., Park, N., & Seligman, M. E. P. (2005a). Assessment of character strengths. In G. P. Koocher, J. C. Norcross, & S. S. Hill III (Eds.), *Psychologists' desk reference* (2nd ed., pp. 93–98). New York: Oxford University Press.

Peterson, C., Park, N., & Seligman, M. E. P. (2005b). Orientations to happiness and life satisfaction: The full life versus the empty life. *Journal of Happiness Studies, 6*, 25–41.

Peterson, C., Park, N., & Seligman, M. E. P. (2006). Greater strengths of character and recovery from illness. *Journal of Positive Psychology, 1*, 17–26.

Peterson, C., Ruch, W., Beerman, U., Park, N., & Seligman, M. E. P. (2007). Strengths of character, orientations to happiness, and life satisfaction. *Journal of Positive Psychology, 2*, 149–156.

Peterson, C., Park, N., Hall, N., & Seligman, M. E. P. (2009). Zest and work. *Journal of Organizational Behavior, 30*(2), 161–172.

Rachels, J. (1999). *The elements of moral philosophy* (3rd ed.). New York: McGraw-Hill.

Rowe, G., Hirsh, J. B., & Anderson, A. K. (2007). Positive affect increases the breadth of attentional selection. *Proceedings of the National Academy of Sciences of the United States of America, 104*, 383–388.

Ryff, C. D. (1989). Happiness is everything, or is it? Explorations on the meaning of psychological well-being. *Journal of Personality and Social Psychology, 57*, 1069–1081.

Seligman, M. E. P., & Csikszentmihalyi, M. (2000). Positive psychology: An introduction. *American Psychologist, 55*, 5–14.

Seligman, M. E. P., Steen, T. A., Park, N., & Peterson, C. (2005). Positive psychology progress: Empirical validation of interventions. *American Psychologist, 60*, 410–421.

Seligman, M. E. P., Rashid, T., & Parks, A. C. (2006). Positive psychotherapy. *American Psychologist, 61*, 774–788.

Sigerist, H. E. (1941). *Medicine and human welfare*. New Haven: Yale University Press.

Snyder, C. R., & Lopez, S. J. (Eds.). (2002). *Handbook of positive psychology*. New York: Oxford University Press.

Stein, N., Folkman, S., Trabasso, T., & Richards, T. A. (1997). Appraisal and goal processes as predictors of psychological well-being in bereaved caregivers. *Journal of Personality and Social Psychology, 72*, 872–884.

U.S. Public Health Service. (1999). *Mental health: A report of the surgeon general*. Rockville: U.S. Public Health Service.

Waugh, C. E., & Fredrickson, B. L. (2006). Nice to know you: Positive emotions, self-other overlap, and complex understanding in the formation of new relationships. *Journal of Positive Psychology, 1*, 93–106.

Waugh, C. E., Otake, K., Hejmadi, A., & Fredrickson, B. (2006). *Induced positive emotions expand self-other overlap in three cultures*. Manuscript in preparation.

World Health Organization (2004). *Promoting mental health: Concepts, emerging evidence, practice* (Summary report). Geneva: World Health Organization.

Modern Economic Growth and Quality of Life: Cross-Sectional and Time Series Evidence

6

Richard A. Easterlin and Laura Angelescu

Introduction

This chapter provides a selective survey of cross-sectional and time series evidence on the empirical relation between quality of life and modern economic growth. The phenomenon of modern economic growth, so-named by Nobel Laureate Simon Kuznets (1966), marks a new epoch in the economic history of humankind, and first appeared on the world scene in the latter part of the eighteenth century in northwestern Europe. It may be defined as a rapid and sustained rise in real output per head and attendant shifts in production technology, factor input requirements, and the resource allocation of a nation. "Rapid and sustained" is taken here to mean an average growth rate of real GDP per capita that approaches 1.5% per year or more over at least half a century. A rate of 1.5% per year is about the average in the half century before World War I for the group of 15 nations that were the leaders in modern economic growth. It is unprecedented in human history—projecting real per capita output backward from, say 1850, at a 1.5% annual rate would in a matter of a few centuries yield income levels well below the margin for human survival. In the last half of the twentieth century, growth rates in many parts of the developed and developing world have substantially exceeded 1.5% per year.

The basis of modern economic growth is a sweeping change in the technology by which goods are produced (Easterlin 1996). In every country that has developed, essentially the same methods of production have been employed, marked by a dramatic rise in the ratio of physical and human capital to unskilled labor, the use of inanimate energy and mechanization, growth of scale in many industries, and the development of high transportation and communication density. Adoption of this new technology has invariably been accompanied by a shift in the allocation of resources out of agriculture to the industry and service sectors, and a redistribution of labor force to geographic areas favorably situated for the new methods of production.

Quality of life [QoL] embraces the multiple dimensions of human experience that affect well-being. QoL is captured in both objective and subjective indicators. Objective indicators are those external to the individual and encompass measures of material living levels and their components, as well as family life, physical and mental health, work, environment, and so on. The measures relate both to circumstances whose increase raises QoL, such as level of nutrition or life expectancy, and to "bads," such as pollutants and crime, whose increase lowers QoL. Subjective measures are self-reports of personal well-being, as obtained in surveys of happiness, general life satisfaction, prevalence of positive and negative moods, and the like.

Much of the literature relating economic growth to quality of life examines cross-sectional (point-of-time) relationships, usually how countries at different levels of real GDP per capita differ in regard to various QoL indicators, where GDP per capita (or a variant thereof) is taken as a summary index of the level of economic development. Almost always, the data in these studies relate to recent experience—the past few years, the latest decade, or at most the last 40 or 50 years. In these

R.A. Easterlin (✉) • L. Angelescu
University of Southern California, Department of Economics,
Los Angeles, CA, USA
e-mail: easterl@usc.edu

K.C. Land et al. (eds.), *Handbook of Social Indicators and Quality of Life Research*,
DOI 10.1007/978-94-007-2421-1_6, © Springer Science+Business Media B.V. 2012

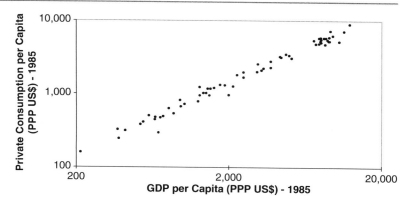

Fig. 6.1 Private consumption per capita and GDP per capita, 64 countries, 1985 (Source: Heston et al. 2002)

cross-sectional studies, positive correlations are often taken as signifying causal relations running from economic growth to QoL. A much more limited set of studies of economic growth and QoL has been based on time series evidence. These studies seek to throw light on the extent to which changes in QoL actually accompany the process of modern economic growth. In what follows, we survey both the cross-sectional and time series evidence, taking up first, objective indicators, and then subjective. We omit indexes that arbitrarily combine indicators from different realms of life such as the Human Development Index (UNDP 2006). Although such measures provide a useful corrective to reliance on a single measure of welfare such as per capita income, the composite indexes suffer from the lack of a theoretical basis for defining the scope and weighting of the indicators included. Even more important, such composite measures, including those combining subjective with objective indicators (Hagerty and Veenhoven 2006) obscure recognition that the components reflect different dimensions of QoL and very likely result from different causal mechanisms.

Objective Indicators

Cross-Sectional Patterns

A wide range of QoL indicators—economic, social, and political—is significantly associated with levels of real GDP per capita in point-of-time comparisons of countries at different levels of economic development. What follows is a small sample of such indicators, chosen partly on the basis of broad societal scope and the availability of observations for a large number of countries, but, more importantly, with a view to ranging across a variety of economic, social, and political conditions.

Consumption Levels

Higher income allows people to satisfy their needs better, and one would expect, therefore, that consumption would be higher in richer countries. This pattern is indeed observed in cross-sectional data (Fig. 6.1). The data for the 64 countries in the figure are the best estimates of quantitative differences in consumption among countries because they are derived using price comparisons for individual goods that cover the entire range of goods included in final consumption expenditure and GDP. According to the estimates, per capita consumption in the five richest countries averages 26 times that of the five poorest. In practical terms, this translates into economic differences in the necessities of life on the order of tenfold for food, 25-fold for clothing, and 73-fold for shelter (Fig. 6.2). Differences in food consumption, in turn, translate into sizeable nutritional differences, as reflected in energy and protein intake, and fruits and vegetables consumption per capita (Fig. 6.3).

The difference between rich and poor is even more pronounced when one goes further up the pyramid of material needs and looks at the consumption of durables. Radios, cars, and television sets are all much more plentiful in higher-income countries (Fig. 6.4). While cars and TV sets are luxuries in most Third World countries, they are part of everyday life in the richer ones, where the question is often not whether a household owns one but rather how many.

One of the main characteristics of modern economic growth is the introduction of new goods. The consumer durables just discussed—cars, radios, and TV sets—were new goods introduced over the course of the first

Fig. 6.2 Food, clothing, and shelter consumption per capita and GDP per capita, 64 countries, 1985 (Source: Heston et al. 2002)

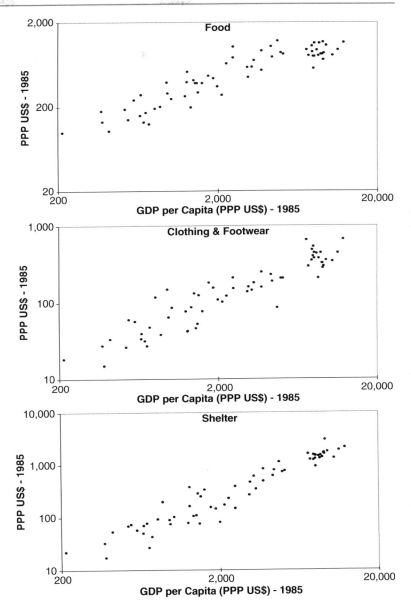

half of the twentieth century. Examples of their counterparts at the start of the twenty-first century are cellular phones and the Internet. These even newer goods are already becoming commonplace in developed countries (Fig. 6.5). In poorer areas of the world, however, they are for most persons a thing of the future.

The repeated positive association with higher income observed here for a wide range of consumer goods raises serious doubts about Ronald Inglehart's assertion (1988, p. 1203) that since World War II, a new generation of individuals has emerged in the richer countries characterized by "postmaterialist" values that have, in his words, "tended to neutralize the emphasis on economic accumulation." Neither the data reflecting satisfaction of basic food needs nor those for the consumption of less essential consumer goods and services give any indication of a tapering off of the growth of consumption in richer societies.

Higher income is also sometimes accompanied by an increase in the so-called "bads," showing that economic growth is not costless. Probably the most prominent "bad" is pollution. If we look, for

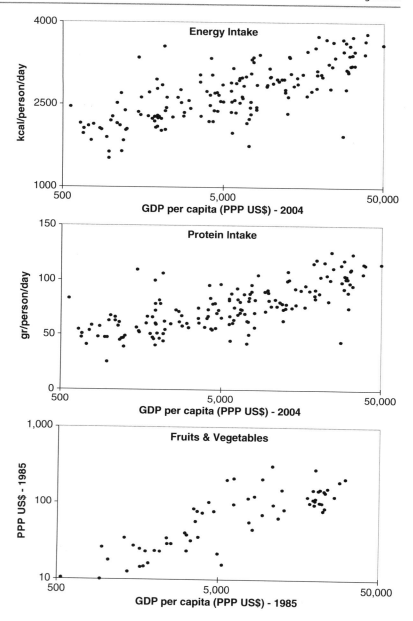

Fig. 6.3 Energy intake and protein intake, 162 countries, 2000–2002, and fruits and vegetables consumption per capita, 64 countries, 1985, and GDP per capita (Source: FAO (2004) for energy intake and protein intake, UNDP (2006) for GDP per capita, and Heston et al. (2002) for fruits and vegetables consumption)

example, at the cross-sectional relationship between GDP per capita and carbon dioxide emissions, we notice a high positive correlation (Fig. 6.6). This strong relationship is hardly surprising given that cars, a salient feature of high-income consumption, are among the main sources of such emissions. Shafik (1994) also reports a very strong positive relationship between income and carbon dioxide emissions. (Holtz-Eakin and Selden's 1995 analysis suggests that there is a diminishing marginal propensity to emit carbon dioxide, but there is little evidence of this in the figure.)

Some argue that, in general, the relation between environmental quality and economic growth is U-shaped, that "environmental quality may deteriorate during a period in which developing countries begin to industrialize, but at some point this deterioration is stopped and reversed as income rises" (Portney 2000).

Fig. 6.4 Radios per capita, 113 countries; cars per capita, 98 countries; and TV sets per capita, 107 countries, and GDP per capita, 1990 (Source: Easterly 1999)

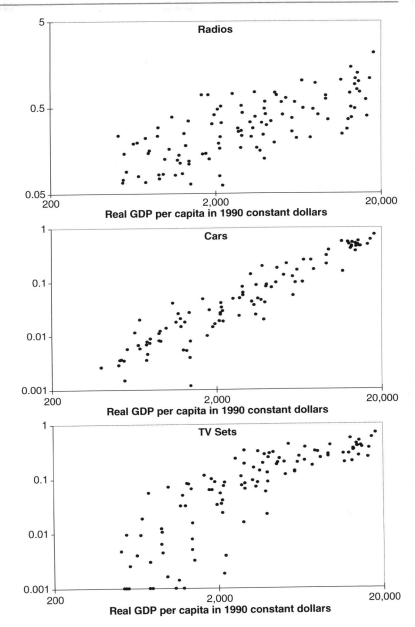

Grossman and Kruger (1991) provide some supporting evidence of this U shape in data on air quality in selected cities in developed and developing countries during the period 1977–1988, but a thorough test of the hypothesis remains to be done.

The flip side of higher food consumption reveals another "bad" associated with economic growth—the detrimental diet choices that people in richer countries may make, reflected in their much higher intake of fat (Fig. 6.7). The result is new and growing health problems that these countries are facing, such as obesity and high blood pressure (Offer 2006; Oswald and Powdthavee 2007).

Taken together, these pieces of cross-sectional evidence confirm that richer countries lead the way when it comes to the quantity and quality of consumption. The positive impact of greater consumption on QoL, however, is offset to some extent by negative effects brought about by that consumption, such as new environmental and health problems.

Fig. 6.5 Cellular subscribers per 1,000 people, 146 countries, and Internet users per 1,000 people, 168 countries, and GDP per capita, 2003 (Source: UNDP (2006) for cellular subscribers and GDP per capita and World Bank (2006) for Internet users)

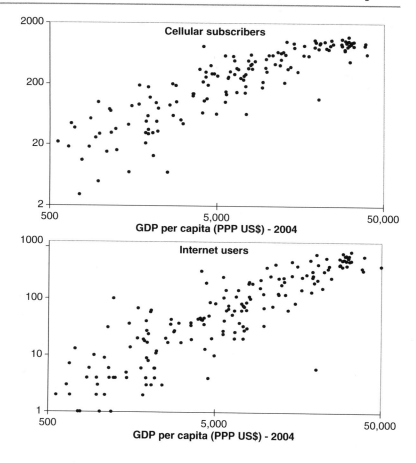

Fig. 6.6 Carbon dioxide emissions and GDP per capita, 109 countries, 1990 (Source: Easterly 1999)

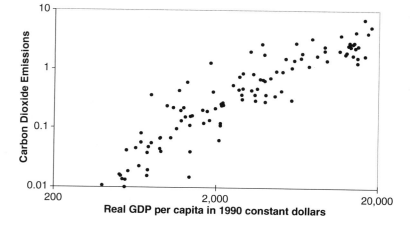

Geographic Distribution

The new technologies underlying modern economic growth dramatically alter the location of economic activity and, in consequence, where people live. Prior to the onset of economic growth, manufacturing is typically carried on with hand tools in shops and homes for limited local markets, and is, in consequence, widely dispersed among towns and villages. With the shift to mechanization and factory production, a strong trend toward geographic centralization of production sets in, with location in cities and towns with good access to transportation increasingly favored (Easterlin 1999).

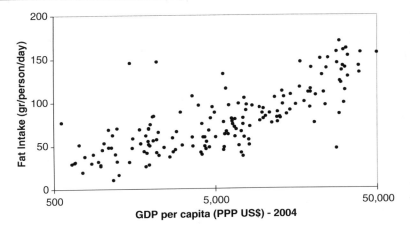

Fig. 6.7 Fat intake (g/person/day) and GDP per capita, 162 countries, 2000–2002 (Source: FAO (2004) for fat intake and UNDP (2006) for 2004 GDP per capita)

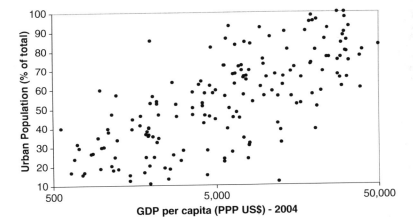

Fig. 6.8 Urban population (% of total) and GDP per capita, 172 countries, 2003 (Source: UNDP 2006)

This shift in the locational distribution of economic opportunity is reflected in the cross-sectional patterns of urbanization (Fig. 6.8).

Whether urbanization of the population is a positive or negative change in QoL is debatable. Although there are analysts who praise the benefits of urban life, such as opera, theater, and spectator sports that require a large population base to sustain them, surveys suggest that a fair proportion of urban dwellers would prefer a rural environment (Fuguitt and Zuiches 1975; Fuguitt and Brown 1990). The suburbanization movement that emerged in the twentieth century with the advent of motor vehicles is arguably a reflection of this preference to live in a more rural-type setting. If this is so, the twenty-first century's emerging Internet technology may lead to a further gradual relaxation of the trend toward population centralization, just as the earlier innovation of motor vehicles promoted suburbanization.

Social Indicators

Representative social indicators of quality of life such as life expectancy and education also exhibit a strong cross-sectional correlation with GDP per capita.

Life expectancy at birth is the average number of years a group of individuals can expect to live. It is determined by considering a fictitious generation that at every age from birth until the age of the maximum life span has a risk of death observed at that age in the year when the indicator is calculated. It is often taken as a proxy, more generally for health. The high positive association of life expectancy with GDP per capita (Fig. 6.9), coupled with higher levels of food, clothing, and housing consumption made possible by higher income, leads naturally to the inference that "Wealthier is Healthier" (Pritchett and Summers 1996). As has been seen, however, increased pollution and adverse dietary changes may also accompany economic growth,

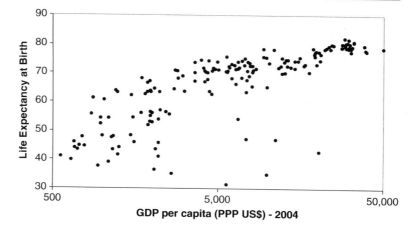

Fig. 6.9 Life expectancy at birth and GDP per capita, 172 countries, 2003 (Source: UNDP 2006)

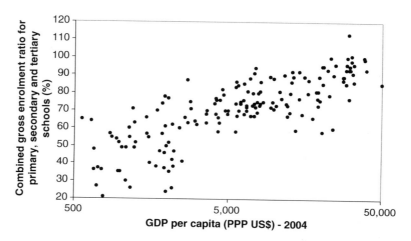

Fig. 6.10 Combined gross enrollment ratio for primary, secondary and tertiary schools (%) and GDP per capita, 169 countries, 2003 (Source: UNDP 2006)

raising some doubts about the simplistic association of greater health with higher income. Indeed, in the nineteenth century, the concentration of population in cities and towns induced by modern economic growth increased exposure to disease (Schofield and Reher 1991). Some experts assert flatly that "low mortality for all will not come as an unplanned spinoff from economic growth" (Caldwell 1986).

A strong positive cross-sectional relationship also exists between GDP per capita and education, as measured by the gross school enrollment ratio (Fig. 6.10). Again, an argument might be made that modern economic growth is the cause of the association because higher per capita income would increase the demand for schooling by individual consumers. But governments too may have an interest in schooling, based on ideological, humanistic, and nationalistic concerns, and act to promote education independently of the level of income. Moreover, some might argue that the empirical association reflects the opposite direction of causality—that education leads to economic growth (Easterlin 1981).

The fertility rate is not often used as a quality of life measure, but it is surely indicative of a major change in women's roles. This point is made vividly by a commentator on the impact of the fertility decline on English working-class women:

> The typical working class mother of the 1890's, married in her teens or early twenties and experiencing ten pregnancies, spent about fifteen years in a state of pregnancy and in nursing a child for the first years of its life. She was tied, for this period of time, to the wheel of childbearing. Today, for the typical mother, the time so spent would be about four years. A reduction of such magnitude in only two generations in the time devoted to childbearing represents nothing less than a revolutionary enlargement of freedom for women. (Titmuss 1966, p. 91)

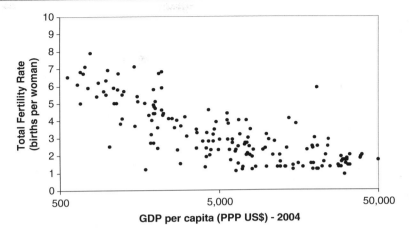

Fig. 6.11 Total fertility rate (Births per woman) and GDP per capita, 167 countries, 2003 (Source: UNDP 2006)

The cross-sectional evidence reveals a very strong negative correlation between GDP per capita and the fertility rate (Fig. 6.11). Just as longer lives and better education are indicators of improved QoL, so too is a lower rate of childbearing, for it means that women are freer to choose what to do with their lives. As in the case of life expectancy and education, however, whether the fertility decline is chiefly caused by economic growth is open to question.

Political Indicators

The relevance of political democracy to quality of life is suggested by Alex Inkeles (1991, p. x) who writes: "[D]emocratic systems give people a greater sense of freedom and, I would argue, more actual freedom, to influence the course of public events, express themselves, and realize their individual human potential." The proposition that economic growth promotes political democracy is often termed the "Lipset hypothesis" (Lipset 1959). It is illustrated here in terms of the "polity composite index." This index is calculated from the Polity IV dataset as the difference between democracy and autocracy measures, both of which range from 0 to 10 (Marshall and Jaggers 2004). The Polity IV democracy index is derived from the coding by knowledgeable scholars of a country's situation with regard to the following: competitiveness of political participation, the openness and competitiveness of executive recruitment, and constraints on the chief executive. The Polity IV autocracy index is similarly based on scoring countries according to competitiveness of political participation, the regulation of participation, the openness and competitiveness of executive recruitment, and constraints on the chief executive. The polity composite index is normalized to lie between 0 and 1, with 1 being the highest rating on political democracy. When 1990s data for this measure are plotted against GDP per capita, there is evidence of a positive relationship (Fig. 6.12).

Human rights and political democracy tend to go together, so one would expect a positive cross-sectional association also to exist between human rights and GDP per capita. This, in fact, turns out to be the case (Fig. 6.13). In the figure, the measure of human rights is based on 40 indicators from the major United Nations human rights treaties—for example, freedom to peacefully associate and assemble, freedom from torture, and the right to peaceful political opposition (Humana 1992). The results are graded into four categories or levels ranging from unqualified respect for a specific right to a constant pattern of violations.

Barro (1997, p. 52), using an index of political rights similar to these two measures and controlling for numerous other factors thought to determine democracy, concludes that "the cross-country evidence examined in this study confirms that the Lipset hypothesis is a strong empirical regularity. In particular, increases in various measures of the standard of living tend to generate a gradual rise in democracy."

Thus, contemporary cross-sectional evidence indicates that a number of important social and political indicators, as well as economic measures, are significantly related statistically to levels of GDP per capita. For the social and political measures, the strength of the relationship, measured, say, by ordinary least squares regressions, is sometimes not as great as for the economic measures, but typically, it is highly significant.

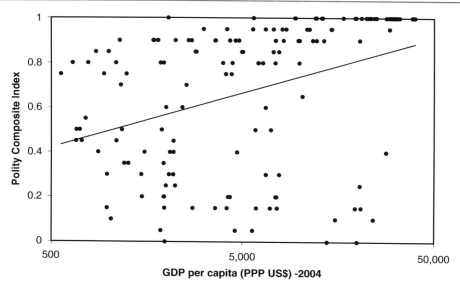

Fig. 6.12 Polity composite index and GDP per capita, 152 countries, 2004 (Source: UNDP (2006) for GDP and Marshall and Jaggers (2004) for the polity composite index)

Fig. 6.13 Human rights rating and GDP per capita, 85 countries, 1992 (Source: Easterly (1999))

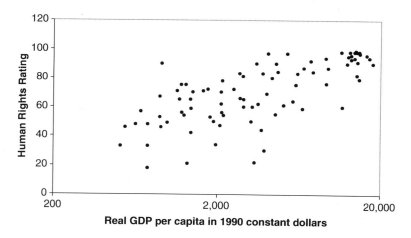

Time Series

Cross-sectional comparisons of QoL indicators with GDP per capita, such as those summarized above, give seemingly strong evidence that economic growth has brought about sweeping changes in QoL—most good, but some, bad. Correlation does not mean causation, however, and if economic growth is the moving force behind the observed changes in QoL, then one should find that the cross-sectional associations above are actually replicated in the historical experience of countries undergoing modern economic growth. One would expect, for example, that the takeoff into modern economic growth, which is marked by a noticeable increase in the growth rate of GDP per capita, would be accompanied by similar takeoffs in the various economic, social, and political indicators just surveyed. Is this, in fact, the case? As will be seen, the answer, in general, is yes for measures directly related to economic performance, such as consumption and urbanization, but no for social and political indicators. The implication with regard to causation is that factors other than economic growth play an important part in the advances in indicators of QoL in the social and political realms.

Consumption Levels

Insofar as quality of life embraces material subsistence, there can be little doubt that modern economic growth has brought about a major long-term improvement because the food, clothing, and shelter available to the

6 Modern Economic Growth and Quality of Life: Cross-Sectional and Time Series Evidence

Table 6.1 Consumer goods of the 1990s nonexistent or rare two centuries ago[a]

Household furnishings	Kitchen equipment	Personal care, health
Electric lighting (99)	Electric/gas range (99)	Eyeglasses
Running water (99)	Electric/gas oven (99)	Contact lenses
Indoor flush toilet (99)	Electric/gas refrigerator (99)	Artificial limbs
Electric/gas hot water heater (92)	Coffee maker (99)	Safety razor
Air conditioning (76)	Microwave oven (91)	Vitamins
Ceiling fan (60)	Dishwasher (48)	Painkillers
Floor coverings	Freezer (35)	Antiallergenics
Bedsprings	Outdoor gas grill (28)	Antidepressants
Household cleaning	Toaster	Exercise equipment
Vacuum cleaner (92)	Waffle iron	Quartz, digital watch
Clothes washer (82)	Food processor	*Food, tobacco*
Clothes dryer (74)	Blender	Canned foods
Electric iron	Friction matches	Frozen foods
Cleaning preparations	*Communications*	Prepared cereals and mixes
Transportation	Telephone (95)	Margarine
Automobile (92)	Cordless phone (61)	Chewing gum
Jet airplane flight	Answering machine (58)	Cigarettes
Motorcycle	Personal computer (40)	Pocket lighter
Bicycle	Laser printer (38)	
Recreation	Cellular phone (33)	
Radio (98)	Pages	
Color television (97)	Fax machine (6)	
Video cassette recorder (82)	Photocopier (4)	
Stereo equipment (69)	Mechanical pen/pencil	
Camcorder (26)	*Clothing*	
Movies	Synthetic fibers	
Motorboat	Elastic goods	
Jet ski	Sewing machine	
Camera, roll film		

Source: Easterlin (1996, p. 160), Cox and Alm (1999, p. 26), United States Census Bureau (2005)
[a]Number in parentheses are percent of households with item for goods for which data are available

average household have risen at rates never before known. Since the major part of GDP consists of consumption, time series evidence on aggregate consumption along with GDP would be redundant. But a sense of the enormous transformation in material living levels, qualitative as well as quantitative, can be readily obtained from a simple contrast of living conditions in the late eighteenth century in, even then, relatively rich United States, with the situation today. Everyday life two centuries ago was most akin to what we currently know as "camping out." At that time, among the rural population (95% of the total), housing typically consisted of one-story houses with one or two rooms and an attic under the rafters. Frequently, there was no flooring except the hard earth. A fireplace with a chimney provided heating and cooking. Toilet facilities consisted of outdoor privies. Water and wood had

to be fetched. Transportation consisted of a horse and wagon (Brady 1972; cf also Lebergott 1993, 1996).

The qualitative change from that world to the United States' current panoply of consumer goods—cars and planes, electrical appliances and running water, telecommunications and computers, pharmaceuticals and health care, and the phenomenal array of food and clothes—is literally incredible. Writing more than three decades ago about living levels in the United States, economic historian Dorothy S. Brady made this point simply and effectively: "Today, the great majority of American families live on a scale that compares well with the way *wealthy* families lived 200 years ago" (1972, p. 84, emphasis added). Brady's point is readily apparent if we consider the long list of consumer goods that are common today but were either nonexistent or rare two centuries ago (Table 6.1).

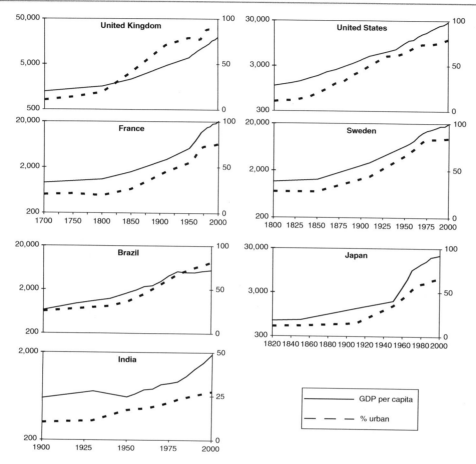

Fig. 6.14 Real GDP per capita and percent of population in urban places in seven countries (GDP in 1990 international Geary–Khamis dollars) (Source: GDP per capita from Maddison (2003). Percent urban from UN (2005) and UN (2004) (http://esa.un.org/unpp) from 1950 to 2000. Previous years for (1) the United Kingdom and France obtained by extrapolation to 1700 based on change in percent urban in Bairoch (1988), 215–221; (2) the United States obtained by extrapolation to 1800 based on change in percent urban in U.S. Census Bureau (1961), 1–4; (3) Sweden and Japan by extrapolation to 1800 based on change in percent urban in Bairoch (1988), 221; (4) Brazil obtained by extrapolation to 1900 based on change in percent urban in Merrick and Graham (1979); (5) India by extrapolation to 1900 based on change in percent urban in Bairoch (1988), 407)

If quality of life is identified with the amount and kinds of goods available to the average consumer, then there can be little question that economic growth has wrought a phenomenal advance.

Geographic Change

The strong centralizing force on the location of economic activity of the new production methods underlying modern economic growth is apparent in the historical experience of a wide range of countries. Figure 6.14 gives time series of the proportion of population in urban areas and GDP per capita for seven countries for which reasonably good and fairly long historical data are available. Although the data are imperfect, the parallel between rapid growth of GDP per capita and urbanization noted in the cross section is apparent in every country (see also Easterlin 1996, Figs. 3.1–3.3). This sharp rise in urbanization with the onset of modern economic growth must be seen against a backdrop of centuries of low levels of urbanization—on the order of 10–15%—with little sizeable change (Fig. 6.15). Modern economic growth has reversed the residential pattern that existed since the beginning of settled agriculture some 10,000 years ago—from a situation where most people lived in rural areas to one where most now live in urban centers or their suburban and ex-urban appendages.

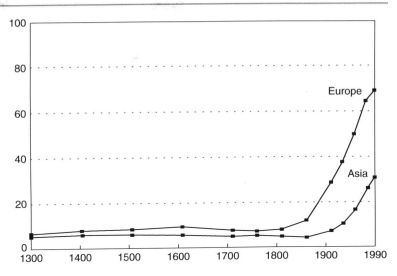

Fig. 6.15 Percentage of population in urban areas, Europe, and Asia, 1300–1990 (Source: United Nations 1977)

Table 6.2 Turning points in demographic measures and growth of GDP per capita in seven countries

	(1)	(2)	(3)	(4)	(5)
	Approximate turning point			Deviation from turning point in GDP per capita, years	
	GDP per capita	Life expectancy at birth (e_0)	Total fertility rate (TFR)	e_0 (2)–(1)	TFR (3)–(1)
United Kingdom	1820	1871	1881	+51	+61
France	1820	1893	1881	+73	+61
United States	1830	1890	1830	+60	0
Sweden	1850	1875	1885	+25	+35
Japan	1870	1923	1950	+53	+80
Brazil	1900	1940	1962	+40	+62
India	1945	1945	1967	0	+22

Source and notes: Easterlin (2000, 2003). The turning point in real GDP per capita is the date at which an increase occurs in the growth rate over at least half a century to around 1% per year or more. The turning point in life expectancy is the date at which a marked improvement (10 years or more) takes place over a period of half a century. The turning point in the total fertility rate is the date at which a decline of around one child per woman takes place within three decades

Social Change

The broad social indicators of QoL previously surveyed also show marked change in countries that have experienced economic growth, but a correlation in time between these indicators and economic growth is much less apparent than in the cross-sectional data. A concise base line for comparing the timing of major changes in the social indicators with economic growth is the date of the takeoff into modern economic growth, that is, the time when the growth rate of GDP per capita over a period of at least half a century reveals a marked increase to a magnitude approaching 1.5% per year or more. Column 1 of Table 6.2 lists such turning points for the seven countries of Fig. 6.14. Although precise dating of the takeoff into modern economic growth is not possible because the evidence available is fragmentary, the dates given in the table agree reasonably well with qualitative impressions in descriptive economic histories of these countries. The gradual spread of modern economic growth from Western Europe to, in rough order, its overseas offshoots, the rest of Europe, Japan, Latin America, and the rest of Asia is also reflected in a very approximate way by the seven countries listed. Our interest here is whether major social indicators of quality of life—life expectancy, fertility, and education—also exhibit marked

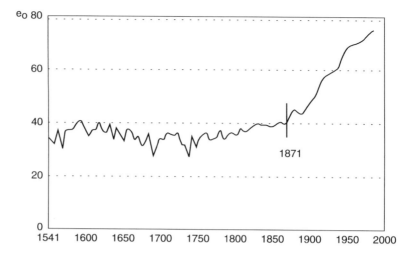

Fig. 6.16 Life expectancy in England and Wales since the sixteenth century. (Source: 1541–1871, Wrigley and Schofield (1981, p. 230); 1871 to 1945–1947, Keyfitz and Flieger (1968, pp. 36–9); 1950–1955 to 1990–1995, United Nations (1995))

turning points and, if so, whether these turning points are reasonably concurrent with those for modern economic growth shown in the table.

On the question of whether significant turning points in major social indicators are apparent, the answer, as previously suggested, is yes. An illustration of such a turning point is given in Fig. 6.16 for life expectancy at birth in Great Britain. This figure is based on an exceptional time series of annual data going all the way back to 1541, the product of the prodigious labor of two British economic historians (Wrigley and Schofield 1981). The abrupt upturn in the series around 1871 is readily apparent to the naked eye.

Thanks to the research efforts of demographers who have produced similar but somewhat shorter historical time series not only for life expectancy, but also childbearing, similar turning points in both life expectancy and fertility can be dated for all seven of the countries under consideration here. The first three columns of Table 6.2 bring together the turning points in these demographic measures along with those for GDP per capita; the last two columns, those in which we are especially interested, present the deviations of the turning points of the demographic series from that in GDP per capita.

Clearly, the typical pattern in this group of countries is that the upturn in life expectancy lags that in GDP per capita by a considerable number of years, and the downturn in fertility, usually by even more. A few exceptions are apparent, however. In India, the takeoffs in life expectancy and GDP per capita are concurrent; in the United States, the onset of fertility decline and rapid growth of GDP per capita also occur together.

Moreover, although the typical pattern for the present set of countries is for takeoffs in the demographic indicators to lag that in economic growth, a broader country sample would show that this is not always the case. In sub-Saharan Africa marked upturns in life expectancy in the last half of the twentieth century have occurred in the absence of a takeoff into economic growth (Easterlin 2000), and indications of fertility downturns are also starting to appear. Thus, the association between the demographic measures, on the one hand, and economic growth, on the other, that one would expect based on the cross-sectional data is not usually found in time series data.

Scholars of the history of education have not produced historical series of school enrollment, literacy, or educational attainment comparable to those that demographers and economic historians have constructed for life expectancy and fertility. Nevertheless, enough fragmentary data are available to assess the proposition that in the countries under study here, a takeoff in universal schooling occurred at the same time as the onset of modern economic growth.

Table 6.3 gives the school enrollment and literacy rate in each of our seven countries at or around the time of takeoff into modern economic growth. Although these schooling rates are fairly rough estimates, the sizeable magnitudes of the extent of schooling in most of these countries at the dates listed contrast strikingly with the worldwide state of very low school enrollment and literacy well into the twentieth century (Easterlin 1965). Clearly, in most of the countries in the table schooling was already well advanced before the takeoff into modern economic growth. The contrast with

6 Modern Economic Growth and Quality of Life: Cross-Sectional and Time Series Evidence

Table 6.3 School enrollment rate and adult literacy at or near the turning point in GDP per capita in seven countries

	(1)	(2)	(3)	(4)	(5)
	Turning point in GDP per capita	School enrollment rate		Adult literacy rate	
		Date	Percent	Date	Percent
United Kingdom	1820	1830	42	1850	68
France	1820	1830	39	1850	58
United States	1830	1830	56	1850	77
Sweden	1850	1830	66	1850	90
Japan	1870	1830	30	1850	26
Brazil	1900	1910	12	1950	49
India	1945	1950	20	1950	19

Source: Easterlin (1996, 2000, 2003)

the patterns for life expectancy and fertility is noteworthy. Whereas the demographic indicators for these countries typically lag substantially the onset of modern economic growth, a considerable growth of schooling occurred in a number of these countries before the takeoff into economic growth, and probably considerably before, because the initial expansion of schooling often occurred rather slowly. Equally noteworthy is the similarity that the pattern for education shares in common with those for life expectancy and fertility, namely that the advent of rapid improvement in the indicator often does not occur concurrently with that in GDP per capita. For education, as for the demographic indicators, the simple association between economic growth and quality of life evident in the cross section is not reproduced in the time series data.

Political Democracy

Historical measures of political democracy are scarce, but one available for the countries included here is "legislative effectiveness," an indicator of whether a legislature already exists and how important a role it plays in political decision making, based on the judgments of knowledgeable scholars (Banks 1971). For all of the seven countries under study here, a legislature already existed at or near the takeoff into modern economic growth, and the legislature was at least partly effective (Table 6.4). This central institution of political democracy was clearly not an effect of economic growth in these countries, but must have arisen from forces operating prior to the onset of modern economic growth.

This does not mean that political democracy is an invariable antecedent of modern economic growth. In

Table 6.4 Legislative effectiveness rating[a] at or near turning point in GDP per capita in seven countries

	(1)	(2)	(3)
	Turning point in GDP per capita	Legislative effectiveness	
		Date	Rating
United Kingdom	1820	1820–1829	1.0
France	1820	1820–1829	0.7
United States	1830	1820–1829	1.0
Sweden	1850	1820–1829	0.7
Japan	1870	1885	0.7
Brazil	1900	1895–1905	0.7
India	1945	1950–1959	1.0

Source: Easterlin (2000, 2003)
[a]Scaled as follows by scholars with specialized knowledge of the political histories of the individual countries:
Effective legislature=1.0
Partially effective legislature=0.7
Ineffective legislature=0.3
No legislature exists=0

the last half of the twentieth century, economic growth has occurred at an unprecedented rate in most of the less developed world outside of sub-Saharan Africa under circumstances where legislative restraints on the executive branch of government have typically been quite limited or nonexistent (Table 6.5, col. 1). Moreover, despite unprecedentedly high rates of economic growth in this period in many less developed areas, there is no clear-cut movement toward political democracy in these areas. In China, other parts of east Asia, and northern Africa, where effective legislatures have been virtually nonexistent, economic growth has averaged between 2% and 4% per year (columns 2 and 3). In contrast, India, which also has had an economic growth

Table 6.5 Growth rate of real GDP per capita and legislative effectiveness, major less-developed areas, ca. 1950–1994

	(1)	(2)	(3)
	Growth rate of GDP per capita (percent per year)	Legislative effectiveness	
		1950–1959	1990–1994
China	3.8	0.2	0.3
Asia, except China and India	3.7	0.5	0.5
India	2.2	1.0	1.0
Northern Africa	2.1	0.3	0.3
Latin America	1.6	0.7	0.7
Sub-Saharan Africa	0.5	0.5	0.4

Source: Easterlin (2000). For definition of legislative effectiveness, see Table 6.3. Values shown are averages of annual data for indicated period. For regions, measures are weighted averages (by population) of country values. Unweighted averages give similar results

rate exceeding 2%, already had an effective legislature at the start of its takeoff into modern economic growth. Thus, there is little in the experience of the last half of the twentieth century, or the longer historical experience represented by the seven countries studied here, to suggest that the current cross-sectional association between economic growth and political democracy is indicative of a corresponding systematic linkage in historical time.

The frequent contradiction noted here between cross-sectional and time series evidence has been pointed out by others. A study by William Easterly (1999) brings together from a variety of sources 81 indicators of quality of life for the years 1960, 1970, 1980, and 1990 for a large number of countries worldwide. The indicators range across seven areas, several of which have been partly touched on above: (1) individual rights and democracy, (2) political instability and war, (3) education, (4) health, (5) transport and communication, (6) inequality across class and gender, and (7) "bads"—indicators of the prevalence of crime, terrorism, pollution, work injuries, and suicide. (The "bads" are scaled so that a diminution is positively correlated with growth.) This innovative study considers both cross-sectional and time series relationships to real GDP per capita of these indicators. The findings are much like those we have already pointed out. Although there is a strong cross-sectional association between these indicators and real GDP per capita, the time series relationships are quite mixed. Easterly finds that the effect on the indicators of exogenous shifts over time—those due to factors other than economic growth—is typically quite strong compared with the effect of economic

growth. Using three different econometric techniques to assess the role of GDP per capita versus exogenous factors in explaining the change in the various indicators, he concludes that GDP per capita has an impact on QoL that is significant, positive, and more important than exogenous factors only for from 6 to 32 out of the total of 81 indicators, depending on the technique of analysis. There are only three of 81 indicators in all three econometric methodologies "for which growth is the primary life-improving and significant determinant: calorie intake, protein intake, and telephones" (p. 262). (Note that two of these three relate to consumption, and the third, to communications density.) Easterly concludes that "the evidence that life gets better during growth is surprisingly uneven" (p. 268). A similar conclusion comes from two papers by Charles Kenny (2005, 2006) that consider both quantitative and qualitative evidence, more limited in range, but extending over a substantially longer time period.

What conclusion emerges from this survey of objective QoL measures? The answer, we believe, is that so far as objective indicators of material living levels are concerned, economic growth, on balance, raises QoL, but there are sometimes significant "bads" associated with this consumption, such as rising pollution and obesity. With regard to where people live, economic growth is clearly responsible for the strong centralization of population in urban places, but whether this is taken as an improvement in QoL is debatable. Finally, when it comes to social and political indicators, an examination of historical experience reveals noticeable timing differences in their improvement from that in GDP per capita, and raises serious doubt that economic

6 Modern Economic Growth and Quality of Life: Cross-Sectional and Time Series Evidence

Table 6.6 Cigarette consumption per person 18 years or older, United States, 1900–2000

	(1)
Year	Cigarette consumption per person 18 years or older
1900	54
1905	70
1910	151
1915	285
1920	665
1925	1,085
1930	1,485
1935	1,564
1940	1,976
1945	3,449
1950	3,522
1955	3,597
1960	4,171
1965	4,259
1970	3,985
1975	4,123
1980	3,851
1985	3,461
1990	2,827
1995	2,515
2000	2,092

Source: U.S. Dept. of Agriculture Economic Research Service (2002)

growth has been the primary factor in QoL advances in the social and political realms.

This is not the place to discuss causal factors that are at work other than economic growth, and these factors would doubtless vary according to the indicator under discussion. But it is clear that one determinant of quality of life, public policy, often plays an important causal role independently of economic growth. A simple illustration is provided by another QoL indicator, per capita cigarette consumption. As indicated earlier, measures of quality of life include "bads," whose increase reduces quality of life. Cigarette consumption is clearly one of these. In the United States, following the introduction of the cigarette in the late nineteenth century, per capita consumption rose nearly 80-fold from 1900 to the early 1960s (Table 6.6). This trend is partly a reflection of rising income associated with economic growth, and partly of the impact on consumption of new goods generated by technological advances associated with economic growth. But since its peak in the early 1960s,

per capita consumption has steadily declined, and by 2000, consumption was down by one half from the early 1960s and back to the level prevailing at the start of World War II. This decline is clearly due to the breakthrough in knowledge that established the adverse effect on health of cigarette smoking and the dissemination of this knowledge via public health policies and the health industry. Cross-sectional data underscore this conclusion (Fig. 6.17). Unlike the previous graphs, a plot of male adult smoking against GDP per capita does not reveal a strong positive association across countries. To the naked eye, there is no clear relationship, and a fitted regression, in fact, reveals a slightly negative but statistically significant association. This result is because the high-income countries are those who have first acted vigorously via public policy to curtail smoking. Had this graph been plotted with 1960s data, the more common consumption pattern would have prevailed—high levels of GDP per capita associated with higher prevalence of smoking.

An implication of the evidence of cigarette consumption is that "bads" associated with economic growth—air pollution, obesity, and the like—are amenable to correction with appropriate public policies. But what the evidence on smoking illustrates more generally is the important role that public policy may play in influencing QoL. The cigarette experience is a contemporary example of the central role of public policy in promoting health and life expectancy more generally. The great breakthroughs in health knowledge came with the sanitation movement and validation of the germ theory of disease in the middle and latter half of the nineteenth century. This knowledge led to the development of a new technology for controlling contagious disease, and this technology was very largely implemented by public policy through the establishment of a public health system (Easterlin 2004, Chaps. 6, 7). In like manner, the disjunction between the advance of schooling and growth of GDP per capita is arguably a reflection of the important and independent role played by governments in establishing universal schooling. If social and political indicators of QoL are, at present, positively associated with GDP per capita, it is often because the countries that first implemented the new production technology underlying modern economic growth were also the first to introduce, often via public policy, new advances in knowledge in the social and political realms.

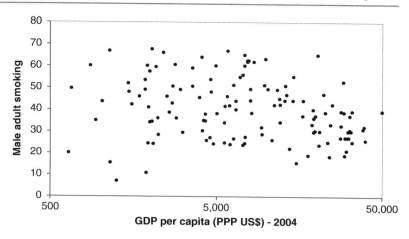

Fig. 6.17 Male adult smoking and GDP per capita, 131 countries, 1997–2003 (Source: Mackay and Eriksen (2002), and UNDP (2006))

Subjective Indicators

Subjective indicators of QoL are obtained from surveys in which respondents report on their feelings of well-being, that is, their *subjective* well-being (SWB). Two measures are commonly used to study the relation between economic growth and SWB. The first is happiness. A typical survey question is that used in the United States General Social Survey (GSS): Taken all together, how would you say things are these days—would you say that you are very happy, pretty happy, or not too happy? To facilitate analysis, the responses are often assigned integer values, with a range from least satisfied or happy equal to 1, up to the total number of response options (in the present example, 3). Another often-used question relates to general life satisfaction. In the German Socio-Economic Panel Survey, for example, the following question is asked: We would like to ask you about your satisfaction with your life in general. Please answer according to the following scale where "0" means completely dissatisfied, "10" means completely satisfied: How satisfied are you with your life all things considered?

Over the half century since such survey questions were introduced, a substantial methodological literature has developed regarding the reliability, validity, and comparability of the answers to such questions (Frey and Stutzer 2002a, b; Kahneman et al. 1999; Veenhoven 1993). The consensus is that the responses, although not without their problems, are meaningful and reasonably comparable among groups of individuals. Perhaps the main reason for this is that in answering such questions, people everywhere tend to take into account the same types of things in assessing their well-being. These are the things that occupy most of their time and are somewhat within their control, namely making a living, raising a family, health, and work.

In what follows, we look first at studies examining the relation between SWB and economic growth at a point in time, where economic growth is, as above, indexed by real GDP per capita. Then we consider how SWB changes over time as countries experience rising GDP per capita.

Cross-Sectional Patterns

The generally accepted cross-sectional finding on the relation between happiness and GDP per capita is that happiness is lower in poorer countries and increases at a diminishing rate as the level of GDP per capita increases. Scholars in psychology, sociology, economics, and political science who have made major contributions to the study of SWB concur on this assertion (Diener et al. 1993; cf. also Diener and Biswas-Diener 2002; Veenhoven 1991; Frey and Stutzer 2002a; Inglehart 1997, 2000; Layard 2005). The policy appeal of this generalization is great because it implies that raising the incomes of poor countries will raise their well-being considerably, while an increase of equal dollar amount for rich countries will have only a small or negligible effect on happiness. The typical basis for this generalization is a simple bivariate comparison of happiness or life satisfaction with GDP or GNP per capita without controls for other possible determinants

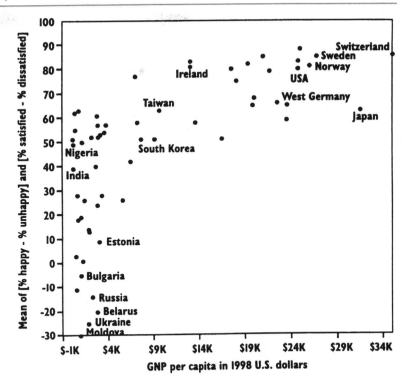

Fig. 6.18 Subjective well-being and GNP per capita, 60 countries, ca, 1990–1996 (Source: Inglehart (2000), p. 217)

of SWB, using averages for a number of countries at a single point (or period) in time, as illustrated in Fig. 6.18. A curve fitted to the data in the figure would imply that among countries with real GNP per capita less than $9,000, happiness rises rapidly as one goes from poorer to slightly richer countries. In contrast, among countries where GNP per capita exceeds $9,000, there is little improvement in happiness as affluence grows.

Similar comparisons within countries of happiness with household income have yielded the same diminishing returns pattern and are thought to buttress the cross-country findings. Figure 6.19, for example, presents data on mean happiness and mean income in the United States for persons arrayed from low to high in terms of household income. The diminishing happiness returns pattern in the figure is typical of within-country comparisons of happiness and income at a point in time (cf. Argyle 1999). The within-country pattern resembles that in cross-country comparisons of the type illustrated by Fig. 6.18. Clearly, in the cross section, both within- and across-country studies point to a diminishing returns relation of happiness to real GDP per capita.

Time Series

If there are diminishing returns to income in terms of happiness, as the cross-sectional studies suggest, then the point-of-time pattern should be reproduced as a country actually experiences rising GDP per capita (Easterlin 2005a). Empirical verification of the cross-sectional relation with time series data has been handicapped by a lack of historical series for SWB. The earliest study, one of the United States from 1946 through the early 1970s found a pattern of no significant trend in happiness as GDP per capita increased. As shown in Fig. 6.20, this result has subsequently been found to prevail for a later period as well (Easterlin 1974, 2005b).

Studies of other high-income nations also suggest that typically, SWB does not increase as GDP per capita grows (Inglehart and Klingemann 2000; Diener and Oshi 2000; Blanchflower and Oswald 2004). This is not to say that SWB is necessarily constant as GDP per capita rises. In the initial study of the United States, there is a growth in happiness from around 1946–1960, followed by a return by the early 1970s to the 1946

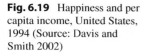

Fig. 6.19 Happiness and per capita income, United States, 1994 (Source: Davis and Smith 2002)

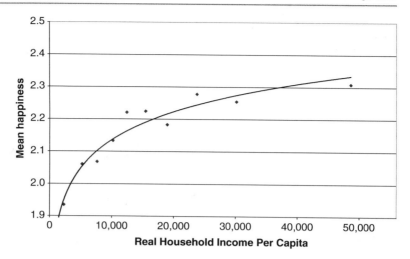

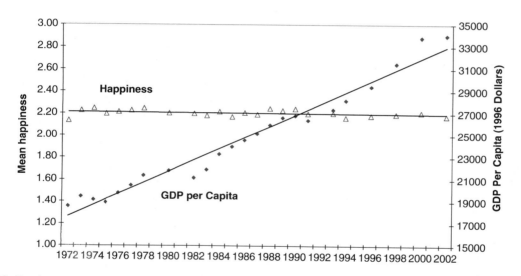

Fig. 6.20 Happiness and real GDP per capita, United States, 1972–2002 (Source: Davis and Smith 2002; U.S. Census Bureau 2003)

level (Easterlin 1974). Studies of European countries sometimes find increasing SWB accompanying economic growth in one country, constancy of SWB in another, and declining SWB in a third. On average, however, there is no significant improvement in SWB as GDP per capita grows.

The increase in GDP per capita in such time series studies is fairly substantial—often a doubling or more. The usual constancy of SWB in the face of rising GDP per capita has typically been reconciled with the cross-sectional pattern in Fig. 6.18 on the grounds that the time series observations for developed nations correspond to the upper-income range of the cross-sectional studies where happiness changes little or not at all as real income rises.

The first serious challenge to this interpretation of the cross-sectional results was found in SWB data for Japan covering the period from the late 1950s to the late 1980s (Easterlin 1995). In the late 1950s, Japan was poorer than were many developing countries at the end of the twentieth century. Subsequently, Japan's GDP per capita multiplied a phenomenal fivefold in three decades, at that time a record rate of economic growth. If Japan had followed the pattern observed in the

6 Modern Economic Growth and Quality of Life: Cross-Sectional and Time Series Evidence

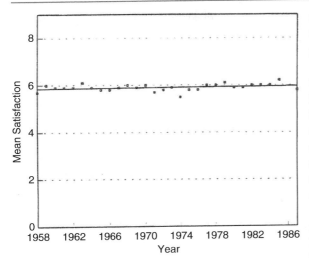

Fig. 6.21 Mean subjective well-being, Japan 1958–1987 (Source and notes: Veenhoven (1993). An ordinary least squares regression is fitted to the data; the coefficient of mean satisfaction on year is not statistically significant)

Table 6.7 Correlations of happiness with GDP per capita for 21 countries, classified by statistical significance and level of country's development in 1996

Level of development	(1) Number of countries	(2) Positive	(3) None	(4) Negative
		Significance of coefficient		
All countries	21	6	14	1
High	5	2	3	0
Medium	7	2	4	1
Low	9	2	7	0

Source: Easterlin (2005b)

cross-sectional data, SWB should have risen noticeably over this period as Japan progressed from a poor to a rich nation. In fact, Japan's SWB remained constant, following the horizontal time series pattern usually observed in the more developed nations (Fig. 6.21).

In a more comprehensive recent study of time series data, Hagerty and Veenhoven (2003) claim to find support—though of a somewhat mixed nature—for a positive association between happiness and income, not only in poor, but rich countries as well. They bring together data for 21 countries, nine of whom are classified as low income, covering periods ranging from 11 to 38 years. They state (p.12) that "wealth is positively correlated with happiness for 14 of the 21 countries...." As they recognize, however, this generalization is not based on statistical significance. When account is taken of significance, one obtains the results in Table 6.7. In two thirds of the 21 nations, there is no significant relation between happiness and GDP per capita; six have a positive relation, and one, negative.

In Hagerty and Veenhoven's group of poorer countries, the typical result is the same as for their higher-income countries—no improvement in happiness as GDP per capita grows. Indeed, among their low-income countries, the proportion with a significant positive coefficient, two out of nine, is less than in the middle- or high-income group, the opposite of what one would expect based on the diminishing returns relationship observed in cross-sectional studies.

The rates of economic growth per decade for the 21 nations in the Hagerty–Veenhoven analysis range from a low of −9% to a high of 88%. If one selects seven European Union members plus the United States, who are highly integrated economically and culturally, one finds they are all clustered together with very similar economic growth rates, from 16% to 23% per decade, over almost 25 years. Does happiness rise in these countries, and, if so, at similar rates? The answer is no. In three of these countries happiness increases, in four it is unchanged, and in one it declines. The disparate trends in happiness for these countries suggest that, since economic growth is so much alike, the different trends in happiness must be due to factors other than economic growth.

Recently, limited evidence has started to become available for China, a low-income country of special interest because of its phenomenal rate of economic growth. In the short period from 1994 to 2005, average real income in China increased by 250%. In the same period, the proportion of survey respondents satisfied "with the way things are going in your life today" fell from almost 80 to under 70%. (Kahneman and Krueger 2006, p. 16). The evidence for China is consistent with that for other countries, both rich and poor—economic growth is not typically accompanied by greater happiness.

A very recent working paper by Stevenson and Wolfers (2008) claims to find a positive association between happiness and economic growth. Their analysis, however, fails to differentiate between the short-term and long-term relation of subjective well-being and GDP per capita. It is well established that fluctuations in economic conditions affect subjective well-being (Di Tella et al. 2001). This is strikingly so for the transition countries of central and Eastern Europe since 1990, where the shorter term contraction and expansion movement has often lasted more than a decade

(Easterlin 2009). When the observations for these countries are deleted from the Stevenson–Wolfers analysis (Stevenson and Wolfers 2008, Fig. 15), their significant positive relation between subjective well-being and GDP per capita no longer holds.

The limited evidence so far available thus suggests that in both rich and poor countries, economic growth does not raise subjective well-being (for more recent evidence, see Easterlin 2010, Chaps. 3–5 and Easterlin and others 2010). Moreover, the fact that countries with similar rates of economic growth may have quite different happiness trends implies that factors other than economic growth are important in determining what happens to subjective well-being. Clearly, there is need for more comprehensive time series studies that examine the effect on happiness, not just of economic growth but the variety of factors at work, such as health, family circumstances, unemployment, and the like, including the effects of public policies. But the results for subjective indicators, like those for objective indicators, caution against the use of cross-sectional patterns to infer time series relationships between economic growth and quality of life.

independently of economic growth, and is by no means an inevitable accompaniment.

As the QoL criteria are broadened to encompass objective indicators in the social and political areas, such as health, education, and political and human rights, the central role of economic growth becomes even more dubious. This is made clear by the typical failure of time series evidence to reproduce off-cited cross-sectional patterns. Economic growth may make possible advances in the social and political realms by making more resources available, but the evidence makes it clear that such a result is not sure to occur.

Finally, if one turns to subjective measures of well-being rather than objective indicators, the breakdown between economic growth and quality of life becomes even greater. Although the evidence remains limited, the common pattern both in rich and poor countries is that typically, increases in per capita income ranging from a doubling to quintupling fail to raise levels of happiness and life satisfaction. People may have many more goods and a much wider variety, but whether that means they find their lives more satisfying remains questionable.

Conclusion

Although this survey is far from exhaustive, what can be said, by way of brief summary, on the relation between QoL and modern economic growth as evidenced by the cross-sectional and time series data assembled here?

If one focuses on objective indicators and material well-being, then there can be no disputing that modern economic growth has improved quality of life. With economic growth come markedly larger amounts of food, clothing, and shelter per capita, as well as sweeping qualitative changes in the level of living. If, however, it is recognized that modern economic growth has also been the prime mover in the concentration of population in cities, large and small, then reservations start to arise about the benefits of economic growth because of the congestion and air, water, and noise pollution fostered by urban concentrations. To this must be added the negative spin-offs of ever-rising consumption, such as carbon dioxide emissions of motor vehicles and increased fat accompanying higher food intake. Of course, appropriate public policies may offset these "bads," as has happened in regard to cigarette smoking. But public policy often operates

References

Argyle, M. (1999). Causes and correlates of happiness. In D. Kahneman, E. Diener, & N. Schwarz (Eds.), *Well-being: The foundations of hedonic psychology* (pp. 353–373). New York: Russell Sage.

Bairoch, P. (1988). *Cities and economic development*. Chicago: University of Chicago Press.

Banks, A. S. (1971). *Cross-polity time series data*. Cambridge: The MIT Press.

Barro, R. J. (1997). *Determinants of economic growth: A cross-country empirical study*. Cambridge: The MIT Press.

Blanchflower, D. G., & Oswald, A. (2004). Well-being over time in Britain and the USA. *Journal of Public Economics, 88*, 1359–1386.

Brady, D. S. (1972). Consumption and the style of life. In L. E. Davis, R. A. Easterlin, & W. N. Parker (Eds.), *American economic growth: An Economist's history of the united states* (pp. 61–89). New York: Harper and Row.

Caldwell, J. C. (1986). Routes to Low mortality in poor countries. *Population and Development Review, 12*(2), 171–220.

Cox, W. M., & Alm, R. (1999). *Myths of rich and poor*. New York: Basic Books.

Davis, J. A., & T. W. Smith. (2002). *General social surveys, 1972–2002*. [machine-readable data file] Chicago: National Opinion Research Center.

Di Tella, R., MacCulloch, R., & Oswald, A. (2001). Preferences over inflation and unemployment: Evidence from surveys of happiness. *The American Economic Review, 91*(1), 335–341.

Diener, E., & Biswas-Diener, R. (2002). Will money increase subjective well-being? A literature review and guide to needed research. *Social Indicators Research, 57*, 119–169.

Diener, E., & Oshi, S. (2000). Money and happiness: Income and subjective well-being across nations. In E. Diener & E. M. Suh (Eds.), *Culture and subjective well-being* (pp. 185–218). Cambridge: The MIT Press.

Diener, E., Sandvik, E., Seidlitz, L., & Diener, M. (1993). The relationship between income and subjective well-being: Relative or absolute? *Social Indicators Research, 28*, 195–223.

Easterlin, R. A. (1965). A note on the evidence of history. In C. A. Anderson & M. J. Bowman (Eds.), *Education and economic growth* (pp. 422–429). Chicago: Aldine.

Easterlin, R. A. (1974). Does economic growth improve the human Lot? In P. A. David & M. W. Reder (Eds.), *Nations and households in economic growth: Essays in honor of Moses Abramovitz*. New York: Academic.

Easterlin, R. A. (1981). Why isn't the whole world developed. *The Journal of Economic History, XLI*(1), 1–19.

Easterlin, R. A. (1995). Will raising the incomes of all increase the happiness of all? *Journal of Economic Behavior and Organization, 27*, 1–34.

Easterlin, R. A. (1996). *Growth triumphant: The twenty-first century in historical perspective*. Ann Arbor: University of Michigan Press.

Easterlin, R. A. (1999). Twentieth century American population growth. In S. Engerman & R. E. Gallman (Eds.), *The Cambridge economic history of the United States, vol. III. The twentieth century*. New York: Cambridge University Press.

Easterlin, R. A. (2000). The worldwide standard of living since 1800. *Journal of Economic Perspectives, 14*(1), 7–26.

Easterlin, R. A. (2003). Living standards. In J. Mokyr (Ed.), *Oxford encyclopedia of economic history* (Vol. 3). Oxford: Oxford University Press.

Easterlin, R. A. (2004). *The reluctant economist: Perspectives on economics, economic history, and demography*. New York: Cambridge University Press.

Easterlin, R. A. (2005a). Diminishing marginal utility of income? Caveat Emptor. *Social Indicators Research, 70*, 243–255.

Easterlin, R. A. (2005b). Feeding the illusion of growth and happiness: A reply to Hagerty and Veenhoven. *Social Indicators Research, 74*, 429–443.

Easterlin, R. A. (2009). Lost in transition: Life satisfaction on the road to capitalism. *Journal of Economic Behavior and Organization, 71*, 130–145.

Easterlin, R. A. (2010). *Happiness, growth, and the life cycle*. New York: Oxford University Press.

Easterlin, R. A., Angelescu, L., Switek, M., Sawangfa, O., & Zweig, J. S. (2010). The happiness income paradox revisited. *Proceedings of the National Academy of Sciences, 107*, 22463–22468.

Easterly, W. (1999). Life during growth. *Journal of Economic Growth, 4*, 239–276.

FAO, Food and Agricultural Organization of the United Nations. (2004). *FAO statistical yearbook 2005–6* (Vol. 2). Roma: FAO.

Frey, B. S., & Stutzer, A. (2002a). *Happiness and economics*. Princeton: Princeton University Press.

Frey, B. S., & Stutzer, A. (2002b). What can economists learn from happiness research? *Journal of Economic Literature, XL*, 402–435.

Fuguitt, G. V., & Brown, D. L. (1990). Residential preferences and population redistribution 1972–1988. *Demography, 27*(4), 589–600.

Fuguitt, G. V., & Zuiches, J. J. (1975). Residential preferences and population distribution. *Demography, 12*(3), 491–504.

Grossman, G., & Kruger, A. (1991). *Environmental impacts of a north American free trade agreement*. Princeton: Princeton University.

Hagerty, M. R., & Veenhoven, R. (2003). Wealth and happiness revisited – growing national income *does* go with greater happiness. *Social Indicators Research, 64*, 1–27.

Hagerty, M. R., & Veenhoven, R. (2006). Rising happiness in nations 1946–2004: A reply to Easterlin. *Social Indicators Research, 79*, 421–436.

Heston, A., Summers, R., & Atten, B. (2002). *Penn world tables version 6.1*. Philadelphia: Center for International Comparisons at the University of Pennsylvania (CICUP).

Holtz-Eakin, D., & Selden, T. (1995). Stoking the fires: CO_2 Emissions and economic growth. *Journal of Public Economics, 57*, 85–101.

Humana, C. (1992). *World human rights guide* (3rd ed.). Oxford: Oxford University Press.

Inglehart, R. (1988). The renaissance of political culture. *American Political Science Review, 82*(4), 1203–1230.

Inglehart, R. (1997). *Modernization and postmodernization: Cultural, economic, and political change in 43 societies*. Princeton: Princeton University Press.

Inglehart, R. (2000). Globalization and postmodern values. *The Washington Quarterly, 23*(1), 215–228.

Inglehart, R., & Klingemann, H.-D. (2000). Genes, culture, democracy, and happiness. In E. Diener & E. M. Suh (Eds.), *Culture and subjective well-being* (pp. 165–183). Cambridge: The MIT Press.

Inkeles, A. (Ed.). (1991). *On measuring democracy: Its consequences and concomitants*. New Brunswick: Transaction Publishers.

Kahneman, D., & Krueger, A. B. (2006). Developments in the measurement of subjective well-being. *Journal of Economic Perspectives, 20*, 3–24.

Kahneman, D., Diener, E., & Schwarz, N. (Eds.). (1999). *Well-being: The foundations of hedonic psychology*. New York: Russell Sage.

Kenny, C. (2005). *There's more to life than money: Examining the link between income, health and education*. Mimeo: World Bank.

Kenny, C. (2006). Were people in the past poor and miserable? *Kyklos, 59*, 275–306.

Keyfitz, N., & Flieger, W. (1968). *World population*. Chicago: University of Chicago Press.

Kuznets, S. (1966). *Modern economic growth: Rate, structure and spread*. New Haven/London: Yale University Press.

Layard, R. (2005). *Happiness: Lessons from a new science*. New York: Penguin Press.

Lebergott, S. (1993). *Pursuing happiness*. Princeton: Princeton University Press.

Lebergott, S. (1996). *Consumer expenditures. New measures & old motives*. Princeton: Princeton University Press.

Lipset, S. M. (1959). Some social requisites of democracy: Economic development and political legitimacy. *American Sociological Review, 59*(February), 1–22.

Mackay, J., & Eriksen, M. (2002). *The tobacco atlas*. Geneva: World Health Organization.

Maddison, A. (2003). *The world economy: Historical statistics* (CD-ROM). Paris: Organization for Economic Co-operation and Development.

Marshall, M. G., & Jaggers, K. (2004). *Political regime characteristics and transitions, 1800–2002* (Polity IV Project). College Park: University of Maryland.

Merrick, T. W., & Graham, D. H. (1979). *Population and economic development in brazil: 1800 to the present*. Baltimore: Johns Hopkins University Press.

Offer, A. (2006). *The challenge of affluence: Self-control and well-being in the United States and Britain since 1950*. Oxford: Oxford University Press.

Oswald, A. J., & Powdthavee, N. (2007). Obesity, unhappiness, and the challenge of affluence: Theory and evidence. *The Economic Journal, 117*, F441–F454.

Portney, P. R. (2000). Environmental problems and policy: 2000–2050. *Journal of Economic Perspectives, 14*(1), 199–206.

Pritchett, L., & Summers, L. H. (1996). Wealthier is healthier. *Journal of Human Resources, XXXI*(4), 841–868.

Schofield, R., & Reher, D. (1991). The decline of mortality in Europe. In R. Schofield, D. Reher, & A. Bideau (Eds.), *The decline of mortality in Europe* (pp. 1–17). Oxford: Clarendon.

Shafik, N. (1994). Economic development and environmental quality: An econometric analysis. *Oxford Economic Papers, 46*, 757–773.

Stevenson, B., & Wolfers, J. (2008). Economic growth and subjective well-being: Reassessing the Easterlin Paradox. *Brookings Papers on Economic Activity, 39*(1 (Spring)), 1–87.

Titmuss, R. M. (1966). *Essays on the welfare state*. London: Unwin University Press.

UNDP (UN Development Program). (2006). *Human development report, 2005*. Oxford: Oxford University Press for UNDP.

United Nation. (1995). *Demographic indicators 1950–2050 (1994 revision)*. New York: United Nations.

United Nations. (1977). *Population bulletin of the United Nations, No. 8. 1976*. New York: United Nations.

United Nations. (2004). *World urbanization prospects: The 2003 revision*. New York: United Nations. http://esa.un.org/unpp

United Nations. (2005). *World population prospects: The 2004 revision*. New York: United Nations. http://esa.un.org/unpp

United States Census Bureau. (1961). *United States census of population: 1960. Number of inhabitants, United States summary* (Final Report PC(1)-1A). Washington, DC: United Sates Government Printing Office.

United States Census Bureau. (2003). *Statistical abstract of the United States: 2003* (123rd ed.). Washington, DC: GPO.

United States Census Bureau. (2005). *Statistical abstract of the United States: 2006* (125th ed.). Washington, DC: GPO.

United States Department of Agriculture Economic Research Service. (2002). *Tobacco outlook report*. Washington, DC: United States Department of Agriculture Economic Research Service.

Veenhoven, R. (1991). Is happiness relative? *Social Indicators Research, 24*, 1–34.

Veenhoven, R. (1993). *Happiness in nations, subjective appreciation of life in 56 nations 1946–1992*. Rotterdam: Erasmus University.

World Bank (2006). *World development indicators online*. Downloaded at publications.worldbank.org/WDI/

Wrigley, E. A., & Schofield, R. S. (1981). *The population history of England 1541–1871*. Cambridge: Harvard University Press.

National Accounts of Well-Being

Ed Diener, Ph.D. and William Tov, Ph.D.

National Well-Being Accounts

Over the past decades, there have been periodic national and international surveys of subjective well-being, including assessments of life satisfaction, but these measures have not been used systematically by policymakers. In a 2004 article in *Psychological Science in the Public Interest*, Diener and Seligman argued that nations should establish regular assessments of well-being to complement the economic indicators (e.g., GDP, savings rates, consumer confidence) and objective social indicators (e.g., crime rates, longevity, rates of infant mortality). They recommended that policymakers be informed by national measures of well-being because economic and objective social indicators can omit much of what is important and can even mislead us about much of what we value. The authors further noted that there has been a serious disconnect over the years between the increase in economic variables such as per capita income and the lack of growth in life satisfaction, as well as increasing rates of depression. As nations grow wealthy, differences in well-being are

To appear in:
Encyclopedia of Quality of Life
Kenneth Land, Editor

E. Diener, Ph.D. (✉)
Department of Psychology, University of Illinois,
603 E. Daniel Street, Champaign, IL 61820, USA

The Gallup Organization, Washington, DC, USA
e-mail: ediener@uiuc.edu; EDiener@s.psych.uiuc.edu

W. Tov, Ph.D.
School of Social Sciences, Singapore Management University,
Singapore, Singapore

less frequently due to differences in income and more frequently due to other factors such as social relationships, enjoyment at work, feelings of security and belonging, the lack of serious stressors, and possessing meaningful long-term values and goals. Monitoring well-being at a national level will alert the citizenry to important information beyond economic growth that should help guide policy.

Subjective well-being is known colloquially as "happiness" and refers to the various ways in which people evaluate their lives positively. In the emotional realm, it involves positive feelings and experiences in relation to what is happening and few negative or unpleasant experiences. In terms of conscious thought, it involves judging life to be satisfying and fulfilling. Because subjective well-being is a state in which a person feels and believes that life is going well, it reflects the many different values that are strived for by the individual. Unlike economic indicators, which locate a person's well-being primarily in the material realm of marketplace production and consumption, well-being indicators assess the full range of inputs to the quality of life, from social relationships to spirituality and meaning, from material consumption to feelings of relaxation and security.

The goals of national accounts of well-being would be to inform policymakers about groups and situations where misery should be alleviated, to educate the citizenry about factors that will enhance their well-being, and to place well-being in the spotlight so that economic impact is not the only consideration when governmental policies are debated. Business and other organizations, as well as individuals and governments, could use the information provided by indicators of well-being. Because well-being indicators can include

K.C. Land et al. (eds.), *Handbook of Social Indicators and Quality of Life Research*,
DOI 10.1007/978-94-007-2421-1_7, © Springer Science+Business Media B.V. 2012

both broad evaluations such as life satisfaction, and judgments of narrower experiences such as feelings of enjoyment at work, the indicators can give a broad assessment of how the lives of target groups are doing, as well as specific information about domains where quality of life could be improved. In both cases, well-being indicators reflect how positively or negatively people are experiencing their lives, and such experiences reflect a core aspect of quality of life that should be of utmost concern to policymakers.

Historical Context

In the early phases of the industrial revolution, when meeting the basic needs of the citizenry for food and shelter was of paramount concern, economics was of primary importance and helped to dramatically increase the quality of life. However, economic indicators by themselves do not provide a complete assessment of whether nations are flourishing. Industrially developed societies now have the means to fulfill the basic needs of their citizens, and a continuing emphasis primarily on economic growth might lead to ever-greater material consumption and production but little increase in well-being. Beyond money, people seek happiness, meaning, engagement, and satisfaction, and these are influenced by many other factors besides material wealth. In order to build societies in which well-being is widespread, we must measure it directly rather than relying solely on economic indicators as a major proxy.

Before his assassination, Robert F. Kennedy eloquently stated the premise underlying national indicators of well-being:

Too much and too long, we seem to have surrendered community excellence and community values in the mere accumulation of material things….The Gross National Product includes air pollution and advertising for cigarettes, and ambulances to clear our highways of carnage. It counts special locks for our doors, and jails for the people who break them. The GNP includes the destruction of the redwoods and the death of Lake Superior. It grows with the production of napalm and missiles and nuclear warheads.

And if GNP includes all this, there is much that it does not comprehend. It does not allow for the health of our families, the quality of their education, or the joy of their play. It is indifferent to the decency of our factories and the safety of our streets alike. It does not include the beauty of our poetry or the strength of our marriages, or the intelligence of our public debate or the integrity of our public officials.

GNP measures neither our wit nor our courage, neither our wisdom nor our learning, neither our compassion nor our devotion to our country. It measures everything, in short, except that which makes life worthwhile.[1]

The indicators of well-being advocated in this chapter are able to reflect the full range of things that make life worthwhile—from the integrity and security of our neighborhoods to the compassion and wisdom of our citizens. A severe limitation of economic measures is that they emphasize what is traded in recordable market activities, overlooking crucial aspects of the quality of life such as social relationships, religion, and moral values. Because the broad spectrum of well-being measures includes our emotional reactions as well as our satisfaction with diverse areas of life, they can more fully assess the range of factors influencing our quality of life, aside from economic production and consumption.

In the following chapter, we elaborate on the concept of subjective well-being and discuss why it will capture those aspects of life so beautifully articulated by Kennedy. We will describe various conceptions of the good life and discuss whether subjective well-being is truly desirable. Next, we discuss the various components of subjective well-being and how each is measured. We also assess the validity of self-reports of well-being. We then describe the relevance of well-being to governmental policymaking. Finally, we consider various concerns about national accounts of well-being. We argue that although well-being measures are not perfect, they have sufficient validity to warrant their use by policy leaders.

Conceptions of Well-Being

Since time immemorial, philosophers, religious leaders, and ordinary people have pondered what makes a good life. In the Confucian ideal, a person's responsibilities to others and society figure prominently in defining the good life. In the view of Aristotle, happiness (called eudaimonia) consisted of virtuous actions

---

[1] Robert F. Kennedy. Address to an election rally at the University of Kansas, on March 18, 1967.

that fulfill the full spectrum of human potential. The idea of subjective well-being has some roots in Greek hedonism. Although some early hedonists were concerned with the immediate pursuit of bodily pleasures, later refinements of hedonism emphasized the inclusion of mental and spiritual pleasures and the careful selection of pleasures so as to enhance long-term well-being. The utilitarian philosophers followed in this tradition and defined the good society as one that provided the most happiness for most people.

Modern conceptions of well-being include elements from each of the traditions above. As noted earlier, subjective well-being encompasses a range of indications that one's life is going well. Although pleasure is included as one aspect of subjective well-being, the concept is much broader in that it includes purpose, meaning, and feelings of fulfillment. Furthermore, it is recognized that long-lasting pleasant feelings usually emerge from making progress toward important goals and values. Thus, subjective well-being is not mere hedonism: people do not merely want to feel happy, they want to feel positively because they are achieving the things they believe are valuable and worthwhile. True subjective well-being then not only consists of pleasant emotional feelings but also the judgment that one's life is worthwhile and that the pleasant feelings are due to living a life that one believes is good. In addition, healthy social relationships in which one is both supported by and supportive of others, as advocated by Confucius, are seen as important causes of well-being. Thus, subjective well-being is a concept that includes all the various ways that a person evaluates his or her life in a positive manner.

Desirability of Subjective Well-Being

If policymakers are to give serious consideration to well-being indicators, an important question is whether subjective feelings and thoughts of well-being are indeed desirable. People do value states such as happiness. Across the world, college students believe that happiness is one of the most important values (Diener 2000). People are often motivated to select activities that produce pleasant feelings and avoid unpleasant experiences unless there are compelling reasons to undergo them. Although philosophers differ on what they consider to be the "good life," it is widely assumed that it must contain some form of subjective well-being in which the person

evaluates his or her *own* life in a positive way. After all, a virtuous or otherwise good life is not complete if the person feels miserable, or even only neutral. Without positive experiences and thoughts about our lives, we would be but robots or computers.

Besides feeling good, it turns out that happiness has other benefits, while chronic unhappiness can be detrimental. In terms of health, negative emotions such as stress, frustration, chronic anxiety, and anger can lower our immune strength, contribute to cardiovascular disease, and foster other health problems. It appears that both morbidity and mortality are related to the frequent and prolonged experience of unpleasant emotions. Although brief experiences of unpleasant emotions can be natural and adaptive in certain situations, the long-term experience of negative emotions seems to take a toll on physical health and can also contribute to mental health problems. More serious forms of unhappiness such as depression can substantially raise the risk of health problems such as the recurrence of a heart attack.

The effects of pleasant emotions on health are, at this time, more uncertain than the effects of unpleasant emotions, although there are some data suggesting that pleasant emotions can foster health and longevity. Outside of the realm of physical health, there is accumulating evidence that positive emotions have adaptive value and that people who chronically experience frequent pleasant affect tend to have beneficial outcomes in several areas of life. Such "happy" individuals are not only more likely to be successful in their own lives but also more likely than unhappy people to act in ways that benefit their communities and societies. For instance, happy people are more likely to get married, to remain married, and to be happily married—factors which contribute to a stable society.

People who tend to chronically experience positive emotions are more likely to earn higher salaries, to receive higher supervisor ratings at work, and are better organizational citizens (for instance, helping others at work). They are more likely to trust others in their communities and be involved in volunteer work. People who are happy are more likely to be sociable and amiable, and to like and be liked by others more than people who are unhappy. Furthermore, happy people are more likely to have self-confidence and be leaders. Finally, there is some evidence that the subjective well-being of citizens may facilitate support for democratic governance (Inglehart and Klingemann 2000; Tov and

Diener 2008). Thus, happiness is not just a private affair that feels good to the individual; it is in the best interest of societies that citizens be happy.

Thus, happiness not only feels good but also fosters effective functioning. However, this does not mean that people should be elated all of the time. Most happy people are rarely elated or intensely happy; milder levels of pleasant moods are the norm, with intense pleasant emotions being a rarity. Furthermore, happy people do experience unpleasant emotions—they get sad, angry, and fearful on the appropriate occasions, and these emotions can facilitate adaptive functioning. Nevertheless, the desirable society is one in which situations evoking negative emotions are infrequent. It is becoming increasingly clear that the good society is not only one that allows individuals to pursue happiness but also one that arranges many conditions that are conducive to happiness, such as providing the strong health, transportation, and governance structures that sustain the stability and quality of life.

It has been objected that governments should not intervene in the happiness of individuals because subjective well-being is a private affair, and governments should not interfere with the lives of its citizens. This overlooks the fact that governments already intervene in numerous ways in everyday life. Economic affairs that might be seen as private matters are partly shaped by governmental policies concerning taxation, tariffs, interest rates, minimum wage laws, and limits on work hours. The intended use of well-being indicators is not to invite greater intrusion upon individual lives but to provide information that makes governmental intervention beneficial. Furthermore, some of the greatest successes of governments have been in areas—such as public health—which were once seen as private affairs. Governments cannot make citizens happy; individuals must do this for themselves. But governments can, in many ways, provide the circumstances that allow this to occur. In addition, evidence of the social benefits of well-being has mounted to the point that one can question whether happiness is only an individual concern. Governments are unlikely to create policies that directly produce cheer and joviality, but they can take steps to insure that citizens are generally pleased with their lives and that existing conditions facilitate a preponderance of pleasant emotions as people work, love, and play.

Another objection to making well-being a policy concern stems from the perception of happiness as a hedonistic state of pleasure that should not be the goal of individuals with serious values and goals. Some think of pleasant emotions in purely hedonistic terms, but we reiterate that people feel positive emotions when they are achieving their goals and values and not simply "having fun" or experiencing physical pleasure. That is, feeling contented, joyful, satisfied, and pleased results from doing things we value and do not arise *solely* from involvement in entertaining activities. Thus, long-term levels of pleasant emotions reflect something deeper than pure hedonism—that people are making progress toward things they value. Loving and caring for others, trusting and wanting to help others, engagement in interesting work, and joy over a job well-done are all positive emotions that result from people's deeply held values.

In conclusion, people around the globe believe that happiness is important. It is not the only thing that is important—people have other values as well. But happiness can reflect progress toward those values. Furthermore, people who are frequently in pleasant states and are satisfied with their lives tend to be more effective and successful and act in ways that benefit society. Of course, happiness is not a sufficient guarantor of productive and caring citizens, but it is one very helpful, facilitative factor. Having discussed briefly the nature and implication of well-being, we turn next to the specific components of well-being. Understanding the multifaceted nature of well-being is critical if it is to be measured in ways that are useful to policymaking decisions.

Components of Subjective Well-Being

Although terms such as "subjective well-being" and "happiness" imply that it is a single entity, in actuality, it is a broad concept that includes a number of diverse elements, which together form well-being. No single concept represents the full nature of well-being, and the various types of well-being correlate only moderately with each other. Just as a person's financial well-being cannot be fully described by income and must also include savings, debt, cost of living, and so forth, a person's subjective well-being cannot be fully assessed by a single measure such as life satisfaction. Although something can be learned from such a measure, a complete rendering of subjective well-being requires the assessment of several different factors.

On-line Versus Recall Measures

People can evaluate life at the moment—how they feel right now—or they can reflect back over life and report how they felt over some period of time such as the past year. This distinction turns out to be critical because the average of on-line momentary reports is not always identical to people's recall of their experience. Both types of measures can provide important insights into well-being. When people report their "on-line" momentary moods and emotions, fewer memory biases are present—individuals are simply reporting how they feel at the moment, and therefore, less information must be considered. When such reports are averaged over time or across certain types of activities or situations, one can obtain important information about how a person is feeling in various situations on average. However, when people *recall* how they felt over time, there can be discrepancies from the on-line reports, owing to their individual self-concepts, beliefs, and expectancies. For example, recalling how one felt during the past month could be influenced by one's mood at the moment or one's expectations about situations; individuals can also selectively forget certain experiences. Thus, recall measures are only modestly accurate at estimating people's ongoing experiences of well-being, and the two types of measures provide related but distinct information about well-being.

When do the two types of measures diverge? We know that certain cultural groups diverge more on recall measures than on on-line measures of well-being, suggesting that either memory or self-presentation may selectively alter the reports of some groups more than others. For example, although European Americans often report more happiness than Asian Americans and Japanese, this difference is larger in recall measures of the past week than in on-line measures taken on a daily basis (Oishi 2002). When people evaluate past episodes such as a vacation, they may misremember their experiences in accordance with their *overall* impression of the event. There is also evidence that happier people may recall their moods as being more positive while unhappy people may recall their moods as being more negative than they were on-line. People may *remember* being happier with their partner than they report on-line when a relationship is going well, but not when the relationship is unrewarding.

In light of the discrepancy that can occur between on-line reports and recall measures, should we restrict ourselves to the on-line measures only? Not necessarily. As mentioned earlier, on-line and recall measures do correlate at moderate to strong levels, meaning that the recall measures can provide a quick approximation of people's experiences. Oftentimes, a recall measure will provide the best prediction of future behavior because it partly reflects what people expect from themselves and their environment. However, on-line measures can more accurately depict people's true experiences in various activities, with less distortion from their expectations. Although on-line measures can be expensive if they are collected over a period of weeks, estimates of on-line moods and emotions can be made based on systematic recall of experiences during previous days. When on-line and recall measures converge, they offer stronger evidence for the conclusions to be drawn. When the two types of measures diverge, as they occasionally do, they can give insights into the variables that affect each score. A complete accounting of people's subjective well-being will include both on-line estimates and recall measures as each type of measure has its strengths.

Broad Versus Narrow Measures

Well-being measures can also focus on satisfaction with broad aspects of life (e.g., one's work or marriage) or narrower aspects of life (e.g., commuting to work, one's work supervisor, or one's home). Oftentimes, the narrow measures are less influenced by self-concept or personal expectations because they are more grounded in actual experiences with concrete aspects of life. Furthermore, the narrow measures can often point more clearly to policy interventions because of their specific focus, whereas the broad measures may be too vague to suggest particular policies that are likely to influence them with any certainty. Consequently, narrow measures might also be more appropriate for monitoring the impact of policy interventions. Thus, in designing national accounts of well-being, it will be useful to include or even focus on specific aspects of life. Nevertheless, broad measures may still be useful in capturing a wide range of factors (e.g., personality, values, etc.) that narrow measures do not assess due to their limited scope.

Structure of Well-Being Concepts

Additional aspects of well-being must also be distinguished. First, the pleasantness and unpleasantness of emotional experience (i.e., their valence) are not necessarily polar opposites—they represent distinct aspects of experience. The frequent experience of pleasant affect does correlate with the infrequent experience of unpleasant affect, but the two are only modestly inversely related. Thus, individuals might experience very little of either type, while others may frequently experience both. Moreover, a person who experiences a decrease in negative emotions will not invariably experience an increase in positive emotions—the two can occur somewhat independently. Second, the emotional aspects of well-being are distinguishable from the cognitive aspects. Cognitive judgments, such as life satisfaction or satisfaction with one's work, do not map perfectly onto a person's emotions—one can be relatively satisfied and yet not experience high levels of positive emotions. Thus, a complete assessment of subjective well-being requires more than a simple life satisfaction or happiness question; well-being is a multifaceted phenomenon and requires multipronged assessment.

Combining the various aspects of well-being (e.g., temporality, broadness, valence, emotions, and cognition), both Dolan (Dolan and White 2006) and Diener and his colleagues (Kim-Prieto et al. 2005) have developed a temporal model of well-being, starting at external events and circumstances and moving through experience to recall and global evaluations. This model is represented in Table 7.1 and provides one useful way of sampling the domain of well-being measures. In the upper regions of the table, positive and negative emotions are shown as they occur in a temporal sequence beginning with instigating events and proceeding to global judgments. Various positive and negative feelings can be assessed at different stages of the temporal sequence. After individuals experience an event, they can recall and evaluate it. Each of these different facets of well-being can be relevant to quality of life.

In the next region of the table below emotions, we show the various types of cognitive judgments that can be made about one's life—from life satisfaction to narrower judgments about specific domains such as work, health, and marriage. Finally, the table includes other types of well-being such as optimism and trust in others. These too are forms of well-being because they reflect evaluations of various aspects of a person's past, present, and future life. What the table clearly indicates is that a thorough assessment of well-being requires the measurement of many concepts, just as the assessment of health must include many different types of measures. A thermometer, X-ray, blood pressure cuff, and eye examination can all yield valuable information about health that is relatively independent of the other measures. However, just as a few measures can often give a reasonably good estimate of a person's health, a few measures of subjective well-being can often yield summary scores that reveal much about how individuals feel about their lives. Thus, certain summary measures can be quite useful, but more specific measures are needed for a full assessment of well-being.

Although national surveys tend to emphasize broad, general questions, the model in Table 7.1 helps us evaluate well-being concepts at each of the temporal stages in terms of their relevance to policy questions. Although trait-like, "in general," evaluations tend to dominate measures of well-being, on-line measures and perceptions of domains will often be very relevant to policy discussions. Thus, Table 7.1 is valuable in alerting researchers to the fact that there are important aspects of well-being that are not captured by broad survey questions about happiness and life satisfaction. Comprehensive, national accounts of well-being should therefore consist of a variety of measures in order to reflect a range of well-being components.

Validity of Self-Report Measures of Well-Being

A basic question about the validity of measures is "Valid for what?" In the case of well-being indicators, we want measures that accurately reflect people's experiences of their lives as desirable—to fully capture the concept of "utility" as used by economists. The strongest form of validity is to build a theoretical network in which the properties of the measures are completely understood. In this endeavor, we review the evidence supporting the validity of self-report measures of well-being. We also discuss how the scaling of such measures can be validly interpreted.

Table 7.1 Various well-being concepts

	Events and circum-stances ("objective" measures)	Perceptions of events, domain perception, including appraisals and standards	Reactions to events and circumstances	Later recall of reactions and experiences	Trait-like, global, life, and other evaluative responses
Temporal model of affect (moods and emotions)					
Positive (pleasant) emotions					
Joy Enjoyment, fun Interested Elated, ecstatic Calm, relaxed Affectionate, caring Loving, warm Happy, pleased Proud, pride Grateful, thankful Optimistic Active, energetic Awe, wonder Optimism Nostalgia, reminiscence Etc.	Pleasant situations, interesting work and leisure activities, and times when the person accomplishes his or her goals. These situations are often captured by economic and social indicators	People's evaluations of the positive aspects of their lives, as in reports of satisfaction (see below)	Daily reconstruc-tion method (DRM) and on-line experience sampling methods (ESM)	Recall of pleasant feelings during periods such as the past month or past year or a specific activity such as work or a vacation	Reports of the person's positive experiences "in general"
Negative (unpleasant) emotions					
Anger, rage, irritation Sad, melancholy, depressed Fearful, anxious Worried, stressed Guilt, shame Jealous, envious Frustrated Regret, rumination Pessimism Etc.	Unpleasant situations, boring work, and times when the person fails to accomplish his or her goals. External or "objective" measures of adverse situations	People's evaluations of the negative aspects of their lives, as in reports of dissatisfaction (see below)	Daily reconstruc-tion and on-line experience sampling methods of unpleasant feelings	Recall of unpleasant feelings during specific periods such as the past month or past year or a specific activity such as work or a vacation	Reports of the person's negative experiences "in general"
Cognitive judgments of life and various aspects of life					
Judgments of life as: Satisfying Purposeful Meaningful And so forth	Respondents make broad judgments about their lives as a whole, evaluating their lives in general terms				
Judgments of life domains: Work Social relationships Health Leisure Income Housing And so forth	Respondents offer evaluations of specific aspects of their lives that may be broader (e.g., work) or narrower (e.g., income at work), in terms of liking, satisfaction, desire to change, and so forth				
Judgments of self-domains: Self-efficacy Ability to help one's group Respect from one's group Family is doing well And so forth	Respondents offer evaluations of aspects of their own functioning, and the functioning of the groups that are central to their identity				
Motivational and other concepts reflecting well-being					
Engagement	The person finds activities, such as work, to be worthwhile, interesting, and involving				
Optimism	The person believes that generally good things will happen in his or her future, although recognizing that some bad events are inevitable				
Trust	The person, in general, trusts others in his or her community				
Positive energy	The person feels energetic and has the energy necessary to work for her or his goals and values				

Convergence with Other Measures

Self-reports of well-being tend to correlate with other types of measures of "happiness," which suggests that they have some degree of validity. The other forms of measurement of well-being are diverse, including:

A. Biological measures of positive and negative states (prefrontal cerebral brain asymmetry, hormone levels such as cortisol, immune system strength, cardiovascular system parameters, wound healing, and so forth). Biological indicators often correlate modestly with self-reports of well-being, in part, because the biological measures reflect many factors besides happiness. However, the correlations are consistent and understandable and therefore lend substantial support to the validity of self-report scales.

B. Informant reports (family and friends reporting on the happiness of a target person). When individuals who know a respondent are queried about how happy they believe the person is, those reports correlate with the self-reports of the respondent. When a number of informant reports are averaged together to reflect a broader view of the target's happiness, they often correlate moderately with the target's own assessment.

C. Reaction time (people react quickly to positive information about their lives). There is some evidence that happy people are more likely to attend to positive information and respond more quickly to positive characteristics that might be associated with their lives.

D. Memory (happy people remember more positive than negative events from their lives). The validity of the self-report measures of well-being is supported by the fact that people reporting themselves to be happy are more likely to remember many positive events from periods of their lives such as the past year and have a difficult time remembering many negative events from the same period.

E. Open-ended questions and interviews. In a few studies, respondents have been intensively interviewed after answering the self-report scales. Even when interviewers do not know the respondent's answers to the self-report scales, their judgments about the respondent's happiness converge with the answers given to the scales.

F. Smiling and behavior. People who are happy have been found to smile more often and to behave in other ways indicating a positive mood (e.g., being more sociable, having an open posture).

G. Experience-sampling (on-line) measures. We can reduce certain measurement artifacts such as memory biases by sampling people's moods and emotions at various moments in their everyday lives. Measures might be taken at random times during waking hours over a week or through systematic recall of moods and events at the end of each day. When such measures are taken and averaged, they correlate at moderate to substantial levels with broader, global reports of well-being collected from a one-time survey.

Correlations between well-being self-report scales and the alternative measures of happiness range from modest (.20) to moderate (.50) and are almost always positive. The moderate size of the correlations is to be expected because the measures weight different aspects of well-being—self-reports reflect people's labeling of their experience; informant reports reflect perceptions by others of people's behaviors; smiling is heavily influenced by sociability and social norms; and biological measures reflect various physiological systems that underlie or have indirect effects on the components of well-being. Furthermore, each of the alternative measures suffers from its own shortcomings, which further reduces the correlations. Nevertheless, the correlations are consistent enough to indicate that self-report survey measures of well-being have a degree of validity.

Prediction of Outcomes

At times, skeptics ask what well-being predicts, and the answer is—many things. For instance, low life satisfaction is associated with increased risk for suicide. At both the national and individual levels, several studies have shown that measures of life satisfaction predict suicide and are associated with suicidal ideation and behavior. As we mentioned earlier, self-reported well-being and ill-being measures also predict positive outcomes such as sociability, advancement at work, trust in others, prodemocratic attitudes, volunteering, higher income, and certain health outcomes. Thus, not only do the measures correlate with other assessments of well-being per se but also they predict behaviors that follow from well-being and ill-being.

Stability over Time and Responsiveness to Major Life Events

There tends to be a substantial amount of stability in well-being measures when they are assessed at various points in time, for example several months apart. This stability is due largely to the stability of people's temperaments as well as their life circumstances, both of which can affect their feelings of well-being. However, when substantial changes in life circumstances occur, such as the death of a spouse, unemployment, or severe disability, well-being *does* change. Again, the pattern of change in the self-report measures of well-being suggests a degree of validity for the measures.

Understandable Patterns of Findings That Replicate

Measures of well-being show a pattern that is readily comprehensible, usually forming a predictable pattern that replicates across studies. For instance, lower levels of subjective well-being appear in very poor nations or very poor neighborhoods relative to more affluent areas. Well-being levels are also low in nations that have undergone a rapid deterioration in conditions, such as the former Soviet bloc countries. In contrast, high levels of well-being exist among democratic societies and those in which interpersonal trust is also high. Although there are anomalous findings in the literature on well-being, most findings are replicable and understandable.

At the individual level, the correlates of reported subjective well-being also show a predictable pattern. For example, individual poverty correlates with low levels of well-being. However, beyond a certain level of affluence, further increases in income make only a small difference to well-being. Other factors such as disabilities that interfere with the person working, the death of a spouse, and being laid off from one's job all lower people's life satisfaction. Not all of the observed patterns have been expected, but there are enough replicable patterns in the well-being data associated with important differences in life circumstances to give a degree of confidence in the well-being scales.

At the same time, the well-being measures reveal patterns of well-being and ill-being that are not always self-evident from common sense alone. For example, the impact of unemployment on well-being can last a few years, and levels of well-being do not necessarily completely recover even after regaining employment.

Cardinality and Interpersonal Comparability of Scores

The measures of well-being that are most likely to be used by policymakers are large-scale surveys of populations in which respondents use rating scales to report on various aspects of their subjective well-being. Can we compare the scores of different individuals; does one person's "3" exceed another person's "4"? Important evidence that well-being scores *can* be compared across individual respondents is that the scales frequently correlate with predictors such as income as well as with other measures of well-being. If the scores were not comparable across individuals, predictable correlations would not arise. How individuals use the scales may be relatively similar to each other though not exactly the same. For example, a person reporting an "8" on a 10-point happiness scale is virtually always happier than someone who reports a "3," and the latter is much more likely to suffer from clinical depression. However, a person who reports a "7" might not invariably be less happy than a person who reports an "8." Thus, the scales are likely to be approximately ordinal in nature and comparable across individuals at that level.

The interval nature of well-being data can be examined through statistical methods such as Item Response Theory. Occasionally, scale adjustment based on these methods leads to altered conclusions about the well-being of groups. However, the use of nonparametric ordinal statistics to treat well-being data has typically not led to different conclusions from those based on parametric statistics that assume equal scale intervals. More research in this area is needed. What can be said is that most conclusions based on correlations remain the same whether one assumes cardinal (interval) scaling or not, but that conclusions based on the means of groups might change for groups that are not very dissimilar after adjustments for interval scaling are made. In the future, researchers should more frequently examine the scale properties of various scale items within different cultural and sociodemographic groups. It may be that respondents who are less familiar with survey formats are prone to using the scales in idiosyncratic ways. However, such analyses are best accomplished when multi-item scales are employed.

In conclusion, there is broad evidence that well-being measures have validity. Even though the measures are subjective and refer to private internal experiences that are not directly accessible to others, a wide range of evidence converges on the conclusion that the self-report scales do assess important aspects of people's experience and how they feel and think about their lives. Just as with measures in other fields such as economics or chemistry, the self-report scales of subjective well-being have imperfections and limitations. However, we are increasingly coming to understand these shortcomings, which means that we can correct for them and take them into account.

Policy Uses of National Accounts of Well-Being

Now that we have discussed the concept of subjective well-being, its measurement, and validity, we come to the question of the policy uses of well-being. Why might policymakers want to use surveys of well-being to inform policy decisions? First, as we will soon elaborate, the economic measures that are the mainstay of policy decision-making do not capture many important aspects of life. To reiterate, well-being is extremely important to people but is only modestly assessed by variables such as income. Second, various forms of subjective well-being predict positive outcomes for the individual and society. Thus, not only is subjective well-being valued by most people but it also yields important benefits. Although the good society requires a number of other elements, feelings of well-being are a critical component. Thus, it is to the advantage of societies to monitor subjective well-being and take measures where possible to enhance it.

The Limits of Economic Measures

In order to understand the role in policy of accounts of well-being, it is important to understand the limitations of the regnant economic indicators. The economic model is built on the idea of a rational consumer, who spends their time and money in a way that maximizes "utility" (approximately equivalent to happiness or well-being). Within the constraints of their resources, according to this model, people work to earn money, spending it through acts of consumption intended to maximize well-being. If individuals are informed and have free choice, then they will make choices that they believe will maximize feelings of well-being. In many economic models, people make a tradeoff between work and leisure, with the former being undesirable and the latter being desirable, that is just offset by the amount of pleasure they can acquire by purchasing goods and services.

Although there is substantial validity in the economic view of people, there are also many shortcomings. For one thing, people do not always act in their own best interests in a "rational" way. For instance, repeatedly in laboratory experiments, it has been shown that people will forego their own best interests to punish "cheaters," even though they themselves have absolutely nothing to gain. The moral action, in this case, trumps people acting in their own best monetary interests. Outside the laboratory, people often help others even when it is not in their "rational" best interest to do so. In these instances, the economic measures can omit important aspects of quality of life. Similarly, there are data to show that choices are not always transitive, as assumed by models of rational choice. Just because a person chooses A over B, and B over C, does not mean they will inevitably choose A over C. Thus, people do not always make rational choices in a way assumed by economic theory. A related problem is that choices are seen as good in economic models because with more choices, the person has the potential for greater utility. However, Schwartz and Ward (2004) have gathered compelling evidence suggesting that too many choices can interfere with well-being rather than enhance it.

Another limitation of the economic model is that people do not always make choices that will maximize their well-being. Hsee and Zhang (2004) have shown that when people choose among goods, they tend to use criteria that are not necessarily relevant to how the product will be *experienced*. That is, the factors that influence the choice are not always the factors that influence the enjoyment of the selected product. Similarly, Wilson and Gilbert (2005) have shown that people sometimes are not fully able to forecast their own happiness. For example, they may overemphasize how they expect to feel *immediately after* a choice is made and not fully realize how they will experience something different after the initial phase of excitement. Thus, choice is not always rational, nor does it inevitably lead to the most well-being or happiness. National accounts of well-being could help educate citizens about their choices, in addition to complementing economic indicators in terms of policy formation.

Well-being measures might also be useful in showing that work can be enjoyable and rewarding. In economic models, work is considered a cost that must be undergone to accrue money for buying things that are of utility; it is not considered that work itself can have utility. Yet, people spend many waking hours at work, and most people enjoy their work to some extent—some finding it to be extremely rewarding. By viewing work as aversive, economists develop models of human behavior that are insufficient in understanding people's behavior and motivations. Thus, well-being measures at work can aid in *both* the creation of more satisfying and productive work environments as well as the development of more adequate economic models. For example, we know that unemployment can be quite aversive to those laid off and lead to significant drops in life satisfaction. This does not square with the idea that unemployment simply results from people *choosing* to trade unpleasant work activity for more leisure, thereby sacrificing income to gain free time. In fact, we know that unemployed people are often quite unhappy, not only because they have lost the self-respect that comes from doing an activity valued by society but also because they have lost an activity that they often find enjoyable. Findings such as those on unemployment and subjective well-being can help behavioral scientists improve economic models and aid policymakers and organizational leaders in increasing quality of life. Factors such as job security, variety at work, and health-care benefits can be compared with increases in income in terms of how they affect well-being.

Finally, though economic measures are presumed to be more objective than well-being measures, they are not perfectly so. It is often not recognized that survey data contribute to the index of gross national product (GNP) and that what enters into the GNP is based on a number of subjective choices. For example, although volunteer work and homemaking can produce substantial amounts of goods and services, economists often omit them from the GNPs of most societies. There are black markets and "gray markets" of illegal or off-the-books economic activities that must be approximated rather than measured directly. Expenses forced on a society by bad circumstances (e.g., jails and police to counter crime) contribute to GNP in addition to expenditures on desirable products (e.g., parks, the arts, university education). Because economic measures by themselves provide an incomplete assessment of the quality of life, well-being measures have a clear place in policy discussions. Next, we outline three criteria that well-being indicators should meet in order to best complement economic indicators.

Requirements of Measures to be Useful for Policy Analyses

In order to be useful in policy debates, well-being measures must have a number of properties besides validity. In the first place, the measures must assess factors that are seen as a legitimate concern of the government. If the citizenry believes that the government should not intervene to change certain subjective states, then well-being measures would be fruitless because policy interventions would be unlikely to occur. For example, it might be a common belief among citizens that government action to alleviate misery is more justifiable than government actions to create feelings of fun among citizens, and in this case, measures of unhappiness would be more likely to influence policy debates. If the measures are used to create policies to increase the well-being of certain target groups, such as the elderly or disadvantaged groups, a prerequisite is that the citizenry accept policies aimed at helping these groups.

A related requirement is that the measures concern subjective states that are amenable to influence by government policies. If policymakers have no resources or ability to intervene and increase happiness in a certain domain, the well-being measures are unlikely to have much impact. For example, policies that regulate work hours could directly affect job satisfaction and indirectly affect marital satisfaction, but policies designed to increase romantic love between spouses would be difficult to administer as well as unlikely to be accepted by citizens. There are additional factors such as cultural norms and individual personality that influence well-being but may not be appropriate targets for intervention (these and other concerns are discussed later in the chapter). In other words, the most useful measures of well-being are those that are relevant to potential policy concerns.

Finally, the measures of well-being should capture patterns that are not fully reflected in economic and social indicators. If accounts of subjective well-being suggest that crime harms well-being or that poverty decreases well-being, then the measures are useful because they validate the use of the other indicators. However, if the measures of well-being capture information that goes beyond the economic and objective social indicators, they are much more valuable. For instance, indicators about poverty and crime do not convey the same information as measures about trust and involvement with one's community. The latter type of knowledge could aid individuals and governments in making choices that truly maximize well-being. Policies designed to reduce poverty and crime, though important, may not necessarily improve the quality of relationships in a community. Thus, where economic indicators offer an incomplete picture of well-being, national accounts of subjective well-being can add valuable information.

Implications of Using Well-Being Measures for Policy Decisions

Such uses of the national measures of well-being apply both at the level of individual education and choice as well as at the level of society. Some uses might be quite focused, as in providing information about a specific policy under consideration. However, broad measures could also be relevant for more extensive debates about the overall priorities of the society.

One value of the indicators, especially when published in public forums, is to draw attention and inspire discussion. Topics and concerns that are assessed and discussed in the public media tend to draw people's attention. Thus, when we, as a society, publish economic indicators on a daily basis, people tend to think about economic growth. If we were to publish indicators about national well-being, people, including policymakers, would think about well-being and discuss the well-being of groups that appeared deficient. Especially fine-grained indicators such as work engagement and satisfaction in different industries and work activities can illuminate the areas in which we are successful, as well as those needing interventions.

A primary purpose of the national accounts of well-being would be to educate individuals about when and where people experience high versus low levels of well-being. For instance, the measures might show that people are unhappy when commuting to and from work and therefore could alert individuals to information that is relevant when they seek a residence. Similarly, people might be tempted to purchase a home in the path of an airport runway approach because of lower real estate prices. However, if it is found that well-being suffers in such an area due to aircraft noise, homebuyers could make more informed decisions about whether they are truly making a good purchase.

A second area where the national accounts of well-being can be useful is in making adjustments to numbers that are relevant to the administration of government policies (Dolan and White 2007). There are areas such as crime victimization and government expenditures where the evaluation of outcomes is not provided by the market. For instance, crime victimization is not given a value in the marketplace. Although the costs of victimization could be quantified through payment for physical and mental health services, not all crime victims may seek or be able to afford treatment. If policymakers relied only on these "objective" data, they might underestimate the impact of crime in their community and misallocate funds for relevant programs. Well-being measures, however, might reveal less satisfaction with work and family or a reduced sense of trust in one's community. Thus, well-being indicators could provide another measure of the impact of crime victimization that would assist the courts and other agencies.

In a similar vein, formulas for health expenditures or for research on specific illnesses might be based in part on the amount of misery that various ailments are thought to cause. Such accounts can provide a more accurate view of how well-being and ill-being are affected by disease and thereby assist in making more valid adjustments to expenditure formulas than other methods based on guessing or intuition. Another example of a specific policy use of the well-being measures is to adjust government employee salaries. Government employees often receive benefits such as greater job security that those in the private sector do not receive. The value of these benefits can be gauged through well-being measures to help adjust salaries outside of the private sector. These examples are meant to indicate the types of specific, concrete uses to which well-being measures might be put rather than to actually argue for their use in these specific cases.

Yet another area where well-being measures can be a useful input to policy decisions is in evaluating the impact of government expenditures such as on parks, health care, freeways, and the environment. Currently, spending in these areas occurs within the context of political dialogue in which economists have substantial input concerning the costs of these expenditures. Economists argue that people's choices reflect their values and desires and, therefore, that people express their personal desires through their expenditures or political actions. However, the political process is complicated by competing constituencies attempting to influence outcomes. Thus, government expenditures alone poorly reflect the desires of significant segments of the population. On that account, well-being measures can serve as a very useful source of information. For instance, the impact of parks or the length of commuting on the well-being of a community can be an important consideration for policy debates.

At the broadest level, the well-being measures can help the citizens of a society weigh their priorities. For example, if mental illness is one of the biggest causes of suffering in wealthy nations, the amount of expenditures in this area might be increased. If people who work fewer hours are happier in a nation, business and government leaders might take steps to reduce the work week. If incomes are rising steeply, but levels of well-being are flat or declining, citizens may think about their personal and national priorities and whether changes are needed. Richard Layard (2005) has argued that measures of well-being can reorient the priorities of societies away from a strict emphasis on economic growth. Such measures will not provide automatic solutions to societal problems, but like economic indicators, they can be a very important source of information. Indeed, in economically developed nations, the well-being indicators might even be more informative than economic indices. Well-being indicators can also add to economic indices by reflecting the interplay of various domains on people's experiences. For example, the work context may influence the family context, and economic indicators might fail to capture this. Individuals might choose to work overtime to earn more money, but their family lives might suffer as a consequence. These "externalities" (unintended consequences of economic activities) might include greater delinquency among children who remain unsupervised by overworked parents. Such consequences are more likely to be reflected in well-being indicators, whereas they might be overlooked by economic measures alone.

There are a number of marketplace areas where the economic focus on "revealed preferences," choices made by producers and consumers, can be extended substantially by adding survey measures of well-being. For example, the impact of inequality, inflation, and unemployment are instances in which economic measures do not fully reflect how well-being is affected by economic factors. Similarly, how changes in income aspirations influence well-being is important in part because they can predict future economic behavior. Furthermore, the impact of behaviors such as smoking, alcohol consumption, volunteering, and working a second job on well-being is of interest both to policymakers and economists.

Finally, well-being measures can help evaluate the impact of various "dilemmas of the commons." Such dilemmas arise from collective actions over which no single individual has full control. For example, the threat of pollution occurs when large numbers of people drive inefficient automobiles. Nevertheless, there is little incentive for any single person to buy nonpolluting cars if they are more expensive to operate or purchase. The economic model does not fully appraise the situation because the acts of individual consumers have so little effect that people may not weigh it in their personal decisions. However, the effects of pollution can harm the well-being of the community, and this effect can show up in people's evaluations of their lives and environments. Such information could enable individuals to better weigh the costs and benefits of purchasing more fuel-efficient cars.

Specific Examples of Well-Being Measures That Are Relevant to Policy Issues

Different measures of well-being are likely to be relevant to different policy questions. For example, a general measure of life satisfaction might be relevant to policy questions about inequality because large differences between social classes in happiness and contentment can lead to societal instability. More specific measures related to income satisfaction or housing satisfaction, however, might lead to more concrete insights into possible policy alternatives. Below, we give some examples of policy questions, and the potential types of well-being measures that might be most relevant to those issues:

Noise Abatement Measures near an Airport
- Moods of those living in landing/take-off paths (e.g., feeling rested or tired)

Carpooling Lanes
- People's moods when driving alone versus carpooling with others

- People's moods and emotions who commute long or short to work (e.g., at work, during commute, and at home)

State-Supported Day Care for Elderly Alzheimer Patients
- Moods and emotions of Alzheimer caregivers when patient is in daycare or at home
- Life satisfaction of caregivers when respite care is provided or not provided

Minimum Wage Laws
- Life satisfaction among people earning the minimum wage
- Income satisfaction among various groups, including low-wage earners

Wage and Hour Regulations and Systems
- The happiness and life satisfaction of workers who are forced to work overtime, or who voluntarily work overtime
- The work satisfaction of workers who have various flextime arrangements

Allocating Health Research Money or Health-Care Expenditures
- An unhappiness index of people with various medical problems

Age of Retirement
- Life satisfaction of workers at various ages, including people who are elderly
- Work satisfaction of retired workers who return to work
- Moods and emotions at work versus leisure of retired versus working senior citizens

Taxes on Cigarettes
- Moods and emotions of those who reduce their tobacco consumption
- Moods and emotions of those who quit smoking
- Life satisfaction of smokers versus nonsmokers, controlling for other factors
- Health satisfaction of people in households with or without smokers

Schools and Age Boundaries (e.g., Grades K-8 Versus Grades 1–5 and Middle School)
- How much children enjoy school and look forward to school
- Engagement and interest in various school activities and subjects
- On-line measures of moods and emotions in school
- Satisfaction with school, friends, and classmates
- Life satisfaction in various schools or school districts

Parks and Recreation
- Are parks more crucial to well-being in areas where dwellings have no yards?
- Life satisfaction and happiness when parks are plentiful or rare in a city

Setting Social Security Benefits
- Is there a life satisfaction curve in retirement relating well-being to income, such that income differences make only smaller differences above some minimal inflection point?

We are not pretending that we necessarily have pinpointed the precise best measures for each policy issue. Instead, we are trying to convey the fact that multiple types of well-being measures might be relevant to the same policy and that different types of measures might be most relevant to different policy questions. Naturally, economic measures such as the costs of various policy alternatives will also be quite relevant. Nonetheless, the well-being measures can, in many cases, add substantially to the information that policymakers need.

Concerns About National Accounts of Well-Being

In the previous section, we saw the range of measures that might be employed in national accounts of well-being. We now move to the concerns that might be raised when implementing such measures within the context of large-scale national surveys and utilizing them for policy decisions.

Measurement Artifacts

Although there is substantial support for the validity of self-reports of well-being, there are, nevertheless, contaminating influences on these measures that have nothing to do with the actual experience of subjective well-being. We discuss a number of measurement artifacts and evaluate the extent to which they threaten the validity of well-being measures.

Item-Order Effects The order of items in a survey influences how people respond to those items. For example, one item might make salient certain information that otherwise would not have been considered when responding to a later item. Alternatively, an earlier question might change how the respondent interprets the *meaning* of a subsequent question. Interpretive effects and priming (salience) effects can bias responses to well-being questions. These effects are usually not large, but they can be statistically significant. One solution is to insure that the items always stay in the same order in surveys that are to be compared with one another. Another solution is to systematically vary item order and analyze whether this produces any effects.

Contamination by Current Mood A respondent's mood at the time of the survey can influence the responses given. For example, individuals in an unusually good mood might report that their job is very satisfying, although in a more normal mood, this might not be their typical response. These mood effects have been found to be small in most research, although sometimes, they are statistically significant. Like item-order, the effects are difficult to predict ahead of time because respondents may themselves correct their answers so as to not let mood be a factor. In some cases, they may even overcorrect for their mood. Surveys should not be conducted when broad groups of people are likely to be in an unusually bad or good mood. For example, a survey might not be representative of normal well-being if it were administered immediately after a large disaster or during a national event such as a soccer championship. As long as unusual times are avoided when taking the survey, current mood effects are likely to be random across respondents and will not bias responses for the sample as a whole. On the other hand, governments may want to collect data on current mood some time after a disaster and make comparisons across different areas to help plan for needed services. Because current mood is grounded in immediate experience rather than recall, it can serve as a useful measure of well-being.

Number-Use and Other Scaling Effects Some individuals may use extreme numbers in responding, whereas other individuals may prefer the middle range on a scale. Some individuals may treat certain numbers as wider categories than other numbers, or be attracted to specific values such as the midpoint of the scale or a popular number such as "7." *Item Response Theory* is a form of scale analysis that is designed to examine the issue of number use and how respondents use scales. Furthermore, some forms of response scales are more impervious than others to differences in scale use. For instance, dichotomous items that ask respondents whether they are in *either* a bad mood *or* a good mood

yield less information, but are also less likely to be influenced by number use than a similar question using a 1–10 scale. It pays to be aware of the possibility of scale use differences and to inspect the data for such patterns.

Mode of Administration Mode of administration refers to whether self-report responses are collected in face-to-face interviews, over the phone, or via the Internet; whether respondents can see a "show card" with the possible responses or only hear the response alternatives; and so forth. If respondents cannot see the response alternatives, responding will entail a memory load, and the ability to handle this will vary across individuals, thereby influencing responses. Although the effects are not always large, the mode of administration can affect mean levels of well-being responses. For example, people may report being happier in face-to-face interviews than in phone interviews or anonymous questionnaires, and these effects can differ among groups. Thus, it is important to keep mode of administration as constant as possible for all respondents if they are to be compared with one another.

Social Desirability A common concern in survey research is that respondents may construct responses to impress the researcher—such responses are usually culturally desirable or intended to form a certain type of impression. The concept of social desirability seems deceptively simple but is, in fact, conceptually complex and has been difficult to assess and control. "Social desirability scales" such as the Marlowe–Crowne have not proven useful because they capture substantive personality differences between people that should not be thought of as response artifacts. For example, individuals' social desirability scores correlated with their well-being as reported by close others (Diener et al. 1991b). Furthermore, people who answer in a socially desirable way in one domain may not necessarily respond in a socially desirable way in another domain. One method of assessing social desirability at the group level is to administer questionnaires to some respondents in an anonymous written format and compare the answers to respondents who were interviewed face-to-face, with the idea that the interview is likely to enhance socially desirable responding.

Translation Across Languages Although severe concerns have been expressed about the equivalence of measures when they are translated into different languages, little research has, in fact, been conducted on this topic, and the research that has been done to date has not shown serious difficulties with translated scales. It has been found that people in different language areas of Switzerland produce scores that are very similar to other Swiss groups. In my (Diener) laboratory, Shao (1993) used a strategy of asking bilinguals to respond to the Satisfaction with Life Scale in both English and Mandarin but in random orders spaced weeks apart. Few differences were produced by which language was used. In another study, Kuppens et al. (2006) found that the structure of emotions across regions of the world, using college-student subjects, was the same for major emotions, with a clear positive affect and negative affect cluster appearing in every region and language.

One strategy for dealing with translation is the translation/back-translation method, although this approach is controversial owing to the fact that exact wording in back-translation might not be optimal in terms of conveying the concepts involved. Another strategy is to use multiple words and items in order to insure that the general concept is conveyed in each language. Yet another method is to empirically compare the scales by having bilinguals at each research site, take the scales in the various languages, and compare the results.

Although the issue of measurement artifacts deserves further systematic research, it does not preclude the valid assessment of well-being through self-report and across nations. As with measurement, in general, researchers should attend to and address possible artifacts when possible. Self-reports of well-being are valid but should continue to be refined and improved as they are used in national surveys.

Cultural response bias is a more important concern and is discussed later.

Objective Versus Subjective Measures

A related concern in the measurement and use of national accounts of well-being is that they are too "subjective," whereas economic and social indicators are more "objective" and therefore more reliable. This claim rests on the assumption that other people cannot *see* another person's subjective well-being, whereas interobserver agreement can be achieved with economic and objective social indicators because everyone can observe the phenomena in question. There are a number of fallacies in this reasoning.

The first fallacy in this objective–subjective dichotomy is that economic measures consist solely of factors that are observable, whereas well-being measures are concerned only with unobservable factors. On the contrary, economic indicators include variables such as consumer confidence, as well as estimates of unobserved factors such as the "shadow economy" (economic activity occurring outside of the government's surveillance). Conversely, as we noted earlier, "subjective" variables such as life satisfaction may have objectively observable manifestations such as patterns of brainwave or immune activity.

Another fallacy is that examining unobservable phenomena is unscientific. It should be noted that the most sophisticated of the sciences is built on concepts and phenomena (e.g., black holes, quarks) that are not directly observable but are inferred from various indirect measures. In the same way, measures of well-being can triangulate an underlying phenomenon by observing various indirect manifestations of it (e.g., individuals' behavior, their ability to rapidly produce positive thoughts, their descriptions of their feelings, and so forth).

A final fallacy is that "objective" economic measures are more accurate than "subjective" well-being measures. However, *both* objective and subjective measures may include errors of measurement. While people might lie and say that they are happy when in fact they are not, economists may overlook productive activity because people avoid reporting it or because the system of recording such activity is faulty. Employment figures derived from surveys may require employers to estimate their workforce and payroll by categorizing their employees in ways that may not be consistently understood across businesses. Finally, it should be noted that the economic measures are filled with subjective choices. Economists decide whether household production should be included in the measures or not. A slew of productive activities, such as volunteer behavior, may not be included in the economic measures simply because it was decided not to include them.

The Issue of Paternalism

Another concern about national indicators of well-being is that they will foster a paternalistic attitude in which governments interfere in the lives of individuals, either by telling them how to live life or creating policies that have unwanted impacts on individuals. However, it is important to note that governments already intervene in many aspects of modern life, through taxes, laws, and other policies. The intention of well-being indicators is not to bolster paternalism or governmental intrusion but rather to guide and improve the widespread intervention that already occurs and will continue to occur in the future. Economic measures are based on similar reasoning—governments enact numerous regulations that affect the lives and economic activities of their citizens, and these measures simply help to enlighten such policies. Moreover, both economic and well-being measures can be used by businesses and individuals to make decisions.

If government intervention is a fact of everyday life, do the measures of well-being facilitate a degree of interference in personal lives that is not inherent in the economic measures? For example, might changing interest rates to spur economic productivity be less intrusive than policies designed to enhance social relationships? Not necessarily. First, economic interventions such as work hour laws and minimum wage laws are to some extent designed to enhance well-being. Policies related to day care or nursing homes will certainly influence people's social lives and well-being. Whether policies are paternalistic or not will be a feature of specific policies and the behaviors they affect rather than whether the outcomes concern subjective well-being or economics.

A related objection to national accounts of well-being is that they might put pressure on people to be happy or act happy. The idea that people might be pressured to be happy is a misconception of what subjective well-being entails. Because subjective well-being is the feeling that life is going well, most people find it desirable. Not everyone might want to feel giggly and cheerful, of course, but all people want to believe that their life is proceeding as desired. Similarly, a person need not act cheerful in order to have high subjective well-being, and there is nothing in the measures to suggest that people should jaunt about in euphoric reverie. People can achieve subjective well-being by working toward their goals with meaning and purpose and by achieving their values. For some people, this will mean being joyful or happy; for others, this might result in feelings of contentment, satisfaction, and fulfillment. The way to avoid a "happiology" measure of cheerfulness

that is burdensome to many is to create measures of well-being that include fulfillment, interest, trust in others, and attainment of one's goals.

The Limited Sphere of Policymaking: Top-Down Versus Bottom-Up Influences

Some factors that influence well-being may fall outside of the province of policymakers. The experience of objectively good events can contribute to well-being and is referred to as a "bottom-up" process. However, one of the major discoveries in the research on subjective well-being is that a considerable amount of happiness is based on "top-down" influences—how the person tends to *interpret* events.

These factors, such as temperament and cultural norms, lie outside of the control of governments and organizations. This is no different from the economic indicators. Policy leaders can influence money supply, interest rates, and other factors that have an impact on the economy. At the same time, there are factors that are largely outside of leaders' control, such as people's conscientiousness and work ethic or their desire to save money. We now briefly discuss the implications of top-down influences for policy uses of well-being.

Temperament People's temperament or predisposition tends to substantially influence how happy they are. Their upbringing, which includes cultural influences, can also color their evaluation of their lives and the events happening to them. Twin studies also reveal greater similarity in well-being between identical twins than fraternal twins, suggesting the presence of genetic influences. Differences in temperament raise important issues for the measurement of well-being, but they do not completely override the effects of circumstances. Recall that the effects of life events like unemployment and widowhood produce substantial drops in well-being across participants. Because policymakers have little control over temperament and can primarily influence only the structure of external circumstances, it will be important to separate the types of influences that cause specific scores on well-being scales.

Cultural Differences The culture in which people are raised can influence their outlook on the world and the degree to which they evaluate events in a positive way. There appear to be differences in well-being between nations that are due not just to income but to culture as well. For example, East Asians report lower levels of well-being than one might expect based on the objective standard of living in Pacific Rim nations, whereas Latin Americans often report higher levels of well-being than one might expect based on objective conditions in those nations. Perhaps because self-criticism is taught in many East Asian cultures and because social closeness and support is a prominent feature in Latin American nations, the two regions of the world differ on feelings of well-being. However, there is also some evidence that these cultural differences are larger on global measures of well-being than in on-line experience-sampling measures, suggesting that some of the cultural differences might be due to recall and self-concept rather than to actual experience per se. Individuals in cultures that tend to take a critical stance toward life may report lower well-being than respondents in cultures where a more celebratory approach is taken. These differences may not be artifactual in that they can lead to differences in behavior and health, but as yet we know little of how cultural differences in well-being relate to differences in life outcomes. Along with temperament, cultural influences on well-being are important considerations—especially in a multicultural context.

One concern in making comparisons across nations or cultures, which represents additional challenges beyond comparing individuals within a culture, is whether the emotions or feelings composing well-being differ. For example, perhaps in one society, feelings of power are desirable while in another society, feelings of compassion are more desirable and pleasant. Research, to date, suggests that there are certain core emotions that are considered pleasant or unpleasant in all regions of the world. For example, feelings of joy, happiness, and contentment are probably felt as pleasant everywhere, whereas feeling sad, angry, and fearful are felt as unpleasant everywhere. It may be that when these emotions are felt, it is because an evaluation of events has been made suggesting that things are good or bad in the person's life. However, other emotions such as pride seem to differ substantially in how they are evaluated across cultures. Thus, cross-national and cross-cultural differences in well-being must be interpreted cautiously. Such differences can be adequately understood only after intensive study of the structure of well-being within each cultural area.

Varying Standards Can Be Used in Computing Well-Being

Probably, one of the biggest advantages in using well-being measures is also one of the biggest sources of confusion—the fact that different people often use different standards when they evaluate their lives (Michalos 1985). For example, a wealthy individual might be dissatisfied with their income because they compare it to even richer neighbors or because they cannot afford a private jet. In contrast, a poor person might be very satisfied with even a tenth of that income. How can government policies be used to enhance well-being when people's reports of their subjective well-being can depend on such drastically different standards? Note that there is a parallel situation in economics, where government policies to increase national wealth must contend with vast differences in incomes between individuals and where policies to increase wealth might help some individuals more than others.

Because people can use different standards in judging their satisfaction with various aspects of their lives, satisfaction reports must be interpreted appropriately. In some cases, we might question why people have what appear to be inappropriately high standards. If people have very high and unrealistic standards that lead them to dissatisfaction, this can negatively affect their behavior. For instance, dissatisfied people may be more likely to quit their jobs, go on strike, or steal from the workplace. Thus, it is important to determine the sources of dissatisfaction. We might, in some cases, want to assess the standards themselves. Certainly, caution is required in comparing the satisfaction of groups that might have quite different standards.

Nonetheless, we know that the evaluation of other factors seems to entail *inherent* standards in which social comparisons are less relevant. For example, people like interesting, engaging activities, and they dislike pain. People enjoy the support and respect of others. They can judge whether they are hungry or full, whether they are interested or bored, and whether they are happy or sad without reference to others. One strength of the well-being research is that it informs us of those domains of life that are subject to easily shifting comparison standards and those that are likely to reflect needs that are universal to all humans.

One challenge in the measurement of well-being for policy purposes is to examine the standards people are using and determine the policy implications. Furthermore, when standards are extremely high and unrealistic, governments may be faced with destructive dissatisfaction that leads to social breakdown. Thus, although government policies will normally be directed at the factors that influence quality of life in a particular realm, in some instances, they might be directed at the standards used by people. However, there is a danger in governments manipulating people's standards in order to avoid the need for improving social conditions. Thus, like economic indicators, the measures of well-being must be used with care and do have the potential for misuse.

Focus on Misery Eradication?

Some have maintained that the job of governments is to focus on the eradication of misery and, therefore, that well-being measures should be composed of assessments of ill-being such as depression, anxiety, and pain. Indeed, most large-scale surveys, to date, have included primarily measures of psychological and physical symptoms, including mental states such as depression and stress. However, the belief that governments will not be concerned with interventions once life reaches a neutral point is not true. Governments will be interested in life satisfaction, contentment, affection, and joy in part because such states often have positive outcomes such as an enthusiastic and productive workforce, a citizenry that largely trusts their neighbors and leaders, and ultimately, the social stability that is the underpinning of democratic governance. Furthermore, governments at both national and local levels have shown themselves to be interested in improving life beyond neutrality and not just in eradicating misery.

Although the elimination of unhappiness may take priority for both individuals and governments, both are also interested in moving upward even after reaching the neutral point. Take for example, policies of national governments—the creation of national parks, the establishment of national holidays and festivities, support for the arts, building universities, and exploring outer space—that are clearly designed for positive betterment rather than eliminating some clear and present misery. Similarly, local governments such as municipalities build parks and sponsor parades, give monetary support both to youth athletics and professional sports, attract tourists, and underwrite biking trails and adult self-development classes. Many of the miseries are declining. For instance, hunger has been greatly reduced, and food is available to eradicate starvation around the globe; many diseases have been conquered, and others have been greatly diminished. Misery will often have the first attention of governments. But as miseries are reduced, governments will increasingly move toward increasing positive well-being, and therefore, the well-being indicators must include the full range of well-being, not just negative measures.

Conclusions and Future Directions

There is a substantial amount of valid variance in measures of well-being. Although there are certain measurement artifacts such as current-mood and item-order effects, these can often be controlled or assessed and usually produce small effects. More research needs to be conducted on some artifacts across cultures such as scale usage.

A much more challenging problem with measures of well-being, when used in the policy arena, is to separate top-down from bottom-up effects. After all, governments are much more likely to endeavor to change the environment to enhance well-being than to change people's personalities or cultural norms about emotional feelings. Despite the fact that there are strong indications that the measures have a moderate level of validity, there is also clear evidence that the measures can be influenced by individual differences in personality, cultural norms for the expression and experience of emotion, and by people's desire to appear happy. A major challenge, therefore, is to determine when differences in well-being are due to personality and culture, to environmental circumstances, or some interaction of these factors. This determination will make the measures much more useful to policymakers.

In our laboratory, we view the difference between on-line reports and global reports, as well as the difference between satisfaction with narrow and broad domains, as possible ways to disentangle bottom-up and top-down influences. In addition, we advocate the use of multimethod research in which self-reports of well-being are supplemented by other methods (e.g., biological measures, informant reports, and speeded memory measures). This approach is perhaps most likely to help disentangle various influences on well-being measures. Nevertheless, it is difficult to use these measures in large-scale surveys of nations, and therefore, developing easier methods of assessing bottom-up well-being is essential.

Besides measurement issues, there are conceptual challenges in using well-being for policy purposes. A prime issue is that of habituation, aspiration level, or "adaptive preferences." Because people very often adapt to some degree to their circumstances and adjust their aspirations to be realistic, people in very different life circumstances may score equally high on certain measures of well-being. This represents a challenge for using well-being in policy debates because we would prefer that the measures reflect circumstances that should be the targets of policy rather than internal factors. Thus, this issue is related to the top-down effects of personality and culture discussed earlier.

Just as with economic measures, there are shortcomings and questions for future research. Nonetheless, we are now at the point where the well-being measures show enough validity to be used in policy debates, and the relevance of these indicators to many policy issues is quite clear. Thus, it is an opportune time to initiate national indicators of subjective well-being.

References

Diener, E. (1984). Subjective well-being. *Psychological Bulletin, 95*, 542–575.

Diener, E. (1995). A value based index for measuring national quality of life. *Social Indicators Research, 36*, 107–127.

Diener, E., & Fujita, F. (1995). Methodological pitfalls and solutions in satisfaction research. In A. C. Samli & M. J. Sirgy (Eds.), *New dimensions in marketing/quality-of-life research* (pp. 27–46). Westport: Greenwood Press.

Diener, E., & Oishi, S. (2003). Are Scandinavians happier than Asians? Issues in comparing nations on subjective well-being. In F. Columbus (Ed.), *Politics and economics of Asia.* Hauppauge: Nova.

Diener, E., & Suh, E. (1997). Measuring quality of life: Economic, social, and subjective indicators. *Social Indicators Research, 40*, 189–216.

Diener, E., Sandvik, E., & Pavot, W. (1991a). Happiness is the frequency, not the intensity, of positive versus negative affect. In F. Strack, M. Argyle, & N. Schwarz (Eds.), *Subjective well-being: An interdisciplinary perspective* (pp. 119–139). New York: Pergamon.

Diener, E., Suh, E. M., Lucas, R. E., & Smith, H. E. (1999). Subjective well-being: Three decades of progress. *Psychological Bulletin, 125*, 276–302.

Diener, E., Napa-Scollon, C. K., Oishi, S., Dzokoto, V., & Suh, E. M. (2000). Positivity and the construction of life satisfaction judgments: Global happiness is not the sum of its parts. *Journal of Happiness Studies, 1*, 159–176.

Diener, E., Scollon, C. N., & Lucas, R. E. (2004). The evolving concept of subjective well-being: The multifaceted nature of happiness. In P. T. Costa & I. C. Siegler (Eds.), *Advances in cell aging and gerontology* (app, Vol. 15, pp. 187–220). Amsterdam: Elsevier.

Kahneman, D., Krueger, A. B., Schkade, D. A., Schwarz, N., & Stone, A. A. (2004). A survey method for characterizing daily life experience: The day reconstruction method. *Science, 306*, 1776–1780.

Larsen, R. J., Diener, E., & Emmons, R. A. (1985). An evaluation of subjective well-being measures. *Social Indicators Research, 17*, 1–18.

Larsen, R. J., Diener, E., & Lucas, R. (2002). Emotion: Models, measures, and individual differences. In R. Lord, R. Klimoski, & R. Kanfer (Eds.), *Emotions at work* (pp. 64–106). San Francisco: Jossey-Bass.

Lucas, R. E., Diener, E., & Suh, E. (1996). Discriminant validity of well-being measures. *Journal of Personality and Social Psychology, 71*, 616–628.

Lucas, R. E., Diener, E., & Larsen, R. J. (2003). Measuring positive emotions. In S. J. Lopez & C. R. Snyder (Eds.), *Positive psychological assessment: A handbook of models and measures* (pp. 201–218). Washington, D.C.: American Psychological Association.

Menzel, P., Dolan, P., Richardson, J., & Olsen, J. A. (2002). The role of adaptation to disability and disease in health state valuation: A preliminary normative analysis. *Social Science & Medicine, 55*, 2149–2158.

Oishi, S. (2002). The experiencing and remembering of well-being: A cross-cultural analysis. *Personality and Social Psychology Bulletin, 28*, 1398–1406.

Oishi, S., & Diener, E. (2001). Re-examining the general positivity model of subjective well-being: The discrepancy between specific and global domain satisfaction. *Journal of Personality, 69*, 641–666.

Pavot, W., & Diener, E. (1993). Review of the satisfaction with life scale. *Psychological Assessment, 5*, 164–172.

Pavot, W., Diener, E., & Suh, E. (1998). The temporal satisfaction with life scale. *Journal of Personality Assessment, 70*, 340–354.

Sandvik, E., Diener, E., & Seidlitz, L. (1993). Subjective well-being: The convergence and stability of self-report and non-self-report measures. *Journal of Personality, 61*, 317–342.

Schimmack, U., & Oishi, S. (2005). The influence of chronically and temporarily accessible information on life satisfaction judgments. *Journal of Personality and Social Psychology, 89*, 395–406.

Schimmack, U., Diener, E., & Oishi, S. (2002). Life-satisfaction is a momentary judgment and a stable personality characteristic: The use of chronically accessible and stable sources. *Journal of Personality, 70*, 345–384.

Scollon, C. N., Kim-Prieto, C., & Diener, E. (2003). Experience sampling: Promises and pitfalls, strengths and weaknesses. *Journal of Happiness Studies, 4*, 5–34.

Scollon, C. N., Diener, E., Oishi, S., & Biswas-Diener, R. (2004). Emotions across cultures and methods. *Journal of Cross-Cultural Psychology, 35*, 304–326.

Scollon, C. N., Diener, E., Oishi, S., & Biswas-Diener, R. (2005). An experience sampling and cross-cultural investigation of the relation between pleasant and unpleasant affect. *Cognition and Emotion, 19*, 27–52.

Vitterso, J., Røysamb, E., & Diener, E. (2002). The concept of life satisfaction across cultures: Exploring its diverse meaning and relation to economic wealth. In E. Gullone & R. Cummins (Eds.), *Social indicators research book series: The universality of subjective wellbeing indicators* (pp. 81–103). Dordrecht: Kluwer.

Vitterso, J., Biswas-Diener, R., & Diener, E. (2005). The divergent meanings of life satisfaction: Item response modeling of the satisfaction with life scale in Greenland and Norway. *Social Indicators Research, 74*, 327–348.

Wirtz, D., Kruger, J., Scollon, C. N., & Diener, E. (2003). What to do on spring break? The role of predicted, online, and remembered experience in future choice. *Psychological Science, 14*, 520–524.

Further Reading

Diener, E. (2000). Subjective well-being: The science of happiness and a proposal for a national index. *American Psychologist, 55*, 34–43.

Diener, E., & Seligman, M. E. P. (2004). Beyond money: Toward an economy of well-being. *Psychological Science in the Public Interest, 5*, 1–31.

Diener, E., Sandvik, E., Pavot, W., & Gallagher, D. (1991b). Response artifacts in the measurement of subjective well-being. *Social Indicators Research, 24*, 35–56.

Dolan, P., & White, M. P. (2006). Dynamic well-being: Connecting indicators of what people anticipate with indicators of what they experience. *Social Indicators Research, 75*, 303–333.

Dolan, P., & White, M. P. (2007). How can measures of subjective well-being be used to inform public policy? *Perspectives on Psychological Science, 2*, 71–85.

Hsee, C. K., & Zhang, J. (2004). Distinction bias: Misprediction and mischoice due to joint evaluation. *Journal of Personality and Social Psychology, 86*, 680–695.

Inglehart, R., & Klingemann, H.-D. (2000). Genes, culture, democracy, and happiness. In E. Diener & E. M. Suh (Eds.), *Culture and subjective well-being* (pp. 185–218). Cambridge: MIT Press.

Kim-Prieto, C., Diener, E., Tamir, M., Scollon, C., & Diener, M. (2005). Integrating the diverse definitions of happiness: A time-sequential framework of subjective well-being. *Journal of Happiness Studies, 6*, 261–300.

Kuppens, P., Ceulemans, E., Diener, E., & Kim-Prieto, C. (2006). Universal intracultural and intercultural dimensions of the recalled frequency of emotional experience. *Journal of Cross-Cultural Psychology, 37*, 491–515.

Layard, R. (2005). *Happiness: Lessons from a new science.* New York: Penguin.

Michalos, A. C. (1985). Multiple Discrepancies Theory (MDT). *Social Indicators Research, 16*, 347–413.

Schwartz, B., & Ward, A. (2004). Doing better but feeling worse: The paradox of choice. In P. A. Linley & S. Joseph (Eds.), *Positive psychology in practice* (pp. 86–104). Hoboken: Wiley.

Shao, L. (1993). *Multilanguage comparability of life satisfaction and happiness measures in mainland Chinese and American students.* Master's thesis, University of Illinois, Urbana-Champaign.

Tov, W., & Diener, E. (2008). The well-being of nations: Linking together trust, cooperation, and democracy. In B. A. Sullivan, M. Snyder, & J. L. Sullivan (Eds.), *Cooperation: The political psychology of effective human interaction* (pp. 323–342). Malden: Blackwell.

Wilson, T. D., & Gilbert, D. T. (2005). Affective forecasting: Knowing what to want. *Current Directions in Psychological Science, 14*, 131–134.

Time Use as a Social Indicator

John P. Robinson and Steven Martin

Time figures prominently in the structure and quality of people's lives. It is experienced not only in terms of the familiar American phrase "Time is money" but also in terms of the increased years of life expectancy, the decreased hours in the workweek, and the decreased days of work layoffs/strikes that analysts have used to document the increased quality of life (QOL) in society over the last 100 years.

This chapter examines various ways that time enters into such quality of life concerns, but unlike the above aggregate indicators, it focuses on the lives of individuals—usually in the form of 24 h time diaries collected from nationally representative samples. It examines two basic areas:

1. *Objective time*: Simple documentation and accounting of the hours and minutes spent on various daily activities, like paid work, TV viewing and time alone. This has become more prominent as more government agencies conduct time-diary surveys, as in the American Time-Use Survey (ATUS 2011) described below.
2. *Subjective time*: Survey questions on how people perceive their time use and how they feel about and value the way they spend their time. Since most government agencies shy away from using subjective questions, most data here come from time studies done in academic settings.

This review will also examine the intersections of the two, such as whether particular ways of spending time seem to translate into higher qualities of life

(QOL), such as whether people who work longer hours (or watch more TV) report their lives as being more satisfying or being more stressed.

Some distinctions in the types of time-use indicators and their QOL implications are discussed, in the context of social indicator questions in general. Simple diary figures by themselves generally do not have immediate QOL implications, in that analysts cannot assume a person's QOL would rise or fall as they spent more time eating or traveling. In contrast, analysts generally seem more ready to draw such QOL implications, as when parents spend more time with their children or people have more free time available. Support for some such conclusions is provided in the second part of this review on subjective indicators.

While most of the examples cited in this review refer to US data, it is also the case that time-use data are now collected routinely by central statistical offices in most European and other Western countries, and their work is often also supplemented by subjective time questions in these countries. The most comprehensive archive of multinational diary data and articles is located at the University of Oxford and can be accessed via its website www.timeuse.org. Table 8.1 below illustrates of the types of multinational output possible from this data archive (Gershuny 1990).

Objective Time

There are several ways of objectively measuring people's use of time and the time spent on various activities. The most common, until recently, was to ask them directly in the form of "stylized" time estimate questions, such as "How many hours did you spend working

J.P. Robinson (✉) • S. Martin
Department of Sociology, University of Maryland,
College Park, MD, USA
e-mail: robinson@socy.umd.edu

K.C. Land et al. (eds.), *Handbook of Social Indicators and Quality of Life Research*,
DOI 10.1007/978-94-007-2421-1_8, © Springer Science+Business Media B.V. 2012

at your job last week?" or "How many hours a day do you watch television?". These have the advantage of being simple, direct, and relatively inexpensive to ask, with respondents providing answers in a few seconds. Examples include time spent working (from the Current Population Survey (CPS 2011)), doing volunteer work, traveling, and watching television. Putnam (2000), for instance, drew on trends from several activities or time-estimate questions to support his argument about declining social capital in America. However, evidence described below indicates such time-estimate questions may not provide valid estimates of actual time spent (e.g., Chase and Godbey 1983), and when aggregated across all activities add up to more than the 168 h available (Hawes et al. 1975; Verbrugge and Gruber-Baldine 1993).

Other measurement methods involve more "observational" approaches, using clocks and stopwatches to quantify anthropologists' field notes (e.g., McSweeney 1980). Prominent examples in the US context include Levine's (1997) recording of walking speeds or time to conduct simple economic transactions at a bank or post office across different cities and countries, and Barker and Wright (1951) extremely detailed account of "One Boy's Day." A related method involves observations "on site," as in Hadaway et al.'s (1993) head counts of attendees at churches and Barker and Barker's (1961) head counts at various "behavior settings" in small towns. Television rating firms often verify program ratings by "telephone coincidental" surveys, asking those who answer what they were doing and what programs they were watching when the phone rang. Perhaps the most extensive and intensive example of time observation is from Holmes and Bloxham (2009), using observers who "shadow" respondents and electronically record their media and other daily activities every 10 s across the day.

Another holistic approach is the Experimental Sampling Method (ESM) pioneered by Csikszentmihalyi (1991) and his colleagues, in which participants report on their activities at 10–30 random moments during a day when alerted by an electronic beeper. This approach has the additional QOL advantage of asking beeped participants how they were feeling when the beeper went off. This provides the basis for Kubey and Csikszentmihalyi (1990) critique of the low QOL surrounding most TV viewing and for Csikszentmihalyi and Larsen (1984) insightful depiction of the complex emotional lives of teenagers. A limitation of the ESM technique is that it also has only been used with convenience samples with limited generalizability, and it is unlikely to achieve high cooperation rates from respondents in more typical survey settings. That is why it has not been used to generate population estimates of time use. That problem has been largely overcome in the major method reviewed and cited here, namely, the time diary.

Time-Diary Methodology

The time diary is a micro-behavioral technique for collecting self-reports of an individual's daily behavior in an open-ended fashion on an activity-by-activity basis. Individual respondents keep or report these activity accounts for a short, manageable period, such as a day or a week—usually across the full 24 h of a single day. In that way, the technique capitalizes on the most attractive measurement properties of the time variable, namely:

- All 24 h of daily activity is potentially recorded, including activities in the early morning hours, when few respondents are awake.
- The 1,440 min of the day is equally distributed across respondents, thereby preserving the "zero sum" property of time that allows various trade-offs between activities to be examined—that is, if time on one activity increases, it must be zeroed out by decreases in some other activity.
  - Respondents are allowed to use a time frame and an accounting variable that is highly familiar and understandable to them and accessible to the way they probably store their daily events in memory.

The open-ended nature of activity reporting means that these activity reports are automatically geared to detecting new and unanticipated activities (for example, in past decades, new activity codes had to be developed to accommodate aerobic exercises, use of E-mail, I-pods, and other new communications technologies).

The measurement logic behind the time-diary approach follows that employed in the first American diary study, done as part of the most extensive and well-known of diary studies—the 1965 Multinational Time Budget Study of Szalai (1972). In that study, about 2000 respondents aged 19–65 in urban employed households from each of 12 different countries kept a diary account of a single day. The same diary procedures and activity codes were employed in each country. Respondents were chosen in such a way that each day

8 Time Use as a Social Indicator   161

Fig. 8.1 Time diary question wording

	Next, I would like to ask you about the things you did yesterday. I want to know only the specific things you did yesterday, not the things you usually do. Let's start at midnight [fill day of week before diary day], that is, the night before last.
Q1)	What were you doing [fill in day of week before diary day] at midnight?
	***If person reported traveling, ask question Q2B
Q2A)	Where were you?
Q2B)	How were you traveling?
Q3)	What time did you finish?
Q4)	At any time while you were (REPEAT ACTIVITY) did you do anything else? (like talking, reading, watching tv, listening to the radio, eating, or caring for children)
Q5)	While you were (REPEAT ACTIVITY) who was with you?
Q6)	What did you do next?

Source: CATI Transcript, 1998-99 Family Interaction, Social Capital, and Trends in Time Use Study.

of the week was equivalently represented, but usually only in one season (mainly the fall of 1965); in subsequent US studies, all seasons of the year were covered as well (Robinson and Godbey 1999).

In each of the US time-diary studies, a standard series of questions has been used by sequentially "walking" respondents through a 24-h period. Question wording from one recent diary study is shown in Fig. 8.1. Starting at some point in the diary day (usually midnight or 4 a.m. of the diary day), the respondent is asked "What were you doing?" (Q1). Responses to this query are commonly known as "primary" activities because they are thought to be the most salient or determining activity for respondents at the time. Respondents are also asked, "Did you do anything else?" (Q4) at the same time you did each "primary activity." These "anything else" reports are referred to as "secondary" activities because they capture time spent in simultaneous "multitasking" activities that are presumably not the major focus of attention (Scheuch 1972). For example, respondents might report getting a child dressed for school (primary activity) while also listening to the radio (secondary). Respondents also

report the location of each (primary) activity (Q2A) and identify the other people present during the activity (Q5). Figure 8.2 shows the diary entries for one respondent in this study, an employed married woman aged 43 with two children under age 18, who completed her diary in late June. As the recounting of her day began at midnight, she was working for the subsequent 20 min (until 12:20 a.m.). She then drove home, which took 40 min, where she watched half an hour of TV (while also engaged in cleaning up her home), followed by 45 min of dishwashing. She went to sleep at 2:15 a.m. and got up at 7:45 a.m., whereupon she drank coffee and then got her 16-year-old son out of bed.

She ate lunch at noon, and subsequently did another hour and a half of house cleaning and dusting, and watched another half hour of TV. That was followed by an hour of bill paying and another hour of TV viewing. She then took a half hour each for showering and for dressing, prior to an hour's dinner with her husband and children. At that point (6:30 p.m.), she drove back to work, where she worked again until midnight.

Totaling up her day, she put in 6.5 h of paid work and 6.3 h of housework. Getting her children up took

Married woman, aged 43, with two children < age 18 (diary completed on a Thursday in June)					
What did you do?	**Time Began**	**Time Ended**	**Where Were You:**	**With Whom?**	**Doing Anything Else?**
Working	Midnight	12:20	Work	Coworker (s)	No
Traveling home from work	12:20	1:00	Car	—	Listening to the radio
Watching TV	1:00	1:30	Home	—	Cleaning house
Washing dishes	1:30	2:15	Home	—	No
Sleeping	2:15	7:45	Home	—	No
Drinking coffee	7:45	8:15	Home	Spouse	Talking
Woke 16-year old son up	8:15	8:30	Home	Children	No
Washing clothes	8:30	11:00	Home	Children	Additional clothes care
Watching TV	11:00	11:30	Home	—	Additional clothes care
Woke 14-year old daughter up	11:30	12:00	Home	Children	Watching TV
Eat lunch	12:00	12:30	Home	Children	Watching TV
Cleaned up and dusted	12:30	2:00	Home	—	Clothes care
Watching TV	2:00	2:30	Home	Children	No
Paid bills	2:30	3:30	Home	—	Watching TV
Watching TV	3:30	4:30	Home	—	Clothes care
Bathing/showering	4:30	5:00	Home	—	No
Dressing	5:00	5:30	Home	Children	Watching TV
Eating dinner	5:30	6:30	Home	Spouse, Children	Talking
Traveling to work	6:30	7:00	Car	—	Listening to the radio
Working	7:00	Midnight	Work	Coworker(s)	Visiting and socializing

Source: 2000 National Survey of Parents.

Fig. 8.2 Sample of completed time diary

another 0.8 h. She spent only 5.5 h sleeping, 1.5 h eating, and an hour grooming. She watched 2.5 h of TV, which was her only free time during the day. She was on the road for 1.2 h and at her workplace for 6.5 h, and she spent the remaining 16.3 h of the day at home, mostly with her children when she was not alone.

The task of keeping the diary may create some recall difficulties, but is fundamentally different from the task of making long-term time estimates. The diary keeper's task is to recall one day's activities in sequence, which should be similar to the way the day was structured chronologically for the respondent and to the way most people store their activities in memory. Rather than having to consider a long time period, the respondent needs to focus attention only on a single day (yesterday). Rather than working from some list of activities whose meanings vary from one respondent to another, respondents simply describe their day's activities in their own words.

The diary technique also presents respondents with a task that gives them little opportunity to distort activities in order to present themselves in a particular light. They are given few clues about a study's interest in one activity or another, because the diary is simply intended as a complete record of any and all activities on that day. Some respondents may wish to portray themselves as hard workers or light television viewers, but in order to do so, they must also fabricate the activities that precede and follow the one they want to misreport. Further, it is only a one-day account, and on any given day respondents probably realize that they may work less or watch television more than usual. Moreover, respondents are not pressured to report an activity if they cannot recall it or do not wish to report it.

Automatic procedures can be built into the diary recording procedures conducted by Computer Assisted Telephone Interviewing (CATI) to facilitate complete and reliable reporting. Whenever respondents report consecutive activities that involve different locations, for example, they can be reminded that there needs to be some travel episode to connect them. Activity periods that last more than 2 hours automatically involve the probe "Were you doing anything else during that time or were you doing (*activity*) for the entire time?" Moreover, all periods across the day must be accounted for, in order that the diary account does total to all 1,440 min of the day (across the 24 h).

Activity Coding: The largely open-ended diary reports are coded using a basic activity coding scheme like that developed for the 1965 Multinational Time Budget Research Project (by Szalai 1972). As shown in outline form in Fig. 8.3, the Szalai code first divides activities into non free-time activities (codes 00–54,59) and free-time activities (codes 55–58, 60–99); non free-time activities are further subdivided into paid work (including commuting, which is usually referred to as "contracted time" in the time-diary literature), into three categories of family care (housework, childcare, and obtaining goods and services, or unpaid work that is often referred to as "committed time" in the literature), the three basic aspects of personal care (sleeping, eating, and grooming), and educational activities. The remaining free-time activities are coded under the five general headings of (1) information seeking (including the Internet), (2) organizational activity, (3) entertainment and socializing, (4) recreation, and (5) communications. The main value of the open-ended diary approach is that activities can be recorded or recombined, depending on the analyst's unique assumptions or purposes.

Activity categories are typically coded in minutes per day and then converted into hours per week after ensuring that all days of the week were equally represented. In other words, the sampling units are person-days rather than persons, since the latter were only interviewed about a single day's activities. The diary data in these studies were weighted by demographic variables to match the March Current Population Survey characteristics on gender, age, education, employment status, and the like and to provide equal representation of all 7 days of the week.

The Szalai code has several attractive features. First, it has been tested, found to be reliable, and has been used in several countries around the world. Second, and because of this, extensive prior national normative data are available for comparison purposes. Third, it can be easily adapted to include new code categories of interest to researchers who are looking into different scientific questions from various disciplines. The location coding can be aggregated to estimate time spent in travel, outdoors, or at home, all important parameters for analyzing time-use trends.

Moreover, the ten main headings can also be conveniently split into the four "super categories" identified by Aas (1978):

1. Paid "contracted" work (codes 01–09)
2. Unpaid "committed" work (10–19,20–29,30–39)
3. Personal care (40–49)
4. Free time (codes 60–69,70–79,80–89,90–99)

Under nine of these ten main headings in Fig. 8.3, there is a second_9 code to capture the travel associated with each category, so that it can be added together to total all travel during the day. It can also be added to the activity group (shopping, socializing) to give a fuller measure of the total time spent for that purpose.

When aggregated, then, activity-diary data have been used to provide generalizable national estimates of the full range of alternative daily activities in a society, from *contracted* paid work time for an employer, to the *committed* time for unpaid housework and family caregiving, to *personal* care for body and mind, and to all the types of activities that take place in *free* time. The multiple uses and perspectives afforded by time-diary data have led to a recent proliferation of research and literature in this field. Comparable national time-diary data have been collected in more than 40 countries over the last two decades, including virtually all Eastern and Western European countries. In the USA, the first national diary study was conducted in 1965, and it has then been replicated every decade in 1975, 1985, 1995, and 1998–2001. Since 2003, the American Time-Use Survey (ATUS 2011) has been collecting diary data continuously by US Census Bureau for the Bureau of Labor Statistics (BLS)—with samples of more than 12,000 respondents per year leading to an overall sample base of more than 100,000 respondents since 2003. The ATUS has expanded the list of activity categories to more than 400.

00-49 Nonfree Time

00-09 Paid Work
00	(Not Used)
01	Main Job
02	Unemployment
03	(Not Used)
04	(Not Used)
05	Second Job
06	Eating at work
07	Before/after work
08	Breaks
09	Travel/to-from work

10-19 Household Work
10	Food Preparation
11	Meal Cleanup
12	Cleaning House
13	Outdoor Cleaning
14	Clothes Care
15	Car repair
16	Other Repairs
17	Plant care, gardening
18	Pet care
19	Other Household

20-29 Child Care
20	Baby care
21	Child care
22	Helping/teaching
23	Talking/reading
24	Indoor playing
25	Outdoor playing
26	Medical care-child
27	Other child care
28	(Not used)
29	Travel/child care

30-39 Obtaining Goods/Services
30	Everyday (food) shopping
31	Durable/house shop
32	Personal services
33	Medical appointments
34	Govt/financial services
35	Repair services
36	(Not Used)
37	Other services
38	Errands
39	Travel/goods and services

40-49 Personal Needs and Care
40	Washing, hygiene, etc.
41	Medical care
42	Help and care to others
43	Meals at home
44	Meals out
45	Night sleep
46	Naps/day sleep
47	Dressing/grooming etc.
48	Private, no report (sex)
49	Travel/Personal care

50-99 Free Time

50-59 Educational
50	Students classes
51	Other classes
52	Homework
_53_	**Internet (WWW) us**_e_
54	Library use
55	Other education
56	**Email/IM**
57	**Computer games**
58	**Other computer use**
59	Travel/education

60-69 Organizational
60	Professsional/Union
61	Special interest
62	Political/civic
63	Volunteer helping
64	Religious groups
65	Religious practice
66	Fraternal
67	Child/youth/family
68	Other organizations
69	Travel/organizational

70-79 Entertainment/social
70	Sports events
71	Entertainment
72	Movies (not videos)
73	Theater
74	Museums
75	Visiting
76	Parties
77	Bars/lounges
78	Telephone/Cell phone
79	Travel/social

80-89 Recreation
80	Active Sports
81	Outdoor
82	Walking/hiking
83	Hobbies
84	Domestic crafts
85	Art
86	Music/drama/dance
87	Games
88	Other recreation
89	Travel/recreation

90-99 Communications
90	Radio
91	TV + videos
92	Records/tapes
93	Read Books
94	Read Magazines/etc
95	Reading newspaper
96	Conversations (face-to-face)
97	Writing letters
98	Think/relax
99	Travel/communication

Fig. 8.3 The Szalai 1966 two-digit activity code (updated)

Methodological Evidence on the Accuracy of Time Diaries

Two important properties of social-science measures are reliability and validity. Reliability refers to the ability of a measurement instrument to provide consistent results from study to study or under different conditions (telephone vs. mail; open code vs. closed code); that is, do we get similar results using the same diary approach? Validity refers to the ability of an instrument to provide data that agree with estimates provided by other methods (such as observation or beepers).

Reliability

Estimates from time diaries have been found to produce reliable and replicable results at the aggregate level. For example, Robinson (1977) found a 95 correlation between time-use patterns found in the 1965 national time diaries ($n=1,244$) and the aggregate figures for the single site of Jackson, Michigan ($n=788$). Similar high correspondence was found for the American data and for time-diary data from Canada, both in 1971 and in 1982 (Harvey and Elliot 1983).

Reliability was also noted using different diary approaches. Thus, a correlation of .85 was found between time expenditure patterns found in the 1965–1966 US Jackson time study using the "tomorrow approach" (in which respondents filled out their diary for the following day), and time expenditures for a random one-tenth of the sample, who also filled out a "yesterday diary" (a diary for the previous day). This indicates that respondent yesterday diaries, which can be obtained in a single interview, generate the same basic figures as the more expensive tomorrow diary, which requires another visit by the interviewer. In a smaller replication study in Jackson (MI) in 1973, an aggregate correlation of .88 was obtained between these same measures (Robinson 1977), another indicator that not much daily activity is missed in either diary approach.

Further support for the reliability of the diaries comes from convergent time figures obtained from the telephone, mail-back, and personal interviews in the 1985 national study; and from the overall national results and those obtained in 1986 in Jackson, Michigan, in 1987–1988 in California, and in 1986 and 1992 in Canada (Robinson and Godbey 1999, Appendices A, B and C)

Validity

Almost all diary studies depend on the self-report method rather than on some form of observation. Thus, questions arise about the accuracy of the diaries. Several studies bear directly on the validity of the time diary, in the sense of there being an independent source or quasi-observer of reported behavior.

The first of these studies involved the low TV viewing figure from the 1965 time diaries relative to standard television rating-service figures. In a small-scale study (Bechtel et al. 1972), the television-viewing behavior of a sample of 20 households was monitored over a week's time by means of a video camera. The camera was mounted on top of that set, thus allowing the video camera/microphone to record all the behavior that took place in front of the television screen. The results indicated that both rating-service methods of television exposure (the Nielsen audimeters, which electronically measured the TV channel the set is tuned to, and the paper-and-pencil viewing diaries) produced estimates of viewing that were 20–50% higher than primary or secondary viewing activities reported in time diaries or observed by the camera (Allen 1968).

Three more general validity studies examined the full range of activities, not just television viewing, and employed larger and more representative samples. A 1973 random sample of 60 residents of Ann Arbor and Jackson, Michigan kept beepers for a 1-day period and reported their activity whenever the beeper was activated (some 30–40 times across the day). Averaged across all 60 respondents (and across waking hours of the day), the correlation of activity durations from the beeper and from the diaries was .81 for the Ann Arbor sample and .68 for the Jackson sample (Robinson 1985). In a second study, a telephone sample of 249 respondents interviewed as part of a 1973 national panel survey were asked to report their activities for a designated particular "random hour" during the previous day—with no hint from the interviewer about what they had previously reported for that hour in their diary. An overall correlation of .81 was found between the two aggregate sets of data—that is, between the activities reported in the random hours and in the diary entries for those same random hours (Robinson 1985). In a third study, Juster (1985) compared the "with whom" reports in the 1975–1976 diaries of respondents with those of their spouses across the same day. Juster found more than 80% agreement between these independently obtained husband and wife diaries about the presence or absence of their spouse during daily activities, and in a separate analysis, a .92 correlation between time spent on various home energy-related activities and aggregate time-of-day patterns of energy use measured by household utility meters.

More recently, some preliminary studies using the "shadow" technique have been conducted with student samples. The students shadow someone they know across an 8–12-h period of the waking day, recording all the things each person did during that observation period. The next day, that student then asks the shadowed person for an unrehearsed account of the same activities. Although the samples so far have been very small and highly unrepresentative, with some highly variable individual reporting, agreement at the aggregate level on most activities across the day is ±10%. While some respondents have difficulty recalling their activities, people who overestimate, say housework, seem to be balanced out by those who underestimate housework. In other words, there do not seem to be activities that are systematically overestimated or underestimated, despite these individual errors in recall. As noted above, far more sophisticated "shadow" studies of nonstudent populations are being collected by Holmes and Bloxham (2009).

Methodological studies in other countries further attest to the basic generalizability of time-diary data (e.g., Gershuny 2000; Michelson 1978). Nonetheless, further careful and well-controlled methodological studies need to be conducted to provide more definitive evidence on diary measurement properties.

Diary-Estimate Comparisons

Given the extensive prior reliance on time-estimate questions ("How many hours did you spend _____?") prior to the greater availability of diary data, the question arises about how well the two compare on a side-by-side basis. There are seven activities in particular on which extensive estimate questions are available for the USA:

1. *Work*: Like their counterpart government agencies in most Western countries, the US Bureau of Labor Statistics (BLS) has been regularly collecting data on estimated work hours from very large national samples of workers. Robinson and Bostrom (1994) reported that BLS estimated work hours were a little higher than work hours reported in time diaries, particularly for those workers estimating longer work hours. Robinson and Gershuny (1994) replicated these findings for 12 other Western countries. Jacobs (1998) argued that these differences could be explained by the well-known phenomenon of "regression to the mean," as did Frazis and Stewart (2004). The debate continues in (Robinson et al. 2011).

2. *Housework*: Marini and Shelton (1993) and Press and Townsley (1998) both reported that housework time estimates from the National Survey of Families and Households (NSFH) were considerably higher than those reported in separate time-diary studies. Bianchi et al. (2006) replicated these results for men and women in a national survey that collected diary and estimate questions from the same respondents, allowing direct comparisons on detailed housework activities (e.g., cooking, cleaning). For each activity, the estimates were more than 50% higher than the diaries, even after "multitasking" was included. Again, the discrepancy was higher the higher the respondents' housework estimates.

3. *Sleep*: The National Sleep Foundation (2007) reported Americans estimating they obtained less than 7 h of sleep per day, even lower than what they reported in their 2002 survey. In contrast, diary studies find sleep hours closer to 8 h per day (for those aged 18–64), going back to the first diary study in the 1960s. The result has been replicated in Canada as well as other Western countries (Michelson and Robinson 2010).

4. *Free Time*: Harris (1987) reported that Americans estimated they had only 17 h of free time per week compared to 26 h in the 1960s, although Hamilton (1991) noted the wording of his question had changed. Nonetheless, other surveys have also found estimates of less than 20 h, while the free time as measured in time diaries consistently totals more than 35 h per week (Robinson and Godbey 2005; Aguiar and Hurst 2009; Bureau of Labor Statistics 2011).

5. *Television*: The major free-time activity by all time-diary accounts is television viewing, which according to the latest Bureau of Labor Statistics (2011) ATUS data averages about 16 weekly hours. If one were to add in the approximately 5 diary hours of viewing as a secondary activity, that would add to 21 h per week, which is almost exactly the figure that is implied by General Social Survey (GSS) respondents, who, since 1972, have consistently

estimated that they watch 3 h per day. (Both figures are only about half as high as the 35 weekly hours as reported by Nielsen (1999), the TV industry's main rating service.)

6. *Religion*: Diary, as well as observational studies (Hadaway et al. 1993), suggest that attendance at religious services is over-reported in traditional survey-estimate questions, such as asked in the General Social Survey (Presser and Stinson 1998).

7. *Volunteering*: The Bureau of Labor Statistics (2011) ATUS figures put formal volunteering at about 1 h per week, which is quite close to the figure generated in their separate estimate survey (Bureau of Labor Statistics 2009). Earlier surveys by the Gallup organization put the figure at closer to 1.8–2.4 h per week (Independent Sector 2001).

Taken together then, these diary-estimate comparisons suggest a familiar pattern to survey methodologists, one of "social desirability." In America, as well as other societies, where keeping busy is a "badge of honor" (Social Research 2005), one might expect survey respondents to self-report higher levels of their work, housework, religious attendance and volunteering hours (for the Gallup questions) and to underestimate their sleep and free time. The case of TV (and volunteering for the two BLS studies) provides notable exceptions. More detailed evidence will also be needed to examine this hypothesis more definitively.

Sample Bias

One of the controversies surrounding time-diary data collections is whether certain types of individuals (e.g., busy people) fail to respond to the diary. This is part of a larger debate about the validity of estimates of time use from the diary and disputed claims about whether Americans are working more (e.g., Schor 1991) or less (Robinson and Godbey 1999; Aguiar and Hurst 2009). There is a small methodological literature on this issues, which includes comparisons with CPS estimates, but again what is needed are studies involving more direct observational or work diaries to compare with workweek estimates. Gershuny (2000) has recently noted that participating in a time-diary survey requires more time and effort of respondents compared to participation in other types of surveys, and time-diary surveys in general have higher nonresponse rates than other survey types. Consequently, the issue

of nonresponse bias is a potential problem because it is possible that busy individuals may opt out of participation in a time-diary survey, especially one that requires completion of a weekly time diary. However, based on a detailed comparison of participation rates in 19 activities for individuals from a 1987 survey who elected to participate in a weekly time-diary survey, and individuals from the same survey who elected not to participate in the weekly time-diary survey, Gershuny (2000: 268) concludes that nonresponse was not associated with an individual's activity patterns, "in particular the general state of busyness or otherwise—of sampled individuals." Along the same line is Abraham et al. (2006) finding that ATUS diary keepers did not differ markedly from non-keepers on various demographic factors obtained earlier from both groups.

Earlier Diary Surveys in the United States: There have been roughly decade-interval (1965, 1975, 1985, 1992–1995, 1998–2001) national time-diary surveys by academic survey firms from which to make trend comparisons with the current American Time-Use Survey (ATUS 2011). The ATUS has also collected its "yesterday" diaries, based on the recall of what respondents did the previous day.

1965 US Time-Use Study: In the fall of 1965, as part of a multinational time-use study, the University of Michigan Survey Research Center (SRC) surveyed 1,244 adult respondents, ages 18–64, who kept a single-day "tomorrow" diary in the fall of 1965 (and Spring of 1966). The interviewer visited respondents and explained the procedure then left the diary to be filled out for the following day. The interviewer then returned on the day after the "diary day" to collect the completed diary.

1975 US Time-Use Survey: In the fall of 1975, the SRC personally surveyed 1,519 adult respondents and 887 of their spouses, who provided retrospective "yesterday" diaries. These respondents were subsequently reinterviewed across the winter, spring, and summer months of 1976, mainly by telephone.

1985 US Time-Use Survey: In 1985, the University of Maryland SRC collected single-day diaries from more than 5,300 respondents across the year employing the same basic open-ended diary approach as the 1965 and 1975 studies, using personal, telephone, and mail-back diaries for either yesterday or tomorrow.

1990s *US Time-Diary Collections*: Two national diary studies were conducted by the Maryland SRC by national random digit dial telephone procedures, one between 1992 and 1994 with 9,386 respondents and the second one in 1995 with 1,200 respondents. All interviews in both phases used the retrospective diary (or yesterday) method for the previous day. Two further yesterday studies were conducted by the University of Maryland, one in 1998 ($n=1,200$) and the other in 1999–2001 ($n=978$), in addition to the Sloan Foundation's National Survey of Parents ($n=1,200$) in 2000 (Bianchi et al. 2006).

2003–present *Bureau of Labor Statistic's ATUS*: The Bureau of Labor Statistics has now collected over 100,000 daily diaries continuously across the year since 2003, using the telephone yesterday method with a CPS sample and a more detailed set of activity categories, as described at www.bls/tus.gov and archived at www.atus-x.

A detailed comparison of the methods and results of these US time-series data can be found in Fisher et al. (2007). Parallel data from more than 30 other countries can be found at www.timeuse.org.

Trends and Patterns in Time Use

Robinson and Godbey (1999) provide a list of the 22 main uses of time recorded in prior research and a standard set of predictor variables used in studies of time use. In most studies, the activities or uses of time (such as work or TV viewing) are dependent variables— or the behavior to be predicted—whereas the demographic characteristics (such as gender and marital status) are the independent variables (the factors that predict activity). Researchers are interested in assessing the extent to which the six categories of background factors can predict the four major types of time: *contracted* (paid work) time, *committed* (family care) time (mainly divided into core housework and cleaning, childcare, and shopping), *personal care* (sleeping, eating, and grooming), and the remaining activities that comprise *free time* (dominated by TV viewing, which takes up almost half of that free time).

The predictor variables can be grouped into six categories:

1. Birth factors: The factors one is born with (e.g., gender, race, and age).

2. Status factors: The factors that reflect one's social status or standing (e.g., education, income, and occupation).
3. Role factors: The various roles one undertakes and performs (e.g., as an employee, spouse, or parent).
4. Location factors: The effects of where one lives (e.g., by region, living in urban vs. rural areas, type of housing).
5. Temporal factors: The year, season, or day of the week of the diary.
6. Geo-cultural factors: Such as the country lived in or access to technology.

Variations by these six sets of factors demonstrate the ways that time use is powerfully shaped by factors such as life course stage, gender, and access to social and economic resources.

In terms of the main *trends* in US time use since 1965 (the "year" variable), most notable overall activity *increases* are found in childcare, TV viewing, and fitness activities. The most notable *decreases* are found in paid work for men, housework for women (men's housework, by contrast, has nearly doubled), eating, and reading (mainly of newspapers). The main shifts in housework occurred between 1965 and 1975 (Gershuny and Robinson 1998; Bianchi et al. 2000).

There is little evidence in these diaries of other expected changes—even those considered to be "common knowledge," such as historical increases in average paid work hours or decreases in free time, childcare, social visiting, relaxing, or (non-newspaper) reading— or of age per se as a major predictor of time.

Among some key findings by demographic background obtained by time-use researchers for *birth factors* are:

1. *Gender*: The largest shift here is the above-noted activity of housework, whereby men's share increased from 15% in 1965 to about 35% today (with the notable exception of laundry). This is part of a larger picture of increased "gender convergence" and "time androgyny," in that women are doing more of the activities that men dominated before, primarily for paid work but also for the former "male" activities of education, TV viewing, and fitness activity (Fisher et al. 2006; Robinson and Godbey 1999). In contrast, the gender gap in childcare, grooming, reading, and hobbies has declined.
2. *Age*: Between the ages of 18 and 64, the main age differences are predicted by role factors, such as those due to the increase in housework and childcare

that accompany marriage and parenthood. Thus, people over the age of 64 spend more time sleeping, but that is because so few of them are working. One major age shift is the decline in paid work time by those ages 55–64, many of whom are taking early retirement. Another is that those under age 30 are going to college in greater numbers today than in the past.

3. *Race*: Since 1965, Blacks have consistently spent more time in grooming, religion, and TV viewing, whereas Whites spend more time in housework, reading, and visiting. Thus, there is little closing of the race gap to parallel the closing of the gender gap. Moreover, the above differences by race are not explained by education or other demographic differences between the races.

In terms of the three main indicators of one's *social status*:

4. *Education*: There is an increasing tendency for a greater number of work hours and less sleep for the college educated, along with higher figures for reading and attending social events (such as the arts or sporting events). By far the most dramatic educational difference is for lower levels of TV viewing among the college educated; the amount of time college-educated people spend watching TV is about half of that for those with less than a high school degree (Robinson and Godbey 1999).

5. *Income*: Differences by income parallel those for education and are often simply a function of education.

6. *Occupation*: Differences by occupation are also largely confounded with education, but Robinson and Gershuny (2009) have taken advantage of the detailed ATUS occupation codes to identify several occupation differences that are not explained by the above two status factors—such as the higher time reading and attending arts events by teachers and lawyers, and the higher TV times by construction workers.

In terms of the three main *role* factors:

7. *Employment*: Whether one is currently employed is probably the most significant predictor of time use, particularly as work hours increase. Sleep is the major activity affected; housework and childcare are cut by a third, and TV viewing decreases dramatically as well.

8. *Marriage*: Getting married also reduces most free-time activities, mainly due to increased housework and other family-care activities (but more for wives than for husbands).

9. *Parenthood*: Surprisingly, having children has less time effect than getting married, but it still means more housework and shopping and less free time and TV viewing for mothers (Bianchi et al. 2006).

Locational and seasonal predictors seem to have much less impact than those above, and those that are found tend be a function of them, such as higher TV viewing in the South due to lower education levels there. Few notable regional differences emerge, nor is there much evidence of a more hectic lifestyle in more urban areas. Outside of less housework among dwellers of apartments or trailers, housing type has little relation to ways of spending time.

Likewise, little effect of seasonal differences is found, much as for regional differences that may reflect climatic/weather differences. There are major and obvious differences by day of the week, with weekends meaning decreased work and more time for sleep and TV.

Another primary factor linked to time use is technology. Although the development of "time-saving" appliances in the twentieth century might lead one to believe that time use has changed as a result, the few time studies conducted to date suggest that consumers seem to use their "hassle-saving" features instead— that is, to increase outputs from the technology rather than to save time (Robinson and Godbey 1999; Morgan et al. 1965). The major exception is television, which has truly revolutionized time, mainly away from other media like radio, movies, and newspapers, but also from socializing, hobbies, and sleep (Robinson and Godbey 1999). The temporal impact of the Internet is dwarfed by comparison with TV, and it does not appear to have replaced particular other activities (Robinson and Martin 2009).

Cross-National Results

Finally, multinational research reveals surprising convergences across most of the more than 30 countries studied (some identified below), although most of them are developed, Western societies in Europe (which can afford to conduct expensive time-diary surveys). For example, Bittman (2000) found similar increases in free time since the 1960s in other countries, much as in the United States. In an analysis of all productive activity (contracted and committed time together) in

Table 8.1 Average weekly hours for whole population: age 18–64 (from Fisher and Robinson 2011)

| Population aged 18–64 | Oceania, North/South America | | | | Central Europe | | | | |
Hours per week	Australia	Brazil	Canada	USA	Belgium	France	Germany	Nethlnd	UK
Paid work (away from home)	26.1	25.8	28.7	28.6	18.8	22.1	20.4	18.7	23.0
Paid work at home	2.0	2.6	NA	1.6	1.1	1.3	1.2	1.1	2.1
Study and job or skill training	0.7	2.1	1.0	1.1	2.0	1.9	1.6	1.6	0.9
Homework	0.9	1.2	1.2	0.9	1.2	1.2	0.7	0.9	0.4
Commuting, job/study/travel	3.2	5.8	3.0	2.5	3.2	2.8	3.0	2.8	3.2
Cooking and food related	6.1	5.0	4.7	3.5	5.8	6.0	4.9	6.4	6.0
All other housework/repairs, garden	7.2	6.2	8.9	7.8	8.8	7.9	8.4	7.1	6.9
Shop, service, other domestic	4.6	3.2	3.6	3.7	4.2	4.7	4.8	4.3	4.8
Housework/personal care travel	2.7	1.4	2.4	4.3	1.5	0.1	2.5	2.1	2.2
Physical/medical child care	2.2	1.4	1.9	2.0	1.3	1.9	1.3	2.1	2.3
Interactive/other child care	3.2	0.7	1.0	2.0	0.7	0.9	0.9	1.9	1.4
Child care-related travel	0.8	0.5	0.6	0.6	0.4	0.5	0.4	0.7	0.9
Petcare	0.6	0.1	0.5	0.4	0.4	0.6	0.4	1.2	0.4
Organisational/voluntary activity	1.3	3.2	3.2	3.6	0.8	1.3	2.2	3.2	1.5
Sleep and naps	58.7	56.4	58.4	58.6	58.3	61.1	57.3	59.5	58.8
Wash, dress, other personal care	6.2	7.2	4.5	5.6	5.1	5.0	6.1	6.1	5.4
Meals (at home/pack lunch)	6.7	7.1	6.8	5.8	11.0	12.4	10.9	9.0	8.8
Walking (including walking dogs)	0.7	0.7	0.6	0.5	1.8	1.9	1.9	NA	1.9
Sports and other exercises	1.9	0.9	2.5	1.6	1.5	1.1	1.6	1.8	1.3
Restaurants, bar, pub, café	1.3	2.6	2.3	1.8	1.5	3.2	0.8	1.9	1.1
Party, visits socialise away	2.2	2.4	1.5	0.5	4.4	3.2	4.6	8.2	5.3
Party, visits socialise at home	0.4	2.9	4.0	6.1	2.5	1.8	3.3	2.9	1.9
Leisure away from home	2.5	0.6	3.5	1.1	1.3	1.4	1.6	1.1	0.9
Other travel	2.0	2.0	1.0	2.2	5.0	3.6	4.2	3.0	3.3
Relax, do nothing	1.5	1.6	1.9	1.9	3.0	0.7	1.8	1.4	2.2
Computing/internet (games)	0.4	0.5	1.7	1.2	2.8	0.6	2.0	1.8	1.2
Television	12.3	14.3	13.6	15.4	15.4	13.2	12.1	8.1	15.6
Radio, Ipod, other audio	2.3	0.4	2.1	0.7	0.5	0.4	0.6	4.0	0.7
Read	2.2	0.7	0.2	1.9	2.5	2.2	3.9	3.7	2.5
Other leisure and hobbies	4.6	1.3	2.2	0.3	1.1	3.0	2.2	1.4	0.7
Unrecorded time	0.5	5.8	0.2	0.1	0.1	NA	0.4	0.0	0.4
Free time	34.8	NA	37.3	35.3	43.4	36.3	41	39.3	39
Total	168	168	168	168	168	168	168	168	168

NA no data available

12 countries, Goldschmidt-Claremont (1995) found the same basic equality of men and women in overall hours spent on such activities. Another study found the same pattern of increased father childcare across six Western countries since 1990 (France being a notable exception), much as was reported in a 2004 study (Gauthier et al. 2004) for many other countries over this period. Robinson and Godbey (1999) found many similarities in both the trends and predictors of time use in Japan, Russia, and Canada. Gershuny (2000) has extended these results to more than 15 other countries.

These national differences are summarized for 23 countries from the Oxford University archive in Table 8.1 to illustrate the extent to which multinational cooperation and comparisons and opportunities are now possible (Fisher and Robinson 2011). A simplified way of summarizing these multinational data is provided by the Multidimensional Scaling (MDS) program in SPSS (Arthur 2004) in Fig. 8.4. Here, it can be seen that the Table 8.1 time-use differences indicate a notable stamp of geographical and cultural similarities on daily life, much as Converse (1972:150) concluded

Northern Europe/Nordic			Eastern Europe						South Europe/Mediterranean			Asia	
Finland	Norway	Sweden	Bulgaria	Estonia	Latvia	Lithuania	Poland	Sloven	Italy	Spain	Turkey	Japan	Korea
22.2	24.5	26.7	23.7	27.1	29.3	24.9	20.1	23.6	23.6	24.6	20.8	32.2	26.0
2.1	1.2	1.2	0.2	1.5	2.6	5.6	3.5	1.1	0.5	0.7	NA	1.9	0.2
1.8	1.4	1.4	0.6	1.1	1.9	2.0	2.0	1.5	1.1	2.0	2.8	4.1	2.0
0.7	0.8	0.7	0.5	0.5	0.7	0.7	1.3	1.6	1.4	1.2	NA	1.1	0.4
2.5	3.2	2.9	2.8	3.3	4.3	3.4	2.9	2.9	3.5	3.6	NA	4.7	6.0
5.1	5.6	5.8	8.6	7.4	5.7	7.0	8.2	7.2	7.1	7.1	8.9	5.7	5.8
7.7	6.3	6.8	11.6	9.5	7.7	9.6	8.1	11.9	8.9	6.7	7.5	6.0	6.4
3.9	4.1	4.2	1.8	3.5	2.6	2.0	2.9	2.5	3.6	4.3	1.6	3.0	3.9
1.8	1.6	2.2	1.9	2.1	2.5	2.2	2.1	1.9	1.8	1.3	NA	1.4	1.8
1.9	2.3	2.0	1.1	0.0	1.1	1.4	1.8	1.4	1.5	2.1	3.4	0.8	1.5
0.8	0.8	0.9	1.1	0.9	0.6	0.8	1.6	1.1	1.2	0.6	NA	1.1	1.3
0.2	0.4	0.6	0.1	0.2	0.2	0.1	0.2	0.2	0.5	0.6	NA	0.4	0.6
0.4	0.1	0.2	0.1	0.2	0.1	0.1	0.2	0.2	0.1	0.1	NA	0.1	NA
2.0	1.5	1.6	1.1	1.8	1.4	1.9	2.9	1.4	1.8	1.4	4.4	0.6	1.7
59.0	56.2	56.4	62.4	59.5	59.9	58.9	58.7	58.1	57.3	59.0	59.3	53.7	54.4
4.9	5.5	5.3	4.4	6.2	4.7	6.4	6.1	4.7	7.1	5.6	18.8	7.7	8.8
8.4	8.5	10.3	12.6	8.4	9.8	10	10.4	9.6	11.7	11.3	NA	13.1	11.6
2.0	1.8	2.0	2.1	1.6	1.9	1.2	2.1	2.5	2.3	3.9	NA	2.1	1.4
2.3	2.1	2.0	0.9	1.1	1.5	1.1	1.1	1.6	1.3	1.3	0.8	0.0	1.4
0.7	0.9	0.4	1.8	0	0.5	0.1	0.2	0.6	1.5	0.9	NA	2.6	NA
3.7	5.6	4.1	2.6	2.3	2.7	2.5	3.4	4.1	4.6	5.1	0.4	0.0	3.5
2.6	6.5	3.2	1.9	1.4	1.4	1.5	2.8	2.9	1.9	1.4	8.3	0.0	1.4
0.7	0.9	0.7	0.1	0.6	0.7	0.2	0.4	0.6	0.7	0.8	NA	0.0	2.7
4.2	4.1	4.6	2.4	2.6	3.1	2.8	3.1	3.2	4.7	3.3	9.3	2.7	2.7
2.1	1.3	2.6	0.9	1.8	2.1	1.2	1.3	3.4	3.3	2.7	4.0	0.9	1.2
0.9	1.3	1.4	0.1	0.4	0.5	0.8	1.1	0.7	0.7	1.1	NA	1.2	2.8
14.7	12.6	11.9	16.6	15.4	13.8	15.3	15.3	13.2	10.6	12.0	13.8	13.9	14.6
0.9	0.7	0.5	0.5	0.7	0.5	0.6	0.9	0.6	0.4	0.4	0.5	0.9	0.2
4.9	3.7	3.3	2.0	4.1	2.8	2.5	2.6	2.5	2.0	1.6	1.3	2.0	1.8
1.8	2.1	1.6	1.3	1.3	1.0	0.9	0.5	1.0	1.0	1.1	2.1	3.5	1.9
1.1	0.4	0.5	0.2	1.5	0.4	0.3	0.2	0.2	0.3	0.2	NA	0.6	NA
42.6	44	38.8	33.4	34.8	32.9	31	35	37.1	35.3	35.8	NA	30.4	35.6
168	168	168	168	168	168	168	168	168	168	168	168	168	168

in his earlier application of MDS to 1965 multinational diary data:

> All that entered the computer were 455 proportions indicating how people at 15 anonymous sites distributed their 24-h day across 37 disparate and unidentified activity categories. It is remarkable that statistical compression of these raw data yields anything resembling a physical map.

The more than 10 h a week in TV viewing in most countries in Table 8.1 also reinforces the conclusion that TV has had a greater impact on daily use of time than any other household technology, and that it continues to dominate free time in most countries. The much lower time spent with IT suggests that TV use has not been greatly displaced by the Internet and personal computers (Robinson and Martin 2009). Main gains in viewing time occurred in the United States in the 1970s, coincident with the arrival of color TV, and it has made persistent but smaller inroads on free time since then. As was true 40 years ago, these diary studies show that lower TV time is correlated with more time at work and more travel and that TV is viewed more by people who are at

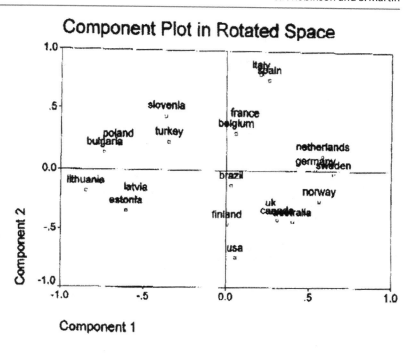

Fig. 8.4 MDS mapping of country similarity based on the diary data in Table 8.1 (From Robinson and Gershuny 2009)

home and who have more free time and sleep. Early casualties of TV, such as sleep and reading, are now correlated with more viewing.

QOL Implications: While the QOL or positive benefits of engaging in particular daily activities are often not obvious, social observers seem to concur that increases in daily activities like childcare, volunteering and other potentially altruistic behaviors, as well as free time represent improvements in a person's or society's QOL, while increases in time spent on routine housework, repair activities, and TV viewing are seen as less desirable, with empirical support for many of these assumptions provided in Table 8.2 in the next section.

US Trends in Time Use: As noted above, diary data have been collected at roughly 10-year intervals since 1965 and have shown some consistent trends since then. The major overall trend has been in the form of a gender switch—paid work declines for men in contrast to paid work increases for women, coupled with increased housework for men and a large decrease in housework for women. Moreover, there is also more general gender convergence evident in many other personal and free-time activities as well (Robinson and Godbey 1999). Overall, there seems little evidence of a more hectic lifestyle, say in terms of less free time or declining sleep (Robinson and Caporaso 2009).

Other major general increases (for both men and women) are evident for childcare, TV viewing, fitness activities, and relaxing (and free time in general), in contrast to notable decreases in newspaper reading, hobbies, and work breaks. Many of these changes for those aged 18–64 are reported in Robinson and Godbey (1999), which covers most activities reported in diaries. Also available are activities for which estimate trend data are also available, mainly from the General Social Survey (GSS), the Survey of Public Participation in the Arts (SPPS), the Panel Study of Income Dynamics (PSID), and organizations interested in particular activities (like sleep or volunteering).

The General Social Survey (GSS): There are several GSS activities for which estimate data are available: work, TV and newspaper use, religious attendance, sex, and several other types of social interaction. Analyses in Robinson and Martin (2008) show the direction of 1972–2000 trends for many of these behaviors, particularly the declines in newspaper reading and church attendance (Presser and Stinson 1998) and little consistent change in social activity. However, the GSS data show no change in TV viewing hours over the 1972–2004 period, in contrast to the 70% increase in viewing found in the 2005 diaries compared to 1965. The PSID housework decline for women and increase

8 Time Use as a Social Indicator

Table 8.2 Enjoyment ratings from diary activities vs. in general (on a scale from 10=enjoy a great deal to 0=dislike a great deal)

10-Enjoy a Great Deal

!	(1985 Diary average=7.0)	1975 General (average=6.8)
!		
!	9.3 Sex	
!	9.2 Play sports	
!		
!	8.7 Play children	8.9 Childcare
!	8.5 Church, religion	
!	8.5 Sleep	8.6 Play with children
!	8.2 Meals away	8.0 Social, talk
!	8.2 Socialize, visit others	*8.0 Work*
!	8.0 Socialize with family	
!	8.0 Work breaks	
!		
!	7.9 Reading	7.5 Sleep
!	7.8 Meals at home	7.4 Eating
!	****7.8 TV**	7.4 Wash, dress
!	7.4 Hobbies, crafts	7.3 Church, religion
!	7.2 Exercise	7.0 Reading
!	7.2 Baby care	
!	7.2 Organizations	
!	**7.0 Work*	
!	7.0 Bathing	
!		
!	6.6 Cooking	6.8 Hobbies
!	6.6 Other shopping	6.5 Play sports
!	6.4 Childcare	6.5 Cultural events
!	6.4 Help others	6.2 Cooking
!	6.3 Work commute	
!	6.1 Dressing	
!		
!	5.8 Other housework	****5.9 TV**
!	5.5 Grocery shopping	
!	5.5 Home repairs	5.1 Home repairs
!	5.2 Pay bills, financial, etc.	5.0 Organizations
!	5.0 Yardwork	
!		
!	4.9 Clean house	4.6 Grocery shop
!	4.9 Laundry	4.3 Other shop
!	4.8 Health care, doctor	4.2 Clean house
!	4.7 Car repair	
!		
!		

0- Dislike a Great Deal

1985 and 1975 national data, from Robinson and Godbey (1999), Appendix O
* ** Discrepancy between general and diary ratings (See text)

for men is quite consistent with that shown in the diaries (Juster et al. 2003).

We now turn to a different type of data, one that attempt to provide greater insight into the meanings of these time measures, and their QOL implications.

Subjective Time Measures

Subjective time measures in this review fall into three categories:

1. *Affect*: Enjoyment and satisfaction, with questions about how much pleasure respondents obtain from specific activities or their lives more generally. See Table 8.2.
2. *Time pressure*: Perceptions of time pressure and stress, with questions about feeling rushed, time crunch and personal stress, or spending enough time with one's spouse or children.
3. *Output*: Questions related to outputs from time inputs, such as being more satisfied with house cleanliness, how well one's children are doing in life. These have supplemented with more objective measures of output, like grades in school and house cleanliness.

Turning to each of these topics in more detail

Affect

As reflected in Table 8.2, the data concerning activity satisfaction are obtained in two ways:

1. As rated in "*real time*" that is integrated as part of the time diary, as a follow-up question after each reported activity.
2. As rated in *general*, as in the survey question "On a scale from __ to __ how much do you enjoy doing _____(activity)?" In both cases, respondents give ratings on a 1–5, 1–7, or 0–10 rating scale, with higher scores indicating more positive affect.

Table 8.2 shows differences in ratings in the diary vs. in general rating contexts. Interestingly, these diary ratings of some activities in the first column differ significantly from the responses derived from the general survey questions in the second column. For example, respondents rated their diary work time enjoyed an average of about one point *lower* on these 0–10 scales than when asked about their work in general, and the particular TV programs they watched as one point *higher* than TV viewing in general. Nonetheless, there was much more convergence on other activities, such as ratings of childcare and socializing being toward the most enjoyable end of the scale vs. housework and repair activities being at the bottom. Nonetheless, it does appear that the general ratings may not reflect fluctuations in feelings as people engage in these activities in "real time." Kahneman et al. (2004) and Krueger et al. (2009) have published important new arguments about the need for approaching QOL national measurement using the real-time subjective ratings in the diary, arguing that the general measures fail to capture actual emotions. They suggest these as supplemental measures to the Gross Domestic Product (GDP) to more fully reflect a country's QOL.

At the same time, the general ratings did perform well in the 1975 study in being a major predictor of diary times, indicating a reassuring example of attitudes predicting behavior (activity). In this case, the prediction task was not a simple one since it involved predicting diary times of TV, housework, sleep, etc. in Wave 3 of the study, based on enjoyment ratings given 3 months earlier in Wave 2. Another more general activity-affect question asks respondents whether to make forced-choice judgments, as in the question, "Do you enjoy yourself more at work, or in your free time, or are they about the same?" In one national survey, as might be expected, more respondents chose free time (30%) than work (15%), but most respondents (55%) rated them as equally enjoyable. This suggests the assumption of those social observers that people who go to work just to make the income to enjoy themselves in their free time and to buy things may not realize that work is not the daily scourge it is often made out to be subjective QOL questions, the main one of interest here being how happy respondents feel in general. One may not be surprised to find there is a connection between the two, but it turns out to be a rather robust and monotonic (Robinson and Martin 2008). That is, GSS respondents who report more hours of TV per day report being progressively less happy, for example (similar to the findings of Kubey and Csikszentmihalyi (1990), who examined the relation in far more detail).

Activities and Affect in the General Social Survey (GSS): As noted above, the GSS has been regularly asking behavior questions on several activities (TV, religious attendance, social visiting, and the like) since 1972. It has also asked these same respondents several

those who more often attend religious services, read the newspaper, and socialize with relatives, neighbors, and friends report being progressively more happy. Moreover, these relations are not explained after major demographic predictors of happiness (like marriage, gender, and education) are taken into account. This suggests that there is something involved in doing these activities that makes people happier, or that happy people enjoy them more, or more likely both.

Time Pressure

A separate issue regarding the time-QOL connection involves feelings of time pressure, of being rushed or under stress, with the general assumption that the less of this in one's life the better. These mainly have come in the form of single questions asked in separate surveys, so that little is known about their interconnection. Nonetheless, they do provide important insights into how time and life are experienced.

Rushed: Perhaps the oldest and most well-known of these questions was asked in the first American time diary in 1965, and it has since been asked in more than 10 national surveys in the interim (Robinson and Godbey 1999, Chap. 15). The question asks respondents how rushed they generally feel, and it shows a significantly increase in proportions (from 24% to 38% for those aged 18–64) of Americans who said they "always" feel rushed between 1965 and early 1990s. Since then, there seems no significant increase in such feelings. This is perhaps the most persuasive evidence of overwrought or overworked Americans, countering the time-diary figures which show increased free time.

The availability of the rushed item in the 1982, 1998, and 2004 GSS surveys also makes it possible to replicate the Campbell et al. (1976) finding of an inverse curvilinear relation between feeling rushed and positive life affect, with those in the middle (saying they are only "sometimes" rushed) reporting higher life satisfaction (Robinson and Martin 2008). A companion item to the rushed question asks respondents the opposite questions of how often they "....have time on their hands you don't know what with." In line with the rushed item trends, those saying "almost never" have risen from 48% in the 1960s and 1970s to about 60% in the 1990s, and those on the other end (who say "quite often" having time on their hands) dropped from 15% to less than 10%.

Stress: Given the great medical concern and societal attention paid to the stressful lifestyles in America, it is surprising that so little data using standardized trend questions on stress. The National Center for Health Statistics did include a direct question on perceived stress in its very large 1985 and 1995 surveys, and it did find a significant rise from 50% to 56% between 1986 and 1993, but then a surprising decline to 48% in 1995 (paralleling the 1995 decline in feeling always rushed). Unfortunately, this question appears not to have been asked since then to track recent levels of stress.

Time Crunch Scale: Robinson and Godbey (1999) report results from a 1993 national survey that developed a 10-item measure of feelings of time pressure, with an average of about 33% of respondents agreeing with these items (about the same proportion as who describe themselves as always rushed). As with the rushed and stress questions, women and those aged 25–44 were most likely to respond being under more time crunch.

Other Questions: Another single item asked respondents in 1992 whether they would be willing to give up a day's pay to get a day off from work, to which nearly 50% said "Yes," and that proportion has remained at that level since then. On a more balanced question, only 13% of respondents said they would like to work fewer hours compared to 35% who wanted more work—and 52% who said the same work hours. That latter result is in keeping with the 23% of workers in both 1975 and in 1998 who reported being "very tired" at the end of a workday, again suggesting workers face little overall time problems with their work

Time pressure concerns are also evident in questions asking respondents whether they have more or less free time than 5 years previously, and here far more respondents say "less" free time than "more." In family surveys, when asked whether they spend enough time with their children, most parents say "not enough," even though mothers (but especially fathers) are spending more time with their children than 10 or 20 years ago (Bianchi et al. 2006). Parallel questions about time with one's spouse or by oneself drew similar or higher

levels "not enough time" responses. Other GSS questions have asked perceptions of how well balanced one's work and family lives were. Robinson (1977) found that less than 30% of wives said they wished their husbands would help them more with the housework or with childcare, and that has not changed much since then.

Outputs from Time Inputs

Here, there are concerns about the productivity or consequences of various ways of spending time. Does one feel that the hours devoted to an activity have any parallel in terms of output? Thus, one set of survey questions has asked parents about how well their children are doing in life, about their satisfaction with the amount of time the family spends together, or about awareness of where their children are at times when they are not with them (Bianchi et al. 2006). Other survey items have asked how satisfied respondents are with the cleanliness of their homes, or the quality of the family meals (Juster and Stafford 1985).

A few studies have examined time's relations with more objective measures of output. Schuman et al. (1985) found little relationship between study time and grades in school. Robinson and Godbey (1999) similarly found little relation between time spent on housework and respondent satisfaction with household cleanliness or ratings of that cleanliness by the respondent or by the interviewer who observed the dwelling; nor did they find that presence of household appliances helped reduce housework time, perhaps because it is the busier and more ambitious families that buy the technology in the first place, as found earlier in Morgan et al. (1965). In another comparison, they found, other factors equal, respondents who reported longer work hours were slightly more likely to attend arts events or to engage in sex. In general, these analyses support Parkinson's (1962) most insightful observation that "Work expands to fill the time available for its completion." It is surprising that so few studies have been done on this topic, given the many unfounded work policies and decisions based on the assumption that more work time means higher output.

Some more promising advances in linking time to output and welfare have been recently proposed by economists. Bittman and Ironmonger (2011) have presented a typology outlining options to simply placing monetary values on work, unpaid work and free time, one that moves beyond the initial strategy of valuing time in terms of the implicit wage rate of the individual. Folbre (2009) has elaborated ways in which time-use data can improve both subjective and objective measures of living standards, pointing out flaws in ways conventional economics values different activities. In their recent prizewinning book, *Discretionary Time: A New Measure of Freedom*, Goodin et al. (2008) assert that time is an inherently superior metric compared to money, reversing the usual process of valuing time in dollars and instead expressing money in terms of the time required to earn it. Their arguments are built around the central idea that the *ability to choose* how one allocates one's time lies at the core of a positive notion of freedom: The authors develop a new standard of welfare from the idea of escape from the "realm of necessity," by defining "discretionary time" as what is left after necessary minimum time that must be devoted to personal care, paid work, and nonmarket work. Discretionary time thus represents an advance over the more conventional category of "free time" as a new metric of welfare.

On the negative end of the welfare scale, there is the concern about the possible negative impacts of time spent eating. Zick and Stevens (2011) report that while time spent eating as a primary activity has remained the same or declined over previous decades, eating time as a secondary activity has risen significantly—particularly as an accompaniment to TV viewing. In Australia, Brown et al. (2011) present evidence that TV viewing is accompanied by increased consumption of high-calorie snack foods. The ATUS has begun questions about food consumption and fitness activity to provide further evidence on daily activity and obesity (Janes et al. 2011).

Summary and Conclusions

While the diary is one of many options in ways to measure how people spend time objectively, research with time diaries thus far has produced a body of rich and insightful results. That promises to increase in the future given the availability of continuous, large-sample, and high-quality government data, as in the many and varied application of ATUS studies in the USA in (Robinson and Godbey 2005).

Diary data have raised serious issues about the accuracy of data obtained by more traditional "time estimate" questions, both in terms of simple amounts of time spent and in trends in these amounts across recent decades. Research done with diaries supports the conclusion that the time estimates are open to the common survey problem of social desirability (Krosnick 1999). While more definitive methodological research is needed as these ATUS data are more widely used, the diary method has showed promising results in terms of the major criteria of reliability and validity. It also needs to be noted that, although most of the data reviewed here are for those aged 18–64, the ATUS diary data are available for senior citizens aged 65+ (Robinson and Godbey 1999; Robinson 2010) and to young children (as reviewed in Raley 2006; Hofferth 2001; Robinson and Godbey 1999), often again with surprising results (such as that American children report less than an hour a day doing school homework or doing household work).

Diary trends since the first national US diary study in 1965 indicate a number of surprising societal changes, particularly in the converging lifestyles of men and women, who are now doing more equal amounts of not just paid work and housework but most personal and free-time activities as well. Diary trends also indicate more TV viewing, childcare, and fitness activity, which has been offset by decreases in housework, eating meals, and newspaper reading. There also appears to be a notable increase in secondary activities, which evidence of increased multitasking (mainly involving TV, radio and other newer media). This is reflected as well in the 20 percentage point increase in the proportion of respondents who say they are often doing two or more activities at once (Bianchi et al. 2006).

A major problem with the present ATUS data collection, however, is that it includes few of these subjective questions that are necessary to interpret and give meaning to any changes or levels of time that are observed. However, this ATUS survey is currently asking respondents about how people *feel* about the activities they are engaged in using the measures developed by Krueger et al. (2009) to help understand whether their activity choices might improve their QOL.

Based on these subjective data, it could be taken as an encouraging sign that the trends in US diary hours do follow a generally hedonistic direction, in that Robinson and Godbey (1999) find people report spending increased time on activities they find more enjoyable (like childcare and free-time activities) and less time on the things they don't like to do (especially housework). Along the same line, Bianchi et al. (2006) report increased time spent on childcare, especially interactive or "fun" activities with one's child. Moreover, these same long-term *time* trends are found in other countries as well (Bittman 1998; Gershuny 2000). Conversely, time spent on the most enjoyable activity of sex has not been increasing since 1989, even given the increase in Viagra, Internet services and pornography, and other marital aids (Robinson 2010).

Policy Issues: Time diaries provide clear evidence of several social inequalities. In the case of the division of housework between men and women, Fig. 8.1 shows that both men and women rate housework as quite low in terms of enjoyment. Yet women continue to do twice as much of it. However, it is hard to imagine what type of policy would offset this imbalance, outside of providing counselors to help individual couples to make better arrangements for themselves.

The "Take back your time" movement (DeGraff 2003) proposed that American workers stop all paid work after mid-October, so that their total annual work hours would be equivalent to those of European workers. Yet, Hochschild (1997) found in one company that it was other workers themselves who sabotaged innovative family-friendly policies to reduce work hours. The National Sleep Foundation has raised alarms about sleep deprivation as a national crisis, although time diaries show no decline in sleep over the last 40 years—which holds steady at the legendary 8 h a night. The "turn off your TV" movement has designated one week a year for people to leave their sets off and to instead participate in more potentially gratifying activities. However, Table 8.2 suggests that, although people rate TV in general as relatively low on the fun meter, the programs they watched on the diary day rated far higher in enjoyment.

Of all the potential policy issues related to time use, what seems most impressive is the largely anecdotal data on the meager, marginal outputs that workers produce and obtain for their inputs of work time. These data largely suggest that the same work productivity can be achieved with 20–50% less time spent on the job (Parkinson 1962; Schor 1991; Schuman et al. 1985) and that many workers put in simple "face time" to impress their employers.

This inability of diary data to speak directly to the quality of people's lives and to guide policy to improve that life quality remains the major limitation of time use research and a major area for future studies. The findings reported in Table 8.2 represent an important first step toward gaining more nuanced insights into time-use statistics, but a new study design—such as a "representative ethnography" that combines the insights of observation with the generalizability of representative sampling of respondents could provide more enlightened meanings (Robinson and Meadow 1982). Diary data allow researchers to document what people are doing, yet scholars need to find out more about why, with whom, for whom, and to what ends people are using their time.

References

Aas, D. (1978). Studies of time use: Problems and prospects. *Acta Sociologica, 2*, 123–141.

Abraham, K., Maitland, K., & Bianchi, S. (2006). Nonresponders to the ATUS. *Public Opinion Quarterly, 70*(5), 676–703.

Abraham, K., Helam, S., & Presser, S. (2009). How social processes distort measurement: The impact of nonresponse on estimates of volunteer work in the united states. *The American Journal of Sociology, 114*, 1129–1165.

Aguiar, M., & Hurst, E. (2007). Measuring trends in leisure: The allocation of time over five decades. *Quarterly Journal of Economics, 122*(3), 969–1006.

Aguiar, M., & Hurst, E. (2009). A summary of trends in American time allocation. *Social Indicators Research, 92*, 70–80.

Allen, C. L. (1968). Photographing the TV audience. *Journal of Advertising Research, 8*(1), 8.

American Time-Use Survey (2011). www.bls.gov/atus.

Arthur, M. (2004). *SPSS handbook*. New York: Research Methods.

Barker, R., & Barker, L. (1961). Behavior units for the comparative studies of cultures. In B. Kaplan (Ed.), *Studying personality cross-culturally*. Evanston: Row, Peterson.

Barker, R., & Wright, H. (1951). *One boy's day: A specimen record of behavior*. New York: Harper and Brothers.

Bechtel, R., Achepohl, C., & Akers, R. (1972). Correlates between observed behavior and questionnaire responses in television viewing. In E. A. Rubenstein, G. A. Comstock, & J. P. Murray (Eds.), *Television and social behavior, reports and papers* (Television in day to day life: Patterns and use, Vol. 4, pp. 274–344). Washington, D.C.: GPO.

Bianchi, S., et al. (2000). Is anyone doing the housework? *Social Forces, 79*, 191–228.

Bianchi, S., Robinson, J., & Milkie, M. (2006). *Changing rhythms of American family life*. New York: Russell Sage.

Bittman, M. (1998). The land of the long lost weekend: Trends in free time among working age Australians, 1974–1992. *Society and Leisure, 21*(2), 353–379.

Bittman, M. (2000). Now it's 2000: Trends in doing and being in the new millennium. *Journal of Occupational Science, 7*, 108–117.

Bittman, M., & Ironmonger, D. (2011). Conference overview. *Social Indicators Research, 101*, 173–183.

Brown, J., Nicholson, J., Broom, D., & Bittman, M. (2011). Television viewing by school-age children: Associations with physical activity, snack food consumption and unhealthy weight. *Social Indicators Research, 101*, 221–225.

Bureau of Labor Statistics. (2009). www.bls.gov.

Bureau of Labor Statistics. (2011). *Volunteering in the United States (2010)* www.bls.gov.

Campbell, A., Converse, P., & Rodgers, W. (1976). *The quality of American life*. New York: Russell Sage.

Chase, D., & Godbey, G. (1983). The accuracy of self-reported participation rates: A research note. *Leisure Studies, 2*, 231–233.

Converse, P. (1972). Country differences in time use. In A. Szalai (Ed.), *The use of time* (pp. 145–178). The Hague: Mouton.

CPS. (2011). *Current population survey*. www.census.gov/cps.

Csikszentmihalyi, M. (1991). *Flow: The psychology of optimal experience*. New York: Harper Collins.

Csikszentmihalyi, M., & Larsen, R. (1984). *Being adolescent*. New York: Basic Books.

DeGraff, J. (2003). *Take back your time*. New York: Berrett-Koehler.

DeGrazia, S. (1962). *Of time, work, and leisure*. New York: Twentieth Century Fund.

Fisher, K., & Robinson, J. (2011). Daily life in 23 countries. *Social Indicators Research, 101*, 195–204.

Fisher, K., Egerton, M., Gershuny, J., & Robinson, J. (2006). Gender convergence in the American heritage time-use survey. *Social Indicators Research, 82*, 1–33.

Fisher, K., et al. (2007). Gender convergence in the American heritage time-use study. *Social Indicators Research, 82*, 1–33 (with Kimberly Fisher, Muriel Egerton and Jonathan Gershuny).

Folbre, N. (2009). Time use and living standards. *Social Indicators Research, 93*(1), 77–83.

Frazis, H., & Stewart, J. (2004). What can time-use data tell us about hours at work. *Monthly Labor Review, 127*(12), 3–9.

Gauthier, A. H., Smeeding, T. M., & Furstenberg, F. F., Jr. (2004). Are parents investing less time in children? Trends in selected industrialized countries. *Population and Development Review, 30*, 647–671.

Gershuny, J. (1990). *The multinational longitudinal time budget data archive*. European Foundation for the Improvement of Living and Working Conditions, Dublin.

Gershuny, J. (1992). Are we running out of time? *Future, 24*, 3–22.

Gershuny, J. (2000). *Changing times: Work and leisure in postindustrial society*. Oxford: Oxford University Press.

Gershuny, J., & Robinson, J. (1998). Historical changes in the household division of labor. *Demography, 25*(47), 537–553.

Goldschmidt-Claremont. (1995). *Measures of unrecorded activities in fourteen countries* (Human Development Report #20) New York: United Nations.

Goodin, R. E., Rice, J. M., Parpo, A., & Eriksson, L. (2008). *Discretionary time: A new measure of freedom*. Cambridge: Cambridge University Press.

Hadaway, C. I., Marler, P., & Chaves, M. (1993). What the polls don't show: A closer look at U.S. Church attendance. *American Sociological Review, 58*, 741–752.

Hamilton, R. (1991). Work and leisure. *Public Opinion Quarterly, 55*, 347–356.

Harris, L. (1987). *Inside America*. New York: Vintage.

Harvey, A., & Elliot, D. (1983). *Time and time again*. Ottawa-Hull: Employment and Immigration Commission.

Hawes, D., Talarzyk, W., & Blackwell, R. (1975). Consumer satisfactions from leisure time pursuits. In M. Schlinger (Ed.), *Advances in consumer research*. Chicago: Association for Consumer Research.

Hochschild, A. (1997). *The time bind*. New York: Henry Holt and Company.

Hochschild, A., & Machung, A. (1989). *The second shift: Working parents and the revolution at home*. New York: Viking.

Hofferth, S. (2001). How American children spend their time. *Journal of Marriage and Family, 63*, 295–308.

Holmes, M., & Bloxham, M. (2009). An observational method of time-use research. *Social Indicators Research, 93*, 245–248.

Independent Sector. (2001). *Giving and volunteering in the United States*, Washington, D.C. www.Independent Sector.org.

Jacobs, J. (1998). Measuring time at work. *Monthly Labor Review, 121*, 42–53.

Janes, M., Hamrick, K., & Lacey, J. (2011). Exercise, eating patterns, and obesity: Evidence from the ATUS and its eating & health module. *Social Indicators Research, 101*, 215–219.

Juster, F. T. (1985). The validity and quality of time use estimates obtained from recall diaries. In F. T. Juster & F. P. Stafford (Eds.), *Time, goods, and well-being* (pp. 63–92). Ann Arbor: Institute for Social Research, University of Michigan.

Juster, F. T., & Stafford, F. P. (1985). *Time, goods, and well-being*. Ann Arbor: Survey Research Center, Institute for Social Research, University of Michigan.

Juster, F. T., Ono, H., & Stafford, F. (2003). An assessment of alternative measures of time use. *Sociological Methodology, 33*, 19–54.

Kahneman, D., Krueger, A. B., Schkade, D. A., Schwarz, N., & Stone, A. A. (2004). A survey method for characterizing daily life experience: The day reconstruction method. *Science, 306*(5702), 1776–1780.

Krosnick, J. (1999). Question framing. In J. Robinson et al. (Eds.), *Measures of political attitudes*. San Diego: Academic.

Krueger, A., et al. (2009). Time use and subjective well-being in the US and France. *Social Indicators Research, 92*, 10–20.

Kubey, R., & Csikszentmihalyi, M. (1990). *Television and the quality of life*. Hillsdale: Lawrence Erlbaum.

Levine, R. (1997). *A geography of time*. New York: Basic Books.

Marini, M., & Shelton, B. A. (1993). Measuring household work: Recent experience in the United States. *Social Science Research, 22*, 361–385.

McSweeney, B. (1980). Lack of time as an obstacle to women: The case of upper Volta. *Comparative Education Review, 24*(2), 124–139.

Michelson, W. (1978). *Public policy in temporal perspective*. The Hague: Mouton.

Michelson, W. (2006). *Time use: Explanations and explorations in the social sciences*. New York: Pergammon.

Morgan, J., et al. (1965). *Productive Americans*. Ann Arbor: Institute for Social Research.

Morgan, J. N., Sirageldin, I., & Baerwaldt, N. (1966). *Productive Americans*. Ann Arbor: Institute for Social Research, University of Michigan.

National Sleep Foundation (2007). *Women and sleep*. National Sleep Foundation.org

Nielsen/NetRatings. (1999). *TV viewing in Internet households. A report by Nielsen Media Research.* Retrieved from http://www.nielsen-netratings.com/.

Parkinson, C. N. (1962). *Parkinson's law.* New York: Penguin.

Press, J., & Townsley, K. (1998). Work and housework among husbands and wives. *Gender and Society, 42*(2), 188–218.

Presser, S., & Stinson, L. (1998). Estimating the bias in survey reports of religious attendance. *American Sociological Review, 63*(1), 136–152.

Putnam, R. D. (2000). *Bowling alone: The collapse and revival of American community.* New York: Simon & Schuster.

Raley, S. (2006). Children's time use. In S. Bianchi, J. Robinson, & M. Milkie (Eds.), *Changing rhythms of American family life.* New York: Russell Sage.

Robinson, J. P. (1977). *How Americans use time: A social-psychological analysis of everyday behavior.* New York: Praeger.

Robinson, J. P. (1985). The validity and reliability of diaries versus alternative time use measures. In F. T. Juster & F. P. Stafford (Eds.), *Time, goods, and well-being* (pp. 33–62). Ann Arbor: Survey Research Center, Institute for Social Research, University of Michigan.

Robinson, J. (2010). Sex, arts and verbal abilities: Three further indicators of how American life has Not improved. *Social Indicators Research, 99*(1), 1–12.

Robinson, J. (2011). IT, TV and time displacement: What Alexander Szalai anticipated but couldn't know. *Social Indicators Research, 101*, 193–206.

Robinson, J. P., & Bostrom, A. (1994). The overestimated workweek? what time diary measures suggest. *Monthly Labor Review, 117*(8), 11–23.

Robinson, J., & Caporaso, A. (2009). Senioritis in repose. *e International Journal of Time Use Research (eIJTUR), 6* December, 306–313 (with Andrew Caporaso).

Robinson, J. P., & Gershuny, J. I. (1994). Measuring hours of paid work: Time diary versus estimate questions. In *Bulletin of labor statistics* (pp. xi–xvii). Geneva: International Labor Office.

Robinson, J. P., & Gershuny, J. I. (2009). *Visualizing multinational differences in daily life.* Paper presented at the 2010 IATUR conference in Paris, July 2009.

Robinson, J. P., & Godbey, G. (1999). *Time for life: The surprising ways Americans use their time* (2nd ed.). University Park: Pennsylvania State University Press.

Robinson, J. & Godbey, G. (2005). Busyness as usual. *Social Research, 72*, 407–426.

Robinson, J., & Land, K. (2008). Social indicators and quality of life. In W. Donsbach & M. Traugott (Eds.), *Handbook of public opinion research.* Thousand Oaks: Sage Publications.

Robinson, J., & Martin, S. (2008). What do happy people do? *Social Indicators Research, 89*, 565–571.

Robinson, J., & Martin, S. (2009). (2008) "Of time and television". *The Annals of Social and Political Science (The End of Television), 265*(September), 74–87 (with Stephen Martin).

Robinson, J., & Martin, S. (2010). IT use and declining social capital: More cold water from the GSS and ATUS. *Social Science Computer Review, 29*(1), 45–63 (with Steven Martin).

Robinson, J. P., & Meadow, R. (1982). *Polls apart.* Cabin John: Seven Locks Press.

Robinson, J., & Michelson, W. (2010). Sleep as a victim of the time crunch – a multinational analysis. *e International Journal of Time-Use Research, 7*(November), 61–72 (with William Michelson).

Robinson, J., Martin, S., Glorieux, I., & Mirren, J. (2011). The overestimated workweek revisited. *Monthly Labor Review*, (June), pp. 1–13

Scheuch, E. (1972). The time-budget interview. In A. Szalai et al. (Eds.), *The use of time* (pp. 69–89). Mouton: The Hague.

Schor, J. (1991). *The overworked American.* New York: Basic Books.

Schuman, H., Walsh, E., Olson, C., & Etheridge, B. (1985). Effort and reward: The assumption that college grads are affected by quantity of study. *Social Forces, 63*, 945–966.

Social Research (2005) *Busyness* Special Issue

Szalai, A. (1966). Trends in comparative time budget research. *American Behavioral Scientist, 29*, 3–8.

Szalai, A. (1972). *The use of time.* The Hague: Mouton.

Szalai, A., S. Ferge, et al. (1966, September). *The multinational comparative time-budget research project: Report on the organization, methods, and experiences of the pilot study, 1965–1966, and the preliminary results of 13 parallel time-budget surveys.* Contributions to the round table on time-budgets at the VIIth world congress of sociology, Evian, 1966.

Verbrugge, L., & Gruber-Baldine, D. (1993). *Baltimore study of activity patterns.* Ann Arbor: Institute of Gerontology, University of Michigan.

Walker, K. (1969). Homemaking still takes time. *Journal of Home Economics, 61*(October), 621–624.

Walker, K., & Woods, M. (1976). *Time use: A measure of household production of family goods and services.* Washington, D.C.: American Home Economics Association.

Zick, K., & Stevens, R. (2011). Time spent eating and its implications for Americans' energy balance. *Social Indicators Research, 101*, 267–273.

Issues in Composite Index Construction: The Measurement of Overall Quality of Life

9

Michael R. Hagerty and Kenneth C. Land

"Are you better off now than 4 years ago?" Asked by numerous politicians since Ronald Reagan famously posed it as a candidate in the 1980 Presidential Election in the United States, this question invites voters to make a complex and perilous series of judgments to estimate *overall quality of life* (*QOL*) in their country. Each citizen must, at least informally, engage in the following activities: (1) Select the indicators that are most important to her or him, (2) obtain data from social reports or other news sources on the progress of those indicators, and (3) integrate those indicators across disparate domains to achieve a judgment of overall progress on QOL.

It is clear that science can help citizens with the first two tasks by collecting reliable and valid indicators related to QOL and by disseminating those indicators widely in social reports to facilitate citizens' judgments. But for some very good reasons, social scientists have been reluctant to help in the third task of summarizing those indicators into a composite QOL index (for brevity below, the term "QOL index" often is used to reference a "composite QOL index"). These reasons are: First, constructing a QOL index requires "comparing apples to oranges" because the indicators have no common unit (how does one combine longevity measured in years with income measured in dollars?); second, it requires knowledge of how each

citizen selects and weights indicators to arrive at their overall judgment; and third, it requires that citizens are sufficiently homogenous that a single QOL index would be accepted by a majority of citizens, because it approximates their own individual QOL judgments. And underlying these concerns is a worry that constructing a QOL index could become "politicized" or manipulated for short-term political gain at the expense of long-term scientific credibility.

This chapter outlines the progress that social science research has made on these questions in the last 50 years, and proposes some principles for developing QOL indices that help assure acceptance by citizens and resistance to politicization. We begin by reviewing three composite indices from economics that have achieved these goals in the United States (similar indices have been developed in many other countries). We then describe seven principles to guide the developments of QOL indices. This is followed by a review of 14 existing QOL indices which we evaluate with respect to these principles. We then state several common criticisms of composite indices and solutions thereto. The chapter concludes with several recommendations with respect to the construction of QOL indices.

Three Composite Indices of the Economy

The use of composite indices of various aspects of economic activity and conditions has a long history from which a number of lessons can be learned. We review three economic indices: the Dow-Jones Industrial Average, the Consumer Price Index, and the Consumer Sentiment Index.

M.R. Hagerty
University of California, Graduate School of Management, Davis, CA, USA
e-mail: mrhagerty@ucdavis.edu

K.C. Land (✉)
Department of Sociology, Duke University, Durham, NC, USA
e-mail: kland@soc.duke.edu

K.C. Land et al. (eds.), *Handbook of Social Indicators and Quality of Life Research*,
DOI 10.1007/978-94-007-2421-1_9, © Springer Science+Business Media B.V. 2012

The Dow-Jones Industrial Average (DJIA). The Dow-Jones Industrial Average is probably the index most quoted by print and electronic media in the USA. It was created in 1882 for investors who wanted to "see the forest instead of the trees" as a simple way to gauge overall movement in the New York Stock Exchange. It originally included only nine railroad stocks, a steamship line, and a communications company. Today, it includes 30 large "industrial" companies (including WalMart). The bundle of stocks is picked *subjectively* by editors of the Wall Street Journal, and is modified periodically to "reflect the current economy." Originally, the calculation was a simple average of the prices of the stocks, divided by their number. Today, the editors have modified the simple average to a "price-weighted" average, with adjustments for prices when a stock "splits" (e.g., a two-for-one split in which owners of 100 shares have 200 shares after the split). Among all stock market indices, the DJIA is the least representative and uses the simplest calculation. Despite these weaknesses, it is nevertheless the most frequently quoted and most easily understood.

The Consumer Price Index (CPI-U). The Consumer Price Index-Urban is published by the Bureau of Labor Statistics as an estimate of the cost of living in urban areas in the USA. It is probably the second most-often quoted index by the media in the USA, not because it is less important than the DJIA, but because it is updated over a month rather than every day. The BLS monitors prices for 211 items in 38 geographic areas, and maintains 8,018 "disaggregated" price indices, including, for example, the price of apples in Chicago. The creation of an index would seem straightforward, since all items are measured in the common unit "dollars." But despite the common metric, the *weights* for each item must be determined. The proper weight should reflect the fact that apples contribute far less than household rent in calculating CPI, because a "representative" family allocates far more of their budget to rent than to apples. The natural weight would be the proportion of the average family's budget that is devoted to that item in that month. The problem is that full-scale surveys of family budgeting and "representative consumer baskets of goods" occur only every 2–5 years. Hence the "constant weights" must be modified by estimates to predict how families will allocate their purchases every month. The index must be shown to be robust to errors in estimating how families allocate their purchases

each month, and considerable research has investigated the properties of various indices when faced with real consumer decisions. This research has focused on two areas: the problem of how consumers substitute purchases when the *price* of one item rises and the problem of how consumers substitute purchases when the *quality* of one item rises.

An example of price substitution is that consumers will purchase less beef when its price increases and will instead purchase more of substitutes, such as chicken. Hence, a simple constant-weight average index overstates the true cost of living. Research has shown that geometric averages/means are more robust to substitution errors than arithmetic averages/means, so the CPI-U now uses geometric averages[1] of prices in each of the 8,018 price series. The CPI-U however still uses fixed weights based on surveys that are at least 2 years old. To remedy this, the BLS now offers a "chained" CPI-U that updates weights dynamically each month using the most recent batch of surveys.

It is worth noting that the CPI is a weighted average, where the weights have been constant for long periods. Only recently has the CPI made incremental improvements by estimating dynamically changing weights. The QOL indices that we review later are similarly of this general form: weighted averages with constant weights. It is also worth noting that CPI research has not allowed "the perfect to be enemy of the good," but has published indices for over 50 years that had known errors, because constant weights are a first approximation to dynamic weights. Finally, the CPI research has sought to compare proposed indices with how individuals actually behave, and whether the aggregate index successfully predicted families' substitution behavior. A similar approach with respect to QOL indices will be described below.

The Consumer Confidence Index (CCI). The CCI was introduced in 1952 by the University of Michigan's Survey Research Center. It consists of a five-question battery in monthly consumer surveys. The questions are:

- "We are interested in how people are getting along financially these days. Would you say that you (and your family living there) are better off or worse off financially than you were a year ago?"

---

[1]The geometric mean $\tilde{X}_n$ of n positive numbers $X_1, X_2, ..., X_n$ is the positive nth root of their products, that is, $\tilde{X}_n = \left(\prod_{i=1}^{n} X_i \right)^{1/n}$.

- "Now looking ahead—do you think that a year from now you (and your family living there) will be better off financially, or worse off, or just about the same as now?"
- "Now turning to business conditions in the country as a whole—do you think that during the next 12 months we'll have good times financially, or bad times or what?"
- "Looking ahead, which would you say is more likely—that in the country as a whole we'll have continuous good times during the next 5 years or so, or that we will have periods of widespread unemployment or depression, or what?"
- "About the big things people buy for their homes—such as furniture, a refrigerator, stove, television, and things like that. Generally speaking, do you think now is a good or a bad time for people to buy major household items?"

The CCI is calculated in the following way: For each of the five questions which comprise the index, the proportion of unfavorable responses is subtracted from the proportion of favorable responses—to give the favorable balance of opinion—and then 100 is added to each balance. The resulting five figures are then averaged with equal weights to form the Index of Consumer Sentiment.

These three economic indices draw on over 100 years of experience and research. In the next section, we generalize from this research and over 30 years of QOL studies to formulate desirable principles for constructing QOL indices. Later sections will apply these criteria to existing QOL indices.

Principles for Constructing a Composite QOL Index

We state *seven principles for constructing QOL indices* and then consider their implications. Some are well known, but some are relatively new.[2]

The first principle is that each of the subseries that compose an index should be reliable and valid. This criterion is well known, and a review of QOL indices by Hagerty et al. (2001) concludes that most social reports can now boast many reliable and valid indicators. In the case of the DJIA, validation implies that it must correlate with the overall movements of the New York Stock Exchange and with gross domestic product 6 months in the future. In the case of QOL indices, the subseries could be validated to assure that they correlate with global measures of QOL, such as surveys of citizens' average happiness, frequency of smiling, lack of revolutionary or separatist political movements, and eventually, with brain imaging that displays positive emotion.

Second, to improve transparency, the QOL index should not be reported alone, but as part of a report that shows each underlying subseries. For example, the subseries of the CPI are reported at the same time as the CPI itself, and many users calculate an alternate "core" CPI by deleting the more volatile food and fuel series, because previous research shows that the core CPI is more stable and is a better predictor of next month's CPI.

Third, the QOL report should disaggregate the index for population subgroups. The CPI-U is calculated for all urban dwellers (the best known CPI series), but it is also calculated for rural dwellers and wage earners. This is likewise important in QOL reports, because informed citizens, policy decisions, and government programs require knowledge of whether some groups (e.g., the elderly, children, minorities, immigrants) are disadvantaged and may require help.

Fourth, an index should be robust to incomplete data or other data problems. In the CPI, research has shown that the chained CPI is a robust index even when updated surveys of family purchases are not available. In a QOL index, some series may be available monthly (e.g., earnings per family), but others are available only yearly (e.g., inequality), and each is reported with varying accuracy. Research to determine the robustness of a QOL index in these situations is warranted.

Fifth, the index should reflect the best model of how people actually make QOL judgments for themselves. Among economic indices, the CCI assumes that people can form judgments about their likelihood of earning and spending more money next year, and that a simple average of these perceptions predicts families' future purchasing. In the case of QOL indices, we can rely on research over the last

---

[2]These principles are consistent with guidelines for constructing composite indicators of all types such as those summarized in Nardo et al. (2005), but are focused on QOL measurement and its unique, substantive features.

30 years into how individuals make their personal judgments of QOL, described later.

Sixth, the index should reflect the weights that citizens give to individual subseries. The CPI achieves this by national surveys of families and the proportion of their budget spent on each category. In the case of a QOL index, if citizens tend to place high importance on the health domain and only moderate importance on inequality, then a composite QOL index should reflect this, with a unit change in (standardized) health causing a larger change in the composite index than a unit change in (standardized) inequality.

Seventh, an index should be accepted by a large majority of citizens. By accepted, we mean that most citizens trust it and endorse its use by political decision makers, because the index is a good approximation to the QOL judgments that the citizens themselves would make. In the case of the DJIA, vast numbers of investors show acceptance by using it to make individual buy/sell decisions daily (even though it is known to represent only a few large stocks and is an imperfect predictor of future activity), and the Bureau of Economic Research uses such indices to predict future economic activity. Despite its flaws, the DJIA shows acceptance by millions of decision makers.

The first four principles for constructing QOL indices are widely known and honored. In a review of extant QOL indices, Hagerty et al. (2001) proposed similar criteria and showed that many existing QOL indices conform to these goals. However, the last three criteria have been formalized fairly recently, in response to a call by Land (2004) for "evidence-based" QOL indices. These last three criteria (especially that the QOL index be accepted by a majority of citizens) have always been implicitly employed by past researchers, but only recently have the methods and measurements for predicting citizen acceptance been formalized. Hence we elaborate in more detail the last three principles for constructing QOL indices.

Principle 5: How people actually make QOL judgments for themselves. A long stream of research has concluded that a simple weighted average model predicts individuals' overall judgments of their QOL from satisfaction with their individual domains (Campbell et al. 1976; Cummins 1996; Veenhoven 1993). Though in some studies the direction of causality is ambiguous ("top-down" models predict that higher overall affect

causes higher ratings of individual domains), researchers agree that if actual conditions in a domain improve, then the change in overall rating of QOL is well predicted by a linear (weighted) additive model (Lucas et al. 2003; Sastre 1999). Another caveat is that if the weights contain excessive error in measurement (e.g., if weights are measured at the individual level rather than aggregated over larger samples), then an equal-weight model will perform as well or better than a weighted model.

Acknowledging these caveats, we accept the weighted average model as a good description of citizens' QOL judgment model, and define citizen i's importance weight as w_{ik} and citizen i's overall QOL judgment for country n as Q_{in}. Then we can predict their QOL judgments with the *weighted average model* (*WAM*):

$$Q_{in} = \sum_{k=1}^{K} w_{ik} x_{kn}, \quad w_{ik} > 0, \quad \text{for} \quad n = 1,\ldots,N \text{ countries}, \quad (9.1)$$

where x_{kn} is the score for the kth social indicator of country n, and K is the total number of social indicators that citizens use to make their judgments of QOL.[3] Adopting this additive model also benefits the fourth principle in constructing QOL indices, since it is well known that additive models are quite robust to errors in measurement.

Note that the weighted average model of Eq. 9.1 can be viewed as a logarithmic transformation of the weighted product method for composite index construction studied by Munda and Nardo (2003; see also Nardo et al. 2005). Using notation similar to that of Eq. 9.1, the *weighted product* (*WP*) *model* can be written as

$$Q_{in} = \prod_{k=1}^{K} x_{kn}^{w_{ik}}, \quad w_{ik} > 0, \quad \text{for} \quad n = 1,\ldots,N \text{ countries}. \quad (9.2)$$

In a recent contribution to the literature on methods of composite index construction, Zhou et al. (2010) studied the WP model and proposed a multiplicative optimization extension thereof by application of data envelopment analysis (DEA)-type methods to determine

---

[3] As research progresses, this model may be modified to include substitutability or complementarity between social indicators that would require modeling *interactions* among indicators. For example, an individual with higher average income may consider life expectancy more important than an individual with very low income (as life becomes more "worth living," longer life may be more valuable).

the values of weights of individual indicators in a composite index such as the life expectancy, education, and gross domestic product per capita indicators used to calculate the Human Development Index (described later in this chapter). The DEA method originally was developed for efficiency analysis in economics and management science (Charnes et al. 1978, 1994; Land et al. 1993). It transforms a multiplicative optimization problem into a series of linear programming problems (Dantzig 1963) in which weights for composite scores are determined by internal comparisons of each of a set of entities with each other with respect to their efficiency in producing outputs (e.g., consumer products) from given levels of inputs (e.g., labor, capital).

Zhou et al. (2010) applied DEA to calculate two sets of weights for the component indicators of a composite QOL index—a set of "best" weights for each entity calculated in comparison to the "best practice" entity or entities on each specific indicator and a set of "worst" weights calculated in comparison to the "worst practice" entity or entities on each specific indicator. They then calculate composite index scores for each entity being compared as weighted averages of logarithmic transformations of the two sets of weights, and, in the absence of "decision makers or analysts [having] no particular preference" (Zhou et al. 2010, p. 173) for one set of weights or the other, suggest equal weighting as a "fairly neutral choice." Zhou et al. suggest that this extension of the WP method can provide an alternative to subjectively determined weights for composite indices. In an empirical application, Zhou et al. show that the ranks of most of 27 countries in the Asia and Pacific region given by the conventional Human Development Index remain unchanged when they are ranked by composite indices based on the multiplicative optimization method. This relatively new approach to the development of weights for composite indices merits additional analysis and study. For instance, given the logarithmic relationship between the models of Eqs. 9.1 and 9.2, it is entirely possible that citizens as well as decision makers and analysts use an informal version, or at least some approximation thereto, of the equal weighting of "best practice" (distance from the best performing unit(s)) and "worst practice" (distance from the worst performing unit(s)) relative rankings to arrive at composite index scores/summary judgments.

Principle 6: Citizens' importance weights for subseries. Given that we know *how* citizens form QOL

judgments, the next obvious question is *which* social indicators do citizens use to determine QOL. Fortunately, the answer has been found to be roughly consistent over 30 years and in over 30 studies reviewed by Cummins (1996). Table 9.1 displays some of these studies and gives the mean importance weights averaged from surveys of US citizens. Column (a) contains the domains of life and mean importances (weights of relative importance) from the pathbreaking study by Campbell et al. (1976). Consistent with later studies, they found that health tends to be rated highest life domain (area), followed by family life, extent of civil rights allowed by the national government, friendships, housing, job, community, and leisure activities. To address the concern that the "stated importance" of domains might differ from the "real" importance, Campbell et al. (1976) showed a close correlation between the stated importances in Table 9.1a and regression coefficients predicting stated QOL from life domains, demonstrating convergent validity for the weights in Table 9.1.

Table 9.1b contains the average importance weights from the US responses to an international online survey in 2005 of current readers of *The Economist* magazine. Respondents were asked to rate the importance of ten social indicators on a 5-point scale, where 5 denoted "Very important" and 1 denoted "Unimportant." Finally, Table 9.1c contains mean importance weights for US citizens from the World Values Survey (WVS) (Inglehart 2000), which asks respondents in 50 countries to rate the importance of: family, friends, leisure time, politics, work, and religion. The exact wording to the questions in 1995 was, "Please say, for each of the following, how important it is in your life. Would you say xxx is very important (3), rather important (2), not very important (1), or not at all important (0)?" The scale is usually assumed to be equal interval, (hence the codes are equal interval), and the anchoring at "not at all important" may be assumed to represent a weight of near zero.

In summary, a fairly useful and predictive model of how people make their own QOL judgments using the weighted average model has been developed and validated empirically. And importance weights have been found to be relatively consistent in 30 years of surveys. According to the fifth and sixth principles, then, a QOL index should be a weighted average of the major domains, with weights approximating those in Table 9.1. The final principle uses this information to estimate acceptance of the QOL index by citizens.

Table 9.1 Mean ratings of importance of domains in USA from (a) Campbell, Converse, and Rodgers (CCR) (1976 Table 3–5), (b) The Economist Intelligence Unit (EIU) (2005), and (c) World Values Survey (WVS) (Inglehart 2000)

(a) CCR (1976)		(b) EIU (2005)		(c) WVS (1999)	
"Health"	3.63[a]	"Your health"	4.68	–	
"Marriage"	3.56	–[b]			
"Family life"	3.54	"Family relations"	4.47	"Family"	2.94
"National government"	3.46	"Degree of political and civil liberty in your county"		"Politics"	1.68
		"Degree of social equality in your country"			
		"Degree of gender equality in your country"			
"Friendships"	2.92	–		"Friends"	2.65
"Housing"	2.90	"Material well-being"	3.50		
"Job"	2.81	"Job satisfaction"		"Work"	2.31
		"Job security"			
"Community"	2.79	"Social and community activities"	3.51	–	
"Religious faith"	2.65	–		"Religion"	2.37
"Nonwork activities"	2.21	–		"Leisure time"	2.29
"Financial situation"	2.06	–		–	
"Organizations"	.99	–			
N		994		1,502	

[a]Mean ratings from Campbell, Converse, and Rodgers were reversed by subtracting them from five so that higher ratings indicate higher importances, to be consistent with other studies in table
[b]Indicates that domain was not rated in study

Principle 7: Assuring acceptance by citizens. Final acceptance of any index by the public is a complex process of demonstrating unbiasedness, credibility, and usefulness to citizens, together with extensive publicity. Moller and Dickow (2002) outline how this was achieved in South Africa during its democratic transition. While some of these factors are outside the control of social scientists, the properties of unbiasedness and usefulness can and should be built into a QOL index by adopting the following proposition as closely as possible: An index will be unbiased and useful if the index summarizes a large amount of data in a way that closely mimics the judgment of a citizen if she were to read the entire report and make her own judgment of QOL.

Hagerty and Land (2007) formalized this proposition by defining a quantitative measure of agreement between an index and a citizen *i*'s actual judgment of QOL. They considered several measures and recommend the simple correlation coefficient between the citizen *i*'s actual QOL judgments and the index's ratings. As this correlation increases, agreement between the two increases, with maximum agreement yielding a correlation of +1. They denote this correlation as A_{Qi}, for the agreement (correlation) between a QOL index and person *i*'s actual judgments of QOL. Critical values of this measure are +.7 (the common requirement for reliability between two raters) and 0 (the point above which the QOL index at least agrees *in direction* with the individual's actual ratings). Hence, if agreement A_{Qi} is at least above zero, then the QOL index agrees in direction with the individual's ratings, and both would agree on whether "things are getting better or worse."

Ideal data to calculate agreement would use surveys of citizens' actual judgments of various countries' QOL. Then the agreement A_{Qi} could be calculated as the simple correlation between the proposed index and each individual's actual QOL judgments. To our knowledge, such data do not yet exist (though they would be relatively easy to collect). However, Hagerty and Land use next-best data to calculate agreement with some real QOL indices—survey data on *importance weights* that citizens report.

The research then extrapolates citizens' QOL judgments using the linear model in Eq. 9.1 which is known to fit well.

Using this method, they calculated average agreement between the Human Development Index (which uses equal weights) and the actual weights surveyed from a sample of 1,502 US citizens in the World Values Survey (Inglehart et al. 2000). As noted above, the average weights from the WVS are given in Table 9.1c. Mean agreement between the HDI index ratings of QOL and the 1,502 individuals' ratings (predicted from their weights) was $+.97$ (standard error of estimate $=.04$).

This is remarkably high, and Hagerty and Land go on to probe why agreement should be so high even though the equal weighting in the HDI differs from the unequal weights that citizens report in the WVS. Using the weighted average model of QOL judgments of Eq. 9.1, they prove mathematically that several factors unexpectedly affect agreement for any index. Specifically, they show that agreement will be higher when (1) the index is based on cross-sectional data rather than time-series data, (2) the distribution of citizens' weights is unimodal rather than bimodal (as in abortion where conflict is much higher because weights are extreme and bimodal), (3) the distribution of citizens' weights is not negatively correlated across indices (people who highly value one indicator always place a very low value on another indicator), and (4) citizens' weights are all positive (or all negative) for each indicator. The HDI and the WVS conform to all four of these properties. Hence the agreement induced by the equal weight in HDI is quite high compared to the unequal weights that citizens report in the WVS.

Why should these four properties influence distortion so greatly? The first property states that cross-sectional indices (such as the HDI, Estes' Index of Social Progress, and Veenhoven's Happy Life Expectancy, all of which are described in the next section of the chapter) will show high agreement, regardless of differences in citizens' weights. The intuitive reason behind this is that all citizens are likely to agree (regardless of their importance weights) that Somalia currently has lower QOL than Canada. Hence, any citizen with positive weights (greater than zero and less than one) will create high agreement and high correlation with QOL ratings by the index. The technical

reason behind this is that agreement A can be written as a simple matrix product:

$$A_{Qi} = \mathbf{W}_Q^* \mathbf{R}_x \mathbf{W}_i^*, \tag{9.3}$$

where $\mathbf{R}_x$ is the correlation matrix between the K social indicators, $\mathbf{W}_Q^*$ are the weights (standardized) that the QOL index uses, and $\mathbf{W}_i^*$ are the importance weights (standardized) applied by person i. Equation 9.3 shows that the correlation A_{Qi} between the index and any individual is a function *not only of the weights*, but also is moderated by the correlations among the social indicators $\mathbf{R}_x$. When the intercorrelations $\mathbf{R}_x$ are high (as they are in the HDI and other cross-sectional indices), Hagerty and Land prove that agreement will be high *regardless* of whether the weights for the index differ much from the weights for the average citizen, as in the case for the HDI.

Even though Hagerty and Land's first property states that cross-sectional QOL indices create the highest agreement, it is crucial for policy makers to also have QOL indices that are based on time series for a single country, because national debates more often focus on time-series analyses ("Are you better off than 4 years ago?") than on cross-sectional analyses ("Are we better off than Somalia?"). This type of data results in many more negative correlations among indicators, which tend to decrease agreement in QOL indices.[4] Therefore, Hagerty and Land assessed distortion for a time-series index, the Index of Social Health (ISH) by Miringoff and Miringoff (1999). They show that the correlation among the 16 social indicators often yielded large negative correlations (e.g., life expectancy above age 65 is negatively correlated ($r=-.85$) with average weekly earnings in the USA since 1970). The question then is whether these negative correlations give rise to a QOL index with agreement too low for a majority of citizens to endorse. Hagerty and Land first examined a

---

[4] The reason for negative correlations is due in part to "restriction of range" problems (e.g., life expectancy varied far less in the USA since 1970 than it does in a cross-sectional sample of nations, where Somalia has a life expectancy of only 40 years). Negative correlations are also due to preferences of individual nations. For example, the USA seems to prefer higher GDP/capita at the expense of some loss in equality, compared to European nations. Such a policy could result in negative correlation between these indicators as inequality is pushed up in order to gain GDP/capita.

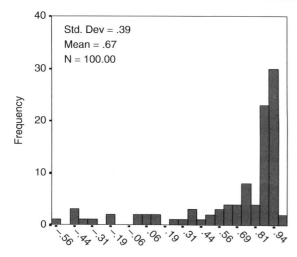

Fig. 9.1 Distribution of agreement $A_{E,i}$ between the equal-weight QOL index of the Index of Social Health and 100 simulated individuals with uniformly distributed weights

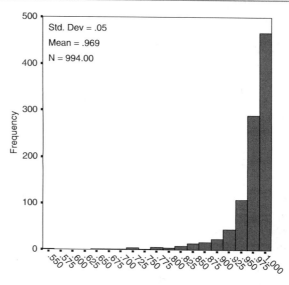

Fig. 9.2 Distribution of agreement $A_{E,i}$ between the equal-weight QOL index of the Index of Social Health and the 994 actual US respondents of the EIU survey

"benchmark" case simulating 100 citizens' weights to be uniformly distributed[5] across each of the 16 attributes. The results are shown in Fig. 9.1, where the distribution of correlations between the QOL index (with equal weights) and the 100 simulated individuals is plotted. Despite the fact that the correlations *among the indicators* are negative due to the time-series nature of the index, the correlations between the QOL index and the 100 individuals show that most have very high agreement with the QOL index with equal weights. The average agreement $A_{E,i}$ is .67, and over 50% of simulated individuals have agreement $A_{E,i}$ greater than +.7, the typical value that psychologists chose to show high reliability between raters. Hence, the equal-weighting index for the ISH would induce sufficient agreement to correctly capture more than 50% of these simulated citizens' QOL judgments.

Hagerty and Land compared this "benchmark" case of uniformly distributed weights to actual surveys of weights from the WVS and *The Economist* Intelligence Unit (EIU). Figure 9.2 shows the distribution of correlations $A_{E,i}$ between the QOL index for ISH (with equal weights) and the 994 US respondents to the EIU survey. Mean agreement is +.96, and over 90% of respondents displayed correlations higher than .7. Hence, not only a majority, but a supermajority of the EIU respondents would accept this equal-weighted index for ISH. Figure 9.2 shows higher agreement between the QOL index and respondents because the real respondents in Fig. 9.2 are not uniformly distributed, but have sharply unimodal distributions.

The second property that increases agreement is whether the distribution of citizens' actual weights is unimodal as opposed to bimodal. The intuitive reason behind this is that, when weights are unimodal, a single index can be constructed near the mean to capture the weights of most citizens. In contrast, a polarized indicator such as "number of abortions performed" is likely to have weights that are highly bimodal, with some citizens extreme on one side, others extreme on the other side of the distribution, and fewer in the middle. In actual surveys of weights, Hagerty and Land calculate that all distributions they examined for citizens in 40 countries are unimodal rather than bimodal distributions, increasing the likelihood of agreement by an index. (In fact, if an indicator is as

---

[5] A uniform distribution of citizen's importance weights ensures that any proportion between 0 and 1 has equal likelihood of being chosen and assigned to an index component for a simulated individual. In fact, as noted in the text, empirical distributions of importance weights show that some values are more likely to occur than others. Therefore, the assumption of a uniform distribution represents an extreme that is used to ascertain whether or not the resulting index is highly correlated with the QOL index.

highly polarized as abortion, we recommend that it *not* be included in the index because it decreases the chance of agreement, though it should be included in the social report).

The third property that increases agreement is whether the distribution of citizens' weights is negatively correlated for many indicators. In such a case, people who highly value one indicator would always place a very low value on another indicator. Interestingly, Hagerty and Land have found no such negative correlations in the WVS or the EIU surveys, increasing the likelihood of agreement.

The last property that increases agreement is whether every citizen weights an indicator with a positive number. For instance, no one prefers lower life expectancy over higher life expectancy. This property seems quite reasonable for most social indicators (health, income, housing, job satisfaction), and in fact, most surveys do not allow negative weights (Inglehart 2000; Campbell et al. 1976). In contrast, including an indicator such as the number of abortions is likely to create this condition. Such a condition generates more radical differences among individual citizens, and results in lower agreement for any QOL index. Hence we recommend not including any indicators where some citizens hold positive weights but others hold negative weights (though of course all indicators should be included in the larger social report).

Optimal weights for a QOL index. Analyzing a weighted average model of QOL judgment of the form of Eq. 9.1, Hagerty and Land (2007) show mathematically that: (1) *if a survey is available to measure the distribution of citizens' importance weights for each indicator, then agreement is maximized when the index is constructed using the mean weights of citizens.* But, since such surveys are often not available, they also prove that (2) *constructing an index with equal weights produces what in statistics is termed a minimax estimator (that is, equal weighting will minimize maximum possible disagreements).* We note that many of the indices reviewed in this chapter already use equal weighting, but the reasoning behind equal weighting was never well justified. In the context of the weighted average model of QOL judgments of Eq. 9.1, the proofs of Hagerty and Land (2007) now place current practice on a sound theoretical footing, and show how it is possible to further increase acceptance through surveys.

Review of Existing QOL Indices

Having articulated several principles for QOL index construction, we can now review and evaluate a number of existing QOL indices. Composite indicators of QOL have historical roots in economics, where Bentham's social welfare function simply added the individual happiness of each person to get total social welfare. Sen (1993) continues this research stream, provides a set of minimal requirements for a summary utility index to exist, and helped develop the Human Development Index. Kahneman et al. (2004) propose a formal set of National Well-Being Accounts that adds results from psychology to the economic framework, which we review below. In the area of sociology, Land (2000: 2687) documents the rapid growth of QOL indices:

> With the tremendous increase in the richness of social data available for many societies today as compared to two or three decades ago, a new generation of social indicators researchers has returned to the task of summary index construction. Some examples: (1) at the level of the broadest possible comparisons of nations with respect to the overall quality of life, the *Human Development Index* (United Nations Development Programme 1993), *Diener's (1995) Value-Based Index of National Quality-of-Life,* and *Estes' (1988; 1998) Index of Social Progress*; and (2) at the level of comparisons at the national level over time in the United States, the *American Demographics Index of Well-Being* (Kacapyr 1996), *the Fordham Index of Social Health* (Miringoff and Miringoff 1996), and the *Genuine Progress Indicator* (Redefining Progress 1995).

The QOL indices he cites vary on number of indicators, whether they incorporate only "objective" indicators such as crime rate or "subjective indicators" such as social surveys, whether they are cross-sectional (multiple countries at one point in time) or time series (one country at multiple points in time), and the weights they assign to social indicators. Each will be briefly described here. A summary of each index is given in Table 9.2. Further detail on many of these indices is provided by Hagerty et al. (2001).

1. *The Human Development Index (HDI).* The HDI is a combination of three indicators measured cross-sectionally for each of a set of countries: longevity, knowledge (literacy, weighted 2/3, and years of schooling, weighted 1/3), and income. Sen's capability approach to QOL is used, described as "a process of enlarging people's choices" (United Nations Development Program 1990: 10).

Table 9.2 Fourteen current QOL indices and some of their properties

Index name	Disaggregates into subseries (domains)?	Disaggregates into subpopulations?	Standardizes each indicator?	Construction of index	Reflects citizens' importance weights?
Human Development Index UNDP (2001)	Yes, income, education, health	Yes, in later indices for the poor and women	Yes: Max-Min. Income is log not linear.	Additive with equal weights. Log (income) + education + health	No survey, but experts preview
Genuine Progress Indicator Redefining Progress (1995)	Yes	No	Yes: to dollars	Additive with equal weighting for all money units	No
Index of Economic Well-Being Osberg and Sharpe (2000).	Yes, income, investment, inequality, insecurity	No	Yes	Additive with unequal weights	No, though does sensitivity analysis on alternate weights
National Well-Being Index Kahnemann et al. (2004)	Yes, 19 domains considered	Possible, but not reported	Yes: to affect on 6 point scale	Additive with weights equal to time spent on that activity	Yes, time-use survey
Money Magazine Guterbock (1997)	Yes, 40 indicators, heavily weighted to economic conditions	No	Proprietary and unknown	Proprietary and unknown, but includes cost of housing, amenities, etc.	Yes, through a reader-convenience sample of 250. Also allows readers to input their own weights
Index of Social Progress Estes (1997)	Yes	No, though some indicators include only at-risk population	Yes	Additive with equal weights	Yes, panel of expert citizens
Index of Social Health Miringoff and Miringoff (1999)	Yes, 16 indicators. But not calculated over entire population. Includes vulnerable subgroups only	No, though some indicators describe only vulnerable subgroups	Yes: Max-Min	Additive with equal weights	No, fails to include GDP, average life expectancy
Happy Life-Expectancy Veenhoven (1996)	Yes, subjective happiness, life expectancy	No, though possible	No: cardinal measurement of both domains	Multiplicative with equal weights	No

M.R. Hagerty and K.C. Land

American Demographics Index of Well-Being Kacapyr (1997)	Yes: reports individual indicators	No	Yes	Additive with equal weights	No
Netherlands' Living Conditions Index Boelhouwer and Stoop (1999)	Yes, reports individual indicators but not sub-groups	Yes, reports by province	Yes	Additive with equal weights	No
Economist Intelligence Unit Economist Intelligence Unit (2005)	Yes	Not reported: subgroup data from some countries not available	Yes	Additive with unequal weights	Yes, but convenience sample of readers
Australian Quality of Life Index	Yes, standard of living, health, relationships, what they are achieving in life, safety, community connection, future security	Yes	Yes	Additive with equal weights	No
Child and Youth Well-Being Index Land et al. (2001, 2007)	Yes, seven domains: material well-being, social relationships, health and safety, educational attainments, place in community, and emotional/spiritual well-being	Yes, by race and ethnic group	Yes	Additive with equal weights	No, but reviewed by experts
Kids Count Index (Annie E. Casey Foundation)	Yes	Yes	Yes	Additive with equal weights	No, but reviewed by experts

A maximum and minimum value is selected for each variable, and by a formula the indicators are transformed to range from zero to one, and averaged to produce the HDI. Longevity is life expectancy at birth, which is the average years of life of persons who died in the year of reference. The knowledge variable is a combination of adult literacy—the percent of adults who can read and write—and years of schooling attained by the adult population. Income originally was the log of the per capita gross domestic product. Subsequently, the GDP/capita was modified by using an Atkinson formulation that "the higher the income relative to the poverty level, the more sharply the diminishing returns affect the contribution of income to human development" (United Nations Development Program 1993: 91).

Each HDI indicator is standardized in the sense that it is assigned a value between 0 and 100, where 0 represents the lowest-ranking country and 100 the highest-ranking country. The use of minimum and maximum values is faulted when standardization is performed each year. The case is cited of a country that raises its life expectancy to increase the minimum value; with the maximum country remaining constant, the transformed values would still range the same and would not reflect the leap in longevity (Trabold-Nubler 1991: 239). The solution suggested for this problem is to select minimum and maximum values that are absolute (constant) and will not be surpassed by the developing countries over the next decade or two (Trabold-Nubler 1991: 241).

2. *The Genuine Progress Indicator* (*GPI*). The GPI (Redefining Progress 1995) was developed from an economic background, and attempts to value all of its indicators in dollar terms from 1950 to present. It broadens the conventional gross domestic product framework to include the contributions of the family and community realms, and of the natural habitat, along with conventionally measured economic production. The GPI takes into account more than 20 aspects of economic life that GDP ignores (value of time spent on household work, parenting, and volunteer work; the value of services of consumer durables; and services of highways and streets). Subtractions are defensive expenditures due to crime, auto accidents, and pollution; social costs, such as the cost of divorce,

household cost of pollution, and loss of leisure; and depreciation of environmental assets and natural resources, including loss of farmland, wetlands, old growth forests, reduction in the stock of natural resources, and the damaging effects of wastes and pollution.

There are serious problems with the assumptions and valuation techniques used to estimate many of the resource and environmental variables in the GPI. For example, the value of the loss of wetlands becomes unrealistically larger and larger over time and gives a strong downward bias to the index. For this reason, the index in its current form is not a reliable measure of QOL or genuine progress. Also, the economic statistics are difficult to disaggregate to subgroups such as the poor, disabled, etc.

3. *The Index of Economic Well-Being* (*IEWB*). The IEWB was developed by Osberg and Sharpe (2000) and is posted at www.csls.ca. Though it is derived from strictly economic theory, it does not attempt to measure QOL in dollars, and integrates four major QOL domains: average consumption flows (including personal consumption flows adjusted for the underground economy, the value of increased longevity, changes in family size which affect the economies of scale in household consumption, cost of commuting, household pollution abatement, auto accidents, crime, changes in working time, government services, and the value of unpaid work), aggregate accumulation of productive stocks (net capital physical stock, including housing stocks, the stock of research and development, value of natural resources stocks, the stock of human capital, the level of foreign indebtedness, and the net changes in the value of the environment due to CO_2 emissions), inequality in the distribution of individual incomes (measured by the Gini coefficient for after-tax household income and the intensity of poverty incidence and depth, defined as the product of the poverty rate and the poverty gap), and insecurity in the anticipation of future incomes (change over time in the economic risks associated with unemployment, illness, "widowhood," and old age). The weights attached to each of these four components of economic well-being can vary, depending on the values of different observers, though for most of their publications, the weights assigned are [.4, .1, .25, .25].

The IEWB has been estimated at the national and international level and can be disaggregated to the province level, so it can help policy makers at these levels in program and policy development. However, it is difficult to disaggregate it to special populations, such as the elderly or immigrants because government statistics do not break out these groups.

4. *National Well-Being Accounts (NWBA)*. An attempt to concatenate economic with psychological theory was made by Kahneman et al. (2004) with their proposed National Well-Being Accounts; see also the chapter by Diener and Tov in this *Handbook*. It is proposed to use time diaries to track citizens' positive and negative affect (pleasant and unpleasant emotions) during each of 19 activities (intimate relations, socializing after work, dinner, lunch, relaxing, exercise, praying, socializing at work, watching TV, phone at home, napping, cooking, shopping, computer at home, housework, childcare, evening commute, working, and morning commute). It is likely that some of these activities can be combined, since they are similar and contain similar affect.

The NWBA approach assumes that well-being is separable over time, so that average affect can be weighted by time and added to get overall well-being for one person, and averaged to get average well-being for the population. The resulting index is standardized because affect is measured on a seven-point scale. It can be computed for any subpopulation because it is survey-based. The model is a weighted additive, where the weights are time spent in each activity. The Bureau of Labor Statistics now publishes the monthly American Time Use Survey, though it does not currently collect affect ratings for each activity. Kahneman et al. argue that this index is consistent with economic theory and should be acceptable to economic experts. It remains to be fully developed, implemented, and reported on a continuing basis.

5. *Money Magazine's "Best Places" (MBP)*. With subscription and individual sales each month of almost two million copies, *Money* Magazine could be said to be the most prolific distributor of QOL information today with its annual Best Places survey. *Money* uses a three-step process in developing its rankings each year (Guterbock 1997). In the first stage, 250 *Money* readers are surveyed to determine the importance weights of more than 40 criteria used in choosing a city to live. In the second stage, current statistical data for each city are collected on a wide range of empirical indicators. While the full list of indicators is not disclosed, some examples offered by *Money* include the following: (1) number of doctors per capita, (2) violent crime rate from the FBI Uniform Crime Reports, (3) the cost-of-living index from the American Chamber of Commerce Research Association, (4) recent job growth, (5) future job growth estimates, (6) typical price of a three-bedroom home and its property tax from twenty-first century Real Estate brokers, and (7) housing appreciation rate over the past 12 months from twenty-first century. In the third stage, the individual indicators are aggregated into nine broad categories matching categories previously derived in the first stage.

Guterbock (1997) does a masterful job of "retro-engineering" the skimpy data provided by *Money* over 10 years and succeeds in deducing the flawed weighting scheme for the variables used. Aside from being atheoretical, the problem with the index appears to be the overweighting given to the economic conditions of the 300 cities in the USA that are ranked in this index (Guterbock 1997). We applaud the use of surveys to assess citizens' weights for this QOL index. However, we show later that the inclusion of indicators, such as "housing prices," is likely to increase distortion and reduce public acceptance of this index as a QOL index.

6. *Estes' Index of Social Progress (ISP)*. In a series of publications dating back to 1984, Richard J. Estes (1984, 1998) has developed an "Index of Social Progress" (ISP) and applied it to a number of nation-states around the world as well as to groups of states in particular regions of the world. The purpose of the ISP is to (1) identify significant changes in the "adequacy of social provision" occurring throughout the world and (2) assess national and international progress in providing more adequately for the basic social and material needs of the world's growing population.

The ISP consists of 46 social indicators that have been subdivided into ten subindexes: Education, Health Status, Women Status, Defense Effort, Economics, Demographic, Geography, Political

Participation, Cultural Diversity, and Welfare Effort. All of the 46 component indicators of the ISP are "objective" indicators, such as "percent adult illiteracy," "life expectation in years," "real gross domestic product per head," and "violations of political rights index." Estes has computed the ISP on 10 and 5-year intervals from 1970 to 1995.

Due to the number and redundancy of the component indicators of the ISP, Estes has subjected them to a two-stage varimax factor analysis in which each indicator and subindex was analyzed for its relative contribution toward explaining the variance associated with changes in social progress over time. Standardized scores of the component indicators then were multiplied by the factor loadings to create weighted subindex scores which then were summed to obtain the "Weighted Index of Social Progress" (WISP).

7. *The Index of Social Health (ISH)*. The Index of Social Health was developed by the Fordham Institute for Innovation in Social Policy (Miringoff and Miringoff 1996, 1999). They include 16 measures as time series since 1970, composed of: infant mortality (as reported by the National Center for Health Statistics), child abuse (from National Committee to Prevent Child Abuse), children in poverty (measured by the Census Bureau), teenage suicide, drug abuse (percent of teenagers using any illicit drug in the past 12 months, measured by the federally sponsored study "Monitoring the Future"), high-school dropout rate, teenage births, unemployment, average weekly earnings, health insurance coverage (now measured by the Census Bureau), poverty among those over 65, life expectancy at age 65, violent crime rate, alcohol-related traffic fatalities, housing affordability (measured by the housing affordability index of the National Association of Realtors), and gap between rich and poor (measured by the Gini coefficient from the Census Bureau). See Miringoff and Miringoff (1999) for complete details.

Note that these 16 components are *not* organized into the usual domains. Instead, they organize the components by age groupings, with the first three pertaining to children, the next four to youth, the next three to adults, the next two to the aging, and the last five to all age groups.

However, the authors fail to address the question of whether these measures are valid. That is, how well do these 16 components correlate with peoples' experienced quality of life? This is probably the weakest part of their project. In Miringoff and Miringoff (1999), only one page is devoted to discussing why they chose the 16 components of their index, and no validation studies are cited.

The index applied equal weights to all 16 components after (roughly) standardizing each. By standardizing, we mean that they attempt to put the components on a comparable scale, ranging from zero (worst performance since 1970) to one (best performance since 1970). But instead of using the usual statistical method of computing z-scores (subtract the mean and divide by the standard deviation), they subtract the minimum and divide by the range. Statisticians do not use this procedure because it has poor statistical properties: It is vulnerable to outliers, and will vary with the number of years in the sample (Hagerty 1999). On the other hand, explaining their index to lay people is easier than explaining standardized scores.

8. *Veenhoven's Happy Life-Expectancy Scale (HLE)*. The computation of Happy Life-Expectancy consists in multiplying "standard" life expectancy in years with average happiness as expressed on a scale ranging from zero to one. For example,

> Suppose that life-expectancy in a country is 50 years, and that the average score on a 0–10 step happiness scale is 5. Converted to a 0–1 scale, the happiness score is then 0.5. The product of 50 and 0.5 is 25. So happy life-expectancy in that country is 25 years. This example characterizes most of the poor nations in the present day world. If life-expectancy is 80 years and average happiness 8, happy life-expectancy is 64 years (80×0.8). This example characterizes the most livable nations in the present day world. (Veenhoven 1996: 29)

Veenhoven validates the HLE by showing positive correlations (controlling for a country's affluence) for HLE and many social indicators (e.g., purchasing power, state expenditures as a percent of GDP, percent literate).

A potential problem for HLE is that it changes very slowly, so that country rankings will not change much each year. It may be considered a very useful "output" or "outcome" measure, but it is missing the "throughput" measures of a county's performance on the other domains (freedom, family and job satisfaction, etc.).

9. *American Demographics' Index of Well-Being (AD-IWB)*. The *American Demographics* magazine

published the Index of Well-Being for the United States from February 1996 to December 1998. The Index, however, covers the period April 1990 to July 1998. It was a monthly composite of five indicators and was unique in that it was updated every month, with subseries updated monthly by government sources. The five areas were monitored with 11 monthly time series: consumer attitudes (Consumer Confidence Index and Consumer Expectations Index), income and employment opportunity (real disposable income per capita and employment rate), social and physical environment (number of endangered species, crime rate, and divorce rate), leisure (168 less weekly hours worked and real spending on recreation per capita), and productivity/technology (industrial production per unit of labor and industrial production per unit of energy). Each component was "benchmarked" to an April 1990 level of 100. The separate reporting of each component and the socioeconomic forces undergirding the change were an important, informative feature of the Index. The weights for each element of each component were determined "by fitting a trend line to the series from 1983 to 1997. Then the larger the monthly deviations from that trend, the smaller the weight given to the data series. Specifically, the weight given to a data series was inversely proportional to the variance from its own trend, which means that data series with relatively smaller fluctuations around their trends were given more importance in the index. The weights were normalized so that they sum to unity" (e-mail communication 4/9/99). The author further explains, "Every component of my index gets the weight it deserves because a 10% change in consumer attitudes is equivalent to a 0.2% change in the leisure sector based on past trends. The 10% move in consumer attitudes gets a 1% weight while the 0.2% move in leisure gets a 50% weight. After applying the weights, both moves are seen to be equivalent" (e-mail communication 4/9/99). Thus, by the above-described device, change in the Index was influenced equally by each of the five components.

The AD-IWB employed a weighting scheme unique among QOL studies. The purpose was to equalize the influence on change, rather than the influence of the item upon the output of QOL.

10. *The Netherlands' Living Conditions Index (LCI)*. The Netherlands Social and Cultural Planning Office (Boelhouwer and Stoop 1999) has developed the Living Conditions Index (LCI). Its base year is 1974, with annual updates since then. It was designed for the specific purpose of public policy "to reflect conditions in areas that are influenceable by government policy" (p. 51). The LCI index is reported as a single index (=100 in 1997), but can be broken down into its components of: housing, health, purchasing power, leisure activities, mobility, social participation, sport activity, holidays, education, and employment. The specific indicators have changed over the years to address new public policy problems. The authors argue strongly that only objective indicators should be included in the index, because only these are controllable by public policy. Nevertheless, they also collect measures of overall happiness in order to validate their LCI against perceived happiness. These simple correlations in 1997 were all significant and in the expected direction (see their Table III). Further, their LCI is more reliable than the separate components, because the correlation of LCI with happiness is higher than the correlation of any of the separate components. Hence, the separate domains are not redundant, but provide some additional predictive validity. However, a multiple regression should be reported in order to sort out which domains add significant explanation to LCI and happiness. Unequal weights are assigned in computing the LCI by factor-analyzing the components and using the loadings on the first factor as weights. However, this could be improved by using the weights from a multiple regression in predicting happiness. The resulting weights would make LCI the best forecast of subjective happiness.

11. *The Economist Intelligence Unit's Quality of Life Index (EIU-QOLI)*. The Economist Intelligence Unit (2005) published their first QOL index, composed of ten publicly available series. The domains are: material well-being (in GDP PPP $), health (in life expectancy), political stability and security (Economist ratings), family life (in divorce/1000), community life (church or trade union attendance), climate and geography (in latitude), job security (unemployment rate), political freedom (ratings by Freedom House), and gender equality (ratio of

average male to female earnings). The index is a weighted average model, with weights derived from a multiple regression predicting life satisfaction in 74 countries where data were available. These scores are then related in a multivariate regression to various factors that have been shown to be associated with life satisfaction in many studies. As many as nine factors survive in the final estimated equation (all except one are statistically significant; the weakest, gender equality, falls just below). Together these variables explain more than 80% of the intercountry variation in life-satisfaction scores. Using beta coefficients from the regression to derive the weights of the various factors, the most important were health, material well-being, and political stability and security. These were followed by family relations and community life. Next in order of importance were climate, job security, political freedom, and finally gender equality. No subgroups within countries were calculated. Data are not available for subgroups from many of those countries.

12. *The Australian Unity Wellbeing Index (AUWBI).* Cummins et al. (2005) have developed a continuing survey sampling 2,000 Australian citizens semiannually and have created two indices called the Personal Wellbeing Index and the National Wellbeing Index. The Personal Wellbeing Index is the average level of satisfaction across seven aspects of personal life—health, personal relationships, safety, standard of living, achieving, community connectedness, and future security. The National Wellbeing Index is the average satisfaction score across six aspects of national life—the economy, the environment, social conditions, governance, business, and national security. Both indices are based on subjective indicators measuring satisfaction with each domain. Each indicator is a single item in the survey, rating satisfaction on a 0–10. The scores are then combined across the seven domains to yield an overall Index score, which is adjusted to have a range of 0–100. Hence each series is already standardized.

The indices are embedded in an extensive social report that disaggregates the indices by domain and by subpopulations, examines trends over time, and relates changes to changes in current events and changes in demographics. The index currently extends from April 2001 and is in its 16th wave.

As more waves are collected, time-series analysis correlating the subjective measures with official objective statistical series can be done.

13. *The Child and Youth Well-Being Index (CWI).* The Foundation for Child Development Child and Youth Well-Being Index Project (Land et al. 2001; Land et al. 2007) calculates changes in the QOL of children and youth in the USA. A general description of the Index, annual reports, charts and tables, and scientific papers are posted at www.soc.duke.edu/~cwi/. The CWI is composed of 28 national-level Key Indicator time series since grouped into seven domains that are based on Cummins' (1996) review of subjective well-being studies: family economic well-being, social relationships (with family and peers), health, safety/behavioral concerns, educational attainments, community connectedness (participation in schooling or work institutions), and emotional/spiritual well-being. It uses equal weights of Key Indicators within domains and equal weights of the seven domains to calculate a composite QOL index for children and youth. Annual changes are indexed from two base years, 1975 and 1985. Trends for children's QOL are plotted from the base years. The trends are broken down by race and ethnicity, by infancy, childhood and adolescence, and by each of the seven domains. In Land et al. (2007), some evidence of the external validity of the CWI is provided in the form of a high correlation with trends in overall life satisfaction of high school seniors from 1975 to 2003. Annual reports on the CWI are broadly disseminated to the American public by the Foundation for Child Development and have resulted in much print and electronic media coverage.

14. *Kids Count Index (KCI).* In collaboration with the CWI Project, the Annie E. Casey Foundation has developed a Kids Count Index to estimate changes in the QOL of children and youth in each of the 50 states of the USA. The index includes ten indicators, which have not been subdivided into domains (the authors say that ten indicators are few enough in number to make domains unnecessary). The indicators are: percent of low-birth-weight babies, infant mortality rate, child death rate (ages 1–14), teen death rate (ages 15–19), teen birth rate, high-school dropout rate, idle teens, parental underemployment, child poverty rate, and children in

single-parent households. The indicators are each standardized and equally weighted to create the index. They calculate change over time as a change in indicator from baseline, relative to baseline year of 1990. One of their stated goals is to generate publicity for the plight of children using scientifically generated data. They are indeed achieving their goal of publicity, citing over 1,160 newspaper articles referencing the index, 509 television interviews, and hundreds of radio interviews, and over 750,000 internet visits per year. Interestingly, they report that the state's rank is listed in the headline of the newspaper article 36% of the time, and is mentioned in the body of the article in 62% of articles.

Common Criticisms of Indices and Recommended Solutions

An index of QOL is a relatively novel concept to journalists and laymen, and they will have questions to assess whether the index is credible, unbiased, and informative. Below are some typical criticisms and solutions that are commonly posed.

1. *"A composite index can obscure whether some indicators have moved in opposite directions."* We agree that this is a danger, and remind critics that every summary statistic suffers this drawback. This problem can easily be remedied by including discussion in a companion social report on which indicators are improving, and which are declining, both of which are important information for citizens and policy analysts. A QOL index is not intended to stand alone, but must be accompanied by a social report that examines trends in each subseries.

2. *"A composite index could obscure sub-group comparisons, such that disadvantaged populations may be worse off even when the average QOL index improves."* Again, we agree that this is a danger, and our principles recommend that the social report disaggregates measures of conditions for disadvantaged groups. Such breakdowns for the elderly, children, and minorities in the social report already are standard practice in the Swedish and German social reports. In summary, composite indices are quite useful to *begin* a report, but should not *end* the reporting.

3. *"Composite indices may be appropriate for unidimensional phenomena such as the CPI, but they cannot capture multi-dimensional concepts such as Quality of Life."* We agree that developing indices for multidimensional phenomena is more difficult than for unidimensional concepts. But citizens and decision makers are already making these judgments without the help of science to make political decisions and to draft laws. The words "quality of life" are invoked more than 20 times per week on the floor of the US Congress (GPO 1999), with varying definitions and no measurements. Citizens and decision makers would certainly benefit from scientific attempts to capture QOL, by improving the reliability and validity of subseries, by reducing perceptual biases to which humans are prone, and by providing a common language to discuss which indicators should be included and how they should be weighted for each application. This chapter provides seven principles for achieving this.

4. *"A composite index could be dominated by a single indicator. If the index assigns very high weight to one domain, then the index will be driven by that domain only, and the index would be distorted."* This is a potential danger, and a section of the social report (1) must show how each subseries is standardized to prevent one subseries from dominating, and (2) must justify what weights are applied. In the absence of surveys of citizens or decision makers to assess their weights, an easy way to avoid this problem is simply to apply equal weights to all indicators, which Hagerty and Land (2007) mathematically proved to be the minimax solution that minimizes maximum distortion of the index.

5. *"A composite index may not reflect the 'true' weights that citizens actually apply to social indicators."* Johansson (2002) warns that even surveys of citizens' weights may not be correct because citizens' weights may *change* as they discuss the issues and listen to candidates. Such dynamically changing weights are likely to occur for some indicators and instances, and, as surveys become better at measuring weights, it would be informative to track any changes in weights during an electoral cycle. Such a development parallels the history of the CPI, which was initiated with static weights but was modified to dynamic weights as research progressed.

6. *"A composite index provides an 'easy way out' for citizens and policy makers to avoid reading the entire report."* We have no doubt that many citizens

will only hear the "headlines" of any report because they are "satisficers" with limited time, memory, and cognitive skills. To serve them best, we should develop a QOL index that as closely as possible mimics their own judgments if they were to read the entire report. And of course we encourage them to read the report for themselves to understand the movement of subseries and their causes.

7. "*A composite QOL index raises the specter that the government begin 'social planning' where bureaucrats push citizens into programs they have not helped design.*" We strongly reject this type of social planning, and instead suggest that a QOL index should be used to hold agencies *accountable* for improving QOL for citizens in their purview.

8. "*If composite QOL indices are so valuable, why doesn't the government officially adopt a QOL index?*" Federal/national governments will probably be the last organizations to adopt QOL indices, because they require acceptance by the largest number of people. But smaller government units have already adopted QOL indicators. (Miringoff and Miringoff (1999) count 11 states and 28 communities). One federal government has already adopted a QOL index (Netherlands LCI), and another country is evaluating a candidate QOL index (Canadian Index of Wellbeing 2009). As experience and credibility with QOL systems grow among local governments and nongovernmental organizations, we expect federal governments to eventually adopt not just one, but a "family" of QOL indices similar to those for the CPI, each appropriate for different subpopulations or situations. This is part of the movement toward evidence-based measures of QOL.

Conclusions

Seven principles for constructing QOL indices have been stated and described above. Based on these principles, several recommendations can be made:

1. We recommend that the social indicators be integrated into a QOL index using the weighted average model, since it well captures the QOL judgments made by real citizens. The model also is robust to errors in measurement.

2. We recommend that the weights used be proportional to surveys of citizens' own weights for the various indicators, some of which are given in Table 9.1. This procedure maximizes agreement between citizens and the index, and has the further advantage of protecting the index from political manipulation of the weights and indicators. If surveys of citizens' weights are not available, then equal weighting minimizes the worst disagreements.

3. We recommend that the set of indicators span the major domains of QOL shown in Table 9.1 or at least as many thereof as possible (the exact name of each domain has not been standardized, nor is this essential). Again, this assures that domains that citizens designate as important are included in the index.

4. We recommend that an indicator be rejected for use in the QOL index (though should be kept in the larger social report) when some citizens place negative weights but other citizens place positive weight on it. As discussed above, "number of abortions" per year may be positively weighted by some as "freedom from government interference," but negatively by others as murder. Inclusion of such an indicator would decrease agreement by all citizens and lead to lower acceptance. We stress that not all social indicators should be included in a QOL index. A more subtle example of an indicator that should not be included is "average price of a 3-bedroom home" in *Money* magazine's index. Some people (homeowners) would place a high positive weight on this, but others (homebuyers) would place a high negative weight. In fact, this is an example of a zero-sum negotiation game where every gain for a buyer is a loss for the seller, and joint gains are always zero regardless of the price. Negotiation researchers (Pruitt and Kim 2004; Carnevale and Pruitt 1992) recommend instead including indicators that allow positive joint gains to enhance the framing of shared interests. Much research has shown that this increases the likelihood of agreement and increases joint gains in negotiations. Applying these principles to the *Money* magazine example, a simple "laddering" procedure ("what deeper goals are you trying to achieve with lower housing prices/higher housing prices?") could replace the single zero-sum attribute (price) with two shared goals: lower cost per square foot of new construction and higher personal income. Both of these new indicators would conform to our assumptions and would result in higher likelihood of agreement.

5. We recommend that an indicator be rejected for use in a QOL index (though should be kept in the larger social report) when the indicator is a "policy indicator" rather than a "goal" or "outcome" indicator. An example of a "policy indicator" is tax policy, where conservatives place a negative weight on average tax burden, and liberals tend to place a positive weight. Tax policy is better viewed as a means to an end, and a successful QOL index would again apply laddering to include the end-state variables (e.g., better health care, education, pollution control, and economic growth). These examples clarify that a QOL index would *not* remove the need for policy analysis and political discussion, but would better *focus* policy analysis and politics by forcing proponents to estimate each policy's results on the QOL index.

Using these recommendations and the seven principles for constructing a QOL index, our review suggests that it is quite feasible to create QOL indices that are reliable and valid, robust to errors, and well accepted by the public because they capture the QOL judgments that a citizen would make if she were to read the entire report. Such "evidence-based" principles would help prevent the political manipulation of weights and indicators and would strengthen the democratic process.

References

Boelhouwer, J., & Stoop, I. (1999). Measuring well-being in the Netherlands: The SCP index from 1974 to 1997. *Social Indicators Research, 48*, 51–75.

Campbell, A., Converse, P. E., & Rodgers, W. L. (1976). *The quality of American life*. New York: Russell Sage.

Canadian Institute of Well Being. (2009). *How are Canadians really doing? A closer look at select groups* (Special Report, December 2009). http://ciw.ca/Libraries/Documents/ACloserLookAtSelectGroups_FullReport.sflb.ashx.

Carnevale, P. J., & Pruitt, D. G. (1992). Negotiation and mediation. *Annual Review of Psychology, 43*, 531–582.

Charnes, A., Cooper, W. W., & Rhodes, E. L. (1978). Measuring the efficiency of decision making units. *European Journal of Operational Research, 2*, 429–444.

Charnes, A., Cooper, W. W., Lewin, A. Y., & Seiford, L. M. (Eds.). (1994). *Data envelopment analysis: Theory, methodology, and application*. Boston: Kluwer Academic.

Cummins, R. A. (1996). The domains of life satisfaction: An attempt to order chaos. *Social Indicators Research, 38*, 303–328.

Cummins, R. A., Woerner J., Tomyn, A., Gibson, A., & Knapp T. (2005). *The wellbeing of Australians – Personal relationships* (Australian Unity Wellbeing, Index: Report 14).

Melbourne: Australian Centre on Quality of Life, School of Psychology, Deakin University. ISBN 1 7415 6024 1, http://www.deakin.edu.au/research/acqol/index_wellbeing/index.htm.

Dantzig, G. B. (1963). *Linear programming and extensions*. Princeton: Princeton University Press.

Diener, E. (1995). A value based index for measuring national quality of life. *Social Indicators Research, 36*, 107–127.

Economist Intelligence Unit. (2005). The economist intelligence unit's quality of life index. *The world in 2005*, pp. 1–5. http://www.economist.com/media/pdf/QUALITY_OF_LIFE.pdf.

Erickson, R. (1993). Descriptions of inequality: The Swedish approach to welfare research. In M. Nussbaum & A. Sen (Eds.), *The quality of life*. Oxford: Clarendon.

Estes, R. J. (1984). *The social progress of nations*. New York: Praeger.

Estes, R. J. (1988). *Trends in world social development*. New York: Praeger.

Estes, R. J. (1997). Social development trends in Europe, 1970–1994: Development prospects for the new Europe. *Social Indicators Research, 42*, 1–19.

Estes, R. J. (1998). Social development trends in transitional economies, 1970–1995. In R. H. Kempe, Sr. (Ed.), *Challenges of transformation and transition from centrally planned to market economies* (pp. 13–30). United Nations: United Nations Centre for Regional Development.

Government Printing Office (GPO). (1999). *Congressional register searchable website*. http://www.access.gpo.gov.

Guterbock, T. M. (1997). Why money magazine's 'Best places' keep changing. *Public Opinion Quarterly, 61*, 339–355.

Hagerty, M. R. (1999, February) Comment on the construction of the forham index of social health. social indicators network news. *Working group 6 of international Sociological association, 57*, p 10.

Hagerty, M. R., & Land, K. C. (2007). Constructing summary indices of quality of life: A model for the effect of heterogeneous importance weights. *Sociological Methods and Research, 35*, 455–496.

Hagerty, M. R., Cummins, R. A., Ferriss, A. L., Land, K., Michalos, A. C., Peterson, M., Sharpe, A., Sirgy, J., & Vogel, J. (2001). Quality of life indexes for national policy: Review and agenda for research. *Social Indicators Research, 55*, 1–96.

Inglehart, R., et al. (2000). *World values surveys and european values surveys, 1981–1984, 1990–1993, and 1995–1997*. [Computer file]. ICPSR version. Ann Arbor: Institute for Social Research [producer]. Ann Arbor: Inter-university Consortium for Political and Social Research [distributor].

Johansson, S. (2002). Conceptualizing and measuring quality of life for national policy. *Social Indicators Research, 58*, 13–32.

Kacapyr, E. (1996). *Economic forecasting*. M. E. Sharpe.

Kacapyr, E. (1997, October). Are we having fun yet? *American Demographics, 19*, 28–29.

Kahnemann, D., Krueger, A. B., Schkade, D., Schwarz, N., & Stone, A. (2004). Toward national well-being accounts. *American Economic Association Papers and Proceedings, 94(2)*, 429–434.

Land, K. C. (2000). Social indicators. In E. F. Borgatta & R. V. Montgomery (Eds.), *Encyclopedia of Sociology* (Revth ed., pp. 2682–2690). New York: Macmillan.

Land, K. C. (2004). An evidence-based approach to the construction of summary quality-of-life indices. In W. Glatzer, M. Stoffregen, & S. von Below (Eds.), *Challenges for quality of life in the contemporary world* (pp. 107–124). New York: Kluwer.

Land, K. C., Lovell, C. A. K., & Thore, S. (1993). Chance-constrained data envelopment analysis. *Managerial and Decision Economics, 14*(November-December), 541–554.

Land, K. C., Lamb, V. L., & Mustillo, S. K. (2001). Child and youth well-being in the United States, 1975–1998: Some findings from a new index. *Social Indicators Research, 56*, 241–320.

Land, K. C., Lamb, V. L., Meadows, S. O., & Taylor, A. (2007). Measuring trends in child well-being: An evidence-based approach. *Social Indicators Research, 80*, 105–132.

Lucas, R. E., Clark, A. E., Georgellis, Y., & Diener, E. (2003). Reexamining adaptation and the set point model of happiness: Reactions to changes in marital status. *Journal of Personality and Social Psychology, 84*, 527–539.

Miringoff, M. L., Miringoff, M. L., & Opdycke, S. (1996). Monitoring the nation's social performance: The index of social health. In E. F. Zigler, S. L. Kagan, & N. W. Hall (Eds.), *Children, families, and government* (pp. 10–30). New York: Cambridge University Press.

Miringoff, M. L., & Miringoff, M. L. (1999). *The social health of the nation: How American is really doing.* New York: Oxford University Press.

Moller, V., & Dickow, H. (2002). The role of quality of life surveys in managing change in democratic transitions: The South African case. *Social Indicators Research, 58*(1–3), 267–292.

Munda, G., & Nardo, M. (2003). *On the methodological foundations of composite indicators used for ranking countries.* Paper presented at the First OECD/JRC workshop on composite indicators of country performance. JRC, Ispra

Nardo, M., Saisana, M., Saltelli, A., Tarantola, S., Hoffman, A., & Giovannini, E. (2005). *Handbook on constructing composite indicators: Methodology and user guide.* Paris: Organization for Economic Co-operation and Development.

Osberg, L., & Sharpe, A. (2000, November). *International comparisons of trends in economic well-being.* Paper presented at the annual meeting of the American Economic Association, Boston.

Pruitt, D. G., & Kim, S. H. (2004). *Social conflict: Escalation, stalemate, and settlement* (3rd ed.). New York: McGraw Hill.

Redefining Progress. (1995). *The genuine progress indicator: Summary of data and methodology.* San Francisco: Redefining Progress.

Sastre, M. T. M. (1999). Lay conceptions of well-being and rules used in well-being judgments among young, middle-aged, and elderly adults. *Social Indicators Research, 47*, 203–231.

Sen, A. (1993). Capability and well-being. In A. Sen & M. C. Nussbaum (Eds.), *The quality of life* (pp. 30–53). Oxford: Clarendon.

Trabold-Nubler, H. (1991). The human development index: A new development indicator? *Intereconomics, 26*, 236–243.

United Nations Human Development Program. (1990). *Human development report.* New York: Oxford University Press.

United Nations Human Development Program. (1993). Human development index: Survey of recent reviews. *Human development report.* New York: Oxford University Press.

United Nations Development Program. (2001). *Human development report.* New York: Oxford University Press.

Veenhoven, R. (1993) Happiness in Nations, Rotterdam: Risbo. Data available from web-site: http://www.eur.nl/fsw/research/happiness.

Veenhoven, R. (1996). Happy life-expectancy: A comprehensive measure of quality of life in nations. *Social Indicators Research, 39*, 1–58.

Zhou, P., Ang, B. W., & Zhou, D. Q. (2010). Weighting and aggregation in composite index construction: A multiplicative optimization approach. *Social Indicators Research, 96*, 169–181.

Measuring the Quality of Life and the Construction of Social Indicators

10

Filomena Maggino and Bruno D. Zumbo

Introduction

Complexity and the Process of Measurement

As is evident from even a cursory review of the research literature and current practices, the well-being of societies represents a multidimensional concept that is difficult and complex to define. Its quantitative measurement requires a multifaceted approach and a multipurpose methodology that is a mix of many approaches and techniques founded upon statistical indicators. The main notion that should be kept in mind in order to measure societal well-being from a quantitative perspective, using statistical indicators, is *complexity*. The complexity stems from the reality to be observed, and affects the measuring process and the construction of the indicators. Therefore, complexity should be preserved in analyzing indicators and should be correctly represented in telling stories from indicators.

In considering the topics we wished to include in this chapter, we chose to be inclusive with an eye toward integrating a vast body of methodological literature. Our aim in this chapter is to disentangle some important methodological approaches and issues that should be considered in measuring and analyzing quality of life from a quantitative perspective. Due to space limitations, relative to the breadth and scope of the task at hand, for some issues and techniques, we will provide details, whereas for others, more general integrative remarks. The chapter is organized as follows. The first section (comprised of three sub-sections) deals with the conceptual definitions and issues in developing indicators. The aim of this first section, like the chapter as a whole, is to provide a framework and structure. The second section (comprised of three sub-sections) is an overview of the analytic tools and strategies. The third, and final, section (comprised of two sub-sections) focuses on methodological and institutional challenges.

Given that our primary purpose is to catalog and organize the complex array of foundational methodological issues, analytic tools, and strategies, we will make extensive use of figures and tables whose primary purpose is to list and contrast concepts, issues, tools, and strategies. Table 10.1 provides an overview of the questions and issues one faces one when one is dealing with the first stage in developing indicators: the conceptual definitions, framework and structure. Table 10.2 provides an overview of the questions and issues surrounding the analytic tools and strategies. Tables 10.1 and 10.2 also provide a type of "advanced or graphic organizer" for the first and second sections of the chapter and as such are meant to help the reader catalog and retain some order in the complex array of ideas, tools, and strategies found when one aims to measure quality of life and one considers the construction of social indicators.

F. Maggino (✉)
Università degli Studi di Firenze, Florence, Italy
e-mail: filomena.maggino@unifi.it

B.D. Zumbo
University of British Columbia, Vancouver, Canada
e-mail: bruno.zumbo@ubc.ca

K.C. Land et al. (eds.), *Handbook of Social Indicators and Quality of Life Research*,
DOI 10.1007/978-94-007-2421-1_10, © Springer Science+Business Media B.V. 2012

Table 10.1 An overview of the questions and issues when dealing with conceptual definitions

	Conceptual definition (framework and structure)
How can the complexity be conceptually designed?	
1. Hierarchical design	Indicators should be developed through a *logical modeling process* conducting from concept to measurement. Given its features, this logical design is defined *hierarchical*, since each component is defined and finds its meaning in the ambit of the preceding one. Conceptually, the hierarchical design is characterized by the following components: (i) the conceptual model, (ii) the areas to be investigated, (iii) the latent variables, and (iv) the basic indicators
	The hierarchical design is completed by defining the <u>relationships between</u>:
	• *Each variable and the corresponding indicators*. These relations define the *model of measurement*
	• *Basic indicators*. In this perspective, two different states can be identified:
	○ Indicators are related to each other and relate to the same latent variable (in other words, they contribute to the definition of same variable); in these cases, the indicators are called *constitutive*
	○ Indicators are not related to each other and relate to different latent variables; in this case, the indicators are called *concomitant*
	• *Latent variables*. These relations are defined in the ambit of the conceptual model and identify the structural pattern. The analysis of this kind of relationships is accomplished by *modeling the indicators*
How can the indicators be conceptually defined?	
2. Model of measurement	The model of measurement can be conceived through two different conceptual approaches:
	• *Reflective approach*. the basic indicators are seen as functions of the latent variable, whereby changes in the latent variable are reflected (i.e., manifested) in changes in the observable indicators
	• *Formative approach*. a latent variable construct can be defined as being determined by (or *formed* from) a number of basic indicators
How can the indicators be consistently organized?	
3. system of indicators	A *system of indicators* represents the fulfillment of the conceptual framework and allows an organizational context to be defined in order to allow methodological supports and structured and systematic data management in a long-term longitudinal perspective
	This is particularly demanding with reference to subjective data, which require a great use of resources (beyond a solid survey research methodology)

Developing Indicators, Conceptual Definition, Framework and Structure

An Introduction to This Section: Developing and Managing Indicators

The *process of measurement* in the social sciences requires a robust conceptual definition, a consistent collection of observations, and a consequent analysis of the relationship between observations and defined concepts. The measurement objective that relates concepts to reality is represented by *indicators*. From this perspective, an indicator is not a simple crude bit of statistical information but represents a measure organically connected to a conceptual model aimed at knowing different aspects of reality. In other words, a generic index value can be converted into an "indicator," when its definition and measurement occur in a sphere of operation or influence (i.e., the ambit) of a conceptual model and are connected to a defined aim. As such, indicators can be considered *purposeful statistics* (Horn 1993). As Land (1971, 1975) reminds us, a statistical index can be considered an "indicator" when: (1) it represents a component in a model concerning a social system, (2) it can be measured and analyzed in order to compare the situations of different groups and to observe the direction (positive or negative) of the evolution along time (time series analysis), and (3) it can be aggregated with other indicators or disaggregated in order to specify the model.

Far too often, however, indicators are developed and used without consideration of the conceptual

Table 10.2 An overview of the questions and issues surrounding the analytic tools and strategies

II. Analytic tools and strategies	
The consistent application of the hierarchical design actually leads to a parceled picture, with reference to the conceptual model, and consequently produces a compound data structure. In order to reconstruct a meaningful and interpretable picture, data needs to be managed pursuing different technical goals:	
– Reducing data structure	
– Combining indicators	
– Modeling indicators	
The different analytic and technical strategies to be adopted in these respects constitute a "composite" *process*, carried out through subsequent/consecutive steps (MULTISTAGE) and different/alternative analytic approaches (MULTITECHNIQUE).	
☞ *How can the observed picture be reconstructed?*	
1. Reducing data structure	Since data structure shows:
	– Basic indicators, stratified with reference to the identified variables
	– Cases, stratified with reference to the standard unit (e.g., Individuals vs. Cities)
	Data reduction has the following goals:
	(1) *Reconstructing the conceptual variables by aggregating basic indicators* through different logics:
	a. Aggregating basic indicators referring to the same variable (*reflective logic*);.
	b. Aggregating indicators creating a new conceptual variable (*formative logic*),
	Since both kinds of aggregation process are carried out at micro level (e.g., for each individual), the following reduction step needs to be accomplished
	(2) *Defining macro-units by aggregating single cases*: the aggregating process aims at leading information observed at micro-level to the proper and identified macro level of interest (*definition of macro-units*). identifying the proper aggregation criterion should take into account the nature of measured characteristics (e.g., compositional, contextual, and so on) requiring different analytic approaches
Traditional approach:	The two goals are usually carried out through traditional and consolidated analytic approaches and based upon linear statistics
Alternative approach: This stage allows the system of indicators to be operational.	New methodologies have been proposed allowing discrete ordinal data to be dealt with, especially when evaluation, comparisons and rankings are of concern. Such methodologies are based on Partially Ordered SEt Theory (POSET theory), part of Discrete Mathematics that offers many tools and results to explore and analyze the structure of discrete datasets, like that of interest in the present study. Posets of finite cardinality can be conveniently depicted by means of certain directed acyclic graphs, called Hasse diagrams

(continued)

Table 10.2 (continued)

II. Analytic tools and strategies

✍ *How can the whole picture be simplified and shown?*

2. *Combining indicators*	Sometimes, also after the data reduction process has been accomplished, the complexity of the system of indicators may require particular combinations in order to (Noll 2009)

– Answer the call by "policy makers" for condensed information
– Improve the chance to get into the media (compared to complex indicator systems)
– Allow multidimensional phenomena to be transformed into uni-dimensional
– Allow situations to be more easily compared across time
– Compare cases (e.g., Nations) in a transitive way (ranking).
– Allow clear cut answers to questions like the following:

    a. Are living conditions getting better or worse across time?
    b. Do people living in city a enjoy a better quality of life than those living in city b?
    c. Is population subgroup x better off than population subgroup y?

Depending on the particular need, different approaches can be adopted:

– *Dashboards* allow indicators to be represented in a single graphical solution and the complex relationships among indicators to be communicated

– *Benchmarking* through

    ○ *Composite indicators* can represent useful approaches aimed at summarizing indicators
    ○ *Partial order sets*: new approaches based upon the *POSET* theory can be fruitfully applied through getting over the methodological critical aspects shown by composite indicators

✍ *How can the whole picture be explained?*

3. *Modeling indicators*	This stage is aimed at analyzing different aspects of the defined model (e.g., objective and subjective indicators) in order to find explanations by identifying the proper analytic approaches

Table 10.3 A structured plan to aid in developing and managing indicators

definition of the phenomenon and a logical cohesion of the conceptual definition and the analytic tools and strategies. In our experiences, the lack of any logical cohesion is often masked by the use and application of sophisticated procedures and methods that can deform reality producing distorted results.

Table 10.3 is an organization tool and structured plan to aid in developing and managing indicators that are able to (1) represent different aspects of the reality, (2) picture the reality in an interpretable way, and (3) allow meaningful stories to be told. We can see in Table 10.3 that the conceptual definition (framework and structure) shapes both how one develops indicators and the analytic tools and strategies. In terms of developing indicators, one does so through a hierarchical design, which leads to defining a measurement model and eventually to developing a system of indicators. Likewise, one manages indicators in terms of reducing the data structure, combining indicators, and modeling the indicators.

Table 10.4 is the advanced organizer for the developing indicators, conceptual definition (framework and structure) section. We can see that there are three sections: (1) hierarchical design which leads to (2) the choice of a measurement model, and eventually to (3) the system of indicators.

Defining the Hierarchical Design

Indicators should be developed, following Lazarsfeld's model (1958), through a *hierarchical design* requiring the definition of the following components: (a) conceptual model, (b) areas, (c) latent variables, (d) basic indicators, and (e) observed variables. We will describe each of these in turn below.

Conceptual Model

The definition of the conceptual model represents a process of abstraction, a complex stage that requires the identification and definition of theoretical constructs that have to be given concrete references wherein they can be applied. In the social sciences, the description of concepts varies according to (1) the researcher's point of view, (2) the objectives of the study, (3) the applicability of the concepts, and (4) the sociocultural, geographical, and historical context. Examples include concepts such as health, education, well-being, income, production, and trade.

The process of conceptualization allows us to identify and define the:
(a) Model aimed at data construction
(b) Spatial and temporal ambit of observation
(c) Aggregation levels (among indicators and/or among observation units)
(d) Approach aimed at aggregating the basic indicators and the techniques to be applied in this perspective (weighting criteria, aggregation techniques, etc.)
(e) Interpretative and evaluative models

Areas

The areas (in some cases named "pillars") define in general terms the different aspects that allow the phenomenon to be clarified and specified consistently with the conceptual model. The process of defining areas can be time-consuming and exacting, especially with complex constructs, and requires a systematic review and analysis of the relevant research literature.

Latent Variables

Each variable represents one of the aspects to be observed and confers an explanatory relevance onto the corresponding defined area (see Zumbo 2007, 2009). The identification of the latent variable is founded on theoretical and statistical assumptions (e.g., homogeneity, dimensionality) as empirical commitments so that the defined variable can reflect the nature of the considered phenomenon consistently

Table 10.4 On overview of developing indicators, conceptual definition (Framework and structure)

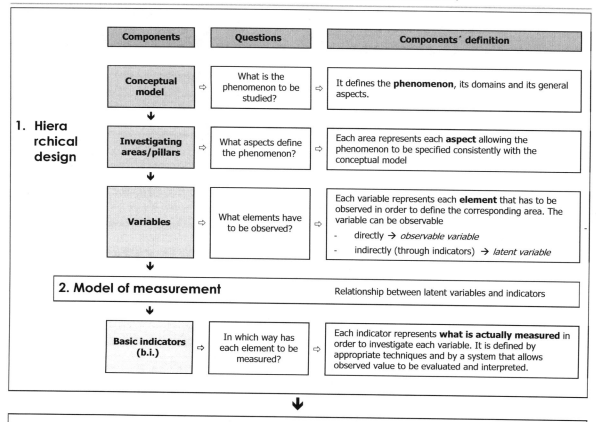

with the conceptual model. However, even if we are able to identify a variety of diverse variables, we have to accept the possibility that maybe no set of variables can perfectly capture the concept to be measured (e.g., social or economic well-being; Sharpe and Salzman 2004).

Basic Indicators

Each basic indicator (e.g., an item, in subjective measurement) represents what can be actually measured in order to investigate the corresponding variable.[1] This means that each observed element represents not a direct measure of the variable but an *indicator*[2] of the reference variable (De Vellis 1991). The hierarchical process allows a meaningful and precise position to be attributed to each indicator inside the model. In other words, each indicator takes on and gains its own meaning, and consequently can be properly interpreted because of its position inside the hierarchical structure; each indicator represents a distinct component of the phenomenon within the hierarchical design. The possibility to define and to consider alternative forms for each indicator has to be evaluated.

According to a simple and relatively weak strategy, each latent variable is defined by a single element (*single indicator approach*). This strategy, applied because of its thrifty and functional capacity, requires the adoption of robust assumptions. The adoption of single indicators presents a risk since it is rarely possible to define the direct correspondence between one latent variable and one indicator. In other words, the variable is not always directly observable through

---

[1] In specific cases, some variables can be directly measured (e.g., some objective information). In this case, variable and indicator coincide.

[2] In data analysis, indicators/items are technically defined "variables"; consequently, these are conceptually different from "latent variables."

a single indicator. In fact, defining and adopting the single indicator approach can produce a wide and considerable amount of error that leads to problems concerning:

(a) *Precision* (*reliability*), since the measurement through one single indicator is strongly affected by random error[3]
(b) *Accuracy* (*validity*), since the chance that one single indicator can describe one latent complex variable is highly dubious and questionable
(c) *Relationships* with the other variables
(d) *Discriminating* and *differentiating* among observed cases, for example, individuals

This is precisely why, in many cases, the presence of complex latent variables requires the definition of several basic indicators. This can be done by adopting the *multiple indicators approach,* which considers the multiple indicators as *multiple measures* (Sullivan and Feldman 1981). Multiple indicators contribute to the measurement of the major aspects of the variable because each basic indicator may correspond to one particular aspect of the latent variable. This approach allows for the inherent variability in the defined latent variable to be covered. In addition, this approach allows the problems produced by the single indicators approach to be avoided, or at least for their significance and weight to be reduced. In technical terms, the complete group of basic indicators referring to one variable represents a *set of indicators*, while the complete group of indicators defining an area is called a set of *thematic indicators*.

The hierarchical design can be drawn also through sub-designs (e.g., each area could require sub-areas), and its logic can be applied both at the micro and macro level.

Observed Variables

Some variables can be observed and directly measured. Consequently, they do not need any indicator (e.g., age, level of education).

Defining the Model of Measurement

The model of measurement can be conceived through two different conceptual approaches (Blalock 1964; Diamantopoulos and Siguaw 2006): models with reflective or formative indicators. Figure 10.1 is a statistical description of the two models.

Model of reflective indicators. This model is also sometimes referred to as the *top-down* explanatory approach. In this case, latent variables are measured by indicators assumed to be *reflective* in nature. In other words, the indicators are seen as functions of the latent variable, whereby changes in the latent variable are reflected (i.e., manifested) in changes in the observable indicators.[4] Structural relationships are identified among latent constructs by statistically relating covariation between the latent variables and the observed variables or indicators, measuring these latent, unobserved variables. If variation in an indicator X is associated with variation in a latent construct Y, then exogenous interventions that change Y can be detected in the indicator X. Most commonly, this relationship between latent variable and indicator is assumed to be *reflective*. That is, the change in X is a reflection of (determined by) the change in the latent construct Y. With reflective (or *effect*) measurement models, causality flows from the latent variable to the indicators.

Models with formative indicators. This model is sometimes referred to as the *bottom-up* explanatory approach. In this case, indicators are viewed as causing—rather than being caused by—the latent variable. The indicators are assumed to be *formative* (or causal) in nature. Changes in formative indicators, as firstly introduced by Blalock (1964), determine changes in the value of the latent variable. In other words, a latent variable can be defined as being determined by (or *formed* from) a number of indicators. In this case, causality flows from the indicator to the latent variable. A classic example of formative indicators is socioeconomic status (SES), where indicators such as education, income, and occupational prestige are items that cause or form the latent variable SES. If an individual loses his or her job, the SES would be negatively affected. However, saying that a negative change has occurred in an individual's SES does not imply that

---

[3]By using multiple measures, random errors tend to compensate each other. Consequently, the measurement turns out to be more accurate. The greater the error component in one single measure, the larger the number of required measures needs to be.

[4]As pointed out, the proposed model is conceptually related to latent structural models that find analytic solutions through the application of the structural equations method (Asher 1983; Bartholomew and Knott 1999; Blalock 1964, 1974; Bohrnstedt and Knoke 1994; Lazarsfeld and Henry 1968; Long 1993a, 1993b; Maggino 2005a; Netemeyer et al. 2003; Saris and Stronkhorst 1990; Sullivan and Feldman 1981; Werts et al. 1974).

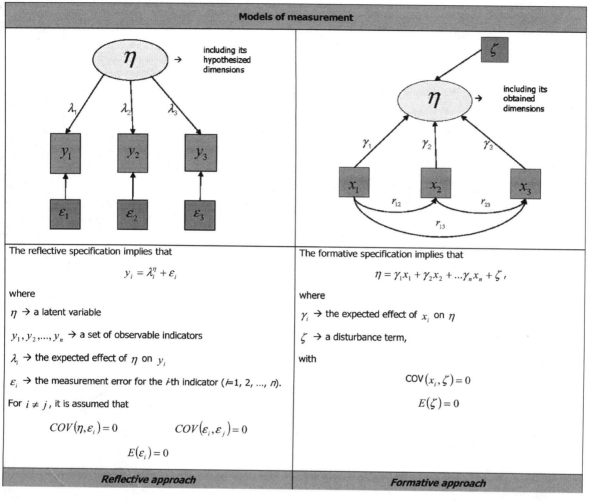

Fig. 10.1 Description of formative and reflective measurement models

there was a job loss. Furthermore, a change in an indicator (say income) does not necessarily imply a similar directional change for the other indicators (say education or occupational prestige).

Traditionally, the reflective view is seen related to the development of scaling models applied especially (as we will see) in subjective measurement (*scale construction*), whereas the formative view is commonly seen in the development of *synthetic indicators* based on both objective and subjective measurements. As Zumbo (2007) notes, the reflective model is most often cast as factor analysis whereas the formative models as principal components analysis.

The distinction between formative and reflective indicators and the necessity of a proper specification are important in order to correctly assign meaning to the relationships implied in the structural model. As Zumbo (2007) states, there are no empirical tests of whether a latent variable is reflective or formative; the exception is the vanishing tetrads test of Bollen and Teng (2000). It should be noted that, although it is often presented as evidence, computing a principal components analysis (PCA) is not sufficient evidence that one has formative indicators, nor does fitting a factor analysis model provide sufficient evidence to claim one has reflective indicators—that is, as is often evidenced in practice, both PCA and factor analysis may fit the same data equally well. Bollen and Lennox (1991) suggest that a good place to start, and often the only thing available, is a literal thought experiment.

10 Measuring the Quality of Life and the Construction of Social Indicators

Table 10.5 Possible outcomes in deciding between reflective and formative indicators

		'Correct' auxiliary theory	
		reflective	formative
Choice of the perspective	reflective	*correct decision*	**Type I error**
	formative	**Type II error**	*correct decision*

Zumbo (2007) added that one can also supplement this thought experiment with a content validation study wherein one asks subject matter experts to consider and rate whether the items (or indicators) are effects or causes; that is, whether the variable is a measure or index, respectively. One can build on the methodologies described for content validity by incorporating questions about whether an item should be considered a cause or effect indicator using methodology in content validity including the coefficients, designs, etc. Also, one could investigate the source of the decision of effects vs. causes by talk-aloud protocols and/or by conducting multidimensional scaling of the subject matter experts' judgments. These approaches aid one in determining whether one has reflective or formative indicators. What Zumbo was suggesting is an extension of Bollen and Lennox's thought experiment to include data from subject matter experts.

In deciding between formative and reflective indicators, four different situations can be theoretically identified (Diamantopoulos and Siguaw 2006), as represented in Table 10.5.

Two outcomes are desirable and correspond to the correct adoption of the measurement perspective (operationalization) following the correct conceptualization of the construct of interest. The other two outcomes correspond to wrong choices. In particular, two types of error may occur. Type I occurs when a reflective approach has been adopted, although a formative approach would have been theoretically appropriate for the construct. Type II occurs when a formative approach has been adopted even if the nature of the construct requires a reflective operationalization (a synthetic indicator construction procedure is adopted in place of a scaling model). This error can lead to identification problems.

Developing a System of Indicators

The application of the hierarchical design, strictly connected to the definition of a proper conceptual framework, leads to the consistent definition of a set of indicators (single and synthetic indicators). Each indicator measures and represents a distinct constituent of the observed phenomenon. Consequently, the set of indicators does not represent a pure and simple collection of indicators but provides researchers with information that is bigger than the simple summation of the elements. If the structure is systematized also in time perspective, the set of indicators can be characterized as a *system of indicators*.

The basic requirements defining a system of indicators are synthesized by Noll (2004) and depicted in Table 10.6.

Defining a system of indicators can be seen as the realization of a demanding (in terms of resources and skills) study to be conducted through several stages. There are several risks one may face in developing a system of indicators. That is, the set of identified indicators may be poor (i.e., limited) or poorly defined and unable to fit the conceptual framework, goals, and objectives; also, the data are not reliable; the indicators may not allow local realities to be compared (e.g., explanatory variables are not measured); and the system's results are not able to produce effects on the strategic, decision, and planning processes.

Systems of indicators can be utilized for both scientific and operational (e.g., public policy) goals. In particular, systems of indicators turn out to be useful whenever a process involves a composite evaluation (policy and technique). In this sense, a system of indicators can represent an important and valid support to individuals involved in decision processes. Decision makers need to know and manage a composite mosaic of information in order to define and evaluate priorities to be translated into actions.

Main Functions

Systems of indicators can be distinguished according to the functions for which they have been created (Berger-Schmitt and Noll 2000; Land 2000; Noll 1996). The different functions, illustrated in Table 10.7, can be thought of in cumulative terms since each of them requires the previous one/s.

Crucial Elements

The main elements that make a system of indicators work are (1) aims, (2) structure, (3) analytic approaches, and (4) the interpretative and evaluative models (Noll 1996; Berger-Schmitt and Noll 2000).

Table 10.6 Noll's requirements defining a system of indicators

Characteristics	– *Objectivity.* Provided information should turn out to be equal or comparable, independently from who are the users
	– *Quantification.* Provided values should be quantitative—obtained through standardized procedures and measures; this allows results to be reported with more precision and detail, and data to be analyzed through complex methods
	– *Efficiency and fidelity.* Methods, techniques and instruments that allowed data and results to be obtained have to be communicated and publicized
	– *Economicity.* The system has to produce simple,
	– standardized, available and up-to-datable information
	– *Generalization and exportability.* The system has to allow its generalization to other similar context
	– *Joint development.* The system has to be developed in a shared way by all the "actors"
Formal criteria to respect:	– Comprehensiveness – Nonredundancy
	– Consistency – Parsimoniousness
Key elements:	– *Conceptual framework* requested in order to identify and justify the selection of dimensions to be measured
	– Definition and selection of the *dimensions to be measured*
	– *System architecture* requested in order to support the basic structure and to define measurement procedures
	– Identification of *units to be monitored*
	– Organization of *measuring and monitoring procedures*

Aims

One of the main requirements of a system of indicators is reference to the aims of its construction. Concerning this, we can distinguish between:

1. *Conceptual aims* (*goals*) that represent broad statements concerning what has to be achieved or what is the problem to be faced. Usually goals are placed at a macro level (national, international, etc.).
2. *Operational aims* (*objectives*) that represent the instruments identified in order to attain the conceptual aims. Objectives can have different temporal prospects (monthly, four-monthly, annual, bi-annual, etc.).
3. *Planning aims* (*actions*) that represent the specific activities identified to accomplish objectives. They can include developments and infrastructural changes in policies, in institutions, in management instruments, etc.

Each goal, objective and action has:

1. Corresponding *targets*, representing those elements allowing each goal, objective and action to find measurable criteria and to define a *timetable*.

2. Corresponding *indicators* defined in order to assess progress towards the target with goals and objectives and the accomplishment of actions[5]; these indicators can be distinguished in Table 10.8.

These indicators can be combined in order to define composite measures (efficacy/efficiency indicators).

Structure

The design through which data are collected and systematized defines the structure of the system. The structure can be:

1. *Vertical.* Data are collected from local levels (e.g., regions) in order to be systematized (aggregated) at a higher level (e.g., country). This structure allows policy goals to be implemented, according to local information.
2. *Horizontal.* Data are collected only at one level (e.g., regional) and allow particular observational

---

[5] Another nonalternative classification distinguishes them with reference to their polarity, *positive* or *negative* quality of life observations (see the contribution to this by Alex Michalos in Sirgy et al. 2006).

Table 10.7 The various functions of systems of indicators

Description and explanation functions	*Monitoring.* This basic function concerns and refers to the capacity of the system to: – Identify and clearly define the existing problems, – Draw promptly attention to new problems and to formulate questions – Control and identify the main critical points of the system – Measure changes over time if any (economic, social, etc.) – Improve all these capacities This function requires timing and frequencies of observation to be defined in order to evaluate any change *Reporting.* In this case the system plays an important role of explanation by meeting the need to – *Describe* the situation, condition, and dynamics of a certain reality (a country, an institution, etc.); in this perspective, the system answers question like "what is going on?" – *Analyze* the existing relationships between different components; in this perspective, the system answers questions like "in which way did it happen?" In this function, description and analysis are strictly related to reporting function, as synthetically represented below (Noll 2009; Berger-Schmitt and Noll 2000) $$monitoring + analysis + interpretation = reporting$$
Evaluation functions	*Forecasting.* The systematic use of indicators allows the effects attributable to change in a series to be documented and consequently trends in observed reality to be forecasted. This function, representing a natural consequence of the reporting function, increases the probability of reaching some results by allocating resources and planning efficient procedures *ex-ante*. (Cannavò 2009) *Accounting.* A system can represent a useful means of *accounting*, by which it is possible to measure and make systematically available data in order to support decisions concerning the allocation and destination of resources (financial and others) In particular, this function allows the development of a system allowing decision makers to (Cannavò 2009): – Control ex post the suitability of the defined standards and of the planned resource flows – Evaluate efficiency and correctness of the defined procedures – Test adequacy and actual attainment of results *Program management and performance evaluation.* Systems of indicators represent valid supports to *project management since* they allow specific strategic programs to be evaluated with reference to their realization at the present, their capacity to meet particular and specific purposes, and the prescription of future actions. In the ambit of strategic programs, indicators must allow the following assessments: – Evaluation of the present state (where are we now?) – Identification of the priorities and the actions to be pursued (where do we want to go?) – Evaluation of adequacy (are we taking the right path to get there?) – Evaluation of progress towards goals and objectives by quantifying the strategic performances (are we there yet? Can differences be observed?) Since these systems are constructed with reference to specific programs, they cannot be generalized. In this perspective, this important function can play an important role in policy analysis (policy guidance and directed social change) by allowing problem definition, policy choice and evaluation of alternatives, and program monitoring (Land 2000) *Assessment.* A system can represent valid support to assessment procedures (certification and accountability). In this case, the goal may be to certify or judge subjects (individuals or institutions) by discriminating their performances or to infer functioning of institutions, enterprises, or systems

ambits (environment, education) to be monitored and compared.

3. *Local.* This structure is typically designed in order to support local decision processes. This kind of system is characterized by two levels:

   (a) Internal, when the indicators are aimed at monitoring the internal organization of the level

   (b) External, when the indicators refer to parameters existing at higher levels (e.g., transportation)

Analytic Approaches

Indicators have to be placed in an analytic context, consistently with aims and structure. In this perspective, different analytic approaches can be distinguished.

Interpretative and Evaluative Models

The observed results can be interpreted only according to a specific frame of reference. This can also include particular *standard-values*, which can be defined a

Table 10.8 Indicators and corresponding function

Indicators		Function
– Input	→	Measuring resources available in the system and indicating some sort of inputs into a process
– Process (intermediate output)	→	Monitoring the basic progress of implementing the actions defined and outlined at strategic levels
– Output/outcome	→	Monitoring direct results of actions
– Impact	→	Monitoring progress and improvement towards goals and objectives achievement

priori, according to the objectives or empirical observations (e.g., surveys). In certain cases, along with general standards, differential standards can be defined with reference to different groups (e.g., for males and females). Comparisons among groups are possible according to the availability of a unique scale for the observed and standard values.

The Indicators in a System

Selection

Different issues need to be addressed when selecting and managing indicators, especially when this is carried out within a complex system allowing for functions such as monitoring, reporting and accounting. Michalos (in Sirgy et al. 2006) identified 15 different issues related to the combination of social, economic, and environmental indicators. As Michalos states, the issues collectively yield over 200,000 possible combinations representing at least that many different kinds of systems (Sirgy et al. 2006). The 15 different issues are:

1. Settlement/aggregation area sizes: e.g., the best size to understand air pollution may be different from the best size to understand crime.
2. Time frames: e.g., the optimal duration to understand resource depletion may be different from the optimal duration to understand the impact of sanitation changes.
3. Population composition: e.g., analyses by language, sex, age, education, ethnic background, income, etc. may reveal or conceal different things.
4. Domains of life composition: e.g., different domains like health, job, family life, housing, etc. give different views and suggest different agendas for action.

5. Objective vs. subjective indicators: e.g., relatively subjective appraisals of housing and neighborhoods by actual dwellers may be very different from relatively objective appraisals by "experts."
6. Positive vs. negative indicators: negative indicators seem to be easier to craft for some domains, which may create a biased assessment, e.g., in the health domain measures of morbidity and mortality may crowd out positive measures of well-being.
7. Input vs. output indicators: e.g., expenditures on teachers and school facilities may give a very different view of the quality of an education system from that based on student performance on standardized tests.
8. Benefits and costs: different measures of value or worth yield different overall evaluations as well as different evaluations for different people, e.g., the market value of child care is far below the personal, social or human value of having children well cared for.
9. Measurement scales: e.g., different measures of well-being provide different views of people's well-being and relate differently to other measures.
10. Report writers: e.g., different stakeholders often have very different views about what is important to monitor and how to evaluate whatever is monitored.
11. Report readers: e.g., different target audiences need different reporting media and/or formats.
12. Conceptual model: e.g., once indicators are selected, they must be combined or aggregated somehow in order to get a coherent story or view.
13. Distributions: e.g., because average figures can conceal extraordinary and perhaps unacceptable variation, choices must be made about appropriate representations of distributions.
14. Distance impacts: e.g., people living in one place may access facilities (hospitals, schools, theaters, museums, libraries) in many other places at varying distances from their place of residence.
15. Causal relations: before intervention, one must know what causes what, which requires relatively mainstream scientific research, which may not be available yet.

Choices and options selected for each issue have implications for the other issues. The issues are not mutually exclusive and are not expected to be exhaustive as others can be identified. Dealing with these issues is merely a technical problem to be solved by statisticians or information scientists. However, the construction of

10 Measuring the Quality of Life and the Construction of Social Indicators

Table 10.9 Attributes of quality of an indicator

(I) Methodological soundness

This characteristic refers to the idea that the methodological basis for the production of indicators should be attained by following internationally accepted standards, guidelines, or good practices. This dimension is necessarily dataset-specific, reflecting different methodologies for different datasets. The elements referring to this characteristic are (i) concepts and definitions, (ii) scope, (iii) classification/sectorization, and (iv) basis for recording. Particularly important is the characteristic of *accuracy and reliability*, referring to the idea that indicators should be based upon data sources and statistical techniques that are regularly assessed and validated, inclusive of revision studies. This allows accuracy of estimates to be assessed. In this case accuracy is defined as the closeness between the estimated value and the unknown true population value but also between the observed individual value and the "true" individual value. This means that assessing the accuracy of an estimate involves analyzing the total error associated with the estimate: sampling error and measurement error

(II) Integrity

Integrity refers to the notion that indicator systems should be based on adherence to the principle of objectivity in the collection, compilation, and dissemination of data, statistics, and results. The characteristic includes institutional arrangements that ensure
(1) Professionalism in statistical policies and practices
(2) Transparency
(3) Ethical standards

(III) Serviceability

Comparability is a particular dimension of serviceability. It aims at measuring the impact of differences in applied concepts and measurement tools/procedures
– *Over time*, referring to comparison of results, derived normally from the same statistical operation, at different times
– *Between geographical areas*, emphasizing the comparison between countries and/or regions in order to ascertain, for instance, the meaning of aggregated indicators at the chosen level
– *Between domains*. This is particularly delicate when involving subjective measurement (e.g., cultural dimensions)

(IV) Accessibility

Accessibility relates to the need to ensure
(1) Clarity of presentations and documentations concerning data and metadata (with reference to the information environment: data accompanied with appropriate illustrations, graphs, maps, and so on, with information on their quality, availability and—eventual—usage limitations)
(2) Impartiality of access
(3) Pertinence of data
(4) Prompt and knowledgeable support service and assistance to users in other words, it refers also to the physical conditions in which users can obtain data: where to go, how to order, delivery time, clear pricing policy, convenient marketing conditions (copyright, etc.), availability of micro or macro data, various formats (paper, files, cd-rom, internet...), etc.

indicators of well-being and quality of life is essentially a political and philosophical exercise, and its ultimate success or failure depends on the negotiations involved in creating and disseminating the indicators, or the reports or accounts that use those indicators. (Michalos, in Sirgy et al. 2006). Within a system, we consider also the difficulties related to the availability of indicators (across time and space) and in harmonizing different data sources and levels of observation.

Quality

Many international institutions, such as the World Bank and UNESCO (Patel et al. 2003) and Eurostat (2000) have tried to identify the attributes of *quality* that indicators (and approaches aimed at their management) should possess and need to be considered in the process of developing of new indicators or of selecting available indicators. Tables 10.9 and 10.10, respectively,

list the attributes of a good indicator and what a good indicator should be.

Although it does not represent a dimension of quality in itself, prerequisites of quality refers to all those (institutional or not) preconditions and background conditions allowing for quality of statistics. In other words, indicator construction is not simply a technical problem but should become part of a larger debate concerning how to construct indicators obtaining a larger legitimacy to be promoted. These prerequisites cover the following elements:
1. Legal and institutional environment, allowing
   (a) Conceptual framework to be defined
   (b) Coordination of power within and across different institutions to be framed
   (c) Data and resources to be available for statistical work
2. Quality awareness informing statistical work

Table 10.10 What a good indicator should be

An indicator should be			With reference to its capacity and possibility to		
	Clear	Meaningful		*Define and describe* (concepts, definitions, and scopes)	
	Appropriate	Accurate			
	Exhaustive	Well-designed			
	Measurable	Stable		*Observe* unequivocally and stably (in terms of space and time)	*(I)* Methodological soundness
	Reliable	Rigorous		Record by a *degree of distortion as low as possible* (explored through statistical and methodological approaches)	
	Valid	Precise			
	Repeatable	Exact			
	Robust	Faithful			
	Transparent	With ethical standards		*Adhere* to the principle of objectivity in the collection, compilation, and dissemination	*(II)* Integrity
	Consistent	Pertinent		*Reflect adequately the conceptual model* in terms of aims, objectives and requirements underlying its construction (knowing, monitoring, evaluating, accounting, …)	
		Coherent			
	Relevant			Meet current and potential users' needs. It refers to whether all indicators that are needed are produced and the extent to which concepts used (definitions, classifications etc.) Reflects user needs. The identification of users and their expectations is therefore necessary.	
	Practicable	Up-to-datable		*Be observed* through realistic efforts and costs in terms of development and data collection (for example, short time between observation and data availability)	*(III)* Serviceability
	Revisionable				
	Well-timed	Timely		Reflect the length of time between its availability and the event or phenomenon it describes	
		Periodic			
	Regular	Punctual		Reflect the time lag between the release date of data and the target date when it should have been delivered	
	Comparable	Disagregable		*Be analyzed* in order to record differences and disparities between units, groups, geographical areas and so on, by employing the available information as much as possible	
	Discriminant	Thrifty			
	Believable	Comprehensible		*Be spread* that is, it has to be easily findable, accessible, useable, analyzable, and interpretable in order to gain also users' confidence (*brand image*)	*(IV)* Accessibility
	Accessible	Simple			
	Interpretable	Manageable			

Analytic Tools and Strategies

The consistent application of the hierarchical design actually leads to a parceled picture, with reference to the conceptual model, and consequently produces a compound data structure. In order to reconstruct a meaningful and interpretable picture, data needs to be managed pursuing different technical goals: reducing data structure, combining indicators, and modeling indicators

The different analytic and technical strategies to be adopted in these respects constitute a "composite" *process*, depicted in Table 10.11, carried out through subsequent/consecutive steps (multistage—MS) and different/alternative analytic approaches (multitechnique—MT). We discuss each of these strategies in turn below.

Reducing Data Structure

When indicators are developed according to a conceptual framework, dealing with a multidimensional construct and evaluating multiple aspects to be observed at different levels (individual, community, national, and global), the collected data produce a subsequent data structure which turns out to be very complex and needs to be reduced in some way. In particular, the information

Table 10.11 The compositive process of the different analytic and technical strategies

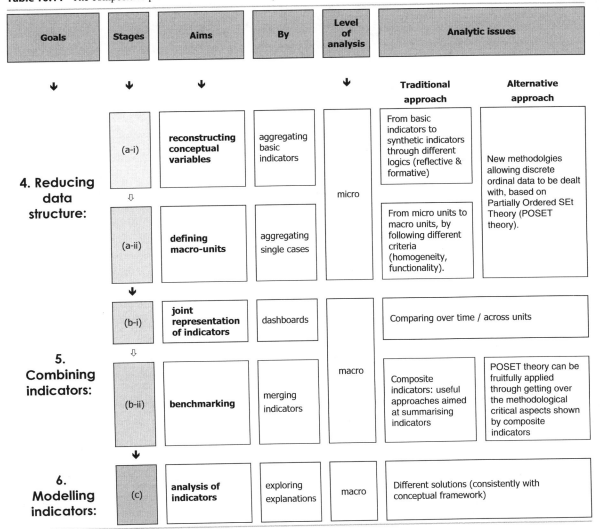

Table 10.12 Traditional approach to data reduction

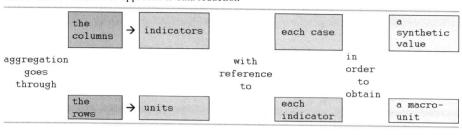

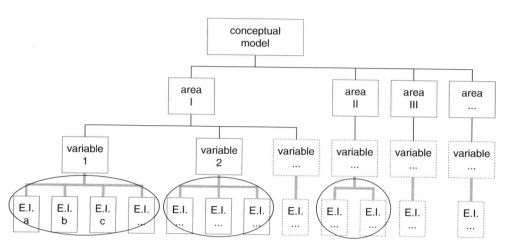

Fig. 10.2 An example in which the indicators that will make up three different synthetic indicators

collected at the micro-level needs to be aggregated at a proper scale (spatial or temporal), in order to accomplish a correct analysis and obtain a composite picture (e.g., national).

With reference to this goal, two different approaches can be identified. While the first one turns out to be very traditional (and known), the second one applies a different analytic approach, quite new with reference to data reduction perspective.

Traditional Approach

In reducing the data structure, the traditional approach proceeds through the following logic (Table 10.12).

Aggregating Indicators and Creating Synthetic Indicators

In order to better manage the complexity of the measured data, analytic models are required providing for significant data aggregations at different levels in order to ensure correct and different comparisons, transversal (between groups, regions) and longitudinal at both micro and macro levels.

In other words, the complexity of this structure can be reduced by defining and applying additional models. The purpose of these models is—through the definition and adoption of particular assumptions—to condense and synthesize the dimension by referring to the *multiple measures*.

The construction of synthetic indicators should be consistent with the adopted measurement model. In this context, the traditional distinction between formative and reflective is particularly important since aggregation of indicators has to be consistently accomplished. In other words, indicators can be aggregated into complex structures through a consistent methodology according to two different criteria: (1) *reflective criterion* and (2) *formative criterion*. In both cases, the condensation of basic indicators, considered multiple measures, produces new synthetic values obtained by applying the appropriate aggregating model. Each synthetic indicator tries to re-establish the unity of the described concept by the corresponding latent variable. In Fig. 10.2, one finds the indicators that will make up three different synthetic indicators.

In this context, the traditional distinction between formative and reflective is particularly important because aggregation of indicators has to be consistently accomplished. In other words, indicators can be aggregated in order to define a synthesis through a consistent methodology according to two different criteria: reflective and formative criteria.

1. The reflective criterion

    Since the indicators are seen as functions of the latent variable, the procedure aimed at aggregating has to take into account the main specific properties of the reflective indicators, which can be synthesized as follows (Diamantopoulos and Winklhofer 2001):

    (a) Indicators are interchangeable (the removal of an indicator does not change the essential nature of the underlying construct).

    (b) Correlations between indicators are explained by the measurement model.

    (c) Internal consistency is of fundamental importance: two uncorrelated indicators cannot measure the same construct.

    (d) Each indicator has error term (ε).

    (e) The measurement model can be estimated only if it is placed within a larger model that incorporates effects of the latent variable.

As a result, the reflective criterion can be accomplished through a statistical approach consistent with the traditional specification used in *factor models*, where an observed measure is presumed to be determined by latent factors. The fundamental equation of the factor model (for m indicators) is the following:

$$\sigma_{x_i}^2 = \sum_{j=1}^{m} \lambda_{x_i\xi_j}^2 + \delta_{x_i}^2$$

where

$\sigma_{x_i}^2$ total variance of indicator x_i

$\lambda_{x_i\xi_j}$ factor loading of indicator x_i with reference to latent variable ξ_j

$\delta_{x_i}^2$ uniqueness (specific variance + error) of indicator x_i

2. The formative criterion

    Since the indicators are viewed as causing—rather than being caused by—the latent variable, the procedure aimed at aggregating has to take into account the main specific properties of the formative indicators, which can be synthesized as follows (Diamantopoulos and Winklhofer 2001):

    (a) The indicators are not interchangeable (omitting an indicator is omitting a part of the construct).

    (b) The correlations between indicators are not explained by the measurement model.

    (c) There is no reason that a specific pattern of signs (i.e., positive vs. negative) or magnitude (i.e., high vs. moderate vs. low); in other words, internal consistency is of minimal importance: two uncorrelated indicators can both serve as meaningful indicators of the construct.

    (d) Indicators do not have error terms; error variance is represented only in the disturbance terms (ζ).

As a result, the formative criterion can be accomplished through a statistical approach consistent with a principal components specification, where the latent variable is defined as a linear combination of basic (manifest) indicators:

$$\eta = \gamma_1 x_1 + \gamma_2 x_2 + ... \gamma_n x_n + \zeta$$

where

η latent variable

γ_i the expected effect of x_i on η

$\eta\zeta$ the disturbance term

Traditionally, the reflective view is seen related to the development of scaling models applied especially in subjective measures (*scale construction*), whereas the formative view is commonly seen in the development of *synthetic indicators* based on both objective and subjective measurements.

In both cases, the aggregation of basic indicators, considered multiple measures, produces new synthetic values. Each synthetic indicator tries to re-establish the unity of the defined concept described by the corresponding latent variable.

Aggregating Observed Units and Defining Macro Units

This aggregation perspective aims at condensing values observed at micro/lower levels (usually, individual) to higher levels in order to produce new meaningful units, identified according to different kinds of scales. Generally, the macro units refer to preexistent/predefined partitions, such as identified *groups* (social, generation, etc.), *areas* (geographical, administrative, etc.), and *time periods* (years, decades, etc.).[6]

The aggregation can be accomplished through either an additive or compositional approach. The *additive approach* is characterized by a single-value synthesizing the values observed at micro level; this is usually done by averaging individual values at the level of interest (country, region, social group, and so on). According to the number of involved indicators, the single synthetic value could be represented by a simple descriptive statistical index, univariate (mean, median) or multivariate (centroid). The *compositional approach* is characterized by obtaining macro-units' values by aggregating individual values in a certain number of homogeneous subgroups. This approach is based upon the *homogeneity* criterion: within each level of aggregation (area, group, and so on), individuals' values are aggregated (or averaged) only if cases are homogeneous according to the involved indicators. Each level is then represented by a profile of values, component values (generally proportions or incidences) describing the subgroups. Each subgroup represents a macro unit defined in terms of a *typology*.[7] The sum of component values is constant. Each typology will be considered in the context of the successive higher-level analysis through the component value.

As seen in Table 10.13, in both cases the solution has to be reached consistently with the nature of data (qualitative or quantitative) and by taking into account the number of indicators to be aggregated.

Simultaneous Aggregation of Indicators and Units

Through particular combined analytic processes, the simultaneous aggregation of indicators and cases can be accomplished. These approaches have great potentialities since they simultaneously allow data reduction and synthesis to be reached, simultaneously for both cases and indicators:

(A) *A tandem analysis*, which is realized by combining Principal Components Analysis and a clustering algorithm; the latter is applied to the synthetic scores obtained through the application of the former. In this perspective *Cluster Analysis* can also be combined with *Multidimensional scaling* (MDS) (Nardo et al. 2005a, b). This approach could turn out to be difficult since the identification of homogeneous groups relies on the quality of the synthetic scores previously obtained.

(B) *A factorial k-means analysis*, which is realized by simultaneously combining a discrete clustering model (*partitioning method* like *K Means method*) and a continuous factorial model (Principal Components Analysis) in order to identify the best partition of the objects. In particular, the partition is described by the best orthogonal linear combinations of the variables (factors) according to the least-squares criterion. The use of a fast alternating least-squares algorithm allows applications to large data sets (Nardo et al. 2005a, b).

---

[6] Aggregation of scores collected at micro levels is a well-known issue in many scientific fields, like economics and informatics, where particular analytic approaches are applied (e.g., probabilistic aggregation analysis). In econometric fields, particular empirical methodologies have been developed, allowing the explanation of systematic individual differences (*compositional heterogeneity*) that can have important consequences in interpreting aggregated values (Stoker 1993).

Other attempts aimed at weighting average values by different criteria can be identified (Kalmijn and Veenhoven 2005; Veenhoven 2005).

[7] Identification of typologies requires particular analytic approaches, allowing homogeneous groups among individual cases to be identified (Aldenderfer and Blashfield 1984; Bailey 1994; Corter 1996; Hair et al. 1998; Lis and Sambin 1977):

– *Segmentation analysis*, which can be conducted through different procedures (*Hierarchical Cluster Analysis, Q Analysis*)

– *Partitioning analysis*, which can be conducted through different procedures, like K Means Methods, Iterative Reclassification Methods, "Sift and Shift" Methods, Convergent MethodsEach analytic approach produces results that vary according to the decisions made in terms of (1) selected indicators, (2) measures used in order to evaluate proximities between individual-points, (3) method used in order to assign individual-points to a group, (4) criterion used in order to determine the number of groups, and (5) criterion used in order to check the interpretability of the groups.

Combining Indicators

Joint Representation of Indicators: Dashboards

Dashboards represent useful tools aimed at simultaneously representing, comparing and interpreting indicators' values through an analogical perspective, by setting them on a standardized scale, and by representing them on a color scale (e.g., a green-to-red color scale). Several software programs (free or not) can be used in

Table 10.13 An overview of aggregation approaches based on the nature of the data

				aggregation approach			
				additive		compositional	
				involved indicators			
				single ↓	multiple ↓	single ↓	multiple ↓
nature of data	qualitative	disjointed	labels →	mode		incidences	typologies
		ordinal	natural / conventional order →	median	L1 – median	incidences	typologies
	quantitative	discrete	natural numbers →	median	L1 – median	incidences	typologies
		continuous	real numbers →	mean	centroide	incidences	Typologies

order to carry out the graphical representation through different images:

Whichever representation form is adopted, indicators' values are displayed through

1. Separated values (values are not aggregated), allowing weak and strong points to be identified.
2. Colors, allowing the analysis of relative performance (value to be displayed relatively to an expected value or a given level/targets).
3. Distributions, allowing assessment indicators' meaningfulness, outliers identification, etc.
4. Scatterplot graph, allowing simple correlation analysis between the indicators to be visualized. This function allows synergies (indicators whose "desirable" values are positively correlated) and potential conflicts (e.g., environment vs. many economic and social variables) to be identified.

Through the graphical display, dashboards allow comprehensive monitoring and evaluation of programs, performances or policies, since:

1. Highly complex systems of indicators can be represented by taking into account the hierarchical design.
2. Easy communications are possible through a catchy and simple graphical representation.
3. Indicators can be related to weights interpreted in terms of:
   (a) *Importance* (reflected by the size of the segments)
   (b) *Performance result* (reflected by the color, interpretable in terms of "good vs. bad")
4. Performances of different cases can be compared.

Of course, a dashboard does not allow complex analysis concerning relationships between indicators and comparisons of performance over time (trends) or across units (inter-cases comparisons). Dashboards can be useful in creating composite indicators.

Benchmarking: Merging Indicators
Traditional Approach: Composite Indicators

The previous procedures allow one to reduce the complexity of data by aggregating basic indicators (*construction of synthetic indicators*), and aggregating units/cases (*definition of macro units*).

Although the reduction process has been accomplished, the indicators consistently obtained through the hierarchical design remain a complex system. Sometimes, the complexity of the system of indicators may require indicators allowing measures that are more comprehensive. This need can emerge in order to (Noll 2009):

(a) Answer the call by "policy makers" for condensed information
(b) Improve the chance of getting into the media (compared to complex indicator systems)
(c) Allow multidimensional phenomena to be converted to unidimensional
(d) Allow situations to be compared across time more easily
(e) Compare cases (e.g., nations) in a transitive way (ranking and benchmarking)
(f) Allow clear cut answers to defined questions related to change across time, difference between groups of population or comparison between cities, countries, and so on

Composite indicators can provide useful approaches. A composite indicator synthesizes a number of values expressed by the indicators that constitute it (Booysen

2002; Nardo et al. 2005a; Sharpe and Salzman 2004) and re-establish the unity of the concept described in the hierarchical design. The aggregating process allows a somewhat faithful description of the reality, but an "indication" that will be more or less accurate, meaningful, and interpretable depending on the defined hierarchical design and the applied methodology.

Functions of Composite Indicators

Each composite indicator can be classified according to several criteria.

Purposes

The indicators can be distinguished according to their *purpose*, which can be:

- *Descriptive*, when the indicators are aimed at describing and knowing a particular reality (for example, quality of life). These indicators are said to be informative and baseline-oriented; in other terms, they allow changes across time, differences between geographical areas, and connections between social processes to be pointed out.
- *Explicative*, when the indicators are aimed at interpreting reality.
- *Predictive*, when the indicators help to delineate plausible evolutionary trends that it is possible to describe in terms of development or decrement; these indicators require strong prediction models and continuous observations across time.
- *Normative*, when the indicators are aimed at supporting, guiding, and directing decisions and possible interventions (policies) concerning problems to be solved. The normative function needs the definition of particular reference standards defined in terms of time, territory, etc.; the reference values allow the evaluation of the attainment of defined goals.
- *Problem-oriented*, when the indicators are defined as a function of a specific hypothesis of research and analysis aimed at identifying contexts, kinds, and severities of specific problems (for example the lack of quality of life conditions among immigrants).
- *Evaluating*, which can be distinguished as:
  - *Practical*: indicators interfacing with observed process (e.g., in an organization)
  - *Directional*: indicators testing if the observed condition is getting better or not
  - *Actionable*: indicators allowing change effects to be controlled

Governance Contexts

The indicators can be distinguished according to the *context* in which they are created, used, and interpreted. From this perspective, we can identify different contexts. For example:

- *Public debates*. In this case, the indicator/s have the function of informing, stimulating, forming, and developing particular sensitivity.
- *Policy guidance*. In this case, the indicators/s can support particular policy decisions.
- *Administrative guidance*. In this case, the indicator/s can support the evaluation of the different impacts of different alternatives.

Perspectives of Observation

The indicators can be distinguished according to different *perspectives of observation*. For instance, in the ambit of quality of life, a complex indicator that measures through

- A *conglomerative* approach measures overall well-being, where increases in well-being of the best-off can offset decreases in well-being of the worst-off.
- A *deprivational* approach measures only the welfare of the worst-off (Anand and Sen 1997).

Anand and Sen (1997) argued that the conglomerative and deprivational perspectives are not substitutes for each other, and proposed a *complementary* approach. "We need both, for an adequate understanding of the process of development. The plurality of our concerns and commitment forces us take an interest in each." The adoption of a complementary approach allows us to construct indices of social and economic well-being that should reflect the aggregated and disaggregated approaches. According to this methodology, conglomerative and deprivational indices should be constructed separately side-by-side along the lines of the United Nations Development Programme indicators (Sharpe and Salzman 2004).

Forms of Observation

The indicators can be distinguished according to the different *forms of observation*. In this perspective, we can distinguish between:

- *Status indicators*, which measure the reality in a particular moment; they allow for cross-comparisons between different realities. These indicators can produce cross data that need to be carefully managed since different realities cannot always be directly compared; this is particularly true in the case of subjective characteristics observed in different geographical, social, cultural, political, environmental, and administrative conditions.

- *Trend indicators*, which measure reality across time; they require a defined longitudinal observational design (for example, repeated surveys on particular populations). These indicators can produce *time series* that need to be carefully managed since the observed moments could reveal themselves to be incomparable and/or the defined indicators could reveal themselves as non applicable after some time.

Levels of Communication

The indicators can be distinguished according to the different *levels of communication*. It regards the target group to which the final indicator will be communicated. From this perspective, indicators can be classified as:

- *Cold indicators*. In this case, the indicators have a high level of scientific quality and show a high level of complexity and difficulty.
- *Hot indicators*: In this case, the indicators are constructed at a low level of difficulty and show a high level of understanding. It is unusual for these indicators to be used in a policy context.
- *Warm indicators*. In this case, the indicators show a good balance between quality, comprehensibility, and resonance.

Methodological Issues

The construction of composite indicators requires a particular methodology and specific techniques aimed at:

1. Verifying the dimensionality of selected indicators (*dimensional analysis*)
2. Defining the importance of each indicator to be aggregated (*weighting criteria*)
3. Identifying the technique for aggregating the indicator values into the composite indicator (*aggregating-over-indicators techniques*)
4. Assessing the robustness of the composite indicator in terms of capacity to produce correct and stable measures (*uncertainty analysis, sensitivity analysis*)
5. Assessing the discriminant capacity of the composite indicator (*ascertainment of selectivity* and *identification of cut-point or cut-off values*)

Selecting Indicators Leading to Dimensional Analysis

This analysis aims at selecting the indicators to be included in the composite, showing the best statistical characteristics.

From this perspective, *dimensional analysis* mainly allows the *dimensionality* of the conceptual construct, which the composite is based on, to be identified. In other words, dimensional analysis allows the analysts to investigate the level of complexity by which the composite indicator has to be constructed.

Actually, the results lead to a further selection of indicators before going through the construction of the composite indicator. From the statistical point of view, the selection should avoid superimposition and redundancies among indicators. However, in selecting the indicators also other criteria should be taken into account. In short, the criteria are:

- *Redundancy*. In building a composite indicator, two indicators showing a very high correlation are considered redundant; it is recommended to select only one of them.
- *Comparability*. When two indicators are redundant, it is recommended to select the one allowing trend analysis and wide comparisons.
- *Political impact*. If two indicators convey strong political messages, they can be both included in the final list.
- *Availability*. Indicators which prove to be available for a large number of cases are preferable.

Dimensional analysis can be performed through different approaches (Alt 1990; Anderson 1958; Bolasco 1999; Cooley and Lohnes 1971; Corbetta 1992, 2003; Cox and Cox 1994; Hair et al. 1998; Kruskal and Wish 1978; Maggino 2004a, b, 2005a; Sadocchi 1981). Among them, the following methods are the more commonly used:

- *Correlation analysis*. It is useful in order to select indicators that are not redundant and to avoid multicollinearity (*double counting*) in composite indicator construction (Nardo et al. 2005a).
- *Principal component analysis*. The main goal of principal component analysis is to describe the variation of a data set using a number of scores that is smaller than the number of the original indicators. This approach is very often applied to test dimensional structures, even though this practice is strongly criticisable. This is done following the idea that this approach can be assimilated to Factor

Analysis. The two approaches are actually, however, very different from each other. In particular, the main goal of Principal Component Analysis is not to test a (dimensional) model but simply to decompose the correlations among indicators in order to condense the variance among all the indicators as much as possible by calculating new linear variables, defined components.

– *Multidimensional scaling*. It allows the underlying dimensionality to be tested and for the creation of a geometrical multidimensional representation (*map*) of the complete group of indicators (Cox and Cox 1994; Kruskal and Wish 1978; Torgerson 1958).

– *Cluster analysis*. In this context, it can be useful to identify meaningful groupings among indicators (Aldenderfer and Blashfield 1984; Bailey 1994; Corter 1996; Hair et al. 1998; Lis and Sambin 1977; Maggino 2005a).

In some cases, methods related to a reflective model of measurement can be carefully used, like:

– *Performance analysis (Item Response Theory)*. When the indicators refer to performance variables, a particular analysis, derived directly from the application of *Item Response Theory* (related to the reflective model of measurement), allows the indicators that better discriminate among units to be selected. In particular, the identified indicators can be distinguished from each other in terms of difficulty and discriminant capacity (Andersen 1972, 1973; Andrich 1988; Bock and Aitken 1981; Hambleton et al. 1991; Lord 1974, 1984; Ludlow and Haley 1995; McDonald 1989; Rasch 1960; Rupp et al. 2004; Rupp and Zumbo 2003, 2006; Sijtsma and Molenaar 2002; Swaminathan and Gifford 1982, 1985, 1986).

– *Factor analysis*. It allows the hypothesized dimensional structure underlying the group of indicators (latent structure analysis) to be tested; it is based upon the assumption that the total variance of each indicator is produced by a linear combination of different variance components (additive assumption), *common variance* (due to the dimensional structure), *specific variance* (due to the specificity variance of each indicator), and *error*. Actually, factor analysis allows the common variance (*communality*) to be estimated (Kim and Mueller 1989a; b; Marradi 1981).

In some cases, the approaches can be combined (e.g., *tandem analysis* or *factorial k-means analysis*, Nardo et al. 2005a).

Weighting Criteria

Since not necessarily all the identified indicators contribute with the same importance to the measurement and evaluation of the latent variable, a weighting system needs to be defined in order to assign a weight to each indicator before proceeding to the indicators aggregation.

When an implicit weighting system cannot be identified, a criterion has to be adopted in order to define a weighting system, which can reproduce as accurately as possible the contribution of each indicator to the construction of the composite indicator. From this perspective, the definition of the weighting system can constitute an improvement and refinement of the adopted model of measurement.

From the technical point of view, the weighting procedure consists in defining and assigning a weight to each indicator. The weight will be used in the successive computation of the individual aggregate score; in particular, each weight is multiplied for the corresponding individual value of the indicator.

In order to proceed with the definition of a differential weighting system, the analyst needs to take into account (Nardo et al. 2005a):

• The defined rationale and theoretical structure which the conceptual construct and, consequently, the composite indicator are based on
• The meaning and the contribution of each indicator to the aggregation
• The quality of data and the statistical adequacy of the indicators

In this sense, apart from the applied approach, the defined weights represent judgment values.

The researcher has to carefully evaluate and make formally explicit not only the methodology to be adopted but also the results that would have been obtained with other methodologies, also reasonably applicable.

The identification of the procedure for identifying the weights needs to distinguish between *equal weighting* (*EW*)[8] and *differential weighting* (*DW*). The composite indicator will be strongly influenced by

---

[8]Equal weighting does not necessarily imply unitary weighting.

whichever choice is made concerning this. Cases' positions can sharply change by simply changing the weights assigned to each indicator.

The adoption of the *differential weighting* procedure does not necessarily correspond to the identification of different weights but rather to the selection of the most appropriate approach in order to identify the weights among the following (Nardo et al. 2005a):

1. *Statistical methods*:
   (a) Correlation
   (b) *Principal Component Analysis* (PCA)
   (c) *Data Envelopment Analysis* (DEA)
   (d) *Unobserved Components Models* (UCM).

The adoption of statistical methods in weighting components of social indices has to be considered carefully since, by removing any control over the weighting procedure from the analysts, it gives a false appearance of mathematical objectivity that is actually difficult to achieve in social measurement (Sharpe and Salzman 2004).

2. *Multiattribute models*:
   (a) *Multiattribute decision making* (in particular, *Analytic Hierarchy Processes*—AHP) (Yoon and Hwang 1995),
   (b) *MultiAttribute Compositional Model* (in particular, *Conjoint Analysis*, CA),[9]

3. *Subjective methods*. New perspectives have been introduced recently showing the possibility involves more individuals (experts or citizens) in the process of defining weighting systems for social indicators. These approaches are defined from the perspective of giving more legitimacy to social indicators by taking into account citizens' importance (values) and not—as usually done in the past—statistical importance.[10]

Assigning differential weights can be just as doubtful, especially when the decision is not supported by:

- Theoretical reflections that endow a meaning on each indicator or consider its impact on the synthesis
- Methodological concerns that help to identify the proper techniques, consistently with the theoretical structure

Table 10.14 Aggregating table according to a typical compensatory approach (additive technique)

		B		
		1	*2*	*3*
A	*4*	5	6	7
	3	4	5	6
	2	3	4	5
	1	2	3	4

In any case, we have to consider that a whole set of weights able to express in a perfect way the actual and relative contribution of each indicator to the measurement does not exist.

Independently from the approach adopted in order to define them, the weights can be kept constant or can be changed according to particular considerations concerning each application. In both cases, the researcher needs to rationalize the choice. The former approach can be adopted when the aim is to analyze the evolution of the examined QOL ambit. The latter can be adopted when the aim—for example—concerns the definition of particular priorities. Please see Russell et al. (2006) for a discussion of whether weighting captures what is important in the phenomenon.

Techniques for Aggregating Indicators

The choice of the aggregating technique must be consistent with the adopted aggregation model. In particular, it has to consider the adopted assumptions concerning the level of complexity of the composite indicator (*dimensionality*) expressed in terms of homogeneity among indicators to be aggregated, and the relationship between these indicators and the latent variable.

Moreover, the choice must take into account the specific characteristics of each technique; in particular, we have to consider if the technique:

(a) Admits compensability among the indicators to be aggregated
(b) Necessitates comparability among indicators
(c) Necessitates a homogeneity in the levels of measurement of the indicators

(a) An aggregating technique is *compensatory* when it allows low values in some indicators to be compensated by high values in other indicators. In the typical aggregating table (see Table 10.14), we can observe all the possible synthetic values, obtainable by aggregating two indicators (*A* and *B*) using simple addition (additive technique).

---

[9]Hair et al. (1998); Louviere (1988); Malhotra (1996). A particular example of Conjoint Analysis application to QOL measurement see Maggino (2005b).

[10]Hagerty and Land (2007); Maggino (2008a, b, 2009); Maggino and Ruviglioni (2008a, b, 2009).

Table 10.15 Aggregating table according to a typical compensatory approach (multiplicative technique)

		B		
		1	**2**	**3**
	4	4	8	12
A	**3**	3	6	9
	2	2	4	6
	1	1	2	3

Some of the obtained synthetic values, even if completely identical, are obtained through different original indicators. This means that obtained aggregated values do not allow us to return to the original unit's profile since the same synthetic values are obtained through different combinations of scores. In other words, two units with different realities turn out to be identical and indistinct.

By using the same data reported in the previous table, all the possible synthetic values can be observed, obtainable by aggregating two indicators (A and B) using the multiplicative techniques (following the geometrical approach)—see table 10.15.

Table 10.15 suggests that the multiplicative technique is compensatory as well, especially with reference to indicators showing low values.

Generally, in order to make multiplicative functions more manageable, the values of involved indicators are logarithmically transformed (summing up logarithm values corresponds to multiplying the original values). However, this procedure has to be followed with caution since it can also produce problems of interpretation.

If compensability is admitted, a unit showing a low value for one indicator will need higher values on the others in order to obtain a higher synthetic value. From this perspective, a compensatory technique can be useful in some contexts especially when the purpose of applying indicators is to stimulate behaviors aimed at improving the overall performance by investing in those areas showing lower values.

All this highlights how important the choice of the aggregating technique is in order to avoid inconsistencies between the weights previously chosen—in terms of theoretical meaning and importance—and the way these weights are actually used. In other words, in order to continue interpreting the weights as "importance coefficients," a noncompensatory aggregating procedure has to be preferred, such as a noncompensatory multicriteria approach, like multi-criteria analysis (MCA) (Nardo et al. 2005a).

(b) *Comparability* refers to the distributional characteristics of indicators, in particular to directionality and functional form.

– *Directionality* concerns the direction by which each indicator measures the concept (i.e., positive or negative). In some cases, it could be necessary to make the directionality of the whole group of indicators uniform before starting the aggregation process. In order to make the directionalities uniform, the indicators to be transformed should be submitted to the reflection procedure:

$$\left[\left(higher \cdot value \cdot observed\right)+1\right]$$
$$-\left(individual \cdot unit's \cdot original \cdot value\right)$$

– *Functional forms* represent the changes in a variable that are valued at different levels. If changes are valued in the same way, regardless of level, then the functional form is linear. If changes are valued differently, according to the level, the functional form is not linear. In other words, in some cases the same absolute differences between observed values are valued differently and consequently can have different meaning (e.g., a change of 100 euros in terms of income can have a different meaning if it occurs at a high or at a low level of income).

In interpreting the level of a variable, two issues arise:

– Are absolute values of a variable proportional in importance with reference to the measured concept?

– Are changes in the values of a variable of equal importance at various levels of the variable?

According to the response to these questions, the functional forms will be linear or nonlinear (Sharpe and Salzman 2004). Consequently, the most convenient interpretation and analytic treatment can be identified. If changes (Nardo et al. 2005a) are more significant at lower levels of the indicator, the functional form should be concave down (e.g., log or the nth root); on the opposite, if changes are more important at higher levels of the indicator, the functional form should be concave up (e.g., exponential or power).[11] Both the functional forms are nonlinear by definition.

---

[11] The standard choice is for log as the concave down function and power as the concave up function.

- Applying the appropriate functional form helps to better interpret the changes in the indicator. Many indicators commonly taken into account in social and economic indices show nonlinear functional forms, such as per capita GDP, measures of unemployment, poverty gaps and rates, measures of inequality such as ratios of high and low incomes, and environmental depletion (Sharpe and Salzman 2004).[12]

(c) *Homogeneity* refers to the level of measurement adopted by the whole group of indicators. Almost all the aggregating techniques require homogeneous scales. Some techniques exist allowing the indicators' original scales to be transformed into an interpretable common scale. In order to select the proper approach, the data quality and properties and the objectives of the indicator should be taken into account.

The literature offers several *aggregation techniques* (Nardo et al. 2005a). The linear aggregation approach (additive technique) is the most widely used. By contrast, multiplicative techniques (following the geometrical approach) and the technique based upon multicriteria analysis (following the noncompensatory approach) allow the difficulties caused by compensation among the indicators to be overcome (Table 10.16):

Assessing Robustness

(A) Uncertainty and sensitivity analysis

As we have seen, in order to proceed in aggregating multiple measures many choices have to be taken; these decisions can influence the robustness, which is the capacity of the composite indicator to produce correct and stable measures (Edward and Newman 1982; Nardo et al. 2005a; Saisana et al. 2005; Saltelli et al. 2004; Sharpe and Salzman 2004; Tarantola et al. 2000). Assessing the robustness allows us to evaluate the role and the consequences of the subjectivity of the choices made with reference to: (a) the model to estimate the measurement error; (b) the procedure for selecting the indicators; (c) the procedure for data management (missing data imputation, data standardization and normalization, etc.); (d) the criterion for weight assignment; and (e) the aggregation technique used.

In order to evaluate the robustness of the composite indicator, a specific analytic procedure can be employed dealing with all the choices that can represent possible sources of uncertainty. In other words, the robustness is assessed by testing and comparing all the possible different performances that would have been obtained through different decisions along all the construction process of the composite indicator. In particular, the procedure allows us to: evaluate the applicability of the model of measurement and the factors that contribute to the variability of the composite score, detect the choices producing values as stable as possible, understand the performance of the adopted model, and ascertain the quality of the adopted model. This procedure, which can be included in the wider field of the *what-if analysis*, is conducted through two stages; each stage corresponds to a different analytic methodology (Nardo et al. 2005a):

1. *Uncertainty analysis.* This method aims at analyzing to what extent the composite indicator depends on the information composing it. In order to evaluate how the uncertainty sources influence the synthetic score obtained, the procedure identifies different scenarios for each individual case; each scenario corresponds to a certain combination of choices that produces a certain synthetic value.

2. *Sensitivity analysis.* This method aims at evaluating the contribution of each identified source of uncertainty by decomposing the total variance of the synthetic score obtained; to this end, the procedure tests how much the synthetic score is sensitive to the different choices (small differences reveal low sensitivity).

The two approaches, generally treated in separate contexts, are very popular in any scientific field that requires the development and assessment of models (financial applications, risk analyses, neural networks); in addiction, the *uncertainty analysis* is adopted and applied more frequently than the *sensitivity analysis* (Jamison and Sandbu 2001). The iterative and synergic application of both the procedures have been revealed to be

---

[12] Anand and Sen (1997) state that, in measures of poverty deprivation "the relative impact of the deprivation … would increase as the level of deprivation becomes sharper". According to this motivation, the UNDP develops measures of deprivation and inequality that more heavily penalize countries with higher indicators of deprivation in absolute value terms. For example, a decrease of 5 years of life expectancy from a base level of 40 is more heavily penalized than the same decrease beginning at a level of 80 (Sharpe and Salzman 2004).

Table 10.16 An overview of aggregation approaches

			Aggregating approaches			
			1. Linear aggregation		2. Geometrical aggregation	3. Noncompensatory aggregation
			Simple additive	Cumulative		
Assumptions	Dimensionality	Relationships between indicators	Uni	Uni	Uni	Multi
	Model of measurement	Relationship between indicators and latent variable	Monotonic	Differential relationship	Monotonic	
	Compensation	Among indicators	Admitted	Not admitted (scalability of indicators)	Admitted	Not admitted
	Homogeneity	Of the level of measurement	Requested	Requested	Requested	Not requested

useful and powerful (Saisana et al. 2005; Saltelli et al. 2004; Tarantola et al. 2000) in developing aggregated measures.[13]

(B) Assessing discriminant capacity

Assessing the discriminant capacity (Maggino 2007) of the composite indicator requires exploring its capacity in:

- Discriminating between cases and/or groups. This can be accomplished by applying the traditional approaches of statistical hypothesis testing.
- Distributing all the cases without any concentration of individual scores in a few segments of the continuum. To this end, some coefficients were defined (Guilford 1954; Maggino 2003, 2007).
- Showing values that are interpretable in terms of selectivity through the identification of particular values or reference scores. It allows the interpretation of the individual scores and eventually the selection of individual cases according to particular criteria; the reference scores are called *cut-points* or *cut-offs*, referring respectively to continuous and discrete data. The selection of these reference scores is particularly useful when the composite indicator is applied for diagnostic and screening purposes.[14]

Criticisms of Composite Indicators

Despite its spreading, the composite indicator approach is currently being deeply criticized as inappropriate and often inconsistent (Freudenberg 2003). Critics point out conceptual, methodological, and technical issues especially concerning the difficulty in conveying into unidimensional measures all the relevant information pertaining to phenomena which are complex, dynamic, multidimensional, full of ambiguities, and nuances, and which are represented by data being sensitive and qualitative (even when quantitatively measured) and containing errors and approximations.

In other words, a composite indicator is hardly able to reflect the complexity of a socioeconomic phenomenon and to capture the complexity of the variables' relationships. This incapacity is related to the

---

[13] The possibility of applying techniques such as *cluster analysis* should not be ignored since these techniques allow different and alternative typologies to be evaluated among the observed cases.

[14] *Receiver operating characteristic* or *relative operating characteristic analysis* represents a valid method to be applied in order to test the discriminant capacity of a composite indicator. This analysis, connected directly to cost/benefit analysis in the

area of *diagnostic decision making*, allows the relationship between sensitivity and specificity to be studied and analyzed in order to identify discriminant *cut-point*, *cut-off*, or *operating-point*.

ROC analysis is realized by studying the function that relates:

- The probability of obtaining a "true alarm" among cases that needs an action (→ sensitivity → *hit rate* → **HR**).
- The probability of obtaining a "false alarm" among cases that do not need an action (→ 1-specificity → *false alarm rate* → **FAR**).

In order to study this relationship, two rates are computed for each *cut-point*. An optimal curve can be obtained by defining many *cut-points* along the supposed continuum of the composite indicator.

The procedure was conceived during the Second World War in order to study and improve the reception of radars and sonars. (Peterson, W. W., Birdsall, T. G., & Fox, W. C. (1954). *The theory of signal detectability*. Institute of Radio Engineers Transactions, PGIT-4, 171–212.).

comprehensiveness and complexity of the phenomenon that should be covered by the composite indicators.

Those who maintain composite indicators stress they are simple to build and to communicate and based on "objective" computation tools. Although objectivity is always invoked as an essential requirement, in practice the procedures for computing composite indicators are far from being "aseptic." Generally, they comprise different stages (Nardo et al. 2005a, b; Sharpe and Salzman 2004), each introducing some degree of arbitrariness to make decisions concerning:

– The *analytic approach* to determine the underlying dimensionality of the available elementary indicators and the selection of those to be used in the evaluation process (*dimensional analysis*)
– The choice of the *weights* used to define the importance of each elementary indicator to be aggregated (*weighting criteria*);
– The aggregation technique adopted to synthesize the elementary indicators into composite indicators. (*aggregating-over-indicators techniques*).
– *The choice of the models and conceptual approaches* in order to assess:
  (a) The robustness of the synthetic indicator in terms of capacity to produce correct and stable measures (*uncertainty analysis, sensitivity analysis*)
  (b) The discriminant capacity of the synthetic indicator (*ascertainment of selectivity* and *identification of cut-point or cut-off values*)

Even though some decisions are strictly technical, it is quite difficult to make these decisions objective since they may involve different kinds of concerns. Generally, they are taken through a process accepted and shared by the scientific community.

Indicators selection. Selecting the indicators to be included in the composite represents a fundamental stage of the construction process since it operationally defines the latent concept that the composite is supposed to measure (formative logic). From the statistical point of view, this stage aims at:

– Exploring the level of complexity of the concept (dimensionality) as it is measured by the identified indicators
– Selecting the indicators showing the best statistical characteristics

The two goals are pursued contextually through traditional analytic approaches. Beyond the criticisms previously expressed concerning the metrics of data, the application of the traditional dimensional procedures puts other doubts, especially from the statistical logic point of view.

– *Factor Analysis.* It can be applied only to test the hypothesized dimensionality and to select the indicators that best fit the dimensional structure. In particular, it allows the hypothesized dimensional structure underlying the group of indicators (latent structure analysis) to be tested; it is based upon the assumption that the total variance of each indicator is produced by a linear combination of different variance components (additive assumption), *common variance* (due to the dimensional structure), *specific variance* (due to the specificity variance of each indicator), and *error*. Actually, factor analysis allows the common variance (*communality*) to be estimated (Kim and Mueller 1989a, b).
– *Principal Component Analysis.* The main goal of principal component analysis is to describe the variation of a data set using a number of scores that is smaller than the number of the original indicators. This approach is very often applied to test dimensional structures by assimilating it to factor analysis, even though this practice is strongly criticizable. In fact, the main goal of principal component analysis is not to test a (dimensional) model but simply to decompose the correlations among indicators in order to condense the variance among all the indicators as much as possible by calculating new linear variables, defined components.

Irrespective of the statistical tool adopted, dimensionality reduction raises some relevant questions, concerning its consequences on the composite indicator construction. If the concept to be measured turns out to be actually unidimensional, computing a single composite indicator could be justifiable. But when concepts are truly multidimensional, then singling out just one, albeit composite, indicator is very questionable. The nuances and ambiguities of the data would in fact be forced into a conceptual model where all the features affecting the multidimensionality are considered as noise to be removed. Moreover, synthetic scores could be biased towards a small subset of elementary indicators, failing to give a faithful representation of the data. Please see Zumbo and Rupp (2004) and Zumbo (2007) for a synthesis of the field and recommendations from a psychometric point of view.

Weighting indicators. When constructing indicators, particular attention is paid to the weighting process, which aims at assigning different *importance* to the elementary indicators to be aggregated. The necessity of choosing weights based on objective principles is frequently asserted (Nardo et al. 2005a, b; Ray 2008; Sharpe and Salzman 2004), leading to a preference for statistical tools like correlation analysis, principal component analysis, or data envelopment analysis, to mention a few. However, adopting purely statistical methods in weighting components of social indices must be carefully considered. Removing any control over the weighting procedure from the analyst, it gives a possibly false appearance of objectivity that is actually difficult to achieve in social measurement (Sharpe and Salzman 2004). Moreover, since defining weights is often interpreted from the perspective of identifying personal and social *values*, the procedure should necessarily involve individuals' contributions in attributing importance to different domains. Sometimes, the choice and decision could be shared by a larger community (involving individuals in the process of social indicators construction). If indicators concern societal well-being, their construction turns out to be not just a technical problem, being part of a larger debate aimed at obtaining a larger *legitimacy*. From this perspective, the weighting issue can be even considered as a leverage of democratic participation in decisions ("res publica"). Hagerty and Land (2007) stressed how building composite indicators should take into account and maximize the agreement among citizens concerning the importance of each elementary indicator. Choosing consistent weighting criteria is thus a subtitle issue, largely subjective and possibly data independent.

Aggregating indicators. Further criticisms concern the aggregating process, which raises methodological difficulties (Munda and Nardo 2008) encountered to get unidimensional scores out of multidimensional data, and which raises methodological difficulties when dealing with ordinal data. The process is in fact quite controversial since:

– The indicators to be aggregated are rarely homogeneous in many respects (metrics, directionality, functional form, …) and need not share common antecedents (Howell et al. 2007).
– The aggregating technique might introduce implicitly meaningless compensations and trade-offs among indicators.

– It is not clear how to combine ordinal variables, using numerical weights.

Methodological difficulties rise particularly when ordinal indicators are to be aggregated into a composite indicator, to get unidimensional scores for comparing and ranking statistical units. Unidimensional scores are usually computed through weighted averages of the ordinal evaluation variables, as in the quantitative case. As a matter of fact, this leads to highly controversial results, since weighted averages cannot be consistently computed over ordinal variables and different choice of the scaling tools would imply very different final conclusions (moreover, scaling tools tend to impose a quantitative latent model to data, which is often forced, arguable, and not fully justifiable on any epistemological basis).

Composite indicators represent the mainstream approach to socioeconomic evaluation (Maggino and Fattore 2011; Fattore et al. 2011), yet the discussion above shows how many critical issues affect their computation. The difficulties are even greater when ordinal variables are dealt with, since statistical tools based on linear metric structures cannot, strictly speaking, be applied to nonnumeric data. In a sense, socioeconomic analysis faces an impasse: (1) implicitly or not, it is generally taken for granted that "evaluation implies aggregation"; thus (2) ordinal data must be scaled to numerical values, to be aggregated and processed in an (formally) effective way; Unfortunately, (3) this often proves inconsistent with the nature of the phenomena and produces results that may be largely arbitrary, barely meaningful, and interpretable. Realizing the weakness of the outcomes based on composite indicator computations, statistical research has focused on developing alternative and more sophisticated analytic procedures, but almost always assuming the existence of a cardinal latent structure behind ordinal data. The resulting models are often very complicated and still affected by the epistemological and technical issues discussed above. The way out of this impasse can instead be found realizing that evaluation need not imply aggregation and that it can be performed in purely ordinal terms. This is exactly what poset theory allows.

Assessing robustness. This stage aims at proving that the results obtained through the composite are not affected by the choices made along the process. The assessment is accomplished by applying uncertainty and sensitivity analysis. It could be interpreted as an attempt to objectify the choices, turned which were inevitably subjective. Actually, this stage aims at defending the choices through evidence. However, this approach does not require a methodological defense of the choices, in terms of scientific responsibility.

Traditional statistical data analysis procedures, based upon linear mathematical instruments, are hardly applicable for data discrete in their nature. New challenges and perspectives are emerging aimed at improving technical tools and strategies with reference to:

- Reducing data structure in order to aggregate units and indicators.
- Combining indicators.
- Communicating the "picture" obtained through the indicators (correctly and significantly representing and showing results).

These new challenges and perspectives should take into account:

- Nature of data (generally ordinal)
- Process and trends of phenomena (not always linear but more frequently monotonic)

By considering all this, new challenges and perspectives can be identified in order to improve the technical strategies allowing social indicators to be constructed and managed.

Modeling Indicators

Dealing with a comprehensive conceptual framework requires exploring possible explanations of the relationships among the indicators, which conceptually model and hierarchically design the variables.

From this perspective, a proper analytic approach should be identified according to the defined conceptual framework. The feasibility of different statistical approaches needs to be considered by taking into account their specific assumptions. The goal is to identify a procedure able to yield results, not only statistically valid and consistent with reference to the defined conceptual framework, but also easy to be read and interpreted at policy level.

Structural Models Approach

With reference to the causal explanatory perspective, we can refer to *structural equation modeling* (SEM), which, as known, represents a statistical technique for testing and estimating causal relationships using a combination of statistical data and qualitative causal assumptions.

SEM is considered a confirmatory rather than an exploratory approach. It usually starts with a hypothesis, represented as a model, operationalizes the constructs of interest with a measurement instrument, and tests the model.

The causal assumptions embedded in the model often have falsifiable implications, which can be tested with empirical data. SEM can also be used inductively by specifying the model and using data to estimate the values of free parameters. Often the initial hypothesis requires adjustment in light of model evidence, but SEM is rarely used purely for exploration.

SEM models allow unreliability of measurement in the model to be explicitly captured and, consequently, structural relations between latent variables to be accurately estimated.

Given its specific assumptions, this approach can be adopted only in the presence of a strong conceptual interpretative framework concerning the causal relationships between objective and subjective indicators. In other words, it requires a strong acceptance of the direction of the relationships among objective and subjective indicators.

Moreover, as shown above, two possible directions can be defined in casual explanation of well-being, *bottom-up* and *top-down*, which, however, are not separately able to explain completely the relationships between the observed variables. This means that causal effects can emerge in both directions. Diener (1984) suggested using both *bottom-up* and *top-down* approaches in order to examine the causal directions of well-being. Consequently, the application of a model allowing bidirectional effects to be estimated, has to be used on with extreme caution (Scherpenzeel and Saris 1996) and requires longitudinal data and analyses. The caution should increase especially in the presence of both objective and subjective indicators.

Multilevel Approach

Multilevel analysis refers to statistical methodologies, first developed in the social sciences, which analyze outcomes simultaneously in relation to determinants measured at different levels (for example, individual, workplace, neighborhood, nation, or geographical region existing within or across geopolitical boundaries) (Goldstein 1999; Hox 1995; Krieger 2002).

This approach can be applied from the perspective of integrating objective and subjective indicators by assuming that people living in the same territory (e.g., city or region) share the same macro-level living conditions (objective quality of life) that contribute together with the micro-level living conditions (objective quality of life) to subjective well-being. If the conceptual model is clearly specifiable and acceptable with reference to which variables are to be included in the study and at which level, these analyses can potentially assess whether individuals' well-being is influenced by not only "individual" or "household" characteristics but also "population" or "area" characteristics (Krieger 2002). In fact, this approach assumes that structural characteristics of territories come before individual living conditions and that both precede subjective well-being. The goal is to describe the relationships between subjective well-being ("outcome" variable), territorial characteristics (macro-level living conditions: socio-economic conditions, demographic trend, and so on) and individual objective characteristics (micro-level living conditions: sex, religion, family composition, level of education, and so on).

The general analytic framework could be multiple regression; subjective well-being is regressed on territorial and individual characteristics. If the goal is to evaluate the importance of territorial characteristics on subjective well-being, we could aggregate individual data at a territorial level, but—as we know—this could result in the well-known *ecological fallacy*. In fact, the correlation between the observations resulting from the multilevel structure (the individuals in the same territory present the same values concerning the territory characteristics) of data make the outcomes of the same territory more homogeneous than those yielded by a random sample of individuals drawn from the whole population. This higher homogeneity is naturally modeled by a positive within-territory correlation among individual levels of subjective well-being in the same territory. This problem can be avoided by applying a variance components model.

In statistics, a *variance components model*, also called *random effect/s model*, is a kind of *hierarchical linear model*. These models (along with generalized linear mixed models, nested models, mixed models, random coefficient, random parameter models, split-plot designs) are part of *multilevel models* (Raudenbush and Bryk 2002), which are statistical models of parameters that vary at more than one level.

These models can be seen as generalizations of linear models (also extendible to nonlinear models)[15] and represent more advanced forms of simple linear regression and multiple linear regression. They are appropriate for use with nested data. In particular, they assume that the data describe a hierarchy of different populations whose differences are constrained by the hierarchy.

In other words, multilevel analysis allows variance in outcome variables to be analyzed at multiple hierarchical levels, whereas in simple linear and multiple linear regression all effects are modeled to occur at a single level.

For example, in educational research, where data are often considered as pupils nested within classrooms nested within schools, it may be necessary to assess the performance of schools teaching by one method against schools teaching by a different method. It would be a mistake to analyze these kinds of data as though the pupils were simple random samples from the population of pupils taught by a particular method. Pupils are taught in classes, which are in schools. The performance of pupils within the same class will be correlated, as will the performance of pupils within the same school.

Conceptually, the model is often viewed as a hierarchical system of regression equations. For example, assume we have data in J groups or contexts and a different number of individuals N_j in each group. On the individual (lowest) level, we have the dependent variable Y_{ij} and the explanatory variable X_{ij}, and on the group level, we have the explanatory variable Z_j. Thus, we have a separate regression equation in each group:

$$Y_{ij} = \beta_{0j} + \beta_{1j} X_{ij} + e_{ij} \qquad (10.1)$$

The β_j are modeled by explanatory variables at the group level:

$$\beta_{0j} = \gamma_{00} + \gamma_{01} Z_j + u_{0j} \qquad (10.2)$$
$$\beta_{1j} = \gamma_{10} + \gamma_{11} Z_j + u_{1j} \qquad (10.3)$$

---

[15]Multilevel analysis has been extended to include multilevel structural equation modeling, multilevel latent class modeling, and other more general models.

Substitution of (10.2) and (10.3) in (10.1) gives:

$$Y_{ij} = \gamma_{00} + \gamma_{10}X_{ij} + \gamma_{01}Z_j + \gamma_{11}Z_jX_{ij} + u_{1j}X_{ij} + u_{0j} + e_{ij} \quad (10.4)$$

In general, there will be more than one explanatory variable at the lowest level and also more than one explanatory variable at the highest level. Assume that we have P explanatory variables X at the lowest level, indicated by the subscript p ($p = 1,\ldots, P$), and Q explanatory variables Z at the highest level, indicated by the subscript q ($q = 1, \ldots, Q$). Then, Eq. 10.4 becomes the more general equation:

$$Y_{ij} = \gamma_{00} + \gamma_{p0}X_{pij} + \gamma_{0q}Z_{qj} + \gamma_{pq}Z_{qj}X_{pij} + u_{pj}X_{pij} + u_{0j} + e_{ij} \quad (10.5)$$

Multilevel analysis generally uses maximum likelihood (ML) estimators, with standard errors estimated from the inverse of the information matrix. Computing the ML estimates requires an iterative procedure. (Bryk and Raudenbush 1992; Goldstein 1999; Hox 1995).

Even if the multilevel approach presents logic and analytic solutions acceptable from the statistical point of view, this method should be considered carefully in the context of quality of life. For instance, when the territorial characteristics do not affect individuals in the same manner and with the same degree (territorial heterogeneity), some authors (Rampichini and Schifini 1998) suggest introducing a new level in the hierarchy, represented by individuals within each territory. For example, different clusters of individuals could be identified sharing the same living conditions at a micro level. This could lead to results in which similar clusters are in different territories.

Life-Course Perspective

Life-course perspective refers to a conceptual model that considers well-being status at any given individual state (age, sex, marital status) not only reflecting contemporary conditions but also embodying prior living circumstances. This means that we could try to study people's developmental trajectories (environmental and social) over time, by considering also the historical period in which they live, in reference to their society's social, economic, political, and ecological context. This approach assumes that some components can exist which can determine an effect, at a sensitive or "critical" period of an individual's life, having a lifelong significance. The interest could be oriented to analyzing which of these processes are reversible and what the role of objective micro or macro level characteristics is.

This perspective deserves particular attention and consideration. Its limit is mainly represented by the difficulty of obtaining detailed and consistent individual longitudinal data and by the complexity of managing, analyzing, and modeling these kinds of data. According to its characteristics, this approach turns out to be useful for studying clinical data.

Bayesian Networks Approach

A Bayesian network is a graphical model representing a certain reality described by variables. The goal is to explore the relationships among the variables of interest through probabilities.[16]

This model has several *advantages* for data analysis:

1. The model encodes dependencies among all variables, it readily handles situations where some data entries are missing.
2. It is adaptable since it can be used to learn causal relationships, and hence can be used to gain understanding about a problem domain and to predict the consequences of intervention.
3. It has both a causal and probabilistic semantics, it is an ideal representation for combining prior knowledge (which often comes in causal form) and data.

---

[16]Bayesian networks are based upon the concept of conditional probability. *Conditional probability* is the probability of some event *A*, given the occurrence of some other event *B*. Conditional probability is written $P(A|B)$, and is read "the probability of *A*, given *B*." The conditional and marginal probabilities of two random events are related in probability theory by *Bayes' theorem* (often called *Bayes' law* after Rev Thomas Bayes). It is often used to compute posterior probabilities given observations. For example, a patient may be observed to have certain symptoms. Bayes' theorem can be used to compute the probability that a proposed diagnosis is correct, given that observation.

As a formal theorem, Bayes' theorem is valid in all common interpretations of probability. However, it plays a central role in the debate around the foundations of statistics: frequentist and Bayesian interpretations disagree about the ways in which probabilities should be assigned in applications. According to the frequentist approach, probabilities are assigned to random events according to their frequencies of occurrence or to subsets of populations as proportions of the whole. In the Bayesian perspective, probabilities are described in terms of beliefs and degrees of uncertainty.

4. It offers an efficient and principled approach aimed at data overfitting.

5. Since a Bayesian net only relates nodes that are probabilistically related by some sort of causal dependency, an enormous saving of computation can result. There is no need to store all possible configurations of states. All that is needed to store and work with is all possible combinations of states between sets of related parent and child nodes (families of nodes).

6. It can be useful in assisting decision making. If some states lead to "positive" results (e.g., pleasure), while others to negative outcome (e.g., pain), it is possible to implement the model in order to maximize the former and minimize the latter. There is a science of decision making that mixes probability with measurements of value. It is called *decision theory* or *utility theory*. Bayesian networks are easily extended to computing utility, given the degree of knowledge we have on a situation, and so they have become very popular in business and civic decision making as much as in scientific and economic modeling.

Some *limitations* can be identified.

1. The remote possibility that a system's user might wish to violate the distribution of probabilities upon which the system is built.

2. The computational difficulty of exploring a previously unknown network.

3. The quality and extent of the prior beliefs used in Bayesian inference processing. A Bayesian network is only as useful as this prior knowledge is reliable. Either an excessively optimistic or pessimistic expectation of the quality of these prior beliefs will distort the entire network and invalidate the results. Related to this concern, there is the selection of the statistical distribution induced in modeling the data. Selecting the proper distribution model to describe the data has a notable effect on the quality of the resulting network.

Traditional exploratory approaches, such as clustering and mapping approaches, multidimensional analysis, correspondences analysis (Aldenderfer and Blashfield 1984; Bailey 1994; Corter 1996; Hair et al. 1998; Lis and Sambin 1977), should be added to the approaches presented above. The approaches are all practicable but in view of their application, their capability to meet assumptions and to fit the needs of the conceptual framework need to be explored.

Closing Remarks

Methodological Challenges in Indicators Construction for the Measurement of Societal Well-Being

Actually, even a quick check of the academic literature allows us to see a long tradition and intense research work existing in the field of measuring societal well-being through complex approaches. Sometimes, this tradition has been set in the hard economic perspective that considers economic indicators as the main and unique approach allowing progress to be measured.

The recent debates on different perspectives in measuring societal well-being led to different scenarios also in academic research. Some challenges can be drawn:

1. Concerning the *conceptual model*:
   (a) More attention and efforts are needed in order to:
      – Better define *sustainability*, in particular on its relationship with quality of life
      – Join the concept of sustainability (more related to the future generations dimension) with the concept of *vulnerability* (more related to the future of present generations dimension)
   (b) *Subjective indicators* should not be seen as antithetical to objective indicators but as an important tool allowing information to be added, which cannot be provided by objective measures. In both perspectives, the measurement process needs

An agreement on what and how to measure

A clear conceptual framework clarifying the relationship between objective and subjective measures and their integration

2. Concerning *methodological issues*:
   (a) It is impossible to assess complex phenomena with a single indicator (even using a composite indicator) and it is necessary to define and deal with *sets of indicators*.
   (b) As regards *subjective indicators*, it is important to
      – define *accurate measures* (e.g., notable academic research exists in the field of scaling techniques)
      – improve and enhance *existing data sources*
   (c) More work should be done on *reliability* of indicators and *their comparative capacity* among countries, across time to deal with different levels of analysis.

3. Concerning *strategic issues*:
   (a) More attention should be paid in order to improve
       - *Quality* of indicators
       - *Legitimacy*, trust, authority and credibility of indicators of well-being of societies

There is a great need for exchanging information and dialog on these issues between different actors and within different research contexts.

Institutional Challenges: National Statistical Offices and the Measurement of Societal Well-Being

As we have seen, measuring and monitoring well-being of societies requires a complex and comprehensive framework and integrated approaches at conceptual and methodological levels. This perspective is urged not only by researchers belonging to academics but also by other organizations and institutions.

Also, the awareness aroused by many people directs us toward a more comprehensive approach in measuring societal well-being. The Report of Commission on the Measurement of Economic Performance and Social Progress (Stiglitz et al. 2009)—chaired by Joseph E. Stiglitz—represents further evidence of that and proposes the following 12 recommendations (Table 10.17):

As a consequence, measuring and monitoring societal well-being creates a great need for statistics but statistics with new and shared working models.

Moreover, this will require huge investments in order to carry out needed survey projects (systematic or finalized) and systematic control on data quality.

Managing this complexity requires the involvement of different governance levels, which represents a new challenge for statistics and for the statistical offices.

Following the OECD Istanbul Declaration—signed by representatives of the European Commission, the Organisation for Economic Cooperation and Development, the Organisation of the Islamic Conference, the United Nations, the United Nations Development Programme and the World Bank, during the II OECD World Forum on "Statistics, Knowledge and Policy" (2007)—societies urge statistical offices, public and private organizations, and academic experts to work

Table 10.17 Twelve recommendations from the report of the commission on the measurement of economic performance and social progress

1	When evaluating material well-being, look at income and consumption rather than production
2	Emphasize the household perspective
3	Consider income and consumption jointly with wealth
4	Give more prominence to the distribution of income, consumption and wealth
5	Broaden income measures to nonmarket activities
6	Quality of life depends on people's objective conditions and capabilities. Steps should be taken to improve measures of people's health, education, personal activities and environmental conditions. In particular, substantial effort should be devoted to developing and implementing robust, reliable measures of social connections, political voice, and insecurity that can be shown to predict life satisfaction
7	Quality of life indicators in all the dimensions covered should assess inequalities in a comprehensive way
8	Surveys should be designed to assess the links between various quality of life domains for each person, and this information should be used when designing policies in various fields
9	Statistical offices should provide the information needed to aggregate across quality of life dimensions, allowing the construction of different indexes
10	Measures of both objective and subjective well-being provide key information about people's quality of life. Statistical offices should incorporate questions to capture people's life evaluations, hedonic experiences and priorities in their own survey
11	Sustainability assessment requires a well-identified dashboard of indicators. The distinctive feature of the components of this dashboard should be that they are interpretable as variations of some underlying "stocks." A monetary index of sustainability has its place in such a dashboard but, under the current state of the art, it should remain essentially focused on economic aspects of sustainability
12	The environmental aspects of sustainability deserve a separate follow up based on a well-chosen set of physical indicators. In particular there is a need for a clear indicator of our proximity to dangerous levels of environmental damage (such as associated with climate change or the depletion of fishing stocks)

alongside representatives of their communities to produce high-quality, facts-based information that can be used by all segments of society to form a shared view of societal well-being and its evolution over time.

A possible model could be that aimed at involving different public corporations operating in statistical areas and interacting in order to define an organic system, operating as a coordinated network organization (*statistical offices network*). Such a network's activities should be structured in nodes and needs to be:

– Aimed at defining clear statistical goals and programs
– Organized at different levels (national, regional or local)
– Planned with special reference to data production, in order to avoid redundancies, to rationalize the network and to qualify the nodes
– Harmonized with reference to statistical functions, by overcoming fragmentation, diversity and super-impositions at different network levels
– Adjusting forms of communication and involvement for different actors

These actions could be conceived at a:

– *General level,* since they should define norms concerning the statistical functions to be considered as a public service providing common and multifunctional wealth. Statistics should be considered in terms of knowledge and assessment
– *Specific level,* since they should promote (1) increasing the production of data and indicators at local levels; (2) interacting and integrating different data bases and data sources; and (3) developing appropriate analytic methods.

Some risks arise, related to the lack of coordination (the activities could turn out to be dispersed, fragmented, marginalized and excessively differentiated) and reciprocal knowledge of each node's activities.

In order to avoid that, the network requires:

– New professionals to be defined.
– New competences to be developed.
– A system of statistical data certification to be implemented.
– A strong support from administrative sectors to be assured.

All these efforts should aim at splitting the role of official statisticians from "information providers" to "knowledge builders."

References

Abbey, A., & Andrews, F. M. (1985). Modeling the psychological determinants of life quality. *Social Indicators Research, 16,* 1–34.

Aldenderfer, M. S., & Blashfield, R. K. (1984). *Cluster analysis* (Sage university paper series on quantitative applications in the social sciences, series no. 07–044). Beverly Hills: Sage.

Alt, M. (1990). *Exploring hyperspace. A non-mathematical explanation of multivariate analysis.* New York/London: McGraw-Hill.

Anand, S., & Sen, A. (1997). *Concepts of human development and poverty: A multidimensional perspective* (Human development papers 1997). New York: UNDP.

Andersen, E. B. (1972). The numerical solution of a set of conditional estimation equations. *Journal of the Royal Statistical Society, Series B, 34,* 42–54.

Andersen, E. B. (1973). A goodness of fit test for the Rasch model. *Psychometrika, 38,* 123–140.

Anderson, T. W. (1958). *An introduction to multivariate statistical analysis.* New York/London/Sidney: Wiley.

Andrews, F. M., & Withey, S. B. (1976). *Social indicators of well-being: Americans' Perceptions of life quality.* New York: Plenum Press.

Andrich, D. (1988). *Rasch models for measurement* (Sage university paper series on quantitative applications in the social sciences, series no. 07–068). Newbury Park: Sage.

Asher, H. B. (1983). *Causal modelling* (Sage university paper series on quantitative applications in the social sciences, series no. 07–003). Newbury Park: Sage.

Bamber, D. (1975) The area above the ordinal dominance graph and the area below the receiver operating characteristic graph. *Journal of Mathematical Psychology, 12:* 387–415.

Bailey, K. D. (1994). *Typologies and taxonomies. An introduction to classification techniques* (Sage university paper series on quantitative applications in the social sciences, series no. 07–102). Thousand Oaks: Sage.

Bartholomew, D. J., & Knott, M. (1999). *Latent variable models and factor analysis, Kendall's library of statistics* (Vol. 7). London: Arnold Publishers.

Bottarelli, E., & Parodi, S. (2003). Un approccio per la valutazione della validità dei test diagnostici: le curve R.O.C. (Receiver Operating Characteristic)". *Ann. Fac. Medic. Vet. di Parma,* XXIII: 49–68 (www.unipr.it/arpa/facvet/annali/2003/49.pdf)

Berger-Schmitt R., & Noll, H. -H. (2000). *Conceptual framework and structure of a European system of social indicators* (EuReporting working paper no. 9). Mannheim: Centre for Survey Research and Methodology (ZUMA) – Social Indicators Department

Bezzi, C., Cannavò, L., & Palumbo, M. (2009). *Gli indicatori sociali e il loro uso valutativo.* Milano: Franco Angeli Editore.

Blalock, H. M. (1964). *Causal inferences in nonexperimental research.* Chapel Hill: University of North Carolina Press.

Blalock, H. M. (Ed.). (1974). *Measurement in the social sciences. Theories and strategies.* Chicago: Aldine Publishing Company.

Bock, R. D., & Aitken, M. (1981). Marginal maximum likelihood estimation of item parameters: An application of an EM algorithm. *Psychometrika, 46*, 443–459.

Bohrnstedt, G. W., & Knoke, D. (1994). *Statistics: A tool for social data analysis*. Itasca: Peacock Publishers.

Bolasco, S. (1999). *Analisi multidimensionali dei dati. Metodi, strategie e criteri di interpretazione*. Roma: Carocci.

Bollen, K. A., & Lennox, R. (1991). Conventional wisdom on measurement: A structural equation perspective. *Psychological Bulletin, 10*, 305–314.

Booysen, F. (2002). An overview and evaluation of composite indices of development. *Social Indicators Research, 59*, 115–151.

Bryk, A. S., & Raudenbush, S. W. (1992). *Hierarchical linear models: Applications and data analysis methods*. Thousand Oaks: SAGE.

Campbell, A., Converse, P. E., & Rodgers, W. L. (1976). *The quality of American life*. New York: Russell Sage.

Cannavò, L. (2009). Dell'incertezza e della complessità: gli indicatori tra ricerca valutazione. In C. Bezzi, L. Cannavò, & M. Palumbo (Eds.), *Gli indicatori sociali e il loro uso valutativo*. Milano: Franco Angeli Editore.

Cooley, W. W., & Lohnes, P. R. (1971). *Multivariate data analysis*. New York/London/Sidney: Wiley.

Coombs, C. H., Dawes, R. M., and Tversky, A. (1970) *Mathematical psychology: An elementary introduction*. Englewood Cliffs: Prentice-Hall, Inc.

Corbetta, P. (1992). *Metodi di analisi multivariata per le scienze sociali*. Bologna: Il Mulino.

Corbetta, P. (2003). *Metodologia e tecniche della ricerca sociale*. Bologna: Il Mulino.

Corter, J. E. (1996). *Tree models of similarity and association* (Sage university paper series on quantitative applications in the social sciences, series no. 07–112). Thousand Oaks: Sage.

Costa, P. T., & McCrae, R. R. (1980). Still stable after all these years: personality as a key to some issues in adulthood and old age. In P. B. Baltes & O. G. Brim (Eds.), *Life span development and behaviour* (pp. 65–102). New York: Academic.

Costanza, R., Fisher, B., Ali, S., Beer, C., Bond, L., Boumans, R., et al. (2007). Quality of life: An approach integrating opportunities, human needs, and subjective well-being. *Ecological Economics, 61*, 267–276.

Cox, T. F., & Cox, M. A. A. (1994). *Multidimensional scaling*. London: Chapman & Hall.

Cummins, R. A. (1993). *Comprehensive quality of life scale for adults (ComQol-A4)*. Melbourne: Deakin University, School of Psychology.

Cummins, R. A. (1995) On the trail of the gold standard for subjective well-being. *Social Indicators Research, 35*: 170–200.

De Vellis, R. (1991). *Scale devolopment. Theory and applications* (Applied social research methods series, Vol. 26). London: SAGE.

Diamantopoulos, A., & Siguaw, J. A. A. (2006). Formative versus reflective indicators in organizational measure development: A comparison and empirical illustration. *British Journal of Management, 17*, 263–282.

Diamantopoulos, A., & Winklhofer, H. M. (2001). Index construction with formative indicators: An alternative to scale development. *Journal of Marketing Research, 38*, 269–277.

Diener, E. (1984). Subjective well-being. *Psychological Bulletin, 95*, 542–575.

Diener, E., & Suh, E. (1997). Measuring quality of life: economic, social, and subjective indicators. *Social Indicators Research, 40*, 189–216.

Drenowski, J., & Wolf, S. (1966). *The level of living index*. Geneva: United Nations Research Institute for Social Development.

Drewnowski, J. (1970). *A planning model for social development*, Unrisd, (Report n.70.5), Geneva.

Easterlin, R. A. (1974). Does economics growth improve the human lot? Some empirical evidence. In P. A. David & M. W. Reder (Eds.), *Nations and households in economic growth; essays in honor of Moses Abramowitz* (pp. 89–125). New York: Academic.

Edward, W., & Newman, J. R. (1982). *Multiattribute evaluation* (Sage university paper series on quantitative applications in the social sciences, series no. 07–026). Newbury Park: Sage.

Egan, J. P. (1975) *Signal detection theory and ROC analysis*. New York: Academic Press.

Engel, U., & Reinecke, J. (1996). *Analysis of change*. Berlin/New York: Walter de Gruyter.

Epidemiological Bullettin. (2002). Introduction to social epidemiology. *Epidemiological Bullettin, 23*(1). http://www.paho.org/English/sha/be_v23n1-socialepi.htm

Erikson, R. (1993). Descriptions of inequality: The Swedish approach to welfare research. In M. Nussbaum & A. Sen (Eds.), *The quality of life* (pp. 67–83). Oxford: Oxford University Press.

Eurostat. (2000). *Definition of quality in statistics and standard quality report*, Eurostat.

Fattore, M., & Maggino, F. (2011). Socio-economic evaluation with ordinal variables: Integrating counting and poset approaches in *Statistica & Applicazioni* (forthcoming).

Fattore, M., Maggino, F., & Colombo, E. (2011). From composite indicators to partial orders: Evaluating socio-economic phenomena through ordinal data. In F. Maggino & G. Nuvolati (Eds.), Quality of Life: reflections, studies and researches in Italy. *Social Indicators Research Series* (forthcoming).

Firebaugh, G. (1997). *Analyzing repeated surveys* (Sage university paper series on quantitative applications in the social sciences, series no. 07–115). Newbury Park: Sage.

Freudenberg, M. (2003). *Composite indicators of country performance: a critical assessment* (STI working paper, 2003/16, Industry Issues). Paris: OECD. url: http://www.olis.oecd.org/olis/2003doc.nsf/43bb6130e5e86e5fc12569fa005d004c/8bb0f462911c2cc6c1256ddc00436279/$FILE/JT00153477.DOC

Frisch, M. B. (1998). Quality of life therapy and assessment in health care. *Clinical Psychology: Science and Practice, 5*, 19–40.

Ghiselli, E. E. (1964). *Theory of psychological measurement*. New York/London: McGraw-Hill.

Giovannini, E. (2007). *The role of statistics in a globalised world: risks and challenges*. Paper presented at the DGINS (Directors-General of the National Statistical Institutes) Conference, 20–21 September 2007, Budapest, Hungary

Glenn, N. D. (1977). *Cohort analysis* (Sage university paper series on quantitative applications in the social sciences, series no. 07–005). Newbury Park: Sage.

Global Water Partnership - Technical Committee. (2004). *Monitoring and evaluation indicators for Integrated Water Resources Management strategies and plans*, http://www.gwpforum.org/gwp/library/Tec_brief_3_Monitoring.pdf

Goldstein, H. (1999). *Multilevel statistical models*. London: Arnold Publisher. http://www.arnoldpublishers.com/support/goldstein.htm.

Green, D. M., & Swets, J. A. (1966) *Signal detection theory and psychophysics*. New York: Wiley.

Greenley, J. R., Greenberg, J. S., & Brown, R. (1997). Measuring quality of life: A new and practical survey instrument. *Social Work, 42*, 244–254.

Guilford, J. P. (1954). *Psychometric methods*. New York/London: McGraw-Hill.

Hagerty, M. R., & Land, K. C. (2007). Constructing summary indices of quality of life: A model for the effect of heterogeneous importance weights. *Sociological Methods and Research, 35*, 455–496.

Hair, J. F., Anderson, R. E., Tatham, R. L., & Black, W. C. (1998). *Multivariate data analysis* (5th ed.). Upper Saddle River: Prentice-Hall.

Hambleton, R. K., Swaminathan, H., & Rogers, H. J. (1991). *Fundamentals of item response theory* (Measurement methods for the social sciences series, Vol. 2). London: SAGE.

Hanley, J. A., & McNeil, B. J. (1982) The meaning and use of the area under a receiver operating characteristic (ROC) curve. *Radiology, 143*: 29–36.

Headey, B., Veenhoven, R., & Wearing, A. (1991). Top-down versus bottom-up theories of subjective well-being. *Social Indicators Research, 24*, 81–100.

Horn, R. V. (1993). *Statistical indicators*. Cambridge: Cambridge University Press.

Howell, R. D., Breivik, E., & Wilcox, J. B. (2007). Reconsidering formative measurement. *Psychological Methods, 12*, 205–218.

Hox, J. J. (1995). *Applied multilevel analysis*. Amsterdam: TT-Publikaties.

Jamison, D., & Sandbu, M. (2001). WHO ranking of health system performance. *Science, 293*, 1595–1596.

Kalmijn, W. M., & Veenhoven, R. (2005). Measuring inequality of happiness in nations: In search for proper statistics. *Journal of Happiness Studies, 6*, 357–396.

Kim, J.-O., & Mueller, C. W. (1989a). *Introduction to factor analysis: What it is and how to do it* (Sage university paper series on quantitative applications in the social sciences, series no. 07–013). Newbury Park: Sage.

Kim, J.-O., & Mueller, C. W. (1989b). *Factor analysis: Statistical methods and practical issues* (Sage university paper series on quantitative applications in the social sciences, series no. 07–014). Newbury Park: Sage.

Kozma, A., Stone, S., Stones, M. J., Hannah, T. E., & McNeil, K. (1990). Long- and short-term affective states in happiness: Model, paradigm and experimental evidence. *Social Indicators Research, 22*, 119–138.

Krieger, N. (2002). A glossary for social epidemiology. *Epidemiological Bullettin, 23*(1). http://www.paho.org/English/sha/be_v23n1-glossary.htm.

Kruskal, J. B., & Wish, M. (1978). *Multidimensional scaling* (Sage university paper series on quantitative applications in the social sciences, series no. 07–011). Newbury Park: Sage.

Lance, C. E., Mallard, A. G., & Michalos, A. C. (1995). Tests of the causal directions of globallife facet satisfaction relationships. *Social Indicators Research, 34*, 69–92.

Land, K. C. (1971). On the definition of social indicators. *The American Sociologist, 6*, 322–325.

Land, K. C. (1975). Social indicator models: An overview. In K. C. Land & S. Spilerman (Eds.), *Social indicator models* (pp. 5–36). New York: Russell Sage.

Land, K. C. (2000). Social indicators. In Borgatta, E. F., & Montgomery, R. V (Eds.), *Encyclopedia of sociology*, rev edn. New York: Macmillan

Lazarsfeld, P. F. (1958). Evidence and inference in social research. *Daedalus, 87*, 120–121.

Lazarsfeld, P. F., & Henry, N. W. (1968). *Latent structure analysis*. Boston: Houghton M Company.

Lis, A., & Sambin, M. (1977). *Analisi dei cluster*. Padova: CLEUP.

Little, R. J. A., & Rubin, D. B. (1987). *Statistical analysis with missing data* (Wiley Series in Probability and Mathematical Statistics). New York: Wiley.

Long, J. S. (1993a). *Confirmatory factor analysis. A preface to LISREL* (Sage university paper series on quantitative applications in the social sciences, series no. 07–033). Newbury Park: Sage.

Long, J. S. (1993b). *Covariance structure models. An introduction to LISREL* (Sage university paper series on quantitative applications in the social sciences, series no. 07–034). Newbury Park: Sage.

Lord, F. M. (1974). Estimation of latent ability and item parameters when there are omitted responses. *Psychometrika, 39*, 29–51.

Lord, F. M. (1984). Standard errors of measurement at different ability levels. *Journal of Educational Measurement, 21*, 239–243.

Louviere, J. J. (1988). *Analyzing decision making: Metric conjoint analysis*. Newbury Park: Sage.

Ludlow, L. H., & Haley, S. M. (1995). Rasch model logits: Interpretation, Use and trasformation. *Educational and Psychological Measurement, 55*, 967–975.

Lyubomirsky, S., King, L. A., & Diener, E. (2005). The benefits of frequent positive affect: Does happiness lead to success? *Psychological Bulletin, 131*, 803–855.

Maggino, F. (2003). *Method effect in the measurement of subjective dimensions*. Firenze: Firenze University Press, Archivio E-Prints.

Maggino, F. (2004a). *La misurazione nella ricerca sociale. Teorie, strategie, modelli*. Firenze: Firenze University Press, Archivio E-Prints.

Maggino, F. (2004b). *I modelli di scaling. Confronto tra ipotesi complesse per la misurazione del soggettivo*. Firenze: Firenze University Press, Archivio E-Prints.

Maggino, F. (2005a). *L'analisi dei dati nell'indagine statistica*. Firenze: Firenze University Press.

Maggino, F. (2005b). *The importance of quality-of-life dimensions in Citizens' preferences: An experimental application of conjoint analysis*. Firenze: Firenze University Press, Archivio E-Prints.

Maggino, F. (2007). *La rilevazione e l'analisi statistica del dato soggettivo*. Firenze: Firenze University Press.

Maggino, F. (2008a). *Choice of weights for subjective variables*, invited paper at the "Conference on Composite Score" (ESADA, Universitat Ramon Llull, Barcelona, 14–15 February 2008), Chair: Prof. W.Saris

Maggino, F. (2008b). *Towards more participative methods in the construction of composite indicators. The case of obtaining* weights: from "objective" to "subjective" approaches, invited paper presented at the International Seminar on "Involving citizens/communities in measuring and fostering well-being and progress: towards new concepts and tools", Council of Europe (Strasbourg, 27–28 November, 2008).

Maggino, F. (2009). *Towards more participative methods in the construction of social indicators: survey techniques aimed at determining importance weights*, paper to be presented at the 62nd conference of the World Association for Public Opinion Research "Public Opinion and Survey Research in a Changing World" (Swiss Foundation for Research in Social Sciences – University of Lausanne – 11–13 September 2009 – Lausanne – Switzerland).

Maggino, F. (forthcoming). *Obtaining weights: from objective to subjective approaches in view of more participative methods in the construction of composite indicators.*

Maggino, F. & Ruviglioni, E. (2008a). *Choice of subjective weights for subjective variables. Identifying subjective/individualized weights for comparing well-being among group and individuals*, paper presented at the session on "Social Indicators" organized by Heinz-Herbert Noll (GESIS-ZUMA, Mannheim) at the VII International Conference on Social Science Methodology (1–5 September 2008, Campus di Monte Sant'Angelo, Naples).

Maggino, F. & Ruviglioni, E. (2008b). *Choice of subjective weights for subjective variables. Identifying subjective/individualized weights for comparing well-being among group and individuals*, paper presented at the IV International Conference on Quality of Life Research – QOL 2008 – "Quality of Life Improvement through Social Cohesion", Conference organized by the Department of Statistics of Wroclaw University of Economics (15–18 September 2008, Wroclaw).

Maggino, F. & Ruviglioni, E. (2009) *Obtaining weights: from objective to subjective approaches in view of more participative methods in the construction of composite indicators*, paper presented at the Seminar on "*New Techniques and Technologies for Statistics (NTTS)*" – EUROSTAT (18–20 February 2009 – Brussels – Belgium).

Malhotra, N. K. (1996). *Marketing research: An applied orientation.* Englewood Cliffs: Prentice-Hall International, Inc.

Mallard, A. G. C., Lance, C. E., & Michalos, A. C. (1997). Culture as a moderator of overall life satisfaction relationships. *Social Indicators Research, 40*, 259–284.

Marradi, A. (1981). Factor analysis as an aid in the formation and refinement of empirically useful concepts. In E. F. Borgatta & D. J. Jackson (Eds.), *Factor analysis and measurement in sociological research.* London: SAGE.

Maslow, A. H. (1954). *Motivation and personality.* New York: Harper and Brothers.

Max-Neef, M. (1992). Development and human needs. In P. Ekins & M. Max-Neef (Eds.), *Real life economics: Understanding wealth creation* (pp. 97–213). London: Routledge.

McDonald, R. P. (1989). Future directions for item response theory. *International Journal of Educational Research, 13*, 205–220.

Menard, S. (1991). *Longitudinal research* (Sage university paper series on quantitative applications in the social sciences, series no. 07–076). Newbury Park: Sage.

Michalos, A. C. (1985). Multiple discrepancies theory (MDT). *Social Indicators Research, 16*, 347–413.

Michalos, A. C. (1992). Use and abuses of social indicators. *Sinet 32.*

Michalos, A. C. (2008). Education, happiness and wellbeing. *Social Indicators Research, 87*, 347–366.

Nardo, M., Saisana, M., Saltelli, A., Tarantola, S., Hoffman, A., & Giovannini, E. (2005a). *Handbook on constructing composite indicators: Methodology and userguide.* OECD, Statistics Working Paper

Nardo, M., Saisana, M., Saltelli, A., & Tarantola, S. (2005b). *Tools for composite indicators building.* European Commission, EUR 21682 EN, Institute for the Protection and Security of the Citizen, JRC, Ispra.

Netemeyer, R. G., Bearden, W. O., & Sharma, S. (2003). *Scaling procedures: Issues and applications.* Thousand Oaks: Sage.

Noll, H. -H. (1996). *Social indicators and social reporting: The international experience*, http://www.ccsd.ca/noll1.html

Noll, H. -H. (2004). *Social indicators and indicators systems: tools for social monitoring and reporting*, Paper presented at OECD, World Forum "Statistics, knowledge and policy", Palermo, 10–13 November 2004.

Noll, H. -H. (2009). *Measuring and monitoring the quality of life*, Lecture at the Università degli Studi di Firenze, April 23–24, 2009. http://www.gesis.org/forschung-lehre/veranstaltungen/veranstaltungs-archiv/zentrum-fuer-sozialindikatorenforschung/quality-of-life/

Nussbaum, M., & Glover, J. (1995). *Women, culture, and development: A study of human capabilities.* Oxford: Oxford University Press.

Organisation for Economic Cooperation and Development. (2007). *Istanbul Declaration*, II OECD World Forum on "Statistics, Knowledge and Policy", June, 27–30, Istanbul. http://www.oecd.org/document/51/0,3343,en_21571361_31938349_37115187_1_1_1_1,00.html

Patel, S., Hiraga, M, Wang, L., Drew, D., & Lynd, D. (2003). *A framework for assessing the quality of education statistics*, World Bank, Development Data Group and UNESCO, Institute for Statistics.

Rampichini, C., & Schifini, S. (1998). A hierarchical ordinal probit model for the analysis of life satisfaction in Italy. *Social Indicators Research, 44*, 5–39.

Rasch, G. (1960). *Probabilistic models for some intelligence and attainment tests.* Copenhagen: Danish Institute for Educational Research.

Raudenbush, S. W., & Bryk, A. S. (2002). *Hierarchical linear models: Applications and data analysis methods* (2nd ed.). Newbury Park: Sage.

Rubin, D. B. (1987). *Multiple imputation for nonresponse in survey* (Wiley Series in Probability and Mathematical Statistics). New York: Wiley.

Rupp, A. A., & Zumbo, B. D. (2003). Which model is best? robustness properties to justify model choice among unidimensional IRT models under item parameter drift. *Alberta Journal of Educational Research, 49*, 264–276.

Rupp, A. A., & Zumbo, B. D. (2006). Understanding parameter invariance in unidimensional IRT models. *Educational and Psychological Measurement, 66*, 63–84.

Rupp, A. A., Dey, D. K., & Zumbo, B. D. (2004). To bayes or not to bayes, from whether to when: Applications of Bayesian methodology to modeling. *Structural Equation Modeling, 11*, 424–451.

Russell, L. B., Hubley, A. M., Palepu, A., & Zumbo, B. D. (2006). Does weighting capture what's important? Revisiting subjective importance weighting with a quality of life measure. *Social Indicators Research, 75*, 141–167.

Sadocchi, S. (1981). *Manuale di analisi statistica multivariata per le scienze sociali*. Milano: Franco Angeli Editore.

Saisana, M., Saltelli, A., & Tarantola, A. (2005). Uncertainty and sensitivity techniques as tools for the analysis and validation of composite indicators. *Journal of the Royal Statistical Society A, 168*, 1–17.

Sakitt, B. (1973). Indices of discriminability, *Nature, 241*: 133–134.

Saltelli, A., Tarantola, S., Campolongo, F., & Ratto, M. (2004). *Sensitivity analysis in practice. A guide to assessing scientific models*. Chichester: Wiley, http://webfarm.jrc.cec.eu.int/uasa/doc/forum-tutorial/WU082-FM.pdf.

Saris, W. E., & Stronkhorst, L. H. (1990). *Causal modelling in nonexperimental research. An introduction to the LISREL approach*. Amsterdam: Sociometric Research Foundation.

Scherpenzeel, A., & Saris, W. (1996). Causal direction in a model of life satisfaction: The top-down/bottomup controversy. *Social Indicators Research, 38*, 161–180.

Sen, A. (1993). Capability and well-being. In M. Nussbaum & A. Sen (Eds.), *The quality of life* (pp. 30–53). Oxford: Clarendon.

Sharpe, A., & Salzman, J. (2004). *Methodological choices encountered in the construction of composite indices of economic and social well-being*. Ottawa: Center for the Study of Living Standards.

Sijtsma, K., & Molenaar, I. W. (2002). *Introduction to nonparametric item response theory* (Measurement methods for the social sciences series, Vol. 5). London: SAG.

Sinden, J. A. (1982). Application of quality of life indicators to socioeconomic problems: An extension of Liu's method to evaluate policies for 26 Australian towns. *American Journal of Economics and Sociology, 41*, 401–420.

Simpson, A. J., & Fitter, M. J. (1973) What is the best index of detectability? *Psychological Bulletin, 80*: 481–488.

Sirgy, M. J., Michalos, A. C., Ferriss, A. L., Easterlin, R. A., Patrick, D., & Pavot, W. (2006). The quality-of-life (QOL) research movement: Past, present, and future. *Social Indicators Research, 76*, 343–466.

Stiglitz J. E., Sen, A., & Fitoussi, J.-P. (Eds.) (2009) *Report by the commission on the measurement of economic performance and social progress*, Paris. http://www.stiglitz-sen-fitoussi.fr/en/index.htm

Stoker, T. M. (1993). Empirical approaches to the problem of aggregation over individuals. *Journal of Economic Literature, 31*, 1827–1874.

Stones, M. J., Hadjistavropoulos, T., Tuuko, H., & Kozma, A. (1995). Happiness has trait-like and state-like properties: A reply to Veenhoven. *Social Indicators Research, 36*, 129–144.

Sullivan, J. L., & Feldman, S. (1981). *Multiple indicators. An introduction* (Sage university paper series on quantitative applications in the social sciences, series no. 07–015). Newbury Park: Sage.

Swaminathan, H., & Gifford, J. A. (1982). Bayesian estimation in the Rasch model. *Journal of Educational Statistics, 7*, 175–192.

Swaminathan, H., & Gifford, J. A. (1985). Bayesian estimation in the two-parameter logistic model. *Psychometrika, 50*, 349–364.

Swaminathan, H., & Gifford, J. A. (1986). Bayesian estimation in the three-parameter logistic model. *Psychometrika, 51*, 589–601.

Tarantola, S., Jesinghaus, J. M., & Puolamaa, M. (2000). Global sensitivity analysis: A quality assurance tool in environmental policy modelling. In A. Saltelli, K. Chan, & M. Scott (Eds.), *Sensitivity analysis* (pp. 385–397). New York: Wiley.

Torgerson, W. S. (1958). *Theory and methods of scaling*. New York/London/Sydney: Wiley.

Tucker, L., & MacCallum, R. (1993). Exploratory factor analysis, Book Manuscript, Retrieved in 2008, from: http://www.unc.edu/~rcm/book/factornew.htm

United Nations Development Programme. (2007). *Human development report 2007*. New York: Oxford University Press.

Veenhoven, R. (2002). Why social policy needs subjective indicators. *Social Indicators Research, 58*, 33–45.

Veenhoven, R. (2005). Inequality of happiness in nations. *Journal of Happiness Studies, 6*, 351–355.

Veenhoven, R. (2009). Well-being in nations and well-being of nations. Is there a conflict between individual and society. *Social Indicators Research, 91*, 5–21.

Werts, C. E., Linn, R. L., & Jöreskog, K. G. (1974). Quantifying unmeasured variables. In H. M. Blalock (Ed.), *Measurement in the social sciences: Theories and strategies*. Chicago: Aldine Publishing Company.

Yoon, K. P., & Hwang, C.-L. (1995). *Multiple attribute decision making* (Sage university paper series on quantitative applications in the social sciences, series no. 07–104). Thousand Oaks: Sage.

Zapf, W. (1975). Systems of social indicators: Current approaches and problems. *International Social Science Journal, 27*, 479–498.

Zapf, W. (1984). Individuelle Wohlfahrt: Lebensbedingungen und Wahrgenommene Lebensqualität. In W. Glatzer e & W. Zapf (Eds.), *Lebensqualität in der Bundesrepublik* (pp. 13–26). New York/Campus: Frankfurt a. M.

Zumbo, B. D. (2007). Validity: Foundational issues and statistical methodology. In C. R. Rao & S. Sinharay (Eds.), *Handbook of statistics* (Psychometrics, Vol. 26, pp. 45–79). Boston: Elsevier.

Zumbo, B. D. (2009). Validity as contextualized and pragmatic explanation, and its implications for validation practice. In R. W. Lissitz (Ed.), *The concept of validity: Revisions, new directions and applications* (pp. 65–82). Charlotte: Information Age Publishing.

Zumbo, B. D., & Rupp, A. A. (2004). Responsible modeling of measurement data for appropriate inferences: Important advances in reliability and validity theory. In D. Kaplan (Ed.), *The SAGE handbook of quantitative methodology for the social sciences* (pp. 73–92). Thousand Oaks: Sage.

Quality of Life Well-Being in General Medicine, Mental Health and Coaching

11

Michael B. Frisch

Introduction

The pervasive lack of articulated theory and the methodological inconsistency within and across healthcare disciplines (e.g., social work, nursing, psychology, medicine, and gerontology) have resulted in quality of life (QOL) being equated with diverse constructs. Depending on the study, QOL refers to

- Sex
- Pain
- Level of fatigue
- Life satisfaction
- Subjective well-being (SWB) or happiness
- Objective living conditions and circumstances (e.g., housing, standard of living), behaviors such as attending sporting events that a researcher (rather than a respondent) deems as "healthy" or "good"
- Impairments in "functional ability" presumably caused by a particular disease or disorder
- Behavioral competencies needed to gain satisfaction in valued areas of life
- Self-esteem
- Personal control
- Mortality of disease
- Symptoms of psychological disturbance (e.g., depression and anxiety) and/or physical illness (Bowling 1991; Brundage et al. 2011; Soh et al. 2011; Salek 1998; Spilker 1996; Stewart and King 1994)

M.B. Frisch (✉)
Baylor University, Waco, TX, USA
e-mail: Michael_B_Frisch@baylor.edu

In addition, polyglot QOL scales add to the theoretical confusion by confounding these diverse constructs in single measures which are proliferating (Salek 1998).

The inconsistency in measuring and conceptualizing QOL threatens to trivialize the field in the eyes of clients or consumers and their families, third-party payers, and regulators who, at present, are willing to consider QOL in determining the cost-effectiveness of treatments and health plans (Frisch 1998, 2006; Diener and Seligman 2004; Dimsdale and Baum 1995; Gladis et al. 1999). In particular, an explicit, comprehensive, and testable theory seems to be an essential prerequisite for further advances in the understanding, assessment, and intervention of QOL problems in healthcare as well as in nonclinical, positive psychology settings (Danovitch and Endicott 2008).

This chapter reviews the history of QOL in medicine mental health and organizational coaching (Biswas-Diener and Dean 2007), presents one possible unifying theory based on research in QOL, well-being, and social indicators, and then concludes with guidelines for how this theory or any other theory can be used to guide medical/mental health coaching assessment and treatment planning for individual patients and clients. The reader is referred to Salek's (1998) comprehensive sample of QOL instruments for general use as well as scores of measures designed for use with particular diseases such as cancer, COPD, diabetes, etc. The focus in this chapter will be on more generic or nondisease-specific measures that can be used across different disease entities.

K.C. Land et al. (eds.), *Handbook of Social Indicators and Quality of Life Research*,
DOI 10.1007/978-94-007-2421-1_11, © Springer Science+Business Media B.V. 2012

A History of the Quality of Life (QOL) Concept

QOL refers to the degree of excellence in life (or living) relative to some expressed or implied standard of comparison, such as most people in a particular society (Oxford English Dictionary 1989; "quality" entry; also see Veenhoven 1984; for similar definition). The degree, grade, or level to which "the best possible way to live" or "the good life" is attained can range from high to low or good to poor (Veenhoven 1984). Usually, QOL is explicitly or implicitly contrasted with the quantity of life (e.g., years), which may or may not be excellent, satisfying, or enjoyable. The Stoic philosopher Seneca (c. 4 b.c.–65 a.d.) clearly valued quality over quantity: "… it matters with life as with play; what matters is not how long it is, but how good it is" (Hadas 1958, p. 63). In this vein, popular definitions center on excellence or goodness in aspects of life that go beyond mere subsistence, survival, and longevity; these definitions focus on "domains" or areas of life that make life particularly enjoyable, happy, and worthwhile, such as meaningful work, self-realization (as in the full development of talents and capabilities), and a good standard of living. These popular definitions and the origins of the phrase, QOL, may stem from the increased affluence and college education in Western societies following World War II and the accompanying fundamental attitude shift away from an emphasis on material wealth toward a concern with QOL issues (Campbell 1981; Patterson 1996). Cross-cultural studies support the view that this shift in values continues to characterize postmodern, Western affluent societies (Diener and Suh 2000; Inglehart 1990).

Popular definitions of QOL found their way into political discourse, resulting in efforts by affluent Western governments to study and improve the QOL of their citizenry through a series of national QOL surveys begun in the United States in 1959 (e.g., Cantril 1965; Gurin et al. 1960). Sociologists and economists created the "Social Indicators Movement," in part, to supplement "objective" indices of QOL (e.g., material well-being) with "subjective" measures of "well-being," "perceived QOL," life satisfaction, and personal happiness. Little correlation between objective and subjective indices QOL was found (e.g., Michalos 1991; Myers and Diener 1995; see Davis and Fine-Davis 1991, for an international review).

As with the fields of sociology and economics, the discussion of QOL issues in general medicine is a post-World War II phenomenon, dating from 1948 (Dimsdale and Baum 1995) but beginning in earnest during the 1960s (Kaplan 1988). Until recently, QOL was equated with symptoms of disease (or morbidity) and length of survival from an illness (or mortality; Taylor 2002). While current conceptualizations include the constructs of happiness, well-being, SWB, and life satisfaction, most emphasis is placed on behavioral competencies or "functional ability" (e.g., Dimsdale and Baum 1995; Soh et al. 2011; Spilker 1996; Ware 2004), which is often unrelated to happiness (e.g., Diener et al. 1999; Frisch 1998a; Safren et al. 1997). Functional ability can be defined as perceived behavioral competencies, that is, clients' or medical patients' perceived ability to function effectively and successfully in valued areas of daily life. Functional ability includes social role performance (e.g., as a parent, spouse, employee) and the daily living skills needed for dressing, eating, transportation, handling money, maintaining a home or apartment, and the like.

QOL theory and measurement in gerontology began in the 1960s as part of an effort to define and foster "successful aging" (Baltes and Baltes 1990; George and Bearon 1980). QOL in gerontology has been defined primarily as life satisfaction that is the primary outcome of successful aging from a variety of theoretical perspectives (Abeles et al. 1994; George and Bearon 1980). Gerontologists also define QOL in terms of functional ability and, to a lesser extent, happiness, pain, energy level, personal control, and self-esteem (Stewart and King 1994).

Clinical and health psychologists have only recently begun to recognize the potential contribution of QOL theory and research both to the clinical enterprise (Frisch 2006; Frisch et al. 1992; Kazdin 1993a, b, 1994; Ogles et al. 1996; Safren et al. 1997) and to non-clinical coaching interventions (Frisch et al. 1992; Frisch 1998, 2006, 2009).

Frisch's QOL/WB Theory

Frisch's (1998, 2006) QOL theory attempts to address the inconsistency and confusion in the literature in health-related quality of life. Key terms are explicitly defined. The theory consists of an empirically based and empirically validated model of QOL and life satisfaction applicable to general medical, mental health and coaching purposes.

Defining Happiness, Well-Being, and QOL

The terms *quality of life, perceived quality of life, subjective well-being (SWB), well-being, happiness,* and *life satisfaction* have been used interchangeably, and inconsistently, in the literature. However, each term has unique theoretical nuances (Campbell et al. 1976; Diener 1984; Diener and Seligman 2004). The global constructs of SWB and happiness are equivalent and have, for the most part, been defined in terms of affect, cognition, or a combination thereof (e.g., Andrews and Robinson 1991; Diener 1984; Diener et al. 1999, 2003; Lyubomirsky et al. 2005). Affective theorists define SWB as either positive affect alone or as a preponderance of positive affect (such as joy, contentment, or pleasure) over negative affect (such as sadness, depression, anxiety, or anger) in an individual's experience (e.g., Andrews and Robinson 1991; Bradburn 1969).

The Life Satisfaction Approach

Cognitive theorists use the "life satisfaction approach" to SWB, defining happiness in terms of cognitive judgments as to whether a person's needs, goals, and wishes have been fulfilled (Campbell et al. 1976; Cantril 1965). Thus, life satisfaction is defined as a "cognitive judgmental process dependent upon a comparison of one's circumstances with what is thought to be an appropriate standard" (Diener et al. 1985a, p. 71)—the smaller the perceived discrepancy between one's aspirations and achievements, the greater the level of satisfaction, according to this approach (Diener et al. 2003; Frey and Stutzer 2001).

QOL as the Life Satisfaction Part of Happiness

A consensus has emerged among some researchers who have found evidence for the cognitive theory of emotion, in general, and SWB, in particular, supporting a combined cognitive-affective theory or definition of SWB based upon numerous studies, including factor-analytic and large-scale national and cross-cultural studies (e.g., Andrews and Withey 1976; Diener 1984; Diener and Larsen 1993; Tay and Diener 2011; Headey and Wearing 1992; Lazarus 1991; Michalos 1991; Veenhoven 1984; also see the cognitive theories of emotion posited by Beck and his colleagues; Clark and Beck 1999; by Lazarus 1991). According to this view, SWB and well-being are synonymous with personal happiness. Personal happiness, in turn, is defined in terms of three parts: life satisfaction, positive affect, and negative affect. In high SWB or happiness, there is high life satisfaction and a preponderance (in duration) of positive versus negative affective experience in consciousness. That is, our conscious experience consists of much more positive than negative emotional experiences (Diener 1984; Diener et al. 1999). In other words, our degree of happiness is a positive function of the degree of life satisfaction and of the extent of positive affect preponderance in a person's daily experience (Diener & Tay, 2011).

QOL theory further assumes that the affective components of happiness stem largely from our cognitively based life satisfaction judgments or appraisals as when we feel happy, secure, and relieved once our standards for satisfying work have been met. In keeping with the cognitive theorists who take the "life satisfaction approach" just discussed in QOL theory, life satisfaction refers to our subjective evaluation of the degree to which our most important needs, goals, and wishes have been fulfilled. Thus, the perceived gap between what we have and what we want to have in valued areas of life determines our level of life satisfaction or dissatisfaction.

Finally, in QOL theory, QOL is equated with life satisfaction (see Fig. 11.1 and Table 11.1). In support of this view, QOL in psychology and psychiatry and to a lesser extent in general medicine and cancer treatment is often equated with life satisfaction (e.g., Danovitch and Endicott 2008; Ferrans 2000; Frisch 1998a, 2000; Rabkin et al. 2000; Snyder et al. 2000). When not defined solely in terms of life satisfaction, life satisfaction is almost always a component of QOL theories and assessments (e.g., Gladis et al. 1999; Spilker 1996). Interestingly, QOL in gerontology is often equated with life satisfaction; indeed, life satisfaction is the primary outcome of "successful aging" from a variety of theoretical perspectives (e.g., George and Bearon 1980; Stewart and King 1994).

Further Support for the Life Satisfaction Approach to Happiness and QOL

Life satisfaction is also emphasized over positive and negative affect in QOL theory for pragmatic reasons. Practically speaking, life satisfaction is less susceptible

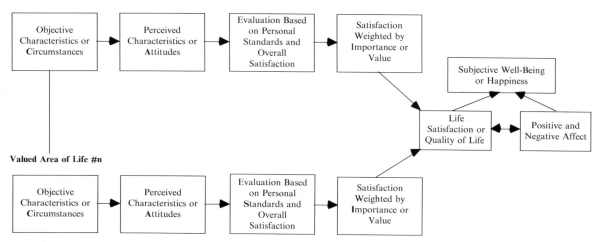

Fig. 11.1 CASIO model of life satisfaction, happiness, and positive psychology intervention. Note: The "O" element of CASIO refers to the assumption that overall satisfaction may be increased by boosting satisfaction in *any* valued area of life, even areas *O*ther than those of immediate concern. Interventions in any CASIO element may boost happiness in an area of life like love or work. In Beck's cognitive theory, moderate to high happiness or life satisfaction may be seen as part the positive schema cluster called the *constructive mode*

to momentary online mood fluctuations and irrelevant contextual effects than is positive or negative affect (Diener 2003). Additionally, life satisfaction is much easier to measure than the preponderance of positive over negative affect experiences over time (e.g., Campbell et al. 1976; Diener et al. 2003; Diener and Larsen 1993; Michalos 1991); this may explain the predominance of life satisfaction measures in the American Psychiatric Association's listing in their *Handbook of Psychiatric Measures* and the relative exclusion of behavioral functional ability measures, which are relegated to chapters on functioning rather than QOL (Danovitch and Endicott 2008).

Life satisfaction may best reflect the concepts of happiness and QOL because life satisfaction best reflects the philosophical notion of the "good life" according to Veenhoven (1993), because it reflects enduring and longstanding well-being—Seligman (2002) would say "authentic happiness"—and because it is highly individualistic and flexible: "a strength of the life satisfaction measure is its flexibility because people can consider or ignore information that they personally consider to be relevant or irrelevant. Therefore, the measure is idiographic in that the individual respondent, not the experimenter, can weigh information in whatever way the individual prefers" (Diener et al. 2003, p. 24).

Life Satisfaction as a Predictor of Health Problems and Health-Related Expenditures as Well as Future Job Performance and Satisfaction

Besides the reasons just cited, the relative emphasis on life satisfaction over affect in QOL theory reflects the plethora of predictive validity studies whose findings support the view that low life satisfaction may predict a number of problems and maladaptive behaviors (with adaptive behaviors and outcomes associated with moderate to high satisfaction):

- Job performance and satisfaction as much as 5 years in advance (Judge and Hulin 1993; Judge and Watanabe 1993)
- Job accidents, unit profitability, and productivity (Harter et al. 2002)
- School performance (e.g., academic retention and functioning in school; Frisch et al. 2005; Valois et al. 2001; Zullig et al. 2001)
- Health (Diener and Chan 2011)
- Healthcare expenditures (e.g., treatment costs; Moreland et al. 1994; Stewart et al. 1992; Ware 1986)
- Suicide (Koivumaa-Honkanen et al. 2001)
- Deaths due to fatal injuries (Koivumaa-Honkanen et al. 2002)

11 Quality of Life Well-Being in General Medicine, Mental Health and Coaching

Table 11.1 The 16 areas of life that may constitute a person's overall quality of life

Health is being physically fit, not sick, and without pain or disability

Self-esteem means liking and respecting yourself in light of your strengths and weaknesses, successes and failures, and ability to handle problems

Goals-and-values/spiritual life (A person's goals-and-values or philosophy of life may or may not include spiritual life.) Goals-and-values are your beliefs about what matters most in life and how you should live, both now and in the future. This includes your goals in life, what you think is right or wrong, and the purpose or meaning of life as you see it

Spiritual life may or may not be an important part of a person's *goals-and-values. Spiritual life* refers to spiritual or religious beliefs or practices that you pursue on your own or as part of a like-minded spiritual community

Money (or *standard of living*) is made of the money you earn, the things you own (like a car or furniture), and believing that you will have the money and things that you need in the future

Work means your career or how you spend most of your time. You may work at a job, at home taking care of your family, or at school as a student. Work includes your duties on the job, the money you earn (if any), and the people you work with

Play (or *recreation*) means what you do in your free time to relax, have fun, or improve yourself. This could include watching movies, visiting friends, or pursuing a hobby like sports or gardening

Learning means gaining new skills or information about things that interest you. Learning can come from reading books or taking classes on subjects like history, car repair, or using a computer

Creativity is using your imagination to come up with new and clever ways to solve every day problems or to pursue a hobby like painting, photography, or needlework. This can include decorating your home, playing the guitar, or finding a new way to solve a problem at work

Helping (social service and civic action) means helping others (not just friends or relatives) in need or helping to make your community a better place to live. Helping can be done on your own or in a group like a church, a neighborhood association, or a political party. Helping can include doing volunteer work at a school or giving money to a good cause

Love (or *love relationship*) is a very close romantic relationship with another person. Love usually includes sexual feelings and feeling loved, cared for, and understood

Friends (or *friendships*) are people (not relatives) you know well and care about who have interests and opinions like yours. Friends have fun together, talk about personal problems, and help each other out

Children include a measure of how you get along with your child (or children). Think of how you get along as you care for, visit, or play with your child (or children)

Relatives mean how you get along with your parents, grandparents, brothers, sisters, aunts, uncles, and in-laws. Think about how you get along when you are doing things together like visiting, talking on the telephone, or helping each other

Home is where you live. It is your house or apartment and the yard around it. Think about how nice it looks, how big it is, and your rent or house payment

Neighborhood is the area around your home. Think about how nice it looks, the amount of crime in the area, and how well you like your neighbors

Community is the whole city, town, or rural area where you live (not just your neighborhood). Community includes how nice the area looks, the amount of crime, and how well you like the people. It also includes places to go for fun like parks, concerts, sporting events, and restaurants. You may also consider the cost of things you need to buy, the availability of jobs, the government, schools, taxes, and pollution

- Response of depressed clients to pharmacotherapy and the need of both medication and psychotherapy treatments for some depressed clients (Miller et al. 1998)
- "Chronic pain syndrome" (Dworkin et al. 1992)
- Cardiovascular diseases such as myocardial infarction (Vitaliano et al. 1994; for a review)
- Other physical illnesses such as respiratory tract infections and colds in both healthy individuals and those afflicted with cancer (Anderson et al. 1994)

- Willingness to participate in prevention programs aimed at eliminating unhealthy behaviors like smoking (Wagner et al. 1990)
- Adolescent substance abuse (Gilman and Huebner 2000)
- Adolescent and adult violent and aggressive behaviors (Valois et al. 2001)
- Peer relationship problems in adolescents (Ford et al. 1997; Gilman and Huebner 2000)
- Impulsive, reckless behavior such as unsafe sex practices (Kalichman et al. 1997)

- Somatoform disorders (Baruffol et al. 1995; Lundh and Sinonsson-Sarnecki 2001)
- Anxiety disorders (Baruffol et al. 1995)

Major Depression—Initial Onset and Relapse

In one of the few prospective studies of its kind, Lewinsohn and his colleagues (Lewinsohn et al. 1991) found that low life satisfaction preceded or predicted episodes of clinical depression in an undepressed subsample of community volunteers. Participants evidenced low life satisfaction just prior to the onset of clinical depression. Life satisfaction ratings tended to worsen during the depressive episode, only to move up into the average or normal range once the depression abated. Low life satisfaction was the only variable found to be "prodromal, or an early manifestation, of depression's onset" (p. 163) both in this study and in a prospective study of depressive relapse that followed clients who had been successfully treated for depression (Gonzales et al. 1985). The results of these studies were corroborated and extended in a prospective study of 184 randomly selected community volunteers in which levels of life satisfaction assessed 2 years earlier significantly predicted the onset of DSM depressive, anxiety, and somatoform disorders (Baruffol et al. 1995). The authors concluded that low life satisfaction is a major risk factor for psychological disturbance.

Besides identifying risks for health problems and related expenditures, life satisfaction seems to predict a person's ability to function in major life tasks or social roles such as work. Life satisfaction relates to and, at times, predicts a person's satisfaction at work—in the context of school, "work" includes the ability to stay in school and complete a degree, that is, academic retention—making QOL measures a potential screening device for employers and schools since those satisfied with their life generally are more likely to be successful in and satisfied with their work (see Diener et al. 1999; for review and Frisch et al. 2005; for an original research study on the topic). Life satisfaction seems to be discriminable from the constructs of psychiatric symptoms, negative and positive affect, depression, and anxiety in both clinical and nonclinical samples, making it less likely that the relationships reviewed here merely reflect the influence of a third

variable-like depression (Crowley and Kazdin 1998; Diener 2000; Frisch et al. 1992; Gonzales et al. 1985; Headey et al. 1993; Lewinsohn et al. 1991; Lucas et al. 1996; McNamara and Booker 2000; Schimmack et al. 2002; Snyder et al. 2000).

Model of Life Satisfaction and QOL Interventions (CASIO)

The CASIO model of life satisfaction is, in many ways, the centerpiece of QOL theory. Figure 11.1 presents the "CASIO" model of life satisfaction that is then joined with "Positive and Negative Affect" to explain the concept of SWB or personal happiness. The CASIO model of life satisfaction is used as the basis for many of the QOL interventions that make up Quality of Life Therapy and Coaching since intervention in any CASIO element may lead to greater happiness in an area of life; for this reason, CASIO is also called Five Paths to Happiness in QOLTC (Frisch 1998b, 2006).

The "CASIO" model in Fig. 11.1 is a linear, additive model of life satisfaction based on the work of Campbell et al. (1976), which assumes that an individual's overall life satisfaction consists largely of the sum of satisfactions with particular "domains" or areas of life deemed important by the individual. (Those areas most closely related to personal goals are usually deemed considered most important; Diener et al. 2003.) This additive assumption has been empirically validated in numerous studies and reviews (e.g., Andrews and Withey 1976; Campbell et al. 1976; Davis and Fine-Davis 1991; Diener and Diener 1995; Diener and Larsen 1984; Diener and Oishi 2003; Diener et al. 1999, 2003; Evans 1994; Groenland 1990; Headey et al. 1985; Headey and Wearing 1992; Kozma and Stones 1978; Linn and McGranahan 1980; McGee et al. 1990; Michalos 1983, 1991; Rice et al. 1992; Szalai and Andrews 1980). For example, when asked about the source of their global life satisfaction judgments, research participants spontaneously – without any prompts – and consistently report basing these judgments on their satisfaction with particular domains or areas of their life that they deem important such as romantic relationships, family, health, and finances (Schimmack et al. 2002).

A corollary to the additive assumption is that satisfying areas of life may compensate for areas of dissatisfaction or low satisfaction (e.g., Campbell et al. 1976; Diener et al. 2003; Frisch 1998b). For example, some

CASIO Elements of QOL Theory

As illustrated in Fig. 11.1, a person's satisfaction with a particular area of life is made up of four parts: (1) the objective characteristics or circumstances of an area, (2) how a person perceives and interprets an area's circumstances, (3) the person's evaluation of fulfillment in an area based on the application of standards of fulfillment or achievement, and (4) the value or importance a person places on an area regarding his or her overall happiness or well-being.

The *C* in the CASIO Model: Objective Characteristics and Living Conditions

Objective life circumstances or living conditions refer to the objective physical and social characteristics of an area of life whose effects on life satisfaction and SWB are cognitively mediated. According to Michalos (1991), about half of the SWB equation reflects persons' perception and evaluation of their circumstances, while their actual or objective circumstances constitute the other half. The objective characteristics of an area of life contribute to satisfaction judgments, such as when a person's satisfaction with work is based on the work itself, pay, relationships with coworkers and bosses, the work environment, and job security (Diener and Larsen 1984; Diener et al. 2003; Frisch 1998b).

The role of perceptions and satisfaction judgments may help to explain the lack of significant correlations between objective and subjective indices of QOL such as wealth and housing after years of research carried out as part of the Social Indicators Movement (Michalos 1991; Myers and Diener 1995; see Davis and Fine-Davis 1991; for a review of the Social Indicators Movement). By way of illustration, two people in identical circumstances will often respond differently to the circumstances as in the case of two janitors, one who appreciates his work conditions and enjoys his work, and another who sees the work as beneath her.

In QOL theory, objective living conditions vary in their "rewardingness" or potential for yielding human fulfillment or satisfaction. Reasonable rewardingness in a living environment is a prerequisite for QOL enhancement. When individuals accurately perceive the objective characteristics of an area of life as extremely impoverished or destructive to their well-being, efforts to alter or remove themselves from the environment should take precedence over purely cognitive coping efforts, a point lost in some purely cognitive formulations of depression and SWB. This does not, however, preclude biased interpretations of accurately perceived situations to enhance self-esteem and optimism, which is reflected in the *A* in the CASIO model (Taylor and Brown 1988).

A in CASIO Model: Attitude

In addition to objective characteristics, individuals' subjective perception of an area's characteristics will also influence their satisfaction with the area as when they distort the objective reality of a situation in either a positive or negative way. In addition to this "reality testing" aspect, the Attitude component of CASIO satisfaction judgments includes how a person interprets reality or a set of circumstances once it is perceived. This interpretation includes deciding the implications that a given set of circumstances has for a person's self-esteem (e.g., causal attributions) and present or future well-being (Lazarus 1991).

The *S* in the CASIO Model: Standards of Fulfillment

The evaluated characteristics of an area of life in Fig. 11.1 refer to the application of personal standards to the perceived characteristics of an area. Specifically, the perceived characteristics of an area of life are evaluated through the application of standards of fulfillment that reflect a person's goals and aspirations for that particular area of life (Diener et al. 2003). That is, a person decides whether his or her needs and aspirations have been met in a valued area of life. The level of achievement of standards for key characteristics in an area of life is combined subjectively via a "hedonic calculus" (Andrews and Withey 1976) to form an overall judgment of satisfaction for a particular area of life (i.e., "Overall Satisfaction" with the area in Fig. 11.1).

People will feel more satisfied when they perceive that their standards of fulfillment have been met and less satisfied when they have not been met (Diener et al. 2003; Schimmack et al. 2002). The standards, aspirations, and goals an individual holds for an area of life can dwarf the influence of objective living conditions in determining their satisfaction with an area as when goals and standards are set unrealistically high (i.e., not commensurate with functional abilities or the potential rewardingness of a given environment to provide rewards), a common scenario in depression (see, e.g., Ahrens 1987; Bandura 1986; Rehm 1988).

The *I* in the CASIO Model: Weighing Area Satisfaction by Importance

QOL theory proposes that a person's satisfaction with a particular area of life is weighed according to its importance or value to the person before the area's satisfaction enters into the subjective "equation" of overall life satisfaction (see Fig. 11.1). Thus, satisfaction in highly valued areas of life is assumed to have a greater influence on evaluations of overall life satisfaction than areas of equal satisfaction judged of lesser importance. For example, a person equally satisfied with work and recreational pursuits who values work more highly will have his or her overall judgments of life satisfaction influenced more by work than recreational satisfaction. In QOL theory, the value or importance attributed to specific domains or areas of life reflects a person's most cherished goals and values; it also can dramatically affect overall judgments and ratings of satisfaction. In a clinical or coaching intervention context, life satisfaction may increase when an extremely important area of dissatisfaction is de-emphasized as less important in the process of reexamining life priorities as when persons who are exposed to unsolvable problems at work relegate work to a marginal place in their life and commit themselves instead to being a better spouse or parent or vice versa (Frisch 2006).

The *O* in the CASIO Model: Overall Satisfaction

Since individuals' overall satisfaction in life reflects, in part, the sum of satisfactions in all valued areas of life, they may boost their overall satisfaction by increasing satisfaction in any or all areas they value, even areas that are not of immediate concern or that have not been considered recently. The gist of the *O* positive psychology strategy is to focus on these areas of lesser concern or focus in order to increase overall positive affect.

Life Satisfaction Approach to Happiness

There are implications of the CASIO model of life satisfaction. As noted previously, QOL theory maintains that happiness comes largely from having needs,

wants, and goals fulfilled in the areas of life that we care about; this includes satisfaction and happiness as we meet subgoals along the way. While real-time or online *flow* experiences may not generate happiness or its elements – life satisfaction, positive over negative affect, *at the time* (Seligman 2002), a deep sense of satisfaction or contentment follow such experiences. As, for example, when therapists "at the top of their game" see clients all day only to feel content and at times joyful at the end of the day, reflecting on their use of skill with challenging clients in the service of therapeutic goals. Similarly, parents playing with their children, teens doing challenging homework all evening, and a guitarist practicing all afternoon on a complex piece of music, experience satisfaction and/or other elements of happiness at the conclusion of their labors and for as long as the related memories persist and are recalled even savored, perhaps as a way to bask or self-soothe oneself with pleasant memories of engaging and challenging activities.

Our level of satisfaction with an area of life that we care about, along with our emotions about the area, tells us if we are making progress toward long-term goals and short-term subgoals. Thus, our feelings and satisfaction with an area tell us our progress and prospects, they tell us our progress in gaining fulfillment so far, and they tell us our prospects for future fulfillment in the area.

Happiness Ingredients

Overall happiness may be likened to a salad or a stew with different ingredients for different people and tastes. QOL theory assumes that a finite number of areas of human aspiration and fulfillment may be identified that will be applicable to both clinical and nonclinical populations; numerous researchers have found support for this assumption (e.g., Andrews and Withey 1976; Campbell et al. 1976; Diener 1984; Headey and Wearing 1992; Veenhoven 1984, 1993). That is, people tend to want the same things, although the areas valued by a particular individual will vary as will the subjective importance of those areas to that individual's overall life satisfaction or happiness. Thus, an area of life such as work may be highly valued by one individual but judged irrelevant to overall happiness by another who is retired.

Based upon an exhaustive review of the literature in general, "cognitive mapping" studies of human concerns (Andrews and Inglehart 1979; Andrews and

Withey 1976) and studies identifying particular areas of life associated with overall life satisfaction and happiness (e.g., Andrews and Withey 1976; Campbell et al. 1976; Cantril 1965; Diener 1984; Flanagan 1978; Inglehart 1990; Michalos 1991; Veenhoven 1984), a comprehensive list of human concerns, "domains," or areas of life was developed; evidence for the importance of these chosen domains has accumulated since 1994 and the publication of the Quality of Life Inventory or QOLI® by Pearson Assessments. An effort was made to be comprehensive but to limit the areas of life to those empirically associated with overall satisfaction and happiness. The 16 potential "Valued Areas of Life" – see Fig. 11.1 – related to overall life satisfaction are listed in Table 11.1 (and make up the QOLI; Frisch 1994, 2004a, 2009).

The Importance of Weighting Satisfaction by Importance: Theory

The weighting of an area's satisfaction by its importance to an individual is considered essential according to many theorists in the fields of both quality of life/SWB and clinical psychology/psychiatry. Indeed, satisfaction in areas of life deemed unimportant or "goal irrelevant" should have no influence on overall life satisfaction or SWB according to these theorists (Campbell et al. 1976;Diener et al. 1985a, 2003, 2004; Frisch 1998a; Flanagan 1978, 1982; Ferrans and Powers 1985; Lazarus 1991; Pavot and Diener 1993; also see Abramson et al. 1989; Bandura 1986; Clark et al. 1999) who make the same point with respect to the impact of life events on measures of negative well-being and clinical depression. Also see Pelham (1995) who makes the same point with respect to self-esteem judgments – weighted esteem of self-aspects is more strongly related to global self-esteem that unweighted esteem of self-aspects judgments.

By omitting importance ratings in theories and scale scoring schemes, researchers, clinicians, and coaches will allow unimportant – or relatively unimportant – areas to be weighed the same as a client's most cherished areas of life since all domains are considered to be of equal value; this may lead to distortions and inaccuracies in estimates of overall life satisfaction, SWB, or QOL, along with a misunderstanding of a person's fundamental values and goals in life. For example, scale items about satisfaction with marriage, children, or work are assumed important in unweighted scoring schemes or theories even when a respondent is widowed, childless, and retired, respectively, and no longer interested in these areas.

The Importance of Weighting Satisfaction by Importance: Research

Weighing satisfaction by importance is an implicit part of the process of making global satisfaction judgments according to empirical findings. Studies of source reports support the view that individuals estimating their SWB vary systematically in their valuing – or importance ratings – of different life domains such as work, health, leisure, school, or love life (e.g., Schimmack et al. 2002; Schwarz and Strack 1999). Furthermore, only valued domains, that is, domains cited in source reports of overall life satisfaction judgments, impact overall life satisfaction judgments; unimportant domains seem to have no impact on such overall ratings. Finally, Schimmack et al. (2002) also found that weighing domain satisfaction judgments by importance improves the relationship between domain satisfaction and global life-satisfaction, presumably by reflecting the domains that really matter to a person's overall quality of life (also see Campbell et al. 1976).

Risk and Protective Factors for Life Satisfaction and High QOL: "Top-Down" and "Bottom-Up" Influences on Life Satisfaction

In keeping with findings that support both approaches, the QOL theory of life satisfaction is both a top-down and bottom-up theory (Diener and Larsen 1993). Rewarding or pleasurable objective life circumstances and events foster life satisfaction as do superordinate cognitive styles and traits. Individual difference or environmental variables that increase the probability for high life satisfaction are called protective factors, while factors that decrease the probability for high life satisfaction are called vulnerability or risk factors. The vulnerability factors proposed by QOL theory are supported by research findings (for reviews see Argyle 2001; Clark et al. 1999; Diener 1984; Diener and Seligman 2004; Headey and Wearing 1992) and include:
- Inadequate coping skills or functional abilities, especially social skills related to valued areas of life.
- Any of the following generalized cognitive styles or personality traits: neuroticism/negative affectivity,

self-focused attention, trait low self-esteem, self-blame and criticism for negative outcomes, the depressive or pessimistic attributional style for interpreting the causes of negative events (i.e., internal, stable, and global attributions for negative events), negative cognitive schemas, low self-efficacy, pessimism, introversion – especially low sociability and low interpersonal warmth, low hope, and perfectionism or the tendency to set unrealistically high standards for personal accomplishment or satisfaction in valued areas of life.

- Biological (heritable) vulnerabilities to anxiety, depression, and low trait SWB/unhappiness; exaggerated neuroendrocrine reactions to stress, including the stress of repeated frustration in gaining life satisfaction (Lazarus 1991).
- Social isolation or lack of social support, especially close friends, mates, or confidants.
- Early experiences with loss, uncontrollable events, and unpredictable events (e.g., Barlow 2002).
- Negative parenting experiences with unengaged, neglectful or overprotective, and emotionally reactive caretakers who may model ineffective coping skills or who fail to foster autonomy and self-efficacy (e.g., Barlow 2002).
- A low frequency of pleasant events, which is often indicative of unrewarding life circumstances, inadequate functional/coping abilities or both.

Protective factors or "immunities" to low life satisfaction simply consist of the opposites of vulnerabilities or risk factors (e.g., adequate coping and interpersonal competencies, optimism, high self-esteem).

QOL Is More than Functional Ability or Impairment

Functional ability can be defined as perceived behavioral competencies, that is, clients' or medical patients' perceived ability to function effectively and successfully in valued areas of daily life. From the psychological perspective of QOL theory, particular functional impairments may or may not discourage, demoralize, or ruin individuals' basic contentment or QOL, suggesting the need to assess life satisfaction, or SWB first and foremost (Diener et al. 1999; Diener 2000; Frisch 1998b, Soh et al. 2011) in order to assess QOL and to gain the needed context for understanding assessments of objective circumstances and functional abilities. For example, even clients who value the ability to drive (or walk more than one mile) equally can be expected to differ to the extent that driving (or walking) restrictions affect their satisfaction with life; one person may be devastated while another, who pursues interests close to home or lives in a self-contained retirement community, may suffer little, if any, impairment in life satisfaction or SWB. Very often the impact of problems in abilities/functioning or in objective living circumstances will be drastically tempered by the cognitive aspects of the last four CASIO elements along with other psychological risk and protective factors proposed by QOL theory and described later in the chapter. As Taylor (2002) asserts, QOL in medicine should consist of patients' reports of their subjective experience (e.g., life satisfaction) rather than behavioral or functional ability measures alone.

QOL Is Not Defined in Terms of Symptoms or Morbidity

The entire rationale for QOL assessment rests upon the discriminability of the construct from morbidity; otherwise this "extra" assessment would be a waste of time, yielding no additional information than that gleaned from symptom measures. When QOL and symptoms are confounded, valuable information may be lost according to Gladis et al. (1999) who present compelling evidence for the discriminability of life satisfaction from depressive symptoms (also see Lewinsohn et al. 1991; Gonzales et al. 1985). Unfortunately, some health-related QOL measures still confound psychiatric symptoms with the QOL components of SWB and functional ability as in the case of the Global Assessment of Functioning (GAF) Scale or Axis V of the DSM-IV-TR (American Psychiatric Association 2000; see Bowling 1991; Spilker 1996; for other examples).

How to Do QOL Assessments: Integrating QOL with Traditional Health/Medical Assessments

As early as 1992, psychologists decried the exclusive emphasis on psychiatric symptoms of "ill-being" to the neglect of positive mental health and functioning (Frisch et al. 1992). Now, leaders from opposing theoretical camps in clinical psychology, psychiatry, health psychology, and general medicine encourage the development of nonpathology-oriented measures of

11 Quality of Life Well-Being in General Medicine, Mental Health and Coaching

Table 11.2 Essential constructs for integrated quality of life and clinical or medical assessment

Coaching or nonclinical assessments are identical to clinical assessments of those with a DSM disorder except for the omission of the first-order construct of symptoms of disorder or disease. Despite this omission, Coaching requires a medical evaluation or report from a client's personal physician to the effect that no serious physical or psychiatric problems are evident that would militate against doing Coaching.
First-order constructs
It is recommended that these constructs be assessed at the outset for all clients or patients
• Symptoms of disorder or disease
• Overall indicator of well-being, quality of life
Area-based or domain-based measures whose overall scores are explained in terms of specific areas of life like work, relationships, and recreation are preferred because they suggest areas of intervention
Second-order CASIO constructs (Assess these constructs only when particular areas of dissatisfaction or low satisfaction (e.g., love, work, and recreation) are the focus of treatment or intervention as when overall quality of life is found to be low.)
• Objective circumstances or living conditions (related to areas of dissatisfaction or low satisfaction)
• Cognitive constructs related to areas of dissatisfaction (including perception of and interpretation of objective circumstances, goals or standards of fulfillment for areas, and personal importance or value of areas)
• Personal competencies or "functional abilities" related to areas of dissatisfaction (e.g., social skills for relationships, budgeting for money or standard of living, and daily living skills for health and personal safety)

QOL, SWB, life satisfaction, positive psychology, and "positive mental health" to augment those that focus on negative affect and symptoms (see Diener and Seligman 2004; Frisch 1998a). For example, some cognitive-behavioral, psychodynamic, and humanistic theorists agree that a client's happiness or satisfaction with life is an essential criterion for mental health and for a positive outcome in psychotherapy, and that happiness or satisfaction with life should be routinely assessed by researchers and clinicians alike (Berzon 1998; Danovitch and Endicott 2008; Fava and Ruini 2003; Frisch 1992; Kazdin 1993a, b, 1994, 2003; Seligman 2002; Strupp 1996; Strupp and Hadley 1977). For example, according to Alan Kazdin, "there are few constructs as clinically important as quality of life," and that "measures of quality of life add an important domain to treatment (outcome) evaluation since clinicians are usually interested in improving patients' quality of life as a result of either psychological or medical treatment" (1993b, p. 296). Similarly, Strupp and his colleagues (Strupp 1996; Strupp and Hadley 1977) maintain that contentment, satisfaction, or SWB is the most important criteria of "mental health" and positive outcome in psychotherapy from a client's perspective (see also Ogles et al. 1996): "the individual wishes first and foremost to be happy, to feel content. He or she thus defines mental health in terms of highly subjective feelings of well-being, feelings that have an incontrovertible validity of their own" (Strupp 1996, p. 1019).

The World Health Organization defines health as "a state of complete physical, mental, and social well-being and not merely the absence of disease or infirmity" (World Health Organization 1948). In keeping with this definition, the goal of healthcare today is to improve clients' QOL in addition to affecting a biological cure for physical illness or disability (Hyland 1992; Muller et al. 1994). QOL is increasingly viewed as an essential health care outcome or "medical endpoint" which is at least as important as symptomatic status and survival in evaluating the effectiveness of any health care intervention. For this reason, general medicine and health psychology researchers are saying that biological measures of health should be supplemented with QOL and happiness measures to adequately represent the health of an individual or a group (American College of Physicians 1988; Berzon 1998; Diener and Seligman 2004; Faden and Leplege 1992; Fallowfield 1990; Frisch et al. 1992; Ogles et al. 1996; Palfreyman et al. 2010).

QOL theory defines *positive mental health* as happiness with its core constituents of life satisfaction and preponderance in the frequency of positive affect experiences over negative affect. Either happiness overall or one of its core constituents qualifies as an indicator of positive mental health in QOL theory.

In keeping with Frisch's (2006) QOL theory, in general, and the CASIO model of life satisfaction, in particular and in keeping with current findings in the fields of QOL and SWB reviewed here, Table 11.2 lists the essential constructs for assessment in psychology, coaching, and medicine. These constructs are based on a definition of health as the absence of physical disease or disability along with the presence of positive mental health and QOL to a level commensurate with well-functioning and nonclinical peers. As part of an initial and general macroanalysis (Emmelkamp 1982) or overview, it is recommended that the clinician construct a comprehensive list of psychological disturbances and physical diseases or disabilities from which a client suffers. The client's level of QOL or life satisfaction should also be assessed to determine whether it falls within or above the average or normal range of the client's well-functioning nonclinical peers. Only if a client's QOL is significantly lower than his or her peers (i.e., one or two standard deviations below the mean for functional peers; Ogles et al. 1996) will the assessment of second-order constructs (see Table 11.2) and subsequent QOL interventions be necessary. The clinician, with the client's consent, may choose to treat or intervene in any specific area of life dissatisfaction deemed relevant to the client's symptoms. In general, people whose life satisfaction scores are average or above enjoy a good QOL and are mentally healthy (e.g., positive mental health) to the point where further QOL assessment and intervention may be unnecessary (Frisch 1994).

Implicit in this recommended assessment procedure is the assumption that clinical significance refers to both (1) clinically meaningful and relevant constructs (such as QOL) that reflect how clients feel and function in everyday life, and (2) the extent to which treatment-related change in these clinically significant, relevant, and important constructs indicates moving into the average range or level for nonclinical well-functioning peers (Kazdin 1992, 2003; Ogles, et al. 1996; Ogles et al. 2001; also see Kazdin for review of other methods).

Screening for Psychological Disturbances and Symptoms

Clinical, health, and positive (with clinical training) psychologists may quickly and efficiently screen for psychological disturbances and symptoms by utilizing a symptom checklist such as the SCL-90-R (Derogatis and Lynn 1999) or the Frisch Essential Symptom Scale (FESS) (Frisch 2002). A clinical interview with the client, and, when possible, significant others (e.g., spouse) is also recommended; this interview should yield a comprehensive listing of symptoms as revealed by the client's behavior during the interview, presenting complaints, current medications, response to

stressful life events, and history (e.g., psychiatric, medical, family, and social). The goal of this phase of assessment of first-order constructs (Table 11.2) is to generate a comprehensive list of possible psychiatric symptoms and associated DSM-IV-TR disorders.

Next, potential DSM-IV-TR diagnoses can be conclusively ruled in or out by directly questioning patients with respect to the criteria for each suspected disorder as spelled out in the DSM. Time can be saved by asking patients about "essential" symptoms first, as in the case of major depressive disorder where either anhedonia or depressed mood must be present, making it unnecessary to inquire about other depressive symptoms when these two are absent (Frisch 2000; Othmer and Othmer 1994). When it comes to diagnosing psychological disturbances, informal but direct questioning about specific DSM-IV-TR criteria may be adequately reliable and is certainly less time consuming and costly than standardized, structured diagnostic interviews, according to Lambert and his colleagues (Ogles et al. 1996).

Screening for Nonpsychiatric or General Medical Conditions

Nonpsychiatric or general medical conditions can be assessed via clients' personal physicians, an important step in clinical or coaching assessment. Symptoms of physical disease or disability revealed by clients should be corroborated through consultation with their physician.

QOL is the second first-order construct listed in Table 11.2. Clients' level of life satisfaction or QOL can be assessed through use of a brief screening measure. In cases where clients' overall QOL is not commensurate with well-functioning peers, further assessment is called for to (1) identify the sources of dissatisfaction and (2) assess the second-order constructs (Table 11.2) associated with each area of dissatisfaction. The former can be accomplished by using a domain- or area-based QOL screening measure (examples appear later in this chapter). The latter constitutes a microanalysis (Emmelkamp 1982) or functional analysis, which specifies the reasons for and parameters (e.g., controlling variables, causes) of low satisfaction in a particular area of life. Initial, domain-based QOL assessment can also be viewed as screening for "problems in living" which can be as important as symptom screenings (Frisch 1992). An urgent need exists for brief measures of problems in living (Othmer and Othmer 1994).

Assessing Second-Order Constructs

Multimodal assessments can be used for assessing and changing the second-order constructs (Table 11.2). For example, role-play assessments have been invaluable in assessing both patient's social capabilities and actual behavior in real-life situations (Frisch and Higgins 1986). Both the objective circumstances and clients' personal competencies in conducting relationships can be assessed by observing the interaction of those who are dissatisfied with their relationships with their "antagonists" (e.g., family members, coworkers) in sessions. Clients' problem-solving ability, standards of fulfillment, perceptions, and goals for particular areas of life can be assessed via interview and various instruments such as the Vision Quest and "What's Wrong?" exercises in the Toolbox (Frisch 2006). Home visits can be helpful in assessing the objective living conditions of clients reporting dissatisfaction with their surroundings, especially for older patients (Frisch 2006). Clinicians may simply discuss the Areas of Life to Consider for Greater Happiness handout in the Toolbox with clients gain information on particular areas of life (Frisch 2006).

Based on a sample of 281 outpatients, Frisch (1992, 1994, 2009) has identified the specific and recurrent, or typical, reasons (i.e., second-order factors) clients give for dissatisfaction with each of the sixteen areas of life in QOL theory and the QOLI. For example, patients dissatisfied with their level of self-esteem usually feel inadequate because of their failure to meet their standards of performance and success in highly valued areas of life, such as work, school, parenthood, love relationship, or weight control. These possible explanations for unhappiness in specific areas of life can be presented to clients by therapists as a start in identifying the second-order constructs that explain dissatisfaction in a particular area for a particular client. The CASIO model (Fig. 11.1) is often discussed with clients as part of a collaborative effort to identify their reasons for their dissatisfaction with particular areas of life.

Once a client's QOL and symptomatic status are comprehensively assessed, the process of clinical case conceptualization and treatment planning can be advanced through the final two steps of case conceptualization and establishing intervention priorities and strategies. One parsimonious approach to case conceptualization involves applying both the Beck model for any DSM disorder (Clark and Beck 1999) and, at the same time, invoking QOL theory in the form of the CASIO model to explain dissatisfaction in valued areas of life that may or may not have contributed to clients' DSM disorders.

The Steps in QOL Assessment

Step 1 – Assess Clients' Overall QOL: QOL theory of assessment – also called QOLTC for Frisch's Quality of Life Therapy and Coaching, Frisch 2006 – begins with an evaluation of a clients' overall life goals and overall QOL compared to nationwide norms to determine whether their QOL is substandard. Client feedback can be very motivating as in those cases in which clients acclimated to misery in a high-stress job deny their misery only to find themselves in the low or very low range on a test like the QOLI that puts them at risk for a host of physical and psychological maladies. The QOLI or a similar instrument is administered before treatment, at 3-week intervals during treatment, and at the end of treatment, as well as at follow-ups or booster sessions. The QOLI yields an overall score, a profile of specific areas of happiness and unhappiness that make up the overall score, and a list of problems that hurt or hinder satisfaction in specific areas of life.

Step 2 – Life (or Lifetime) Goal Assessment: The second step involves the assessment of life goals. Implementing life goal assessment involves administering: QOLI, The Vision Quest Exercise, Happiness Pie Exercise (Optional), (Optional) (see Frisch 2006; Miller and Frisch 2009).

Step 3 – Assess Specific Areas of Life or "Domains" Contributing to Clients' Overall QOL: Step 3 involves finding which specific areas of life contribute to overall unhappiness or dissatisfaction. As a follow-up to assessing clients' overall QOL with nationwide norms, it is important to know which specific areas of life are assets or strengths to clients (strengths are areas of happiness or satisfaction) and which areas are contributing to unhappiness (weaknesses are areas of dissatisfaction or unhappiness) and thus, are good targets for intervention.

Step 4 – Finding the Causes of Dissatisfaction in Particular or Specific Areas of Life: Once identified, each specific area of dissatisfaction can be analyzed or assessed in terms of the CASIO model to see which CASIO factors are causing the dissatisfaction and how. This can be accomplished by asking clients why they feel dissatisfied with an area. Another optional way that each area of dissatisfaction in life can be analyzed is by using the What's Wrong? (see Frisch 2006). It can also help to know clients' Vision Quest goals. For example, dissatisfaction with health on the QOLI can be better understood in the context of a goal for health cited in Vision Quest of "quitting smoking and losing weight."

Step 5 – Medical Consultation or Report from a Physician: In QOLTC, a medical consultation or report from the client's personal physician is sought to be sure that the client is free from major physical or psychological disturbances that would require treatment by mental health and general medicine professionals in addition to any positive psychology intervention program. In cases of serious physical illness or disability, QOLTC is often conducted as a behavioral medicine treatment aimed at improving or sustaining clients' overall QOL even though the QOLTC interventions do not directly impact the disease or disability. In these situations, close and frequent consultation is a must between therapists and physicians along with taking great care to tailor interventions to clients' unique physical constraints and limitations.

Step 6 – Screening for Psychiatric or DSM Disorders: In clinical situations, clients are evaluated for DSM symptoms and disorders as well as their QOL. Therapists with training in assessment and psychopathology can administer this screening themselves. Where possible, time is saved by using brief symptom or essential symptoms measures such as the FESS (Frisch 2002, 2006).

Step 7 – Sharing an Integrated Case Conceptualization and Treatment/Intervention Plan with Clients: Although not technically part of the assessment phase of QOLTC, in the next step in the process of QOLTC, the results of the initial assessment are integrated via the ACT Model of Case Formulation (see Frisch 2006). The resulting case conceptualization and treatment/intervention plan is then shared with clients to build their understanding and motivation for treatment and to bring a common understanding to clients and therapists as to what the clients' assets and problems are and what intervention plan would best serve the clients' goals.

Sharing Case Conceptualizations with Clients and Patients

Once a QOLTC assessment is complete, the results of QOL, DSM, and medical assessments are integrated via the ACT Model of Case Formulation (see Frisch 2006), a part of QOL theory and QOLTC. QOL areas of growth that are not a problem to clients may be listed alone or in addition to problems areas as in dissatisfaction with play or recreation. The resulting case conceptualization and treatment/intervention plan are then shared with clients to build their understanding and motivation for treatment and to bring a common understanding to clients and therapists as to what the clients' assets and problems are and what intervention plan would best serve clients' goals. Many wonder why this step is necessary since it delays treatment and intervention.

The Need for Sound Case Conceptualization and Formulation

Too often, therapists are taught to blindly apply treatment or coaching techniques to particular problems and disorders, skipping the important first step of case formulation and conceptualization. Authors from all major schools of psychotherapy and coaching have criticized this approach to treatment planning as simplistic and superficial (e.g., see Kazdin 1993a, 2003; Persons et al. 2001; Strupp and Binder 1984). Therapist-scholars are not the only ones insisting on thoughtful case conceptualizations as a prerequisite to adequate treatment planning and implementation. Increasingly, licensing boards for all coaching and mental health professions (including psychology, psychiatry, and social work) are requiring candidates for licensure to show the ability to conceptualize cases as a necessary first step in treatment planning (Othmer and Othmer 1994). Assessing this ability has become de rigueur in oral exams for licensure in which test cases are presented to candidates in order to assess their "in the trenches" conceptualization skills.

The essential problem with assigning treatments or interventions to specific disorders or positive psychology areas of life without prior case conceptualization or formulation is that the unique causal factors or dynamics of a case are ignored. Without considering the unique factors responsible for a particular client's problems, the therapist or coach runs the risk of choosing interventions that fail because they do not address the root causes of the client's problems. At best, this may result in ineffective treatment; at worst, the intervention may be iatrogenic, making the client worse, that is, more unhappy and with a more severe DSM disorder than prior to treatment.

A simple listing of positive psychology targets for intervention, QOL problems, or DSM disorders, does not address the issue of etiology, that is, how the problems develop, how the problems are maintained, and how they interrelate. In fact, many diagnostic systems such as the DSM-IV-TR are designed to be atheoretical and agnostic with respect to the issue of etiology. Psychopathology research has repeatedly supported the view that most diagnoses and clinical problems represent the "final common pathway" for multiple causes that vary from client to client. The same can be said for QOL problems or areas for growth. Thus, for example, in unhappiness or dissatisfaction with *Love*, the CASIO dynamics or causes may be completely different for different clients as when one couple struggles with impossibly high standards adopted from the media, for example, norms for sexual athleticism and infidelity – an S problem in CASIO terms – and another couple suffers because neither partner makes the relationship a priority for time and effort, a decidedly I problem in CASIO terms. Without considering the CASIO and other factors unique to each client, or in this case, couple, the "wrong" interventions aimed at the wrong factors could easily be applied as when I-oriented CASIO interventions are applied for S-oriented CASIO problems.

Brief Case Conceptualization

Sharing a case conceptualization with clients may be as simple as going over a QOLI profile to show clients how their particular areas of dissatisfaction contribute to an overall unhappiness in CASIO terms, followed by an examination of how Five Path or CASIO strategies could improve clients' satisfaction in these valued areas of life. Alternatively, positive psychology areas of growth that are not a problem to clients may be directly plugged into the Five Path exercise. For example, Work may be the focus of a Five Path or CASIO intervention effort to boost satisfaction and productivity even though this is not a problem per se but only an area for growth. This approach can be applied for coaching clients who do not have a specified DSM disorder.

Well-Being Intervention: Quality of Life Therapy and Coaching or QOLTC

With three supportive randomized controlled trials conducted by different laboratories (Abedi and Vostanis, 2010; Rodrigue and others, 2005, 2006, 2011), including two grant-supported studies by the USA's National Institute of Health, Quality of Life Therapy and Coaching or QOLTC (Frisch 1998, 2006) is an "evidence-based" well-being intervention program in the strict sense of the word, according to M.E.P. "Marty" Seligman (2011) and Ed Diener (2011, personal communication, September 29, 2011) and others (Biswas-Diener 2010; Biswas-Diener & Dean, 2007; Todd B. Kashdan, personal communication, July 25, 2011; Furey 2007; Magyar-Moe, 2009). The term well-being is used synonymously with quality of life and positive psychology in much of this intervention literature.

Quality of Life Therapy and Coaching is "manualized" in the form of a book entitled Quality of Life Therapy (Frisch 2006), providing step-by-step instruction in assessing, tailoring interventions, and monitoring progress, outcome, and follow-up with the evidence-based well-being assessment, the Quality of Life Inventory or QOLI (Frisch et al., 2005). Quality of Life Therapy and Coaching aims to help coaching or clinical clients achieve positive life goals by matching goals with interventions in any one of the following sixteen areas of life said to comprise human happiness and meaning (after considering genetic contributions): Goals-and-Values (which may include Spiritual Life), Self-Esteem, Health, Relationships (with friends, lovers, children, relatives, etc.), Work and Retirement, Play, Helping or Service, Learning, Creativity, Money or Standard of Living, and Surroundings—Home, Neighborhood, Community. The precise definition of these areas can be found in Table 11.1. While tested with clinical populations (for example, Grant et al., 1995; Magyar-Moe, 2009), Quality of Life Therapy and Coaching is also used in professional-, organizational-, and executive-coaching (Biswas-Diener, 2010; Dean & Biswas-Diener, 2007; Rodrigue and others, 2011; Seligman 2011). The approach is informed by the longstanding social indicators literature as well as the field of positive psychology/well-being (Biswas-Diener & Dean, 2007; Diener, 2006; Furey 2007; Land, 2006).

A cornerstone of Quality of Life Therapy and Coaching is the QOLI® or Quality of Life Inventory, an empirically validated well-being assessment used throughout Quality of Life Therapy and Coaching in planning and evaluating interventions. The QOLI yields an overall domain-based life satisfaction score as well as a profile of satisfaction in each of the sixteen areas of life addressed in QOLTC. This profile reveals areas of dissatisfaction which are in need of remediation and well-being intervention. The QOLI® was used in the first trial of Quality of Life Therapy and Coaching and in all subsequent randomized controlled trials; in each case it was sensitive to intervention related changes. Psychometric research on the QOLI is extensive, including the author's research and test manuals (Frisch, 1994, 2009; Frisch et al., 1992, 2005) as well as independent studies and evaluations by other researchers at other laboratories (for example, Biswas-Diener, 2010; Biswas-Diener and Dean, 2007; Danovitch and Endicott 2008; Henning and others, 2007; Scogin and others, 2007; Kazdin, 1993, 2003; Ogles, Lambert and Masters, 1996; McAlinden and Oei , 2006; Persons and Bertagnolli, 1999; Eng, Coles, Heimberg, & Safren, 2001, 2005 and ; Peterson, 2006).

Quality of Life Therapy and Coaching has been taught as part of the curriculum of the Masters in Applied Positive Psychology Programs at the University of Pennsylvania and the University of East London along with Baylor University, the University of Utah, and programs of the International Society for Quality of Life Studies, the American Psychological Association, the British Psychological Society, and Ben Dean's online MentorCoach program in well-being intervention. QOLTC is one of the few comprehensive and step-by-step approaches to well-being or quality of life intervention which have also been evaluated as evidence-based or empirically validated (for example, Seligman, 2011). Additional trials of Quality of Life Therapy and Coaching are underway in several labs, including that of James R. Rodrigue of Beth Israel and Harvard Medical Center of Boston, MA in the USA.

References

Abedi, M. R., & Vostanis, P. (2010). Evaluation of Quality of Life Therapy for parents of children with obsessive-compulsive disorders in Iran. *European Child and Adolescent Psychiatry*. doi:10.1007/s00787-010-0098-4.

Abbe, A., Tkach, C., & Lyubomirsky, S. (2003). The art of living by dispositionally happy people. *Journal of Happiness Studies: An Interdisciplinary Forum on Subjective Well-Being, 4*, 385–404.

Abeles, R. P., Gift, H. C., & Ory, M. G. (Eds.). (1994). *Aging and quality of life*. New York: Springer.

Abramson, L. Y., Seligman, M. E. P., & Teasdale, J. D. (1978). Learned helplessness in humans: A critique and reformulation. *Journal of Abnormal Psychology, 87*, 49–74.

Abramson, L. Y., Metalsky, G. I., & Alloy, L. B. (1989). Hopelessness depression: A theory-based subtype of depression. *Psychological Review, 98*, 358–372.

Ahrens, A. H. (1987). Theories of depression: The role of goals and the self-evaluation process. *Cognitive Therapy and Research, 11*, 665–680.

American College of Physicians. (1988). Comprehensive functional assessment for elderly patients. *Annals of Internal Medicine, 109*, 70–72.

American Psychiatric Association. (2000a). Diagnostic and statistical manual of mental disorders (4th ed., TR). Washington, DC: American Psychiatric Association.

American Psychiatric Association. (2000b). *Handbook of psychiatric measures*. Washington, DC: American Psychiatric Association.

American Psychological Association. (2002). Ethical principles of psychologists and code of conduct. *American Psychologist, 57*(12), 1060–1073.

Anderson, B. L., Kiecolt-Glaser, J. K., & Glaser, R. (1994). A biobehavioral model of cancer stress and disease course. *American Psychologist, 49*, 389–404.

Andrews, F. M. (1974). Social indicators of perceived quality of life. *Social Indicators Research, 1*, 279–299.

Andrews, F. M., & Inglehart, R. F. (1979). The structure of well-being in nine western societies. *Social Indicators Research, 6*, 73–90.

Andrews, F. M., & Robinson, J. P. (1991). Measures of subjective well-being. In J. P. Robinson, P. R. Shaver, & L. S. Wrightsman (Eds.), *Measures of personality and social psychological attitudes* (pp. 61–114). San Diego: Academic.

Andrews, F. M., & Withey, S. B. (1976). *Social indicators of well being: American's Perceptions of life quality*. New York: Plenum Press.

Argyle, M. (1999). Causes and correlates of happiness. In D. Kahneman, E. Diener, & N. Schwarz (Eds.), *Well-being: The foundations of hedonic psychology* (pp. 61–84). New York: Russell Sage.

Argyle, M. (2001). *The psychology of happiness* (2nd ed.). London: Routledge.

Aristotle. (2000). *Nicomachean ethics*. (R. Crisp, Ed. & Trans.). New York: Cambridge University Press. (Original work published 0000).

Arns, P. G., & Linney, J. A. (1995). Relating functional skills of severely mentally ill patients to subjective and societal benefits. *Psychiatric Services, 46*, 260–265.

Awad, A. G. (1992). Quality of life of schizophrenic patients on medications and implications for new drug trials. *Hospital and Community Psychiatry, 43*, 262–265.

Babigian, H. M., Cole, R. E., Reed, S. K., Brown, S. W., & Lehman, A. F. (1991). Methodology for evaluating the Monroe-Livingston capitation system. *Hospital and Community Psychiatry, 42*, 913–919.

Baltes, P. B., & Baltes, M. M. (Eds.). (1990). *Successful aging: Perspectives from the behavioral sciences*. New York: Cambridge University Press.

Bandura, A. (1986). *Social foundations of thought and action: A social-cognitive theory*. Englewood Cliffs: Prentice-Hall.

Barlow, D. H. (2002). *Anxiety and its disorders: The nature and treatment of anxiety and panic* (2nd ed.). New York: Guilford Press.

Barlow, D. H., Allen, L. B., & Choate, M. L. (2004). Toward a unified treatment for emotional disorders. *Behavior Therapy, 35*, 205–230.

Baruffol, E., Gisle, L., & Corten, P. (1995). Life satisfaction as a mediator between distressing events and neurotic impairment in a general population. *Acta Psychiatrica Scandinavica, 92*, 56–62.

Baumeister, R. F. (1991). *Escaping the self: Alcoholism, spirituality, masochism, and other flights from the burden of selfhood*. New York: Basic Books.

Beck, A. T. (1979). *Cognitive therapy and the emotional disorders*. New York: Plume.

Beck, J. S. (1995). *Cognitive therapy: Basics and beyond*. New York: Guilford Press.

Beck, A. T. (1996). Beyond belief: A theory of modes, personality, and psychopathology. In P. M. Salkovskis (Ed.), *Frontiers of cognitive therapy* (pp. 1–25). New York: Guilford Press.

Beck, A. T. (1999). *Prisoners of hate: The cognitive basis of anger, hostility, and violence*. New York: Harper Collins Publishers.

Beck, A. T., Rush, A. J., Shaw, B. F., & Emery, G. (1979). *Cognitive therapy of depression*. New York: Guilford Press.

Beck, A. T., Wright, F. D., Newman, C. F., & Liese, B. S. (1993). *Cognitive therapy for substance abuse*. New York: Guilford Press.

Beck, A. T., Freeman, A. A., Davis, D. D., & Associates. (2004). *Cognitive therapy of personality disorders* (2nd ed.). New York: Guilford Press.

Ben-Porath, Y. S. (1997). Use of personality assessment instruments in empirically guided treatment planning. *Psychological Assessment, 9*, 361–367.

Berzon, R. A. (1998). Understanding and using health-related quality of life instruments within clinical research studies. In M. J. Staquet, R. D. Hays, & P. M. Fayers (Eds.), *Quality of life assessment in clinical trials* (pp. 3–15). Oxford: Oxford University Press.

Bigelow, D. A., Brodsky, G., Stewart, L., & Olson, M. (1982). The concept and measurement of quality of life as a dependent variable in evaluation of mental health services. In G. J. Stahler & W. R. Tash (Eds.), *Innovative approaches to mental health evaluation* (pp. 345–366). New York: Academic.

Biswas-Diener, R. (2010). *Practicing positive psychology coaching*. Hoboken, NJ: Wiley.

Biswas-Diener, R., & Dean, B. (2007). *Positive psychology coaching*. Hoboken, NJ: Wiley.

Biswas-Diener, R., Vitterso, J., & Diener, E. (2003). *Most people are pretty happy, but there is cultural variation: The Inughwit, the Amish, and the Maasai*. Manuscript submitted for publication.

Bowlby, J. (1985). The role of childhood experience in cognitive disturbance. In M. J. Mahoney & A. Freeman (Eds.), *Cognition and psychotherapy* (pp. 181–200). New York: Plenum Press.

Bowling, A. (1991). *Measuring health: A review of quality of life measurement scales*. Philadelphia: Open University Press.

Bradburn, N. M. (1969). *The structure of psychological well-being*. Chicago: Aldine.

Brickman, P., & Campbell, D. T. (1971). Hedonic relativism and planning the good society. In M. H. Appley (Ed.), *Adaptation-level theory* (pp. 287–305). New York: Academic.

Brickman, P., Coates, D., & Janoff-Bulman, R. (1978). Lottery winners and accident victims: Is happiness relative? *Journal of Personality and Social Psychology, 36*, 917–927.

Brief, A. P., & Nord, W. R. (1990). Work and nonwork connections. In A. P. Brief & W. R. Nord (Eds.), *Meanings of occupational work* (pp. 171–199). Lexington: Lexington Books.

Brown, D. (1995). A values-based model of facilitating career transitions. *Career Development Quarterly, 44*, 4–11.

Brownell, K. D. (2004). *The LEARN®program for weight management* (10th ed.). Dallas: American Health Publishing Company.

Brundage, M., Bass, B., Davidson, J., Queenan, J., Bezjak, A., Ringash, J., et al. (2011). Patterns of reporting health-related quality of life outcomes in randomized clinical trials: Implications for clinicians and quality of life researchers. *Quality of Life Research: An International Journal of Quality of Life Aspects of Treatment, Care and Rehabilitation, 20*(5), 653–664.

Burns, D. (1999). *Feeling good* (Rev. ed.). New York: HarperCollins.

Campbell, A. (1981). *The sense of well-being in America*. New York: McGraw-Hill.

Campbell, A., Converse, P. E., & Rogers, W. L. (1976). *The quality of American life*. New York: Russell Sage.

Cantril, H. (1965). *The pattern of human concerns*. New Brunswick: Rutgers University.

Carlbring, P., Westling, B. E., Ljungstrand, P., Ekselius, L., & Andersson, G. (2001). Treatment of panic disorder via the internet: A randomized trial of a self-help program. *Behavior Therapy, 32*, 751–764.

Carver, C. S., & Scheier, M. F. (1990). Origins and functions of positive and negative affect: A control-process view. *Psychological Review, 97*, 19–35.

Chambliss, C. H. (2000). *Psychotherapy in managed care: Reconciling research and reality*. Boston: Allyn & Bacon.

Clark, D. A., & Beck, A. T. (1999). *Scientific foundations of cognitive theory and therapy of depression*. New York: Wiley.

Clark, M. P., & Mason, T. W. (2001). Implementation of a comprehensive system of program evaluation: The Iowa State University experience. *Journal of College Student Development, 42*, 28–35.

Clark, L. A., Vittengl, J., Kraft, D., & Jarrett, R. B. (2003). Separate personality traits from states to predict depression. *Journal of Personality Disorders, 17*, 152–172.

Cleary, P. (1996). Future directions in quality of life research. In B. Spilker (Ed.), *Quality of life and pharmacoecomonics in clinical trials* (2nd ed., pp. 73–78). New York: Lippincott-Raven Press.

Coan, R. W. (1977). *Hero, artist, sage, or saint?: A survey of views on what is variously called mental health, normality, maturity, self-actualization, and human fulfillment*. New York: Columbia University Press.

Coleman, R. (1992). *Lennon: The definitive biography*. New York: Perennial Currents.

Colozzi, E. A., & Colozzi, L. C. (2000). College students' callings and careers: An integrated values-oriented perspective. In D. A. Luzzo (Ed.), *Career counseling of college students:*

An empirical guide to strategies that work (pp. 63–91). Washington, DC: American Psychological Association.

Cornell, J. E., Saunders, M. J., Paunovich, E. D., & Frisch, M. B. (1997). Oral health quality of life inventory (OH-QoL). In G. Slade (Ed.), *Assessing oral health outcomes: Measuring health status and quality of life* (pp. 135–149). Chapel Hill: University of North Carolina Press.

Cottraux, J. (1993). Behavioral psychotherapy applications in the medically ill. *Psychotherapy and Psychosomatics, 60*, 116–128.

Cowen, E. (1991). In pursuit of wellness. *American Psychologist, 46*, 404–408.

Crits-Christoph, P., & Connolly, M. B. (1997). Measuring change in patients following psychological and pharmacological interventions: Anxiety disorders. In H. H. Strupp, L. M. Horowitz, & M. J. Lambert (Eds.), *Measuring patient changes in mood, anxiety, and personality disorders: Toward a core battery* (pp. 155–190). Washington, DC: American Psychological Association.

Crowley, M. J., & Kazdin, A. E. (1998). Evaluation in clinical practice: Clinically sensitive and systematic methods of treatment delivery. *Journal of Child and Family Studies, 7*, 233–251.

Crowne, D. D., & Marlowe, D. (1960). A new scale of social desirability independent of psychopathology. *Journal of Counseling Psychology, 24*, 349–354.

Csikszentmihalyi, M. (1990). *Flow: The psychology of optimal experience*. New York: Harper & Row.

Csikszentmihalyi, M. (1997). *Finding flow: The psychology of engagement with everyday life*. New York: Basic Books.

Csikszentmihalyi, M., & Hunter, J. (2003). Happiness in everyday life: The uses of experience sampling. *Journal of Happiness Studies, 4*, 185–199.

Cummins, R. A. (2003). Normative life satisfaction: Measurement issues and homeostatic model. *Social Indicators Research, 64*, 225–256.

Cushman, A. (1992). Are you creative? *Utne Reader, 50*, 52–60.

Danovitch, I., & Endicott, J. (2008). Quality of life measures. In A. J. Rush & H. A. Pincus (Eds.), *Handbook of psychiatric measures* (2nd ed., pp. 125–140). Washington, DC: American Psychiatric Association.

Davis, E. E., & Fine-Davis, M. (1991). Social indicators of living conditions in Ireland with European comparisons. *Social Indicators Research, 25*, 103–365.

Davison, G. C., Neale, J. M., & Kring, A. M. (2004). *Abnormal psychology* (9th ed.). Hoboken: Wiley.

DeNeve, K. M., & Cooper, H. (1998). The happy personality: A meta-analysis of 137 personality traits and subjective well-being. *Psychological Bulletin, 124*, 197–229.

Denney, D. R., & Frisch, M. B. (1981). The role of neuroticism in relation to life stress and illness. *Journal of Psychosomatic Research, 25*, 303–307.

Derogatis, L. R., & Lynn, L. L. (1999). Psychological tests in screening for psychiatric disorder. In M. E. Maruish (Ed.), *The use of psychological testing for treatment planning and outcome assessment* (2nd ed., pp. 41–80). Mahwah: Erlbaum.

DeRubeis, R. J., Tang, T. Z., & Beck, A. T. (2001). Cognitive therapy. In K. S. Dobson. *Handbook of cognitive-behavioral therapies* (2nd ed., pp. 349–392). New York: Guilford Press.

Diamond, R., & Becker, M. (1999). The Wisconsin quality of life index: A multidimensional model for measuring quality of life. *Journal of Clinical Psychiatry, 60*, 29–31.

Dickens, C. (1947). *The personal history of David Copperfield*. Oxford: Oxford University Press.

Diener, E. (1984). Subjective well-being. *Psychological Bulletin, 95*, 542–575.

Diener, E. (2000). Subjective well-being: The science of happiness and a proposal for a national index. *American Psychologist, 55*, 34–43.

Diener, E. (2003). What is positive about positive psychology: The curmudgeon and Pollyanna. *Psychological Inquiry, 14*, 115–120.

Diener, E. (2006). Foreword. In M. B. Frisch (Ed.), *Quality of life therapy* (pp. vii–viii). Hoboken, NJ: Wiley.

Diener, E., & Diener, M. (1995). Cross-cultural correlates of life satisfaction and self-esteem. *Journal of Personality and Social Psychology, 68*, 653–663.

Diener, E., & Larsen, R. J. (1984). Temporal stability and cross-situational consistency of affective, behavioral, and cognitive responses. *Journal of Personality and Social Psychology, 47*, 580–592.

Diener, E., & Larsen, R. J. (1993). The experience of emotional well-being. In M. Lewis & J. M. Haviland (Eds.), *Handbook of emotions* (pp. 405–415). New York: Guilford Press.

Diener, E., & Oishi, S. (2003). Are Scandinavians happier than Asians? Issues in comparing nations on subjective well-being. In E. Columbus (Ed.), *Politics and economics of Asia*. Hauppauge: Nova Science.

Diener, E., & Seligman, M. E. P. (2002). Very happy people. *Psychological Science, 13*, 81–84.

Diener, E., & Seligman, M. E. P. (2004). Beyond money: Toward an economy of well-being. *Psychological Science in the Public Interest, 5*(1), 1–31.

Diener, E., & Chan, M. Y. (2011). Happy people live longer: Subjective well-being contributes to health and longevity. *Applied Psychology: Health and Well-Being, 3*(1), 1–43.

Diener, E., & Suh, E. M. (Eds.). (2000). *Culture and subjective well-being*. Cambridge: MIT Press.

Diener, E., Emmons, R. A., Larsen, R., & Griffen, S. (1985a). The satisfaction with life scale. *Journal of Personality Assessment, 49*, 71–75.

Diener, E., Horwitz, J., & Emmons, R. A. (1985b). Happiness of the very wealthy. *Social Indicators Research, 16*, 263–274.

Diener, E., Suh, E. M., Lucas, R. E., & Smith, H. L. (1999). Subjective well-being: Three decades of progress. *Psychological Bulletin, 125*, 276–302.

Diener, E., Diener, M., Tamir, M., Kim-Prieto, C., & Scollon, C. (2003). *A time-sequential model of subjective well-being*. Unpublished paper, Champaign.

Diener, E., Scollon, C., & Lucas, R. E. (2004). The evolving concept of subjective well-being: The multifaceted nature of happiness. In P. T. Costa & I. C. Siegler (Eds.), *The psychology of aging*. New York: Elsevier Publishing.

Dimsdale, J. E., & Baum, A. (Eds.). (1995). *Quality of life in behavioral medicine research*. Hillsdale: Erlbaum.

Donahue, E. M., Robins, R. W., Roberts, B. W., & John, O. P. (1993). The divided self: Concurrent and longitudinal effects of psychological adjustment and social roles on self-concept differentiation. *Journal of Personality and Social Psychology, 64*, 834–846.

Dworkin, R. H., Hartstein, G., Rosner, H. L., Walther, R. R., Sweeney, E. W., & Brand, L. (1992). A high-risk method for studying psychosocial antecedents of chronic pain: The prospective investigation of herpes zoster. *Journal of Abnormal Psychology, 101*, 200–205.

Easterbrook, G. (2004). *The progress paradox: How life gets better while people feel worse.* New York: Random House Trade Paperbacks.

Eickman, L. S. (2004). *Eating disorders, cognitive behavior therapy, and beyond: Innovation and critical analysis of cognitive behavioral therapy for treating eating disorders in a college counseling center.* Unpublished Manuscript, Baylor University at Waco.

Eidelson, R. J., & Eidelson, J. I. (2003). Dangerous ideas: Five beliefs that propel groups toward conflict. *American Psychologist, 58*, 182–192.

Ellwood, P. M. (1988). Shattuck lecture – Outcomes management: A technology of patient experience. *New England Journal of Medicine, 23*, 1549–1556.

Emmelkamp, P. M. (1982). *Phobic and obsessive-compulsive disorders: Theory, research and practice.* New York: Plenum Press.

Emmons, R. A. (1986). Personal strivings: An approach to personality and subjective well-being. *Journal of Personality and Social Psychology, 47*, 1105–1117.

Emmons, R. A., & McCullough, M. E. (2003). Counting blessings versus burdens: An experimental investigation of gratitude and subjective well-being in daily life. *Journal of Personality & Social Psychology, 84*(2), 377–389.

Endicott, J., Nee, J., Harrison, W., & Blumenthal, R. (1993). Quality of life enjoyment and satisfaction questionnaire: A new measure. *Psychopharmacology Bulletin, 29*, 321–326.

Eng, W., Coles, M. C., Heimberg, R. G., & Safren, S. A. (2001a). Quality of life following cognitive behavioral treatment for social anxiety disorder. *Depression and Anxiety, 13*, 192–193.

Eng, W., Heimberg, R. G., Hart, T. A., Schneider, F. R., & Liebowitz, M. R. (2001b). Attachment in individuals with social anxiety disorder: The relationship among adult attachment styles, social anxiety, and depression. *Emotion, 1*, 365–380.

Etcoff, N. (1999). *Survival of the prettiest.* New York: Doubleday.

Evans, D. R. (1994). Enhancing the quality of life in the population at large. *Social Indicators Research, 33*, 47–88.

Faden, R., & Leplege, A. (1992). Assessing quality of life: Moral implications for clinical practice. *Medical Care, 30*, 166–175.

Fallon, P., Katzman, M. A., & Wooley, S. C. (1994). *Feminist perspectives on eating disorders.* New York: Guilford Press.

Fallowfield, L. (1990). *The quality of life: The missing measurement in health care.* London: Souvenir Press.

Fava, G. A., & Mangelli, L. (2001). Assessment of subclinical symptoms and psychological well-being in depression. *European Archives of Psychiatry and Clinical Neuroscience, 251*(8), 1147–1152.

Fava, G. A., & Ruini, C. (2003). Development and characteristics of a well-being enhancing psychotherapeutic strategy: Well-being therapy. *Journal of Behavior Therapy and Experimental Psychiatry, 34*, 45–63.

Feinberg, J. (1992). *Freedom and fulfillment.* Princeton: Princeton University Press.

Ferrans, C. E. (2000). Quality of life as an outcome of cancer care. In C. Yarbro, M. Frogge, & M. Goodman (Eds.), *Cancer nursing: Principles and practice* (5th ed., pp. 243–258). Boston: Jones and Bartlett.

Ferrans, C. E., & Powers, M. J. (1985). Quality of life index: Development and psychometric properties. *Advances in Nursing Science, 8*, 15–24.

Ferrans, C. E., & Powers, M. J. (1992). Psychometric assessment of the quality of life index. *Research in Nursing and Health, 15*, 29–38.

Fibel, B., & Hale, W. D. (1978). The generalized expectancy for success scale: A new measure. *Journal of Consulting and Clinical Psychology, 46*, 924–931.

Finley, J. (Producer). (2003). *Christian meditation: Entering the mind of Christ* (CD Recording No. AF00679D). Boulder: Sounds True.

Flanagan, J. C. (1978). A research approach to improving our quality of life. *American Psychologist, 33*, 138–147.

Flanagan, J. C. (1982). Measurement of quality of life: Current state of the art. *Archives of Physical Medicine and Rehabilitation, 63*, 56–59.

Folkman, S., & Moskowitz, J. T. (2000). Positive affect and the other side of coping. *American Psychologist, 55*, 647–654.

Ford, A. A. (2004). *The quest for egalitarian relationship: Charles Dickens and the pseudo-sibling romance.* Unpublished dissertation, Baylor University, Waco.

Ford, J. D., & Kidd, P. (1998). Early childhood trauma and disorders of extreme stress as predictors of treatment outcome with chronic posttraumatic stress disorder. *Journal of Traumatic Stress, 11*, 743–761.

Ford, J. D., Fisher, P., & Larson, L. (1997). Object relations as a predictor of treatment outcome with chronic posttraumatic stress disorder. *Journal of Consulting and Clinical Psychology, 65*, 547–559.

Foster, R. J. (1988). *A celebration of discipline.* San Francisco: Harper San Francisco.

Frank, J. D., & Frank, J. B. (1993). *Persuasion and healing: A comparative study of psychotherapy* (3rd ed.). Baltimore: The Johns Hopkins University Press.

Freud, S. (1989). Civilization and its discontents. In P. Gay (Ed.), *The Freud reader* (pp. 722–772). New York: Norton.

Frey, B. S., & Stutzer, A. (2001). *Happiness and economics: How the economy and institutions affect human well-being.* Princeton: Princeton University Press.

Frisch, M. B. (1992). Use of the quality of life inventory in problem assessment and treatment planning for cognitive therapy of depression. In A. Freeman & F. Dattilio (Eds.), *Comprehensive casebook of cognitive therapy* (pp. 27–52). New York: Plenum Press.

Frisch, M. B. (1993). The quality of life inventory: A cognitive-behavioral tool for complete problem assessment, treatment planning, and outcome evaluation. *Behavior Therapist, 16*, 42–44.

Frisch, M. B. (1994). *Manual and treatment guide for the quality of life inventory or QOLI®.* Minneapolis: Pearson Assessments (formerly, National Computer Systems).

Frisch, M. B. (1998a). Documenting the effectiveness of employee assistance programs. *Employee Assistance Research, 2*, 2–5.

Frisch, M. B. (1998b). Quality of life therapy and assessment in health care. *Clinical Psychology: Science and Practice, 5*, 19–40.

Frisch, M. B. (2000). Improving mental and physical health care through quality of life therapy and assessment. In E. Diener & D. R. Rahtz (Eds.), *Advances in quality of life theory and research* (pp. 207–241). New York: Kluwer.

Frisch, M. B. (2002). A quick screen for DSM-IV disorders: The essential symptom approach. In L. VandeCreek & T. Jackson (Eds.), *Innovations in clinical practice: A source book* (pp. 375–384). Sarasota: Professional Resources Press.

Frisch, M. B. (2004a). Use of the QOLI or quality of life iInventory in quality of life therapy and assessment. In M. R. Maruish (Ed.), *The use of psychological testing for treatment planning and outcome assessment: Vol. 3. Instruments for adults* (3rd ed., pp. 749–798). Mahwah, NJ: Erlbaum.

Frisch, M. B. (2004b). *Teaching positive psychology*. Invited paper presented to the Third Annual International Positive Psychology Summit, Washington, DC.

Frisch, M. B. (2006). *Quality of life therapy: Applying a life satisfaction approach to positive psychology and cognitive therapy*. Hoboken: Wiley.

Frisch, M. B. (2009). *Quality of life inventory handbook: A guide for laypersons, clients, and coaches*. Minneapolis, MN: NCS Pearson.

Frisch, M. B., & Froberg, W. (1987). Social validation of assertion strategies for handling aggressive criticism: Evidence for consistency across situations. *Behavior Therapy, 2*, 181–191.

Frisch, M. B., & Gerrard, M. (1981). Natural helping systems: A national survey of Red Cross volunteers. *American Journal of Community Psychology, 9*, 567–579.

Frisch, M. B., & Higgins, R. L. (1986). Instructional demand effects and the correspondence among self-report, naturalistic, and role-play measures of social skill as influenced by instructional demand. *Behavioral Assessment, 8*, 221–236.

Frisch, M. B., & Jessop, N. S. (1989). Improving WAIS-R estimates with the Shipley-Hartford and Wonderlic personnel tests: Need to control for reading ability. *Psychological Reports, 65*, 923–928.

Frisch, M. B., & MacKenzie, C. J. (1991). A comparison of formerly and chronically battered women on cognitive and situational dimensions. *Psychotherapy, 28*, 339–344.

Frisch, M. B., & McCord, M. (1987). Sex role orientation and social skill: A naturalistic assessment of assertion and conversational skill. *Sex Roles, 17*, 437–448.

Frisch, M. B., & Sanford, K. P. (2005). *Construct validity and the search for a unidimensional factor solution: Factor analysis of the quality of life inventory in a large clinical sample.* Unpublished paper, Baylor University, Waco.

Frisch, M. B., Elliot, C. H., Atsaides, J. P., Salva, D. M., & Denney, D. R. (1982). Social skills and stress management training to enhance patients' interpersonal competencies. *Psychotherapy: Theory, Research, and Practice, 19*, 349–358.

Frisch, M. B., Cornell, J., Villanueva, M., & Retzlaff, P. J. (1992). Clinical validation of the quality of life inventory: A measure of life satisfaction for use in treatment planning and outcome assessment. *Psychological Assessment: A Journal of Consulting and Clinical Psychology, 4*, 92–101.

Frisch, M. B., Clark, M. P., Rouse, S. V., Rudd, M. D., Paweleck, J., & Greenstone, A. (2005). Predictive and treatment validity of life satisfaction and the quality of life inventory. *Assessment, 12*(1), 66–78.

Fromm, E. (1956). *The art of loving.* New York: Harper & Row.

Fuhrer, M. J. (2000). Subjectifying quality of life as a medical rehabilitation outcome. *Disability and Rehabilitation, 22*, 481–489.

Furey, R. (2007). Beyond feeling better: Adding happiness to the treatment plan. *PsycCRITIQUES* [serial online], *52*(5).

Gablik, S. (1991). *The reenchantment of art.* New York: Thames and Hudson.

Gatchel, R. J. (2002). Psychophysiological disorders: Past and present perspectives. In R. J. Gatchel & E. B. Blanchard (Eds.), *Psychophysiological disorders* (2nd ed.). Washington, DC: American Psychological Association.

Geigle, R., & Jones, S. B. (1990). Outcomes measurement: A report from the front. *Inquiry, 27*, 7–23.

George, L., & Bearon, L. (1980). *Quality of life in older persons.* New York: Human Sciences Press.

George, M. S., Ketter, T. A., Parekh, P. I., Horowitz, B., Herscovitch, P., & Post, R. M. (1995). Brain activity during transient sadness and happiness in healthy women. *American Journal of Psychiatry, 152*, 341–351.

Gilman, R., & Huebner, E. S. (2000). Review of life satisfaction measures for adolescents. *Behavior Change, 3*, 178–183.

Gladis, M. M., Gosch, E. A., Dishuk, N. M., & Crits-Christoph, P. (1999). Quality of life: Expanding the scope of clinical significance. *Journal of Consulting and Clinical Psychology, 67*, 320–331.

Goleman, D. (1995). *Emotional intelligence: Why it can matter more than IQ.* New York: Bantam Books.

Gonzales, L. R., Lewinsohn, P. M., & Clarke, G. N. (1985). Longitudinal follow-up of unipolar depressives: An investigation of predictors of relapse. *Journal of Consulting and Clinical Psychology, 53*, 461–469.

Gottman, J. M. (1994). *What predicts divorce.* Hillsdale: Erlbaum.

Gottman, J. M., & Silver, N. (1999). *The seven principles for making marriage work.* New York: Crown.

Grady, K. L., Jalowiec, A., White-Williams, C., Pifarre, R., Kirklin, J. K., Bourge, R. C., & Costanzo, M. R. (1995). Predictors of quality of life in patients with advanced heart failure awaiting transplantation. *Journal of Heart and Lung Transplantation, 14*, 2–10.

Grant, G., Salcedo, V., Hynan, L. S., & Frisch, M. B. (1995). Effectiveness of quality of life therapy. *Psychological Reports, 76*, 1203–1208.

Grebner, S., Semmer, N. K., & Elfering, A. (2003). *Working conditions and three types of well-being. A longitudinal study with self-report and rating data.* Manuscript submitted for publication.

Groenland, E. (1990). Structural elements of material well-being: An empirical test among people on social security. *Social Indicators Research, 22*, 367–384.

Gurin, G., Veroff, J., & Feld, S. C. (1960). *Americans view their mental health.* New York: Basic Books.

Guyatt, G. H., & Jaeschke, R. (1990). Measurements in clinical trials. In B. Spilker (Ed.), *Quality of life assessment in clinical trials.* New York: Raven.

Guyatt, G. H., Walter, S., & Norman, G. (1987). Measuring change over time: Assessing the usefulness of evaluative instruments. *Journal of Chronic Disease, 40*, 171–178.

Hadas, M. (Ed.). (1958). *The stoic philosophy of Seneca: Essays and letters of Seneca.* New York: Doubleday.

Hagerty, M. R. (2000). Social comparisons of income in one's community: Evidence from national surveys of income and happiness. *Journal of Personality and Social Psychology, 78*, 746–771.

Harter, J. K., Schmidt, F. L., & Hayes, T. L. (2002). Business-unit-level relationship between employee satisfaction, employee engagement, and business outcomes: A meta-analysis. *Journal of Applied Psychology, 87*, 268–279.

Hayes, S. C., Nelson, R. O., & Jarrett, R. B. (1987). The treatment utility of assessment: A functional approach to evaluating assessment quality. *American Psychologist, 42*, 963–974.

Headey, B., & Wearing, A. (1992). *Understanding happiness: A theory of subjective well-being*. Melbourne: Longman Cheshire.

Headey, B. W., Holmstrom, E. L., & Wearing, A. J. (1985). Models of well-being and ill-being. *Social Indicators Research, 17*, 211–234.

Headey, B., Kelley, J., & Wearing, A. (1993). Dimensions of mental health: Life satisfaction, positive affect, anxiety, and depression. *Social Indicators Research, 19*, 63–82.

Heimberg, R. G. (2002). Cognitive-behavioral therapy for social anxiety disorder: Current status and future directions. *Biological Psychiatry, 51*, 1101–1108.

Helliwell, J. E. (2003). How's life? Combining individual and national variables to explain subjective well-being. *Economic Modeling, 20*, 331–360.

Henning, E., Turk, C., Mennin, D., Fresco, D., & Heimberg, R. (2007). Impairment and quality of life in individuals with generalized anxiety disorder. *Depression and Anxiety, 24*(5), 342–349.

Herr, E. L., & Cramer, S. H. (1992). *Career guidance and counseling through the life span* (4th ed.). New York: HarperCollins.

Hibbard, M. R., Gordon, W. A., & Kotherap, L. M. (2000). Traumatic brain injury. In F. M. Dattilio & A. Freeman (Eds.), *Cognitive-behavioral strategies in crisis intervention* (2nd ed., pp. 219–242). New York: Guilford Press.

Hightower, N. (2002). *Anger busting 101: The new ABC's for angry men & the women who love them*. Houston: Bayou Publishing.

Hohmann, A. A. (1996). Measurement sensitivity in clinical mental health services. In L. I. Sederer & B. Dickey (Eds.), *Outcome assessment in clinical practice* (pp. 161–168). Baltimore: Williams & Wilkins.

Hope, D. A., Heimberg, R. G., Juster, H. R., & Turk, C. L. (2000). *Managing social anxiety: Client workbook*. San Antonio: Psychological Corporation.

Horowitz, L. M., Strupp, H. H., Lambert, M. J., & Elkin, I. (1997). Overview and summary of the core battery conference. In H. H. Strupp, L. M. Horowitz, & M. J. Lambert (Eds.), *Measuring patient changes in mood, anxiety, and personality disorders: Toward a core battery* (pp. 11–56). Washington, DC: American Psychological Association.

Huebner, E. S. (1994). Preliminary development and validation of a multidimensional life satisfaction scale for children. *Psychological Assessment, 6*, 149–158.

Huebner, E. S., Drane, W., & Valois, R. F. (2000). Levels an demographic correlates of adolescent life satisfaction reports. *School Psychology International, 21*, 281–292.

Hughes, G. J. (2001). *Aristotle on ethics*. London: Routledge.

Hyland, M. E. (1992). A reformulation of quality of life for medical science. *Quality of Life Research, 1*, 267–272.

Inglehart, R. (1990). *Culture shift in advanced industrial society*. Princeton: Princeton University Press.

Jacobson, N. S., & Christensen, A. (1996). *Integrative couple therapy*. New York: Norton.

Jacobson, N. S., & Margolin, G. (1979). *Marital therapy*. New York: Brunner/Mazel.

Jacobson, N. S., & Truax, P. (1991). Clinical significance: A statistical approach to defining meaningful change in psychotherapy research. *Journal of Consulting and Clinical Psychology, 59*, 12–19.

Jahoda, M. (1958). *Current concepts of positive mental health*. New York: Basic Books.

Jakubowski, P., & Lange, A. J. (1978). *The assertive option*. Champaign: Research Press.

Jarrett, R. B., Kraft, D., Doyle, J., Foster, B. M., Eaves, G., & Silver, P. C. (2001). Preventing recurrent depression using cognitive therapy with and without a continuation phase. *Archives of General Psychiatry, 58*, 381–387.

Jenkins, C. D. (1992). Assessment of outcomes of health intervention. *Social Science and Medicine, 35*, 367–375.

Johnson, J. R., & Temple, R. (1985). Food and drug administration requirements for approval of new anticancer drugs. *Cancer Treatment Report, 69*, 1155–1157.

Judge, T. A., & Hulin, C. L. (1993). Job satisfaction as a reflection of disposition: A multiple source causal analysis. *Organizational Behavior and Human Decision Processes, 56*, 388–421.

Judge, T. A., & Watanabe, S. (1993). Another look at the job satisfaction-life satisfaction relationship. *Journal of Applied Psychology, 78*, 939–948.

Judge, T. A., Thoreson, C. J., Bono, J. E., & Patton, G. K. (2001). The job satisfaction-job performance relationship: A qualitative and quantitative review. *Psychological Bulletin, 127*, 376–407.

Kahneman, D. (1999). Objective happiness. In D. Kahneman, E. Diener, & N. Schwarz (Eds.), *Well-being: The foundations of hedonic psychology* (pp. 3–25). New York: Russell Sage.

Kahneman, D., Diener, E., & Schwarz, N. (Eds.). (1999). *Well-being: The foundations of hedonic psychology*. New York: Russell Sage.

Kalichman, S. C., Kelly, J. A., Morgan, M., & Rompa, D. (1997). Fatalism, current life satisfaction, and risk for HIV infection among gay and bisexual men. *Journal of Consulting and Clinical Psychology, 65*, 542–546.

Kaplan, R. M. (1988). Health-related quality of life in cardiovascular disease. *Journal of Consulting and Clinical Psychology, 56*, 382–392.

Kassinove, H., & Sukhodolsky, D. G. (1995). Anger disorders: Basic science and practice issues. In H. Kassinove (Ed.), *Anger disorders: Definition, diagnosis, and treatment*. Washington, DC: Taylor & Francis.

Katschnig, H. (1997). How useful is the concept of quality of life in psychiatry. In H. Katschnig, H. Freeman, & N. Sartorius (Eds.), *Quality of life in mental disorders* (pp. 3–16). New York: Wiley.

Katschnig, H., & Angermeyer, M. C. (1997). Quality of life in depression. In H. Katschnig, H. Freeman, & N. Sartorius (Eds.), *Quality of life in mental disorders* (pp. 137–148). New York: Wiley.

Kazdin, A. E. (1992). *Research design in clinical psychology* (2nd ed.). New York: Macmillan.

Kazdin, A. E. (1993a). Evaluation in clinical practice: Clinically sensitive and systematic methods of treatment delivery. *Behavior Therapy, 24*, 11–45.

Kazdin, A. E. (1993b). Treatment of conduct disorder: Progress and directions in psychotherapy research. *Development and Psychopathology, 5*, 277–310.

Kazdin, A. E. (1994). Methodology, design, and evaluation in psychotherapy research. In A. E. Bergin & S. L. Garfield (Eds.), *Handbook of psychotherapy and behavior change* (4th ed., pp. 19–71). New York: Wiley.

Kazdin, A. E. (2003). *Research design in clinical psychology* (4th ed.). Boston: Allyn & Bacon.

Keane, T., & Solomon, S. (1996). *Assessment of PTSD: Report on the NIMH/National Center for PTSD Consensus Conference.* Washington, DC.

Keen, S. (1994). *Hymns to an unknown God.* New York: Bantam.

Kocsis, J. H., Zisook, S., Davidson, J., Shelton, R., Yonkers, K., Hellerstein, D. J., Rosenbaum, J., & Halbreich, U. (1997). Double-blind comparison of sertraline, imipramine, and placebo in the treatment of dysthymia: Psychosocial outcomes. *American Journal of Psychiatry, 154,* 390–395.

Koivumaa-Honkanen, H., Honkanen, R., Viinamaki, H., Heikkila, K., Kaprio, J., & Koskenvuo, M. (2001). Life satisfaction and suicide: A 20-year follow-up study. *American Journal of Psychiatry, 158,* 433–439.

Koivumaa-Honkanen, H., Honkanen, R., Koskenvuo, M., Viinamaki, H., & Kaprio, J. (2002). Life dissatisfaction as a predictor of fatal injury in a 20-year follow-up. *Acta Psychiatrica Scandinavia, 105,* 444–450.

Kolotkin, R. L., Head, S., Hamilton, M., & Chie-Kit, J. T. (1995). Assessing impact of weight on quality of life. *Obesity research, 3,* 49–56.

Koocher, G. P., & Keith-Spiegel, P. (1998). *Ethics in psychology: Professional standards and cases* (2nd ed.). New York: Oxford University Press.

Kornfield, J. (2000). *After ecstasy, the laundry: How the heart grows wise on the spiritual path.* New York: Bantam Books.

Kozma, A., & Stones, M. J. (1978). Some research issues and findings in the study of psychological well-being in the aged. *Canadian Psychological Review, 19,* 241–249.

Kozma, A., Stone, S., & Stones, M. J. (2000). Stability in components and predictors of subjective well-being. In E. Diener & D. R. Rahtz (Eds.), *Advances in quality of life theory and research* (pp. 13–30). New York: Kluwer.

Land, K. C. (2006). Quality of Life Therapy for All!: A review of Frisch's approach to positive psychology, Quality of Life Therapy. *SINET (Social Indicators Network News), 85,* 1–4.

Lazarus, R. S. (1991). *Emotion and adaptation.* New York: Oxford University Press.

Lazarus, R. S., & Folkman, S. (1984). *Stress, appraisal, and coping.* New York: Springer.

Lehman, A. F., Ward, N. C., & Linn, L. S. (1982). Chronic mental patients: The quality of life issue. *American Journal of Psychiatry, 139*(10), 1271–1276.

Lewinsohn, P., Redner, J., & Seeley, J. (1991). The relationship between life satisfaction and psychosocial variables: New perspectives. In F. Strack, M. Argyle, & N. Schwartz (Eds.), *Subjective well-being* (pp. 141–169). New York: Plenum Press.

Lewis, R. W. B. (2001). *Dante.* New York: Viking.

Linn, J. G., & McGranahan, D. A. (1980). Personal disruptions, social integration, subjective well-being, and predisposition toward the use of counseling services. *American Journal of Community Psychology, 8,* 87–100.

Loftus, E., & Ketcham, K. (1994). *The myth of repressed memory.* New York: St. Martin's Griffin.

Lowman, R. (1993). *Counseling and psychotherapy of work dysfunctions.* Washington, DC: American Psychological Association.

Lucas, R. E., Diener, E., & Suh, E. (1996). Discriminant validity of well-being measures. *Journal of Personality and Social Psychology, 71,* 616–628.

Lucas, R. E., Clark, A. E., & Georgellis, Y. (2003). Reexamining adaptation and the set point model of happiness: Reactions to changes in marital status. *Journal of Personality & Social Psychology, 84*(3), 527–539.

Ludden, J., & Mandell, L. (1993). Quality planning for mental health. *Journal of Mental Health Administration, 20,* 72–78.

Luminet, O. (2004). Measurement of depressive rumination and associated constructs. In C. Papageorgiou & A. Wells (Eds.), *Depressive rumination: Nature theory and treatment* (pp. 187–215). Chichester: Wiley.

Lundh, L., & Sinonsson-Sarnecki, M. (2001). Alexithymia, emotion, and somatic complaints. *Journal of Personality, 69,* 483–510.

Luzzo, D. A. (Ed.). (2000). *Career counseling of college students: An empirical guide to strategies that work.* Washington, DC: American Psychological Association.

Luzzo, D. A., & McWhirter, E. H. (2001). Sex and ethnic differences in the perception of educational and career-related barriers and levels of coping efficacy. *Journal of Counseling & Development, 79*(1), 61–67.

Lykken, D. (1999). *Happiness: The nature and nurture of joy and contentment.* New York: St. Martin's Griffin.

Lyubomirsky, S., & Tkach, C. (2004). The consequences of dysphoric rumination. In C. Papageorgiou & A. Wells (Eds.), *Depressive rumination: Nature theory and treatment* (pp. 21–42). Hoboken: Wiley.

Lyubomirsky, S., Sheldon, K. M., & Schkade, D. (2005). Pursuing happiness: The architecture of sustainable change. *Review of General Psychology, 9*(2), 111–131.

Lyubomirsky, S., King, L., & Diener, E. (in press). Happiness is a good thing: A model of the benefits of chronic positive affect. *Psychological Bulletin.*

Magyar-Moe, J. L. (2009). *Therapist's guide to positive psychological interventions.* New York: Academic.

Maslow, A. (1982). *Toward a psychology of being* (2nd ed.). New York: Van Nostrand Reinhold.

Matarazzo, J. D. (1992). Psychological testing and assessment in the 21st century. *American Psychologist, 47,* 1007–1018.

McAlinden, N., & Oei, T. (2006). Validation of the Quality of Life Inventory for patients with anxiety and depression. *Comprehensive Psychiatry, 47*(4), 307–314.

McCrae, R. R., & Costa, P. T., Jr. (1990). *Personality in adulthood.* New York: Guilford Press.

McCrae, R. R., Costa, P. T., Jr., Ostendorf, F., Angleitner, A., Hrebícková, M., Avia, M. D., Sanz, J., Sánchez-Bernardos, M. L., Kusdil, M. E., Woodfield, R., Saunders, P. R., & Smith, P. B. (2000). Nature over nurture: Temperament, personality, and lifespan development. *Journal of Personality and Social Psychology, 78,* 173–186.

McGee, H. M., O'Boyle, C. A., Hickey, A., O'Malley, K., & Joyce, C. R. B. (1990). Assessing the quality of life of the individual: The SEIQoL with a healthy gastroenterology unit population. *Psychological Medicine, 21,* 749–759.

McGregor, I., & Little, B. R. (1998). Personal projects, happiness, and meaning: On doing well and being yourself. *Journal of Personality and Social Psychology, 74,* 494–512.

McKnight, D. L., Nelson, R. O., & Hayes, S. C. (1984). Importance of treating individually assessed response classes in the amelioration of depression. *Behavior Therapy, 15*(4), 315–335.

McLean, P. D., & Hakstian, A. R. (1979). Clinical depression: Comparative efficacy of outpatient treatments. *Journal of Consulting & Clinical Psychology, 47*(5), 818–836.

McMillan, D., & Fisher, P. (2004). Cognitive therapy for depressive thinking. In C. Papageorgiou & A. Wells (Eds.), *Depressive rumination: Nature theory and treatment* (pp. 241–258). Hoboken: Wiley.

McNamara, J. R., & Booker, D. J. (2000). The abuse disability questionnaire: A new scale of assessing the consequences of partner abuse. *Journal of Interpersonal Violence, 15*, 170–183.

Meehl, P. E. (1992). Factors and taxa, traits and types, differences of degree and differences in kind. *Journal of Personality, 60*, 117–174.

Mehnert, T., Krauss, H. H., Nadler, R., & Boyd, M. (1990). Correlates of life satisfaction in those with disabling conditions. *Rehabilitation Psychology, 35*, 3–17.

Meichenbaum, D. (1994). *Clinical handbook for assessing and treating PTSD*. Waterloo: Institute Press.

Mendlowicz, M. V., & Stein, M. B. (2000). Quality of life in individuals with anxiety disorders. *American Journal of Psychiatry, 157*, 669–682.

Merton, T. (1996a). *Contemplative prayer*. New York: Doubleday.

Merton, T. (1996b). *Life and holiness*. New York: Doubleday.

Michalos, A. C. (1983). Satisfaction and happiness in a rural northern resource community. *Social Indicators Research, 13*, 225–252.

Michalos, A. C. (1991). *Global report on student well-being: Vol. I. Life satisfaction and happiness*. New York: Springer.

Miller, W. R., & Rollnick, S. (2002). *Motivational interviewing* (2nd ed.). New York: Guilford Press.

Miller, I. W., Keitner, G. I., Schatzberg, A. F., Klein, D. N., Thase, M. E., Rush, A. J., Markowitz, J. C., Schlager, D. S., Kornstein, S. G., Davis, S. M., Harrison, W. M., & Keller, M. B. (1998). The treatment of chronic depression: Pt. 3. Psychosocial functioning before and after treatment with sertraline or imipramine. *Journal of Clinical Psychiatry, 59*, 608–619.

Miller, W. R., Rollnick, S., & Conforti, K. (2002). *Motivational interviewing: Preparing people for change* (2nd ed.). New York: Guilford Press.

Miller, C. A., & Frisch, M. B. (2009). *Creating your best life: The ultimate life list guide*. New York: Sterling Publishing.

Millon, T. (1987). *Manual for the MCMI-II*. Minneapolis: National Computer Systems.

Mirin, S. M., & Namerow, M. J. (1991). Why study treatment outcome? *Hospital and Community Psychiatry, 42*, 1007–1012.

Moras, K. (1997). Toward a core battery for treatment efficacy research on mood disorders. In H. H. Strupp, L. M. Horowitz, & M. J. Lambert (Eds.), *Measuring patient changes in mood, anxiety, and personality disorders: Toward a core battery* (pp. 301–338). Washington, DC: American Psychological Association.

Moreland, K. L., Fowler, R. D., & Honaker, L. M. (1994). Future directions in the use of psychological assessment for treatment planning and outcome evaluation: Recommendations and predictions. In M. E. Maruish (Ed.), *The use of psychological testing for treatment planning and outcome assessment* (pp. 581–602). Hillsdale: Erlbaum.

Morganstern, J., Labouvie, E., McCrady, B. S., Kahler, C. W., & Frey, R. M. (1997). Affiliation with alcoholics anonymous after treatment: A study of its therapeutic effects and mechanisms of action. *Journal of Consulting and Clinical Psychology, 65*, 768–777.

Mother Teresa. (1985). *Words to love by*. Notre Dame: Ave Maria Press.

Muller, A., Montaya, P., Schandry, R., & Hartl, L. (1994). Changes in physical symptoms, blood pressure, and quality of life over 30 days. *Behavior Research and Therapy, 32*, 593–603.

Myers, D. G. (1993). *The pursuit of happiness*. New York: Avon.

Myers, D. G. (2000). *The American paradox*. New Haven: Yale University Press.

Myers, D. G. (2004). *Psychology* (7th ed.). New York: Worth.

Myers, D. G., & Diener, E. (1995). Who is happy? *Psychological Science, 6*, 10–19.

Nelson-Gray, R. O. (1996). Treatment outcome measures: Nomothetic or idiographic? *Clinical Psychology: Science and Practice, 3*, 164–167.

Newman, F. L., Ciarlo, J. A., & Carpenter, D. (1999). Guidelines for selecting psychological instruments for treatment planning and outcome assessment. In M. E. Maruish (Ed.), *The use of psychological testing for treatment planning and outcome assessment* (2nd ed., pp. 153–170). Mahwah: Erlbaum.

Nhat Hanh, T. (1999). *The heart of Buddah's teaching*. New York: Broadway Books.

Nozick, R. (1989). *The examined life*. New York: Simon & Schuster.

Ogihara, T., Ozawa, T., & Kuramoto, K. (1991). Usefulness of the beta-blocker carteolol and its effect on quality of life in elderly hypertensive patients. *Current Therapeutic Research, 49*, 38–46.

Ogles, B. M., Lambert, M., & Masters, K. (1996). *Assessing outcome in clinical practice*. Boston: Allyn & Bacon.

Ogles, B. M., Lunnen, K. M., & Bonesteel, K. (2001). Clinical significance: History, application, and current practice. *Clinical Psychology Review, 21*, 421–446.

Othmer, E., & Othmer, S. C. (1994). *The clinical interview using DSM-IV* (Vol. 1). Washington, DC: American Psychiatric Press.

Oxford English Dictionary. (1989). Oxford, England: Oxford University Press.

Palfreyman, S., Tod, A., Brazier, J., & Michaels, J. (2010). A systematic review of health-related quality of life instruments used for people with venous ulcers: An assessment of their suitability and psychometric properties. *Journal of Clinical Nursing, 19*(19–20), 2673–2703.

Papageorgiou, C., & Wells, A. (2004). Nature, functions, and beliefs about depressive rumination. In C. Papageorgiou & A. Wells (Eds.), *Depressive rumination: Nature theory and treatment* (pp. 3–20). Hoboken: Wiley.

Patterson, J. T. (1996). *Grand expectations: The United States, 1945–1974*. New York: Oxford University.

Paunovic, N., & Ost, L. (2001). Cognitive-behavior therapy vs. Exposure therapy in the treatment of PTSD in refugees. *Behaviour Research and Therapy, 39*, 1183–1197.

Pavot, W., & Diener, E. (1993). Review of the satisfaction with life scale. *Psychological Assessment, 5*, 164–172.

Pelham, B. W. (1995). Self-investment and self-esteem: Evidence for a Jamesian model of self-worth. *Journal of Personality and Social Psychology, 69*, 1141–1150.

Pennebacker, J. W., & Stone, L. D. (2004). Translating traumatic experiences into language: Implications for child abuse and long-term health. In L. J. Koenig & L. S. Doll (Eds.), *From child sexual abuse to adult sexual risk: Trauma, revictimization, and intervention* (pp. 201–216). Washington, DC: American Psychological Association.

Perls, F. S. (1971). *Gestalt therapy verbatim*. New York: Bantam Books.

Persons, J. B. (1989). *Cognitive therapy in practice: A case formulation approach*. New York: W. W. Norton & Company.

Persons, J. B., & Bertagnolli, A. (1999). Inter-rater reliability of cognitive-behavioral case formulations of depression: A replication. *Cognitive Therapy and Research, 23,* 271–283.

Persons, J. B., Davidson, J., & Thompkins, M. A. (2001). *Essential components of cognitive-behavior therapy for depression*. Washington, DC: American Psychological Association.

Peterson, C. (2006). Back cover. In M. B. Frisch (Ed.), *Quality of life therapy* (pp. back cover of book). Hoboken, NJ: Wiley.

Peterson, C., & Seligman, M. E. P. (Eds.). (2004). *Character strengths and virtues: A handbook and classification*. New York: Oxford University Press.

Petry, N. M., Petrakis, I., Trevisan, L., Wiredu, G., Boutros, N. N., Martin, B., et al. (2001). Contingency management interventions: From research to practice. *American Journal of Psychiatry, 158,* 694–702.

Plato. (2001). *Plato's republic* (B. Jowett, Trans.). New York: Agora Publications..

Pohl, R. B., Wolkow, R. M., & Clary, C. M. (1998). Sertraline in the treatment of panic disorder: A double-blind multicenter trial. *American Journal of Psychiatry, 155,* 1189–1195.

Putnam, R. (2001). *Bowling alone: The collapse and revival of American community*. New York: Simon & Schuster.

Rabkin, J. G., Griffin, K. W., & Wagner, G. (2000). Quality of life measures. In A. J. Rush & H. A. Pincus (Eds.), *Handbook of psychiatric measures*. Washington, DC: American Psychiatric Association.

Rapaport, M. H., Endicott, J., & Clary, D. M. (2002). PTSD and quality of life: Results across 64 weeks of sertraline treatment. *Journal of Clinical Psychiatry, 63,* 59–65.

Rehm, L. P. (1988). Self-management and cognitive processes in depression. In L. B. Alloy (Ed.), *Cognitive processes in depression* (pp. 143–176). New York: Guilford Press.

Reich, R. B. (2000). *The future of success*. New York: Vintage Press.

Reisman, J. M. (1966). *A history of clinical psychology* (Enlarged Ed.). New York: Irvington.

Reynolds, D. S. (1996). *Walt Whitman's America: A cultural biography*. New York: Vintage.

Rice, R. W., Frone, M. R., & McFarlin, D. B. (1992). Work-nonwork conflict and the perceived quality of life. *Journal of Organizational Behavior, 13,* 155–168.

Rodrigue, J. R., Baz, M. A., Widows, M. R., & Ehlers, S. L. (2005). A randomized evaluation of quality of life therapy with patients awaiting lung transplantation. *American Journal of Transplantation, 5*(10), 2425–2432.

Rodrigue, J. R., Widows, M. R., & Baz, M. A. (2006). Caregivers of patients awaiting lung transplantation: Do they benefit when the patient is receiving psychological services? *Progress in Transplantation, 16,* 336–342.

Rodrigue, J. R., Mandelbrot, D. A., & Pavlakis, M. (2011). A psychological intervention to improve quality of life and reduce psychological distress in adults awaiting kidney transplantation. *Nephrology Dialysis Transplantation, 26*(2), 709–715. doi:10.1093/ndt/gfq382.

Rouse, S. V., Butcher, J. N., & Miller, K. B. (1999). Assessment of substance abuse in psychotherapy clients: The effectiveness of the MMPI-2 substance abuse scales. *Psychological Assessment, 11,* 101–107.

Rush, A. J. (2000). *Sequenced treatment alternatives for resistant depression: STARD research protocol*. Unpublished manuscript.

Rush, A. J., & Kupfer, D. J. (2001). Strategies and tactics in the treatment of depression. In G. O. Gabbard (Ed.), *Treatments of psychiatric disorders* (3rd ed., Vol. 2, pp. 1417–1442). Washington, DC: American Psychiatric Association.

Russell, B. (1958). *The conquest of happiness*. New York: Liveright Publishing Corporation.

Safren, S. A., Heimberg, R. G., Brown, E. J., & Holle, C. (1997). Quality of life in social phobia. *Depression and Anxiety, 4,* 126–133.

Salek, S. (Ed.). (1998). *Compendium of quality of life instruments*. New York: Wiley.

Sarason, S. B. (1990). *Challenge of art to psychology*. New Haven: Yale University Press.

Schimmack, U., Diener, E., & Oishi, S. (2002). Life-satisfaction is a momentary judgment and a stable personality characteristic: The use of chronically accessible and stable sources. *Journal of Personality, 70,* 345–385.

Schipper, H., Clinch, J., & Powell, V. (1990). Definitions and conceptual issues. In B. Spilker (Ed.), *Quality of life assessments in clinical trials*. New York: Raven.

Schnurr, P. P., Friedman, M. J., Lavori, P. W., & Hsieh, F. Y. (2001). Design of Department of Veterans Affairs Cooperative Study No. 4230: Group treatment of posttraumatic stress disorder. *Controlled Clinical Trials, 22,* 74–88.

Schwartz, R. C. (2001). *Introduction to the internal family systems model*. Oak Park: Trailheads Publications.

Schwarz, N., & Strack, F. (1999). Reports of subjective well-being: Judgmental processes and their methodological implications. In D. Kahneman, E. Diener, & N. Schwarz (Eds.), *Well-being: The foundations of hedonic psychology* (pp. 61–84). New York: Russell Sage.

Scogin, F., Morthland, M., Kaufman, A., Burgio, L., Chaplin, W., & Kong, G. (2007, December). Improving quality of life in diverse rural older adults: A randomized trial of a psychological treatment. *Psychology and Aging, 22*(4), 657–665.

Seeman, J. (1989). Toward a model of positive health. *American Psychologist, 44,* 1099–1109.

Segal, Z. V., Williams, J. M. G., & Teasdale, J. F. (2002). *Mindfulness-based cognitive therapy for depression: A new approach to preventing relapse*. New York: Guilford Press.

Seligman, M. E. P. (2002). *Authentic happiness*. New York: Free Press.

Seligman, M. E. P. (2011). *Flourish*. New York: Free Press.

Shafranske, E. P. (1996). Introduction: Foundation for the consideration of religion in the clinical practice of psychology. In E. P. Shafranske (Ed.), *Religion and the clinical practice of psychology* (pp. 1–20). Washington, DC: American Psychological Association.

Shehan, C. L. (1984). Wives' Work and psychological well-being: An extension of Gove's social role theory of depression. *Sex Roles, 11,* 881–899.

Sheldon, K. M., & Elliot, A. J. (1999). Goal striving, need-satisfaction, and longitudinal well-being: The self-concordance model. *Journal of Personality and Social Psychology, 76,* 482–497.

Sheldon, K. M., & Houser-Marko, L. (2001). Self-concordance, goal-attainment, and the pursuit of happiness: Can there be an upward spiral? *Journal of Personality and Social Psychology, 80*, 152–165.

Sheldon, K. M., Elliot, A. J., Kim, Y., & Kasser, T. (2001). What is satisfying about satisfying events? Testing 10 candidate psychological needs. *Journal of Personality and Social Psychology, 80*, 325–339.

Shiner, R. L. (2003). *Development and happiness*. Paper presented at the second International Positive Psychology Summit, Washington, DC.

Sijie, D. (2001). *Balzac and the little Chinese seamstress*. (I. Rilke, Trans.). New York: Anchor Books.

Simon, L. (1998). *Genuine reality: A life of William James*. New York: Harcourt Brace.

Simpson, J. A., & Weiner, E. S. (Eds.). (1989). *The Oxford English dictionary* (2nd ed.). Oxford: Oxford University Press.

Sirgy, M. J. (2002). *The psychology of quality of life*. Dordrecht: Kluwer.

Snyder, C. R., & Lopez, S. (Eds.). (2002). *Handbook of positive psychology*. New York: Oxford University Press.

Snyder, A. G., Stanley, M. A., Novey, D. M., Averill, P. M., & Beck, J. G. (2000). Measures of depression in older adults with generalized anxiety disorder: A psychometric evaluation. *Depression and Anxiety, 11*, 114–120.

Soh, S., McGinley, J., & Morris, M. (2011). Measuring quality of life in Parkinson's disease: Selection of-an-appropriate health-related quality of life instrument. *Physiotherapy, 97*(1), 83–89.

Spilker, B. (1996). *Quality of life and pharmacoecomonics in clinical trials* (2nd ed.). New York: Lippincott-Raven Press.

Stanard, R. P. (1999). The effect of training in a strengths model of case management on client outcomes in a community mental health center. *Community Mental Health Journal, 35*, 169–179.

Sternberg, R.-J. (2003). *TI: Wisdom, intelligence, and creativity synthesized*. New York: Cambridge University Press.

Stewart, A. L., & King, A. C. (1994). Conceptualizing and measuring quality of life in older populations. In R. P. Abeles, H. C. Gift, & M. G. Ory (Eds.), *Aging and quality of life* (pp. 27–54). New York: Springer.

Stewart, A. L., Ware, S. E., Sherbourne, C. D., & Wells, K. B. (1992). Psychological distress/well-being and cognitive functioning measures. In A. L. Stewart & J. E. Ware (Eds.), *Measuring functioning and well-being: The medical outcomes study approach* (pp. 102–142). Durham: Duke University Press.

Strupp, H. H. (1996). The tripartite model and the consumer reports study. *American Psychologist, 51*, 1017–1024.

Strupp, H. H., & Binder, J. L. (1984). *Psychotherapy in a new key: A guide to time-limited dynamic psychotherapy*. New York: Basic Books.

Strupp, H. H., & Hadley, S. W. (1977). A tripartite model of mental health and therapeutic outcomes. *American Psychologist, 32*, 187–196.

Suldo, S., & Huebner, E. S. (2005). *Very satisfied youth: Advances in quality of life research*. New York: Springer.

Sullivan, M. (1992). Quality of life assessment in medicine: Concepts, definitions, purposes, and basic tools. *Nordic Journal of Psychiatry, 46*, 79–83.

Szalai, A., & Andrews, F. M. (Eds.). (1980). *The quality of life: Comparative studies*. Beverly Hills: Sage.

Tatarkiewicz, W. (1976). *Analysis of happiness*. Hague: Martinus Nijhoff.

Taylor, S. E. (2002). *Health psychology*. New York: McGraw-Hill.

Taylor, S. E., & Brown, J. D. (1988). Illusion and well-being: A social psychological perspective on mental health. *Psychological Bulletin, 103*, 193–210.

Tay, L., & Diener, E. (2011). Needs and subjective well-being around the world. *Journal of Personality and Social Psychology, 101*(2), 354–365.

Telch, M. J., Schmidt, N. B., Jaimez, T. L., & Jacquin, K. M. (1995). Impact of cognitive-behavioral treatment on quality of life in panic disorder patients. *Journal of Consulting and Clinical Psychology, 63*, 823–830.

Terry, D. J., Mayocchi, L., & Hynes, G. J. (1996). Depressive symptomotology in new mothers: A stress and coping perspective. *Journal of Abnormal Psychology, 105*, 220–231.

Truong, M. (2003). *The book of salt*. Boston: Houghton Mifflin.

Turk, D. L., Mennin, D. S., Fresco, D. M., & Heimberg. R. G. (2000, November). *Impairment and quality of life among individuals with Generalized Anxiety Disorder*. Paper presented at the annual meeting of the Association for Advancement of Behavior Therapy, New Orleans.

Twenge, J. M. (2000). The age of anxiety? The birth cohort change in anxiety and neuroticism, 1952–1993. *Journal of Personality and Social Psychology, 79*, 1007–1021.

Vaillant, G. (2002). *Aging well*. New York: Basic Books.

Valois, R. F., Zullig, K. J., Huebner, E. S., & Drane, J. W. (2001). Relationship between life satisfaction and violent behaviors among adolescents. *American Journal of Health Behavior, 25*, 353–366.

Veenhoven, R. (1984). *Conditions of happiness*. Boston: Reidel.

Veenhoven, R. (1993). *Happiness in nations: Subjective appreciation of life in 55 nations 1986–1990*. Rotterdam: RISBO—Erasmus University.

Veenhoven, R. (1996). Developments in satisfaction research. *Social Indicators Research, 37*, 1–46.

Veenhoven, R. (1999). Quality-of-life in individualistic society: A comparison of 43 nations in the early 1990's. *Social Indicators Research, 48*, 157–186.

Veenhoven, R. (2003a). Arts of living. *Journal of Happiness Studies, 4*, 373–384.

Veenhoven, R. (2003b). Hedonism and happiness. *Journal of Happiness Studies, 4*, 437–457.

Vitaliano, P. P., Dougherty, C. M., & Siegler, I. C. (1994). Biopsychosocial risks for cardiovascular disease in spouse caregivers of persons with Alzheimer's disease. In R. P. Abeles, H. C. Gift, & M. G. Ory (Eds.), *Aging and quality of life* (pp. 145–159). New York: Springer.

Wagner, E. H., Schoenbach, V. J., Orleans, C. T., Grothaus, L. C., Saunders, K. W., Curry, S., & Pearson, D. C. (1990). Participation in a smoking cessation program: A population-based perspective. *American Journal of Preventive Medicine, 6*, 258–266.

Walker, A. (1982). *The color purple*. New York: Harcourt.

Walker, L. E. A. (1994). *Abused women and survivor therapy*. Washington, DC: American Psychological Association.

Ware, J. E. (1986). The assessment of health status. In C. H. Aiken & D. Mechanic (Eds.), *Applications of social science to clinical medicine and health policy* (9th ed.). New Brunswick: Rutgers University Press.

Ware, J. E. (2004). SF-36 health survey update. In M. R. Maruish (Ed.), *The use of psychological testing for treatment planning and outcome assessment: Vol. 3. Instruments for adults* (3rd ed., pp. 693–718). Mahwah: Erlbaum.

Warr, P. (1999). Well-being and the workplace. In D. Kahneman, E. Diener, & N. Schwarz (Eds.), *Well-being: The foundations of hedonic psychology* (pp. 392–412). New York: Russell Sage.

Warren, R. (2002). *The purpose-driven life*. Grand Rapids: Zondervan.

Watson, G. (1930). Happiness among adult students of education. *Journal of Educational Psychology, 21*, 79–109.

Wells, A., & Papageorgiou, C. (2004). Metacognitive therapy for depressive rumination. In C. Papageorgiou & A. Wells (Eds.), *Depressive rumination: Nature theory and treatment* (pp. 259–273). Chichester: Wiley.

Wenger, N. K., & Furberg, C. D. (1990). Cardiovascular disorders. In B. Spilker (Ed.), *Quality of life assessments in clinical trials*. New York: Raven.

Wessman, A. E., & Ricks, D. F. (1966). *Mood and personality*. New York: Holt, Rienhart, & Winston.

Williams, R. (1998). *Anger kills: Seventeen strategies for controlling the hostility that can harm your health*. New York: HarperTorch.

Witkiewitz, K., & Marlatt, G. A. (2004). Relapse prevention for alcohol and drug problems. *American Psychologist, 59*, 224–235.

Wolfe, T. (1988). *The bonfire of the vanities*. New York: Bantam.

Woody, S. R., & Adessky, R. S. (2002). Therapeutic alliance, group cohesion, and homework compliance during cognitive-behavioral group treatment of social phobia. *Behavior Therapy, 33*, 5–27.

World Health Organization. (1948). World Health Organization constitution. In *Basic documents*. Geneva: World Health Organization.

Wortman, C. B., & Silver, R. C. (1987). Coping with irrevocable loss. In A. Baum, C. J. Frederick, I. H. Frieze, E. S. Shneidman, & C. B. Wortman (Eds.), *Cataclysms, crises, and catastrophes: Psychology in action* (pp. 185–235). Washington, DC: American Psychological Association.

Yalom, I. (1980). *Existential psychotherapy*. New York: Basic books.

Yardley, J. K., & Rice, R. W. (1991). The relationship between mood and subjective well-being. *Social Indicators Research, 24*, 101–111.

Zullig, K. J., Valois, R. F., Huebner, E. S., Oeltmann, J. E., & Drane, J. W. (2001). Relationship between perceived life satisfaction and adolescents' substance abuse. *Journal of Adolescent Health, 29*, 279–288.

Education and Quality of Life

12

Jason D. Edgerton, Lance W. Roberts, and Susanne von Below

The Importance of Education and Its Connection to Quality of Life

The purpose of formal education, of schooling, can be broadly conceptualized as fourfold—socialization, allocation, economic production, and legitimation—with each process interrelating with the others.

Socialization

Schooling is a primary means for the transmission of culture and passing along of values, knowledge, and skills deemed important in a society and for the responsible participation of citizens within that society. This socialization function has, in recent decades, increasingly come to encompass training and preparation for productive employment in the globalizing "knowledge economy." Critical theorists point to the "hidden curriculum" embedded within the formal education system which instills in students the patterns of thought and behavior compatible with modern capitalist society. Others point to the upper and middle-class values (e.g., achievement orientation, extended time horizon) imbuing formal education and

the cultural, material, and social advantages incumbent upon their acquisition.

Allocation

The formal education system is also a means of rationing opportunity, of differentiating and allocating individuals into different positions within a society's social stratification structure; attainment of educationally contingent credentials is linked to occupational trajectory, income, and attendant life chances. Depending on the chosen theoretical perspective, the formal education system can be seen as promoting social mobility or curtailing it, the weight of empirical evidence suggests it does both to varying degrees (Hout and DiPrete 2006). Functionalist and liberal approaches see stratification as an inevitable feature of education as an allocative mechanism; individuals of differing ability and motivation are sorted out according to the needs of society and/or the economy. Critical approaches emphasize the allocative inequities within education systems, contending that formal education systems tend to reproduce existing social inequalities. Functionalist and liberal accounts emphasize the notion of equal educational opportunity; all children should have access to public education, but that ultimately meritocratic competition will ensure that the "cream rises to the top." Critics see claims of equal opportunity as illusory and argue that children are already on unequal footing when they enter the formal education system and that these disparities tend to grow and multiply at successive levels, such that over their educational careers, those from privileged backgrounds experience a cumulative advantage over their less fortunate peers.

J.D. Edgerton (✉) • L.W. Roberts
University of Manitoba, Winnipeg, Canada
e-mail: j_edgerton@umanitoba.ca

S. von Below
Assistant Head, Statistics and International Comparative Analyses, German Federal Ministry of Education, University of Manitoba, Winnipeg, Canada

K.C. Land et al. (eds.), *Handbook of Social Indicators and Quality of Life Research*,
DOI 10.1007/978-94-007-2421-1_12, © Springer Science+Business Media B.V. 2012

Employment and Economic Development

Increasingly education is seen as vital cog in a country's economic engine, both in terms of training, and research and development. One prominent economic rationalist approach, *human capital theory*, focuses on returns to investment in education: education and training (human capital[1]) increase worker productivity and hence the value of educated workers. Thus, individuals who invest time, energy, and money into education do so with the expectation of securing a better job and enhanced lifetime earnings. At the individual level, increasing education (human capital) increases worker productivity and thus garners better employment and income for the individual. At the social or aggregate level, general increments in the stock of human capital are supposed to increase overall productivity, prosperity, and social cohesion (OECD 1998, 2001). Many governments have embraced this policy rationale even though definitive evidence of the macro-level effects of human capital investment remains rather elusive (e.g., Barro 2001; McMahon 1997, 1999, 2000; Helliwell 2001; Sweetman 2002; Krueger and Lindahl 2001).

Legitimation of Knowledge and Status

A contrarian screening or signaling hypothesis exists which questions the strength of the education-productivity relationship. This hypothesis argues that it is just as likely that it is not the increased level of knowledge *per se* that enhances a person's educational returns but rather what the attainment of a particular credential signifies to employers about the characteristics of a potential employee (i.e., that they have the value orientations, motivation, habits, etc., sought by or familiar to the employer). A related aspect of such credentialism is professionalization, by which certain occupational groups seek to elevate the status of their work (and corresponding level of compensation). This is done by, among other means, establishing institutionalized authority over a specialized area of knowledge and practice (such as medicine or accountancy) and limiting

professional membership by requiring certain higher education credentials. This gatekeeping function is a form of social selection that contributes to the stratification within society, as various occupational groups seek to establish or maintain the relative advantages of institutionally sanctioned expertise. Accordingly, the acquisition of certain education-contingent professional credentials has a potent effect on a person's standing within society's socioeconomic structure.

From this brief review of the basic purposes of formal education within modern western society, it is apparent that schooling is integrally related to life chances, both in terms of those who are afforded (and equipped to capitalize on) educational opportunity and those who are excluded from or afforded less opportunity. Indeed, there is a vast body of literature documenting various aspects of this relationship across regional, national, and international contexts. It follows that if education affects life chances, then it also has the potential to affect quality of life. The contemporary tendency to view education as remedy for various social and economic ills is testament to its perceived importance to quality of life. For example, the Organization for Economic Cooperation and Development (OECD) enthusiastically advocates investment in human capital as a strategy for overcoming labor market challenges in the global economy, increasing individual opportunity and national economic productivity, as well as contributing to the resolution of a host of social problems (OECD 1998, 1999a, 2001).

UNESCO (2000: 8) also underscores the fundamental nature of the connection between quality of life and education in its assertion that

> ...all children, young people and adults have the human right to benefit from an education that will meet their basic learning needs in the best and fullest sense of the term, an education that includes learning to know, to do, to live together and to be. It is an education geared to tapping each individual's talents and potential, and developing learners' personalities, so that they can improve their lives and transform their societies...Without accelerated progress towards education for all, national and internationally agreed targets for poverty reduction will be missed, and inequalities between countries and within societies will widen.

Defining Quality of Life

The term "quality of life" (QoL) is rendered somewhat problematic by its broad application in different contexts for different purposes by analysts working within

---

[1] Human capital is succinctly defined by the OECD (1998: 9) as "the knowledge, skills, competences, and other attributes embodied in individuals that are relevant to economic activity." Highest level of education attained and/or number of years of schooling are the most common operational definitions of human capital.

various distinct academic disciplines (Rapley 2003; Phillips 2006).[2] While the generic connotations of the term may be cursorily familiar to most people, its multidimensional and multidisciplinary scope makes more precise conceptualization a task rife with inconsistency and ambiguity. At base, ascertaining quality of life involves some assessment of welfare, whether of the individual or of the collective, and this assessment typically involves objective (i.e., measurable in terms of quantity or frequency) and subjective (i.e., measurement contingent on the perception of the particular individual) indicators. Defining what constitutes welfare or the requisite conditions for the "good life" is itself a value-laden enterprise and underscores the normative footings of quality of life research (particularly the search for "objective" indicators). Often, which indicators—subjective or objective—and which level of aggregation—e.g., individual, family, community, nation—a researcher is interested in depend on the discipline within which that researcher is working. One of the characteristic difficulties in QoL research is that subjective and objective indicators are often poorly correlated, and so it is common practice to include both in research (Rapley 2003; Cummins 1997). Subjective measures typically involve self-report surveys or interviews. Common examples of objective measures include per capita income, life expectancy, morbidity rates, literacy rates, average or median level of educational attainment, and unemployment rates.

Given space considerations, the present chapter will primarily focus on the relationship between education and quality of life outcomes at the individual/familial level. Circumscribing our topic in this way also aids the choice of a definition of quality of life. Rapley (2003) considers a number of proposed definitions of quality of life at various levels of aggregation. He suggests that the most influential individual-level definition of quality of life is that posited by Robert Cummins (and operationalized by the Comprehensive Quality of Life Scale[3]). Cummins (1997: 132) defines quality of life in

terms of both subjective and objective dimensions, with each dimension consisting of seven domains: "material well-being, health, productivity, intimacy, safety, community, and emotional well-being. Objective domains comprise culturally relevant measures of objective well-being. Subjective domains comprise domain satisfaction weighted by their importance to the individual." These domains each contribute to overall quality of life. Cummins (1996) conducted a meta-analysis of 32 articles purporting to measure variously 173 dimensions of quality of life (invoking 351 labels) and found that the seven COMQoL dimensions incorporated 83% of the dimensions reported. Haggerty et al. (2001) review 22 prominent QoL indexes and conclude that the seven domains posited by Cummins currently provide the most useful standardized taxonomy for discussing QoL domains.

This chapter uses (with slight modifications) these 7 QoL domains—Material Well-being/Standard of Living, Productivity/Achieving in Life, Emotional Well-being/Resiliency, Health, Community, Relationships/Intimacy, Personal Safety/Future Security—as an heuristic framework to organize an overview of research (primarily in the fields of economics, psychology, and sociology) conducted since 1990 on the relationship between education and quality of life.[4] It should be noted that while we have in several sections drawn attention to the importance of comparison across national contexts, the preponderance of research considered here is focused on the United States. We will first briefly mention education as an indicator of quality of life (output or outcome), and then we will offer a more extensive review of evidence on education as a cause (throughput) of quality of life.

---

[2] See Sirgy et al. (2006) for an overview and progress report of QoL research across several prominent fields of inquiry.

[3] The ComQoL was abandoned in 2001 due to persistent problems with the instrument (see Cummins 2002). Cummins and associates subsequently established the International Wellbeing Group that is developing a new quality of life measurement, the Personal Wellbeing Index (International Wellbeing Group 2006). In the PWI, the original ComQoL domains have been modified slightly and an eighth added. Thus, the PWI quality of life domains

are standard of living, health, achieving in life, relationships, safety, community-connectedness, future security, and spirituality/religion. While the PWI itself is intended only to measure subjective satisfaction within these domains, one of the criteria for domain selection was commensurability with objective measurement (or at least the possibility of objective measurement when suitable indicators are established) of each domain as well (International Wellbeing Group 2006).

[4] The literature review was conducted using the following databases: Education: A SAGE Full-text Collection, Psychology: A SAGE Full-text Collection, Sociology: A SAGE Full-text Collection, ERIC, CSA Sociological Abstracts, EconLit, and PsychINFO. In addition to quality of life, other potentially equivalent keywords used in the search included wellbeing, wellness, standard of living, happiness, subjective wellbeing, life satisfaction, benefits.

Education as Quality of Life Indicator

Extending from the belief in education as integral to life chances is the assumption that educational indicators (e.g., enrolment rates, average scores on standardized achievement tests) are also social indicators or markers of the distribution of living conditions within a society. Social indicators are statistical tools useful to policymakers for monitoring various aspects of social systems and for guiding the implementation and evaluation of policies directed at improving and maintaining quality of life (Ferris 1988; Land 2000). Numerous indexes of quality of life or well-being include education as an indicator, for example, the Human Development Index (UNHDP 2003), Quality of Life (Diener 1995), and Index of Social Progress (Estes 1997) each incorporate some measure of educational participation and literacy rates. Other prominent examples of QoL measures that variously incorporate education indicators include Johnston's (1988) QoL Index, the International Living Index (see Haggerty et al. 2001), Miringoff's Index of Social Health (Miringoff et al. 1996, Miringoff and Miringoff 1999), Michalos' (1980–82) North American Social Report, Netherland's Living Conditions Index (Boelhouwer and Stoop 1999), and the Swedish ULF system (Haggerty et al. 2001). The rest of this chapter will focus on education not as a macro-level indicator of quality of life but rather as a primary factor affecting and affected by individuals' quality of life, both directly and indirectly.

Education Effects by Quality of Life Domain

Achieving in Life

Level of educational attainment itself is an indicator of achievement in that particular levels of educational credentials are associated with particular levels of educational attainment or performance. In the labor market, individual academic credentials signify to employers a particular history of achievement or performance by their holder and by extension, the future performance potential of that individual as an employee. More specific vocational credentials may signify that an individual is formally qualified (i.e., has completed the requisite training) for a particular job.

It follows that educational achievement is crucial to occupational status attainment as well. Hauser et al. (2000: 197) analyzed several national survey datasets from the USA and concluded that the net effect of education on occupational status (controlling for mother's and father's education levels, family head's occupational status, and several other relevant social background variables) is much greater for high school and postsecondary education than for sub-high school levels of education. Similarly, using longitudinal data from the Wisconsin Longitudinal Survey, they document a substantial and enduring positive effect for post-high school education on occupational status over the lifespan, adjusting for social background, ability, and various socialpsychological variables (Hauser, et al. 2000: 225).[5]

Pascarella and Terenzini (2005) identify several net effects of higher education on labor market success. With regard to occupational status, they find that a bachelor's degree provides a substantial advantage over a high school diploma. An associate (i.e., 2-year) degree provides a moderate status advantage, while lesser amounts of postsecondary education or sub-baccalaureate credentials, such as vocational diplomas, provide a modest advantage. In terms of labor force attachment, their gathered evidence generally indicates a positive association between amount of postsecondary education and workforce participation and, conversely, a negative association between amount of postsecondary education and likelihood of unemployment. As well, workers with postsecondary education are more likely to rise to supervisory roles (Ross and Reskin 1992; Bound et al. 1995; Krahn 2004).

Intergenerational Effects

In all OECD countries, educational achievement is strongly linked to the occupations, education, and economic status of students' parents, although the magnitude of the relationship differs across counties (UNICEF 2002). There is a well-documented positive relationship between parental education and child education level and cognitive development (Wolfe and Haveman 2001). Conversely, poor education is associated with a

---

[5] Hauser and Sewell have developed a socialpsychological model to account for impact of social background and education on occupational status (Hauser et al. 2000: 209–210; Sewell and Hauser 1992a; b).

number of detrimental intergenerational consequences (Haveman and Wolfe 1994, 1995; Maynard and McGrath 1997: 127). Wolfe and Haveman (2001) observe that there are two paths of influence generally identified in the literature, a direct path (via better choices and investments by parents) and an indirect path (contextual effects—such as better quality human and social capital—of the neighborhoods in which children are raised). They review a number of studies and conclude there seems to be a strong relationship between number of years of parental schooling and several important outcomes for their offspring such as school performance, teenaged childbearing, health, and criminal behavior. As well, Wolfe and Haveman (2001; Ginther et al. 2000) identify a "persistent" (although not unanimous) pattern of findings linking neighborhood contextual variables with offspring outcomes such as schooling, teenaged childbearing, and criminal activity.

Parental postsecondary attendance has a net positive effect on the high school math and science scores of a child. The effect seems to be largely accounted for by the relatively learning-enriched or intellectually stimulating home environment ("learning capital") provided by more educated parents (Pascarella and Terenzini 2005: 590; Feinstein et al. 2004). Educated parents are not only more likely to cultivate the disposition and the capacity to learn but are also more apt to ingrain an appreciation and enjoyment of learning along higher achievement expectations (Krahn 2004). Reared in more cognitively enriching home environments from an early age (UNICEF 2002), children from socioeconomically advantaged backgrounds enter formal schooling with a greater "readiness to learn." Conversely, Miech et al. (2001) found that children from lower SES backgrounds are more likely to enter the education system with lower levels of self-regulation[6] which is associated negatively with school adjustment outcomes—even when family background is controlled for. Haas (2006) found that socioeconomic disadvantage is associated with poorer childhood health, which, in turn, has significant negative effects on educational attainment and adult socioeconomic status (occupational earnings, wealth) over the life course.

More educated parents are also more likely to settle in neighborhoods where not only are there more stimulating and supportive public resources, but where their children interact—in school and out—with peers primed in similarly enriched home environments and frequently exposed to high-achieving adult role models (Feinstein et al. 2004). There is also some evidence that student's performance is affected by peer grouping, with students benefiting from immersion in context of high performing peers and high expectations (Davies 1999; Ho and Willms 1996; Frempong and Willms 2002; Feinstein et al. 2004).

Furthermore, the early educational advantage tends to persist at successive educational levels (Kerckhoff and Glennie 1999). Students whose parents attended postsecondary institutions are more likely to pursue postsecondary education themselves, more likely to attain a first degree, and are more likely to continue on to graduate or professional school. For instance, students whose parents attended a postsecondary educational institution are twice as likely to complete a bachelor's degree as first generation students (those whose parents did not attend). While students whose parents hold bachelor degrees are five times as likely as first generation students to also earn one (Pascarella and Terenzini 2005). The children of university-educated parents are also much more likely to enter into managerial or professional occupations (Krahn 2004).

Material Well-Being/Standard of Living

Space limitations prevent a comprehensive treatment of the socioeconomic returns to education literature, so we will content ourselves with touching on some of the basic findings. Educational attainment directly effects occupational status (one's initial level of entry and subsequent stability of attachment to the labor market), and both contribute to determining how much one earns (Tachibanaki 1997). OECD data on employment and unemployment rates by level of education generally demonstrate this, as seen in Tables 12.1 and 12.2. On average across OECD countries, the probability of unemployment decreases while the probability of employment increases with higher levels of education. In terms of earnings premiums for higher levels of education, Table 12.3 shows that, on average, across OECD countries, those with less than upper secondary

---

[6] "Specifically, self-regulation refers to processes, such as the tendency to maintain attention on a task and to suppress inappropriate behavior under instructions" (Miech et al. 2001: 103).

Table 12.1 Trends in unemployment rates by educational attainment (1991–2004)

Number of 25- to 64-year-olds in unemployment as a percentage of the labor force aged 25–64, by level of educational attainment[a]

		1995	1998	2000	2001	2002	2003	2004
OECD average	Below upper secondary	10.8	9.5	9.1	8.9	9.4	10.2	10.4
	Upper secondary and postsecondary non-tertiary	7.3	6.4	5.8	5.6	5.9	6.2	6.2
	Tertiary education	4.6	4.1	3.6	3.3	3.8	4.0	3.9

Source: Table A8.4a in OECD (2006)
[a]International Standard Classification of Education (ISCED), see Appendix for definitions of educational levels

Table 12.2 Trends in employment rates by educational attainment (1991–2004)

Number of 25- to 64-year-olds in employment as a percentage of the population aged 25–64 by level of educational attainment

		1995	1998	2000	2001	2002	2003	2004
OECD average	Below upper secondary	57	57	57	57	57	56	56
	Upper secondary and postsecondary non-tertiary	73	75	75	75	75	74	74
	Tertiary education	84	85	85	85	84	83	84

Source: Table A8.3a in OECD (2006).

Table 12.3 Relative earnings of the population with income from employment

By level of educational attainment and gender for 25- to 64-year-olds and 30- to 44-year-olds (upper secondary education = 100)

		Below upper secondary education	Postsecondary non-tertiary education	Tertiary-type B education	Tertiary-type A and advanced research programs	All tertiary education
Australia	2001	77	NA	106	148	133
Belgium	2002	91	NA	114	152	132
Canada	2001	79	105	115	177	143
Czech Rep.	1999	68	NA	151	180	179
Denmark	2001	87	118	114	127	125
Finland	2001	95	NA	121	181	150
France	2002	84	NA	125	167	150
Germany	2002	78	116	120	161	146
Hungary	2001	77	131	164	210	210
Ireland	2000	87	82	124	163	149
Italy	2000	78	NA	NA	138	138
Korea	1998	78	NA	106	147	135
Netherlands	1997	85	121	139	144	144
New Zealand	2001	74	NA	NA	133	133
Norway	2002	85	125	155	135	137
Portugal	1999	62	NA	141	192	178
Spain	2001	78	NA	95	141	129
Sweden	2001	89	127	110	148	135
Switzerland	2003	76	112	141	168	158
UK	2001	67	NA	128	174	159
USA	2002	71	120	118	195	186
Average		79	116	126	161	150

NA not applicable or data not available
Source: Table A11.1a in OECD (2006)

education earn 21% less than individuals with upper secondary education (i.e., high school diploma); individuals with postsecondary but non-tertiary education earn 16% more. Individuals with type B tertiary education (i.e., technical/vocational training) earn 26% more than those with upper secondary education while those with type A tertiary education (usually university) enjoy the greatest advantage of all, earning 61% more. The table also indicates that the steepness of this educational-level earnings gradient varies substantially across countries.

Card (1998) conducted an extensive review of the economic literature pertaining to the impact of education on earnings and concluded that "A unifying theme in much of this work is that the return to education is not a single parameter in the population, but rather a random variable that may vary with other characteristics of individuals, such as family background, ability, or level of schooling" (Card 1998: 2). Thus, while the weight of evidence points toward a causal link, the relationship is far from straightforward as the effect of education on earnings is variously conditioned by a host of other variables. Yet as complicated as the picture can become, as Soloman and Fagano (1997: 826) aptly summarize, "everything else being equal, those with more and better education seem to earn more."

Consistent with this, Pascarella and Terenzini (2005) identify an income premium related to higher educational attainment. Using data from representative nationwide samples, Pascarella and Terenzini estimate the general premium for a bachelor's degree (compared to a high school diploma) in the USA to be about 37% for men and about 39% for women. They estimate the hourly wage premium to be about 28% for men and about 35% for women.

Pascarella and Terenzini (2005) also find evidence of a credentialing effect. The term credentialing effect[7] is used to denote the earnings advantage that accrues to those who complete a degree compared to others who have the same amount of credits or courses but no degree. Pascarella and Terenzini estimate that men with a bachelor's degree earn, on average, about 15% more than men with 4 years of university credit but no

degree. For women, they estimate the average advantage at about 12%. The average earnings advantage for men who complete a 2-year associate degree is 9% over men with 2 years of postsecondary course credit but no degree. For women, the estimated average advantage is about 11%. Heckman et al. (1996) findings suggest the credentialing effect represents only a small proportion of the relationship between educational attainment and earnings. Their results indicate a statistically significant credentialing effect, but they also found an enduring net return to years of schooling.

Another important source of evidence regarding the effects on education on earnings comes from longitudinal studies. Grubb (1993) analyzed data from the 1972 National Longitudinal Survey (NLS) in the USA and found an earnings advantage related to higher education (even after correcting for factors such as socioeconomic status, race, ability, work experience, and access to on-the-job training). For males, about one half of the earnings advantage offered by obtaining a 4-year bachelor degree (compared to just high school completion) is due to the additional schooling itself; for females, extra schooling accounts for about a third of the advantage. He found that while community college (2-year) degrees offer a return, it is less than for 4-year degrees and is due mostly to increased access to jobs that offer greater opportunity for on-the-job training rather than the additional schooling per se.

Kane and Rouse (1995) also utilize the 1972 NLS data to estimate the annual returns (% increase in income) to community college and 4-year university degrees to be 7% and 28% respectively for men and 26% and 39% for women. They also find evidence of returns for those who completed some course credits but not a degree, the rate of return per completed credit was higher for university courses than community college ones, and higher for women than men. Kane and Rouse also analyzed data from a different survey, the National Longitudinal Survey of Youth (NLSY), and found somewhat different results in that male college and university dropouts held an earnings advantage over their high school graduate counterparts while female dropouts did not.

Murname et al. (1995) found that the net wage gap between university graduates and high school graduates increases over the career span. Arias and McMahon

---

[7] Also called the "sheepskin effect" (Card 1998: 7).

(1997) used cross-sectional earnings data (1967–1995) from the Current Population Survey (CPS) to estimate "dynamic rates of return." Their findings indicate that the earnings premium for completing a university degree is increasing relative to the rate of return for only partially completing a degree (i.e., earning some credits). The cumulative nature of this economic gap is evident in Land and Russell's (1996) finding (using 7 years of panel data from the Survey of Income and Program Participation) that households with a highly educated head have more wealth (net assets) than households with a poorly educated head.

Two important "third" variables to be considered when examining the education-income relationship are family background and ability. First, individuals with higher education tend to have parents with higher education as well. It might be that the income advantage results from family background (for instance, from having a parent with connections). Second, it can be argued that those who attain higher levels of education do so because they have greater ability and that those individuals would earn higher wages even without higher schooling. In short, it might actually be underlying ability—not education—that is responsible for higher income.

Intrafamily comparisons provide an opportunity to control for family background effects on earnings.[8] For example, Ashenfelter and Zimmerman (1997) estimated the relationship of educational attainment differences to income differences between fathers and sons. They found that a 1-year difference in educational attainment resulted in a 5-percent difference in wage rates. Altonji and Dunn (1996) looked at siblings and found that an additional year of schooling translated into a 3.7-percent increase in earnings among brothers and a 6.3-percent increase among sisters.

Identical twin studies are a useful method for isolating the effect of schooling on earnings from the effects of both family background and ability differentials. The rationale behind such studies is that studying genetically identical individuals raised in the same family provides increased control (sometimes referred to as a "natural experiment") over variance due to disparities in social background and ability. Hence, "contrasts of the wage differences of identical twins with their education differences may provide a particularly useful way to isolate the causal effect of schooling on earnings" (Ashenfelter and Rouse 1998: 281). If there are earnings differences between identical twins with differing levels of education, the difference is presumed not to be due to genetically determined ability, and we can be more confident that schooling does indeed affect earnings over and above any contribution by family background or ability. Ashenfelter and Rouse (1998) estimate an earnings advantage of about 8% per extra year of schooling for the more educated twin (adjusted upward to 9.9% when accounting for family background and measurement error in the self-reported education variable). Similarly, Miller et al. (1995) found an adjusted income (log of annual earnings) advantage of 4.5% per extra year of schooling among another sample of twins.

Although the above discussion of returns to education has focused almost exclusively on findings in the American context, there is evidence from other countries as well—for examples, see Asplund and Pereira (1999) for a review of European evidence, see Johnes (1993) for evidence from developing countries, see Blundell et al. (2000) and Chevalier et al. (2002) for UK evidence. But cross-national comparison also adds to the complexity of the emerging picture since the transition from school to work is not uniform across nations. For example, Sullivan and Smeeding (1997) utilize Luxembourg Income study (LIS) data (1989–1994) to compare the educational attainment-income gradient across eight nations. They conclude that "among advanced economies there is no obvious relationship between the degree of earnings inequality and the percentage of the labor force attaining higher levels of education. Countries differ substantially both in the way in which they organize their educational systems and the way in which they integrate the educational system with the labor market" (p. 513). Thus, we can add institutional features of the linkages between national education systems and labor markets to the list of important variables that condition the education-earnings relationship.

Similarly, Kerckhoff (2000, 2001) concludes that various institutional features of education systems determine their "capacity to structure" students' transition into the workforce. Müller and Shavit (1998), for example, analyze data and case studies from 13

---

[8] The outcome variable in the monetary return to education is typically the average log hourly wage.

developed countries in an effort to examine the importance of three institutional characteristics of national education systems—vocational specificity of credentials, standardization of credentials, and degree of stratification within the education system. Educational systems vary in terms of the extent to which they focus on specialist versus generalist education credentials. Some systems ("qualificational") are characterized by a high degree of specialized vocational training, while others ("organizational") offer a more generalized (academic) education aimed at providing a basic set of skills that are widely transferable across vocational settings, to be fine-tuned by on the job learning. Educational systems also vary in terms of degree of formal stratification and standardization. For instance, the German system is a qualificational one that is highly stratified in that it sorts students from early on into differing educational trajectories leading either to an academic track or a vocational track in which specialized training is linked to particular vocations. The German credential system is also characterized by a high degree of standardization of credentials. Employers are more involved in determining and sanctioning the skill requirements of a particular credential, with the result that a specific credential from different schools has uniform meaning. The USA, on the other hand, is an organizational system where credentials tend to be more generic, formal sorting begins later, and credentials are much less uniform in their value and meaning. In the USA, a credential is typically not considered specialized preparation for a particular job (although there are exceptions such as professional schools or vocational training programs) but rather a broad indication (a signal) of the ability and potential of that individual. The process of matching skills to job requirements is much more "a trial-and-error process" in North America (Heinz 1999).

Müller and Shavit (1998) found that while there were some significant differences among the 13 countries studied, there were also some important commonalities such as educational credentials are positively linked with occupational prestige; the marginal returns to postsecondary education are greater than for lower level education; educational attainment is an important determinant of labor force participation; and educational attainment (particularly postsecondary) is associated with lower risk of unemployment. One of the most notable differences between countries concerned is the magnitude of the effects of credentials on occupational outcomes, with some countries exhibiting a more rigid credential contingent occupational hierarchy than others.

Conventional human capital theory holds that it is the skill-imparting, productivity-enhancing aspects of education that lead to the earnings advantage enjoyed by the more educated. But some scholars argue that there is more to the equation, making the case for the importance of the socialization aspects of schooling in the determination of labor market success as well (Bowles and et al. 2001a, b; Farkas 1996; Heckman 2000; Rosenbaum 2001). Bowles and Gintis (2000) conducted a meta-analysis of 25 studies that looked at the schooling-earnings connection and found that cognitive skills were only part of the equation; formal education imparts not only skills but also instills the attitudes and habits valued by employers. They call these qualities (e.g., trustworthiness, identification with company or management goals, diligence, future-orientation, strong sense of self-efficacy) "incentive-enhancing preferences."

Thus, it may be that those individuals who succeed in higher education (which rewards many similar preferences or habits of conduct) may be more prepared to succeed within the similar incentive structure of a demanding high performance (and hence higher paying) workplace. A higher level of education is associated with enhanced "psychological capital," that is, the motivational and attitudinal orientation—particularly high self-esteem and internal locus of control—likely to lead to higher wage employment (Goldsmith et al. 1997). These habits, skills, and styles associated with school and occupational success are also referred to by some analysts as "cultural capital" (e.g., Farkas 1996, 2003; Lareau 2001; Lareau and Weininger 2003).

Further evidence for the importance of such non-cognitive skills (or "soft skills"[9]) in the labor market comes from studies by Heckman and colleagues (Cameron and Heckman 1993; Heckman and Rubinstein 2001) which reveal that while GED (Graduate Education Development) certificate holders exhibit substantially superior cognitive skills than other high school dropouts, they do not experience a

---

[9] See also Duncan and Dunifon (1998).

corresponding earnings advantage. Part of the reason appears to be related to behavioral issues such as delinquency and crime. Thus, the authors suggest that the GED sends a "mixed signal" in the job market—that the individual has the cognitive capacity to complete high school but may be lacking other attitudinal and behavioral qualities that are valued by the employer.

Emotional Well-Being

There is an abundance of evidence pointing to a positive correlation between education and psychological health and well-being. Educational achievement is associated directly with increased self-esteem and indirectly via effect of earnings. Education is associated with an increased sense of self-efficacy, and self-efficacy is associated with numerous physical and mental benefits (see Ross and Van Willigen 1997). "Emotional resilience" or the ability to cope with adversity and stress is related to self-efficacy and self-esteem both of which can be enhanced through education and successful learning (Hammond 2004). Schooling can also help foster the acquisition of adaptive skill sets—such as problem-solving skills and communication skills—that contribute to resilience (Howard et al. 1999). There is evidence that undesirable events and adverse experiences have greater negative emotional repercussions for lower SES individuals compared to those with higher SES (e.g., McLeod and Kessler 1990). Ranchor et al. (1996) found an association between SES, especially education level and significant variation in coping styles and resources, with lower SES individuals being disadvantaged along several psychosocial dimensions (negative self-esteem, social desirability, hostility, social support).

de Ridder (1995: 313) found that level of educational attainment influenced beliefs related to SES differences in vulnerability to psychological distress. She defined beliefs as "lay theories" or "cultural models" held by the individual that are shaped by their social group and social position, and which "reflect the generalized experiences about the meaning of stressful events, their impact on health, and their controllability." Similarly, a previous interview study ($n = 10$) conducted by de Ridder (cited in de Ridder 1995: 322) found that "lower educated participants were more easily agitated by daily hassles, thought them very unpleasant and disruptive, and felt they had no control," compared to more highly educated participants who "…limited their definition of stress to severe problems for which no solution was available; daily hassles were considered part of their normal routine." As well, more educated respondents "thought of stress more positively: although they agreed that stress was potentially harmful in specific situations, in many cases, they also considered it a challenge, as they felt able to control or solve the situation."

Many studies have found the effects of education on psychological health are mediated by work conditions (e.g., Lennon 1994; Link et al. 1993). Individuals with higher education are more likely to be involved in work with greater intrinsic and extrinsic rewards. For example, more educated individuals are less likely to be involved in alienating repetitive labor and more likely to be involved in work that permits greater autonomy (developing and reinforcing feelings of self-efficacy), creativity, more novelty and opportunity for continued learning and personal growth (Mirowsky and Ross 2003, 2005; Ross and Wu 1995; Schieman 2002), and greater social support which enhances resilience to psychological distress, depression, and anxiety (Ross and Van Willigen 1997).

Although people who are college educated rate higher on a wide range of quality of life indicators (e.g., income, self-efficacy, social support network, mortality risk, perceived health status, time spent in developmentally enriching activities with children), they do not consistently express a higher degree of satisfaction with their lives (Ross and Van Willigen 1997; Pascarella and Terenzini 2005). It seems that with increased educational attainment and socioeconomic status come higher expectations, people's sense of life satisfaction is affected by their rising frame of reference and the tendency to recalibrate expectations upward at each level of achievement and acquisition. Education may also open one's eyes to a wider range of possibilities as well as raising the standards by which one evaluates satisfaction in various domains of life. As well, people tend to compare their circumstances not with those below them but rather with their status peers and those above them. There are several different accounts of the relative nature of satisfaction such as congruity theory (Wilson et al. 1973), multiple discrepancies theory (Michalos 1985, 2008), and judgment theory (Meadow et al. 1992).

On the other hand, there is some affirmative evidence regarding the effects of education on reported happiness. Blanchflower and Oswald (2001) looked at multiyear cross-sectional data from the USA (GSS) and Great Britain (Eurobarometer Survey) and found that educational attainment is associated positively with happiness even when family income is controlled. There is also some indication that education may be indirectly related to life satisfaction in later adulthood. Fernandez-Ballesteros (2001: 27) found that more educated individuals with higher incomes report higher levels of participation in physical, cultural, and social activities which are positively associated with life satisfaction.

Gerdtham and Johannesson (2001) also found that reported happiness increased with education and income, as well as with self-rated health status.[10] Meeks and Murrell (2001) suggest that the lifelong health advantage associated with educational attainment is mediated by "trait negative affect." That is, higher educational attainment is inversely associated with levels of enduring negative effect; low negative affect is, in turn, associated with better health and greater life satisfaction in older adults—or what the authors term "successful aging." Successful aging is contingent on a "life history of successful adaptation" which results from the interplay of inherited and learned psychological attributes, degree of life adversity, and available resources. Educational attainment is positively related to successful adaptation along each of these dimensions (e.g., high intelligence, high level of aspiration and motivation, enhanced socioeconomic opportunities and outcomes).

Health

The positive association between education and health is well documented. For example, Bound et al. (1995) found that more educated men were generally less likely to report having health problems such as severe chronic pain, hearing and vision problems, arthritis or functional limitations on daily activities, while individuals who attended or graduated college have a lower risk profile for cancer and coronary heart disease (Pascarella and Terenzini 2005). There is also consid-

erable evidence to suggest that such education-related health disparities grow across the lifespan (Mirowsky and Ross 2003; O'Rand 2001; Prus 2004; Ross and Wu 1995, 1996). Mirowsky and Ross (2005: 27) observe that the cumulative health-related consequences of education are evident at various levels, "… from the socioeconomic (employment, job quality, earnings, income, and wealth) and behavioral (habits such as smoking or exercising, beliefs such as perceived control over one's own life, personal relationships) to the physiological (blood pressure, cholesterol levels, aerobic capacity), anatomical (body fat, joint deterioration, arterial fatty plaque) and perhaps intracellular (insulin resistance, free radical damage)." They also note that in addition to permeating most aspects of life, many of these consequences of educational attainment are reciprocal in nature, mutually conditioning and compounding the effects of one another, good and bad, such that disparities grow over time.

Mirowsky and Ross (2003) found evidence of substantial socioeconomic disparities in health which increase across the lifespan. Modest education-contingent socioeconomic disparities upon initial entrance into the workforce compound over time, as do related health disparities. Specifically, they found that persons with college degrees have lower levels of impairment across the lifespan; the increase in impairment with aging was steeper for those with less than high school compared to those with college degrees, thus resulting in an increasing impairment gap across the lifespan. Although the gap continues to grow after age 65, the rate of divergence attenuates (see also Ross and Wu 1996). Prus (2004) found that the education-contingent gap in both subjective health and functional health grew across the adult life course up until age 79 (survey data was aged capped at age 79).

Higher education typically leads to occupations that involve less health risk and provide greater financial capacity to purchase better housing, nutrition, and health care, all of which are directly linked with health status (Roberge et al. 1995). Indirect psychosocial effects emanate from one's position in the socioeconomic structure (sense of personal agency, coping skills, social support) and from lifestyle preferences and practices (recreational activities, diet, smoking, access to health care information, and services). Even so, there is evidence that educational attainment is predictive of health even when income is controlled for. For example, Meeks and Murrell (2001) found that

---

[10] There is some evidence for the positive effects of happiness on health (Veenhoven 2008).

education accounts for variation in health (and life satisfaction) above and beyond that predicted by income, but the reverse does not hold for income net of education.

Grossman and Kaestner (1997) review a number of American studies that point to years of formal education as the most important socioeconomic correlate of good health, more important than either occupation or income (both of which are partially determined by education). This relationship holds across a number of health indicators, including mortality rates, morbidity rates, self-rated health status, and physiological measures, regardless of whether analyzed at the group or individual level. Using structural equation modeling and the National Health Interview Survey, Lynch (2006) found that only about 30% of the effect of education on self-rated health is accounted for by income, but that this indirect effect of education through income is increasing across cohorts.

As with emotional well-being, many of the effects of education on physical health are mediated by workplace conditions. Less educated have more physically demanding jobs with increased risk of negative physical consequences (although less than in the past). In addition, some of the same workplace conditions that affect psychological health also impact physical health. For example, the fact that more educated individuals are less likely to be involved in alienating repetitive labor and more likely to be involved in work that develops and reinforces feelings of self-efficacy or personal control (Mirowsky and Ross 2003, 2005; Ross and Wu 1995; Ross and Van Willigen 1997). A greater sense of self-efficacy, or the belief in one's ability to initiate action and effect outcomes, is also associated with better health outcomes. There is also some evidence that the salutary effects associated with the more autonomous, less routinized employment afforded by higher educational attainment may actually be even greater for women than men. Due to their traditionally disadvantaged status within society, women may reap amplified health benefits from educationally augmenting their socioeconomic position (Reynolds and Ross 1998; Schieman 2002).

Many of the positive effects of education on health stem from the increased likelihood of adopting or initiating proactive health measures, which prevents and/ or forestalls many ailments. If individuals believe they have some control over the conditions of their life, including their health, they are more likely to participate in health-promoting lifestyles and activities. Education increases the capacity to produce healthy outcomes via "learned effectiveness," education imparts analytical and problem-solving skills that transfer to various aspects of life including health maintenance (Mirowsky and Ross 2005). For instance, education is associated with increased likelihood of adaptive response in the wake of health crisis such as quitting smoking after a heart attack (Wray et al. 1998).

More educated individuals live healthier lifestyles including moderation in consumption and regular exercise (Ross and Wu 1995; Mirowsky and Ross 1999) due to access to better information for health management, greater proficiency at integrating information into lifestyle decisions, greater resources to facilitate health-promoting activities (e.g., money to buy equipment, gear, memberships, more flexible schedule to fit exercise in), and to procure health professional assistance when needed. For example, college graduates spend more time on fitness activities than those with lower educational attainment (Robinson and Godbey 1997). Similarly, Kenkel (1991) found an education-contingent difference in exercise time of about 17 min per day per extra year of schooling.

In general, the more educated are less likely to smoke (Bound et al. 1995; Sander 1995b; Zhu et al. 1996; Kenkel 1991). If they do smoke, the more educated tend to smoke less per day, with each additional year of schooling reducing average daily cigarette intake by 1.6 for men and 1.1 for women (Kenkel 1991). The more educated are also more likely to quit smoking than those with less education (Sander 1995a; Zhu et al. 1996). Those with more education are also less likely to be heavy drinkers than their less educated counterparts (Kenkel 1991).

Parental education is also associated with various child and adolescent health outcomes. Several studies by Edwards, Shakotko, and Grossman (cited in Grossman and Kaestner 1997: 94) find that parental educational attainment, particularly mother's, has positive and statistically significant effects on a number of health indicators in childhood and adolescence. For example, children and adolescents of better educated mothers have better oral health and less likelihood of obesity or anemia than those of less well-educated mothers.

Further to the body of research on the relationship between education and health, there are also studies looking at the relationship between education and longevity. Numerous studies have found a positive relationship between education and life expectancy (e.g., Rogot et al. 1992; Crimmins and Saito 2001). Connected to this is a relationship between education and decreased morbidity (Crimmins and Saito 2001). Individuals with less health problems over the lifespan enter their later years in better health and tend to live longer. As cohorts age, education's association with health and longevity grows stronger. Individuals with higher socioeconomic status experience a "compression of morbidity" into a short period in the final years of life, whereas lower status individuals are more likely to start experiencing health problems from middle age onward (Mirowsky and Ross 2005: Prus 2004). Educational attainment is negatively related to mortality across the lifespan (Guralnik et al. 1993; Kaplan and Keil 1993). There is a growing socioeconomic disparity in mortality rates (Lauderdale 2001; Bartley et al. 1998). Manton et al. (1997) studied National Long Term Care Surveys in the USA from 1982 to 1991 and found that persons with 8 or more years of education had advantages in terms of level of functioning and longevity over those with less than 8 years of education. The longevity advantage at age 65 for educated women was 7 years and 2 years for men.

Explaining the relationship between education, health, and longevity. Ross and Wu (1995) contend that education affects health along three basic fronts: work and socioeconomic conditions (income security, nature of work, satisfaction with work, access to quality health care, etc.), socialpsychological resources (self-efficacy, social support network, etc.), lifestyle (exercise, diet, smoking, health monitoring, etc.). Mirowsky and Ross (2003, 2005) offer a more comprehensive cumulative advantage/disadvantage model to account for the positive effects of education on health. They suggest that the lifelong health advantage afforded by greater educational attainment is due to three interrelated processes: permeation, accumulation, and amplification. First, *the differential effects of education permeate most aspects of life* such as the conditions of one's work; rewards from work; interpersonal relationships; habits; economic capacity; social, psychological, and informational resources; security; sense of autonomy. For example, more educated individuals are less likely to be involved in work that involves repetitive task performance, or is physically demanding, and tend to have higher degree of autonomy. The more educated also tend to earn more and so are less likely to experience economic stress and more able to pur-

chase goods and services (e.g., food, heath care, housing) that produce good health. Second, *consequences accumulate over the lifespan.* For example, the health consequences of habits and lifestyles (diet, exercise, smoking) accumulate over the lifespan, both positive (e.g., lung capacity, muscle mass) and negative (e.g., excess body fat, fatty plaque in blood vessels, decreasing bone density). Third, *cumulative outcome differentials condition and amplify each other, with advantages concentrating in some individuals and disadvantages concentrating in others, such that disparities grow over the lifespan.* For example, over time regular exercise and a healthy diet produce beneficial accumulations (low body fat and high aerobic capacity), thereby reinforcing those healthy behaviors and the sense of control over one's health, while lack of exercise and poor diet produce harmful accumulations (high body fat and low aerobic capacity) which perpetuate those unhealthy behaviors (e.g., the more body fat one has, the more difficult physical activity becomes, not exercising results in increased fat and further aversion to exercise) and diminishes the sense of control over one's health and undermines further effort. Thus, to the degree that educational attainment is associated with increased sense of control over one's health (via successful engagement in health-promoting behaviors), the educationally advantaged are likely to enjoy corresponding health advantages.

The cumulative nature of socioeconomic health disparities is highlighted by Mirowsky and Ross's (2005) concept of "cascading structural amplification." It captures the "slippery slope" nature of socioeconomic health disadvantage, in which a sequence of circumstances unfolds leading the less educated down a path of mounting health problems: low education leads to poor income, economic hardships are rendered more difficult by inadequate coping skills (due to educational deficits), and economic hardships exacerbate health issues (do not live in neighborhood with recreational facilities, cannot afford healthy food or exercise gear/equipment or memberships, lack information about health-promoting behaviors or opportunities, no peer support, etc.).

Another suggested mechanism by which education effects health is *rate of time preference*, or one's time orientation. Adoption of a longer time horizon is assumed to be associated with health-promoting behavior. Just as the propensity to delay gratification is conducive to time (and monetary) investment in education (and hence greater educational attainment), it may also be related to inclination to invest time (and money) in health management (Fuchs 1982 in Grossman and Kaestner 1997). There is some suggestion that the education-time preference relationship is reciprocal; that is, more educated parents tend to instill a more future-oriented time preference in their children to begin with, and this preference is further reinforced by successful educational attainment (Leigh 1998). Either way, it may be that the majority of education's positive effect on health is a function of education's effect on time preference—individuals with a longer time horizon may be more willing to invest proactively in the maintenance of their health. Thus, to the degree that education alters time preference toward the future, it also improves health.

Mirowsky and Ross (2005) suggest that the more educated are more proficient at producing health outcomes due to generally enhanced analytical and problem-solving skills ("learned effectiveness") which they apply to health maintenance. Similarly, Grossman and Kaestner (1997) observe that the more educated tend to be "more efficient producers of health" than less educated individuals. This efficiency effect is twofold: "allocative efficiency" pertains to the augmentation of knowledge afforded by education—better educated individuals typically have access to greater amounts of health relevant knowledge and are more inclined to appreciate its import. "Productive efficiency" refers to the greater efficacy of the better educated in producing positive health outcomes than the poorly educated, given that both have the same information. More educated individuals have greater familiarity with the knowledge production process which may translate into greater trust in "expert" recommendations and greater likelihood of compliance. That is, more educated individuals may be more likely (and better equipped) to comprehend the relevance of expert recommendations and to be more effective in mitigating risk accordingly (Smith 1997).

It should also be noted that there is also research that suggests that the pattern of the relationship between education and health across the lifespan is not linear. For example, Lynch (2006) found that the relationship between education, income, and health varies across the lifespan and across cohorts and that the relationship between these variables peaks at different times. In his sample, the relationship between education and income peaked around age 81, the relationship between income and health peaked around age 56, and the total effect of education (including indirect effects through income) on health peaked around age 46. His results suggest that the cumulative health advantage associated with education grows into middle age and then tapers off into old age.

Community

Ross and Van Willigen (1997) found that the well-educated reported a higher level of social support. Further to this, there was a strong association between the non-alienated work typical of the well-educated and perceptions of social support. They suggest that the non-alienated work environments characterized by non-routine, autonomous, creative work and opportunities for personal growth and learning also foster supportive relationships among coworkers, colleagues, and bosses.

According to the 1987 GSS, individuals with higher levels of educational attainment report having membership in a greater variety of volunteer groups and participating in more organized activities (Smith 1995). Postsecondary graduates exhibit higher levels of involvement in civic and community groups. Pascarella and Terenzini (2005) report that, compared to high school graduates, individuals with a bachelor degree were 1.8 times more likely to participate regularly in political activities, 2.4 times as likely to be involved in community welfare groups, and 1.8 times as likely to be highly committed to community leadership. Such engagement with community causes and organizations may also foster introduction to influential social networks that are less accessible to the less educated.

Curtis et al. (2004) analyzed Canadian data from the World Values Survey and found individuals with higher levels of education reported greater involvement in public protest, in community interest groups, as well as in supporting social movements. Utilizing data from Statistics Canada's National Survey of Giving, Volunteering, and Participation, they also found that the more educated were more likely to report voting and participation in volunteer activities.

In recent years, the notion of social capital has been broadly deployed to describe various dimensions of "community." While human capital resides in individuals, social capital resides in relationships. There are two basic approaches to conceptualizing social capital (see

Portes 2000); one school sees social capital as a second order property of individuals embedded in social networks, while the other sees it as a collective property of communities and nations.[11] The following discussion of returns to social capital is conducted with reference to the former (more instrumental) understanding, the social networks (or social resources) approach. Burt (2000) pithily characterizes the basic notion of network social capital theory as "[b]etter connected people enjoy higher returns." Flap (1999: 7) describes social capital as "social networks and the resources of others an actor can call upon [which] can be considered a social resource…another means for that actor to improve or defend his conditions of living." There is considerable evidence that social capital, in the form of social resources, significantly affects status attainment (Lin 1999). Social resources are resources activated through one's direct and indirect contacts. The potential utility of such resources is related to one's position within particular social networks (i.e., status, connections, and influence). Not all networks are created equal: some networks (comprised predominantly of socioeconomically advantaged groups) are richer in social resources (more diverse, higher caliber connections) than others. Structural constraints and homophily (like affiliating with like) contribute to the maintenance of this network inequality, such that the level of social resources (and potential status outcomes) available to the individual is substantially impacted by one's social background (Lin 2000) and resulting social capital disparities tend to be cumulative in nature (Granovetter 1995). Some individuals and families are embedded in richer networks with greater access to information and opportunity, not only from their own social network, but via complimentary cross connections with other networks (Burt 2000). Lai et al. (1998) found evidence that occupational attainment (current job status) is significantly influenced by level of education but also by the social resources of contacts mobilized in the job search. The caliber of contacts (i.e., the richness of contact social resources) available to a person, in turn, derives from "positional advantages" related to family background (parental resources), education, and network resources.

Lin (2000: 484) observes that human capital and social capital can be seen as reciprocally related in that "[w]ell-connected parents and social ties can … enhance the opportunities for individuals to obtain better education, training, and skill and knowledge credentials. On the other hand, it is clear that human capital induces social capital. Better educated and better trained individuals tend to move in social circles and clubs rich in resources." One compelling question that then emerges from this insight—the convertibility of capital forms—concerns the relative importance of human versus social capital to status outcomes. For example, Boxman et al. (1991) found an inverse relationship between the two forms of capital, where the effect of human capital on income was strongest when social capital was low and weakest when social capital was high. Consistent with this, Flap and Boxman (1999) found that for top managers, social capital had a positive effect on income regardless of the level of human capital and that the effect of human capital diminished as the level of social capital increased. Flap and Boxman (2001) also found that social capital had a positive effect on income, prestige of job attained, and likelihood of informal job searching (i.e., those with greater social capital are more likely to attempt to invoke it via informal job searches). Taken together, these results suggest that level of human capital is most important to status attainment for those with lesser levels of social capital, but that its importance diminishes as one's level of social capital increases. Thus, while education may facilitate entrance to a socioeconomic trajectory, beyond a certain threshold, accumulated social capital (i.e., access to information and influential connections) carries greater weight and further advantage. Or put another way, returns to education may be limited without sufficient social capital.[12]

As previously discussed in the section on intergenerational effects of academic achievement, there is some evidence of "neighborhood effects" due to factors such as disparities in the quality of resources available

---

[11] Portes (1998, 2000) and others (e.g., Morrow 1999) argue that, increasingly, the application of the social capital as collective property approach is being uncritically stretched beyond the limits of its usefulness and as, a result, is become increasingly vague, all encompassing, and of dubious analytical value.

[12] Mouw (2003) contends that evidence for the positive effects of network social capital on labor market outcomes is—upon closer inspection—confounded and that while the utility of influential contacts is intuitively appealing, better evidence is still required to substantiate proponents' claims regarding social capital mechanisms.

to families and "collective socialization." Children in neighborhoods with less well-developed infrastructure (libraries, family resource centers, literacy and after school programs, cultural amenities like museums, and recreational facilities) may lag behind their peers from more affluent neighborhoods in terms of social and physical development and school-readiness (Brooks-Gunn et al. 1993, 1996; Neuman and Celano 2001). Brooks-Gunn et al. (1993) also find evidence consistent with the notion of "collective socialization" which highlights the importance of neighborhood adult role models and extra-familial monitoring or informal social control (Sampson 2001) to children's psychosocial development. Exposure to high-achieving adult role models has positive effects on student conduct, attitudes, and expectations regarding education and occupational options. Ainsworth (2002) reported that prevalence of high-status residents is strongly predictive of increased time spent on homework and higher math/reading test scores, results consistent with the collective socialization thesis.

Children's educational outcomes can also be impacted (above and beyond individual family background influences) by the makeup of the student population at their school (Strand 1997; Feinstein et al. 1999; Robertson and Symons 2003). Indeed, there is a substantial body of evidence that "the average socioeconomic status of a child's class or school has an effect on his or her outcomes, even after taking account of (individual-level) ability and socioeconomic status" (Willms 2001: 25). For example, Ho and Willms (1996), utilizing a large representative sample of US middle school students, found that both advantaged and disadvantaged students achievement in mathematics and reading improves when they attend schools with higher average socioeconomic status. Mayer (2002) found that increased economic segregation (the affluent concentrating in particular areas and the poor in others) in the USA increased the educational attainment gap (the gradient) between socioeconomically advantaged and disadvantaged students.[13] Thus, "economic segregation in one generation contributes to economic inequality in the next generation" (p. 167) via perpetuation of disparities in educational and occupational opportunities.

Ho and Willms (1996) also found that parental involvement in schooling (i.e., volunteering, attending parent teacher organization meetings) has a positive effect on student achievement, and parental involvement tends to be higher in high socioeconomic status schools (although they did not find significant family-level SES-contingent differences in extent of parental involvement). Furthermore, their results show that socioeconomic gradients (SES-contingent differences in achievement) tend to be shallower in schools with high parental involvement. A number of studies (e.g., Barnard 2004; Fan and Chen 2001; Feuerstein 2000; Jeynes 2003; Steinberg et al. 1992; McWayne et al. 2004) document the importance of parental involvement (variously measured) to academic achievement, and while Ho and Willms (1996) found no family-level SES differences in parental involvement, other studies (e.g., Lee and Bowen 2006) indicate a positive relationship between parental education and parental involvement. Hill et al. (2004) found that parental involvement by more educated parents tended to increase their children's level of academic aspiration, school behavior, and achievement, but that parental involvement by lower educated parents only raised academic aspirations without significantly improving school behavior or achievement.

Sampson and colleagues (Sampson et al. 1997, 1999), in an attempt to augment the generic social capital metaphor, posit the related, but more circumscribed, notion of "collective efficacy." They (Sampson et al. 1999: 635) conceive collective efficacy as "…a task-specific construct that relates to the shared expectations and mutual engagement by adults in the active support and social control of children." They argue that collective efficacy places more emphasis on the "agentic" dimensions of community social relations and—consonant with the social network "instrumental" approach to social capital—focuses on the purposeful mobilization of resources toward desired (child and youth) outcomes. In a study utilizing survey data from residents in 342 Chicago neighborhoods, Sampson et al. (1999) found neighborhood affluence to be positively related to collective efficacy, as well as to "reciprocated exchange" (the intensity of interfamily and adult involvement in childrearing), and "intergenerational closure" (extent to which adults and children in a neighborhood are linked to one another).

While Ainsworth (2002) found that neighborhood characteristics predicted educational outcomes almost

---

[13] Similar results emerged when she conducted the analysis at the level of census tracts and at the level of school districts.

Intimate Relationships

Marriage

Schooling has a positive influence on success in making choices involving marriage and family size by allowing better access to information for decision-making (Wolfe and Haveman 2001: 228). More educated individuals are more likely to be married, and marriage is negatively related to various forms of distress, although the effect of education on this is modest at best (Ross and Van Willigen 1997: 287).

Berrington (2001) found that enrollment in education was a strong inhibitor of marriage among young adults. Level of education is an especially important determinant of marital status for women. Women with less education tend to marry and have children earlier than more educated women. Higher educational attainment gives more educated women greater earning power which equals greater economic independence and greater freedom in deciding whether to marry or not. Accordingly, marriage and childbearing tend to occur later for more educated women. As well, women with little or no educational credentials are more likely to marry early than are men of similar educational standing. (Blackwell and Bynner 2002).

Marriage Dissolution

There is evidence of an educational effect on divorce, and this effect is stronger for women than for men. More educated women are generally less likely to divorce than women with lower levels of education (Tzeng 1992). Less educated women are more likely to marry and have children earlier, and early mar-

riage is related to higher likelihood of divorce (Blackwell and Bynner 2002: 9; also see Berrington and Diamond 1999). As well, women's level of educational attainment and employment status are important moderators of the consequences of divorce for children (Kiernan 1996). More educated women (particularly those employed in well-paying jobs before marital dissolution) tend to be better protected from economic hardship postseparation. (Bianchi et al. 1999).

Educational homogamy effects marital stability. Couples in which the wife has a higher level of educational attainment than the husband are about 28% more likely to divorce than couples where each member has the same level of education; when husbands have a higher level of education than their wives, couples are 20% more likely to divorce than couples with the same level of education (Tzeng 1992).

Education may enhance communication skills which protect against marriage breakdown. But in the case of divorce, education is also positively associated with ability to cope with divorce (Blackwell and Bynner 2002: 10).

Parenthood

Education is positively associated with delayed motherhood and negatively associated with fertility rate, especially among college educated women (Rindfuss et al. 1996). That is, less educated women are more likely have children earlier (Blackwell and Bynner 2002), while more educated women are more likely to delay motherhood (Heck et al. 1997; Ekert-Jaffé et al. 2002). The birth rate among American women over the age of 30 has increased in recent decades only among those with 4-year university degrees (Martin 2000). This finding is consistent with the notion that more educated women are waiting (perhaps to establish careers) before having children.

The increased opportunity cost for more educated higher earning women is an important factor in delayed childbearing. So is a shift in preference among more educated parents from quantity to quality, that is, toward greater intensity of investment in fewer children, with the expectation that "higher expenditures of time and money [will] raise the future productivity of the child in the workforce and in everyday life" (Greenwood 1997: 506).

Kieran (1997) identifies a number of benefits associated with delayed marriage and/or parenthood,

---

[14] Strong correlations for peer group are confounded by inadequate control for self-selection.

such as enhanced financial capacity to improve quality of housing, consumer goods and leisure activities and decreased likelihood of marital breakdown. As well, delayed childbearing also often affords greater opportunity for women to become established in their careers or employment situations which increases resilience to economic hardship in the case of marital dissolution.

Teens (especially girls) with lower academic performance are more likely to experience early parenthood and attendant social disadvantages (Kiernan 1997). Teen parents are more likely to drop out of high school, lack parenting skills, and live in poverty (Maynard and McGrath 1997). Children born to adolescent mothers are academically and behaviorally disadvantaged relative to children born to older mothers (Dahinten et al. 2007) and are more likely to become teen parents themselves (Maynard and McGrath 1997; Kiernan 1997).

Child Welfare

Numerous familial outcomes are associated with level of educational attainment, including poverty, out-of-wedlock childbearing, early parenthood, and child abuse and neglect. All these outcomes are less prevalent among high school graduates than among early school leavers (Maynard and McGrath 1997: 130). Wolfe and Haveman (2001: 230) review a number of studies and also conclude that there exists generally a strong relationship between number of years of parental schooling and several important outcomes for their offspring such as schooling, teenaged childbearing, health, and criminal behavior. Higher parental education is associated with ability to pay for better quality childcare and residence in communities with more extensive social service and educational resources, positive peer groups, and lower crime (Maynard and McGrath 1997: 133).

While many of the child welfare benefits of education cited by Maynard and McGrath appear to be mediated by the positive effect of more schooling on income, there are also parental education effects above and beyond the monetary advantage. Higher parental education is associated with greater access to knowledge about the developmental needs of children, greater propensity to seek out and implement new childcare information (Greenwood 1997), increased quality of parent-child interaction, and less negative and more positive parenting behaviors (Feinstein et al. 2004), greater probability of parental involvement with child's school, of reading to a child, and of helping with homework (Pascarella and Terenzini 2005).

Personal Safety/Future Security

As we have seen, educational disadvantage generally translates into socioeconomic disadvantage. Such disadvantaged persons are disproportionately exposed to various types of risk. They are more exposed to economic risks such as unemployment, job insecurity, and general economic hardship (Abbot et al. 2006; Furlong and Cartmel 1997; Perrons 2000); to environmental hazards such as pollutants and toxins, proximity to polluting industries, and insalubrious "ambient conditions" such as poor housing quality (Evans and Kantrowitz 2002; Lester et al. 2001; Liu 2001; Mohai and Bryant 1992); and are often less well equipped to deal with negative events or circumstances (e.g., lack of marketable credentials, insufficient financial management knowledge, inadequate financial resources for relocation, limited psychosocial coping skills).

Some aspects of the safety domain dovetail with the health domain in that socioeconomic disparities in safety are related to numerous disparities in health. As Evans and Kantrowitz (2002: 204) contend, much of the "…link between SES and health derives from multiple exposures to a plethora of suboptimal environmental conditions…The poor are most likely to be exposed not only to the worst air quality, the most noise, the lowest-quality housing and schools, etc., but of particular consequence, also to lower-quality environments on a wide array of multiple dimensions." For example, as noted before, higher educated individuals are also less likely to have physically demanding jobs which are associated with various negative effects on health (Bound et al. 1995). Cubbin and Smith (2002: 365)—after reviewing a number of studies examining the relationship between socioeconomic status and injury—conclude that "SES has a strong inverse association with the risk of both homicide and unintentional injuries in all ages; as individual or area SES decreases, the risk of homicide or unintentional injury increases." In a similar vein, Adler et al. (1994: 18) observe that "…components of SES, including income, education, and occupation, shape one's life course and are enmeshed in key domains of life, including (a) the physical environment in which one lives and works and associated exposure to pathogens, carcinogens, and other environmental hazards; (b) the social environment and associated vulnerability to interpersonal aggression and violence as well as degree of access to social resources and supports...."

More educated individuals are less likely to suffer the stress of economic hardship. The least qualified workers are the most vulnerable to unemployment during economic downturns (Gangl 2001). Moreover, those with higher educational attainment have greater "ability to benefit from disequilibria" (Bowles et al. 2001a). In simple terms, they are better positioned to take advantage of/profit from market trends and cycles (i.e., to extract rents) or, conversely, to protect themselves and their families from economic trends and cycles. Someone with a MBA is generally better positioned to repackage him/herself in a changing labor market (or migrate to a different market for new opportunities) than is a manual laborer with grade 10 education. Such market resilience may also be enhanced by a strong sense of agency/self-efficacy and a more future-oriented time preference, both characteristics that are associated with higher educational attainment. As well, there is some indication that even when income is low, education decreases the likelihood of economic hardship by improving household budget management (Mirowsky and Ross 1999). This difference may be related to the efficiency advantages ("learned effectiveness") apparent among the more educated in health maintenance (Grossman and Kaestner 1997; Gilleskie and Harrison 1998; Mirowsky and Ross 2005) and environmental risk-averting behavior (Smith 1997). The better educated are likely to have access to more relevant knowledge, to trust it, and, given equal information, to be more proficient at generating positive outcomes than those with less education. This learned effectiveness advantage may apply in financial management just as it does in health management.

There is also some indication of a negative relationship between education and crime (Tauchen et al. 1994; Lochner and Moretti 2004). Over two thirds of incarcerated men in the USA in 1993 had not graduated high school (Freeman 1996). The inhibitory effect of education on crime seems to be primarily explained in terms of increasing the cost opportunity—those with more education and higher wages are more risk averse—although there may also be effects related to missed learning as well as peer influence and lifestyle factors associated with non-completion of high school

(Lochner 2004). Consistent with this, several studies (e.g., Freeman 1996; Machin and Meghir 2000; Gould et al. 2002) have found negative relationships between wages and criminal activity, although the empirical relationship is not clear-cut (Lochner 2004).

Methodological Considerations

This chapter, although by no means exhaustive, has sampled a fairly diverse body of research from multiple disciplines intent on identifying various connections between education and an assortment of quality of life outcomes. These studies vary in the degree to which they attempt to account for threats to the validity of their findings. While an in-depth discussion of the strengths and weaknesses of each study is beyond the objectives of this chapter, in this section, we will briefly touch upon some prominent threats to validity that should be kept in mind when looking at returns to education research. The two most common sets of concerns pertain to (a) the spuriousness of reported educational effects due to inadequate consideration of antecedent or intervening "third" variables and (b) issues regarding the valid and reliable measurement of educational attainment.

"Third" Variables

In short, failure to adequately control for the influence of important third variables may lead to overestimation or underestimation of the effects of education on observed outcomes. That is, the more potentially confounding antecedent or intervening variables controlled for, the more confident one can be that the observed relationship is in fact valid and that the difference (or some significant portion thereof) observed in the outcome/dependent variable is due to the effect of the predictor/independent variable. In addition to level of educational attainment, there are a host of variables that might plausibly influence some of the quality of life outcomes in question. The most prominent factors are family background and ability as well as a number of variables pertaining to mental and physical health and psychological attributes (preferences) such as motivation, aspirations, and time orientation. Additionally, the benefits of education may transpire via both direct and indirect effects. For example, education has a substantial indirect effect on health through income and wealth. Studies vary in terms of how many and how well they control for these variables, but no study can incorporate them all. A notable shortcoming of many studies is that they do not partial income out when looking at the relationship between education and various quality of life outcomes. The basic idea behind the most common approach for estimating the influence of so-called third variables (alternative explanations) is to compare the estimates of the effect of educational attainment on a target outcome when a particular variable (or set of variables) is controlled for versus when it is not controlled for. The observed difference in educational effects provides an approximate indication of the influence on returns to education of the variable(s) in question. Practical limitations (e.g., most available datasets are cross sectional rather than longitudinal and/or are not likely to include measures of all plausible control variables) prevent any study from adequately considering all potentially confounding variables, so we are left to weigh the balance of complimentary and contradictory findings across a body of studies as best we can. We also, of course, need to exercise due caution in making causal connections due to the correlational nature of most of the returns to education research.

A classic example of the third variable issue is evident in the study of the education-income relationship. Two prominent third variables that must be considered are family background and ability. First, individuals with higher education tend to have parents with higher education as well. It could be that the income advantage results from family background factors (i.e., financial, cultural, and social capital advantages received from well-educated, affluent parents). Second, it can be argued that those who attain higher levels of education do so because they have greater ability and that those individuals would earn higher wages even without higher schooling. In short, it might actually be underlying ability—not education—that is responsible for higher income. In addition to statistically controlling for factors such as gender, race, and SES, sometimes preexisting groups can be incorporated into a study in order to increase control over outcome-relevant variance. For instance, intrafamily comparisons provide an opportunity to control for family background effects on earnings while identical twin studies are a useful (though impractical) method for isolating the effect of schooling on earnings from not only family

background variation but also variation in individual ability.

A related source of confounding variance in returns to education research is "selection bias." The alternative explanation offered by the selection hypothesis is that individuals from higher SES backgrounds, with higher ability, exhibiting a particular cluster of psychological attributes and robust health are more likely to attain (to be selected into) higher levels of education; thus, these factors account for part (some would argue most) of the effects of educational attainment. For example, there is some indication that the positive association between educational attainment and health is due not to the effects of education on health status but rather to the effects of health (particularly in the school years) on educational attainment: individuals with better health are more apt to persist in school and to reach higher levels of educational attainment (Grossman and Kaestner 1997). The basic question concerns the influence of selection versus social causation (i.e., education causes adult outcomes such as health status). Haas (2006) found that poorer childhood health was negatively associated with educational attainment and lifelong returns to education (adult occupational SES, earnings, and wealth), a finding consistent with the selection hypothesis. But he also found that the association between SES and adult health persisted above and beyond such selection effects; that is, adult SES had some significant effect on adult health regardless of childhood health. In sum, he found support for both selection and social causation. So while there is evidence of a selection bias in effect, this bias does not appear to fully account for the observed relationship between education and various quality of life outcomes.

Measuring Educational Attainment

Educational attainment is often measured by number of years/grades or highest degree obtained, but as numerous commentators have pointed out such measures do not adequately capture all the relevant aspects of education, such as variation in quality of education (Behrman et al. 1997), or the value of different credentials that require the same years of schooling, nor do such attainment indicators apply with equal accuracy across different national contexts (Kerckhoff et al. 2002). National education systems vary along a number of important dimensions such as extent of formal stratification (i.e., tracking or streaming), degree of standardization and credential specialization, and articulation with the labor market (Kerckhoff 2001; Müller and Shavit 1998; Sullivan and Smeeding 1997). For example, years of schooling is a more valid measurement of education in the USA than in many European countries with much more differentiated credential systems and multiple pathways of school-to-work transition. As well, utilizing years of schooling assumes that the effect of educational attainment is linear and that the returns to schooling increase linearly per additional year of education. But there is also evidence of nonlinear effects such as the credentialing or sheepskin effect, where inordinate wage premiums are often evident for degree holders in comparison to nondegree holders with similar total years of schooling (Card 1998; Pascarella and Terenzini 2005).

Two of the most widely used standards for classifying educational credential across countries are the ISCED (International Standard Classification of Education) and CASMIN (Comparative Analysis of Social Mobility in Industrial Nations) schemes. Traditionally, CASMIN fits the education credential systems of some countries better (many European countries) while the ISCED appears to better fit other countries (e.g., the USA) although there are examples of CASMIN being modified to incorporate these other countries (Kerckhoff et al. 2002; Müller and Shavit 1998). Another approach being developed by OECD/INES mitigates the incommensurate credentials problem by taking a broader picture of what education actually provides individuals. This new approach is based on the notion that schooling imparts more than just academic skills to students and thus seeks to augment measurement of curricular subjects (i.e., math, science, and reading literacy) with measurement of "cross-curricular competencies," or knowledge and skills that transcend specific subject areas (OECD 1997; Peschar 2004). Cross-curricular competencies are conceived as those competencies (life skills) required by individuals in order to be responsible, productive, fully functioning members of society. Four important cross-curricular competency domains have currently been identified: civics, problem-solving, self-related cognitions, oral and written communication. The OECD's Programme for International Student Assessment has incorporated self-regulated cognitions (learning) and problem-solving items into subsequent

cycles. Other similar efforts at developing indicators of the general life skills imparted by schooling are also underway (e.g., Hautamaki 1998; Meijer et al. 2001). More comprehensive sets of indicators may provide a more multidimensional understanding of how schooling contributes to preparing students to meet the personal, social, and economic challenges of modern life. For example, it may help further clarify the extent to which the positive effect of education on earnings is due to the cultivation of cognitive versus noncognitive skills.

Conclusion

This chapter has reviewed a wide array of research on the impact of educational attainment on quality of life. Adopting Cummins' (1996, 1997) quality of life schema as a heuristic framework, we looked at educational effects in seven broad life domains: *achieving in life, material well-being/standard of living, emotional well-being/resiliency, physical health, community, intimate relationships, and personal safety/future security*. Of course, no life domain is an island; each exists jointly with the others. Accordingly, the effects of educational attainment on QoL are multidimensional (cutting across life domains) and often reciprocal (conditioning of and conditioned by domains) in nature. In light of this, we deem it useful at this juncture to give some consideration to the dynamic nature of the relationship between education and quality of life.

Behrman et al. (1997: 3) suggest there are basically three underlying pathways by which schooling imparts benefits: (a) improving the stock of knowledge and the analytical skills individuals use to guide their behavior, (b) altering individuals' preferences, and (c) altering the constraints/opportunities presented to individuals.

(a) Enhancing Knowledge and Cognitive Development

Pallas (2000: 505) sums up key findings in this area as indicating that "individuals with more schooling have access to a richer array of information than those with less schooling. They know more about their social, cultural, and political worlds, and they can apply that knowledge to shape their futures." In short, more educated individuals are able to bring more information to bear in decision-making situations, thus, on the whole, improving the quality of those decisions.

Pascarella and Terenzini (2005) reviewed a host of studies from the 1990s that compared freshmen to seniors in terms of a number of basic dimensions of learning and cognitive development. In addition to statistically significant gains in fundamental knowledge domains such as English, Mathematics, Science, and Social Sciences, senior university students also demonstrated statistically significant improvements over their freshman counterparts in terms of general intellectual sophistication. That is, they exhibited greater propensity for critical thought and more advanced critical thinking skills, greater reflective judgment-thinking ("the ability to use reason and evidence to address ill-structured problems"), and greater epistemological sophistication or maturity. Evident long-term effects are that, compared to high school graduates, postsecondary graduates are not only "more knowledgeable and more proficient at becoming informed" but that they are also better equipped and more amenable to lifelong learning and continued intellectual growth.

There are numerous benefits to enhanced cognitive proficiency, some of which are related to productivity, employment, and earnings and some of which are related to other aspects of life quality, such as health. For example, there is strong suggestion that the more educated, due to greater access to information and greater proficiency at analyzing and implementing new information, are "more efficient producers of health" (Grossman and Kaestner 1997). Education imparts analytical and problem-solving skills ("learned effectiveness") that transfer to various aspects of life including health maintenance (Mirowsky and Ross 2005). More educated individuals have greater familiarity with the knowledge production process which may translate into greater trust in "expert" recommendations and greater likelihood of compliance. Thus, more educated individuals are more likely (and better equipped) to comprehend the relevance of expert recommendations and to be more effective in mitigating risk accordingly (Smith 1997).

This increased receptivity to learning is a primary consequence of the socialization effect of schooling. In addition to introducing new knowledge and training the mind to approach information, problems and ideas with more sophistication, schooling also shape individual preferences.

(b) Changing Preferences

When economists talk of an individual's preferences, they are essentially talking about a constellation of personal attributes or tendencies, such as an individual's general values orientation or priorities—the motives, attitudes, and ethics that guide individual conduct (what psychologists would see as facets of personality). Development of preferences occurs in concert with cognitive development, the two manifesting synergistically as habits of mind and behavior.[15] Thus, preferences include a host of possible personal traits such as work ethic, primary incentives, desire for autonomy, comfort with delayed gratification, political beliefs, and various lifestyle choices such as diet and leisure activities.

Level of education also has an effect on the values and practices that parents model for their children. Lareau (2000, 2003) has provided ethnographic evidence of important differences between middle- and working-class parents in childrearing practices and value orientations that translate into advantageous educational outcomes for middle-class children. Middle-class parents tend to be more hands on in their children's education, provide greater extracurricular learning opportunities, encourage analytical thought, impart greater achievement motivation, and model social skills (such as self-assertiveness and negotiation) conducive to success within "the rules of the game" that constitute formal education and later occupational contexts. Kohn (1969) observed an association between education and valuing autonomy even when controlling for subsequent occupation; increasing level of education was associated with increasing prioritization of autonomy. One of the aspects of autonomy that is most important to individual psychological health is control over the work process (Kohn 1976; Kohn and Schooler 1982).[16] A notable corollary

---

[15] Farkas (2003: 556) notes that a growing body of research suggests that "[p]atterns of habitual behavior, particularly the extent of conscientiousness or good work habits, developed from birth through adolescence, in conjunction with the cognitive skills developed alongside these behaviors, determine school success and schooling and occupational attainment. These skills and habits then combine with skills and habits developed on the job to determine employment and earnings success."

[16] Kohn et al. (1990) found that while the significant relationship between level of education and priority given to autonomy held in the USA, it was not evident in Japan or Poland.

of the desire for autonomy is self-efficacy or belief in one's ability to exert control over valued outcomes.

Formal education instills an analytical and problem-solving orientation that leads to a greater sense of personal agency or self-efficacy which strengthens resolve to initiate action and to better manage various aspects of one's life such as health status (Mirowsky and Ross 1999, 2005). Similarly, Goldsmith et al. (1997) found that higher educational attainment is associated with enhanced "psychological capital," the motivational and attitudinal requisites—particularly high self-esteem and internal locus of control—leading to higher wage employment. Pascarella and Terenzini (2005), in their extensive review of the literature on the affects of college, conclude that numerous studies indicate that postsecondary education has a net effect (i.e., persists after a number of potentially confounding variables are controlled) on student self-concept. As well, they identify a small but significant and long-term increase in university students' internal locus of control (perception of internal or self-control versus external or other-control of one's life) as well as fairly consistent indications of improved social skills and social self-confidence.

Pascarella and Terenzini (2005) also find evidence that attainment of university education is positively associated with increased valuation of the intrinsic rewards of work such as interesting tasks, freedom to use one's skills and talents, and involvement in decision-making. They also observe an association between university attendance and long-term changes in graduates' "sociopolitical attitudes and values and civic community engagement." Enduring changes include increased likelihood of voting and direct participation in the political process, as well as involvement in civic and community initiatives (Pascarella and Terenzini 2005).

Another important preference that is affected by education is what economists term "rate of time preference." Basically, this construct refers to the relative value an individual places on immediate versus future consumption or gratification, or even more pointedly, their degree of "patience" (Becker and Mulligan 1997). People vary in their capacity to forgo more immediate consumption, to invest time, effort, and money with the promise of greater payoff (pleasure or "utilities") in the future. While some argue that a lower rate of time preference for the present (longer time horizon) increases the level of formal schooling attainment, Becker and Mulligan (1997: 736) suggest that schooling enhances the ability to delay gratification because it teaches problem-solving and abstract thinking skills such as scenario simulation, and consequently, "educated people should be more productive at reducing the remoteness of future pleasures." As well, they suggest that education increases patience indirectly via its positive effect on earnings in that those with greater wealth are better positioned to cultivate long-term returns. Others suggest that the relationship between education and time preference is probably one of reciprocal effects: the ability to delay gratification enhances educational attainment, and greater educational attainment enhances ability to delay gratification (Leigh 1998). Thus, more educated parents tend to cultivate a more future-oriented time preference in their children to begin with, and this preference is further reinforced by successful educational attainment. Health status, occupational prestige, income, and credit rating are examples of areas in one's life potentially affected by one's time preference.

(c) Lessening Constraints and Increasing Opportunities

Learning begets learning, schooling provides access to substantive knowledge, but it also creates awareness of and potential access to further learning opportunities, thereby broadening the aspirational horizon of students. For instance, successful students, as they advance, become introduced to previously unknown educational and occupational options. Or academic success may lead to financial assistance such as scholarships and bursaries that enable a student to further their education beyond what their financial resources might otherwise afford.

Higher educational attainment also leads to occupations that are more likely to provide the opportunity for continued refinement of the cognitive and interpersonal skills developed in school. As well, occupations requiring higher education credentials tend to provide relatively high earnings which, in turn, enable access to wider range of material and nonmaterial resources and opportunities linked to an array of positive long-term outcomes (Pascarella and Terenzini 2005). Higher earnings enable individuals to live in safer, better-resourced (libraries, schools, recreational facilities, etc.) communities and to afford healthier lifestyles (e.g., healthier food, gym memberships, exercise equipment, personal trainers, etc.). In addition, there are intergenerational repercussions, in that offspring of highly educated parents are more likely to attain high levels of education (and attendant benefits) themselves.

The effects of education on a broad spectrum of life outcomes are mediated by workplace conditions. For example, better educated individuals are generally less likely to be employed in dangerous working conditions and generally have better access to non-alienated work (less routinized and monotonous, greater autonomy, variety, and creativity) which decreases physical and mental distress (Ross and Van Willigen 1997) and the level of satisfaction derived from work (Ross and Reskin 1992).

These three pathways are interrelated; change or development in one is accompanied by change or development in the others, and each—to varying degrees—affects aspects of quality of life, within and across specific domains and in general. Thus, like a series of feedback loops, the effects of education in one domain may impact and be impacted by the effects of education in other domains. By way of simple illustration, remaining in school improves an individual's knowledge base and the analytical tools they bring to bear upon a range of circumstances, which may produce more successful responses (e.g., school achievement, task performance at work) and thus better opportunities (scholarship, promotion to a better paying job), which may, in turn, reshape individual preferences (reinforces hard work ethic, expands time horizon), which may increase the probability of the person pursuing further schooling (either initially or via upgrading) thereby increasing occupational and economic status. Of course, this example ignores a number of other factors that may differentially impinge upon individual educational trajectories (e.g., family background, ability, gender, race, school resources, etc.). The array of combinations of factors that could plausibly affect the educational attainment-quality of life relationship is sizeable and remains a primary challenge to researchers.

None of the returns to education studies considered here has incorporated the full breadth of plausibly influential variables into its design; social reality is too complex. Studies vary in the number of plausible influences they attempt to account for and in the rigor with which they do so. Practical and methodological limitations persist (e.g., selection bias and appropriate

measurement of education), but viewed across the laminate profile of a large number of studies, certain patterns become apparent. Schooling does affect (and is affected by) individual quality of life by enhancing knowledge and analytical capacity, shaping preferences, and expanding opportunities. These changes feed off one another and have repercussions across all seven life domains examined; change along one pathway can affect the other pathways and one or more domains which can, in turn, affect each other.

Schooling is positively associated with achieving in life; in simple terms, success breeds success; those who do well in school are likely to continue onto higher levels of educational attainment which is associated with higher socioeconomic attainment (occupational status, income, etc.). Concomitant with enhanced achievement, schooling also raises material well-being by increasing economic returns. While factors such as family background, ability, and health influence educational attainment and its effect on economic returns, there is strong evidence for an effect of schooling on earnings net of these factors. The exact mechanism by which education enhances economic returns is still not completely clear. Some findings suggest that education increases the productivity of workers by increasing knowledge and skills, while other findings are more consistent with the notion that education socializes individuals into the values, habits, and attitudes favored by employers as conducive to successful performance. From the studies reviewed here, it seems that both views contribute something integral to the answer that is emerging and will continue to emerge as the breadth and sophistication of available data keeps growing.

Education also benefits psychological and physical health. While there is evidence of direct (net of other factors) health benefits to education (such as greater health knowledge and "learned effectiveness" and increased psychological resiliency via a greater compliment of coping skills), many of the salutary effects of education are indirect consequences of work, whether it be the actual conditions of the workplace (autonomy, nature of tasks and relationships, opportunity for continued learning, and personal fulfillment) or the socioeconomic repercussions (occupational prestige, financial resources to pursue other interests, etc.). The various health advantages related to education and socioeconomic status are cumulative in nature, growing across (and extending) the lifespan. Part of the association between health and education seems to be due to the effect of early health on subsequent school attainment, but education still appears to provide significant health benefits above and beyond this selection effect.

There also seem to be indications of positive associations between education and richer social networks and social resources (social capital) as well as context effects related to neighborhood of residence and schoolmates, although contradictory results also exist which suggest such connections may be spurious. Again, the complexity of social reality and the difficulty associated with accounting for all plausible influences presents a stern test for scientific consensus.

Our review also looked at a number of studies pointing to a positive association between education and various dimensions of intimate relationships such as later onset of marriage and parenthood, greater parental resources and skills, and better child welfare. The benefits to women appear particularly strong in a number of respects: delayed marriage and/or motherhood are associated with higher educational attainment, greater economic resources, and more personal freedom for women, and educational attainment is negatively associated with teen parenthood (the disadvantages of which—such as poverty—seem to fall disproportionately upon young mothers). Lastly, in the domain of personal safety/future security, it appears that education is associated with decreased likelihood of exposure to an assortment of economic, social, and environmental risks and that when such stressors are encountered, the more educated are better equipped to effectively cope or adapt.

In sum, while there are still numerous questions and gaps remaining, the case for the positive effects of educational attainment on quality of life is in the balance very convincing. But it remains incumbent upon researchers to keep striving toward the increasingly comprehensive data required to bring the blurry aspects into focus. For example, one increasingly popular research strategy, necessarily given short shrift in this chapter, is cross-national comparison. Studying the differences and similarities between the institutional features of national educational systems promises to further reveal significant insights into the importance of societal and institutional context in determining quality of life returns to education.

Appendix

International Standard Classification of Education (ISCED): The International Standard Classification of Education (ISCED-97) is used to define the levels and fields of education used as part of the OECD's system of education indicators (OECD 2006). For details on ISCED 1997 and how it is nationally implemented, see *Classifying Educational Programmes: Manual for ISCED-97 Implementation in OECD Countries* (OECD 1999b). Levels include *Pre-primary education (ISCED 0), Primary education (ISCED 1), Lower secondary education (ISCED 2), Upper secondary education (ISCED 3), Postsecondary non-tertiary level of education (ISCED 4), Tertiary-type A education (ISCED 5A), Tertiary-type B education (ISCED 5B),* and *Advanced Research Qualifications (ISCED 6).*

Upper secondary education (ISCED 3): Upper secondary education (ISCED 3) corresponds to the final stage of secondary education in most OECD countries. Instruction is often more organized along subject matter lines than at ISCED level 2, and teachers usually need to have a higher level, or more subject-specific, qualifications than at ISCED 2. The entrance age to this level is typically 15 or 16 years. There are substantial differences in the typical duration of ISCED 3 programs both across and between countries, typically ranging from 2 to 5 years of schooling. ISCED 3 may either be "terminal" (i.e., preparing the students for entry directly into working life) and/or "preparatory" (i.e., preparing students for tertiary education). Programs at level 3 can also be subdivided into three categories based on the degree to which the program is specifically oriented toward a specific class of occupations or trades and leads to a labor-market relevant qualification: general, pre-vocational or pre-technical, and vocational or technical programs.

Postsecondary non-tertiary level of education (ISCED 4): Postsecondary non-tertiary education straddles the boundary between upper secondary and postsecondary education from an international point of view, even though it might clearly be considered upper secondary or postsecondary programs in a national context. Although their content may not be significantly more advanced than upper secondary programs, they serve to broaden the knowledge of participants who have already gained an upper secondary qualification. The students tend to be older than those enrolled at the upper secondary level.

Tertiary-type A education (*ISCED 5A*): Tertiary-type A programs (ISCED 5A) are largely theory based and are designed to provide sufficient qualifications for entry to advanced research programs and professions with high skill requirements, such as medicine, dentistry, or architecture. Tertiary-type A programs have a minimum cumulative theoretical duration (at tertiary level) of 3 years full-time equivalent, although they typically last 4 or more years. These programs are not exclusively offered at universities. Conversely, not all programs nationally recognized as university programs fulfill the criteria to be classified as tertiary-type A. Tertiary-type A programs include second degree programs like the American Master. First and second programs are subclassified by the cumulative education of the programs, i.e., the total study time needed at the tertiary level to complete the degree.

Tertiary-type B education (*ISCED 5B*): Tertiary-type B programs (ISCED 5B) are typically shorter than those of tertiary-type A and focus on practical, technical, or occupational skills for direct entry into the labor market, although some theoretical foundations may be covered in the respective programs. They have a minimum duration of 2 years full-time equivalent at the tertiary level.

References

Abbot, D., Jones, A., & Quilgars, D. (2006). Social inequality and risk. In P. Taylor-Gooby & J. Zinn (Eds.), *Risk in social science* (pp. 228–247). New York: Oxford University Press.

Adler, N. E., Boyce, T., Chesney, M. A., Cohen, S., Folkman, S., Krahn, R. L., & Syme, S. L. (1994). Socioeconomic status and health: The challenge of the gradient. *American Psychologist, 49*, 15–24.

Ainsworth, J. W. (2002). Why does it take a village? The mediation of neighborhood effects on educational achievement. *Social Forces, 81*(1), 117–152.

Altonji, J., & Dunn, T. (1996). The effects of family characteristics on the return to education. *The Review of Economics and Statistics, 78*, 692–704.

Arias, O., & McMahon, W. H. (1997). *Dynamic rates of return to education in the US* (Working Paper No. 96–0142). Urbana: Office of Research, College of Commerce and Business Administration, University of Illinois.

Ashenfelter, O., & Rouse, C. (1998). Income, schooling, and ability: Evidence from a new sample of identical twins. *Quarterly Journal of Economics, 113*(1), 253–284.

Ashenfelter, O., & Zimmerman, D. (1997). The estimates of the return to schooling from sibling data: Fathers, sons, and brothers. *Review of Economics and Statistics, 79*, 1–9.

Asplund, R., & Pereira, P. (1999). *Returns to human capital in Europe: A literature review.* Helinski: ETLA 9 The Research Institute of the Finnish Economy/Taloustieto Oy.

Barnard, W. M. (2004). Parent involvement in elementary school and educational attainment. *Children and Youth Services Review, 26*, 39–62.

Barro, R. J. (2001). Education and economic growth. In J. F. Helliwell (Ed.), *The contributions of human and social capital to sustained economic growth and well-being: International symposium report.* Canada/Paris: Human Resources Development Canada and OECD.

Bartley, M., Blane, D., & Smith, G. D. (1998). Beyond the black report. *Sociology of Health & Illness, 20*(5), 563–577.

Becker, G. S., & Mulligan, C. B. (1997, August). The endogenous determination of time preference. *Quarterly Journal of Economics, 112*(3), 729–759.

Behrman, J. R., Crawford, D. L., & Stacey, N. (1997). Introduction. In J. R. Behrman, D. L. Crawford, & N. Stacey (Eds.), *The social benefits of education* (pp. 1–9). Ann Arbour, MI: University of Michigan Press.

Berrington, A. (2001). Entry into parenthood and the outcome of cohabiting partnerships in Britain. *Journal of Marriage and Family, 63*, 80–96.

Berrington, A., & Diamond, I. (1999). Marital dissolution among the 1958 British birth cohort: The role of cohabitation. *Population Studies, 53*, 19–38.

Bianchi, S. M., Subaiya, L., & Kahn, J. R. (1999). The gender gap in the economic well-being of nonresident and custodial mothers. *Demography, 36*, 195–203.

Blackwell, L., & Bynner, J. (2002). *Learning, family formation and dissolution* (Wider benefits of learning research report no. 4). London: Center for Research on the Wider Benefits of Learning, Institute of Education.

Blanchflower, D. J., & Oswald, A. J. (2001). *Well-being over time on Britain and the USA* (NBER Working Paper 7487). Cambridge, MA: National Bureau of Economic Research.

Blundell, R., Dearden, L., Goodman, A., & Reid, H. (2000). The returns to higher education in Britain: Evidence for a British cohort. *The Economic Journal, 110*, 82–99.

Boelhouwer, J., & Stoop, I. (1999). Measuring well-being in the Netherlands: The SCP index from 1974 to 1997. *Social Indicators Research, 48*, 51–75.

Bound, J., Schoenbaum, M., & Waidmann, T. (1995). Race and education difference in disability status and labor force attachment in the health and retirement survey. *Journal of Human Resources, 30*, S227–S269.

Bowles, S., & Gintis, H. (2000). Schooling, intelligence, and income in America. In K. Arrow, S. Durlauf, & S. Bowles (Eds.), *Meritocracy and inequality* (pp. 119–136). Princeton, NJ: Princeton University Press.

Bowles, S., Gintis, H., & Osborne, M. (2001a). *The determinants of individual earnings: Skills, preferences, and schooling.* Unpublished paper, University of Massachusetts.

Bowles, S., Herbert, G., & Melissa, O. (2001b). Incentive-enhancing preferences: Personality, behavior and earnings. *The American Economic Review, 92*(2), 155–158.

Boxman, E. A. W., De Graaf, P. M., & Flap, H. D. (1991). The impact of social and human capital on the income attainment of Dutch managers. *Social Networks, 13*, 51–73.

Brooks-Gunn, J., Duncan, G. J., Klebanov, P. K., & Sealand, N. (1993). Do neighborhoods influence child and adolescent development? *The American Journal of Sociology, 99*(2), 353–395.

Brooks-Gunn, J., Klebanov, P. K., & Duncan, G. J. (1996). Ethnic differences in children's intelligence scores: Roles of economic deprivation, home environment, and maternal characteristics. *Child Development, 67*, 396–408.

Burt, R. S. (2000). The network structure of social capital. In R. I. Sutton & B. M. Staw (Eds.), *Research in organizational behaviour* (pp. 345–423). Greenwich, CT: JAI Press.

Cameron, S., & Heckman, J. (1993). The non-equivalence of the high school equivalents. *Journal of Labor Economics, 11*(1), 1–47.

Card, D. (1998). *The causal effect of education on earnings.* University of California (Working paper no.2). Berkeley: Center for Labor Economics.

Chevalier, A., Conlon, G., Galinda-Rueda, F., & McNally, S. (2002). *The returns to higher education teaching.* London: Centre for Economics of Education, London School of Economics.

Cook, T. D., Herman, M. R., Phillips, M., & Settersten, R. A., Jr. (2002). Some ways in which neighborhoods, nuclear families, friendship groups, and schools jointly affect changes in early adolescent development. *Child Development, 73*(4), 1283–1309.

Crimmins, E. M., & Saito, Y. (2001). Trends in healthy life expectancy in the United States, 1970–1990: Gender, racial and educational differences. *Social Science & Medicine, 52*, 1629–1641.

Cubbin, C., & Smith, G. S. (2002). Socioeconomic inequalities in injury: Critical issues in design and analysis. *Annual Review of Public Health, 23*, 349–375.

Cummins, R. A. (1996). The domains of life satisfaction: An attempt to order chaos. *Social Indicators Research, 38*, 303–328.

Cummins, R. A. (1997). Assessing quality of life. In R. I. Brown & R. I. Brown (Eds.), *Quality of life for people with disabilities* (pp. 116–150). Cheltenham: Stanley Thornes.

Cummins, R. A. (2002). *Vale ComQol: Caveats to using the comprehensive quality of life scale: Welcome the personal wellbeing index.* Melbourne: Deakin University. http://acqol. deakin.edu.au/instruments/Caveats_ComQol_scales.doc.

Curtis, J., Grabb, E., Perks, T., & Chui, T. (2004). Political involvement, civic engagement, and social inequality. In J. Curtis, E. Grabb, & N. Guppy (Eds.), *Social inequality in Canada: Patterns, problems, and policies* (4th ed., pp. 431–449). Scarborough: Prentice Hall Allyn and Bacon Canada Inc.

Dahinten, S. V., Shapka, J., & Willms, J. D. (2007). Adolescent children of adolescent mothers: The impact of family functioning on trajectories of development. *Journal of Youth and Adolescence, 36*(2), 195–212.

Davies, S. (1999). Stubborn disparities: Explaining class inequalities in schooling. In J. Curtis, E. Grabb, & N. Guppy (Eds.), *Social inequality in Canada: Patterns, problems, and policies* (3rd ed.). Scarborough: Prentice Hall Allyn and Bacon Canada Inc.

de Ridder, D. T. D. (1995). Social status and coping: An exploration of the mediating role of beliefs. *Anxiety, Stress, and Coping, 8*, 311–324.

Diener, E. (1995). A value based index for measuring national quality of life. *Social Indicators Research, 36*, 107–127.

Duncan, G. J., & Dunifon, R. (1998). 'Soft-skills' and long-run market success. In S. W. Polacheek (Ed.), *Research in labour economics* (Vol. 17, pp. 123–150). Stamford, CT: JAI Press.

Duncan, G. J., Boisjoly, J., & Mullan Harris, K. (2001). Sibling, peer, neighbor, and schoolmate correlations as indicators of the importance of context for adolescent development. *Demography, 38*(3), 437–447.

Ekert-Jaffé, O., Joshi, H., Lynch, K., Mougin, R., & Rendall, M. (2002). Fertility, timing of births and socio-economic status in France and Britain: Social policies and occupational polarization. *Population, 57*(3), 475–507, (Paris: Institut National d'Études Démographiques).

Estes, R. J. (1997). Social development trends in Europe, 1970–1994: Development prospects for the new Europe. *Social Indicators Research, 42*(1), 1–19.

Evans, G. W., & Kantrowitz, E. (2002). Socioeconomic status and health: the potential role of environmental risk exposure. *Annual Review of Public Health, 23*, 303–331.

Fan, X. T., & Chen, M. (2001). Parental involvement and students' academic achievement: A meta-analysis. *Educational Psychology Review, 13*, 1–22.

Farkas, G. (1996). *Human capital or cultural capital? Ethnicity and poverty groups in an urban school district.* New York: Aldine de Gruyter.

Farkas, G. (2003). Cognitive skills and non-cognitive traits and behaviors in stratification processes. *Annual Review of Sociology, 29*, 541–562.

Feinstein, L., Robertson, D., & Symons, J. (1999). Pre-school education and attainment in the NCDS and the BCS. *Education Economics, 7*(3), 209–234.

Feinstein, L., Kathryn, D., & Ricardo, S. (2004). *A model of the inter-generational transmission of educational success* (Wider benefits of learning research report no. 11). London: Center for Research on the Wider Benefits of Learning, Institute of Education.

Fernandez-Ballesteros, R., Zamarron, M. D., & Ruiz, M. A. (2001). The contribution of socio-demographic and psychosocial factors to life satisfaction. *Ageing and Society, 21*(1), 25–43.

Ferris, A. L. (1988). The uses of social indicators. *Social Forces, 66*, 601–617.

Feuerstein, A. (2000). School characteristics and parent involvement: Influences on participation in children's schools. *The Journal of Educational Research, 94*, 29–39.

Flap, H. D. (1999). Creation and returns of social capital: A new research program. *The Tocqueville Review, 20*(1), 5–26.

Flap, H. D., & Boxman, E. A. (1999). Getting a job among managers. In R. Leenders & S. Gabbay (Eds.), *Corporate and social capital and liability* (pp. 197–216). New York: Kluwer Academic.

Flap, H. D., & Boxman, E. A. (2001). Getting started: The influence of social capital on the start of the occupational career. In N. Lin, K. S. Cook, & R. S. Burt (Eds.), *Social capital: Theory and research* (pp. 159–184). New York: Aldine de Gruyter.

Freeman, R. (1996). Why do so many young American men commit crimes and what might we do about it? *Journal of Economic Perspectives, 10,* 25–42.

Frempong, G., & Willms, J. D. (2002). Can school quality compensate for socioeconomic advantage? In J. Douglas Willms (Ed.), *Vulnerable children: Findings from Canada's national longitudinal survey of children and youth* (pp. 277–303). Edmonton: University of Alberta Press.

Furlong, A., & Cartmel, F. (1997). *Young people and social change: Individualization and risk in late modernity.* Buckingham: Open University Press.

Gangl, M. (2001). Changing labour markets and early career outcomes: Labour market entry in Europe over the last decade. *Work, Employment and Society, 16*(1), 67–90.

Gerdtham, U. G., & Johannesson, M. (2001). The relationship between happiness, health, and socioeconomic factors: results based on Swedish microdata. *Journal of Socio-Economics, 30,* 553–557.

Gilleskie, D., & Harrison, A. (1998). The effect of endogenous health inputs on the relationship between health and education. *Economics of Education Review, 17,* 279–297.

Ginther, D., Haveman, R., & Wolfe, B. (2000). Neighborhood attributes as determinants of children's outcomes: How robust are the relationships? *Journal of Human Resources, 35*(4), 603–642.

Goldsmith, A., Veum, J., & Darity, W. (1997). The impact of psychological and human capital on wages. *Economic Inquiry, 35*(October), 815–829.

Gould, E., Mustard, D., & Weinberg, B. (2002). Crime rates and local market conditions in the United States: 1974–1994. *The Review of Economics and Statistics, 84,* 45–61.

Granovetter, M. (1995). *Getting a job: A study of contacts and careers* (2nd ed.). Chicago: University of Chicago Press.

Greenwood, D. T. (1997). New developments in the intergenerational impact of education. *International Journal of Educational Research, 27*(6), 503–511.

Grossman, M., & Kaestner, R. (1997). Effects of education on health. In J. R. Behrman, D. L. Crawford, & N. Stacey (Eds.), *The social benefits of education* (pp. 69–123). Ann Arbour, MI: University of Michigan Press.

Grubb, W. N. (1993). The varied economic returns to postsecondary education. *Journal of Human Resources, 28,* 365–382.

Guralnik, J., Land, K., Blazer, D., Fillenbaum, G., & Branch, L. (1993). Educational status and active life expectancy among older Blacks and Whites. *The New England Journal of Medicine, 329,* 11–116.

Haas, S. A. (2006). Health selection and the process of social stratification: The effect of childhood health on socioeconomic attainment. *Journal of Health and Social Behavior, 47,* 339–354.

Haggerty, M. R., Cummins, R. A., Ferriss, A. L., Land, K., Michalos, A. C., Peterson, M., Sharpe, A., Sirgy, J., & Vogel, J. (2001). Quality of life indexes for national policy: Review and agenda for research. *Social Indicators Research, 55*(1), 1–96.

Hammond, C. (2004). Impacts of learning on well-being, mental health and effective coping. In T. Schuller, J. Preston, C. Hammond, A. Brasset-Grundy, & J. Bynner (Eds.), *The benefits of learning: The impact of education on health, family life, and social capital* (pp. 37–56). New York: RoutledgeFarmer.

Hauser, R. M., Warren, J. R., Huang, M.-H., & Carter, W. Y. (2000). Occupational status, education, and social mobility. In K. Arrow, S. Durlauf, & S. Bowles (Eds.), *Meritocracy and inequality* (pp. 89–117). Princeton, NJ: Princeton University Press.

Hautamaki, J. (1998). *Learning to learn as part of cross-curricular competencies. Studies of 6th and 9th graders in Finland.* Helsinki: Center for Educational Assessment, University of Helsinki.

Haveman, R. B., & Wolfe, B. (1994). *Succeeding generations: On the effects of investments in children.* New York: Russell Sage.

Haveman, R., & Wolfe, B. (1995). The determinants of children's attainments: A review of methods and findings. *Journal of Economic Literature, 33,* 1829–1878.

Heck, K. E., Schoendorf, K. C., Ventura, S. J., & Kiely, J. L. (1997). Delayed childbearing by education level in the United States, 1969–1994. *Maternal and Child Health Journal, 1*(2), 81–88.

Heckman, J. (2000). Policies to foster human capital. *Research in Economics, 54,* 3–56.

Heckman, J. J., & Rubinstein, Y. (2001). The importance of non-cognitive skills: Lessons from the GED testing program. *The American Economic Review, 91*(2), 145–149.

Heckman, J., Layne-Farrar, A., & Dodd, P. (1996). Does measured school quality really matter? An examination of the earnings-quality relationship. In G. Burtless (Ed.), *Does money matter: The effect of school resources on student achievement and adult success* (pp. 192–289). Washington: Brookings Institution Press.

Heinz, W. R. (1999). Introduction: Transitions to employment in a cross-national perspective. In W. R. Heinz (Ed.), *From education to work: Cross-national perspectives* (pp. 1–21). New York: Cambridge University Press.

Helliwell, J. F. (Ed.) (2001) *The contributions of human and social capital to sustained economic growth and well-being: International symposium report.* Ottawa/Paris: Human Resources Development Canada and OECD.

Hill, N. E., Castellino, D. R., Lansford, J. E., Nowlin, P., Dodge, K. A., Bates, J. E., & Pettit, G. S. (2004). Parent academic involvement as related to school behavior, achievement, and aspirations: Demographic variations across adolescence. *Child Development, 75*(5), 1491–1509.

Ho, E., & Willms, J. D. (1996). The effects of parental involvement in on eighth grade achievement. *Sociology of Education, 69*(2), 126–141.

Hout, M., & DiPrete, T. A. (2006). What have we learned: RC28's contributions to knowledge about social stratification. *Research in Social Stratification and Mobility, 24*(1), 1–20.

Howard, S., Dryden, J., & Johnson, B. (1999). Childhood resilience, review and critique of the literature. *Oxford Review of Education, 25*(3), 307–323.

International Wellbeing Group. (2006). *Personal wellbeing index.* Melbourne: Australian Centre on Quality of Life, Deakin University (http://www.deakin.edu.au/research/acqol/instruments/wellbeing_index.htm.).

Jeynes, W. H. (2003). A meta-analysis—The effects of parental involvement on minority children's academic achievement. *Education and Urban Society, 35,* 202–218.

Johnes, G. (1993). *The economics of education.* London: Macmillan.

Johnston, D. F. (1988). Toward a comprehensive "quality of life" index. *Social Indicators Research, 20,* 473–496.

Kane, T. J., & Rouse, C. E. (1995). Labour market returns to two- and four-year college. *The American Economic Review, 85,* 600–614.

Kaplan, G., & Keil, J. (1993). Socioeconomic factors and cardiovascular disease: A review of the literature. *Circulation, 88,* 90–105.

Kenkel, D. (1991). Health behavior, health knowledge, and schooling. *Journal of Political Economy, 99*(2), 287–305.

Kerckhoff, A. C. (2000). Transition from school to work in comparative perspective. In M. T. Hallinan (Ed.), *Handbook of the sociology of education* (pp. 453–474). New York: Kluwer Academic/Plenum Publishers.

Kerckhoff, A. C. (2001). Education and social stratification processes in comparative perspective [Extra Issue]. *Sociology of Education,* 78: 3–18.

Kerckhoff, A. C. Dietrich-Ezell, & Brown, J. S. (2002). Toward an improved measure of educational attainment in stratification research. *Social Science Research, 31,* 99–123.

Kerckhoff, A. C., & Glennie, E. (1999). The Mathew effect in American education. *Research in Sociology of Education and Socialization, 12,* 35–66.

Kiernan, K. (1996). Lone motherhood, employment and outcomes for children. *International Journal of Law, Policy and the Family, 10,* 233–249.

Kiernan, K. (1997). Becoming a young parent: a longitudinal study of associated factors. *The British Journal of Sociology, 48,* 406–428.

Kohn, M. L. (1969). *Class and conformity: A study in values.* Chicago: University of Chicago Press.

Kohn, M. L. (1976). Occupational structure and alienation. *The American Journal of Sociology, 82,* 111–130.

Kohn, M. L., & Schooler, C. (1982). Job conditions and personality: A longitudinal assessment of their reciprocal effects. *The American Journal of Sociology, 87,* 1257–1286.

Kohn, M. L., Naoi, A., Schoenbach, C., Schooler, C., & Slomcyzynski, K. M. (1990). Position in the class structure and psychological functioning in the United States, Japan, and Poland. *The American Journal of Sociology, 95,* 964–1008.

Krahn, H. (2004). Choose your parents carefully: Social class, post-secondary education and occupational outcomes. In J. Curtis, E. Grabb, & N. Guppy (Eds.), *Social inequality in Canada: Patterns, problems, and policies* (4th ed., pp. 187–203). Scarborough: Prentice Hall Allyn and Bacon Canada Inc.

Krueger, A. B., & Lindahl, M. (2001). Education for growth: Why and for whom? *Journal of Economic Literature, 39*(4), 1101–1136.

Lai, G. W., Lin, N., & Leung, S. (1998). Network resources, contact resources, and status attainment. *Social Networks, 20*(2), 159–178.

Land, K. C. (2000). Social indicators. In E. F. Borgatta & R. Montgomery (Eds.), *Encyclopedia of sociology* (pp. 2682–2690). New York: Macmillan Reference USA.

Land, K. C., & Russell, S. T. (1996). Wealth accumulation across the life course: Stability and change in sociodemographic covariate structures of net worth data in the Survey of Income and Program Participation, 1984–1991. *Social Science Research, 25,* 334–353.

Lareau, A. (2000). *Home advantage: Social class and parental intervention in elementary education.* New York: Rowman and Littlefield Publishers, Inc.

Lareau, A. (2001). Linking Bourdieu's concept of capital to the broader field. In B. J. Biddle (Ed.), *Social class, poverty, and education* (pp. 77–100). New York: RoutledgeFalmer.

Lareau, A. (2003). *Unequal childhoods: Class, race and family life.* Berkely and Los Angeles: University of California Press.

Lareau, A., & Weininger, E. (2003). Cultural capital in educational research: A critical assessment. *Theory and Society, 32,* 567–606.

Lauderdale, D. S. (2001). Education and survival: Birth cohort, period, and age effects. *Demography, 38,* 551–561.

Lee, J.-S., & Bowen, N. K. (2006). Parent involvement, cultural capital, and the achievement gap among elementary school children. *American Educational Research Journal, 43*(2), 193–218.

Leigh, J. P. (1998). The social benefits of education: A review article. *Economics of Education Review, 17*(3), 363–368.

Lennon, M. C. (1994). Women, work, and well-being: The importance of work conditions. *Journal of Health and Social Behavior, 35,* 235–247.

Lester, J. P., Allen, D. W., & Hill, K. M. (2001). *Environmental injustice in the United States: Myths and realities.* Boulder, CO: Westview Press.

Lin, N. (1999). Social networks and status attainment. *Annual Review of Sociology, 23,* 467–488.

Lin, N. (2000). Inequality in social capital. *Contemporary Sociology, 29*(6), 785–795.

Link, B. G., Lennon, M. C., & Dohrenwend, B. P. (1993). Socioeconomic status and depression: The role of occupations involving direction, control, and planning. *The American Journal of Sociology, 98,* 1351–1387.

Liu, F. (2001). *Environmental justice analysis: Theories, methods and practice.* Boca Raton, FL: Lewis Publishers.

Lochner, L. (2004). Education, work and crime: A human capital approach. *International Economic Review, 45*(3), 811–843.

Lochner, L., & Moretti, E. (2004). The effect of education on crime: Evidence from prison inmates, arrests, and self-reports. *The American Economic Review, 94,* 155–189.

Lynch, S. M. (2006). Explaining life course and cohort variation in the relationship between education and health: The role of income. *Journal of Health and Social Behavior, 47,* 324–338.

Machin, S., & Meghir, C. (2000). *Crime and economic incentives* (IFS Working Papers W00/17). London: Institute for Fiscal Studies.

Manton, K., Stallard, E., & Corder, L. (1997). Education-specific estimates of life expectancy and age-specific disability in the U.S. elderly population. *Journal of Aging and Health, 9,* 419–450.

Martin, S. P. (2000). Diverging fertility among U.S. women who delay childbearing past age 30. *Demography, 37*(4), 523–533.

Mayer, S. E. (2002). How economic segregation affects children's educational attainment. *Social Forces, 81*(1), 153–176.

Maynard, R. A., & McGrath, D. J. (1997). Family, structure, fertility, and child welfare. In J. R. Behrman, D. L. Crawford,

& N. Stacey (Eds.), *The social benefits of education* (pp. 125–174). Ann Arbour, MI: University of Michigan Press.

McLeod, J. D., & Kessler, R. C. (1990). Socioeconomic status differences in vulnerability to life events. *Journal of Health and Social Behavior, 31*, 162–172.

McMahon, W. W. (1997). Conceptual framework for measuring the total social and private benefits of education. *International Journal of Educational Research, 27*(6), 453–481.

McMahon, W. W. (1999). *Education and development: Measuring the social benefits*. New York: Oxford University Press.

McMahon, W. W. (2000). The impact of human capital on non-market outcomes and feedbacks on economic development: Techniques for measurement and estimates of impacts of education in OECD countries. In J. F. Helliwell (Ed.), *The contributions of human and social capital to sustained economic growth and well-being: International symposium report*. Canada/Paris: Human Resources Development Canada and OECD.

McWayne, C., Hampton, V., Fantuzzo, J., Cohen, H. L., & Sekino, Y. (2004). A multivariate examination of parent involvement and the social and academic competencies of urban kindergarten children. *Psychology in the Schools, 41*, 363–377.

Meadow, H. L., Mentzer, J. T., Rahtz, D. R., & Sirgy, M. J. (1992). A life satisfaction measure based on judgement theory. *Social Indicators Research, 26*, 23–59.

Meeks, S., & Murrell, S. A. (2001). Contribution of education to health and life satisfaction in older adults mediated by negative affect. *Journal of Aging and Health, 13*(1), 92–119.

Meijer, J., Elshout-Mohr, M., & van Hout-Wolters, B. H. A. M. (2001). An instrument for the assessment of cross-curricular skills. *Education Research and Evaluation, 7*(1), 79–107.

Michalos, A. C. (1980–1982). *North American Social Report* 1–5. Dordrecht: Reidel.

Michalos, A. C. (1985). Multiple discrepancies theory (MDT). *Social Indicators Research, 16*, 347–413.

Michalos, A. C. (2008). Education, happiness and wellbeing. *Social Indicators Research, 87*(3), 347–366.

Miech, R., Essex, M. J., & Goldsmith, H. H. (2001). Socioeconomic status and the adjustment to school: The role of self-regulation during early childhood. *Sociology of Education, 74*(2), 102–120.

Miller, P., Mulvey, C., & Martin, N. (1995). What do twin studies reveal about the economic returns to education? A comparison of Australian and American findings. *The American Economic Review, 85*, 586–599.

Miringoff, M. L., & Miringoff, M. L. (1999). *The social health of the nation: How America is really doing*. New York: Oxford University Press.

Miringoff, M. L., Miringoff, M. L., & Opdycke, S. (1996). Monitoring the nation's social performance: The index of social health. In E. F. Zigler, S. L. Kagan, & N. W. Hall (Eds.), *Children, families, and government* (pp. 10–30). New York: Cambridge University Press.

Mirowsky, J., & Ross, C. E. (1999). Economic hardship across the life course. *American Sociological Review, 64*, 548–569.

Mirowsky, J., & Ross, C. E. (2003). *Education, social status, and health*. New York: Aldine de Gruyter.

Mirowsky, J., & Ross, C. E. (2005). Education, cumulative advantage, and health. *Ageing International, 30*(1), 27–62.

Mohai, P., & Bryant, B. (1992). Environmental racism: Reviewing the evidence. In P. Mohai & B. Bryant (Eds.), *Race and the incidence of environmental hazards: A time for discourse*. Boulder, CO: Westview Press.

Morrow, V. (1999). Conceptualising social capital in relation to the well-being of children and young people: A critical review. *The Sociological Review, 47*(4), 744–765.

Mouw, T. (2003). Social capital and finding a job: Do contacts matter? *American Sociological Review, 68*, 868–898.

Müller, W., & Shavit, Y. (1998). The institutional embeddedness of the stratification process. In Y. Shavit & W. Müller (Eds.), *From school to work: A comparative study of educational qualifications and occupational destinations* (pp. 1–48). Oxford: Clarendon.

Murname, R. J., Willett, J. B., & Levy, F. (1995). The growing importance of cognitive skills in wage determination. *The Review of Economics and Statistics, 77*, 251–266.

Neuman, S. B., & Celano, D. (2001). Access to print in low-income and middle income communities: An ecological study of four neighbourhoods. *Reading ResearchQuarterly, 36*(1), 8–26.

O'Rand, A. M. (2001). Stratification and the life course: The forms of life course capital and their interrelationships. In R. H. Binstock & L. K. George (Eds.), *The handbook of aging and the social sciences* (5th ed., pp. 197–216). NY: Academic.

Organization for Economic Co-operation and Development (OECD). (1997). *Prepared for life? How to measure Cross-Curricular Competences. Centre for Educational Research and Innovation*. Paris: OECD.

Organization for Economic Co-operation and Development (OECD). (1998). *Human capital investment: An international comparison*. Paris: Centre for Educational Research and Innovation and OECD.

Organization for Economic Co-operation and Development (OECD). (1999a). *Overcoming exclusion through adult learning*. Paris: Centre for Educational Research and Innovation and OECD.

Organization for Economic Co-operation and Development (OECD). (1999b). *Classifying educational programmes: Manual For ISCED-97 implementation in OECD countries*. Paris: OECD.

Organization for Economic Co-operation and Development (OECD). (2001). *The well-being of nations: The role of human capital*. Paris: Centre for Educational Research and Innovation and OECD.

Organization for Economic Co-operation and Development (OECD). (2006). *Education at a glance OECD indicators 2006*. Paris: Centre for Educational Research and Innovation and OECD.

Pallas, A. M. (2000). The effects of schooling on individual lives. In M. T. Hallinan (Ed.), *Handbook of sociology of education* (pp. 499–525). New York: Klewer Academic/Plenum Publishers.

Pascarella, E., & Terenzini, P. (2005). *How college affects students: A third decade of research*. San Francisco: Jossey-Bass.

Perrons, D. (2000). Living with risk: Labour market transformation, employment policies and social reproduction in the UK. *Economic and Industrial Democracy, 21*, 283–310.

Peschar, J. L. (2004). Cross-curricular competencies: Developments in a new area of educational outcome indicators.

In J. Moskowitz & M. Stephens (Eds.), *Comparing learning outcomes: International assessment in educational policy* (pp. 45–67). Ottawa/Paris London: RoutledgeFarmer.

Phillips, D. (2006). *Quality of life: Concept, policy and practice.* New York: Routledge.

Portes, A. (1998). Social capital: Its origins and applications in modern sociology. *Annual Review of Sociology, 24,* 1–24.

Portes, A. (2000). The two meanings of social capital. *Sociological Forum, 15*(1), 1–12.

Prus, S. G. (2004). A life course perspective on the relationship between socio-economic status and health: Testing the divergence hypothesis. *Canadian Journal on Aging, 23*(suppl 1), 145–153.

Ranchor, A. V., Bouma, J., & Sanderman, R. (1996). Vulnerability and social class: Differential patterns of personality and social support over the social class. *Personality and Individual Differences, 20,* 229–237.

Rapley, M. (2003). *Quality of life research: A critical introduction.* Thousand Oaks: Sage.

Reynolds, J. R., & Ross, C. E. (1998). Social stratification and health: Education's benefits beyond economic status and social origin. *Social Problems, 45,* 221–247.

Rindfuss, R. R., Morgan, S. P., & Offut, K. (1996). Education and the changing age pattern of American fertility: 1963–1989. *Demography, 33,* 277–290.

Roberge, R., Berthelot, J., & Wolfson, M. (1995). Health and socio-economic inequalities. *Canadian Social Trends, 7*(2), 15–19, (Statistics Canada Catalogue No. 11–008E).

Robertson, D., & Symons, J. (2003). Do peer groups matter? Peer group versus schooling effects on academic attainment. *Economica, 70,* 31–53.

Robinson, J. P., & Godbey, G. (1997). *Time for life: The surprising ways Americans use their time.* University Park, PA: Pennsylvania State University Press.

Rogot, E., Sorlie, P. D., & Johnson, N. J. (1992). Life expectancy by employment status, income, and education in the national longitudinal mortality study. *Public Health Reports, 107,* 457–461.

Rosenbaum, J. (2001). *Beyond college for all: Career paths for the forgotten half.* New York: Russell Sage.

Ross, C. E., & Reskin, B. (1992). Education, control at work, and job satisfaction. *Social Science Research, 21,* 134–148.

Ross, C. E., & Van Willigen, M. (1997). Education and the subjective quality of life. *Journal of Health and Social Behavior, 38,* 275–297.

Ross, C. E., & Wu, C.-L. (1995). The links between education and health. *American Sociological Review, 60,* 719–745.

Ross, C. E., & Wu, C.-L. (1996). Education, age, and the cumulative advantage in health. *Journal of Health and Social Behavior, 37,* 104–120.

Sampson, R. (2001). How do communities undergird or undermine human development? relevant contexts and social mechanisms. In A. Booth & N. Crouter (Eds.), *Does it really take a village: Community effects on children, adolescents, and families* (pp. 3–31). Mahway, NJ: Lawrence Erlbaum.

Sampson, R. J., Raudenbaush, S., & Earls, F. (1997). Neighborhoods and violent crime: A multilevel study of collective efficacy. *Science, 277,* 918–924.

Sampson, R. J., Morenoff, J. J., & Earls, F. (1999). Beyond social capital: Spatial dynamics of collective agency for children. *American Sociological Review, 64,* 633–660.

Sander, W. (1995a). Schooling and quitting smoking. *The Review of Economics and Statistics, 77,* 191–199.

Sander, W. (1995b). Schooling and smoking. *Economics of Education Review, 14,* 23–33.

Schieman, S. (2002). Socioeconomic status, Job conditions, and well-being: Self-concept explanations for gender-contingent effects. *The Sociological Quarterly, 43*(4), 627–646.

Sewell, W. H., & Hauser, R. M. (1992a). The influence of the American occupational structure on the Wisconsin model. *Contemporary Sociology, 21*(5), 598–603.

Sewell, W. H., & Hauser, R. M. (1992b). *A review of the Wisconsin longitudinal study of social and psychological factors in aspirations and achievements, 1963–1993* (CDE working papers, no. 92–1). Madison, Wisconsin: Center for Demography and Ecology, University of Wisconsin-Madison.

Sirgy, M. J., Michalos, A. C., Ferriss, A. L., Easterlin, R. A., Patrick, D., & Pavot, W. (2006). The quality-of-life (QOL) research movement: Past, present, and future. *Social Indicators Research, 76,* 343–466.

Smith, T. W. (1995). Some aspects of measuring education. *Social Science Research, 24,* 215–242.

Smith, V. K. (1997). Feedback effects and environmental resources. In J. R. Behrman, D. L. Crawford, & N. Stacey (Eds.), *The social benefits of education* (pp. 175–218). Ann Arbour, MI: University of Michigan Press.

Soloman, L. C., & Fagano, C. L. (1997). Benefits of education. In L. J. Saha (Ed.), *International encyclopedia of the sociology of education* (pp. 819–829). New York: Pergamon.

Steinberg, L., Lamborn, S. D., Dornbusch, S. M., & Darling, N. (1992). Impact of parenting practices on adolescent achievement: Authoritative parenting, school involvement and encouragement to succeed. *Child Development, 63,* 1266–1281.

Strand, S. (1997). Pupil progress during key stage 1: A value added analysis of school effects. *British Educational Research Journal, 23*(4), 471–488.

Sullivan, D. H., & Smeeding, T. M. (1997). Educational attainment and earnings inequality in eight nations. *International Journal of Educational Research, 27*(6), 513–525.

Sweetman, A. (2002). Working smarter: education and productivity. *The Review of Economic Performance and Social Progress,* 157–180.

Tachibanaki, T. (1997). Education, occupation, and earnings. In L. J. Saha (Ed.), *International encyclopedia of the sociology of education* (pp. 293–297). New York: Pergamon.

Tauchen, H., Witte, A. D., & Griesinger, H. (1994). Criminal deterrence: Revisiting the issue with a birth cohort. *The Review of Economics and Statistics, 76,* 399–412.

Tzeng, M.-S. (1992). The effects of socioeconomic heterogamy and changes on marital dissolution for first marriages. *Journal of Marriage and Family, 54,* 609–619.

UNESCO. (2000, April 26–28). *The Dakar Framework for Action—Education for All: Meeting our Collective Commitments,* Adopted by the World Education Forum, Dakar.

UNHDP. (2003). *United Nations Human Development Report 2003.* New York: Oxford University Press Inc.

UNICEF Innocenti Research Centre. (2002). *A league table of educational disadvantage in rich nations* (Innocenti Report Card No. 4). Florence: UN Children's Fund.

Veenhoven, R. (2008). Healthy happiness: effects of happiness on physical health and the consequences for preventive health care. *Journal of Happiness Studies, 9*(3), 449–469.

Willms, J. D. (2001). Three hypotheses about community effects. In J. F. Helliwell (Ed.), *The contributions of human and social capital to sustained economic growth and well-being: International symposium report* (pp. 251–271). Ottawa/Paris: Human Resources Development Canada and OECD.

Wilson, A., Rosenblood, L. K., & Oliver, P. R. (1973). Congruity theory and linear models of attitude change. *Canadian Journal of Behavioural Science, 5*, 399–409.

Wolfe, B., & Haveman, R. (2001). Accounting for social and non-market benefits of education. In J. F. Helliwell (Ed.), *The contributions of human and social capital to sustained economic growth and well-being: International symposium report* (pp. 221–250). Ottawa/Paris: Human Resources Development Canada and OECD.

Wray, L. A., Herzog, A. R., Willis, A. J., & Wallace, R. B. (1998). The impact of education and heart attack on smoking cessation among middle-aged adults. *Journal of Health and Social Behavior, 39*(4), 271–294.

Zhu, B., Giovano, G., Mowery, P., & Eriksen, M. (1996). The relationship between cigarette smoking and education revisited: Implications for categorizing persons' educational status. *American Journal of Public Health, 86*, 1582–1589.

Review of Research Related to Quality of Work Life (QWL) Programs*

13

M. Joseph Sirgy, Nora P. Reilly, Jiyun Wu, and David Efraty

Introduction

In the last few decades, we have witnessed a trend indicating that many corporations are increasingly implementing job satisfaction and empowerment programs (e.g., Wilkinson 1998). These programs promote employee well-being in the workplace and are often the result of management's self-interest to promote profitability. Management has found that programs designed to increase job satisfaction and empower employees *may* increase employee productivity and job performance (e.g., Armenakis and Bedeian 1999; Greenhaus et al. 1987; O'Toole and Ferry 2002; Petty et al. 1984). In turn, higher levels of productivity and performance serve to increase the organization's economic well-being.

From this perspective, management views employee participation in organization development activities as means to higher financial returns. While an economic orientation may remain a necessity for business organizations, it need not preclude a focus on employee well-being. Quality of work life (QWL) programs can result in job satisfaction and quality of life (QOL, i.e., life satisfaction, happiness, and subjective well-being). The often-overlooked non-financial consequences of QWL programs are commendable ends in and of themselves (Wolf 1971).

At the core of the QWL movement is the satisfaction of employees' needs through organization development (e.g., McGregor 1960). Though QWL has been associated with employee productivity, job satisfaction, organizational commitment, and low turnover rates, QWL researchers have shown that QWL plays an important role in life satisfaction and QOL (e.g., Ilies et al. 2009; Kabanoff 1980; Lawler 1982; Lee et al. 2002; Near et al. 1980; Sirgy et al. 2001). The current review links QWL research to overall QOL.

Both QWL and QOL represent conditions of work life and life in general. QWL programs can contribute to QOL through satisfaction of basic and growth needs in a variety of life domains: work, family, leisure, and spiritual, among others. The thread that binds a QWL program to QOL is the affect associated with the multiple domains that comprise work and nonwork activities. The most typical indicator of this affect is self-reported satisfaction.

Job satisfaction is viewed as an attitude or, more recently, an emotional state (Weiss et al. 1999) associated with one's job experiences, whereas life satisfaction is considered to be associated with evaluations of all salient life domains are cognitively integrated (summed or averaged). Given that job satisfaction is positively related to life satisfaction

---

*This chapter is significantly adapted and updated from the following publication by the same authors: Sirgy, M. J. Reilly, N., Wu, J., & Efraty, D. (2008). A work-life identity model of well-being: Towards a research agenda linking quality-of-work-life (QWL) programs with quality of life (QOL). *Applied Research in Quality of Life*, 3(3), 181–202.

M.J. Sirgy (✉)
Department of Marketing, Virginia Polytechnic Institute and State University, Blacksburg, VA 24061-0236, USA
e-mail: sirgy@vt.edu

N.P. Reilly
Department of Psychology, Radford University, Radford, VA, USA

J. Wu
Rhode Island College, Providence, Rhode Island, USA

D. Efraty
University of Houston-Downtown, Houston, TX, USA

K.C. Land et al. (eds.), *Handbook of Social Indicators and Quality of Life Research*,
DOI 10.1007/978-94-007-2421-1_13, © Springer Science+Business Media B.V. 2012

(e.g., $r = +.44$; Kantak et al. 1992; Tait et al. 1989), it should follow that perceptions of QWL and QOL should also tend to be positively related because affective reactions to work experiences spill over or spread to nonwork domains, and vice versa. While Judge and Watanabe (1993) have argued that some people can segment their feelings or compensate for divergent affective reactions across life domains, they estimate that 68% of people experience reciprocal *spillover* between job satisfaction and life satisfaction (see also Rain et al. 1991; Rice, et al. 1985; Staines 1980).

The spillover from one's experience in a particular life domain (e.g., work life, leisure life, family life, spiritual life) to one's satisfaction/dissatisfaction with life in general may be affected by a variety of moderators. For example, a study conducted by Efraty et al. (1999) has shown that the spillover between job satisfaction and life satisfaction is moderated by organizational commitment. That is, employees who reported a higher level of organizational commitment experienced greater spillover than those who expressed lower levels of commitment. The authors explained this finding using the saliency bias hypothesis. Spillover of affect from one life domain to another is more likely to occur when the domain is considered highly salient in the mind of that individual than when that domain is not considered salient. Specifically, employees who regard their jobs to be very important in their lives at large are likely to experience heightened satisfaction or dissatisfaction with their jobs, which in turn spills over to other nonwork domains and affect life satisfaction in general.

Interestingly, both job and life satisfaction share a substantial dispositional component (e.g., Diener et al. 1999; Hart 1999; Heller et al. 2002). A top-down approach to the study of job and life satisfactions suggests that common traits (e.g., positive and negative affectivity) influence both. In fact, although personality removes a huge chunk of the variance from the job-life satisfaction relationship, the link still remains. It is interesting to note that situational influences on subjective well-being (a bottom-up approach) have been found to account for a significant amount of variance in subjective well-being (see Diener et al. 1999; also see Sirgy 2002). QWL programs traditionally assume a bottom-up approach to fostering productivity and satisfaction.

This chapter is designed to review the research related to QWL programs. There are many QWL programs. We will discuss some of them in terms of two major categories: QWL programs that affect *work-related* role identities and QWL programs that impact *nonwork* identities.

Satisfaction in Work Life and Spillover to Overall Life

QWL programs related to work life can be categorized into four major groups: (1) QWL programs related to the work environment, (2) QWL programs related to job facets, (3) QWL programs related to management/supervisory duties and responsibilities, and (4) QWL programs related to corporate policies dealing with employee pay and promotion. We will discuss selected

Table 13.1 QWL policies and programs that satisfy employee needs in work life

The work environment	Job facets	Management/supervisory duties and responsibilities	Corporate policies related to employee pay and promotion
• Decentralized organizational structures	• Participation in decision-making and high-involvement programs	• TQM	• Promotion opportunities from within
• Teamwork	• Job enrichment programs	• Performance feedback and role clarity	• Pay and incentive plans
• Parallel structures and quality circles	• Programs to enhance occupational status and prestige	• Ethical supervisory behavior	
• Ethical corporate mission and culture		• Co-leadership	
• The organization's work schedule			

QWL Programs Related to the Work Environment

We identified several QWL programs related to the work environment. These are decentralized organizational structures, teamwork, parallel structures and quality circles, and ethical corporate culture.

Decentralized Organizational Structures

Based on the assumption that bureaucratization is positively associated with job dissatisfaction and off-the-job alienation, Efraty and Sirgy (1995) conducted a study showing workers in a decentralized bureaucracy experience greater spillover (between job satisfaction and life satisfaction) than workers in a centralized bureaucracy. Decentralized bureaucracies allowed workers to enjoy greater work discretion and less immediate supervision. Work discretion and low levels of supervision serve to reduce work role stress, which in turn help reduce negative self-evaluations in work life. This, of course, serves to reduce spillover of negative affect from work life to overall life, thus decreasing the likelihood of diminishing employee QOL. Furthermore, greater work discretion and less immediate supervision serve to enhance the value of the work role identity, which in turn leads to positive self-evaluations. Increases in positive self-evaluations in relation to the work role identity (and decreases in negative self-evaluations) contribute to higher levels of subjective well-being or QOL through spillover.

Teamwork

A team is a small group of people with complementary skills, who work together to achieve a common goal for which they are collectively accountable (Brill 1976). Teamwork, characterized by reciprocal trust and respect among team members, serves to enhance both QWL and QOL (e.g., Lee and Chang 2008; Nandan and Nandan 1995; Qvale and Hanssen-Bauer 1990; Richardson and West 2010). Teamwork can be induced through role clarification, problem solving, goal clarification and prioritization, and conflict resolution.

Teamwork promotes work role identity by providing employees with greater work resources to achieve work role expectations (than non-teamwork) through the participation required by goal setting, problem solving, goal clarification and prioritization, and conflict resolution. Achieving work role expectations, in turn, serves to increase positive self-evaluations. The latter generates positive affect in the work domain, which in turn spills over to overall life and thus increases subjective well-being. One can also argue that teamwork serves to reduce work demands by shifting this responsibility to the team and away from the self. This serves to decrease negative self-evaluations that may arise when work role expectations are not met.

Parallel Structures and Quality Circles

Jobs generating higher levels of involvement involve *parallel structures*, also known as "collateral structures," "dualistic structures," or "shadow structures" (e.g., Galbraith 1998). Jobs with parallel structures provide an alternative setting to address problems and propose innovative solutions free from the formal organization structure. *Quality circles* are an example of parallel structures. Quality circles consist of small groups of 13–15 employees who volunteer to meet periodically, usually once a week for an hour or so, to identify and solve productivity problems (Galbraith 1998). These group members make recommendations for change, but decisions about implementation of their proposals are reserved for management.

Parallel structures, characterized in terms of voluntary employee meetings to identify and discuss problems at work, serve to enhance employee–work environment fit and need satisfaction in the work domain. Just in the same way that teamwork is hypothesized to affect QOL, parallel structures promote the work role identity. It does so by providing the employee with additional resources to meet work demands. Doing so increases the likelihood of positive self-evaluations in work life (as a direct result of meeting work role expectations), which in turn spills over to overall life. Furthermore, parallel structures reduce work role stress by shifting responsibility of task completion away from the self and toward the group.

Ethical Corporate Mission and Culture

An ethical corporate mission and culture are important in enhancing work-related identity by generating positive affect that spills over to the other life domains. The results of a 2-year empirical study based on face-to-face interviews showed that employees believe that being associated with an ethical organization gives them a sense of meaning and purpose in their work (Mitroff and Denton 1999). The study uncovered five basic designs or models in which organizations can contribute meaning and a sense of purpose in work. These are the *religious-based organization* (e.g., church-affiliated and -run businesses), the *evolutionary organization* (a firm that begins with a strong association with a particular religion and over time evolves to a more ecumenical position), the *recovering organization* (an organization that focuses on helping people solve certain problems and in doing so fosters a sense of spirituality), the *socially responsible organization* (firms in which their founders or heads are guided by strong spiritual principles that they apply directly to their business for the betterment of society), and the *values-based organization* (the founders or managers are guided by general philosophical principles or values that are not aligned or associated with a particular religion or spirituality).

Organizations with a high ethical corporate mission and culture may provide a better person-environment fit than organizations with a low ethical mission and culture, as organizational characteristics can affect person-environment fit (e.g., Fletcher et al. 2008). For evidence of how a caring, ethical organization contributes to employee higher-order need satisfaction, see literature review by Giacalone and Jurkiewicz (2002). Also see de Klerk (2005), Duchon and Plowman (2005), Fry (2005), Gavin and Mason (2004), Jurkiewicz and Giacalone (2004), Kinjerski and Kolodinsky et al. (2008), Milliman et al. (2003), and Pawar (2009), Skrypnek (2004).

Many employees may desire to engage in tasks that can contribute to the betterment of the human condition. An ethical organization places demands on their employees that are more congruent with the employees' work role identity (in the role of a "do-gooder") than other organizations. Also, ethical organizations may provide more work resources to meet the demands of the "do-gooder" than other organizations. Such organizations increase the value of the work role identity in the sense that employees feel that their work is meaningful because they help others. Under these conditions, employees are likely to experience high levels of positive self-evaluations, which in turn contribute to subjective well-being.

QWL Programs Related to the Job

Several QWL programs are related to the job. These are participation in decision-making/high-involvement programs and job enrichment programs.

Participation in Decision-Making and High-Involvement Programs

In a seminal study, Teas et al. (1979) found that participation in decision-making and high-involvement programs contribute positively and significantly to work satisfaction (see Levine 1995; Stairs and Gaplin 2010 for reviews). High-involvement programs act as a conduit to help employees express their thoughts and feelings in important organizational decisions, and this input is likely to influence the final management decision. High-involvement programs afford employees with a greater sense of meaningfulness in their work activities, which increases the value of their work role identity.

Job Enrichment Programs

Job design is the process of defining the job tasks and work arrangements necessary to accomplish them. This process may determine the amount of satisfaction that workers experience at work. As noted by Schermerhorn et al. (2003, p.153), the best job design is always one that meets organizational requirements for high performance, offers a good fit with individual skills and needs, and provides opportunities for job satisfaction. Enriched jobs enhance motivation to work, as prescribed by the Job Characteristics Model (Hackman and Oldham 1980). This model identifies five job characteristics that are essential for job design—skill variety, task identity, task significance, autonomy, and feedback. If these job characteristics are present, they are likely to enhance the meaningfulness of work, experienced responsibility for outcomes and knowledge of actual results, as well as work outcomes such as intrinsic work motivation, quality of work performance, and satisfaction with the work.

The Job Characteristic Model allows for individual differences that moderate the match between the worker and the job (e.g., Blood and Hulin 1967; Hulin and Blood 1968). Specifically, the model describes the effects of the following moderators:

1. *Growth need strength* refers to the worker's need for growth opportunities. The model prescribes that only individuals with high growth needs will favor enriched jobs that, for example, provide a

high level of autonomy in decision-making. Those with low growth need strength might experience stress in response to an enriched job. Workers whose competencies and skills match the requirements of enriched jobs are likely to welcome the job redesign. Those who are deficient in the required skills are not likely to feel good about the enriched design.

2. *Context satisfaction* refers to worker satisfaction with various "context" (environmental) aspects of the work setting such as satisfaction with salary, working conditions, salary, supervision, etc. According to the model, workers who are satisfied with the job context are more likely to support and favor enriched jobs.

QWL Programs Related to Management Duties/Responsibilities and Supervisory Behavior

Several QWL programs relate to management duties and responsibilities. These include total quality management, performance feedback and role clarity, and ethical supervisory behavior.

Total Quality Management (TQM)

The idea underlying TQM is that all members of the organization are committed to high-quality results, continuous improvement, and customer satisfaction. TQM also prescribes employee involvement and empowerment. Popovich-Hill and Hubbard (1995) conducted a study in the hospitality field to examine the effect of TQM on QOL. They found that indeed TQM had a positive impact on work and life satisfaction (see also Ugboro and Obeng 2000). Ooi et al. (2008) also found that when TQM is conducted as teamwork, it significantly increases job satisfaction. TQM allows employees to assume multiple role identities within the work domain, including the role of planner, team member, coordinator, communicator, producer, and responsible party. Engaging in multiple identities at work provides added meaning and value to the overall work role. Furthermore, fulfillment of these varied roles is likely to satisfy more needs, which in turn translates into positive self-evaluations contributing to subjective well-being.

Performance Feedback and Role Clarity

The seminal study by Teas et al. (1979) found that salespeople's need fulfillment is directly related to role clarity and performance feedback; higher levels of role clarity and performance feedback lead to higher levels of job satisfaction. Role clarity and performance feedback help employees meet their work role expectations. Meeting those expectations generate positive self-evaluations, which in turn contribute to subjective well-being. Performance feedback and role clarity facilitate learning and enhance job performance.

Ethical Supervisory Behavior

Employees view their jobs as purposeful and meaningful when their immediate supervisor treats them honestly, fairly, and with care. Thus, ethical supervisory behavior promotes the work role identity by heightening the importance of the work role. Meeting those work role expectations are then likely to generate higher levels of positive self-evaluations than meeting expectations that are less important. More positive self-evaluations in the work domain contribute significantly to subjective well-being.

Ethical supervisory behavior affects work satisfaction through perceptions of procedural justice. That is, employees feel dissatisfied with their work when they perceive that their supervisors are not living up to their own role expectations of what a "good and ethical supervisor" should do. In a classic sociological analysis of the effects of supervisory style, Hopper (1965) has shown that close or punitive supervision becomes frustrating to subordinates when it violates the subordinates' normative expectations of authority. More recently, the literature on organizational justice (e.g., Cropanzano et al. 2002) provides more evidence to support this contention. In role theory terms, feelings of inequity translate to role stress, which contribute to negative self-evaluations adversely influencing subjective well-being.

Corporate Policies Related to Employee Pay and Promotion

In this section, we will discuss two sets of QWL programs related to employee promotion and incentives, namely promotion from within and incentive plans.

Promotion from Within

Self-actualization, according to Maslow (1954), is the desire to become more and more from what one is to anything that one is capable of becoming. Promotion and career progress are important in that regard.

Progressive companies have promotion-from-within programs (Messmer 2004). This means that open positions are filled, whenever possible, by qualified candidates from within the company. Promotion-from-within programs serve to enhance the value of the work role identity and promote multiple work role identities (e.g., specialist, team player, and supervisor/manager). Meeting the needs of more role identities and highly valued role increases the likelihood of experiencing positive self-evaluations at work, which in turn contributes significantly to subjective well-being.

Pay and Incentive Plans

Diener et al. (2010) tested the relationship between income and happiness. Specifically, income was found to be related to well-being in that general life satisfaction was influenced by people's contentment with their standard of living and their ability to fulfill their desire for luxury goods. However, it is not income that contributes to well-being per se but the social resources associated with income (e.g., purchase power of goods and services that provide status and prestige to the individual) (cf. Bozionelos and Nikolaou 2010).

There is a popular assumption that employees who draw higher *pay* are happier in their life and work. Judge et al. (2010) carried out a meta-analysis on this issue. They assessed 86 studies looking specifically at the correlations between employees' compensation/pay and their job satisfaction. Across studies a key finding emerged: There is a modest and positive relationship between pay level and both satisfaction with the job as a whole and with pay specifically. Thus, one can argue that pay does indeed enhance the value of the work role identity, which in turn contributes to positive self-evaluations at work leading to subjective well-being. However, it should be noted that evidence suggests that the well-being effect generated by increases in pay is short-lived (cf. Maraist et al. 1999; Wyld and Maurin 2011).

There are many incentive plans that organizations use to reward their employees and satisfy employee needs for self-actualization, self-esteem, and social recognition. These include individual incentive programs, group incentive programs, and profit-sharing plans. *Individual incentive programs* give income over and above base salary to employees who meet work-related role expectations. Merit pay can be construed as a type of an individual incentive program. Much evidence has shown that individual incentive programs are directly linked to job performance (e.g., Tharp 1985). These programs are perceived as the outcome of meeting role demand, which in turn contributes to positive self-evaluations and positive affect in the work domain, spilling over to subjective well-being.

Group incentive programs give pay over and above base salary to all team members when the team collectively meets a project goal. There seems to be much evidence suggesting that group incentive programs serve to improve job performance and employee productivity (e.g., Bartol and Hagmann 1992), which in turn serve to enhance work satisfaction. This occurs as a result of recognizing the group incentive as an outcome of meeting role demand.

Profit-sharing plans are organization-wide incentive programs that provide employees with a share of the firm's profits. There are many forms of profit-sharing plans such as stock options, stock appreciation rights, performance achievement plans, restricted stock plans, phantom stock plans, and book value plans (see Redling 1982, for a review). One can easily argue that profit-sharing plans go a long way to enhance satisfaction in the work domain as well as nonwork domains (e.g., family life, leisure life, social life). Profit sharing is a means to generate more resources to promote role identity at work and outside of work.

Satisfaction in Nonwork Life and Spillover to Overall Life

QWL programs that promote nonwork role identities and need satisfaction are grouped in three categories. The first is alternative work arrangements, the second is components of employee's compensation package, and the third is ancillary programs. Table 13.2 summarizes the QWL programs related to nonwork life.

Alternative Work Arrangements

Alternative work arrangements involve a QWL program designed to minimize work—family conflict and help employees balance the demands of their work and family lives (Quick et al. 1997). Greenhaus and Beutel (1985) suggested that the most common type of work-family conflict is time-based conflict, experienced when the time devoted to one role makes the fulfill-

Table 13.2 QWL policies and programs that satisfy employee needs in nonwork life (e.g., family, leisure, financial, health, spiritual, community)

Alternative work arrangements	Employment benefits	Ancillary programs
• Work at home	• Health benefits	• Childcare programs
• Flextime	• Retirement benefits	• Elder care programs
• Compressed workweek	• Supplemental pay benefits	• Fitness programs
• Part-time work arrangements		• Social programs and events
• Job sharing		• EAPs and counseling services
		• Innovative programs

ment of the other difficult. Common programs are those that manipulate work arrangements such as full-time work-at-home, part-time work-at-home, flextime, compressed workweek, and part-time work arrangements (e.g., Duxbury and Haines 1991; Schermerhorn et al. 2003). Alternative work arrangements typically affect life satisfaction by reducing work-family conflict, which in turn enhances satisfaction with work and family life (e.g., Higgins and Duxbury 1992; Kopelman et al. 1983). For comprehensive overviews of alternative work arrangements, refer to the studies conducted by Baltes et al. (1999), and Baltes et al. (2010), Frone and Yardely (1996), Parker and Wall (1998).

Work at Home

Full-time (or part-time) work at home—sometimes referred to as "teleworking," "telecommuting," and "flexiplace"—involves allowing employees to fulfill their job duties and responsibilities from their home, thus spending significantly more time at home than at the office. Madsen (2003) conducted a survey to investigate the differences in work-family conflict between full-time worksite employees and full-time teleworking employees. The study results indicated that teleworkers had lower levels of work-family conflict in various dimensions. Research has shown that multiple roles involving both work and family may decrease stress because of increased opportunities for need satisfaction (e.g., Valdez and Gutek 1989). It may be that work at home contributes to QOL by reducing conflict between family and work roles; work at home serves to reduce the work role demand and concomitant stress and enhances multiple role identities—work and family roles (Batt and Valcour 2003; Hill et al. 2003).

Flextime

Flextime refers to the use of flexible work schedules to help employees integrate work and life demands

(Kossek et al. 1999). A variation of flextime is "flexyears." Under this program, employees can choose (at 6-month intervals) the number of hours they want to work each month over the next year (International Management 1982). Research has shown many firms use flextime; however, a majority of surveyed managers expressed more concerns about flextime than other forms of alternative work arrangements (e.g., part-time work and leave of absence). Why? Perhaps because of possible lower levels of employee productivity. With respect to the effect of flextime on nonwork life, Lucas and Heady (2002) conducted a survey of 125 full-time employed commuters from Atlanta, Georgia, the city with the largest average commute distance in the world. They found that commuters with flextime reported less stress and fewer feelings of time urgency than those without flextime. Thus, flextime provides employees with resources allowing them to engage in work and nonwork roles with less stress. By the same token, flextime allows employees to engage in work and nonwork roles with relative ease, thus satisfying more needs.

Furthermore, one can argue that flextime is likely to benefit certain kind of employees more than others. Using data from the 1997 Current Population Survey Work Schedules Supplement of the US Census Bureau, Sharpe et al. (2002) have shown that flextime is used more for married males, non-Hispanic whites, those with relatively higher levels of education and income, those with preschool-aged children, managers or professionals, and employees of the federal government than other demographic segments.

Studies have shown that the use of flextime at work is an effective strategy that helps employees manage demand of both work and family role by reducing role conflict, thus enhancing subjective well-being (e.g., Rau and Hyland 2002).

Compressed Workweek

A compressed workweek refers to working more hours during the day but taking longer weekends (or days off) to allow the employee to spend more time on non-work matters. Much research has shown that employees gain from compressed workweek. For example, one study reported a 20% reduction in commuter trips (Northrup 1991). Another study has shown that childcare expenses can be reduced significantly by adopting a compressed workweek (Solomon 1991). A recent study shows that the alternative schedule reduces work-family conflict and has positive and long-lasting effects on both the organization and the employees. These positive effects may be due to reducing stress from commuting and the financial burden of childcare (Facer and Wadsworth 2008).

Furthermore, Latack and Foster (1985) reported that overall reactions to compressed workweeks are favorable for employees who are allowed to participate in the decision to adopt them, who have their jobs enriched as a result of the new schedule, and who have strong higher-order needs. Saltzstein et al. (2001) found that compressed workweek contributes to work-life balance. However, the same study also noted that its effects are most positive when the employee is in need of childcare assistance.

Part-Time Work Arrangements

Part-time work arrangements refer to working less than the traditional 40 h/week. Part-time work arrangements, characterized by working part time to allow the employee to spend more time with family members, serve to reduce work-related stress by reducing work role demands; it helps meet role demand in the context of both work and family roles, decreases conflict between work and family roles, enhances multiple role identities, and helps promote the family caretaker role by enhancing its perceived value. Doing so increases (decreases) the likelihood of positive (negative) self-evaluations in work and family roles, contributing to subjective well-being.

However, the effect of this QWL program may be limited to certain types of employees. For example, Booth and Van Ours (2009) found that part-time women are more satisfied with working hours than full-time women. Farber (1999) found that most people take part-time jobs when they get laid off or lose their full-time job. Thus, a part-time job for these workers becomes a point of transition to finding a full-time job. Therefore, future research could further investigate the QOL effectiveness of this QWL program in relation to employees who voluntarily choose this program versus those who are laid off or lose their full-time jobs. Other moderators may include lone mothers and culture. Specifically, Gill and Davidson (2001) found that lone mothers in management and professional occupations were less able to take advantage of part-time work arrangements because of greater financial pressures. Lone mothers reported higher levels of pressure from workload and the home-work balance than other women.

With respect to culture as a moderator, Wharton and Blair-Loy (2002) conducted a cross-national study of finance professionals interested in working part time. Hong Kong respondents expressed more interest in part-time work than their British and American counterparts. Perhaps the Chinese culture places more priority on the family role identity than the British and American culture. If so, we can expect that the effectiveness of this QWL program would be greater in places such as China and Hong Kong than in Britain and the USA.

Job Sharing

Job sharing refers to situations in which specific job-related duties and responsibilities are shared between two or more employees (Voydanoff 1989). About 10% of firms questioned in a survey conducted by Solomon (1994) indicated that they allow for job sharing. Job sharing has become increasingly popular recently, especially in industries hard hit by unemployment and job losses. An example of such an industry is travel and tourism because of the September 11, 2001 attacks (Sherwyn and Sturman 2002). Some large companies have created job-sharing programs such as the Barclay Bank in the UK (Human Resource Management Digest 2003), where there is a national online job-sharing register to help employees find a potential job-share partner. Job sharing may serve to enhance family well-being. Job sharing promotes the development of one's work role identity as well as at least one valued nonwork role identity—that of a parent, spouse, or caretaker—by providing resources that reduce the conflict between the two.

As with part-time employment, Gill and Davidson (2001) found that lone mothers in management and professional occupations were less able to take advantage of job sharing, perhaps because of greater financial pressures.

Employment Benefits

A majority of companies in the USA offer at least some employment benefits to their employees (Grossman and Magnus 1988). For example, about 92% of medium and large firms and 69% of small firms provide health insurance. Most firms also provide retirement/pension benefits—88% of large firms, 78% of medium-sized firms, and 73% of small businesses. Social security is legally required and contributes toward most employees' retirement income (Grossman and Magnus 1988). A discussion of employment benefits in terms of insurance benefits, retirement benefits, and supplemental pay benefits follows.

Insurance Benefits

There are essentially three types of insurance benefits provided to employees in the USA: worker's compensation, life insurance, and medical/health insurance. *Worker's compensation* is a program that provides income and medical benefits to work-related accident victims or their dependents regardless of fault. Some companies have instituted rehabilitation programs for injured employees (Bialk 1987). These include exercise programs, career counseling to guide injured workers into less strenuous jobs, and nursing assistance. Obviously, one can predict that the worker's compensation program provides the injured employees a living allowance to satisfy basic needs affecting family's finances and health. Thus, worker's compensation can be construed as a QWL program that helps people meet demand of their roles as a financial provider and family caretaker and obviously applies only to people who are accident victims.

Life insurance and *hospitalization/medical/disability insurance* work similarly. One interesting area of research that may have a significant effect on employee QOL is the "pre-existing condition" exclusion. For example, Madrian (1994) assessed the effect of health insurance (provided by US employers) on job mobility and found that in many instances, employees are "locked" into their jobs because of "pre-existing condition" exclusions. The pre-existing conditions on their health insurance make it expensive for some employees with chronic health problems to relinquish their current health insurance (cf. Buckley and Van Giezen 2004). One can easily argue that the traditional health insurance requiring no pre-existing conditions is very negative on QOL, especially for those employees with chronic illness.

Retirement Benefits

Most US companies offer at least three forms of retirement benefits: social security, pension plans, and early retirement. *Social Security* in the USA provides three types of benefits: (1) retirement benefits, (2) survivor's or death benefits, and (3) disability payments (Dessler 1997, p. 518). Thus, social security benefits help employees meet demand of their roles as a financial provider and family caretaker.

US employers offer a variety of *pension plans*. As with social security, pension plans help employees meet demand of their roles as a financial provider and family caretaker. Many large companies in the US also offer *early retirement* windows in which specific employees (often age 50+) are eligible to participate. Early retirement plans vary considerably, but most involve a combination of improved or liberal pension benefits plus a cash payment (Karoly and Rogowski 1994). How does the QOL of early retirees change after retirement? Perhaps employees who do not regard their work role as central to their self-concept and identity are likely to benefit more from an early retirement program.

Supplemental Pay Benefits

This program involves payment to employees for time off for holidays, vacations, jury duty, funerals, military duty, illness, sabbaticals, and maternity leave. It also includes unemployment insurance payments for laid-off or terminated employees, and it contributes to employee well-being in the same way that insurance and retirement benefits do. Furthermore, one can argue that unemployment insurance tends to benefit employees who are heads of households, particularly those with large families.

The average number of annual *vacation* days is generally high in industrialized countries. For example, the US average is about 10 days/year, 30 in Sweden and Austria, 25 in France, and 20–25 in the UK, Spain, Norway, Finland, and Belgium (Matthes 1992). Vacation allows employees to reduce work role stress and promote nonwork roles in family, social, leisure, and cultural life. It would be fruitful to investigate the QOL impact of variations in vacation days in relation to different population groups. Career-oriented professionals with stronger work role identities—or few nonwork identities—may not need long vacations.

With respect to *sick leave*, most employers grant full pay for a specified number of days—usually up to 12 days/year. Some employers offer a buyback of unused sick leave at the end of the year by paying their employees a daily equivalent pay for each sick leave day not used (Bunning 1988). A buyback option may serve to promote the work role identity by rewarding work. It would be fruitful to investigate variations of sick leave programs on different employee groups. For example, a buyback of unused sick leave may contribute more to subjective well-being for employees who view their jobs as a way to make a living (and of lower socioeconomic status) than career-oriented professionals (and higher socioeconomic status).

Over 100 countries have enacted some form of *parental leave* policies, with most assuring at least 2–3 months of paid job absences (Ruhm 1998). A study of parental leave in Europe has shown that parental leave serves to increase the employment rate of women (Ruhm 1998). Parental leave may contribute to QOL by enhancing the role of parent in family life. Most significantly, parental leave works well for mothers and fathers of infants or children who suffered from physical and/or emotional trauma.

Severance pay—a one-time payment when terminating an employee—varies from 3 to 4 days wages to several months of wages. Many countries have laws that force employers to provide severance pay under conditions of plant closings and downsizing (Dessler 1997, p. 511). Having severance pay serves to reduce work role stress. Thus, employees, in their role of being financial providers to their families, can deal with job layoffs in case of plant closings, downsizing, etc.

Ancillary Programs

There are many ancillary programs found in the QWL literature designed to meet employee nonwork needs. These include childcare programs, elder care programs, fitness programs, social programs and events, employee assistance programs, and innovative programs.

Childcare Programs
Many large employers offer subsidized childcare assistance in the form of covering the full or partial cost of childcare or providing childcare services at the work site (Blain and Haywood 2004). Subsidized day care is becoming increasingly popular in the USA (Bureau of National Affairs 1988). Research has uncovered the positive effects of subsidized childcare to those organi-

zations having them. These organizational effects include increased ability to attract employees, lower absenteeism, improved morale, favorable publicity, and lower turnover, among others (e.g., Campbell and Campbell 1988; Peterson and Massengill 1988; Quick et al. 1997).

Ezra and Deckman (1996) used data from the 1991 Survey of Federal Employees to investigate how the use of family friendly policies (e.g., childcare programs, flextime) affects federal employees' satisfaction with their jobs and work-family balance. The study found that on-site childcare programs help employees, particularly mothers, face the demands of both work and family better. Ostensibly, this is due to the fact that the needs of both work and nonwork roles are simultaneously met and work-family conflict is reduced.

More recently, studies have shown that the use of childcare services at work is an effective strategy that helps employees manage demand of both work and family role by reducing role conflict, thus enhancing subjective well-being (e.g., Rau and Hyland 2002).

Elder Care Programs
These programs are designed to help employees who take care of their elderly parents. Many companies offer a variety of plans such as company-sponsored elder care centers and subsidies to help employees cover the cost of placing their parents into an elder care center (e.g., Earhart et al. 1993). Elder care programs have the potential to enhance QOL of employees who have parents in need in significant ways. They do so by minimizing the conflict between the work role and the caretaker role. The same mediation and moderation logic applied to childcare also applies to elder care.

Fitness Programs
The scope of employee fitness programs ranges from company-paid memberships at private fitness clubs to complete on-site facilities. Falkenberg (1987) reviewed much of the evidence available concerning the effects of employee fitness programs on employee well-being and the organization. The effects include the following:

- Higher-fitness levels reduce stress and improve health.
- Long-term participation in fitness programs changes employee mental state (i.e., employees show less signs of depression and anxiety).
- Short-term participation in fitness programs affects mood states (i.e., stimulates positive feelings about

one's self and generates feelings of muscular endurance and increased physiological arousal that translate into feelings of exhilaration and relaxation).

Falkenberg argued that much of the evidence points out that employee fitness programs serve to reduce stress symptoms, absenteeism, and lateness. Reduction of stress occurs when employees exercise during demanding work periods, which may serve to reduce stress in both work and nonwork roles. Reduced absenteeism and lateness occur when employees are better able to schedule work and nonwork activities.

Social Programs and Events

Some employers provide various social and recreational opportunities for their employees. These include company-sponsored athletic events, dance clubs, annual summer picnics, craft activities, employee retreats, and parties (Bureau of National Affairs 1992). QOL is likely to be impacted through the social life domain. That is, employees' QOL is enhanced through these QWL programs by increasing social and leisure well-being.

Consider the following seminal study by Kohn and Schooler (1982). These researchers have shown that providing tangible social support on the job can reduce the negative impact associated with stress at work.

Employee Assistance Programs (EAPs)

EAPs are services that provide employees with counseling or treatment for problems such as alcoholism, gambling, or stress (e.g., Employee Benefits 2005; Rockett 2004). One study estimated that 50–75% of all large US companies offer variations of EAP programs (Hellan 1986).

In the hospitality industry, Tse and Jackson (1990) argued that alcohol abuse is more likely because the work environment encourages drinking. The environment associated with food, drink, and entertainment is conducive to drinking alcohol. The environment is also quite stressful because service is time pressured. EAPs combating alcohol abuse can play a significant role in employee life satisfaction.

In general, one might argue that EAPs help employees better fulfill their work roles and their nonwork roles as well as reduce work and nonwork role stress. In addition to enhancing employees' QOL, EAPs contribute to the financial health of employers. Evidence suggests that EAPs reduce health costs, improve productivity, decrease absenteeism, decrease employee turnover, and increase employee morale and job satisfaction (e.g., Rockett 2004).

Innovative Benefits

One study of innovative benefits (Dessler 1997, p. 527; The Research Staff of Hewitt Associates 1995) found Canadian companies offer benefits such as
- Lakefront vacations
- Weight loss programs
- Child adoption assistance
- Company country club membership
- Season tickets to cultural activities and events such as the ballet, theaters, concerts, and museums
- Lunch-and-learn programs (employees can attend talks on a variety of subjects such as stress management, weight control, computer literacy, fashion, and travel)
- Home assistance program (monetary assistance to help employees purchase a home)
- Subsidized employee transportation (e.g., car pooling systems)
- Food services (coffee wagons, vending machines, and cafeteria services)
- Executive perks (e.g., company car, chauffeured limousine, security system, company plane, yacht, executive dining room, liberal expense account, club membership, and credit cards, among others)

Summary and Conclusion

QWL deals with the interface between employee role identities and work resources. QWL programs serve to enhance QOL by (1) providing appropriate work resources to meet the expectations of employee role identities, (2) reducing role conflict in work and nonwork life, (3) enhancing multiple role identities, (4) reducing role demands, (5) reducing stress related to work and nonwork role identities, and (6) increasing the value of the role identity. Specifically, we describe a variety of QWL programs related to work life (decentralized organization structures, teamwork, parallel structures, ethical corporate mission and culture, the organization work schedule, etc.) and nonwork life (work at home, flextime, compressed workweek, part-time work arrangements, job sharing, etc.) and review the evidence in the research literature.

This chapter is designed to motivate industrial/organizational psychologists, management scholars, and QOL researchers to engage in research to further develop a theory of the QWL-QOL relationship. We believe that the QWL programs discussed in this chapter can play a significant role in employee life satisfaction, happiness, and subjective well-being. Such concepts are very important in organizational research for theoretical and practical purposes (e.g., Ashkanasy 2011; Blanchflower and Oswald 2011; Judge and Kammeyer-Mueller 2011). Future research should systematically and methodically test the QOL effects of these QWL programs. Different QWL programs tend to affect different role identities in different ways. Some meet multiple roles. Some are effective in generating more resources, facilitating the realization of role expectations. Some are effective in reducing conflict within a specific role identity or between two or more role identities. Others are designed to clarify and articulate role expectations to match work and nonwork demands.

Furthermore, one should not expect that the various QWL programs discussed in this chapter have equivalent QOL effects across the board. Of course not! QOL effects of these programs are likely to be moderated by a set of sociocultural, demographic, and dispositional factors that deserve attention. Future research should investigate the moderating effects of the QWL-QOL relationship in systematic and programmatic ways guided by well-established QOL theory.

References

Armenakis, A. A., & Bedeian, A. G. (1999). Organizational change: A review of theory and research in the 1990s. *Journal of Management, 25*(3), 293–315.

Ashkanasy, N. M. (2011). International happiness: A multilevel perspective. *Academy of Management Perspectives, 25*(1), 23–29.

Baltes, B. B., Briggs, T. E., Huff, J. W., Wright, J. A., & Neuman, G. A. (1999). Flexible and compressed workweek schedules: A meta-analysis of their effects on work-related criteria. *Journal of Applied Psychology, 84*, 496–513.

Baltes, B. B., Clark, M. A., & Chakrabarti, M. (2010). Work-life balance: The roles of work-family conflict and work-family facilitation. In P. A. Linley, S. Harrington, & N. Garcea (Eds.), *Oxford handbook of positive psychology and work* (pp. 201–212). Oxford: Oxford University Press.

Bartol, K., & Hagmann, L. (1992). Team-based pay plans: A key to effective teamwork. *Compensation and Benefits Review, 24*, 24–29.

Batt, R., & Valcour, P. M. (2003). Human resources practices as predictors of work-family outcomes and employee turnover. *Industrial Relations, 42*, 189–220.

Bialk, B. S. (1987). Cutting workers' compensation costs. *The Personnel Journal, 66*(7), 95–97.

Blain, J., & Haywood, J. (2004). The rise of employer-sponsored childcare. *The British Journal of Administrative Management, 41*, 24–26.

Blanchflower, D. G., & Oswald, A. J. (2011). International happiness: A new view on the measure of performance. *Academy of Management Perspectives, 25*(1), 6–22.

Blood, M. R., & Hulin, C. L. (1967). Alienation, environmental characteristics and worker responses. *Journal of Applied Psychology, 51*, 284–290.

Booth, A. L., & Van Ours, J. C. (2009). Hours of work and gender identity: Does part-time work make the family happier? *Economica, 76*(301), 176–196.

Bozionelos, N., & Nikolaou, I. (2010). Happiness around the world: Is there more to it than money? *Journal of Management Perspectives, 24*(4), 96–98.

Brill, N. I. (1976). *Teamwork: Working together in the human services*. Philadelphia: J. B. Lippincott Company.

Buckley, J. E., & Van Giezen, R. W. (2004). Federal statistics on healthcare benefits and costs trends: An overview. *Monthly Labor Review, 127*(11), 43–56.

Bunning, R. (1988). A prescription for sick leave. *The Personnel Journal, 67*(8), 44–49.

Bureau of National Affairs. (1988). Child care benefits offered by employers. *Bulletin to Management,* 84–85.

Bureau of National Affairs. (1992). Employee benefit costs. *Bulletin to Management,* 12–14.

Burke, P. J. (1991). Identity processes and social stress. *American Sociological Review, 56*, 836–849.

Campbell, T. A., & Campbell, D. E. (1988). Employers and childcare. *The Personnel Journal, 67*(4), 84–87.

Cropanzano, R., Ambrose, M. L., Greenberg, J., & Cropanzano, R. (2002). Procedural and distributive justice are more similar than you think: A monistic perspective and research agenda. In *Advances in organizational justice*. Palo Alto: Stanford University Press.

de Klerk, J. J. (2005). Spirituality, meaning in life, and work wellness: A research agenda. *International Journal of Organizational Analysis, 13*(1), 64–88.

Dessler, G. (1997). *Human resource management* (7th ed.). Upper Saddle River: Prentice-Hall.

Diener, E., Suh, E. M., Lucas, R. E., & Smith, H. L. (1999). Subjective well-being: Three decades of progress. *Psychological Bulletin, 125*(2), 276–302.

Diener, E., Ng, W., Harter, J., & Arora, R. (2010). Wealth and happiness across the world: Material prosperity predicts life evaluation, whereas psychological prosperity predicts positive feeling. *Journal of Personality and Social Psychology, 99*, 52–61.

Duchon, D., & Plowman, D. A. (2005). Nurturing spirit at work: Impact on work unit performance. *The Leadership Quarterly, 16*, 807–833.

Duxbury, L., & Haines, G., Jr. (1991). Predicting alternative work arrangements from salient attitudes: A study of decision-makers in the public sector. *Journal of Business Research, 23*, 83–97.

Duxbury, L., & Higgins, C. A. (1991). Gender differences in work-family conflict. *Journal of Applied Psychology, 76*(1), 60–74.

Earhart, K., Middlemist, R. D., & Hopkins, W. (1993). Elder care: An emerging employee assistance issue. *Employee Assistance Quarterly, 8*(3), 1–10.

Efraty, D., & Sirgy, M. J. (1995). Occupational prestige and bureaucratization effects on the spillover between job satisfaction and life satisfaction: A re-conceptualization. In M. J. Sirgy & A. C. Samli (Eds.), *New dimensions of marketing/quality-of-life research* (pp. 253–266). Westport: Quorum Books.

Efraty, D., Sirgy, M. J., & Claiborne, C. B. (1991). The effects of personal alienation on organizational identification: A quality-of-work life model. *Journal of Business and Psychology, 6*, 57–78.

Efraty, D., Sirgy, M. J., & Siegel, P. (1999). The job/life satisfaction relationship among professional accountants: Psychological determinants and demographic differences. In E. Diener & D. Rahtz (Eds.), *Advances in quality of life studies* (pp. 129–157). Dordrecht: Kluwer Academic Publishers.

Employee Benefits. (2005). Buyer guide: Employee assistance programs. *Employee Benefits, 13*(January), 47.

Ezra, M., & Deckman, M. (1996). Balancing work and family responsibilities: Flextime and childcare in the federal government. *Public Administration Review, 56*(2), 174–180.

Facer, R. L., II, & Wadsworth, L. (2008). Alternative work schedules and work-family balance: A research note. *Review of Public Personnel Administration, 28*(2), 166–177.

Falkenberg, L. E. (1987). Employee fitness programs: Their impact on the employee and the organization. *Academy of Management Review, 12*(3), 511–522.

Farber, H. S. (1999). Alternative and part-time employment arrangements as a response to job loss. *Journal of Labor Economics, 17*(4), 142–170.

Fletcher, T. D., Major, D. A., & Davis, D. D. (2008). The interactive relationship of competitive climate and trait competitiveness with workplace attitudes, stress, and performance. *Journal of Organizational Behavior, 29*(7), 899–922.

Frone, M. R., & Yardely, J. K. (1996). Workplace family-supportive programs: Predictors of employed parents' importance ratings. *Journal of Occupational and Organizational Psychology, 69*(4), 351–367.

Fry, L. W. (2005). Toward a theory of ethical and spiritual well-being, and corporate social responsibility through spiritual leadership. In R. Giacalone, C. Jurkiewicz, & C. Dunn (Eds.), *Positive psychology in business ethics and corporate responsibility* (pp. 47–83). Greenwich: Information Age Publishing.

Galbraith, R. (1998). *Designing organizations*. San Francisco: Jossey-Bass.

Gavin, H. G., & Mason, R. O. (2004). The virtuous organization: The value of happiness in the workplace. *Organizational Dynamics, 33*(4), 379–392.

Giacalone, R. A., & Jurkiewicz, C. L. (Eds.). (2002). *Handbook of workplace spirituality and organizational performances*. Armonk: M.E. Shape.

Gill, S., & Davidson, M. J. (2001). Problems and pressures facing lone mothers in management and professional occupations – a pilot study. *Women in Management Review, 16*(7/8), 383–400.

Greenhaus, J. H., & Beutell, N. J. (1985). Sources of conflict between work and family roles. *Academy of Management Review, 10*, 76–88.

Greenhaus, J. H., Bedian, A. G., & Mossholder, K. W. (1987). Work experiences, job performances, and feelings of personal and family well-being. *Journal of Vocational Behavior, 31*, 200–215.

Grossman, M., & Magnus, M. (1988). The boom in benefits. *Personnel Journal, 67*, 51–59.

Hackman, J. R., & Oldham, G. R. (1980). *Work redesign*. Reading: Addison-Wesley.

Hart, P. M. (1999). Predicting employee life satisfaction: A coherent model of personality, work and non-work experiences, and domain satisfactions. *Journal of Applied Psychology, 84*(4), 564–584.

Hellan, R. T. (1986). Employee assistance: An EPA update: A perspective for the '80s. *The Personnel Journal, 65*(6), 51.

Heller, D., Judge, T. A., & Watson, D. (2002). The confounding role of personality and trait affectivity in the relationship between job and life satisfaction. *Journal of Organizational Behavior, 23*, 815–835.

Higgins, E. T. (1989). Self-discrepancy theory: What patterns of belief cause people to suffer? In L. Berkowitz (Ed.), *Advances in experimental social psychology* (Vol. 22, pp. 93–135). San Diego: Academic.

Higgins, C. A., & Duxbury, L. E. (1992). Work-family conflict: A comparison of dual career and traditional-career men. *Journal of Organizational Behavior, 13*, 389–411.

Hill, E. J., Ferris, M., & Martinson, V. (2003). Does it matter where you work? A comparison of how three work venues (traditional office, virtual office, and home office) influence aspects of work and personal/family life. *Journal of Vocational Behavior, 63*, 220–241.

Hopper, E. (1965). Some effects of supervisory style: A sociological analysis. *The British Journal of Sociology, 16*, 189–205.

Hulin, C. H., & Blood, M. R. (1968). Job enlargement, individual differences and worker responses. *Psychological Bulletin, 69*, 41–55.

Human Resource Management Digest. (2003). Barclays pioneers a job-share register. *Human Resource Management Digest, 11*(2), 14–17.

Ilies, R., Wilson, K. S., & Wagner, D. T. (2009). The spillover of daily job satisfaction onto employees' family lives: The facilitating role of work-family integration. *Academy of Management Journal, 52*(1), 87–102.

International Management. (1982). After flexible hours, now it's flex year. *International Management*, 31–32.

Judge, T. A., & Kammeyer-Mueller, J. D. (2011). Happiness as a societal value. *Academy of Management Perspectives, 25*(1), 30–41.

Judge, T. A., & Watanabe, S. (1993). Another look at the job satisfaction-life satisfaction relationship. *Journal of Applied Psychology, 78*, 939–948.

Judge, T. A., Piccolo, R. F., Podsakoff, N. P., Shaw, J. C., & Rich, B. L. (2010). The relationship between pay and job satisfaction: A meta-analysis of the literature. *Journal of Vocational Behavior, 77*(2), 157–167.

Jurkiewicz, C. L., & Giacalone, R. A. (2004). A values framework for measuring the impact of workplace spirituality and organizational performance. *Journal of Business Ethics, 49*, 129–142.

Kabanoff, B. (1980). Work and non-work: A review of models, methods, and findings. *Psychological Bulletin, 88*, 60–77.

Kantak, D. M., Futrell, C. M., & Sager, J. K. (1992). Job satisfaction and life satisfaction in sales force. *Journal of Personal Selling & Sales Management, 12*(1), 1–7.

Karoly, L., & Rogowski, J. A. (1994). The effect of access to post-retirement health insurance as the decision to retire early. *Industrial and Labor Relations, 48*(1), 103–123.

Kinjerski, V. M., & Skrypnek, B. J. (2004). Defining spirit at work: Finding common ground. *Journal of Organizational Change Management, 17*(1), 26–42.

Kohn, M. L., & Schooler, C. (1982). Job conditions and personality: A longitudinal assessment of their reciprocal effects. *The American Journal of Sociology, 87*, 1257–1286.

Kolodinsky, R. W., Giacalone, R. A., & Jurkiewicz, C. L. (2008). Workplace values and outcomes: Exploring personal, organizational, and interactive workplace spirituality. *Journal of Business Ethics, 81*, 465–480.

Kopelman, R., Greenhaus, J., & Connolly, T. (1983). A model of work, family, and inter-role conflict: A construct validation study. *Organizational Behavior and Human Performance, 32*, 198–215.

Kossek, E. E., Barber, A. E., & Winters, D. (1999). Using flexible schedules in the managerial world: The power of peers. *Human Resource Management, 38*(1), 33–47.

Large, M. D., & Marcussen, K. (2000). Extending identity theory to predict differential forms and degrees of psychological distress. *Social Psychology Quarterly, 63*(1), 49–59.

Latack, J., & Foster, L. (1985). Implementation of compressed work schedules: Participation and job re-design as critical factors for employee acceptance. *Personnel Psychology, 38*(1), 75–92.

Lawler, E. E., III. (1982). Strategies for improving the quality of work life. *American Psychologist, 37*, 486–493.

Lee, Y., & Chang, H. (2008). Relations between teamwork and innovation in organizations and the job satisfaction of employees: A factor analytic study. *International Journal of Management, 25*(3), 732–739.

Lee, M. D., MacDermid, S. M., & Buck, M. (2000). Organizational paradigms of reduced-load work: Accommodation, elaboration, and transformation. *Academy of Management Journal, 43*, 1211–1226.

Lee, D.-J., Sirgy, M. J., Efraty, D., & Siegel, P. (2002). A study of quality life, spiritual well-being, and life satisfaction. In R. A. Giacalone & C. L. Jurkiewicz (Eds.), *Handbook of workplace spirituality and organizational performances* (pp. 209–230). Armonk: M.E. Shape.

Levine, D. I. (1995). *Reinventing the workplace: How business and employees can both win*. Washington, DC: Brookings Institutions.

Lucas, J. L., & Heady, R. B. (2002). Flextime commuters and their driver stress, feelings of time urgency, and commute satisfaction. *Journal of Business and Psychology, 16*(4), 565–571.

Madrian, B. C. (1994). Employment-based health insurance and job mobility: Is there evidence of job-lock? *Quarterly Journal of Economics, 109*(1), 27–54.

Madsen, S. R. (2003). The effects of home-based teleworking on work-family conflict. *Human Resource Development Quarterly, 14*(1), 35.

Maraist, C. C., Davison, H. K., Brief, A. P., Dietz, M., & O'Shea, D. P. (1999). *Does pay matter? The effects of work on subjective well-being*. Paper presented at the annual meeting of the Society for Industrial and Organizational Psychology, Atlanta, Georgia.

Maslow, A. H. (1954). *Motivation and personality*. New York: Harper.

Matthes, K. (1992). In pursuit of leisure: Employees want more time off. *HR Focus*, no. 7.

McGregor, D. (1960). *The human side of enterprise*. New York: McGraw-Hill.

Messmer, M. (2004). Recognizing potential stars by promoting from within. *Strategic Finance, 86*(4), 9–11.

Milliman, J., Czaplewski, A. J., & Ferguson, J. (2003). Workplace spirituality and employee work attitudes: An exploratory empirical assessment. *Journal of Organizational Change Management, 16*, 426–447.

Mitroff, I. I., & Denton, E. A. (1999). A study of spirituality in the workplace. *Sloan Management Review, 40*(4), 83–92.

Nandan, S., & Nandan, M. (1995). Improving quality of care and quality of work life through interdisciplinary health care teams. In H. L. Meadow, M. J. Sirgy, & D. Rahtz (Eds.), *Developments in quality-of-life studies in marketing* (Vol. 5, pp. 80–86). Illinois: Academy of Marketing Science and the International Society for Quality-of-Life Studies.

Near, J. P., Rice, R. W., & Hunt, G. R. (1980). The relationship between work and non-work domains: A review of empirical research. *Academy of Management Review, 5*, 415–429.

Northrup, H. (1991). The twelve hour shift in the North American Mini-steel industry. *Journal of Labor Research, 12*(3), 261–278.

O'Toole, R. E., & Ferry, J. L. (2002). The growing importance of elder care benefits for an aging workforce. *Compensation & Benefits Management, 18*(1), 40–44.

Ooi, K., Arumugam, V., The, P., & Alain, Y. (2008). TQM practices and its association with production workers. *Industrial Management & Data Systems, 108*(7), 909–927.

Parker, S. K., & Wall, T. D. (1998). *Job and work design: Organizing work to promote well-being and effectiveness*. San Francisco: Sage.

Pawar, B. S. (2009). Workplace spirituality facilitation: A comprehensive model. *Journal of Business Ethics, 90*(3), 375–386.

Peterson, D. J., & Massengill, D. (1988). Childcare programs benefit employers, too. *Personnel, 65*(5), 58–62.

Petty, M. M., McGee, G. W., & Cavender, J. W. (1984). A meta-analysis of the relationships between individual job satisfaction and individual performance. *Academy of Management Review, 9*, 712–721.

Popovich-Hill, P., & Hubbard, S. S. (1995). Quality of life in the workplace: The role of internal marketing. In H. L. Meadow, M. J. Sirgy, & D. Rahtz (Eds.), *Developments in quality-of-life studies in marketing* (Vol. 5, pp. 133–137). Dekalb: Academy of Marketing Science and the International Society for Quality-of-Life Studies.

Quick, J. C., Quick, J. D., Nelson, D. L., & Hurrell, J. J., Jr. (1997). *Preventive stress management in organizations*. Washington, DC: American Psychological Association.

Qvale, T. U., & Hanssen-Bauer, J. (1990). Implementing QWL in large scale project organizations: 'Blue Water' site design in the Norwegian Offshore Oil Industry. In H. L. Meadow & M. J. Sirgy (Eds.), *Quality-of-life studies in marketing and management* (pp. 519–535). Blacksburg: Virginia Tech, Center for Strategy and Marketing Studies.

Rain, J. S., Lane, I. M., & Steiner, D. D. (1991). A current look at the job satisfaction/life satisfaction relationship: Review and future considerations. *Human Relations, 44*, 287–307.

Rau, L. B., & Hyland, M. M. (2002). Role conflict and flexible work arrangements: The effects of applicant attraction. *Personnel Psychology, 55*, 111–136.

Redling, E. (1982). The 1981 tax act: Boom to managerial compensation. *Personnel, 57*(March–April), 26–35.

Rice, R. W., McFarlin, D. B., Hunt, R. G., & Near, J. (1985). Organizational work and the perceived quality of life: Toward a conceptual model. *Academy of Management Review, 10*(2), 296–310.

Richardson, J., & West, M. A. (2010). Dream teams: A positive psychology of team working. In P. A. Linley, S. Harrington, & N. Garcea (Eds.), *Oxford handbook of positive psychology and work* (pp. 235–249). Oxford: Oxford University Press.

Rockett, R. (2004). Increases sales of EAP and work-life benefits. National Underwriter. *Life and Health, 104*(30), 20.

Ruhm, C. J. (1998). The economic consequences of parental leave mandates: Lessons from Europe. *Quarterly Journal of Economics, 113*(1), 285–315.

Saltzstein, A. L., Ting, Y., & Saltzstein, G. H. (2001). Work-family balance and job satisfaction: The impact of family-friendly policies on attitudes of federal government employees. *Public Administration Review, 61*, 452–467.

Schermerhorn, J. R., Hunt, J. G., & Osborn, R. N. (2000 & 2003). *Organizational behavior*. New York: Wiley.

Sharpe, D. L., Hermsen, J. M., & Billings, J. (2002). Factors associated with having flextime: A focus on married workers. *Journal of Family and Economic Issues, 22*(1), 51.

Sherwyn, D., & Sturman, M. C. (2002). Job sharing: A potential tool for hotel managers. *The Cornell Hotel and Restaurant Administration Quarterly, 43*(5), 84–92.

Sirgy, M. J. (2002). *The psychology of quality of life*. Dordrecht: Kluwer Academic Publishers.

Sirgy, M. J., Efraty, D., Siegel, P., & Lee, D. (2001). A new measure of quality of work life (QWL) based on need satisfaction and spillover theories. *Social Indicators Research, 55*, 241–302.

Solomon, C. M. (1991). 24-employees. *The Personnel Journal, 70*(8), 56–62.

Solomon, C. M. (1994). Job sharing: One job, double headache? *The Personnel Journal, 73*(September), 88–96.

Staines, G. (1980). Spillover versus compensation: A review of the literature on the relationship between work and nonwork. *Human Relations, 33*, 111–129.

Stairs, M., & Gaplin, M. (2010). Positive engagement: From employee engagement to workplace happiness. In P. A. Linley, S. Harrington, & N. Garcea (Eds.), *Oxford handbook of positive psychology and work* (pp. 155–172). Oxford: Oxford University Press.

Stryker, S., & Serpe, R. (1994). Identity salience and psychological centrality: Equivalent, redundant, or complementary concepts? *Social Psychology Quarterly, 57*, 16–35.

Tait, M., Padgett, M. Y., & Baldwin, T. T. (1989). Job and life satisfaction: A re-evaluation of the strength of the relationship and gender effects as a function of the date of the study. *Journal of Applied Psychology, 74*(3), 502–507.

Teas, R. K., Wacker, J. G., & Hughes, E. (1979). A path analysis of causes and consequences of salespeople's perception of role clarity. *Journal of Marketing Research, 16*, 355–369.

Tharp, C. (1985). Linking annual incentive awards to individual performance. *Compensation and Benefits Review, 17*(November-December), 38–43.

The Research Staff of Hewitt Associates. (1995). *Innovative benefits*. Toronto: Canada: Hewitt Associates.

Tse, E., & Jackson, G. A. (1990). Alcohol abuse in the workplace: Challenges and strategic implications for the hospitality industry. In H. L. Meadow & M. J. Sirgy (Eds.), *Quality-of-life studies in marketing and management* (pp. 215–226). Blacksburg: Virginia Tech, Center for Strategy and Marketing Studies.

Ugboro, I. O., & Obeng, K. (2000). Top management leadership, employee empowerment, job satisfaction, and customer satisfaction in TQM organizations: An empirical study. *Journal of Quality Management, 5*(2), 247–272.

Valdez, R. L., & Gutek, B. A. (1989). Family roles: A help or hindrance for working women? In B. A. Gutek & L. Larwood (Eds.), *Women's career development*. Newbury: Sage Publications.

Voydanoff, P. (1989). Work and family: A review and expanded conceptualization. In E. B. Goldsmith (Ed.), *Work and family: Theory, research, and applications*. Newbury Park: Sage Publications.

Weiss, H. M., Nicholas, J. P., & Daus, C. S. (1999). An examination of the joint effects of affective experiences and job beliefs on job satisfaction and variations in affective experiences over time. *Organizational Behavior and Human Decision Processes, 78*, 1–24.

Wharton, A. S., & Blair-Loy, M. (2002). The "overtime culture" in a global corporation: a cross-national study of finance professionals' interest in working part-time. *Work and Occupations, 29*(1), 32–65.

Wilkinson, A. (1998). Empowerment: Theory and practice. *Personnel Review, 27*, 40–56.

Wolf, W. B. (1971). The professor of management: The academy of management and professionalism. *Academy of Management Proceedings, 31*, 1–6.

Wyld, D. C., & Maurin, R. (2011). Does more money buy happiness on the job? *Journal of Management Perspectives, 25*(1), 101–102.

Spirituality, Religiosity, and Subjective Quality of Life

14

Ralph L. Piedmont and Philip H. Friedman

Because large numbers of people across the globe profess a belief in God and consider themselves to be religious (e.g., Dogan 2003; Gallup 1995), spirituality and religiosity are of great interest to researchers and clinicians in the social and medical sciences. The pervasive influence of these constructs in society in general, and the day-to-day lives of people in particular, make them obvious targets for scientific scrutiny. What influence do these constructs exert on our physical and psychological equilibrium? A fast-growing research literature continues to document significant empirical relations between religious and spiritual variables (i.e., spiritual constructs) and salient mental and physical health outcomes (Koenig 1997; Koenig et al. 2000; Miller and Thoresen 2003; Thoresen 1999). This interest is truly interdisciplinary in nature and generating a vast empirical literature (Dy-Liacco et al. 2003). A recent, focused PsycINFO search (September 8, 2009) on the number of times the terms quality of life (QOL) and spirituality or religion appeared in a scientific article returned over 32,000 citations. The purpose of this chapter is to provide a general review of the literature on QOL and its relations to the spiritual/religious relying mostly on research conducted in the USA. Because numerous literature reviews already exist in this area (e.g., Koenig et al. 2000; Sawatzky et al. 2005), this chapter will focus on distilling key conceptual and empirical findings rather than merely recounting

all the results from this very large literature. The chapter will conclude by identifying current issues in the field relevant to researchers worldwide and outlining potentially useful directions for future research. But before beginning, it is necessary to define the key variables of this chapter: religiosity and spirituality.

Quality of Life, Spirituality, and Religiosity Defined

In examining quality of life (QOL), this chapter takes a rather broad perspective. QOL can be divided into objective (qualities associated with specific, verifiable outcomes, such as death rates) and subjective (qualities associated with personal perspectives on self-functioning, such as satisfaction with life) types of outcomes. The main focus of this report will be to examine how religious and spiritual constructs, and their measurement, are related to subjective QOL indices. The question to be addressed is, "To what extent does religious involvement and spiritual experience contribute to perceived increases in satisfaction with life and other mental health outcomes?" This perspective works out of our interest in learning how spirituality and religiosity become involved in (or moderate) the motivational struggle of individuals to create a sense of well-being and happiness in their lives. Not covered in this review is how negative aspects of spirituality (e.g., spiritual struggles, religious crises) impact these outcomes (see Piedmont et al. 2007 for one perspective on this). However, some attention will be given to how spiritual constructs relate to objective outcomes surrounding physical health. This is a result of many studies including both types of QOL indicators

R.L. Piedmont (✉)
Department of Pastoral Counseling, Loyola University, Maryland, 8890 McGaw Road, Suite 380, Columbia, MD 21045
e-mail: rpiedmont@loyola.edu

P.H. Friedman
Foundation for Well-Being, Institute for Transpersonal Psychology, Palo Alto, CA, USA

K.C. Land et al. (eds.), *Handbook of Social Indicators and Quality of Life Research*, DOI 10.1007/978-94-007-2421-1_14, © Springer Science+Business Media B.V. 2012

in their designs, and is included to give the reader some sense of the predictive value of spiritual constructs across a number of important life outcomes.

Despite widespread usage, spirituality and religiosity do not have any universally accepted definitions (e.g., Miller and Thoresen 2003). Scott (cited in Hill et al. 2000) identified 31 different definitions of religiousness and 40 for spirituality, which she classified into nine different content areas (e.g., experiences of connectedness, systems of thought or beliefs, and capacities for transcendence). Nonetheless, spirituality and religiosity are seen by many as conceptually sharing much in common (e.g., Hill and Pargament 2003), and some researchers prefer to interpret these two dimensions as being quite similar (e.g., Zinnbauer et al. 1999). Musick et al. (2000) have noted that in samples of adults, these two terms are highly related to one another. They questioned whether there is a meaningful distinction between these two constructs or if any disparities are "… simply an artifact of the wishes of researchers hoping to find such differences" (p. 80).

Nonetheless, there are those who emphasize the distinctiveness between these two constructs (e.g., Piedmont 2001; Piedmont and Leach 2002). Here, spirituality is viewed as an attribute of an individual (much like a personality trait) while religiosity is understood as encompassing more of the beliefs, rituals, and practices associated with an institution (Miller and Thoresen 1999, p. 6). Religiosity is concerned with how one's experience of a transcendent being is shaped by, and expressed through, a community or social organization. Spirituality, on the other hand, is most concerned with one's personal relationships to larger, transcendent realities, such as God or the Universe. Clarifying spirituality and religiosity in terms of *personal* versus *social* orientations has some value for the field and helps to promote clarity in discussing these terms. Although these concepts are highly correlated, there is empirical support for their discriminant validity (e.g., Piedmont et al. 2009). For the purposes of this report, spirituality and religiosity will be defined in this manner. Accordingly, each construct's relationship to QOL will be examined separately.

Religiosity and QOL

One direct and simple assessment method for researching religiosity has been to correlate the frequency of religious participation with a variety of outcomes. "Frequency of Church Attendance" is perhaps the most widely used index in this area [and has been shown to be a strong predictor of physical and mental health outcomes (George et al. 2002)], although other behavioral exemplars include "Frequency of Prayer," "Frequency of Reading Religious Literature," and "Frequency of Watching Religious Programs." For well over 30 years, researchers have been able to document the linkage between involvement in religious activities and other theological, attitudinal, and behavioral outcomes (see Dittes 1969 for an early overview of research in this area). Perhaps the most important are the consistent findings in the medical literature of significant relationships between involvement in religious activities and a variety of physical health outcomes, such as reduced blood pressure and less hypertension, increased immune functioning, and a reduced risk of mortality (Koenig et al. 1998; Powell et al. 2003; Seeman et al. 2003).

The facilitative effects of religious activity have also been documented with mental health outcomes as well. Koenig et al. (2000) noted in their review that despite early research (e.g., in the 1950s and 1960s) that claimed no positive effect for religion on mental health, better designed and implemented research of the last 20 years has shown quite consistent positive findings (see Koenig et al. 2000 for a comprehensive review of this literature). Religious involvement has been consistently related to greater life satisfaction, hope, optimism, and purpose in life. Koenig and Larson also noted that religious involvement has been related to a faster resolution of depressive episodes and that religious interventions helped depressed individuals recover faster than those receiving either a secular intervention or no intervention at all. In their review of the literature, Ellison and Levin (1998) noted the prospective, positive impact that religious involvement has on well-being, depression, and stress experience. Although religion may protect us from negative mental health outcomes, it does not seem to prevent physical diseases or to improve recovery time from an acute illness (see Powell et al. 2003). The benefits for religious involvement have been found for minority and elderly groups as well, suggesting that religion's impact is universal and not a consequence of social privilege or cultural ethos. The effect of religious involvement occurs even when physical and social factors are controlled.

While this literature provides consistent support for religion as a relevant factor in human mental health and well-being, a number of conceptual and empirical questions and issues remain. The key conceptual question is, "Why does religious involvement have this impact on functioning?" One answer is that being involved in a religious group may have required behavior and dietary patterns that are associated with good physical health (e.g., abstaining from smoking and drinking). Some religions may have very specific rules about health habits (e.g., Seventh-Day Adventists), and most religions teach followers to respect and care for their bodies because the body is "the temple for the soul" (George et al. 2002). Research has shown that more religiously involved individuals tend to not smoke or smoke less than nonreligious individuals (Koenig et al. 1998) or that religiously committed adolescents are less likely to exhibit delinquent behaviors (e.g., stealing personal property, using drugs, sexual promiscuity; Johnson et al. 2001). Of course, as Ellison and Levin (1998) pointed out, those who are attracted to religion may have risk-averse personalities to begin with, leading them to avoid potentially toxic behaviors and to seek the safety of supportive religious groups.

Other reasons for the value of religion could be the higher levels of social support that adherents experience. Religion certainly involves social contact in terms of formal worship services and informal "fellowship" activities (e.g., prayer groups, ministry activities) that provide individuals with opportunities for developing interpersonal contacts that can increase self-esteem, assist in managing stress, and promote positive feelings. These groups can be helpful in modeling (and reinforcing) a more positive lifestyle and for providing emotional and physical support that, according to Powell et al. (2003, p. 49), "may allay feelings of isolation, low control, and despair and improve one's sense of self-efficacy."

Clearly, conceptual models are needed to help articulate the pathways by which religious involvement impacts quality of life outcomes. However, it will be important that researchers demonstrate that religiosity is not mediated away by these non-spiritual mechanisms. As Hill and Pargament (2003, p. 66) argued, we must not overlook the "possibility that something inherent within the religious and spiritual experience itself contributes to or detracts from physical and mental health." Although we will have more to say on this later in the chapter, it is important to note that to be considered ultimately useful, it will need to be shown that religiosity is not merely a stand-in variable for other variables that are themselves the causal

agents for positive mental health (like social support). In other words, religiosity will need to be shown to have its own effect on mental health *independent* of these other variables. As a non-reducible quantity, it will need to be examined and understood in its own right (see Johnson et al. 2001 who demonstrated that religion's impact on delinquency was independent of other related predictors, such as social control and socialization).

Empirically, an important issue to be addressed concerns the measurement of religious qualities. As Gorsuch (1988) pointed out, there was a heavy reliance on very simple, single-item measures of religiosity, the most common being religious affiliation. Such a variable is too simplistic and insensitive for useful research purposes. Merely using religious affiliation tends to lump together those who are active and involved in their faith with those who are not. Single-item measures of religious behaviors also have psychometric problems, most notably a lack of conceptual richness and limited reliability. Clearly, there is a need to use multi-item measures where both a construct's conceptual bandwidth can be fully implemented and the psychometric utility of the scale can be measured. Numerous measures of religiosity have been developed (see Hill and Hood 1999 for a compendium of instruments), although many lack developed validity evidence. Multi-item scales, such as the *Multidimensional Measurement of Religiousness/ Spirituality* (MMRS; Fetzer Institute/National Institute on Aging Working Group 1999) or the *Religious Commitment Inventory-10* (RCI-10; Worthington et al. 2003) can help develop more sophisticated theories of what religiosity is, and what about it makes it such a useful and robust predictor of QOL outcomes.

Spirituality and QOL

Emmons and Paloutzian (2003) noted that measures of spiritual constructs have literally exploded over the past two decades possibly because they attempt to answer why numinous qualities (e.g., feelings of awe, hallowedness, and sacredness) are related to such diverse psychological outcomes. Spirituality is frequently interpreted as an internal process of the person. It represents an inner search for something transcendent or sacred. At least implicitly, most spirituality scales are measures of some internal motivation that propel individuals toward specific, identifiable goals (e.g., Emmons 1999). Cast in this light, measures of spirituality represent one psychological source underlying religious behavior that carries potential explanatory power both conceptually and empirically. In their meta-analysis of the literature on religiosity and mental health, Hackney and Sanders (2003) found that the more a spiritual measure captured intrinsic motivational styles (e.g., personal devotion versus involvement in institutional religion), the stronger the empirical link with mental health outcomes. Thus, this enhanced predictive validity suggests that measuring spirituality may be a better approach to understanding the numinous in this area.

There exists a wide range of spiritual constructs that capture diverse facets. A review of all these constructs is beyond the scope of this single chapter. However, some dimensions of spirituality have received much empirical and conceptual attention in the literature, and this section will examine these more salient constructs. Four general areas of spiritual constructs that have garnered significant interest from the field and accrued a sizable body of research are reviewed in this section.

Intrinsic-Extrinsic Religiousness

Perhaps the most well-known set of religious/spiritual constructs are the intrinsic and extrinsic religious orientations developed by Allport and Ross (1967). The Religious Orientation Scale (ROS) was developed out of Allport's (1950) original ideas about religion and its relationship to important social attitudes, most notably prejudice. Allport understood religion to be a master motive, a psychological force that found its origins at the center of the individual and served to organize and direct the psychic system. As Allport noted (1950, p. 142):

> It [religiosity] is the portion of personality that arises at the core of the life and is directed towards the infinite. It is the region of mental life that has the longest-range intentions, and for this reason is capable of conferring marked integration upon personality, engendering meaning and peace in the face of tragedy and confusion in life.

Allport made an important distinction between this "mature" motive and more "immature" religious motives that are more self-seeking and utilitarian in nature. The ROS was developed to operationalize these motives. Intrinsically religious individuals "find their master motive in religion. Other needs, strong as they may be, are regarded as of less ultimate significance, and they are, so far as possible, brought into harmony with the religious beliefs and prescriptions...it is in this sense that he *lives* his religion" (Allport and Ross 1967, p. 434; italics in original). As such, intrinsic religiosity represents more of spiritual quality than a religious involvement dimension. Donahue (1985) noted that intrinsic religiosity (I) relates to a number of outcomes, including being ideologically tolerant and unprejudiced, better levels of mental health, regular church attendance, and being more mature. Extrinsic religiosity (E) reflects a more utilitarian and instrumental view of religion; it is something that can be used to obtain satisfaction for other needs (e.g., security, social status, and self-justification; Allport and Ross 1967). Donahue noted that E was positively related to prejudice, dogmatism, trait anxiety, and fear of death. E captures that aspect of "religion that gives religion a bad name" (Donahue 1985, p. 416).

Research using the ROS has shown it to have a number of psychometric issues. First, although I and E were originally conceptualized to be opposite poles of the same dimension, empirically, they turn out to be independent of one another. Second, the E dimension has also been shown to capture two distinct facets: social (involved in religion for interpersonal contact) and personal (using religion for personal needs and security). Third, there were concerns about the level of language in the scale, making it unsuitable for less educated samples. As such, a number of different revisions to this scale have occurred. There is the "Age-Universal version" (Gorsuch and Venable 1983) that is appropriate for use with individuals as young as fifth grade and another version, the "I/E-Revised" (Gorsuch and McPherson 1989), that aims to provide a more stable assessment of the two E facets. Trimble (1997) noted that over 150 research studies have been done using various versions of these instruments, making the ROS perhaps the most researched scale to date. Although the ROS has been shown early on to be a good predictor of prejudice and religious attitudes, later work has demonstrated that the I/E domains correlated with important psychosocial outcomes such as sexual attitudes (Haerich 1992), altruism (Trimble 1997), purpose in life (Batson et al. 1993), and mental health (Ventis 1995).

The value of the ROS is that it takes a multidimensional approach to understanding religiousness that captures both its positive and negative aspects. The mutual orthogonality of the I and E dimensions makes possible a fourfold typological classification of one's religious orientation. Individuals can be classified as being "high" or "low" on each of these two dimensions. Those high on I and low on E are considered "intrinsics," while those high on E and low on I are "extrinsics." Those high on both domains are referred to as "indiscriminately pro-religious" and those low on both are "nonreligious." This typology appreciates the interactional nature of these two dimensions and enables one to decompose curvilinear effects into more conceptually manageable pieces. It enables a more precise evaluation of the spiritual motivations underlying various social behaviors. Although a relatively "old" instrument in the field, the ROS (and its variants) continues to have relevance for research in this area.

Religious Coping

As noted above, Allport (1950) believed that spirituality represented a core aspect of human personality, one that organized and directed the agentic flow of behavior. Spirituality is a way by which individuals create a sense of purpose and meaning for their lives (Frankl 1966; Piedmont 2001, 2004a). Thus, it is particularly interesting and conceptually valuable to examine the role of spirituality in the coping process. Stress, disease, and loss threaten our basic sense of psychological integrity and physical mortality, and they present the strongest challenges to our world view. Does spirituality mitigate the potentially dysphoric effects of negative life events? If so, what is it about spirituality that keeps the fabric of our inner worlds intact in the face of such disequilibria? These are the questions that research on spiritual coping attempts to answer. In the process, such research hopes to demonstrate the resiliency that high levels of spirituality provide.

One of the most frequently employed measures of spiritual coping is the *Religious Problem Solving Scale* (RPSS; Pargament et al. 1988). The RPSS identifies three religiously based problem-solving styles. These are: the *deferring*, where the individual defers the responsibility of problem-solving to God; the *self-directing*, in which it is the individual's responsibility to solve problems; and the *collaborative*, in which the responsibility for the problem-solving process is held jointly by the individual and God (Hill and Hood 1999

provide a review of this instrument). Research has provided support for the utility of the scale. The factor structure has been shown to generalize well to religious samples (e.g., Fox et al. 1998), although it has not always been recovered in general adult samples (e.g., Nairn and Merluzzi 2003). Nonetheless, research has shown that the RPSS does predict important outcomes such as burnout (Rodgerson and Piedmont 1998) and positive adjustment to cancer (Nairn and Merluzzi 2003). Most importantly, these studies have also shown that the predictive effects of the RPSS were not completely mediated by other potential predictors, such as personality and self-efficacy.

Although this work helped to document the importance of religion in the coping process, it was not sufficient for identifying which specific components of spirituality were involved in coping. Further, there was also a need to recognize specifically that religion could have both positive and negative effects on coping and QOL. As such, Pargament developed another measure of religious coping, the RCOPE (Pargament et al. 2000), that includes very specific coping behaviors. As Pargament et al. noted, "It is not enough to know that an individual prays, attends church, or watches religious television. Measures of religious coping should specify *how* the individual is making use of religion to understand and deal with stressors" (2000, p. 521, italics in original). The RCOPE contains five content domains: meaning, control, comfort/spirituality, intimacy/spirituality, and life transformation. Each domain has from 3 to 6 subscales that contain very specific coping behaviors that are both positive (e.g., "Sought God's love and care," "Tried to build a strong relationship with a higher power") and negative (e.g., "Wondered if God really cared," "Felt punished by God for my lack of devotion"). The goal of the scale was to identify those elements of religious coping helpful in managing stress and those that may hinder positive adaptation.

Ano and Vasconcelles (2005) provided a meta-analysis of research using this multifaceted approach to religious coping. They found in their analysis of 49 studies (containing 105 effects) that positive coping techniques were indeed related to positive psychological adjustment and that negative religious coping behaviors were related to negative outcomes (cumulative effect sizes were .33 and .22, respectively). Although no effort was made to assess potential mediation effects, these results show the RCOPE to have a small-to-medium predictive effect. Lewis et al. (2005) showed that the short form of the RCOPE significantly predicted happiness even after controlling for levels of intrinsic religiosity. Thus, religious coping may have something to contribute to QOL over and above general measures of spirituality. Certainly more research is warranted on this scale, but it does provide a significant enhancement to our thinking about religion's effect on behavior—that there exists the possibility that certain aspects of religiosity can exert a negative influence on adaptation.

Overall, the area of stress and coping provides an interesting context for examining the role of religion and spirituality in daily life. Efforts at charting this influence focus on specific actions, behaviors, and attitudes that are religiously oriented. What is most engaging is the openness to consider the negative aspects of religion and spirituality. What form(s) of the spiritual is (are) associated with impaired functioning? If spirituality does create a durable sense of personal meaning, then in addition to understanding how a positive spiritual orientation creates cohesiveness under stress circumstances, we need also to consider how a negative spirituality can create a sense of personal meaning that can maintain a dysfunctional style of life even under adaptive circumstances (see, e.g., Stifler et al. 1993).

Spiritual Transcendence

For Piedmont (1999, 2001), spiritual transcendence represents a universal human capacity to stand outside of one's own immediate existence and to view life from a broader, more integrative whole. To varying degrees, we begin to realize that there is a larger meaning and purpose to life. Because spirituality is concerned with how individuals create ultimate meaning for their lives, it is not surprising that some see it as a central organizing aspect of personality (Allport 1950; Batson et al. 1993) and as such, should be related to a variety of constructs that impact the quality and satisfaction people derive for their lives.

The *Spiritual Transcendence Scale* (STS), which is a part of the *Assessment of Spirituality and Religious Sentiments* (ASPIRES) scale (Piedmont 2004a), was developed to conceptualize spirituality as a motivational aspect of the individual. Rather than viewing spirituality as a cognitive schema (Beit-Hallahmi 1989;

Worthington et al. 1996), a way of being (Elkins 1988), or way of understanding (Wong 1998), the STS defines spirituality as a nonspecific affective force that drives, directs, and selects behaviors (Piedmont 2004a). As an intrinsic source of motivation, spirituality would be a relatively stable construct over time and would impel individuals toward identifiable goals (Emmons 1999). Spirituality would operate in ways consistent with other motivational traits, such as extraversion, power, affiliation, and conscientiousness.

The STS scale comprises three correlated facets, labeled *Connectedness* (feelings of belongingness to a larger human reality that cuts across generations and groups), *Prayer Fulfillment* (the ability to create a personal space that enables one to feel a positive connection to some larger reality), and *Universality* (the belief in a larger meaning and purpose to life). These facet scales evidence differential patterns of relationships to a variety of psychosocial outcomes in both normal and clinical samples (Piedmont 2001, 2004b).

There are three important findings concerning the STS that are relevant for this discussion. First, as a motivational variable, the STS has shown itself related to a wide number of important outcomes such as well-being, life satisfaction, coping ability, interpersonal style, and psychological growth and maturity (Piedmont 2001) as well as being relevant to predicting levels of burnout and job satisfaction among clergy (Golden et al. 2004). Bartlett et al. (2003) demonstrated the predictive value of spiritual transcendence for predicting well-being among chronic arthritis sufferers. The STS scales have also been shown to predict coping ability and improvement in both substance abuse (Piedmont 2004b) and gambling (Walsh 2001) samples. Most importantly, Piedmont (2006) has shown that the predictive effects of the STS were not mediated by other relevant predictors, like personality, nor were they product of some methodological artifact due to correlated method error. Thus, spiritual transcendence makes a unique predictive contribution to our understanding of how individuals manage the many stressors in their lives.

Second, the STS was developed to capture an aspect of spirituality that was nondenominational in nature and that captured a universal aspect of human functioning. It is hypothesized that spiritual transcendence is an intrinsic, and unique, aspect of humanity. As such, the STS should be a relevant predictor of outcomes for individuals across both religious groups and cultures. A growing body of research is demonstrating the utility of the STS as a generalizable construct.

Goodman et al. (2005) gave the ST scales to a sample of conservative, reformed, and orthodox Jews. She found the ST scales to be reliable in all three samples and to significantly predict outcomes. Piedmont and Leach (2002) gave the ST scales and elements of the religiosity scale (in English) to an Indian sample of Hindus, Muslims, and Christians. The ST scales evidenced alpha reliabilities comparable to those found in the USA. Further, the ST scales were found to evidence significant incremental validity over the FFM personality domains in predicting emotional well-being and psychological maturity. Cho (2004) translated the ST items into Korean and distributed the form to middle-aged married couples. The ST scales were found to significantly predict fear of intimacy. Wilson (2004) gave the ST scales in English to a sample of aboriginal Canadians who were receiving inpatient treatment for alcoholism. The ST scales were found to be quite reliable, and the overall score correlated significantly with other measures of spirituality and ethnic identity. Piedmont (2007) translated the ST scales into Tagalog, a native language of the Philippines. Alpha reliabilities were comparable with American samples, save Connectedness, which was much lower in both the self- and observer-rating versions. However, test-retest reliabilities were found to be very high for all scales. The ST scales were also found to evidence significant incremental validity over the FFM personality domains in predicting measures of well-being, life satisfaction, and world view, among others. Finally, Rican and Janosova (2010) translated the ASPIRES into Czech and administered it to a large sample of secular Czech youth who largely reject organized religion. Here, again, the factor structure, independence from established personality measures, and incremental validity were found to hold. These findings are evidence that the STS represents a universal quality of human behavior and that the model of spirituality represented by the STS has relevance across cultures, religions, and languages.

Third, as a motivational variable, spirituality needs to be considered as a causal input into one's psychological system. In other words, levels of spirituality will have a direct impact on how other aspects of one's inner world will function. Increasing levels of spirituality will bring about a corresponding improvement in feelings of well-being, coping ability, and life satisfaction.

Little research has been done on causal modeling spiritual constructs, but that which has been accomplished supports the causal precedence of spirituality (e.g., Dowling et al. 2004). Dy-Liacco et al. (2005) examined a variety of causal models using the STS, religiosity, world view, and well-being. They found the best empirical support for those models that used the STS as the predictor of these constructs. Piedmont et al. (2009), using SEM, examined the STS in relation to measures of well-being and psychological growth (e.g., self-actualization and purpose in life). Two models were examined, one where spirituality was viewed as a product of these constructs (i.e., happy, mature people also had a better sense of spirituality) and the other where spirituality was the predictor (i.e., a more developed sense of personal meaning and connection with a transcendence reality led to higher levels of psychological maturity and personal well-being). Again, the best empirical support was found for those models that viewed spirituality as the causal predictor.

Forgiveness and Gratitude and QOL

The field of positive psychology focuses on people's strengths rather than their weaknesses, on building the best things in life rather than repairing the worst, and on fulfilling the lives of normal people rather than healing the wounded. In their groundbreaking book, Peterson and Seligman (2004) focused on those character strengths and virtues that are believed to be the bedrock of the human condition. For the purposes of this chapter, we will focus only on two: forgiveness and gratitude. Although it is certainly possible to experience forgiveness and gratitude without any professed religious affiliation, the inner experience of forgiveness and gratitude would appear to be a relevant correlate to any definition of spirituality. Almost all well-known spiritual teachers from many traditions emphasize forgiveness and gratitude as key virtues to be cultivated (e.g., Rye et al. 2001).

Forgiveness

The research on forgiveness to date indicates that the more forgiving a person has been, the less negative affect (e.g., depression, anger, anxiety), and the higher levels of well-being, quality of life, and life satisfaction experienced (Friedman 2010; Friedman and Toussaint 2006; Toussaint and Friedman 2008;

Toussaint and Webb 2005; see also Worthington 2005 for an overall review). However, there are many types of forgiveness (e.g., forgiveness of self, forgiveness of others, forgiveness of circumstances or situations, forgiveness of God, asking for forgiveness), and each appears to have somewhat different effects on QOL outcomes. It is important in examining this literature to consider how these factors moderate the findings. For example, Toussaint et al. (2001) found in a national probability sample that forgiving oneself and others was *positively* related to life satisfaction, but seeking forgiveness was *negatively* related to life satisfaction. Krause and Ellison (2003) found that forgiving others was positively related in older adults to life satisfaction and negatively related to depressive affect, depressive somatic symptoms, and death anxiety. On the other hand, being forgiven by God had no relationship to depressive somatic symptoms and was a significantly weaker correlate of these outcomes. Thus, the type of forgiveness serves as a salient moderator of forgiveness' effect.

Another distinction to consider is whether a scale captures state or trait forgiveness. State measures of forgiveness deal with forgiveness of a particular person or situation. Changes in these state measures may enhance quality of life variables without necessarily enhancing either a general disposition to forgiveness or enhancing spirituality. Changes in trait or dispositional measures of forgiveness may enhance *both* quality of life and level of spirituality if the change is substantial. In those studies where both types of measures were included, they showed different results. For example, state forgiveness but not trait forgiveness positively related to existential well-being (Rye et al. 2001), while in a study by McCullough et al. (2001), state forgiveness was not related to life satisfaction cross-sectionally or longitudinally. In a series of studies using the Heartland Forgiveness Scale (Thompson et al. 2005), a trait measure of forgiveness, the researchers distinguished between forgiveness of self, forgiveness of others, and forgiveness of circumstances. The results indicated that high levels of dispositional forgiveness were predictive of low depression, anger, and anxiety and increased satisfaction with life. However, when controlling for each type of forgiveness, they found that forgiveness of self accounted for unique variance in depression, anxiety, and satisfaction with life but not in anger. Forgiveness of others (circumstances) accounted for unique variance in anger.

Forgiveness of circumstances predicted all four aspects of psychological well-being (depression, anxiety, anger, and life satisfaction) above and beyond the prediction by self and other forgiveness. These researchers concluded that forgiveness of self and situations appeared to be more strongly related to aspects of psychological well-being than forgiveness of others.

Forgiveness as currently studied is operationalized as a multidimensional construct, and research has shown that different types of measures have very different patterns of correlation with external QOL criteria. Findings are, on the surface, inconsistent, but it is clear that many factors, such as age, health status, race, and type of instrument, moderate the observed effects. Also, a comprehensive theory of forgiveness is needed that can relate these different forgiveness constructs together (see Jampolsky 1999 and the Foundation for Inner Peace 1975 for non-dualistic approaches to forgiveness theory). Finally, it should be noted that most existing measures of forgiveness are secular in orientation. Only one subscale of the RCOPE (summarized above) measures forgiveness, through an explicit assessment of appeals to either God or spiritual helpers to aid in forgiving or release of resentments. Further research needs to be done that compares the role of spiritually oriented measures with secular scales to understand better conceptual differences and to examine the relative predictive validity of QOL outcomes.

Gratitude

Gratitude, like forgiveness, has been studied extensively in recent years and can be considered both an inner experience and an attitude. Emmons and McCullough (2003, 2004) have shown that people with a strong disposition to gratitude have the capacity to be empathetic and to take the perspective of others. Grateful people are also considered to be more generous and helpful by people in their social networks (McCullough et al. 2002). In addition, McCullough et al. indicated that those who regularly engaged in religious activities such as prayer and reading religious materials were more likely to be grateful, to acknowledge a belief in the interconnectedness of life, and to possess a commitment and responsibility to others.

In recent series of studies by Emmons and colleagues (Emmons and McCullough 2003, 2004) employing the Gratitude Questionnaire-6 (GQ6; a brief six-item measure of gratitude), they indicated that grateful people reported higher levels of positive emotions, life satisfaction, vitality and optimism, and lower levels of depression and stress (see also Watkins et al. 2003; Watkins 2004). Interestingly, this research found that measures of negative affect such as anxiety and irritability did not correlate with measures of gratitude. This has led some to conclude that the disposition toward gratitude appears to increase pleasant feelings more than it diminishes unpleasant emotions (Emmons and McCullough 2003, 2004).

Watkins et al. (2003) indicated that there was a positive correlation between gratitude and internal locus of control, divine control, and intrinsic religious orientation and a negative correlation with extrinsic religious orientation. They interpret this to mean that grateful people are more likely to feel in control of their destiny through the actions of a divine entity that is interested in their well-being. McCullough et al. (2002) found small but significant correlations between self and informant's ratings of gratitude with self-transcendence, importance of religion, frequency of religious attendance, religious friends, reading scripture, prayer, and relationship with God (correlations ranged from .16 to .32). Both sets of authors indicated that there is a negative relationship between gratitude and narcissism. Clearly, gratitude has very strong associations with spiritual and religious motivations and behaviors. However, much of this research has been done with college students, thereby limiting the generalizability of their findings.

Toussaint and Friedman (2008) showed in a sample of psychotherapy clients strong significant correlations (most $rs > .50$) between both gratitude and measures of well-being, quality of life, life satisfaction, positive affect, positive beliefs, cognitive balance, affective balance, optimism, self-worth, hope, and happiness. However, Friedman also found moderate-to-strong negative correlations between gratitude and various measures of negative affect, especially depression, anger, anxiety, and vulnerability (rs ranging from $-.40$ to $-.70$). Perhaps for those who might benefit most from a gratuitous perspective, the associations may be equally strong for positive and negative psychological affects.

Summary

Positive psychology represents a more secular approach to addressing human kind's ultimate sense of self. Although spiritual and positive psychological constructs have much in common, research is needed to better understand how these two sets of constructs overlap with each other. To what extent do they represent redundant concepts? What unique insights do they contribute? As this short review noted, there exists quite a bit of variability in the predictiveness of forgiveness and gratitude. Especially regarding the former, much more conceptual and empirical work needs to be done that examines the various aspects of forgiveness (e.g., forgiveness of others versus forgiveness of self) and their personological implications. Gratitude represents a more circumscribed construct that can be easily measured. However, its relationship with QOL needs to be examined across more demographically diverse samples.

Current Issues

There should be little doubt, given this review, that spiritual constructs are relevant dimensions for understanding a wide range of salient mental and physical health outcomes. Certainly, current scales can adequately measure spirituality and religiosity. What is particularly exciting about this research is that spirituality and religiosity represent psychological aspects of the individual not contained in the models and measures employed by traditional physical and social scientists. Thus, a consideration of one's spirituality represents an entirely new dimension of the person that has the potential for significantly changing how we think about ourselves and, most importantly, for identifying new pathways for making interventions into peoples' lives. To accomplish this will require much more work. As the field struggles to exploit its potential, there are numerous challenges to its growth. This section will outline four issues that the field is currently struggling with and will need to be addressed.

Defining the Basic Constructs of the Field

The current data suggest that religiosity and spirituality, although highly related, are not interchangeable constructs. Although the field has had difficulty in defining these concepts, with some believing that a single overall definition is impossible, or inappropriate (e.g., Hill, et al. 2000), the basic scientific need for accurate description and definition of spiritual constructs still remains. If religiosity and spirituality are such complex phenomena that they defy concise description, then they offer little hope for truly expanding our understanding of people. As Hill et al. (2000, p. 65) noted,

> Without a clearer conception of what these terms mean, it may be difficult to know with any precision or reliability what researchers attribute to them. Also, communication within the social scientific study of these constructs and across other disciplines may be impaired by a lack of common understanding and clinical agreement. Finally, without common definitions within psychological as well as sociological research, it becomes difficult to draw general conclusions from various studies. Therefore, these definitions are in dire need of empirical grounding and improved operationalization.

In their review of the literature on spirituality and QOL, Sawatzky et al. (2005) empirically documented this problem by showing that although there are many spirituality scales that carry the same or similar names, they are assessing very different qualities. It is critical for the field to find ways to operationalize these constructs in order to promote consistency and understanding (e.g., Sperry 2005). Koenig (2008), an active researcher in the field of spirituality and health, has provided an overview of some of these definitional issues and the impact they have on the field's development. He asserted that if the field cannot create a unique, clear construct, the use of religious and spiritual constructs should be eliminated from research altogether.

Measurement Properties of Scales

The field is plagued by a lack of substantial validity information for many of the assessment instruments that are available (e.g., Gorsuch 1984; Slater et al. 1994). A perusal of the compendium of measures of religiosity presented by Hill and Hood (1999) shows that of the 126 instruments presented, 40 (32%) provide no psychometric data beyond the original study. Thus, many measures are developed, but there is little follow-through in the scientific community to develop these instruments.

Ideally, empirical parameters need to be developed for defining what is and is not spiritual. To do so would require an evaluation of spiritual constructs within larger personality models, like the Five-Factor Model of Personality (FFM; Digman 1990; McCrae and John 1992). The FFM represents a comprehensive, empirically developed, taxonomy of traditionally defined personality dimensions. Locating spiritual scales within the context of this model would help to determine the extent to which the scale captures already established personality dynamics and to what extent it represents something different. MacDonald (2000) provides a good example of this type of research. He jointly factor analyzed a number of putative spiritual scales along with markers of the FFM domains. He was able to recover the five personality dimensions, but his results also indicated that many of the spiritual and religious scales defined additional factors independent of the personality domains. Perhaps one way to define what is spiritual is to demonstrate that a scale is independent of personality and correlated to those qualities that constitute this independent dimension (see also Piedmont 2001; Piedmont et al. 2009).

Methodological Issues

There is no doubt that spiritual constructs have important relationships with a variety of physical and mental QOL indicators. However, these findings do not go unchallenged. Sloan and colleagues have criticized this research on the basis of numerous methodological and statistical shortcomings (Sloan and Bagiella 2002; Sloan et al. 2001). One of the concerns centers on the lack of evidence documenting the predictive power of religious and spiritual variables over and above other established constructs, like social support. This failure to demonstrate incremental predictive validity for spiritual and religious constructs raises important concerns about their construct validity (see Joiner et al. 2002). The question arises as to what degree spiritual constructs are merely the "religification" (Van Wicklin 1990) of already existing personality constructs. As Buss (2002) noted, "Religious phenomena may simply parasitize existing evolved mechanisms or represent byproducts of them" (p. 203).

Still other criticisms have centered on the empirical robustness of the findings. Sloan et al. also argued that these mostly zero-order relationships fail to control for the multiple comparisons that are performed in such studies, thus increasing the likelihood for Type I errors. Smith (2001) argued that the observed relationships with health outcomes may be artifactual—the product of a singular reliance on self-report data. For him, correlated method error (e.g., acquiescence, social desirability) may be responsible for the findings.

Three other issues need to be considered when examining studies in this area. The first concerns the magnitude of effect often noted between religious/spiritual constructs and measures of QOL, which are clearly low to moderate in magnitude. In a meta-analytic study on the relationship between spirituality and QOL, Sawatzky et al. (2005) found an overall relationship of $r = .34$ (CI: .28–.40). In another meta-analysis of religious coping's relations to psychological adjustment, Ano and Vasconcelles (2005) found effects of .33 for positive religious coping (CI: .30–.35) and .22 for negative religious coping (CI: .19–.24). These findings mirror still others that examined spirituality in national and cross-national samples (e.g., Diener and Clifton 2002; Ferriss 2002). Small-to-moderate effect sizes do not diminish the importance of spiritual constructs to understanding QOL outcomes; however, it should remind researchers that these constructs are not going to single-handedly answer all our questions about QOL.

A second, related issue concerns the impact of spirituality on QOL outcomes across various cultures. Most research in this report has focused on various US samples. However, it needs to be determined whether these effects can generalize globally. Diener and Clifton (2002) examined the relationship between religiosity and well-being in both US and international probability samples. Aside from observing mostly small associations, they did note that religiosity's effect did vary across communist versus noncommunist countries, with the former evidencing no associations. Clearly, cultural and societal conditions impact the benefits of religion and research needs to understand the complex role that context plays in how people experience spirituality (see Tarakeshwar et al. 2003).

The third issue concerns the potential problem of criterion contamination. Measures of spirituality that have been shown to correlate with QOL outcomes may contain items that are themselves QOL-related. As such, any observed association has less to do with the role of spirituality as a predictor than the correlation being the result of a statistical artifact; the two scales correlate because they share similar items. For example, the *Spiritual Well-Being Scale* (Paloutzian and Ellison 1991) is noted as being one of the most widely used scales for research and clinical purposes (Boivin et al. 1999). It contains items such as "I feel that life is a positive experience," "I feel very fulfilled and satisfied with life," and "I feel good about my future," all of which are themselves indicators of a positive QOL. Therefore, it is not surprising that this measure can correlate very strongly with self-reported measures of satisfaction with life and QOL (e.g., $r > .50$; Matheis et al. 2006).

These are core issues that the field needs to address. Science demands that its models be parsimonious and that our constructs represent reliable effects. These criticisms here of mediation, small effect size, cultural relativity, statistical conclusion invalidity, and correlated method error are serious hurdles that must be jumped before the wider social and physical sciences will recognize spiritual constructs as substantive constructs. Piedmont (2006) conducted a series of Structural Equation Model (SEM) analyses in American and Philippine samples to examine exactly these issues. He found that spirituality was *not mediated* by personality in predicting a variety of QOL outcomes, including well-being, psychological maturity, and world view. These findings were observed with both self-report and observer rating data, and across two relatively distinct cultural groups. Researchers interested in examining religious and spiritual effects need to routinely control for potential mediators, such as the personality dimensions of the FFM which are also important predictors of QOL outcomes (see Piedmont 2001).

Identifying Causal Pathways

A key empirical question that is emerging in the field concerns the causal relationships between them and other psychological constructs. As Hackney and Sanders (2003) discussed in their meta-analysis, although most studies frame their emphasis in terms of the effects of spirituality and religiousness on various outcomes, the correlational nature of these studies leaves open the possibility that good QOL predisposes people to spiritual and religious involvement rather than the other way around. This is an important issue that speaks to the ultimate value of the spiritual constructs. If one's spiritual orientation develops out of one's sense of personhood, then it is one's level of psychological adjustment that forms the experiences of the transcendent. Thus, unhappy people will tend to have unhappy relationships with the transcendent. Like any other behavior, relationships with some ultimate reality are reflections of more basic psychological dynamics. From this perspective, spiritual constructs are merely the reflection of already established psychological constructs (e.g., Joiner et al. 2002), or are just a conduit or method by which individuals are able to activate other psychological mechanisms that are adaptive (e.g., Fredrickson 2002).

However, if spirituality and religiosity are "inputs" into our psychological system, then they become important conduits through which growth and maturity can be focused. In this scenario, the quality of one's relationship to the transcendent has important implications for our own psychological sense of stability (Piedmont 2005). Therefore, disturbances in our relationship to the transcendent would have serious repercussions for the rest of our mental world. Demonstrating the causal precedence of spiritual constructs would enable their use as explanatory constructs in larger models of QOL. If religious and spiritual constructs do play a significant role in driving adaptation and growth, then this creates the possibility for a whole new class of potential therapeutic strategies based on these types of dynamics (e.g., Murray-Swank 2003; Piedmont 2004b). At a minimum, it would demand that any model of human behavior must include spiritual constructs if that model were to be comprehensive (Piedmont et al. 2009).

Directions for Future Research

We believe that this is an exciting time to be involved in research on spirituality and religiosity and its linkages to important life outcomes, such as QOL. Never has there been more interest in the field than now. There are a variety of measures, a growing (interdisciplinary) empirical literature, and openness in the scientific community to examine the possible contribution of spirituality. As noted above, there certainly are methodological and conceptual issues confronting researchers in this area as they struggle to document the relevance of spirituality and religiosity. However, we would like to say a few words about the directions the field should move toward as the scientific discussion evolves.

Theoretical Models

Having demonstrated that spiritual constructs have something important to say about QOL, it is now important to begin to integrate these findings within larger mainstream models of well-being, coping ability, personality development, and mental/physical health (to name but a few). We need to develop a conceptual depth to our understanding of spirituality that is consistent with current theoretical models of human functioning. Future work will have to begin to identify: (a) how spiritual and religious variables develop and are expressed over the life course; (b) those factors, both internal and environmental, that influence the expression of religious sentiments and spiritual motivations; and (c) the pathways by which spiritual and religious constructs impact, and are impacted by, psychological processes and dynamics. Peterson and Seligman (2004) attempted to integrate spirituality within a larger psychological model of character strengths and virtues. Such a process helps to elaborate the types of properties spirituality has and the role it plays in the psychic life of the individual. Paloutzian and Park (2005) provide another effort to outline how spirituality can be integrated into psychological study at all different levels, from the neurological to the intra-psychic to the organizational and social. There are many levels of analysis where a consideration of the spiritual and religious can be included. Such conceptual developments are needed.

More Sophisticated Statistical Models

The development of better theories will help to identify the many relevant variables that need to be considered when conducting research in this area. As such, research will need to implement multivariate designs that will be able to address more sophisticated questions about incremental validity, mediation, and construct dimensionality (e.g., Dy-Liacco et al. 2005; Piedmont 2006). Unfortunately, the field has an over reliance on cross-sectional, correlational data. Batson (1997, p. 6) has argued, "In research methods, the psychology of religion is about 30 years behind other areas of psychology." Few studies adjust for Type I error due to multiple comparisons, statistically control for other relevant mediators, or apply multivariate or SEM techniques to model building/testing questions. There is a very strong reliance on correlational-type data (Dy-Liacco et al. 2003). To move forward, the field will need to employ more sophisticated analytic techniques (including more experiments) that will examine more complex conceptual questions related to systems and processes.

Longitudinal and Cross-Observer Data

What is the role and impact of spiritual and religious constructs over the life span? How does a spiritual orientation develop? When does it develop? How does it become expressed over time? These are important questions that need to be answered. Few research studies take such a perspective, although there are exceptions (see, e.g., Pargament et al. 2004; Wink and Dillon 2003). As people age, does what constitutes spirituality change? Do we need different scales to measures spirituality at different age ranges? Piedmont (1999) has hypothesized that spiritual transcendence increases as people get older, a result of a more active concern over personal mortality. He provided data showing a significant age effect, and also that different aspects of spirituality were relevant for younger as opposed to older individuals (Piedmont 2004a, b). Brennan and Mroczek (2002) described statistical procedures (i.e., latent growth curve and individual growth curve analyses) for examining changes in spirituality over time at both the aggregate and individual levels. These statistical techniques can be helpful in charting the natural developmental changes that may occur on spiritual dimensions. It also needs to be determined whether different spiritual constructs have similar or different trajectories over the life span.

Related to the use of longitudinal data is the need to include other sources of information beyond mere self-report, specifically, the need to include observer ratings in studies of spiritual and religious constructs. As noted above, the almost singular reliance on self-report data raises questions of acquiescence effects and correlated method error as explanations for observed findings. It is important that the fields develop and validate observer rater versions of their self-report instruments (see Piedmont 2004a). In this manner, ratings of individuals' spirituality can be obtained from knowledgeable others (e.g., parents, spouses, close friends, etc.). Showing that these observer ratings of spirituality converge with self-rated scores would overcome these two criticisms. More importantly, showing significant convergence between self- and observer-rated scores of spirituality provides evidence of consensual validation for the spiritual construct. Such cross-observer convergence demonstrates that people share an understanding of what "spirituality" means and can identify dispositions, behaviors, and goals toward which this construct directs the individual. Without such agreement, spiritual and religious constructs must be viewed as solipsistic aspects of the individual—labels applied to idiosyncratic aspects of the person that may have limited interpretive and predictive value.

Cross-Cultural and Multi-faith Approaches

It has long been known that the majority of measures designed to assess spirituality are rooted in Christian-based perspectives (Gorsuch 1984; Slater et al. 2001), reflecting mostly a mainline Protestant orientation (Gorsuch and Miller 1999). Although Christianity may be the mainstream faith orientation in America, it certainly does not represent, nor speak for, other faith traditions. Piedmont and Leach (2002) have noted that this lack of theological pluralism undermines both the scientific endeavor to understand the basic elements of spirituality and efforts to develop a comprehensive model of spiritual development and experience that would have ecological validity.

Although there is clear value for understanding the spiritual and religious dynamics of specific religious groups and cultures (Moberg 2002), there is a twofold value for attempting to understand what is common across different groups. First, it needs to be known to what extent spirituality is an innate aspect of the individual. Does spirituality represent a fundamental motivational aspect of the individual that orients him or her to specific types of outcomes? Or is spirituality really a specific, context-dependent response to organized religion? (Also implied in this question is the more fundamental etiological question, "What came first, religion or spirituality?" See Piedmont et al. (2009) for an empirical analysis of this question.) If spirituality is a motivation, then there should be some basic qualities of spirituality that are consistent across all spiritually mature individuals regardless of their religious affiliation. We can see support for this proposition with only a casual perusal of history; individuals such as Jesus (a Jew), Buddha (an Eastern Philosopher), Gandhi (a Hindu), and Mother Teresa (a Catholic) all share many of the same qualities and dispositions, yet they come from very different time periods and different faith backgrounds. What is this basic quality, and how does it come to influence behavior? What resources does it provide for coping, adapting, and thriving?

The second advantage of cross-cultural and cross-faith research is that it will begin to show that spiritual constructs are a universal aspect of the human experience. More than that, spirituality may represent a *uniquely* human quality. Only our species evidences any concern for, sensitivity to, or celebration of the sacred. There are no animal models for spirituality. Every human culture across history has reserved a significant place for religious and spiritual endeavors. The little cross-cultural research that has been done (e.g., Cho 2004; Piedmont 2007) has indicated that broad concepts of spirituality generalize well to different faiths and cultures. In fact, many of the spiritual concepts used in research in the USA and Europe have been found in other languages that do not share a common etymological root with English. This is evidence that all cultures are led toward and encounter similar spiritual realities.

Finally, very little research has been conducted on spiritual masters or teachers from a variety of spiritual or religious traditions around the world. This would appear to be essential if we are to understand the highest and best there is in spirituality and religiosity, especially if we are to see it as a major strength and virtue. Most research to date has been done with college students, adolescents, normal adults, and the elderly, many of whom except for the college students are in some state of distress, illness, or injury. Such an approach may shed new insights into spirituality and its related dynamics. Perhaps what may be the ultimate gift from the study of spirituality would be the identification of those core, common, qualities that unite all people in a common quest for understanding the human experience and its ultimate meaning.

Conclusions

Despite the many issues and challenges facing the field of religious and spiritual research, it is hoped that these data persuasively demonstrate the value of such constructs for understanding people and the quality of their lives. Spiritual constructs do have something to add to scientific models of human behavior. The information contained in spiritual variables is non-redundant with extent constructs in the social and physical sciences. The spiritual domain represents a new, untapped "frontier" of insights into people that science needs to exploit. Such efforts would open the door to potentially new types of paradigms for conceptualiz-

ing our inner worlds and for developing positive, durable interventions that address the central existential (and personality-organizing) questions of personal meaning and ultimate purpose.

References

Allport, G. W. (1950). *The individual and his religion*. New York: Macmillan.

Allport, G. W., & Ross, J. M. (1967). Personal religious orientation and prejudice. *Journal of Personality and Social Psychology, 5*, 432–443.

Ano, G. G., & Vasconcelles, E. B. (2005). Religious coping and psychological adjustment to stress: A meta-analysis. *Journal of Clinical Psychology, 61*, 461–480.

Bartlett, S. J., Piedmont, R. L., Bilderback, A., Matsumoto, A. K., & Bathon, J. M. (2003). Spirituality, well-being and quality of life in persons with rheumatoid arthritis. *Arthritis Care and Research, 49*, 778–783.

Batson, C. D. (1997). An agenda item for psychology of religion: Getting respect. In B. Spilka & D. N. McIntosh (Eds.), *The psychology of religion: Theoretical approaches*. Boulder: Westview Press.

Batson, C. D., Schoenrade, P., & Ventis, W. L. (1993). *Religion and the individual: A socio-psychological perspective*. New York: Oxford University Press.

Beit-Hallahmi, B. (1989). *Prolegomena to the psychological study of religion*. Lewisburg: Bucknell University Press.

Boivin, M. J., Kirby, A. L., Underwood, L. K., & Silva, H. (1999). Spiritual well-being scale. In P. Hill & R. Hood Jr. (Eds.), *Measures of religiosity* (pp. 382–385). Birmingham: Religious Education Press.

Brennan, M., & Mroczek, D. K. (2002). Examining spirituality over time: Latent growth curve and individual growth curve analyses. *Journal of Religious Gerontology, 14*, 11–29.

Buss, D. M. (2002). Sex, marriage, and religion: What adaptive problems do religious phenomena solve? *Psychological Inquiry, 13*, 201–203.

Cho, I. (2004). *An effect of spiritual transcendence of fear of intimacy*. Unpublished Masters thesis, Torch Trinity Graduate School of Theology, Seoul, Korea.

Diener, E., & Clifton, D. (2002). Life satisfaction and religiosity in broad probability samples. *Psychological Inquiry, 13*, 206–209.

Digman, J. M. (1990). Personality structure: Emergence of the five-factor model. *Annual Review of Psychology, 41*, 417–440.

Dittes, J. E. (1969). Psychology of religion. In G. Lindzey & E. Aronson (Eds.), *Handbook of social psychology* (Vol. 5, pp. 602–659). Reading: Addison-Wesley Publishing Co.

Dogan, M. (2003). Religious beliefs in Europe: Factors of accelerated decline. *Research in the Social Scientific Study of Religion, 14*, 161–188.

Donahue, M. J. (1985). Intrinsic and extrinsic religiousness: Review and meta-analysis. *Journal of Personality and Social Psychology, 48*, 400–419.

Dowling, E. M., Gestsdottir, S., Anderson, P. M., von Eye, A., Almerigi, J., & Lerner, R. M. (2004). Structural relations among spirituality, religiosity, and thriving in adolescence. *Applied Developmental Science, 8*, 7–16.

Dy-Liacco, G. S., Piedmont, R. L., Leach, M. M., & Nelson, R. W. (2003). A content analysis of research in the social scientific study of religion from 1997 to 2001: Where we have been and where we hope to go. *Research in the Social Scientific Study of Religion, 14*, 277–288.

Dy-Liacco, G. S., Kennedy, M. C., Parker, D. J., & Piedmont, R. L. (2005). Spiritual transcendence as an unmediated causal predictor of psychological growth and worldview among Filipinos. *Research in the Social Scientific Study of Religion, 16*, 261–286.

Elkins, D. N. (1988). Towards a humanistic-phenomenological spirituality: Definition, description, and measurement. *Journal of Humanistic Psychology, 28*, 5–18.

Ellison, C. G., & Levin, J. S. (1998). The religion-health connection: Evidence, theory, and future directions. *Health Education and Behavior, 25*, 700–720.

Emmons, R. A. (1999). *The psychology of ultimate concerns: Motivation and spirituality in personality*. New York: Guilford Press.

Emmons, R. A., & McCullough, M. E. (2003). Counting blessings versus burdens: An experimental investigation of gratitude and subjective well-being in daily life. *Journal of Personality and Social Psychology, 84*, 377–389.

Emmons, R. A., & McCullough, M. E. (2004). *The psychology of gratitude*. New York, NY: Oxford University Press.

Emmons, R. A., & Paloutzian, R. F. (2003). The psychology of religion. *Annual Review of Psychology, 54*, 377–402.

Ferriss, A. L. (2002). Religion and the quality of life. *Journal of Happiness Studies, 3*, 199–215.

Fetzer Institute/National Institute on Aging Working Group. (1999). *Multidimensional measurement of religiousness/spirituality for use in heath research*. Kalamazoo: Fetzer Institute.

Foundation for Inner Peace. (1975). *A course in miracles*. Glen Ellen: Author.

Fox, C. A., Blanton, P. W., & Morris, M. L. (1998). Religious problem solving scale: Three styles revisited. *Journal for the Scientific Study of Religion, 37*, 673–677.

Frankl, V. F. (1966). Self-transcendence as a human phenomenon. *Journal of Humanistic Psychology, 6*, 97–106.

Fredrickson, B. L. (2002). How does religion benefit health and well-being? Are positive emotions active ingredients? *Psychological Inquiry, 13*, 209–213.

Friedman, P. (2010). *The forgiveness solution*. San Francisco: Conari Press.

Friedman, P., & Toussaint, L. (2006). The relationship between forgiveness, gratitude, distress, and well-being: An integrative review of the literature. *International Journal of Healing and Caring-Online, 6*(2), 1–10.

Gallup, G. (1995). *The Gallup poll: Public opinion 1995*. Wilmington: Scholarly Resources.

George, L. K., Ellison, C. G., & Larson, D. B. (2002). Explaining the relationship between religious involvement and health. *Psychological Inquiry, 13*, 190–200.

Golden, J., Piedmont, R. L., Ciarrocchi, J. W., & Rodgerson, T. (2004). Spirituality and burnout: An incremental validity study. *Journal of Psychology and Theology, 32*, 115–125.

Goodman, J. M., Britton, P. J., Shama-Davis, D., & Jencius, M. J. (2005). An exploration of spirituality and psychological

well-being in a community of orthodox, conservative, and reform Jews. *Research in the Social Scientific Study of Religion, 16*, 63–82.

Gorsuch, R. L. (1984). Measurement: The boon and bane of investigating religion. *American Psychologist, 39*, 228–236.

Gorsuch, R. L. (1988). Psychology of religion. *Annual Review of Psychology, 39*, 201–221.

Gorsuch, R. L., & McPherson, S. E. (1989). Intrinsic/extrinsic measurement: I/E-Revised and single item scales. *Journal for the Scientific Study of Religion, 29*, 348–354.

Gorsuch, R. L., & Miller, W. R. (1999). Assessing spirituality. In W. R. Miller (Ed.), *Integrating spirituality in treatment: Resources for practitioners*. Washington, DC: American Psychological Association.

Gorsuch, R. L., & Venable, G. D. (1983). Development of an "age universal" I-E scale. *Journal for the Scientific Study of Religion, 22*, 181–187.

Hackney, C. H., & Sanders, G. S. (2003). Religiosity and mental health: A meta-analysis of recent studies. *Journal for the Scientific Study of Religion, 42*, 43–55.

Haerich, P. (1992). Premarital sexual permissiveness and religious orientation: A preliminary investigation. *Journal for the Scientific Study of Religion, 31*, 361–365.

Hill, P. C., & Hood, R. W., Jr. (1999). *Measures of religiosity*. Birmingham: Religious Education Press.

Hill, P. C., & Pargament, K. I. (2003). Advances in the conceptualization and measurement of religion and spirituality: Implications for physical and mental health research. *American Psychologist, 58*, 64–74.

Hill, P. C., Pargament, K. I., Hood, R. W., McCullough, M. E., Swyers, J. P., Larson, D. B., & Zinnbauer, B. J. (2000). Conceptualizing religion and spirituality: Points of commonality, points of departure. *Journal for the Theory of Social Behavior, 30*, 51–77.

Jampolsky, G. (1999). *Forgiveness: The greatest healer of all*. Hillsboro: Beyond Words Publishing, Inc.

Johnson, B. R., Jang, S. J., Larson, D. B., & De Li, S. (2001). Does adolescent religious commitment matter? A reexamination of the effects of religiosity on delinquency. *Journal of Research in Crime and Delinquency, 38*, 22–43.

Joiner, T. E., Perez, M., & Walker, R. L. (2002). Playing devil's advocate: Why not conclude that the relation of religiosity to mental health reduces to mundane mediators? *Psychological Inquiry, 13*, 214–216.

Koenig, H. G. (1997). *Is religion god for your health? The effects of religion on physical and mental health*. Binghamton: Haworth Press.

Koenig, H. G. (2008). Concerns about measuring "spirituality" in research. *The Journal of Nervous and Mental Disease, 196*, 349–355.

Koenig, H. G., George, L. K., Hays, J. C., Larson, D. B., Cohen, H. J., & Blazer, D. G. (1998). The relationship between religious activities and blood pressure in older adults. *International Journal of Psychiatry in Medicine, 28*, 189–213.

Koenig, H. G., McCullough, M. E., & Larson, D. B. (2000). *Handbook of religion and health*. New York: Oxford University Press.

Krause, N., & Ellison, C. G. (2003). Forgiveness by God, forgiveness of others, and psychological well-being in late life. *Journal for the Scientific Study of Religion, 42*, 77–93.

Lewis, C. A., Matlby, J., & Day, L. (2005). Religious orientation, religious coping, and happiness among UK adults. *Personality and Individual Differences, 38*, 1193–1202.

MacDonald, D. A. (2000). Spirituality: Description, measurement, and relation to the five-factor model of personality. *Journal of Personality, 68*, 153–197.

Matheis, E. N., Tulsky, D. S., & Matheis, R. J. (2006). The relation between spirituality and quality of life among individuals with spinal cord injury. *Rehabilitation Psychology, 51*, 265–271.

McCrae, R. R., & John, O. P. (1992). An introduction to the five-factor model and its applications. *Journal of Personality, 57*, 415–433.

McCullough, M. E., Bellah, C. G., Kilpatrick, S. D., & Johnson, J. L. (2001). Vengefulness: Relationships with forgiveness, rumination, well-being, and the big five. *Personality and Social Psychology Bulletin, 27*, 601–610.

McCullough, M. E., Emmons, R. A., & Tsang, J. (2002). The grateful disposition: A conceptual and empirical topography. *Journal of Personality and Social Psychology, 82*, 112–127.

Miller, W. R., & Thoresen, C. E. (1999). Spirituality and health. In W. Miller (Ed.), *Integrating spirituality into treatment* (pp. 3–18). Washington, DC: American Psychological Association.

Miller, W. R., & Thoresen, C. E. (2003). Spirituality, religion, and health: An emerging research field. *American Psychologist, 58*, 24–35.

Moberg, D. O. (2002). Assessing and measuring spirituality: Confronting dilemmas of universal and particular evaluative criteria. *Journal of Adult Development, 9*, 47–60.

Murray-Swank, N. (2003). *Solace for the soul: An evaluation of a psycho-spiritual intervention for female survivors of sexual abuse.* Unpublished doctoral dissertation, Bowling Green State University, Bowling Green, Ohio

Musick, M. A., Traphagan, J. W., Koenig, H. G., & Larson, D. B. (2000). Spirituality in physical health and aging. *Journal of Adult Development, 7*, 73–86.

Nairn, R. C., & Merluzzi, T. V. (2003). The role of religious coping in adjustment to cancer. *Psycho-Oncology, 12*, 428–441.

Paloutzian, R., & Ellison, C. W. (1991). *Manual for the spiritual well-being scale.* Nyack: Life Advance, Inc.

Paloutzian, R., & Park, C. (2005). *The handbook of the psychology of religion and spirituality.* New York: Guilford.

Pargament, K. I., Kennell, J., Hathaway, W., Grevengoed, N., Newman, J., & Jones, W. (1988). Religion and the problem-solving process: Three styles of coping. *Journal for the Scientific Study of Religion, 27*, 90–104.

Pargament, K. I., Koenig, H. G., & Perez, L. M. (2000). The many methods of religious coping: Development and initial validation of the RCOPE. *Journal of Clinical Psychology, 56*, 519–543.

Pargament, K. I., Koenig, H. G., & Tarakeshwar, N. (2004). Religious coping methods as predictors of psychological, physical and spiritual outcomes among medically ill elderly patients: A two-year longitudinal study. *Journal of Health Psychology, 9*, 713–730.

Peterson, C., & Seligman, M. E. P. (2004). *Character strengths and virtues: A handbook and classification.* Washington, DC: American Psychological Association.

Piedmont, R. L. (1999). Does spirituality represent the sixth factor of personality? Spiritual transcendence and the five-factor model. *Journal of Personality, 67*, 985–1013.

Piedmont, R. L. (2001). Spiritual transcendence and the scientific study of spirituality. *Journal of Rehabilitation, 67*, 4–14.

Piedmont, R. L. (2004a). *Assessment of spirituality and religious sentiments, technical manual.* Baltimore: Author.

Piedmont, R. L. (2004b). Spiritual transcendence as a predictor of psychosocial outcome from an outpatient substance abuse program. *Psychology of Addictive Behaviors, 18*, 213–222.

Piedmont, R. L. (2005). The role of personality in understanding religious and spiritual constructs. In R. Paloutzian & C. Park (Eds.), *The handbook of the psychology of religion and spirituality.* New York: Guilford.

Piedmont, R. L. (2006). Spirituality as a robust empirical predictor of psychosocial outcomes: A cross-cultural analysis. In R. Estes (Ed.), *Advancing quality of life in a turbulent world.* New York: Springer.

Piedmont, R. L. (2007). Cross-cultural generalizability of the spiritual transcendence scale to the Philippines: Spirituality as a human universal. *Mental Health, Religion, and Culture, 10*, 89–107.

Piedmont, R. L., & Leach, M. M. (2002). Cross-cultural generalizability of the spiritual transcendence Scale in India: Spirituality as a universal aspect of human experience. *American Behavioral Scientist, 45*(12), 1888–1901.

Piedmont, R. L., Hassinger, C. J., Rhorer, J., Sherman, M. F., Sherman, N. C., & Williams, J. E. G. (2007). The relations among spirituality and religiosity and Axis II functioning in two college samples. *Research in the Social Scientific Study of Religion, 18*, 53–73.

Piedmont, R. L., Ciarrocchi, J. W., Dy-Liacco, G., & Williams, J. E. G. (2009). The empirical and conceptual value of the spiritual transcendence and religious involvement scales for personality research. *Psychology of Religion and Spirituality, 1*, 162–179.

Powell, L. H., Shahabi, L., & Thoresen, C. E. (2003). Religion and spirituality: Linkages to physical health. *American Psychologist, 58*, 36–52.

Rican, P., & Janosova, P. (2010). Spirituality as a basic aspects of personality: A cross-cultural verification of Piedmont's model. *The International Journal for the Psychology of Religion, 20*, 2–13.

Rodgerson, T. E., & Piedmont, R. L. (1998). Assessing the incremental validity of the religious problem solving scale in the prediction of clergy burnout. *Journal for the Scientific Study of Religion, 37*, 517–527.

Rye, M. S., Loiacono, D. M., Folck, C. D., Olszewski, B. T., Heinm, T. A., & Madia, B. P. (2001). Evaluation of the psychometric properties of two forgiveness scales. *Current Psychology: Developmental, Learning, Personality, Social, 20*, 260–277.

Sawatzky, R., Ratner, P. A., & Chiu, L. (2005). A meta-analysis of the relationship between spirituality and quality of life. *Social Indicators Research, 72*, 153–188.

Seeman, T. E., Dubin, L. F., & Seeman, M. (2003). Religiosity/spirituality and health: A critical review of the evidence for biological pathways. *American Psychologist, 58*, 53–63.

Slater, W., Hall, T. W., & Edwards, K. J. (2001). Measuring religion and spirituality: Where are we and where are we going. *Journal of Psychology and Theology, 29*, 4–21.

Sloan, R. P., & Bagiella, R. (2002). Claims about religious involvement and health outcomes. *Annals of Behavioral Medicine, 24*, 14–21.

Sloan, R. P., Bagiella, R., & Powell, T. (2001). Without a prayer: Methodological problems, ethical challenges, and misrepresentation in the study of religion, spirituality, and medicine. In T. G. Plante & A. C. Sherman (Eds.), *Faith and health: Psychological perspectives* (pp. 339–354). NY: Guilford Press.

Smith, T. W. (2001). Religion and spirituality in the science and practice of health psychology: Openness, skepticism, and the agnosticism of methodology. In T. G. Plante & A. C. Sherman (Eds.), *Faith and health: Psychological perspectives* (pp. 355–380). New York: Guilford Press.

Sperry, L. (2005). Is a consensus definition of spirituality possible? Theory construction in spirituality-oriented psychotherapy. *Research in the Social Scientific Study of Religion, 16*, 207–220.

Stifler, K., Greer, J., Sneck, W., & Dovenmuehle, R. (1993). An empirical investigation of the discriminability of reported mystical experiences among religious contemplatives, psychotic inpatients, and normal adults. *Journal for the Scientific Study of Religion, 32*, 366–372.

Tarakeshwar, N., Stanton, J., & Pargament, K. (2003). Religion: An overlooked dimension in cross-cultural psychology. *Journal of Cross-Cultural Psychology, 34*, 377–394.

Thompson, L. Y., Snyder, C. R., Hoffman, L., Michael, S. T., Rasmussen, H. N., Billings, L. S., Heinze, L., Neufeld, J. E., Shorey, H. S., Roberts, J. C., & Robert, D. E. (2005). Dispositional forgiveness of self, others, and situations: The heartland forgiveness scale. *Journal of Personality, 73*, 313–359.

Thoresen, C. E. (1999). Spirituality and health: Is there a relationship? *Journal of Health Psychology, 4*, 291–300.

Toussaint, L., & Friedman, P. (2008). Forgiveness, gratitude, and well-being: the mediating role of affect and beliefs. *Journal of Happiness*. doi:10.1007/s10902-008-9111-8.

Toussaint, L., & Webb, J. R. (2005). Forgiveness, mental health and well-being. In E. L. Worthington Jr. (Ed.), *Handbook of forgiveness*. New York: Routledge.

Toussaint, L., Williams, D. R., Musick, M. A., & Everson, S. A. (2001). Forgiveness and health: Age differences in a U.S. probability sample. *Journal of Adult Development, 8*, 249–257.

Trimble, D. E. (1997). The religious orientation scale: Review and meta-analysis of social desirability effects. *Educational and Psychological Measurement, 57*, 970–986.

Van Wicklin, J. F. (1990). Conceiving and measuring ways of being religious. *Journal of Psychology and Christianity, 9*, 27–40.

Ventis, W. L. (1995). The relationship between religion and mental health. *Journal of Social Issues, 51*, 33–48.

Walsh, J. (2001). *Spirituality and recovery from pathological gambling*. Unpublished doctoral dissertation, Loyola College in Maryland

Watkins, P. (2004). Gratitude and subjective well-being. In R. A. Emmons & M. E. McCullough (Eds.), *The psychology of gratitude*. New York, NY: Oxford University Press.

Watkins, P., Woodward, K., Stone, T., & Kolts, R. (2003). Gratitude and happiness: Development of a measure of gratitude and relationships with subjective well-being. *Social Behavior and Personality, 31*, 431–452.

Wilson, T. (2004). *Ethnic identity and spirituality in the recovery from alcoholism among aboriginal Canadians*. Unpublished Master's Thesis, University of Windsor, Ontario, Canada.

Wink, P., & Dillon, M. (2003). Religiousness, spirituality, and psychosocial functioning in late adulthood: Findings from a longitudinal study. *Psychology and Aging, 18*, 916–924.

Wong, P. T. P. (1998). Meaning centered counseling. In P. T. T. Wong & P. S. Fry (Eds.), *The human quest for meaning* (pp. 395–435). Mahwah: Erlbaum.

Worthington, E. L. (2005). *Handbook of forgiveness*. New York: Routledge.

Worthington, E. L., Kurusu, T. A., McCullough, M., & Sandage, S. J. (1996). Empirical research on religion and psychotherapeutic processes and outcomes: A 10-year review and research prospectus. *Psychological Bulletin, 119*, 448–487.

Worthington, E. L., Wade, N. G., Hight, T. L., Ripley, J. S., McCullough, M. E., Berry, J. W., Schmitt, M. M., Berry, J. T., Bursley, K. H., & O'Connor, L. (2003). The religious commitment inventory—10: Development, refinement, and validation of a brief scale for research and counseling. *Journal of Counseling Psychology, 50*, 84–96.

Zinnbauer, B. J., Pargament, K. I., & Scott, A. B. (1999). The emerging meanings of religiousness and spirituality: Problems and prospects. *Journal of Personality, 67*, 889–920.

Consumer Well-Being (CWB): Various Conceptualizations and Measures

15

Dong-Jin Lee and M. Joseph Sirgy

Introduction

The effect of marketing on consumers' quality of life has interested many scholars (Sirgy 2001; Sirgy and Lee 2008; Sirgy et al. 2008b). Marketing influences consumers' quality of life in large part because it directly affects satisfaction in the consumer life domain and indirectly in other life domains such as work life, family life, leisure life, financial life, among others (Day 1978, 1987; Leelakulthanit et al. 1991; Lee and Sirgy 1995; Sirgy 2001; Samli et al. 1987). While there have been various efforts to measure consumer well-being (CWB), limited attention has been given to describing and understanding the theoretical underpinnings of the available CWB measures.

Speaking of CWB measures, some of the existing measures come from the public sector, others from the academic sector. For example, the US Bureau of Labor Statistics has its popular Consumer Price Index, essentially a CWB measure. The United Nations Development Programme has its Total Consumption Expenditures Index. The US Better Business Bureau has a CWB measure based number of consumer complaints (against individual businesses) filed in various local offices around the US Consumer Union has its own measure of CWB based on experts' judgment of product quality. Brand quality ratings are reported in their monthly publication of *Consumer Reports* (Sirgy and Lee 2008).

There also have been many conceptualizations and measures of CWB published in marketing, business, and QOL scientific journals stemming from the academic world. For example, studies have captured CWB by measuring satisfaction with shopping (Meadow and Sirgy 2008), satisfaction with possessions (Nakano et al. 1995), or both (Day 1987; Leelakulthanit et al. 1991). Lee et al. (2002) have developed a CWB measure that taps five dimensions of marketplace experiences ranging from shopping to disposal of consumer goods. The measures is based on the notion that the psychosocial phenomenon of CWB reflects satisfaction and dissatisfaction stemming from one's aggregate experience of consumer goods and services within a given macromarketing system. In addition, CWB has been conceptualized in terms of community well-being, the level of need satisfaction, and perception of value, bottom-up spillover, among others.

There are many different conceptualizations and measures of CWB, and as a result, marketers and policymakers often do not know how to choose a CWB measure most suitable for their task. Hence, the main goal of this paper is to identify various CWB measures and classify them based on their theoretical foundations. Thus, we make an attempt to provide a detailed and comprehensive treatment of CWB measures and their underlying conceptual models. Doing so can help marketers and policymakers choose appropriate and effective CWB measures to gauge the effectiveness of marketing and policy programs.

D.J. Lee (✉)
School of Business, Yonsei University, Seoul, South Korea
e-mail: djlee@base.yonsei.ac.kr; djlee81@yonsei.ac.kr

M.J. Sirgy
Department of Marketing, Virginia Tech, Blacksburg, VA 24060-0236, USA
e-mail: sirgy@vt.edu

K.C. Land et al. (eds.), *Handbook of Social Indicators and Quality of Life Research*,
DOI 10.1007/978-94-007-2421-1_15, © Springer Science+Business Media B.V. 2012

However, before we begin describing the various conceptualizations and measures of CWB, we need to ensure that the reader understands the distinction between CWB and consumer satisfaction.

The Distinction Between CWB and Consumer Satisfaction

There is a plethora of research in consumer satisfaction with varied conceptualizations and measures. For a good literature review of this research, we recommend the reader to examine Richard Oliver's book on *Satisfaction: A Behavioral Perspective on the Consumer* (Oliver 1997, 2009). However, for readers who are not very familiar with the consumer satisfaction literature, we will describe one particular measure that we think is representative of the vast literature on consumer satisfaction, namely the University of Michigan's *American Consumer Satisfaction Index* (ACSI) (Fornell 1992; Fornell et al. 1996).

The university (through its College of Business' National Quality Research Center) has been measuring national consumer satisfaction since 1994 (www. theacsi.org). The National Quality Research Center reports ACSI levels quarterly in manufacturing durables such as automobiles, personal computers, household appliances and consumer electronics, and e-business. The ACSI measure is based on the notion that customer satisfaction is determined mostly by perceived value, perceived quality, and customer expectations. The Center conducts a survey of actual users of major brands in various product categories. The survey includes questions capturing customer expectations, perceived quality, value perceptions, satisfaction, customer complaints, and customer loyalty (Fornell 1992; Szymanski and Henard 2001). The exact measurement constructs are shown in Table 15.1.

We view the ACSI measure as highly representative of consumer satisfaction conceptualizations and measures. Much of consumer satisfaction research is guided by the theoretical notion that consumer satisfaction plays a major role in customer loyalty, repeat purchase, and positive word-of-mouth communications (e.g., Fornell 1992; Fornell et al. 1996; Szymanski and Henard 2001). Of course, the goal is to enhance consumer satisfaction for the purpose of ensuring higher levels of repeat patronage, ergo sales, market share, and profit.

In contrast, the concept of CWB is inherently guided by a different meta-level concept, namely the

Table 15.1 The measurement constructs involved in the ACSI

1. Expectation
   - Customer expectation about overall quality
   - Customer expectation about reliability
   - Customer expectation about customization
2. Performance
   - Perception of overall quality
   - Perception of reliability
   - Perception of customization
3. Value
   - Price given quality
   - Quality given price
4. Consumer satisfaction
   - Overall satisfaction
   - Satisfaction against expectation
   - Satisfaction against the ideal
5. Customer loyalty
   - Repurchase likelihood
   - Price tolerance (increase) given repurchase
   - Price tolerance (decrease) to induce repurchase
6. Customer complaints

Source: Fornell et al. (1996)

link between CWB and quality of life. In other words, all the conceptualizations and measures of CWB we review in this chapter are grounded on the implicit or explicit assumption that high levels of CWB lead to higher levels of consumer's quality of life—higher levels of life satisfaction, overall happiness with life, absence of ill being, societal welfare, etc.

Various Conceptualization and Measures of CWB

We identified several conceptualizations and resulting measures of CWB from both public and academic sectors. Contributions from the public sector encompass contributions from the business community, NGOs, and government agencies. In contrast, academic contributions entail conceptualizations and measures developed by academicians and published in academic journals. These contributions are all summarized and captured in Table 15.2.

Contributions from the Public Sector

We will describe in this section several important contributions of conceptualizations and measures of CWB that were established in the public sector. These are the

15 Consumer Well-Being (CWB): Various Conceptualizations and Measures

Table 15.2 Various conceptualizations and resulting measures of CWB

Contributions from the public sector	Contributions from the academic sector
• The Cost of Living Model	• The Shopping Satisfaction Model
• The Consumption Equity Model	• The Possession Satisfaction Model
• The Consumer Complaint Model	• The Acquisition/Possession Satisfaction Model
• The Quality Model	• The Consumer Life Cycle Model
	• The Community Model
	• The Need Satisfaction Model
	• The Perceived Value Model
	• The Bottom-Up Spillover Model
	• The Marketers' Orientation Model
	• The Materialism Model
	• The Globalization Model

Table 15.3 Product categories captured by the consumer price index for urban consumers

1. Food and beverages
Food: food at home/food away from home
Alcoholic beverages
2. Housing
Shelter
Fuels and utilities
Household furnishings and operations
3. Apparel
4. Transportation
Private transportation
Public transportation
5. Medical care
Medical care commodities
Medical care service
6. Recreation
7. Education and communication
Education
Communication
8. Other goods and services
Tobacco and smoking products
Personal care

Source: http//:www.bls.gov/cpi/home

Cost of Living Model, the Consumption Equity Model, the Consumer Complaint Model, and the Quality Model (Sirgy and Lee 2008).

The Cost of Living Model

An aspect of purchasing goods and services is consumers' experiences with prices of the goods and services they spend and changes of these prices over time. The *Consumer Price Index* (CPI) measures changes in the cost of living over time. Specifically, the CPI captures changes in prices of goods and services at the national level over time (http//:www.bls.gov/cpi/home). CPI ratings are reported overall as well as by household expenditure category. These are food at home, food away from home, alcoholic beverages, housing, apparel and services, transportation, health care, entertainment, personal care products and services, reading, education, tobacco products and supplies, personal insurance and pensions, and miscellaneous. Details regarding the CPI are shown in Table 15.3.

The assumption here is that increases in prices of goods and services (i.e., inflation) decrease CWB in relation to the acquisition of goods and services. This is because inflated prices make the purchase of needed goods and services unaffordable.

Samli (2003) argued that there is also hidden inflation that has the same effect of inflation but not captured in the CPI. For example, many firms reduce the quantity of staples in the package without increasing the price of the marketed item. This practice is equivalent to raising the product's price, but it is not incorporated in the CPI. This type of hidden inflation negatively affects the well-being of consumers, especially those with limited and fixed incomes such as the poor and elderly.

The Consumption Equity Model

The United Nations Development Programme (UNDP) uses a variety of indicators and data to compare countries and world regions in their state of consumption (UNDP 1998). The goal is to identity and measure equities and inequities in the consumption of goods and services that meet basic needs.

QOL researchers at the UNDP define QOL partly in terms of satisfaction of basic needs. Human development, in their view, involves not only satisfaction of basic needs but also equity in basic need satisfaction among different population segments. Researchers at the UNDP believe that countries should strive to increase or decrease consumption of goods and services to satisfy basic needs as a direct function of a ratio of total consumption expenditures and size of population. Thus, countries that are consuming too much (in relation to their population size) should decrease their rate of consumption, whereas countries consuming too little should increase their rate of consumption. Establishing a semblance of equity in consumption of goods and services that meet basic needs equates with human development, ergo QOL enhancement (Ruger 2008; Sirgy et al. 2011b)

The UNDP developed a measure based on this consumption equity concept, namely the Total Consumption Expenditure Index (TCEI). The TCEI is a composite of consumption of cars, paper products, telephone connections, electricity, total energy, meat, fish, and cereals. Thus, a TCEI score of a given country refers to the summary of all expenses across various expenditure categories.

The UNDP divides countries in terms of their GDP and compares the total consumption expenditure of the richest nations (20% of all countries fall in this bracket) to the middle 60% and the poorest 20%. The typical finding is that the richest countries consume around 85% of total consumption expenditure. A high level of total consumption expenditure at the country level represents a high CWB at the macro level.

The Consumer Complaint Model

The US Better Business Bureau (BBB) developed a CWB measure based on complaint data. Consumers from any region of the USA call or write to the BBB and register a complaint against a company for any problem related to the company's products and services. The data are compiled by company name. Consumers who want to purchase a product or service can call their local BBB office (or access their database through the Internet) to find out whether customers of particular brands and firms have complained about a brand or firm in question. Consumer complaints for a specific companies and brands are aggregated across all BBB communities. A high level of complaints in relation to a specific company or brand represents a lower level of CWB—specific to that company and brand (Sirgy et al. 2007).

Table 15.4 represents a sample of consumer complaints filed at the Better Business Bureau (http://www.thelocalbbb.com). The top 10 categories of fraud complaints include Internet actions, home shopping, Internet services, lotteries, foreign money offers, loan services, telephone services, among others.

The Quality Model

Consumer Reports (www.consumerreports.org), a monthly publication of the Consumer Union, provides expert assessments of quality for a variety of products and services. Common dimensions of quality include

Table 15.4 The top 10 categories of consumer fraud complaints in 2003

1. Internet auctions—15%
2. Shop-at-home/catalog sales—9%
3. Internet services and computer complaints—6%
4. Prizes, sweepstakes, and lotteries—5%
5. Foreign money offers—4%
6. Advance fee loans and credit protection—4%
7. Telephone services—3%
8. Business opportunities and work-at-home plans—2%
9. Magazine buyers clubs—1%
10. Office supplies and services—1%

Source: http://www.thelocalbbb.com/alerts/alerts.html?newsid=312&newstype=1

Table 15.5 Quality dimensions used by consumer reports in experts' ratings of automobiles

• Child-safe power windows
• Dealer discounts and incentives
• Features
• Financing options
• Fuel economy
• Headlights
• Hoses and belts, inspecting
• Hybrid gas-electric
• Incentives and dealer discounts
• Insurance
• Interior detailing
• Keys, electronic, hacked
• Kid friendly
• Load capacity
• Maintenance
• Tires
• Owner satisfaction

Source: http://www.consumerreports.org

experts' ratings of product reliability, durability, and safety. Furthermore, Consumer Reports include owner satisfaction as another dimension of product quality. A high level of positive assessment for a specific product represents a higher CWB. Table 15.5 shows how *Consumer Reports* rate quality of various automobile models and brands (Sirgy and Lee 2008).

Contributions from the Academic Sector

We will describe in this section several important contributions of conceptualizations and measures of CWB that were established in the academic sector. These are

Table 15.6 Meadow's overall consumer satisfaction

Item used to capture satisfaction with retail establishments in the local area: "How was your experience with retail institutions in purchasing the following products?" (very dissatisfied/very satisfied)

- Food
- Housing
- Household operations
- Household furnishing
- Clothing and accessories
- Personal care
- Medical care
- Recreation
- Transportation
- Education

Source: Meadow and Sirgy (2008)

the Shopping Satisfaction Model, the Possession Satisfaction Model, the Acquisition/Possession Model, the Consumption Satisfaction Model, the Consumer Life Cycle Model, the Community Model, the Need Satisfaction Model, the Perceived Value Model, the Bottom-up Spillover Model, the Marketers' Orientation Model, and the Globalization Model (see Table 15.2).

The Shopping Satisfaction Model

Meadow and Sirgy (2008) generated a measure of CWB called *Overall Consumer Satisfaction-Composite* (OCSC). This measure is based on consumers' experiences with retail institutions in purchasing food, housing, household operations, household furnishings, clothing and accessories, personal care, medical care, recreation, transportation, and education. This approach focused on capturing overall *acquisition* or shopping satisfaction (Sirgy and Lee 2008).

The author used a sample of 249 elderly consumers to demonstrate that life satisfaction (or subjective quality of life) can be predicted significantly from satisfaction with a variety of retail establishments in the local area. Table 15.6 shows the exact items used in capturing satisfaction with various retail establishments in the local area.

The Possession Satisfaction Model

Other researchers have focused on *possession of material things* to capture CWB. For example, Nakano et al. (1995) examined consumers' overall satisfaction with their material possessions and standard of living. As part of a larger investigation of

consumer socialization, Nakano et al. (1995) used a two-question measure to capture CWB, namely: "How do you feel about your standard of living—the things you have like housing, car, furniture, recreation, and the like?" and "How do you feel about the extent to which your physical needs are met?" CWB is conceptualized as the composite of a set of these items. In sum, CWB is construed in terms of satisfaction with one's ownership of consumer durables and other material possessions.

Sirgy et al. (1998a, b) focused on the material life domain, a psychological construct that groups consumer experiences related to the possession of economic goods. The authors hypothesized that satisfaction with material possessions influences overall life satisfaction. It was further hypothesized that the degree of influence material satisfaction has on life satisfaction is moderated by materialism (i.e., emotional involvement with material possessions). Specifically, satisfaction with material possessions more strongly influences life satisfaction for materialistic than for non-materialistic individuals. Furthermore, satisfaction with material possessions was hypothesized to be influenced by materialism. That is, those who are materialistic are more likely to be dissatisfied with their possessions because they have high possession expectations. The model's constructs were operationalized in the context of a survey that was administered to about 300 college students. The data provided general support for the model. The CWB measure used in the Sirgy et al.'s study is shown in Table 15.7.

The Acquisition/Possession Satisfaction Model

Day (1978, 1987) and Leelakulthanit et al. (1991) conceptualized the consumer life domain as having two dimensions: *acquisition* and *possession* of consumer goods and services related to those goods. The *acquisition* dimension refers to experiences related to the purchase of consumer goods and services associated with these goods. Examples include assortment, quality, and price of goods available in local stores; the attractiveness of the local stores; the courtesy and helpfulness of personnel in the local stores; and after-purchase service provided by the local stores (e.g., warranty policies, return policies). In contrast, the possession dimension focuses on experiences related to material possessions (e.g., house/apartment, furniture, car/truck, clothing/accessories, savings, etc.). See Table 15.8.

Table 15.7 Sirgy et al.'s material possessions measure of CWB

"If you own any of the following items, please indicate the extent to which you are satisfied/dissatisfied with possessing or owing something—a classic car or a piece of property—even though you never use. Or they might be pleased both to own and to use the thing. On these items, indicate only how you feel about owning the item, not how you feel about using or consuming it. Respond only to the items you own"

1. House or condominium
2. Consumer electronics (CD player, TV, VCR, computers, etc.)
3. Furniture and/or appliances
4. Private transportation (cars, trucks, motorcycles, and bicycles)
5. Clothing, accessories, and jewelry
6. Savings and investments

Scale: 1 = awful, 2 = bad, 3 = unsatisfactory, 4 = neutral, 5 = satisfactory, 6 = good, 7 = wonderful; 0 = no opinion, missing value
Source: Sirgy et al. (1998b)

Table 15.8 The Leelakulthanit, Day, and Walters' CWB measure

1. *Satisfaction with material possessions*
   (a) House/apartment
   (b) Furniture
   (c) Car/truck
   (d) Clothing and accessories
   (e) Savings and investments
2. *Satisfaction with acquisition/consumption*
   (a) Selection of merchandise in stores
   (b) Quality of goods
   (c) Prices charged
   (d) Attractiveness/ambience of stores

Scale: 1 = extremely pleased, 7 = extremely displeased
Source: Leelakulthanit et al. (1991)

Leelakulthanit et al. (1991) found a significant relationship between possession satisfaction and life satisfaction. This finding was more pronounced for older and low-income people than counterpart segments.

The Consumer Life Cycle Model

Lee et al. (2002) conceptualized CWB in terms of consumer satisfaction with varied marketplace experiences. These experiences involve acquisition (or shopping for goods and services in the local area), possession (product ownership), consumption (use of goods and services), maintenance (repair and servicing of consumer durables), and disposal (selling, trading-in, or junking of consumer durables) (cf. Sirgy et al. 2008a, b). The theoretical assumption is that consumers experience satisfaction and dissatisfaction in relation to acquisition, possession, consumption, maintenance, and disposal of consumer goods or services, and that overall satisfaction with these marketplace experiences influences overall life satisfaction.

In relation to *acquisition satisfaction*, Lee et al. defined this concept as satisfaction related to shopping and other activities involved in the purchase of consumer goods and services. Specifically, seven factors of the acquisition experience (that play a significant role in CWB) were identified—factors such as satisfaction with the quality, prices, hours, and services of stores in the local area (see Table 15.9).

In relation to *possession satisfaction,* the authors have focused on certain consumer goods (e.g., car, house, furniture, and household appliances) and the extent to which ownership of these goods contribute significantly to quality of life. *Possession satisfaction* was defined as satisfaction that results from the ownership of consumer goods, and was measured with six single-item scales that tap satisfaction with major classes of possessions such as house or condominium, consumer electronics, and private transportation (see Table 15.9).

With respect to *consumption satisfaction,* the authors defined this dimension as satisfaction resulting from the use of consumer goods and services. It is closely related to but distinct from possession satisfaction, the difference being that possession satisfaction focuses on positive affect that flows from ownership *per se* whereas consumption satisfaction focuses on satisfaction that flows from the actual use or *consumption* of the product. Satisfaction was measured for 11 major categories of consumer goods and services that have proven to influence the quality of life (e.g., healthcare services, banking/insurance services, and consumer electronics). See Table 15.9.

Turning to *maintenance satisfaction,* the authors defined this concept as satisfaction consumers experience when they seek to have a possession repaired or

15 Consumer Well-Being (CWB): Various Conceptualizations and Measures

Table 15.9 The Lee et al.'s CWB measure

1. *Acquisition satisfaction*

"Please indicate how satisfied or dissatisfied you are with the shopping in your community. Respond to each of the following aspects of the shopping environment in your community:"

- (a) Quality of goods available in local stores
- (b) Prices charged in local stores
- (c) Attractiveness or ambiance of local stores
- (d) Courtesy or helpfulness of store personnel
- (e) Hours that the stores are open
- (f) Store refund/replacement policies for defective goods
- (g) Availability of goods you want in local stores

[*Scale*: 1 = awful, 2 = bad, 3 = unsatisfactory, 4 = neutral, 5 = satisfactory, 6 = good, 7 = wonderful, 0 = no opinion, missing value]

2. *Possession satisfaction*

"If you own any of the following items, please indicate the extent to which you are satisfied/dissatisfied with possessing or owning them. Note that a person might like owning something—a classic car or a piece of property—even though they never use it. Or they might be pleased both to own and to use the thing. On these items, indicate only how you feel about *owning* the item, not how you feel about using or consuming it. Respond only to the items you own."

- (a) House or condominium
- (b) Consumer electronics (CD player, TV, VCR, computers, etc.)
- (c) Furniture and/or appliances
- (d) Private transportation (cars, trucks, motorcycles, and bicycles)
- (e) Clothing, accessories, and jewelry
- (f) Savings and investments

[*Scale*: 1 = awful, 2 = bad, 3 = unsatisfactory, 4 = neutral, 5 = satisfactory, 6 = good, 7 = wonderful, 0 = no opinion, missing value]

3. *Consumption satisfaction*

"If you own any of the items shown below, please indicate the extent to which you are generally satisfied/dissatisfied with using or consuming them. Since we sometimes use things, we do not own or own things or service we do not use, it should be possible to separate our general satisfaction in using a thing from our satisfaction in owning it. On items shown below, indicate only how you generally feel about *using or consuming* the item, not how you feel about owning it. Respond only to the items that you use."

- (a) Health-care services (doctors, dentists, optometrists, etc.)
- (b) Banking/insurance services
- (c) Personal care services (barbers, hairdressers, manicurists, etc.)
- (d) Restaurants
- (e) Food and grocery items
- (f) Consumer electronics (CD player, TV, VCR, computers, etc.)
- (g) Furniture and/or appliances
- (h) Private transportation (cars, trucks, motorcycles, and bicycles)
- (i) Clothing, accessories, and jewelry
- (j) Utilities (electricity, telephone, etc.)
- (k) Savings and investments

[*Scale*: 1 = awful, 2 = bad, 3 = unsatisfactory, 4 = neutral, 5 = satisfactory, 6 = good, 7 = wonderful, 0 = no opinion, missing value]

4. *Maintenance satisfaction*

Satisfaction with repair services

"Please indicate how satisfied or dissatisfied you are with the repair services available to you. Examples of repair organizations would include car garages, plumbing services, electricians, appliance and shoe repair shops, etc. How do you feel about the following aspects of repair services available to you?"

- (a) Quality of the service provided by most repair organizations
- (b) The skill of the people who do the repairs
- (c) The availability of services when you need them
- (d) The price the repair organizations usually charge for their services
- (e) The speed of service or promptness of most repair organizations
- (f) The honesty of the people who do the repairs

(continued)

Table 15.9 (continued)

(g) The range of choices available when picking a repair service

(h) The level of appropriateness to your questions or complaints

(i) The accuracy of price estimates given before the service is provided

[*Scale*: 1 = awful, 2 = bad, 3 = unsatisfactory, 4 = neutral, 5 = satisfactory, 6 = good, 7 = wonderful, 0 = no opinion, missing value]

Satisfaction with materials and services for do-it-yourself repairs

"People who do their own repair work often require materials and services that help them get the job done. Please indicate how you feel about the materials and services available in your community."

(a) Price of replacement parts and tools

(b) Quality of advice or assistance provided by retailers, friends, or others in the community

(c) The completeness and intelligibility of owner's manuals or assembly instructions

(d) Availability of necessary replacement parts and tools

(e) The technical support provided by manufacturers

(f) Quality of replacement parts and tools

(g) Availability of "how-to-repair" workshops

(h) The availability of stores specializing in parts and tools, i.e., places such as auto parts, building supplies, and hardware stores

[*Scale*: 1 = awful, 2 = bad, 3 = unsatisfactory, 4 = neutral, 5 = satisfactory, 6 = good, 7 = wonderful, 0 = no opinion, missing value]

5. *Disposition satisfaction*

"For various reasons, people may be more or less happy with the disposability of a product. If you use any of the following products, please indicate the extent to which you are satisfied/dissatisfied with the product class when you dispose of the product or its package. Respond only to items that you use."

(a) Food (milk, canned foods, cookies, carbonated drinks, etc.)

(b) Personal care products (toothpaste, shampoo, deodorant, etc.)

(c) Cleaning and home maintenance products (detergents, window sprays, vacuum bags, air fresheners, paint, etc.)

(d) Paper products

(e) Baby car e product (diapers, baby wipes, talcum powder, Vaseline, etc.)

(f) Automotive products (oil, oil filters, antifreeze, car wax, batteries, tires, etc.)

(g) Lawn and yard (leaves, grass, dead wood, etc.)

[*Scale*: 1 = awful, 2 = bad, 3 = unsatisfactory, 4 = neutral, 5 = satisfactory, 6 = good, 7 = wonderful, 0 = no opinion, missing value]

Source: Lee et al. (2002)

cleaned. The authors conceptualized maintenance satisfaction as having two major subdimensions—satisfaction with maintenance and repairs provided by service vendors in the community (i.e., *repair services*), and satisfaction with services that facilitate maintenance and repair by the owners themselves (i.e., *do-it-yourself support services*). They identified nine aspects of repair services that affect quality of life, such as availability and price of maintenance/repair services and the honesty of service providers (see Table 15.9).

Finally, with respect to *disposal satisfaction,* the authors defined this concept as the degree of satisfaction consumers feel with the disposability of their products such as the convenience and ease of disposal and the environmental friendliness of the product at the time of disposal. Disposal satisfaction was captured using seven categories of consumer goods for which respondents rated their satisfaction with product disposability such as food, personal care, and automotive products (see Table 15.9).

In a survey of 298 university students, the proposed measure was found to have predictive validity in relation to life satisfaction for three dimensions (acquisition, possession, and consumption). Satisfaction in the consumer life domain was demonstrated to be an important component of life satisfaction. This measure was modified and further validated using large-scale samples in a variety of countries (see Sirgy et al. 2008a, b for the modified measures).

The Consumer Life Cycle Model has been used in other product-specific contexts such as personal transportation and housing. With respect to *personal transportation*, Lee and Sirgy (2004) found that consumer's perceived QOL impact of current vehicles is largely determined by satisfaction with purchase, preparation for personal use, ownership, use, and maintenance (i.e., various experiences across the consumer life cycle with a particular product). See this CWB measure in Table 15.10. The authors also hypothesized that

Table 15.10 The Sirgy and Lee CWB measure in relation to personal transportation

1. *Acquisition—the prepurchase and purchase of the vehicle*
   (a) The anticipation felt before you purchased your vehicle[a]
   (b) Looking at different cars at dealerships and other places
   (c) The information obtained about the different brand/model options
   (d) Pulling the vehicle off the lot/away from the sales location for the first time
   (e) The vehicle and options you were able to pick from at the buying location
   (f) Your interaction with the person or salesperson you bought the vehicle from
   (g) The arrangements of payment for the vehicle
   (h) The price negotiations with the salesperson you bought the vehicle from
   (i) Financing options available
   (j) Dealing with the bank or finance company

2. *Preparation—after buying the vehicle, you prepared to use it by getting insurance, tags, etc.*
   (a) Information concerning the vehicle (car manual)
   (b) Information concerning the insurance
   (c) Information concerning license and tags
   (d) The explanation of warranty and contract information about the vehicle
   (e) The amount of time it took to file all paperwork at the dealership
   (f) The time and effort spent at the DMV or the agency responsible for tags and registration
   (g) The financial cost of getting the vehicle registered
   (h) The financial cost of insurance
   (i) Having the vehicle ready for use by the dealer (or person you bought the vehicle from) right after purchase[a]

3. *Possession—the ownership experience with the vehicle*
   (a) Seeing your vehicle out in public
   (b) Seeing your vehicle at your residence
   (c) Showing your car to your friends and co-workers
   (d) The knowledge that the vehicle is yours
   (e) Your status of the brand, make, and model
   (f) The rate of depreciation of your vehicle
   (g) Damage or theft of the vehicle or parts[a]

4. *Consumption—the use of the vehicle*
   (a) Overall performance of the vehicle
   (b) Reliability of the vehicle
   (c) Functionality of the vehicle
   (d) Comfort of the vehicle
   (e) The vehicle's fuel economy
   (f) The engine power of the vehicle
   (g) The vehicle's safety features
   (h) The vehicle's performance after wear and tear

   (i) The vehicle's performance in rough terrain
   (j) The vehicle's performance in inclement weather
   (k) Overall driving enjoyment[a]

5. *Maintenance—the maintenance and repair experience*
   (a) Learning how to fix your vehicle
   (b) Spending time repairing or doing preventative maintenance on your vehicle
   (c) Saving money by working on the car yourself or finding someone who does the job right for the right price
   (d) Keeping your vehicle running right
   (e) The cost of repairs when your vehicle breaks down
   (f) The availability of parts for your vehicle
   (g) Continually fixing faulty parts
   (h) The durability of your vehicle[a]
   (i) Keeping the vehicle's exterior looking good[a]

6. *Disposition—the selling or "junking" of the vehicle*
   (a) Money lost or gained in selling the vehicle
   (b) Being the salesperson for the vehicle
   (c) Listing or advertising the vehicle for sale
   (d) Mental relief of having your old vehicle sold or passed on to others
   (e) The thought of no longer having your old vehicle— your sentiment toward your vehicle
   (f) Resale value of your vehicle's brand
   (g) The time it took to find a buyer
   (h) Junking the vehicle (i.e., no sale could be made)
   (i) Loss of asset

[a]Items deleted
Scale: 1 = felt very negative, 5 = felt very positive
Source*: Sirgy and Lee (2003)

perceived QOL impact of one's previously owned vehicle is also determined by satisfaction with the disposal (trade-in, selling, or junking) of that vehicle. Survey results provided validational support for this CWB measure.

In relation to *housing*, Grzeskowiak et al. (2006) developed and tested a model of housing well-being guided by the consumer life cycle model. Housing well-being refers to the home resident's cumulative positive and negative affect associated with house purchase, use, maintenance, ownership, and selling—the more positive (and the less negative) affect associated with these experiences, the greater the housing well-being. It was also hypothesized that

- Satisfaction with quality of life impact of home is mostly influenced by satisfaction with home use and home ownership.
- Satisfaction with home use is mostly influenced by satisfaction with home maintenance, neighborhood, and community.

- Satisfaction with home ownership is mostly influenced by satisfaction with home maintenance and neighborhood.
- Satisfaction with home maintenance is mostly influenced by satisfaction with home preparation, home purchase, and neighborhood.
- Satisfaction with neighborhood is mostly influenced by satisfaction with community and home purchase.
- Satisfaction with home purchase is mostly influenced by satisfaction with home preparation and sale of previous home.

This model was tested using a sample of 193 homeowners in the USA and 285 Korean homeowners. The results provided support for the nomological validity of the housing well-being measure (Grzeskowiak et al. 2006). See this CWB measure in Table 15.11.

The Community Model

The CWB measure developed by Sirgy and colleagues (Sirgy et al. 2000, 2010a, b; Sirgy and Cornwell 2001) is based on the notion that CWB is a direct function of community residents' satisfaction with a variety of retail and service establishments in the local area. Through a community residents' survey, survey respondents are asked to express their satisfaction/dissatisfaction with a variety of retail and services establishments available in the local area. These establishments include banking/savings services, insurance services, taxi/private transportation, restaurants/night clubs, department stores, drug stores/supermarkets, specialty stores, health-care services, telephone services, electricity services, gas/oil services, real estate services, home repair services, day care services, nursing homes/retirement

Table 15.11 The Grzeskowiak et al. measure of CWB in relation to housing

1. Satisfaction with home purchase

Satisfaction with real estate agent (search process)

(a) The real estate agent was attentive

(b) The real estate agent was highly knowledgeable

(c) The real estate agent saved us much time and effort

(d) The real estate agent was very helpful

(e) The real estate agent identified suitable homes

(f) The real estate agent helped us negotiate with the seller

(g) The real estate agent was unreliable[a]

(h) The real estate agent was complacent[a]

(i) The real estate agent had incomplete or inadequate information on homes, mortgage companies, loan officers, home inspection companies, closing attorneys, and title companies[a]

(j) The real estate agent had inadequate information on the strengths and weaknesses of the homes shown[a]

(k) We got a good deal negotiating directly with the home seller—without the help of a real estate agent[b]

Satisfaction with home inspection (selection of home)

(a) The home inspector was good

(b) The home inspector focused on unimportant home features[a]

(c) The home inspector missed substantial faults and defects in the house[a]

(d) The home inspector overlooked future costs of repair[a]

(e) The cost of the home inspection was expensive[b]

Satisfaction with closing process

(a) The closing was very cumbersome[a]

(b) The closing had a lot of steps[a]

(c) I felt in the dark going through closing[a]

(d) It took too long to close[a]

(e) The fees we paid to the closing attorney (or title company) were high[a]

(f) The closing attorney (or title company) has a good reputation[b]

Satisfaction with loan officer

(a) The loan officer was easy to work with

(b) The loan officer was trustworthy

(c) The loan officer was knowledgeable

Satisfaction with loan process

(a) Obtaining the mortgage loan was long and tedious[a]

(b) It was difficult obtaining the mortgage loan[a]

(c) We felt quite apprehensive waiting for the loan approval[a]

Satisfaction with financing cost

(a) We got a good interest rate on the mortgage loan

(b) We paid a high interest rate on the mortgage loan[a]

2. Satisfaction with home preparation

Satisfaction with home design

(a) The architect respected our own design ideas

(b) We designed large and spacious rooms

(c) The entire experience with planning and designing our own home allowed us to feel very creative

(d) We felt good by coming up with remodeling ideas[b]

Satisfaction with home personalization

(a) We managed to personalize our own home

(b) We initiated our own projects

(c) We designed things around the house to match the family needs

Satisfaction with homebuilder

(a) The homebuilder was a good contractor

(b) The homebuilder was a pleasure to work with

(c) We had to stay on top of the homebuilder to make sure that things get done right and on time[a]

(d) The homebuilder neglected to do things because he thought that they were not needed without consulting with us[a]

(e) We managed to save money by contracting out on our own[b]

(continued)

15 Consumer Well-Being (CWB): Various Conceptualizations and Measures

Table 15.11 (continued)

Satisfaction with development experience

(a) We appreciated the development experience because it gave us a chance to contribute our own ideas to making the house livable

(b) We became aware of many energy conservation issues while going through the building process

Satisfaction with building yourself

(a) Building our own home ourselves made us more confident of the quality issues

(b) A significant advantage of building our own home was the fact that we moved at our own pace

(c) A bad thing about building our own home is the fact that some things had to be done over[a]

(d) We felt that landscaping was like a hobby for us[b]

(e) A significant advantage of building our own home was the fact that we built more for less money[b]

(f) Building our own home made it easier to get things done because we were in charge. It took longer to build our own home than we expected[b]

3. Satisfaction with home use

Satisfaction with home spaces (size)

(a) The house was spacious

(b) We can entertain many guests in the house

(c) The house has plenty of rooms for various needs

(d) The family room is good for entertaining and get-togethers

(e) The house is good for entertaining

(f) The house is not built to meet our family needs[a]

(g) We do not have enough bathrooms in the house[b]

(h) We have too much space—more than we need[b]

(i) Some rooms are too large, not space efficient[b]

(j) The kitchen is spaciousness enough[b]

(k) The car garage is a waste of space[b]

Satisfaction with living environment (yard)

(a) The environment around the house is beautiful

(b) The yard is nice; it is a good place for our children to play

(c) The family enjoys the yard very much

(d) The yard is well maintained

(e) The yard has a nice picnic area, good for outdoor cooking

(f) The yard has a nice picnic area, good for entertaining

(g) The yard has nice big trees[b]

(h) The house is set off from traffic[b]

(i) The house is in town, it is conveniently located[b]

(j) The yard is dangerously close to the road[b]

Satisfaction with home layout

(a) The layout of the house makes it easy to maintain

(b) The house is quite open, so we can easily monitor the children

(c) The laundry room is conveniently located

(d) The kitchen layout is convenient

(e) The bedrooms are close together and cozy[b]

(f) The stairs are difficult to climb, especially for older people[b]

(g) The house needs a foyer[b]

(h) The laundry area is not where it should be[b]

Satisfaction with home quality

(a) The house is well built

(b) The house is comfortable

(c) The building of the house is of low quality, necessitating excessive upkeep[a]

(d) The house does not consume much energy[b]

(e) The craftsmanship involved in building the house is below expectations[b]

Satisfaction with home amenities

(a) The guest area is convenient and self-contained

(b) The master bathroom has separate sinks for couple

(c) The house has a library; it is a quiet place

(d) The house has an exercise room

(e) The house has a sunroom[b]

(f) The intercom in the house makes the house attractive[b]

Satisfaction with home appliances

(a) The kitchen appliances are nice

(b) The fixtures around the house are nice

(c) The kitchen is easy to keep clean

4. Satisfaction with neighborhood

Satisfaction with rules and regulations

(a) We have a neighborhood committee that enforces rules to keep homes and yards attractive

(b) We have landscaping guidelines

(c) Our homeowners' association addresses issues important to the neighborhood

(d) The homeowners' association serves to maintain neighborhood safety and quality

(e) Our homeowners' association addresses common goals and lifestyle needs

(f) The neighborhood committee restricts our freedom to do what we like to do with our homes and yards

(g) Our neighborhood has good amenities[b]

Satisfaction with neighborhood social life

(a) The neighbors are nice

(b) We usually visit with our neighbors

(c) We have good friends in the neighborhood

(d) Our neighbors are dependable and helpful

(e) The neighbors usually plan social events

(f) Our neighbors are lively people

(g) People living in our neighborhood do not care for each other[a]

Satisfaction with neighborhood externalities

(a) Our neighbors are good

(b) Our neighbors are quiet

(c) Our neighbors are noisy[a]

(d) Our neighborhood has the ideals of both city and country features

(continued)

Table 15.11 (continued)

(e) Our neighborhood is safe

(f) The house is located out in the country, but close to city[b]

(g) The yard has a small lawn[b]

(h) Our neighborhood is quiet; we do not have many kids[b]

(i) The house is in close proximity to other houses[b]

Satisfaction with neighborhood problems

(a) Our neighborhood is a gated community[a]

(b) Dogs are a nuisance in our neighborhood; they run loose and bark constantly[a]

(c) We have heavy traffic through the neighborhood, cars speeding dangerously[a]

(d) Our neighborhood is expanding too rapidly—uncontrolled growth[a]

(e) We have tensions among neighbors such as older neighbors blocking plans for children's park[a]

(f) The house is close to crop fields that have pollutant fertilizers[a]

(g) The house is close to college housing facilities, which is bad[a]

(h) Our neighborhood is located close to schools[b]

(i) We have a problem with wildlife in our neighborhood—wildlife causes fear[b]

(j) We have a problem with wildlife in our neighborhood—wildlife eats plants and garden vegetables[b]

(k) The house is not located conveniently—it is difficult to get to places[b]

5. Satisfaction with community

Satisfaction with infrastructure

(a) We have good hospitals and clinics close by to where we live

(b) We have good schools in the community

(c) Where we live is convenient to work, schools, shopping, downtown, and interstate

Satisfaction with lifestyle

(a) The community holds charity benefits events to raise money for needy

(b) The community has good parks and recreation facilities and programs

(c) Living in our community is conducive to healthy family lifestyle

(d) We have walking trials in the community

(e) Our community is not overcrowded[b]

(f) The community is becoming increasingly crowded[b]

(g) Our community has experienced increases in crime[b]

6. Satisfaction with home maintenance

Satisfaction with ongoing maintenance requirements

(a) Our house is easy and inexpensive to maintain

(b) Our house is aging requiring constant repairs[a]

(c) There is a lot of wear and tear around the house[a]

(d) The lawn is low maintenance

(e) The yard has a simple layout easy to maintain

(f) The flowers and shrubs around the house are hard to keep up[a]

(g) Our house takes a lot of time and effort to keep it maintained[a]

(h) It is harder on the owner to keep up with home maintenance and repairs as owners grow older[a]

(i) We constantly have to do maintenance work around the house to stay up on it[a]

(j) The yard is a lot of work[a]

(k) The house has high maintenance needs[a]

(l) The house has a small lawn that is easily manageable[b]

(m) We get family help to do home repairs[b]

Satisfaction with present maintenance requirements

(a) The house is built using high quality materials making it easy for us to maintain

(b) We might not have bought the house we are currently living in if we knew the extent of needed repairs[a]

(c) The exterior of the house is made out of wood; we would prefer brick[a]

(d) The house is in constant need of repair[a]

(e) Most of the homes in the neighborhood are in good condition requiring little maintenance and repairs

(f) We used subcontractors we know as highly qualified and trustworthy when we did home repairs and/or renovations

(g) We have to take care of home repairs ourselves because we own our own house—we do not have a landlord

(h) We do a lot to maintain the investment value of our home

(i) It is satisfying to work in the garden; it is a hobby

(j) The master bath is not too big to keep clean[b]

Satisfaction with home repairs or renovation

(a) There are mold spores in the house[a]

(b) The house has too many porches requiring high maintenance[a]

(c) There are lots of construction activities in the neighborhood making the appearance of the neighborhood looking bad[a]

(d) The roads in the neighborhood are not government maintained[a]

(e) Much of the exterior of the house is maintained by the homeowners' association[a]

(f) The subcontractors we hired to do home repairs or renovations did not do a good job[a]

(g) The subcontractors we hired to do home repairs or renovations take a long time to complete the job[a]

(h) We have a home warranty to take care of all major home repairs[b]

Satisfaction with yard work

(a) The grass is brown because we cannot water it constantly due to drought and water restrictions[a]

(b) The lawn is in bad condition[a]

(continued)

15 Consumer Well-Being (CWB): Various Conceptualizations and Measures

Table 15.11 (continued)

(c) Many of the lawns and homes in the neighborhood are unkept, requiring much maintenance[a]

(d) The lawn is not properly graded[a]

(e) The lawn is well irrigated; it is a healthy lawn

(f) It is cheaper to maintain the yard on our own than having someone else do it[b]

7. Satisfaction with home ownership

Satisfaction with value appreciation

(a) The property value in the area around our house is high, which is good for us

(b) We have built quite a bit of equity in the house

(c) Our house has appreciated significantly in value

Satisfaction with financial burden

(a) The bad thing about real estate investment is the capital gains tax[a]

(b) The bad thing about owning a home is that we have to pay for all the repairs, unlike rentals[a]

(c) Another bad thing about owning a home is the real estate taxes we have to pay every year[a]

(d) Another bad thing about owning a home is the mortgage—it can be steep[a]

(e) The good thing about owning a home is that the mortgage payments are reduced over time[b]

(f) The good thing about owning a home is that we get tax benefits from the interest rate we pay on the mortgage[b]

Satisfaction with gratification of ownership

(a) Another advantage of owning a home is privacy. We cannot get the kind of privacy we need by renting an apartment

(b) We feel a sense of pride owning our own home

(c) It is important to know that we own our own home

(d) Owning our own home gives us a feeling of independence

(e) Owning our own home is security for the future

(f) The good thing about owning a home is the ability to design the home for all kinds of hobbies[b]

(g) Home ownership brings with it many headaches, burdens, and responsibilities[b]

8. Satisfaction with sale of previous home

Satisfaction with listing agent

(a) The listing agent was dependable

(b) The listing agent helped us with negotiating with potential homebuyers

(c) The listing agent did not do a good job screening potential homebuyers[a]

(d) The listing agent did not give us adequate advance notice to show the house[a]

(e) The listing agent acted unprofessionally[a]

(f) The listing agent charged us an unreasonable fee[a]

(g) We received lower appraisal than expected from the listing agent[a]

Satisfaction with closing

(a) The closing attorney (title company) was not on top of things[a]

(b) The closing attorney (title company) charged us an unreasonable fee[a]

(c) The needed home repairs to sell the house were handled by knowledgeable, dependable workers

(d) The needed home repairs to sell the house were handled by unprofessional people; the work was low quality[a]

(e) The home repair firm charged us an unreasonable fee[a]

(f) The closing attorney (title company) did a good job overall[b]

Satisfaction with financial proceeds

(a) We made a good profit selling the house

(b) We made a lower profit than expected on the sale of the house[a]

[a]Indicates reversed coded scale items
[b]Indicates items that cross-loaded with other factors and were deleted from further analysis
Scale: 5-point Likert-type scale (1 = strongly disagree; 5 = strongly agree)
Source: Grzeskowiak et al. (2006)

community-type services, private schools, spectator sports, TV stations, radio stations, local newspaper, automobile care services, realtors, investment services, legal services, and entertainment (see Table 15.12).

Results of two major surveys have shown that a composite measure of satisfaction/dissatisfaction with those retail and service establishments in the local area plays a major and significant role in predicting satisfaction with the community at large and one's satisfaction with life overall (Sirgy et al. 2010a, b).

The Need Satisfaction Model

Based on need hierarchy theory (Maslow 1954, 1970), human development needs encompass a wide range of needs grouped in terms of two major categories, namely high-order and lower-order needs. Higher-order needs include the need for self-actualization, esteem, knowledge, and beauty or aesthetics. Lower-order needs include physiological, economic, and social. The basic postulate of the need satisfaction model of CWB is that consumer goods and services that serve to meet the full spectrum of human development needs should be rated highly in terms of CWB than goods and services that satisfy only a small subset of needs (Sirgy et al. 2010a, b).

This theoretical perspective was used by Sirgy et al. (2006b) in developing a CWB measure specifically for personal transportation. They conducted a set of three studies that validated the CWB measure. The measure is based on the theoretical notion that the welfare of consumers of personal transportation vehicles is enhanced when the consumption of the vehicle meets the full spectrum of human developmental needs (i.e., safety, economic, family, social, esteem, actualization, knowledge, and aesthetics needs). Table 15.13 shows the measurement items of this measure.

To test the predictive (nomological) validity of the CWB measure, the authors hypothesized that CWB with personal transportation—the extent to which one's personal transportation vehicle meets one's various developmental needs such as safety, economic, family,

Table 15.12 The Sirgy et al.'s community-based services measure of CWB

Satisfaction with individual government services

(a) Fire services

(b) Rescue services

(c) Police services

(d) Sanitation services

(e) .....

Satisfaction with individual business services

(a) Banking/savings

(b) Insurance

(c) Restaurant/night clubs

(d) Day-care services

(e) .....

Satisfaction with individual nonprofit services

(a) Alcohol/drug

(b) Crisis intervention

(c) Adoption/foster care

(d) Family planning services

(e) .....

Satisfaction with community conditions

(a) Government services in general

(b) Business services in general

(c) Nonprofit services in general

(d) Quality of environment in the community (air, water, land, etc.)

(e) The rate of change to the natural landscape (deforestation, housing/commercial development, loss of agricultural land, ridgeline development, etc.)

(f) Race relations in the community

(g) Cost of living in the community

(h) Crime in the community

(i) Ties with people in the community

(j) One's neighborhood

(k) One's housing conditions

Scale: +3 = delighted, +2 = pleased, +1 = mostly satisfied, 0 = mixed feelings, −1 = mostly dissatisfied, −2 = unhappy, −3 = terrible, X = never thought about it or no opinion

Sources: Sirgy and Cornwell (2001), and Sirgy et al. (2000)

Table 15.13 The need satisfaction measure of CWB in relation to personal transportation

Personal transportation needs satisfaction

(a) I feel very safe in my car

(b) My car is economical

(c) My car satisfies my family needs

(d) My car meets my social needs

(e) The image of my car shows status and prestige to others

(f) My car does not let me down when I use it for daily and weekly activities

(g) My car reflects who I am

(h) My car reflects who I would like to be

(i) My car is beautiful, inside and out

Need satisfaction with vehicle design characteristics

(a) My car has good brakes

(b) My car handles well in bad weather

(c) My car is very efficient on gas mileage

(d) My car is spacious enough to fit my entire family

(e) I show off my car to my friends because of its great looks

(f) My car hardly breaks down

(g) The design of my car has the look that reflects who I am

(h) The design of the car has an image that reflects the kind of person I would like to be

(i) My car has a beautiful interior

(j) My car has a beautiful exterior

Need satisfaction with car insurance and agent services

(a) I have good insurance protecting me from accident damages

(b) I feel secure in my car because I know my insurance would take care of everything if I get injured

(c) What I pay for my car insurance is reasonable. I have no complaints here

(d) My car insurance accommodates my family needs

(e) If I had a car accident I would not have to miss work, thanks to my insurance

Need satisfaction with vehicle warranty, repair, and maintenance services

(a) The car manufacturer has a great warranty making me feel that I have a safe car

(continued)

Table 15.13 (continued)

(b) I trust the safety of my car because I trust the mechanics who service it

(c) I trust the auto servicing place; they do not rip me off

(d) I do not worry about the car breaking down when a family member takes the car. This is because I trust the mechanics who service it

Need satisfaction with dealer/financial services

(a) I trust the safety of my car because I trust the salesperson who helped me pick the right car

(b) I am not dissatisfied with the interest (or price) charged by the car dealer (or financial lender)

(c) My car dealer helped me pick the best car for my family needs

Scale: 1 = strongly disagree to 5 = strongly agree
Source: Sirgy et al. (2006b)

social, esteem, actualization, knowledge, and aesthetics needs—is likely to be determined by need satisfaction with vehicle design characteristics, warranty and maintenance services, insurance policy and agent services, and dealer and financial services. Furthermore, it was hypothesized that higher levels of CWB with personal transportation should lead to higher levels of overall vehicle satisfaction and brand loyalty. These hypotheses were tested through three separate studies with samples taken from the USA, Korea, and Germany. The results of the three studies provided support for the nomological validity of the CWB measure.

The Perceived Value Model

Sirgy et al. (2006a) reported a study that involved the development of an Internet well-being measure. The measure was designed for possible use by government agencies and industry associations that are directly involved with the promulgation of the Internet. The Internet well-being measure is based on the theoretical notion that the perception of the overall impact of the Internet on users of the Internet is determined by their perceptions of the impact of the Internet in their life domains such as consumer life, work life, leisure life, social life, education life, community life, sensual life, among others. In turn, the perception of impact of the Internet in a given life domain (e.g., consumer life, work life) is determined by perceptions of benefits and costs of the Internet within that domain. Thus, the Internet well-being measure is a composite of value perception of consumers across various life domains. A high level of value perception represents a high level of Internet well-being.

The authors reported a study involving a focus group to identify all the perceived benefits and costs within salient life domains of college students. A literature search was conducted to identify studies that examined the quality of life impact of the Internet in a variety of life domains. They then tested nomological validity of the measure through two surveys at two major universities (one in the USA and the other in Korea). The statistical analysis allowed them to identify those measurement items that are most predictive, and therefore considered as nomologically valid. The retained measurement items of this CWB measure are shown in Table 15.14.

The Bottom-Up Spillover Model

The essence of the Bottom-up Spillover Model is the notion of a satisfaction hierarchy, and that positive and negative affect spills from concrete events to life domains (e.g., work life, leisure life, family life, social life, love life) to overall life. Thus, specific events housed in a given life domain may affect life satisfaction through a "bottom-up spillover" of affect (Diener 1984; Sirgy 2002; Sirgy et al. 2010a, b). There are many advocates of the bottom-up approach (e.g., Heady et al. 1985). Many studies have been conducted using the bottom-up approach. For example, a recent study has measured life satisfaction of Calcutta (India) residents and their satisfaction with various life domains. The study indicated that satisfaction with material possessions, family life, self-development, and local government administration had a significant effect on life satisfaction of the Calcutta residents.

A number of CWB measures in health care and travel and tourism were developed guided by the Bottom-up Spillover Model. In relation to *health care*, Rahtz and colleagues (Rahtz and Sirgy 2000; Sirgy et al. 2004) hypothesized that community residents' satisfaction with health-care services available within their community affects community QOL and life satisfaction. Furthermore, it was hypothesized that the bottom-up spillover from community QOL to life satisfaction is greater for those individuals with low personal health satisfaction, lower income, and old age. That is, the degree of bottom-up spillover from the community QOL to life satisfaction is likely to be greater when consumers are highly involved in the community QOL due to their bad health condition,

Table 15.14 The Sirgy, Lee, and Bae CWB measure in relation to the Internet

1. *Perceived benefits of the Internet in consumer life*
   (a) The anonymity/impersonality of the Internet helps me with shopping because there are no salespeople to contend with
   (b) Buying on the Internet is very convenient
   (c) The Internet allows consumers to be a savvy shopper—that is to do a good job shopping around
   (d) The Internet helps achieve greater product and service customization—that is, people, products, and services that better match their needs.
   (e) The Internet helps consumers find rare items
   (f) Seeing the product in virtual reality helps with shopping

2. *Perceived costs of the Internet in consumer life*
   (a) Shopping on the Internet comes with it the risk of being deceived
   (b) Shopping on the Internet comes with it the risk of receiving a wrong item when ordered
   (c) Shopping on the Internet comes with it the risk of fraud
   (d) A negative feature of shopping on the Internet is the lack of tangibility—that is, the consumer cannot touch and feel the product
   (e) Another negative feature associated with the Internet shopping is the delay of gratification—that is, the consumer has to wait until the product is delivered by mail before consumption
   (f) Lack of assistance from sales people is a negative feature of Internet shopping
   (g) Unwanted advertising (SPAM) is another negative feature of Internet shopping
   (h) A shortcoming of the Internet is the lack of security of financial information and transactions
   (i) Another shortcoming of the Internet is the loss of privacy arising from financial transactions—potential use of personal information by unknown entities
   (j) There is a concern that computer thieves and hackers can access personal information from financial transaction machines located everywhere (e.g., gas stations, restaurants, grocery stores)
   (k) Unwanted advertising (SPAM) distracts and interferes with financial transactions over the Internet

3. *Perceived benefits of the Internet in work life*
   (a) The Internet makes work more flexible—that is, employees can complete work anytime if there is access to Internet
   (b) The Internet allows employees to telecommute; thus, employees can be more mobile
   (c) The Internet is an effective means of communication
   (d) The Internet is an inexpensive means of communication
   (e) The Internet helps access information about business threats—information about competitors, changing environment, etc.
   (f) The Internet helps access about business opportunities—information about custom distributors, suppliers, etc.

4. *Perceived costs of the Internet in work life*
   (a) Besides the benefits of the Internet at work, Internet comes with it certain costs as managers have higher work expectations because Internet is supposed to enhance work productivity
   (b) Another possible cost is the decrease in productivity due to the integration of personal leisure and work life such as reading and sending personal e-mails while at work
   (c) Technical problems arising from system compatibility (such as compatibility of files in attachments to e-mail messages)
   (d) Problems with ergonomics: typing too much on the computer while using Internet lead to physical aches and health problems
   (e) Unwanted advertising (SPAM) is irritating and distracting at work

5. *Perceived benefits of Internet in leisure life*
   (a) The Internet allows convenient access to information related to personal interest
   (b) The Internet allows the user to be better educated on topics of personal interest
   (c) The Internet allows access to games, recreational activities, and entertainment programs
   (d) The Internet allows the user to maintain a leisure lifestyle anywhere such as listening to one's favorite radio stations and reading one's favorite newspaper away from home

6. *Perceived costs of the Internet in leisure life*
   (a) The Internet has its costs too such as being addicted to surf the net
   (b) The Internet can be irritating and frustrating at times due to technical difficulties and the time it takes to access certain websites
   (c) Using the Internet is time-consuming, responding to all the e-mail messages one reads thus taking away from leisure time
   (d) Using the Internet is time-consuming, responding to all the e-mail messages one reads thus taking away from leisure time

7. *Perceived benefits of the Internet in social life*
   (a) The Internet helps people communicate with family and friends by making it easy and convenient
   (b) The Internet helps people communicate with family and friends by making it inexpensive
   (c) The Internet helps with group communications
   (d) E-mail helps with communication by taking messages while one is away
   (e) The Internet provides opportunities to meet new people

8. *Perceived costs of the Internet in social life*
   (a) The Internet allows strangers to intrude into people's lives
   (b) The Internet is a poor substitute for face-to-face social interactions

(continued)

Table 15.14 (continued)

(c)	Communicating through the Internet increases the chance of miscommunication and lack of body language (body language is known to enhance communication effectively)
(d)	The Internet puts more pressure on people to communicate because it makes communication easy
(e)	Unwanted advertising (SPAM) interferes with social communication on the Internet
9.	Perceived benefits of the Internet in education life
(a)	The Internet provides easy access to educational opportunities such as taking a distance learning class
(b)	The Internet provides easy access to information necessary for educational projects and assignments
(c)	The Internet facilitates communication with professors and instructors
(d)	The Internet facilitates communication with other students involved in group projects
(e)	The Internet helps increase student productivity—helps students accomplish more course-related work in a shorter time
10.	Perceived costs of the Internet in education life
(a)	The Internet has its shortcoming too. One shortcoming is work interruption due to technical difficulties such as certain servers going down
(b)	Another shortcoming associated with the Internet is professor and instructors expect more from students because they assume that students can accomplish a great deal with the help of the Internet
(c)	Students are overwhelmed with too much information on Internet-information overload
11.	Perceived benefits of the Internet in community
(a)	The Internet provides access to information about one's community, community services, and community activities
(b)	The Internet provides access to community residents to pay for community services such as payment of water, sewage, car tags, and personal property taxes
12.	Perceived benefits of Internet in sensual life
(a)	The Internet provides access to sensual and erotic images

Scale used to capture responses to the measures is a 5-point Likert-type scale: 1 = strongly disagree, 5 = strongly agree
Source: Sirgy et al. (2006a)

lower income, and their age. Results of two major surveys provided good support of the model (Rahtz and Sirgy 2000; Rahtz et al. 2004). See measurement items pertaining to this CWB measure in Table 15.15.

In addition, Sirgy et al. (1994) tried to demonstrate bottom-up spillover from hospital satisfaction to life satisfaction. They tested a conceptual spillover model surmising that hospital satisfaction spills over to community life affecting community health-care satisfaction, which in turn spills over to health life affecting personal health satisfaction, which in turn spills over unto the most super ordinate life domain affecting overall life satisfaction. The model was tested using a telephone survey of 400 community residents. The study findings supported a slight variation of the spillover model. Specifically, hospital satisfaction was found to be highly predictive of both community health-care satisfaction and personal health satisfaction. Both community health-care satisfaction and personal health satisfaction were highly predictive of life satisfaction. The measure used to capture hospital satisfaction involved one indicator: "How do you feel about hospital [name] in general?" A seven-point Delighted-Terrible scale was used to capture the satisfaction responses.

In relation to *travel and tourism services*, Neal et al. (1999) hypothesized that travelers' overall life satisfaction is derived from satisfaction with the primary life domains (e.g., family, job, health). Specifically, overall life satisfaction is derived from two sources of satisfaction, namely, satisfaction with non-leisure life domains and satisfaction with leisure life. Satisfaction with leisure life is derived from satisfaction with leisure experiences that take place at home and satisfaction with travel/tourism experiences. Satisfaction with travel/tourism experiences results from satisfaction with trip reflections of the traveler (e.g., what the traveler remembers regarding perceived freedom from

Table 15.15 The community health-care measure of CWB

1. Satisfaction with individual health care services in a community

$$\mathbf{IHS} = \sum \mathbf{IHS}_i (i = 1 \text{ to } n) \text{ where}, \mathbf{IHS}_i = \mathbf{Q}_i \times \mathbf{I}_i \times \mathbf{U}_i \times \mathbf{K}_i$$

$\mathbf{IHS}_i$ = *satisfaction* with the community health-care program/service in question

$\mathbf{Q}_i$ = satisfaction with *quality* of the community health-care program/service in question

"How satisfied are you with the *quality* of this health service in the community?" "Very satisfied" responses were coded as +2, "satisfied" as +1, "somewhat satisfied" as 0, "not very" as −1, and "not at all" as −2

(continued)

Table 15.15 (continued)

I_i = perceived *importance* of the community health-care service/program in question

"How *important* is this _____ [name of the health-care program or service] to you in the community?" Responses were tapped on a scale having five categories—"very important," "important," "somewhat important," "not very," and "not at all." "Very important" responses were coded as 1.0, "important" as 0.8, "somewhat important" as 0.6, "not very" as 0.4, and "not at all" as 0.2

U_i = past *use* of the community health-care program/service in question

"Concerning the use of _____ [name of the health-care program or service]." This statement was followed by four response categories: "I have used" (coded as 1.0), "A family member has used" (coded as 0.85), "A friend has used" (coded as 0.5), and "I do not know of anyone who used this service" (coded as 0.25)

K_i = knowledge of the availability of the health service/program in question in the community

"How much knowledge about available _____ [name of the health-care program or service] would you say you have?" Responses were tapped on a scale involving five categories—"a large amount," "a fair amount," "some," "very little," and "none." "A large amount" responses were coded as 1.0, "a fair amount" as 0.8, "some" as 0.6, "very little" as 0.4, and "none" as 0.2.

- Satisfaction with Women's Health Service
- Satisfaction with Children's Health Services
- Satisfaction with Elderly Health Services
- Satisfaction with Physical Fitness Programs and Facilities
- Satisfaction with Outpatient Services
- Satisfaction with Cancer Services
- Satisfaction with Alcohol and Drug Rehabilitation Services
- Satisfaction with Heart Disease Services
- Satisfaction with Diabetes Services
- Satisfaction with Obstetrics
- Satisfaction with Physical Rehabilitation Services
- Satisfaction with Psychiatric/Mental Health Services
- Satisfaction with Home Health Services
- Satisfaction with Overnight/Long-term Hospital Care
- Satisfaction with Emergency/Emergency Room Services

2. Overall satisfaction with community health care services

"In general, how satisfied are you with the overall quality of health care available in this area?," "How satisfied are you with the overall quality of health care that you personally have received in the area?," and "How satisfied, would you say, most of your friend, neighbors, and other family members living in the area are with the overall quality of health care available in this area?" Responses were tapped on a scale involving five categories—"very satisfied," "satisfied," "somewhat satisfied," "not very," and "not at all"

3. Community QOL

"Overall, how satisfied are you with the community in which you live?" "Delighted" (coded as 7), "pleased" (coded as 6), "mostly satisfied" (coded as 5), "mixed or equally satisfied and dissatisfied" (coded as 4), "mostly dissatisfied" (coded as 3), "unhappy" (coded as 2), "terrible" (coded as 1), "neutral or neither satisfied nor dissatisfied" (coded as missing data), and "never thought about it" (coded as missing data)

Source: Rahtz and Sirgy (2000) and Rahtz et al. (2004)

control, perceived freedom from work, involvement, arousal, mastery, and spontaneity experienced during the trip) and satisfaction with travel/tourism services. Satisfaction with travel/tourism services was hypothesized further to be derived from satisfaction with the service aspects of travel/tourism phases—pre-trip services, en-route services, destination services, and return-trip services. See the measurement items of these CWB-related constructs in Table 15.16.

The model was tested using a study of university faculty and staff, and the results were supportive of the model. The original model was extended by hypothesizing the moderation effect of length of stay (Neal et al. 2004). Specifically, the authors expected that the hypothesized relationships in the model are likely to be more evident in relation to travelers who have more time to experience the tourism services than those who do not. A survey of 815 consumers of travel/tourism services who reside in Southwest Virginia was conducted. As predicted, the data confirmed hypotheses as established in the original model. Satisfaction with tourism services affects travelers' QOL through the

15 Consumer Well-Being (CWB): Various Conceptualizations and Measures

Table 15.16 Neal et al.'s CWB measure in relation to travel and tourism services

1. *Satisfaction with travel/tourism services related to the pre-trip*

    (a) I was satisfied with the quality of service provided by travel and tourism professionals (e.g., travel agents, ticket agents, hotel reservation clerks) while planning the trip

    (b) Making travel and accommodation arrangements for this trip was basically problem free (e.g., travel agents were knowledgeable, I was not put on hold for long periods of time)

    (c) The cost of the services provided by travel and tourism professionals in helping me with the travel logistics was reasonable and well worth it

2. *Satisfaction with travel/tourism services related to the en-route trip*

    (a) I was pleased with the quality of the services provided in transit to the vacation site

    (b) My travels to the vacation site were basically problem free (e.g., the plane seats were as reserved, the train seats reclined properly, the bus driver did not get lost)

    (c) The cost of travel to the vacation site was reasonable and well worth it

3. *Satisfaction with travel/tourism services at the destination site*

    (a) Tourist services at the vacation site (e.g., regarding activities, tourist attractions, restaurants, hotels) were comprehensive and of high quality. These services made the trip a richer experience for me

    (b) Tourist services provided at the vacation site were basically problem free (e.g., the hotel room reserved was available at check-in time, the food was acceptable)

    (c) The cost of tourist services at the vacation site was reasonable and well worth it

4. *Satisfaction with travel/tourism services related to the return trip*

    (a) I was satisfied with the quality of the services provided by those who assisted me on the way home (e.g., flight attendants, cabin stewards, bus drivers, ticket agents)

    (b) My return travels were basically problem free (e.g., the plane seats were comfortable, we returned on time)

    (c) The cost of travel home from the vacation site was reasonable and well worth it

5. *Satisfaction with travel/tourism services related to the trip in general*

    (a) In general, I was pleased with the quality of the travel and tourism services related to this vacation trip

    (b) The travel and tourism services related to this vacation trip were basically problem free

    (c) The cost of the travel and tourism services related to this vacation trip was reasonable and well worth it

6. *Trip reflections*

    (a) On this trip, I *felt free* to do the kinds of things I cannot do at home

    (b) On this trip, I *felt free* from the controls of other people. I felt in control of my movements and actions

    (c) On this trip, I *felt free* from the pressures of life

    (d) I needed to *get away from work and relax*. This trip helped me to rejuvenate

    (e) On this trip, I felt *far away from the drudgery of work*

    (f) I was feeling overworked and emotionally exhausted. This trip helped me *to get away from the stresses and strains of work*

    (g) On this trip, I became *emotionally involved and engaged* with people and things. This experience was very pleasant for me

    (h) This trip allowed me to *get close* to my spouse, children, relatives, and/or friends. It was very much worthwhile

    (i) On this trip, I was able to *reestablish a dwindling relationship* with people for whom I care a lot

    (j) On this trip, I managed to *do exciting things*. I experienced a lot of thrills. This experience has been enriching

    (k) On this trip, I established friendships with one or more new people. This was *exciting*

    (l) Indeed to make some new friends

    (m) On this trip, I got involved with an exciting activity. I felt *alive*

    (n) On this trip, I was able to pursue a passionate interest. This experience was *thrilling*

    (o) On this trip, I had a chance to *master* a hobby or sport. I had wanted to do this for a long time but never had the chance

    (p) On this trip, I was able to *sharpen my skills* on a passionate hobby or sport. This was very rewarding to me

    (q) On this trip, I felt *spontaneous*. This experience has enriched me in ways I never expected

    (r) One cannot afford to be spontaneous in everyday life. But one needs to be spontaneous once in a while. This trip allowed me to do just that, *be spontaneous*

    (s) On this trip, I enjoyed getting to do things on the "*spur of the moment*"

7. *Satisfaction with the general trip experience*

    (a) All in all, I feel that this trip has *enriched my life*. I am really glad I went on this trip

    (b) On this trip, I *accomplished the purpose of the vacation*. This experience has enriched me in some ways

    (c) This trip was *rewarding* to me in many ways. I feel much better about things and myself after this trip

8. *Satisfaction with leisure experiences at home*

    (a) I do things that are fulfilling when I am off work

    (b) Lately, I have been feeling very good about the way I spend my leisure time after work

    (c) Leisure time after work is very important to me

(continued)

Table 15.16 (continued)

9. *Satisfaction with leisure experiences at large*

   (a) Recently, I have been spending quality leisure time in general (e.g., going on vacations, relaxing round the house, enjoying a hobby)

   (b) I am the kind of person who knows how to enjoy leisure time anytime and anywhere

   (c) I am generally happy with the quality of my leisure time

All items in table were measured with a 5-point Likert-type scale with 1 = strongly disagree, 5 = strongly agree)
Sources: Neal et al. (1999, 2004)

mediating effects of satisfaction with travel/tourism experiences and satisfaction with leisure life. Furthermore, the moderating effect of length of stay was confirmed by the data. Sirgy et al. (2010a, b) found that travel trip influences life satisfaction through tourists' experiences of positive and negative affect associated with a recent tourist trip couched within various life domains (e.g., social life, leisure life, family life, cultural life, health and safety, love life, work life, and financial life). In sum, this replication and extension study provided additional validational support of the original tourism services satisfaction measure in relation to QOL-related measures.

The Marketer's Orientation Model

The basic assumption of the Marketer's Orientation Model is that CWB is directly a function of marketers' action to enhance the QOL of their customers (Lee et al. 1998). That marketers' orientation toward enhancing their customers' QOL is pivotal and that it should be studied as a CWB phenomenon. As such, Lee and Sirgy (1999) examined the effects of moral philosophy and ethnocentrism on quality of life orientation in international marketing. International quality of life (IQOL) orientation refers to marketers' disposition to make decisions to enhance the well-being of consumers in foreign markets while preserving the well-being of other stakeholders. See items of the IQOL orientation measure in Table 15.17.

It was hypothesized that marketers' moral philosophy and ethnocentrism influence the development of marketers' IQOL—the higher the IQOL orientation of international managers, the higher their moral idealism, the higher their moral relativism, and the lower their ethnocentrism. Also, it was hypothesized that American managers are likely to score higher on moral

Table 15.17 The IQOL orientation measure

I. *Enhancement of consumers' well-being in foreign markets*

   1. I believe the primary mission of the multinational corporation operating in a foreign country is (a) to maximize short-term profits from that country and (b) to enhance the well-being of target consumers of that country

   2. Regarding market selection of a product in a foreign country, I believe the multinational corporation should target (a) the most profitable market segment in that country and (b) market segments that have the greatest potential to enhance the well-being of target consumers in that country

   3. I believe that the multinational corporation in a foreign country should develop new products to (a) maximize short-term profit from that country and (b) enhance the well-being of consumers in that country

II. *Preservation of other stakeholders' well-being in host countries*

   1. Regarding organizational stakeholders of the multinational corporation operating in foreign countries (e.g., local government, local community, local environment), I believe (a) the impact of a product on the local community and environment is of secondary importance compared to short-term profitability of the product, and (b) reducing potential negative side effects to the local community and environment is a major responsibility of the multinational corporation

   2. With respect to distribution in a foreign country, I believe (a) it is acceptable for the multinational corporation to distribute excess inventory through unauthorized dealers in that foreign country, and (b) the multinational corporation should use only legal channels to maximize product accessibility

   3. Regarding channel members within a foreign country, I believe: (a) the multinational corporation operating in a foreign country should strive to gain power over channel members in that foreign country, and (b) the multinational corporation should treat channel members in a foreign country as vital stakeholders of the firm

Source: Lee and Sirgy (1999) and Lee et al. (1998)

relativism but lower on moral idealism compared to their Korean counterparts. Also, Korean managers were expected to be more ethnocentric than American managers. Survey data were collected from business professionals in the USA and Korea. The survey results provided support for the hypothesized relationships and the IQOL measure. In relation to marketing orientation model of consumer well-being, Sirgy and Lee (2008) argued that well-being marketing is a philosophy grounded in business ethics. Specifically, well-being marketing is based on duty of beneficence and non-maleficence.

The Materialism Model

Belk (1984, p. 291) defined materialism as the importance a consumer attaches to worldly possessions. At the highest levels of materialism, such possessions assume a central place in a person's life and are believed to provide the greatest source of satisfaction and dissatisfaction in life. However, religious teachers (e.g., Jesus, Mahavira) and philosophers (e.g., Hegel 1977/1807) have long affirmed that the joys of the intellect and the spirit exceed those of material possessions, that true satisfaction in life comes from the former, not the latter. For example, Fromm (1976) distinguishes among three levels of existence: having, doing, and being. *Having* is the lowest of the three states, reflecting preoccupation with acquiring material possessions. In *doing*, people focus on action rather than consumption or possession. *Being*, Fromm's highest level of existence, refers to finding serenity and satisfaction in one's identity as a free being, in *who* one is rather than in what one *does* or *has*.

The empirical record supports the position of the religious teachers and philosophers. Several studies have examined the relationship between materialism and happiness or life satisfaction (e.g., Belk 1984, 1985; Dawson and Bamossy 1991; Richins 1987; Richins and Dawson 1992). All have demonstrated a negative correlation between those constructs. In a meta-analysis of studies treating the correlation, Wright and Larsen (1993) found a medium-sized negative effect across all data points, demonstrating the robustness of the relationship (cf. Fournier and Richins 1991). Sirgy (1998) explained this relationship by arguing that materialistic people tend to have inflated and unrealistic desires and expectations of being financially affluent, and they feel dissatisfied with their income and financial status because of these inflated and unrealistic desires and expectations. This dissatisfaction with their standard of living contributes to feelings of dissatisfaction with life.

Ahuvia and Wong (2002) argued that some materialism constructs emphasize affective responses while others emphasize cognitive beliefs. For example, Ger and Belk's (1996) and Belk's (1985) materialism measure focuses on affect. Belk (1985) defines materialism as a personality trait involving envy, nongenerosity, and a chronic concern that one's possession may be lost or stolen. In contrast, Richins and Dawson's (1992) materialism measure focuses on cognitive beliefs.

Table 15.18 Richins and Dawson's materialism measure

Success
• I admire people who own expensive homes, cars, and clothes
• Some of the most important achievements in life include acquiring material possessions. I do not place much emphasis on the amount of material objects people own as a sign of success (reverse coded)
• The things I own say a lot about how well I am doing in life
• I like to own things that impress people
• I do not pay much attention to the material objects other people own (reverse coded)

Centrality
• I usually buy only the things I need (reverse coded)
• I try to keep my life simple, as far as possessions are concerned (reverse coded)
• The things I own are not all that important to me (reverse coded)
• I enjoy spending money on things that are not practical
• Buying things gives me a lot of pleasure
• I like a lot of luxury in my life
• I put less emphasis on material things than most people (reverse coded)

Happiness
• I have all the things I really need to enjoy life (reverse coded)
• My life would be better if I owned certain things I do not have
• I would not be any happier if I owned nicer things (reverse coded)
• I would be happier if I could afford to buy more things
• It sometimes bothers me quite a bit that I cannot afford to buy all the things I would like

Note: Responses are recorded on 5-point Likert scales ranging from "strongly disagree" (1) to "strongly agree" (5)
Source: Richins and Dawson (1992)

Richins (1994, 1987) views materialism as a personal value system in which materialistic people believe that money is the key to happiness. Materialistic people allow material possessions to play a central role in their lives, and they judge success in life by income and possessions. The items used in Richins and Dawson's (1992) materialism measure are shown in Table 15.18.

Guided by Richins' conceptualization of materialism, Sirgy et al. (1998a, b) hypothesized that television viewership influences materialism and dissatisfaction with standard of living, which, in turn, contributes to feelings of dissatisfaction with life. The authors collected data from five countries to examine the issue in a variety of cultural and media environments.

The countries and types of samples were USA (consumer panel and college students), Canada (urban households), Australia (urban households), Turkey (urban households), and China (urban households). The results were generally consistent with the hypotheses. Overall, the results show that television viewership, at least in the USA, may play a significant role in making people unhappy with their lives. Much of television advertising reinforces material consumption and possession with images of the "good life." Thus, television advertising contributes to *terminal materialism*—materialism for the sake of materialism. The authors conclude by encouraging advertising professionals to make a concerted effort creating ads that reflect *instrumental materialism*—materialism for the sake of meeting essential and basic needs—and to shy away from ads that reflect terminal materialism. This study was replicated and extended reinforcing the findings of the previous study (Sirgy et al. 2011a, b).

The Globalization Model

Sirgy et al. (2004, 2007) developed a set of theoretical propositions to explain the impact of globalization on a country's quality of life (QOL). They described how globalization impacts the quality of life of residents of a country by articulating the globalization construct (in terms of inflows and outflows of goods, services, capital, technology, and people). They also articulated the country's QOL construct in terms of *consumer*, economic, social, and health well-being, and showed how globalization may impact a country's QOL. It was argued that globalization increases CWB at the country level. This is because globalization increases accessibility to lower-priced, high-quality imports and, thus, increases consumer spending power. Also, globalization increases consumer choice and motivates domestic firms to be more competitive.

The focus here is how CWB was conceptualized and measured in the context of the globalization model. According to the authors, a country characterized as high on CWB is one in which most of its people's basic needs are met and have access to goods and services to meet their non-basic needs. This definition of CWB was further operationalized through two dimensions and corresponding indicators: satisfaction of basic needs and access to goods and services related to non-basic needs. Indicators of *satisfaction of basic needs* were identified in terms of housing quality [e.g., number of persons per room (−), housing amenities such as plumbing and heat (+)], quality of infrastructure (e.g., availability and quality of public transportation, telecommunications, public safety, water, and energy), and other welfare measures. Indicators of *access to goods and services related to non-basic needs* include the Consumer Confidence Index (CCI), the Consumer Expectations Index (CEI), the Consumer Price Index (CPI), and other cost of living measures.

Conclusion

The main purpose of this chapter is to review various measures of CWB. We first started out by making the distinction between consumer satisfaction and CWB. We argued that much of consumer satisfaction measurement research is guided by the notion that consumer satisfaction leads to brand loyalty and repeat purchase. In contrast, research in CWB is guided by the notion that higher levels of CWB contribute to higher levels of life satisfaction.

We then reviewed CWB conceptualizations and measures widely used in the public sector. The Cost of Living Model is based on the notion that CWB is higher when a country registers low inflation (low CPI). The Consumption Equity Model is based on the notion that a country should consume in direct proportion to the size of its population to achieve global consumption equity. Additionally, the Quality Model and the Consumer Complaint Model are based on the notion that CWB is high when quality of consumer goods and services is high (as indicated in *Consumer Reports*) and low complaints filed against individual companies and brands at the Better Business Bureau (Sirgy and Lee 2008).

Following this, we reviewed a set of CWB conceptualizations and measures as developed in the academic sector. Academic research on that topic shows that CWB is high when consumers are satisfied with marketplace experiences such as shopping in the local area, preparing or assembling consumer goods for personal use, owning durable goods, using goods and services to satisfy their needs, maintaining and repairing goods they own, and disposing those goods after consumption. That is, high CWB reflects a high level of satisfaction with various marketplace experiences—from shopping to disposal.

CWB was also conceptualized and measured in terms of need satisfaction and perception of value.

15 Consumer Well-Being (CWB): Various Conceptualizations and Measures

That is, CWB is high when a particular good or service serves to satisfy human needs better and satisfy a spectrum of needs, compared to situations in which a good or service satisfies a need less intensely and only one particular need (or a small set of needs). Also, CWB is high when consumers perceive greater value in various life domains—more benefits and less costs in each domain.

The Bottom-Up Spillover Model posits that CWB does play an important role in overall life satisfaction, because satisfaction with particular marketplace experiences does spill over to other life domains and to overall life. These "bottom-up" spillover consumer goods and services influence overall life satisfaction.

We also described other conceptualizations of CWB including materialism and marketers' orientation. CWB, conceptualized as materialism, is argued to be high when materialism is low, because high levels of materialism leads to low levels of life satisfaction. The marketers' orientation concept defines CWB from the vantage point of the marketer. Certain marketers are motivated to practice the kind of marketing that enhances CWB while other marketers practice marketing for the sole purpose of meeting organizational goals such as higher levels of sales, profit, and market share.

References

Ahuvia, A. C., & Wong, N. (2002). Personality and value based materialism: Their relationship and origins. *Journal of Consumer Psychology, 12*, 389–402.

Belk, R. W. (1984). Three scales to measure constructs related to materialism: Reliability, validity, and relationship to measure of happiness. *Advances in Consumer Research, 12*, 265–280.

Belk, R. W. (1985). Materialism: Trait aspects of living in the material world. *Journal of Consumer Research, 12*, 265–280.

Belk, R. W. (1995). Collecting as luxury consumption: Effects on individuals and households. *Journal of Economic Psychology, 16*, 477–490.

Dawson, S., & Bamossy, G. (1991). If "we are what we have", what are we when we don't have? *Journal of Social Behavior and Personality, 6*, 363–384.

Day, R. L. (1978). Beyond social indicators: Quality of life at the individual level. In F. D. Reynolds & H. C. Barksdale (Eds.), *Marketing and the quality of life* (pp. 11–18). Chicago: American Marketing Association.

Day, R. L. (1987). Relationship between life satisfaction and consumer satisfaction. In A. C. Samli (Ed.), *Marketing and the quality-of-life interface* (pp. 289–311). Westport: Quorum Books.

Diener, E. (1984). Subjective well-being. *Psychological Bulletin, 95*, 542–575.

Fornell, C. (1992). A national customer satisfaction barometer: The Swedish experience. *Journal of Marketing, 56*, 6–21.

Fornell, C., Johnson, M. D., Anderson, E. W., Cha, J., & Bryant, B. E. (1996). The American customer satisfaction index: Nature, purpose, and findings. *Journal of Marketing, 60*, 7–18.

Fournier, S., & Richins, M. L. (1991). Some theoretical and popular notions concerning materialism. *Journal of Social Behavior and Personality, 6*, 403–414.

Fromm, E. (1976). *To have or to be*. New York: Harper and Row.

Ger, G., & Belk, R. W. (1996). Cross-cultural differences in materialism. *Journal of Economic Psychology, 17*, 55–77.

Grzeskowiak, S., Sirgy, M. J., Lee, D.-J., & Claiborne, C. B. (2006). Housing well-being: Nomological (predictive) validation study. *Social Indicators Research, 79*, 503–541.

Heady, B. W., Holmstrom, E. L., & Wearing, A. J. (1985). Models of well-being and ill-being. *Social Indicators Research, 17*, 211–234.

Hegel, G. W. F. (1977, 1807). *Helgel's phenomenology of spirit*. Oxford: Oxford University Press.

http://www.bls.gov/cpi/home: Consumer Price Index Detailed Report Tables 1–29, June 2005

http://www.consumerreports.org, The Consumer Reports

http://www.thelocalbbb.com/alerts/alerts.html, The Better Business Bureau

Lee, D.-J., & Sirgy, M. J. (1995). Determinants of involvement in the consumer/marketing life domain in relation to quality of life: A theoretical model and research agenda. In H. L. Meadow, M. J. Sirgy, & D. Rahtz (Eds.), *Developments in quality of life studies in marketing* (pp. 13–18). Blacksburg: Academy of Marketing Science.

Lee, D.-J., & Sirgy, M. J. (1999). International marketers' quality-of-life orientation: A measure and validational support. *Journal of Business Ethics, 18*, 73–89.

Lee, D.-J., & Sirgy, M. J. (2004). Quality of life (QOL) marketing: Proposed antecedents and consequences. *Journal of Macromarketing, 24*, 44–58.

Lee, D.-J., Sirgy, M. J., & Su, C. (1998). International quality-of-life orientation: The construct, its antecedents, and consequences. *Research in Marketing, 14*, 151–184.

Lee, D.-J., Sirgy, M. J., Larsen, V., & Wright, N. D. (2002). Developing a subjective measure of consumer well-being. *Journal of Macromarketing, 22*, 158–169.

Leelakulthanit, O., Day, R., & Walters, R. (1991). Investigating the relationship between marketing and overall satisfaction with life in a developing country. *Journal of Macromarketing, 11*, 3–23.

Majumdar, R. (1997). Impact of marketing on the quality of life. In H. L. Meadow (Ed.), *Developments in quality-of-life studies* (Vol. 1, p. 53). Blacksburg: International Society for Quality-of-Life Studies.

Maslow, A. H. (1954, 1970). *Motivation and personality*. New York: Harper.

Meadow, H. L., & Sirgy, M. J. (2008). Developing a measure that captures elderly's well-being in local marketplace transactions. *Applied Research in Quality of Life, 3*, 63–80.

Nakano, N., MacDonald, M., & Douthitt, R. (1995). Toward consumer well-being: Consumer socialization effects of work experience. In M. J. Sirgy, H. L. Meadow, D. Rahtz, & A. C. Samli (Eds.), *Developments in quality-of-life studies in marketing* (pp. 107–111). Dekalb: Academy of Marketing Science.

Neal, J., Sirgy, M. J., & Uysal, M. (1999). The role of satisfaction with leisure travel/tourism services and experiences in satisfaction with leisure life and overall life. *Journal of Business Research, 44*, 153–163.

Neal, J., Sirgy, M. J., & Uysal, M. (2004). Measuring the effect of tourism services on travelers' quality of life: Further validation. *Social Indicators Research, 69*, 243–277.

Oliver, R. (1997). *Satisfaction: A behavioral perspective on the customer.* New York: McGraw Hill.

Oliver, R. (2009). *Satisfaction: A behavioral perspective on the customer* (2nd ed.). New York: Mc-Graw Hill.

Rahtz, D., & Sirgy, M. J. (2000). Marketing of health care within a community: A quality-of-life/need assessment model and method. *Journal of Business Research, 48*, 165–176.

Rahtz, D., Sirgy, M. J., & Lee, D.-J. (2004). Further validation and extension of the quality-of-life/community healthcare model and measures. *Social Indicators Research, 69*, 167–198.

Richins, M. L. (1987). Media, materialism, and human happiness. In M. Wallendorf & P. Anderson (Eds.), *Advances in consumer research* (pp. 352–356). Provo: Association for Consumer Research.

Richins, M. L. (1994). Value things: The public and private meanings of possessions. *Journal of Consumer Research, 21*, 504–521.

Richins, M. L., & Dawson, S. (1992). A consumer value orientation for materialism and its measurement: Scale development and validation. *Journal of Consumer Research, 19*, 303–316.

Ruger, J. P. (2008). Ethics in American health: Ethical approaches to health policy. *American Journal of Public Health, 98*, 1751–1756.

Samli, A. C. (2003). The consumer price index and consumer well being: Developing a fair measure. *Journal of Macromarketing, 23*, 105–111.

Samli, A. C., Sirgy, M. J., & Meadow, H. L. (1987). Measuring marketing contribution to quality of life. In A. C. Samli (Ed.), *Marketing and quality of life interface* (pp. 3–14). Westport: Quorum Books.

Sirgy, M. J. (1998). Materialism and the quality of life. *Social Indicators Research, 43*, 227–260.

Sirgy, M. J. (2001). *Handbook of quality-of-life research: An ethical marketing perspective.* Dordrecht: Kluwer Academic Publishers.

Sirgy, M. J. (2002). *The psychology of quality of life.* Dordrecht: Kluwer Academic Publishers.

Sirgy, M. J., & Cornwell, T. (2001). Further validation of the Sirgy et al.'s measure of community quality of life. *Social Indicators Research, 56*, 125–143.

Sirgy, M. J., & Lee, D.-J. (2003). Developing a measure of consumer well being in relation to personal transportation. *Yonsei Business Review, 40*, 73–101.

Sirgy, M. J., & Lee, D.-J. (2008). Well being marketing: An ethical philosophy for consumer goods firms. *Journal of Business Ethics, 77*, 377–403.

Sirgy, M. J., Hansen, D. E., & Littlefield, J. E. (1994). Does hospital satisfaction affect life satisfaction? *Journal of Macromarketing, 14*, 36–46.

Sirgy, M. J., Lee, D.-J., Kosenko, R., Meadow, H. L., Rahtz, D., Cicic, M., Jin, G. X., Yarsuvat, D., Blenkhorn, D. L., &

Wright, N. (1998a). Does television viewership influence and propagate dissatisfaction with standard of living and overall life? *Journal of Advertising, 27*, 125–142.

Sirgy, M. J., Lee, D.-J., Larsen, V., & Wright, N. (1998b). Satisfaction with material possessions and general well-being: The role of materialism. *Journal of Consumer Satisfaction, Dissatisfaction and Complaining Behavior, 11*, 103–118.

Sirgy, M. J., Rahtz, D., Cicic, M., & Underwood, R. (2000). A method for assessing residents' satisfaction with community-based services: A quality-of-life perspective. *Social Indicators Research, 49*, 279–316.

Sirgy, M. J., Rahtz, D., & Lee, D.-J. (2004). Further validation and extension of the quality of life community healthcare model and measures. *Social Indicators Research, 69*, 167–198.

Sirgy, M. J., Lee, D.-J., & Bae, J. (2006a). Developing a subjective measure of Internet well being: Nomological (Predictive) Validation. *Social Indicators Research, 78*, 205–249.

Sirgy, M. J., Lee, D.-J., & Kressmann, F. (2006b). A need-based measure of consumer well-being (CWB) in relation to personal transportation: Nomological validation. *Social Indicators Research, 79*, 337–367.

Sirgy, M. J., Lee, D.-J., & Rahtz, D. (2006c). Macro measures of consumer well being (CWB): A critical analysis and research agenda. *Journal of Macromarketing, 26*, 27–44.

Sirgy, M. J., Lee, D.-J., Miller, C., Littlefield, J. E., & Atay, E. G. (2007). The impact of exports and imports on a country's quality of life. *Social Indicators Research, 83*, 245–281.

Sirgy, M. J., Lee, D.-J., Grzeskowiak, S., Chebat, J. C., Herrmann, A., Hassan, S., Hegazi, I., Ekici, A., Webb, D., Su, C., & Montana, J. (2008a). An extension and further validation of a community-based consumer well-being measure. *Journal of Macromarketing, 28*, 243–257.

Sirgy, M. J., Lee, D.-J., & Rahtz, D. (2008b). Research on consumer well being: Overview of the field and introduction to the special issue. *Journal of Macromarketing, 27*, 341–3490.

Sirgy, M. J., Kruger, P. S., Lee, D.-J., & Yu, G. B. (2010a). How does a travel trip affect tourists' life satisfaction? *Journal of Travel Research, 50*, 261–275.

Sirgy, M. J., Widgery, R., Lee, D.-J., & Yu, G. B. (2010b). Developing a measure of community well being based on perceptions of impact in various life domains. *Social Indicators Research, 96*, 295–311.

Sirgy, M. J., Gurel-Atay, E., Webb, D., Cicic, M., Husic, M., Herrmann, A., Hegazy, I., Lee, D-J., & Johar, J. S. (2011a). Linking advertising, materialism, and life satisfaction. *Social Indicators Research* (online).

Sirgy, M. J., Lee, D.-J., & Yu, G. B. (2011b). Consumer sovereignty in healthcare: Fact or fiction. *Journal of Business Ethics, 101*, 459–474.

Szymanski, D. M., & Henard, D. H. (2001). Customer satisfaction: A meta-analysis of the empirical evidence. *Journal of the Academy of Marketing Science, 29*, 16–35.

United Nations Development Programme. (1998). *Human development report 1998.* New York: Oxford University Press.

Wright, N. D., & Larsen, V. (1993). Materialism and life satisfaction: A meta-analysis. *Journal of Consumer Satisfaction, Dissatisfaction and Complaining Behavior, 6*, 158–165.

Perceived Quality of Life of Children and Youth

16

E. Scott Huebner, Rich Gilman, and Claudia Ma

Research on the quality of life (QOL) of adults has flourished during the last several decades, capturing the attention of a variety of scientific disciplines, such as economics, medicine, political science, psychology, and sociology. QOL conceptualizations, measurement techniques, and intervention strategies have developed from two traditions: objective and subjective QOL. Controversy has ensued regarding the importance of each and the relationships between them. Proponents of the objective QOL indicators strategy focus on population-based measures related to various objective criteria for "good" lives, such as frequencies of teen births, risk behaviors, and poverty levels. On the other hand, proponents of the subjective indicators perspective focus on models and measures that incorporate individuals' subjective perceptions and evaluations of key indicators of life quality, such as life satisfaction or perceived quality of life (PQOL) with respect to individuals' *overall* lives or specific life domains (e.g., family relationships, school experiences, living environments). Because research with adults reveals that objective and subjective indicators (e.g., physician vs. self-ratings of physical health) are distinguishable

from one another, researchers have concluded that objective and subjective indicators reflect distinct but complementary QOL information (Diener and Suh 1997). Thus, a full understanding of the QOL of children and youth requires multiple indicators drawn from both traditions. Land et al. (2007) provide a notable example of the benefits of integrating the two approaches in the construction and validation of the Child and Youth Well-Being Index. Furthermore, the studies of Ben-Arieh and Goerge (2001) and Fattore et al. (2007) underscore the importance of contextual factors in the development of child well-being indexes, including grounding the indicators in the experiences of children.

Although research with adults has burgeoned over the years, research with children and youth has lagged significantly behind, particularly with respect to PQOL. Large-scale studies have been particularly absent. The typical study has involved small-scale, convenience samples, limiting the generalizability of the findings. Most studies of the PQOL of children have also employed global measures of PQOL. Such measures can be useful; nevertheless, they fail to differentiate a variety of specific domains (e.g., family, friends, school, self, living environment) that have been demonstrated to be important to children across the age range of 8–18 (Gilman et al. 2000; Huebner 1994; Seligson et al. 2003). Under some circumstances, global scores may mask differences observable in domain-level scores. For example, Antaramian et al. (2008) found that adolescents' reports of family satisfaction (but not general life satisfaction) were related to their family structure (intact vs. nonintact families).

Thus, although current findings on the PQOL of children are promising, much more research is needed

---

E.S. Huebner (✉) • C. Ma
Department of Psychology, University of South Carolina, Columbia, SC, USA
e-mail: Huebner@sc.edu; claudia.lindner@gmail.com

R. Gilman
Cincinnati Children's Hospital Medical Center, University of Cincinnati, Cincinnati, OH, USA

to approach such laudable goals as "to inform decision-makers concerning the identification of variabilities within the population, inequities, public needs and trends" (Campbell 1976). For example, similar to a proposal for national longitudinal databases to monitor the PQOL of adults (Diener 2000), Huebner et al. (2004b) have argued for the development of ongoing, large-scale youth PQOL studies as part of comprehensive health-care assessments and interventions.

Although conceptually differentiable from measures of psychopathology, PQOL reports have been found to be inversely related to child reports of mental and physical health problems, risk behaviors (e.g., alcohol and drug use, risky sexual behavior), and school-related problems (see Gilman and Huebner 2003 and Huebner et al. 2006 for reviews). Importantly, PQOL has been shown to be more than an epiphenomenon; PQOL can influence adaptive outcomes. For example, PQOL has been shown to serve as a cognitive mediator of the relationship between parenting behavior and adolescents' externalizing and internalizing behavior (Suldo and Huebner 2004a). Similarly, PQOL mediates the relationship between the frequency of stressful life events and internalizing behavior in adolescents (McKnight et al. 2002). Additionally, Suldo and Huebner (2004b) found that adolescent PQOL moderated the relationship between stressful life events and subsequent increases in externalizing behavior problems. That is, the effects of stressful life events were significantly greater among students with low PQOL. Finally, in a longitudinal study of adolescents, lower levels of global PQOL predicted an increased likelihood of being victimized by peers (Martin et al. 2008). In short, efforts to promote PQOL are likely to be more than simple hedonistic pursuits. Rather, such efforts should facilitate adaptive outcomes in children and youth.

Measurement of Child PQOL

Similar to what has been noted in the adult literature, research on the measurement of PQOL among children has paled in comparison with studies investigating child and adolescent psychopathology (Rich 2003). PQOL has been associated with the absence of symptoms of psychopathology, such as mental distress (Frisch 1999; Keyes 2005). The assumption that psychological distress and PQOL occupy two ends of a bipolar continuum has been repeatedly called into question (Jahoda 1958;

Keyes 2006; Seligman and Csikszentmihalyi 2000). For example, in a sample of elementary school children, Greenspoon and Saklofske (2000) found that assessments incorporating measures of psychological distress and PQOL could reliably differentiate elementary school children into four distinct categories, with placement determined by level of endorsement (high vs. low) within each dimension (psychopathology vs. PQOL). Thus, categories ranged from high psychopathology—high PQOL to low psychopathology—low PQOL, the latter category demonstrating that children who do not endorse symptoms of psychopathology do not necessarily endorse high PQOL levels. This group may reflect the lives of children whose personal and environmental resources and assets, although adequate, are challenged by various acute and/or chronic stressors (Masten 2001). Subsequent research has demonstrated that the group of students who report low PQOL, without clinical levels of psychological symptoms, reveal not only social deficits but academic and physical health deficits compared to students in the other three groups (Suldo and Shaffer 2008). Students in this group display lower levels of school engagement and GPA (Antaramian et al. 2010). In this regard, using measures of PQOL in conjunction with measures of psychopathology appears needed to more comprehensively describe children's overall adaptation (Lopez et al. 2003).

Such assessment of PQOL has been advocated for a number of professional settings, including medical (Fallowfield 1994), school (Baker et al. 2003), public health (Huebner et al. 2004b), and child clinical settings (Kazdin 1993). To this end, substantial progress has been made in the construction of various child PQOL measures designed for use with general (i.e., nonclinical) populations as well as specific populations, including children experiencing psychiatric disorders (Bastiaansen et al. 2004), trauma stemming from sexual abuse (Valente 2005), and medical conditions such as cancer (Detmar 2005) and chronic asthma (Chan et al. 2005). Although PQOL measures have been administered to both general and clinical samples on occasion, the specificity of the items comprising the clinical scales often limits their applicability to general samples of youth. In this section, findings related to generic PQOL measures will be described. Readers interested in reviews of clinical PQOL measures should consult Quittner et al. (2003) and Matza et al. (2004) for additional information.

PQOL measures have been developed for use with children ranging between the ages of 8 and 18. Reviews of the psychometric properties of select measures can be found in Bender (1997), Gilman and Huebner (2000), and Huebner (2004). In general, extant measures largely reflect research and clinical interest in assessing PQOL at its most global (i.e., life as a whole) level or across specific domains. In the former case, global measures require the computation of a single PQOL score, based on domain-free items (e.g., "I like my life as a whole"). Presumably, this single score includes an individual's unique combination of objective (e.g., income) and subjective factors (e.g., perceived competence and coping efficacy), and their interaction with more stable and dispositional aspects such as personality and temperament (see Lent 2004). Examples of global PQOL instruments include the *Satisfaction with Life Scale* (SWLS: Diener et al. 1985) and the *Students' Life Satisfaction Scale* (SLSS: Huebner 1991a, b). Such measures are often administered when researchers prefer that respondents define their own criteria for their overall PQOL.

In contrast, multidimensional PQOL measures yield domain-specific scores as we well as an overall (general) score. Examples of these measures include the *Multidimensional Students' Life Satisfaction Scale* (MSLSS; Huebner 1994a), the *Brief Multidimensional Students' Life Satisfaction Scale* (BMSLSS: Seligson et al. 2003), and the *Comprehensive Quality of Life Scale—Fifth Edition* (ComQol-S5: Cummins 1997), which is now *The Personal Well-being Index—School Children*, 3rd Ed, 2005 (see http://www,deakin.edu.au/research/acqol/instruments/PWI/PWI-school.pdf). For these multidimensional measures, the number and types of domains are based on criteria selected by the researcher(s) and may differ given fundamentally different conceptualizations of what constitutes life quality. As one example, the MSLSS assesses five specific domains believed most important in a child's life (school, living environment, self, family, and friends), while the Com-Qol-S5 assesses seven different domains (material well-being, health, productivity, intimacy, safety, place in community, and emotional well-being). Depending upon the researchers' interests, inclusion of many different domains could be considered appropriate (Frisch 1999). Nevertheless, the number and weighting of the specific domains is important to consider when interpreting "total" or general life satisfaction scores, which are derived from some combination of the lower-order domains. For example, a total PQOL score derived from a simple summation of items across five domains may or may not be comparable to a total PQOL score derived from a weighted combination of lower-order scores across seven domains.

A number of theories have been proposed regarding the relationship between domain-specific PQOL and global PQOL scores (see Lance et al. 1989; Lance et al. 1995), with most comprising either a "top-down" or a "bottom-up" approach. In the former case, the level of global PQOL determines how quality of life is perceived within specific relevant domains, while the opposite is found for the bottom-up approach. Research findings have been inconclusive, despite the implications for clinical practice, both among adults (Frisch 2006; Lent et al. 2005) and children (Huebner 2004).

Psychometric Qualities of Self-Report Child PQOL Measures

Given the recency of interest in PQOL among children, the first step in this line of research has relied on self-report scales (Diener 2003). At present, there is sufficient evidence to conclude that child and adolescent PQOL self-reports yield adequate validity and reliability across the ages of 8–18 (Gilman and Huebner 2000; Huebner 2004). For example, many of the PQOL measures converge with each other, as well as with constructs that are conceptually similar. Specifically, Dew and Huebner (1994a) reported that the SLSS and the PLSS correlated at .58, while the SLSS and a brief version of the MSLSS (i.e., BMSLSS) correlated at .66 (Seligson et al. 2003). The SWLS showed a correlation of .42 with a one-item satisfaction measure (Leung and Leung 1992), and a correlation of .71 with a measure of happiness among an adolescent sample (Neto 1993). These relationships indicate that although a moderate (but significant) degree of variance is shared between PQOL scales, the proportion of unshared variance is large enough to indicate that the scales assess PQOL in a somewhat different manner. Evidence of criterion-related validity has also been demonstrated for the PQOL measures, including significant, positive correlations with hope (Valle et al. 2004), sense of mastery (Sam 1998), self-esteem (Huebner et al. 1999; Marriage and Cummins 2004), and social support (Petito and Cummins 2000). Further, PQOL measures evidence negative associations with negative affect (Seligson et al. 2003), external locus of control (Huebner et al. 2000b), depression (Adelman et al. 1989), and anxiety (Gullone and Cummins 1999).

Reports obtained by general PQOL measures have yielded a reasonable degree of temporal stability. For example, a correlation of .81 was obtained for the MSLSS across a 4-week period (Huebner et al. 1998), while the Com-Qol yielded a coefficient of .73 across the same time span (Cummins 1997). Global and general PQOL measures have reported stability estimates ranging from .53 for a 1-year period (Huebner et al. 2000b) to .85 (time span not reported; Adelman et al. 1989).

Perhaps most important in terms of assessing PQOL among children is the construct validity of the measures. It should be noted that among most measures, the use of exploratory factor analyses (i.e., principal axis and principal components) or demonstrations of convergent and discriminant validity has been used to support the underlying conceptual model of a particular instrument (see Gilman and Huebner 2000). Confirmatory factor analyses have rarely been used to substantiate the invariance of the factor structure beyond the exploratory phase of development. Further, few studies have investigated the factor invariance of a PQOL measure across different groups of children, which would indicate that the PQOL measures are assessing a "psychological universal" (Diener 1994, p. 112). Nevertheless, the limited research that has been conducted generally supports the hypothesized factor structures of most PQOL measures. For example, results from exploratory factor analyses have supported a one-factor model for the SWLS (Neto 1993) and the SLSS (Gilman and Huebner 1997), but not for the Perceived Life Satisfaction Scale (Adelman et al. 1989), the latter finding suggesting that the PLSS may be multidimensional rather than unidimensional in nature (Huebner and Dew 1993). For the multivariate measures, convergent and discriminant validity for the Com-Qol (Gullone and Cummins 1999) and exploratory and confirmatory analyses for the MSLSS (Huebner 1994a; Gilman et al. 2000) have been used as support for construct validity. Further, the factor structure of some PQOL measures appears to be invariant across disparate groups. For example, Atienza et al. (2003) reported that the SWLS yielded a unidimensional factor structure among Spanish youth that was consistent with that obtained among American youth. Similar findings were noted between Korean and American youth on the MSLSS (Park et al. 2004), and a separate study supported the MSLSS factor structure among American, Chinese, Israeli, Croatian, and Irish adolescents (Gilman et al. 2008). Nevertheless, both the Park et al. and

Gilman et al. studies reported slightly lower reliabilities on the self-satisfaction domain of the MSLSS for youth in some nations, and Atienza et al. reported different factor loadings of the SWLS across gender. These findings suggest that interpretation of particular PQOL items may vary with respect to culture.

One reason for differences in PQOL results across disparate groups may be the manner in which the instruments, most of which were originally written for English speaking children, are interpreted among non-English speaking children. However, few differences have been found in the psychometric properties of PQOL scales when the items are translated from English. For example, translation of the MSLSS into Hebrew (Schiff et al. 2006), Chinese (Tian et al. 2003), and Korean (Park et al. 2004) has yielded comparable psychometric properties in comparison to American youth. Likewise, the SWLS has yielded similar psychometric properties among Spanish speaking youth (Atienza et al. 2003), as has the MSLSS (Casas et al. 2001). Thus, differences in PQOL reports do not appear to be influenced by translation. Nevertheless, although these studies provide support for the further study of PQOL across cultures and nations, additional research incorporating more complex procedures, such as multigroup confirmatory factor analyses and item response theory, is necessary to better determine how various PQOL measures are interpreted by non-English speaking children.

Although the stability coefficients of PQOL instruments across various time spans suggest that PQOL reports are influenced by personal dispositional factors, they are also sensitive to changes in internal and/or environmental conditions. Similar to findings in the adult literature (Diener et al. 1999), PQOL measures appear sensitive to psychosocial interventions. For example, two studies administered the MSLSS to adolescents who were first entering residential treatment settings (Gilman and Barry 2003; Gilman and Handwerk 2001), with both revealing that PQOL significantly decreased during the first month of stay, but incrementally and significantly increased during the following 3 months of treatment. Farrell et al. (2003) reported that of six outcome measures to assess the treatment effects of a violence prevention program for rural adolescents, a PQOL measure was the most sensitive. Finally, Bearsley and Cummins (1999) reported significant changes in the Com-Qol subscales among adolescents who experienced significant disruptions in their living situation (i.e., homelessness). These findings suggest that PQOL measures are sensitive enough to capture fluctuations in perceived life quality due to changes in some life circumstances.

Alternative Forms of PQOL Measurement

Findings obtained from extant PQOL measures are based on self-reports, introducing the possibility of item misinterpretation or social desirability. In general, the findings for each scale largely attenuate such concerns. For example, the wording of items for each measure is intentionally simple so as to be interpretable across a wide array of age groups. For instance, MSLSS were written to be readable at the late first-to-second grade level, thus facilitating easy interpretation for youth of third grade level and above. Further, the internal consistency of the PQOL scales is considered adequate for research purposes, with the estimates usually ranging between .70 and .85 (see Gilman and Huebner 2000). Such findings suggest that youth respond to the items in a relatively consistent manner. Nevertheless, the internal consistency estimates can differ for youth from different nationalities (see Huebner et al. 2006), suggesting that items can be interpreted differently based on cultural nuances.

With respect to social desirability, studies often report correlations between PQOL and social desirability that are mild to moderate at best (Gilman and Barry 2003; Huebner 1991a; Huebner et al. 1998). If anything, given the nature of the construct under study, social desirability may reflect substantive individual differences that should be taken into account (Diener et al. 1999). Indeed, studies that are statistically controlled for social desirability do not improve correlations between social desirability and external criteria (e.g., Dew 1996), suggesting that social desirability does not indicate a serious threat to the validity of PQOL scales.

Nevertheless, as studies evolve from descriptive analyses of factors that contribute to high life quality among youth to more complex, theory-driven analyses, alternative forms of PQOL measurement will need to be considered. Some promising methods have been developed and implemented for youth populations. The use of experience sampling methodology (ESM) is one example. ESM involves repeated assessment of states, such as flow, a variable related to QOL, may be obtained throughout random periods in the course of a youth's day. These methods have been used in the context of various school settings (Shernoff et al. 2003), extracurricular activities (Larson 2000), child and family interactions (Rathunde 1997), and living situations (Asmussen and Larson 1991). Other methods have included reports by others (e.g., peers, parents) to corroborate PQOL self-reports. Findings have been generally positive in this regard. For example, using the SLSS, Dew and Huebner (1994a) obtained a moderate correlation ($r = .48$) between PQOL reports of high school students and their parents' estimates of their youths' PQOL. Similar correlations were noted between middle school students and their parents using the same scale (Gilman and Huebner 1997). Self-other correlations of this magnitude are not relegated to global PQOL measures. For example, correlations between adolescent and parent reports on the MSLSS ranged from .41 to .55 across the five domains of the scale (Huebner et al. 2002). Collectively, these findings support the association of parent-student PQOL reports, with correlations higher than what has been found among measures that assess psychopathology (e.g., Achenbach et al. 1987).

Levels of Child PQOL

Similar to studies of adults, most children and adolescents report positive levels of satisfaction with their overall lives as well as with specific domains. For example, in a study of more than 5,000 South Carolina (USA) adolescents, 26% reported that they were "delighted" with their lives overall, 29% reported "pleased," 18% reported "mostly satisfied," 16% reported "mixed," 4% reported "mostly dissatisfied," 3% reported "unhappy," and 4% reported "terrible" (Huebner et al. 2000a). Of five domains (family, friends, school, self, and living environment), satisfaction with the school domain was rated the lowest, with 9% of the students indicating "terrible," 7% indicating "unhappy," and 7% indicating "mostly dissatisfied." Similar findings were observed in a large-scale survey of middle schoolers in South Carolina as well (Huebner et al. 2005) and with studies of younger children in the USA and elsewhere (e.g., Korea, Spain) (see Huebner et al. 2006, for a review). Thus, although normative levels of PQOL are above the neutral point, indicating that most children are happy, there are significant numbers of youth who are not happy with their overall lives or with specific aspects of their lives.

A related point concern is whether there is a point in the PQOL continuum that yields diminishing positive returns. Incorporating Lazarus' (1991) theory of coping as a framework, it may be that the establishment of a positive mental "set point" serves as a signal against which ongoing cognitive appraisals, affective states, and environmental circumstances are compared. Although individuals who maintain a positive set point tend to garner positive psychological and psychosocial benefits throughout their lives (Lyubormirsky et al. 2005; Myers and Diener 1995), it has also been speculated that extreme PQOL levels above this set point may indicate unrealistic or distorted cognitive or emotional systems, which may result in maladaptive behaviors (Baumeister 1989; Boyd-Wilson et al. 2004; Taylor et al. 2000). That is, considering the stresses of day-to-day living that tend to keep this set point in check, extreme PQOL reporting may indicate naïveté at best and "smug complacency, obnoxious arrogance, and lack of motivation" at worst (Friedman et al. 2002, p. 355).

Although research is in its most preliminary stages for both adults and children, there is evidence to suggest that individuals at the extreme high end of the PQOL continuum obtain psychological, psychosocial, and psychoeducational benefits that are not observed even among individuals reporting "average" PQOL levels. For example, Diener and Seligman (2002) found that over a 2-month period, "very happy people" (i.e., college students) rated themselves and were rated by others as more social and extraverted, and they reported less psychological distress than individuals at the extreme low end of the continuum. Similar results were obtained by Friedman et al. (2002). Recent studies have found similar results among children. For example, Gilman and Huebner (2006) found that adolescents who were placed at the extreme positive end of the PQOL continuum (based on their global PQOL scores as indexed by the SLSS) reported significantly higher interpersonal and intrapersonal functioning than adolescents reporting extremely low PQOL scores. Further, compared to youth reporting "average" levels of PQOL, students with extremely high PQOL reported significantly lower scores on measures of interpersonal stress, anxiety, and depression, and higher scores on measures of hope, internal locus of control, self-esteem, and (positive) attitudes toward teachers. Suldo and Huebner (2006) reported similar findings in which very

high adolescent PQOL was associated with high social support and perceived competence, and virtually no psychopathology. Thus, evidence for limitations associated with high levels of PQOL has not been provided for children to date. Furthermore, these studies demonstrated that PQOL reports illuminate differences in adjustment that are not revealed by measures of psychopathology alone.

Correlates of PQOL

The correlates of PQOL among children can be organized within the ecological framework introduced by Bronfenbrenner (1979). This ecological approach examines children's PQOL vis-à-vis the major personal and environmental systems and reflects the multiplicity of interactive influences of the various systems.

Bronfenbrenner identified four different system levels: the micro-, meso-, exo-, and macrolevels. Belsky (1980) added the ontogenic level to the model. For the purposes of this review, the antecedents and correlates of children's PQOL can be organized into (1) the ontogenic system, which represents influential current and historical psychological characteristics of children; (2) the microsystem, which characterizes the immediate forces of family, friends, religious groups, and neighbors; (3) the exosystem and mesosystem, which involve settings that do not contain the children but that have indirect and/or interactive effects on them; and (4) the macrosystem, which involves overarching institutional patterns of the culture, including cultural and religious beliefs and values.

The Ontogenic Level Factors

At the core of the ecological paradigm are the ontogenic level factors that relate to child PQOL. In this level, the assumption is that individual differences affect children's PQOL. This model is transactional, which implies that not only is the child influenced by her or his environmental systems, but also that environmental systems are in turn affected by characteristics of the child, including PQOL.

Ontogenic factors include individual difference factors, such as personality characteristics, and historical factors, such as age.

Age

The findings for age have been equivocal. Studies that consist of American youth samples have consistently shown that age has no significant impact on children's global PQOL (Dew and Huebner 1994a; Gilman and Huebner 1997; Wilson et al. 1997). On the other hand, cross-cultural findings with non-American samples have reported conflicted findings. Man (1991) found that younger Hong Kong students in secondary schools reported higher levels of PQOL than older students. Chang et al. (2003) found that global PQOL tends to decline from childhood to adolescence. Park and Huebner (2005) found that an increase in age among South Korean students in secondary schooling is related to a decrease in both global and domain-specific PQOL. On the other hand, age differences have been reported for some specific domains, such as satisfaction with school experiences among American students (Huebner et al. 2000a; Okun et al. 1990; Nickerson and Nagle 2004).

Personality

Personality variables are strongly related to child and youth PQOL. Children who report high degrees of global PQOL are those who also report high self-esteem, extraversion, and internal locus of control (Huebner 1991a, b). Other studies have demonstrated that global and domain-specific self-concepts also correlated highly with reports of global PQOL among children and adolescents (Dew and Huebner 1994a; Gilman and Huebner 1997; McCullough et al. 2000; Terry and Huebner 1995). Fogle et al. (2002) found that global PQOL was associated with high levels of extraversion and perceived social self-efficacy, with social self-efficacy mediating the relationship between extraversion and PQOL.

Causal attribution, a cognitive variable, is also a key correlate of PQOL, linking personality to PQOL (Cheng and Furnham 2001; Rigby and Huebner 2005). In their sample of high school students, Rigby and Huebner (2005) found that students with an adaptive attribution style demonstrated higher global PQOL than students with a maladaptive attribution style. Furthermore, an adaptive attributional style partially mediated the relationship between emotional stability and PQOL. In other words, high school students who scored higher in emotional stability were more likely to make adaptive attributions, which were associated with higher PQOL.

Numerous studies show that children with lower global PQOL display negative behaviors that are associated with unfavorable outcomes. Low PQOL has been associated with a variety of psychopathological problems, such as depression, anxiety, and conduct disorder (Huebner and Alderman 1993; Greenspoon and Saklofske 1997; Huebner et al. 2000b; Suldo and Huebner 2004b; Valois et al. 2001). In a study of American school-aged students (ages 8–19), Adelman et al. (1989) found that students who were referred for mental health services demonstrated lower PQOL than nonreferred students. Newcomb et al. (1986) found that early alcohol usage was associated with dissatisfaction with peers and that this early dissatisfaction with peers preceded an increase in young adult alcohol usage. Students with low global PQOL may also be at risk for inappropriate dieting behaviors, unhealthy weight perceptions, and lack of physical exercise (see Huebner et al. 2004a, b for a review). Furthermore, poor physical health in adolescents is associated with a lower PQOL (Zullig et al. 2005).

Microsystem Level Factors

This system characterizes the influence of immediate environmental forces such as family, peers, and school, on children's PQOL. The factors subsumed under this level represent the interactions between child characteristics and these immediate environmental influences.

Family and Parental Factors
Parent Attachment

Child PQOL has been found to be positively associated with the quality of parent/child relationship (Leung and Leung 1992; Dew and Huebner 1994a). More specifically, one area that has been explored is the relationship between PQOL and the quality of the parent attachment relationship, that is, the extent to which the child feels securely attached to her or his parents. Several studies have demonstrated robust relationships between adolescent PQOL and a secure attachment with parents (Armsden and Greenberg 1987; Bradford and Lyddon 1994; Nickerson and Nagle 2004; Ma and Huebner 2008). In one study exploring the relationship between parent and peer attachment and PQOL, Nickerson and Nagle (2004) found that quality of parent attachment significantly predicted the level of PQOL of students in grades 4–8 and explained more variance in global PQOL than quality of peer attachment. Furthermore, parental trust was the most significant component of the attachment-global PQOL relationship. Grossman and Rowat (1995) concluded that a lack of paternal involvement and children's perception of poor relationship between their parents resulted in a negative effect on child PQOL.

Family Structures

Few studies have examined the relationship between family structures and global PQOL. Of the studies available, Demo and Acock (1996) reported that adolescents from the USA (ages 12–18) who resided with both parents reported higher PQOL. Similarly, Antaramian et al. (2008) found that adolescents from two-parent families reported higher family life satisfaction.

Parent-Child Relations

In examining the nature of parent-child relationships, parenting style plays a key role in predicting a child's global PQOL. Petito and Cummins (2000) demonstrated that authoritative parenting style was positively related to global PQOL among a group of adolescents from ages 12–17. In a similar study, Suldo and Huebner (2004a) investigated the relationship between dimensions of authoritative parenting styles (i.e., social support, strictness-supervision, and psychological autonomy granting) with global PQOL. Collectively, all three components of authoritative parenting styles significantly predicted global PQOL and contributed 26% of variance. Furthermore, when examining each component individually in terms of its predictive power, parental social support emerged as the strongest predictor of global PQOL, whereas strictness-supervisions and psychological autonomy granting accounted for a smaller amount of variance.

The importance of parent-child relationships is supported across cultures. For example, parent-adolescent disagreements are negatively related to PQOL in adolescents from European and Vietnamese-American cultures (Phinney and Ong 2002), and also among Chinese youth (Shek 1997).

Peer Factors

The sources of individual differences in PQOL also include the perceived quality of peer support. Dew and Huebner (1994a) found that children with higher levels of satisfaction with their peer relationships reported higher levels of global PQOL. Children who were not accepted by peers were found to express greater dissatisfaction (Green et al. 1980). Nickerson and Nagle (2004) found that peer attachment significantly predicted specific PQOL domains among different age groups. In their sample of children from ages 13 to 15, peer attachment significantly predicted global PQOL along with specific domains of PQOL (living environment satisfaction, self-satisfaction, school satisfaction). In the sample of children from ages 8 to 11, peer attachment significantly predicted specific domains of PQOL (living environment satisfaction and self-satisfaction). In the sample of children from ages 11 to 14, only one specific domain of PQOL, self-satisfaction, significantly predicted peer attachment. Their study also demonstrated that among the specific dimensions of peer attachments, peer trust was the most predictive dimension of PQOL.

The relative importance of peer attachments may vary as a function of gender and age, however. Ma and Huebner (2008) found that peer attachment mediated the relationship between parent attachment and PQOL in early adolescent age students, but only for females. The relationship between peer attachment and global PQOL was nonsignificant for male students, suggesting that peer relationships are much more critical to female students' PQOL, at least in early adolescence.

The quality and types of social experiences appear to have impact on children's global PQOL. Martin and Huebner (2007) investigated the interrelationship among positive social experiences, also known as prosocial experiences, peer victimization experiences, and global PQOL among middle school students. Specifically, they found that for both males and females, overt and relational victimization were significantly correlated with global PQOL. Additionally, prosocial experiences uniquely predicted global PQOL, above and beyond variance related to victimization experiences.

School Factors
School Performance

In general, PQOL appears unrelated to intellectual ability and modestly related at best to indicators of school performance, such as grades (Gilman and Huebner 2006; Huebner and Alderman 1993; Huebner 1991b; Leung and Leung 1992). One study found no significant mean difference in levels of global PQOL between a group of students deemed at academic risk and a group of normally achieving students (Huebner and Alderman 1993). The finding was also consistent for a sample of Chinese youths (Leung and Leung 1992). To the contrary, another study of Chinese students found that academic test scores were more predictive of children's than adolescents' PQOL (Chang et al. 2003). As suggested by the authors, this particular finding might be due to the uniqueness of Hong Kong's educational system, where children are exposed to more strict and elaborate testing sequences than adolescents. However, it is also possible that Asian students derive higher levels of global PQOL from positive school experiences due to the Asian culture's relatively high demands and expectations for children's school success. Relatedly, Park and Huebner (2005) found that Korean students' (mean age = 15) global PQOL was significantly related to their satisfaction with their school experiences, whereas American students' satisfaction with their school experiences did not contribute as much variance to their global PQOL.

Activities
Participation in school activities has demonstrated correlations with PQOL. Gilman (2001) investigated the relationship between structured extracurricular activities (SEA) and domain-specific PQOL reports. SEAs were defined as structured activities in which individuals remain actively engaged and mentally stimulated (e.g., participating in sports versus watching television). In his study, Gilman found that of the six PQOL domains, only the school domain demonstrated significant correlations with the frequency of SEA participation. Specifically, students who were involved in more self-selected structured extracurricular activities reported higher school satisfaction than students with fewer structured extracurricular activities. In a recent study using a sample of 490 students from grades 6 through 12 (mean age = 14.45), Gilman and Huebner (2006) investigated the relationship between the frequency of participation in structured extracurricular activities (SEAs) and students' *global* PQOL. The results demonstrated that students with "high" and "average" levels of PQOL reported participation in a higher number of SEAs than students with "low" levels of global PQOL.

School Perceptions and Engagement
An emerging body of literature provides evidence that school is also important to children's global PQOL (see Suldo et al. 2006, for a review). Students' levels of global PQOL are significantly related to several motivational variables, including students' *perceptions* of their academic abilities, teacher and classmate support,

and general satisfaction with school. Students who report higher levels of PQOL feel they can succeed with their schoolwork, perceive their teachers to be caring and supportive, and evaluate their schooling experiences positively. Students with high levels of *school* PQOL, in particular, also demonstrate fewer behavior problems, as well as higher grades and greater levels of participation (Baker et al. 2000; Huebner and Gilman 2006). Even among students as young as kindergarten age, lower levels of school satisfaction at the beginning of the year predict lower levels of engagement near the end of the year, which in turn predict decreased standardized academic test performance (Ladd et al. 2000).

Neighborhood Factors
Research suggests that neighborhood characteristics are significant predictors of global PQOL (e.g., Barresi et al. 1984; Morris and Winter 1978; Sirgy et al. 2000), especially variables centered around neighborhood support (Oberle et al. 2011). With respect to children and youth, Sam (1998) found that adolescents living in a relatively homogenous ethnic community or neighborhood reported higher PQOL than those living is ethnically diverse areas. Similar findings were reported by Neto (2000) with a sample of adolescents from immigrant backgrounds. Homel and Burns (1989) found that children who lived in nonresidential areas of inner cities, increasing the risk of social isolation, reported lower PQOL than children who lived in residential areas. Additionally, opportunities to bond with nonfamilial adults in the neighborhood were associated with higher PQOL (Paxton et al. 2006).

Chronic and Acute Life Events
In general, life events that are acute (e.g., death in the family) or chronic (e.g., living in a poor quality neighborhood) have modest to moderate levels of influence on children's PQOL (Ash and Huebner 2001; McCullough et al. 2000). In other words, stressful life events are related to PQOL, but not as strongly as might be expected (McCullough et al. 2000; McKnight et al. 2002). In one study, it was found that the relationship between chronic stressors and adolescents' global PQOL was partially mediated by locus of control orientation (Ash and Huebner 2001), suggesting that chronic stressors exert their effects on PQOL primarily through changes in children's cognitions. Furthermore, in the same study, it was found that acute stressors contributed 9.5% of the variance in PQOL reports, and the addition of chronic

stressors contributed an additional 19% of variance in PQOL reports, underscoring the importance of ongoing daily events in children's lives. In addition, chronic positive experiences were found to be a significant predictor of global PQOL above and beyond acute positive experiences in life. In a similar study, it was found that both acute and chronic life events added significant variance to the prediction of PQOL (McCullough et al. 2000). The frequencies of stressful life events also predicted an additional 3% of variance in PQOL, over and above what personality variables predicted (McKnight et al. 2002). Nevertheless, as with adults, life experiences account for modest amounts of variance in the PQOL of children and youth.

Mesosystem and Exosystem Level Factors

The systems include settings that exert indirect rather than direct influences on children's experiences. In Bronfenbrenner's own words, they "comprises the linkages and processes taking place between two or more settings, at least one of which does not contain the developing person, but in which events occur that indirectly influence processes within the immediate setting in which the developing person lives" (Bronfenbrenner 1989, p. 227). Examples would include home-school and school-community interactions and their impact on PQOL for children. Studies of PQOL at these levels of Bronfenbrenner's framework have rarely been conducted.

Macrosystem Level Factors

The macrosystem includes, but is not limited to, the cultural variables that influence the individual. It also can be thought of as "a societal blueprint for a particular culture or subculture" (Bronfenbrenner 1989, p. 228). This system includes cultural beliefs that children and adolescents have adopted regarding family values and cultural norms. The macrosystem also includes economic, educational, legal, and political systems. Research on child and youth PQOL at this level has also been sparse; however, preliminary findings are reported below.

Gender
Similar to findings for students' age, findings for students' gender have also been mixed. The majority of

studies consisting of American youth samples reported that global PQOL is not significantly related to gender (Huebner 1991a, b, c; Wilson et al. 1997). Cross-culturally, gender differences have been reported in samples of Turkish students residing in Netherlands (Verkuyten 1986) and Portuguese students (Neto 1993). Similar to findings with respect to age differences, gender differences have been reported for specific domains, such as school satisfaction in US students (Huebner et al. 2000a; Huebner 1994a, b; Nickerson and Nagle 2004).

Socioeconomic Status (SES)
Although the majority of the studies have found nonsignificant correlations between SES and global PQOL (Gilman and Huebner 1997; Sam 1998; Wilson et al. 1997; Huebner 1991a, b, c), these studies have also been limited mostly to samples of American youth. Among a sample of Latino students, Rodriguez et al. (2003) found that SES was a significant predictor of PQOL. As Veenhoven (1988) suggested, the significance of SES for individuals' PQOL may have different bearings under divergent circumstances and cultures. In a society where a high standard of living is important, the relationship between SES and PQOL might be more pronounced (Grob et al. 1996). In a sample of Chinese college students, Tong and Song (2004) found that SES was a significant predictor of global PQOL. They found that low-SES Chinese students scored lower on global PQOL than their average-SES Chinese peers.

Ethnic Differences
The findings for the associations between race and global PQOL among American students have been mixed. Studies have found no difference in mean levels of overall PQOL between African-American students and Caucasian students (Huebner 1995; Huebner et al. 2000a, b). However, Gilman (2001) found that African-American students with medium and high levels of social interest reported higher PQOL than their Caucasian counterparts.

In general, cross-cultural studies have reported that most children and adolescents are satisfied with their lives. These findings are generated from samples of Canadian students (Greenspoon and Saklofske 1997), Chinese students (Leung and Leung 1992; Chang et al. 2003), Spanish students (Casas et al. 2001), and Korean students (Park and Huebner 2005). Neto (1995) found that young Portuguese living in France did not differ in levels of global PQOL from young Portuguese living in Portugal. Sam (1998) found that Vietnamese, Pakistanis, Turks, and Chileans did not differ in global PQOL from Norwegian adolescents. However, Gilman et al. (2008) found that although most of the youth in their samples of students from Ireland, USA, China, and South Korea reported positive PQOL, there were some exceptions for some specific domains, including satisfaction with school (Ireland, South Korea, USA), living environments (China, South Korea), self (South Korea), and general PQOL (South Korea).

Others

Cultural experiences may have profound influences on an individual's PQOL. Although few research studies have been directly devoted to the study of cultural beliefs of children and their relations to global PQOL, cross-cultural studies have found that members of Eastern cultures are more likely to emphasize the collectivist ideology, where harmony with group members is key. On the other hand, the self is considered primary in Western cultures, and personal characteristics such as attributes and goals are more valued and valid in predicting PQOL (Suh et al. 1998). A comparison of youth from Korea versus the USA showed similarities and differences in the associations between domain-specific PQOL reports and global PQOL reports across the two groups (Park and Huebner 2005). In this study, cross-cultural comparisons were made on PQOL scores between 472 Korean students (ages 12–17) and 543 US students. The results showed that in general, Korean students scored lower PQOL than US students across all specific domains of PQOL (i.e., family, school, living environment, self) and global PQOL. Specifically, the largest statistically significant difference was detected for the self domain, with US students reporting higher scores than Korean students. The study also investigated the correlation of specific PQOL domains with global PQOL across the two cultures. The findings revealed that different domains of PQOL served as correlates of global PQOL. Specifically, the self domain contributed more variance to global PQOL for US students than for Korean students, while the school domain was a stronger predictor of global PQOL for the Korean students.

In another large-scale cross-cultural study, Grob et al. (1999) examined the relationship between subjective well-being and agentic variables (strain, global coping, emotion-oriented coping, problem-oriented coping) for 3,250 adolescent students residing in Eastern and Western European countries and the USA. The main goal of the study was to determine whether predictors of the subjective well-being are of the same kind and hold the same predictive power across Western and Eastern countries. The study reported several intriguing findings. First, in general, adolescent students from both macrocontexts (Western and Eastern countries) reported overall high mean levels of subjective well-being. Second, a closer examination revealed that students from all Western countries, with exception of France, reported significant higher subjective well-being ratings than their Eastern countries' counterparts. Third, for adolescents from the Western countries, problem-oriented coping was more significantly positively associated with subjective well-being than for adolescents from Eastern countries. In this large-scale cross-cultural study, adolescents from both macrocontexts shared more similarities than differences in their overall level of well-being. This conclusion was expected given the commonalities among the Western and Eastern countries in terms of ethnic makeup and religious beliefs. Taken together, this may inform the findings of Park and Huebner (2005) with Korean and US students. Thus, future studies of children's PQOL should attend to the importance of how differences in cultural norms, ideology, and practices may influence the antecedents and consequences of individual differences in children's PQOL.

Conclusions

Based on this review, the following conclusions appear warranted regarding child PQOL (ages 8–18):

1. Although the development of PQOL measures appropriate for children has only recently been undertaken, there is promising, preliminary support for the convergent and discriminant validity of PQOL measures. The lack of research with children younger than the age of 8 is notable. Researchers will need to develop measures that are suitable to younger children.

2. Most children report global PQOL scores in the positive range (i.e., above a neutral point). That is, most children are happy. PQOL is variable across specific domains; some groups of children may not show a positive "set point" in relation to specific domains. Significant numbers of children and youth may report greater dissatisfaction in some areas of

their lives (e.g., secondary level US students' reports of satisfaction with their school experiences).

3. Demographic relationships appear to account for modest amounts of variance in child PQOL reports, except perhaps in the case of those children and youth suffering from extreme poverty or other extremely negative conditions (e.g., adjudicated youth).

4. Ontogenic (i.e., intrapersonal and developmental history) variables, including personality, cognitive, and affective variables, relate strongly to child PQOL. The influence of personality variables on PQOL appears to be mediated by cognitive factors, such as perceptions of self-efficacy and attribution processes. The study of developmental history variables awaits long-term longitudinal studies of children's well-being (see below).

5. Environmental events and experiences relate significantly to child PQOL. Personal and environmental variables appear to interact to determine child PQOL. The influence of environmental variables on PQOL also appears to be mediated by cognitive factors, such as self-efficacy. Research supports the importance of *multiple* contextual factors, ranging from the family to the peer group and school and neighborhood (Oberle et al. 2011). Studies have yet to explore interactions among major environmental systems (e.g., community-school relations).

6. Interpersonal relationships, especially family relationships, are of paramount importance to high PQOL in children and adolescents. Satisfying family relationships are important across all ages studied (ages 8–18). Peer relationships and experiences are critical as well, but may be differentially related to gender and age.

7. Extant measures of PQOL differentiate several groups of children in expected ways (e.g., students with emotional disabilities, adjudicated youth). Students with lower global PQOL are more likely to display a variety of mental health, physical, and school-related problems.

8. The meaning and correlates of PQOL likely differ across race, culture, nation, and developmental level.

9. PQOL is not an epiphenomenon; global PQOL influences important child outcomes, such as peer victimization (Martin et al. 2008) and withdrawal of parental emotional support (Saha et al. 2010).

Taken together, these studies indicate support for the study of child PQOL. Although such research is just beginning, the preliminary findings are consistent with studies of adults and with complex models of the antecedents and consequences of individual differences in life satisfaction, including personality/temperament factors, environmental factors, cognitive mediators, and behavioral consequences (see Lent 2004). Nevertheless, given that children have less control over their lives than adults, it seems likely that developmental differences related to cognitive, social-emotional, and physical maturation interacting with related environmental experiences likely play some moderating role in the determination, expression, and consequences of PQOL across the developmental trajectory from childhood to adulthood. The relevance of particular domains of PQOL is likely also subject to developmental considerations (see Gilligan and Huebner 2007).

Implications for Research and Policy

Future child and adolescent PQOL research should address several neglected issues. First, theory-based research is needed to direct future studies. Although this line of inquiry is in an early stage of development, the derivation of testable theories of child PQOL is a key next step. To date, few theory-based studies have appeared in the literature. Second, the development of psychometrically sound, child-focused PQOL measures has also begun only recently. As recommended by Gilman and Huebner (2000), existing child-focused PQOL measures would benefit from rigorous studies of basic psychometric properties, including evaluations of normative samples, reliability, and validity. Additionally, research is needed to more thoroughly assess the effects of response distortions, importance ratings, developmental changes, cultural differences, and disabilities on child PQOL ratings. Third, research on child PQOL has been limited mostly to cross-sectional research. Studies of the correlates of PQOL offer a useful initial step; however, the advancement of PQOL research requires longitudinal and/or experimental studies to clarify the directionality of relationships. Studies, such as those by Martin et al. (2008), Shek (1998), and Suldo and Huebner (2004b), in which low PQOL was shown to precede the occurrence of psychopathological behaviors and victimization experiences, offer needed information regarding the directionality of PQOL effects as well as potential support for dual-factor models of mental health (Greenspoon and Saklofske 2000; Suldo and Shaffer 2008). Given the importance of the school context in the lives of children and youth, increasing attention to studies of transactional relationships between PQOL and school experiences should shed considerable light on the range of effects of PQOL in this age group.

Fourth, studies of the usefulness of PQOL reports as indicators of intervention effects would be beneficial. Although some studies suggest that PQOL reports may operate as useful outcome measures (e.g., Farrell et al. 2003; Gilman and Handwerk 2001), much additional research is needed. For an excellent example from the adult PQOL literature, Frisch et al. (2005) demonstrate effective strategies for conducting treatment sensitivity research that would be applicable to children as well.

Finally, cross-cultural research is essential for investigating the universality of findings related to the nature, determinants, and consequences of individual differences in child PQOL reports. Research with adults has underscored the importance of caution with respect to generalizing across different racial, cultural, and national groups. To date, few cross-national and/or cross-cultural studies of children and adolescents have been conducted. Nevertheless, preliminary work suggests important cultural differences with regard to individual's attribution processes as well as in norms for expressing negative emotions and cognition (Grob et al. 1999).

In conclusion, PQOL research with children and adolescents has yielded rich findings. Overall, PQOL appears to be a meaningful construct with children as early as approximately 8 years of age. PQOL is related to wide array of important variable, indicating the central importance of the construct for child development. Nevertheless, using Bronfenbrenner's ecological (1989) framework, limitations of the existing body of research are apparent. To date, studies of PQOL in children and youth have emphasized more proximal variables to the relative neglect of more distal meso-, exo-, and macrosystem variables. Continued research in these neglected areas appears warranted to capture the full complexity of child and youth PQOL. Such ecological research that is informed by developmental considerations should be particularly crucial.

Child PQOL literature suggests social policy implications. Layard (2005) has offered provocative suggestions for national policies based on well-being research. In general, Layard's suggestions for policy making are aimed at promoting optimal well-being at the macrosystemic level through attention to the major child supports (microsystemic environments of family, school, community) that appear to help shape child well-being and competence.

Particularly pertinent are his suggestions for family policies that relate to the welfare of children. Consistent with the findings of the central importance of families to child and adolescent PQOL across the full range of development, Layard suggests the need to develop policies that protect and support the development of healthy children and families, including compulsory prenatal and parenting classes, more family-friendly policies at work (flexible work hours, parental leave options), increased availability of high-quality child care (priced in relation to income), and changes in public attitudes toward the responsibilities of raising children, geographical mobility, and educational goals for their children. In doing so, children's most proximal environmental experiences should be characterized by fewer family stresses, marital discord, family breakups, and so forth that impede healthy child development and PQOL. With respect to educational goals, Layard argues that the school curriculum should incorporate moral education activities throughout a child's school years, leading to the "development of a sense of purpose wider than oneself" (p. 234), consistent with findings that child and youth PQOL is associated with positive interpersonal behaviors. Specifically, curricular activities should include topics such as control over negative emotions, parenting, mental illness, and citizenship. Specific recommendations for addressing such topics are elaborated upon by various educational scholars in Gilman et al. (2009).

The broad-based QOL perspective that incorporates children's perceptions of their well-being in addition to the traditional objective QOL perspective draws attention to the advantages of monitoring child well-being (including PQOL) on a national, if not, international basis. The developing research base provides important insights into new ways of defining and understanding the determinants and consequences of child and youth QOL and well-being, including the child's subjective perspective, to help optimize the functioning of all citizens. For example, policies based on QOL research that provide more optimal environments for children should likely in turn lead to the promotion of an "upward spiral" (Fredrickson 1998), that is, more positive primary environmental systems (e.g., healthy families, stronger communities, safe and healthy schools).

Of course, such broad-based interventions need to be accompanied by comprehensive research and evaluation efforts to systematically evaluate their effectiveness so that science is informed by practice (policy) as well as practice is informed by science.

References

Achenbach, T. M., McConaughy, S. H., & Howell, C. T. (1987). Child/adolescent behavioral and emotional problems: Implications of cross-informant correlations for situational specificity. *Psychological Bulletin, 101*, 213–232.

Adelman, H. S., Taylor, L., & Nelson, P. (1989). Minors' dissatisfaction with their life circumstances. *Child Psychiatry and Human Development, 20*, 135–147.

Antaramian, S. J., Huebner, E. S., & Valois, R. F. (2008). Adolescent life satisfaction. *Applied Psychology: Health and Well-Being, 57*, 112–126.

Antaramian, S. J., Huebner, E. S., Hills, K. J., & Valois, R. F. (2010). A dual-factor model of mental health: Toward a more comprehensive understanding of youth functioning. *The American Journal of Orthopsychiatry, 80*, 462–472.

Armsden, G. C., & Greenberg, M. T. (1987). The inventory of parent and peer attachment: Relationships to well-being in adolescence. *Journal of Youth and Adolescence, 16*, 427–454.

Ash, C., & Huebner, E. S. (2001). Environmental events and life satisfaction reports of adolescents: A test of cognitive mediation. *School Psychology International, 22*, 320–336.

Asmussen, L., & Larson, R. (1991). The quality of family time among young adolescents in single-parent and married-parent families. *Journal of Marriage and the Family, 53*, 1021–1030.

Atienza, F. L., Balaguer, I., & Garcia-Merita, M. (2003). Satisfaction with life scale: Analysis of factorial invariance across sexes. *Personality and Individual Differences, 35*, 1255–1260.

Baker, J. A., Dilly, L. J., Aupperlee, J. L., & Patil, S. A. (2000). The developmental context of school satisfaction: Schools as psychologically healthy environments. *School Psychology Quarterly, 18*, 206–221.

Barresi, C. M., Ferraro, K. F., & Hobey, L. (1984). Environmental satisfaction, sociability, and well-being among the urban elderly. *International Journal of Aging & Human Development, 18*, 227–293.

Bastiaansen, D., Koot, H. M., Bongers, I. L., Varni, J. W., & Verhulst, F. C. (2004). Measuring quality of life in children referred for psychiatric problems: Psychometric properties of the PedsQL-super(TM) 4.0 generic core scales. *Quality of Life Research: An International Journal of Quality of Life Aspects of Treatment, Care, and Rehabilitation, 13*, 489–495.

Baumeister, R. F. (1989). The optimal margin of illusion. *Journal of Social and Clinical Psychology, 8*, 176–189.

Bearsley, C., & Cummins, R. A. (1999). No place called home: Life quality and purpose of homeless youths. *Journal of Social Distress and the Homeless, 8*, 207–226.

Beh-Arieh, A., & George, R. (2001). How do we monitor the state of our children. *Children and Youth Services Review, 23*, 603–631.

Belsky, J. (1980). Child maltreatment: An ecological integration. *American Psychologist, 35*, 320–335.

Bender, T. A. (1997). Assessment of subjective well-being during childhood and adolescence. In G. Phye (Ed.), *Handbook of classroom assessment: Learning, achievement, and adjustment* (pp. 199–255). San Diego: Academic.

Boyd-Wilson, B. M., McClure, J., & Walkey, F. H. (2004). Are well-being and illusory perceptions linked? The answer may be yes, but…. *Australian Journal of Psychology, 56*, 1–9.

Bradford, E., & Lyddon, W. J. (1994). Assessing adolescent and adult attachment: An update. *Journal of Counseling and Development, 73*, 215–219.

Bronfenbrenner, U. (1979). *The ecology of human development: Experiments by nature and design*. Cambridge: Harvard University Press.

Bronfenbrenner, U. (1989). Ecological systems theory. *Annals of Child Development, 6*, 187–249.

Campbell, A. (1976). Subjective measures of well-being. *American Psychologist, 31*, 117–124.

Casas, F., Alsinet, C., Rosich, M., Huebner, E. S., & Laughlin, J. E. (2001). *Cross-cultural investigation of the multidimensional students life satisfaction scale with Spanish adolescents*. Paper presented at the Third Conference of the International Society for Quality of Life Studies, Girona, Spain.

Chan, K. S., Mangione, S. R., Burwinkle, T. M., & Varni, J. W. (2005). The PedsQLTM: Reliability and validity of the short-form generic core scales and asthma module. *Medical Care, 4*, 256–265.

Chang, L., McBride-Chang, C., Stewart, S. M., & Au, E. (2003). Life satisfaction, self-concept, and family relations in Chinese adolescents and children. *International Journal of Behavioral Development, 27*, 182–189.

Cheng, H., & Furnham, A. (2001). Attributional style and personality as predictors of happiness and mental health. *Journal of Happiness Studies, 2*, 307–327.

Cummins, R. A. (1997). *Manual for the comprehensive quality of life scale-student (Grades 7–12): ComQol-S5* (5th ed). Deakin University, Melbourne: School of Psychology.

Demo, D., & Acock, A. (1996). Family structure, family process, and adolescent well-being. *Journal of Research on Adolescence, 6*, 457–488.

Detmar, S. (2005). Children with cancer: The quality of life. *Quality of Life Research: An International Journal of Quality of Life Aspects of Treatment, Care and Rehabilitation, 14*, 1649–1650.

Dew, T. (1996). *Preliminary development and validation of a multidimensional life satisfaction scale for adolescents*. Unpublished doctoral dissertation, University of South Carolina, Columbia, SC.

Dew, T., & Huebner, E. S. (1994). Adolescents' perceived quality of life: An exploratory investigation. *Journal of School Psychology, 31*, 185–199.

Diener, E. (1994). Assessing subjective well-being: Progress and opportunities. *Social Indicators Research, 31*, 103–157.

Diener, E. (2000). Subjective well-being: The science of happiness and a proposal for a national index. *American Psychologist, 55*, 34–43.

Diener, E. (2003). What is positive about positive psychology: The curmudgeon and the pollyanna. *Psychological Inquiry, 14*, 115–120.

Diener, E., & Seligman, M. E. P. (2002). Very happy people. *Psychological Science, 13*, 81–84.

Diener, E., & Suh, E. (1997). Measuring quality of life: Economic, social, and subjective indicators. *Social Indicators Research, 40*, 189–216.

Diener, E., Emmons, R. A., Larsen, R. J., & Griffin, S. (1985). The satisfaction with life scale. *Journal of Personality Assessment, 49*, 71–75.

Diener, E., Suh, E. M., Lucas, R. E., & Smith, H. L. (1999). Subjective well-being: Three decades of progress. *Psychological Bulletin, 125*, 276–302.

Fallowfield, L. (1994). An overview of quality of life measurements. In W. E. Dodson & M. R. Trimble (Eds.), *Epilepsy and quality of life* (pp. 85–98). New York: Raven.

Farrell, A. D., Valois, R. F., & Meyer, A. L. (2003). Impact of the RIPP violence prevention program on rural middle school students. *Journal of Primary Prevention, 24*, 143–167.

Fattore, T., Mason, J., & Watson, E. (2007). Children's conceptualization of their well-being. *Social Indicators Research, 80*, 5–29.

Fogle, L. M., Huebner, E. S., & Laughlin, J. E. (2002). The relationship between temperament and life satisfaction in adolescence: Cognitive and behavioral mediation models. *Journal of Happiness Studies, 3*, 373–392.

Fredrickson, B. (1998). What good are positive emotions? *Review of General Psychology, 2*, 300–319.

Friedman, E. T., Schwartz, R. M., & Haaga, D. A. F. (2002). Are the very happy too happy? *Journal of Happiness Studies, 3*, 355–372.

Frisch, M. (2006). *Quality of life therapy: Applying a life satisfaction approach to positive psychology and cognitive therapy.* New York: John Wiley and Sons.

Frisch, M. B. (1999). Quality of life assessment/intervention and the Quality of Life Inventory (QOLI). In M. R. Maruish (Ed.), *The use of psychological assessment for treatment planning and outcome assessment* (Vol. 2, pp. 1227–1331). Hillsdale: Erlbaum.

Frisch, M. B., Clark, M. P., & Rouse, S. V. (2005). Predictive and treatment validity of life satisfaction and the quality of life inventory. *Psychological Assessment, 12*, 66–78.

Gilligan, T., & Huebner, E. S. (2007). Initial development and validation of the multidimensional students life satisfaction scale-adolescent version. *Applied Research in Quality of Life, 2*, 1–16.

Gilman, R. (2001). The relationship between life satisfaction, social interest, and frequency of extracurricular activities among adolescent students. *Journal of Youth and Adolescence, 30*, 749–767.

Gilman, R., & Barry, J. (2003). Life satisfaction and social desirability among adolescents in a residential treatment setting: Changes across time. *Residential Treatment for Children and Youth, 21*, 19–42.

Gilman, R., & Handwerk, M. L. (2001). Changes in life satisfaction as a function of stay in a residential setting. *Residential Treatment for Children and Youth, 18*, 47–65.

Gilman, R., & Huebner, E. S. (1997). Children's reports of their life satisfaction: Convergence across raters, time, and response formats. *School Psychology International, 18*, 229–243.

Gilman, R., & Huebner, E. S. (2000). Review of life satisfaction measures for adolescents. *Behaviour Change, 17*, 178–195.

Gilman, R., & Huebner, E. S. (2003). A review of life satisfaction research with children and adolescents. *School Psychology Quarterly, 18*, 192–205.

Gilman, R., & Huebner, E. S. (2006). Characteristics of adolescents who report very high life satisfaction. *Journal of Youth and Adolescence, 35*, 311–319.

Gilman, R., Huebner, E. S., & Laughlin, J. E. (2000). A first study of the multidimensional students' life satisfaction scale with adolescents. *Social Indicators Research, 52*, 135–160.

Gilman, R., Huebner, E. S., Tian, L., Park, N., O'Byrne, J., Schiff, M., Sverko, D., & Langknecht, H. (2008). Cross-national adolescent multidimensional life satisfaction reports: Analyses of mean scores and response style differences. *Journal of Youth and Adolescence, 37*, 142–154.

Gilman, R., Huebner, E. S., & Furlong, M. J. (2009). *Handbook of positive psychology in the schools.* New York: Routledge.

Green, K. D., Forehand, R., Beck, S. J., & Vosk, B. (1980). An assessment of the relationship among measures of children's social competence and children's academic achievement. *Child Development, 51*, 1149–1156.

Greenspoon, P. J., & Saklofske, D. H. (1997). Validity and reliability of the multidimensional students' life satisfaction scale with Canadian children. *Journal of Psychoeducational Assessment, 15*, 138–155.

Greenspoon, P. J., & Saklofske, D. H. (2000). Toward an integration of subjective well-being and psychopathology. *Social Indicators Research, 54*, 81–108.

Grob, A., Little, T. D., Wanner, B., Wearing, A. J., & Euronet. (1996). Adolescent well-being and perceived control across fourteen sociocultural contexts. *Journal of Personality and Social Psychology, 71*, 785–795.

Grob, A., Stetsenko, A., Sabatier, C., Botcheva, L., & Macek, P. (1999). A cross-national model of subjective well-being in adolescence. In F. Alsaker (Ed.), *The adolescent experience: European and American adolescents in the 1990s* (pp. 115–130). Mahwah: Erlbaum.

Grossman, M., & Rowat, K. (1995). Parental relationships, coping strategies, received support, and well-being in adolescents of separated or divorced and married parents. *Research Nurse Health, 18*, 249–261.

Gullone, E., & Cummins, R. A. (1999). The comprehensive quality of life scale: A psychometric evaluation with an adolescent sample. *Behaviour Change, 16*, 127–139.

Homel, R., & Burns, A. (1989). Environmental quality and the well-being of children. *Social Indicators Research, 21*, 133–158.

Huebner, E. S. (1991a). Initial development of the students' life satisfaction scale. *School Psychology International, 12*, 231–240.

Huebner, E. S. (1991b). Correlates of life satisfaction in children. *School Psychology Quarterly, 6*, 103–111.

Huebner, E. S. (1991c). Further validation of the students' life satisfaction scale: The independence of satisfaction and affect ratings. *Journal of Psychoeducational Assessment, 9*, 363–368.

Huebner, E. S. (1994a). Preliminary development and validation of a multidimensional life satisfaction scale for children. *Psychological Assessment, 6*, 149–158.

Huebner, E. S. (1994b). Conjoint analyses of the students' life satisfaction scale and the Piers-Harris self-concept scale. *Psychology in the Schools, 31*, 273–277.

Huebner, E. S. (1995). The students life satisfaction scale: An assessment of. psychometric properties with black and white elementary school students. *Social Indicators Research, 34*, 315–323.

Huebner, E. S. (2004). Research and assessment of life satisfaction of children and adolescents. *Social Indicators Research, 66*, 3–33.

Huebner, E. S., & Alderman, G. L. (1993). Convergent and discriminant validation of a children's life satisfaction scale: Its relationship to self- and teacher-reported psychological problems and school functioning. *Social Indicators Research, 30*, 71–82.

Huebner, E. S., & Dew, T. (1993). Is life satisfaction multidimensional? The factor structure of the perceived life satisfaction scale. *Journal of Psychoeducational Assessment, 11*, 345–350.

Huebner, E. S., & Gilman, R. (2006). Students who like and dislike school. *Applied Research in Quality of Life, 1*, 139–150.

Huebner, E. S., Laughlin, J. E., Ash, C., & Gilman, R. (1998). Further validation of the multidimensional students' life satisfaction scale. *Journal of Psychoeducational Assessment, 16*, 118–134.

Huebner, E. S., Gilman, R., & Laughlin, J. E. (1999). A multimethod investigation of the multidimensionality of children's well-being reports: Discriminant validity of life satisfaction and self-esteem. *Social Indicators Research, 46*, 1–22.

Huebner, E. S., Drane, J. W., & Valois, R. F. (2000a). Levels and demographic correlates of adolescent life satisfaction reports. *School Psychology International, 21*, 281–292.

Huebner, E. S., Funk, B. A., & Gilman, R. (2000b). Crosssectional and longitudinal psychosocial correlates of adolescent life satisfaction reports. *Canadian Journal of School Psychology, 16*, 53–64.

Huebner, E. S., Brantley, A., Nagle, R. J., & Valois, R. F. (2002). Correspondence between parent and adolescent ratings of life satisfaction for adolescents with and without mild mental disabilities. *Journal of Psychoeducational Assessment, 20*, 20–29.

Huebner, E. S., Suldo, S. M., Smith, L. C., & McKnight, C. G. (2004a). Life satisfaction in children and youth: Empirical foundations and implications for school psychologists. *Psychology in the Schools, 41*, 81–93.

Huebner, E. S., Valois, R. F., Suldo, S. M., Smith, L. C., McKnight, C. G., Seligson, J. L., & Zullig, K. J. (2004b). Perceived quality of life: A neglected component of adolescent health assessment and intervention. *Journal of Adolescent Health, 34*, 270–278.

Huebner, E. S., Valois, R. F., Paxton, R. J., & Drane, J. W. (2005). Middle school students' perceptions of quality of life. *Journal of Happiness Studies, 6*, 15–24.

Huebner, E. S., Suldo, S., & Gilman, R. (2006). Life satisfaction. In G. Bear & K. Minke (Eds.), *Children's needs-III* (pp. 357–368). Bethesda: National Association of School Psychologists.

Jahoda, M. (1958). *Current concepts of positive mental health.* New York: Basic Books.

Kazdin, A. (1993). Adolescent mental health: Prevention and treatment programs. *American Psychologist, 48*, 127–141.

Keyes, C. L. M. (2005). Mental illness and/or mental health? Investigating axioms of the complete state model of health. *Journal of Counseling and Clinical Psychology:, 17*, 539–548.

Keyes, C. L. M. (2006). Mental health in adolescence: Is America's youth flourishing? *The American Journal of Orthopsychiatry, 76*, 395–402.

Ladd, G. W., Buhs, E. S., & Seid, S. M. (2000). Children's initial sentiments about kindergarten: Is school liking an antecedent of early classroom participation and achievement? *Merrill-Palmer Quarterly, 46*, 255–279.

Lance, C. E., Lautenschlager, G. J., Sloan, C. E., & Varca, P. E. (1989). A comparison between bottom-up, top-down, and bidirectional models of relationships between global and life facet satisfaction. *Journal of Personality, 57*, 601–624.

Lance, C. E., Mallard, A. G., & Michalos, A. C. (1995). Tests of the causal directions of global-life facet satisfaction relationships. *Social Indicators Research, 34*, 69–92.

Land, K. C., Lamb, V. L., & Meadows, S. O. (2007). Measuring trends in child well-being: An evidence-based approach. *Social Indicators Research, 80*, 105–122.

Larson, R. W. (2000). Toward a psychology of positive youth development. *American Psychologist, 55*, 170–183.

Layard, R. (2005). *Happiness: Lessons of a new science.* New York: Penguin Press.

Lazarus, R. S. (1991). *Emotion and adaptation.* New York: Oxford University Press.

Lent, R. W. (2004). Toward a unifying theoretical and practical perspective on well-being and psychosocial adjustment. *Journal of Counseling Psychology, 51*, 482–509.

Lent, R. W., Singley, D., Sheu, H. B., Gainor, K. A., Brnenner, B. R., Treistman, D., & Ades, L. (2005). Social cognitive predictors of domain and life satisfaction: Exploring the theoretical precursors of subjective well-being. *Journal of Counseling Psychology, 52*, 429–442.

Leung, J., & Leung, K. (1992). Life satisfaction, self-concept, and relationship with parents in adolescence. *Journal of Youth and Adolescence, 21*, 653–665.

Lopez, S. J., Snyder, C. R., & Rasmussen, H. N. (2003). Striking a vital balance: Developing a complementary focus on human weakness and strength through positive psychological assessment. In C. R. Snyder & S. J. Lopez (Eds.), *Positive psychological assessment: A handbook of models and measures* (pp. 3–20). Washington: American Psychological Association.

Lyubormirsky, S., King, L. A., & Diener, E. (2005). The benefits of frequent positive affect: Does happiness lead to success? *Psychological Bulletin, 131*, 803–855.

Ma, C., & Huebner, E. S. (2008). Attachment and life satisfaction among early adolescents: Some relationships matter more to girls than boys. *Psychology in the Schools, 45*, 177–190.

Man, P. (1991). The influence of peers and parents on youth life satisfaction in Hong Kong. *Social Indicators Research, 24*, 347–365.

Marriage, K., & Cummins, R. A. (2004). Subjective quality of life and self-esteem in children: The role of primary and secondary control in coping with everyday stress. *Social Indicators Research, 66*, 107–122.

Martin, K., & Huebner, E. S. (2007). Peer victimization, prosocial experiences, and emotional well-being of middle school students. *Psychology in the Schools, 44*, 199–208.

Martin, K., Huebner, E. S., & Valois, R. F. (2008). Does life satisfaction predict victimization experiences in adolescents? *Psychology in the Schools, 45*, 705–714.

Masten, A. S. (2001). Ordinary magic : Resilience processes in development. *American Psychologist, 56*, 227–238.

Matza, L. S., Swensen, A. R., Flood, E. M., Secnik, K., & Leidy, N. K. (2004). Assessment of health-related quality of life in children: A review of conceptual, methodological, and regulatory issues. *Values in Health, 7*, 72–92.

McCullough, G., Huebner, E. S., & Laughlin, J. E. (2000). Life events, self-concept, and adolescents' positive subjective well-being. *Psychology in the Schools, 37*, 281–290.

McKnight, C., Huebner, E. S., & Suldo, S. M. (2002). Relationships among stressful life events, temperament, problem behavior, and global life satisfaction. *Psychology in the Schools, 39*, 677–687.

Morris, E. W., & Winter, M. (1978). *Housing, family, and society.* New York: Wiley.

Myers, D. G., & Diener, E. (1995). Who is happy? *Psychological Science, 6*, 10–19.

Neto, F. (1993). The satisfaction with life scale: Psychometric properties in an adolescent sample. *Journal of Youth and Adolescence, 22*, 125–134.

Neto, F. (1995). Predictors of satisfaction with life among second-generation migrants. *Social Indicators Research, 35*, 93–116.

Neto, F. (2000). Satisfaction with life among adolescents from immigrant families in Portugal. *Journal of Youth and Adolescence, 30*, 53–67.

Newcomb, M. D., Bentler, P. M., & Collins, C. (1986). Alcohol use and dissatisfaction with self and life: A longitudinal analysis of young adults. *Journal of Drug Issues, 63*, 479–494.

Nickerson, A., & Nagle, R. J. (2004). The influence of parent and peer attachments on life satisfaction in middle childhood and early adolescence. *Social Indicators Research, 66*, 35–60.

Oberle, E., Schonert-Reichl, K. A., & Zumbo, B. D. (2011). Life satisfaction in early adolescence: Personal, neighborhood, school, family, and peer influences. *Journal of Youth and Adolescence, 40*, 889–901.

Okun, M., Braver, M. W., & Weir, R. (1990). Grade level differences in school satisfaction. *Social Indicators Research, 49*, 419–428.

Park, N., & Huebner, E. S. (2005). A cross-cultural study of the levels and correlates of life satisfaction among adolescents. *Journal of Cross-Cultural Psychology, 36*, 444–456.

Park, N., Huebner, E. S., Laughlin, J. E., Valois, R. F., & Gilman, R. (2004). A cross-cultural comparison of the dimensions of child and adolescent life satisfaction reports. *Social Indicators Research, 66*, 61–79.

Paxton, R., Valois, R. F., Huebner, E. S., & Drane, J. W. (2006). Opportunities for adult bonding/meaningful neighborhood roles and life satisfaction among middle school students. *Social Indicators Research, 79*, 291–312.

Petito, F., & Cummins, R. A. (2000). Quality of life in adolescents: The role of perceived control, parenting style, and social support. *Behaviour Change, 17*, 196–207.

Phinney, J., & Ong, A. (2002). Adolescent-parent disagreements and life satisfaction in families from Vietnamese and European American backgrounds. *International Journal of Behavioral Development, 26*, 556–561.

Quittner, A. L., Davis, M. A., & Modi, A. C. (2003). Health-related quality of life in pediatric populations. In M. C. Roberts (Ed.), *Handbook of pediatric psychology* (Vol. 3, pp. 696–709). New York: Guilford Press.

Rathunde, K. (1997). Family context and the development of undivided interest: A longitudinal study of family support and challenge and adolescents' quality of experience. *Applied Developmental Science, 5*, 158–171.

Rich, G. J. (2003). The positive psychology of youth and adolescence. *Journal of Youth and Adolescence, 3*, 1–3.

Rigby, B., & Huebner, E. S. (2005). Do causal attributions mediate the relationship between personality characteristics and life satisfaction in adolescence? *Psychology in the Schools, 42*, 91–99.

Rodriguez, N., Mira, C. B., Meyers, H. F., Morris, J. K., & Cardoza, D. (2003). Family or friends: Who plays a greater supportive role for Latino college students? *Cultural Diversity & Ethnic Minority Psychology, 9*, 236–250.

Saha, R., Huebner, E. S., Suldo, S. M., & Valois, R. F. (2010). A longitudinal study of parenting behavior and adolescent life satisfaction. *Child Indicators Research, 3*, 149–156.

Sam, D. L. (1998). Predicting life satisfaction among adolescents from immigrant families in Norway. *Ethnicity & Health, 3*, 5–18.

Schiff, M., Nebbe, S., & Gilman, R. (2006). Life satisfaction among Israeli children in residential treatment care. *British Journal of Social Work, 36*, 1325–1343.

Seligman, M. E. P., & Csikszentmihalyi, M. (2000). Positive psychology: An introduction. *American Psychologist, 55*, 5–14.

Seligson, J. L., Huebner, E. S., & Valois, R. F. (2003). Preliminary validation of the Brief Multidimensional Students' Life Satisfaction Scale (BMSLSS). *Social Indicators Research, 61*, 121–145.

Shek, D. T. (1997). The relation of parent-adolescent conflict to adolescent psychological well-being, school adjustment, and problem behavior. *Social Behavior and Personality, 25*, 277–290.

Shek, D. T. (1998). Adolescent positive mental health and psychological symptoms in a Chinese context. *Psychologia, 41*, 217–225.

Shernoff, D. J., Csikszentmihalyi, M., Schneider, B., & Shernoff, E. S. (2003). Student engagement in high school classrooms from the perspective of flow theory. *School Psychology Quarterly, 18*, 158–176.

Sirgy, M., Rahtz, D., Cicic, M., & Underwood, R. (2000). A method for assessing residents' satisfaction with community-based services: A quality-of-life perspective. *Social Indicators Research, 49*, 279–316.

Suh, E., Diener, E., Oishi, S., & Triandis, H. C. (1998). The shifting basis of life satisfaction judgments across cultures: Emotions versus norms. *Journal of Personality and Social Psychology, 74*, 482–493.

Suldo, S. M., & Huebner, E. S. (2004a). The role of life satisfaction in the relationship between authoritative parenting dimensions and adolescent problem behavior. *Social Indicators Research, 66*, 165–195.

Suldo, S. M., & Huebner, E. S. (2004b). Does life satisfaction moderate the effects of stressful life events on psychopathological behavior in adolescence? *School Psychology Quarterly, 19*, 93–105.

Suldo, S. M., & Huebner, E. S. (2006). Is extremely high life satisfaction during adolescence advantageous? *Social Indicators Research, 78*, 179–203.

Suldo, S. M., & Shaffer, E. J. (2008). Looking beyond psychopathology: The dual-factor model of mental health in youth: Associations with education, social, and physical health outcomes. *School Psychology Review, 37*, 52–68.

Suldo, S. M., Riley, K. N., & Shaffer, E. J. (2006). Academic correlates of children and adolescents' life satisfaction. *School Psychology International, 27*, 567–582.

Taylor, S. E., Kemeny, M. E., Reed, G. M., Bower, J. E., & Gruenwald, T. L. (2000). Psychological resources, positive illusions, and health. *American Psychologist, 55*, 99–109.

Terry, T., & Huebner, E. S. (1995). The relationship between self-concept and life satisfaction in children. *Social Indicators Research, 35*, 29–52.

Tian, L., Wang, L., & Gilman, R. (2003). Advances in western research on life satisfaction of among adolescents. *Chinese Mental Health Journal, 17*, 814–816.

Tong, Y., & Song, S. (2004). A study on general self-efficacy and subjective well-being of low SES college students in a Chinese university. *College Student Journal, 38*, 637–642.

Valente, S. M. (2005). Sexual abuse among boys. *Journal of Child and Adolescent Psychiatric Nursing, 18*, 10–16.

Valle, M. F., Huebner, E. S., & Suldo, S. M. (2004). Further evaluation of the children's hope scale. *Journal of Psychoeducational Assessment, 22*, 320–337.

Valois, R. E., Zullig, K., Huebner, E. S., & Drane, J. W. (2001). Relationships between life satisfaction and violent behavior among adolescents. *American Journal of Health Behavior, 25*, 353–366.

Veenhoven, R. (1988). The utility of happiness. *Social Indicators Research, 20*, 333–354.

Verkuyten, M. (1986). Impact of ethnic and sex differences on global self-esteem among adolescents in the Netherlands. *Psychological Reports, 59*, 446–467.

Wilson, S. M., Henry, C. S., & Peterson, G. W. (1997). Life satisfaction among low-income rural youth from Appalachia. *Journal of Adolescence, 20*, 443–459.

Zullig, K. J., Valois, R. F., Huebner, E. S., & Yoon, J. W. (2005). Adolescent health-related quality of life and perceived satisfaction with life. *Quality of Life Research, 14*, 1573–1584.

The Quality of Life of Adults

17

Elizabeth Eckermann

Are Adults a 'Specific' Population?

This chapter explores the quality of life of adults. 'Adults' are not commonly identified as a 'specific population' other than as distinct from children and adolescents. Rather, adult life and experiences are regularly assumed to be, and presented as, the 'norm' in research and in the undifferentiated application of research to services and policy. Critique of the validity and reliability of research, and its application to concrete situations, often rests on the inappropriate transposing of findings from a specific population to other populations or, in fact, to the entire population. For example, research on the eating habits of middle-aged males was used to develop the universal public health message 'eat less fat, salt and sugar' which has had unintended consequences on the well-being of adolescent girls who took the message too literally (Eckermann 1997). Thus, in considering the quality of life of adults, we need to identify the conditions and experiences adults share in common. However, we also need to be cognizant of the biological, psychological, geographical, historical, cultural, religious, social, political and economic circumstances that differentiate their experiences of the world and cause divergent quality of life outcomes.

Most of the literature on the quality of life of adults qualifies the word adult, e.g. 'handicapped adults', 'older adults' and 'adults with chronic illness'. In fact, the only journal which addresses quality of life issues and that does not qualify the word 'adult' is the *Journal of Adult Development*. Psychology is the only discipline that has acknowledged adults as a separate population group. This is hardly surprising. Since most of the measurement tools for QOL come from psychology, researchers in the discipline have had to consider the appropriateness of domains of life to particular age groups. For example, the Personal Wellbeing Index (International Wellbeing Group 2006) has separate measurement tools and manuals for adults (PWI-A), school-aged children (PWI-SC) and pre-school children (PWI-PS).

For the purposes of this chapter, 'adults' will be defined as all persons aged 18–65 years. The 18 and 65 years' cut-off points are purely instrumental to avoid repeating material covered in other chapters. Age will be the only criterion for inclusion or exclusion; other specific populations about whom chapters appear in this volume will not be excluded. However, generational and other differences within this very broad age range will be identified.

Is there anything unique about quality of life outcomes, experiences and issues for people aged 18–65 years that distinguishes them from children and adolescents and older people and overrides other dimensions of difference such as class, ethnicity and gender? Certainly there are factors that may contribute to shared experiences for this age group, such as issues of work/leisure balance (Fine-Davis et al. 2004) and generational squeeze between older parents and a younger generation (Vanderbeck 2007). However, there are more factors dividing than uniting this specific population. For example, the diversification of family structures (Kaufmann 2002; ABS 2006) as well as of work

E. Eckermann (✉)
Deakin University, Geelong, VIC, Australia
e-mail: Liz.eckermann@deakin.edu.au

K.C. Land et al. (eds.), *Handbook of Social Indicators and Quality of Life Research*,
DOI 10.1007/978-94-007-2421-1_17, © Springer Science+Business Media B.V. 2012

situations and environments (Japanese Ministry of Finance 2006) means that life experiences and circumstances vary enormously in the 18–65 age group.

The quality of life of adults has been shown to vary markedly across the dimensions of sex and gender socialisation (Ostlin et al. 2006; UNICEF 2006; Eckermann 2000), ethnicity and race (Cummins et al. 2002), culture (Lau et al. 2005), religion, socioeconomic class and social status (Green 2006), geographic location (Cummins et al. 2002), health status, personality and emotional state (Spiro and Bosse 2000), as well as across generations within the 18–65 age range (Levenson 2000). These aspects of social location cause differentiation in both objective and subjective dimensions of well-being. I will examine the work-life balance as a possible point of convergence of adult quality of life and lifespan and gender as possible points of divergence. Before exploring the convergence and divergence of quality of life experiences amongst adults, it is necessary to specify how the concept of quality of life is being used in this chapter.

Defining and Measuring Quality of Life

Quality of life consists of objectively measurable variables such as standard of living as well as more nebulous concepts such as freedom, happiness, art, environmental health and innovation, as represented in the Bhutanese concept of Gross National Happiness (Layard 2005). However, quality of life is defined differently across the disciplines which regularly use the concept, and even within disciplines, according to the reason for measuring it. The key disciplines utilising the concept of quality of life are, inter alia, philosophy, medicine, economics, psychology, sociology, political science, law and business studies.

Philosophy has the oldest claim on the term. Researchers from the philosophical traditions range from those who see traditional philosophical debates (dating back to Aristotle in the fourth century BCE) about 'the good life' and what constitutes the human subject as 'the underpinning for quality of life research' (Iseminger 1997; Saugstad 2000; Ventegodt et al. 2003) to those who propose an emerging meaning for quality of life as 'fitness' or 'a multidimensional set of values, unique to each organism, person and context' (Chris Lucas 2002 http://www.calresco.org/lucas/qol.htm). Researchers from the Quality of Life Research Centre

in Copenhagen based their Danish Quality of Life Survey on basic philosophical questions using the validated SEQOL questionnaire of more than 300 questions (Ventegodt et al. 2003). The definition of quality of life that best represented what they were trying to assess was simply 'being' (Ventegodt et al. 2003). Another key synonym in philosophical research using the concept of quality of life is 'happiness'. Aristotle in his *Nicomachean Ethics* used the Greek term 'eudaimonia', which translates to 'happiness' in English. The *Journal of Happiness Studies*, which started in 2000 as an 'interdisciplinary forum on subjective well-being', attests to how this philosophical definition now pervades all disciplines.

Medical definitions of quality of life vary from broad hedonistic definitions such as the patient's ability to enjoy normal life activities and 'the overall enjoyment of life' (lymphomainfo.healthology.com/focus_article.asp), to more functional ones such as 'an evaluation of health status relative to the patient's age, expectations, and physical and mental capabilities' (www.oncura.com/glossary.html) and 'the level of comfort, enjoyment, and ability to pursue daily activities', a definition which is often used in deciding on treatment options (www.oralchemo.org/html/en/services/glossary.html). In the past, many medical uses of the term tended to rely on medical assessments, on behalf of patients, rather than on self-assessment. For example, Disability Adjusted Life Years (DALYs) and Quality Adjusted Life Years (QALYs), which used professional assessments of the impact of disability, were the main measures of quality of life used in medicine until the mid-1990s. However, more recently, especially for large-scale national surveys and cross-cultural medical research, subjective measures of quality of life (e.g. the SF-36 and WHOQOL) have been used routinely. In 1993, Ware and associates developed the Short Form-36 Health Survey Questionnaire (SF-36) which was used extensively in national health surveys and is now 'the most frequently used measure of generic health status across the world' (Bowling 2005:63). In the same year, researchers from the World Health Organization collaborated with 15 centres across the globe to develop two measures of quality of life, a long-form WHOQOL-100 and a short-form WHOQOL-BREF. The WHOQOL Group defined quality of life as 'an individual's perception of their position in life in the context of the culture and value systems in which they live and in relation to their goals, expectations, standards and concerns'(WHOQOL 1993:1). Thus, for the WHOQOL group, quality of life is

> a broad-ranging concept incorporating in a complex way the person's physical health, psychological state, level of independence, social relationships, personal beliefs and their relationship to salient features of the environment. This definition reflects the view that QOL refers to a subjective evaluation which is embedded in a cultural, social, and environmental context. As such, QOL cannot be simply equated with the terms 'health status', 'life-style', 'life satisfaction', 'mental state', or 'well-being'. Rather, it is a multidimensional concept incorporating the individual's perception of these and other aspects of life.

(http://www.coag.uvic.ca/documents/research_snapshots/Quality_Life_Definitions_Measurement_Application.htm)

The trajectory in the use of the term has been similar for economists, but they continue to use DALYs and QALYs as the gold standards in evaluating health outcomes. Basically this involves combining mortality and morbidity data rather than incorporating subjective assessments. Economics tends to view quality of life as a residual concept, encompassing all aspects of outcomes that do not have a monetary value. For example, the official definition of quality of life in the UK GCSE Economics curriculum is 'a measure of the standard of living which considers non-financial factors' (www.tutor2u.net/economics/gcse/revision_notes/key_terms.htm).

There has been some use by economists of scales such as AQOL (Australian Quality of Life measure), SF-36 and HUI versions 1, 2 and 3 (Health Utility Index). However, in contrast to developments in other disciplines, objective conditions of life are still emphasised, and amongst health economists in particular, a clinical focus prevails.

Sociologists and political scientists have also tended to emphasise the contextual objective measures of the conditions of life as the key features of quality of life (Pusey 2003) but do take account of subjective assessments. They tend to disaggregate global quality of life findings by gender, socioeconomic and other social and economic dimensions of differentiation and focus on the incommensurability between objective and subjective measures (Eckersley 2006; Eckermann 2000). For example, Pusey's (2003) study of middle Australia found that despite significant economic growth and 'reform' over the last two decades of the twentieth century, 'middle Australians' were deeply dissatisfied with their lot in life. Eckersley (2006) and Eckermann

(2000) similarly argue that objective and subjective indicators of quality of life are frequently at odds.

Psychology is the discipline which has produced the most prolific output on quality of life, and most measures of quality of life emerged from psychology. Comprehensive reviews of many of these definitions and measures are provided by Bowling (2005) and researchers from the Canadian University of Victoria's Centre on Ageing (2005) (http://www.coag.uvic.ca/documents/research_snapshots/Quality_Life_Definitions_Measurement_Application.htm) and in the chapters in Volumes I and II of this handbook. The contribution that psychology has made to quality of life research is to insist on (and respect as scientific) subjective measures of well-being. All psychologists working in the field accept that quality of life is multidimensional; they just have differing ideas about which domains of life are core to subjective well-being. Some argue that a spiritual dimension is important (Haas 1999; WHOQOL 1993), others emphasise human rights (Schalock 2000) and most argue that the various 'domains in aggregate must represent the total construct' (Hagerty et al. 2001:7).

Thus, despite three decades of extensive research on quality of life, and the formation of several international multidisciplinary societies (the International Society for Quality of life Studies[ISQOLS], the International Society for Quality of Life Research [ISOQOL]) and many interdisciplinary journals, 'the wider research community has accepted no common definition or definitive theoretical framework of quality of life' (Bowling 2005:7). However, Bowling argues that quality of life refers to the 'goodness of life', so it implies a positive model rather than deficit model of life. In this respect, it reflects the WHO (1947) definition of health as 'state of complete physical, mental and social well-being rather than an absence of disease or infirmity'.

Bowling (2005) argues that 'what matters in the twenty-first century is how the patient feels, rather than how professionals think they feel. Symptom response or survival rates are no longer enough … therapy has to be evaluated in terms of whether it is more or less likely to lead to an outcome of life worth living in social and psychological, as well as physical, terms' (Bowling 2005:1) and from the perspective of the person being assessed. Davis and Fine-Davis (1991) reiterate this point arguing that there is 'no consistent relationship between objective social conditions …and perceived well-being', which is why most researchers now tend to measure subjective and objective dimensions of quality of life separately and do not expect commensurability. For example, Cummins (2000) in the Australian Unity Wellbeing Index measures Personal Wellbeing Index, a totally subjective assessment, separately from the National Wellbeing Index, a more objective overview.

The first common feature across the definitions referred to above is the adoption of a positive stance on the 'goodness of life'. All share an 'implicit critique of traditional indicators of success and progress (which are often deficit measures)'. Second, all acknowledge, albeit with differing degrees of insistence, 'the need to take account of both subjective and objective aspects of human experience in assessing wellbeing' (Cummins 2000 www.deakin.edu.au/acqol). These are the two elements that are used to inform a definition in this chapter. I use the Australian Centre on Quality of Life generic definition of quality of life as follows: 'Quality of life is both objective and subjective. Each of these two axes comprises several domains which, together, define the total construct. Objective domains are measured through culturally relevant indices of objective well-being. Subjective domains are measured through questions of satisfaction' (Cummins 2000, www.deakin.edu.au/acqol). Obviously, which domains are included in any measurement tool varies with the purposes for which the research is being undertaken (Cummins 2000, www.deakin.edu.au/acqol).

The dimensions along which the quality of life issues of adults converge and diverge are discussed using the above definition as a guide. I start with the dimension most likely to represent convergence of experiences, the work-life balance.

Work-Life Balance

The age range 18–65 years is the expected work span in most countries where life expectancy exceeds 70 years, unemployment is at relatively low levels and child labour has been 'officially' abolished. Thus, in such countries, juggling work/leisure activities is the sphere where one would expect most overlap in the experience of adults. Fine-Davis et al.'s (2004) comparative analysis of working parents juggling work and family life in France, Italy, Ireland and Denmark found some shared issues across the 4 European countries.

However, major differences also emerged in the quality of life of parents of young children, depending on the level of gender equity in household division of labour and social policies to support working parents, which prevailed in each country. Fine-Davis et al.'s findings have been reinforced in more recent research.

Shepanski and Diamond's (2007) research on work-life balance in Australia found that the marked economic prosperity over the past 30 years in Australia has 'come at a price' and that 'only one quarter of those surveyed think that life is getting better' (Shepanski and Diamond 2007:13–14). Although the improved objective economic conditions should have provided the potential for enhanced quality of life, the 'harsh reality' is that the large proportion of the population that works asocial hours (long hours, weekends and nights and often on a casual basis) suffers 'relational breakdown and dysfunction' (Shepanski and Diamond 2007:13). The specific outcomes include increased morbidity, 'strained family relationships' and 'parenting marked by anger, inconsistency and ineffectiveness', all of which ultimately lead to reduced well-being for their children. These problems affect all levels of society and override the socioeconomic class impact on health and well-being (Shepanski and Diamond 2007:13)

To the statement 'A government's prime objective should be achieving the greatest happiness of the people, not the greatest wealth', 77% of the surveyed population of Australia in 2006 agreed. To the question 'What is the most important thing for your happiness?', about '60% of surveyed Australian cited partner/spouse and family', and 'a further 8% specified community and friends' (Shepanski and Diamond 2007:14). This finding is repeated in other research in Australia (Evans and Kelley 2004) and across the globe. The strong 'connection between changing working patterns and a general decline in wellbeing associated with relationships' (Shepanski and Diamond 2007:14) both within the family and outside the family suggests that this may be one of the key areas of convergence in adult experience of quality of life.

Shepanski and Diamond's study supports conclusions drawn by Pusey and Eckersley several years earlier. Pusey's (2003) study of middle Australia also found that despite significant economic growth and 'reform' over the last two decades of the twentieth century, 'middle Australians' were deeply dissatisfied with their lot in life. Eckersley (2006:256) explains this apparent anomaly, suggesting that juggling the work-life balance is part of a wider phenomenon of alienation. He argues that for most of the twentieth century, in many countries, rising material circumstances were important in increasing life expectancy and reducing morbidity. By the end of the century, this connection was broken by a culture of excessive individualisation and materialism such that there is now an inverse relationship between material conditions of life and quality of life. 'Materialism and individualism are (currently in most Western countries) detrimental to health and well-being' (Eckersley 2006:252). He suggests that 'individualization has transformed identity from a "given" into a "task"..'a fate, not a choice so we cannot choose not to play the game' (Eckersley 2006:254). Individuals in their quest for a 'separate self' increase 'objective isolation' and 'subjective loneliness'. In the process, they experience a 'loss of moral clarity, a heightened moral ambivalence and ambiguity a ...dissonance between ... professed values and lifestyles and a deep cynicism about social institutions' (Eckersley 2006:254), which alienate them from governments, communities, their families and friends.

The question we now need to ask, against this backdrop of widespread dissatisfaction, is how is it that in large quality of life studies such as the Australian Unity Wellbeing Index (Cummins 2000) and in series of surveys, most respondents score quite highly on subjective well-being measures such as the Personal Wellbeing Index? Do factors such as gender, stage of adulthood and cultural traditions play a role?

Lifespan Effect: Continuous or Major Transitions?

There is ample evidence to support the argument that quality of life issues, and outcomes, vary across the lifespan (Merluzzi and Nairn 1999; Lang and Heckhausen 2001; Helson et al. 2002; Staudinger et al. 2003; Isaacoqitz et al. 2003; Jokisaari 2004; Wrosch et al. 2005; An and Cooney 2006; Oswald 2008; Blanchflower and Oswald 2008). There is some debate as to whether this is a continuous process or whether there are specific biological, psychological and social transitions in the life trajectory that make it possible to identify a generational effect (Turner 1994; Riggs and Turner 2000). Riggs and Turner's (2000) study of an elite group of the baby boomer generation (born 1945–1950), which is often referred to as the privileged

or 'lucky generation', points to particular generational experiences (such as being born in the aftermath of the Second World War) that made them as a cohort, and have a view of life which differed significantly from elites from subsequent generations.

Researchers from psychology and sociology have suggested that major transitions in a person's life can cause dramatic changes (in either a positive or negative direction) in both the subjective and objective domains of well-being (Williams 2005; Muehrer and Becker 2005). Examples include the first sexual encounter, leaving school, entering the workforce, starting tertiary education, becoming unemployed, death of a relative, having an organ transplant (Muehrer and Becker 2005), leaving home, sudden financial independence, sudden financial dependence, marriage or first cohabitation with a partner, gaining voting and drinking rights, birth of the first child, divorce, menopause, sudden incapacitation (Mezey et al. 2002), retirement and birth of the first grandchild (Williams 2005). The palliative care literature is replete with evidence of the impact on quality of life, both positive and negative, of transition to incapacity and the role of resilience in maintaining good quality of life even in the face of major adversity (Mezey et al. 2002).

Adaptation and resilience, 'the ability to bounce back or cope successfully despite substantial adversity' (Rutter 1985 quoted in Earvolino-Ramirez 2007) is often associated with childhood, and the popular phrase 'children are so resilient' implies that adults are not (Earvolino-Ramirez 2007:73). However, increasingly the term resilience is used to refer to adult experiences too and the capacity of adults to adapt to, and be positive in the face of, major life transitions. A Resilience Scale for Adults (RSA) has been developed (Friborg et al. 2003). The role of resilience in helping people cope with the 11 September 2001 attacks on the World Trade Center in New York and the Pentagon in Washington has been explored in detail (Fredrickson et al. 2003). The evidence suggests that some aspects of resilience increase with age and with exposure to adverse circumstances and resilience has an important gender dimension (Carver 1998; Riggs and Turner 2000; Cummins 2011). In particular, the baby boomer generation (who are now in their late 50s and early 60s) seems more resilient, and optimistic, than subsequent generations, and women within that generation were more inclined to be resilient and optimistic than men (Riggs and Turner 2000:89; Cummins 2006).

The most recent research on generational effects across the lifespan is by Oswald (2008). Their research across 80 countries revealed that levels of happiness and life satisfaction across the lifespan can be represented as a U-curve with levels being their lowest between 44 and 46 years but increasing to almost the same high levels as for 20-year olds by the time people reach 70 years. This U-bend is thought to override any cohort, employment status, income and parenting status effect (Oswald 2008; Blanchflower and Oswald 2008). The research on affective changes with age by Stone et al. (2010), summarised in the Editorial of the Economist (2010, p. 3), suggests that

> enjoyment and happiness dip in middle age, then pick up; stress rises during the early 20s, then falls sharply; worry peaks in middle age, and falls sharply thereafter; anger declines throughout life; sadness rises slightly in middle age and falls thereafter.

Gender and QOL

Reviews of quality of life measures up until 2000 argued that there was very little sex difference in quality of life outcomes. This was largely due to a lack of sex disaggregation of quality of life findings and the absence of any significant gender analysis of the outcomes and experiences. However, more recent research has identified significant gender differences (Cummins 2006; Fine-Davis et al. 2004) at several levels. Fine Davis et al. noted the differential quality of life outcomes (using both objective and subjective indicators) across the four European countries according to each country's traditional practices in the household division of labour and in the government's policies on supporting gender equity. Thus, differentials are located in relationship practices at the household level and policy at the state level.

Cummins (2006) observed sex differences in quality of life outcomes in the last sets of large-scale data using the Personal Wellbeing Index. Despite less favourable objective conditions, women consistently report higher levels of subjective well-being. Undertaking a gender analysis of these differences between the sexes points to resilience as a key factor in producing differential outcomes between men and women (Earvolino-Ramirez 2007). Gender acts in interesting ways in health and well-being. Evidence points to women's longevity compared to men in most countries of the world but greater morbidity levels for females (UNICEF 2006). However, when it comes to quality of life, we get some complicated findings. The Longitudinal Study on Women's Health (Women's Health Australia) and other large-scale social surveys tell us that women's objective conditions of life still seem to be worse than men's (disposable income, job opportunities, access to power and decision-making, leisure time, competing roles). Some quality of life measures, especially those which examine both objective conditions and subjective perceptions, show that women's quality of life is lower than men's. However, the Personal Wellbeing Index (Cummins 2000) looks only at subjective measures and consistently reveals higher scores for women than men. The concept of resilience, which is so central to the theory behind the Index (Homeostatic Theory), is the most plausible explanation for such differences. Women appear to be more resilient than men in difficult circumstances. Maybe it is because they have had more practise. The greater emphasis on emotional literacy in the gender socialisation of girls appears to equip females of all ages to battle through difficult times and to draw others into the problem-solving process. In contrast, masculine socialisation has tended to emphasise independence and going it alone. It is of little wonder that men are less satisfied with their levels of social connectedness when they discover that the fortress response to problems does not work.

Conclusions

Stage of lifespan and gender are not the only factors which lead to differential quality of life experiences. Lau et al. (2005) found significant differences in personal well-being scores, using the PWI, between Australian adults and Chinese adults from Hong Kong, which they attributed to a cultural bias against reporting positive states of being amongst Hong Kong Chinese. These differences are also evident in the range of domains that different countries request to add to the International Wellbeing Index and their differential scores on the PWI. Even within countries, there are significant differences in PWI scores according to geographical location. The Australian Unity Wellbeing Index Report 13.1 (Feb. 2006) used a sample of 22,829 respondents to assess geographical differences in personal well-being. The two domains that were most sensitive to geographical influence were

17 The Quality of Life of Adults

community connection and feelings of safety. Personal well-being was significantly higher in non-metropolitan areas as a result of high scores on these two domains. External circumstances such as socioeconomic class and poverty across nations (Cummins 2002) are also important variables in differential experiences of quality of life, but this issue has been explored elsewhere in this handbook. Similarly, personality characteristics (especially neuroticism and extroversion) obviously impact on well-being and quality of life.

There are factors which unite adults aged 18–65 years in terms of quality of life experiences, but there are more factors which divide them. The three key messages which emerge from this review of quality of life in adults are:

- The importance of disaggregating all data collected by sex, age or generation, socioeconomic status, geographical location, ethnicity and health status
- The need to undertake analysis to understand those differences, for example, using gender analysis to understand sex differences
- The need to avoid extrapolating findings from specific populations (such as university students) to other populations (all adults) or the entire population
- The need to question popular assumptions about the relationship between ageing and quality of life

This chapter should be read in conjunction with the chapters on specific populations that also address quality of life in adults such as adults with disabilities and adults from the diversity of cultural background covered in Volume III.

References

ABS. (2006). *Australian social trends 2006*. Canberra: Australian Bureau of Statistics.

An, J. S., & Cooney, T. M. (2006). Psychological well-being in mid to late life: The role of generativity development and parent-child relationships across the lifespan. *International Journal of Behavioral Development, 30*(5), 410–421.

Blanchflower, D. G., & Oswald, A. J. (2008). Is well-being U-shaped over the life cycle? *Social Science & Medicine, 66*(8), 1733–1749.

Bowling, A. (2005). *Measuring health* (3rd ed.). Berkshire: Open University Press.

Carver, C. S. (1998). Resilience and thriving: Issues, models and linkages. *Journal of Social Issues, 54*, 245–266.

Cummins, R. (2000). Objective and subjective quality of life: An interactive model. *Social Indicators Research, 52*, 55–72.

Cummins, R. A. (2002). Subjective well-being from rich and poor. In W. Glatzer (Ed.), *Rich and poor disparities, perceptions, consequences* (pp. 137–156). Dordrecht: Kluwer.

Cummins, R. A. (2006). *Australian unity wellbeing index: Report 14.1 – "Fifth anniversary special report – summarising the major findings"*, Melbourne: Australian Centre on Quality of Life, School of Psychology, Deakin University. ISBN 1 74156 0454, http://www.deakin.edu.au/research/acqol/index_wellbeing/index.htm

Cummins, R. A., Eckersley, R., Pallant, J., & Davern, M. (2002). The international wellbeing group and the Australia unity wellbeing index. *Social Indicators Network News, 69*, 8.

Davis, E. E., & Fine-Davis, M. (1991, September). Social indicators of living conditions in Ireland with European comparisons. Special edition, *Social Indicators Research, 25*(2–4), 103–365.

Earvolino-Ramirez, M. (2007). Resilience: A concept analysis. *Nursing Forum, 42*(2), 73–82.

Eckermann, E. (1997). Foucault, embodiment and gendered subjectivities: The case of voluntary self starvation. In A. Petersen & R. Bunton (Eds.), *Foucault, health and medicine* (pp. 151–169). London: Routledge.

Eckermann, E. (2000). Gendering indicators of health and well being: is quality of life gender neutral? *Social Indicators Research: An International and Interdisciplinary Journal for Quality of Life measurement: Special Issue: Quality Of Life in OZ, 52*(1), 29–54.

Eckersley, R. (2006). Is modern Western culture a health hazard? *International Journal of Epidemiology, 35*, 252–258.

Editorial. (2010). The U-bend of life: Why, beyond middle age, people get happier as they get older. *The Economist* December 16. http://www.economist.com/nodel/17722567/print

Evans, M., & Kelley, J. (2004). *Effect of family structure on life satisfaction, Australian evidence* (Working Paper No. 24/04 ISSN 1447–5863). Melbourne Institute of applied economic and Social research, University of Melbourne.

Fine-Davis, M., Fagnani, J., Giovannini, D., Hojgaard, L., & Clarke, H. (2004). *Father and mothers: Dilemmas of the work-life balance: A comparative study in four European countries* (Social indicators research series, Vol. 21). Dordrecht: Kluwer.

Fredrickson, B. L., Tugade, M. M., Waugh, C. E., & Larkin, G. R. (2003). A prospective study of resilience and emotions following the terrorist attacks on the United States on September 11th, 2002. Journal of Personality and Social Psychology, 84(2), 365–376. doi:10.1037/0022-3514.84.2.365.

Friborg, O., Hjemdal, O., Rosenvinge, J., & Martinussen. (2003). A new rating scale for adult resilience: What are the central prospective resources behind healthy adjustment. *International Journal of Methods in Psychiatric Research, 12*(2), 65–76.

Green, M. (2006). *Perceptions of quality of life: The relative influence of race and class*. Paper presented at the annual meeting of the American Sociological Association, San Francisco, CA. August 14, 2004. *Online <.PDF>*. 2006–10–05 http://www.allacademic.com/meta/p110247_index.html

Haas, M. (Ed.). (1999). The Singapore puzzle. Westport and London: Praeger.

Hagerty, M. R., Cummins, R. A., Ferris, A. L., Land, K., Michalos, A. C., Peterson, M., et al. (2001). Quality of life indexes for national policy: Review and agenda for research. *Social Indicators Research, 55*, 1–91.

Helson, R., Jones, C., & Kwan, V. S. Y. (2002). Personality change over 40 years of **adult**hood: Hierarchical linear modeling analyses of two longitudinal samples. *Journal of Personality and Social Psychology, 83*(3), 752–766.

http://www.coag.uvic.ca/documents/research_snapshots/Quality_Life_Definitions_Measurement_Application.htm 1 May 2011

International Wellbeing Group. (2006). *Personal wellbeing index*. Melbourne: Australian Centre on Quality of Life, Deakin University. (http://www.deakin.edu.au/research/acqol/instruments/wellbeing_index.htm.)

Isaacoqitz, D. M., Vaillant, G. E., & Seligman, M. E. P. (2003). Strengths and satisfaction across the adult lifespan. *International Journal of Aging & Human Development, 57*(2), 181.

Iseminger, K. A. (1997). *Philosophy as an underpinning for quality of life research*. Doctoral thesis, State University of New York at Buffalo, New York.

Japanese Ministry of Finance. (2006). *Changes in Japan's economic society*. Tokyo: Ministry of Finance, Government of Japan.

Jokisaari, M. (2004). Regrets and subjective well-being: A life course approach. *Journal of Adult Development, 11*(4), 281–288.

Kaufmann, F. (2002). *Family life and policies in Europe*. Oxford: Oxford University Press.

Lang, F. R., & Heckhausen, J. (2001). Perceived control over development and subjective well-being: Differential benefits across adulthood. *Journal of Personality and Social Psychology, 81*(3), 509–523.

Lau, A. L. D., Cummins, R. A., & McPherson, W. (2005). An investigation into the cross-cultural equivalence of the personal wellbeing index. *Social Indicators Research, 72*(3), 403–430.

Layard, R. (2005). *Happiness: Lessons from a new science*. New York/London: Penguin Press, London.

Levenson, R. W. (2000). Expressive, physiological, and subjective changes in emotion across adulthood. In S. H. Quails & N. Abeles (Eds.), *Psychology and the aging revolution: How we adapt to longer life* (pp. 123–140). Washington, DC: American Psychological Association.

Lucas, C. (2002). *Quality of life* http://www.calresco.org/lucas/qol.htm

lymphomainfo.healthology.com/focus_article.asp

Merluzzi, T. V., & Nairn, R. C. (1999). Adulthood and aging: Transitions in health and health cognition. In *Life span perspectives on health and illness* (pp. 189–206). Mahwah: Lawrence Erlbaum Associates Publishers.

Mezey, M., Dubler, N., Mitty, E., & Brody, A. (2002). What impact do setting and transitions have on the quality of life at the end of life and the quality of the dying process? *The Gerontologist, 42*, 54–67.

Muehrer, R., & Becker, B. (2005). Life after transplantation: New transitions in quality of life and psychological distress. *Seminars in Dialysis, 18*(2), 124–131(8), Blackwell Publishing.

Ostlin, P., Eckermann, E., Mishra, U. S., Nkowane, M., & Wallstram, E. (2006). Gender and health promotion: A multisectoral policy approach. *Health Promotion International, 21*(1), 25–35. Oxford: Oxford University Press. ISSN 1460–2245.

Oswald, A. (2008). U curve in happiness—bottoms at 44 years.

Pusey, M. (2003). *The experience of middle Australia: The dark side of economic reform*. Melbourne: Cambridge University Press.

Riggs, A., & Turner, B. S. (2000). Pie-eyed optimists: Baby-boomers the optimistic generation? *Social Indicators Research, 52*, 73–93.

Rutter, M. (1985). Resilience in the face of adversity: Protective factors and resistance to psychiatric disorder. *British Journal of Psychiatry, 147*, 598–611.

Saugstad, A. (2000). *Philosophy and the good life*. http://goinside.com/00/9/good.html 8 May 2011

Schalock, R. L. (2000). Three decades of quality of life. *Focus on Autism & Other Developmental Disabilities, 15*(2), 116–127.

Shepanski, P., & Diamond, M. (2007). *An unexpected tragedy: Evidence for the connection between working patterns and family breakdown in Australia*. Sydney: Relationships Forum.

Spiro, A., & Bosse, R. (2000). Relations between health-related quality of life and well-being: The gerontologist's new clothes. *International Journal of Aging & Human Development, 50*, 297–318.

Staudinger, U. M., Bluck, S., & Herberg, P. Y. (2003). Looking back and looking ahead: adult age differences in consistency of diachronous ratings of subjective well-being. *Psychology and Aging, 18*(1), 13–24.

Stone, A. A., et al. (2010, June). A snapshot of the age distribution of psychological well-being in the United States. Proceedings of the National Academy of Sciences of the United States of America, 107(22).

Turner, B. S. (1994). The postmodernisation of the life course: Towards a new social gerontology. *Australian Journal on Ageing, 13*(3), 109–111.

UNICEF. (2006). *The state of the world's children 2007: Women and children, the double dividend of gender equality*. New York: UNICEF.

Vanderbeck, R. M. (2007). Intergenerational geographies: Age relations. *Segregation and Re-engagements Geography Compass, 1*(2), 200–221. doi:10.1111/j.1749–8198.2007.00012.x.

Ventegodt, S., Merrick, J., & Andersen, N. J. (2003). Measurement of quality of life II. From the philosophy of life to science. *The Scientific World Journal, 3*, 962–971.

Ware, J. E., Snow, K. K., Kosinski, M., & Gandek, B. (1993). *SF-36 health survey: Manual and interpretation guide*. Boston: The health Institute, New England Medical Center.

WHOQOL Group. (1993). *WHOQOL study protocol*. Geneva: Division of Mental Health, WHO.

Williams, D. (2005). *Life events and career change: Transition psychology in practice*. Paper presented to the British Psychological Society's Occupational Psychology Conference, January 1999. Updated April 9, 2005.

World Health Organization (WHO). (1947). *Constitution of the world health organization*. Geneva: WHOpubs.

Wrosch, C., Bauer, I., & Scheier, M. F. (2005). Regret and quality of life across the adult life span: The influence of disengagement and available future goals. *Psychology and Aging, 20*(4), 657–670.

www.oncura.com/glossary.html

www.oralchemo.org/html/en/services/glossary.html

www.tutor2u.net/economics/gcse/revision_notes/key_terms.htm

Cross-National Comparisons of Quality of Life in Developed Nations, Including the Impact of Globalization

18

Wolfgang Glatzer

Development, Globalization, and the Quality of Life

More than 2,000 years ago, it seemed as if the main regions on earth were rather equal in respect to their economic power, but then, a development process took place characterized by growth, differentiation, and inequality. The economic growth was not continuous. There was a slow growth in the first millennium and a rapid growth after 1820 when industrialization came into power (Maddison 2001). The growth tendency was accompanied by an increasing disparity between richer and poorer regions. The world map of the distribution of wealth (measured by GDP per capita) shows that Europe was leading and "the Western offshoots" which are constituted by the USA, Canada, Australia, and New Zealand, belonged also to the most wealthy world regions (Maddison 2001, p. 264). In terms of Gross Domestic Product (GDP), they were part of the highly developed areas of the world, and only a few additional countries of the world like Japan attained similar economic success.

Many nations joined and are still joining the path of industrialization and economic growth. This has been accompanied by a challenging discussion about the reasons for different developmental paths in terms of performance and exploitation.

The ongoing, long-term process of the developed world is often defined as modernization, and in its latest stage, it is characterized as globalization. This is a worldwide process of increasing interdependency of people, goods, capital, and information. New features of the modern world in recent decades result from the enforcement of international networks in economic, social, and cultural terms. The arguments that globalization influences quality of life are often to be found in the sense that "globalization brings good and bad news" (Henderson 2002). As described sometimes, a "global village" seems to emerge, but it is also shown that developments are running in different directions; inconsistencies and ambivalences are characterizing the world of the twenty-first century (Camfield 2004).

Aside from the highly developed countries, we find many less-developed countries especially in Africa and South America and also a number of better-off countries; for example, the tiger countries in Southeast Asia. Due to the availability of scarce resources like oil, there are also newcomers among the wealthy countries. Nevertheless, this chapter is concentrated on countries with the experience of a long-term industrialization and modernization.

Beginning in the 1960s of the last century, the question of quality of life arose due to continuing economic success. The social costs of economic growth got more and more into public awareness, especially the environmental damages and the loss of future resources. Also, the doubts grew that increasing GDP at a high level could not contribute to increasing quality of life. Already in the last century, conventions about national accounts were developed worldwide for measuring economic activities and wealth, but this was not the

W. Glatzer (✉)
Department of Social Sciences, Goethe-University
Frankfurt/Main, Frankfurt, Germany
e-mail: glatzer@soz.uni-frankfurt.de

K.C. Land et al. (eds.), *Handbook of Social Indicators and Quality of Life Research*,
DOI 10.1007/978-94-007-2421-1_18, © Springer Science+Business Media B.V. 2012

same for measuring quality of life. Nevertheless, a number of different concepts for defining and measuring quality of life in objective as well as in subjective terms are now available (Nussbaum and Sen 1993; Offer 1996; Rapley 2003).

One question is the same for modernization and globalization as it is for quality of life: Is there one pattern or are there some competing models or perhaps a multi-variety? The discussion of this issue will be kept to the end of this chapter. First, there is the issue of definitions.

Definitions of Quality of Life in the Developed World

While the term quality of life was already mentioned in the 1920s (by Cecil Pigou), the character of this as a societal goal was attained later in the 1970s (Glatzer et al. 2004). The process of discussing and defining quality of life began in the USA earlier than in Europe. There was one very significant difference: in the USA, a strong preference for the subjective approach to quality of life gained acceptance whereas in Europe—at least in Scandinavia and to a certain degree in Central Europe—more emphasis was given on objective indicators which measure social conditions independent from individual awareness. In both areas, more and more concepts (and also indicators) were developed, which are roughly shown in the scheme below.

As shown in Overview 18.1, quality of life and social well-being are basically defined as a constellation of components which can consist of objective living conditions and/or of subjectively perceived well-being. Experts from the social and natural sciences usually monitor the objective living conditions, which exist to a certain degree independently from the awareness of the population exposed to them. Their range may vary from the personal context through the community domain to the world's environmental conditions. Some approaches prefer to focus on social problems, preferably on poverty, social exclusion, and social inequality.

Subjectively perceived well-being consists of evaluations made by individuals; subjective quality of life is here in the eye of the beholder. Investigations of the subjective perceptions of well-being have demonstrated that it is a multifaceted concept. It has a positive side, which is mostly described in terms of satisfaction, happiness, and others. Its negative side is defined in terms of worries, anxieties, and further aspects. For the

subjectively perceived part of reality, there are comprehensive concepts like satisfaction with life as a whole and happiness in general; these concepts can be deconstructed down to many life domains.

The relationship between objective conditions and subjective perceptions is usually not very strong, and there are typical constellations of good and bad levels. For example, the type of quality of life called well-being is described as good conditions and good feelings whereas deprivation is characterized by low levels of living conditions and bad feelings of the people exposed to them. Dissonance—good conditions with bad feelings—and adaptation—bad conditions with good feelings—are the inconsistent types (Zapf 1987, p. 17).

Several investigations have shown that negative well-being is only modestly correlated with positive well-being. This means some people are satisfied and happy though they have a high burden of worries, while others are unhappy though they have only few worries. In consequence, subjective well-being is a somewhat complicated and ambivalent concept.

In addition to positive and negative dimensions of well-being, another dimension has to be regarded: future expectations: It is a very different experience if somebody in a bad situation looks optimistic into the future compared with them seeing no way out. This is the reason why future expectations should also be emphasized as a component of quality of life. Optimism and pessimism become an essential part of the concept of quality of life.

Objective Measurement of Quality of Life

In the tradition of objective measurement, there are a few approaches which are designed and implemented in a worldwide perspective. Comprehensive indices have been developed and counted for most countries (Sharpe 1999; Noll 2004). The most interesting indicators are the Human Development Index (HDI), Human Well-being Index (HWI), and the Weighted Index of Social Progress (WISP). Beside these well-documented well-being indicators, there are additional ones presented in newspapers, in journals, and on Internet pages often with a scientific origin. The three indicators named above play a significant role in scientific discussion, and they are statistically available for all the developed countries are included in this chapter. Often, the main indicators are not seen as sufficient, and therefore a

18 Cross-National Comparisons of Quality of Life in Developed Nations, Including the Impact of Globalization

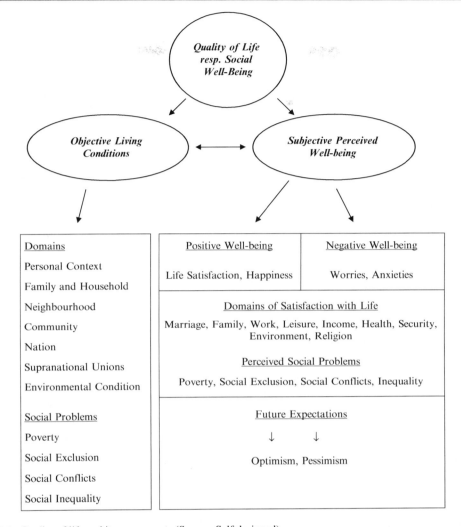

Overview 18.1 Quality of life and its components (Source: Self designed)

number of satellite indicators are added in order to give a more detailed picture of the conditions in societies.

Human Development: The Human Development Index (HDI)

The concept of human development was derived by the United Nations. It is embedded in a broader goal discussion about millennium development goals, human development, and human rights (Human Development Report 2005). Certain components, which are related to the concept of quality of life, are defined as key capabilities for human development. They concern preferably three goal areas which are:

- To lead a long and healthy life
- To acquire knowledge
- To have access to resources needed for a decent standard of living

Thus, only three components—length of life, knowledge enlargement, and standard of living—are the main criteria for quality of life. Additionally in the concept, but not considered essential conditions for human development, are environmental sustainability, the protection of personal security, and political rights as well as equity and gender equity.

According to the HDI, the three goal areas are operationalized in the following way:

- A long and healthy life as measured by life expectancy at birth

Overview 18.2 Human development index (*HDI*) for developed countries 2003 (Source: Human Development Report 2007/2008, p. 229)

European Countries

Highest HDI-Values

Norway (0,968)	Iceland (0,968)
Ireland (0,959)	Sweden (0,956)
Switzerland (0,955)	Netherlands (0,953)
France (0,952)	Finland (0,952)
Spain (0,949)	Denmark (0,949)
Austria (0,948)	United Kingdom (0,946)
Belgium (0,946)	Luxembourg (0,944)
Italy (0,941)	Germany (0,935)
Greece (0,926)	Slovenia (0,917)
Portugal (0,897)	Czech Republic (0,891)
Malta (0,878)	Hungary (0,874)
Poland (0,870)	Slovakia (0,863)
Lithuania (0,862)	Estonia (0,860)
Latvia (0,855)	Croatia (0,850)
Bulgaria (0,824)	

Lowest HDI-Values

North America, Australia, Japan

Australia (0,962)
Canada (0,961)
Japan (0,953)
United States (0,951)
New Zealand (0,943)

- Knowledge as measured by the adult literacy rate (with two-thirds weight) and the combined primary, secondary, and tertiary gross enrollment ratio (with one-third weight)
- A decent standard of living as measured by GDP per capita[1]

The HDI indicator is available for many countries. Its range varies from 0.968 for the best countries (Iceland and Norway) to 0.336 for the weakest country (Sierra Leone) (Human Development Report 2007/2008, p. 229–232). In the concept of the United Nations, the value of 0.800 marks the border between "high human development" and "medium human development." Among the countries classified as highly developed, we find 70 countries, among them are all European countries and the other highly industrialized countries (see Overview 18.2).

According to the HDI of 2005, Norway and Iceland are the most highly developed countries in the world followed by two non-European countries—Australia and Canada. Ireland, Sweden, and Switzerland closely follow. A little bit lagging behind are Japan, then the USA, and New Zealand. It is remarkable that they score higher than the bigger European countries like Germany and Great Britain. Within the European countries, there is a downward shift from the northern through the central and southern to the eastern countries.

With such well-documented data, it is possible to show for each country what the different indicators contribute to the overall indicator. For example, the good position of the USA in relation to Germany and the UK is due to their high GDP index and not so much to their life expectancy index and their education index. Thus, the superior position of the USA is mainly a consequence of its economic success.

As the time series of the HDI go back to the year 1975, it is possible to demonstrate how the leading position of the USA at the beginning of these international comparisons has changed. Indeed, in 1975, only one European country—namely Denmark—showed a slightly higher HDI than the USA. Between 1975 and 1990, only few changes in the relative positions of the European countries and the USA occurred, but from 1995 onward, more and more European countries claimed a level equivalent to that of the USA, and today, there are eight European countries above the level of the USA. Additionally, Australia and Canada have also surpassed the USA. Thus, the USA lost its leading position to several European and non-European nations in the past two decades.

Additional Comparisons: The human development concept goes far beyond the HDI. Quality of life indicators in the core sense are enlarged through indicators of negative well-being and social problems. In consequence within the HDI approach, significant satellite

---

[1] To calculate the HDI, an index is developed for each of the three dimensions, which ranges from 0 (minimum value) to 100 (maximum value). The HDI is the simple average of the three index values.

indicators are related to human poverty, unemployment, the impact of HIV/Aids on health, and to victimization, but also female economic activity and the mechanization of everyday life are included into the presentation.

Output indicators from a comprehensive collection of development indicators enlarge the picture given by the HDI. The good position of the USA as measured by the HDI is challenged by the Human Poverty Index for developed countries (declared as HPI-2) which includes the population below the poverty line as well as some additional aspects. This shows that no country in Europe shows a higher Human Poverty Index than the USA. That is, the high economic success of the USA in terms of GDP is accompanied by overproportional poverty in terms of HPI. This can be further demonstrated by the percentage of income that goes to the lowest 10% of a country's population. Again, there is no country in Europe which gives such a small share to the poor as the USA. Additionally, there is no country in Europe which leaves a higher income share to the top 10% than the USA (it is 30% of total income). But some of the European countries are not very far behind on this measure.

Another important indicator for quality of life and economic performance is the unemployment rate, which is in the European context is related to social exclusion. It is not always defined and counted in fully comparable ways among the countries; this requires expansion.

A further problem of comparability is that yearly results of the unemployment rate sometimes vary by chance. Because of this, it is better to compare the whole decade from 1991 to 2001. On this measure, the average unemployment rate shows the USA to be in a medium position. Most of the smaller European countries have a lower value than the USA, but the bigger countries such as France, Germany, the UK, Spain, and Italy are above. Far above are the newcomers in the European Union like Poland and Slovenia who had much lower unemployment rates in the decades before the dissolution of the Soviet Empire but which are now much higher. Overall it can be said that unemployment is an increasing burden in Europe, more so than in the USA.

The goal of leading a long and healthy life has been challenged by the HIV virus, which remains a continuing danger. The impact on a society is shown by the proportion of people living with HIV/AIDS, as a percentage of adults aged between 15 and 49 (United Nations 2005, p. 258). The figure for the USA (0.61%)

is higher than for all European countries in 2001. Only Spain, Italy, and Portugal get near to the USA, whereas Northern Europe and Central Europe show very low figures. Clearly, in terms of HIV/Aids risk, the USA has worse conditions compared to Europe.

Security, which is a high value on both continents, is expected to be different due to the differences in societal conditions and the respective approaches to law and punishment. One outcome measure for security is the percentage of people victimized by crime as a percent of the total population measured in representative surveys. These data refer to people victimized by one or more of the following 11 crimes: robbery, burglary, car theft, car vandalism, bicycle theft, sexual assault, theft from car, theft of personal property, assault, and threats, and theft of motorcycle or moped (United Nations 2005, p. 308/9). The position of the USA in the International Crime Victim Surveys from the years 1995 to 1999 is above some of the European countries, the highest of which are Portugal (15.5%), Switzerland (18.2%), Austria (18.8%), and Finland (19.1%). Many European countries are close to the USA with 21.1%, but some have significantly higher values. The percentage of victims of crime varies substantially across the European countries, such that the USA does not constitute an exceptional case.

The human development approach as a whole is in the tradition of social reporting broad and flexible; its index is rather narrow and a compromise between traditional and rising concerns.

Well-Being Assessment: The Human Well-Being Index (HWI)

The approach called "well-being assessment" is concerned especially with the relationship between people and the ecosystem and how they affect one other (Prescott-Allen 2001). This form of assessment is related to human concerns in five dimensions, as:

- *Health and population* are related to the goal of people enjoying long lives in good health while keeping their numbers within the bounds of human and natural resources.
- *Wealth,* in terms of private and national wealth, implies that individuals and households have the material goods and income to secure basic needs and decent livelihoods and that the community has the resources to support enterprise and maintain prosperity.

Overview 18.3 Human well-being index (*HWI*) for developed countries 2000 (Source: Prescott-Allen 2001, p. 150–152)

European Countries		North America, Australia, Japan
Highest HWI-Values		
Norway (82)	Finland (81)	
Denmark (81)	Iceland (80)	Japan (80)
Austria (80)	Belgium (80)	
Sweden (79)	Switzerland (78)	Australia (79)
Netherlands (78)	Luxembourg (77)	Canada (78)
Germany (77)	Ireland (76)	
France (75)	Italy (74)	United States (73)
Spain (73)	United Kingdom (73)	New Zealand (73)
Portugal (72)	Slovenia (71)	
Greece (70)	Czech Republic (70)	
Malta (70)	Hungary (65)	
Poland (65)	Estonia (62)	
Latvia (62)	Lithuania (61)	
Slovakia (61)	Bulgaria (58)	
Croatia (57)		
Lowest HWI-Values		

- *Knowledge* assures that people have the capacity to innovate and cope with change, live well and sustainably, and fulfill their potential, and *culture* is concerned with avenues for spiritual growth, creativity, and self-expression.
- *Community* means freedom and governance, where human rights are fully respected, and individuals are free to choose which decisions are made and who should make them as well as peace and order. Communities coexist peacefully and protect their members from crime and violence.
- *Household and gender equity* assures that benefits and burdens are shared fairly among households, all groups, and between males and females.

The index constructed for these dimensions runs from 0 to 100[2]: In practice, the countries attain values between 3 (Sierra Leone) and 82 (Norway). On the basis of the well-being index, the differences between the nations are described in qualitative terms: "good," "fair," "medium," "poor," and "bad." All the developed countries are classified as fair. Worldwide, there are only two "good" countries which belong to the Nordic countries namely Norway and Finland. Denmark also scores 71 in

the table below. For a more detailed analysis, it may be useful to show the differences between the USA and Germany, which is the biggest country in the EU, for the domains of human well-being. Germany is better off in respect to "community" and "equity" whereas the USA scores higher on "wealth" and "knowledge." "Health" is about the same in both countries. These comparisons give hints where all the 180 countries of the world have their advantages and their deficits.

An enlightening view on the differences between Europe and North America is attained when the European countries are separated into the group above and the group below the USA, which rates 73 points on the HWI scale. There is a very clear result in the sense that compared to the HDI, the HWI positions more European countries above the level of the USA. According to the concept of the HWI, all countries of Northern and Western Europe together with Italy and Spain are better-off than the USA. All the Eastern and the remaining Southern European countries are less advanced than the USA.

The perspective of this approach is in the course of the argument broadened into the ecosystem. The well-being method starts with the intention of covering both people and the ecosystem and ascribes equal weight to them. Again, as in the case of the HDI approach, there is an enlargement of dimensions with emphasis on ecosystem well-being, which is in the end combined into a comprehensive index. The flexibility of the approaches for enlarging demands is rather high (Overview 18.3).

---

[2] The construction of the HWI is as a composite index, where each country is positioned in a range between 0 and 100, the best and the worst empirical value. Using benchmarks, which were developed by the author, the different countries of the world are evaluated from fair/good to bad (Prescott-Allen 2001).

Overview 18.4

Overview 18.4 Weighted index of social progress (*WISP*) for developed countries 2000 (Source: Estes 2004, p. 132; http://www.sp2.upennn.edu/~restes/WISP2000/Table %2045c00pdf, 11.10.2011)

European Countries

Highest WISP-Values

		North America, Australia, Japan
Denmark (107)	Sweden (107)	
Norway (104)	Finland (101)	
Austria (100)	Luxembourg (100)	
Germany (100)	Iceland (98)	
Italy (98)	Belgium (97)	
United Kingdom (96)	Spain (96)	
Netherlands (95)	France (94)	
Ireland (94)	Switzerland (93)	New Zealand (93)
Hungary (91)	Portugal (90)	Japan (91)
Greece (90)	Bulgaria (89)	Australia (89)
Czech Republic (88)	Slovakia (87)	Canada (86)
Poland (85)	Slovenia (85)	United States (85)
Estonia (81)	Latvia (77)	
Lithuania (74)	Croatia (70)	

Lowest WISP-Values

Social Progress: The Weighted Index of Social Progress (WISP)

Social progress is a very traditional goal, which is used as final objective (Estes 1984, p. 17). The starting idea is to define indicators which are clearly accepted as signs of progress if they move to the better. Altogether there are 40 indicators as measures of progress. An aggregation of the 40 indicators to ten subindices is performed. Many more dimensions are included than in the previous approaches. The WISP is finally computed with weights for the dimensions derived from a factor analysis.

The areas of the subindices are Education, Health Status, Women Status, Defense Effort; Economic Sub-index; Demographic Sub-index; Environmental Sub-index; Social Chaos Sub-index; Cultural Diversity Sub-index; Welfare Effort Sub-index (Overview 18.4).

The four North European countries are at the top of world social leaders: Denmark, Sweden, Norway, and Finland with index values of 101–107. The middle-performing countries include Estonia, Romania, and others. The lowest value in Europe was attained for Albania (63), one of the socially least development countries. Germany is the reference point with the index value of 100. The order of countries is changing compared with HDI and HWI. Most astonishing is that the USA is now in a rather low position just above some East European countries (Estes 1988, 1997).

Overall, it turns out that the Northern European, followed by Western European countries, are the top ones according to the WISP. The leading position of the northwest of Europe is the result of the influence of a broad variety of societal dimensions. As in respect to HDI and HWI, the highest score for the USA can be found in the economic subindex whereas the lowest score shows up in the poverty burden. While Europe as a whole scores higher than the USA, due to the higher scores of the West and the North, South and the East Europe are below the scores of the USA.

The WISP has been computed between 1970 and 2000. Consequently, there are results in long-term perspective as follows:

The USA and the regions of Europe had improved between 1970 and 1990 according to the WISP, but they have lost indicator points between 1990 and 2000. Thus, two decades of success were followed by one decade of backward movement.

Comparisons Between Objective Comprehensive Indices

Looking at the previous sections, one could argue that it is possible to create statistically rather different results. But despite different indicators, the similarities are also striking. Northern European countries are always at the top of the measures of well-being. However, depending on the type of index used, the USA may be above Europe, on the middle level of Europe or behind Europe. This is no arbitrariness. The point is that we have first to define our values and criteria, and then we can estimate the well-being of our nations. If values and criteria are different, then the outcomes are different. The HDI contains only three criteria and gives a high weight to GDP (one-third); HWI uses around ten criteria, and WISP uses about 40 indicators concerning many soft social domains and giving only marginal weight to conventional GDP. The rather high scores for the USA depend to a high degree on the emphasis on economic indicators.

Subjective Measurement of Quality of Life

The approach of subjective perception of quality of life developed on the basis of survey research and was, in the beginning, mainly elaborated in the USA. But not much time elapsed until most of the Europeans and also the Australians utilized the subjective approach. There are now a large number of indicators for the perceived quality of life. One of the main steps forward in this research field was the central archive, built at Rotterdam, called the World Database of Happiness (Veenhoven 1984, 2005a, b). This constitutes a systematic collection of subjective indicators and statistics from all over the world. In the following account, three types of indicators are illustrated as the Overall Satisfaction with Life (OSL) as a one-item indicator, the Affect Balance Scale (ABS) as an indicator which contains positive and negative dimensions of affect, and the Personal Well-being Index (PWI) as a multi-domain indicator.

Satisfaction and Happiness: Overall Satisfaction with Life (OSL)

Both satisfaction with life and happiness are often conceived as a concept in the sense of a subjective overall evaluation of life. They are regarded as the most simple and efficient measures of how a population perceives its quality of life. It is an astonishing performance of our brain to express satisfaction for all the aspects of life in one evaluation. No other term than satisfaction could be used for evaluating the mood at a dinner, the beauty of one's spouse, the attractiveness of a region, and the tensions in the world system. Of course, satis-

faction is a subjective expression, and it is not always absolutely sure that people give the "true" answer. The answer to the question "how satisfied are you, all in all, with your life" seems, after long scientific experience, the best description that we can get with respect to a personal assessment of life for a large number of people. And the answer scale from 0 to 10 seems to have the most useful capabilities.

Examples for this kind of survey question have been collected in the World Database of Happiness (Veenhoven 2005a, b), and some are available on the Internet for accounting procedures as the World Value Surveys (Halman et al. 2008). These data about life satisfaction allow international comparisons, based on the same scales, investigating the satisfaction hierarchy of countries, regarding the satisfaction distribution in the countries, and showing changes in the past decades. According to these data rather stable pattern have emerged.

The Satisfaction Hierarchy of Developed Countries

It is a privilege of the small countries in Europe to show the highest satisfaction level for their population (compare Delhey 2004). The indicators at the change of the last century show the top satisfaction countries: Switzerland, Denmark, and Malta joined by Ireland, Iceland, and Austria which are followed by the Netherlands and Luxembourg. All these countries have less than ten million inhabitants, and this suggests that small countries are more easily able to develop high satisfaction levels. A big country like the USA or Germany has never attained the satisfaction level of small countries like Denmark, which is often the highest. It must be a specific advantage connected with the size of small countries which produces high satisfaction, among them surely the feelings of identity and of belonging together.

The USA is a nation which shows relatively high satisfaction but below the small European countries and Canada. All the bigger countries of Europe have a lower satisfaction level than the USA: Germany, Great Britain, France, Italy, Spain. Below all the West European and North American countries is the satisfaction level of Japan. Below the Japanese satisfaction level, we find only some East European countries (Overview 18.5).

The European Union as a whole contains very different satisfaction levels; the range of European countries is broader than the range of the remaining developed

Overview 18.5 Overall satisfaction with life (*OSL*) for developed countries 1999/2000 (Mean Values on Satisfaction Scale: 11-point scale from 0 (dissatisfied) to 10 (fully satisfied) Source: The Value Surveys 1981–2004 (http://www.jdsurvey.net/bdasepjds/QuestionMarginals.jsp 06.06.2008))

Highest OSL-Values

European Countries		North America, Australia, Japan
Switzerland (8,39)	Denmark (8,24)	
Malta (8,21)	Ireland (8,17)	
Iceland (8,05)	Austria (8,02)	
Netherlands (7,88)	Luxembourg (7,87)	
Finland (7,78)	Norway (7,66)	Canada (7,80)
Belgium (7,65)	Sweden (7,65)	United States (7,65)
Germany (7,45)	United Kingdom (7,40)	Australia (7,55)
Slovenia (7,23)	Italy (7,17)	
Spain (7,09)	Czech Republic (7,06)	
Portugal (7,06)	France (6,78)	
Greece (6,67)	Croatia (6,46)	Japan (6,48)
Poland (6,37)	Slovakia (6,03)	
Estonia (5,90)	Hungary (5,69)	
Bulgaria (5,34)	Latvia (5,27)	
Lithuania (5,09)		

Lowest OSL-Values

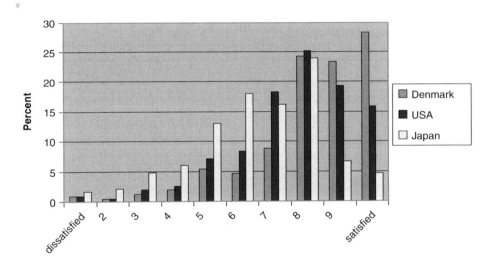

Overview 18.6 The distribution of life satisfaction scores measured with a ten-point scale in Denmark, the USA, and Japan 1999/2000 (Source: The Value Surveys 1981–2004 (http://www.jdsurvey.net/bdasepjds/QuestionMarginals.jsp 06.06.2008))

countries. This hierarchy among developed countries is rather stable between different surveys.

The Distributions of Satisfaction Scores Within Nations

The question of how satisfaction scores are distributed indicates the potentials of satisfaction and dissatisfaction in society. Among the developed countries, we do not find a low satisfaction level. We know for sure that all developed countries show a negatively skewed distribution with the most numerous values in the positive area. This means that in all these societies, the satisfied fraction overwhelms the dissatisfied fraction. We never find a bipolar distribution or a right skewed distribution which probably would be an indicator of far-reaching political instability and confrontation. The left skewed distribution represents a mixture of satisfaction and dissatisfaction which allows dissatisfaction of some few individuals. Nevertheless, it leads to a rather stable situation in the society. The following table exhibits the distribution of satisfaction scores for three types of countries: Denmark for a rather high satisfaction, the

USA for a middle satisfaction, and Japan for a relatively low satisfaction among the developed countries (Overview 18.6).

The question of inequality of satisfaction takes us a step further. Satisfaction could be equally or unequally distributed, and it is a core question to find out whether the distributions are developing in the direction of more or less equality. It is a deep philosophical-political question as to whether it is more important that people should *feel* equal in subjective terms or if people should *be* equal in objective terms.

Most people in the highly developed world reached about the same satisfaction level from 1981 to 2000 (Overview 18.7). This is especially true for Denmark with the highest level, the USA as the biggest country in the middle of the satisfaction scale, and Japan at the end (see Overview 18.8).

The stability of satisfaction in the societal average does not mean that the individuals are stable in respect to their quality of life. Many individuals may change while the whole society remains stable. If the same number of individuals increase their satisfaction as reduce their satisfaction, this could sum up to no change of the societal satisfaction level.

	1981	1990	1995	2000
Denmark	84	86		86
Canada	82	83		81
Australia	83		77	
USA	77	81	78	79
Germany	71	71	70	80
Spain	57	67	55	65
Japan	54	53	58	53

Overview 18.7 Satisfaction with life in developed nations from 1981 to 2000 (Explanation: Different researchers prefer different representations of the same indicator dimension. Most often, they give the mean for the satisfaction scale from 0 to 10; the table here shows another possibility, the percentage of respondents who score higher than 5. The idea here is to show the satisfied share of the population. Source: World Value Surveys 1981–2004, Online)

Historical Comparisons of Perceived Quality of Life

The content of quality of life was some time ago not a developed concept, even though questions in relation to perceived quality of life already emerged more than 50 years ago (see Overview 18.9). One set of internationally comparable data goes back to 1975, with data from Gallup surveys. Quality of life was examined by using an 11-point response scale (see Overview 18.8). Researcher discovered a higher satisfaction with life in the USA than in the European Union.

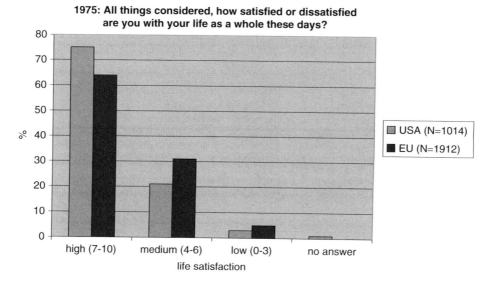

Overview 18.8 Perceived quality of life in Europe and the USA 1975

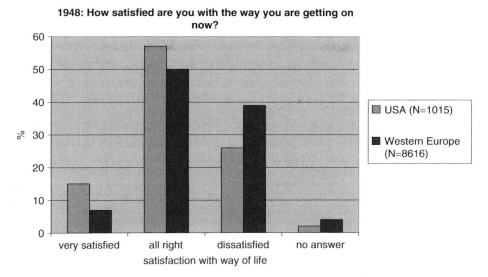

Overview 18.9 Perceived quality of life in Europe and the USA 1948

Even earlier, in 1948, a three-step way of life satisfaction scale was used, which is today unusual. The question was related to the "satisfaction about the way of getting on." Satisfaction is much higher in the USA compared with Western Europe. This is reasonable in the light of postwar conditions, which were much more destructive for Europe than for the USA.

Affect: The Affect Balance Scale (ABS)

Another type of multidimensional construct for measuring quality of life in international terms is the Affect Balance Scale, which was used in the context of early, more psychological investigations of quality of life (Bradburn 1969). As with the Personal Well-Being Index, the Affect Balance Scale is multidimensional but in a different way; it is not only related to positive life dimensions but also includes negative affect in the recent past experience of individuals. It is a ten-item rating scale including five statements reflecting positive feelings and five statements reflecting negative feelings. The items are related to a high degree to positive and negative events in everyday life, which happen usually to everybody. The answers to the questions are offered in a yes or no format. Respondents are asked to focus on feelings that they have experienced during the past few weeks.

The questions reflecting positive feelings are:

- Pleased about having accomplished something?
- That things were going your way?
- Proud because someone complimented you on something you had done?
- Particular excited or interested in something?
- On top of the world?

The questions reflecting negative feelings are:

- So restless that you could not sit long in a chair?
- Bored?
- Depressed or very unhappy?
- Very lonely or remote from other people?
- Upset because someone criticized you?

Source: Bradburn 1969, p. 3 ff

The list of items makes clear that the concern is more on psychological rewards, which most people experience in everyday life. The concept is related to "process benefits" (Juster) and is not taking account of the evaluation of living conditions. The average score on the scale between −5 and +5 on the Affect Balance Scale at the top is 2.9 for Sweden and at the bottom is 0.39 for Japan.[3] It is only partially the same order as overall satisfaction with life. If the index is regarded with respect to its separate positive and negative parts,

---

[3] A score on the Positive Affect Scale is obtained by summing up ratings for the 5 positive affect questions; the score for the Negative Affect Scale is obtained by summing up the ratings for the 5 negative affect questions. The Affect Balance Scale score is computed by subtracting Negative Affect Scale scores from Positive Affect Scale scores. Scores range then from −5 (lowest affect balance score) to +5 (highest affect balance score).

Overview 18.10 Affect balance values for selected countries around 1990 (Source: World Happiness Data Bank)

European Countries		North America, Australia, Japan
Highest ABS-Values		
Sweden (2,9)	Iceland (2,53)	
Norway (2,31)		Canada (2,31)
Ireland (2)		United States (2,21)
Denmark (1,93)		Australia (2,04)
Netherlands (1,86)	Austria (1,77)	
United Kingdom (1,7)	Slovenia (1,53)	
Poland (1,46)	Germany West (1,42)	
Portugal (1,36)	France (1,33)	Japan (1,39)
Finland (1,18)	Italy (1,24)	
Latvia (0,92)	Hungary (0,86)	
Estonia (0,77)	Czech Republic (0,76)	
Spain (0,73)	Lithuania (0,6)	

Lowest ABS-Values

it is evident that in the USA, people have on average a much higher positive affect, but the negative affect is similar to other countries. The Affect Balance Scale shows that the negative burden of life and the positive side of life vary somewhat independently. The different patterns that Bradburn's Affect Balance Scale is indicating for the various societies of the world reflect mainly their differences in their cultures of everyday life (Overview 18.10).

Perceived Well-Being: The Personal Well-Being Index (PWI)[4]

In the debate about quality of life, there are always voices saying that it is not possible to reduce quality of life to one dimension. Indeed, one item alone can never meet the differentiation and intricacy of subjective well-being. Moreover, a certain number of items would lead to a more informative representation of subjective well-being. One of the most interesting approaches in the line of a deconstruction of life satisfaction is the differentiation between personal and national well-being as shown in the items of Overview 18.11. The Personal Well-Being Index (PWI) contains eight items, and its

complement, the National Well-Being Index (NWI), consists of six items (Cummins et al. 2003; Lau 2005).[5] According to the underlying idea, a small number of items should be developed that represent a big share of the variance of quality of life. The list of countries included is up to now ad hoc (Cummins et al. 2004).

The answers are counted on an 11-point scale from 0 to 10, where 0 means completely dissatisfied and 10 means completely satisfied. A lot of tests were conducted using this measurement instrument, and they showed adequate construct validation for the well-being scale (Cummins 2004).

The results after some years of research are special for subjective multi-item scales. First, there are the same dimensions which receive a lot of positive resonance in nearly all countries. Second, it is shown that the various indicators behave differently in direction and magnitude. Third, there are different levels between personal well-being and national well-being, which are both measured by *a multi-item index*. Fourth, in the Australian time series, the influence of major international events is documented. It works sometimes in unexpected directions: For example, the disaster in one

---

[4] The list includes over 50 countries, and these can be viewed at http://www.deakin.edu.au/research/acqol/inter_wellbeing/index.htm. The international comparisons are mainly in respect to reliability and validity of the data.

[5] The Personal Well-Being Index is related to a theory of homeostasis of subjective well-being. According to this theory, subjective well-being is actively managed by a system that strives to maintain the individual level of happiness close to a genetically determined set point. But it is no problem to regard the concept of the PWI independent from this theoretical contribution.

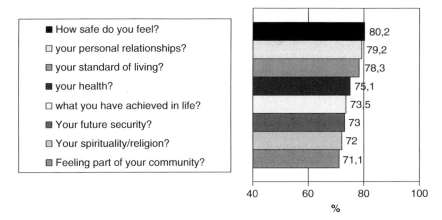

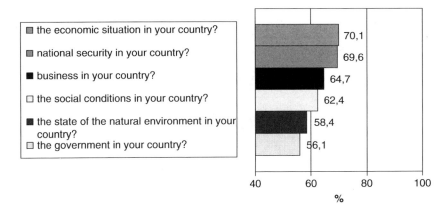

Overview 18.11 Personal well-being index and national well-being index 2007 (Percentage: Share of respondents who tell to be satisfied between 7 and 10. Source: Cummins et al. (2007), p. 4)

country—September 11th in the USA—contributed to higher satisfaction in Australia because people were stimulated to develop more internally cohesion. So national comparisons may be used to detect the influence of world events between nations.

Comparisons of Different Subjective Measures

In the subjective dimension, we find similar results over many years, from a number of surveys and across different scales. The conclusion is that these results are rather good indicators for the perceived quality of life. Various tests for reliability and validity support this view. Obviously, a broader battery of indicators gives a more adequate picture for a whole nation than a single indicator.

With the growing awareness of the subjective dimension, there emerged various needs for subjective data. Two data archives should be mentioned: The World data archive of happiness at Rotterdam collects all the relevant subjective data in a systematic manner. Another enterprise is the World Values Survey. It collects self-produced data, which are related to a certain degree to the perception of quality of life.

Overview 18.12 Happy life expectancy (*HLE*) for developed countries 1995–2005 (Source: http://worlddatabaseofhappiness.eur.nl/hap_nat/findingreports/RankReport2006)

European Countries

Highest HLE-Values

		North America, Australia, Japan
Switzerland (63,9)	Denmark (62,7)	
Iceland (62,2)	Austria (61,0)	Australia (60,7)
Sweden (60,8)	Finland (59,8)	Canada (59,8)
Norway (59,4)	Luxembourg (59,0)	
Netherlands (58,7)	Ireland (58,3)	New Zealand (57,8)
Malta (58,2)	Belgium (57,0)	United States (57,0)
Germany (56,1)	United Kingdom (55,0)	
Italy (54,2)	Spain (53,4)	
France (51,4)	Slovenia (50,4)	Japan (50,4)
Greece (49,6)	Czech Republic (47,9)	
Portugal (45,7)	Poland (43,2)	
Croatia (42,6)	Hungary (40,2)	
Slovakia (39,4)	Estonia (35,8)	
Lithuania (33,2)	Latvia (32,9)	
Bulgaria (30,0)		

Lowest HLE-Values

The creation of new data for quality of life reveals that the Northern European countries again attain the best indicator values. There seem to exist societal conditions which are close to the needs and values of the people in these countries, and therefore life is perceived of better quality.

New Approaches of Societal Analysis

Whereas the monitoring of societal trends has a longer history, the survey-based investigation of the subjective dimension is a rather new perspective on societies. The investigation of this dimension is accompanied by new approaches for societal analysis. Three such approaches will be described in the following: One novelty concerns indicators which combine objective and subjective dimensions of reality. Another approach is the distribution of subjective data in a society especially in respect to inequality. Finally, the concomitants of subjective well-being including its ecological impact are now on the research agenda.

Combinations of Objective and Subjective Data

The combination of objective and subjective data into one index happens seldom. The reason is presumably that it is necessary to bring together data from different sources and in each case one has to find a common denominator. One example for such an approach is the Happy Life Expectancy (HLE), which was developed by Ruut Veenhoven (1996). Until recently, the data are available for 91 countries. This index combines, on the objective side, the average length of life in years with, on the subjective side, the average appreciation of life on a scale from 0 to 1. The result of a multiplication of these two parameters is the HLE index, designed to indicate happy life years (Overview 18.12).

In this approach, the highest available value is attained for Switzerland with 63.9 years of happy life expectancy, and the lowest value is found in Bulgaria with 30.0 years. Above 60 years counts as "top," below 25 years is defined as "bottom," and in between as middle range. According to the results of the previous indicators, most of the top countries are again in North European (Denmark, Iceland, Sweden), but here are joined by Switzerland, Austria, and Australia, being above the benchmark indicator of 60 years. The USA belongs to the middle range, as does also Germany and the UK, and somewhat behind these countries we find Japan. Eastern European countries and Baltic countries are at the bottom of the European level. No developed country is rated as "bottom." These results do not differ fundamentally from the quality of life indicators presented before.

Overview 18.13 Inequality of happiness (*IOH*) in developed countries 1995–2005 (IOH value: Standard deviation of four-step satisfaction scale. Source: http://worlddatabaseofhappiness.eur.nl/hap_hat/findingreports/RankReport2006–3.htm)

European Countries

Highest IOH-Values

		North America, Australia, Japan
Netherlands (1,5)	Switzerland (1,7)	Australia (1,7)
Finland (1,7)	Sweden (1,8)	
Iceland (1,8)	Denmark (1,8)	
Austria (1,9)	Norway (1,9)	
Ireland (2,0)	Germany (2,0)	
Belgium (2,0)	Malta (2,0)	
United Kingdom (2,1)	Luxembourg (2,1)	Canada (2,1)
Italy (2,1)	Spain (2,1)	Japan (2,1)
France (2,2)	Slovenia (2,2)	United States (2,1)
Portugal (2,2)	Czech Republic (2,2)	New Zealand (2,3)
Greece (2,4)	Hungary (2,4)	
Estonia (2,4)	Latvia (2,5)	
Croatia (2,5)	Slovakia (2,6)	
Bulgaria (2,7)	Poland (2,7)	
Lithuania (2,8)		

Lowest IOH-Values

Inequality of Subjective Well-Being in Societies

The discovery of the new dimension of subjective well-being has also led to the question of its inequality inside the countries. Analogously to income inequality, there is assumed an inequality of satisfaction (Veenhoven 2005a, b). Since each individual has their own satisfaction score, the degree of inequality can be measured and related to objective measures like income. It is argued that the inequality of a feeling is a better expression of the tensions of a society than the inequality of income which—measured by experts—is perhaps not well perceived by people (Overview 18.13).

The result is that the small countries in North and Central Europe demonstrate low inequality of life satisfaction. Also Switzerland and Australia belong to the "top" group with low inequality of life satisfaction. The big countries of Europe are similar to the big non-European countries. The past socialist countries in Eastern Europe and the Baltic area have the highest standard deviation for their satisfaction scores. No developed country has a standard deviation for its perceived life quality above 3. The comparison over time shows that there is a trend toward more equality of life satisfaction though it is known that in the economic area, trends to more inequality are present. The social consequences of this newly discovered inequality should be regarded more carefully in the future.

Ecological Efficiency and Quality of Life

There are many possibilities for correlating quality of life with other variables. One ecologically oriented example is an index, called the (Un)Happy Planet Index, which is an index of human well-being and environmental impact. The basic issue being addressed is "what goes in (natural resources), and what comes out (human lives of differing length and happiness)." The political challenge, then, is whether "it is possible to live long, happy lives with a much smaller environmental impact" (Marks et al. 2006, p. 2/3). In fact, this is no pure output measure as are the indicators in previous sections. It is a measure for environmental efficiency. "It is the first ever index to combine environmental impact with well-being to measure the environmental efficiency with which country by country, people live long and happy lives" (Marks et al. 2006, p. 1). This index includes on the objective side, life expectancy, and on the subjective side, overall life satisfaction; the sum is divided by a measure for the economic footprint. This footprint is a complex concept insofar it measures how much land area is required to sustain a given population at present levels of consumption, technological development, and resource efficiency. Its accounting unit is global average hectares.

This style of thinking and counting leads to surprising results for the 180 countries of the world: Vanuatu, Colombia, and Costa Rica are—especially due to their low footprint—the best countries. The first developed

Country	GDP 2005	HDI 2005	HWI 2000	WISP 2000	OSL 2000	ABS 1995	HLE 1995	Average
Iceland	4	1	4	7	3	2	2	1,9
Norway	2	1	1	3	8	3	8	3,7
Denmark	5	13	2	1	1	8	1	4,4
Sweden	10	6	7	1	9	1	4	5,4
Austria	6	14	5	5	4	10	3	6,7
Ireland	3	5	12	12	2	6	10	7,1
Canada	7	4	9	19	6	3	6	7,7
Finland	11	10	2	4	7	18	6	8,3
Netherlands	9	7	9	11	5	9	9	8,4
Australia	12	3	7	17	11	7	5	8,9
USA	1	11	15	20	9	5	11	10,3
UK	8	15	17	9	13	11	13	12,3
Germany	15	17	11	6	12	14	12	12,4
Japan	13	7	5	14	20	15	17	13
France	14	9	13	12	19	15	16	14
Italy	16	16	14	7	15	17	14	14,1
Spain	17	12	15	9	16	24	15	15,4
Slovenia	18	18	19	20	14	12	17	16,9
Portugal	20	19	18	16	17	19	20	18,4
Czech Rep.	19	20	20	18	17	23	19	19,4
Poland	24	22	21	20	21	13	21	20,3
Hungary	21	21	21	14	23	21	22	20,4
Estonia	22	24	25	23	22	22	23	23
Latvia	25	25	24	24	24	20	25	23,9
Lithuania	23	23	23	25	25	25	24	24

Overview 18.14 Objective and subjective indicators for quality of life and economic performance (Sources: Compilation from the Overviews 18.2/18.3/18.4/18.5/18.10/18.12 (GDP values are per capita))

countries on the scale are Malta (40), Austria (61), Iceland (64), and the position of the biggest developed country, the USA, is position 150. A country is well-off if it achieves, with a low ecological footprint, high values for length and happiness of life. These results are challenging to a high degree, and this concept should be adopted in replication studies. While the developed countries attain high values in the goal dimension, their ecological footprints are to the heaviest in the world. Thus, the message of this study is to improve ecological efficiency to reduce the ecological footprint.

Comparative Results for the Quality of Life in the Developed World

Quality of life research is engaged in an ongoing process of clarifying its measurement procedures and ultimately, defining the comparative situation of life quality in countries and on continents (Diener 2006). The conclusions in methodological respects are:
– Quality of life is from a cross-cultural standpoint a multivaried concept and affords inevitably political

and cultural decisions about its relevant components in developed societies.
– For different views on reality, there are objective and subjective perspectives available, and both are differentiated within themselves. The decision between the preference for an objective and a subjective approach or a combination of both is never avoidable. Cross-cultural comparisons are elaborated with objective indicators (HDI, WBI, WISP), subjective indicators (OSL, ABS, PWI), and combined indicators (HLE). Each index leads to specific results for the different developed societies.
– The various comprehensive indexes contain between one and forty subindices, and this is decisive for the results, which are obtained for the number and type of traits of developed societies and finally their similarities and differences. Only an obligatory constellation of values and criteria measured by one set of indicators would lead to a consistent evaluation of our societies. The different measurement procedures for quality of life indicators as for traditional wealth measures influence to a certain degree the statistical results (Overview 18.14).

There is significant evidence that quality of life is highest in the small North European countries; Iceland, Norway, Denmark, and Sweden show the best average value for six Quality of Life Indexes and also GDP per capita. These are the only countries which take one to three times the number one position on the different quality of life scales. This leading group of countries is joined by Austria and Ireland. The best non-European country Canada is followed by Finland and the Netherlands. Interestingly, the high-population countries (more than 50 million inhabitants) the USA, Germany, the UK, Japan, and France are at a similar level in the middle of the hierarchy. The exception is the first position of the USA in respect to GDP per capita, which documents its extraordinary economic performance. In the lower area of the quality of life scales are countries situated in the South of Europe (Italy, Spain) followed by the East (Czech Republic, Poland, Hungary) and finally the Baltic countries (Estonia, Latvia, Lithuania). There is a clear picture of stages going down from Northern Europe to Southern Europe and then to Eastern Europe and there again up to the Baltic states, which reflects, to a certain degree, the different histories of the regions.

An explanation of this picture is also enhanced by attention to the different types of welfare states: the social democratic welfare states of Northern Europe are at the top, the conservative and liberal welfare states of Central Europe are in the middle, and the rudimentary welfare states of Southern and Eastern Europe are in the low stratum of the well-being hierarchy. Another remarkable point is that, in general, the level of well-being of the big countries (above 50 million inhabitants) is never at the top. These big countries show normally a significant heterogeneity between their regions. Consequently, there is a tendency for large countries that their average indicators for their whole area are neither at the top nor at the bottom of well-being.

The differing relative positions for the various countries confirm that economic success and quality of life are rather different dimensions and also objective and subjective measurement leads to different results. All the scales and indicators represent different views of the countries. Nevertheless, they represent structural features of the respective societies on the path of globalization, which are slowly transformed by people and politics.

References

Bradburn, N. M. (1969). *The structure of psychological well-being*. Chicago: Aldine.

Camfield, L. (2004). Subjective measures of well-being in developing countries. In W. Glatzer, S. von Below, & M. Stoffregen (Eds.), *Challenges for quality of life in the contemporary world*. Dordrecht/Boston/London: Kluwer.

Cummins, R. A., Eckersley, R., Palant, J., Van Vugt, J., & Misajon, R. (2003). Developing a national index of subjective wellbeing: The Australian unity wellbeing index. *Social Indicators Research, 64*, 159–190.

Cummins, R. A., et al. (2004). *The international wellbeing index: A psychometric progress report*. A psychometric progress report. http://www.deakin.edu.au/research/acqol/iwbg/correspondence/2004/International-Wellbeing-Index.ppt, 10.10.2011

Cummins, R. A., et al. (2007). *Australian unity wellbeing index* (Report 18). Australian Centre on Quality of Life. Melbourne: Deakin University.

Diener, Ed. (2006). Guidelines for national indicators of subjective well-being and ill-being. *Journal of Happiness Studies, 7*, 397–404.

Delhey, J. (2004). *Life satisfaction in an enlarged Europe*. Dublin: European Foundation for the Improvement of Living and Working Conditions. Dublin

Estes, R. (1984). *The social progress of nations*. New York: Praeger.

Estes, R. (1988). *Trends in world social development—the social progress of nations 1970–1987*. Westport/London: Praeger.

Estes, R. J. (1997). Social development trends in Europe 1970–1994: Development prospects for the new Europe. *Social Indicators Research, 42*(1), 1997.

Estes, R. (2003). At the crossroads: Development challenges of the new century. Dordrecht: Kluwer Academic Publishers. http://www.sp2.upenn.edu/restes/WISP2000/Table%205%20WISP%20Scores%20and%20Ranks%20For%20All%20Countries.pdf. Accessed 10 October 2011.

Glatzer, W., von Below, S., & Stoffregen, M. (2004). *Challenges for quality of life in the contemporary world*. Dordrecht/Boston/London: Kluwer.

http://us.oneworld.net/article/report-measures-human-development-trends-us

Halman, L. et al. (2008). *Changing values and beliefs in 85 countries*. Leiden: Brill.

Henderson, H. (2002). *Globalization and quality of life. Talking points for the Calvert group press briefing*. National Press Club, Washington, DC. http://www.hazelhenderson.com/recentPapers/Calvert%20Press%20Briefing%20tlk%20pnts.html, 10.10.2011

Human Development Report. (2007/2008). United Nations Development Programme.

Lau, A. L. D. (2005). *The international wellbeing group and the international wellbeing index*. http://www.rs.polyu.edu.hk/rs/peole/rsalau_IWG.htm, 04.11.2004

Lau, A. L. D., Cummins, R. A., & McPerson, W. (2005). An investigation into the cross-cultural equivalence of the personal wellbeing index. *Social Indicators Research, 72*, 403–430.

Maddison, A. (2001). *The world economy: A millenial perspective.* Paris: OECD.

Marks, N., Saaman, A., Simms, A., & Thompson, S. (2006). *The (un-)happy planet—An index of human wellbeing and environmental impact.* (http://www.happyplanetindex.org/public-data/files/happy-planet-index-first-global.pdf, 10.10.2011)

Noll, H. H. (2004). Social indicators- and quality-of-life research: Background, achievements and current trends. In N. Genov (Ed.), *Advances in sociological knowledge over half a century* (pp. 151–181). Wiesbaden: VS Verlag für Sozialwissenschaften.

Nussbaum, M. C., & Sen, A. (1993). *The quality of life.* Oxford: Clarendon.

Offer, A. (1996). *Pursuit of the quality of life.* Oxford: Oxford University Press.

Prescott-Allen, R. (2001). *The wellbeing of nations—a country-by-country index of quality of life and the environment.* Washington/Covelo/London: Island Press.

Rapley, M. (2003). *Quality of life research.* London/New Dehli: Sage Publications/Thousand Oaks.

Sharpe, A. (1999). *A survey of indicators of economic and social well-being.* Ottawa: Centre for the Study of Living Standards.

United Nations Development Programme. (2003). *Human development report 2003.* Oxford: University Press, New York, Oxford.

United Nations Development Programme. (2005). *Human development report 2005.* New York.

Veenhoven, R. (1984). *Conditions of happiness.* Dordrecht/ Boston: D.Reidel.

Veenhoven, R. (1996). Happy life-expectancy—A comprehensive measure of quality-of-life in nations. *Social Indicators Research, 39,* 1–58.

Veenhoven, R. (2005a). http://www.worlddatabaseofhappiness. eur.nl/

Venhoven, R. (2005b). Return of inequality in modern society? Test by dispersion of life-satisfaction across time and nations. *Journal of Happiness Studies, 6,* 457–487.

Veenhoven, R. (2006). Average happiness in 95 nations 1995–2005. World Database of Happiness, RankReport 2006. worlddatabaseofhappiness.eur.nl, 10.12.2008.

World Value Survey www.worldvaluesurvey.org

Zapf, W. (Ed.). (1987). German social report. Living conditions and subjective well-being, 1978–1984. *Social indicators research, 19(1),* pp. 1–171.

Quality of Life in Developing Countries

19

Laura Camfield

Introduction

The increasing use of population level indicators of subjective quality of life (QoL) and individual QoL measurement in developing countries should improve international and local understanding of the challenges faced by people in these environments, and the policies and interventions that will best help people meet them (Camfield and McGregor 2009). This increase has become possible through greater sophistication in measurement, combined with a substantial body of multidisciplinary research into local conceptions of quality of life from sources as diverse as development ethics and participatory development practice. Whether researchers are exploring QoL quantitatively or qualitatively, they all share an interest in what it means for different people to live well or badly in their environment. However, in the past research on measurement and meaning has often been separated, and one of the aims of this chapter is to explore ways in which they can be brought together.

Whilst studying subjective QoL alone is not sufficient to gain a rounded picture of people's lives, it is an area that has historically been underdeveloped in developing countries in comparison to objective work (e.g. household surveys).[1] It has also become an ethical priority as it reflects a growing interest in how people in developing countries view themselves, their lives, their immediate surroundings and their larger social situation. For example, recent research on the role of core affect and the homeostasis of subjective well-being (SWB) in keeping responses to 'global' life satisfaction questions stable and positive[2] may provide a fresh perspective on the problem of adaptation or 'false consciousness' (Scott 1975; Lockwood 1981; Sen 1984, Clark 2007). For QoL researchers, working in very different environments can throw their normative assumptions and measurement practices into sharp relief, increasing the salience of issues such as the effect of adaptation and the accessibility of reference groups and frames on people's responses. General methodological issues also become more acute. For example, the extent to which QoL measures are 'appropriate technologies' (i.e. work equally well in resource-poor environments), the challenges of translation and the ethics of research with people who are relatively poor (in terms of both resources and time) and powerless.

To make what would otherwise be a very general review more accessible (i.e. 'QoL in 84 per cent of the world'[3]), I used Bangladesh as a concrete example to see how it might benefit from access to accurate, non-economic measures, and the discursive space offered by a concept of QoL.[4] Whilst there is a strong tradition of participatory development research in Bangladesh,

---

[1] There are notable exceptions to this, for example, the work of Moller et al. in South Africa.

L. Camfield (✉)
School of Development Studies, University of East Anglia,
Norwich, NR4 7TJ, UK
e-mail: l.camfield@uea.ac.uk

---

[2] See Cummins 2002a; Russell 2003; Davern and Cummins 2005.

[3] The estimate takes a cut-off of 0.89 in the Human Development Index (HDR 2005) to exclude OECD members or 'highly developed' countries.

[4] Bangladesh was 139th in the Human Development Index, has a per capita income of $1,770 PPP and was categorised by Transparency International (2003) as the most corrupt country in the world.

K.C. Land et al. (eds.), *Handbook of Social Indicators and Quality of Life Research*,
DOI 10.1007/978-94-007-2421-1_19, © Springer Science+Business Media B.V. 2012

supported by international donors, there has been little work specifically on QoL. The subfield of health-related QoL (HRQoL) is the exception to this with both adaptation of international measures (e.g. SF-36, Ahmed et al. 2002, WHOQOL-Bref, Izutsu et al. 2005) and development of native ones (Nilsson et al. 2005).

In addition to illustrations from Bangladesh, there are examples of prominent and interesting work in boxes throughout the text. We also discuss the work of the multidisciplinary Wellbeing in Developing Countries Research Group (WeD) in Bangladesh, Ethiopia, Peru and Thailand (www.welldev.org.uk)

The first section of the chapter summarises the advantages of QoL research in developing countries for residents, policymakers and practitioners. It then outlines the main issues around exploring and defining QoL, and the role of qualitative and participatory work in this process. Finally, it reviews previous and ongoing work on using, developing and adapting measures of subjective QoL in developing countries.

What QoL Measurement Has to Offer Developing Countries

QoL is a dynamic and holistic concept that incorporates the material, relational and cognitive/affective dimensions of people's lives. This includes the creation of meaning and forming of standards, which are not individual processes. The openness of the concept enables the understanding of people's lives in their own terms. For example, rather than rush to measurement, researchers need first to ask people what a good quality of life or 'living well' means to them, here and now. The term QoL implies support for research providing a socially and culturally embedded view of people's lives that throws up questions rather than answers. For example: What do people value? What do they aspire to? How do they remain resilient when reality falls short of their aspirations?

If we look at poverty and development not as ends in themselves but in terms of their effect on QoL, a number of things become apparent. First, people may not experience themselves as poor, and their labelling may come from a form of 'focusing illusion' where the researcher only sees their most visible attribute (Schkade and Kahneman 1998). Second, where people characterise themselves as poor, it may be for different reasons than the researcher might imagine. For example,

the participatory research conducted in Armenia by 'Consultations with the Poor' (discussed in Sect. "Exploring Local Understandings of QoL: The Contribution of Participatory Research") found that single pensioners were consistently ranked as the poorest because of their isolation, despite the fact that their income levels were no lower than average. Material poverty also does not mean that people then see their lives in terms of lack or deprivation, or are happy to be represented in this way. To rephrase Kahneman (originally talking about people with paraplegia, another group whose QoL has been misrepresented by 'experts'):

> Everyone is surprised by how happy [the poor] can be. The reason is that they are not [poor] full time. They do other things. They enjoy their meals, their friends. They read the news. It has to do with the allocation of attention
>
> (Kahneman in Wallis 2005)

Studying the QoL rather than the poverty of people in developing countries enables researchers to explore what poor people have and are able to do, rather than focusing on their deficits (Lawson et al. 2000; Camfield and McGregor 2005). This will produce more credible and respectful representations of people's lives to inform development policy and practice, hopefully leading to development that creates the conditions for people to experience good QoL, rather than undermining their existing strategies.

Although individual QoL measures are relatively new to this field, they have a number of advantages over qualitative methods. For example, (a) they do not require special expertise to use or analyse, (b) they are quick to administer and so take less time from the researcher and the respondent[5] (reducing costs on both sides), (c) they can be combined with other methods (e.g. as a module in a household survey[6]) and (d) they may have more credibility with policymakers than participatory methods, despite having the same subjective element (White and Pettit 2005).

At the population level, subjective indicators of QoL can address topical issues (e.g. changes in government

---

[5] See Davis et al. 1999 for the time cost of participatory work. Household surveys, although regarded as a 'necessary evil' by researchers, are also notoriously time-consuming.

[6] The WeD group's Resources and Needs Questionnaire included a global happiness question and five questions on domain satisfaction designed to address basic need fulfilment (Guillen-Royo and Velazco 2005).

policy or short-term political conflict[7]), generate longitudinal data sets to explore the effect of processes such as globalisation and provide accurate data for planning. They have been included in population surveys by both governments and international bodies, initially in the United States (Campbell 1981) and Europe (e.g. Germany, Glatzer and Zapf 1984), but more recently in Latin America, Asia and Africa (see Møller 2005, and surveys such as World Values, International Social Survey Program, Comparative Study of Electoral Systems, Latino barometer, Afro barometer, East Asia barometer, Asia barometer, Arab barometer, Global barometer, Social Weather Station, etc.). These indicators explore QoL in terms of satisfaction with different areas of life (or domains, e.g. material, financial, social and political) and also include questions about other subjective variables like trust, optimism and 'anomie' (Huschka and Mau 2005; Alkire 2007). Standard questions about happiness and life satisfaction are a routine part of these data sets and have been collated by Veenhoven for comparative purposes in the World Database of Happiness (http://www.eur.nl/fsw/research/happiness/).

The presence of international longitudinal data on people's reports of their subjective well-being has also enabled interesting theorising on topics such as the marginal utility of increased national income (e.g. Easterlin and Angelescu 2009) and the effect of political change in South Africa and the former Russian republics (e.g. Møller 2001; Inglehardt and Klingemann 2000[8]).

Individual QoL measures can assist needs assessment, planning, monitoring and evaluation. For example, individualised QoL measures could help establish local priorities in local-level planning systems, or warn where poorly designed interventions might have negative consequences for the QoL of people they are intended to benefit (Copestake and Camfield 2010). Data from these measures could also help development policymakers and practitioners to choose between types of intervention, and justify these decisions in terms of outcomes and the efficiency of resource allocation

(see the 3D Human Wellbeing (McGregor and Sumner 2009) and Wellbeing and Poverty Pathways www.wellbeingpathways.org approaches).

Exploring and Defining QoL in Developing Countries

Extensive research has demonstrated that well-being, happiness and having a good quality of life are concepts that are understood across cultures, even though they may not be encapsulated in a single word or phrase. For example, in Bangladesh, QoL requires several sentences to convey the same meaning (Nilsson et al. 2005), and in Thailand the best translation is 'kin dee, yu dee' (eat well, live well). However, this does not mean that QoL, as it is operationalised in QoL measures, is equally universal. According to Schmidt and Bullinger (2007), because 'Quality of life instrument development has so far mainly evolved from developed countries and has only subsequently been applied to developing countries', quality of life measures tend to 'reflect the values and concerns of clinicians, patients and the general public of the country of origin'. This problem is more colourfully expressed by the veteran QoL researcher Hunt who observes that

> The ethnocentricity of assuming that a measure developed in, say, the USA, or England, will be applicable (after adaptation) in pretty much any country or language in the world . . . is highlighted if one imagines the chances of a health questionnaire developed in Bali, Nigeria, or Hong Kong being deemed suitable for use in Newcastle, Newark, or Nice.
>
> (1999, p. 230)

One of the problems with much individual QoL measurement (and here I mainly refer to HRQoL, as this is where the bulk of this work has taken place) is that measures are based on the idea that people can easily articulate their inner feelings and experiences. This is a skill that may be more common among educated, middle-class, Anglo-Saxon researchers than the people they are working with. It is more difficult to measure intangible or social aspects of people's experiences, which may account for the focus on 'physical function' as the most concrete and generalisable aspect of health (e.g. Leplege and Hunt 1997). However, even within health care the importance of social and environmental factors has been acknowledged and is

---

[7]For example, the lowest SWB score ever recorded (1.6 on a 10-point scale) occurred following the overthrow of the government of the Dominican Republic.

[8]Inglehardt and Klingemann (2000) observed a decline in the reported SWB of Russians from 70% to 38% between 1981 and 1996 whilst GDP per capita remained roughly the same.

supported by many population and patient surveys[9] (e.g. Bowling 1995; McDowell and Newell 1996).

Another concern is the possible normativity of substantive concepts of QoL or well-being. For example, the selected domains of quality of life may act as standards to which the individual is expected to live up (Mozes and Maor's *Good Life Questionnaire* gives examples of what should count as a 'purposeful life plan' as opposed to mere 'hedonism' (1999)). This problem can even extend to the scales used. For example, respondents appear to use the range of values provided on the scale as a normative frame of reference in estimating the frequency with which they perform activities such as watching television. This results in higher frequency reports along scales that present high rather than low values (Schwarz et al. 1985).

The lack of explicit conceptual foundations has also been a problem with measures of HRQoL, as publications tend to report their psychometric properties rather than their 'conceptual latent model' (Sartorius and Kuyken 1993).[10] This also decreases the likelihood of a successful translation. For example, Bowden and Fox-Rushby's evaluation of the translation and adaptation of the nine most common HRQoL measures[11] demonstrated a near-universal focus on measurement and scale equivalence rather than conceptual equivalence (2003). This is obviously problematic as items require careful translation to ascertain that they can work as well in African and/or South Asian languages as they do in European ones. Items on social relationships or emotions even pose problems translating between European languages. For example, in the USA, 'social activities' (items 6 and 10 of the SF-36) means different activities with different people, whilst in Russia it means 'to participate in political meetings or act like a trade union leader' (IQOLA, unpublished report).

The challenge of translation extends beyond vocabulary to the tacit models underlying the measures,

which exemplify the operation of Lukes's second and third levels of power (1986). Their imposition of models developed in one type of society on others with significant cultural and material differences risks not only setting the agenda in terms of what QoL is to encompass, but also of shaping the ways in which it can be thought about in the first place. An example is the Cartesian dualism of separate physical and psychological domains, and the way the social domain, if it has been included, is represented as external to the person. Research to develop a HRQoL measure for elderly people in rural Bangladesh observed that people's concepts of QoL were both holistic and 'embedded in social relations'[12] (Nilsson et al. 2005, p. 371):

> It was clear that elderly people saw [physical, psychological, social, spiritual, economic, and environmental] dimensions as closely intertwined, and not as separate aspects of their lives
>
> (Ibid., p. 303)

The problem is most acute with eudaemonic measures of SWB, which seem closer to measures of psychological well-being than SWB. Christopher (1999) has criticised Ryff's (1989) measure of SWB on the basis that its six factors (self-acceptance, personal growth, purpose in life, positive relations with others, autonomy, happiness and environmental mastery) reflect its development as part of a North American project looking at resilience in older adults. He suggests that Ryff's definition of autonomy as 'internal control' reveals the individualism of the society the measure was developed in, since in other societies, secondary control through acceptance and harmonisation is more common, and autonomy is often exercised through relationships (Devine et al. 2007). Christopher identified other culturally specific assumptions, for example, a self that was 'always-already' there (not constituted through relations with others) and can exist outside society, and the implicit rejection of 'conformity', or 'pro-solidarity behaviour' as it might be more positively described.

Developing this theme further, Markus and Kitayama (1991) argue that SWB cannot be studied cross-culturally because its definitions are culturally rooted 'moral visions'. For this reason, measures of SWB that ask directly about people's satisfaction with life or happiness are more commonly used in developing

---

[9]The failure to fully acknowledge the importance of these areas could also be explained by resistance from powerful stakeholders as valued aspects of life such as 'feeling a sense of identity or belonging' tend not to be affected by medical interventions!

[10]See Keedwell and Snaith 1996; Ziebland et al. 1993; Fox-Rushby and Bowden [unpublished].

[11]The Dartmouth COOP/WONCA Charts, Nottingham Health Profile, Sickness Impact Profile, SF-36, Quality of Wellbeing Scale, and the WHOQOL, and the health economic measures 15-Dimensional Measure, Health Utilities Index and EuroQol.

[12]This was also found by the WeD exploratory QoL research in Bangladesh (Choudhury 2005).

countries, as they do not have the same problems with content. However even 'formal' accounts of well-being contain assumptions like 'feeling happy is universally important', and 'subjects have authority over their own wellbeing', which in this context may be equally problematic (Tiberius 2004). Kitayama and Markus maintain that the concept of happiness is less relevant to societies they define as 'collectivist' (using Triandis's bipolar classification system; Triandis 1994) because it is founded in individual judgments. They suggest that in collectivist societies it should be redefined as the realisation of social harmony (2000). The influential development economist Amartya Sen has also questioned the validity of subjective judgements on the basis of a post-famine health survey of widows in India, which showed significant disparities between self-reports and external observations (1984, p. 309), claiming that 'if a starving wreck, ravished by famine, buffeted by disease, is made happy through some mental conditioning (say, via the "opium" of religion), the person will be seen as doing well on this mental states perspective' (ibid., p. 188).

Unfortunately I do not have space to explore the contribution of cross-cultural psychology to understanding QoL in developing countries. However, I will briefly note debates around the validity of the binary distinction between individualism and collectivism (Matsumoto 1999; Oyserman et al. 2002), and how this might influence people's experiences of positive and negative affect.

Collectivism and Individualism were originally distinguished by Hofstede (1980) and Triandis (1994), and have since become organising metaphors for work in cross-cultural psychology and QoL. Individualism is hypothesised to be most common in North America and Europe, whilst collectivism is more common in East Asia and Latin America, and low in North America and Europe. Individualists are said to maintain an emotional distance from the in-group, give primacy to their personal goals and regulate their behaviour according to their attitudes. Collectivists, in contrast, value harmony and the integration of the family, use in-group norms to define themselves and regulate their behaviour, and make strong distinctions between the in-group and the out-group. For example, 'Western individualists' apparently see their behaviour as less important than their thoughts and feelings and as a function of their personal attributes and dispositions, whilst 'East Asian collectivists' attend to situational factors like norms, roles and obligations (Fiske et al. 1998).

Oyserman et al. (2002) have criticised the use of this distinction to explain every difference, for example, development of political systems, as they feel it has replaced the study of specific, local phenomena and blocked the exploration of other foundational cultural schemes such as 'uncertainty avoidance' (Hofstede 1980). Oyserman et al.'s (2002) meta-analysis of 83 different studies reported that contrary to popular belief both African Americans and Latin Americans were higher in individualism than European Americans. Japanese and Koreans were also no higher in collectivism, although the differences in individualism were more difficult to interpret.

Notwithstanding this critique, there has been much interesting work in this area; for example, experimental research using priming for interdependence or independence (linked respectively to collectivism and individualism) has produced effects that mirror previously identified cultural differences on these axes[13] (Oyserman et al. 2002). Research on differences in self-esteem at the national level suggests that self-esteem and self-consistency are less important in East Asia (Diener and Suh 2000), and that the size of the correlation between self-esteem and life satisfaction varies with the degree of individualism (Diener and Diener 1995). Self-esteem and perceived emotional support are reported to be equally predictive of life satisfaction in Japan and Philippines, but not in the USA, where emotional support has an ambivalent meaning (Uchida et al. 2001). Japanese respondents also report more self-esteem decreasing situations than Americans, and are more likely to interpret situations as self-esteem decreasing (Kitayama 2002).

In the area of emotions, individualists are apparently more likely to use emotions than norms to judge life satisfaction, and as a result emotions and life satisfaction correlate better in individualist cultures (Suh et al. 1998; Oishi et al. 1998; Eid and Diener 2001). There is also a weaker relationship between life satisfaction and emotion ambivalence or conflict in collectivist cultures (Suh 1994). However, emotional norms are important in all cultures: The valuing of pride in USA and Australia and guilt in Taiwan and China has a significant effect on sources of self-esteem (Eid and Diener 2001). More importantly perhaps for developing countries, Diener and Fujita suggest that life satisfaction relates more to

---

[13] For example, German respondents primed for interdependence react in a similar way to Chinese ones, and also perceive the behaviour of others in a similar way.

perceived resources than emotions (1995, p. 926), a proposition that the WeD research described in the final section is able to test as it combines a household survey with measures of aspirations (WeDQoL goals), emotions (PANAS) and life satisfaction (SWLS).

Emotion or affect is also culturally mediated. For example, Diener et al. (1998) observed that pleasant affect is experienced more frequently in cultures where it is valued. Mean national life satisfaction can similarly be predicted on whether the average respondent thinks it is good to be satisfied. In countries where the majority of people affirm that high life satisfaction is desirable, their most satisfactory domains will be the strongest predictor of their overall score. But in countries where high life satisfaction is undesirable, there is a stronger correlation between people's least satisfactory domains and life satisfaction (ibid.; confirmed by Schimmack et al. (2002) in Ghana, Japan, Mexico, Germany and the USA). Psychological research on emotions has been extended to Sub-Saharan Africa where Kim-Prieto and Eid (2004) observed emotional norms that appeared to be specific to this region (e.g. the existence of significant groups of people who thought all positive emotion was undesirable).

Uchida et al.'s (2004) review concluded that whilst the experience of happiness appeared to be universal, there were differences in meanings, motivations and predictors that merited qualitative study. For example, in North America, happiness was defined as personal achievement and was best predicted by self-esteem, whilst in East Asia it was characterised as interpersonal connectedness, and best predicted by whether the person perceived themselves as embedded in social relationships. Other important differences were whether happiness was pursued through personal achievement or social harmony and, if it was achieved, whether this was attributed to the individual (internally) or their relationships (externally). Happiness has also been studied within QoL. For example, Lau et al. (2005) experimented with the addition of a 'satisfaction with happiness' item to the Hong Kong version of the Personal Wellbeing Index (*PWI*),[14] which only increased the amount of explained variance in global

life satisfaction by 1%. The same addition in Australia increased it by 14%, with a corresponding effect on the profile of domain contributions.

This example of differing priorities in countries at a relatively similar stage of economic development[15] underlines the need for iteration between universal and local definitions of QoL. This will not only prevent measures being biased towards concerns that have little relevance locally, but also the incorporation of biases on the part of the respondents from adaptation, or the limited availability of reference groups (what Appadurai (2004) characterises as 'poverty of aspiration'). Rapley (2003) argues that for QoL to be measurable, it needs to be defined locally in a way that reflects people's lived experience of the concept. He describes this as a 'meaning-based' approach to understanding QoL, which is developed from people's experiences in a subjective and holistic way, as opposed to the 'function-based' approach of HRQoL. It is certainly obvious when a measure has been 'compiled' by researchers in developed countries with minimal local participation. Many of the normative reference points for functional scales may be irrelevant (e.g. the WHOQOL-100 asks about your 'satisfaction with the social care services', which are not available in the majority of developing countries), or inappropriate (the SF-36 asks about physical activities like running, which would be considered undignified for an older person in South Asia, Nilsson et al. 2004).

Evidence from qualitative and quantitative studies of QoL and well-being also shows small but important differences in the things people value, associated with characteristics such as age, gender, religion and location. This throws into question the value of 'universal' measures, especially if they could be better described as 'native' scales for North America and Europe. For example, within HRQoL there has been a move towards items and modules specific to countries, conditions and population groups such as the elderly. There has also been greater individualisation through individualised QoL measures and computer-based administration.

There are strong arguments for scales specifically for use in developing countries, which are part methodological and part based on observed differences in areas of importance. For example, Veenhoven (1991) and

---

[14]The item on happiness had previously been omitted because (a) it conflated affective and cognitive, as satisfaction was seen as a combination of the two (Okun and Stock 1987), and (b) it was not amenable to objective measurement. It was also difficult to translate because satisfaction and happiness are interchangeable in Chinese.

[15]In 2003, Hong Kong's GDP per capita was US$26,632, and Australia's was $27,179, and their respective HDI scores were 0.916 and 0.955.

Oishi et al. (1999) report a higher correlation between satisfaction with income and life satisfaction in poorer countries, suggesting that income may be more important for the poor than the rich due in part to its relationship to basic need satisfaction. Cummins (2005, p. 3) has also identified money as 'the most flexible resource in terms of its capacity as an external buffer' because it 'allows people to minimize the negative potential inherent within their environment'. The utility of money is supported by Lau et al.'s (2005) validation of the *PWI* in Hong Kong, which observed a smaller number of differences in domain scores for the high-income group, suggesting that income has a stabilising effect across all domains.

Whilst a negative relationship between wealth and happiness has been observed for poor countries (e.g. Schyns 2003), this may be due to inequality in distribution, or the confounding of the relationship in rich countries by factors such as increased human rights. Diener and Diener suggest that

> Overall, people in poor countries are less satisfied with their lives compared to people living in rich countries, but factors other than economy determine the wellbeing of people in these countries. In rich countries, on the other hand, there is a small tendency for national wealth to be a better predictor of self-reported satisfaction with life
>
> (1995, p. 96)

These dynamics are illustrated at the micro-level in the box below, which describes the results from the WeD group's exploratory work on the perceived determinants of QoL in Bangladesh.

Living Well in Bangladesh (see Choudhury 2005)

The initial, exploratory phase of the WeD QoL research in Bangladesh generated a large amount of data on the characteristics of well-being at individual, household and community levels.[16] It also collected more personal data on hopes, fears, sources of happiness and unhappiness, happy and unhappy memories and coping strategies. This section reports the data from three questions: (1) What are the characteristics of a man/woman who lives well? (2) When were you happiest? (3) What are the characteristics of a man/woman who is an ideal person and respected by all?

All respondents mentioned good health and following the teachings of Islam as characteristics of people who were living well. Education in general was significant for men and younger women, and being able to educate your children was important for women.

Older men and women felt that having personal wealth or income (i.e. not being dependent) was an important element for a good life; however, their rationale for this was slightly different. Older men associated personal wealth with being able to live an honest life, live in peace with others, buy land and conduct business. However, older women saw it as a means of having more power and respect in their son's household. Both groups wanted to be provided for and cared for by their sons. A dutiful son was also a source of pride and respect, especially if they were employed or made a good living. The quality of the relationship with sons and daughter-in-laws was also important for older women, even more than being materially provided for. Young men characterised living well as being educated, inheriting wealth, being employed and having good health, all of which contributed to securing or improving incomes. Young women focused on good health and household incomes, but were also concerned with the health and upbringing of their children.

The happiest episodes of life for Bangladeshi men and women of all ages were characterised by the following: (a) no worries or responsibilities, (b) no need to work, (c) all their wants fulfilled, (d) economic solvency or self-sufficiency, (e) enjoying close relationships with family members and (f) celebrating their own or their family's achievements. For this reason a quarter of respondents described childhood and youth as their happiest period as they were cared for by their parents, and did not have to work, or worry about meeting daily needs. Similarly a fifth of male respondents characterised student or school life as their happiest period, and this was equally true of younger women. Younger women fondly

---

[16]Qualitative and quantitative data were collected from 68 men and women, primarily distinguished by age and socioeconomic status. The respondents were living in six peri-urban, rural and urban sites, which were chosen for their relative proximity to the capital.

(continued)

(continued)

recalled life before marriage because they were able to continue their education and live with their parents, and men described it as a time of economic solvency and peace. Older and younger women also recalled early married life as a happy period because it was associated with economic solvency, freedom, independence and close relationships with their spouses.[17] Other memories related to specific incidents such as meeting national figures, earning the community's respect or completing a training course. They also related to other periods when the respondent had no worries or responsibilities or immediately prior to migration (if the respondent was a young man).

The most important characteristic of a man/woman who is an ideal person/respected by all was being benevolent and altruistic, named by over 90% of focus groups. Approximately three-quarters of respondents also mentioned being educated, practising religion and having a good character. Being honest was also important (63% of respondents), as was being respectful towards others (44%), well behaved and courteous (44%) and giving good advice (31%). These characteristics appeared to be equally valued by men and women, and older and younger age groups. In contrast to the results from the other WeD countries, in Bangladesh people did not explicitly value receiving help or support from others, possibly because of the detrimental effect on people's status of being a dependent or 'client'. Supporting your family was also not mentioned, which may be an example of how core values are often inarticulable.

---

[17]Periods when they had a close relationship with their spouse were also sources of happy memories for some men.

The preceding section highlights the importance of identifying local differences in the conceptualisation and weighting of QoL before developing a measure. Whilst this could be a lengthy process, much material already exists from qualitative and participatory work investigating the determinants of QoL and well-being in developing countries, which is described in the next section.

Exploring Local Understandings of QoL: The Contribution of Participatory Research

The most comprehensive attempt to explore poor people's understandings of well-being was the 'Consultations with the Poor' study which was carried out in over 50 countries with developing and transition economies. The first two volumes were entitled 'Can Anyone Hear Us?' (Narayan and Walton 2000) and 'Crying Out for Change' (Narayan et al. 2000), which foreground their emancipatory aims. They were supplemented by a review of participatory research on criteria for poverty, ill-being or vulnerability (Brock 1999). The sources of well-being were grouped under five headings: *Material* (having a secure livelihood and fulfilment of your basic needs), *Physical* (health, strength and appearance), *Security* (including peace of mind), *Freedom of choice and action* (including self-development and mobility) and *Social well-being* (good family and community relationships). Two key themes emerged from the syntheses: First, the importance of people's assets and capabilities, and second, whether they were embedded in enabling or disabling relationships, as these were not only intrinsically valuable, but also affected their access to income. The syntheses also noted the following: (a) the adverse impact of national shocks and policy changes, (b) the culture of inequality and exclusion in government service agencies and (c) widespread inequality between men and women, which increased female vulnerability.

Brock's (1999) separate review covered participatory research with 58 groups of children and adults in 12 developing countries. In rural areas the criteria for ill-being primarily related to food security, followed by lack of work, money and assets (predominantly land). In urban areas the primary concern was the immediate living environment, for example, housing that was crowded and unsanitary, poor access to water, dirty and dangerous streets and violence inside and outside the household. Lack of land was also an issue, in so far as it affected housing. Rural and urban areas noted poor health as both a cause and effect of ill-being. In urban areas this was related to the quality of the housing, and in rural ones to water quality. Participants also noted the vulnerability of particular groups (e.g. households with an elderly or female head, or large numbers of dependents), and individuals at different stages in the life cycle (e.g. new daughter-in-laws).

Brock's review foregrounds experiential aspects of poverty which impact on people's agency and mobility such as fear, dependence, shame and hopelessness. Participants recounted not feeling accepted or respected by others, and feeling powerless in front of officials. People experienced reductions in their choices—participants in a participatory exercise in South West China distinguished between what they 'could do' in the past, and now 'have to' or 'are forced to' do (Herrold 1999 in Brock 1999). They were also less able to avoid relationships of dependency—in Sri Lanka the definition of being rich was that 'you don't have to stretch out your hand to other people', which reflects a common ideal of self-sufficiency among rural households. Although the experience of lack of control limits people's choices and opportunities for action, it does not appear to be as central to conceptions of poverty as dysfunctional family or community relationships—for example, where people are embedded in communities that have been corroded by poverty, or the social dislocation caused by outmigration on a large scale.

Whilst the scale and breadth of the 'Consultations with the Poor' project is exciting, the individual country studies were of variable quality (Cornwall and Fujita 2007), which reduces their utility to people developing measures. It is worth bearing in mind that not only is the quality of participatory work variable, but it often starts with the value-laden term 'poverty' and so misses the opportunity to understand people's lives in their own terms (Cooke and Kothari 2001; White and Pettit 2005). As I suggested in the introduction, a more open-ended approach enables the inclusion of some of the compensatory richness of people's lives, which helps explain their resilience, even in the most hostile environments.

The WeD approach to QoL is based on the assumption that people reflect on the quality of their experiences, to a greater or lesser degree, according to their cultural context. The goal of the WeD QoL research was to produce a methodology that creates a space for self-evaluation. This would enable people to tell us what they value, what they have experienced, how satisfied they are with what they have, and what they can do and be. The first phase of the QoL research explored these topics qualitatively (see the box with data from Bangladesh and Jongudomkarn and Camfield 2006 for further details). Read as a whole, the data provide a rounded picture of people's lives, which focuses on their aspirations and values. The methodology attempted to avoid normative accounts by supplementing questions about what it means to live well with ones on personal sources of happiness and happy memories.

The qualitative QoL data suggest that the most important areas of life for people in all countries are *close relationships* (family, 'natal' family and partner), followed by *material well-being* (income, assets, satisfaction of basic needs, home and community environment, and access to local services), and *relationships with the community and the wider world* (e.g. with relatives living in the city or overseas, or the regional government). *Religion* (e.g. believing in God or the human potential for enlightenment, conducting acts of worship and living ethically) appeared to be very important in Bangladesh and Thailand and fairly important in Ethiopia. Similarly, *education* for themselves and their children was a priority for people in Bangladesh and Ethiopia, although apparently not in Thailand, or rural and urban areas of Peru.

We compared responses to questions about people's goals from Ethiopia and Bangladesh, as these are countries at a similar stage of development. The main priorities for respondents from Bangladesh were maintaining family harmony, getting salaried employment and being educated. For respondents from Ethiopia they were having your own home, enough to eat and drink and being respected by your neighbours. However, the greatest differences were not between people from different countries, but between men and women of different ages whose different identities or experiences cause them to value very different things. For example, in Thailand the older generation wanted to be healthy and able to attend the temple or mosque, whilst young men wanted good jobs and motorbikes. Similarly, young men in Bangladesh were the only group whose hopes for the future focused on themselves (e.g. 'becoming rich'), rather than the happiness and prosperity of their children.

The work of Rozel-Farnworth (2009) in developing a 'QoL toolkit' with smallholder organic farmers in Madagascar provides another link between participatory and QoL research. She aimed to produce a toolkit that was simple, flexible and open, acknowledging that well-being is a process of becoming so needs to be studied with dynamic methods. The methods also needed to be specific enough to produce unique meanings in particular situations, and universal enough to speak to other stakeholders (e.g. the German consumers at the other end of the organic supply chain). Her methodology emphasised relatively long engagement in the field, the use of local interviewers who were fluent in French and Malagasy and flexible use of methods to ensure the best fit with the emergent themes.

The methods used by Rozel-Farnsworth were primarily participatory (Chambers 1997), although she also contrasted the self-reported health status of farmers and plantation workers with proxy ratings from healthcare workers to explore how priorities differed for the two groups. Her methods included 'dream mapping', where different individuals drew maps of the area they thought of as their community and indicated the things they wanted to change; seasonal and historical calendars; daily activity diagrams; transect walks, focusing on well-being in the future and the past; and Gender Access and Control Profiles. She also used a version of Nazarea's (1998) Thematic Apperception Test by giving people eight vague photos of important features of the landscape (e.g. the road from the village or the market) and asking them to tell stories about what the photos evoked for them. One argument against this kind of work is that it does not produce measurements, although quantitative methodologies are now more widely used in participatory research (Chambers 2007). However, it has obvious value as a way of fully understanding local people's realities before developing a measure, and is quicker than long-term ethnographic engagement.

Measuring Subjective QoL in Developing Countries

The main actors in QoL measurement in developing countries are the 'social indicators movement' (see Michalos 2004) and HRQoL, where cross-cultural assessment of individual QoL is well established (see Schmidt and Bullinger 2007). These comprise people from the following disciplines: economics (especially development and 'happiness' economists), psychology (health and social psychologists), social policy, community development and, most recently, development studies. There are three main forms of measure, used at population and individual levels, which I introduce here and then discuss in detail:

- *Global, single-item, unidimensional,* e.g. the Global Happiness Question (*GHQ*) used in the Barometer surveys of social and political attitudes.
- *Global, multiple-item, unidimensional,* e.g. the Satisfaction with Life Scale (*SWLS*, Diener et al. 1985), which measures satisfaction with life as a whole.
- *Profile, multidimensional,* with either overlapping or independent domains. For example, the Sarason Social Support Questionnaire (*SSQ*, Sarason et al. 1987), or the World Health Organization Quality of Life Measure-100 item (*WHOQOL-100*, WHOQOL Group 1995). Profile measures are usually phrased in terms of satisfaction with specific domains of life, but they can use other question stems (e.g. only half of questions in the WHOQOL are phrased in terms of satisfaction).

Global, Single-Item Measures

These measure people's happiness and satisfaction with their life as a whole, mainly using 3-, 4- or 10-point scales.[18] Their advantage is that they are quick and simple to administer, and are easy both for respondents to understand and researchers to analyse.

They can, however, have a high ratio of error variance to true variance (Larsen and Fredrickson 1999). For this reason they have been comprehensively critiqued by Schwartz and Strack who conclude that 'there is little to be learned from self-reports of global wellbeing' (1991, p. 80). Schwartz and Strack provide an impressive list of possible sources of bias, including the weather, time of enquiry, various features to which interviewer draws subject's attention, interview context (e.g. a person who uses a wheelchair in the same room) and the way the questions were set up (ibid.). Mood also appears to be a stronger determinant of global life satisfaction than satisfaction with specific domains. This may actually be a point in favour of

---

[18]See World Database of Happiness Item Bank, http://www1.eur.nl/fsw/happiness/hap_quer/hqi_fp.htm

GHQs as it may indicate that they tap 'core affect' which Cummins and Davern describe as the source of stability for judgements of SWB (Davern and Cummins 2005, see also Diener et al. 2000). According to Cummins, core affect underpins the homeostatic mechanism that keeps SWB positive and stable; for example, separate studies by Biswas-Diener and Diener in Calcutta (2001) and Rojas in Mexico (2007) found that poor people were only slightly less satisfied with their life as a whole, even though the effect of poverty could be seen across all the domains studied. For this reason Cummins (2004, p. 416) argues that whilst 'SWB is the most insensitive indicator variable it is also the most important since, when it does fall below its normative range, this loss of perceived well-being is experienced as depression'. If depression results from 'homeostatic defeat' as Cummins suggests, and its likely prevalence can be established by population mean scores below 50%, this is very significant as depression has been ranked as the leading cause of lost disability-adjusted life years in developing countries with low mortality and seventh in countries with high mortality (World Health Report 2002).

Cummins's findings are a convincing argument in favour of GHQs, despite the low correlations with domain level measurements. They also contribute to the 'top-down vs. bottom-up' debate, which has been a feature of QoL measurement since its earliest days. To summarise crudely, there are two approaches to QoL, the 'bottom-up' approach which says that life satisfaction is the sum of satisfaction in various domains (e.g. Campbell et al. 1976, Rojas 2007), and the 'top-down' which attributes it to a predispositional trait such as core affect or aspect of personality which influences people's evaluation in specific domains (e.g. Diener et al. 1985). The debate acquires particular salience in developing countries because previously the 'subjective authority' of people was not accepted due to the presumed influence of false consciousness and various forms of adaptation (Camfield and McGregor 2005). Consequently some researchers have interpreted the high SWB scores from many developing nations[19] as confirmation of this hypothesis (e.g. Sen 2002).

Sadly I do not have space to do justice to this debate here (see Heady et al. 1991 and Scherpenzeel and Saris 1996). Nor can I explore its connection to debates on the value of weighting by importance rating (Trauer and MacKinnon 2001; Hsieh 2003, 2004; Russell et al. 2006). Some possible explanations for the lack of correlation are (a) that measures of SWB are unreliable in poorer countries (Vittersø et al. 2002), (b) that the domains specified in measures of SWB are either not exhaustive,[20] or so exhaustive that they are no longer personally relevant or (c) that global life satisfaction, domain specific life satisfaction and objective happiness (defined by Kahneman 1999 as the 'temporal integral of moment based happiness reports') are actually three completely different entities (Diener et al. 2000). I return to this question in the conclusion.

Global single items have been used in large-scale national and international surveys (e.g. the World Values Survey (WVS)). WVS data have been collected in Bangladesh since 1996 and provides an interesting contrast to objective data from the same period. Surprisingly, the decline in happiness in Bangladesh, reported in the WVS from 70.1% in 1996 to 66.6% in 2002, occurred during the same period that the Human Poverty Index fell from 46.5 (1995/1997) to 42.2 (2002), and there was a rise in the Human Development Index from 0.452 to 0.506. The WVS also asked about satisfaction with life as a whole, and these scores show a similar trend from 64.1 to 57.7. The WVS data are consonant with data from the WeD resources and needs questionnaire[21] (2004, $n = 1,500$), which reported a mean of 64.4%, suggesting a real discrepancy between subjective and objective measures of development that merits further investigation.

Some economists also use global, single-item measures, either in combination with questions about satisfaction with consumption or particular 'needs satisfiers', or to calculate people's 'utilities' for different health states (see Fox-Rushby and Bowden unpublished). For example, the understanding of QoL in developing countries has been enhanced by the work of 'happiness economists' on non-material influences on well-being, which is reviewed by Guillen-Royo and Velazco in the section that follows (see also Appendix 1).

---

[19]For example, Nigeria has a per capita income of $328, and according to the UNDP, is one of the 25 least developed countries. Nonetheless, the World Values Survey named it the happiest country in the World in 2000, and 70% of Nigerian respondents described themselves as 'very happy'.

[20]Cummins's review of measures of life satisfaction noted at least 173 different domain names, and suggested the potential number of domains was even larger (1996).

[21]See http://www.welldev.org.uk/research/methods-toobox/ranq-toolbox.htm

Happiness Economics in Developing Countries

Whilst economists have historically assumed that as economies grow so does aggregate utility or well-being, some have moved beyond Samuelson's revealed preferences axiom (1938) and are starting to use self-reported accounts of satisfaction with life or happiness to identify individual well-being (Frey and Stutzer 2002). A precursor to this approach was Easterlin's demonstration that although richer people were happier than poorer ones within countries, economic growth over time did not increase people's self-reported happiness (1974). A wealth of literature has studied the Easterlin 'paradox' since the 1970s; whilst most of it is based in developed countries, there is a growing body of research on happiness determinants in developing countries, which also acknowledges the role of subjective factors in the study of well-being. Examples include Graham and Pettinato (2001) on 17 Latin American countries and Russia; Fafchamps and Shilpi (2003, 2004) on Nepal; Rojas (2005) on Mexico; Knight and Song on rural China (2004); Gandhi Kingdon and Knight on South Africa (2004); and Guillen-Royo and Velazco (2005); Camfield et al. (2010) on Thailand and Bangladesh. All these studies suggest that there is something other than material wealth that matters to the poor and determines their well-being, such as health, unequal income distribution, stable employment, marriage and the quality of relationships (Graham 2005). They also acknowledge the role of social comparison, subjective perceptions and character traits in evaluating well-being.

Some recent empirical studies have analysed the determinants of self-reported happiness using household surveys from developing countries. The following relationship has been generally used in regression analysis:

$$Hi = f(Xi) \qquad (19.1)$$

Expression (19.1) denotes that happiness of individual i (H) is explained by a set of economic and non-economic variables at the respondent and household levels (Xi). The life satisfaction or happiness variable is generally taken from a single-item measure and can be measured on an ordinal or cardinal scale. The table in Appendix 1 summarises the determinants of happiness in some countries in Africa, Asia and Latin America. It also records the econometric methods applied, variables used in the analysis, the sign of the empirical effect found between each variable and

happiness and whether the variable is statistically significant at the 95% level of confidence.

There are two main approaches to the economic analysis of happiness determinants: an ad hoc approach without a unified theoretical foundation and an approach based on economic theory. The majority of empirical studies take the first and consider a wide range of exogenous variables as determinants of happiness, including respondent characteristics, income, relative income, household characteristics, access to assets, as well as basic needs indicators, perceptions variables and access to social resources or networks. Kingdon and Knight (2003) took this approach when estimating well-being regressions for South Africa. The authors found that the best result consisted of variables derived from four different approaches: income, basic needs (or physical functioning), relative (or social functioning) and security.

The second approach uses economic theory (specifically, consumption theory and household models) to identify the variables determining subjective well-being. For example, Fafchamps and Shilpi use reference utility theory to develop a model that explains how isolation, captured as distance to market and proximity to urban centres, affects utility through its effect on consumption and prices for households in Nepal (2003, 2004). Their empirical analysis was focused on life domain satisfactions and did not consider the happiness variable. However, the use of economic theory to identify variables is an innovative line of research that could be further explored.

The most popular econometric method used in estimating happiness functions has been ordinary least squares (OLS) when a cardinal scale is assumed. However, the presence of an ordinal scale in the dependent variable has been addressed with the use of ordered logit or probit models.

Despite differences within studies relating to sample characteristics, methods of analysis and the dependent variable specification, some general conclusions can be drawn. In general, age is negatively associated with self-reported happiness. However other household head characteristics such as education, gender and being self-employed do not present a clear picture across studies. Furthermore, in line with results from happiness research in developed countries, studies about the developing world find a positive and significant relationship between happiness

19 Quality of Life in Developing Countries

and income and marital status (married), and a negative one with being unemployed. Unsurprisingly, material conditions (wealth and assets, as well as the satisfaction of basic needs) and household's wealth perception are also strongly and positively associated with happiness in the studies sampled here.

As mentioned earlier, most economic studies on happiness determinants in developing countries lack a theoretical framework, which weakens their acceptance within the more orthodox economic framework (Fafchamps and Shilpi 2003, 2004, are an exception). There is also a problem related to the goodness of fit of the regression since the independent variables explain less than 20% of the variability in self-reported happiness. The latter could be solved by including explanatory variables that measure the effects of personal traits and by taking into account fixed effects when using either ordinal or cardinal indicators of happiness in panel data on happiness over time.

Global, Single-Item Measures in Survey Research

Happiness economics is still relatively new to QoL, and global single items are more typically used in survey research, often combined with domain-specific indicators. Examples of this work from major world regions are given in the following section.

Southern Africa

According to Møller, head of the South African QoL Trends project, South Africa serves as a 'social laboratory' for studying QoL in developing countries as although it is classified as middle-income country, it is characterised by great inequalities in income and infrastructure, and social and cultural diversity. Consequently the project researchers perceived their first task as 'to define the essence of the good life in South Africa and to develop the method that would tell us to what extent real life matched the good life' (Møller 2007). The research was driven by a desire to 'lend a voice to the invisible people', especially the black and African sector of the population, and demonstrate that illiterate people could participate meaningfully in surveys. The questions were phrased in terms of personal QoL as the researchers wanted people to describe and evaluate their own lives. However, this proved difficult due to the collectivist nature of South African society and people's desire to

take social quality into account. Despite the rhetorical appeal of a single-figure index to rival GDP, they decided a profile measure would be more useful for public policy as this would highlight areas that fell short of people's expectations and/or required immediate attention.[22] The correlation between subjective assessments and objective living conditions in South African samples was so strong that they decided to focus on the former, which had previously been neglected. Interestingly, the data from 1995 suggested that a top-down model had greater explanatory power for both black and white South Africans because the political situation in South Africa meant that life satisfaction was more influenced by positive or negative expectations of the future than current living conditions (what the authors call the 'Mandela factor') (Møller and Saris 2001).

The responsiveness of both domain-specific and global life satisfaction was confirmed by surveys taken immediately after the first open elections in South Africa, where the life satisfaction of all groups had equalised and reached those of Western nations. Life satisfaction then returned to its former levels a few years later when the promised changes had failed to occur. The 'big picture' given by the numbers was enhanced by case studies with particular population groups, for example, 'time use' studies of young and elderly people. The group also addressed 'what would make ordinary South African's happy?' which split along economic lines, with poor South African requesting improvements to their living conditions such as access to jobs, utilities and education, and richer respondents focusing on safety, security and a strong economy. Møller found that global questions on happiness and life satisfaction were so highly correlated that they were interchangeable, so the choice of an indicator depended on the context and the audience (e.g. satisfaction had more authority when communicating with policymakers).[23]

---

[22]See also Hagerty et al.'s review of QoL Indexes for public policy (2001).

[23]The extent of the correlation between these questions is still debated (e.g. Lyubomirsky 2001). For example, Rojas only found a correlation of 0.49 in his data from Mexico city, which led him to conclude that they were separate concepts, with life satisfaction being 'closer to the philosophers' conception of wellbeing as a happy life, which involves a person's judgement of her life' (2007).

Latin America

Rojas, who could be described as a 'happiness economist', uses satisfaction with life as a whole as a proxy for well-being. He characterises well-being as multidimensional (after Hicks (1941)), and as something that occurs in a particular context and culture in relation to other people, and can only be studied interdisciplinarily. His exploration of domain-specific and global life satisfaction across different socioeconomic and demographic groups in two Mexican cities provides empirical support for his 'Conceptual Referent Theory' of well-being (Fuentes and Rojas 2001). This proposes that a person's conceptual referent for a happy life (what they understand by 'being well') plays a part in their judgement of life and happiness and can lead to discrepancies between their objective and subjective well-being (Rojas 2005, 2007, 2009). Rojas's ethical commitment is evidenced by his inferential or 'bottom-up' approach to the data and desire to study a 'person of flesh and blood in her circumstance' (rather than an academic construct). He characterises the researcher's role as understanding, not assessing, since the person surveyed must be the authority on their condition.

The seven domains of satisfaction derived by Rojas's principal components analysis of the Mexican data mirror those of Cummins's meta-analyses of measures of QoL and life satisfaction (1995, 1996). The exception to this is the 'personal' domain, which incorporates time for personal projects and recreation, satisfaction with education and personal growth. However, this echoes Van Praag and Ferrer Carbonell's domain of 'leisure' (2004), and the emphasis put on hobbies and leisure time by Kousa and Mohseni (below). Rojas also found that the domain of community (incorporating indicators relating to environment, safety and trust) did not relate to any of the socioeconomic or demographic indicators.

Another interesting finding was that although the effects of being poor can be seen across all domains except community (especially those that are most significant for life satisfaction), the economically non-poor were only 6% more satisfied with their lives as a whole. Education seemed to be intrinsically valuable in a Mexican urban context as its effect spread across all domains (e.g. the family and personal domains which were very important for life satisfaction), whilst income only affected the economic and job domains.

East Asia

Ibrahim and Chung (2003) measured the QoL of residents on industrial estates in Singapore by collecting personal importance and satisfaction ratings for 18 subjective indicators drawn from an earlier study by Foo (1998). These comprised ten indicators that were characterised as 'personal' (e.g. family life, leisure) and eight as 'external' (e.g. public safety, consumer goods). They also used Foo's method of asking one question on global life satisfaction at the beginning of the survey to reduce bias, and one at the end to enable reflection, and averaging the result to produce an overall life satisfaction score.

The most important indicators were health, family life (also the most important in Foo's study) and public safety. The least important were self-development, religion and politics. People were most satisfied with family life and public safety, and least satisfied with politics, which seems to support arguments against weighting on the basis that satisfaction and importance are highly correlated (e.g. Trauer and Mackinnon 2001). Respondents were also asked an optional open question about which aspect of their lives was least satisfactory and why. A third of respondents nominated the environment, especially heavy pollution, and a sixth nominated lack of leisure time/facilities.

Middle East

Kousha and Mohseni (2000) reported the results of two surveys of Iranians resident in Tehran from 1995 to 1997, which used translated questions from the US General Social Survey (GSS), enabling comparison with the Chicago GSS from 1994. The survey used a 3-point GHQ but had difficulty translating 'happiness', eventually choosing a less formal word that denoted joy and fun. Respondents were also asked about how worried they were at the moment, their level of trust in others, degree of excitement about life and satisfaction in standard domains like 'marriage' and 'family life'.

The study contained an enlightening description of problems with telephone and mail surveys in developing countries (e.g. lack of familiarity with 'junk mail', and people's mail being opened by the post office). This led to their choice of a more reliable, if non-random, snowballing technique. Interestingly, the main determinants of happiness in Tehran were also the areas respondents were least satisfied with (e.g. hobbies and leisure time, and sociopolitical conditions). This differs from the GSS results where the majority of

19 Quality of Life in Developing Countries

Americans were fairly happy with the area they considered most important (marriage), if not quite as happy as the Iranians were.[24] The demographic factors that affected happiness were the same in America and Tehran, but differed in degree of effect, for example, socioeconomic and marital status were not as important as among Americans. Similarly, the determinants of happiness were the same but were differently weighted, so income was most important in Chicago, and hobbies and leisure time in Tehran.

Global, Multi-Item Measures

These are primarily used to measure people's satisfaction with their life 'as a whole' and single psychological traits like anxiety (e.g. the *SWLS*, described below, and the Beck Anxiety Index). Although multi-item measures take longer to administer, they are thought to have greater reliability and validity than single items (Diener et al. 2002). For example, they have less variability due to item-placement effects (Pavot and Diener 1993), or external influences at the time of response. For this reason, the fact that the *SWLS* generally gives lower values for life satisfaction than single items is interpreted as a sign that it is less affected by biases like 'global positivity'[25] (Cummins 1998).

The precision of these measures is enhanced by larger response scales (5, 7 or 11 points, rather than the 3- or 4-point scales used with global single items). However, these can prove a problem for translation and interview administration if scales with adjectival descriptors are used—WeD found 7-point scales challenging in Ethiopia and Bangladesh as Bangla, Amharic and Oromiffa did not have sufficient 'measurement' words to draft meaningful response options. Fortunately Biswas-Diener and Diener's (2001) work in Calcutta suggests that a 3-point scale need not reduce reliability.

Satisfaction with Life Scale (*SWLS*) (Diener et al. 1985)

The *SWLS* is a five-item measure that assesses satisfaction with life 'as a whole' and can be administered in a couple of minutes. It was used in the WeD research and seemed to be popular with respondents in, despite the final item, which is reversed and also very abstract ('If I could live my life over, I would change almost nothing'). The *SWLS* has been used in the majority of developing countries, including Ethiopia, Bangladesh, Zambia, Peru, India, Argentina, Cape Verde, Angola, South Korea, Nepal, South Africa, Taiwan, various Arabic-speaking countries, China and Thailand. Its one-factor structure was shown to fit reasonably well across 41 nations in a study using a student sample (Vitter
sø et al. 2002). The study also observed a 'nested factor' in some countries' data (influencing items 1 and 5), which may relate to differences between nations about the extent to which meeting the ideal standard is defined as satisfaction.[26] Vittersø et al.'s data showed a low correlation with GNP overall (adjusted correlation .25 n.s.), with the strongest correlation for the third item ('I am satisfied with my life'), which was also confirmed as the most central to the scale.

Diener et al. (1995) found that SWB correlated with high income, individualism, human rights and societal equality in a survey of studies using the *SWLS* from 55 nations. The variation within nations was much higher than between them (87% versus 13% of total variance). However, it was still high in relation to the effects of age (0.7%) and gender (1.5%). GNP appeared to explain 17% of variance in *SWLS*, but this reduced to 6% (n.s.) when 'cultural differences in reliability and model fit' were taken into account. The authors explained that 'our study shows that people in poorer nations have less

---

[24]This may be a form of positivity bias where North American survey respondents appear to be more likely to say the things that are going well for them are important.

[25]Global positivity bias is a tendency, particularly common in North America, to respond very positively to questions about happiness or satisfaction with life as a whole; see Strack et al. 1990.

[26]The first item ('in most ways my life is close to my ideal') worked better in richer nations than poor, which the authors suggested could be because 'ideal selves' are more important in rich countries and 'past achievements' in poor ones.

(continued)

(continued)

reliable responses to satisfaction with life measures, and this is an additional explanation of why, in general, wealthy nations score higher on subjective wellbeing scales' as more stable measurement gives higher correlation coefficients (1995, p. 96).

The *SWLS* has been used in a cross-national study with adult participants from the USA, Singapore, Thailand, Japan and Korea examining relationships between materialism, individualism/collectivism and life satisfaction (Wong et al. 2003). A study by Suh et al. across 61 nations demonstrated a relationship between *SWLS* scores and levels of individualism/ collectivism (1998). Another study of attitudes to modernity among Israeli Bedouin women demonstrated a correlation between objective living conditions, attitudes of wives and the wives' perceptions of their husband's attitudes (Kedem-Friedrich and Al-Atawneh 2004). For example, a husband's attitude to his wife's working affected all elements of her SWB to a greater extent than whether she actually worked or not! In an independent confirmation of gap theories of SWB, women were unhappiest if their attitudes were more modern than their husband, or their surroundings.

element of weighting (e.g. the WHOQOL importance scores), as this increases 'face validity'; however its explanatory value is still debated. Alternatively, measures can be entirely individualised, for example, the Cantril Self-Anchoring Striving Scale (Cantril 1965) or Anamnestic Comparative Self-Assessment (Bernheim et al. 2005), which uses person-defined endpoints, or the Global Person Generated Index, *GPGI* (Martin et al. 2010).

Profile measures are most commonly used in HRQoL where a further distinction is made between generic, disease-specific and individualised measures. Generic measures cover all population groups (e.g. the MOS Short-Form 36-Item Health Survey, *SF-36*, Ware and Sherbourne 1992). Disease-specific ones cover people with a specific condition and/or their carers (e.g. the General Measure of the Functional Assessment of Cancer Therapy, *FACT-G*, Cella et al. 1993, and a scale for parents of children with ear, nose and throat infections designed by Berdeaux et al. 1998). Individualised measures come in both disease-specific and generic forms (e.g. the *ADDQoL* for people with diabetes, Bradley et al. 1999, or the Schedule of Individualised QoL, *SEIQoL*, O'Boyle et al. 1992). The most widely used profile measure within international health research is the WHOQOL, which is described in the box below.

Profile Measures

There are two forms of profile measure: first, *overlapping*, which explores different aspects of a complex construct such as social support (e.g. *Social Support Questionnaire*, Sarason et al. 1987), and second, *independent*, which asks the respondents to judge their QoL, or another construct, across a range of separate domains, and does not attempt to produce a total score.[27] Profile measures may include an

---

[27] Some HRQoL researchers have described combining different domains in a single score as 'adding apples and oranges' (Stewart and Ware 1992), especially when questions about levels of functioning are aggregated with how the person feels about the situation (Muldoon et al. 1998). See also Fayers et al. 1997 on the perils of combining causal and indicator variables, and Cummins et al. 2005 for a general critique.

World Health Organization Quality of Life-100 Item (WHOQOL-100) and 26 Item (WHOQOL-Bref)

The WHOQOL Group used a common international protocol to develop two generic profile measures of HRQoL, the WHOQOL-100 and the WHOQOL-Bref. They also developed population-specific modules for older adults (The WHOQOL-OLD Group 2005) and people living with HIV/AIDS (O'Connell et al. 2004), and a module on Spirituality, Religion, and Personal Beliefs (SRPB) has been validated in six countries (The WHOQOL-SRPB Group 2006).

All WHOQOL centres were involved in generating facets, and subsequently items; however,

(continued)

(continued)

the agenda was largely set by the small group of 'experts' who defined the six domains of quality of life (physical, psychological, social, economic, environmental and SRPB).[28] Although there was some iteration between the advisory group and the focus groups, the structure of the instrument did not change substantially (a domain with a single facet was added on SPRB). Questions were drafted by population focus groups (predominantly urban) who suggested locally appropriate ways of asking questions about QoL. Each centre then rank-ordered these questions according to importance to ensure that cross-cultural equivalence was retained. The importance of domains and items was highly equivalent across countries, and subsequent psychometric research has demonstrated the cross-cultural validity of the structure (Power et al. 1999). Items that were only highly important in their countries of origin were retained as national items in the country-specific language version of the WHOQOL but are rarely analysed (e.g. items on energy and food in South-East Asian countries, and security in Israel, Skevington et al. 1999). The WHOQOL also has 100 importance items, but these have proved similarly difficult to analyse (see Skevington et al. 2004). Careful attention was paid to developing cross-culturally comparable response scales by establishing in each country which adjectival descriptors fell at the 25%, 50% and 75% distances between the two ends of each response scale.

The WHOQOL's 'spoke-wheel' development process has been described as the gold standard for international projects (Bowden and Fox-Rushby 2003; Schmidt and Bullinger 2007).

However, it is a resource-intensive process that requires access to translation and transcription facilities, which are not available in many developing countries. Another concern is that the WHOQOL's social domain is also psychometrically weak, largely because it only has three facets.[29] One of these, sexual activity, is prone to missing data even when the questionnaire is self-completed, rather than administered by an interviewer of a different gender or generation, in front of their entire household (Nilsson et al. 2004).

Other reviews have questioned the soundness of the WHOQOL's construct validity,[30] or characterised it as a measure of life satisfaction (slightly unfairly since only half of the items in the WHOQOL-Bref are about satisfaction) (Williams 2000; Hagerty et al. 2001; Cummins et al. 2005). The WHOQOL's use of self-report objective questions could potentially confound subjective measurement (Cummins 2000), as could its use of symptom-oriented variables such as pain, which are causal agents of components of QoL rather than components of QoL (Fayers et al. 1997).

There is a Bangla version of the WHOQOL-Bref, which has been used with urban adolescents in Dhaka (Izutsu et al. 2005). The authors found good discriminant validity, internal consistency and test-retest reliability, but recorded low alphas for social relations (0.28) and physical function (0.58). Nilsson et al. considered using the WHOQOL-100 with older Bangladeshis, but rejected it as too long (2005). They also thought the 5-point scale required a fully functioning memory, and criticised the inclusion of items on sexual function.

---

[28]The WHOQOL-Bref omits the spiritual and economic domains, reducing its utility in developing countries.

---

[29]See O'Carroll et al. 2000; Bonomi et al. 2000; Hagerty et al. 2001.

[30]The extent to which it is based on a comprehensive and coherent theory of QoL.

Profile measures have also been used in general QoL research in developing countries, most notably the Personal Wellbeing Index, *PWI* (Cummins et al. 2003), which is described in the box below.

Personal Wellbeing Index (*PWI*)

The *PWI* is a measure of SWB comprising seven domains: Standard of living, Personal health, Achieving in life,[31] Personal relationships, Personal safety, Community connectedness, and Future security. The domains were proposed as the minimum set of domains that represent the first-level deconstruction of life satisfaction, and this was empirically verified by checking that each domain contributes unique variance when they are collectively regressed against a global life satisfaction question (Thomas 2005 found a correlation of .78 with the *SWLS*).

The global item also helps decide whether a new item should become an additional domain, for example, 'spiritual or religious well-being', which was tested in Australia and failed to make a unique contribution to life satisfaction. The domains can be analysed as a separate variable, or summed to yield an average score that represents SWB. They form a single stable factor and account for about 50% of variance in Australia and other countries.

Two principles lie behind the *PWI*. First, each domain should describe a broad aspect of life which is potentially amenable to subjective and objective measurement. This excludes affective adjectives like Happiness, although this was included experimentally in a comparative study of Australia and Hong Kong (Lau et al. 2005). Second, each domain should describe an unequivocal indicator variable (e.g. 'Satisfaction with your health') rather than a causal variable of QoL (such as 'Satisfaction with your control over your life') for the reasons explained in Fayers et al. (1997). The advantage of this approach was that the end product was theoretically constrained and determined so scale items formed a single tight factor with high construct validity. The approach was also parsimonious, producing the minimum number of domains, and the broad, semi-abstract nature of the chosen domains increases cross-cultural validity.

The *PWI* was created from the Comprehensive Quality of Life Scale (*ComQoL*, Cummins 1997, 2002b), which comprised an objective and subjective measure of QoL and used importance ratings. The *ComQoL* was abandoned in 2001 as the objective scale never factored into seven non-complex domains, despite repeated modification, and the 'multiplicative' method of importance weighting was demonstrated to be psychometrically invalid and have little explanatory power (Trauer and Mackinnon 2001). The *PWI* retained the same question structure and six of the seven domains. The 'happiness' domain was removed for the reason given above, and replaced by 'How satisfied are you with your future security?' The original 7-point Likert scale, which used adjectival descriptors, was replaced with an 11-point End-Defined Response Scale (0–10, 'extremely dissatisfied' to 'extremely satisfied', with a midpoint labelled 'neither satisfied nor dissatisfied'). This optimised the respondent's discriminative capacity, and avoided psychometric confusion from applying adjectival descriptors to an interval scale (Jones and Thurstone 1955).

The *PWI* is often administered alongside the National Wellbeing Index (*NWI*). The results of the two scales cannot be combined, and the usual correlation is around 0.44 (Cummins et al. 2003). The *NWI* comprises six questions about satisfaction with economic situation, state of the environment, social conditions, government, business and national security,[32] and a global question about satisfaction with life in the country where the measure is being administered. Usually scores for the *NWI* are lower than the *PWI*, which is explained by the fact that its relative remoteness from the individual means that satisfaction is not held stable by the homeostatic system, as is hypothesised to occur with the *PWI*. Twelve surveys of the Australian population produced a maximum variation in mean scores of 3.1 percentage points, which supports the stability of SWB (Cummins et al. 2005).

---

[31] This domain was labelled 'Work and productive activity in the measure' in the *PWI*'s predecessor, the *ComQoL* (Cummins 1997).

[32] The last three questions were added in 2002.

(continued)

19 Quality of Life in Developing Countries

(continued)

Currently the International Wellbeing Group has about 100 researchers from over 40 countries, and the scale has been translated into the following languages: Arabic, Chinese (Cantonese and Mandarin), Croatian, Dutch, Italian, Japanese, Mexican, Slovakian and Spanish (Castilian and Argentinean). The *PWI* also has normative data from 14 countries, 8 of which are developing or transition economies (Cummins et al. 2003, 2005).

The scale can be self-completed or interview-administered, and the questions are worded to allow respondents to form a personal interpretation and judgement about them, something that is encouraged by the interview administrator. There are versions of the *PWI* for use with the general adult population (aged at least 18 years), school-age children and adolescents, preschool-age children and people with an intellectual disability or other form of cognitive impairment.

Qualitative support for the *PWI*'s domain structure is provided by the results from the first phase of the WeD QoL research, which show a high degree of consensus (see table in Appendix 2). For example, *Personal relationships* was the most important factor in Bangladesh and Thailand. *Standard of living* was very important in all countries, and aspects relating to this were the two main priorities in Bangladesh, three of the top four in Thailand, and accounted for more than half of the entries for Ethiopia. *Personal health* was featured in all countries except Peru, but was not ranked highly.

Achieving in life also seemed relevant (if interpreted as including education and/or 'exploration'), although interestingly education was not mentioned in Thailand and Peru. *Community connectedness*[33] seemed to be important to everyone except respondents from North East Thailand who focused more on family relationships and to a lesser extent friendships. *Personal safety* was the only domain that did not seem relevant, partly because of the use of the word 'personal', but also because the table only shows data from households and individuals living well. Experiences of insecurity and violence were common responses to questions about living badly or unhappiest experiences, especially in Bangladesh and Peru. It goes without saying that *Future security* is also tremendously important to people living in developing countries, whether interpreted in physical, material or psychological terms. There appeared to be only two important domains omitted from the scale: Religion, which was very important in Bangladesh and Thailand (especially for women and older adults), and fairly important in Ethiopia, and Happiness, including having a sense of meaning. Both of these are currently being tested by the International Wellbeing Group with mixed results (e.g. Lau et al. 2005).

[33]Community connectedness was interpreted as including respect and status, for example, having a 'good appearance' (Ethiopia).

There are currently few QoL measures that have been developed specifically for use in developing countries, and many individual measures of QoL are only available in Western European languages.[34] Therefore, choosing a measure usually also involves translating and adapting it, and this process is described in the following section.

[34]According to Bowden and Fox-Rushby (2003), indigenous South American, South Asian, Arabic and African languages are particularly under-represented.

Adapting Individual Measures of QoL for Use in Developing Countries

Within HRQoL most translation and adaptation has been carried out by international working groups; for example, the International Quality of Life Assessment Group, which works with the *SF-36* (founded 1991); the Functional Assessment of Cancer Treatment Group, which has translated the *FACT* into South Indian, African and most East

Asian languages[35] (founded 1996); and the WHOQOL group (founded 1995). The *SF-36* is also available in Arabic, Japanese, Chinese, Hebrew and Kiswahili, and the Bangla version has been validated with people with disabilities (Hosain et al. 2002) and different socioeconomic statuses[36] (Ahmed et al. 2002). Although adaptation takes place outside the working groups listed above, the results are not always published in international journals, making it difficult to assess its quality. Normative population data is rarely collected in developing countries, which makes meaningful comparison difficult.

A good translation from the original into the 'target' language is a precondition of successful measure adaptation. However, for this to be possible, there needs to be a similar concept of health in both cultures that is used in the same way and has the same relationship to other values. There should also be a comparable system of health care and medical education, assumptions that do not even seem plausible in Europe, let alone internationally (Leplege and Verdier 1995; Anderson et al. 1996). Guyatt (1993) questions the emphasis on transposing a measure from one language to another as closely as possible. He suggests instead that the inconsistencies, ambiguities and untranslatable expressions identified during translation should be used to reformulate the original questionnaire, rather than transfer its problems to a new language.

Whilst there are many different approaches to translation (Acquadro et al. 1996), most authors advise the following: (1) using at least two 'forward' translations with a comparative discussion; (2) being cautious about the use of 'back-translations'[37] as these are often of a lower quality than the original; and (3) checking the translation with a panel of linguists, or more pertinently a focus group of potential respondents. For example, the FACT Group, who have had considerable experience translating between European and East Asian languages, uses forward and back translations (a 'double translation' methodology), consults with an expert advisory committee and also employs linguists to revise the translations.

Translation procedures are more complicated for the WHOQOL Group, and for WeD during the development of the *WeDQoL,* described later in this section, as the iterative development process meant that items had to be translated from a wide variety of languages into English, and then translated into another language with a very different structure (e.g. Thai and Bangla). It would clearly be beneficial in situations like these to have a group of bilingual people from different countries who can discuss each other's translations, and explain the rationale behind their own.

Many different forms of equivalence have been proposed to assess the quality of a translation, but the most comprehensive account is given by Herdman et al. (1998, p. 331) who makes the following distinctions: *Conceptual* (the measure has the same relationship to the underlying concept in both cultures, evidenced by the choice of domains and the emphasis placed on different domains); *Item* (estimates the same parameters on the latent trait being measured and is equally relevant and acceptable in both cultures); *Semantic* (achieves a 'similar effect' on respondents who speak different languages; this should not be confused with a literal translation, which may be meaningless); *Operational* (similar questionnaire format, instructions, mode of administration and measurement method); *Measurement* (psychometric properties are equivalent); and *Functional* (when 'an instrument does what it is supposed to do equally well in two or more cultures').

One of the most important parts of adaptation is the pretesting and piloting, which should be as thorough as that required for the original measure. The following section describes the adaptation of the Global Person Generated Index (*GPGI*)[38] during the first phase of WeDQoL research. This is not presented as an example of best practice, but an account of the reality of adapting a measure in resource-poor environments, without a dedicated team of psychologists or linguists. Our rationale for exploring the individualised QoL measures used within HRQoL was to see if these could be adapted for use in developing countries, as they

---

[35] For example, Pandey et al. 2004 (Malayalam), Mullin et al. 2000 (three African languages).

[36] As with the WHOQOL, the SF-36 social function scale performed poorly, which is especially problematic in Bangladesh as qualitative studies suggest this is the most important area of people's lives.

[37] Translations back into the original language by a native speaker who has not seen the original measure.

[38] The *GPGI* is an extension of the Patient Generated Index (Ruta et al. 1994), which assesses satisfaction with five areas that the respondent identifies as important.

could potentially bridge the gap between the methods familiar to development practitioners and QoL measures. The *GPGI* appeared to be the best fit as it could be administered using participatory techniques that might be more familiar to the respondents, or used as a semi-structured interview schedule. It was piloted in conjunction with the developer in rural and peri-urban sites in Ethiopia, Bangladesh and Thailand (Camfield and Ruta 2007). WeD fieldworkers were given a free hand to interpret and translate a culturally relevant version of the *PGI*. For example, in Bangladesh, the endpoints of the scale, 'good' (bhalo) and 'bad' (kharap), were thought to be too vague, and an alternative wording of satisfaction (shontushtho) and dissatisfaction (oshontushtho) was also tried. There were two separate forward and back translations, but the quality of the translation was most improved by the critical eyes of the field assistants, who in Bangladesh and Ethiopia mostly had English as their second language.

In Ethiopia and Thailand the reception of the *GPGI* was generally positive, especially in comparison with the lengthy semi-structured interview schedules that were administered alongside it. In Bangladesh there was a range of responses from women who immediately said 'I can't do that', to one woman who insisted on filling it in herself.

The first stage of the GPGI involves the respondent identifying up to five areas of their life that are most important to them. Rural respondents found it difficult to think of five important areas (one listed 'kidneys, ears, and eyes'), and many said that their lives were 'very simple' with 'nothing adventurous or complex'. In Bangladesh there seemed to be confusion about what constituted an important area, and people tended to name either goals (e.g. forthcoming exams) or past events (e.g. their father's death). In Ethiopia it was difficult to find a word that meant 'important', and eventually 'wesagn' was used (meaning crucial or needed), which may explain the 'development-oriented' nature of the areas nominated.

The second stage requires respondents to indicate their satisfaction with the areas nominated during the last month using a 10-point scale. The timescale was problematic as respondents found it hard to focus on their QoL in the last month. For example, some respondents spoke of traumatic events occurring several years previously, which were presumably still present in their minds. All countries decided to reduce the original 10-point scale to a 7-point scale, and Bangladesh and Ethiopia recommended reducing it to a 5-point scale in future studies. Thailand experimented with three visual methods to indicate satisfaction: 'moons' (the full moon, a white circle, represented the highest score, and the lunar eclipse, a black circle, represented the lowest), 'smiley faces' (happy-sad) and numbers (labelled from good to bad). Respondents found the visual methods more confusing than the numbers (especially the moons), and it was agreed that any method could be used, providing it was sufficiently well explained.

The third stage requires the respondent to 'spend' points to indicate the relative importance of the nominated areas, which worked best when respondents were given coins to spend. However, there was some confusion between the actual and symbolic value of the coins; for example, in Thailand one respondent gave many coins to the area 'Children', saying 'I must give a lot of money to my children'. Older people also needed a long time to count the coins and make their decision.

After local fieldworkers had piloted it with a range of respondents, the *GPGI* was interview-administered to 240 people from 15 rural, peri-urban and urban sites in Bangladesh, Ethiopia and Thailand. It was accompanied by a semi-structured interview schedule, which enabled the *GPGI* to be validated qualitatively by exploring whether the areas people nominated as important and their appraisals of them differed according to the method used (Camfield and Ruta 2007).

Earlier in the chapter I reported some of the qualitative data from Bangladesh, so I will now briefly review its *GPGI* data. Unfortunately this was the smallest of the country samples as the *GPGI* was only applied in two urban sites in the districts of Manikganj and Dinaspur (Manikganj is near to Dhaka and Dinaspur is relatively remote). Consequently the sample has an unequal balance of men to women (1:4) since in Bangladesh women are rarely seen in public spaces in urban areas (e.g. 'tea shops') and so are less easy to access. More than half of the sample had further or higher education, which is obviously not typical. Less than 5% were farmers, and 9% were over 60. Nearly all respondents nominated their family (including the health of family members), and their children (including their education and future employment) as areas of importance. Over a third of respondents also mentioned being married, and a quarter having money. The data appear to be fairly coherent, but the small size of the sample (evidenced by the large standard deviations) makes it impossible to draw any conclusions.

	Mean	N	Standard deviation
Poor	69.33	10	29.58
Rich	73.75	12	15.14
Illiterate/primary	61.33	5	31.65
Secondary/FE/HE	74.80	17	19.03
Woman	67.78	6	31.62
Man	73.23	16	18.93
Age <39	80.0	10	13.12
Age 40+	66.03	12	25.96
Muslim	72.45	17	24.06
Hindu	69.33	5	17.34
Manikganj	62.83	10	26.94
Dinaspur	79.17	12	15.12

Having explored the challenges of adapting subjective QoL measures, I will now look at the development process and provide some illustrative examples. Two approaches to cross-cultural measure development are described below: first, developing a universal measure that is applicable across all cultures (e.g. the *PWI*), or has a universally applicable core measure with additional nation-, condition- or population-specific modules (e.g. *WHOQOL*), and second, developing individual 'native' scales (e.g. the *KENQOL*, a HRQoL measure specific to Kenya).

Developing Individual Measures of QoL for Use in Developing Countries

'Universal' Measures

Much attention has been paid to cross-cultural measurement in HRQoL research due to interest from international bodies like the WHO, and the organisers of clinical trials[39] (see Schmidt and Bullinger 2007 for a review). Most researchers use a 'sequential' approach where an existing questionnaire is translated from one language to another (e.g. the *SF-36*), although some use a 'parallel' approach where a measure is assembled from existing scales developed in different countries

(e.g. the *EORTC QLQ C-30*. The most rigorous and resource-intensive approach is the 'simultaneous', which involves the cooperative cross-cultural development of a questionnaire and has so far only been used by the WHOQOL group (1995). However, all approaches involve the basic steps of identification of relevant items, translation, pretesting and psychometric validation. These are summarised below, paying particular attention to the challenges of undertaking this process in developing countries.

Items can be identified through focus group discussions (sometimes using participatory methods), semi-structured interviews and participant observation with potential respondents. They can also be identified through literature review and 'expert' consultation; however, this may produce a measure that has lower 'face validity' and credibility with respondents. Focus groups and interviews can be purposively sampled to ensure that important local differences are covered (e.g. caste status in India). Being sensitive to potential group dynamics will enable people to feel comfortable talking in front of, and even contradicting each other, and different perspectives can be articulated. However, some people may not feel confident speaking in focus groups (e.g. those who are very old, poor, low status or in a minority group), although it is particularly important that these people's voices are heard. For this reason, interviews are often preferred, as in close-knit and hierarchical societies the participants and topics of focus groups need to be carefully selected.

Local fieldworkers should be thoroughly trained and supplied with semi-standardised interview schedules and focus group manuals. However, it is also

---

[39] Bowden et al. observed that despite the fact that 71% of mortality in Africa and 39% in South East Asia is attributable to communicable disease, only 3.4% of the HRQoL measures in their review covered this area (2003).

important that the researchers who select the items are present so they understand the background to people's statements and do not misinterpret them. Although recording focus groups and interviews is 'best practice', it does place an extra burden on the fieldworkers, as transcription facilities may not be readily available. Translation may be difficult to arrange, and the results can be variable, even with a bilingual translator working with a native speaker of English.

Once the statements have been selected (usually by two researchers reviewing transcripts or field notes), they are adapted as items. This involves making appropriate modifications to remove redundancy or ambiguity, whilst still capturing their meaning. The items are then combined with an appropriate response scale. The measure can then be pretested with a sample of potential respondents, usually focusing on older and less-educated respondents who are likely to find the questions more difficult to respond to.

The crucial question of how respondents interpret the items is often overlooked, or at least not reported, in accounts of the adaptation and development of measures. Some researchers seem happy to include a large number of items and subsequently eliminate the ones that fail the psychometric tests. However, this risks 'end[ing] up by defining the concept in terms of the indicators that worked', which takes it far away from the ideas expressed in the data, or the theory that the measure was based on (De Vaus 1995, p. 54). Thorough pretesting is essential as it enables researchers to be sure about what is being asked, and answered, and therefore avoid expensive mistakes (Jenkinson 1995; Mallinson 2002; Camfield 2002).

The next section describes the rigorous pretesting of the *KENQOL* HRQoL measure, which used six separate methods to ensure that the measure was capturing 'the self-perceived and locally defined "health" of people in Makueni District, Kenya' (Bowden et al. 2002). The process involved (a) establishing the intended referential and connotative meaning of each question, (b) ensuring that questions were simple and unambiguous, (c) checking if they were locally relevant and obviously related to health, (d) positively phrasing questions to avoid double negatives, (e) making sure they contained only one idea and did not overlap with other questions and (f) using a clear time period.

The appropriateness of questions was judged by 'expanded interviews' where an interviewee responded to three to five questions, followed by a set of probes to investigate the thought processes involved in answering these questions. The interviews are a more structured and thus less cognitively challenging version of the concurrent and retrospective 'think aloud' techniques used in cognitive debriefing (Barofsky 1996). 'Targeted methods' were also used where people with known and opposite characteristics (e.g. rich or poor, sick or well) were asked specific questions to check that these were interpreted in the same way. Two other sets of individuals were asked how they would have answered before and after a development-point project, or during and after an attack of malaria, to qualitatively assess the sensitivity of the questions to change. Respondents were asked to sort questions into groups, using their own or the researchers' categories, to see how questions related to each other. Focus groups were also used to explore the interpretation of words like 'household', time frames like 'last year'[40] and the use of single and plural 'you'. Finally, the results were cross-checked with local academics, key informants and the fieldworkers.

The questionnaire was first piloted domain by domain so the researcher could ask the respondent in detail about their opinion of the questions. For example, did they use the correct forms of address, were the response categories appropriate, what potential problems could they foresee, etc. The interviewer also noted requests for clarification, additional information that could suggest how the question was being interpreted, body language, pauses and emotional responses. Bowden estimated that the process took 6 months of the researcher's time and 12 months of a fieldworker's, but was still worthwhile for both practical and ethical reasons.

For a measure to be used cross-culturally, it needs response categories that can be successfully translated into different languages. Several international working groups have compiled lists of standard scale descriptors (e.g. 'satisfied' or 'fairly satisfied') and after translation have empirically established the distance between them using a Thurstone scaling method. The number of response categories is also a consideration as interview administration of scales with descriptors is time consuming, and there may be a trade-off between precision and respondent fatigue above 3 or 5 points. Fortunately 3-, 5- and 7-point scales are

---

[40] Fieldworkers from the *WeDQoL* piloting in Ethiopia noted that respondents could interpret 'last year' in at least four ways—as a calendar year (Gregorian or Ethiopian), an agricultural year or 12 months since the question was asked.

relatively easy to transpose, so it will still be possible to compare the findings with other studies. The International Wellbeing Group (2005) has circumvented these issues by using an 11-point end-defined response scale, without adjectival descriptors, which has worked well in a number of developing countries.

Practices for psychometric testing to establish the validity and reliability of the measure also vary widely. For example, the FACT Group bases its item analysis on the Rasch model, and uses structural equation models and multivariate statistics to replicate the factor structure of the measure across countries. However, the IQOLA Group (*SF-36*) focuses on the items' discriminant validity and uses item response theory to distinguish patterns of responses to items across cultures (see Schmidt and Bullinger 2007 for further details). Measurement equivalence is obviously important, but cannot replace investigation of the other forms of equivalence specified by Herdman (conceptual, item, semantic, operational and functional) (Bowden and Fox-Rushby 2003a). Conceptual equivalence in particular tends to be assumed rather than tested, and there is little use of qualitative methods.

'Native' Scales

Many of the problems identified in the earlier part of this chapter could be solved by the development of native scales. However, this has been much less common in developing countries, presumably due to resource constraints. Below I briefly describe the development of country or regionally specific measures in Kenya, Hong Kong and Mexico City to highlight the potential of this approach. The WeD research group has done further work in this area, and a detailed description is given at the end of this section.

Fox-Rushby et al. have been developing the *KENQOL* since 1994; the fact that the project is still continuing 11 years later gives some sense of the scale of the enterprise (e.g. Fox-Rushby et al. 1997, 2002, 2003a, b). For example, the local concepts of health that the scale was based upon were identified through extensive qualitative research and long-term participant observation.[41] The *KENQOL* has been designed to access 'those aspects of health that a member of the community could respond to in public to an interviewer who was not necessarily known to them personally' (Bowden et al. 2002, p. 323). It uses a binary response scale, as this fits the nature of the data, and was tested using targeted binary factor analysis with oblique rotation (Fox-Rushby et al. 2003b).

Chan et al. (2004) have developed the *HKQoLOCP* to measure the QoL of older Chinese people living in Hong Kong. The content was generated through focus groups stratified by age and income exploring older people's definitions of QoL, followed by 'expert review'. The 21-item scale covers SWB, health, personal relationships, achievement recognition, finance (one item) and living conditions (one item). It can be applied as both an index and a profile, and the multi-item domains can also be applied as subscales. According to the authors, the respondents placed a 'typically Cantonese emphasis' on eating and family relationships, to the extent that eating correlated highly with all domains, especially SWB and health (0.49 and 0.58, respectively). Living conditions showed the lowest correlation with the QoL composite (0.56), and SWB, the highest (0.82), which is slightly at variance with the findings of Lau et al. (2005) for the *PWI* in Hong Kong where living standards made a significant contribution (0.67).

In order to explore the relationship between SWB and socioeconomic status, and the interaction of poverty, SWB and psychological resources, Lever developed a measure of SWB for the inhabitants of Mexico City (2000, 2004, 2005). SWB was defined as a subjective, multidimensional construct that refers to an individual's level of satisfaction with various aspects of his/her life. The measure was developed through a rigorous process, which included the administration of an open-ended questionnaire to 320 subjects to identify what they thought to be the essential components of QoL (Lever 2000). The final measure has 60 items in 11 domains, e.g. work, children, and uses a 4-point Likert scale to measure levels of satisfaction. It also uses importance to weight domains, but has devised a coding system that combines satisfaction and importance to avoid the problems identified with multiplicative scores.[42]

---

[41]Local concepts of health incorporate contentment, corporeal capability, cleanliness, cooperation and completeness.

[42]The highest number of points—nine—is assigned to areas with the most points for importance and satisfaction, whilst the lowest is assigned to areas with the most points for importance and the least for satisfaction.

Initial results suggested that sociability and close friends were most important for 'general' QoL,[43] followed by family. The centrality of personal relationships reflects the findings of participatory and qualitative explorations of QoL in developing countries. Lever (2004) found significant differences in domain satisfaction by economic group, with the poorest subjects reporting least satisfaction. However, she also observed low correlations between income and SWB.

Bringing the Approaches Together: The WeDQoL

The WeD group have also developed a measure of subjective QoL, the WeDQoL, which bridges the distinction between universal and native scales described earlier in this section. The WeDQoL's development was influenced by the World Health Organization (WHO) definition of quality of life. However, the group modified this to represent subjective quality of life as arising from the disjuncture between what people aspire to and their evaluation of their ability to achieve those aspirations, drawing on Calman (1984) and Michalos (1985). This approach recognises that the goals that people regard as important for their well-being include material items but also relationships, personal qualities and dispositions. Measure development involved a review of existing methods of subjective quality of life used in developing countries, open-ended qualitative research by local fieldworkers in each of the four countries to identify what local people regarded as important goals for their quality of life (Camfield 2006), and the trialling and psychometric validation of the final form of the instrument (Woodcock et al. 2009). The WeDQoL had two components addressing subjective well-being and aspirations:

1. Subjective Well-being

    Adapted versions of two international measures were applied: one capturing satisfaction with life as a whole (SWLS, Diener et al. 1985), and the other feelings or, put more precisely, positive and negative affect (PANAS, Watson 1988). The SWLS was administered with a 3-point scale (5 items, range 5–15) and the PANAS with a 5-point scale. Separate scores were reported for the components of Positive Affect (9 items, range 9–45) and Negative Affect (10 items, range 10–50).

2. Aspirations

    The WeD Quality of Life measure (WeDQoL) Weighted Goal Attainment Scale, or WeDQoL-goals, has two components that measure (1) how necessary an item is to a respondent's well-being and (2) how satisfied they are with this item. The first component is used to weight the second so the final score represents satisfaction with items that are valued by the respondent. In Thailand (Woodcock et al. 2009), the WeDQoL-goals consisted of 51 items and was interview-administered to 369 people, aged between 15 and 89 (mean age 45.7, SD 18.0). Respondents rated the perceived necessity for well-being of the 51 goals using a 3-point scale (0–2, where 0 represents 'unnecessary' and 2 'very necessary'). They then rated their satisfaction in achievement of the same goals. The scores for necessity were used to weight the scores for satisfaction so goals that were 'not necessary' were excluded when calculating goal satisfaction, whilst those that were 'very necessary' were given higher weights. The factor analysis of WeDQoL-goals identified three factors which have been labelled by the researchers as 'community/social/health' (23 items, alpha 0.90), 'nuclear family' (6 items, alpha 0.82) and 'house and home' (15 items, alpha 0.80). The 'house and home' factor can be subdivided into two subscales for a more fine-grained analysis: 'basic house and home' (11 items, alpha 0.80) and 'luxury' (4 items, alpha 0.61) (see Appendix 2). The factor scores enable a more reliable representation of the importance a respondent accords to a domain of life, for example, their family, than would be provided by a single item. The WeDQoL-goals was applied in all four countries (see Yamamoto et al. 2008 for Peru; other reports available on request) using a common format with additional country-specific items.

Conclusions

In this chapter I have made a strong case for the expansion of subjective QoL research in developing countries, especially the use of individual QoL measures. I have also outlined the main issues around developing, adapting and using measures of subjective

---

[43]The construct of 'general QoL' excluded work, couple relationship and children, as not all subjects were employed, in relationships or parents.

QoL in developing countries. Measuring people's QoL is clearly an ethical priority as 'GNP per capita is a fairly weak proxy for many of the things commonly associated with the good life' (Kenny 2005, p. 209). However, the measures used need to reflect local understandings of the good life, and should therefore be preceded by extensive qualitative and participatory work. Thorough pretesting is also important, as there is little point in administering a measure if you are not sure what it is measuring. The experience of answering irrelevant or badly drafted questions can visibly reduce the QoL of both researcher and respondent!

Global measures have been criticised for their stability and lack of sensitivity (e.g. Felce 1997). Many different theories have been put forward about the content of the individual's 'evaluative space' when they respond to them (e.g. 'conceptual referent', 'multiple discrepancy' and adaptation theories). However, even on an individual level, they can be valuable as a measure of core affect and disposition to action. For example, Redelmeier and Kahneman (1996) acknowledge that whilst retrospective evaluation of the experience of having a colonoscopy is less accurate than 'online' evaluation, it is still the best predictor of whether people will return for future colonoscopies. Diener et al. (2000) raise the interesting philosophical question of which form of happiness is the 'real' one: 'objective', 'domain-specific' or 'global'. It might be better to reframe this question in terms of what the researcher wants to achieve by assessing someone's QoL. Whilst domain-specific or even objective assessments would give a more accurate evaluation of the person's current state, if the researcher wanted to know their basis for decision making or planning (e.g. 'shall I join this new credit and savings group?'), they might be better off using a global assessment. Similarly, if a policymaker wanted to know about people's satisfaction with their health in order to plan or evaluate an intervention, then a profile measure would be the best choice, and could be supplemented with a global measure to calculate what effect their dissatisfaction with their health was having on their life as a whole. Fortunately, it usually is not necessary to make a choice at all, and the best approaches use a mix of subjective and objective methods in order to assess 'the wellbeing of a person of *flesh and blood* and *in her circumstance* [...], rather than the wellbeing of an academically constructed agent' (Rojas 2007; Camfield et al. 2008).

Acknowledgements Particular thanks to Jackeline Velazco and Monica Guillen-Royo, who wrote the review of happiness economics in developing countries. Thanks also to the Lead Researchers on QoL in the WeD Countries: Kaneta Choudhury and Mohammed Tapan in Bangladesh; Bethlehem Tekola and Ashebir Desalegn in Ethiopia; Jorge Yamamoto and Ana Rosa Feijoo in Peru (who created the *WeDQoL* Peru on which the final *WeDQoL* measure has been based); and Darunee Jongudomkarn, Malee Sabaiying and Sawittri Limchaiarunruang in Thailand. The support of the UK Economic and Social Research Council (ESRC) is gratefully acknowledged. The work was part of the programme of the ESRC Research Group on Wellbeing in Developing Countries.

Appendix 1: Determinants of Happiness in Developing Countries: Summary of Empirical Studies

Country	Latin American	South Africa	Rural China	Mexico	Ethiopia	Thailand
Authors	Graham (2005)	Kingdon and Knight (2003)	Knight and Song (2004)	Rojas (2005)	Guillen and Velazco (2005)	Guillen and Velazco (2005)
Dependent variable	Happiness: 4-point scale	Happiness: 5-point scale	Happiness: 6-point scale	Happiness: 7-point scale	Happiness: 3-point scale	Happiness: 3-point scale
Estimation method	Ordered logit	Ordered probit	OLS	OLS	Ordered probit	Ordered probit
Independent variables	Relationship[a]	Relationship	Relationship	Relationship	Relationship	Relationship
Household head characteristics						
Age	(−)	(+)	(−)	(−)	(−)	(−)
Education	(−)[b]	(+)	(+)	(+)[b]	(−)	(+)[b]
Male	(−)[b]		(−)		(+)[b]	(+)[b]
Married	(+)[b]		(+)	(+)	(+)[b]	(−)[b]
Employment status (self-employed)	(−)				(+)	(−)
Minority	(−)					
Income		(+)	(+)	(+)		
Unemployed	(−)	(−)				
African /coloured/ Indian		(−)				
Household characteristics						
Number of children < 16		(+)				
Urban household		(−)				
Basic needs/assets						
Health index	(+)	(+)	(+)			
Wealth/asset index	(+)				(+)	(+)
Asset value		(+)		(+)		
Household faced food shortage					(−)[b]	(−)
Perception variables						
Household's wealth in village (rich)			(+)		(+)	(+)
Household's wealth in village (above average)			(+)		(+)	(+)
Number of observations	15,209	8,279	9,112	1,540	920	904
Goodness of fit: pseudo R square	0.062	0.09	0.18	0.085	0.14	0.11

[a]The estimated relationship is reported. (+) means a positive or direct relationship between the dependent and independent variables, whilst (−) denotes an indirect or negative relationship
[b]Variable not statistically significant

Appendix 2: Comparison of Characteristics of QoL/Living Well with the Domains of the Personal Wellbeing Index (PWI)

PWI (Cummins et al. 2003)	Bath workshop	Bangladesh	Ethiopia	Thailand	Peru
Personal relationships	Close affiliation (1)	Marriage (7)	Support from natal family	Family relationships (1)	Being in a couple
		Children (5)			Family
		Relationships (3)			Helping each other
Standard of living	Services—formal/informal (4)	Income (1)	Economic stability/need satisfaction	Income, having money (2)	House
	Productive assets (8)	Material goods and environment (2)	Land	Assets, savings, inheritance (3)	Sustenance
	House/shelter (9)		Oxen	Living conditions (8)	Furniture and appliances
			Livestock	Housing (9)	Power supply, water
			Modern agricultural equipment		Material sufficiency (overcoming scarcity)
			Good house		
			Improved local infrastructure		
Personal health	Health (10)	Health (6)	Health	Health, longevity (5)	Rest and recuperation
Achieving in life	Participation/non-participation (6)	Education (4)	Business activities	Job (4)	'Exploration' and purchase and market exchange
			Education (self and children)	Personal qualities	
Community connectedness	Respect/recognition–disrespect/denial (5)	Status (connections) (9)	Good community relationships	Good appearance (7)	Interpersonal/social interaction
Personal safety	No	No	No	No	No
Future security	Security/insecurity (2)	No	No	No	No
	Agency/power/powerlessness (3)				

N.B. The numbers in brackets refer to its importance, where this was analysed

References

Acquadro, C., Jambon, B., Ellis, D., & Marquis, P. (1996). Language and translation issues. In B. Spilker (Ed.), *Quality of life and pharmacoeconomics in clinical trials* (2nd ed., pp. 575–587). Philadelphia: Lippincott-Raven.

Ahmed, S. M., Masud Rana, A. K. M., Chowdhury, M., & Bhuiya, A. (2002). Measuring perceived health outcomes in non-western culture: Does SF-36 have a place? *Journal of Health, Population, and Nutrition, 20*, 334–342.

Alkire, S. (2007). The missing dimensions of poverty data: Introduction to the special issue. *Oxford Development Studies, 35*(4), 347–359.

Anderson, R. T., McFarlane, M., Naughton, M. J., & Shumaker, S. A. (1996). Conceptual issues and considerations in cross cultural validation of generic HRQOL instruments. In B. Spilker (Ed.), *QOL and pharmaceuticals in clinical trials* (2nd ed.). Philadelphia: Lippincott-Raven.

Appadurai, A. (2004). The capacity to aspire. In V. Rao & M. Walton (Eds.), *1060 culture and public action*. Stanford: Stanford University Press.

Barofsky, I. (1996). Cognitive aspects of QOL assessment. In B. Spilker (Ed.), *QOL and pharmacoeconomics in clinical trials* (2nd ed.). Philadelphia: Lippincott-Raven.

Berdeaux, G., Hervie, C., Smajda, C., & Marquis, P. (1998). Parental QoL and recurrent ENT infections in their children: Development of a questionnaire. *Quality of Life Research, 7*, 501–512.

Bernheim, J. L., Theuns, P., Mazaheri, M., Calcoen, P., Heylighen, F., & Rose, M. (2005). Bridging cultural relativity in quality of life by Anamnestic Comparative Self-Assessment (ACSA). *Proceedings Australian Quality of Life Conference*.

Biswas Diener, R., & Diener, E. (2001). Making the best of a bad situation: Satisfaction in the slums of Calcutta. *Social Indicators Research, 55*, 329–352.

Bonomi, A. E., Patrick, D. L., Bushnell, D. M., & Martin, M. (2000). Validation of the United States' version of the World Health Organization Quality of Life (WHOQOL) instrument. *Journal of Clinical Epidemiology, 53*(1), 1–12.

Bowden, A., & Fox-Rushby, J. A. (2003). A systematic and critical review of the process of translation and adaptation of generic health-related quality of life measures in Africa, Asia, Eastern Europe, the Middle East, South America. *Social Science & Medicine, 57*, 1289–1306.

Bowden, A., Fox-Rushby, J. A., Nyandieka, L., & Wanjau, J. (2002). Methods for pre-testing and piloting survey questions: Illustrations from the KENQOL survey of HR-QoL. *Health Policy and Planning, 17*, 322–330.

Bowling, A. (1995). A survey of the public's judgments to inform scales of QOL. *Social Science & Medicine, 41*, 1411–1417.

Bradley, C., Todd, C., Gorton, T., Symonds, E., Martin, A., & Plowright, R. (1999). The development of an individualised questionnaire measure of perceived impact of diabetes on quality of life: the ADDQoL. *Quality of Life Research, 8*, 79–91.

Brock, K. (1999). *It's not only wealth that matters—It's peace of mind too: A review of participatory work on poverty and ill-being*. A study prepared for the World Development Report 2000/01. Washington, DC: PREM, World Bank.

Calman, K. C. (1984). QOL in cancer patients a hypothesis. *Journal of Medical Ethics, 10*, 124–127.

Camfield L. (2002). *Measuring quality of life in dystonia: An ethnography of contested representations*. PhD thesis.

Camfield, L. (2006). *Why and How of Understanding 'Subjective' Well-being: Exploratory work by the WeD group in four developing countries*. Well-being in Developing Countries Working Paper 26.

Camfield, L., Guillen-Royo, M. & Velazco, J. (2010). Does need satisfaction matter for psychological and subjective wellbeing in developing countries: A mixed-methods illustration from Bangladesh and Thailand. *Journal of Happiness Studies, 11*(4):497–516.

Camfield, L., & McGregor, J. A. (2005). Resilience and wellbeing in developing countries. In M. Ungar (Ed.), *Handbook for working with children and youth pathways to resilience across cultures and contexts*. Thousand Oaks: Sage.

Camfield, L., & McGregor, J. A. (2009). Editorial. Quality of life and international development policy and practice. *Applied Research in Quality of Life, 4*(2), 129–134.

Camfield, L., & Ruta, D. (2007). 'Translation is not enough': Using the Global Person Generated Index (GPGI) to assess individual quality of life in Bangladesh, Thailand, and Ethiopia. *Quality of Life Research, 16*(6), 1039–1051.

Camfield, L., Crivello, G., & Woodhead, M. (2008). Well-being research in developing countries: Reviewing the role of qualitative methods. *Social Indicators Research, 90*(1), 5–31.

Campbell, I. (Ed.). (1981). *The quality of American life*. New York: Russell Sage.

Campbell, A., Converse, P. E., & Rogers, W. L. (1976). *The quality of American life: Perceptions, evaluations, and satisfactions*. New York: Russell Sage.

Cantril, H. (1965). *The pattern of human concerns*. New Brunswick: Rutgers University Press.

Cella, D. F., Tulsky, D. S., & Gray, G. (1993). The Functional Assessment of Cancer Therapy (FACT). Scale: Development and validation of the general measure. *Journal of Clinical Oncology, 11*, 572–597.

Chambers, R. (1997). *Whose reality counts? Putting the first last*. London: Intermediate Technology. 297 pp.

Chambers, R. (2007). *'Who counts? The quiet revolution of participation and numbers' (IDS Research Summary of IDS Working Paper 296)*. Brighton: IDS.

Chan, A. C. M., Phillips, D. R., Cheng, S.-T., Chi, I., & Ho, S. Y. S. (2004). Constructing a quality of life scale for older Chinese people in Hong Kong (HKQoLOCP). *Social Indicators Research, 69*, 279–301.

Choudhury, K. (2005). *Quality of life—Phase 1 Report Bangladesh (rural sites)*. Unpublished, Wellbeing in Developing Countries Research Group, Bangladesh.

Christopher, J. C. (1999). Situating psychological wellbeing: Exploring the cultural roots of its theory and research. *Journal of Counseling and Development, 77*, 141–152.

Clark, D. A. (2007). *Adaptation, poverty and well-being: Some issues and observations with special reference to the capability approach and development studies*. GPRG-WPS-081.

Cooke, B., & Kothari, U. (Eds.). (2001). *Participation: The new tyranny?* London: Zed Books.

Copestake, J., & Camfield, L. (2010). Measuring multidimensional aspiration gaps: A means to understanding cultural aspects of poverty. *Development Policy Review, 28*(5), 617–633.

Cornwall, A., & Fujita, M. (2007). The politics of representing "the poor". In J. Moncrieffe & R. Eyben (Eds.), *The power of labelling. How people are categorised and why it matters.* London: Earthscan.

Cummins, R. (1995). On the trail of a gold standard for subjective wellbeing. *Social Indicators Research, 35,* 179–200.

Cummins, R. A. (2005). Caregivers as managers of subjective wellbeing: A homeostatic perspective. *Journal of Applied Research in Intellectual Disabilities, 18*(4), 335–344.

Cummins, R. A. (1996). The domains of life satisfaction: An attempt to order chaos. *Social Indicators Research, 38,* 303–332.

Cummins, R. (1997). *"Comprehensive quality of life scale—Adult", manual* (5th ed.). Melbourne: Deakin University.

Cummins, R. (1998). The second approximation to an international standard for life satisfaction. *Social Indicators Research, 43,* 307–334. Dordrecht: Kluwer Academic.

Cummins, R. A. (2000). Personal income and subjective wellbeing: A review. *Journal of Happiness Studies, 1,* 133–158.

Cummins, R. (2002a). Normative life satisfaction: Measurement issues and a homeostatic model. *Social Indicators Research, 64,* 225–256.

Cummins, R. A. (2002b). *Vale ComQol: Caveats to using the comprehensive quality of life scale: Welcome the personal wellbeing index.* Melbourne: Deakin University. http://acqol.deakin.edu.au/instruments/Caveats_ComQol_scales.doc.

Cummins, R. A. (2004). *The international wellbeing index: A psychometric progress report.* Paper presented at Sixth Conference of The International Society for Quality of Life Studies, Philadelphia, US.

Cummins, R. A., Eckersley, R., Pallant, J., van Vugt, J., & Misajon, R. (2003). Developing a national index of subjective wellbeing: The Australian Unity Wellbeing Index. *Social Indicators Research, 64*(2), 159–190.

Cummins, R. A., Davern, M., Okerstrom, E., Lo, S. K., & Eckersley, R. (2005). *Report 12.1 Australian Unity Wellbeing Index: Special report on city and country living.* Melbourne: Australian Centre on Quality of Life.

Davern, M., & Cummins, R. A. (2005). *Subjective wellbeing as an affective construct.* Unpublished.

Davis, J., Richards, M., & Cavendish, W. (1999). *Beyond the limits of PRA? A comparison of participatory and conventional economic research methods in the analysis of Ilala palm use in South-Eastern Zimbabwe* (Working Paper). London: ODI.

de Vaus, D. A. (1995). *Surveys in social research* (4th ed.). London: UCL Press/Taylor and Francis.

Devine, J., Camfield, L., & Gough, I. (2007). Autonomy or dependence—or both? Perspectives from Bangladesh. *Journal of Happiness Studies, 9*(1), 105–138.

Diener, E., & Diener, C. (1995). The wealth of nations revisited: Income and quality of life. *Social Indicators Research, 36,* 275–286.

Diener, E., & Fujita, F. (1995). Resources, personal strivings, and subjective wellbeing: A nomothetic and idiographic approach. *Journal of Personality and Social Psychology, 68,* 926–935.

Diener, E., & Suh, E. M. (2000). Measuring SWB to compare the QoL of cultures. In E. Diener & E. M. Suh (Eds.), *Subjective wellbeing across cultures* (pp. 1–12). Cambridge: MIT Press.

Diener, E., Emmons, R. A., Larsen, R. J., & Griffin, S. (1985). The satisfaction with life scale. *Journal of Personality Assessment, 49*(1), 71–75.

Diener, E., Diener, M., & Diener, C. (1995). Factors predicting the subjective wellbeing of nations. *Journal of Personality and Social Psychology, 69*(5), 851–864.

Diener, E., Suh, E., Smith, H., & Shao, L. (1995). National differences in reported subjective wellbeing: Why do they occur? *Social Indicators Research, 34,* 7–32.

Diener, E., Gohm, C., Suh, E., & Oishi, S. (1998). Similarity of the relations between marital status and subjective wellbeing across cultures. *Journal of Cross-Cultural Psychology, 31*(4), 419–436.

Diener, E., Scollon, C. K. N., Oishi, S., Dzokoto, V., & Suh, E. M. (2000). Positivity and the construction of life satisfaction judgments: Global happiness is not the sum of its parts. *Journal of Happiness Studies, 1,* 159–176.

Diener, E., Oishi, S., & Lucas, R. E. (2002). Subjective wellbeing: The science of happiness and life satisfaction. In C.R. Snyder & S.J. Lopez (Eds.), *Handbook of Positive Psychology.* Oxford and New York: Oxford University Press.

Easterlin, R. A. (1974). Does economic growth improve the human lot? Some empirical evidence. In P. A. David & M. W. Reder (Eds.), *Nations and households in economic growth.* New York: Academic.

Easterlin, R. A. & Angelescu, L. (2009). *Happiness and growth the world over: Time series evidence on the happiness-income paradox* (IZA Discussion Paper No. 4060).

Eid, M., & Diener, E. (2001). Norms for experiencing emotions: Inter- and intra-national differences. *Journal of Personality and Social Psychology, 81,* 869–885.

Fafchamps, M., & Shilpi, F. (2003, October). *Subjective wellbeing, isolation and rivalry* (mimeo). CSAE, Department of Economics, University of Oxford.

Fafchamps, M., & Shilpi, F. (2004). *Isolation and subjective welfare* (Discussion Paper Series No. 216). University of Oxford: Department of Economics.

Fayers, P. M., Hand, D. J., Bjordal, K., & Groenvold, M. (1997). Causal indicators in quality of life research. *Quality of Life Research, 6,* 393–406.

Felce, D. (1997). Defining and applying the concept of quality of life. *Journal of Intellectual Disability Research, 41*(2), 126–135.

Fiske, A. P., Kitayama, S., Markus, H. R., & Nisbett, R. E. (1998). The cultural matrix of social psychology. In D. T. Gilbert & S. T. Fiske (Eds.), *The handbook of social psychology* (4th ed., Vol. 2, pp. 915–981). New York: McGraw-Hill.

Foo, T. S. (1998). *Measuring the quality of life of Singaporeans.* Singapore: Centre for Real Estate Studies, National University of Singapore.

Fox-Rushby, J., Nzioka, C., Nganda, B., & Mugo, M. *Are health state valuations likely to be understood the same way in Kenya? Moving towards an assessment of conceptual equivalence.* Unpublished.

Fox-Rushby J., Johnson, K., & Mwanzo, I. (1997). Creating an instrument to assess lay perceptions of HRQL: Options and implications. *Quality of Life Research, 6:*633.

Fox-Rushby J. A. (2002) *Disability adjusted life years (DALYs) for decision making: An overview of the literature.* Office of Health Economics, London.

Fox-Rushby, J., Smith, S., Bowden, A. & Lamping, D. (2003a). Understanding the components of HRQL amongst the Kmab of Kenya: Putting a qualitatively derived conceptual model to the psychometric test. *Quality of Life Research, 12,* 861.

Fox-Rushby, J., & Bowden, A. (2003b). Perceived HRQL amongst the Kamba of Eastern Kenya: Socio-economics and demographic variation in KENQOL scores. *Quality of Life Research, 12*, 823.

Frey, B. S., & Stutzer, A. (2002). What can economists learn from happiness research? *Journal of Economic Literature, American Economic Association, 40*(2), 402–435.

Fuentes, N., & Rojas, M. (2001). Economic theory and subjective wellbeing: Mexico. *Social Indicators Research, 53*(3), 289–314.

Glatzer, W., & Zapf, W. (1984). *Lebensqualität in der Bundesrepublik: Objektive Wohlbefinden*. Frankfurt: Campus Verlag.

Graham, C. (2005). *Insights on development from the economics of happiness* World Bank Res Obs, 20(2), 201–231.

Graham, C., & Pettinato, S. (2001). *Happiness and hardship: Opportunity and insecurity in new market economies*. Washington, DC: Brookings Institution Press.

Guillen-Royo, M., & Velazco, J. (2005). *Exploring the relationship between happiness, objective and subjective wellbeing: Evidence from rural Thailand*. Paper presented at the Capabilities and Happiness Conference, June 16–18, 2005.

Guyatt, G. H. (1993). The philosophy of health-related quality of life translation. *Quality of Life Research, 2*(6), 461–465.

Hagerty, M. R., Cummins, R. A., Ferriss, A. L., Land, K., Michalos, A. C., Peterson, M., et al. (2001). Quality of life indexes for national policy: Review and agenda for research. *Social Indicators Research, 55*(1), 1–96.

Heady, B., Veenhoven, R., & Wearing, A. (1991). Top-down versus bottom-up: Theories of subjective wellbeing. *Social Indicators Research, 24*, 81–100.

Herdman, M., Fox-Rushby, J., & Badia, X. (1998). A model of equivalence in the cultural adaptation of HRQL instruments: The universalist approach. *Quality of Life Research, 7*, 323–355.

Herrold, M. (1999). Unpublished notes from a PRA in the Caohai Nature Reserve, China, International Crane Foundation/Yunnan Institute of Geography.

Hicks, J. R. (1941). Education in economics, Manchester Statistical Society, April 30.

Hofstede, G. (1980). *Culture's consequences*. Beverly Hills: Sage.

Hosain, G. M., Atkinson, D., & Underwood, P. (2002). Impact of disability on quality of life of rural disabled people in Bangladesh. *Journal of Health, Population and Nutrition, 20*, 297–305.

Hsieh, Chang-ming. (2003). Counting importance: The case of life satisfaction and relative domain importance. *Social Indicators Research, 61*(2), 227–240. Feb 2003.

Hsieh, Chang-ming. (2004). To weight or not to weight: The role of domain importance in quality of life measurement. *Social Indicators Research, 68*(2), 163–174.

Hunt, S. (1999). The researcher's tale: A story of virtue lost and regained. *Quality of Life Research, 8*(7), 556. In C. R. B. Joyce, C. A. O'Boyle, & H. McGee (Eds.), *Individual quality of life: Approaches to conceptualization and assessment*. Amsterdam: Harwood Academic.

Hunt, S. M., McEwen, J., McKenna, S. P., Williams, J., & Papp, E. (1981). The Nottingham health profile: Subjective health status and medical consultations. *Social Science & Medicine, 19A*, 221–229.

Huschka, D., & Mau, S. (2005). *Aspects of quality of life—Social Anomie in South Africa*. With a foreword by Wolfgang Zapf. WZB Discussion Paper P 2005-002, Berlin.

Ibrahim, M. F., & Chung, S. W. (2003). Quality of life of residents living near industrial estates in Singapore. *Social Indicators Research, 61*(2), 203–225.

Inglehardt, R., & Klingemann, H. D. (2000). Genes, culture, democracy, and happiness. In E. Diener & E. M. Suh (Eds.), *Culture and Subjective wellbeing* (pp. 185–218). Cambridge: MIT Press.

International Wellbeing Group. (2005). *PWI adult manual*. Melbourne: The Australian Centre on Quality of Life, Deakin University.

Izutsu, T., Tsutsumi, A., Islam, A., Matsuo, Y., Yamada H. S. & Kurita, H. et al. (2005). Validity and reliability of the Bangla version of WHOQOL-BREF on an adolescent population in Bangladesh. *Quality of Life Research, 14*, 1783–1789.

Jenkinson, C. (1995). Evaluating the efficacy of medical treatment: Possibilities and limitations. *Social Science & Medicine, 41*(10), 1395–1401.

Jones, L. V., & Thurstone, L. L. (1955). The psychophysics of semantics: An experimental investigation. *Journal of Applied Psychology, 39*(1), 31–36.

Jongudomkarn, D., & Camfield, L. (2006). Exploring the quality of life of people in North Eastern and Southern Thailand. *Social Indicators Research, 78*, 489–530.

Kahneman, D. (1999). Objective happiness. In D. Kahneman, E. Diener & N. Schwarz (Eds.), Well-being: Foundations of hedonic psychology (pp. 3–25). New York: Russell Sage Foundation Press.

Kahneman, D. (2005). The New Science of HAPPINESS, By: Wallis, Claudia, Coady, Elizabeth, Cray, Dan, Park, Alice, Ressner, Jeffrey. Time, 0040781X, 1/17/2005, Vol. 165(3)

Kedem-Friedrich, P., & Al-Atawneh, M. (2004). Does modernity lead to greater wellbeing? Bedouin women undergoing a sociocultural transition. *Social Indicators Research, 67*(3), 333–351.

Keedwell, P., & Snaith, R. P. (1996). What do anxiety scales measure? *Acta Psychiatrica Scandinavica, 93*, 177–180.

Kenny, C. (2005). Why are we worried about income? Nearly everything that matters is converging. *World Development, Elsevier, 33*(1), 1–19.

Kim-prieto, C., & Eid, M. (2004). Norms for experiencing emotions. *Journal of Happiness Studies, 5*(3), 241–268.

Kingdon, G., & Knight, J. (2003). *Wellbeing poverty versus income poverty and capabilities poverty?* (CSAE WPS/2003–16). Global Poverty Reduction Group, Centre for the Study of African Economies.

Kingdon, G., & Knight, J. (2004). *Community, comparisons and subjective wellbeing in a divided society*. Presented at Northeast Universities Development Consortium Conference, HEC Montréal, October 1–3.

Kitayama, S. (2002). Culture and basic psychological processes: Toward a system view of culture. *Psychological Bulletin, 128*, 189–196.

Kitayama, S., Markus, H. R., & Kurokawa, M. (2000). Culture, emotion, and wellbeing: Good feelings in Japan and the United States. *Cognition and Emotion, 14*, 93–124.

Knight, J., & Song, L. (2004). *Subjective wellbeing and its determinants in rural China* (Mimeo).

Kousha, M., & Mohseni, N. (2000). Are Iranians happy? A comparative study between Iran and the United States. *Social Indicators Research, 52*(3), 259–289.

Larsen, R. J., & Fredrickson, B. L. (1999). Measurement issues in emotion research. In D. Kahneman, E. Diener, & N. Schwartz (Eds.), *Wellbeing: The foundations of hedonic psychology* (pp. 40–60). New York: Russell Sage Foundation.

Lau, A. L. D., Cummins, R. A., & McPherson, W. (2005). An investigation into the cross-cultural equivalence of the personal wellbeing index. *Social Indicators Research, 72*, 403–430.

Lawson, C. W., McGregor, J. A., & Saltmarshe, D. K. (2000). Surviving and thriving: Differentiation in a peri-urban community in Northern Albania. *World Development, 28*(8), 1499–1514.

Leplege, R., & Hunt, S. (1997). The problem of QOL in medicine. *Journal of the American Medical Association, 278*, 47–50.

Leplege, A., & Verdier, A. (1995). The adaptation of health status measures: Methodological aspects of the translation procedure. In A. Shumaker Sally & A. Berzon Richard (Eds.), *The international assessment of health related quality of life theory, translation, measurement and analysis*. Oxford: Rapid Communications.

Lever, J. P. (2000). The development of an instrument to measure quality of life in Mexico City. *Social Indicators Research, 50*(2), 187–208.

Lever, J. P. (2004). Poverty and subjective wellbeing in Mexico. *Social Indicators Research, 68*(1), 1–33.

Lockwood, D. (1981). The weakest link in the chain? Some comments on the Marxist theory of action. In R. I. Simpson (Ed.), *Research in the sociology of work* (Vol. 1, pp. 435–481). Greenwich: JAI Press.

Lukes, S. (1986). *Power*. Oxford: Basil Blackwell.

Lyubomirsky, S. (2001). Why are some people happier than others? The role of cognitive and motivational processes in wellbeing. *American Psychologist, 56*, 239–249.

Mallinson, S. (2002). Listening to respondents: A qualitative evaluation of a health status questionnaire. *Social Science & Medicine, 54*(1), 11–21.

Markus, H. R., & Kitayama, S. (1991). Culture and the self: Implications for cognition, emotion, and motivation. *Psychological Review, 98*(2), 224–253.

Martin, F., Camfield, L., & Ruta, D. (2010). The global person generated index. In V. R. Preedy & R. R. Watson (Eds.), *Handbook of disease burdens and quality of life measures* (pp. 59–72). New York: Springer.

Matsumoto, D. (1999). Culture & self: An empirical assessment of Markus & Kitayama's theory of independent & interdependent self construals. *Asian Journal of Social Psychology, 2*, 289–310.

McDowell, I., & Newell, C. (1996). *Measuring health*. Oxford: Oxford University Press.

McGregor, J. A., Sumner, A. (2009). *After 2015: '3D Human Wellbeing'*. IDS In Focus Policy Briefings 9.2, Brighton: Institute of Development Studies.

Michalos, A. (1985). Multiple discrepancy theory. *Social Indicators Research, 16*, 347–413.

Michalos, A. C. (2004). Social indicators research and health related quality of life research. *Social Indicators Research, 65*(1), 27–72.

Møller, V. (2001). Happiness trends under democracy: Where will the new South African set-level come to rest? *Journal of Happiness Studies, 2*(1), 33–53.

Møller, V. (2005). Resilient or resigned? Criminal victimisation and quality of life in South Africa. *Social Indicators Research, 72*(3), 263–317.

Møller, V. (2007). Researching quality of life in a developing country: Lessons from the South African case. In I. Gough & J. A. McGregor (Eds.), *Wellbeing in developing countries:*

New approaches and research strategies. Cambridge: Cambridge University Press.

Møller, V., & Saris, W. E. (2001). The relationship between subjective wellbeing and domain satisfactions in South Africa. *Social Indicators Research, 55*(1), 97.

Mozes, B., & Maor, Y. (1999). Developing the concept of a new tool assessing a different type of generic quality of life: The "Good Life Questionnaire". *Quality of Life Research, 8*(7), 571.

Muldoon, M.F, Barger, S.D, Flory, J.D., Manuck, S.B. (1998). What are quality of life measurements measuring? BMJ 316 (7130): 542

Mullin V., Cella D., Chang C-H., Eremenco S., Mertz M., Lent L., Falkson C. & Falkson G. (2000). Development of 3 African language translations of the FACT-G. *Quality of Life Research, 9*, 139–149.

Narayan, D., & Walton, M. (2000). *Can anyone hear us? (Voices of the Poor Study)*. Oxford: Oxford University Press.

Narayan, D., Walton, M., & Chambers, R. (2000). *Crying out for change (Voices of the Poor Study)*. Oxford: Oxford University Press.

Nilsson, J., Parker, M. G., & Kabir, Z. N. (2004). Assessing health-related quality of life among older people in rural Bangladesh. *Journal of Transcultural Nursing, 15*, 298–307.

Nilsson, J., Grafstro, M., Zamand, S., & Kabir, Z. N. (2005). Role and function: Aspects of quality of life of older people in rural Bangladesh. *Journal of Aging Studies, 19*, 363–374.

O'Boyle, C. A., McGee, H., Hickey, A., O'Malley, K., & Joyce, C. R. B. (1992). *Individual quality of life in patients undergoing hip replacement*. Lancet, 339, 1088–91.

O'Carroll, R. E., Smith, K., Couston, M., Cossar, J. A., & Hayes, P. C. A. (2000). Comparison of the WHOQOL-100 and the WHOQOL-BREF in detecting change in quality of life following liver transplantation. *Quality of Life Research, 9*(1), 121–124.

O'Connell, K., Saxena, S., & Skevington, S. M., for the WHOQOL-HIV Group (2004). WHOQOL-HIV for quality of life assessment among people living with HIV and AIDS: Results from a field test. *AIDS Care, 16*(7), 882–889.

Okun, M. A., & Stock, W. A. (1987). The construct validity of subjective well-being measures: An assessment via quantitative research syntheses. *Journal of Community Psychology, 15*, 481–492.

Oishi, S., Schimmack, U., Diener, E., & Suh, E. M. (1998). The measurement of values and individualism-collectivism. *Personality and Social Psychology Bulletin, 24*(11), 1177–1189.

Oishi, S., Diener, E. F., Lucas, R. E., & Suh, E. M. (1999). Cross cultural variations in predictors of life satisfaction: Perspectives from needs and values. *Personality and Social Psychology Bulletin, 25*, 980–990.

Oyserman, D., Coon, H. M., & Kemmelmeier, M. (2002). Rethinking individualism and collectivism: Evaluation of theoretical assumptions & meta-analyses. *Psychological Bulletin, 128*, 3–72.

Pandey, M., Thomas, B. C., Ramdas, K., Eremenco, S., & Nair, M. K. (2004). Reliability & validity of the Malayalam functional assessment of cancer therapy for head & neck cancer. *The Indian Journal of Medical Research, 120*, 51–55.

Pavot, W., & Diener, E. (1993). The affective and cognitive context of self-reported measures of subjective wellbeing. *Social Indicators Research, 28*, 1–20.

Power, M., Bullinger, M., Harper, A., on behalf of the WHOQOL Group. (1999). The World Health Organization WHOQOL-100: Tests of the universality of quality of life in 15 different cultural groups world-wide. *Health Psychology, 18*(5), 495–505.

Rapley, M. (2003). *Quality of life research—A critical introduction.* London: SAGE Publication.

Redelmeier, D. A., & Kahneman, D. (1996). Patients' memories of painful medical treatments: Realtime and retrospective evaluations of two minimally invasive procedures. *Pain, 66*(1), 3–8.

Rojas, M. (2005). A conceptual-referent theory of happiness: Heterogeneity and its consequences. *Social Indicators Research, 74*, 261–294.

Rojas, M. (2007). The complexity of wellbeing: A life-satisfaction conception and a domains-of-life approach. In I. Gough & J. A. Mcgregor (Eds.), *Wellbeing in developing countries: New approaches and research strategies.* Cambridge: Cambridge University Press.

Rojas, M. (2009). Enhancing poverty-abatement programs: A subjective well-being contribution. *Applied Research in Quality of Life, 4*(2), 179–199.

Rozel-Farnworth, C. (2009). Well-being is a process of becoming: Respondent-led research with organic farmers in Madagascar. *Social Indicators Research, 90*(1), 89–106.

Russell, J. (2003). Core affect and the psychological construction of emotion. *Psychological Review, 110*(1), 145–172.

Russell, L. B., Hubley, A. M., Palepu, A., & Zumbo, B. (2006). Does weighting capture what's important? Revisiting subjective importance weighting with a QoL measure. *Social Indicators, 75*(1), 141–167.

Ruta, D. A., Garratt, A. M., Leng, M., Russell, I. T., & MacDonald, L. M. (1994). A new approach to the measurement of QOL. The patient-generated index. *Medical Care, 32*(11), 1109–1126.

Ryff, C. D. (1989). Happiness is everything, or is it? Explorations on the meaning of psychological wellbeing. *Journal of Personality and Social Psychology, 57*(6), 1069–1081.

Samuelson, P. (1938). A note on the pure theory of consumers' behavior. *Economica NS, 5*, 61–71.

Sarason, I. G., Sarason, B. R., Shearin, E. N., et al. (1987). A brief measure of social support. Practical and theoretical implications. *Journal of Social Personal Relationships, 4*, 497–510.

Sartorius, N., & Kuyken, W. (1993) Translation of health status instruments. In J. Orley & W. Kuyken (Eds.), *Proceedings of the Joint Meeting Organised by the World Health Organization and the Foundation IPSEN* (pp. 3–18). Paris: Springer-Verlag.

Scherpenzeel, A. C., & Saris, W. E. (1996). Causal direction in a model of life-satisfaction: The top-down/bottom-up controversy. *Social Indicators Research, 38*, 161–180.

Schimmack, U., Diener, E., & Oishi, S. (2002). Life satisfaction is a momentary judgment and a stable personality characteristic: The use of chronically accessible and stable sources. *Journal of Personality, 70*(3), 345–384.

Schkade, D. A., & Kahneman, D. (1998). Does living in California make people happy? A focusing illusion in judgments of life satisfaction. *Psychological Science, 9*(5), 340–346.

Schmidt, A., & Bullinger, M. (2007). Cross-cultural quality of life assessment approaches and experiences from the health care field. In I. Gough & J. A. Mcgregor (Eds.), *Wellbeing in developing countries: New approaches and research strategies.* Cambridge: Cambridge University Press.

Schwarz, N., & Strack, F. (1991). Evaluating one's life: A judgment model of subjective wellbeing. In F. Strack, M. Argyle, & N. Schwarz (Eds.), *Subjective wellbeing: An interdisciplinary perspective* (International series in experimental social psychology, Vol. 21, pp. 27–47). Elmsford: Pergamon Press.

Schwarz, N., Hippler, H. J., Deutsch, B., & Strack, F. (1985). Response categories: Effects on behavioral reports and comparative judgments. *Public Opinion Quarterly, 49*, 388–395.

Schyns, P. (2003). *Income and life satisfaction – A cross-national and longitudinal study.* PhD thesis, Eburon, Delft.

Scott, J. C. (1975). Exploitation and rural class relations: A victim's perspective. *Comparative Politics, 7*, 489–532.

Sen, A. (1984). *Resources, values and development.* Oxford: Blackwell.

Sen, A. K. (2002). Health: perception versus observation. *British Medical Journal, 324*, 860–861.

Skevington, S. M., Bradshaw, J., & Saxena, S. (1999). Selecting national items for the WHOQOL: Conceptual and psychometric considerations. *Social Science and Medicine, 48*, 473–487.

Skevington, S. M., O'Connell, K., & The WHOQOL Group. (2004). Can we identify the poorest quality of life? Assessing the importance of quality of life using the WHOQOL-100. *Quality of Life Research, 13*(1), 23–34.

Stewart, A. L., & Ware, J. E. (1992). *Measuring functioning and well-being: The medical outcomes study approach.* Durham, NC: Duke University Press.

Strack, F., Schwarz, N., Chassein, B., Kern, D., & Wagner, D. (1990). Salience of comparison standards and the activation of social norms: Consequences for judgements of happiness and their communication. *British Journal of Social Psychology, 29*(4), 303–314.

Suh, E. (1994). *Emotion norms, values, familiarity, and subjective wellbeing: A cross-cultural examination.* Unpublished master's thesis, University of Illinois at Urbana-Champaign.

Suh, E., Diener, E., Oishi, S., & Triandis, H. C. (1998). The shifting basis of life satisfaction judgements across cultures: Emotions versus norms. *Journal of Personality and Social Psychology, 74*, 482–493.

The WHOQOL-OLD Group. (2005). Development of the WHOQOL-Old module. *Quality of Life Research, 14*(10), 2197–2214.

The WHOQOL-SRPB Group. (2006). A cross-cultural study of spirituality, religion and personal beliefs as components of quality of life. *Social Science & Medicine, 62*, 1486–1497.

Thomas, J. (2005). Satyananda yogic lifestyle and subjective wellbeing (unpublished). www.deakin.edu.au/research/acqol/.../2005/paper-thomas-2005.doc.

Tiberius, V. (2004). Cultural differences and philosophical accounts of wellbeing. *Journal of Happiness Studies, 5*, 293–314.

Trauer, T., & Mackinnon, A. (2001). Why are we weighting? The role of importance ratings in quality of life measurement. *Quality of Life Research, 10*, 577–583.

Triandis, H. C. (1994). *IND-COL.* Unpublished research scale.

Uchida, Y., Kitayama, S., Mesquita, B., Reyes, J. A. (2001) Interpersonal sources of happiness: The relative significance in three cultures. *13th Annual convention of the American Psychological Society*, Toronto, Canada, June.

Uchida, Y., Norasakkunkit, V., & Kitayama, S. (2004). Cultural constructions of happiness: Theory & empirical evidence. *Journal of Happiness Studies, 5*, 223–239.

van Praag, B. M. S., & Ferrer-i-Carbonell, A. (2004). *Happiness quantified: A satisfaction calculus approach*. Oxford: Oxford University Press.

Veenhoven, R. (1991). Is happiness relative? *Social Indicators Research, 24*, 1–34.

Vitterso, J., Roysamb, E., & Diener, E. (2002). The concept of life satisfaction across cultures: Exploring its diverse meaning and relation to economic wealth. In E. Gullone & R. A. Cummins (Eds.), *The universality of subjective wellbeing indicators* (pp. 81–103). Dordrecht, Netherlands: Kluwer Academic Publishers.

Wallis, C. (2005). The new science of happiness. Time magazine.

Ware, J. E., & Sherbourne, C. D. (1992). The MOS 36-item short-form health survey (SF-36): I. Conceptual framework and item selection. *Medical Care, 30*, 473–483.

Watson, D. (1988). Development and validation of a brief measure of positive and negative affect. *Journal of Personality and Social Psychology, 54*, 1063–1070.

WeD-Ethiopia (2004). *Exploratory phase of the QoL research in Ethiopia* (Draft Country Report). Addis Ababa, January.

White, S., & Pettit, J. (2005). Participatory approaches and the measurement of human wellbeing. In M. McGillivray (Ed.), *Measuring human wellbeing*. Oxford: WIDER/Oxford University Press.

WHOQOL Group. (1995). The World Health Organization Quality of Life assessment (WHOQOL): Position paper from the World Health Organization. *Social Science & Medicine, 41*, 1403–1409.

Williams, J. I. (2000). Ready, set, stop: Reflections on assessing quality of life and the WHOQOL-100 (U.S. version). World Health Organization Quality of Life. *Clinical Epidemiology, 53*(1), 13–17.

Wong, N., Rindfleisch, A., & Burroughs, J. E. (2003). Do reverse-worded items confound measures in cross-cultural consumer research? The case of the material values scale. *Journal of Consumer Research, 30*, 72–91.

Woodcock, A., Camfield, L., McGregor, J.A., & Martin, F. (2009). Validation of the WeDQoL-Goals-Thailand measure: Culture-specific individualised quality of life. *Social Indicators Research, 94*(1), 135–171.

Yamamoto, J., Feijoo, A. R., & Lazarte, A. (2008). Subjective wellbeing: An alternative approach. In J. Copestake (Ed.), *Wellbeing and development in Peru: Global and local views confronted*. New York: Palgrave Macmillan.

Ziebland, S., Fitzpatrick, R., & Jenkinson, C. (1993). Tacit models of disability underlying health status instruments. *Social Science & Medicine, 37*(1), 69–75.

Economies in Transition: Revisiting Challenges to Quality of Life

20

Richard J. Estes

Introduction

"Economies in Transition" (hereafter referred to as "EITs") consist of 31 geographically dispersed nations (International Monetary Fund 2010) with a combined population of 1,916 million—approximately 27.8% of the world's total in 2010 (UNPOP 2010). EITs are located in East and Southeast Asia ($N=4$), Central and Eastern Europe ($N=10$), and Central Asia ($N=11$). They also include China, Turkey, the Russian Federation, and the three Baltic States of Estonia, Latvia, and Lithuania. Other countries are regarded as EITs, but the challenges associated with their development have tended to be longer in duration (e.g., Brazil, India, Indonesia, and Mexico, among others). The majority of countries classified as EITs in this study are relatively young—most having achieved their independence only since the collapse of the former Soviet Union in December 1991. The social, political, and economic transitions for some of the study's EITs began earlier than 1991, but owing to their long histories, large geographic territories, and current political complexities, their transition process has moved more slowly, i.e., the Russian Federation (1917), Turkey (1923), and China (1949).

Though improving, income poverty remains pervasive in certain EIT subgroups (especially within member nations of the Commonwealth of Independent States) in comparison with their pre-transition economic status (UNDP 2010b; World Bank 2010). All of the EITs struggle with profound uncertainties associated with their transformation (Jacobsson 2010; Moran et al. 2006; Weingast and Wittman 2006); indeed, throughout the social histories of most EITs, and with the exception of those located in Central and Eastern Europe, few have had prior experience with the private ownership of the means of production or with democratically elected political systems[1] (Graham and Lindahl 2010; Svetlicic and Rojec 2003; Watts and Walstad 2002; Young et al. 2002). Political transparency and the participation of people in what previously had been regarded as "affairs of *the* state" have proven especially challenging for the successor states to the former Soviet Union, including for the Russian Federation (Weingast and Wittman 2006; Wejnert 2002). As a result, high levels of public corruption and at least semi-autocratic political systems continue to prevail in many of the Asian and Commonwealth of Independent States (CIS) EITs (Freedom House 2010; Transparency International 2010). The majority of EITs also are struggling with creation of the "political space" needed for the emergence of a viable civil society as partners with governments in promoting broad-based social development goals (Anheier et al. 2010; Singh 2003).

The economic challenges confronting the EITs are compounded by the high levels of competition associated with globalization (Friedman 2005; Stiglitz 2002, 2010). This is especially problematic in EITs with few

R.J. Estes (✉)
School of Social Policy & Practice, University of Pennsylvania, Philadelphia, PA, USA
e-mail: restes@sp2.upenn.edu

[1] China (1949) and the Russian Federation (1917) are still in the process of transitioning from state-controlled political systems. The transition to participatory democratic political systems is proving to be especially difficult for both countries, albeit their transformation to open market economic systems has been quite rapid.

K.C. Land et al. (eds.), *Handbook of Social Indicators and Quality of Life Research*,
DOI 10.1007/978-94-007-2421-1_20, © Springer Science+Business Media B.V. 2012

or no natural resources. As one consequence of this dilemma, some EITs are experiencing net outward population flows of their youngest and best educated citizens whose advanced technical skills easily can be sold in global labor markets[2]; other EITs, however, are experiencing the return of members of their diaspora, e.g., China and India (International Labour Organization 2010; IOM 2010).

Further, many of the EITs also are experiencing significant challenges in achieving their health, education, and related social objectives. Lack of attention to these sectors is resulting in higher than pre-transition levels of infant and child mortality, higher rates of maternal deaths, more restricted roles for women in public life, and, for some, reduced levels of average life expectation (UNDP 2010a; WHO 2010). Post-transition approaches to housing, education, and transportation also are under assault in many EITs as they seek to respond to increasing public demands in these sectors with market solutions. Environmental pollution (OECD 2010; WRI 2010), declining public sector investment in industrial and physical infrastructure (World Bank 2010), and sharply reduced social welfare expenditures (UNDP 1999; USDHHS 2010) also are major challenges confronting some EITs.

The preceding forces have combined to produce higher levels of income poverty in many "Middle Performing" EITs for the very old and the very young as well as for those struggling with chronic illnesses (UNDP 1999). Further, infectious diseases, including HIV/AIDS, are undermining the development capacity of many EITs and are forcing them to redirect a disproportionate share of their discretionary resources to tertiary health care rather than to broad-based social development initiatives (OSI 2005; UNDP 2010b; WHO 2010).

Other EITs, however, are beginning to experience meaningful progress toward their transition goals, and as a result, highly favorable patterns of political, social, and economic development are beginning to emerge for their countries (Graham and Lindahl 2010; Koyuncu et al. 2010; Peerenboom 2007; Rumer 2005; UNDP 2010b). Effective multi-party political systems exist in the most socially progressive EITs (Freedom House 2010) as do local, national, and international networks of non-governmental organizations (Anheier et al. 2010). These critical structural innovations have been created despite continuing high levels of public corruption (Transparency International 2010). But for most EITs, their new, still emerging, "social architecture" is very much a work in progress with the result that comparatively few experience confidence concerning the eventual outcomes of their transition efforts. Even so, the difficult process toward establishing more open economic and political systems is continuing within the subgroup of EIT social leaders (SLs), and the results of their efforts are reflected in measurable advances in the overall quality of life of their populations (Jeffries 2003; OECD 2010; UNDP 2010b; World Bank 2004).

This chapter explores the extent to which the EITs are succeeding in advancing their transformative social, political, and economic goals. In particular, the chapter reports the results of a comprehensive survey of the comparative successes and failures of 31 EITs for the 20-year period 1990–2010. More specifically, this chapter (1) reports the results obtained through application of a statistically weighted version of the author's previously developed *Weighted Index of Social Progress* (WISP) to an analysis of social development trends in EITs for 1990–2010; (2) using the WISP, identifies current EIT *social development leaders* (SLs) and *Middle Performing Countries* (MPCs); (3) using WISP scores as a point of reference, provides more recent social indicator data for the 5-year period 2005–2010; and (4) serves as a baseline against which future developments in the EITs can be assessed (ala Estes 1998, 2007).

Methodology

The present study is the twelfth in a series of analyses of global and regional social development trends, including two earlier reports that focused on the development dilemmas confronting the EITs (Estes 1998, 2007). The purpose of all 12 studies has been (1) to identify significant changes in "adequacy social provision"[3] throughout the world and (2) to assess national and

---

[2]Unfortunately, some young people migrating from their countries – mostly young women and children – do so under criminal circumstances, often as victims of human trafficking (U.S. Department of State 2010).

[3]"Adequacy of social provision" refers to the changing capacity of governments to provide for the basic social, material, and other needs of the people living within their borders, e.g., for food, clothing, shelter, and access to at least basic health, education, and social services, etc. (Estes 1988).

20 Economies in Transition: Revisiting Challenges to Quality of Life

international progress in providing more adequately for the basic social and material needs of the world's growing population. This chapter reports a time-series analysis of the development performances of 31 Economies in Transition (EITs) over the 20-year period beginning 1990. Throughout the chapter, data are reported for four levels of analysis: (1) development trends occurring within the EITs vis-à-vis those of other geopolitical groupings of nations, (2) social patterns for the EITs as a group, (3) EIT subgroup variations in development, and (4) development trends occurring in each of the 31 EITs.

Index of Social Progress (ISP)

The primary instrument used in this study is the author's extensively pre-tested "Index of Social Progress" (ISP). In its present form, the ISP consists of 41 social indicators that have been subdivided into 10 subindexes (Table 20.1): *Education* (*N*=4), *Health Status* (*N*=7), *Women Status* (*N*=5), *Defense Effort* (*N*=1), *Economic* (*N*=5), *Demographic* (*N*=3), *Environmental* (*N*=3), *Social Chaos* (*N*=5), *Cultural Diversity* (*N*=3), and *Welfare Effort* (*N*=5).[4] All 41 of the ISP's indicators have been established to be reliable indicators of social development; indeed, most are used routinely by other scholars of comparative national and international development (UNDP 2010; World Bank 2010; WRI 2010).

Weighted Index of Social Progress (WISP)

Owing to the volume of data gathered for this analysis only statistically weighted index (WISP) and subindex scores are reported in this chapter. The study's statistical weights were derived through a two-stage principal components and varimax factor analysis in which indicator and subindex scores were analyzed separately for their relative contribution toward explaining the

---

[4]For methodological reasons, the ISP's 41 indicators are divided between positive and negative indicators of social progress. On the Education Subindex, for example, higher *adult illiteracy* rates are negatively associated with social progress, whereas gains in *primary school enrollment* levels are positively associated with overall improvements in development. Thus, the ISP has been structured to achieve a balance between negative and positive factors that influence development.

Table 20.1 Indicators on the Weighted Index of Social Progress (WISP) by subindex, 2010 (41 indicators and 10 subindexes)

Subindex indicators
Education subindex (*N*=4)
Public expenditure on education as percentage of GDP, 2008–2009 (+)
Primary school completion rate, 2008–2009 (+)
Secondary school net enrolment rate, 2008–2009 (+)
Adult literacy rate, 2008 (+)
Health Status subindex (*N*=6)
Life expectation at birth, 2008 (+)
Infant mortality rate, 2008–2009 (−)
Under-5 child mortality rate, 2008 (−)
Physicians per 100,000 population, 2005–2008 (+)
Percent of population undernourished, 2006–2008 (−)
Public expenditure on health as percentage of gross domestic product, 2008–2009 (+)
Women Status subindex (*N*=5)
Female adult literacy as percentage of male literacy, 2009 (+)
Contraceptive prevalence use among married women, 2008 (+)
Life time risk of maternal death, 2005 (+)
Female secondary school enrollment as percentage of male enrolment, 2008 (+)
Seats in parliament held by women as percentage of total, 2010 (+)
Defense Effort subindex (*N*=1)
Military expenditures as percentage of GDP, 2009 (−)
Economic subindex (*N*=5)
Per capita gross domestic product (as measured by PPP), 2009 (+)
Percent growth in gross domestic product (GDP), 2009 (+)
Unemployment rate, 2006–2008 (−)
Total external debt as percentage of GNI, 2009 (−)
GINI Index Score, most recent year 2005–2009 (−)
Demography subindex (*N*=3)
Average annual rate of population growth, 2009 (−)
Percent of population aged <15 years, 2009 (−)
Percent of population aged >64 years, 2009 (+)
Environmental subindex (*N*=3)
Percentage of nationally protected area, 2004–2008 (+)
Average annual number of disaster-related deaths, 2000–2009 (−)
Per capita metric tons of carbon dioxide emissions, 2007 (−)
Social Chaos subindex (*N*=6)
Strength of political rights, 2010 (−)
Strength of civil liberties, 2010 (−)
Number of internally displaced persons per 100,000 population, 2009 (−)
Number of externally displaced persons per 100,000 population, 2009 (−)
Estimated number of deaths from armed conflicts (low estimate), 2006–2007 (−)
Perceived corruption index, 2009 (+)

(continued)

Table 20.1 (continued)

Subindex indicators
Cultural Diversity subindex ($N = 3$)
Largest percentage of population sharing the same or similar racial/ethnic origins, 2009 (+)
Largest percentage of population sharing the same or similar religious beliefs, 2009 (+)
Largest share of population sharing the same mother tongue, 2009 (+)
Welfare Effort subindex ($N = 5$)
Age First National Law—Old Age, Invalidity & Death, 2010 (+)
Age First National Law—Sickness & Maternity, 2010 (+)
Age First National Law—Work Injury, 2010 (+)
Age First National Law—Unemployment, 2010 (+)
Age First National Law—Family allowance, 2010 (+)

variance associated with changes in social progress over time. Standardized indicator scores ($N=41$) were multiplied by their respective factor loadings, averaged within their subindex, and the average subindex scores ($N=10$), in turn, were subjected to a second statistical weighting. The resulting values from this two-stage statistical weighting process formed the basis for computing the composite Weighted Index of Social Progress (WISP) scores as summarized in Table 20.2.[5] Statistically unweighted Index of Social Progress (ISP) scores are reported on the author's project website for those investigators who may wish to reanalyze the data using their own system of statistical weights.[6]

Data Sources

The majority of the data used in this analysis were obtained from the annual reports supplied by individual countries to specialized agencies of the United Nations, the United Nations Development Programme (2010a, b), the World Bank (2010), the Organization for Economic Cooperation and Development (OECD 2010), and the International Social Security Association (ISSA 2010; USDHHS 2010). Data for the *Environmental* subindex were obtained from the World Resources Institute (WRI 2010), the United Nations Commission on Sustainable Development, and the World Bank. Data

for the *Social Chaos* subindex were obtained from Amnesty International (2010), Freedom House (2010), the International Federation of Red Cross and Red Crescent Societies, the Stockholm International Peace and Research Institute (SIPRI 2010), and Transparency International (2010). Data for the *Cultural Diversity* subindex were gathered from the *CIA World Factbook* (2011), the *Encyclopedia Britannica* (2010), and the work of independent scholars in the fields of comparative linguistics, religion, and ethnology. The formal social welfare programs data were obtained from policy reports prepared by the U.S. Social Security Administration (USDHHS 2010).

Country Selection

Thirty-one Asian, Central and Eastern European (CEE), Commonwealth of Independent States (CIS), as well as Russia, Turkey, and the three Baltic States were selected for inclusion in the current analysis (Table 20.3). Countries with missing, inadequate, incomplete, or seriously distorted data were excluded from the analysis.[7]

Time Frames

Index and subindex findings are reported separately for the EITs for three discrete time periods, i.e., 1990, 2000, and 2010. In addition to the WISP data reported for these time periods, additional social indicator data for the EITs are summarized in Tables 20.5–20.8 for 2005–2010. Figures 20.1–20.6 provide both global and group WISP indicator scores for the EITs for the study's entire 20-year time period.

Development Trends of EITs Relative to Those of Other Major World Regions

Figures 20.1 and 20.2 summarize the study's major findings on the WISP for all 161 countries included in the author's comprehensive analysis of worldwide

---

[5] A fuller description of these procedures is summarized in Estes (1988), pp. 199–209.

[6] http://www.sp2.upenn.edu/restes/WSS09.html

[7] Owing to problems of data availability, three EITs were excluded from the present analysis – Bosnia-Herzegovina, Serbia, and Montenegro.

Table 20.2 Statistical weights used in constructing the Weighted Index of Social Progress

$$\text{WISP2010} = \Big\{ \big[(\text{Factor } 1)*.697\big] + \big[(\text{Factor } 2)*.163\big] + \big[(\text{Factor } 3)*.140\big] \Big\}$$

where:

$$\text{Factor } 1 = \big[(\text{Health}*.92) + (\text{Education}*.91) + (\text{Welfare}*.72) + (\text{Woman}*.91) +$$
$$(\text{Social Chaos}*.84) + (\text{Economic}*.71) + (\text{Diversity}*.64) + (\text{Demographic}*.93) \big]$$

$$\text{Factor } 2 = \big[(\text{Defense Effort}*.93) \big]$$

$$\text{Factor } 3 = \big[(\text{Environmental}*.98) \big]$$

Table 20.3 Economies in transition grouped by major geographic region ($N = 31$)

Sub-groupings	Countries	
Central and Eastern Europe (CEE) ($N = 10$)	Albania	Macedonia, FYR [#]
	Bulgaria [*]	Poland [*, $]
	Croatia [#]	Romania [*]
	Czech Republic [*, $]	Slovakia [*, $]
	Hungary [*, $]	Slovenia [*, $]
Baltic States ($N = 3$)	Estonia [*, $]	
	Latvia [*]	
	Lithuania [*]	
Turkey ($N = 1$)	Turkey [#, $]	
Russia ($N = 1$)	Russian Federation	
Other Commonwealth of Independent States (CIS) ($N = 11$)	Armenia	Moldova
	Azerbaijan	Tajikistan
	Belarus	Turkmenistan
	Georgia	Ukraine
	Kazakhstan	Uzbekistan
	Kyrgyz Republic	
Selected other Asian Economies in Transition ($N = 5$)	Cambodia**	
	Laos, PDR**	
	Mongolia	
	People's Republic of China Vietnam	

Sources: IMF (2010); OECD (2010); World Bank (2010)

[*] Indicates member states of the European Union ($N = 10$) as of January 2011, [#] Indicates other European countries that are potential candidates for accession to the European Union ($N = 2$), [$] Indicates EIT countries that are members of the Organization for Economic Cooperation & Development as of January 2011 ($N = 7$), [**] Indicates countries classified by the United Nations as "Least Developing" ($N = 2$). All 31 of the countries identified in Table 20.3 are officially classified by the International Monetary Fund as "Economies in Transition" (EIT)

social development trends (Estes 2010). These time-series data cover the period 1970–2010 and reflect comparative WISP performances for six continental groupings, i.e., North America ($N = 2$), Australia–New Zealand ($N = 2$), Europe ($N = 36$), Latin America ($N = 26$), Asia ($N = 45$), and Africa ($N = 50$). The WISP scores for all 161 countries contained in this analysis averaged 43.6, 43.4, 48.1, 48.5, and 48.7 for 1970, 1980, 1990, 2000, and 2010, respectively (Estes 2010).[8]

---

[8] Note: The average scores for each of the WISP's ten subindexes was set at 10.0; thus, the theoretical range of WISP scores is 0.0–100.0, albeit owing to some unusual conditions operating in selected countries, some nations achieved scores that fell outside the theoretical range (Estes 2011).

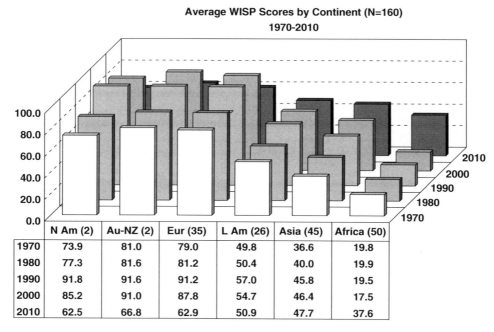

Fig. 20.1 Average WISP scores by continent (N = 160) 1970–2010

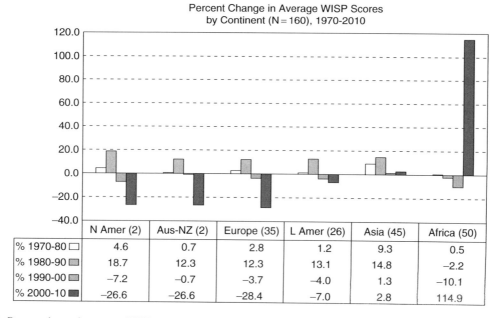

Fig. 20.2 Percent change in average WISP scores by continent (N = 160), 1970–2010

1. The world's most socially developed regions are Australia–New Zealand, Europe, and North America (Fig. 20.1). These regions had already attained the most favorable WISP ratings by 1970; further improvements on the index continued to accrue between 1970–1980 and 1980–1990. Some social improvements also occurred for selected countries included in these clusters between 1990 and 2000,

but as a group, the 39 nations experienced net social losses averaging −3.7 and −28.2, between 1990–2000 and 2000–2010, respectively (Fig. 20.2).

   a. The dramatic WISP losses reported for the world's least socially advanced nations between 2000 and 2010 are directly associated with a protracted period of worldwide economic turmoil brought about by (1) the near-collapse of global financial markets that originated in North America, (2) the actual collapse of at least one large investment bank in the United States, (3) considerable instability in the banking industry virtually everywhere in the Western world, (4) a bursting of the real estate bubbles in North America and Europe, and (5) the imposition by conservative governments in all three subregions of regressive social policies that undermine the secure social safety nets that previously characterized these countries.

   b. In Europe, the "Euro," the common and exclusive currency for 17 member states of the European Union (EU),[9] came under assault with the likely outcome that two or more of the most fiscally vulnerable states may be forced to withdraw from the monetary union, e.g., Greece, Ireland, Portugal, and, possibly, Spain (Aslund 2010; Fidler 2010).

2. The challenges that confronted the world's richest countries between 2000 and 2010 were unparalleled since the period of the Great Depression (1929–1939). These critical financial challenges occurred at the same time that the United States and her allies were engaged in two, largely unfunded, wars in Iraq and Afghanistan—which, on average, cost the United States alone $2.5 thousand million dollars of borrowed money weekly. These expenditures pushed accumulated public debt in the United States to more than $14.4 trillion—an amount equivalent to 100% of the country's annual GDP in 2010.

3. Even with all of the dramatic changes just reported, today, comparatively few differences characterize the overall development profiles of the world's most socially advanced countries—Australia–New Zealand (2010 WISP Average = 66.8), Europe (2010 WISP Average = 62.9), and North America (2010 WISP Average = 62.5).

4. With the exception of the African and Asian regions, all other world regions experienced at least moderate to serious levels of social decline between 2000 and 2010, i.e., −7.0% for Latin America, −26.6% for North America, −26.6% for Australia and New Zealand, and −28.4% for Europe (Fig. 20.2).

5. The remarkable WISP gains reported for Africa's 50 nations for the 2000–2010 time period (+114.9%) are accounted for by (1) the continent's recent ability to exploit the abundant natural resources found in its Northern (primarily oil) and Southern sub regions (mostly gold, diamonds, and other precious minerals) and (2) the significant social gains achieved in Central and Middle Africa associated with implementation of the United Nation's *Millennium Development Campaign* (Estes 2012; UNDESA 1995, 2002; UNDP 1997; World Bank 2006). Though still fragile and reversible, Africa's recent social gains nonetheless are impressive.[10]

6. The social development situation in South America and the Caribbean continues to be perplexing given the group's rich natural resource base and high levels of human capital (ECLAC 2010a, b; World Bank 2010).

   a. Civil unrest, political instability, and high levels of public corruption have combined to deprive many South American and Caribbean countries of the resources needed to advance their development objectives (ECLAC 2010a, b; Human Rights Watch 2010; Transparency International 2010).

   b. Thus, despite impressive gains for a few of the region's countries (most notably, those of Brazil, Chile, Colombia, Mexico, and Peru), development trends in Latin America as a whole advanced slowly between 1970 and 2010, i.e., from a group average WISP score of 49.8 in 1970 to a group average of only 50.9 in 2010 (+2.2%).

7. As reflected in the continental WISP scores reported in Figs. 20.1 and 20.2, considerable variation also exists with respect to Asia's 40-year social development trends. The most significant WISP fluctuations

---

[9]The current "Eurozone" group of countries includes Austria, Belgium, Cyprus, Estonia, Finland, France, Germany, Greece, Ireland, Italy, Luxembourg, Malta, the Netherlands, Portugal, Slovakia, Slovenia, and Spain. The countries currently at greatest risk of being removed from this group are Greece, Ireland, Portugal, and Spain (Editors 2011).

[10]A fuller discussion of positive social development changes occurring among the world's poorest nations is the subject of another recent report prepared by this author (Estes 2012).

are due primarily to the inclusion of China into the United Nations in 1971. With the exception of its political and human rights records (Freedom House 2010; Human Rights Watch 2010), virtually all of the economic developments taking place in China have resulted in dramatic advancements in the country's composite development profile, especially for the country's coastal cities and special economic zones (Guo 2010; Guo and Guo 2010; Zhao and Seng 2010; Peerenboom 2007; Schiere 2010; Zhao and Lim 2010).

a. China's impressive economic successes also are having a positive impact on development trends occurring in her neighboring countries—many of which have entered into formal trade and export agreements with the PRC, e.g., Japan, Malaysia, the Philippines, Taiwan, and Vietnam (Asian Development Bank 2009; World Bank 2010).

b. Through the purchase of bonds and other financial instruments, China also is playing a major role in helping to reduce the sovereign debt crises occurring in Europe (Guo 2010; Kunzmann et al. 2010).

8. WISP scores for the EITs averaged 63.5 in 2000 and 53.9 in 2010 (−15.1%). The development profile of the 31 EITs, therefore, falls between those of South (WISP Avg. 2010=50.9) and North America (WISP Avg. 2010=62.5) for the same time periods.

a. Thus, the EITs achieved at least a moderate level of success on the WISP during the most recent development decade (Table 20.4).

b. However, the legacy of one-party, autocratic, political systems remains strong in many of the Asian and Commonwealth of Independent States EITs and is a factor that keeps some tethered to decades-long traditions of state control over most aspects of economic and political decision-making (Tables 20.7 and 20.8) (Asian Development Bank 2009; Graham and Lindahl 2010; Weingast and Wittman 2006).

c. With the exception of the European EITs (including the Baltic states), most of the EITs have not achieved levels of political freedom found in Northern and Western Europe or other economically advanced countries (Freedom House 2010). Rather, current patterns of political development in the member countries of the CIS more closely approximate those observed for the post-Socialist nations of Asia and those of pre-revolutionary Central and South America.

d. But, still, some EITs achieved substantial social gains between 1990 and 2010, e.g., Croatia (+16 ranks), Uzbekistan (+16 ranks), Vietnam (+13 ranks), Laos (+13 ranks), Czech Republic (+10 ranks), among others (Table 20.4).

In general, then, patterns of world social development between 1970 and 2010 reflect considerable economic turmoil, political instability, and asynchronous development for many of the world's countries. For a minority of countries significant social gains were achieved between 2000 and 2010. Even so, the already socially advanced countries of Europe, Oceania, and North America were able to retain their development leadership positions during this decade (Figs. 20.1 and 20.2).

The situation in Latin America remained relatively unchanged for nearly all four decades covered by the study; however, the region's emerging economies—such as Brazil, Chile, Colombia, Mexico, and Peru—have established new benchmarks for what other countries in the region might be able to achieve for themselves (Editors 2010a; Magnus 2011).

The social situation in Asia generally has been positive due, in large part, to the remarkable economic successes of China and India and, in turn, that of their major manufacturing partners, e.g., India, Indonesia, Japan, Malaysia, the Philippines, and Vietnam (Editors 2010b). These gains are all the more impressive given that the countries represent two of the world's four "population super giants"—three of which are located in Asia, i.e., China (2010 population = 1,339 million), India (2010 population = 1,166 million), and Indonesia (2010 population = 240 million).

However, the most remarkable change in the development profiles summarized in Figs. 20.1 and 20.2 is the 115% increase in WISP scores between 2000 and 2010 reported for the African region. Many factors have contributed to Africa's recent development successes, but nearly all of them can be traced to United Nations *Millennium Development Campaign* which targets the poorest countries of Central and Middle Africa and Central Asia for preferential development assistance (UN 2010a, b, c; UNDP 1997). Thus far, the Campaign is succeeding in achieving many of its important health and educational goals, but others goals are not expected to be achieved fully by the Campaign's planned

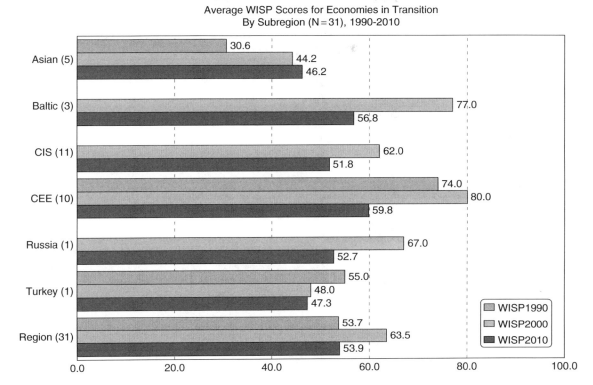

Fig. 20.3 Average WISP scores for economies in transition by subregion ($N=31$), 1990–2010

termination date of 2015 (UN 2010b, c). When combined with the economic successes of the Northern and Southern African subregions recent development successes of Central and Middle Africa are both impressive and historical. And every indication exists for believing that progress in the sectors for Africa will continue over at least the near-term.

Development Trends in the World's Economies in Transition

The study's major 20-year development trends for the EITs are summarized in Figs. 20.3 and 20.4 and Tables 20.4–20.8. WISP scores are reported in these figures for both the EITs as a whole and for each of its six subgroups, i.e., Asia ($N=5$), the Baltic States ($N=3$), the Commonwealth of Independent States (CIS, $N=11$), Central and Eastern Europe (CEE, $N=10$), the Russian Federation ($N=1$), and Turkey ($N=1$). Group-wide performances on the WISP's ten subindexes are reported in Fig. 20.5 for the years 2000 and 2010 along with the percentage change in WISP values over the decade. Country-specific WISP scores for the years 2000 and 2010, including country rank position relative to all 161 countries included in the comprehensive study of world social development, are reported in Table 20.4. Current social indicator data for each country ranked by their overall performance on the WISP are reported in Tables 20.5–20.8. These tables also identify the EIT's 10 *Social Leaders* (SLs) and 21 *Middle Performing Countries* (MPCs); as of 2010, the EITs do not include any *Socially Least Developing Countries* (SLDCs), i.e., failed or failing countries that are on the brink of "social implosion" due to profound economic collapse or political instability, e.g., Afghanistan, Somalia, Sudan, etc. (Ghani and Lockhart 2008; Mallaby 2004).

For comparison purposes, data for each of the social indicators reported in Tables 20.5–20.8 also are reported for the United States.

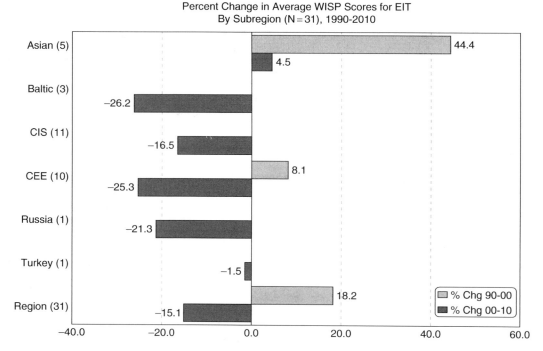

Fig. 20.4 Percent change in average WISP scores for EIT by subregion ($N=31$), 1999–2010

EIT Performances on the WISP

As summarized in Fig. 20.3, EIT performances on the WISP varied widely for each subgroup, i.e., Central and Eastern Europe (2010 WISP Average=59.8), the Baltic States (2010 WISP Average=56.8), the Russian Federation (2010 WISP Average=52.7), the Commonwealth of Independent States (2010 WISP Average=51.8), Turkey (2010 WISP Average=47.3), and the group of selected Asian EITs (2010 WISP Average=46.2).

As with other world regions, average EIT scores for the 2000–2010 time period were at considerable variance with those reported for the 1990–2000 time period (Average WISP Loss=−15.1%). For example, average net gains occurred for the Asian EITs (Average WISP Gain=+4.5%) between 2000 and 2010, whereas significant social losses during the same time period occurred for the Baltic States (Average WISP Loss=−26.2%), the Commonwealth of Independent States (Average WISP Loss=−16.5%), the nations of Central and Eastern Europe (Average WISP Loss=−25.3%), the Russian Federation (Average WISP Loss=−21.3%), and Turkey (Average WISP Loss=−1.5%). The net losses reported for Turkey are judged to be a statistical artifact.

These dramatic shifts in WISP performances for EIT subgroups reflect the high levels of social and economic interdependence that exists between the EITs and other countries (Friedman 2005; Guo 2010; Guo and Guo 2010). The EITs that only recently achieved their independence were impacted significantly more by global economic and political changes than were the EITs that have experienced independence for a longer period of time.

EIT Performances on the WISP Subindexes

The global challenges to the transition process of the EITs are reflected in their subindex scores summarized in Fig. 20.5. Social gains for the EITs as a group are recorded on only two subindexes (i.e., *Social Chaos* and *Environment*), whereas significant social losses took place in the remaining eight sectors measured by the WISP. The magnitude of these social losses will prove difficult for many EITs to overcome in the near term. Specific EIT subgroups, however, including the

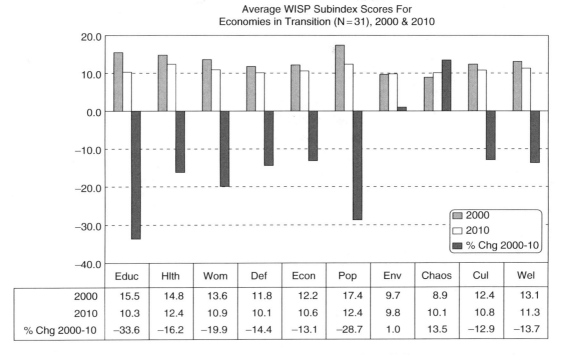

Fig. 20.5 Average WISP subindex scores for economies in transition (*N* = 31), 2000 and 2010

Baltic States and Turkey are expected to rebound more quickly from the challenges posed by the current global economic crises. These reversals in development patterns, though, will be realized only if these EITs sustain the patterns of trade liberalization and democratic political reforms established prior to the economic downturn. For Turkey, the country's more negative WISP profile likely will involve further delays to its gaining entry into the European Union, albeit Turkey already is a member of the Organization for Economic Cooperation and Development (Table 20.3).

EIT Social Leaders (SLs) and Middle Performing Countries (MPCs)

Figure 20.6 and Tables 20.4–20.8 report a range of indicators related to EIT social, political, and economic performances for 2000 and 2010. For comparison purposes, the tables also include values for the same set of indicators for the United States. WISP scores for 2010 are used as the basis for ranking the countries. Thus, the tables identify EIT "Social Leaders" (*N* = 10) and "Middle Performing Countries"

(*N* = 21). Table 20.4, more particularly, reports group and country WISP scores and, for the individual EITs as well as their WISP rank positions for 2000 and 2010. The table also reports changes in WISP rank positions for all EITs for the 10-year period 2000–2010.

The magnitude of the change in WISP rank positions reported in Table 20.4 is used to identify those EITs that experienced the *most positive* and the *most negative* changes in social development for the decade. The WISP ranks for 2010 both order the EITs as a group and serve as a basis for comparing the development performances of the EITs against those of the other countries included in the author's more comprehensive analysis of world social development trends (Estes 2010).

EIT Social Leaders (SLs)

Ten countries are identified in Tables 20.4–20.8 as EIT social leaders (SLs). These countries are classified as SLs on the basis of (1) their exceptional performance on the WISP in 2010 (Average = 61.8) and (2)

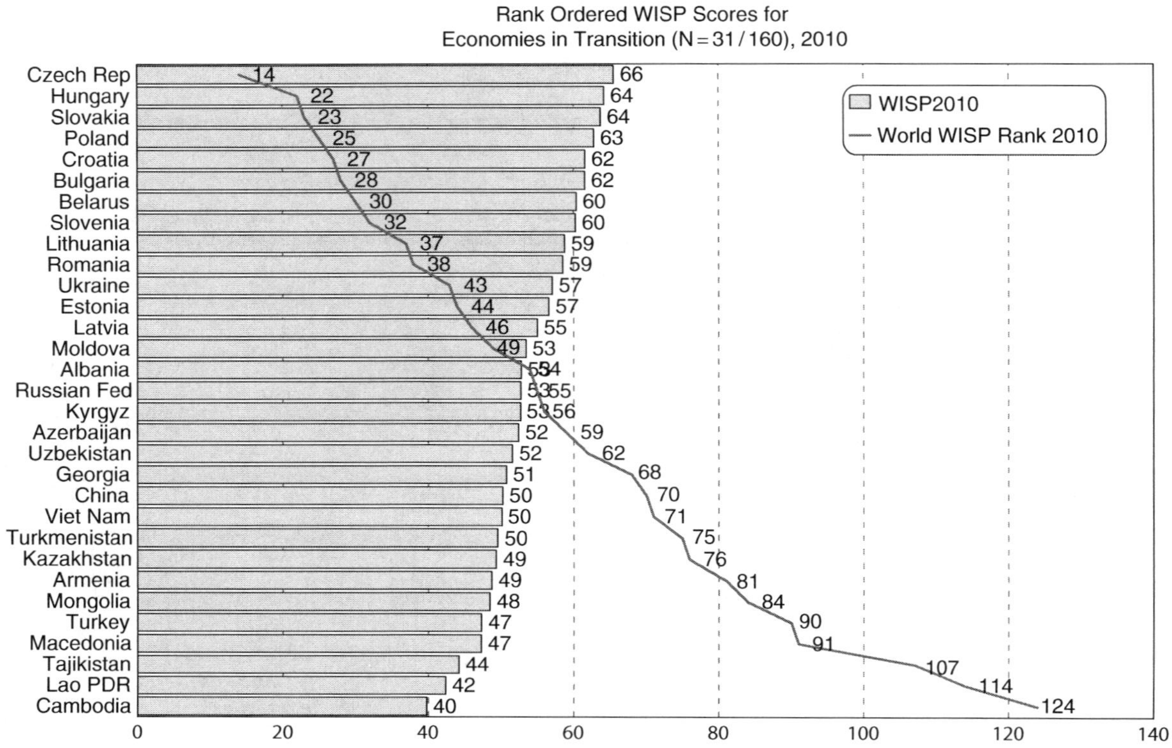

Rank Ordered WISP Scores for Economies in Transition (N = 31 / 160), 2010

Fig. 20.6 Rank ordered WISP scores for economies in transition (N=31/160), 2010

their favorable group outcomes on the social indicators summarized in Tables 20.5–20.8, e.g., highly favorable population growth trends (Table 20.5), generally moderate to strong patterns of economic growth (Table 20.6), increasing progress toward more open and participatory form of governance combined with low level of public corruption (Table 20.7), and increasing allocations of public resources to the health, education, and other social sectors (Table 20.8). The SLs were able to achieve these favorable outcomes at a comparatively rapid pace, even while the many Middle Performing EITs were experiencing slower, often negative, progress toward the same goals. The 10-year social accomplishments of the SLs are all the more impressive given the magnitude their performances in virtually all development sectors measured by the WISP. But progress in social development for many of the SLs also tends to be highly asynchronous, i.e., achieving substantial gains in some sectors but experiencing social losses in others (e.g., China, the Russian Federation).

EIT Middle Performing Countries (MPCs)

The EITs Middle Performing Countries (MPCs) reflect a highly heterogeneous group of countries. They are located in all regions of the world and have populations ranging from a low of 1.3 million for Estonia to a high of 1,339 million for China. Many of the MPCs are governed by one-party autocratic political systems (e.g., China, Turkmenistan, Vietnam). This situation is particularly prevalent among the Asian MPCs which continue to retain post-Socialist style autocratic rule (e.g., Armenia, Tajikistan, Uzbekistan). The majority of these countries made little progress toward their long-term development objectives, and as a result, most achieved only limited progress in the economic factors measured for the 2000–2010 time period. Some of the MPCs also are experiencing continuing high levels of diversity-related social conflict that existed prior to their independence (e.g., Albania, Cambodia, Laos, the Russian Federation). Combined with limited natural resources, or at least limited means for

20 Economies in Transition: Revisiting Challenges to Quality of Life

Table 20.4 WISP scores and WISP rank positions for EITs rank ordered by 2010 WISP scores, 2000 and 2010 ($N=31$)

Countries	WISP 2000 (Base = 161)	WISP00 rank (Base = 161)	WISP 2010 (Base = 161)	WISP10 rank (Base = 161)	Change in WISP rank positions 2000 > 2010 (Base = 161)
EIT social leaders (SLs–WISP range = 59 > 66)					
Czech Republic	88	24	66	14	10
Hungary	91	18	64	22	−4
Slovakia	87	25	64	23	2
Poland	85	27	63	25	2
Croatia	70	43	62	27	16
Bulgaria	89	22	62	28	−6
Belarus	78	33	60	30	3
Slovenia	85	27	60	32	−5
Lithuania	74	39	59	37	2
Romania	77	34	59	38	−4
SL average (N = 10)	**82.4**	**29.2**	**61.8**	**27.6**	**1.6**
EIT middle performing countries (MPCs–WISP range = 40 > 57)					
Ukraine	71	41	57	43	−2
Estonia	81	31	57	44	−13
Latvia	77	34	55	46	−12
Moldova	67	47	53	49	−2
Albania	65	49	53	54	−5
Russia	67	47	53	55	−8
Kyrgyzstan	61	56	53	56	0
Azerbaijan	60	58	52	59	−1
Uzbekistan	52	78	52	62	16
Georgia	63	53	51	68	−15
China	56	69	50	70	−1
Viet Nam	49	84	50	71	13
Turkmenistan	54	71	50	75	−4
Kazakhstan	59	61	49	76	−15
Armenia	65	49	49	81	−32
Mongolia	57	67	48	84	−17
Turkey	48	88	47	90	−2
Macedonia	63	53	47	91	−38
Tajikistan	50	82	44	107	−25
Lao PDR*	21	127	42	114	13
Cambodia*	28	116	40	124	−8
MPCs average (N = 21)	**57.8**	**64.8**	**50.1**	**72.3**	**−7.5**
EITs average (N = 31)	**65.7**	**53.3**	**53.9**	**57.9**	**−4.6**
Standard deviation (N = 31)	**16.8**	**26.6**	**6.7**	**28.7**	**12.6**
United States	**84.8**	**27**	**61**	**29**	**−2**

*Indicates countries officially classified by the United Nations as "least developing"

transporting those natural resources they do have to international markets (e.g., Kyrgyzstan, Mongolia, Uzbekistan), some of the MPCs effectively are not able to participate in global markets on a large scale. The preceding patterns work to the severe disadvantage of land-locked and politically regressive MPCs.

In comparison with the data reported for the group's SLs in Tables 20.5–20.8, the MPCs also are characterized by higher than average rates of infant and child mortality, increased rates of maternal mortality, higher than average rates of preventable infectious diseases, fewer years of average life expectation, and generally

Table 20.5 Selected population-related indicators for economies in transition ranked by WISP score, 2009–2010 ($N=31$)

Countries	Population (millions) 2010	Population growth rate 2009	Age dependent population		Life expectation at birth 2008	Infant mortality 2008–2009	Adult literacy rate 2008
			<15 years 2009	>65 years 2009			
EIT social leaders (SLs–WISP range = 59>66)							
Czech Republic	10.2	−0.1	14	14.9	77.2	2.8	99.0
Hungary	9.9	−0.3	15	16.2	74.0	5.1	99.0
Slovakia	5.4	0.0	15	12.1	74.8	5.8	100.0
Poland	38.5	−0.1	15	13.4	75.5	5.6	99.5
Croatia	4.5	−0.2	15	17.2	75.9	4.5	98.7
Bulgaria	7.2	−0.8	14	17.4	73.3	8.3	98.3
Belarus	9.6	−0.5	15	13.6	70.6	10.9	99.7
Slovenia	2.1	0.1	14	16.2	66.3	29.6	100.0
Lithuania	3.6	−0.5	15	16.2	71.8	5.0	99.7
Romania	22.2	−0.7	15	14.8	73.4	10.0	97.6
SLs total (N = 10)	**113.2**						
SL average (N = 10)	**11.3**	**−0.3**	**14.7**	**15.2**	**73.3**	**8.8**	**99.2**
EIT middle performing countries (MPCs–WISP range = 40 > 57)							
Ukraine	45.7	−0.9	14	15.7	68.3	13.3	99.7
Estonia	1.3	−0.4	15	17.0	74.0	4.4	99.8
Latvia	2.2	−0.6	14	17.3	72.2	7.0	99.8
Moldova	4.3	−1.3	17	11.1	68.4	14.6	98.3
Albania	3.6	0.4	23	9.5	76.6	13.5	99.0
Russia	140.0	−0.5	15	13.1	67.8	11.1	99.5
Kyrgyzstan	5.4	0.9	29	5.2	67.4	32.1	99.3
Azerbaijan	8.2	0.9	24	6.7	70.2	29.6	99.0
Uzbekistan	27.6	1.2	29	4.5	67.8	31.8	99.2
Georgia	4.6	−1.0	17	14.3	71.5	26.0	99.7
China	1,338.6	0.6	20	8.1	73.1	16.6	93.7
Viet Nam	87.0	1.3	25	6.3	74.4	19.5	92.5
Turkmenistan	4.9	1.4	29	4.2	64.8	41.5	99.5
Kazakhstan	15.4	0.5	24	7.1	66.4	25.6	99.7
Armenia	3.0	−0.4	20	11.3	73.5	19.6	99.5
Mongolia	3.0	1.2	26	4.0	66.6	24.3	97.3
Turkey	76.8	1.3	26	5.9	71.9	18.5	87.0
Macedonia	2.1	0.2	18	11.7	74.2	9.8	97.0
Tajikistan	7.4	1.2	36	3.6	66.7	51.8	99.7
Lao PDR*	6.8	1.6	37	3.6	65.0	45.8	69.0
Cambodia*	14.5	2.0	33	3.5	61.0	68.0	77.6
MPCs total (N = 21)	**1802.4**						
MPCs average (N = 21)	**85.8**	**0.5**	**23.4**	**8.7**	**69.6**	**25.0**	**95.5**
EITs total (N = 31)	**1,915.6**						
EITs average (N = 31)	**61.8**	**0.2**	**20.6**	**10.8**	**70.8**	**19.7**	**96.7**
Standard deviation (N = 31)	**238.9**	**0.9**	**7.1**	**5.0**	**4.1**	**15.7**	**6.9**
United States	**307.2**	**1.0**	**20.2**	**12.8**	**78.4**	**6.8**	**7.8**

Data Source: UNDP (2010); World Bank (2010)

*Indicates countries officially classified by the United Nations as "least developing"

20 Economies in Transition: Revisiting Challenges to Quality of Life

Table 20.6 Selected economic indicators for economies in transition ranked by WISP score, 2009–2010 ($N=31$)

Countries	PC GDP (PPP) 2009[a]	% Growth GDP 2009[a]	External debt as % GDP 2009[a]	Unemployment rate 2011[b]	GINI coefficient (varied)
EIT social leaders (SLs–WISP Range = 59 > 66)					
Czech Republic	$25,232	−4.2	39	9.3	25.4
Hungary	$19,764	−6.3	90	11.5	26.9
Slovakia	$22,356	−6.2	55	12.5	25.8
Poland	$19,059	1.7	47	11.8	34.5
Croatia	$19,804	−5.8	94	17.6	29.0
Bulgaria	$12,888	−5.0	105	9.5	29.2
Belarus	$12,569	0.2	16	1.0	28.8
Slovenia	$2,550	−2.2	112	10.6	28.4
Lithuania	$16,746	−15.0	98	16.0	36.0
Romania	$14,198	−8.5	59	8.2	32.1
SL average (N = 10)	**$16,517**	**−5.1**	**71.5**	**10.8**	**29.6**
EIT middle performing countries (MPCs–WISP range = 40 > 57)					
Ukraine	$6,327	−15.1	90	8.4	27.6
Estonia	$19,451	−14.1	118	13.5	35.8
Latvia	$15,411	−18.0	145	19.4	36.3
Moldova	$2,858	−6.5	73	3.4	37.4
Albania	$8,246	2.2	21	12.7	31.1
Russia	$18,945	−7.9	30	7.6	43.7
Kyrgyzstan	$2,287	2.3	68	18.0	33.5
Azerbaijan	$9,652	9.3	6	0.9	**36.5**
Uzbekistan	$2,879	8.1	11	1.1	**36.8**
Georgia	$4,778	−4.0	31	16.4	40.4
China	$6,838	9.1	7	4.3	46.9
Viet Nam	$2,957	5.5	34	6.4	37.8
Turkmenistan	$7,252	8.0	31	60.0	40.8
Kazakhstan	$11,526	1.2	85	5.5	30.9
Armenia	$5,286	−14.4	51	7.1	30.2
Mongolia	$3,527	−1.6	44	2.8	36.6
Turkey	$13,905	−4.7	45	12.4	41.2
Macedonia	$10,822	−0.7	59	33.1	42.8
Tajikistan	$1,975	3.4	34	2.2	32.6
Lao PDR*	$2,259	6.4	55	2.5	34.6
Cambodia*	$1,913	−2.1	38	3.5	44.2
MPCs average (N = 21)	**$7,576**	**−1.6**	**51.2**	**11.5**	**37.0**
EITs average (N = 31)	**$10,460**	**−2.7**	**57.8**	**11.3**	**34.6**
Standard deviation (N = 31)	**$7,137**	**7.6**	**35.4**	**11.4**	**5.8**
United States	**$46,436**	**−2.4**	**100.0**	**5.8**	**40.8**

Data sources:
[a]World Bank (2010)
[b]CIA World Factbook (2011)
*Indicates countries officially classified by the United Nations as "least developing"

lower patterns of per capita income, lower rates of economic growth, and higher levels of public indebtedness (Tables 20.5 and 20.6). On average, the MPCs also experience fewer political freedoms than do their SL counterparts (Table 20.7). And since 2000, social spending has declined more on average within the MPCs than in the SLs (Table 20.8). As is to be expected, these general patterns vary among the individual MPCs, but as a group, they are considerably less developed than the SLs, i.e., WISP scores for the 21 MPCs

Table 20.7 Selected political indicators for economies in transition ranked by WISP score, 2009–2010 ($N = 31$)

Countries	Type of polity 2010[a]	Head of state 2010[a]	Political freedom index (−) 2010[b]	Civil liberties index (−) 2010[c]	Global corruption perceptions index (+) 2009[d]	Global corruption barometer (−) 2010[e]	Failed state index (−) 2010[f]	Percent of parliamentary seats held by women (+) 2010
EIT social leaders (SLs–WISP Range = 59 > 66)								
Czech Republic	Republic	Ceremonial	1.0	1.0	4.9	14	41.5	15.5
Hungary	Republic	Ceremonial	1.0	1.0	5.1	24	50.1	11.1
Slovakia	Republic	Ceremonial	1.0	1.0	4.5	na	48.8	19.3
Poland	Republic	Ceremonial	1.0	1.0	5.0	15	49.0	20.2
Croatia	Republic	Ceremonial	1.0	2.0	4.1	5	59.0	20.9
Bulgaria	Republic	Ceremonial	2.0	2.0	3.8	8	61.2	20.8
Belarus	Republic	Executive	7.0	6.0	2.4	27	78.7	31.8
Slovenia	Republic	Ceremonial	1.0	1.0	6.6	4	36.0	0.0
Lithuania	Republic	Executive	1.0	1.0	4.9	34	47.8	17.7
Romania	Republic	Executive	2.0	2.0	3.8	28	60.2	11.4
SL average (N = 10)			**1.8**	**1.8**	**4.5**	**17.7**	**53.2**	**16.9**
EIT middle performing countries (MPCs–WISP Range = 40 > 57)								
Ukraine	Republic	Executive	3.0	2.0	2.2	34	69.5	8.2
Estonia	Republic	Ceremonial	1.0	1.0	6.6	na	50.7	20.8
Latvia	Republic	Ceremonial	2.0	1.0	4.5	15	55.4	20.0
Moldova	Republic	Ceremonial	3.0	4.0	3.3	37	83.8	25.7
Albania	Republic	Ceremonial	3.0	3.0	3.2	na	67.1	16.4
Russia	Republic	Executive	6.0	5.0	2.2	26	79.0	14.0
Kyrgyzstan	Republic	Executive	6.0	5.0	1.9	na	88.4	25.6
Azerbaijan	Republic	Executive	6.0	5.0	2.3	47	84.4	11.4
Uzbekistan	Republic	Executive	7.0	7.0	1.7	na	90.5	17.5
Georgia	Republic	Executive	4.0	4.0	4.1	3	90.4	5.1
China	Republic	Executive	7.0	6.0	3.6	9	83.0	21.3
Viet Nam	Republic	Executive	7.0	5.0	2.7	44	76.6	25.8
Turkmenistan	Republic	Executive	7.0	7.0	1.8	na	82.5	16.8
Kazakhstan	Republic	Executive	6.0	5.0	2.7	na	72.7	15.9
Armenia	Republic	Executive	6.0	4.0	2.7	22	74.1	8.4
Mongolia	Republic	Executive	2.0	2.0	2.7	48	60.1	4.0
Turkey	Republic	Ceremonial	3.0	3.0	4.4	33	77.1	9.4
Macedonia	Republic	Ceremonial	3.0	3.0	3.8	21	72.7	28.3
Tajikistan	Republic	Executive	6.0	5.0	2.0	na	89.2	17.5
Lao PDR*	Republic	Executive	7.0	6.0	2.0	na	88.7	25.2
Cambodia*	Constitutional Monarchy	Ceremonial	6.0	5.0	2.0	84	88.7	16.3
MPCs average (N = 21)			**4.8**	**4.2**	**3.0**	**32.5**	**77.4**	**16.8**
EITs average (N = 31)			**3.8**	**3.4**	**3.5**	**26.5**	**69.6**	**16.8**
Standard deviation (N = 31)			**2.4**	**2.0**	**1.4**	**19.9**	**16.3**	**7.4**
United States	**Republic**	**Executive**	**1.0**	**1.0**	**7.5**	**5.0**	**35.3**	**16.8**

Sources:

[a]Central Intelligence Agency (2010); Encyclopedia Britannica (2010)

[b]Freedom House (2010). Scores range for 1–7 with 1 representing the most free

[c]Freedom House (2010). Scores range for 1–7 with 1 representing the most free

[d]The degree to which public sector corruption is perceived to exist in 178 countries worldwide

[e]Transparency International (2010). Percent users reporting they paid a bribe to receive attention from at least 1 of 9 different service providers

[f]UNDP (2010)

*Indicates countries officially classified by the United Nations as "least developing"

20 Economies in Transition: Revisiting Challenges to Quality of Life

Table 20.8 Selected central government expenditure priorities of EITs, 2009–2010 ($N=31$)

Countries	General government consumption as % GDP 2008–2009[a]	Public expenditures as % GDP			Military expenditures as % GDP
		Education 2008–2009[b]	Health 2008–2009[b]	Debt-to-GDP 2008–2009	2008–2009[a]
EIT social leaders (SLs–WISP Range = 59 > 66)					
Czech Republic	58.8	4.4	5.8	39.0	1.5
Hungary	59.1	5.4	5.2	90.0	1.3
Slovakia	66.2	3.6	5.2	55.0	1.5
Poland	21.2	4.9	4.6	47.0	2.0
Croatia	46.8	4.7	6.6	94.0	1.8
Bulgaria	49.9	4.1	4.2	105.0	2.3
Belarus	52.9	5.2	4.9	16.0	1.8
Slovenia	47.1	6.0	4.3	112.0	1.5
Lithuania	43.9	4.7	4.5	98.0	1.7
Romania	65.5	4.4	3.8	59.0	1.4
SL average (N = 10)	**51.1**	**4.7**	**4.9**	**71.5**	**1.7**
EIT middle performing countries (MPCs–WISP Range = 40 > 57)					
Ukraine	52.1	5.3	4.0	90.0	2.9
Estonia	45.8	5.0	4.1	118.0	2.3
Latvia	47.7	5.0	3.6	145.0	2.6
Moldova	63.4	8.2	5.2	73.0	0.5
Albania	27.9	2.9	2.9	21.0	2.1
Russia	20.9	3.9	3.5	30.0	4.3
Kyrgyzstan	31.1	6.6	3.5	68.0	3.6
Azerbaijan	43.9	1.9	1.0	6.0	3.5
Uzbekistan	55.6	9.4	2.3	11.0	0.5
Georgia	50.4	2.9	1.5	31.0	5.6
China	22.0	1.9	1.9	7.0	2.0
Viet Nam	36.9	5.3	2.8	34.0	2.2
Turkmenistan	9.6	3.9	1.4	31.0	2.9
Kazakhstan	37.2	2.8	2.5	85.0	1.2
Armenia	17.8	3.0	2.1	51.0	4.0
Mongolia	33.3	5.1	3.5	44.0	1.4
Turkey	39.1	2.9	3.4	45.0	2.8
Macedonia	35.9	3.5	4.7	59.0	2.1
Tajikistan	33.4	3.4	1.1	34.0	2.2
Lao PDR*	21.0	2.3	0.8	55.0	0.4
Cambodia*	13.3	1.6	1.7	38.0	1.2
MPCs average (N = 21)	**35.2**	**4.1**	**2.7**	**51.2**	**2.4**
EITs average (N = 31)	**40.3**	**4.3**	**3.4**	**57.8**	**2.2**
Standard deviation (N = 31)	**15.8**	**1.7**	**1.5**	**35.4**	**1.1**
United States	**36**	**5.3**	**7.1**	**100.0**	**4.6**

Data sources:

[a]Central Intelligence Agency (2010)

[b]World Bank (2010)

*Indicates countries officially classified by the United Nations as "least developing"

averaged 50.1 in 2010 vs. a group average of 61.8 on the WISP for the 10 SLs (Table 20.4).

EITs Experiencing the Most Significant WISP Gains and Losses

The most socially progressive EITs include Croatia (+16 ranks), Uzbekistan (+16 ranks), Vietnam (+13 ranks), Laos (+13 ranks), and the Czech Republic (+10 ranks). Lessor, but important, social gains also were achieved by Belarus (+3 ranks), Lithuania (+2 ranks), Slovakia (+2 ranks), and Poland (+2 ranks). Kyrgyzstan retained its rank position of 56/161 during both 2000 and 2010. The average WISP rank for the SLs in 2010 was 27.6 vs. an average WISP rank of 72.3 during the same period for the MPCs. The differences in the magnitude of average rank positions for the two clusters of EITs are truly dramatic.

The 10-year social gains realized by the EIT social leaders are noteworthy given the high level of political and economic turbulence that characterized the global situation throughout much of the first decade of this century. The SLs significant social gains reflect both a clear sense of their social development objectives and a willingness (and capacity) to make the public investments needed to achieve their objectives. Not surprisingly, five of the ten EIT SLs are now members of the OECD, and eight are members of the European Union (Table 20.3).

Conversely, significant social losses between 2000 and 2010 were experienced by Macedonia (−38 ranks), Armenia (−32 ranks), Tajikistan (−25 ranks), Mongolia (−17 ranks), Kazakhstan (−15 ranks), Georgia (−15 ranks), Estonia (−13 ranks), Latvia (−12 ranks), Russia (−8 ranks), Cambodia (−8 ranks), Bulgaria (−6 ranks), Slovenia (−5 ranks), and Albania (−5 ranks). Lower social losses in WISP ranks occurred for Hungary (−4 ranks), Romania (−4 ranks), Turkmenistan (−4 ranks), Ukraine (−2 ranks), Moldova (−2 ranks), Turkey (−2 ranks), Azerbaijan (−1 rank), and China (−1 rank).

Estonia and Latvia already are members of the European Union; Turkey is a member of the OECD and is under consideration for inclusion in the EU. The social challenges facing all three countries add measurably to the fiscal problems being confronted by the EU and the OECD which have been called upon to help solve the severe financial dislocations confronting Iceland, Ireland, Greece, Portugal, and Spain, among

others (Åslund 2010; Barrios 2010; Gup 2010). The stability of the Euro as a common currency for 17 European countries also is in jeopardy. As of this writing, no solutions to these challenges are self-evident, albeit Germany and France, the EU's two economic engines, have pledged their continuing commitment to avoid EU insolvency. China also has committed itself to purchase as much European sovereign debt as possible (mostly in the form of public bonds) and is engaged in establishing financial partnerships with some of Europe's largest and most fiscally vulnerable companies (Jones 2010; Kunzmann et al. 2010; Sutter 2010). These efforts, however, are perceived by members of the EU to be only temporary given the EU's preference to resolve its financial crises within a regional rather than the international context. Preferences notwithstanding, European nations may find it necessary to enter into a wide range of financial partnerships with entities both within and outside the region in order to regain its economic footing.

EIT Subgroup Performances on the WISP

The States of Central and Eastern Europe (CEE)

The ten countries of Central and Eastern Europe, some of which, as reported in Table 20.3, now are members of either the European Union or the Organization for Economic Cooperation and Development (OECD), or both, attained the highest average WISP scores for 2000 and 2010, i.e., 80.0 and 59.8, respectively. The majority of these countries are truly "European" in their orientation—a factor that contributes to the high levels of social protection, retention of private ownership of the means of production (mostly farms and small businesses) during the Soviet era, and sociopolitical ideologies that have made it easier for many of the CEE states to rejoin the larger group of "European" nations (Ash 2004; Estes 2004; Rifkin 2004). Indeed, average WISP scores for European EITs in 2010 (59.8) closely approximate those reported for all 35 European countries reported in Fig. 20.1 (Average 2010 WISP=62.9, Fig. 20.1 and Table 20.4).

Subindex scores for the ten Central and Eastern European EITs also are highly favorable given that the scores on these subindexes well exceed the average score of 10.0 attained by all 161 countries included in the survey of worldwide social development trends

(Estes 2004).[11] Subindex scores for Central and Eastern European countries were especially strong in the *Health* (2010 SI Average = 14.0), *Population* (2010 SI Average = 13.9), *Welfare Effort* (2010 SI Average = 13.5), *Social Chaos* (2010 SI Average = 12.9), *Women Status* (2010 SI Average = 11.8), *Cultural Diversity* (2010 SI Average = 11.4), and *Economic* (2010 SI Average = 10.8) sectors. Subindex scores on the *Education* (2010 SI Average = 10.7), *Defense Effort* (2010 SI Average = 10.2), and *Environmental* (2010 SI Average = 9.9) subindexes also were higher than EIT group average scores, albeit additional improvements in the *Environmental* subindex would be desirable. No doubt, advances on these subindexes will accelerate as the countries regain their earlier economic footing.

The Baltic States

The three Baltic States of Estonia, Latvia, and Lithuania already are members of the European Union; Estonia is a member of the OECD as well. As a group, the Baltic States attained an average 2010 WISP score of 56.8. This score is comparable to that observed for the EITs of Central and Eastern Europe (Average = 59.8), and much like their CEE counterparts, the Baltic States are European in orientation. As such they share many of the same sociocultural histories previously reported for the CEEs (Estes 2010). They also share many of the same ideologies with the rest of Europe regarding the key to be performed by the state in ensuring the provision of basic services for the aged, poor, and other "socially excluded" populations (Ash 2004; USDHHS 2010; Tables 20.7 and 20.8).

The high subindex scores reported for the Baltic States in Table 20.4 confirm that social development already was well advanced in these countries prior to the beginning of their transition toward market economies and democratic political systems (Table 20.7). Their high subindex scores also reflect considerable ideological unity with the socially advanced nations of Northern, Western, and Southern Europe (Estes 2004; Jacobsson 2010; Wolchick and Curry 2011).

---

[11]The WISP's 10 subindex scores ($N = 161$) were artificially set at a mean of 10.0 with a standard deviation of 1.0. Thus, WISP scores for 2010 ranged from a low of 17.0 to a high of 71.9 (Average = 48.7, SD = 11.8). For the 31 EITs WISP scores, values ranged between 39.8 and 65.5, group WISP average scores = 53.8, and the SD was 6.7.

The only exception to an otherwise impressive pattern of immediate post-transition subindex performances on the WISP for the Baltic States is their comparative poor performance on the *Cultural Diversity* subindex (2010 SI Average = 8.9). The low level of this score vis-à-vis other WISP subindex scores reflects the high levels of cultural diversity that characterizes the Baltic States (e.g., Latvia with its sizeable resident Russian population and Lithuania with its mixture of citizens of Lithuanian, Polish, and Russian extraction), a factor, which for some nations, has tended to slow their rate of national social development (Estes 2004). In any case, as members of the European Union, all of the Baltic States have committed themselves to work toward the social advancement of *all the people* living within their borders.

The Russian Federation

With a WISP score of 52.7 in 2010, social development in the Russian Federation ($N = 1$) is among the lowest reported for the EITs. The Federation's recent performances on the *Welfare Effort* (2010 SI Average = 16.8), *Population* (2010 SI Average = 14.0), *Health* (2010 SI Average = 14.1), and *Women's Status* (2010 SI Average = 10.9) subindexes are solid, however, especially given the enormity of the structural reforms that are required to realize these accomplishments (Table 20.8). Russia's favorable subindex scores in these and other WISP sectors also suggest confirms the emergence of at least the basic elements of a market economy, albeit the role of the state in central economic affairs remains omnipresent (Aslund et al. 2010; Desai and Goldberg 2008).

Levels of *Social Chaos* in the Russian Federation (2010 SI Average = 4.3) remain high (Editors 2008) with the result that only meager social performances are reflected on the Federation's *Cultural Diversity* (2010 SI Average = 8.6), *Environmental* (2010 SI Average = 8.8), and *Defense Effort* (2010 SI Average = 9.3) subindexes. The Federation's subindex scores for the *Education* (2010 SI Average = 9.0) and *Economic* (2010 SI Average = 9.4) sectors are nearly identical and vary only slightly from those reported for other, less developed, countries within the EITs. For example, both sets of scores are substantially below those achieved by the Baltic States and the EITs of Central and Eastern Europe.

Thus, the Russian Federation should be regarded as a country in a "take off" position for achieving higher levels of social development; however, long-standing, primarily internal, struggles suggest that the country's transition to a full market economy and transparent political system over the near-term may be slower than anticipated. In any case, current WISP data make clear that more substantial investments are needed for improving the quality of the country's social infrastructure (Editors 2010c).

The Commonwealth of Independent States (CIS)

All 11 of the Commonwealth of Independent States (CIS), including the Russian Federation which is treated separately above, are included in the present analysis. All 11 states experienced considerable suffering under the tyranny of the Soviet state (Karatnycky 1998). As a result, the majority of CIS nations bear the legacy of comparatively weak social and political institutions (Table 20.7), a tendency toward closed (or at least highly controlled) markets, and a comparatively weak network of non-governmental organizations. Most also struggle with the concept of multi-party democratic governance. Since the collapse of the former Soviet Union in 1991, these nations emerged as fully autonomous nation-states in their own right—albeit all have joined together to form a network of economic alliances between themselves (CIS 2010). The resulting "marriage" from this union has not always been easy, but it follows a familiar path for many of the nations and, therefore, promotes more cooperative patterns of sociopolitical development.

WISP scores for the CIS averaged 51.8 in 2010—a score that continued to place them 4th in overall level of social performance vis-à-vis that of other EITs. WISP scores vary widely for each of the 11 countries (Fig. 20.6) as do their subindex values. Average scores were most favorable for CIS nations on the *Health* (2010 SI Average = 11.9), *Population* (2010 SI Average = 11.8), *Diversity-Related Social Conflict* (2010 SI Average = 11.1), *Welfare Effort* (2010 SI Average = 10.8), *Education* (2010 SI Average = 10.5), *Economic* (2010 SI Average = 10.4), and *Women's Status* (2010 SI Average = 10.4) subindexes—each of which is critical to economic growth and political development. Subindex scores were poorest for CIS on the *Social Chaos* (2010 SI Average = 8.2), *Environmental Effort* (2010 SI Average = 9.7), and *Defense Effort* (2010 SI Average = 9.9) subindexes— sectors that reflect major challenges in dealing with diversity-related issues both within outside the EIT (Amnesty International 2010; Editors 2008; Human Rights Watch 2010; SIPRI 2010).

Turkey

Turkey was the only EIT which experienced net social gains between 2000 and 2010 (+1.5%). Scores for seven of Turkey's WISP subindexes closely approximate or exceed those for the world on average: *Cultural Diversity* (2010 SI Average = 12.4), *Health* (2010 SI Average = 12.0), *Population* (2010 SI Average = 10.0), *Defense Effort* (2010 WISP Average = 9.9), *Economic* (2010 SI Average = 9.3), *Education* (2010 SI Average = 9.3), and *Formal Welfare Effort* (2010 WISP Average = 9.3). Turkey's scores on the other three subindexes were substantially below those recorded for the other EITs and well below those reported for the world as a whole (Estes 2010).

As reported in Fig. 20.6 and Table 20.4 which rank orders the EITs by WISP scores for 2010, Turkey remains one of the least developed of the EITs (Figs. 20.3 and 20.6, Table 20.4). High levels of *Defense* expenditures, *Social Chaos*, and *Environmental* challenges, coupled with the comparatively low status of the country's *Women*, serve as serious impediments to the country's more rapid development. Turkey's comparatively large population size (76.8 million and increasing at the annual rate of 1.3%), high rates of population out-migration (0.6 migrants per 1,000 population), and cultural diversity (70–75% Turkish; 18% Kurdish; 7–12% other minorities) slows the country's pace of development as does its centuries-long political conflicts with neighboring states (SIPRI 2010).

Turkey does aspire, however, to become more socially advanced. The country's relative proximity to important trading centers is an important factor that will facilitate Turkey's further development as will her extensive transportation network and access to multiple warm water seas, including to the Mediterranean. Turkey also is favored by high levels of human capital, an abundance of natural resources and, in its Western regions, European culture (WRI 2010).

Selected Asian EITs

Asian EITs are among the most diverse of the nations included in this analysis (Asian Development Bank 2009). The five Asian EITs include (1) two countries officially designated by the United Nations as "least developing" (LDCs)—Cambodia and Laos; (2) one of world's four population "super giants," i.e., China; (3) geographically large, but sparsely populated, Mongolia; and (4) two nations that have enjoyed only intermittent peace over the past century, i.e., Laos and Vietnam. The combined population of the Asian EITs totals 1,438 million persons, or approximately 75% of the total population of the EITs or 21% of the world's total population (Table 20.5). Fortunately, the pace of social progress in these countries has been rapid having increased their subgroup 2010 WISP scores by 48.5% in just 20 years, i.e., from a group average WISP score of 30.6 in 1990 to 46.2 in 2010 (Figs. 20.3 and 20.4, Table 20.4). The Asian EITs are the only subgroup for which net gains on the WISP were reported for the 2000–2010 time period (Figs. 20.3 and 20.4).

The most important achievements of the Asian EITs on the WISP's ten subindexes, though still low, occurred in the *Economic* (2010 SI Average = 11.6), *Education* (2010 SI Average = 10.9), *Cultural Diversity* (2010 SI Average = 10.3), *Defense Effort* (2010 SI Average = 10.3), *Women Status* (2010 SI Average = 10.2), and *Environmental* (2010 SI Average = 9.9) sectors. Social progress within the Asian EITs remains well below average on the *Population* (2010 SI Average = 9.6), *Health* (2010 SI Average = 8.8), *Social Chaos* (2010 SI Average = 7.9), and *Welfare Effort* (2010 SI Average = 5.9) subindexes.

The development situation of the Asian EITs is troublesome given the size of their total population in combination with the widespread poverty that exists within the subgroup, including in China's Central and Western provinces (Zhao and Seng 2010; UNDP 2010). Years of warfare have depleted the resources of Vietnam, Cambodia, and Laos; these wars are now over, but central government investments in critical social sectors at a level comparable to that of other EITs both within and outside Asia have yet to occur (Table 20.8). The Asian EITs also depend heavily on foreign aid to finance their development. Such dependency, however, as has been found to be the case for Africa (Glennie 2008; Moyo 2009), may well weaken, rather than strengthen, local development capacity (Heckelman 2010).

Clearly, the international focus for the next development decade must focus on helping the Asian EITs, including China (the world's second largest economy after the United States), to stabilize their economies and, as possible, to join the world community as fully equal trading partners. The attainment of such a goal will not be achieved easily given the high levels of mutual distrust, internal tensions, political corruption, and the low starting point from which some of these nations begin (Human Rights Watch 2010).

Discussion

This chapter sought to identify the major development accomplishments and challenges confronting Economies in Transition located in various world regions. In all, data were reported for 31 politically autonomous countries which, in most cases, are succeeding in transforming their approaches to political and economic development toward more open and participatory systems. The data reported in this chapter confirm that many EITs are well along in the transition process, especially the group of ten EIT Social Leaders (SLs). Other EITs, though, still are in a "take off" position vis-à-vis achieving higher levels of social and economic development. The developmental outcomes that might eventually result for these countries are not altogether clear, especially for the Middle Performing Countries (MPCs) located at the lower end of the WISP continuum (Fig. 20.6).

MPCs' social losses are compounded by (1) long-standing patterns of diversity-related social conflict, (2) lack of adequate investments in basic health and education infrastructure, and (3) the comparatively uneasy, sometimes contentious, relationships that exist between lower performing MPCs and their more socially advanced neighbors. The uncertain future of civil society organizations within many of the MPCs adds to the group's development dilemmas, as do the financial crises that currently confront the world's more socially developed countries vis-à-vis their interactions with the MPCs.

Still other EITs are just beginning the process of transforming themselves toward more open and participatory economic and political systems, especially the successor states of the former Soviet Union.

Some of these countries are continuing to invest in highly inefficient state enterprises with the goal of holding on to past patterns of economic development rather than reaching for the future. Inadequate and, in some cases, declining investments in health, education, and social welfare also are interfering with the transition process for some MPCs. Underinvestments in women and children are particularly noteworthy among this group of MPCs. At the same time, many of the MPCs, including the CIS, are holding on to past patterns of high defense spending which, in most cases, contributes to a heightened sense of insecurity among their populations (Table 20.8).

Nonetheless, as a group, ten EITs have been identified as "social leaders" (SLs) in this study. These countries have achieved remarkable progress toward their national development objectives. Most of the progress reported for the SLs took place between 2000 and 2010, but for some, progress accumulated over the entire 20-year period of the study (e.g., the countries of CEE and the Baltic States). A number of factors contributed to social progress of group's social leaders: (1) a comparatively rapid shift toward more open free market approaches to economic development, (2) the adoption of democratic, multi-party, forms of political governance, (3) the creation of "political space" that permitted the emergence of a viable civil society sector, and (4) sustained high investments in social spending. These milestones were not accomplished easily; rather, they required carefully orchestrated actions combined with moderate to high levels of social investments in the health, education, and related social sectors. The majority of the group's SLs also entered into working partnerships with more socially advanced countries both within and outside their subregion, e.g., those EITs that became part of the European Union or Organization for Economic Cooperation and Development, or both. Significant social progress among these SLs also required the reallocation of national resources from defense and military spending to broad-based social development objectives.

But social progress did not occur for all of the EITs. Between 2000 and 2010, 21 EITs, including four SLs, experienced net losses in WISP rank positions relative to all 161 countries included in the more comprehensive study of worldwide social development trends (Table 20.4). Some of these losses were very substantial (Table 20.4) and resulted in reversals of earlier gains in social development.

In general, the following factors contributed to social losses experienced by the EIT's: (1) continuing high levels of diversity-related social conflict, (2) the retention of autocratic political systems, (3) the failure to establish open market economic systems, (4) slow to negative patterns of economic growth, (6) the absence of a viable civil society, (7) limited trading partnerships with more economically advanced neighbors, and (8) continuing high levels of public control over total GDP expenditures. The majority of these countries also failed to achieve important goals in the education, health, social welfare, and related sectors.

In revisiting the social progress attained by the world's EITs, then, one finds highly heterogeneous and asynchronous patterns of social development, i.e., significant social progress occurred for a minority of EITs between 2000 and 2010, whereas the majority of EITs continued to struggle with the challenges associated with the reforms needed to fully implement the economic and political transition process. In the main, the majority of countries in this latter group have had no prior history of private ownership of the means of production (CIS) nor have they experienced the benefits of a fully functioning democratic political system, e.g., China and the Russian Federation.

Thus, three dramatically different clusters of nations exist within the group of 31 EITs: (1) those countries for which the transition process has proven to be exceptionally successful (mostly, 10 countries located in Central and Eastern Europe and the Baltic States), (2) those 11 countries that continue to struggle against what is experienced to be the overly harsh, often unfamiliar, demands of major social reform (mostly, the comparatively resource poor members of the CIS), and (3) those 10 countries that are in a "take off" position vis-à-vis adopting more open approaches to economic development and political reform (mostly, selected nations of Southeast Asia). Given the generally positive 20-year development trends reported in this study for the 31 EITs as a group, this author remains optimistic concerning the future of the EITs, especially given that they possess nearly all of the human and material resources needed to transform their societies into modern nation states.

Acknowledgments Zhou Huiquan (Mary) of the Chinese University of Hong Kong is acknowledged for her research assistance in updating the statistics contained in this chapter.

References

Amnesty International (AI). (2010). *Country reports.* Retrieved January 21, 2011, from http://www.amnesty.org/

Anheier, H., Toepler, S., & List, R. (Eds.). (2010). *International encyclopedia of civil society.* New York: Springer.

Ash, T. G. (2004). *Free world: America, Europe and the surprising future of the West.* New York: Random House.

Asian Development Bank. (2009). *Asian development outlook 2009: Rebalancing Asia's growth.* Manila: Asian Development Bank. Retrieved January 27, 2011, from http://www.adb.org/documents/books/ado/2009/default.asp

Åslund, A. (2010). *The last shall be the first: the East European financial crisis, 2008–10.* Washington, DC: Peterson Institute for International Economics.

Åslund, A., Guriev, S., & Kuchins, A. C. (Eds.). (2010). *Russia after the global economic crisis.* Washington, DC: Peterson Institute for International Economics.

Barrios, S. (Ed.). (2010). *External imbalances and public finances in the EU/European Commission, Directorate-General for Economic and Financial Affairs.* Luxembourg: Publications Office of the European Union.

Commonwealth of Independent States (CIS) (2010). About the Commonwealth of Independent States. Retrieved January 31, 2010, from http://www.cisstat.com/eng/cis.htm

Desai, R. M., & Goldberg, I. (Eds.). (2008). *Can Russia compete?* Washington: Brookings Institution Press.

Economic Commission for Latin America and the Caribbean (ECLAC). (2010a). *Statistical yearbook.* Retrieved January 25, 2011, from http://www.eclac.cl/publicaciones/xml/7/42167/LCG2483b_contenido.pdf

Economic Commission for Latin America and the Caribbean (ECLAC). (2010b). *Latin America and the Caribbean in the world economy 2009–2010: A crisis generated in the centre and a recovery driven by the emerging economies.* Retrieved January 25, 2011, from http://www.eclac.cl/cgi-bin/getProd.asp?xml=/publicaciones/xml/6/40696/P40696.xml&xsl=/comercio/tpl-i/p9f.xsl&base=/tpl-i/topbottom.xsl

Editors. (2008). *The wild south: Russia's treatment of its republics in the Caucasus has turned them into tinderboxes.* Retrieved January 27, 2011, from http://www.economist.com/node/12627992

Editors. (2010a). Commodities alone are not enough to sustain flourishing economies. *Special Report of The Economist,* September 6. Retrieved January 26, 2011, from http://www.economist.com/node/16964094?story_id=16964094

Editors, (2010b). Afloat on a Chinese tide: China's economic rise has brought the rest of emerging Asia huge benefits. But the region still needs the West. *The Economist,* September 2. Retrieved January 25, 2011, from http://www.economist.com/node/16943589?story_id=16943589

Editors. (2010c). Modernizing Russia: Another great leap forward? Modernization is hard to argue with. But it may not be what Russia needs. *The Economist.* March 11, 2010. Retrieved January 25, 2011, from http://www.economist.com/node/15661865

Editors. (2011). *Europe needs growth to prevent a collapse of the Euro. Der Spiegel.* January 11, 2011. Retrieved January 25, 2011, from http://www.spiegel.de/international/business/0,1518,738711,00.html

Encyclopedia Britannica. (2010). Britannica on-line. Retrieved March 1, 2010, from http://www.britannica.com/

Estes, R. J. (1988). *Trends in world social development.* New York: Praeger.

Estes, R. J. (1998). Social development trends in the successor states to the former Soviet Union: The search for a new paradigm. In K. R. Hope Jr. (Ed.), *Challenges of transformation and transition from centrally planned to market economies* (pp. 13–33). Nagoya: United Nations Centre for Regional Development.

Estes, R. J. (2004). Development challenges of the New Europe. *Social Indicators Research, 69,* 123–166.

Estes, R. J. (2007). Development challenges and opportunities confronting economies in transition. *Social Indicators Research, 83,* 375–411.

Estes, R. J. (2010). The world social situation: Development challenges at the outset of a new century. *Social Indicators Research, 98*(3):363–402.

Estes, R. J. (2012). Development trends among the world's socially least developed countries: Reasons for cautious optimism. In B. Spooner (Ed.), *Globalization in progress: Understanding and working with world urbanization.* Philadelphia: University of Pennsylvania Press.

Fidler, S. (2010). The euro's next battleground: Spain. *Wall Street Journal.* February 25. Retrieved January 25, 2011, from http://finance.yahoo.com/banking-budgeting/article/108914/the-euros-next-battleground-spain

Freedom House. (2010). *Freedom throughout the world.* New York: Freedom House.

Friedman, T. L. (2005). *The world is flat: A brief history of the 21st century.* New York: Farrar, Straus, and Giroux.

Ghani, A., & Lockhart, C. (2008). *Fixing failed states: A framework for rebuilding a fractured world.* New York/Oxford: Oxford University Press.

Glennie, J. (2008). *The trouble with aid: Why less could mean more for Africa.* London: Zed Books.

Graham, N. A., & Lindahl, F. (Eds.). (2010). *Political economy of transition in Eurasia.* East Lansing: Michigan State University Press.

Guo, B. (2010). *China's quest for political legitimacy: The new equity-enhancing politics.* Lanham: Lexington Books.

Guo, S., & Guo, B. (Eds.). (2010). *Greater China in an era of globalization.* Lanham: Rowman and Littlefield.

Gup, B. (Ed.). (2010). *The financial and economic crises: an international perspective.* Cheltenham: Edward Elgar.

Heckelman, J. C. (2010). Aid and democratization in the transition economies. *Kyklos, 63,* 558–579.

Human Rights Watch. (2010). *Our work.* Retrieved January 25, 2011, from http://www.hrw.org/en/publications

International Labour Organization. (2010). *Labor migration.* Retrieved January 25, 2011, from http://www.ilo.org/pls/apex/f?p=109:3:3877099091962948::NO::P3_SUBJECT:MIGRATION

International Monetary Fund. (2010). *Transition economies: An IMF perspective on progress and prospects.* Retrieved January 25, 2011, from http://www.imf.org/external/np/exr/ib/2010/110300.htm

International Organization for Migration (IOM). (2010). *World migration report, 2010: The future of migration –*

Building capacities for change. Retrieved January 25, 2011, from http://publications.iom.int/bookstore/index.php?main_page=product_info&cPath=37&products_id=653&language=en

International Social Security Association (ISSA). (2010). *ILO/ World social security report, 2010/11.* Retrieved January 25, 2011, from http://www.issa.int/Resources/overview

Jacobsson, B. (Ed.). (2010). *The European Union and the Baltic States: Changing forms of governance.* London/New York: Routledge.

Jeffries, I. (2003). *The Caucasus and Central Asia republics at the turn of the 21st century: A guide to the economies in transition.* London: Routledge.

Jones, S. (2010). European stocks advance as China helps Europe limit debt crisis. *Bloomberg Businessweek,* December 21. Retrieved January 25, 2011, from http://www.businessweek.com/news/2010–12–21/european-stocks-advance-as-china-helps-europe-limit-debt-crisis.html

Karatnycky, A. (1998). *Nations in transit: From change to permanence.* Retrieved January 29, 2011, from http//www.freedomhouse.org/nit98/karat.html

Koyuncu, C., Ozturkler, H., & Yilmaz, R. (2010). Privatization and corruption in transition economies: a panel study. *Journal of Economic Policy Reform, 13,* 277–284.

Kunzmann, K. R., Schmid, W. A., & Koll-Schretzenmayr, M. (Eds.). (2010). *China and Europe: The implications of the rise of China for European space.* London/New York: Routledge.

Magnus, G. (2011). *Uprising: Will emerging markets shape or shake the world economy?* Chichester: Wiley.

Mallaby, S. (2004). *The world's banker: A story of failed states, financial crises, and the wealth and poverty of nations.* London: Penguin.

Moran, M., Rein, M., & Goodin, R. (Eds.). (2006). *The Oxford handbook of public policy.* New York and Oxford: Oxford University Press.

Moyo, D. (2009). *Dead aid: Why aid is not working and how there is a better way for Africa.* New York: Farrar, Straus, & Giroux.

Open Society Institute (OSI). (2005). *Building open societies, 2005.* Retrieved March 15, 2010 from http://www.soros.org/resources/articles_publications/publications/annual_20060724/a_complete.pdf

Organization for Economic Cooperation and Development (OECD). (2010). *Environment in transition economies.* Retrieved January 25, 2011, from http://www.oecd.org/department/0,3355,en_2649_34291_1_1_1_1_1,00.html

Peerenboom, R. (2007). *China modernizes: Threats to the West or model to the rest?* New York/Oxford: Oxford University Press.

Rifkin, J. (2004). *The European dream: How Europe's vision of the future is quietly eclipsing the American dream.* New York: Penguin.

Rumer, B. (Ed.). (2005). *Central Asia at the end of the transition.* Armonk: M.E. Sharpe.

Schiere, R. (2010). *China's development challenges: Economic vulnerability and public sector reform.* London/New York: Routledge.

Singh, R. S. K. (2003). *Role of NGOs in developing countries: Potential, constraints and policies.* New Delhi: Vedams Books.

Stiglitz, J. E. (2002). *Globalization and its discontents.* New York: W.W. Norton.

Stiglitz, J. E. (2010). *Freefall: America, free markets, and the sinking of the world economy.* New York: W.W. Norton.

Stockholm International Peace Research Institute (SIPRI). (2010). *Statistical yearbook.* Retrieved January 25, 2011, from http://www.sipri.org/

Sutter, R. G. (2010). *Chinese foreign relations: Power and policy since the Cold War* (2nd ed.). Lanham: Rowman & Littlefield.

Svetlicic, M., & Rojec, M. (Eds.). (2003). *Facilitating transition by internationalization: Outward direct investment from Central European economies in transition.* Aldershot: Ashgate.

Transparency International. (2010). *Corruption and the global corruption barometer.* Retrieved January 25, 2011, from http://transparency.org/

U.S. Department of State. (2010). *Trafficking in persons report 2010.* Retrieved January 25, 2011, from http://www.state.gov/g/tip/rls/tiprpt/2010/index.htm

United Nations. (2010a). *The Millennium development goals report, 2010.* Retrieved January 25, 2011, from http://www.un.org/millenniumgoals/pdf/MDG%20Report%202010%20En%20r15%20-low%20res%2020100615%20-.pdf

United Nations. (2010b). *Summit on the millennium development goals: Reports.* Retrieved January 27, 2011, from http://www.un.org/millenniumgoals/reports.shtml

United Nations. (2010c). *Millennium development goals: 2010 progress chart.* Retrieved January 25, 2011, from http://unstats.un.org/unsd/mdg/Resources/Static/Products/Progress2010/MDG_Report_2010_Progress_Chart_En.pdf

United Nations Department of Economic and Social Affairs (UNDESA). (1995). *World summit for social development.* Retrieved January 25, 2011, from http://www.un.org/esa/socdev/wssd/index.html

United Nations Department of Economic and Social Affairs (UNDESA). (2002). *World Summit on Sustainable Development.* Retrieved October 10, 2009 from http://www.un.org/jsummit/

United Nations Development Programme (UNDP). (1997). *Human development to eradicate poverty.* New York: Oxford University Press.

United Nations Development Programme (UNDP). (1999). *The human cost of transition: Human security in South East Europe.* Retrieved January 25, 2011, from http://hdr.undp.org/en/reports/regional/europethecis/name,2799,en.html

United Nations Development Programme (UNDP). (2010a). *Human development report: The real wealth of nations – Pathways to human development.* Retrieved January 25, 2011, from http://hdr.undp.org/en/reports/global/hdr2010/

United Nations Development Programme (UNDP). (2010b). *Regional human development reports for Europe and the Commonwealth of Independent States.* Retrieved January 25, 2010, from http://hdr.undp.org/xmlsearch/reportSearch?y=*&c=r%3AEurope+and+the+CIS&t=*&lang=en&k=&orderby=year

United Nations Population Division (UNPOP). (2010). *Population facts #2010/6,* November 2010. Retrieved January 25, 2011, from http://www.un.org/esa/population/unpop.htm

United States Department of Health and Human Services (USDHHS). (2010). *Social security programs throughout the world.* Retrieved February 1, 2010, from http://www.ssa.gov/policy/docs/progdesc/ssptw/

United States Social Security Administration (USSSA). (2010). *Social security programs throughout the world.* Retrieved January 25, 2011, from http://www.ssa.gov/policy/docs/progdesc/ssptw/

Watts, M., & Walstad, W. B. (Eds.). (2002). *Reforming economics and economic teaching in the transition economies – from Marx to markets in the classroom.* Cheltenham: Edward Elgar.

Weingast, B. R., & Wittman, D. A. (Eds.). (2006). *The Oxford handbook of political economy.* New York/Oxford: Oxford University Press.

Wejnert, B. (Ed.). (2002). *Transition to democracy in Eastern Europe and Russia: Impact on politics, economy and culture.* Westport: Praeger.

Wolchick, S. L., & Curry, J. L. (Eds.). (2011). *Central and East European politics: From communism to democracy* (2nd ed.). Lanham: Rowman & Littlefield.

World Bank. (2004). *Economies in transition: An OED evaluation of World Bank assistance.* Washington: World Bank.

World Bank. (2006). *World development report, 2006: Equity and development.* New York: Oxford University Press.

World Bank. (2010). *World development report, 2010: Development and climate change.* Retrieved January 25, 2011,fromhttp://econ.worldbank.org/WBSITE/EXTERNAL/EXTDEC/EXTRESEARCH/EXTWDRS/EXTWDR2010/0,,contentMDK:21969137~menuPK:5287816~pagePK:64167689~piPK:64167673~theSitePK:5287741,00.html

World Health Organization (WHO). (2010). *The World health report, 2010.* Geneva: World Health Organization.

World Resources Institute (WRI). (2010). *Earth trends/World resources rata CD, 2010.* Washington: World Resources Institute.

Young, A., Teodorovic, I., & Koveos, P. (Eds.). (2002). *Economies in transition: Conception, status and prospects.* River Edge: World Scientific.

Zeng, D. S. (Ed.). (2010). *Building engines for growth and competitiveness in China: Experience with special economic zones and industrial clusters.* Washington: World Bank.

Zhao, L., & Lim, T. S. (Eds.). (2010). *China's new social policy: Initiatives for a harmonious society.* Singapore: World Scientific Press.

Zhao, L., & Seng, L.Y. (Eds.) (2010). *China's new social policy: Initiatives for a harmonious society.* Singapore and Hackensack, NJ: World Scientific.

Quality of Life in Australia

21

Robert A. Cummins, Jacqueline Woerner, Adrian Tomyn, and Adele Gibson-Prosser

Australian Life Quality: An Overview

By almost any measure, the Australian population has high life quality. Australia is a relatively wealthy country, due largely to an abundance of natural resources. It has a Liberal Market Economy (Hall and Soskice 2001); it is classified as high income within the OECD (Organization for Economic Cooperation and Development) countries (World Bank 2007) and has a GDP per capita of about US$39,700 which places it 9th in comparison with other countries (International Monetary Fund 2011). However, its Gini Index is 35.2 (medium) which places it 46th in terms of equality of income distribution, with Sweden on 25.0 and the USA on 40.8.

As one consequence of its wealth, Australian citizens enjoy good medical care and high levels of education. Unemployment has been at about 4–8% over the past decade (Australian Bureau of Statistics 2011c) and only increased to about 6% following the 2009 financial crisis. There is a minimum wage and a social security safety net which provides, at minimum, an income about one third of the average wage. Australia has the second-highest Human Development Index within the list of 124 countries provided by the Human Development Report (2010).

Australia is a young country with an ageing population. It was first colonised by Britain in 1788. Now,

some 22 million people call Australia home, almost all of whom are migrants or the progeny thereof. As a consequence, it is a highly multi-cultural society. About 13% of the population are immigrants who arrived after 1984 (Australian Bureau of Statistics 2007a) and, of these people, 70% are from non-English speaking countries. However, English is the only official language and, according to the 2001 census, the only language spoken at home for around 80% of the population. This imposes an acculturating influence on new arrivals from non-English countries and a unifying influence on the population. The most common other languages spoken at home are Chinese (2.1%), Italian (1.9%) and Greek (1.4%).

Despite substantial immigration, the population grew by only 1.7% during 2009–2010 (Australian Bureau of Statistics 2011a), indicative of an ageing population. While the proportion of people over the age of 65 was 12% in 1997, it is projected to be 18% in 2021 and 26% in 2051 (Australian Institute of Health and Welfare 2002, 2004). The provision of adequate health care to this ageing population is anticipated to strain the resources of Australia's publicly funded, universal health care system, operated by the government authority Medicare Australia (Medicare Australia 2007).

On the negative side, there is a moderate level of crime. In 2009–2010, 6.3% of adults reported being victims of physical or threatened violence during the past year (Australian Bureau of Statistics 2011b), while 0.4% were victims of at least one robbery. In 2007, men were more likely (14%) than women (8%) to be the victim of violence, with younger men (18–24 years) the most likely (31%) to have been a victim (Australian Bureau of Statistics 2007a).

R.A. Cummins (✉) • J. Woerner • A. Tomyn • A. Gibson-Prosser
School of Psychology, Deakin University, Burwood, VIC, Australia
e-mail: Robert.Cummins@deakin.edu.au

K.C. Land et al. (eds.), *Handbook of Social Indicators and Quality of Life Research*,
DOI 10.1007/978-94-007-2421-1_21, © Springer Science+Business Media B.V. 2012

Feelings of safety are generally consistent with these statistics. While most people (86%) feel safe at home, alone and after dark (Australian Bureau of Statistics 2007a), only 48% report feeling safe walking alone in their neighbourhood at night. There are many factors that decrease feelings of safety. The major ones are living in a major city, living in government-subsidised rented accommodation, unemployment, not being proficient in English and being in poor health. Many of these factors are likely to be tied to low income as their root cause.

The indigenous Aboriginal Australians are the most disadvantaged ethnic group. They comprise about 2.5% of the Australian population (Department of Foreign Affairs and Trade 2005) and about 30% of the Northern Territory population. They remain disadvantaged, compared to other Australians, across the full spectrum of social, economic and health areas (Trewin and Madden 2005) despite the provision of substantial 'indigenous-specific' funding (Gardiner-Garden and Park 2007).

In spite of the obvious inequality of opportunity experienced by the Aboriginal population and the medium-range Gini Index, Australians like to think of themselves as egalitarian. A delightful and insightful take on this cultural myth is provided by Poleg (2004) who writes, 'The 19th century English author Marcus Clark exclaimed that the new Australians are "not nations of snobs like the English or of extravagant boasters like the Americans or of reckless profligates like the French; they are simply a nation of drunkards"'. Indeed, they used to be, and the love affair with alcohol has been another defining national characteristic, which now is also taking on mythical status. World Drink Trends (2005) rates Australian total alcohol consumption as the 36th highest among nations. So, there are always two sides to any nation—what the commodities statistics say the nation is and what the people feel themselves to be. The remainder of this chapter will concentrate on the subjective side of life quality.

At a population level, Australian subjective wellbeing (SWB) is always in the top cluster of countries within international comparative surveys (Bergheim 2007; Cummins 1995, 1998). Consistent with this, Australia also has relatively high levels of other commonly measured subjective variables, such as trust between citizens (Bergheim 2007) and low levels of perceived corruption. For example, the General Social Survey (Australian Bureau of Statistics 2007c) found that about half of respondents (54%) felt that 'most people' could be trusted, and they were even more likely to trust their doctor (89%) and local police (76%). The high level of trust in police is a major factor underpinning social stability. While there are many different variables that can be used to describe subjective life quality, the most important and global measure is SWB.

The first systematic measures of SWB in Australia were made by Headey et al. (1984), Headey and Wearing (1989). Members of their Victorian Quality of Life Panel were interviewed four times between 1981 and 1987. They observed that people appeared to have a 'set point' for their SWB, and their findings are discussed further in Cummins (Chap. 4). Then, in 2001, two new surveys were commenced, both of which are extant. One is the Household, Income and Labour Dynamics in Australia (HILDA) Survey (2009), and the other is the Australian Unity Wellbeing Index (2009).

The Australian Unity Wellbeing Index

In 2001, a partnership was established between Deakin University and Australian Unity, a health, finance services and retirement living company. The mutual aim of this partnership was to use the Personal Wellbeing Index (PWI) to monitor the wellbeing of the population. The monitoring instrument, which includes several measures in addition to the PWI, is called the Australian Unity Wellbeing Index. This Index was established as an alternative indicator of population wellbeing to such familiar objective indicators as the economic, health and crime statistics mentioned above. The Australian Unity Wellbeing Index measures quality of life as experienced by the average Australian.

The Index comprises two scales. The Personal Wellbeing Index (International Wellbeing Group 2006) measures subjective wellbeing (SWB) through the average level of satisfaction across seven life domains as: health, personal relationships, safety, standard of living, achieving in life, community connectedness and future security. The National Wellbeing Index is the average satisfaction score across six domains of national life—the economy, the environment, social conditions, governance, business and national security.

The first Index survey, of 2,000 adults from all parts of Australia, was conducted in April 2001. A total of 24 such surveys had been conducted at the time of writing, with the most recent in September 2010.

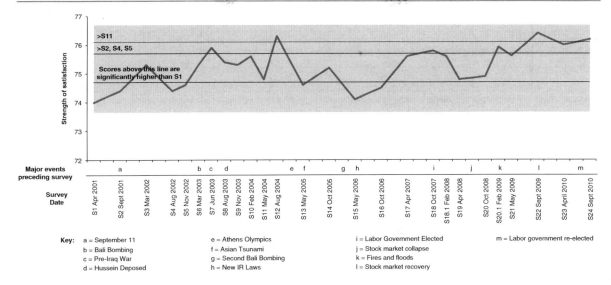

Fig. 21.1 Personal Wellbeing Index

A detailed report is constructed from the results of each survey, and these can be downloaded from the Australian Centre on Quality of Life website at Deakin University (http://www.deakin.edu.au/research/acqol/index.php). A description of changes in the Personal and National Wellbeing Index up to 2007 has been previously published (Cummins et al. 2008), and some data from the PWI are presented in Chap. 20 of this volume to illustrate the functional characteristics of homeostasis. Other results from the Index will be also reported here. First, however, the construction of the PWI will be explained.

Understanding the Personal Wellbeing Index

The PWI has a most unusual construction. It contains a set of domains selected to represent the first-level deconstruction of satisfaction derived from the single item, 'How satisfied are you with your life as a whole?' This question, devised by Andrews and Withey (1976), is the most commonly used measure of SWB and has the desirable characteristic of being both highly personal and highly abstract. As we have argued elsewhere (Cummins et al. 2003b), these two characteristics are essences of the SWB construct. Thus, the criterion for inclusion for each PWI domain is that they individually contribute unique variance, in a multiple regression, where all seven domains are used to predict 'satisfaction with life as a whole' (see the manual for details of this procedure).

Each domain is rated by respondents on a 0–10 end-defined scale (Jones and Thurstone 1955) anchored by 'completely dissatisfied' (0) and 'completely satisfied' (10). The scores are then combined across the seven domains to yield an overall Index score, which is adjusted to have a range of 0–100. The formula for this conversion is provided in the manual.

Each of our 24 surveys is based on a new sample of 2,000 randomly selected adults across Australia. The most remarkable quality of the mean scores, derived from these surveys, is their stability. As will be shown later in Fig. 21.1, all values lie between 73.4 and 76.3 points, giving a total range of 2.9 percentage points. The reason for this stability, as has been argued in Chap. 20 of this Handbook, is the process of subjective wellbeing homeostasis. As in the earlier chapter, this theory will be used to inform the discussion of our results.

The Survey Methodology

Each survey involves a fresh, geographically representative national sample of people aged 18 years or over who are fluent in English. People are surveyed by telephone in a 7–10-min interview, and data collection extends over some 2–3 weeks. In order to ensure an even gender and age distribution, interviewers ask to speak to the person in the house who had the most recent birthday and is at least 18 years old. On average, some 4,500–5,000 calls connect with an eligible respondent, and 2,000 agreed to complete the survey. This gives an effective response rate (completes/(refusals and completes)) of about 42%. This rather low rate reflects, in part, our methodological constraint that an even geographic and gender split is maintained at all times throughout the survey. Thus, some willing respondents are eliminated due to their gender being different from the one required at that time. The reason for this procedure is to ensure that if a major event occurs during the data collection period, its impact can be analysed using representative before and after data.

Initial data screening is completed before data analysis. This involves checking for numbers outside the possible range and also identifying respondents who have consistently scored at the top (10) or the bottom (0) of all PWI domains. These respondents are eliminated prior to further analysis. They either represent a response set or an acquiescent response style typical of people who do not understand the questions (Rosen et al. 1974; Sigelman et al. 1981; Sudman and Bradburn 1974). The proportion of respondents eliminated in this way is about 1%. While their inclusion would have little impact in analyses of the whole sample, in breakdown samples, where the numbers of respondents per cell become much smaller, the impact of such aberrant responses can be considerable.

Unlike gender, the age composition of the sample is not actively managed. However, we normally achieve a breakdown similar to that of the national population as determined by the Australian Bureau of Statistics (Cummins et al. 2003a, Report 5.0).

Presentation of Results and Type of Analysis

In the presentation of results to follow, the statistically significant data trends have been established by analysis of variance. In situations where homogeneity of variance assumptions has been violated, Dunnett's T3 Post-Hoc Test has been used. In the case of t-tests, we have used the SPSS option for significance when equality of variance cannot be assumed. Bonferroni corrections to a criterion of $p < .01$ have been employed where necessary.

More detailed analyses are presented in the cited reports, which also contain the tables of means and standard deviations. The raw data are available from our website: http://www.deakin.edu.au/research/acqol/auwbi/survey-reports/.

All satisfaction values are expressed as the strength of satisfaction on a scale that ranges from 0% to 100% points. The conversion formula is presented in the PWI manual.

An Overview of Changes in the PWI

Changes in the PWI over the 24 surveys to date are shown in Fig. 21.1. The temporal spacing between surveys is shown on the baseline and involves intervals of approximately 3 or 6 months.

The first survey was conducted in April 2001, and the most obvious trend in Fig. 21.1 is the rise in SWB that followed September 11. This rise took the population SWB to a significantly higher level than it had been at the time of the first survey, and this higher level has been generally maintained. In making this determination, a lot of responsibility rests on the first survey being a reliable measure of the pre-September 11 population wellbeing. However, several lines of enquiry have led us to regard this single estimation as being reliable. These are as follows:

1. The results have been carefully checked.
2. Not all of the domains that comprise the PWI have changed over the surveys (Cummins et al. 2008). If this rise was caused by some general sampling phenomenon or method effect, then all of the domains would be expected to rise together.
3. There is no methodological reason to expect the data from Survey 1 to be different from the next two surveys. The data were collected by the same call centre using the same operating procedures and verbal instructions to the respondents.

One plausible reason for this rise, if it is correctly attributed to September 11, is the sense of threat experienced by the Australian population. Even though very few Australians were directly affected by the event, it represented an attack on a strong ally for Australia—the United States of America. The two countries have a long and stable relationship of defence agreements and trade. For example, the USA-Australia alliance under the ANZUS Treaty (Department of External Affairs 1951) binds both countries to recognise that an armed attack in the Pacific area on either one of them endangers the peace and safety of the other. A second alliance, in

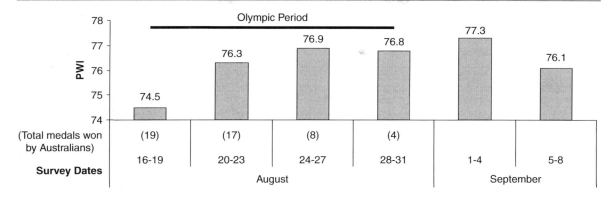

Fig. 21.2 Weekly values for SWB during Survey 12

the form of the Australia-United States Free Trade Agreement (Australian Government – Department of Foreign Affairs and Trade 2005), ensures a preferential trade agreement between the two countries.

While the details of such agreements are of little concern to the majority of the population, the general view of America as a powerful ally is widely held. Thus, the attack on the World Trade Center had far greater impact on the public psyche than an equivalent attack in Russia or China. If it happened in America then, quite conceivably, it could also happen in Australia. Moreover, to reinforce the impact of the event on the public, Australian television played the terrible images of planes hitting the Twin Towers over and over again. The print media and radio were also full of speculations about motives and future scenarios. So, a new idea took shape—that terrorist attacks on such a scale were not just conceivable but real. People had a new source of fear.

When groups are threatened from the outside, they tend to become internally stronger. They engage in behaviour conducive to the creation of bonding social capital (Putnam 2000). This concept was defined originally by Bourdieu (1986) as 'the aggregate of the actual or potential resources which are linked to—membership in a group—which provides each of its members with the backing of the collectively owned capital' (p. 249). This describes the intuitively appealing idea that social networks provide their members with access to the group's shared social and material resources. Thus, social capital is enhanced by circumstances where cooperative relationships are likely to facilitate solutions to collective problems (e.g., Durlauf 2002; Requena 2003). Through this agency, terrorist threats to collective wellbeing may engender bonding social capital, which in turn promotes higher SWB (see Groot et al. 2007).

However, it is not just threat events that apparently cause the wellbeing of Australians to rise. Figure 21.1 shows that one of the highest level of population wellbeing was attained in August 2004 at the time of the Athens Olympics (Survey 12). In some respects, this high level of SWB is an artefact caused by the timing of the data collection. Whereas we normally collect data some time after an event, on this occasion, the period of data collection spanned the Olympic period, and the results are shown below (Fig. 21.2).

Australia achieved spectacular success at the Athens Olympic Games. After the USA, China and Russia, its medal tally ranked fourth. It is evident from Fig. 21.2 that the Personal Wellbeing Index rose during the Olympic period and then started to decrease shortly afterwards. These patterns are statistically weak ($p = .078$ and $p = .017$ respectively), but achieve significance using a one-tail test.

While both threat and enhancement events appear to have caused wellbeing to rise, the reason for each rise should be different. From a sociobiological perspective, a rise in population satisfaction through social bonding would be an adaptive response to threat. The rise in wellbeing due to nationally enhancing events, however, has no such adaptive links and is more simply explained in the personal pride of association with a winning team.

If this interpretation is correct, then there should be a major difference between these two event types, in that the influence of a threat event should be longer lasting. It may be adaptive to maintain a sense of threat for a long period after the event, thereby maintaining alertness to detect a new source of harm and the

Table 21.1 Regression of seven domains against life as a whole (Survey 17)

Variable	LAW	1.	2.	3.	4.	5.	6.	B	β	sr²
1. Standard of living	.568**	.						.285**	.286	.054
2. Health	.371**	.355**	.					.062**	.074	.004
3. Achieving in life	.595**	.459**	.375**	.				.280**	.315	.064
4. Personal relationships	.443**	.309**	.240**	.391**	.			.133**	.175	.025
5. Safety	.298**	.311**	.256**	.245**	.236**	.		.023	.024	.001
6. Community connectedness	.323**	.293**	.195**	.313**	.261**	.325**	.	.037*	.043	.001
7. Future security	.436**	.460**	.272**	.418**	.271**	.425**	.377**	.070**	.079	.004
$R^2 = .511$								Total explained unique variance		.152
Adjusted $R^2 = .509$								Total explained shared variance		.357

*p<.05, **$p < .001$

resources to deal with it. This has been found in relation to the perception of a terrorist threat in Australia (see Cummins et al. 2007b). Enhancement events, on the other hand, may be most adaptive by being transitory. Elevated positive mood inhibits careful information processing (Schwarz 1990) and is therefore undesirable as a chronic condition. If this is so, then the euphoria of Olympic success should be soon submerged within the cauldron of current life realities and other local or international sports carnivals (e.g. football grand finals in September). This is consistent with the trend in Fig. 21.2 showing an apparent return of SWB to lower levels soon after the Athens Olympics were over. In contrast, the influence of the threat events has apparently been much longer lasting.

In summary, it appears that both positive and negative events have acted to raise the wellbeing of the Australian population. So, how can the SWB of the population be further characterised? Clearly, there are many potential avenues. The selection for this chapter has been based on the two domains of life quality that appear to have most relevance as judged by two different techniques. The first is to examine the internal composition of the PWI to see which domains are the strongest contributors to SWB.

An Examination of the PWI

The construction of the PWI, described earlier, is such that the seven individual domains have some degree of autonomy. While each is predominantly driven by core affect (Davern et al. 2007), now called HPMood (Cummins 2010), the domains are individually flavoured

by the cognitive target of each question. Because of this, all of the domains will display a great deal of shared variance, due to the influence of core affect. However, each domain will also contribute unique variance to the parent construct 'life as a whole'. This, after all, is the basic design feature of the scale. An example of a multiple regression to test this proposition is provided in (Table 21.1).

Table 21.1 shows the results of a standard multiple regression where the seven domains are regressed against 'satisfaction with life as a whole'. The sr^2 statistic represents the proportion of unique variance contributed by each domain. It is calculated as the square of the 'part' statistic that can be requested from SPSS in association with a multiple regression. When this value is multiplied by 100, it gives the percentage of unique variance contributed by the item. Thus, satisfaction with standard of living contributes 5.4% of unique variance within the total 50.9% explained variance for this sample.

The strength of contribution by individual domains is concentrated in three domains which are standard of living, achieving and relationships. This shows that these three life areas dominate the contribution of unique variance to subjective wellbeing as measured in this sample. Of the total 15.2% unique variance, these three domains contribute 14.3%. However, the contribution of shared variance through HPMood (35.7%) clearly dominates the composition of SWB (see also Blore et al. 2011; Davern et al. 2007).

The second technique used to determine the most important life domains is to study domain sensitivity within population groups which have the highest and lowest wellbeing.

Identifying the Demographic Groups with the Highest and Lowest SWB

Report 16.1 (Cummins, Walter, and Woerner 2007a) presents an analysis of the cumulative data from 15 surveys. The total number of respondents is about 30,000, and the aim is to identify the demographic sub-groups with the highest and the lowest wellbeing.

The definition of sub-groups was made through the demographic variables of income, gender, age, household composition, relationship status and employment status. While not every combination of demographic variables could be tested due to limitations of cell size, the total number of combinations analysed is 3,277. The SWB of each of these groups was calculated and screened for meeting the criterion for an extreme score.

Extreme group mean scores were initially defined as lying either above 79 points or below 70 points. Both of these values are at least five standard deviations beyond the total sample mean score. That is, using all 15 survey mean scores as data, their grand mean is 74.9 and standard deviation 0.8 points. The extreme groups are, therefore, extreme outliers.

The reports from individual surveys were scored for such groups, with a minimum permitted group size of one respondent. Following this, the data for equivalent groups were combined across surveys.

From this analysis, the 20 highest and 20 lowest groups were identified, with the additional criterion that they contained a minimum of 10 respondents. The corresponding group means were then calculated, and these results are presented in Report 16.1. Following this, in order to increase the reliability of the final groups, a minimum criterion of 20 cases was imposed on each group. This resulted in the identification of six extreme high groups. These are dominated by high income and the presence of a partner. Five extreme low groups were also identified, dominated by very low income, the absence of a partner and unemployment.

As a result of this analysis, the following conclusions were drawn. First, there are two central defining characteristics of people forming the extreme high wellbeing groups. These are living with a partner and having a high household income. Second, the central defining risk factors for people forming the extreme low wellbeing groups are not living with a partner, very low household income and unemployment.

Within both this analysis and the previously reported investigation of the PWI, two life domains are common.

These are money and relationships. Thus, these two domains will be used as the targets of a more detailed study of the life quality of the Australian population in both objective and subjective dimensions.

Economic Wellbeing

Economic wellbeing is defined by the Australian Bureau of Statistics as command over economic resources, while wealth is defined as assets minus liabilities. In 2004, the wealth of the average Australian household was about $500,000 (US$430,000) (Australian Bureau of Statistics 2007b). For most Australians who have their own home, this represents their single biggest asset. For many, it also represents their largest liability. The average mortgage at that time was $113,000, dwarfing other kinds of financial liabilities such as vehicle loans, which averaged $2,700 per household, and credit card debts at $1,900. Thus, the economic wellbeing of people with a mortgage is highly vulnerable to changes in their economic circumstances that may compromise their ability to make loan repayments. Such factors may be housing loan interest rates, income and the cost of living.

On the asset side of the ledger, about 20% of Australians own property in addition to their home, usually a holiday home or an investment property. The next most valuable asset for most Australians is their superannuation, which is compulsory for full-time employees, at an average value of $63,000. This does not mean, however, that everyone is well off. A small proportion of the population controls a large proportion of the national wealth. Many people who are young, renting or single parents struggle to make ends meet. Figure 21.3 comes from Australian Bureau of Statistics (2007e).

The median household net worth of $295,000 (i.e. the midpoint when all households are ranked in ascending order of net worth) is substantially lower than average. Such data distributions are always skewed by the wealthy households. In fact, about 17% of Australian households have a net worth of $50,000 or less, and about 50% of all households have a net worth of $300,000 or less. At the other end of the spectrum, about 10% of the population has a net worth of $1 million or more. This is in accordance with the value of the Gini Index reported earlier.

There are also substantial geographical differences in wealth. The average net worth of a Sydney household in 2003–2004 was $640,600, due largely to the high

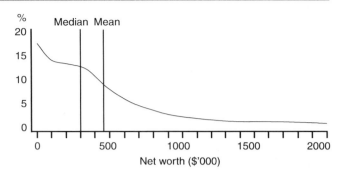

Fig. 21.3 The distribution of household net worth, 2003–2004. *Note*: Households with net worth between $50,000 and $2,050,000 are shown in $100,000 increments

value of property. The net worth of people in rural communities is generally lower than for people in cities, due largely to the lower cost of housing. However, Western Australia is an aberration in this regard. Due to the mining boom in that state, the wealth balance between city and country is reversed. The lowest average net wealth for any geographic group is for Tasmanians not living in Hobart, at $289,000.

Wealth, Age and Relationship Status

Because wealth is the dominance of assets over liabilities, many households with relatively high income have relatively low wealth, especially if they are younger households. Children and mortgages are expensive. Conversely, older households may have relatively low income in their retirement, but have accumulated relatively high net worth over their lifetimes. Thus, for most people, wealth accumulates during their working life and is then utilised during their retirement.

The group with the highest mean household net worth are couples only, aged 55–64. Their mean wealth is $895,000 (Australian Bureau of Statistics 2007e). Many of the people in this group are either nearing the end of their time in the labour force or have recently retired from the labour force; that is, this age group is mainly at the end of the main wealth accumulation period. People over 65 have reduced net worth ($714,000 for couples and $437,000 for lone persons) which reflects two factors. One is the consumption of wealth during retirement, and the other is less opportunity for capital accumulation in earlier decades, due to lower wages and fewer women in the paid work force.

In terms of relationship status, single people aged under 35 have the lowest mean household net worth, at $94,000 (Australian Bureau of Statistics 2007e), followed by single-parent households with dependent children ($158,000). These compare with $518,000 for couple family households with dependent children. This difference is not a function of age since both groups have an average age of about 40 years. Home ownership for single parents is also about half that for the couple parents (39% and 79% respectively).

These differentials are also reflected in the ability to pay off a mortgage. Most people take out a mortgage during their working life and then hope to pay it off by the time they retire. And, indeed, the majority of couples achieve this aim. Of those couples 65 years and over, 85% own their home without a mortgage and another 4% with a mortgage. These proportions drop to 74% and 3% for people living alone, and the order is reversed for single parents with dependent children (11% and 29%).

Satisfaction with Wealth

The other side of the life quality coin is subjective, or how people feel about their material wealth. One of the seven PWI domains asks, 'How satisfied are you with your standard of living?' The pattern for this domain over the 24 surveys is shown below (Fig. 21.4).

Satisfaction with this domain rose significantly immediately following S1. Moreover, this rise has been sustained despite a mixed bag of economic blessings, which will be discussed. The range of scores is 3.5 points between April 2001 (S1:76.3) and September 2009 (S22:79.8). The shape of this response pattern is quite similar to that of the PWI (see earlier), and the correlation with the overall PWI is .85, indicating about 72% shared variance.

It is interesting to note that the rise in satisfaction with standard of living between May 2006 (S15) and

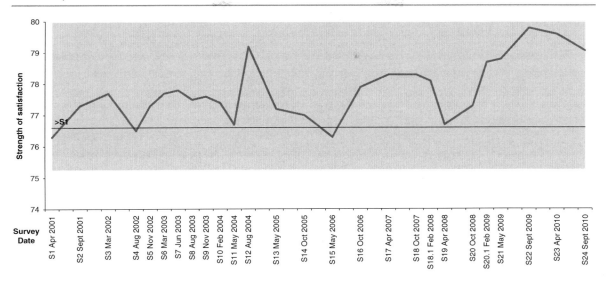

Fig. 21.4 Satisfaction with *standard of living*

October 2007 (S18) occurred despite a succession of 0.25-point rises in interest rates. It is also interesting to note that the rise in wellbeing from April 2008 (Survey 19) commenced in the face of the continuing economic downturn.

There were probably two reasons for this. One was that the various economic stimulus packages released by the government provided households with additional discretionary income. The second was that the poor national economic situation had had a serious negative effect on only a minority of the population. The people personally adversely affected were those who had lost their job or who were reliant on interest from shares or other investments for their income. But these people were in a great minority. While a majority of people had lost wealth with the downturn, for the most part, their investments were intact, and so, they felt they could just wait for the economy to recover. And, in the meantime, if they still had a job and a mortgage, and if their wage has not diminished, then they were better off financially than maybe they had ever been due to the decrease in interest rates and, so, their mortgage payment.

The validity of these changes can be assessed against homeostasis theory. This predicts a strong inverse relationship between changes in the mean and the standard deviation. Because the satisfaction target is quite abstract ('standard of living'), the response will be strongly perfused with HPMood (Blore et al. 2011; Cummins 2010; Davern et al. 2007) and so under considerable homeostatic control. This means that change in satisfaction will be resisted, hence the small degree of variation across the surveys. However, there will be more resistance to upward than to downward movement because the sample is generally sufficiently wealthy to not be in homeostatic defeat. Thus, most people will have a level of satisfaction that is within their set-point range.

When people are operating within their set-point range, their capacity to increase their level of satisfaction on a chronic basis is very limited due to the upper ceiling of the homeostatic range coupled with rapid adaptation to increased wealth (Cummins et al. 2007b). While the lower margin of the range is also defended, there is a limit to the power of homeostasis to defend against really bad economic news. And, if homeostasis is defeated, the control of satisfaction levels pass from homeostasis to the challenging agent. When this occurs, satisfaction is no longer limited to a narrow range, and its value can plummet. This scenario makes the prediction that rises in satisfaction will decrease the sample variance, as a greater proportion of the sample are drawn into the set-point ranges. Falls in satisfaction, on the other hand, will result in increasing variance as respondents leave their range under the influence of homeostatic defeat. In support of this proposition, the correlation between the means and the standard deviations across the 24 surveys is −.76.

Satisfaction with standard of living should also be modifiable, to some measurable extent, by the prevailing economic conditions. This will now be investigated.

Interest Rates

The Reserve Bank of Australia (2011a) is responsible for formulating and implementing monetary policy. The Board's obligations with respect to monetary policy are laid out in the Reserve Bank Act (1959). Section 10(2) of the Act says:

> It is the duty of the Reserve Bank Board, within the limits of its powers, to ensure that the monetary and banking policy of the Bank is directed to the greatest advantage of the people of Australia and that the powers of the Bank... are exercised in such a manner as, in the opinion of the Reserve Bank Board, will best contribute to:
> (a) the stability of the currency of Australia;
> (b) the maintenance of full employment in Australia; and
> (c) the economic prosperity and welfare of the people of Australia.

Monetary policy decisions involve setting the interest rate on overnight loans in the money market. This is the cash rate. Other interest rates in the economy are strongly influenced by this cash rate. The Standard Variable Home Loan rate, for example, mirrors the cash rate almost precisely.

Over the period of these surveys, the cash rate has varied by only 2.0 percentage points, from 4.25 to 6.25 points. Indeed, the rate has remained within this range since December 1996, prior to which it was higher. Perhaps because of this relatively small degree of movement, the cash rate is not significantly related to satisfaction with standard of living. This is true when the actual cash rate at the time of the survey is used ($r=.11$) and when the rates are lagged, by matching each rate with the level of satisfaction in the following survey ($r=-.02$).

Consumer Price Index (CPI)

The Australian Bureau of Statistics (Australian Bureau of Statistics 2007d) is responsible for compiling the Consumer Price Index (CPI). This measures quarterly changes in the price of a 'basket' of goods and services that include the following 11 groups: food, alcohol and tobacco, clothing and footwear, housing, household contents and services, health transportation, communication, recreation, education and financial and insurance services. It is, thus, a measure of inflation, and since 1993, the Reserve Bank of Australia (2007) has set a target for consumer price inflation of 2–3% per annum.

Over the 6-year period from April 2001 to April 2007, the CPI increased from 132.7 to 155.6 points, or 3.8 points per year, which is above the target stated by the RBA above. Moreover, the increases have been very uneven during this period, with the increases between adjacent quarterly surveys ranging from 0.0 points to 0.64 points per month.

These per month rates of increase are significantly correlated with survey mean scores for 'satisfaction with standard of living' in the same period of time ($r=-.53$, $df=15, p<.025$). If the series is lagged, such that the rate of CPI increase is correlated with the survey score in the following time period, the relationship becomes non-significant ($r=.18$). Thus, changes in the rate of inflation are negatively related to satisfaction with standard of living. While this is perfectly logical, it is also the first time that such a relationship has been established.

In summary, despite Australia being a wealthy country, the distribution of income and wealth is far from even across the population. There are identifiable demographic groups, such as single parents, who have low levels of both income and wealth which is, indeed, insufficient to maintain a normal level of SWB on average (see also Cummins Chap. 20). At the level of the whole population, satisfaction with standard of living has significantly fluctuated over the past 6 years. These fluctuations are related to the overall levels of the PWI and also to changes in the rates of inflation.

Relationships

In 2006, the ABS conducted their second General Social Survey (Australian Bureau of Statistics 2007c) which involved a total census of 15,307,000 people aged 18 years and over. The only previous survey of this type had been conducted in 2002. This massive snapshot of the population revealed the most authoritative statements we have concerning the objective nature of relationships in this country. Some of these are as follows:

Contact with Other People

Most people (96%) reported having contact in the previous week (either in person or via telephone, mail or email) with family or friends with whom they did not live. There was no gender difference in this contact and little variation across age groups. Of these people, 79% made their contact in person.

Over a longer 3-month period, most people used a combination of methods to contact family and friends, with fixed telephone being the most common (91%) followed by mobile phone or SMS (77%), followed by the internet (47%) and mail, cards or faxes (31%). The older groups still rely mainly on fixed telephone and standard mail.

This level of connection extends to instrumental support. Most people (93%) reported that they would be able to ask people outside of their household for small favours, such as looking after pets, collecting mail, watering gardens, minding a child for a brief period or borrowing equipment. This same proportion reported that, in a time of crisis, they could get support from outside their household. This support would primarily come from family members (80%) or friends (67%). However, neighbours, work colleagues and various community, government and professional organisations were also regarded as potential sources of support. While there was no gender difference in the perceptions of such support, it was higher in the younger age groups (18–44 years) and lower for people born in non-English-speaking countries.

Household Composition

The description of Australian families as being predominantly 'nuclear' gives a false impression of the complexity of family structures. Over 1,961,000 parents reported that their own children aged 0–24 years were living in another household. Most of these parents (68%) were providing some form of support to their own children, and this is not restricted to the younger children. In Australia, the age at which children become a legal adult is 18 years, and they most commonly stop being dependent on their parents between 18 and 24 years. However, 57% of these adult children are still receiving some form of support from their parents.

The support arrangements included financial support and instrumental support, such as providing transportation. One of the key forms of financial support provided to children aged under 18 years, living elsewhere, is Child Support Payments. These can be paid by mutual agreement or may be imposed by a court order. Of those parents who had children of this age living outside the household, 61% reported making

such payments. Also, about 28% of families were providing support to a relative living outside their household, other than their partner or own child. This was most common in the 55–64-year age range.

Contact Networks

Most people (66%) reported that all or most of their friends were of a similar age. This is more pronounced in the youngest age group of 18–24-year-olds (74%) than for people aged 85+ years (48%). In terms of confidants, 37% felt they could confide in a family member living outside their household while 53% could do so in a friend.

Community participation is quite high, with 63% actively participating in a social group during the last 12 months. This is higher for the youngest age group (67%) and lowest for those aged 75+ years (54%). The most popular type of participation for the 18–24-year group is through sport and physical recreation (44%), while for people aged 75+ years, it is through religious or spiritual organisations. Participation in civic or political groups is not so popular, with a rate of 19% for all persons aged 18 years and over during the previous 12-month period. The groups concerned were most likely to be trade unions and professional and technical associations (7%), environmental or animal welfare groups (5%), followed by body corporate or tenants' associations (4%).

A good sense of connection to other people is engendered through two kinds of voluntary behaviour. One is participation in sport or recreational physical activity. This is quite popular, involving 62% of the sample. The other is voluntary work within organisations. Australia is strong in this area. In 2006, 34% of adults had undertaken some form of voluntary work in the previous 12 months. Women are more likely to be volunteers than men (36 vs. 32%), rates peak at 35–44 years (43%) and are most likely in a couple relationship with dependent children (45%) (Australian Bureau of Statistics 2007a).

Attending events is a weak form of social connection if done alone, but strong if done in the company of friends. Most people (89%) use this form of connection over a 12-month period. The most popular activity is going to the movies (69%), attending sporting events (52%) and visiting libraries (46%), zoological parks and aquariums (41%) and botanic gardens (40%).

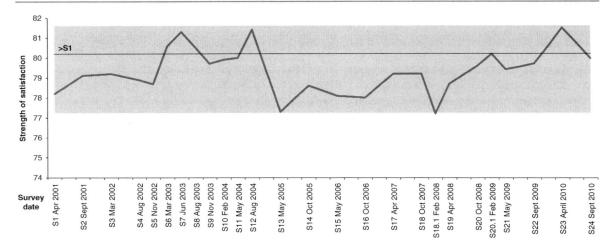

Fig. 21.5 Satisfaction with relationships

This is supported by government expenditure. More than $5.4 billion was spent by the public sector in Australia on cultural activities in 2005–2006 (Australian Bureau of Statistics 2007f). The majority of this funding went to broadcasting and film ($1.2 billion), followed by nature parks and reserves ($1.1 billion), libraries and archives ($576 million) and other museums ($506 million).

One of the factors that make social contacts hard to develop and maintain is relocation, and 43% of the sample had moved home in the 5 years prior to the survey. This was highest (75%) for people aged 25–34 years, people who were renting (84%) and people who are unemployed (62%). The main reason for moving was housing-related (52%) such as moving to a better home or purchasing a home, and for family reasons (26%).

Relationship Satisfaction

We ask, 'How satisfied are you with your relationships?' and the results across the surveys are shown in Fig. 21.5.

This domain did not significantly rise until the period of the pre-Iraq war (Survey 6, March 2003), seemingly in anticipation of the looming war to which Australian troops were to be committed. Such events are likely to constitute a threat to collective wellbeing, which would be expected to engender bonding social capital and enhanced relationship satisfaction.

However, it is not just threat events that are associated with the rise in satisfaction with relationships. Figure 21.5 shows that another peak in satisfaction was attained in August 2004 at the time of the Athens Olympics (Survey 12) and again in Survey 23. These changes mirror SWB (Fig. 21.1), and the correlation between them is .76.

In summary, the General Social Survey of 2006 has provided a view of the population as being quite socially connected, not just within families but also between friends and within the general community. To an extent, this must be facilitated by the complexity of modern family structures, with children being supported in a variety of ways by parents who have separated and with blended families being commonplace. It is also facilitated by a high level of engagement in community activities and substantial government expenditure on the necessary infrastructure. In terms of relationship satisfaction, it appears that this rises in times of national crisis and national celebration. The mechanism for this rise seems likely to be through social bonding and the creation of social capital.

Conclusions

In terms of both objective and subjective measures of wellbeing, Australia has a high level of life quality. In part, this is due to its wealth, but there are also other factors at work. It is a stable democracy, has a basically egalitarian philosophy, if increasingly based in myth, and is generally welcoming of new migrants. It is, thus, free from systematic racial discrimination or sectorial violence. All this is reflected in relatively high and stable levels of subjective wellbeing.

There are, however, pockets of deprivation and low life quality. Most notably, this disadvantage applies quite generally to the indigenous Aboriginal population. The resolution of this imbalance with the non-indigenous population is currently, and must remain, a national priority.

Acknowledgements We thank Ann-Marie James for her assistance with the preparation of this manuscript.

References

Andrews, F. M., & Withey, S. B. (1976). *Social indicators of well-being: American's perceptions of life quality*. New York: Plenum Press.

Australian Bureau of Statistics. (2007a). *3101.0 – Australian Demographic Statistics, Dec 2006*. Retrieved April 7, 2011, from http://www.abs.gov.au/websitedbs/D3310114.nsf/Home/Survey+Participant+Information?OpenDocument.

Australian Bureau of Statistics. (2007b). *4102.0 – Australian Social Trends, 2007*. Retrieved April 7, 2011, from http://www.abs.gov.au/AUSSTATS/abs@.nsf/mf/4102.0?OpenDocument.

Australian Bureau of Statistics. (2007c). *4159.0 – General Social Survey: Summary results*. Retrieved April 7, 2011, from http://www.ausstats.abs.gov.au/ausstats/subscriber.nsf/0/9EBEEE90D2746F45CA2572E20013BD17/$File/41590_2006.pdf.

Australian Bureau of Statistics. (2007d). *6401.0 – Consumer Price Index, Australia, Mar 2007*. Retrieved April 7, 2011, from http://www.abs.gov.au/ausstats/abs@.nsf/mf/6401.0/.

Australian Bureau of Statistics. (2007e). *6554.0 – Household wealth and wealth distribution, Australia, 2003–04*. Retrieved April 7, 2011, from http://www.abs.gov.au/AUSSTATS/abs@.nsf/ProductsbyCatalogue/ABDECB2B70579A67CA25715C001A3C71?OpenDocument.

Australian Bureau of Statistics. (2007f). *Cultural funding by government, Australia, 2005–06*. Retrieved September 30, 2011 http://www.abs.gov.au/ausstats/abs@.nsf/mf/4183.0.

Australian Bureau of Statistics. (2011a). *3218.0 Regional population growth, Australia, 2009–10*. Retrieved April 7, 2011, from http://www.abs.gov.au/ausstats/abs@.nsf/mf/3218.0?OpenDocument.

Australian Bureau of Statistics. (2011b). *4530.0 Crime victimisation, Australia, 2009–10*. Retrieved April 7, 2011, from http://www.abs.gov.au/ausstats/abs@.nsf/mf/4530.0?OpenDocument.

Australian Bureau of Statistics. (2011c). *6105.0 – Australian labour market statistics*. Retrieved April 7, 2011, from http://www.abs.gov.au/ausstats/abs@.nsf/mf/6105.0?OpenDocument.

Australian Government – Department of Foreign Affairs and Trade. (2005). *Australia-United States Free Trade Agreement*. Retrieved April 7, 2011, from http://www.dfat.gov.au/trade/negotiations/us_fta/final-text/index.html.

Australian Institute of Health and Welfare. (2002). *Older Australians at a glance 2002* (3rd ed.). Canberra: AIHW and Australian Department of Health and Ageing, 2002. (AIHW Cat. No. AGE 25.)

Australian Institute of Health and Welfare. (2004). *Australia's Health 2004*. Canberra: AIHW. (AIHW Cat. No. AUS 44.) Retrieved September 30, 2004, from http://www.aihw.gov.au/publication-detail/?id=6442467608

Australian Unity Wellbeing Index. (2009). Melbourne: Deakin University. Retrieved April 7, 2011, from www.deakin.edu.au/research/acqol/index_wellbeing/index.htm.

Bergheim, S. (2007). *The happy variety of capitalism*. Retrieved April 7, 2011, from http://www.dbresearch.com/PROD/DBR_INTERNET_DE-PROD/PROD0000000000209864.PDF.

Blore, J. D., Stokes, M. A., Mellor, D., Firth, L., & Cummins, R. A. (2011). Comparing multiple discrepancies theory to affective models of subjective wellbeing. *Social Indicators Research, 100*, 1–16.

Bourdieu, P. (1986). *Handbook of theory and research for the sociology of education*. Westport, CT: Greenwood Press.

Cummins, R. A. (1995). On the trail of the gold standard for life satisfaction. *Social Indicators Research, 35*, 179–200.

Cummins, R. A. (1998). The second approximation to an international standard of life satisfaction. *Social Indicators Research, 43*, 307–334.

Cummins, R. A. (2010). Subjective wellbeing, homeostatically protected mood and depression: A synthesis. *Journal of Happiness Studies, 11*, 1–17. doi:10.1007/s10902-009-9167-0.

Cummins, R. A., Eckersley, R., Lo, S. K., Okerstrom, E., Hunter, B., & Davern, M. (2003a). *Australian Unity Wellbeing Index: Report 5.0 – The wellbeing of Australians – 1. Personal finances 2. The impact of the Bali Bombing*. Retrieved April 7, 2011 from http://www.deakin.edu.au/research/acqol/index_wellbeing/index.htm.

Cummins, R. A., Eckersley, R., Pallant, J., Van Vugt, J., & Misajon, R. (2003b). Developing a national index of subjective wellbeing: The Australian Unity Wellbeing Index. *Social Indicators Research, 64*, 159–190.

Cummins, R. A., Walter, J., & Woerner, J. (2007a). *Australian Unity Wellbeing Index: Report 16.1. The wellbeing of Australians – Groups with the highest and lowest wellbeing in Australia*. Retrieved September 30, 2011, from http://www.deakin.edu.au/research/acqol/index_wellbeing/index.htm.

Cummins, R. A., Woerner, J., Tomyn, A., Gibson, A., & Knapp, T. (2007b). *Australian Unity Wellbeing Index: Report 17.0. The wellbeing of Australians – Work, wealth and happiness*. Retrieved September 30, 2011, from http://www.deakin.edu.au/research/acqol/index_wellbeing/index.htm.

Cummins, R. A., Mellor, D., Stokes, M. A., & Lau, A. L. D. (2008). Quality of life down-under: The Australian Unity Wellbeing Index. In V. Moller, D. Huschka, & A. C. Michalos (Eds.), *Barometers of quality of life around the globe: How are we doing?* (Social Indicators Research Series 33, pp. 135–159). Dordrecht: Springer.

Davern, M., Cummins, R. A., & Stokes, M. (2007). Subjective wellbeing as an affective/cognitive construct. *Journal of Happiness Studies, 8*, 429–449.

Department of External Affairs. (1951). *Security Treaty between Australia, New Zealand and the United States of America [ANZUS]*. Retrieved April 7, 2011, from http://australian-politics.com/foreign/anzus/anzus-treaty.shtml.

Department of Foreign Affairs and Trade. (2005). *A diverse people*. Retrieved April 7, 2011, from http://www.dfat.gov.au/aib/society.html

Durlauf, S. N. (2002). Bowling alone: A review essay. *Journal of Economic Behavior and Organization, 47*, 259–273.

Gardiner-Garden, J., & Park, M. (2007). *Commonwealth Indigenous-specific expenditure 1968–2006* (Background Note No. 2 2007–08). Parliament of Australia. Retrieved April 7, 2011, from http://www.aph.gov.au/Library/pubs/bn/2007–08/08bn02.htm.

Groot, W., van den Brink, H. M., & van Praag, B. (2007). The compensating income variation of social capital. *Social Indicators Research, 82*, 189–207.

Hall, P. A., & Soskice, D. (2001). *Varieties of capitalism: the institutional foundations of comparative advantage*. Oxford: Oxford University Press.

Headey, B. W., & Wearing, A. J. (1989). Personality, life events, and subjective well-being: Toward a dynamic equilibrium model. *Journal of Personality and Social Psychology, 57*, 731–739.

Headey, B. W., Holmstrom, E. L., & Wearing, A. J. (1984). The impact of life events and changes in domain on well-being. *Social Indicators Research, 15*, 203–227.

Household Income and Labour Dynamics in Australia (HILDA) Survey. (2009). Melbourne: University of Melbourne. Retrieved April 7, 2011, from http://www.melbourneinstitute.com/hilda.

Human Development Report. (2010). *The real wealth of nations: Pathways to human development*. New York: United Nations Development Program.

International Monetary Fund (2011). *World Economic Outlook Database*, October 2010. Retrieved April 7, 2011, from http://www.imf.org/external/pubs/ft/weo/2010/01/weodata/index.aspx.

International Wellbeing Group. (2006). *Personal Wellbeing Index* (4th ed.). Melbourne: Australian Centre on Quality of Life, School of Psychology, Deakin University, ISBN 1 74156 048 9. Retrieved April 7, 2011, from http://www.deakin.edu.au/research/acqol/instruments/wellbeing_index.htm.

Jones, L. V., & Thurstone, L. L. (1955). The psychophysics of semantics: An experimental investigation. *Journal of Applied Psychology, 39*, 31–36.

Medicare Australia. (2007). Retrieved September 30, 2011, from http://www.humanservices.gov.au/corporate/about-us/index

Poleg, D. (2004). *The poppy and the pauper: A short overview of Australian egalitarianism*. Retrieved April 7, 2011, from http://www.drorism.com/australian-egalitarianism.php.

Putnam, R. D. (2000). *Bowling alone: The collapse and revival of American community*. New York: Simon and Schuster.

Requena, F. (2003). Social capital, satisfaction and quality of life in the workplace. *Social Indicators Research, 61*, 331–360.

Reserve Bank Act. (1959). Retrieved April 7, 2011, from http://www.comlaw.gov.au/ComLaw/Legislation/ActCompilation1.nsf/current/bytitle/C276D47C3215A796CA256F71004DA82A?OpenDocument.

Reserve Bank of Australia. (2007). Retrieved April 7, 2011, from http://www.rba.gov.au/Statistics/cashrate_target.html.

Reserve Bank of Australia. (2011a). Retrieved September 30, 2011, from http://www.rba.gov.au/monetary-policy/inflation-target.html

Rosen, M., Floor, L., & Zisfein, L. (1974). Investigating the phenomenon of acquiescence in the mentally handicapped: I – Theoretical model, test development, and normative data. *British Journal of Mental Subnormality, 20*, 58–68.

Schwarz, N. (1990). Feelings as information: informational and motivational functions of aVective states. In E. T. Higgins & R. Sorrentino (Eds.), *Handbook of motivation and cognition* (Vol. 2, pp. 527–561). New York: Guildford Press.

Sigelman, C. K., Schoenrock, C., Winer, J. L., Spanhel, C. L., Hromas, S. G., Martin, P. W., et al. (1981). Issues in interviewing mentally retarded persons: An empirical study. In R. H. Bruininks, C. E. Meyers, B. B. Sigford, & K. C. Lakin (Eds.), *Deinstitutionalization and community adjustment of mentally retarded people* (pp. 114–129). Washington DC: American Association on Mental Deficiency.

Sudman, S., & Bradburn, N. M. (1974). *Response effects in surveys: A review and synthesis*. Chicago: Aldine.

Trewin, D., & Madden, R. (2005). *The Health and Welfare of Australia's Aboriginal and Torres Strait Islander Peoples*. Canberra: Australian Bureau of Statistics. Retrieved April 7, 2011, from http://www.aihw.gov.au/publications/ihw/hwaatsip05/hwaatsip05.pdf.

World Bank (2007). *World Bank list of economies*. Retrieved April 7, 2011, from http://siteresources.worldbank.org/DATASTATISTICS/Resources/CLASS.XLS.

World Drink Trends. (2005). Institute of Alcohol Studies. Retrieved September 30, 2011, from http://www.ias.org.uk/resources/publications/warc/worlddrinks_2005.html.

Quality of Life in East Asia: The Case of Hong Kong

22

Daniel T.L. Shek

Perhaps there is no other research topic like the concept of quality of life (QOL) that has attracted so much research attention from different disciplines. A review of the major databases such as PsycINFO and Medline shows that much research effort has been spent to understand the theoretical and practical aspects of the concept (Shek et al. 2005a). Regarding the essence of the quality of life concept, while there are different definitions of the concept, there is a general agreement among researchers (e.g., Felce and Perry 1995; Wallander et al. 2001) that the concept is multi-dimensional, including material well-being (finance, income, housing quality, transport), physical well-being (health, fitness, mobility, personal safety), social well-being (personal relationships, community involvement), emotional well-being (positive affect, mental health, fulfillment, satisfaction, faith/belief, self-esteem), and productive well-being (competence, productivity). Besides, there are researchers arguing that objective life situation as well as subjective perceptions of an individual in evaluating his/her objective living conditions are important dimensions to be considered (Fahey et al. 2003). Based on the ideas of Veehoven (1996), quality of life is conceptualized in terms of objective living conditions, subjective well-being of an individual, and the perceived quality of a society in this chapter.

In a comprehensive review of QOL studies in the Chinese contexts, Shek and colleagues pointed out that there were several research gaps in the existing literature (Shek et al. 2005a; Shek 2010). These research gaps are summarized as follows:

Gap 1: With reference to ecological conceptions and models, the foci on family quality of life and spirituality are not adequate in the existing literature on quality of life.

Gap 2: While much research has been conducted to examine the quality of life of people in different stages of the life span, such as adulthood in general and old age in particular, there are comparatively fewer research studies on the quality of life of children and adolescents.

Gap 3: Majority of the studies has been conducted in Western contexts based on Western participants, and comparatively fewer studies have been conducted in different Chinese contexts.

Gap 4: While QOL studies in the medical and rehabilitation settings have commonly focused on the physically disadvantaged and intellectually impaired groups, comparatively fewer studies have examined the quality of life of persons experiencing economic disadvantage.

Gap 5: While researchers in different disciplines, including psychology, sociology, social work, education, communication, medicine, and health-related disciplines, have examined the concept of quality of life, dialogues among researchers in different professions are not extensive and forums for exchanges among different professionals are few.

Gap 6: Quality of life studies involving the comparison of different countries within a single study are not widespread.

Gap 7: With reference to the issue of how quality of life at the aggregate level (e.g., community, societal, national,

D.T.L. Shek (✉)
Department of Applied Social Sciences,
Public Policy Research Institute, The Hong Kong Polytechnic University, Hunghom, Hong Kong, PRC
e-mail: daniel.shek@polyu.edu.hk

K.C. Land et al. (eds.), *Handbook of Social Indicators and Quality of Life Research*,
DOI 10.1007/978-94-007-2421-1_22, © Springer Science+Business Media B.V. 2012

regional, international, or global level) can be adequately assessed, there is still the debate surrounding whether objective indicators (such as official statistics) or subjective indicators (such as opinion surveys) are better indicators of quality of life.

In view of the observation that there are relatively fewer QOL studies in different Chinese communities (including Hong Kong), there is a need to take stock of the available studies. As such, there are several objectives of this chapter. First, different sources of data on the quality of life in Hong Kong, including those conducted by the Government, commercial organizations, local as well as international non-governmental organizations, and academics, are briefly described. Second, characteristics of published quality of life studies in Hong Kong captured in the major databases, including PsycINFO, Sociological Abstracts, Social Work Abstracts, Medline, and CINAHL, are discussed. Third, three quality of life research programs involving the collection of trend data over time (Indicators of Social Development Project, Social Development Index Project, and the CUHK Hong Kong Quality of Life Index Project) are described. Fourth, major observations pertinent to the quality of life in Hong Kong are discussed. Finally, methodological issues pertinent to the existing quality of life studies are outlined.

Sources of Data on Quality of Life in Hong Kong

Quality of Life Data Generated by the Government and Government-Related Bodies

As far as the question of "who" conduct quality of life research in Hong Kong is concerned, a survey of the literature shows that there are several sources of the related studies. First, the Government of Hong Kong Special Administrative Region generates data on the quality of life of Hong Kong, and there are several mechanisms involved. First, different Government departments (particularly the Census and Statistics Department) compile statistics on the development of the Hong Kong society and publish research reports based on such statistics. For examples, the Department of Health regularly updates statistics on suicide and mental disorders, the Education Bureau (EDB) keeps statistics based on the student population (such as

students with special needs), and the Environmental Protection Department maintains statistics on the severity of different forms of pollution in Hong Kong. Obviously, such statistics can readily be used as the bases upon which other objective quality of life indicators can be compiled. Second, studies examining the perceptions of Hong Kong people about the Hong Kong society are regularly conducted by different policy bureaus and Government-related organizations. For examples, the Independent Commission against Corruption conducts regular surveys examining the public's perception of the severity of corruption in Hong Kong, the Food and Health Bureau has also examined the public's perception of food safety and the Government's performance in monitoring food safety, and the Home Affairs Bureau has conducted regular opinion polls gauging Hong Kong people's perceptions of different aspects of the Hong Kong society.

Third, many quality of life studies are conducted by advisory committees within the Government. For example, in response to the emergence of the problem of non-engaged youths in Hong Kong, the Commission on Youth carried out several studies to understand the quality of life of this population (Shek and Lee 2004). The Commission on Youth has also examined the emotional quality of life, civic engagement, and social networks of young people in Hong Kong (Commission on Youth 2005, 2010). The study showed that the emotional quality of life of young people in Hong Kong was fairly high and their interpersonal quality of life was acceptable. Another example is that the Elderly Commission has also examined the patterns of elderly suicide in Hong Kong and concluded that elderly suicide rates in Hong Kong were declining (Elderly Commission 2001). The Family Council has recently commissioned several research studies examining adolescent substance abuse, compensated dating, elderly neglect, as well as child neglect. Finally, the Review Panel of the Pilot Project on Child Fatality Review examined the factors leading to child deaths in Hong Kong (Social Welfare Department 2010).

Quality of Life Data Generated by Organizations in the Commercial Sector

There are many studies on the quality of life of Hong Kong conducted by organizations in the commercial sector. Many chambers of commerce in Hong Kong conduct quality of life research. For example, the American Chamber of Commerce in Hong Kong carries out regular business outlook surveys, utilizing indicators including quality of life, freedom of press, and quality of the natural environment (e.g., American Chamber of Commerce 2004, 2008). In another project conducted by the Canadian Chamber of Commerce in Hong Kong in collaboration with the City University of Hong Kong, the Hong Kong Sustainable Development Index was developed. In the baseline survey conducted in 2003, the 10 top priority areas that should be dealt with in Hong Kong included (1) educational system, (2) healthy economy, (3) health and hygiene, (4) environmental protection, (5) caring and ethical employers, (6) urban planning, (7) community spirit and well-being, (8) population policy, (9) civil liberties and human rights, and (10) integration with the Mainland. The respondents were least satisfied with the economy (rank = 10), population policy (rank = 9), caring and ethical employers (rank = 8), and education (rank = 7). Another update in 2008 showed that there was a slight improvement in the overall satisfaction with the development in Hong Kong (Francis 2008).

Besides, some international commercial organizations have also conducted quality of life studies, particularly in the areas of economic confidence and consumer confidence. For example, the Master Card (2010) conducts regular surveys to examine consumer confidence in the Asia Pacific Region in which five selected economic factors are covered in the surveys, including employment, economy, regular income, stock market, and quality of life (Master Index of Consumer Confidence). In a recent survey of consumer confidence in Hong Kong, results showed that sentiments on employment, economy, regular income, and quality of life continued to be very highly optimistic (Master Card 2010). Another example is the Global Consumer Confidence Report conducted by ACNielson (2010) where it was reported that there was a slight decrease in Consumer Confidence Index in Hong Kong after a long period of growth.

Hong Kong. In the social welfare sector, many social welfare organizations have examined quality of life in different social groups, including those populations with special needs. For example, in an attempt to examine stress among young people in Hong Kong, the Hong Kong Federation of Youth Groups (2004) showed that the top ten stresses facing young people included future prospect, examination, self-expectation, job expectation, unemployment, individual finance, time management, parental expectation, poor economy, and relationship with boss. The study also showed that young people's responses to stress were related to a number of psychosocial factors. In another study on the perception of quality of life among the post-1980s, the Hong Kong Federation of Youth Groups (2010) reported that most of the respondents had concerns about the rich–poor gap and social mobility. Other quality of life research conducted by non-government organizations includes the attempts to examine the psychological well-being of adults in Hong Kong. Shek and Tsang (1993) utilized the General Health Questionnaire to examine the mental health of parents with mentally retarded children, and they found that 23.8% of the respondents could be classified as "psychologically at risk." Similarly, based on a sample of working parents in Hong Kong, Shek and Mak (1986) showed that 26.5% of the participants could be regarded as displaying excessive psychological symptoms based on the Chinese General Health Questionnaire.

Perhaps the most comprehensive and systematic study of quality of life in Hong Kong undertaken by the third sector is the Social Development Index (SDI) Project carried out by the Hong Kong Council of Social Service which attempts to capture the quality of life in Hong Kong by utilizing objective statistics and figures (The Hong Kong Council of Social Service 2000, 2002, 2004, 2006; Chua et al. 2010). The Social Development Index is composed of 14 sub-indexes reflecting different aspects of quality of life in Hong Kong. The details of the SDI are described later in this chapter.

Quality of Life Data Generated by Local Non-government Organizations

Many local non-government organizations have conducted research studies on the quality of life in Hong Kong, such as pollution issues and social problems in

Quality of Life Data Generated by International Non-governmental Organizations

In many studies conducted by international non-governmental organizations, quality of life data in

Hong Kong are compared with those of other places of the world. For example, the World Bank compiles the World Development Indicators which describes different aspects of social development, such as distribution of income and poverty. Similarly, the United Nations Development Program publishes the Human Development Report in which the social conditions in different places in the world are described. In the 2010 Human Development Report (United Nations Development Program 2010), Hong Kong was ranked 21st among 169 regions in terms of the Human Development Index (0.862), which was higher than 1980 (0.693), 2000 (0.800) and 2005 (0.842). In addition, Hong Kong was regarded as a place with very high human development.

Many international non-governmental organizations have also conducted quality of life in different countries and places in the world. In a recent study conducted by the New Economics Foundation (2006), results showed that Hong Kong was ranked 88th among 178 countries and places in the world. Although Hong Kong enjoyed a very high level of life expectancy (81.6 which was within the green zone of the traffic light scheme of data coding), Hong Kong people only had a medium level of life satisfaction of 6.6 (within the yellow zone of the traffic light scheme of data coding). Besides, Hong Kong consumed much more resources than other parts of the world, with a score of 4.6 which was in between the "red" and "blood red" zone.

Quality of Life Data Generated by Academic Institutions

There are many types of quality of life studies conducted in Hong Kong from which several attributes can be highlighted. First, quality of life studies in different disciplines, including economics, medicine, geography, psychology, sociology, social work, and education, have been conducted (Shek et al. 2005b). Second, quality of life studies encompassing different domains of quality of life, including objective quality of life (e.g., Chan et al. 2005), subjective quality of life (Shek 2005a) and perceptions of social conditions (e.g., Lau et al. 2005b) have been conducted. With particular reference to the study of psychological well-being, studies on psychological symptoms and positive mental health have been carried out.

Third, quality of life studies based on the general population (e.g., Lau et al. 2005b), populations at the different stages of the life span (e.g., Lau and McKenna 1998; Shek 2005a) and clients with special needs (e.g., Lau and McKenna 2002) have been conducted. Fourth, while some studies were conducted specifically on Hong Kong people (e.g., Shek and Lee 2005), other compared Hong Kong and other countries (e.g., Shek et al. 2005).

What are the conceptual and methodological characteristics of research conducted by academics regarding the quality of life of Hong Kong? A summary of the relevant studies indexed in the major databases can be seen in Table 22.1. To understand the nature of quality of life studies in Hong Kong, Shek and Lee (2007) analyzed published papers on quality of life in Hong Kong in the major databases, including PsycINFO, Sociological Abstracts, Social Work Abstracts, Eric, Medline, and CINAHL. Several dimensions were included in the analyses: (a) type of paper—conceptual (i.e., discussion of conceptual issues only) or empirical paper (i.e., involving the collection of empirical data); (b) conception of quality of life in terms of micro perspective (e.g., individual perceptions such as well-being and subjective satisfaction) or macro perspective (e.g., societal conditions such as poverty); (c) methodology involved—quantitative, qualitative or mixed methodology; (d) stages of the human life span—infancy, childhood, adolescence, adulthood, old age, whole life and others; (e) samples involved—general population or populations with special needs; and (f) whether there were any comparisons of the data collected in Hong Kong with other countries.

Several characteristics can be observed from the review conducted by Shek and Lee (2007). First, most of the existing published studies captured in the major databases were empirical studies. Second, most of the published studies adopted a definition of quality of life from a micro perspective, such as psychological well-being and subjective quality of life. Third, the methodology in most of the published studies was predominantly quantitative in nature. Fourth, as far as the stage of life span covered in these studies is concerned, the review showed that most of the QOL studies concentrated on adults and aged people. Fifth, in contrast to studies based on the general population, there were comparatively more studies focusing on the quality of

22 Quality of Life in Hong Kong

Table 22.1 Number of quality of life studies in the major databases using different search terms

Database and search terms	Year 2005	Year 2011			
		Search anywhere		Search as keywords	
		All publication	Peer-reviewed journal	All publication	Peer-reviewed journal
PsycINFO					
"QOL"	2,063	5,032	4,551	3,918	3,531
"QOL" and "Hong Kong"	35	209	195	52	50
"Quality of life"	17,895	74,192	64,436	29,399	24,508
"Quality of life" and "Hong Kong"	150	2,635	2,298	199	190
Sociological abstracts					
"QOL"	142	262	209	216	168
"QOL" and "Hong Kong"	7	19	17	5	5
"Quality of life"	4,883	7,416	4,992	4,802	2,650
"Quality of life" and "Hong Kong"	105	268	247	58	52
Social work abstracts					
"QOL"	20	31	30	–	–
"QOL" and "Hong Kong"	0	1	1	–	–
"Quality of life"	513	734	666	–	–
"Quality of life" and "Hong Kong"	9	11	11	–	–
Medline					
"QOL"	6,981	10,540	5,940	10,526	5,932
"QOL" and "Hong Kong"	39	134	84	24	49
"Quality of life"	59,406	93,900	49,433	93,041	49,080
"Quality of life" and "Hong Kong"	181	693	418	330	213
ERIC					
"QOL"	56	170	144	170	144
"QOL" and "Hong Kong"	2	5	5	5	5
"Quality of life"	4,675	5,967	1,787	5,960	1,785
"Quality of life" and "Hong Kong"	17	38	32	37	32

life of people with special needs (e.g., cancer patients and people with mental retardation). Finally, very few of the existing published studies included direct comparisons of quality of life findings in Hong Kong with other countries. Generally speaking, these observations are consistent with the observations of Shek et al. (2005a). Of course, the interpretation of the above observations should proceed with caution because some researchers studying quality of life may not term their studies as quality of life studies. One simple example is that while there are many studies on psychological well-being in adolescence, such studies are commonly not regarded as QOL studies by the researchers concerned.

Quality of Life Projects Involving Trend Data

The Indicators of Social Development Project

The Indicators of Social Development Project has been undertaken by The Chinese University of Hong Kong, The Hong Kong Polytechnic University, and The University of Hong Kong with the aim to chart the quality of life and social well-being of the Hong Kong people before and after 1997. To achieve this objective, a series of Social Indicator Surveys have been collected since 1988. To date, a total of 8 surveys were conducted

(Lau et al. 1991, 1992, 1995, 1997, 1999, 2001, 2003, 2005b). In these surveys, around 2,000–5,000 respondents were randomly selected using multistage stratified systematic sampling methods, with 50% or slightly higher response rates in different surveys.

The emphasis of the Social Indicators Surveys is placed on "experience of life" rather than "condition of life." In other words, subjective quality of life is the central focus and the perceptions, values, feelings and aspirations of Hong Kong residents toward various aspects of their lives are examined. There are typically two parts in each survey. In the first part of the study, there is a core component to be answered by all respondents. The questions in the core components are concerned about the respondents' perceived quality of life which remained largely unchanged over time. In the second part of the study, some modules on special topics are included and the questions in each module are answered by a sub-sample of the participants. For example, in the 2004 Social Indicators Survey, four special modules were included. These focus special modules were (a) fertility decline, continuing and life-long education; (b) employment, cross-border activities, and identity; (c) legal culture and political activities; and (d) health and class.

There are several sections in the core component of the questionnaire. For the subjective well-being of the respondents, questions with reference to 20 life domains covering 9 personal life aspects and 11 societal conditions were asked. For each domain, the respondent was asked how satisfied he/she was with reference to a specific domain. The respondent could indicate their level of satisfaction on a 5-point scale ("Very Dissatisfied," "Dissatisfied," "Average," "Satisfied," and "Very satisfied"). For respondents without idea on the subject or unwilling to give their responses, off-scale choices ("Don't know" and "No answer") were provided. The 9 personal life aspects included family life, education attainment, health status, financial situation, job, relationships with friends, relationships with relatives, living environments, and leisure time. For the 11 societal conditions, they included general economic situation, public order, general political situation, performance of the Hong Kong Government, transport, housing, medical services, education, social welfare, employment situation, and recreation facilities. Finally, a question assessing the respondent's global satisfaction with life and a question on the most important ingredient for a happy life

(health, peace of mind, money, having filial children, freedom, love, marriage and family, career, material enjoyment, serving society, and others) were included.

Although the items assessing the 20 life domains represent different items devoted to different aspects of sense of well-being, it would be expected that they should assess the construct of overall quality of life. Actually, Shen and Lai (1999) aggregated the set of responses over the 20 life domains to construct a quality of life measure representing the general sense of well-being of the respondents in Hong Kong.

Besides questions on the respondents' satisfaction with different aspects of life, the following questions are also covered in the core component of the Indicators of Social Development Project:

- Degree of satisfaction with the mass media
- Expectation of the quality of life 3 years later
- Subjective evaluation of the performance of the Hong Kong Government
- Perceived severity of the social problems in Hong Kong (including law and order, housing, transportation, education, employment, young people, medical and health, welfare, pollution, elderly, moral values, income inequality, corruption, and other social problems) and the perceived urgency in tackling each of these problems
- Confidence about different aspects of Hong Kong, including economic prosperity, social stability, personal freedom, protection of human rights, corruption within the Government, rule of law, democratic development, the Chief Executive, public officers who devise policies, and civil servants
- Global confidence about the future of Hong Kong
- Perceived competence of people in Hong Kong to govern Hong Kong
- Chinese Government's respect for the "One country, two systems" arrangement
- Confidence about the future of China
- Perceived trust about the Government of the People's Republic of China (PRC)
- Perceived trust about the Government of the Hong Kong Special Administrative Region
- Perceived fairness of the legal system of Hong Kong
- Perceived identity of being a Chinese person or a Hong Kong person
- Perceived advantages and disadvantages of the increased closeness between Hong Kong and Mainland China

22 Quality of Life in Hong Kong

Table 22.2 Mean global and personal life domain specific satisfaction scores extracted from the reports of the indicators of social development project (Lau et al. 1991, 1992, 1995, 1997, 1999, 2001, 2003, 2005b)

Measures		1990	1993	1995	1997[a]	1997[b]	2001	2004
Global		3.487	3.376	3.397	–	–	3.34	3.34
Personal life domain	Family life	3.689	3.731	3.741	3.82	3.66	3.73	3.73
	Friends	3.689	3.680	3.687	3.74	3.65	3.74	3.74
	Relatives	3.533	3.567	3.583	3.63	3.60	3.66	3.68
	State of health	3.524	3.428	3.471	3.62	3.36	3.49	3.47
	Leisure	3.364	3.297	3.328	3.34	3.37	3.39	3.42
	Job	3.373	3.295	3.299	3.32	–	3.29	3.32
	Dwelling	3.292	3.319	3.361	3.36	3.42	3.48	3.56
	Financial situation	3.185	3.141	3.138	3.23	3.13	3.13	3.14
	Educational attainment	2.860	2.802	2.786	2.88	2.79	2.93	3.01

Note: Global = global satisfaction with life
Personal life domain
Family life = satisfaction with family life
Friends = satisfaction with friends
Relatives = satisfaction with relatives
State of health = satisfaction with state of health
Leisure = satisfaction with leisure
Job = satisfaction with work
Dwelling = satisfaction with dwelling
Financial situation = satisfaction with financial situation
Educational attainment = satisfaction with educational attainment
[a]Economically active respondents
[b]Economically inactive respondents

- Whether one has the right of abode in places outside Hong Kong
- Perceived intention to migrate elsewhere
- Perceived belongingness to Hong Kong
- Perceived social class of the respondent

It is noteworthy that the dataset based on the Indicators of Social Development Project is very substantial and the project itself is also a pioneering project on social indicators research in Hong Kong. Besides, collaboration among the three universities (The Chinese University of Hong Kong, The Hong Kong Polytechnic University, and The University of Hong Kong) is another unique feature of the project. Nevertheless, probably with the exception of the topic on subjective well-being, there are large variations in the topics covered in the eight published reports. Because of this limitation, it is not easy to dig up trend findings to look at changes in quality of life in Hong Kong over time in the reports.

In the latest report on the Indicators of Social Development (Lau et al. 2005b), several observations could be highlighted. First, with reference to global satisfaction about life, there was a "double dip" phenomenon, particularly for satisfaction with the

environmental domains (Tables 22.2 and 22.3). The first dip was between 1990 and 1997, and the second dip was between 1997 and 2004. Actually, while there was a gradual rise in the per capita GDP in this period, such rise in economic condition was not reflected in the global satisfaction index. Second, comparing to 1997, while some social problems were perceived to improve (youth, morale, pollution, public order, transport, and housing) or remained unchanged (elderly and social welfare), some social problems were seen as worse than 1997 (education, unemployment, income inequality, corruption, and health services). Third, subjective quality of life was positively related to the degree of optimism of the respondent (Wong and Zheng 2005). Fourth, throughout the years, the participants perceived individual-related attributes (health, peace of mind, and money) to be the most important ingredients for a happy life.

Social Development Index (SDI)

In contrast to the Indicators for Social Development Project in which surveys were conducted to examine

Table 22.3 Mean public sphere domain specific satisfaction scores extracted from the reports of the indicators of social development project (Lau et al. 1991, 1992, 1995, 1997, 1999, 2001, 2003, 2005b)

Measures	1990	1993	1995	1997[a]	1997[b]	2001	2004
Recreation	3.417	3.413	3.375	3.43	3.45	3.33	3.39
Education	3.208	3.226	3.292	3.32	3.46	3.04	3.06
Economic situation	3.291	3.115	2.713	3.10	3.21	2.40	2.52
Medical services	2.991	3.111	3.168	3.37	3.47	3.43	3.36
Transport	2.889	3.005	2.960	3.28	3.44	3.49	3.51
Government performance	3.062	3.004	2.855	3.13	3.26	2.69	2.52
Employment	3.334	2.966	2.374	2.71	2.54	2.31	2.39
Social welfare	2.884	2.920	2.945	3.00	3.22	3.11	3.17
Housing	2.942	2.859	2.840	2.70	2.91	3.07	3.18
Public order	2.760	2.725	2.886	3.13	3.11	3.09	3.26
Political situation	2.735	2.584	2.690	2.94	3.03	2.80	2.49

Note: Recreation = satisfaction with recreation
Education = satisfaction with education
Economic situation = satisfaction with economic situation
Medical services = satisfaction with medical services
Transport = satisfaction with transport
Government performance = satisfaction with Government performance
Employment = satisfaction with employment
Social welfare = satisfaction with social welfare
Housing = satisfaction with housing
Public order = satisfaction with public order
Political situation = satisfaction with political situation
[a]Economically active respondents
[b]Economically inactive respondents

subjective quality of life, the Social Development Index (SDI) was carried out by the Hong Kong Council of Social Service utilizing objective quality of life indices (Estes 2005; The Hong Kong Council of Social Service 2000). For the first Social Development Index (i.e., SDI-2000), the research was commissioned to Richard Estes (Estes 2005). After the establishment of the framework and database for the SDI, a Social Development Committee was set up by the Hong Kong Council of Social Service, with the author as the chairman of the committee from 2002 to 2005. To date, five reports for the SDI (SDI-2000, SDI-2002, SDI-2004, SDI-2006 and SDI-2008) have been released.

According to Estes (2005), there are several objectives of the initial development of the Social Development Index (SDI-2000) as follows: (1) to create an analytical tool to assess the changing social, political, and economic needs of the HKSAR over time; (2) to analyze Hong Kong's positive and negative development trends for the 19-year period (1981–2000); (3) to assess the quality of life in the "historically vulnerable population groups" of Hong Kong, including women, old people, children, youth, and low-income

households; (4) to assess Hong Kong's social development patterns with reference to other societies both within and outside East Asia; and (5) to collaborate with other concerned parties in Hong Kong to promote more balanced social and economic development in Hong Kong.

The development of the SDI-2000 was a collaborative process involving the researcher, the Hong Kong Council of Social Service, and a panel of experts. After incorporating the views of different stakeholders (such as the panel of experts) and some initial work, the quality of life of Hong Kong indices with reference to 14 sectors (i.e., 14 sub-indexes) involving different indicators were finalized. According to Estes (2005), several criteria were used to select the relevant indicators to be included in each sub-index. These include face validity, construct validity, reliability, representativeness, accuracy, timeliness, availability, and comparability with other measures used in other international and comparative analyses wherever possible. Estes (2005) further argued that the data to be included in the SDI should "1) satisfy at least the minimum requirements of scientific validity and reliability; 2) be collected over the long-term so that the implications of trends, patterns and changes over time can be assessed; and 3) be available to the public" (p. 187–188).

In the SDI, information on 14 sectors (i.e., 14 sub-indexes) involving 47 indicators is described. These 14 sub-indexes include Strength of Civil Sub-index (4 indicators), Political Participation Sub-index (3 indicators), Internationalization Sub-index (3 indicators), Economic Sub-index (3 indicators), Environmental Quality Sub-index (4 indicators), Arts and Entertainment Sub-index (4 indicators), Sports and Recreation Sub-index (3 indicators), Science and Technology Sub-index (2 indicators), Education Sub-index (3 indicators), Health Sub-index (6 indicators), Personal Safety Sub-index (3 indicators), Housing Sub-index (2 indicators), Crime and Public Safety Sub-index (4 indicators), and Family Solidarity Sub-index (3 indicators). The indicators in these 14 sub-indexes can be seen in Table 22.4.

Besides the above 14 sub-indexes, SDI-2000 also covered population-specific sub-indexes for the "historically vulnerable population groups" in Hong Kong (Table 22.5). These include Women's Status Sub-index (5 indicators), Low Income Sub-index (5 indicators), Child Status Sub-index (7 indicators), Young Status Sub-index (7 indicators), and Elderly Status Sub-index (7 indicators). Although these sub-indexes give a fuller picture regarding the quality of life in different population groups in Hong Kong, they were not included in the calculation of the composite SDI score.

According to Estes (2005), data based on the indicators were collected from three main sources: (a) Census and Statistics Department or other government-related bodies of the Hong Kong Government; (b) non-governmental organizations in Hong Kong that were concerned about the development of Hong Kong, such as groups that were concerned about environment human rights and selected other "civil society" organizations; and (c) international organizations such as the United Nations Development Program, the World Bank, the World Health Organization, and other selected international non-governmental organizations that are concerned about social development in different countries in a global context. In the SDI Project, across time data were collected for roughly 400 social, political, and economic indicators. Besides the indicators in the SDI Project, the remaining 320 indicators were placed in a social indicator "data bank" for future use (The Hong Kong Council of Social Service 2000).

Estes (2005) acknowledged several limitations of the SDI. First, only data from public sources were utilized. Second, related changes in the political participation and rule of law domains could not be assessed because there were no reliable data. Third, only objective data were included and no subjective quality of life data were covered in the SDI.

Objective quality of life data were utilized in the Social Development Index, with data in 1981, 1986, 1991, 1996, and 1998 used as the bases of analyses for the SDI-2000. At each time point, quality of life in Hong Kong could be reflected from the following indices: (1) standardized weighted SDI scores for Hong Kong as a whole, with a baseline score of 100 at 1991; (2) the discrete indicators included in the 14 sub-indexes in the SDI, with a baseline score of 100 at 1991; and (3) the discrete indicators included in the sub-indexes for each of five "historically vulnerable" population groups, with a baseline score of 100 at 1991.

Regarding the "change" of quality of life in Hong Kong over time, there are two ways through which the related phenomena can be examined. First, cross-sectional analyses of Hong Kong's development with respect to the discrete indicators in the 14 sub-indexes at each of five points (1981, 1986, 1991, 1996, and 1998) give some idea about the change of quality of life across this time period. Second, the change of the social development in Hong Kong between 1986 and 1996 was assessed by the trend scores. For example, the trend scores at 1998 (i.e., T-1998 scores) were computed with reference to 1986–1996 as the baseline period. The related scores provide an estimate of the *pace* at which changes in development occurred *over time* for each of the SDI's 14 sub-indexes. It should be noted that based on the views of the panel of experts, statistical weights were used to compute the composite SDI and sub-index scores. In the subsequent reports of the SDI (SDI-2002, SDI-2004, SDI-2006, and SDI-2008), similar indices and weights were constructed.

To address the public concern about the lack of measures about the rule of law in Hong Kong, the Hong Kong Council of Social Service has set up an expert panel to develop an additional Rule of Law Sub-index. In contrast to the rest of the sub-indexes in the SDI, the Rule of Law Sub-index was constructed with reference to both quantitative and qualitative data. For the quantitative data, legal statistics related to rule of law in Hong Kong (such as number of judicial review

Table 22.4 Social indicators used to form the SDI-2000 arranged by Development Sector (14 sectors and 47 indicators)

Sector	Indicator
Strength of civil society sub-index (4 indicators)	• No. charitable institutions & trusts qualifying for tax exemption (+)*
	• Private charitable donation as % of GDP (+)
	• Ratio of private charitable donations to government subvention (+)
	• % of work force affiliated with trade unions (+)
Political participation sub-index (3 indicators)	• Turn out in most recent District Board elections (+)
	• Ratio of candidates to territory wide political offices (+)
	• % District Board candidates with political party affiliations (+)
Internationalization sub-index (3 indicators)	• Number of countries that HK residents can travel to without visa (+)
	• Number of registered companies incorporated outside Hong Kong (+)
	• Number of international conferences held in Hong Kong (+)
Economic sub-index (3 indicators)	• Per capita GDP at constant 1990 market prices (+)
	• Gross international reserves (months of import coverage) (+)
	• Percentage of total household income earned by bottom 50% of households (+)
Environmental quality sub-index (4 indicators)	• % of gazetted beaches ranked as poor/very poor (−)
	• Per capita area of public open space (sq. meters) (+)
	• Per capita domestic units fresh water consumption (−)
	• % municipal solid waste recycled (+)
Arts & entertainment sub-index (4 indicators)	• No. buildings and sites declared as monuments (+)
	• No. films produced locally (+)
	• No. books and magazines first published in Hong Kong (+)
	• Attendance at museums & cultural venues/100,000 (+)
Sports & recreation sub-index (3 indicators)	• No. of public sporting facilities (+)
	• Average utilization rate of public sporting facilities (+)
	• Size of delegation participating in major games (+)
Science & technology sub-index (2 indicators)	• No. patents granted to HK entities (residents)
	• No. scientific publications in refereed publications (+)
Education sub-index (3 indicators)	• % age 20+ with upper secondary educational attainment (+)
	• % of persons aged 15 or older having attained tertiary education (+)
	• Adults in continuing education per 100,000 (+)
Health sub-index (6 indicators)	• Average life expectation at birth (+)
	• Infant mortality rate per 1,000 live born (−)
	• Tuberculosis cases per 100,000 population (−)
	• Adults smoking per 100,000 population (−)
	• Deaths from coronary heart diseases/100,000 (−)
	• Suicides per 100,000 adults aged 20+ (−)
Personal safety sub-index (3 indicators)	• Reported food poisoning cases per 100,000 population (−)
	• No. occupational fatalities per 100,000 workers (−)
	• No. traffic fatalities per 100,000 population (−)
Housing sub-index (2 indicators)	• Expenditure on housing as share of total household income (−)
	• No. waiting list applicants for housing authority rental flats (−)
Crime & public safety sub-index (4 indicators)	• Violent crimes per 100,000 population (−)
	• Non-violent crimes per 100,000 population (−)
	• % population reporting victimized by violent crime (−)
	• No. corruption crime convictions per 100,000 (−)
Family solidarity sub-index (3 indicators)	• Marriages per 100,000 persons aged 15+ (+)
	• Divorces as % of marriages (−)
	• Reported domestic violence cases per 100,000 (−)

Note: Plus (+) and minus (−) signs are used to indicate the directional relationship of each indicator to social development.
* For example, a higher number of "charitable institutions and trusts qualifying for tax exemption" is conceptualized as an indication of increased strength of the Civil Society sector which, in turn, is conceptualized as an indication of movement toward a higher level of social development

Table 22.5 Social indicators used to form population-specific sub-indexes for Hong Kong's historically vulnerable population groups (5 sectors involving 31 indicators)

Sector	Indicator
Women's status sub-index (5 Indicators)	• % of women in low-income households (−) • Married women's labor force participation rate (+) • Median women's wages as % of median men's wages, all ages (+) • % women administrators and managers (+) • % District Board political positions occupied (+)
Low income sub-index (5 indicators)	• No. of persons in low-income domestic households/100,000 (−) • % low income household expenditure on housing and food (−) • Unemployment rate of persons in low-income households (−) • Real wage index of wage workers (+) • Homeless persons per 100,000 population (−)
Child status sub-index (7 indicators)	• % children aged 0–14 in low-income households (−) • % children living in single parent households (−) • Under age 5 child mortality per 100,000 (−) • Children aged 2–6 enrolled in kindergarten and child care centers (+) • Child abuse cases per 100,000 (−) • % children immunized against DPT (+) • Children 7–15 arrested per 100,000 (−)
Youth status sub-index (7 indicators)	• % of youth aged 15–19 in low-income households (−) • % of youth aged 15–19 attaining S4 or above (+) • % aged 15–24 studying full-time at tertiary education (+) • Youth unemployment rate (−) • Arrests of persons age 16–20 for violent crimes per 100,000 (−) • Prevalence of drug use among persons 15–19 (−) • Youth suicide rate, aged 10–19 years (−)

cases and number of judges per 1,000,000 persons) were collected. For the subjective perception data, data collected by the Public Opinion Program of The University of Hong Kong on the respondents' perceptions of the rule of law (e.g., ratings by citizens on the impartiality of the court in Hong Kong) were collected. Two groups of informants (personnel in the legal process and law-related organizations) were then invited to weight the indicators for the rule of law. Based on the data collected, the Rule of Law Sub-index was computed based on the weighted raw scores. According to the Hong Kong Council of Social Service (2005), the value of the Rule of Law Sub-index (75 points out of 100) could be regarded to be on the high side in Hong Kong.

In the latest release of the SDI report (SDI-2008), several major observations can be highlighted (Chua et al. 2010). First, there has been a steady increase in social development in Hong Kong. Compared to the scores of 1991 (score = 100), 1996 (score = 122), 1998 (score = 129), 2000 (score = 139), 2002 (score = 144), and 2004 (score = 158), the score of 2006 was 170, which was the highest among these years (see Fig. 22.1). Second, with reference to 1986–1996 as the base years, positive changes in social development were found in different areas in 2006, except family solidarity (Fig. 22.2). Third, despite progress in different domains of social development, it is noteworthy that there has been a substantial drop in family solidarity (Fig. 22.3). Finally, an examination of the trends of social development by sub-indexes in SDI-2000, SDI-2002, SDI-2004, SDI-2006, and SDI-2008 shows that the development of children, youth, and low-income families was recorded to have negative development in all the SDI-reports (Fig. 22.4). An examination of the recent release of the Social Development Index (SDI-2010) showed that the above trends persisted.

The CUHK Hong Kong Quality of Life Index

In contrast to the Indicators of Social Development Project and the Social Development Index in which either official data or survey data are employed, the CUHK Hong Kong Quality of Life Index can be regarded as more comprehensive because both objective and subjective measures are included. According to Chan at al. (2005), the objectives of the CUHK Hong Kong Quality of Life Index are to (1) measure and monitor the quality of life in Hong Kong in the twenty-first century, (2) engage relevant parties in promoting the quality of life in Hong Kong, (3) provide policymakers and the community with useful statistics on the quality of life in Hong Kong, and (4) draw public attention to the issue of quality of life. There are three sub-indexes (socio-cultural sub-index, economic sub-index, and environmental sub-index), including 21 indicators in the CUHK Hong Kong QOL Index (see Table 22.6). According to Chan et al. (2005), these

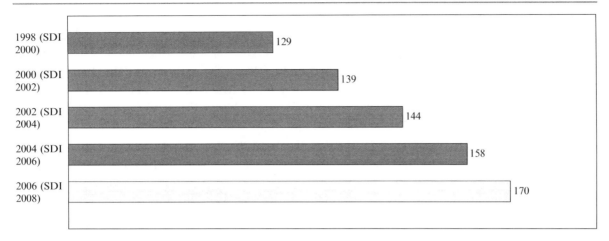

Fig. 22.1 SDI-2000 to SDI-2008 (base year 1991 = 100)

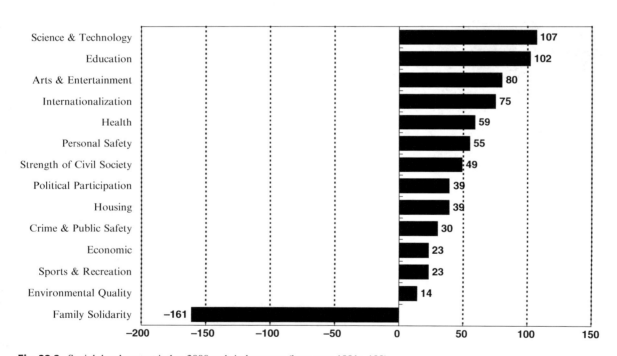

Fig. 22.2 Social development index-2000: sub-index score (base year 1991 = 100)

indicators were selected according to their coverage, measurability, representativeness, and importance to the quality of life in Hong Kong.

For the socio-cultural sub-index, there are 10 indicators. These include standardized mortality rate (per 1,000 standard population), life expectancy at birth, public expenditure on health as a proportion of the GDP, notification rate of notifiable infectious diseases (per 1,000 population), stress index, general life satisfaction index, press freedom index, press criticism index, government performance index, and overall crime rate (per 1,000 population). For the economic sub-index, there are 7 indicators covering housing affordability ratio (annual average of affordable property prices), rental index, unemployment rate, index of current economic conditions, real wage index, public

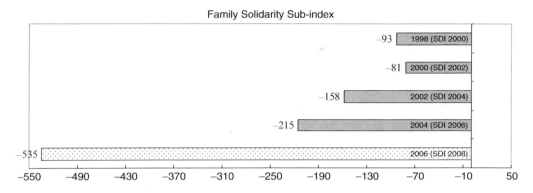

Fig. 22.3 Family solidarity sub-index 2008 (base year 1991 = 100)

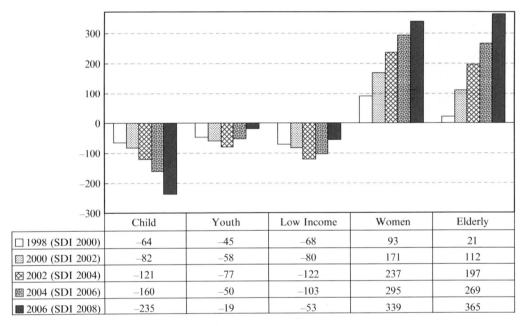

Fig. 22.4 Social development trends for Hong Kong's five population groups (1998, 2000, 2002, 2004 and 2006) (base year 1991 = 100)

expenditure on education as a proportion of the GDP, and age participation rate for first-degree programs and postgraduate programs in local universities. Finally, the environmental sub-index (4 indicators) comprises measures of air index, water index, noise index (per 1,000 population), and recycle rate of municipal solid waste. The definition of the different indicators in the CUHK QOL Index can be seen in Table 22.6.

For each sub-index, a composite QOL score is computed. By summing the QOL scores in these three sub-indexes, a QOL composite index is derived. Taking the year of 2002 as the base year of the study, the CUHK Hong Kong Quality of Life Index of 2002 is 100. If the Index of a year is above 100, it means that the quality of life in Hong Kong in that year is better than that in 2002. If it is below 100, it reveals that the quality of life in Hong Kong in that year is worse than that in 2002. If the Index is 100, it indicates that quality of life in Hong Kong in that year is the same as that in 2002. Hence, among the three subgroups, the socio-cultural sub-index bears the heaviest weight in the composite index, while the environmental sub-index carries the lightest. These sub-indexes allow an in-depth

Table 22.6 Composition of the CUHK Hong Kong quality of life index

Sector	Indicator
Socio-cultural sub-index (10 indicators)	• [a]Standardized mortality rate (per 1,000 standard population)[a] refers to the number of deaths per 1,000 standard population
	• Life expectancy at birth (in years) refers to the life expectancy at birth for males and females
	• Public expenditure on health as a proportion (in %) of the GDP
	• Notification rate of notifiable infectious diseases (per 1,000 population) refers to the number of notified infectious diseases per 1,000 population
	• Stress index refers to the stress that the Hong Kong people are facing (base rate = 100)
	• General life satisfaction index refers to the degree of satisfaction of Hong Kong people with their current lives (base rate = 100)
	• Press freedom index refers to the degree of press freedom in Hong Kong (base rate = 100)
	• Press criticism index refers to the frequency of criticisms by the press of the Hong Kong Corporation, the Hong Kong SAR Government, and the People's Republic of China Government (base rate = 100)
	• Government performance index refers to the degree of satisfaction of Hong Kong people with the performance of the Hong Kong SAR Government (base rate = 100)
	• Overall crime rate (per 1,000 population) refers to the total number of violent and non-violent crimes reported per 1,000 population
Economic sub-index (7 indicators)	• Housing affordability ratio refers to the annual average of affordable property prices (i.e. average property price times 39.9 sq. feet, divided by monthly medium income times 12)
	• Rental index refers to the rental index for the Hong Kong property market
	• Unemployment rate refers to the seasonally adjusted unemployment rate (in %)
	• Index of current economic conditions refers to the public attitude towards economic conditions in Hong Kong
	• Real wage index[b] refers to the real wages for employees up to supervisory level (excluding managerial and professional employees) in all selected industry sectors
	• Public expenditure on education as a proportion (in %) of the GDP
	• Age participation rate for first-degree programs and postgraduate programs in local universities (in %)
Environmental sub-index (4 indicators)	• Air index refers to the daily air pollution index
	• Water index refers to the percentage of rivers in Hong Kong categorized as "good" and "excellent" by the monitoring station
	• Noise index (per 1,000 population) refers to the number of noise complaints received by the Environmental Protection Department and the Police per 1,000 population
	• Recycle rate of municipal solid waste refers to the recycle rate (in %) of solid waste from households and from commercial and industrial sources

[a]Standardized mortality rate is compiled based on the world standard population published in the 1997–1999 World Health Statistics Annual
[b]As from 2001, the real wage index is derived by deflating the nominal wage indices by the 1999/2000-based CPI (A). To facilitate comparison, real wage index prior to 2001 has been re-compiled using the 1999/2000-based CPI (A)

examination of important domains of public concern, while the composite index monitors the overall quality of life.

Among the 21 indicators, six are compiled by the Faculty of Social Science of The Chinese University of Hong Kong. They include the stress index, the general life satisfaction index, the press freedom index, the press criticism index, the government performance index, and the index of current economic conditions. These six indices are measures of individuals' subjective feelings. Among them, four indices of the CUHK

QOL Index (stress, press freedom, government performance, and general life satisfaction) are based on survey data conducted by the Faculty of Social Science, CUHK, involving adults aged 18 and above, and the data were collected through telephone interviews (computer-assisted telephone interviews) using structured questionnaires. The related data were collected from probability samples of Hong Kong residents.

For the stress index, it includes 12 items related to stress ("being able to concentrate on whatever one is doing over past few weeks"; "feeling on the whole that one is doing things well over past few weeks"; "feeling capable of making decisions about things over past few weeks"; "being able to enjoy one's normal day-to-day activities over past few weeks"; "being able to face up to one's problems over past few weeks"; "feeling reasonably happy, all things considered, over past few weeks"; "losing much sleep through worry over past few weeks"; "feeling constantly under strain over past few weeks"; "feeling one could not overcome one's difficulties over past few weeks"; "feeling unhappy and depressed over past few weeks"; "losing confidence in oneself over past few weeks"; "thinking of oneself as a worthless person over past few weeks").

For the general satisfaction index, there are 5 items involved. They are "life being close to ideal in most ways," "conditions of life are excellent", "being satisfied with life", "having secured the most important thing in life", and "would change almost nothing in case of being able to live one's life over".

For the press freedom index, there are 4 items as follows: "when one comments on current affairs, the extent to which one can speak one's mind freely"; "when one criticizes the HKSAR Government, the extent to which one can speak one's mind freely"; "when one criticizes the PRC Government, the extent to which one can speak one's mind freely"; and "when one criticizes big business, the extent to which one can speak one's mind freely". Besides, the respondents are requested to give a score on the degree of press freedom of Hong Kong on a scale from 0 to 10. In short, there are five measures for the press freedom index.

For the government performance index, two measures are used. The participants are asked whether they are satisfied with the performance of HKSAR Government over the last 6 months and rate the performance of HKSAR Government over the last 6 months on a scale from 0 to 10.

The index of current economic conditions is derived from the Quarterly Survey of Consumers that is conducted by the Department of Economics at The Chinese University of Hong Kong. In each quarter, the Department of Economics carries out telephone interviews with a minimum of 500 telephone interviews based on random samples. Two questions are used: "Would you say that you (and your family living there) are better off or worse off financially than you were a year ago?"; "There are big things people buy for their

homes such as furniture and refrigerator, stove, television, and things like that. Generally speaking, do you think now is a good or bad time for people to buy major household items?"

Finally, for the indicator of press criticism, it is constructed from results of content analysis. For example, with reference to the CUHK QOL Index 2003, the news reported by six local newspapers from August 2001 to July 2003 was sampled by the "Constructed Sample Week" method. Each day from Monday to Saturday was randomly selected to construct a sample week in each month. After sampling all the newspapers, the content was analyzed according to their news categories and major geographical locus of concern to measure the extent of press criticism of the Hong Kong Government, the PRC Government, and Hong Kong big business. Fifty samples were analyzed by all coders to determine the inter-coder reliability, which was above 70% for all key variables.

The data on the remaining 15 indicators are obtained from public sources, which include the annual reports of the HKSAR Census and Statistics Department and those of the HKSAR Health Department (for vital statistics, crime statistics, and physical health statistics, etc.), and the quarterly reports of the HKSAR Census and Statistics Department (for wages, price indices, inflation rates, etc.). They are measures of objective environmental conditions.

In the latest release of the CUHK QOL Index, several observations can be highlighted for the year 2009 (Tables 22.7 and 22.8). First, there was a drop in quality of life as far as the overall quality of life is concerned (from 104.83 in 2008 to 102.19 in 2009). Second, with reference to the different sub-domains, while there were increases in QOL scores in the Economic Sub-index (31.15 in 2008 to 31.93 in 2009) and Environmental Sub-index (23.18 in 2008 to 24.05 in 2009), development based on the Social Sub-index (50.50 in 2008 and 46.21 in 2009) deteriorated. Third, regarding the discrete indicators, while there was improvement in several areas (e.g., mortality rate, life expectancy, public expenditure on health, stress index, life satisfaction, Government performance, crime rate, real rental, current economic conditions, public expenditure on education, air index, water index, noise index, and recycle rate of municipal solid waste), the performance in several indicators (infectious diseases, press criticism, housing affordability, unemployment rate, and real wage rate) had deteriorated.

Table 22.7 Data for compiling the "CUHK" Hong Kong Quality of Life Index (2005)

		2002	2003	2004	2005	2006	2007	2008	2009
Social-cultural sub-index									
1.	Standardized mortality rate (per 1,000 standard population)	3.70	3.80	3.80	3.70	3.50	3.50	3.50[a]	3.40[b]
2.	Life expectancy at birth (in years)	F: 84.5	F: 84.3	F: 84.7	F: 84.6	F: 85.5	F: 85.5	F: 85.5[a]	F: 86.1[b]
		M: 78.6	M: 78.5	M: 79	M: 78.8	M: 79.4	M: 79.4	M: 79.3[a]	M: 79.8[b]
3.	Public expenditure on health as a proportion (in percent) of the GDP	2.70	2.70	2.70	2.30	2.10	2.20	2.00	2.30
4.	Notification rate of notifiable infectious diseases (per 1,000 population)	3.73	2.33	2.89	2.91	3.27	3.65	2.38[a]	6.88
5.	Stress index	100.00	88.75	79.51	72.95	74.42	72.91	80.36	80.00
6.	General life satisfaction index	100.00	100.68	105.62	109.94	112.47	110.22	107.57	111.66
7.	Press freedom index	100.00	101.22	100.26	101.43	101.55	103.92	103.64	103.54
8.	Press criticism index	100.00	103.75	91.02	78.82	77.25	81.86	83.65	79.15
9.	Government performance index	100.00	103.23	132.23	169.79	176.29	183.48	130.48	145.10
10.	Overall crime rate (per 1,000 population)	11.18	12.99	11.81	11.37	11.83	11.67	11.25[a]	11.08
Economic sub-index									
11.	Housing affordability ratio	4.68	4.49	5.31	6.22	5.88	6.82	7.67	8.20
12.	Real rental index	87.97	79.67	84.55	93.11	96.68	105.27	107.67	91.70
13.	Unemployment rate	7.34	7.93	6.76	5.55	4.69	3.92	3.68	5.17
14.	Index of current economic conditions	76.55	81.32	99.95	109.75	109.48	116.70	81.55	83.40
15.	Real wage index	117.53	117.70	116.35	115.78	115.48	116.08	116.68	116.30
16.	Public expenditure on education as a proportion (in percent) of the GDP	4.10	4.40	4.40	4.00	3.80	3.50	3.40	4.50
17.	Age participation rate for first-degree programs and postgraduate programs in local universities (in percent)	17.04	17.70	17.50	17.60	18.50	18.70	18.50	18.50
Environmental sub-index									
18.	Air index	46.90	49.93	49.32	45.10	45.68	45.77	44.83	42.26
19.	Water index	74.40	75.60	78.30	80.80	80.80	80.70	81.70[a]	85.03[c]
20.	Noise index (per 1,000 population)	1.84	1.43	1.63	1.24	1.28	1.15	1.07	1.02
21.	Recycle rate of municipal solid waste	36.30	40.82	40.35	43.09	45.59	44.96	47.58[a]	49.67[c]

[a]Revised figure
[b]Provisional figure
[c]Forecasted figure

Major Observations Based on the Quality of Life Studies in Hong Kong

Suppose a lay person asks whether the quality of life of Hong Kong people is "good" or "bad," what answers do we have? In view of the multi-dimensional nature of QOL (e.g., personal, family, and social quality of life) and the different conceptualizations involved, the answer cannot be easily determined. The complexity of the problem is further aggregated by the fact that different methodologies were involved in different studies. In this section, I attempt to highlight the major observations that can be drawn from the existing studies of quality of life in Hong Kong, particularly those involving the collection of trend data.

Observation 1: There Is Progress in the Quality of Life of Hong Kong after 1997

Several sources of evidence suggest that the quality of life of Hong Kong is making steady progress throughout the past decade. First, with specific reference to the

22 Quality of Life in Hong Kong

Table 22.8 Summary of the "CUHK" Hong Kong quality of life index since its establishment in 2002

		2002 (base year)	2003	2004	2005	2006	2007	2008	2009	2009 compared w/2008
Social sub-index										
1.	Standardized mortality rate (per 1,000 standard population)	4.76	4.63	4.63	4.76	5.02	5.02	5.02[a]	5.15[b]	Better
2.	Life expectancy at birth (in year)	4.76	4.75	4.78	4.77	4.81	4.81	4.81[a]	4.84[b]	Better
3.	Public expenditure on health as a proportion (in percent) of the GDP	4.76	4.76	4.76	4.05	3.70	3.88	3.53	4.05	Better
4.	Notification rate of notifiable infectious diseases (per 1,000 population)	4.76	6.55	5.83	5.81	5.35	4.86	6.48[a]	0.74	**Worse**
5.	Stress index	4.76	5.30	5.74	6.05	5.98	6.05	5.69	5.71	Better
6.	General life satisfaction index	4.76	4.79	5.03	5.23	5.35	5.25	5.12	5.31	Better
7.	Press freedom index	4.76	4.82	4.77	4.83	4.83	4.95	4.93	4.93	Same
8.	Press criticism index	4.76	4.94	4.33	3.75	3.68	3.90	3.98	3.77	**Worse**
9.	Government performance index	4.76	4.91	6.29	8.08	8.39	8.73	6.21	6.91	Better
10.	Overall crime rate (per 1,000 population)	4.76	3.99	4.49	4.68	4.48	4.55	4.73[a]	4.80	Better
Social sub-index		**47.62**	**49.44**	**50.65**	**52.01**	**51.59**	**52.00**	**50.50[a]**	**46.21**	**Worse**
Economic sub-index										
11.	Housing affordability ratio	4.76	4.95	4.12	3.19	3.54	2.58	1.72	1.18	**Worse**
12.	Real rental index	4.76	5.21	4.95	4.20	4.00	3.51	3.38	4.29	Better
13.	Unemployment rate	4.76	4.38	5.14	5.92	6.48	6.98	7.13	6.17	**Worse**
14.	Index of current economic conditions	4.76	5.06	6.22	6.82	6.81	7.26	5.07	5.19	Better
15.	Real wage index	4.76	4.77	4.71	4.69	4.68	4.70	4.73[a]	4.71	**Worse**
16.	Public expenditure on education as a proportion (in percent) of the GDP	4.76	4.99	4.99	4.53	4.41	4.06	3.95	5.22	Better
17.	Age participation rate for first-degree programs and postgraduate programs in local universities (in percent)	4.76	4.94	4.89	4.92	5.17	5.22	5.17	5.17	Same
Economic sub-index		**33.32**	**34.30**	**35.02**	**34.27**	**35.09**	**34.31**	**31.15**	**31.93**	**Better**
Environmental sub-index										
18.	Air index	4.76	4.45	4.51	4.94	4.88	4.87	4.97	5.23	Better
19.	Water index	4.76	4.84	5.01	5.16	5.17	5.16	5.23[a]	5.44[c]	Better
20.	Noise index (per 1,000 population)	4.76	5.82	5.30	6.31	6.22	6.54	6.74	6.87	Better
21.	Recycle rate of municipal solid waste	4.76	5.35	5.29	5.65	5.98	5.90	6.24[a]	6.51[c]	Better
Environmental sub-index		**19.04**	**20.46**	**20.11**	**22.06**	**22.25**	**22.47**	**23.18**	**24.05**	**Better**
Quality of life index		**100.00**	**104.20**	**105.78**	**108.34**	**108.93**	**108.78**	**104.83[a]**	**102.19**	**Worse**

Remarks: The higher the score, the better of the performance of the indicator

[a]Revised figure

[b]Provisional figure

[c]Forecasted figure

2009 Human Development Report (United Nations Development Program 2009), it was observed that Hong Kong has progressed steadily in terms of the Human Development Index from 1980 (0.693) to 1995 (0.797), 2005 (0.842), 2009 (0.857), and 2010 (0.862). In addition, Hong Kong was classified as a place with "very high" human development. Second, an examination of the standardized SDI scores which reflected the overall social development in the different years under study showed that there has been gradual progress in the overall quality of life in Hong Kong (Fig. 22.1). The standardized weighted SDI scores were 100 and

170 in 1991 and 2006, respectively. With reference to the different sub-indexes in the SDI, an examination of the patterns in Fig. 22.2 shows that except family solidarity, there has been progress in most of the domains throughout time. Finally, the findings based on the CUHK Hong Kong QOL Index further showed that there was progress in the overall quality of life across time: the overall QOL score was 100 in 2002 and 108.93 in 2006, with a slight drop in recent years. In short, based on the major international and local databases with primarily official statistics, there has been gradual progress in the quality of life in Hong Kong.

Observation 2: Despite the Progress in Hong Kong as a Whole, Quality of Life in Some Social Groups Has Declined

As shown in Fig. 22.4, the development of children, youth, and low-income families has deteriorated throughout time. These observations suggest that although there is global improvement in the quality of life in Hong Kong in the past two decades, some of the groups cannot benefit from the overall progress of the society.

According to the Commission on Youth (2003), the proportion of young people living in low-income households increased in the past decade. In 1991, the percentage of the youth aged 15–19 living in low-income households was 11.0%. However, the rate climbed to 18.3% in 2000. Regarding young people receiving Comprehensive Social Security Assistance, statistics showed that youth poverty in Hong Kong had become serious (Commission on Youth 2003). Based on the statistics of the Social Welfare Department, the number of young CSSA recipients increased substantially between 1996 and 2002, with 40,694 young CSSA recipients in 2002. Using the percentage of young CSSA recipients in relation to total CSSA recipients, the related proportion increased from 5.7% in 1996 to 9.0% in 2002. Similarly, the figures on primary and secondary students applying for School Textbook Assistance Scheme from the Student Financial Assistance Agency also reflect the problem of poverty in young people. With reference to the related statistics in the past 5 years, the general picture is that the number of students who received full textbook allowance have increased for primary school students (from 2% in 1997/1998 school year to 7.7% in 2001/2002) and

for secondary school students (from 1.5% in 1997/1998 school year to 3.1% in 1998/1999). In short, an integration of the statistics from several sources generally suggests that the number of young people experiencing economic disadvantage has increased in the past few years.

In his discussion of social stress in Hong Kong, Shek (2005b) drew the conclusion that "the whole is not equal to the sum total of its parts." That is, while the available epidemiological studies and official statistics can give us some *general* pictures on the social stress confronting the community at large, they may not be able to give us ideas on the social stress in *particular* social groups. Actually, if we focus our attention on the population as a whole, the general impression is that social stress may not be a serious problem for the majority of Hong Kong people. However, this perspective may give a false impression that stress is uniformly distributed in different social groups in Hong Kong. For example, with reference to suicide rates as an indicator of quality of life, while the suicide rates for the whole population is not particular high, elderly suicide rates were found to be higher than all the other age groups in the past two decades (Shek et al. 2005c).

Observation 3: Subjective Quality of Life Has Declined after 1997

With reference to the findings of the Indicators of Social Development Project (e.g., Lau et al. 2005b), it was observed that the global quality of life of people in Hong Kong has declined after 1997. As pointed out by Lau et al. (2005b), in contrast to the gradual rise GDP per capita in Hong Kong in the past decade, the reverse pattern was found for global satisfaction with life. In other words, the betterment of the economic condition is not matched with the rise in subjective quality of life of Hong Kong people. Similar findings are also revealed from the Public Opinion Poll Program (2006) conducted by The University of Hong Kong where public's perceptions of different aspects of the development of Hong Kong are regularly surveyed. The available statistics show that compared with the findings collected in 1997, participants in 2006 perceived democracy, freedom, prosperity, stability, fairness, civilization, and rule of law in Hong Kong to be relatively poorer.

Observation 4: There Are Warning Signals About Declining Quality of Life in Hong Kong

There are several sources of evidence that give warning signals about the declining quality of life in Hong Kong. First, with reference to the Social Development Index, the findings clearly suggest that drop in family solidarity is a problem. In fact, this is the single indicator that has declined in the various reports of the SDI (SDI-2000, SDI-2002, SDI-2004, SDI-2006, SDI-2008, and SDI-2010). Second, with reference to the Indicators of Social Development Project, the respondents perceived deterioration in the domains of education, unemployment, income inequality, corruption, and health services. Third, based on the CUHK Hong Kong QOL Index, it was found that there was deterioration in public expenditure on health as a proportion of the GDP, press criticism index, and housing affordability index.

Although Hong Kong is always proud of its economic growth throughout the years, there is increasing evidence suggesting income inequality is a worsening problem in Hong Kong. If we look at the values of the Gini coefficients over time, it is obvious that the related values have increased throughout the years (0.430 in 1971, 0.429 in 1976, 0.451 in 1981, 0.453 in 1986, 0.476 in 1991, 0.518 in 1996, and 0.525 in 2001, Commission on Poverty 2006). In addition, the unemployment problem among the middle-aged people has continued to be a disturbing social issue in Hong Kong. Because Hong Kong has experienced the difficulty in economic restructuring, unemployment among middle-aged workers is still a big social problem.

Furthermore, some research findings suggest that the price that Hong Kong people have to pay to achieve the "economic miracle" is not low. In a recent study of the working hours among Hong Kong workers, results showed that the working hours in the working force in Hong Kong was the second longest in the world (Union Bank of Switzerland 2006). Furthermore, there are research findings showing that there has been a gradual rise in the suicide rates in Hong Kong. For example, Shek et al. (2005c) showed that there had been a gradual rise in adolescent suicide rates in Hong Kong. Finally, there are research findings suggesting that mental health problems among Hong Kong people are not uncommon. According to the Hong Kong Mood Disorders Centre (2006), it was estimated that significant proportions of people in Hong Kong displayed excessive depressive symptoms (12%), social anxiety symptoms (10%), and psychosomatic symptoms (7%).

Finally, echoing the findings of the SDI that there has been a drop in family solidarity in Hong Kong, there are also research findings showing that the family quality of life in Hong Kong deserves attention. In a recent comparative study between Hong Kong and Shanghai on parenting and parent–adolescent relational qualities, Shek et al. (2006) reported that compared with adolescents in Shanghai, adolescents in Hong Kong reported lower levels of parental behavioral control, a higher level of parental psychological control, and lower levels of parent–adolescent relational qualities.

Observation 5: Perceived Quality of Life Is Related to Factors in Different Systems

With particular reference to those studies examining subjective quality of life, several categories of factors were found to be related to subjective quality of life. First, some personal factors were related to quality of life. For example, age was linearly related to adolescent hopelessness (Shek and Lee 2005), and females generally experienced a higher level of family quality of life (Shek 2002a). Second, Wong and Zheng (2005) presented findings showing that optimism about the future was related to level of perceived satisfaction with the different personal and environmental domains.

Regarding the extra-individual correlates of subjective quality of life, there are several factors involved. First, there is a vast literature suggesting that different family processes such as family functioning and parenting processes are related to subjective well-being of adolescents in Hong Kong (Shek 1999a, b). Second, interpersonal factors (e.g., social capital such as social support) have been found to be related to psychological well-being on the personal level (Shek 2002b). Third, several macrosocial factors were related to subjective quality of life. There are research findings showing that economic disadvantage and poverty are related to adolescent psychological well-being (Shek 2005a). In addition, social class and perceived social class are related to subjective quality of life. Unfortunately, despite the vast literature on the psychosocial correlates on perceived quality of life, few

Observation 6: Quality of Life in Hong Kong Is Better than Quality of Life in China Based on Some Indicators

There are several lines of evidence suggesting that quality of Hong Kong is better than that of Mainland China. Based on the Human Development Report (2010), Hong Kong was superior to China in terms of the Human Development Index. While Hong Kong was regarded as a place with "very high" level of human development, China was regarded as a country with "medium" level of human development. Second, an examination of the available suicide statistics also showed that suicide rates in China were comparatively higher than those of Hong Kong (Shek et al. 2005c). In particular, suicide rates in rural China were alarmingly high. Third, some comparative studies utilizing existing quality of life indexes conducted by the Mainland scholars also revealed that quality of life in Hong Kong was comparatively better than that of Mainland China. Zhu (1996) reported that based on 16 indicators composed by scholars in Mainland China, Hong Kong ranked 25 and China ranked 66 in terms of the overall social development.

Observation 7: There Are Conflicting Pictures Based on Different Studies

While the above observations are based on convergence of research findings in different studies, it should be noted that the pictures derived from the existing quality of life studies are not entirely consistent. While the conclusions based on the objective measures of quality of life suggest that there has been progress in the quality of life of Hong Kong, subjective quality of life studies assessed by the Indicators of Social Development Project generally do not reach similar conclusions. For example, the picture derived from the Human Development Index and the Social Development Index is very positive—that the quality of life in Hong Kong is high and there is much progress in the past two decades. Nevertheless, if we look at the picture based on the subjective quality of life surveys, the picture is less rosy. The findings from the Indicators of Social Development Project are clearly suggesting that despite economic growth in Hong Kong, people have become less satisfied throughout the years. Another example is that although the Social Development Index suggests that education has progressed throughout the year, people were not satisfied with the education system (Lau et al. 2005b). The final example is related to the area of corruption. While Hong Kong ranked 15 in 193 countries in the 2006 Transparent International Corruption Perceptions Index (Transparency International 2006), 76% of the surveyed companies believed they had lost business in the last 5 years because competitors had paid bribes (Control Risks and Simmons and Simmons 2006).

Methodological Issues Deserving Attention

To what extent the pictures on quality of life in Hong Kong based on the existing studies represent the "reality"? It is noteworthy that there are several methodological issues that should be taken into account when the available research findings are interpreted. The first issue is whether the indicators covered in the existing major quality of life databases are representative of the quality of life of people in Hong Kong. Assuming that quantitative approach is a defensible approach that can be used to chart social development, the next question that should be asked is how the indicators are selected. In the Social Development Index, the proposed indicators are based on a thorough literature review and the views of the panels of experts. For the critical theorists, they would probably query whether this would lead to biases of the elites and whether the views of the underprivileged are adequately represented. For theorists adhering to positivism, they would ask whether the indicators used are representative and whether they have construct validity. For the constructivists, they would query whether the inclusion of official statistics would be adequate to reflect the fluid nature of social development. For the Indicators of Social Development Project, one can query why domains such as social justice, spirituality, social harmony, and globalization are not covered in the subjective well-being measures.

Perhaps the most relevant challenge for those subjective quality of life studies is whether the notion of subjective quality of life and its components, which are primarily based on hedonist principles, are most relevant to Chinese people. In the traditional Confucian thoughts, an ideal life is not based on personal satisfaction but one's fulfillment of duties in connection with the five cardinal relations. In the Buddhist thoughts, an ideal life is also not based on personal satisfaction but one's sacrifice and sufferings. In the traditional Taoist thought, an ideal life is again not defined by personal satisfaction but harmony with the self, others, and nature. In addition, as Chinese people are more collectivistic in their orientation of self, it should be asked whether subjective quality of life constructs which are based on the notion of "an autonomous man" are of primary importance to Chinese people (Markus and Kitayama 1991).

The second methodological issue concerns the reliability and validity of quality of life measures, particularly in those quality of life projects involving the collection of trend data. The basic problem is that single-item or single-measure indicators are commonly used to assess different dimensions of quality of life. For example, in the Indicators of Social Development Project, several single-item indicators were used to assess satisfaction of different personal domains (such as satisfaction with friends, family, relatives, etc.) and environmental domains (e.g., transport, Government, etc.). Obviously, while single-item measures have the strengths of convenience and simplicity, the reliability and validity of single-item measures cannot be easily determined. Although Shen and Lai (1999) developed composite measures of quality of life based on factor analysis, these composite indicators were unfortunately not extensively used in the subsequent surveys and analyses. From the perspective of classical test theory, it is maintained that an observed score could be decomposed into three components—true score, score due to random error, and score reflecting systematic error. As single-item measure of subjective quality of life may be highly susceptible to systematic and random errors, the findings based on single-item measure should be interpreted in a cautious manner. For the Social Development Index, although Estes (2005) suggested that reliable and valid measures were used in the SDI, only face validity based on the comments of the panel of experts was examined. The basic question of whether the indicators used can be combined to form the 14 dimensions in the SDI has never been clearly examined.

Based on the argument that multiple item measures are more valid and reliable than single-item measures of quality of life, the third methodological issue concerns the adequacy of locally validated measures of quality of life. A review of the existing literature shows that with a few exceptions (e.g., Lau et al. 2005a; Siu and Shek 2005), there are not many locally validated measures on quality of life, particularly with respect to the general population. Shek (2002c) pointed out that there were few measures of psychosocial functioning of Chinese people. Shek et al. (2005a) also remarked that there were not many locally validated measures of quality of life. Obviously, one important direction for future research in this area is to develop and validate indigenous measures of quality of life.

The fourth methodological issue concerns triangulation of quality of life data. One observation from the quality of life literature in Hong Kong is that there are few attempts integrating quality of life data collected by different methods and from different sources. With reference to the three major databases on quality of life in Hong Kong, while the Social Indicators of Social Development Project is based primarily on subjective quality of life data collected via surveys, the Social Development Index Project is based primarily on official statistics. The CUHK Hong Kong QOL Index incorporates both subjective quality of life data collected via telephone surveys and objective quality of life data collected via review of official statistics.

Borrowing concepts from navigation and military disciplines, Denzin (1978) used the term "triangulation" to argue for the utilization of different types of data based on different methodologies to examine the same phenomenon. The basic belief underlying the concept of triangulation is that there are biases in all types of investigation, and such biases and errors would be revealed and cancelled out when different methods, data sources, and/or investigators are involved. In other words, triangulation refers to the process of seeking convergence of results based on different methods, researchers, and settings on the same phenomenon under observation. Researchers commonly agree that triangulation is an important principle that should be utilized to check the quality of the research data.

Denzin (1978) identified four types of triangulation: triangulation by data sources (i.e., data collected by different persons, times, places, etc.), triangulation by different methods (i.e., different research methods such as observations, interviews, and documents), triangulation by researchers (data collected by different researchers), and triangulation by theory.

Miles and Huberman (1994) added another type of triangulation—triangulation by data types. Obviously, with reference to the above types of triangulation, triangulation of quality of life research findings in Hong Kong is not commonly performed.

The fifth methodological issue is pertinent to the meaning and interpretation of the level and change in quality of life. In the current practice, two approaches are adopted to gauge the level and change in quality of life over time. First, a particular year or period is chosen as the "base year(s)," and the quality of life data in the subsequent years are interpreted to be changing in the positive direction or not with respect to the base year situation. This approach is adopted in the SDI where the scores in different discrete measures were set to be equal to 100. In addition, the trend data are examined with reference to the quality of life in 1986–1996. Similarly, the CUHK Hong Kong QOL Index also adopts this approach where the composite QOL score at 2002 was set to be equal to 100. In the second approach, the meaning of "high" or "low" quality of life is interpreted with reference to the descriptor of the response. For example, if a participant "strongly agrees" that he or she is satisfied with the family, a high level of family quality of life is inferred. This approach is commonly used in those studies in which subjective quality of life is assessed.

Obviously, there are limitations with respect to the above two approaches. In the former approach, while this approach enables researchers to examine the "relative" changes in quality of life, its arbitrariness is beyond doubt. The change or non-change in quality of life will definitely vary if different baseline time points are used. In the latter approach, it hinges upon the question of whether a norm-referenced or criterion-referenced interpretation should be used. In addition, the correspondence between agreement to an item and the actual perceived level of satisfaction is another issue to be considered.

Philosophically, perhaps the most thorny question that the critics may ask is how one can define "positive" or "negative" social development based on the selected indicators. For example, does the increase in divorce rates signify a negative social development? I personally believe it is, but the feminists may not because they would argue that divorce is an indicator reflecting women's liberation. Similarly, does progress in science and technology indicate positive social development?

We might have this belief a century ago. However, when we realize that our working hours increase in a monotonic manner with the progress in science and technology, as in the case of the invention of computer and Internet which enable people to work 24 h a day, we begin to puzzle about the meaning of social development. All these examples point to one important issue underlying the interpretation of findings of the major QOL databases in Hong Kong—the issue of value choices and assumptions.

The sixth methodological issue is pertinent to the magnitude of the response rates in the existing surveys of subjective quality of life. With reference to the Indicators of Social Development Project, an examination of the related response rates in the various surveys reveals that the response rate figures are not impressive and it seems that the response rates have declined across time. The response rates in 1988, 1990, 1993, 1995, 1997, 1999, 2001, and 2004 were 62.7%, 59.2%, 54.9%, 56.4%, 50%, 48.4%, 51.1%, and 46.9%. According to Babbie (1998), "a response rate of at least 50 percent is generally considered *adequate* for analysis and reporting. A response rate of at least 60 percent is considered *good*, and a response rate of seventy percent or more is *very good*" (p. 182). With reference to this rough guideline, it should be noted that the response rates in two surveys were not adequate and the response rates in the rest of the surveys are not on the high side.

The final methodological issue is about the relevance of qualitative studies in the study of quality of life of people in Hong Kong (Lee 1998). An examination of the existing literature on quality of life in Hong Kong shows that they are predominated by quantitative studies in which quantitative methodologies are used. While secondary data analyses (as in the case of the Social Development Index) and social surveys (as in the case of Indicators for Social Development) can generate "objective" profiles and can generate "maps" about quality of life in Hong Kong, the real life experiences of Hong Kong people cannot be properly understood in terms of such "hard" data. According to qualitative researchers, besides the mainstream static pictures, it is equally important to hear the neglected "voices" and the dynamic issues involved. Furthermore, personal experiences painted by "thick description" would help us to understand more the real nature of quality of life of Hong Kong. Of course, according to the social constructionists, it is also important to take into account the social discourse processes involved in the conceptualization, assessment, and interpretation of quality of life of Hong Kong people.

Summary and Conclusions

In summary, the different sources of data pertinent to the quality of life of Hong Kong, including researches conducted by the Government, commercial sector, non-governmental organizations, and academics, are described in this chapter. Based on a review of the published QOL studies captured by the major databases in different academic disciplines, several characteristics of quality of life studies in Hong Kong are identified. These include the predominance of quality of life publications which are empirical, micro, and quantitative in nature, and comparatively more studies are based on adults and people with special needs. In addition, comparison of Hong Kong's situation with other parts of the world is not a regular practice.

Three existing projects (Indicators of Social Development Project, Social Development Index, and the CUHK Hong Kong Quality of Life Index) involving the collection of trend data over time are described in this chapter. With particular reference to the findings generated from this database and other quality of life studies, several observations pertinent to the quality of life of Hong Kong are outlined. These observations include (a) there has been progress in the quality of life in Hong Kong after 1997; (b) despite overall progress in quality of life in Hong Kong, some social groups do not show much improvement; (c) subjective quality of life has dropped after 1997; (d) warning signals about declining quality of life in Hong Kong are existing; (e) there are many psychosocial correlates of subjective quality of life; (f) quality of life in Hong Kong is better than quality of life in China based on some indicators; and (g) there are conflicting pictures based on different studies. Finally, several methodological issues pertinent to the study of quality of life in Hong Kong are outlined which provide some food for thoughts regarding the future direction of quality of life research in Hong Kong.

Acknowledgments The author wishes to thank the Hong Kong Council of Social Service for providing the findings related to the Social Development Index.

References

ACNielsen Company. (2010). *Global consumer confidence report (4th Quarter 2010)*. Retrieved February 14, 2011 from http://au.nielsen.com/site/index.shtml

American Chamber of Commerce in Hong Kong. (2004). *2004 Business outlook survey*. Hong Kong: American Chamber of Commerce in Hong Kong.

American Chamber of Commerce in Hong Kong. (2008). *Third annual survey focuses on air pollution and remedies*. Hong Kong: American Chamber of Commerce in Hong Kong.

Babbie, E. (1998). *Survey research methods*. Belmont: Wadsworth Publishing Company.

Chan, Y. K., Kwan, C. C. A., & Shek, D. T. L. (2005). Quality of life in Hong Kong: The CUHK Hong Kong Quality of Life Index. *Social Indicators Research, 71*(1–3), 259–289.

Chua, H. W., Wong, A. K. W., & Shek, D. T. L. (2010). Social development in Hong Kong: Development issues identified by Social Development Index (SDI). *Social Indicators Research, 95*(3), 535–551.

Commission on Poverty. (2006). *Concept and measurement of poverty*. Retrieved November 17, 2006 from http://www.cop.gov.hk/eng/income_disparity.htm

Commission on Youth. (2003). *Youth in Hong Kong: A statistical profile 2002 (Appendix)*. Hong Kong: Government of the Hong Kong Special Administrative Region.

Commission on Youth. (2005). *Benchmark study on civic engagement and social networks of youths in Hong Kong*. Hong Kong: Home Affairs Bureau, Government of the Hong Kong Special Administrative Region.

Commission on Youth. (2010). *Longitudinal study on civic engagement and social networks of youth in Hong Kong*. Hong Kong: Home Affairs Bureau, Government of the Hong Kong Special Administrative Region.

Control Risks and Simmons and Simmons. (2006). *International business attitudes to corruption – survey 2006*. London: Author.

Denzin, N. K. (1978). *The research act: A theoretical introduction to sociological methods*. New York: McGraw-Hill.

Elderly Commission. (2001). *A multi-disciplinary study on the causes of elderly suicides in Hong Kong*. Hong Kong: Health, Welfare and Food Bureau, Government of the Hong Kong Special Administrative Region.

Estes, R. (2005). Quality of life in Hong Kong: Past accomplishments and future prospects. *Social Indicators Research, 71*, 183–229.

Fahey, T., Nolan, B., & Whelan, C. T. (2003). *Monitoring quality of life in Europe*. Luxembourg: Office for Official Publications of the European Communities.

Felce, D., & Perry, J. (1995). Quality of life: Its definition and measurement. *Research in Developmental Disabilities, 16*, 51–74.

Francis, C. (2008, November 20). *Environment, education top Hong Kong's sustainable development agenda. CityU News Centre*. Retrieved February 14, 2011 from http://www6.cityu.edu.hk/puo/CityUMember/Story/Story.aspx?id=20081120170308

Hong Kong Federation of Youth Groups. (2004). *A study on how Hong Kong young people cope with stress*. Hong Kong: Hong Kong Federation of Youth Groups.

Hong Kong Federation of Youth Groups. (2010). *The Post-80s Generation*. Hong Kong: Hong Kong Federation of Youth Groups.

Hong Kong Mood Disorders Center. (2006). *Surveys on the emotional health of Hong Kong people*. Retrieved November 13, 2006 from http://www.hmdc.med.cuhk.edu.hk/report

Lau, A., & McKenna, K. (1998). Self-perceived quality of life of Chinese elderly people in Hong Kong. *Occupational Therapy International, 5*, 118–139.

Lau, A., & McKenna, K. (2002). Perception of quality of life by Chinese elderly persons with stroke. *Disability and Rehabilitation: An International Multidisciplinary Journal, 24*, 203–218.

Lau, S. K., Lee, M. K., Wan, P. S., & Wong, S. L. (1991). *Indicators of social development: Hong Kong 1988*. Hong Kong: Hong Kong Institute of Asia-Pacific Studies, The Chinese University of Hong Kong.

Lau, S. K., Lee, M. K., Wan, P. S., & Wong, S. L. (1992). *Indicators of social development: Hong Kong 1990*. Hong Kong: Hong Kong Institute of Asia-Pacific Studies, The Chinese University of Hong Kong.

Lau, S. K., Lee, M. K., Wan, P. S., & Wong, S. L. (1995). *Indicators of social development: Hong Kong 1993*. Hong Kong: Hong Kong Institute of Asia-Pacific Studies, The Chinese University of Hong Kong.

Lau, S. K., Lee, M. K., Wan, P. S., & Wong, S. L. (1997). *Indicators of social development: Hong Kong 1995*. Hong Kong: Hong Kong Institute of Asia-Pacific Studies, The Chinese University of Hong Kong.

Lau, S. K., Lee, M. K., Wan, P. S., & Wong, S. L. (1999). *Indicators of social development: Hong Kong 1997*. Hong Kong: Hong Kong Institute of Asia-Pacific Studies, The Chinese University of Hong Kong.

Lau, S. K., Lee, M. K., Wan, P. S., & Wong, S. L. (2001). *Indicators of social development: Hong Kong 1999*. Hong Kong: Hong Kong Institute of Asia-Pacific Studies, The Chinese University of Hong Kong.

Lau, S. K., Lee, M. K., Wan, P. S., & Wong, S. L. (2003). *Indicators of social development: Hong Kong 2001*. Hong Kong: Hong Kong Institute of Asia-Pacific Studies, The Chinese University of Hong Kong.

Lau, A., Cummins, R. A., & McPherson, W. (2005a). An investigation into the cross-cultural equivalence of the Personal Wellbeing Index. *Social Indicators Research, 72*, 403–430.

Lau, S. K., Lee, M. K., Wan, P. S., & Wong, S. L. (2005b). *Indicators of social development: Hong Kong 2004*. Hong Kong: Hong Kong Institute of Asia-Pacific Studies, The Chinese University of Hong Kong.

Lee, M. K. (1998). Qualitative social indicators. In S. K. Lau, P. S. Wen, M. K. Lee, & S. L. Wong (Eds.), *Changing Chinese societies: Social indicators analysis* (pp. 3–18). Hong Kong: Hong Kong Institute of Asia-Pacific Studies, The Chinese University of Hong Kong.

Markus, H., & Kitayama, S. (1991). Culture and the self: Implications for cognition, emotion and motivation. *Psychological Review, 98*, 224–253.

Master Card. (2010). *Master index of consumer confidence*. Retrieved February 14, 2011 from http://www.masterintelligence.com/upload/257/24/3hongkong_cc.swf

Miles, M. B., & Huberman, A. (1994). *An expanded sourcebook: Qualitative data analysis*. Newbury Park: Sage.

New Economics Foundation. (2006). *The happy planet index*. London: New Economics Foundation.

Public Opinion Poll Program. (2006). *Social indicators surveys 1–6/987 to 7–12/06*. Retrieved November 24, 2006 from http://hkupop.hku.hk/chinese/popexpress/socind

Shek, D. T. L. (1999a). Parenting characteristics and adolescent psychological well-being: A longitudinal study in a Chinese context. *Genetic, Social, and General Psychology Monographs, 125*(1), 27–44.

Shek, D. T. L. (1999b). Paternal and maternal influences on the psychological well-being of Chinese adolescents. *Genetic, Social, and General Psychology Monographs, 125*(3), 269–296.

Shek, D. T. L. (2002a). Chinese adolescents' perceptions of family functioning: Personal, school-related, and family correlates. *Genetic, Social, and General Psychology Monographs, 128*(4), 358–380.

Shek, D. T. L. (2002b). Interpersonal support and conflict and adjustment of Chinese adolescents with and without economic disadvantage. In S. P. Shohov (Ed.), *Advances in psychology research* (18th ed., pp. 63–82). New York: Nova Science Publishers.

Shek, D. T. L. (2002c). Special Issue: Research on social work practice in Chinese communities. *Research on Social Work Practice, 12*(4), 485–581.

Shek, D. T. L. (2005a). Economic stress, emotional quality of life, and problem behavior in Chinese adolescents with and without economic disadvantage. *Social Indicators Research, 71*(1–3), 363–383.

Shek, D. T. L. (2005b). Social stress in Hong Kong. In J. Estes (Ed.), *Social development index* (pp. 167–181). Hong Kong: Oxford University Press.

Shek, D. T. L. (2010). Quality of life of Chinese people in a changing world. *Social Indicators Research, 95*(3), 357–361.

Shek, D. T. L., & Lee, B. M. (2004). "Non-engaged" young people in Hong Kong: Key statistics and observations. *International Journal of Adolescent Medicine and Health, 16*(2), 145–163.

Shek, D. T. L., & Lee, B. M. (2007). A comprehensive review of quality of life (QOL) research in Hong Kong. *The Scientific World Journal, 7*, 1222–1229.

Shek, D. T. L., & Lee, T. Y. (2005). Hopelessness in Chinese adolescents in Hong Kong: Demographic and family correlates. *International Journal of Adolescent Medicine and Health, 17*(3), 279–290.

Shek, D. T. L., & Mak, J. W. K. (1986). *A study of life stress of working parents in Hong Kong*. Hong Kong: Hong Kong Christian Service.

Shek, D. T. L., & Tsang, S. K. M. (1993). *Caregivers of preschool mentally handicapped children in Hong Kong. Their stress, coping resources, and psychological well-being*. Hong Kong: Heep Hong Society.

Shek, D. T. L., Chan, Y. K., & Lee, P. S. N. (2005a). Quality of life in the global context: A Chinese response. *Social Indicators Research, 71*(1–3), 1–10.

Shek, D. T. L., Chan, Y. K., & Lee, P. S. N. (Eds.). (2005b). *Social Indicators Research Series (vol. 25): Quality of life research in Chinese, Western and global contexts*. The Netherlands: Springer.

Shek, D. T. L., Lee, B. M., & Chow, J. T. W. (2005c). Trends in adolescent suicide in Hong Kong for the period of 1980 to 2003. *The Scientific World Journal, 5*, 702–723.

Shek, D. T. L., Han, X. Y., & Lee, B. M. (2006). A comparative study on perceived parental control processes and parent-adolescent relational qualities among adolescents in Hong Kong and Shanghai. *Society, 26*, 137–157 (In Chinese).

Shen, S. M., & Lai, Y. L. (1999). Social well-being during the transitional period 1988–1997. In S. K. Lau, M. K. Lee, P. S. Wan, & S. L. Wong (Eds.), *Indicators of social development: Hong Kong 1997* (pp. 1–37). Hong Kong: Hong Kong Institute of Asia-Pacific Studies, The Chinese University of Hong Kong.

Siu, A. M. H., & Shek, D. T. L. (2005). Relations between social problem solving and indicators of interpersonal and family well-being among Chinese adolescents in Hong Kong. *Social Indicators Research, 71*, 517–539.

Social Welfare Department. (2010). *Final report of the review panel of the pilot project on child fatality review*. Hong Kong: Social Welfare Department, Government of the Hong Kong Special Administrative Region.

The Hong Kong Council of Social Service. (2000). *Social development in Hong Kong: The unfinished agenda*. Hong Kong: The Hong Kong Council of Social Service.

The Hong Kong Council of Social Service. (2002). *Social development index 2002 and review of social development 1997–2002*. Hong Kong: The Hong Kong Council of Social Service.

The Hong Kong Council of Social Service. (2004). *Social development index 2004*. Hong Kong: The Hong Kong Council of Social Service.

The Hong Kong Council of Social Service. (2005). *Social development index: Rule of law sub-index 2005 (Final Report)*. Hong Kong: The Hong Kong Council of Social Service.

The Hong Kong Council of Social Service. (2006). *Social development index 2006*. Hong Kong: The Hong Kong Council of Social Service.

Transparency International. (2006). *The 2006 Transparency International Corruption Perceptions Index*. Retrieved November 20, 2006 from http://www.infoplease.com/ipa/A0781359.html

Union Bank of Switzerland. (2006). *Prices and earnings: A comparison of purchasing power around the world*. Zurich: Union Bank of Switzerland.

United Nations Development Program. (2009). *Human development report 2009*. New York: United Nations Development Program.

United Nations Development Program. (2010). *Human development report 2010*. New York: United Nations Development Program.

Veehoven, R. (1996). Happy life-expectancy: A comprehensive measure of quality-of-life in nations. *Social Indicators Research, 39*, 1–58.

Wallander, J. L., Schmitt, M., & Koot, H. M. (2001). Quality of life measurement in children and adolescents: Issues, instruments and applications. *Journal of Clinical Psychology, 57*, 571–585.

Wong, S. L., & Zheng, V. (2005). Social anticipation and social reality. In S. K. Lau, M. K. Lee, P. S. Wan, & S. L. Wong (Eds.), *Indicators of social development: Hong Kong 2004* (pp. 285–328). Hong Kong: Hong Kong Institute of Asia-Pacific Studies, The Chinese University of Hong Kong.

Zhu, Z. F. (1996). New measures to assess social development: Application and social benefits of social indicators. In S. K. Lau, P. S. Wen, M. K. Lee, & S. L. Wong (Eds.), *New frontiers of social indicators research in Chinese societies* (pp. 14–57). Hong Kong: Hong Kong Institute of Asia-Pacific Studies, The Chinese University of Hong Kong.

The Quality of Life of Muslim Populations: The Case of Algeria

23

Habib Tiliouine and Mohamed Meziane

Introduction

It may be relevant to question in the beginning of this chapter whether religion in modern time should be used to classify people and countries so diverse in terms of geography, culture, history, social and political structure, and level of development without committing errors of grave distortions. As a matter of fact, *Islamicity*, as is used here as a reference, has been accepted for labeling populations in international studies. The Organization of Islamic Conference (OIC), for instance, founded on September 25,1969, counts 57 member countries spanning East Asia, South Asia, Southern Europe (Turkey), the Middle East, and in many parts of the African continent from North Africa to sub-Saharan Africa. These countries, which are so heterogeneous, have in common not only the sense of belongingness to this great religion and a glorious past but also a harsh reality of dealing with modern life without losing their Islamic identity. This shared religious identity has also been "reinforced by a new shared experience – the penetration, domination, and (in most areas) the departure of European colonialists" (Lewis 1993, pp. 21–22). Twenty-four Islamic countries did not enjoy freedom from colonization until the second half of the twentieth century. Five of them – Azerbaijan, Kazakhstan, Tajikistan, Turkmenistan, and Uzbekistan – were freed from the former Soviet Union only recently in 1991. The status of other places such as Palestine, Western Sahara, and Chechnya has not yet been decided. Unfortunately all Islamic countries are considered "third world."

Furthermore, due to many reasons, the Muslim identity faces a misunderstanding. The tragic events of September 11 in the USA and afterwards in Spain and England and elsewhere, brought to the surface previously formalized conceptions about Islam and Muslims -- deeply rooted stereotypes and distorted generalizations disseminated in the media and propagated in academic communities. The clash of civilization theory, for instance, argues that "cultural and religious differences are a major cause of international conflict in the post-Cold War era and asserts that Islam in particular encourages Muslim aggressiveness toward non-Muslim peoples" (Tessler 2003). Huntington (1997) openly states: "The underlying problem for the West is not Islamic fundamentalism. It is Islam..." (p. 217). For Tessler, this and similar characterizations are not only troubling but also harmful. They deepen the misunderstanding of Islam and the Muslim world and may lead to policies guided by erroneous assumptions and stereotypes. Using a large part of the data drawn from a variety of Asian and North African populations, collected in the World Value Survey (WVS), Inglehart and Norris (2003) have found, in reply to Huntington, that Muslims and their counterparts in the West both want democracy, yet they are world apart when it comes to attitudes toward divorce, abortion, gender equality, and gay rights.

H. Tiliouine (✉)
Laboratory of Educational Processes and Social Context (Labo-PECS), University of Oran, B.P.1524, Menaouer, Oran 31000, Algeria
e-mail: htiliouine@yahoo.fr

M. Meziane
Department of Psychology and Educational Sciences, University of Oran, Oran, Algeria

K.C. Land et al. (eds.), *Handbook of Social Indicators and Quality of Life Research*,
DOI 10.1007/978-94-007-2421-1_23, © Springer Science+Business Media B.V. 2012

Another consistent thesis emerges from Tessler's analysis using the WVS data. Among ordinary men and women in Western and Muslim populations, political and economic factors play a much more important role in accounting for variance in attitude toward politics, governance, and international relations than religious and cultural predispositions.

These are examples of the ongoing debate regarding the image of Muslims and Islam in modern time. Our chapter will not be directly concerned with this issue. Rather, it will try to shed some light on the quality of life in Muslim populations in the countries that have membership in the OIC. Excluded from our analysis are very large Muslim countries that are not members of the OIC, in addition to those countries having Muslim minorities.

In the first part of this chapter, we will try to broadly define the notion of Islam and look at what is labeled "Islamic traditional perspectives of life and its quality." As Islam emerged from the Arabic peninsula in the sixth century, this religion infiltrated many countries and cultures: the Persians, Indians, Greeks, Romans, Chinese, and so on. This infiltration led to the development and spread of new ways of living, new philosophies, and new ways of governing across different parts of successive Islamic empires. Assuming that quality of life has an important cultural component that should not be neglected, we will apply some of the basic principles in attempt to capture the essence of the Islamic view on this subject.

In the second part, we will look at the quality of life of selected populations using some well-established indicators, both objective and subjective, as well as review available and recent studies on the subject. A final part will deal with recent studies and published data about Algeria, as a case study.

We acknowledge that our account is very limited regarding the number of populations we are dealing with. Besides, the field of study concerning quality of life studies and social indicators is relatively new and has not attracted a many social scientists in Islamic countries to study quality of life issues with sufficient rigor. Our analyses and conclusions are thus based on scarce and limited data.

Part I: Life and Its Quality: The Islamic Perspective

Lewis (1993) states: "…For the Muslim, the Islamic revelation is not a beginning but a completion, the final link in a chain of revelations – and the Islamic community is thus not a new creation but a revival and improvement of something that had existed long before. The history of Islam therefore did not begin with Muhammad; it included the history of the earlier prophets and their missions, and something also of the peoples to whom they were sent" (p. 117). This is true, and we can appreciate this historical notion by understanding the six principles of Islamic dogma. First, the Muslim should believe in One God, Supreme and Eternal, Infinite and Mighty, Merciful and Compassionate, Creator and Provider. Second, he believes in all the messengers of God without any discrimination among them, as well as, all the previous books and revelations. Third, he believes in the angels of God. They are purely spiritual and splendid beings whose nature requires no food or drink or sleep. They have no physical desire of material needs. They spend their days and nights in the service of God. Fourth, he believes in the Last Day of Judgment. This world will come to an end someday, and the dead will rise to stand for their final and fair trial. Everything we do in this world, every intention we have, every move we make, every thought we entertain, and every word we say, all are counted and tabulated. On the Day of Judgment, they will be brought up. People with good record would generously be rewarded and warmly welcomed to the Heaven of God, and those with bad record would be punished and cast into Hell. And finally, the belief that what a human being faces in his life, good or bad, is God's will and should be accepted as so. The true Muslim believes that every person is born "Muslim." This means that the very course of birth takes place in accordance with the Will of God, in realization of His plans, and in submission to His Commands. Then, Muslims believe that Muhammad's mission was to preserve morality in all its forms (other great religions such as Judaism and Christianity).

For Boisard (1979), Islam presupposes three distinct but intimately related tenets. It is a willing submission to a set of laws – moral and cultural rules. It encourages a properly humane heritage. Finally, it defines the position of the believer vis-à-vis the Absolute and enhances solidarity among human beings. As such, it is then a revealed religion, a historical and social phenomenon (pp. 35–37).

In this vein, man enjoys an especially high-ranking status in the hierarchy of all the known creatures. He occupies this distinguished position because he alone is gifted with rational faculties, spiritual aspirations, and power of action. But the more man excels

23 The Quality of Life of Muslim Populations: The Case of Algeria

in rank, the more his responsibility grows. He assumes the role of God's viceroy on earth. His life is then purposeful.

An earthly life of a human being is conceived as a bridge, a transitory stage, or an introduction to the eternal life in the Hereafter. The best use of it, therefore, is to willfully live according to the teachings of God. The importance of knowledge to the Muslim can be captured in the traditional saying "The ink of the scholar is more sacred than the blood of the martyr." The prophet insists that wisdom should be the quest of the believer wherever he may find it (Boisard 1979).

Islam has a whole system of rules and regulations guiding man on how to live his life. As such, man is encouraged to enjoy God's endowments. In a remarkable passage of the Koran, it is said:

> O children of Adam! Wear your beautiful apparel at every time and place of prayer; eat and drink, but waste not by excess, for God loves not wasters. Say: "Who has forbidden the beautiful gifts of God, which he has produced for his servants, and the things, clean and pure (which He has provided) for sustenance?" Say: "They are, in the life of this world, for those who believe, (and) purely for them on the Day of Judgement." Thus do. We explain the Signs in detail for those who understand. Say: "the things that my Lord has indeed forbidden are: shameful deeds, whether open or secret, sins and trespasses against truth or reason; assigning of partners to God -and saying things about God of which you have no knowledge." (Koran, 7, pp. 31–33)

Islam is the religion where moderation is the Golden rule. No "excess" is allowed, even in God's worship. Moreover, everyone has a direct access to God, no mediator is accepted. For this reason, there are no clergymen in Islam. Worship does not imply only to perform the daily due prayers, to give away the compulsory charity (the Alms), fast Ramadan, and go to Mecca pilgrimage, but it encompasses all aspects of life – to live in harmony with oneself, the community and nature. Human "instincts" are not repressed but refined and sublimated. Sex, for instance, is not only allowed but encouraged within the recognized and organized institution of marriage. Divorce is as well accepted when things go wrong.

As a historical and social phenomenon, Islam represents a real revolution in the Arabic peninsula and in the entire region. It was spread quickly, and its message reached the furthest empires and ended face to face with the two superpowers of the time, the Byzantine and the Persian empires.

So, life did not go on as simple as it begun. Early Muslims had to meet the great traditions and the complex systems of thought of its predecessors. Islam represented a cultural revolution through Koran assemblage and *Hadiths* (the Prophets sayings) and their interpretation in light of the new life full of complexities. Islam had to standardize and teach the language of the Koran, Arabic. Besides, early Muslims had to learn to govern the vast territories that embraced Islam, to preserve the Divine message and to refute contrary teachings.

The translation and interpretation of Greek philosophy into Arabic was commented and enriched since the ninth century (Corbin 1964). For instance, Aristotle view of happiness was widely discussed by early Muslim scholars whose writings await to be carefully studied. Ibn Masquawayh (died in 1030) believes that happiness is the ultimate goal and the best good one can reach. According to him, happiness requires things in the body and other things out of it. But in its supreme form, it does not need anything else. He presents two opposing views. The first view makes reference to Aristotle, and the second view reference was made to Pythagoras, Hippocrates, and Plato. For him, Aristotle views happiness based on several criteria: the presence of health, a moderate mood, wealth, a high social status, success, intelligence, and righteous beliefs. The more one acquires these conditions, the more happiness he accumulates. The opposing view treats happiness in the moral sense such as wisdom, courage, chastity, and equity. These virtues are sources of an enduring happiness. Ibn Masquawayh concludes that there are three stages for authentic happiness:

1. The stage where man moderately meets his biological needs.
2. The stage where he progressively exercises self-control and limits himself to meeting necessity needs only.
3. The highest stage where he devotes himself to pious virtue. In this stage, doing good does not need justification. Man does good not to avoid sanctions or to obtain rewards. In this stage, happiness does not vanish due to physical illness or other hardships. This is because man at this stage is fully devoted to God.

It seems that the third stage has been the focus of the Sophist Islamic philosophy. The utmost goal of a Sophist is described through the notion of "melting his will in the will of God, not to accept but what

God wants and not to refuse but what God refuses," (i.e., to be a man of God). In order to be a man of God, man has to meet a set of conditions and perform a number of spiritual practices. Seven stages are enumerated by the Sunni Al-Ghazali (died in December 19, 1111 at the age of 52) in his widely quoted book, *The Revival of Religious Sciences* (Corbin 1964). Nowadays, the *Sophist* tradition continues to enjoy a great popularity in the Muslim world. It gives superiority of the spiritual to that of the physical – devotion to God and his message.

It should be noted that Islamic philosophy had made happiness a central theme of discussion. The voluminous writings on this topic should be critically analyzed in future research.

Part II: Quality of Life in Muslim Countries: Some Objective and Subjective Measures

In this part of the chapter, we examine the quality of life of selected populations using some well-established indicators, both objective and subjective. We also review available and recent studies on the subject.

What Is Meant by Quality of Life?

Quality of life (QOL) has emerged in the last two decades as an integrating concept for addressing the needs and the way of life of many population segments by public policymakers, community developers, and social and behavioral scientists. The World Health Organization (WHO) has been one of the keenest advocates of QOL, which defines health as a state of complete physical, mental, and social well-being, and not merely the absence of disease or infirmity. Reaching this state requires the action of many other social and economic sectors.

So, this concept provides an excellent framework for interdisciplinary, intersectoral research that addresses the determinants of health and well-being in a comprehensive and holistic way. Recent research found important factors that assist in the understanding of the needs and lives of people, paving way to the development of outcome indicators used in the planning and delivery of interventions or services. QOL is thus linked with population health, social development, and community sustainability. Even more, health,

well-being, and QOL have increasingly become interchangeable terms. That is not to say that the medical model of QOL is dominating research in this area. At least two other models are dominant: the economics model and the social sciences model. This latter views QOL as a multidimensional construct influenced by both personal (psychological) characteristics and environmental factors.

Inclusive measures of QOL have become essential, but many issues have not been resolved with regard to this concept. QOL is linked to economic prosperity and regional development as a primary source for community well-being, although research evidence failed to prove such a linear correlation (e.g., Diener and Tov 2004; Diener and Seligman 2004; Hagerty and Veenhoven 2003). Other contributing factors are yet to be fully identified. Research techniques and instruments that might be applicable to di fferent contexts and cultures are still crude instruments and fail to balance objective indicators of QOL with subjective ones.

In spite of these limitations, the QOL research is flourishing. However, QOL of many countries and population segments have not yet been studied. This is mainly due to the lack of competent research institutions and the scarcity of published data concerning these countries and populations segments. This is evident in many Muslim countries. In this context, we are relying on scarce data published by international organizations. The indicators selected here are not country-specific and can be found in the general literature of QOL research. But, when combined, they can be powerful tools to highlight successes and failures and successes of any country. We will begin our discussion with the demographic characteristics of Islamic populations. We will address economic growth and poverty, as in traditionally done classical economics. Doing so may shed some light on what is being achieved economically in these countries relative to other countries. We will examine health provisioning and education because they are necessary components of quality of life. Subjective measures will be used to complement our general assessment of quality of life in the Muslim countries.

It should be noted that the present chapter underwent many revisions. We found it difficult to update all the indicators. The accuracy of the data may also be problematic, mainly because the sample countries generally lack proper research institutions for such data collection.

Sample Countries

All the countries that are included in this analysis are members of the Organization of Islamic Conference (OIC). They constitute a heterogeneous group of countries, but they still have many common characteristics. In some countries, Muslims are less than 50% of the total inhabitants, such as Gabon 1%, Guyana 15%, Mozambique 29%, Suriname 25%, and Uganda 36%. Excluded from our list are countries that are not members of the organization but have a majority of Muslims, such as Central African Republic (55%), Eritrea (80%), Ethiopia (65%), and Tanzania (65%) (based on estimates provided by the CIA World Factbook 2005). The goal here is to concentrate our analysis on a limited number of cases.

As shown in Table 23.1, 57 countries were selected. The total Muslim population of these countries exceeds 1.28 billion inhabitants out of 1.4 billion of Muslims in the world (as the maximum estimated number). Their total area is almost three times that of the United States, United Kingdom, France, and Japan combined. These countries will be compared on a number of dimensions ranging from demographic characteristics to life satisfaction.

It should be noted that not all the countries recognized as Muslims give an equal status to Islam in their constitutions. "Twenty-two of 44 predominantly Muslim countries recognize some constitutional role for Islamic law, principles, or jurisprudence. This includes 18 of the 22 countries where Islam is the religion of the state, as well as four predominantly Muslim countries where a constitutional role for Islam is not the declared state religion" (International Commission on International Religious Freedom March 2005, p. 9). This may demonstrate how diverse Muslim countries are in relation to the status of religion within the formal legal system.

Population Growth in Islamic Countries

It is known that half of the world population live in ten countries. Four of them are predominantly Muslims, with Indonesia, Pakistan, Bangladesh, and Nigeria ranking successively 4th, 6th, 7th, and 9th. Annual population growth rate in Islamic countries is particularly high. Among the 57 countries shown in Table 23.1, annual population growth rates range from a low of 0.1% in Guyana and 0.3% in Kazakhstan to a high of 6.5% in United Arab Emirates and 4.7% in Qatar (between 1975 and 2002).

Total fertility rate (i.e., the number of births per women) is highest in the world (Table 23.1). However, this rate is estimated to slow down by the year 2015 in most of the Islamic countries, except Burkina Faso, Chad, Mali, Mauritania, Niger, Sierra Leone, Suriname, and Uganda, all of them belonging to the poor continent of Africa (Table 23.1). In some of the Islamic countries, the annual population growth rate is expected to sensibly decrease, such as UAE (from 6.5% down to 1.5%), Lebanon (from 4.2% to 1.0%), and Qatar (from 4.7% to 1.3%) (estimates are from 2002 to 2015, see Table 23.1). The rates stay as high as 3% and beyond in the particularly poor regions of Yemen, Niger, Mali, and Burkina Faso (Table 23.1).

The age structure is presently unbalanced. Twelve Muslim countries belong to the group of 21 countries in the world where 45% and more of the total population are less than 14 years olds: Afghanistan (45%), Benin (47%), Burkina Faso (46%), Chad (48%), Gambia (45%), Yemen (47%), and Uganda (50%) (The CIA World Factbook 2005). The ratio of youth to elderly is very high. But, with the increase of life expectancy through greater access to health provisioning (and if the population growth rate slows down), these countries will have to face new challenges of a reversed ratio of elderly to youth. One of the most disturbing social issues of concern is the problem of caring of the elderly. Increased healthcare costs will be a significant economic burden, especially in countries where economic resources are already underprovided.

The data on per capita GDP (see Table 23.1) are catastrophic for many countries. Large segments of these populations are deprived from basic necessities such as proper food, sanitation, education, proper housing, and employment.

Economic Growth and Poverty in Islamic Countries

Economic indicators have been for a long time considered the prime determinants of people's quality of life. This assumption could be easily justified and accepted if the classical economic model of QOL is adopted. Economic indicators reflect the deficiencies in the main sources for basic needs provisioning such as

Table 23.1 Population characteristics and GDP in Islamic countries

Country name	Total population in 2002[a] (millions)	Percentage of muslims[b]	Annual population growth rate[a]		Per capita GDP	
			1975–2002	2002–2015	2002[a]	(year)[c]
Afghanistan	–	100	–	–	–	655 (08)
Albania	3.1	70–75	1.0	0.7	4.830	
Algeria	31.3	99	2.5	1.5	5.760	
Azerbaïdjan	8.3	93.4	1.4	1.0	3.210	
Bahrain	0.7	100	3.5	1.8	17.170	27.943(08)
Bangladesh	143.8	83–85	2.4	1.8	1.700	
Benin	6.6		2.8	2.5	1.070	
Brunei	0.3	63–67	2.9	2.0	19.210	
Burkina Faso	12.6	50	2.7	3.0	1.100	
Cameroon	15.7	55	2.7	1.4	2.000	
Chad	8.3	51–85	2.6	2.9	1.020	
Comoros	0.7	86–98	3.2	2.6	1.690	
Cote d'Ivoire	16.4	60	3.3	1.5	1.520	
Djibouti	0.7	94	4.3	1.5	1.990	1.031 (08)
Egypt	70.5	94	2.2	1.9	3.810	1.949 (08)
Gabon	1.3	01	2.9	1.8	6.590	
Gambia	1.4	90	3.4	2.2	1.690	
Guinea	8.4	85–95	2.7	2.3	2.100	
Guinea-Bissau	1.4	70	3.0	2.9	710	
Guyana	0.8	15	0.1	(.)	4.260	
Indonesia	217.1	88–95	1.8	1.1	3.230	
Iran	68.1	98–99	2.6	1.4	6.690	5.070 (08)
Iraq	–	97	–	–	–	3.524 (08)
Jordan	5.3	92–95	3.7	2.1	4.220	3.257(08)
Kazakhstan	15.5	51.2	0.3	−0.1	5.870	
Kuwait	2.4	85–89	3.3	2.4	16.240	40.485(08)
Kyrgyzstan	5.1	75–76.1	1.6	1.2	1.620	
Lebanon	3.6	60–70	4.2	1.0	4.360	7.659 (08)
Libya	5.4	97–100	3.0	1.8	7.570	14.846 (09)
Malaysia	24.0	52	2.5	1.6	9.120	
Maldives	0.3	100	3.0	2.8	4.798	
Mali	12.6	90	2.6	3.1	930	
Mauritania	2.8	100	2.5	2.7	2.220	
Morocco	30.1	98.7	2.0	1.5	3.810	2.707(08)
Mozambique	18.5	29	2.1	1.5	1.050	
Niger	11.5	80–91	3.3	3.6	800	
Nigeria	120.9	50–75	2.9	2.2	860	
Oman	2.8	75–100	4.1	2.7	13.340	19.102(08)
Pakistan	149.9	97	2.8	2.4	1.940	841(08)
Palestine (occupied territories)	3.4	–	3.7	3.3	–	
Qatar	0.6	100	4.7	1.3	19.844	88.990(08)
Saudi Arabia	23.5	100	4.4	2.5	12.650	18.603(08)
Senegal	9.9	94–95	2.7	2.2	1.580	
Sierra Leone	4.8	60	1.8	2.3	520	
Somalia	–	100	–	–	–	180(08)

(continued)

23 The Quality of Life of Muslim Populations: The Case of Algeria

Table 23.1 (continued)

Country name	Total population in 2002[a] (millions)	Percentage of muslims[b]	Annual population growth rate[a]		Per capita GDP	
			1975–2002	2002–2015	2002[a]	(year)[c]
Sudan	32.9	70–85	2.5	1.8	1.820	1.353(08)
Suriname	0.4	25	0.6	0.7	6.590	
Syria	17.4	90	3.1	2.2	3.620	1.804(08)
Tajikistan	6.2	85–90	2.2	1.2	980	
Togo	4.8	55	2.8	2.2	1.480	
Tunisia	9.7	98	2.0	1.0	6.760	3.796(08)
Turkey	70.3	99.8	2.0	1.2	6.390	
Turkmenistan	4.8	87–89	2.4	1.5	4.300	
Uganda	25.0	36	3.1	3.5	1.390	
United Arab Emirates	2.9	96	6.5	1.5	22.420	64.009(08)
Uzbekistan	25.7	88	2.3	1.4	1.670	
Yemen	19.3	99–100	3.8	3.6	870	926 (09)

Source:
[a]UNDP Human Development Report 2004: 152–155
[b]Estimates vary greatly. The ranges are reported here using diverse sources
[c]World Health Organization, (www.emro.who.int:emrinfo/index.aspx?)

food, clothing, housing, jobs, transport, and so on. But once these basic needs are met to some extent, the fundamentals of psychology teach us that other social and psychological needs come to bear. However, compared to other nations, Muslim countries are lagging behind in terms of economic growth. Few examples may suffice to illustrate this point. GDP per capita figures in 2002 (see Table 23.1) indicate that except for the rich oil-producing countries such as UAE ($22.42), Qatar ($19.84), Kuwait ($16.24), Bahrain ($16.24), and Brunei ($19.210), which are classified as high income group, the situation in some other countries is dramatic: Burkina Faso ($1.10), Chad ($1.02), Guinea-Bissau ($710), Niger ($800), Nigeria ($860), and Yemen ($870).

However, in comparison with the year 2002, some improvements in GDP were noted in 2008 mainly in the oil-producing countries such as Bahrain, Kuwait, and Libya. Decreases in GDP are also noted in poor and unstable countries such as Djibouti, Egypt, Morocco, and Pakistan, and to certain extent Iran (last column in Table 23.1).

The economic performance and future prospects of OIC member countries are largely influenced by economic development in the industrialized countries and the stability of the world economy and finance. The report of the Islamic Development Bank in Jeddah (2005) indicates that about 90% of the OIC

countries trade is being done with other countries, not members of the organization. The same report adds that while member countries in Asia and Africa have somehow sustained their macroeconomic performance, Muslim countries in the Common Wealth of Independent States (CIS), which gained independence following the collapse of the Soviet Union, are facing the prospect of weak macroeconomic performance. News releases of the 2005 conference of the OIC member states mention that the Islamic world is becoming more self-critical, noting that while accounting for 20% of the world's population, Muslim countries contribute only 5% of the world's income. The need for setting up an Islamic common market to promote South-South exchange has been echoed for more than 30 years, but no tangible progress has been made.

All reports on the status of the economic and social development reinforce the realities of widespread poverty, lack of proper health services, and the high rate of illiteracy in the Islamic countries. This is a source of concern to international community. Alan Schwartz wrote in the "New York Times edition" of December 1, 2001 that Sept. 11 has taught the world anew how important it is to take a particular active interest: "If we do not promote economic growth in Muslim nations, we will by default promote growth in the supply of potential terrorists."

Indeed, poverty can be found all over the world, but its scale and prevalence differ across regions and continents. Although it has been defined differently among culturalist and structuralist researchers, poverty implies the presence of deficiencies that threaten physical, psychological, and psychosocial integrity of those suffering from it. It limits individuals' and countries' capacity to make the best use of their resources, both human and material, and may contribute to the widespread of criminal elements and breeding terrorism. As far as Muslim populations are concerned, the scale of poverty is stunning. The figures of Table 23.2 (column 2) represent estimates of the percentage of poor people out of the total population in 37 countries. In 13 countries, more than half of the population is poor, and in 7 out of these 13 countries, poverty afflicts more than 60% of the population, and up to 70% in two countries, Mozambique and Suriname, and 80% in Chad (CIA World Factbook, March 2005).

The Human Poverty Index (HPI) data seem very relevant here (see Table 23.2) as it combine access to safe water, health services, and underweight children under five as measures of standard of living. The results show that out of the 36 Muslim countries for which data are provided, in 14 countries, HPI exceeds 40. In Burkina Faso, Mali, and Niger, the HPI reaches, respectively, up to 65.5, 61.4, and 58.9 (see Table 23.2). In comparison, the figures of the HPI in countries such as France, Germany, Japan, and the USA are, respectively, as low as 10.8, 10.3, 11.1, and 15.8 (UNDP Human Development Report 2004).

The Human Development Index (HDI) as a whole, which includes measures of life expectancy, literacy, education, as well as income, is also low in the majority of Muslim countries. The HDI reaches the lowest levels in the world in cases such as Sierra Leone and Niger. Few small countries are doing better such as UAE, Brunei, Bahrain, Kuwait, and Qatar (see Table 23.2). These five small countries with a total population of 6.9 million (in 2004) are ranked among world countries having very high HDI. In contrast, 18 Muslim countries with a total population of more than 431.6 million are classified in the category of countries with low HDI.

In the Arab world that is synonymous of oil exports, the Arab Human Development Report (UNDP 2003, p. 4) has noted that deprivation in terms of basic human development parameters is about 32.4%, as measured by the HPI. Although Arab countries have the lowest level of dire poverty in the world, it remains the case that one out of every five people lives on less than $2 per day, according to World Bank estimates for the Middle East and North Africa (UNDP 2003, p. 5). Huge disparities within each country and between countries are observed.

However, on a larger scale (i.e., all Muslim countries), some 37% (i.e., 344 million people of the total population of 28 OIC member countries) are suffering from poverty (SESRTCIC 2005). Poverty relationship with lower SWB has been strongly documented by recent research. Diener and Biswas-Diener (2002) have found evidence for a link between extreme relative poverty and lowest SWB or life satisfaction. This link is stronger than the general SWB-income relationship in rich countries

It should be added that an acceptable level of quality of life cannot be realized and economic growth prospects cannot be achieved without a solid infrastructure. If transportation and communication sector, viewed as the backbone of development, may illustrate the failures of the Muslim countries to provide for a decent life for their populace, the figures reported by the Economic and Social Research and Training Center for Islamic Countries Report paint a gloomy picture noting the backwardness of these countries in all: air, land, and sea transport. Muslim states are still lagging behind in information technology and communication.

While the total area of OIC countries is almost three times that of the United States, United Kingdom, France, and Japan put together, the total road network in those four countries amounts to 8.8 million kilometers or three times that of the OICs of 2.9 million kilometers. The OIC railway network is 101,304 km representing half of that of the US, while the total network of the UK, France, and Japan is 72% of that of the OIC region.

Regarding maritime transportation, the 55 OIC nations have a merchant fleet of 2,716 ships, with the highest numbers found in Indonesia, Turkey, Malaysia, Egypt, Iran, and Syria, with these six countries accounting for over 75% of total OIC merchant fleet. OIC fleet merchant amounted to 35.5 million gross registered tons by the end of 2002 accounting for 6% of the world total (SESRTCIC 2005).

The same source indicates that OIC countries have 4,485 airports of which only less than a third have paved runways. The US, in comparison, has four times

23 The Quality of Life of Muslim Populations: The Case of Algeria

Table 23.2 Poverty human development and commitment to education in muslim countries

Country mame	Population below poverty line[a] (2011)[a]	Human poverty index for developing countries HPI-1 (2002)[b]	2007[c] (Rank out of 182 countries)	Human development index HDI (2002)[b] 2002[b]	2007[c] (Rank out of 182 countries)	Adult literacy rate (% age 15 and above) 2002[c]	Education index[c] 2002[b]	2007[c]
Afghanistan	36% (32)	–	59.8 (135)	–	0.352 (181)	–		0.354
Albania	25% (56)	–	4.0 (15)	0.781	0.818 (70)	98.7	0.89	0.886
Algeria	23% (61)	21.9	17.5 (71)	0.704	0.745 (104)	68.9	0.69	0.748
Azerbaijan	11% (84)	–	10.7 (50)	0.746	0.787 (86)	97	0.88	0.881
Bahrain	NA (102)	–	8.0 (39)	0.843	0.895 (39)	88.5	0.85	0.893
Bangladesh	36.3% (30)	42.2	36.1 (112)	0.509	0.543 (146)	41.1	0.45	0.530
Benin	37.4% (28)	45.7	43.2 (126)	0.421	0.492 (161)	39.8	0.44	0.445
Brunei	NA (102)	–	–	0.867	0.920 (30)	93.9	0.87	0.891
Burkina Faso	46.4% (19)	65.5	51.8 (131)	0.302	0.389 (177)	12.8	0.16	0.301
Cameroun	48% (16)	36.9	30.8 (95)	0.501	0.523 (153)	67.9	0.64	0.627
Chad	80% (2)	49.6	53.1 (132)	0.379	0.392 (175)	45.8	0.42	0.334
Comoros	60% (9)	31.4	20.4 (78)	0.530	0.576 (139)	56.2	0.53	0.655
Cote d'Ivoire	42% (23)	45.0	37.4 (119)	0.399	0.484 (163)	49.7	0.47	0.450
Djibouti	42% (23)	34.3	25.6 (86)	0.454	0.520 (155)	65.5	0.52	0.554
Egypt	20% (63)	30.9	23.4 (82)	0.653	0.703 (123)	55.6	0.62	0.697
Gabon	NA (102)	–	17.5 (72)	0.648	0.775 (103)	71.0	0.72	0.843
Gambia	NA (102)	45.8	40.9 (123)	0.452	0.456 (168)	37.8	0.40	0.439
Guinea	47% (17)	–	50.5 (129)	0.425	0.435 (170)	41.0	0.37	0.361
Guinea-Bissau	NA (102)	48.0	34.9 (107)	0.350	0.396 (173)	39.6	0.39	0.552
Guyana	NA (102)	12.9	10.2 (48)	0.719	0.729 (114)	96.5	0.89	0.939
Indonesia	13.3% (78)	17.8	17.0 (69)	0.692	0.734 (111)	87.9	0.80	0.840
Iran	18% (69)	16.4	12.8 (59)	0.732	0.782 (88)	77.1	0.74	0.793
Iraq	25 (56)	–	19.4 (75)	–	–	–	–	0.695
Jordan	14.2% (76)	07.2	6.6 (29)	0.750	0.770 (96)	90.9	0.86	0.870
Kazakhstan	12.1% (81)	–	7.9 (37)	0.766	0.804 (82)	99.4	0.93	0.965
Kuwait	NA (102)	–	–	0.838	0.916 (31)	82.9	0.81	0.872
Kyrgyzstan	40% (25)	–	7.3 (31)	0.701	0.710 (120)	97.0	0.92	0.918
Lebanon	28% (49.)	9.5	7.6 (33)	0.758	0.803 (83)	86.5	0.84	0.857
Libya	NA (102)	15.3	13.4 (60)	0.794	0.847 (55)	81.7	0.87	0.898
Malaysia	5.1% (96)	–	6.1 (25)	0.793	0.829 (66)	88.7	0.83	0.851
Maldives	16% (72)	11.4	16.5 (66)	0.752	0.771 (95)	97.2	0.91	0.885
Mali	36.1% (31)	58.9	54.5 (133)	0.326	0.371 (178)	19.0	0.21	0.331
Mauritania	40% (25)	48.3	36.2 (115)	0.465	0.520 (154)	41.2	0.42	0.541
Morocco	15% (74)	34.5	31.1 (96)	0.620	0.654 (130)	50.7	0.53	0.574
Mozambique	70% (4)	49.8	46.8 (127)	0.354	0.402 (172)	46.5	0.45	0.478
Niger	63% (8)	61.4	55.8 (134)	0.292	0.340 (182)	17.1	0.18	0.282
Nigeria	70% (4)	35.1	36.2 (114)	0.466	0.511 (158)	66.8	0.59	0.657
Oman	NA (102)	31.5	14.7 (64)	0.770	0.846 (56)	74.7	0.71	0.790
Pakistan	24% (58)	41.9	33.4 (101)	0.497	0.572 (141)	41.5	0.40	0.492
Palestine (occupied territories)	60% in W. Bank and 60% in Gaza Strip 70, (4)	–	6.0 (24)	0.726	0.737 (110)	90.2	0.86	0.886
Qatar	NA (102)	–	5.0 (19)	0.833	0.910 (33)	84.2	0.83	0.888
Saudi Arabia	NA (102°)	15.8	12.1 (53)	0.768	0.843 (59)	77.9	0.71	0.828
Senegal	54% (12)	44.1	41.6 (124)	0.437	0.464 (166)	39.3	0.39	0.417

(continued)

Table 23.2 (continued)

Country mame	Population below poverty line[a] (2011)[a]	Human poverty index for developing countries HPI-1 (2002)[b]	2007[c] (Rank out of 182 countries)	Human development index HDI (2002)[b] 2002[b]	2007[c] (Rank out of 182 countries)	Adult literacy rate (% age 15 and above) 2002[c]	Education index[c] 2002[b]	2007[c]
Sierra Leone	70% (3)	–	47.7 (128)	0.273	0.365 (180)	36.0	0.39	0.403
+Somalia	NA (102)	–	–	–	–	–	–	–
Sudan	40 (25)	31.6	34.0 (104)	0.505	0.531 (150)	59.9	0.52	0.539
Suriname	70% (4)	–	10.1 (46)	0.780	07.69 (97)	94.0	0.87	0.850
Syria	11.9% (83)	13.7	12.6 (56)	0.710	0.742 (107)	82.9	0.75	0.773
Tajikistan	60% (9)	–	18.2 (74)	0.671	0.688 (127)	99.5	0.90	0.896
Togo	32% (39)	38.0	36.6 (117)	0.495	0.499 (159)	59.6	0.62	0.534
Tunisia	3.8% (99)	19.2	15.6 (65)	0.745	0.769 (98)	73.2	0.74	0.772
Turkey	17.11 (70)	12.0	8.3 (40)	0.751	0.806 (79)	86.9	0.80	0.828
Turkmenistan	30% (43)	–	–	0.752	0.739 (109)	98.8	0.93	0.906
Uganda	35% (34.)	36.4	28.8 (91)	0.493	0.514 (151)	68.9	0.70	0.698
United Arab Emirates	19.5 (65)	–	7.7 (35)	0.824	0.903 (35)	77.3	0.74	0.838
Uzbekistan	26 (54)	–	8.5 (42)	0.709	0.710 (119)	99.3	0.91	0.888
Yemen	45.2 (21)	40.3	35.7 (111)	0.482	0.575 (140)	49	0.50	0.574

Sources:
[a]CIA World Factbook, 2011
[b]UNDP Human Development Report, 2004 (pp. 246–249; 139–142)
[c]UNDP Human Development Report, 2009 (pp. 176–178)

more paved airports than the entire OIC countries. Only five countries, Pakistan, Turkey, Iraq, Egypt, and Saudi Arabia, have more paved runways compared to the others.

The total OIC number of passenger carriers is 107.6 million, which is less than that in Japan alone. The highest number of kilometers flown was observed in Malaysia, Turkey, Indonesia, Saudi Arabia, and the United Arab Emirates (SESRTCIC 2005).

While there are around 79 million telephone lines in the OIC region which is higher than that of Canada and Japan, there is however a major gap in terms of the number of lines per 100 inhabitants. The OIC average is 6.3 while the world average is 18 per 100 inhabitants. The 83 million cell phones in the OIC region are still lower in terms of subscribers per 100 inhabitants compared to the rest of the word. The number of personal computers is estimated at 25 million which represents 4 percent out of the world total, with 17 million of the total found in Iran, Malaysia, Saudi Arabia, Turkey, and Indonesia.

The situation of the Internet is abysmal, with only 458,432 subscribers, making it 0.3% of the world total (SESRTCIC 2005). Though these figures need updating and many Muslim countries have made important progresses, they give an idea on present challenges facing most of these countries on the way to modernization.

Another important question should be added here: Has Islam anything to do with the slow of economic growth? In other words: Has Islam an adverse impact on the country's economy? This speculation seems groundless because some countries with large proportion of Muslim population are performing well economically – countries such as Turkey, Malaysia, and Indonesia. Furthermore, history teaches us that Muslim countries were at the peak of the world economy for long centuries and that Islam encourages earnings through work within a set of moral guidelines. It is through Muslim business relationships that Islam in its early times reached economic heights such as China.

Knowing that Muslims are nowadays the fastest growing consumer segment worldwide, many researchers are shifting their attention to Islamic ethics and their implications for business (e.g., Rice 1999). Recently, Williams and Zinkin (2010) compared the UN Global Compact ten principles and the tenets of Islam regarding responsible business, and with a couple of exceptions found no divergence between the two. They concluded: "Indeed Islam often goes further and has the advantage of clearer codification of ethical standards as well as a set of explicit enforcement mechanisms" (p. 519).

The economic backwardness of Islamic states should be understood in other ways. Historically speaking, colonization, war conflicts, and exploitation could account for the economic backwardness. Other intrinsic factors are also important, namely type of governance, illiteracy, and internal instability. Most of the economies in Muslim countries are informal, falling between the hands of smugglers and organization monopolies that are run by the few and corrupt at the highest spheres of the state hierarchy. That is, corruption may be a huge factor.

Another factor is the global interconnectedness of the world economy. The global financial crisis of 2008 has proved once again the vulnerability of the current world financial system, which is basically built on speculation. This unprecedented crisis has caused considerable slowdown in economic growth worldwide and has led even those developed countries such as Greece and Ireland to bankruptcy. Its effects are expected to be long lasting especially in our sample countries for their total reliance on developed countries in all aspects of economic life (reports: Naudé 2009; IMF Oct. 2010). The effects of the large increases in food prices and widely consuming products in the world markets are contributing to world poverty. The widespread of civil unrest in the Islamic world since the end of 2010 seems to be partly fuelled by these economic factors. For instance, both the totalitarian regimes of Tunisia and Egypt have already collapsed.

Education and Knowledge in Muslim Countries

The road to development and the path to overcome poverty cannot be conceived without the improvement of the quality of education and the widespread knowledge acquisition among people. An efficient educational system can be a means to expand human capabilities and enhance a strong synergy between education and the economic and social world. In Muslim countries, numerous efforts have been undertaken, mainly in terms of infrastructure. A high degree of quantitative expansion in basic education has been achieved, particularly in the rich oil-producing countries

as may be understood from the Education Index figures in Table 23.2 (UNDP 2004).

The UNDP Education Index measures the country's relative achievement in both adult literacy and combined primary, secondary, and tertiary school enrollment. The differences between Muslim countries are striking with respect to this index too. Meanwhile the best educational outcomes were achieved in 2002 in Turkmenistan and Kazakhstan (0.93), followed by Maldives and Uzbekistan (0.91); it goes as down as 0.16 in Burkina Faso, 0.18 in Niger, 0.21 in Mali, and 0.39 in Senegal and Sierra Leone. The values of the Education Index of 2007 (UNDP 2009), compared to those of 2002 (Table 23.2), indicate that most of the sample countries are making great efforts to deliver education services to their people. However, for reasons which should be studied in future research, the Education Index has slightly decreased in some countries, such as Cameroun, Chad, Guinea, Togo, Cote d'Ivoire, and Maldives. All these are poor countries for which education could play an important role in empowering people facing poverty.

Furthermore, it should be noted that the countries that were liberated from the Soviet Union (e.g., Azerbaijan, Kazakhstan, Kyrgyzstan, Uzbekistan, and Tajikistan) have the highest rate of adult literacy (beyond 95%). In contrast, adult literacy rates in sub-Saharan African states must be a source of worry. They are as low as 12.8% in Burkina Faso and 17.1% Niger. In 15 nations among the 54 countries for which information is provided (Table 23.2), the rate of literacy is lower than 50%, more than half of the population can neither read nor write. These people are the prime targets of unemployment and social exclusion.

Regarding quality education, there are many deficits even in the countries where marked efforts have been made in providing primary and secondary schooling to all children. For this reason the Arab Human Development Report (UNDP 2003) has clearly emphasized that in Arab countries, the most serious problem facing Arab education is its deteriorating quality. This factor undercuts a basic goal of human development, namely to enhance the quality of people's lives and enrich the capabilities of societies (pp. 47–51). This finding among others proves that genuine educational policies should be worked out to improve the Muslim population access to quality education.

Health Provisions in Muslim Countries

As mentioned earlier, the concept of QOL has been developed initially in connection with health research. Good health cannot be conceived unless a variety of other population's needs are met, and it is evident that people who suffer from health problems would not have a peaceful and a productive life. Therefore, the provision for a successful healthcare system is an important means toward development.

The World Health Report (2000) states that "the objective of a good health system is efficacy of two factors: the best attainable average level – *goodness* – and the smallest feasible differences among individuals and groups – *fairness*. Gains in either one of these, with no change in the other, may constitute an improvement, but the two may be in conflict" (Kircaldy et al. 2005, p. 2). Kirkcaldy and colleagues have asserted that if we want to know how good a health system is, one must objectively determine this through its effectiveness and equity, as well as subjectively in terms of well-being of its consumers.

If life expectancy at birth is considered as a product of healthcare, the disparities among Muslim countries are again striking. In 12 countries, life span does not exceed 50 years, with as down as 38.5 years in Mozambique, 41.2 years in Cote d'Ivoire, 45.2 years in Guinea-Bissau, and 45.7 in Uganda. These figures are far behind the world average of 66.9 years (UNDP 2004). In contrast, the same figures exceed 70 years in 19 countries, with the highest in Brunei (76.2), UAE (74.6), Bahrain (73.9), and Albania (73.6) (see Table 23.3).

In comparison, more than 19 countries out of 57 have life expectancy below 60 years in 2007. Table 23.3 (column 3) shows that all the countries in question registered improvements, except the former Soviet Union countries of Kazakhstan, Kyrgyzstan, Tajikistan, Turkmenistan, and Uzbekistan. Moreover, according to the UNDP statistics, Lebanon lost 1.6 years and Mali lost 0.4 years. Whatever the accuracy of these figures might be, they teach us that some improvements are taking place, but very slow – if one considers the troubling figure of 47.3 in Serra Leone, 47.5 in Guinea-Bissau, or 48.1 in Mali, while in the European Union, the corresponding figure is up to 79.0 (UNDP 2009, p. 174).

Although the rich oil-producing countries are among the leading countries in terms of expenditure on health, this is one of the areas where most of their Islamic counterparts fail. Table 23.3 provides an illustration. Two measures of the total expenditure on health as % GDP and Per Capita Expenditure on Health are reproduced from the WHO Report of 2005 and few illustrations concerning 2008 (the last column of Table 23.3). Expenditure on health from GDP ranged between 2% and 12.2% in Iraq and Lebanon in 1998, and 1.5% and 11.5% in 2002 in these two countries, respectively. Although, the increase in the expenditure on health as GDP takes different rates across the countries from 1998 to 2002, an increase is reported in 23 countries, a steadiness in six countries, and a decrease in 25 countries (see Table 23.3).

Meanwhile, the general government expenditure on health from GDP in Muslim countries varied in 2002 between 1.5% and 11.5%, it is as low as US $6 in Sierra Leone and Tajikistan and as high as US $935 Qatar and US $802 in UAE (Table 23.3). The differences are again striking. The few cases reported in Table 23.3 (last column) are illustrations of changes in the value of expenditures. They show that despite net increases in the amounts spent, they still fall short in view of the populations' increasing health needs.

Poverty and its consequences are harming people. For instance, many of the countries in which child mortality rates are high are poor in terms of GDP and continue to face economic downturn. In general, the exclusion from access to health care is commonplace in poor countries. To this, one must add the ill-preparation of health personnel, as well as poor working conditions. Absenteeism is a major issue that affects the already scarce human resource. In Burkina Faso, for example, absenteeism of health district doctors in seven rural districts in 1997 varied between 30% and more than 80% (World health report 2005). However, all these aspects deserve specialized studies to help formulate appropriate development strategies in this area.

Political Life and Freedom in Muslim Countries

Political instability is evident in many parts of the Muslim world. Let us begin here with some of the worst cases. Owing to a precarious economic, social, or security situation, people are often forced to flee their homes in order to find refuge crossing the nearest borders.

Table 23.3 Life expectancy and health expenditure in Muslim countries

Country	Life expectancy at birth in years		Total expenditure on health as % GDP			Per capita expenditure on health at average exchange rate (US$)[c]		
	2002[a]	2007[d]	1998[b]	2002[b]	2009[d] (Rank)	1998	2002	2008 (cases only)
Afghanistan	–	43.6	6	8	7.3 (08)	8	14	48
Albania	73.6	76.5	6.4	6.1		58	94	
Algeria	69.5	72.2	3.8	4.3		62	77	
Azerbaijan	72.1	70.0	4.7	3.7		26	27	
Bahrain	73.9	75.6	4.9	4.4	3.6 (08)	474	517	1.000
Bangladesh	61.1	65.7	3.1	3.1		11	11	
Benin	50.7	61.0	4.5	4.7		18	20	
Brunei	76.2	77.0	3.8	3.5		463	430	
Burkina Faso	45.8	52.7	4.3	4.3		12	11	
Cameroon	46.8	50.9	4.4	4.6		28	31	
Chad	44.7	48.6	5.4	6.5		12	14	
Comoros	60.6	64.9	3.4	2.9		11	10	
Cote d'Ivoire	41.2	56.8	6.4	6.2		54	44	
Djibouti	45.8	55.1	6.3	6.3	8.5 (08)	52	54	88
Egypt	68.6	69.9	5	4.9	6.4 (08)	64	59	124
Gabon	56.6	60.1	4.3	4.3		162	159	
Gambia	53.9	55.7	6.8	7.3		23	18	
Guinea	48.9	57.3	5.3	5.8		24	22	
Guinea-Bissau	45.2	47.5	5.1	6.3		8	9	
Guyana	63.2	66.5	5	5.6		48	53	
Indonesia	66.6	70.5	2.5	3.2		12	26	
Iran	70.1	71.2	5.8	6	6.3(08)	55	104	300
Iraq	–	67.8	2	1.5	2.7(08)	11	11	95
Jordan	70.9	72.4	8.6	9.3	8.5 (08)	144	165	277
Kazakhstan	66.2	64.9	3.8	3.5		53	56	
Kuwait	76.5	77.5	4.4	3.8	2.0 (08)	557	547	1.006
Kyrgyzstan	68.4	67.6	5.8	4.3		20	14	
Lebanon	73.5	71.9	12.2	11.5	8.8(08)	588	568	599
Libya	72.6	73.8	3.7	3.3		210	121	
Malaysia	73.0	74.1	3	3.8		99	149	
Maldives	67.2	71.1	5.5	5.8		108	120	
Mali	48.5	48.1	4.2	4.5		11	12	
Mauritania	52.3	56.6	2.7	3.9		11	14	
Morocco	68.5	71.0	4.4	4.6	5.3 (08)	56	55	144
Mozambique	38.5	47.8	4.1	5.8		9	11	
Niger	46.0	50.8	3.9	4		8	7	
Nigeria	51.6	47.7	5.5	4.7		17	19	
Oman	72.3	75.5	3.7	3.4	2.4 (08)	209	246	458
Pakistan	60.8	66.2	3.5	3.2	2.9(08)	16	13	24
Palestine, Occupied	72.3	73.3	–	–		–	–	
Qatar	72.0	75.5	4	3.1	3.3(08)	736	935	2.935
Saudi Arabia	72.1	72.7	5	4.3	3.3(08)	354	345	621
Senegal	52.7	55.4	4.2	5.1		22	27	
Sierra Leone	34.3	47.3	3	2.9		5	6	
Somalia	–	49.7	2.7	n/a	–	6	n/a	–

(continued)

Table 23.3 (continued)

Country	Life expectancy at birth in years		Total expenditure on health as % GDP			Per capita expenditure on health at average exchange rate (US$)[c]		
	2002[a]	2007[d]	1998[b]	2002[b]	2009[d] (Rank)	1998	2002	2008 (cases only)
Sudan	55.5	57.9	5.2	4.9	3.6(08)	20	19	49
Suriname	71.0	68.8	7.3	8.6		194	197	
Syria	71.7	74.1	5.3	5.1	3.2(08)	57	58	79
Tajikistan	68.6	66.4	3.3	3.3		7	6	
Togo	49.9	62.2	10.5	10.5		35	36	
Tunisia	72.7	73.8	5.9	5.8	6.0(08)	126	126	231
Turkey	70.4	71.7	4.8	6.5		149	172	
Turkmenistan	66.9	64.6	4	4.3		27	79	
Uganda	45.7	51.9	5.4	7.4		15	18	
United Arab Emirates	74.6	77.3	4	3.1	2.4(08)	724	802	1.551
Uzbekistan	69.5	67.6	6.6	5.5		41	21	
Yemen	59.8	62.5	4.9	3.7	5.6(08)	18	23	57

Sources:
[a]Human Development Report 2004 (pp. 139–142)
[b]WHO report 2005 (pp. 192–198)
[c]WHO Report 2005 (pp. 200–203)
[d]Human Development Report 2009 (pp. 171–174)

For instance, following the conflict in the Darfur region of western Sudan, since 2003, 500,000 Sudanese refugees are presently in eight neighboring countries and millions of internally displaced persons, among them 210,000 sought refuge in the already poor country of Chad (UNHCR and the OIC secretariat 2005). After the split up of Sudan into two countries, the situation is not expected to significantly improve soon. Many conflicting issues may fuel tensions, such as borders and the sharing of oil revenues.

Another significant number of Iraqis have taken refuge in neighboring countries and further abroad since the security situation has been not normalized. In Asia, the protracted exile of some 20,000 Muslim refugees of Myanmar in Bangladesh was a major source of concern to UNHCR. Although the vast majority of the initial 250,000 refugees have voluntarily returned to Myanmar, those remaining in Bangladesh have been without a lasting solution for more than a decade (UNHCR and the OIC secretariat 2005). Sahara Occidental in North Africa is another case where thousands of refugees are awaiting a solution in neighboring Algeria, since 1975.

In 2005, the 57 member States of the OIC were hosting about 6.5 million refugees and persons of concern to UNHCR – 38% of the world's total of some 16.9 million (UNHCR and the OIC secretariat 2005). These figures do not include the four million Palestinian refugees (estimated by UNHCR at 4,766,670 refugees in the beginning of 2010) who fall within the specific mandate given by the United Nations General Assembly to the United Nations Relief and Works Agency (UNRWA) for Palestine Refugees.

It should be noted that in nearly all cases, countries hosting large refugee populations are often among the least developed countries and refugee-hosting communities are often located in remote areas where a high level of poverty prevails. Restrictive regulations that limit the freedom of movement and access to education, skills training, and productive livelihoods often face refugees. Consequently, their potential for human growth and development is stifled. Reducing refugees to mere recipients of humanitarian assistance, limit their opportunities to contribute positively to the economy and society of the asylum country. Idleness and dependency can fuel frustration, tension, and even conflict within communities (UNHCR and the OIC secretariat 2005).

Although international agencies should be praised for refugees' assistance, the situation becomes very complicated even if the refugees seek to return home. The subsequent process of the reintegration of returnees poses a considerable challenge as the local environment of postconflict situations is fragile. It becomes clear that strong international financial support, poverty alleviation, and investments in long-term development remain necessary, along with a specific treatment of statelessness. Reports indicate that large numbers of people in the Muslim world continue to live with no formal bond to any states or with no effective citizenship. Reducing and preventing statelessness remain one of the major challenges for many OIC countries and are part of UNHCR's mandate toward stateless persons as provided for by the 1954 Convention relating to the Status of Stateless Persons and the 1961 Convention on the Reduction of Statelessness (UNHCR and the OIC secretariat 2005).

The case of migration to the West and asylum seekers from Islamic countries is subject of wide concern. To this, we can add the brain drain of competencies out of the Muslim world where these highly qualified people are urgently needed. Instability has made the Muslim world an unpleasant place where people could live, work, and invest peacefully. Ratings of the Countries Risk Scale reported by the OECD are discouraging as far as foreign investors in the Muslim world are concerned (OECD 2003).

Furthermore, because of the high figures of illiteracy among the population in most Muslim countries as mentioned earlier, political paternalism is often maintained. According to the large-scale international study of World Values Survey (WVS), Arabs whose large majority are Muslims, value knowledge and good governance strongly but take an ambivalent stand on gender equality (Inglehart and Norris 2003; Tessler 2003). Among the nine regions, Arabs expressed the highest preference for the role of science in the service of humanity. Arabs also topped the list of those supporting the statement that "democracy is better than any other form of government" and expressed the highest level of rejection of authoritarian rule – a strong leader who does not have to bother with parliament and elections (UNDP 2003, p. 19). It seems that political aspirations that value democracy and liberties are popular among Muslims too. Furthermore, school manuals in Muslim countries and Mosques often quote the famous phrase of Omar Ibn Khattab, the second Islamic Khalif: "Since when have you compelled people to enslavement, when their mothers birthed them free?" He is as well the one who have said to his companions: "If you see deviation in me, straighten it out with your

swords." Regardless of the method, the notions of accountability of the rulers to the people and the people's right to take action whenever the rulers have violated their rights have been a traditional Islamic ideal (Raphaeli 2005).

But facts on the ground are again disturbing. In Table 23.4, some illustrations are imported from the growing international literature on this broad subject. Two more major indicators will be cited below: The perceived Corruption Index (PCI) ratings of the year 2002 and 2010 and the state of freedom as estimated in 2003 and 2010.

Corruption ratings relate to perceptions of the degree of corruption as seen by international business people, academics, and risk analysts and range between 10 (highly clean) and 0 (highly corrupt) (Transparency International 2002). None of the Muslim countries is cited among the relatively clean countries from corruption in the world. From Table 23.4, it is apparent that the worst figures are reported in the small rich Arab countries of Bahrain (3.9), Qatar (4.4), Kuwait (4.7), and the UAE (4.8). Whereas, eight points and beyond are found in countries such as Bangladesh (8.7), Nigeria (8.6), Cameroon and Tajikistan (8.2), Indonesia (8.1), and Azerbaijan (8.0). These latter countries are less corrupt than other Muslim countries (Transparency International 2002). In comparison with 2010, the picture generally remained the same with unacceptable levels of corruption (Table 23.4, column 3).

The results of the overall annual evaluation of the state of Global Freedom of the World Survey, however methodologically debatable, may add some clarity to this issue. Two measures are included in the Survey: Political Rights (PR) stands for the free participation in the political process through elections, and Civil Liberties (CL) includes the freedom to develop opinions, institutions, and personal autonomy without interference from the state. It is said that more than 30 judges are included in the ratings process of the target countries. They are analysts/writers and senior-level academic advisors using a variety of sources of information and reports and visits (Freedom House 2003). Although this seems an oversimplification of a complex issue, as far as our sample countries are concerned, the results included in Table 23.4 indicate that among the 56 countries surveyed, five only (Benin, Guyana, Mali, Senegal, and Suriname), with a total population of around 30.3 million, enjoy political rights and civil liberties.

Table 23.4 Estimates of corruption and overall freedom in Muslim countries

Country name	Corruption (scale 0–10)		Overall freedom rating (scale 0–7)[b]					
	2002[a] (ranking)	2010[c] (ranking)	2003 PR	2003 CR	Status of freedom (2003)	2010 PR[c]	2010 CR[c]	Status of freedom (2010)
Afghanistan		1.4 (176)	6	6	Not free	6	6	Not free
Albania		3.3 (87)	3	3	Partly free	3	3	Partly free
Algeria		2.9 (105)	6	5	Not free	6	5	Not free
Azerbaijan	2.0 (95)	2.4 (134)	6	5	Not free	6	5	Not free
Bahrain		4.9 (48)	5	5	Partly free	6 ▼	5	Partly free
Bangladesh	1.2 (102)	2.4 (134)	4	4	Partly free	3 ▲	4	Partly free
Benin		2.8 (110)	2	2	Free	2	2	Free
Brunei		5.5 (38)	6	5	Not free	6	5	Not free
Burkina Faso		3.1 (98)	4	4	Partly free	5 ▼	3 ▲	Partly free
Cameroon	2.2 (89)	2.2 (146)	6	6	Not free	6	6	Not free
Chad		1.7 (171)	6	5	Not free	7 ▼	6 ▼	Not free
Comoros		2.1 (154)	5	4	Partly free	4 ▲	3 ▲	Partly free
Cote d'Ivoire	2.7 (71)	2.2 (146)	6	5	Not free	6	5	Not free
Djibouti		3.2 (91)	5	5	Partly free	5	5	Partly free
Egypt	4.3 (62)	3.1 (98)	6	6	Not free	6	5 ▲	Not free
Gabon		2.8 (110)	5	4	Partly free	6 ▼	5 ▼	Not free
Gambia		3.2 (91)	4	4	Partly free	5 ▼	4	Partly free
Guinea		2.0 (164)	6	5	Not free	7 ▼	6 ▼	Not free
Guinea-Bissau		2.1 (154)	6	4	Partly free	4 ▲	4	Partly free
Guyana		2.7 (116)	2	2	Free	2	3 ▼	Free
Indonesia	1.9 (96)	2.8 (110)	3	4	Partly free	3	4	Free
Iran		2.2 (146)	6	6	Not free	6	6	Not free
Iraq		1.5 (175)	7	5	Not free	5 ▲	6 ▼	Not free
Jordan	4.5 (40)	4.7 (50)	5	5	Partly Free	6 ▼	5	Not free
Kazakhstan	2.3 (88)	2.9 (105)	6	5	Not free	6	5	Not free
Kuwait		4.5 (54)	4	5	Partly free	4	4 ▲	Partly free
Kyrgyzstan		2.0 (164)	6	5	Not free	6	5	Not free
Lebanon		2.5 (127)	6	5	Not free	5 ▲	3 ▲	Partly free
Libya		2.2 (146)	7	7	Not free	7	7	Not free
Malaysia	4.9 (33)	4.4 (56)	5	4	Partly free	4 ▲	4	Partly free
Maldives		2.3 (143)	6	5	Not free	3 ▲	4 ▲	Partly free
Mali		2.3 (143)	2	2	Free	2	3 ▼	Free
Mauritania		2.3 (143)	6	5	Not free	6	5	Not free
Morocco	3.7 (52)	3.4 (85)	5	5	Partly free	5	4 ▲	Partly free
Mozambique		2.7 (116)	3	4	Partly free	4 ▼	5 ▼	Partly free
Niger		2.6 (123)	4	4	Partly free	5 ▼	4	Partly free
Nigeria	1.6 (101)	2.4 (134)	4	4	Partly free	5 ▼	4	Partly free
Oman		5.3 (41)	6	5	Not free	6	5	Not free
Pakistan	2.6 (77)	2.3 (143)	6	5	Not free	4 ▲	5	Partly free
Palestine		–	–	–	–			
Qatar		7.7 (19)	6	6	Not Free	6	5 ▼	Not free
Saudi Arabia		4.7 (50)	7	7	Not free	7	6 ▲	Not free
Senegal	3.1 (66)	2.9 (105)	2	3	Free	3 ▼	3	Free
Sierra Leone		2.4 (134)	4	3	Partly free	3 ▲	3	Partly free
Somalia		1.1 (178)	6	7	Not Free	7 ▼	7	Not free
Sudan		1.6 (172)	7	7	Not free	7	7	Not free

(continued)

23 The Quality of Life of Muslim Populations: The Case of Algeria

Table 23.4 (continued)

	Corruption (scale 0–10)		Overall freedom rating (scale 0–7)[b]					
Country name	2002[a] (ranking)	2010[c] (ranking)	2003 PR	2003 CR	Status of freedom (2003)	2010 PR[c]	2010 CR[c]	Status of freedom (2010)
Suriname		–	1	2	Free	2▼	2	Free
Syria		2.5 (127)	7	7	Not free	7	6▲	Not free
Tajikistan		2.1 (154)	6	5	Not free	6	5	Not free
Togo		2.4 (134)	6	5	Not free	5▲	4▲	Partly free
Tunisia	4.8 (5)	4.3 (59)	6	5	Not free	7▼	5	Not free
Turkey	3.2 (64)	4.4 (56)	3	4	Partly free	3	3▲	Partly free
Turkmenistan		1.6 (172)	7	7	Not free	7	7	Not free
Uganda	2.1 (93)	2.5 (127)	5	4	Partly free	5	4	Partly free
United Arab Emirates		6.3 (28)	6	6	Not free	6	5▲	Not free
Uzbekistan	2.9 (68)	1.6 (172)	7	6	Not free	7	7▼	Not free
Yemen		2.2 (146)	5	5	Partly free	6▼	5	Not free
	Out of 102 countries	Out of 178 countries				▼Decreasing ▲Improving		

Sources:

[a]PCI ranges between 10 (highly clean) and 0 (highly corrupt)–Transparency International 2002 (http://www.transparency.org/policy_research/surveys_indices/cpi/2002)

[b]The World Survey Global Freedom 2003 (www.freedomhouse.org)

[c]http://www.transparency.org/policy_research/surveys_indices/cpi/2010/results

http://www.freedomhouse.org/uploads/fiw10/FIW_2010_Tables_and_Graphs.pdf

All f them are poor, small, and non-Arab countries. The huge majority of 30 countries among the 56 surveyed freedoms are very limited, including the more populous countries such as Turkey and Pakistan. In comparison, up to 2010, eight (08) countries have their general appraisal changed, 03 of them to the worst (Gabon, Jordan, and Yemen), while Indonesia moved from "Partly Free" to "Free", and Lebanon, Maldives, Pakistan, and Togo moved from "Not Free" to "Partly Free." The PR measure has improved in ten countries, decreased in 14 countries, and remained unchanged in 31 countries. Meanwhile, CL measure has improved in 12 countries, decreased in 09 countries, and remained unchanged in 35 countries. Generally, this is not much progress over a time span of 8 years.

In line with these results, some Arab intellectuals are producing compelling jargon and characterizations to portray the realities of their governments. Governments are viewed as a "*black hole,*" and the efforts of some Arab leaders to gain legitimacy are labeled "*legitimacy blackmail.*" In the black hole model, the powers of the ruler are absolute: "A setting in which nothing – in the surrounding social environment – moves and from which nothing escapes." The judiciary

is tamed, the media is dominated, parliament becomes a bureaucratic adjunct, and national wealth is used by the ruler to enrich himself and a coterie of family members, political associates, and friends. This is encouraged through a system of monopoly, a "rentier" model of production, where taxes are not paid, no real separation of powers, the order of succession is determined by the dictators themselves, and corruption is widespread (The Third Arab Human Development Report cited in Raphaeli 2005).

As for the notion of "Legitimacy Blackmail," it portrays that Arab leaders have sought new forms of legitimacy: religious, tribal, and nationalist, instead of gaining it through their people free choice. In some cases, they are presenting themselves as the lesser of two evils: *we may be bad but the alternative is worse* (Raphaeli 2005). The alternative is often presented as religious fundamentalism. Indeed, combating terrorism seems to work in favor of the totalitarian regimes to preserve the status quo which remains in their favor.

Based on the preceding discussion, we concluded that change is needed to realize the legitimate aspirations of the people. The highly controversial UNDP Arab

Human Development Report of 2005 offers three scenarios for change in the Arab World (Raphaeli 2005):
- Maintaining the status quo to which it is referred as the "Impending Disaster Scenario" that will lead to destructive upheavals.
- The "*Izdihar*" alternative that sees the ideal scenario of change is through the provision for "a solid foundation for freedom and good governance."
- The "Halfway House" scenario consists of a gradual and a moderate promotion of reform, incorporating appropriate regional or international initiatives (p. 5).

Up to now, the Iraqi case has taught the world that the ideal change cannot be forced from outside, through military interventions. It must be gradually worked out through the promotion of a culture of human rights respect, freedom, and equity.

It seems that current history is pressing forward, and signs of change are becoming real. Unexpectedly, great revolutions are taking place at least in North Africa and the Middle East. The ongoing events prove that Arab and Islamic populace will not remain silent. While preparing the final version of this chapter, Tunisians and Egyptians have already succeeded in overthrowing the totalitarian regimes that have been in power for long decades (respectively 23 and 31 years). Other Islamic and Arab countries seem to follow such as Yemen, Libya, Bahrain, Oman, and Iran. Although economic factors may partly explain the origin of these changes, the role played by modern communications and media should not be excluded. Social Internet networks have conquered the private space of local regimes' propaganda and allowed people to freely interact. Moreover, in a world that is increasingly becoming "global," some independent TV stations have provided live coverage of almost all important events. These and other factors are speeding up change in Muslim countries.

Subjective Indicators of Quality of Life in Muslim Countries

It is no secret that monitoring societies' progress has been for a long time dominated by the use of objective, mainly economic, measures. The main assumption has been that money automatically boosts life satisfaction and happiness. It should be noted that at the conceptual level, the use of Subjective Well-being (SWB) has been coined to cover the area for which concepts such as life satisfaction and happiness are already interchangeably used. However, a growing body of research has recently challenged such an assumption at the individual, as well as the wider national level. This means that large and measurable slippages exist between economic indicators and subjective indicators (e.g., Diener and Seligman 2004). Trying to answer the question of whether raising incomes of all the people increase their happiness, Hagerty and Veenhoven (2003) described two competing theories: Absolute Utility Theory and Relative Utility Theory. The first theory advocates that additional income allows each person to meet additional needs; consequently, this increases average happiness. Meanwhile, the second theory argues that a rise in income will produce at best short-lived gains in happiness; and therefore raising incomes of all may not increase average happiness. Using survey data from countries with different levels of development, Hagerty and Veenhoven concluded that "increasing national income does go with increasing national happiness, but the short-term effect on happiness is higher than the long-term effect for a given rise in income." Another aspect of the relationship between income and subjective indicators, such as SWB, is that meanwhile a strong correlation is questionable as far as rich countries are concerned; this correlation tends to be stronger for developing countries (Diener and Biswas-Diener 2002; Kenny 2005). These results may prove that income is still a poor substitute of happiness. But taking into account the poor achievements in terms of economic and social development of the Muslim countries that have been discussed earlier, and regardless of the measures used, subjective indicators of well-being are expected to be lower in Muslim countries than those in the more advanced countries. It should be noted that due to the lack of qualified research institutions and the scarcity of publications in the Muslim countries, very limited data are available shedding enough light on people's well-being in those countries.

In regards to the notion that SWB might be in part culturally influenced as revealed by the research conducted by Diener and Tov (2004), we need to acknowledge the role of culture in SWB in Muslim countries. The results reported here still are consistent with our assertion that multifaceted problems linked to underdevelopment in Muslim countries may account for the relatively low levels of life satisfaction. This is reinforced by the recent estimates of the UNDP (2010) concerning perceptions of Individual Well-Being and Happiness in some Islamic nations (see Table 23.5).

Table 23.5 Perceptions of individual well-being and happiness in some Islamic countries

Country name	Overall LS (0–10)	Personal health % of respondents who are satisfied	Standard of living % of respondents who are satisfied	Neg. experience (0 most negative, 100 least negative)
Afghanistan	4.1	79	53	24
Albania	4.6	75	43	20
Algeria	5.6	87	61	33
Azerbaijan	5.3	68	42	21
Bahrain	–	86	66	37
Bangladesh	5.3	73	63	22
Benin	3.0	68	23	24
Brunei	–	–	–	–
Burkina Faso	3.6	70	27	24
Cameroon	3.9	69	40	23
Chad	5.4	69	52	20
Comoros	–	67	23	16
Cote d'Ivoire	4.5	68	17	16
Djibouti	5.7	67	54	27
Egypt	5.8	86	82	33
Gabon	–	–	–	–
Gambia	–	–	–	–
Guinea	4.5	75	27	26
Guinea-Bissau	–	–	–	–
Guyana	6.5	87	64	28
Indonesia	5.7	83	62	13
Iran	5.6	82	55	32
Iraq	5.5	66	41	36
Jordan	5.7	89	72	28
Kazakhstan	6.1	68	51	13
Kuwait	6.6	89	77	24
Kyrgyzstan	5.0	74	48	16
Lebanon	4.7	80	58	39
Libya	–	78	64	–
Malaysia	6.6	87	68	15
Maldives	–	–	–	–
Mali	3.8	71	30	13
Mauritania	5.0	79	47	19
Morocco	5.8	68	71	19
Mozambique	3.8	82	46	22
Niger	3.8	82	52	14
Nigeria	3.8	80	40	23
Oman				
Pakistan	5.4	75	53	32
Palestine	5.0	78	43	45
Qatar	6.7	93	86	26
Saudi Arabia	7.7	84	77	19
Senegal	4.5	68	27	22
Sierra Leone	3.6	47	19	37
Somalia	–	87	73	09
Sudan	5.0	77	64	28

(continued)

Table 23.5 (continued)

Country name	Overall LS (0–10)	Personal health % of respondents who are satisfied	Standard of living % of respondents who are satisfied	Neg. experience (0 most negative, 100 least negative)
Suriname	–	–	–	–
Syria	5.9	89	67	31
Tajikistan	5.1	75	69	21
Togo	2.6	40	11	30
Tunisia	5.9	85	72	30
Turkey	5.5	76	44	28
Turkmenistan	7.2	85	78	15
Uganda	4.5	64	35	31
United Arab Emirates	7.3	98	78	28
Uzbekistan	6.0	79	69	14
Yemen	4.6	80	53	35

Source:
UNDP (2010). Human Development Report, pp. 176–179

It is interesting to note that the highest ratings of life satisfaction are registered in some Gulf rich countries such as Saudi Arabia (7.7), UAE (7.3), Qatar (6.7), Kuwait (6.6), and Malaysia (6.6), but the worst ratings are those of poor African states of Togo (2.6), Benin (3.0), Burkina Faso (3.6), Sierra Leone (3.6), Mali (3.8), and Cameroon (3.9). In general, 20 out of 66 countries have ratings equal or less than the theoretical mean of five points, which is indicative of ill-being.

High correlations could be observed between life satisfaction, satisfaction with personal health, standard of living, and perceptions of own negative experiences in life. Generally, in Muslim countries, these subjective measures are tightly linked to economic aspirations. The data further corroborate the notion that quality of life in Muslim countries should be improved. A list of priorities of the areas of life that need coordinated intervention should be developed through scientific approaches. Humanistic-based policies that boost happiness and morale to break out of the vicious downward spiral of helplessness and underdevelopment are urgently needed. However, we hope that more refined psychological indicators will be used in the future, particularly measures of Eudaemonic Happiness that capture personal growth elements such as personal growth, purpose in life, and the pursuit of excellence and virtue.

It has been argued earlier in this chapter that Islam is not merely a set of beliefs but a code of conduct and a whole lifestyle that embraces almost every aspect of the believer's life. Worship in Islam covers all human actions that are productive and useful to oneself and others. Performing prayers is just a finite part of this system. Unfortunately, Islam itself is misunderstood and, in some cases, abused to justify politically motivated terrorism. The spirituality and peacefulness that Islam propagate are absent from public consciousness. Muslims seem to have surrendered their creative genius of their past. Widespread feelings of deception and reticence have replaced hope and openness.

Part III: The Case of Algeria

In this part, we will focus on the country of Algeria as a case study. The reason for this choice is mainly that the authors of this chapter are natives of Algeria. The goal here is to document, through the use of a variety of objective and subjective indicators, how quality of life can be compromised despite the fact the country is rich in natural resources and, to some extent, has a skilled workforce and a highly aspiring youth population. Again, this case may echo the complex realities of Muslim countries' struggle for modernization.

Algeria, during its recent history, has been unstable. This country underwent a prolonged period of colonization, followed by 27 years of a totalitarian socialist system of governance under the control of a single party. Subsequently, it went through a bloody democratic transition where some of the cruelest atrocities were committed against civilians. It is among the first nations in the world to suffer from the destructive effects of Islamist extremism.

It should be noted that currently, Algeria is considered to be the largest country in Africa, with an area of more than 2,381,000 sq km, populated by about 36 million people (after Sudan became two independent states). It is mostly an Arab and Islamic country – 99% of Algerians are Muslims (see Table 23.1). It has considerable oil and natural gas reserves (the ninth largest natural gas reserves and the second largest gas exporter in the world and ranks 14th for oil reserves), and a geostrategic position, a few kilometers away from the southern coasts of Europe.

During the period of 1954–1962, Algerians fought a fierce battle for independence from the French who have colonized the country since 1832. Algeria was legally annexed to France as a French *Département*, while native citizens had the legal status of "*Indigènes*" (second-class citizens). The war of liberation cost more than a million lives. Before the mass departure of French settlers, the Secret Armed Organization (OAS) led an armed opposition to the independence of Algeria, assassinating intellectuals and destroying the already existing poor infrastructure.

The newly independent state swung into a socialist system of governance, with one of the most totalitarian regimes, under the rules of a single party (FLN, *Front de Libération Nationale*), which held revolutionary and historical legitimacy. From independence to the mid-1980s economic growth averaged 6% annually. This allowed for average expenditures on education and health at about 10% of GDP. Indicators measuring basic needs showed continuous improvement, although rapid population growth slowed down the rate of development.

Between 1977 and 1987, the population grew at an annual average of 3.1% and remained still as high of 2.8% in the late 1980s before tapering off to an average of 2.3% during the 1987–1998 period and 1.5% in 1999–2001. The annual population growth is expected to remain steady at an average rate of 1.5% between 2002 and 2015 (Table 23.1).

In 1986, the price of crude oil fell by almost 50% compared to 1985 (the 1986 oil shock). Algeria underwent a prolonged economic crisis that slashed growth to a mere 1.5% per year on average over 1987–2001, thus contributing to rising unemployment and poverty (IMF 2003, p. 2).

Few months before the fall of the Wall of Berlin, the riots of 1988, coined as "the youth revolution," forced the regime to allow for economic and political reforms; and so, Algeria entered a plural democratic transition phase. A market economy and a multiparty system were established. The latter included the legalization of some religious parties. The first ever local and legislative democratic elections to be organized in the country were dominated by Islamic parties. The first round of legislative elections was won by the FIS (*Islamic salvation Front*) in 1991. The government at that time could not swallow such a vote and decided to nullify the results. Consequently, the country was plunged in an open-ended armed struggle between Islamists' armed groups on the one hand and the army on the other, with much of the civilian population caught in between. Independent press sources indicate that more than 200,000 lives were lost between 1992 and 2002 (Congressional Research Service 2008, *web document*, p. 3: Congressional Research Service 2008, Algeria: Current Issues, Report RS21532, http://wikileaks.org/wiki/CRS-RS21532, consulted on 28.03.2009). The officially announced figure is 100,000 dead and $26 billion worth of damage and the fate of 6,800 is not yet known and labeled "the disappeared" (*les disparus*).

Violence eased after the amnesty of many militia groups when "the civil concord" initiative was approved by a national referendum in September 1999. In another national referendum (September 2005) of what had been labeled "the Charter for Peace and National Reconciliation," 87% of the voters expressed their support to another general amnesty of militia groups. Some financial compensations were granted to the victims of "the National Tragedy." It should be noted that these were the initiatives of President Bouteflika who was first elected for 5 years in 1999, reelected for a second term of office on the April 8, 2004, and is holding office a third term since April 9, 2009 (after the passage of a constitutional amendment allowing him that third mandate).

Up to 2010, the security situation was sensibly calm. A very limited number of terrorists (affiliated since 2006 to Al-Qaida calling themselves Al Qaeda in the Land of the Islamic Maghreb [AQLIM or AQIM]) are presently finding shelter in the extreme southern parts of the country, moving in and out through the vast common borders with African Sahel countries (Niger, Mali, and Mauritania). Their major source of funding comes from kidnapping, mainly Westerners, for ransoms, and through smuggling arms. Another small group is operating in the Kabylie Mountains of the northern regions. One of their important attacks (December 11, 2007) targeted the United Nations headquarters in Algiers, and on September 6, 2007, they attempted to assassinate President Bouteflika.

The economic situation of Algeria remains fragile. One of the reasons is that the country heavily relies on oil and gas exports to finance its development programs. For instance, revenue from oil and gas exports accounts for 60% of the budget, 30% of GDP, and 97% of export earnings in 2007. Additionally, the country was, until recently, "strangled" by a heavy external debt. The Algerian government decided early repayment. Presently, this debt is extremely low at about 1% of GDP (CIA World Factbook, 2011), and according to the IMF's (25.01.2011) estimates, this represents about 2.9% of GDP in 2010 and will decrease down to 2.2% of GDP in 2011.

However, the effects of years of violence are yet felt. The violence has been a factor in the creation of a parallel economy that became dominant (Joffé 2002). A large proportion of the population fled rural areas and villages to settle down in the already crowded cities. During recent years, the government has developed many programs and incentives to stabilize the rural sector (e.g., rural construction assistance and access to investment credit).

Joffé (2002) distinguished between two forms of parallel economies: The first is connected to the regime and integrated into what Algerians themselves define as the "Mafia" – individuals originally part of the Algerian state who exploited their positions for self-interest. The other group comprised smugglers who enjoyed little political weight but exploited the economic opportunities made possible by the growth of violence.

The subsidized private sector made profits with little regard for productivity and national economic development; meanwhile, the public sector suffered massive losses. Over 450,000 workers have lost their jobs in restructuring during the last decade and, even worse, three quarters of the unemployed were under the age of 30, as the labor force was growing by an estimated 250,000 people a year (IMF 2003).

Unemployment rose from 10% in 1985 to close to 30% in 2000. While in 2001, the labor force was estimated at about nine million, about 29% of the population (IMF 2003, p. 2). By the end of 2003, the officially

Table 23.6 The unemployment rate in algeria

Year	Unemployment rate (%)	% Change	Date of information
2003	31.00		2002 est.
2004	26.20	−15.48%	2003 est.
2005	25.40	−3.05%	2004 est.
2006	17.10	−32.68%	2005 est.
2007	15.70	−8.19%	2006 est.
2008	11.80	−24.84%	2007 est.
2009	12.50	5.93%	2008 est.
2010	10.20	−18.40%	2009 est.

Source: CIA World Factbook, December 30, 2010

announced figures to the media indicate that 23.7% are unemployed, whereas Table 23.6 shows a figure of 31%. Meanwhile, unemployment decreased in 2010 to 10.20%. About 21.5% of the unemployed are young (16–25 years old) and a large proportion is women (19.1% compared to 8.1% of men). The National Statistic Office survey showed that unemployment among university graduates reached 21.4% in 2009 and much higher than the 7.3% of people without degrees. Even worse, 33.6% of jobless university degree holders are women (see National Statistic Office: www.ons.dz, accessed on December 19, 2010). These facts can be troubling, but in an economic system dominated by the informal sector, these figures are more problematic.

Furthermore, a large proportion of the Algerian population live in poverty. The percentage of the people below poverty line is reaching 23%, according to recent estimates (CIA World Factbook, 2011). Algeria is ranked 61 among world countries in terms of poverty prevalence (Table 23.2).

It is worth noting that a lot of people with permanent jobs and a regular income are not far from the poverty line, mostly because of rising consumer prices. While the legally binding minimum wage (SNMG, *salaire national minimum garanti*, which is set by the "tripartite" committee that includes the government, the labor union, and employers at the national level, and to which the private sector is also legally bound) remained fixed at DA 4,000 from January 1994 to July 1997, consumer prices recorded a cumulative increase of about 85% during this period. Although SNMG was raised by 50% over 15 months (July 1997–September 1998) to offset the adverse impact of high inflation and was increased again by one-third in 2001 (IMF 2003) until the end of 2003 (AD 8,000 per month is the equivalent of $102 per month at an exchange rate of AD 78.62 = $1 in the last quarter of 2000) (Joffé 2002). It should be noted that the SNMG was raised again in 2004 by AD 2,000 to reach AD 12,000 in 2007 and AD 15,000 in 2009. This means that SNMG was multiplied by three from 1997 to 2009.

The figures reported by Joffé (2002) indicate that average wages in 1997 seem to have been below $200 per month, at a time when the public sector wage – the usually accepted guide to national earnings levels – was $136 per month for a worker, for a technician, it was $186 per month, and for a manager, $227 per month. These wages were increased by 10% since then in response to inflation. However, overall, consumer prices have risen by 66% since 1995, while wages have only risen by 44% over the same period – although inflation is now under control, having steadily fallen from 5.7% in 1997 to 0.3% in 2000 (Joffé 2002) and is officially estimated to have reached 2.3% by the end of 2003 (CNES 2003). The inflation rate was 3% in 2003, 4.5% in 2009, and rose up to 5.7% in 2010, according to CIA World Factbook of December 30, 2010.

During the security crisis of the 1990s, the housing sector was neglected as a major problem in Algeria. The country had one of the highest occupancy ratios in the world. The National Office of Statistics (ONS) figures of 1998 indicate that this ratio was 7.1 persons per housing unit (i.e., 2.6 persons per room). Some two million additional housing units were then required, but state buildings run at just over 130,000 per year, half the required level, and the private but largely publicly financed auto construction sector had fallen prey to massive speculation and scandal (Joffé 2002). According to the state secretary of planning, by the year 2030, Algeria should build the equivalent of the already existing number of houses and infrastructure as the population is estimated to reach 45 million in 2015 (*Le quotidien d'Oran*, the daily newspaper of January 25, 2004).

However, on April 7, 2005, the first anniversary of his reelection, President Bouteflika unveiled *"Le Programme de Soutien à la Croissance Economique."* The government was then committed to spend $55 billion over the period of 5 years (up to 2009) to improve the economic situation of the country. A total of 45.4% of this sum was allocated to improve the living conditions of the population. Most important of all has been the project of constructing one million new housing units. But, the 23,000 local firms' building capacity is very limited. So, openness of the market to international firms was vital. To this date, it seems that Chinese firms are taking the lead. From 1999 to 2008, this effort resulted in the construction of 1,521,384 housing units (Portail du Premier Ministre 2010). This estimate includes the 336,596 units known as "rural constructions" intended to encourage rural populations to stay put (i.e., not to migrate to urban areas). Another major project has been the construction of the East-West highway of 1,216 km. This project managed to create 100,000 jobs (Ministère des Travaux Publics Nov. 2009).

However, profiteers and speculators of the parallel informal economy, backed by a corrupted administration, continue undermining the government efforts at economic reform. Corruption is estimated in 2010 at 2.9 with Algeria ranking 105 out of 178 world countries (Table 23.4).

The age structure of the population remains young. Out of the 32 million inhabitants, more than 11 million were under 17 years old in 2002. In January of this latter year, 32% of the population were 0–14 years old, 23% 15–24 years old, 38% 25–59 years old, and 7% 60+ years old (Ministère de la Santé 2004). It is the Algerian youth who are the prime targets of the deterioration of living standards and unemployment. In this respect, the economic recovery program (*Le programme de soutien à la croissance économique*) projected that by 2009, two million new jobs and 100,000 new small companies and businesses will be created. Moreover, the newly announced development program (*Le plan de développement 2010–2014*) projects the creation of three million new jobs over 4 years. According to news releases by *Le ministre du travail, de l'emploi et de la sécurité sociale* 500,000 new jobs already have been created and 35,000 new small enterprises have been financed by the government in 2010 alone.

However, the troubling fact is that all these projects have not deterred Algerian youth from immigration to the nearest European countries searching for stable jobs and a better life. The government instituted policies to discourage immigration with no avail. It seems that a lot of confidence building is needed to convince Algerian youth to regain trust in their own country's potential.

With regard to the issue of illegal immigration, Algeria has common borders with the poorest sub-Saharan African countries. As such, the country is becoming a crossing border to Europe, with many Africans settling in Algeria awaiting the opportunities to cross to Europe, mainly through Morocco.

Although, School enrollment has increased considerably since the independence (in 2002, it was 93.4% up from 83% in 1998 and 70.4% in 1977), the Algerian educational system at large is not performing up to par (UNESCO 2000). Annual dropouts are estimated at the rate of 500,000–560,000 pupils (CNES 2003). These youth have little chance to find appropriate training or jobs. Even worse, presently, 29% of the total population are students and this segment of the population is estimated to reach 32% by the year 2015 (*Le quotidien d'Oran* newspaper, 25. 01.2004). Illiteracy is high compared to some other Muslim countries with higher HDI ratings (Table 23.2).

Having said this, it should be noted that major changes are taking place since 2001. This is due to the significant improvements of security following the bold initiatives taken by President Bouteflika, and the rise of hydrocarbon export price. The country's money reserves officially has reached $52 billion by the beginning of 2005, up to $61 billion in the first quarter of 2006, and is up to $150 billion by 2010, which gives it more assurance to face future challenges and attract international investors.

During the period of 2010–2014, Algeria has allocated the sum of $286 billion for the development plan (2009–2014). Most important are the creation of three million new jobs and the construction of two million new housing units and more than 1,000 km of new highways.

These future prospects are echoed by the IMF (IMF 2010). IMF foresees an improvement in most economic indicators in 2010–2011, except for the budget balance which is expected to remain negative. GDP is expected to grow to $195 billion in 2010 (relative to $139 billion in 2009 and may reach $171.6 billion in 2011). The growth rate as a whole is expected to be 3.8% in 2010 and 4% in 2011. IMF statistics indicate that after early payment of most of its external debt, Algeria is, by far, the less indebted country in the whole MENA region. Its debt represents only 2.9% of GDP in 2010 and is likely to decrease to 2.2% of GDP in 2011 (IMF 2011, World Economic Outlook update).

Indeed, it may take some time for any population to enjoy the fruits of development efforts. However, studying subjective views and feelings of populations in such contexts can be very helpful for researcher and public policymakers. Economic indicators alone cannot draw a complete picture on how people do perceive change. Subjective measures can produce data guiding further development. Moreover, collecting and disseminating such data in less developed nations can help strengthen the democratization process which is increasingly sought by the Algerian people.

With regard to overall life satisfaction, Algeria's mean score is 5.6 (see Table 23.5) which is moderately low compared to other Arab oil-exporting countries. As will be shown later, this figure is somewhat lower than that of the five Algerian surveys designed to monitor personal and national well-being. The main objectives of our surveys have been to produce large data sets on well-being and its correlates. They were conducted on a regular 18-month interval since October, 2003 by the Laboratory of Educational Processes and Social Context (Labo-PECS) at the University of Oran, Algeria. The Personal Wellbeing Index captures a positive state of mind that enables people to carry out the functions of their daily life in a normal way and be productive and useful. Personal well-being monitoring aims to produce reliable data to supplement traditional economic indicators such as GDP (Tiliouine et al. 2006). Whereas, the National Wellbeing Index captures people's perceptions of the country's performance at large.

The "Algerian Wellbeing" research project has recruited respondents from the Oran region in the first two surveys, but included samples from the Midlands (El-Bayed County, *Wilaya*) on the *Hauts-plateaux* and samples from the Adrar *Wilaya* on the extreme South (Sahara) in the last three surveys. Although these are convenience samples (which limits the generalizability of the findings), the data addresses many research questions, such as the relationships between subjective well-being and factors such as self-perceived health state, religiosity, and other demographic variables. Up to 2010, a total of 13,043 questionnaires have been completed (6,505 male and 6,538 female respondents). All five surveys involved respondents from the general adult population who are 18+ years old when the survey questionnaire was completed (Mean age 30.74, SD 11.9).

Though the survey questionnaires varied in length and content, all surveys included in the beginning items of the International Wellbeing Index (IWI) (IWG 2006, *web document*) as translated into Arabic through the standard method of forward and back translations (Tiliouine et al. 2006). It is worth noting that the IWI comprises two subscales. The Personal Wellbeing Index (PWI) asks how satisfied people are with seven life domains: standard of living, personal health, achievements in life, personal relationships, personal safety, community connectedness, and future security. An eight domain concerning satisfaction with religiosity/spirituality was added (IWG 2006; Tiliouine 2009b).

The National Wellbeing Index (NWI) initially involved three questions about the economic situation, state of environment, and social conditions. In the more recent version, three more items were added – how satisfied people are with government, business, and national security, in their country in general (Tiliouine et al. 2006).

The PWI score is computed from the average satisfaction ratings across the seven or eight domains. Meanwhile, the NWI score is computed as average of satisfaction ratings across the six domains.

This research yielded interesting findings. For instance, Tiliouine (2009a) compared healthy and less healthy groups of respondents. Some marginal differences were found in PWI favoring the healthier group. This effect may be due principally to differences in health satisfaction. A possible interpretation of this finding is that the healthcare system is not performing up to par, a problem that should be addressed by public policymakers. Moreover, the healthier group has scored significantly higher satisfaction with marriage, friendship, and family relationship. This finding raises the question of the direction of causation between the state of health and social relationship.

The multidimensional construct of religiosity was studied in relation to the PWI and health (Tiliouine et al. 2009). The results indicate that, generally, religiosity is ubiquitous among the vast majority of the respondents ($N=2,909$; Survey 3) and has a strong relationship with subjective well-being. This latter relationship is relatively unaffected by dissatisfaction with health. Attempting to explain what about religion that affects subjective well-being, another study was conducted with Muslim college students ($N=494$) (Tiliouine and Belgoumidi 2009). The results show that religious belief and religious altruism significantly contribute to meaning in life. But the results from hierarchical regression analyses indicate that only religious belief makes a significant contribution in both satisfaction with life and

PWI. But, this effect has been almost totally accounted for by meaning in life in the second step. Some of the variance in life satisfaction was due to demographic variables too (Tiliouine and Belgoumidi 2009).

Interestingly, satisfaction with religiosity (which is different from the frequency of religious practice) was found to contributing much variance in satisfaction with life as a whole (Tiliouine 2009b). Thus, the recommendation of adding this item domain to PWI (e.g., Wills 2009) was justified in the context surveying Muslims ($N=2,560$).

In all five studies, the psychometric performance of the IWI was found high in terms of validity, reliability, and sensitivity. These results are comparable to the findings in other countries such as Australia and Hong Kong (IWG 2006). The percentage of the explained variance by the 7 items of PWI in the pooled surveys data reached 45.68 and 57.30 for the 6 items of NWI. These levels are comparable to previous findings documented by the PWI international research team. Principal component factor analysis of the items of each measure separately yielded in each case a single factor with high loadings (PWI item loadings ranged between .57 and .74, those of NWI were from .70 to .80). It should be noted that when all 13 items were factor analyzed together, they confirmed the existence of two separate factors. This is consistent with the initial factor structure firmly established in previous research (Tiliouine et al. 2006; Cummins et al. 2003). The Cronbach Alpha of PWI and NWI were .80 and .85, respectively.

In comparison, the mean score of PWI in 21 surveys in Australia using the same measure ($Mean=74.90$; $SD=.75$) is significant lower than that of Algeria ($Mean=65.19$; $SD=17.16$). This result confirms that subjective well-being is generally lower in developing countries compared to the developed ones (Cummins et al. 2003).

Furthermore, Table 23.7 indicates that health satisfaction registered the highest mean score similar to previous research (Tiliouine et al. 2006, 2009; Tiliouine 2009a, b). This is followed by religiosity satisfaction ($Mean=69.48$; $SD=23.32$; $N=8,680$), which also reinforces previous findings (Tiliouine 2009b). Satisfaction with community connectedness is generally high proving that, as a collectivist culture, feelings of belongingness remain high – despite recent findings (e.g., Cheng et al. 2010) that point to some movement toward more individualistic values.

Table 23.7 Ratings of the International Wellbeing Index and its domains: the pooled five surveys data (2003–2010)

	Variable	N	Mean (0–100)	SD
	Life as a whole	12,985	63.55	25.45
PWI		12,637	65.19	17.16
PWI domains	Standard of living	12,990	62.70	24.84
	Health	12,968	71.19	24.37
	Achievements	12,955	59.60	25.23
	Personal relationships	12,981	67.69	25.26
	Safety	12,972	67.82	26.23
	Community connectedness	12,978	68.89	25.77
	Future security	12,968	58.87	26.28
	Religiosity/spirituality	8,680	69.48	23.32
	Satisfaction with life in Algeria	12,969	56.04	28.01
NWI		12,804	48.28	19.24
NWI domains	Economy in Algeria	12,994	45.87	24.56
	Natural environment	12,997	48.30	25.68
	Social conditions	12,997	44.38	23.51
	Government	12,990	46.41	27.54
	Business	12,984	47.72	24.99
	National security	13,007	57.41	26.41

Table 23.8 Comparisons between gender groups

	Gender	N	Mean	SD	t
Satisfaction with life in general	Male	6,469	62.52	25.98	
	Female	6,516	64.58	24.87	4.61*
PWI	Male	6,307	64.54	17.51	
	Female	6,330	65.84	16.79	4.25*
Satisfaction with life in Algeria	Male	6,474	52.85	28.39	
	Female	6,495	59.21	27.25	13.02*
NWI	Male	6,388	45.94	19.27	
	Female	6,416	50.62	18.92	13.87*

*$p < .0001$

In comparison, the lowest means were obtained in relation to satisfaction with future security ($Mean = 58.87$; $SD = 26.28$) and personal safety ($Mean = 67.82$; $SD = 26.23$), which reveals that security problems remain pervasive. Using the pooled data, we are now conducting additional analyses to draw a realistic picture regarding the stability and change of satisfaction scores during the last 7 years.

The data also show (see Table 23.7) that the lowest scores concern satisfaction with social conditions, followed by the economic situation of the country ($Mean = 44.38$, $SD = 23.51$; $Mean = 45.87$, $SD = 24.56$, respectively). Again, these means echo people's apprehension of the weak economic performance of the country and the discouraging social conditions. Such findings should urge decision makers to develop programs and policies to boost people's trust in their country.

In contrast, the highest scores are of those of satisfaction with natural environment ($Mean = 48.30$, $SD = 25.68$) and business ($Mean = 47.72$, $SD = 24.99$). This latter score may be a response to the provisioning of consumer products in large quantities that the government instituted to stimulate the economy.

The other aspect which deserves attention is gender differences with regard to satisfaction domains. Generally, international research indicates that women response style is slightly different than that of men, and therefore, their satisfaction is a bit higher. This is supported through results shown in Table 23.8, with the largest differences registered with regard to national well-being. Again, comparisons on the basis of individual domains and across time will be conducted in future research.

The last point that we raise here is related to regional differences in both PWI and NWI. First, it may be worth noting that comparisons between the three last surveys proved that the highest satisfaction scores are registered by samples from the Southern areas (Sahara desert), which are the least populous areas and the least modern in both social and economic circumstances. They are followed by the Midlands (Hauts-Plateaux) regions and the more populous and modern Northern areas of Oran. This finding has been consistent across the samples. Women as well as men of the South (Sahara) have higher scores than their women and men counterparts in the other two regions. But, the scores of men and women in the former region are much closer than is the case in the remaining samples (Tiliouine forthcoming). One possible explanation is that in the traditional context of the Sahara, social networks are yet intact. Family structure is also stronger and more extended in the South. Traditional gender roles are firmly maintained. These factors may account for the noted increases in subjective well-being. However, more research is needed to ensure the robustness of these findings.

It could be concluded from the survey results we conducted so far that Algeria achieved significant goals toward modernization in all aspects of life. Among the most significant achievements is reconciliation given the tragedy of past conflicts that cost Algeria 2,000 lives. The recognition of the multicultural and multilingual character of Algeria led the country to avoid much turmoil. But, finding better means to manage the economy of the country through genuine reforms and combating "the politico-financial mafia" remains a significant challenge. Social justice, equity, and hope are a prerequisite for quality of life, which are in short supply in Algeria. Genuine democracy is likely to be the remedy.

Furthermore, successes and failures in all aspects of society should be measured and monitored over time. Independent research institutions that generate reliable data are needed; such data play an important role in informing policymakers and evaluating the impact of policies in place in an effort to modernize the country. The use of both objective and subjective measures is highly recommended because they complement each other.

General Conclusion and Recommendations

Throughout this chapter we were able to demonstrate that Muslim countries are heterogeneous in terms of both economic and social progress. They form at least three main clusters: The small rich, oil-producing countries which are well integrated into the world economy and are enjoying real improvements in both objective and subjective quality of life. Even though political unrest is likely to jeopardize this bliss because of nondemocratic political regimes, note the recent civil unrest (February, 2011) against long-standing monarchies such as those of Bahrain and Oman.

A second group concerns those countries with moderate level development, such as the North African countries. They are more populous, having high population growth, and are faced to a panoply of multifaceted problems, such as low-performing educational and health systems, difficulties in financing development programs, high levels of corruption, and inefficient modes of governance. Social change can bring about a higher quality of life to countries. Change can be in the form of enforcing the rule of law and implementing genuine political reforms.

The third group of Islamic countries comprises the very poor sub-Saharan states. The international community, including the rich Islamic countries should assist them in financing structural economic reform. International aid should encompass long-term investment and capacity building.

Another recommendation (United Nations Report 2005) that can be made with regard to our sample countries is that emphasis should be placed on more equitable distribution of the benefits in an increasingly open world economy. This can be accomplished through promoting democratic participation of all countries in the process that determines an international development agenda. Moreover, democracy and the rule of law should be promoted, and special effort should be made to integrate marginalized groups into society. Equal access to resources and opportunities should help prevent future conflicts.

As many Islamic countries' economies are dominated by a large informal sector, improvements should be made by providing better social welfare programs (i.e., better linkages with the formal sector of society). Opportunities for productive and decent employment should be expanded. Youth should be a focus of employment policies and programs. Those who are able to secure jobs and receive adequate compensation, benefits, and protection under the law should also be empowered to voice their concerns and participate more actively in society (United Nations Report 2005).

However, the world mechanism is grinding away with different speed gears; exclusion seems to be growing in speed and prevalence in a time when the world is increasingly becoming a "small village." This situation must be addressed to maintain world peace and harmony. Collective action is urgently needed to combat disparities among continents and within countries. The recent cases of the bird flu and HIV, H1N1 viruses, natural disasters that hit the globe in the second half of 2005, the financial crisis of 2008, and the Iceland Volcano of 2010, among other challenges, have proved that no single nation can alone counter the consequences of such problems. Furthermore, the world is vulnerable in the face of injustice, racial and ethnic stereotypes, and clash of civilizations. Governments should not repress their people in pretense to address these social ills. We need solutions other than financial and military to enhance humanity at large.

We should add that, while writing these concluding remarks, sweeping changes are unexpectedly taking place in almost the entire Islamic world. For instance, both Tunisia and Egypt have succeeded to overthrow their rulers. People in Libya, Yemen, Bahrain, Oman, and Iran are pressing for political change too. Although it is too early to draw conclusions from these remarkable movements, a number of points could be made:

- In all cases, these changes are led by masses but not in the name of any particular religion, political party, or traditional ideology. The events are led by young women and men longing for freedom and democracy.
- In all cases, nonviolent means are being used by the people to make their voices heard.
- The role of modern communication in creating social change is remarkable. For example, social networks on the Internet are used to rally people and disseminate information. Other media, such independent TV stations, have played an important role in countering government propaganda.
- Finally, religious leaders and political parties are playing a negligible role in these events. This may be a good sign of an end to Islamic religious extremism.

It is interesting to note that the people are brandishing slogans calling for universal values of democracy and justice to prevail.

References

Boisard, M. A. (1979). *L'humanisme de l'Islam*. Paris: Albin Michel.

Cheng, C., Jose, P. E., Sheldon, K. M., Singelis, T. M., Cheung, M. W. L., Tiliouine, H., Alao, A. A., Chio, J. H. M., Lui, J. Y. M., Chun, W. Y., de Zavala, A. G., Hakuzimana, A., Hertel, J., Liu, J. T., Onyewadume, M., & Sims, C. (2010). Sociocultural differences in self-construal and subjective well-being: A test of four cultural models. *Journal of Cross-Cultural Psychology, 20*(10). doi:10.1177/0022022110381117.

CNES (Conseil National Economique et Social). (2003). *Rapport sur la conjoncture économique et social du 1ème semestre 2003*. Alger: CNES.

Congressional Research Service. (2008). Algeria: Current Issues. Report RS21532. http://wikileaks.org/wiki/CRS-RS21532. Accessed 28 March 2009.

Corbin, H. (1964). *Histoire de la philosophie islamique*. Paris: Gallimard.

Cummins, R. A., Eckersley, R., Pallant, J., Van Vugt, J., & Misajon, R. (2003). Development of a national index of subjective wellbeing: The Australian unity wellbeing index. *Social Indicators Research, 64*, 159–190.

Diener, E., & Biswas-Diener, R. (2002). Will money increase subjective wellbeing? A literature review and guide to needed research. *Social Indicators Research, 57*, 119–169.

Diener, E., & Seligman, E. P. (2004). Beyond money: Toward the economy of well-being. *Psychological Science in the Public Interest, 5*(1), 1–31.

Diener, E., & Tov, W. (2004). Culture and subjective well-being. In S. Kitayama, & D. Cohen (Eds.), *Handbook of cultural psychology*. (Draft of 9.6.04, Retrieved June 22, 2005, from Internet: www.psych.uiuc.edu/~ediener

CIA world Factbook. (2005). CIA Publications. (Internet: http://www.cia/publications/factbook/docs/.html)

CIA world Factbook. (2011). CIA Publications. (Internet: http://www.cia/publications/factbook/docs/.html)

Freedom House. (2003). Freedom in the World Survey. (Internet: www.freedomhouse.org)

Freedom House. (2010). Freedom in the World Survey. (Internet: www.freedomhouse.org)

Hagerty, M., & Veenhoven, R. (2003). Wealth and happiness revisited. *Social Indicators Research, 64*, 1–27.

Huntington, S. (1997). *The clash of civilizations and the remaking of world order*. New York: Simon and Schuster.

Ibn Masquawayh (died in 1030). *Tahdib El Akhlaq* (The Refinement of Morals). Rev. Ibn Khatib. Cairo: The Egyptian library (In Arabic).

IMF (International Monetary Fund). (2010). *World economic outlook: Recovery, risk, and balancing*. Washington, DC: IMF.

Inglehart, R., & Norris, P. (2003). The true clash of civilizations. *Foreign Policy, 135*, 63–70. March/April.

International Commission on International Religious Freedom. (2005, March). *The religion-state relationship and the right to freedom of religion or belief: A comparative textual analysis of the constitution of predominantly Muslim countries.* Web document.

Islamic Development Bank. (2005). Inter trade in Muslim countries. (*Web document*: www.isdb.org)

IWG. (2006). International Wellbeing Index. (Web document: http://www.acqol.deakin.edu.au)

IWG (International Well-being Group). (2006). *Personal Wellbeing Index.* Melbourne: Australian Centre on Quality of Life, Deakin University. ISBN No: 1 74156 048 9. Retrieved October 4, 2007, from http://www.deakin.edu.au/research/acqol/instruments/well-being_index.htm

IMF (International Monetary Fund). (2003, March). *Algeria: Selected Issues and Statistical Appendix* (IMF Country Rep. No. 03/69).

IMF (International Monetary Fund). (2011). *World economic outlook update: An update of the key WEO projections.* Retrieved January 25, 2011, from http://ww.imf.org/external/pubs/ft/weo/2011/update/01/pdf/0111.pdf

Joffé, G. (2002). The role of violence within the Algerian economy. *Journal of North African Studies, 7*(1), 29–52.

Kenny, C. (2005). Does development make you happy? subjective wellbeing and economic growth in developing countries. *Social Indicators Research, 73,* 199–219.

Kircaldy, B., Furnham, A., & Veenhoven, R. (2005). Health care and subjective wellbeing in nations. In A. S. G. Antoniou & C. L. Cooper (Eds.), *Research companion to organizational health psychology.* Cheltenham: Edward Elgar Publishers.

Lewis, B. (1993). *Islam in history: Ideas, people, and events in the middle east* (2nd ed.). Chicago: Open Court Publishing Company.

Ministère de la Santé, de la Population et de la Réforme Hospitalière. (2004). *La santé des Algériens et Algériennes.* Alger: Ministère de la santé, de la population et de la réforme hospitalière.

Ministère des travaux Publics. (2009, November). *Demarche et programmes du secteur des travaux publics: Rapport de synthèse.* (www.mtp.gov.dz.DEMARCHE%20%20PROGRAMMES%20TP-V%20FRANCAIS.pdf)

Naudé, W. (2009). The financial crisis of 2008 and the developing countries. Discussion Paper N 2009/01. United Nations University.

OECD. (2003). *Country risk classification of the participants to the arrangement as of 4 April 2003.* (Web document: http://www.oecd.org/dataoecd/37/61/1937723.pdf)

Portail du premier ministre. (2010). *Bilans des réalisations economiques et sociales de la période 1999–2008.* (http://www.cg.gov.dz/media/PDF/Bilanfr.pdf)

Raphaeli, N. (2005). *The Arab development report III: An appeal for openness and freedom.* The Middle East Media Research Institute (MEMRI), Special Dispatch of April 29, 2005 (Website: www.memri.org)

Rice, G. (1999). Islamic ethics and the implications for business. *Journal of Business Ethics, 18*(4), 345–358.

SESRTCIC (Statistical, Economic and Social Research and Training Center for Islamic Countries). (2005). Role of transport and telecommunications in the establishment of an Islamic common market. *Journal of Economic Cooperation among Islamic Countries, 26,* 3.

Tessler, M. (2003). Arab and Muslim political attitudes: Stereotypes and evidence from survey research. *International Studies Perspectives, 4,* 175–180.

Tiliouine, H. (2009a). Measuring satisfaction with religiosity and its contribution to the personal well-being index in a Muslim sample. *Applied Research in Quality of Life, 4*(1), 91–108.

Tiliouine, H. (2009b). Health and subjective wellbeing in Algeria: A developing country in transition. *Applied Research in Quality of Life, 4*(2), 223–238.

Tiliouine, H. (forthcoming). Gender dimensions of quality of life in Algeria. In Eckerman, L. (Ed.). *Gender lifespan and quality of life: An international perspective.* Springer.

Tiliouine, H., & Belgoumidi, A. (2009). An exploratory study of religiosity, meaning in life and subjective wellbeing. *Applied Research in Quality of Life, 4*(1), 109–127.

Tiliouine, H., Cummins, R. A., & Davern, M. (2006). Measuring wellbeing in developing countries: The case of Algeria. *Social Indicators Research, 75,* 1–30.

Tiliouine, H., Cummins, R. A., & Davern, M. (2009). Islamic religiosity, subjective wellbeing, and health. *Mental Health, Religion & Culture, 12*(1), 55–74.

Transparency International. (2002). Corruption Perceptions Index. (http://www.transparency.org/cpi/index.html#cpi)

UNDP. (2004). *Human development report 2004.* New York: United Nations.

UNDP (and Arab Fund for Economic and Social Development, the). (2003). *Arab human development report 2003: Building a knowledge society.* New York: UNDP Regional Bureau for Arab States.

UNDP. (2009). *Human development report.* Overcoming barriers: Human mobility and development. New York: United Nations.

UNESCO. (2000). Education pour tous, Rapports par pays, Algérie. (*Web document*: www.unesco.org)

United Nations High Commissioner for Refugees (UNHCR), in close collaboration with the Organization of the Islamic Conference (OIC) Secretariat (2005). Enhancing Refugee Protection in the Muslim World. Working Document for the OIC *Ministerial Conference on the Problems of Refugees in the Muslim World,* OIC Ministerial Conference on the Problems of Refugees in the Muslim World, November 28–30, 2005.

WHO (World Health Organization). (2005). *The world health report 2005.* Geneva: WHO Publications.

Williams, G., & Zinkin, J. (2010). Islam and CSR: A study of the comparability between the tents of Islam and the UN global compact. *Journal of Business Ethics, 91*(4), 519–533.

Wills, E. (2009). Spirituality and subjective wellbeing: Empirical evidence for a new domain in the PWI index. *Journal of Happiness Studies, 10*(1), 49–69.

Quality of Life in Latin America and the Caribbean

24

Mariano Rojas

Introduction

Latin America and the Caribbean is a vast region with a population above 550 million and with an extension above 20 million square kilometers. It goes from the northern 32° parallel to the southern 56° parallel (not considering Antarctic territories). Many languages are spoken in the region, such as Spanish, Portuguese, French, English, Quechua, Guaraní, Náhuatl, Aymara, and others. As expected, it is a diverse region; there are significant intercountry differences, as well as substantial intracountry disparities. However, albeit it is vague, there is a general idea of the region as a single entity, and most people in the region can identify themselves as Latin-Americans and as Caribbean. This chapter does not aspire to be exhaustive, since it would be almost impossible to encompass all the relevant issues and all the significant research about quality of life in such a vast and diverse region. Hence, this chapter aims to provide a general overview of some relevant issues about quality of life in Latin America and the Caribbean.

Section "The Region" discusses the delimitation of the region. Section "The Quality of Life Situation: Assessment Based on Objective Socioeconomic Indicators" provides a quantitative view of the main quality of life problems in the region. Section "The Quality of Life Situation: Assessment Based on Subjective Well-Being Indicators" follows a subjective well-being perspective to assess the region's situation.

Section "Some Relevant Issues About Latin-American Quality of Life" follows a more qualitative and historical perspective to explain some quality of life problems and to understand the factors that structurally threaten quality of life in the region; it is based on a survey of recent studies. Section "Conclusions" elaborates on the main conclusions.

The Region

There is no clear geographical delimitation for the Latin-American region. Any particular delimitation could be contested. A common delimitation stresses the dominance of a Latin-rooted language in the country; 20 countries would be included on the basis of this criterion. Spanish is widely spoken in Argentina, Bolivarian Republic of Venezuela, Bolivia, Chile, Colombia, Costa Rica, Cuba, Dominican Republic, Ecuador, El Salvador, Guatemala, Honduras, Mexico, Nicaragua, Panama, Paraguay, Peru, and Uruguay; Portuguese is the predominant language in Brazil, and French is spoken in Haiti. However, it is important to remark that many indigenous languages are widely spoken in some countries such as Bolivia, Ecuador, Guatemala, Paraguay, Peru, and Mexico.

The Caribbean region refers to a group of islands in the Caribbean Sea where a Latin language is not widely spoken. Thus, Antigua and Barbuda, Bahamas, Barbados, Dominica, Grenada, Jamaica, Saint Kitts and Nevis, Saint Lucia, Saint Vincent and the Grenadines, and Trinidad and Tobago are included in this region. The Caribbean also incorporates non-Latin-speaking continental countries, such as Belize, Guyana, and Suriname.

M. Rojas (✉)
FLACSO-México & UPAEP, Mexico City, Mexico
e-mail: mariano.rojas.h@gmail.com

K.C. Land et al. (eds.), *Handbook of Social Indicators and Quality of Life Research*,
DOI 10.1007/978-94-007-2421-1_24, © Springer Science+Business Media B.V. 2012

Hence, the broad delimitation for the Latin-American and Caribbean region refers to the area in the American continent that excludes Canada and the United States.[1] This chapter refers mostly to the situation in the Latin-speaking countries, without completely neglecting the situation in the other countries.

In terms of population size, the Latin-American group of countries contains a population of about 575 million people, while the Caribbean group adds less than 7 million people. The largest countries in the region are, by far, Brazil and Mexico, with population figures of 187 million and 106 million people, respectively. Colombia, Argentina, Peru and Venezuela can be considered mid-size countries, with populations in between 25 and 50 million people.

In terms of population size, the first group of countries comprehends a population of about 575 million people, while the second group adds less than 7 million people. The largest countries in the region are, by far, Brazil and Mexico, with population figures of 195 million and 110 million people, respectively. Colombia, Argentina, Peru, and Venezuela can be considered mid-size countries, with populations in between 25 and 50 million people.

Table 24.1 shows a classification of the countries according to the Latin America and Caribbean criterion, as well as their population size.

The Quality of Life Situation: Assessment Based on Objective Socioeconomic Indicators

Economic Situation

This section studies the quality of life situation in Latin America in terms of per capita income figures, income distribution, and poverty and indigence rates. These

---

[1] There is a large group of territories in the geographical region that are under the administration of foreign countries, such as: Anguilla (United Kingdom), Netherlands Antilles (The Netherlands), Aruba (The Netherlands), British Virgin Islands (United Kingdom), United States Virgin Islands (United States), Montserrat (United Kingdom), Puerto Rico (United States), Cayman Islands (United Kingdom), Guadaloupe (France), Martinique (France), French Guyana (France), Turks and Caicos Islands (United Kingdom), Bermudas (United Kingdom), Falkland Islands (United Kingdom), and South Georgia and South Sandwich Islands (United Kingdom).

Table 24.1 Latin America and the Caribbean: population figures in thousands, by country

Latin-American countries	Population	Caribbean countries	Population
Argentina	40,738	Antigua and Barbuda	89
Bolivia	10,031	Bahamas	346
Brazil	195,498	Barbados	257
Chile	17,133	Belize	313
Colombia	46,299	Dominica	67
Costa Rica	4,639	Grenada	104
Cuba	11,203	Guyana	761
Ecuador	13,773	Jamaica	2,730
El Salvador	6,192	Saint Kitts and Nevis	52
Guatemala	14,376	Saint Vincent and the Grenadines	109
Haiti	10,089	Saint Lucia	174
Honduras	7,621	Suriname	524
Mexico	110,675	Trinidad and Tobago	1,344
Nicaragua	5,822		
Panama	3,508		
Paraguay	6,460		
Peru	29,495		
Dominican Republic	9,899		
Uruguay	3,372		
Venezuela	29,043		
Total	**575,866**	**Total**	**6,870**

Source: ECLAC

Note: population in thousands, estimate for 2010

---

indicators are commonly used by economists and by some international organizations.

Per Capita Income. In General, There Is No Productivity Problem

As it is shown in Table 24.2, Latin-American countries have yearly per capita gross domestic products (GDP) that range from about US$ 667.3 dollars in Haiti to a little more than US$ 7,000 dollars in Uruguay and Chile. With the exception of Haiti, all Latin-American countries have per capita GDPs above US$ 1,000 dollars. The average yearly per capita income[2] in the Latin-American region is about US$ 5,637 dollars (almost US$ 15.5 dollars per capita per day). This figure

---

[2] Income and GDP are used as synonymous in this chapter.

Table 24.2 Latin America and The Caribbean: gross domestic product per capita in 2009 in US dollars at current market prices by country

Latin America	GDP per capita	The Caribbean	GDP per capita
Argentina	5,621.6	Antigua and Barbuda	5,807.0
Bolivia	1,410.2	Bahamas	15,851.5
Brazil	6,877.1	Barbados[a]	12,203.1
Chile	7,042.7	Belice[a]	3,636.5
Colombia	4,079.9	Dominica	6,098.6
Costa Rica	5,399.1	Grenada	6,270.5
Cuba	4,817.6	Guyana	2,604.4
Ecuador	3,019.4	Jamaica[a]	5,477.1
El Salvador	3,501.5	Saint Kitts and Nevis	10,485.1
Guatemala	2,596.4	Saint Vincent and the Grenadines	5,514.1
Haiti	667.5	Saint Lucia	5,325.3
Honduras	1,897.5	Suriname	n.a.
Mexico	6,245.5	Trinidad and Tobago[a]	11,475.9
Nicaragua	1,097.4		
Panama	3,954.9		
Paraguay	2,008.3		
Peru	3,294.6		
Dominican Republic	4,444.2		
Uruguay	7,605.3		
Venezuela	6,670.5		
Whole Latin-American region	**5637.39[b]**		
Whole Latin America and The Caribbean region	**5649.02[b]**		

Source: ECLAC, Statistical Yearbook for Latin America and the Caribbean, 2010
[a]Figures at 2008
[b]Population-weighted average

indicates that, on average, Latin-Americans enjoy a relatively adequate standard of living and that production is enough to satisfy, on average, all basic needs. The production situation is dramatically bad in some countries, like Haiti where production is not enough to reach per capita levels of US$ 1.8 dollars per day. Nicaragua and Bolivia have production levels that imply per capita incomes below US$ 4 dollars per day.

Thus, with some exceptions, if income were distributed in an egalitarian way production levels in the Latin-American countries would be enough to satisfy the basic needs of their citizens.

In addition, the economic situation is—on average—relatively comfortable in the Caribbean countries where in general, per capita production levels are considerable higher than in the Latin-American countries. Guyana constitutes an exception in the Caribbean, with a per capita income of US$ 7 dollars per day.

Thus, in general, Latin-American and Caribbean countries do not have a low productivity problem, which could be a serious threat to their quality of life by making it impossible to satisfy people's basic needs. However, there is the perception that the region is vulnerable to recurrent economic crises. Some Latin-American countries have faced deep and widespread economic crises during the last decades, for example, Mexico in 1994, and Brazil and Argentina more recently. These crises have both domestic and international structural causes. Internally, the region is exposed to political uncertainties that do not favor long-term investments projects, as well as to political structures that do not favor pro-egalitarian economic growth. Externally, many economies in the region are closely attached to the economy of the United States.

Economic crises constitute a threat to the quality of life of Latin Americans. Graham and collaborators have studied the relationship between macroeconomic variables and happiness in Latin America. Their analyses use personal cross-country data from the *Latinobarometro* (www.latinobarometro.org) and they follow the pioneer work by Di Tella et al. (1997) on the relationship between happiness and inflation and unemployment rates. Graham and Pettinato (2002a) found that inflation tends to reduce happiness in Latin America, while Eggers and Graham (2004) found that the impact of unemployment on happiness is negative and significant at the 5% or 10% level. Eggers and Graham conjecture that the impact of unemployment on happiness is not more significant because a large proportion of the Latin-American labor force is not in the formal sector and because unemployment is relatively low in Latin America. Graham and Sukhtankar (2004) further study the consequences of Latin-American economic crises on subjective well-being. Their research is based on a contentious but operative definition of economic crisis: countries with negative GDP per capita growth are considered as being in economic crisis, while all other countries are not. They find out that economic crises have "a small adverse impact on personal well-being" (p. 358). In addition, they find out that economic crises

Table 24.3 Latin America: household income distribution indicators selected years

	Quintile 5/Quintile 1	Gini coefficient
Argentina (2005)	21.8	0.52
Bolivia (2002)	44.2	0.61
Brazil (2009)	22.5	0.58
Chile (2009)	14.0	0.52
Colombia (2009)	24.1	0.58
Costa Rica (2009)	16.9	0.50
Ecuador (2009)	13.6	0.50
El Salvador (2009)	12.4	0.48
Guatemala (2002)	18.7	0.54
Haiti	*n.a.*	*n.a.*
Honduras (2002)	26.3	0.59
Mexico (2008)	14.1	0.52
Nicaragua (2005)	16.3	0.53
Panama (2009)	17.6	0.52
Paraguay (2009)	17.1	0.51
Peru (2009)[a]	12.1	0.47
Dominican Republic (2009)	21.9	0.57
Uruguay (2009)	9.2	0.43
Venezuela (2008)	8.9	0.41

Source: ECLAC, Social Perspective 2008–2009
[a]Twenty urban agglomerations

disproportionally affect the well-being of men and people with fixed and limited income.

Income Distribution. There Is a Serious Inequality Problem in the Region

The region faces an acute income distribution problem which makes per capita income indicators a bad proxy for the economic situation of the population. As a matter of fact, regarding income, Latin America is the more unequal region in the world (Lustig 2011).

Table 24.3 shows some income-distribution indicators for the Latin-American countries. The first column shows the ratio of the income earned by households located in the top 20% of the income distribution with respects to the income earned by households located in the bottom 20%. The second column shows the Gini coefficient, which ranges from 0 to 1, 0 showing a perfectly egalitarian distribution and 1 a completely unequal society. It is observed that income distribution is very unequal in Latin-American countries. The Gini coefficient ranges from 0.41 in Venezuela to 0.61 in Bolivia. The richer 20% of households in Bolivia have almost 45 times more income that the poorer 20% of households; this figure is about 37 times in Brazil. The countries with

the lowest GDP per capita in the region (Bolivia, Honduras, Nicaragua and Paraguay) have Gini coefficients above 0.50. Thus, these countries do not only face a low-productivity problem, but their insufficient production is highly concentrated in a few hands; this phenomenon generates vast income exclusion and marginalization.

Hence, Latin America is a region characterized by great intra-country income disparities, which reach polarization levels in many countries.

Inequality, exclusion, and social segregation are entrenched in the region's historical legacy. Spanish and Portuguese colonizers imposed an economic system based on the exploitation of large landholdings and mines through the using of forced indigenous labor (*encomienda* institution) and African slave trade. After independence was reached, which took place for most countries in the early XIX century, the domestic elites developed strong links to the international centers by exporting cheap-labor intensive commodities; it was not in their interest to improve human capital nor to create a society of opportunities (Sokoloff and Engerman 2000; Bourguignon and Verdier 2000). During the last decades, Latin-American countries implemented pro-market reforms in their search for economic development. However, some countries, such as Venezuela, Bolivia, and Ecuador, have just recently deviated from this path. There has been substantial debate about the consequences of pro-market reforms on income distribution with no clear conclusions yet. Behrman et al. (2001) found that pro-market reforms generated both winners and losers, with an increase in wage gaps between skilled and unskilled workers. Lustig (2011) finds a recent tendency toward a more egalitarian income distribution in most Latin-American countries. This tendency is explained by a combination of economic responsible policies with clear political concerns for the distribution of income, as it is shown by moderate leftist administrations.

Graham and Felton (2005) study the well-being impact of an unequal income distribution in Latin America on the basis of information from the *Latinobarometro*. They state that a process of economic growth combined with integration to global markets exposes people to information about international living standards and that this may produce a surge in people's aspirations and a change in their income evaluation norms, which end up affecting their well-being. Graham and Felton use microdata to study the effect of relative-income differences on well being and find that relative income—the gap between each person's income and his/her country's average—matters in Latin America. Thus, inequality significantly matters for the well being of people in the region. They report that "relative income differences have large and consistent effects on well being in the region. Inequality makes those in the highest quintiles roughly 5% happier than the average and those in the poorest quintile 3% less happy, regardless of differences in wealth levels within and across these groups" (p. 1). The positive impact of inequality on the well-being of the wealthier and its negative impact on the well-being of the poorer could emerge from structurally determined low social mobility.[3] Hence, the rich feel that their privileged position is secured, while the poor know that it is almost impossible to get out from their low position. For this reason, the existence of a very unequal distribution does not constitute a main concern for the region's economic elites, which have also exercised substantial political power.

An interesting finding in a Peruvian study is that "almost half of the respondents with the most upward mobility reported that their economic situation was negative or very negative compared to 10 years prior." (Graham 2005, p. 210). Graham uses the term "frustrated achievers" to refer to these persons (Graham and Pettinato 2002b). The paradox of people being frustrated by their performance while enjoying high upward income mobility could be explained because of a change in income evaluation norms. Even though the expenditure of frustrated achievers did substantially increase, this increase was not sufficient to reach the levels of the more affluent groups, whose expenditures were increasing at a faster rate. Another possible explanation mentioned by Graham is that frustrated achievers may feel more vulnerable in a context of reforms and economic volatility.

Hence, unequal income distributions, polarization, and social exclusion threaten the quality of life of Latin

---

[3] Low social mobility in the region is the consequence of a combination of historical and institutional factors, for example: Inheritance plays an important role in economies based on family-owned firms. The economically poor do have fewer opportunities than the rich for accessing high-quality education and health services. Labor markets and economic opportunities are influenced by institutions that favor networks and family links. Furthermore, there is widespread discrimination on the basis of ethnic factors.

Americans in many ways: First, they create a sense of unfairness and exclusion in society: while some people live in opulence, others do not have enough to fully satisfy their basic needs. Second, in a low social-mobility environment these huge intra-country disparities reduce the well-being of those who are in the bottom quintiles. Third, inequality and exclusion in low income countries lead to a large segment of the population being beneath the income-poverty line. Fourth, they contribute to the creation of domestic consumption aspirations which are beyond the economic possibilities of the majority of population. Hence, for this majority of population, their aspirations raise faster than their purchasing capacities. Frustration, low saving rates, and credit-based consumption are the logical consequence of this process. Fifth, the escalation of some social problems—such as crime, violence, corruption, and social fragmentation—could be associated to this polarization. In addition, high polarization is expected to further reduce the chances for upward social mobility, since the productivity of workers is highly determined by the accidental conditions of their birth and upbringing, a factor that used to be partially neutralized by State intervention in areas such as education, health, and nutrition. However, the role of the State has been diminished by pro-market reforms.

Economic Poverty. A Structural Problem

High income poverty is the expected consequence of having a very unequal income distribution in countries where per capita income is not high. Table 24.4 shows historical series for economic poverty and indigence rates (extreme economic poverty) in Latin America as it is defined and measured by United Nations' Economic Commission for Latin-American and the Caribbean (ECLAC). It is observed that 33% of Latin-American population could be considered as economically poor in 2009; thus, about 191 million people lived under the income-poverty line in 2009. Poverty rates are much higher in rural than in urban areas; however, because of a strong process of rural-urban migration during the last 30 years, most poor people are now located in urban rather than rural areas.

It is also observed that poverty rates have declined during the last decade. However, the effect of the recent economic crisis is not fully contemplated by figures shown in Table 24.4.

A look at indigence rates shows that about 13% of Latin Americans live in extreme poverty. They have

Table 24.4 Latin America: economic poverty and indigence rates percentage of people below the poverty and indigence lines

	Poor			Indigent		
	Total	Urban	Rural	Total	Urban	Rural
1980	40.5	29.8	59.9	18.6	10.6	32.7
1990	48.3	41.4	65.4	22.5	15.3	40.4
2000	42.5	35.9	62.5	18.1	11.7	37.8
2002	44.0	38.4	61.8	19.4	13.5	37.9
2009	33.1	27.8	52.8	13.3	8.8	30.0

Source: ECLAC, Social Perspectives 2008–2009. On the basis of special tabulations of data from household surveys conducted in the respective countries

income levels that do not allow for the satisfaction of nutritional needs.

Poverty rates are high everywhere in Latin America; however, the situation is worse in countries such as Bolivia, Guatemala, Honduras, Haiti, Nicaragua, and Paraguay. Countries that show relatively low poverty rates are Uruguay (10%) and Chile (11%). The Caribbean region has relatively low poverty rates, with the notable exception of Suriname.

Thus, Latin America has a serious income-poverty problem. Poverty is widespread in rural areas, while in urban areas, where most of the population lives, it is possible to find whole city settlements under income poverty. This problem emerges from many factors: First, migration from rural to urban areas has been very strong during the last 50 years due to the high concentration of land in a few hands, meager economic opportunities in rural areas, and an urban bias generated by the strategy of industrialization followed from the 1950s to the 1970s. Second, children of early migrants have had difficulties for socially integrating in the urban areas; this difficulty is intensified by a decline in the role of the government as provider of education, nutrition, and health services. Third, unskilled labor has been penalized by the development strategy implemented in the early 1980s. Fourth, the development strategy followed by most Latin-American countries during the last decades mainly pursued economic efficiency, while the task for poverty abatement was left to focalized programs. Hence, neither poverty reduction nor pro-egalitarian growth is a fully incorporated objective of the pro-market development strategies.

Some Latin-American countries have experimented during the last years with focalized poverty-abatement programs. They provide direct transfers to selected people contingent to the families undertaking actions to attain specific health and education goals. For example, transfers are received as long as the family satisfies the requirement of children not dropping out from school. Some well-known focalized programs are *Oportunidades* in Mexico, *Bolsa Familia* in Brazil, and *Familias en Acción* in Colombia. These programs aim to attack vicious loops of poverty that generate within the family space, but they completely neglect the role played by external social and economic conditions in the generation and reproduction of economic poverty.

Looking for an Adequate Development Strategy: Need for Creativity and Autonomy

Perhaps the region's main economic problem resides in the lack of a clear development strategy. The inward-looking development strategy of the 1950s and 1960s was relatively successful at the time, but its benefits exhausted in the 1970s. The State lost credibility due to lack of transparency, corruption, and global economic inefficiencies; thus, large groups of the population question State intervention. However, the market-oriented reforms, privatization, and globalization of the 1980s and 1990s have performed well-beneath expectations, and they are opposed by many in the region.

The disentanglement between the economic-growth strategy and the poverty-abatement and pro-egalitarian income-distribution strategies has important consequences for the well-being of Latin Americans. First, economic growth becomes an inefficient instrument for the abatement of poverty; growth leads to more income, but this income ends up mostly concentrated in small population segments. Under this situation, substantial rates of economic growth would be needed to achieve meager reductions in poverty. Second, the increasing disparity between the income of the poor and the income of the rich is, by itself, a main source of dissatisfaction for the poor. Economic growth leads to poor people having aspirations well beyond their possibilities when it takes place in an unequal society. Third, economic growth is not a sustainable strategy to abate poverty in a world that faces serious depletion of natural resources and of its environment. Fourth, a poverty-abatement program based on direct transfers faces serious political difficulties; the rich end up feeling that the fruits of their effort are being taken away by governments to finance transfers to the poor; hence, the rich develop an anti-governmental and anti-distributional sentiment and end up evading their fiscal responsibilities. On the other hand, some relevant well-being enhancing factors, such as self-esteem and autonomy are not developed by these transfers' program.

An economic-growth strategy that incorporates pro-egalitarian income distribution and poverty abatement criteria is preferred because of the circumstances mentioned above (Rojas 2005c, d). Under this alternative strategy, income-distribution and poverty-abatement concerns are not detached from economic policies. In recent years, some Latin-American countries, such as Argentina, have shown interest in moving toward this kind of strategy. However, local academicians have not been able to advance solid and adequate development-strategy alternatives.

Furthermore, the region seems to lack the autonomy to define its own strategy. The international arena plays an important role in the definition of any development strategy through its international financial, economic, and political organizations, as well as through the direct intervention of foreign aid agencies, multinational companies, and governments. Domestic elites, which exercise immense control on political and economic affairs, are strongly linked to the international spheres of power; their agenda is not necessarily in agreement with the agenda of the large masses of socially excluded people in Latin America (Rojas 2005e). For example, the domestic decisions about issues such as the proper size of the government and its competing activities, the role of privatization and the nature of incentives given to foreign investors, and the degree of insertion into the global economy and the extend of market-oriented reforms are highly dependent on the international arena and on the interests of international players.

Social Indicators

The literature recognizes that the quality of life of a population goes beyond a limited set of economic indicators. This section reviews the Latin-American situation on the basis of some social indicators that are of widespread acceptance as indicators of quality of life.

General Social Indicators

Social indicators in Latin America and the Caribbean regions perform relatively well with respects to world standards. Table 24.5 shows average values for some widely used quality of life indicators.

Table 24.5 Latin America and the Caribbean: general social indicators 2010–2015 period

Life expectancy at birth (number of years)	74.5
Infant mortality rate (rate per 1,000 live births)	25.8
Rate of illiteracy in the population age 15 or over (percentage of the population of the same age)	8.3

Source: ECLAC

Life expectancy at birth is above 73 years old in the region, on average. Some countries such as Costa Rica, Puerto Rico, Cuba, and Chile have life expectancies quite close to 80 years old. Costa Rica and Cuba have a long tradition of solid and widespread social security systems. Life expectancy is very low in Haiti (about 62 years) and Bolivia (67 years).

Infant mortality is also relatively low in the region, with an average rate of 19 per 1,000 live births. Countries like Cuba, Costa Rica, Puerto Rica, Bahamas, Barbados and Chile show rates beneath 10 per 1,000 live births. On the other hand, the situation is dramatically bad in Haiti (42), Bolivia (38), and Guyana (37).

The average illiteracy rate is also relatively low in the region; about 8% of people aged 15 or over in the region are illiterate. Illiteracy rate is an incomplete indicator, since it just refers to a person's capability of reading and writing; functional illiteracy is expected to be much higher. Illiteracy is a serious problem in Haiti (41%), Nicaragua (30%), and Guatemala (25%).

The life expectancy and the illiteracy rate are two components of United Nations' Human Development Index. Latin America and the Caribbean perform relatively well in these components of the Human Development Index, but not so well in the other component of the index (per capita income). This implies that the region's performance is much better when assessed through the Human Development Index than when assessed through the per capita income measure (of widespread use in the economic literature). Bouillon and Buvinic (2003, p. 3) state that "The region's average HDI value is exceeded only by the average for developed countries, and the gap between these two groups has narrowed over time."

Health-Related Indicators

Health indicators are also relatively good in Latin America and the Caribbean. Table 24.6 shows some basic indicators. The proportion of undernourished persons is absolutely high (11%) but still relatively low with respects to other regions of the world. Argentina,

Chile, Costa Rica, Mexico, and Uruguay have figures beneath 5%, while high figures are found in Haiti (50%), Nicaragua (29%), Dominican Republic (26%), El Salvador (25%), and Bolivia (23%).

The indicators referring to environmental health-related conditions, such as access to an improved water source and sanitation are also relatively good for the region.

Table 24.6 Latin America and the Caribbean: health-related indicators

Proportion of undernourished persons[a,b] (percentage of total population)	11.0
Access to an improved water source[c,d] (percentage of total population)	93.0
Access to sanitation[c,d] (percentage of total population)	80.0

Source: FAO (undernourishment), WHO/UNICEF (drinking water, sanitation)
[a]Figure corresponds to Latin-American countries
[b]Figures at 2003
[c]Figure corresponds to Latin-American and Caribbean countries
[d]Figures at 2008

The Quality of Life Situation: Assessment Based on Subjective Well-Being Indicators

Life Satisfaction in Latin-American Countries

Subjective well-being indicators capture the situation in many dimensions of being which are not necessarily considered by commonly used objective indicators. In addition, they do allow for incorporating the heterogeneity across people in their appreciation of the objective conditions. Thus, subjective well-being indicators provide information about the quality of life as people in the region experiences it. In consequence, it is useful to examine the situation of subjective well-being in Latin America. Table 24.7 provides information about life satisfaction and other subjective well-being variables in many Latin-American countries.

Subjective well-being indicators are relatively high in Latin America. As a matter of fact, the large gap which is observed between Latin America and Europe

Table 24.7 Subjective well-being in Latin America: different indicators 2007

	Life satisfaction[a]	Life appreciation[a,b]	Health satisfaction[c]	Economic satisfaction[c]
Argentina	7.1	6.0	85.9	68.4
Bolivia	6.3	5.4	84.2	67.2
Brasil	7.5	6.2	84.5	70.9
Chile	6.5	5.8	69.0	62.4
Colombia	7.4	6.2	84.9	72.2
Costa Rica	8.5	7.4	93.8	85.0
Ecuador	6.4	5.0	80.4	72.1
El Salvador	6.7	5.3	84.3	63.2
Guatemala	7.9	6.4	93.2	84.1
Honduras	7.2	5.2	88.6	70.3
México	7.8	6.6	87.3	75.7
Nicaragua	7.1	4.9	80.4	64.3
Panamá	7.8	6.9	89.8	73.3
Paraguay	6.8	5.2	80.9	58.1
Perú	6.0	5.4	79.9	54.1
Uruguay	6.8	5.7	86.1	62.2
Simple country average	7.1	5.9	84.6	69.0

Source: Rojas (2011), using information from Gallup Poll 2007
[a]Mean values
[b]Corresponds to the best-worst life evaluation question
[c]Percentage of respondents answering 'yes'

on the basis of objective indicators substantially declines when considering subjective well-being indicators. It is widely recognized that most Latin-American countries have subjective well-being indicators which are abnormally high for their corresponding per capita income levels. As a matter of fact, Costa Rica has the highest life satisfaction score in the world according to the 2007 Gallup Poll, much above countries such as Denmark and The Netherlands. Many Latin-American countries outperform the performance of some European countries and of the United States.

It is seen in Table 24.7 that health satisfaction is also good in Latin America, the simple country average for the region is 85%, which means that in each country, on average, only 15% of the population are not satisfied with their health. On the other hand, satisfaction with the economic situation is not so good, a fact that is clearly affected by high income inequality and large segments of the population being in poverty. However, this mix of low economic satisfaction and high life satisfaction indicates that there is more in live than the standard of living, and that Latin Americans do not base their life satisfaction on economic standards alone. This discrepancy between economic indicators (income, economic satisfaction) and life satisfaction points toward the importance of other explanatory factors of subjective well-being, such as human relations (Rojas 2011).

Subjective Well-Being Research in Latin America

On the General Structure of Happiness in Latin America

Graham and Pettinato (2001) use data from the *Latinobarometro* (1997 to 2000) to study the main determinants of happiness in the Latin-American countries; they compare their results to those from industrial economies. Graham and Pettinato find that there are similar age, income, education, marriage, employment, and health effects. Happiness shows a U-shaped relationship with age; a minimum value is reached at an age of about 46 years old. Married people are significantly happier, while there is no significant gender difference. Wealth has a significant and positive effect, as well as being employed. Unemployment and self-employment do have negative effects on happiness; the self-employment effect contrasts with that in advanced industrial economies (where it tends to be positive). Graham and Felton

(2005) argue that while in the advanced industrial economies self-employment is a matter of choice, in Latin America it may be a last-resort option for unemployed people, since Latin Americans rely on an informal job because they do not have access to formal ones. Graham and Felton—on the basis of 2001 Latinobarometro—also find out that those Latin Americans who identify themselves as minority are less happy.

Furthermore, Graham and Pettinato (2002a) tested the Easterlin paradox—which states that wealthy people tend to be happier than poorer ones within countries, but that there is no such relationship among countries or over time—for 17 countries in Latin America. Likewise in Easterlin's studies, Graham and Pettinato found that no relationship between per capita income and average happiness levels does exist in the Latin-American countries.

There Is More in Life Than the Standard of Living

Rojas (2006c) uses a domains-of-life approach to study the sources of life satisfaction in Mexico. A large survey was applied in many states of central Mexico. He constructs domain satisfaction variables on the basis of a large set of questions about satisfaction in specific areas of life. He uses a production–function approach with a flexible specification to estimate the relationship between life satisfaction and satisfaction in domains of life. Rojas finds that satisfaction in the family domain is central for life satisfaction; the estimated coefficient is statistically significant and relatively large in comparison to estimated coefficients for other domains. Satisfaction in health, self, and job domains is also relevant, while economic satisfaction is just slightly relevant. Friends and community satisfaction are irrelevant for working people who are married and have kids—but not so for unmarried people or for married people with no kids.

Furthermore, Rojas (2005b, 2007c) studies the importance of income and education as explanatory variables of satisfaction in domains of life. With respect to income, he finds that the positive impact of higher income is limited to satisfaction in the economic and job domains. These domains are important but not central for life satisfaction. Thus, Rojas concludes that there is more in life than the standard of living and that there are more relevant things. With respect to education, Rojas finds that highly educated people tend to be more satisfied in all relevant domains of life (family, health, self, job, and economic). Hence, education is an important source of life satisfaction because its benefits extend to all relevant domains. Therefore, it is important to promote widespread education—its quantity and its quality—in Latin America, not only because it may be associated to higher income levels but, even more important, because it provides skills and knowledge that is relevant for living a more satisfying life. Hence, the provision of good education should be a central public policy concern in Latin America.

In the same domains-of-life line of research, Rojas (2006b) argues that poverty should be understood in a broader sense, as lack of well-being. Narrow definitions of poverty that tend to over-stress the role played by the economic domain of life do not contribute to the proper design of well-being enhancing social programs.

Communitarian Arrangements in the Family

Rojas (2006a) uses the subjective well-being approach to study what kinds of arrangements prevail in Mexican families. He states that a communitarian family is based on altruistic and solidarity principles, so that household income becomes a "common pot," from which all household members can benefit, independently of their breadwinning status and their personal contribution to household income. Hence, in a communitarian family a person's happiness is related to her household income, but not so to her personal income nor to her family status. On the other hand, individualistic families are based on self-centered and cooperative-bargaining principles. Thus, each person's happiness does depend on her status and personal contribution, and household income is no longer a "common pot" for all household members to equally benefit from. In an extreme case, persons living under individualistic family arrangements could just be considered as housemates.

Using data from Mexico, Rojas (2006a) reaches the following conclusions: first, a person's happiness is related to her household income but not to other income proxies such as personal, household per capita, and household equivalent incomes. Second, a person's breadwinning status—being main, secondary, marginal or no breadwinner—does not matter for the relationship between household income and happiness. These results indicate that Mexican families do follow, in general, communitarian arrangements, which incorporate values such as solidarity and altruism, rather than selfishness and self-centered goals. These

results do imply that by being basically communitarian, families in Latin America can attain greater happiness from a given income with respects to families in individualistic societies.

Furthermore, Rojas (2006a) found that a person's happiness does not decline nor increase as the number of family members raises. However, it was also found that a person's economic satisfaction declines as the size of her family increases (Rojas 2007a). These findings suggest that the financial cost of living in larger families is offset by the benefits from having access to more relational goods and that the institution of the family plays a substantial role in Latin-American countries sustaining happiness levels relatively high for their income.

In addition, Rojas (2010, 2007a) has shown that large Mexican families can attain greater economic satisfaction from a giving household income than the corresponding number of persons living under more individualistic arrangements in smaller families. He has shown that economic poverty figures for Latin America are overestimated because the substantial economies of scales enjoyed by relatively larger and more communitarian families are being neglected by poverty studies.

The Meaning of a Happy Life: The Conceptual-Referent Theory of Happiness

Rojas (2005a) states that persons could have different meanings of what a happy life is, and that these differences in conceptions of happiness could play a role on a person's assessment of her life as a happy one. The conceptual-referent theory of happiness (CRT) studies the conception of what a happy life is people have in mind when making a judgment about their happiness. A typology for conceptual referents of happiness was created on the basis of a survey of philosophical essays.

Rojas (2005a) finds that there are substantial differences across persons in their conception of happiness. Although happiness is a final goal for everybody, not everybody in Mexico has the same notion about what happiness is. Rojas (2007b) studies whether the conceptual referent a person holds has implications for the definition of what are the relevant resources for happiness. If persons assess the goodness of their lives on the basis of different notions of what a happy life is, then it is possible that explanatory factors that are relevant for some people are not so for others. He finds out that income is a relevant variable for a person's happiness if she holds conceptual referents such as 'satisfaction', 'carpe diem', 'enjoyment' and "fulfillment," but not so in other cases. Rojas hypothesizes that the referent a person holds depends on her sociodemographic characteristics, as well as on cultural and upbringing circumstances. Hence, the relevance of alleged explanatory variables of happiness—such as the economic situation—is contingent on cultural and upbringing circumstances, and its universality should not be presumed. The main implication from the analysis is that there may be substantial differences in the conceptual referent a person has across underdeveloped and developed countries; hence, the resources for a good life in so called underdeveloped countries are not the same as in the so called developed ones.

Some Relevant Issues About Latin-American Quality of Life

Globalization and Its Consequences

The economic and social crises of the early 1980s led to a reconsideration of the development strategy in many Latin-American countries. Most countries switched to an outward-looking strategy based on an open economy, export promotion, insertion in the globalization process, privatization of state-owned enterprises and some public services, reduction of State participation in the economy, and larger reliance on the market economy.

After the exhaustion of the inward-looking strategy, the new strategy created high expectations for a prompt and sound development accomplishment in Latin America. However, 25 years after the beginning of the outward-looking and market-oriented development strategy, it is clear that things have not gone as expected. Economic growth has been lower than anticipated, recurring crises are still a threat, income distribution has become more unequal in most countries, polarization and social fragmentation have increased, large segments of the population are socially marginalized and excluded, and the reorientation of social policies associated to a shrinking State—from huge social programs and production-system incorporated redistribution to focalized poverty programs—has led many dimensions of quality of life unattended.

Bouillon and Buvinic (2003) show that the benefits from growth concentrated in regions and localities well integrated into global markets, while already lagging regions did not have the infrastructure or the human capital to take advantage of global market opportunities and pro-market reforms. Moreley (2001) finds that regional income inequality has increased as a consequence of globalization-driven growth.

Saavedra (2003) shows that growth in the 1990s concentrated in capital intensive exports and modern services, and that the generation of unskilled employment was low. Furthermore, the benefits from growth did not spread to all citizens because of an already skewed distribution of education among workers. Hence, workers with little education faced stagnated and even declining real wages. The reinforcement and deepening of labor income inequality in Latin America is also studied by Behrman et al. (2000a, b), they find that the gap in earnings between workers with more and workers with less than post-secondary education has widened; they state that globalization-related growth and pro-market reforms have placed a premium on skilled workers. Menezes-Filho (2003) finds that wage inequality in Brazil intensified in the 1990s because returns to workers with primary and secondary schooling declined while returns to university education increased. Wage inequality is a main source of income inequality in all Latin-American countries, since non-wage income is concentrated in small and rich segments of the population.

It is important to add that globalization and pro-market reforms did not contribute to the improvement of the distribution of education in Latin America. Hence, in an environment of shrinking States, there is little opportunity to make education an important source for income mobility and for a more egalitarian income distribution. Furthermore, in an income and assets concentrated setting—such as the Latin-American case—pro-market reform and privatization have exasperated inequality and social exclusion, by concentrating capital gains in the upper income groups. Thus, together with the deepening of income distribution and marginalization problems, Latin-American countries have also experienced a proliferation of billionaires.

Ethnicity and Exclusion

It is difficult to classify a population according to its ethnicity. Different criteria are used, such as self-assessment ethnicity and spoken-language based ethnicity. Large segments of the Latin-American population are indigenous, especially in countries such as

Mexico, Guatemala and El Salvador (geographical cradle of the Aztec and Mayan cultures) and in Ecuador, Peru and Bolivia (geographical cradle of the Inca culture). Indigenous groups are also important in other Latin-American countries. Afro-descendents are also important in countries such as Brazil, Venezuela, and the Caribbean countries.

The marginalization of ethnic groups from economic and political participation is a fundamental problem for quality of life in Latin America Lucero (2006). Bouillon and Buvinic (2003, p. 3) state that "in Bolivia, Brazil, Guatemala, and Peru the incidence of poverty is twice as high for indigenous and afro-descendents than for the rest of the population."

They also found (2003, p. 4) that "Primary school enrollment rates are lower for children of indigenous families and those of African descent, and youngsters from these families have higher rates of repetition and dropout. Child mortality is also higher among these groups. For instance, among indigenous groups in Guatemala, child mortality is 79 for 1,000 live births, compared to 56 for the rest of the population."

Discrimination against indigenous groups also exists in Latin America. For example, Saavedra et al. (2003) found that white persons enjoy higher access to human capital and physical assets and have higher wages than predominantly indigenous workers in Peru, even after controlling for other explanatory variables. Hall and Patrinos (2004) state that being indigenous increases the probability of being poor in Latin America, even after controlling for other common predictors of poverty. Mezzera (2002) states that afro-descendents earn 50% less than other groups in Brazil—women also earn less, about 30–40% less than other groups. Similar results are found by Arias, Tejerina, and Yamada (2003)

Mega Cities and Urbanization: Advantages and Disadvantages

During the last decades Latin America has experienced a strong process of urbanization. This process is generated by both natural and induced trends; the former originate from the benefits from agglomeration, the later from public policies and development strategies.

Benefits from Urbanization
The benefits from population agglomeration are well-known in the development literature. Urbanization reduces the provision cost of infrastructure (roads, potable water, electricity, and so on) and public services (hospitals, schools, universities, and so on) with respects to rurally-dispersed citizens. Furthermore, economies of agglomeration are also associated to the well-known benefits from "living in cities," such as: access to cultural events, restaurants, large supermarkets, recreational activities, and so on. In addition, people who live in large cities have access to a larger and diversified pool of job opportunities. Up to certain degree, urbanization is expected to be associated to an increase in the quality of life of a country's population. Hence, the existence of a natural trend toward urbanization is of no surprise.

The process of urbanization was also induced by public policies implemented by most Latin-American countries, The import-substitution industrialization strategy followed by most countries from the 1950s to 1980s promoted industrial centers in the urban areas; the urban bias also created strong incentives for rural-urban migration. In addition, strong and centralized political regimes privileged the growth of the country's administrative centers.

In consequence, urbanization rates increased substantially during the last decades of the past century. Urban population in Latin-American was 65.3% of total population in 1980, and it is expected to reach almost 80% in 2015. Some countries show high urban rates; figures for 2005 from the Economic Commission for Latin America and the Caribbean show that Puerto Rico has an urbanization rate of 97.5, Uruguay of 93.1, Argentina of 90.6, Venezuela of 88.8, and Chile of 86.9.

These high rates of urbanization are clearly associated to some quality of life improvements for Latin-Americans. However, there is a generalized sense that in some cases urbanization and agglomeration has gone too far.

There are three mega cities in Latin America, with populations above 12 million: Sao Paolo, Mexico City and Buenos Aires. In addition, Santiago, Rio du Janeiro, Bogotá, Lima, and Guadalajara have populations above 5 million (Source ONU, 2002 Population Reports). Furthermore, cities such as Buenos Aires and Santiago centralize both the economic activity and the population of their countries, they also centralize the country's administrative and public capacity (Gaviria and Stein 1999)

Quality of life in these cities is threatened by factors such as congestion; air pollution; crime; increasing transportation costs in terms of money, time, and stress;

Pollution

A study by the World Health Organization shows that Mexico City has the worst pollution indicators among the largest cities in the world for which data is available. Pollution in Mexico City is worse than in Beijing, Sao Paolo, Cairo, Moscow, Los Angeles, and Yakarta, which are also highly polluted cities. Pollution in Mexico City is associated to a higher than normal incidence of respiratory illnesses such as chronic bronchitis and asthma; it is also associated to high premature-mortality rates. Similar pollution-related health problems are found in Sao Paolo, Lima, and Santiago (Mejía 2005)

Resource Problems

Ezcurra and Mazari-Hiriart (1998) and Saavedra and Cervantes (2003) argue that in some cases the urbanization process has not taken into consideration the regional distribution of natural resources, leading to asymmetries between the regional distribution of the population and economic activity and the distribution of natural resources. For example, in the case of Mexico, water reserves are located in the southern areas of the country, while the population is located in the central areas, and the economic activity in the central and northern areas.

Fragmentation

In addition, Latin-American largest cities are experiencing a process of depersonalization and social fragmentation, which also threatens the quality of life of their inhabitants. The region's inequitable income distribution shows up in urban developments that segment the population on the basis of their social and economic class. The relatively integrated social life that people had in small towns is being replaced in big cities by enclosed residential areas, which not only protect wealthy people from delinquency but also create fragmented neighborhoods. Hence, Latin-American big cities are characterized by the proliferation of residential areas that are internally homogeneous, but highly heterogeneous across quarters. These groups share a common regional space and jurisdiction; however, they are clearly segmented in their social activities (social clubs, schools and universities, working spaces, restaurants). Social fragmentation in large cities is also associated to a general lost of community

purpose. Even though the groups are socially fragmented, they are strongly linked through the economic functioning of societies. For example, enclosed residential areas of high-income groups depend on low-income groups for providing needed services such as guards, gardeners, maids, construction workers, drivers, and so on.

Caldeira (1999) shows that the emergence of enclosed residential areas led to the decline of public recreational areas, as well as to the insecurity of public areas. Rubalcava and Schteingart (2000) and Giglia (2001a, b) studied the emergence of enclosed residential areas in Mexico; in specific, they investigate the disappearance of neighborhoods and their substitution by 'residential solutions' for low-income families and by enclosed residential areas for high-income families. This fragmentation process shows up not only in the residential areas, but also in all social activities. Furthermore, the emergence of enclosed residential areas has led to the deterioration and insecurity of public spaces, such as recreational parks, public streets, and public commercial areas.

In consequence, there is a general sense that urbanization has gone too far in some cases, leading to citizens living their lives in congested, polluted, depersonalized, deteriorated, and unsafe neighborhoods, where there is a lack of general communitarian purpose and a deterioration of interpersonal relations.

Crime and Violence

Crime

Data on crime and violence is partial and fragmentary in Latin America. Furthermore, statistics do not follow homogeneous criteria across countries, and there are reporting flaws everywhere. According to the World Bank (1997), in 1990 the Latin America and Caribbean region had homicide rates more than twice that of the world average: 22.9 per 100,000 versus a worldwide average of 10.7. This is one of the highest homicide rates in the world. Buvinic et al. (1999) state that homicide rates have raised during the last two decades in most Latin-American and Caribbean countries. Rates are substantially high in countries such as Guatemala, El Salvador, Colombia, Peru, and Jamaica.

Buvinic et al. (1999) report that property crimes constitute the larger share of all crimes in most Latin-American and Caribbean countries; these kind of crimes are biased toward people in the higher income quintiles. For example, a Colombian from the highest income quintile has a probability of being a victim of theft of about 15%. The probability for a person in the highest income quintile of being victim of auto theft is about 40% in El Salvador.

Ayres (1998) finds that beyond the direct well-being impact of crime, it also has adverse effects on the region's investment climate and economic growth. Thus, crime affects other relevant factors for quality of life, such as employment and public and private investment. It also affects the perception of safety and the enjoyment of urban and public spaces.

Fajnzylber et al. (1998) investigated the economic factors explaining crime rates in Latin America. They found that economic downturns and an unequal income distribution are main determinants of high crime rates in Latin America. Economic downturns generate a wave of crime which tends to persist even after the economy has reactivated. In a previous study, Fajnzylber (1997) found that inequality in income distribution, but not poverty, is strongly related to the region's high rates of crime and violence. This result is interesting because it shows that a person's relative position is directly important for explaining crime. Buvinic and Morrison (2000) followed a broader perspective to crime; they discuss personal, household, and community and social factors behind crime and violence in Latin America. They state that crime and violence emerge from many sources and in intricate ways.

Crime rates in Latin America are also influenced by historical and institutional factors. The long history of civil conflicts in many Latin-American countries—such as in El Salvador, Guatemala, and Nicaragua—has created environmental conditions that favor crime such as a widespread availability of weapons and an attenuation of inhibitions to violence.

Domestic Violence

It is expected for figures about domestic violence to be flawed because of under-reporting. Furthermore, the legal definition for domestic violence is heterogeneous across countries, and it is subject to some degrees of ambiguity. In addition, people's understanding of what domestic violence is substantially varies across cultures, as well as they report different tolerance levels toward violence. However, it is commonly accepted that there is a domestic violence problem in Latin America. On the basis of local studies across Latin

America, Buvinic et al. (1999, p. 3) conclude that "Anywhere between 30% and 75% of adult women with partners in the region are subject to psychological abuse, and between 10% and 30% suffer physical violence.... violence against children and the elderly are even more scant, but the little available evidence suggests that they too are serious problems."

Domestic violence has enormous repercussions for functionality and social integration of women. Lozano (1997) found that violence against women was the third most important source of disability-adjusted life years for women in Mexico City. Gonzales and Gavilano (1997) found that poverty increases the likelihood of psychological violence in Lima, Peru, but not of physical and sexual violence. They argue that stress-related factors behind poverty may trigger psychological violence.

Drug-Related Violence

A clear threat to the quality of life of Latin-Americans comes from the drug-related business. The region lies just besides the United States, which is the largest drug market in the world and, in consequence, it has become the largest world exporter of marijuana and cocaine. Countries such as Colombia, Mexico, Peru and Ecuador have seriously been affected either as producers or as exporters of drugs. The illegal business of producing, manufacturing and exporting drugs is associated to many quality of life threats, such as drug-related violence, organized crime, raise in domestic consumption of drugs, and the deterioration of the local institutions. The Latin-American Commission on Drugs and Democracy (2008) states that the drug business has weaken the democratic institutions in the region, "the corruption of public servants, the judicial system, governments, the political system, and specially the police forces in charge of enforcing law and order" (LACDD 2008, p. 7). This commission, lead by ex-presidents Gaviria of Colombia, Cardoso of Brazil, and Zedillo of Mexico claims for a new approach on the war on drugs. After four decades, it is clear that the United States' war-on-drugs strategy, which is based on the repression of the supply side, has failed (Hakim 2011). Without any substantial program to reduce the demand for drugs, any repressive strategy, on the supply side will lead to geographical relocations in crop production and manufacturing, greater violence, more spaces for corruption and higher prices of the product which are easily absorbed by a highly inelastic demand. Violence has reached alarming levels in the northern states of

Mexico, where organized groups have also benefited from purchasing and smuggling guns from the United States markets, where purchasing weapons is legal.

Without neglecting the supply side of the market, a new paradigm in the war on drugs must place greater attention to the demand side and to the structural social factors that explain the consumption of drugs.

Conclusions

Quality of life in Latin America and the Caribbean is seriously threatened by a very unequal distribution of income. With some exceptions, mean productivity levels in Latin America are sufficient to guarantee a decent standard of living for all population. However, an unequal income distribution implies that about 40% of Latin-Americans live under the economic poverty line. Furthermore, such an unequal income distribution reflects in social problems such as crime, domestic psychological violence, deterioration of neighborhoods and community sentiments, social fragmentation, depersonalization, lack of social cohesion, and polarization on the role of the government and on the desired development strategy. Income distribution is not only very unequally distributed, but there is also horizontal exclusion, since the income of some ethnic groups fall in the lower quintiles.

It has also been found that an unequal income distribution has a direct impact on subjective well-being because of the low social mobility in the region. The unequal distribution increases subjective well-being for people in the higher income quintiles, while it reduces subjective well-being for people in the lower quintiles.

Some countries do face both a low productivity problem and a very unequal distribution of income and assets. Increasing productivity is an important objective in this case, as well as fostering a more egalitarian distribution of income.

Subjective well-being research shows that life satisfaction is not low in Latin America. It seems that Latin Americans manage to attain life satisfaction even under adverse economic conditions. First, although relevant, the economic domain is not crucial for the life satisfaction of many Latin Americans; it is the family domain the crucial one. Hence, the impact of public policies and development strategies on such an institution as the family should always be taken into consideration. Even though the economic domain is not crucial, its importance raises when income is very low; thus, the importance of increasing production in Latin America should not be neglected, as long as it concentrates in the low income and marginalized groups. Second, Latin-American family arrangements are mostly communitarian, based on solidarity and altruism; these arrangements allow for Latin Americans to attain more satisfaction from a given income. Third, because of upbringing and cultural factors, some Latin Americans do not associate a good life with a wealthy one.

An issue that requires further study refers to the relationship between political power and the propensity to undertake quality of life enhancing policies. It seems that the distribution of power in Latin America implies political equilibriums that do not privilege the quality of life of large masses of population. The problem is structural, since it emerges from colonial factors, as well as from Latin-American position in the international arena. Recent development strategies have performed below expectations, and Latin America's main challenge consists in finding a development strategy that contributes to the quality of life of all its citizens.

References

Arias, O., Tejerina, L., & Yamada, G. (2003). *Education, family background and racial earnings inequality in Brazil.* Working Paper. Poverty and Inequality Unit, Sustainable Development Department, Inter-American Development Bank, Washington, DC.

Ayres, R. L. (1998). *Crime and violence as development issues in Latin America and the Caribbean.* Washington, DC: The World Bank.

Behrman, J. R., Birdsall, N., & Székely, M. (2000a). Intergenerational mobility in Latin America: Deeper markets and better schools make a difference. In N. Birdsall & C. Graham (Eds.), *New markets, new opportunities? Economic and social mobility in a changing world.* Washington, DC: Brookings Institution Press and the Carnegie Endowment for International Peace.

Behrman, J. R., Duryea, S., & Székely, M. (2000b). *Schooling investments and macroeconomic conditions: A micro-macro investigation for Latin America and the Caribbean 1999.* Technical Paper, Inter-American Development Bank, Washington, DC.

Behrman, J., Birdsall, N., & Szekely, M. (2001). *Economic reform and wage differentials in Latin America.* Carnegie Endowment Working Papers, November 2001.

Bouillon, C., & Buvinic, M. (2003) *Inequality, exclusion and poverty in Latin America and the Caribbean: Implications for development,* Inter-American Development Bank.

Bourguignon, F., & Verdier, T. (2000). Oligarchy, democracy, inequality and growth. *Journal of Development Economics, 62*(2), 285–313.

Buvinic, M., & Morrison, A. (2000). *Causes of violence, technical note 3, division of social development, department of sustainable development*, Inter-American Development Bank.

Buvinic, M., Morrison, A., & Shifter, M. (1999). *Violence in Latin America and the Caribbean: A framework for action, technical study, sustainable development department*, Inter-American Development Bank.

Caldeira, T. (1999). Fortified Enclaves: The new urban segregation. In S. M. Low (Ed.), *Theorizing the city. The new urban anthropology reader*. New Brunswick: Rutgers University Press.

Gonzales de Olarte, E., & Gavilano, P. (1997, October). *Poverty and domestic violence against woman in Metropolitan Lima*. Paper presented as part of the Conference Domestic Violence in Latin America and the Caribbean: Costs, Programs and Politics. Inter-American Development Bank. Washington, DC, October 20–21.

di Tella, R., MacCulloch, R., & Oswald, A. (1997). Preferences for inflation and unemployment: Some evidence from surveys of happiness. *The American Economic Review, 91*(1), 335–341.

Eggers, A., & Graham, C. (2004). *The costs of unemployment in Latin America*. Mimeo: The Brookings Institution.

Ezcurra, E., & Mazari-Hiriart, M. (1998). ¿Son Viables las Megaciudades? Las Enseñanzas de la Ciudad de México. *Gaceta Ecológica, 48*, 8–26.

Fajnzylber, P. (1997). *What causes crime and violence?* Washington, DC: World Bank, Office of the Chief Economist, Latin America and the Caribbean.

Fajnzylber, P., Lederman, D., & Loayza, N. (1998). *Determinants of crime rates in Latin America and the world: An empirical assessment*. Washington, DC: The World Bank.

Gaviria, A., & Stein, E. (1999). *Urban concentration in Latin America and the world*. Background paper for the Office of the Chief Economist, Inter-American Development Bank.

Giglia, A. (2001a). Sociabilidad y megaciudades, *Estudios Sociológicos*, El Colegio de México, septiembre–diciembre, 799–821.

Giglia, A. (2001b). *La Nueva segregación urbana, Perfiles Latinoamericanos 19*. México: FLACSO-México.

Graham, C. (2005) Insights on development from the economics of happiness. *World Bank Research Observer, 20*(2), 201–231.

Graham, C., & Felton, A. (2005). *Does inequality matter to individual welfare? An initial exploration based on happiness surveys from Latin America*. The Brookings Institution, Washington, DC, CSED Working Paper No. 38, January.

Graham, C., & Pettinato, S. (2001). Happiness, markets, and democracy: Latin America in comparative perspective. *Journal of Happiness Studies, 2*(3), 237–268.

Graham, C., & Pettinato, S. (2002a). *Happiness and hardship: Opportunity and insecurity in new market economies*. Washington, DC: The Brookings Institution Press.

Graham, C., & Pettinato, S. (2002b). Frustrated achievers: Winners, losers, and subjective well-being in emerging market economies. *Journal of Development Studies, 38*(4), 100–140.

Graham, C., & Sukhtankar, S. (2004). Does economic crisis reduce support for markets and democracy in Latin America? Some evidence from surveys of public opinion and well being. *Journal of Latin American Studies, 36*, 349–377.

Hakim, P. (2011). *Rethinking US drug policy inter American dialogue*. Washington, DC: The Beckley Foundation.

Hall, G., & Patrinos, H. (2004). Overview. In G. Hall & H. Patrinos (Eds.), *Indigenous people, poverty and human development in Latin America: 1994–2004*. Washington, DC: World Bank.

LACDD (2008) *Drugs and democracy: Towards a paradigm shift*. Report of the Latin American Commission on Drugs and Democracy.

Lozano, R. (1997). *La Carga de la Enfermedad y las Lesiones por Violencia contra las Mujeres: El Caso de la Ciudad de México. Documento de la Conferencia Violencia Doméstica en América Latina y el Caribe: Costos, Programas y Políticas*. Banco Inter-Americano de Desarrollo, Washington, DC, 20–21 de octubre.

Lucero, J. A. (2006). *Indigenous political voice and the struggle for recognition in Ecuador and Bolivia*. Background papers, World Development Report 2006: Equity & Development, The World Bank.

Lustig, N. (2011). Tendencias Recientes de la Desigualdad y la Pobreza en América Latina. In M. Puchet, M. Rojas, R. Salazar, G. Valenti, & F. Valdés (Eds.), *América latina: problemas centrales y oportunidades promisorias*. México: FLACSO-México.

Mejía, A. (2005). *Air pollution in urban areas*, LCSEN sector management; manuscript.

Menezes-Filho. (2003). *Education and labor market outcomes in Brazil*. Prepared for the Seminar, Dealing with Risk: Implementing Employment Policies under Fiscal Constrains, 23 March, Milan, Italy.

Mezzera, J. (2002). *Gênero, Raça, Emprego e Rendas*. manuscript.

Moreley, S. (2001). *Distribution and growth in Latin America in an Era of structural reform: The impact of globalization*, Technical Paper No. 184, OECD, Paris.

Rojas, M. (2005a). A conceptual-referent theory of happiness: Heterogeneity and its consequences. *Social Indicators Research, 74*(2), 261–294.

Rojas, M. (2005b). Bienestar Subjetivo y su Relación con Indicadores Objetivos: Consideraciones para la Política Pública. In L. Garduño, B. Salinas, & M. Rojas (Eds.), *Calidad de Vida y Bienestar Subjetivo en México*. México: Plaza y Valdés.

Rojas, M. (2005c). Distribución del Ingreso y Teorías de Justicia. In J. R. Vargas & Y. Xirinachs (Eds.), *La Formación de Economistas: Ensayos en Honor de Pepita Echandi*. Costa Rica: Universidad de Costa Rica.

Rojas, M. (2005d). Qué es Desarrollo Económico? In J. R. Vargas & Y. Xirinachs (Eds.), *La Formación de Economistas: Ensayos en Honor de Pepita Echandi*. Costa Rica: Universidad de Costa Rica.

Rojas, M. (2005e). Una Introducción a la Nueva Economía Política. In J. R. Vargas & Y. Xirinachs (Eds.), *La Formación de Economistas: Ensayos en Honor de Pepita Echandi*. Costa Rica: Universidad de Costa Rica.

Rojas, M. (2006a). Communitarian versus individualistic arrangements in the family: What and whose income matters for happiness? chapter 10. In R. J. Estes (Ed.), *Advancing quality of life in a turbulent world*. Dordrecht: Springer.

Rojas, M. (2006b). Well-being and the complexity of poverty: A subjective well-being approach, chapter 9. In M. McGillivray & M. Clarke (Eds.), *Understanding human well-being*. Tokyo/New York/Paris: United Nations University Press.

Rojas, M. (2006c). Life satisfaction and satisfaction in domains of life: Is it a simple relationship? *Journal of Happiness Studies, 7*(4), 467–497.

Rojas, M. (2007a). Estimating equivalence scales in Mexico: A subjective well-being approach. *Oxford Development Studies, 35*(3), 273–293.

Rojas, M. (2007b). Heterogeneity in the relationship between income and happiness: A conceptual referent theory explanation. *Journal of Economic Psychology, 28*(1), 1–14.

Rojas, M. (2007c). The complexity of well-being: A life-satisfaction conception and a domains-of-life approach, chapter 12. In I. Gough & A. McGregor (Eds.), *Researching well-being in developing countries*. Cambridge: Cambridge University Press.

Rojas, M. (2010). Intra-household arrangements and economic satisfaction: Implications for poverty analysis. *Journal of Happiness Studies, 11*(2), 225–241.

Rojas, M. (2011). Bienestar Subjetivo en América Latina. In M. Puchet, M. Rojas, R. Salazar, G. Valenti, & F. Valdés (Eds.), *América latina: problemas centrales y oportunidades promisorias*. México: FLACSO-México.

Rubalcava, R. M., & Schteingart, M. (2000). Segregación Socioespacial. In G. Garza (Ed.), *La Ciudad de México en el fin del segundo milenio,* México: El Colegio de México – Gobierno del Distrito Federal.

Saavedra, J. (2003). Labor markets during the 1990s. In P. P. Kuczynski & J. Williamson (Eds.), *After the Washington consensus: Restarting growth and reform in Latin America*. Washington, DC: Institute for International Economics.

Saavedra, F., & Cervantes, M. (2003). *Población y Recursos Naturales: El Caso del Agua*. La Situación Demográfica de México 2003. Consejo Nacional de Población, Mexico.

Saavedra, J., Torero, M., & Ñopo, H. (2003). Ethnicity and earnings in urban Peru. In P. P. Kuczynki & J. Williamson (Eds.), *After the Washington consensus: Restarting growth and reform in Latin America*. Washington, DC: Institute for International Economics.

Sokoloff, K. L., & Engerman, S. L. (2000). Institutions, factor endowments, and paths of development in the new world. *Journal of Economic Perspectives, 14*(3), 217–232.

World Bank. (1997). *Crime and violence as development issues in Latin America and the Caribbean. The State of Rio de Janeiro and The Inter-American Development Bank*. Seminar on The Challenge of Urban Criminal Violence. Rio de Janeiro, Brazil, March 2–4.

Quality of Life in Argentina

25

Graciela Tonon

Introduction

This chapter describes the results of several research projects developed by the author studying changes in the level of life satisfaction in Argentina since 2002. Quality of life in Argentina significantly decreased in 2001 as a direct function of the political, economic, and social crisis that besieged the whole country, which resulted in the change of the presidency in December of that year.

In April 2002, we developed a pilot study to test the psychometric properties of the Well-Being Index (IWBG 2001) using 500 residents, living in different parts of the country (age varied between 18 and 67). In 2003, after the change of government, we conducted another study using the same index with 192 people of the same age residing in the Departments of Great Buenos Aires. We conducted another study targeting young people (16–19 years old) in the same region – interviewing 289 hundred teenagers.

As the political climate and social conditions began to change in a positive way (during 2007–2008), we conducted yet another survey involving 976 people in the whole country, using a quality of life measure developed by Paul Anand and his colleagues (Open University, UK). The main objective of this survey was the identification of human capabilities, social

inequalities, and economic opportunities, in addition to mainstream quality of life indicators.

Finally in 2010, we used the ESCVP (Tonon 2009) – a survey instrument to measure the level of satisfaction with quality of life in the country. We surveyed 401 people in May 2010 and 197 people in October 2010 in the Departments of Great Buenos Aires. But, before describing the results of these surveys, we will provide the reader with a brief historical perspective of Argentina.

The National Context in Argentina

To understand the results of our quality of life surveys, we need to understand and acknowledge the national context. During the last decade of the twentieth century and the beginning of the twenty-first century, government used focused social policies. Similarly, Lechner (1996, p. 13) stated that what happened in Latin American countries during that period made people less autonomous and limited in their freedom. Furthermore, the labor market was afflicted by a high level of unemployment, the displacement of jobs, decrease in labor rights, and increase in poverty. As such, people's quality of life was adversely affected.

Since 2003, the situation was changed for the better. Based on information provided by the Statistic National Institute (INDEC), poverty decreased from more than 50% in 2002 to 12% in 2010 and unemployment decreased from 20% in 2002 to 7.5% in 2010 (PNUD Argentina 2010). The new government began to develop universal social policies, increasing access to health and educational services, safeguarding human rights, and improving the economic environment. However, there were significant

G. Tonon (✉)
Faculty of Social Sciences, Universidad Nacional de Lomas de Zamora, Lomas de Zamora, Argentina

Faculty of Social Sciences, Universidad de Palermo, Buenos Aires, Argentina
e-mail: gracielatonon@hotmail.com

K.C. Land et al. (eds.), *Handbook of Social Indicators and Quality of Life Research*,
DOI 10.1007/978-94-007-2421-1_25, © Springer Science+Business Media B.V. 2012

problems too: crime rate was high (INDEC 2007), home ownership was low (INDEC 2001), and difficulties with public transportation continued.

As most of our field data originated from the Departments of Great Buenos Aires, the reader may find it useful to know more about the local areas that were studied (INDEC 2003). The Departments of Great Buenos Aires is the geographic area that surrounds Argentina's capital district; its size is 3,833 km^2 organized in 24 departments. The recent national census (2010) estimated the size of its population as 9,916,715, which is equivalent to fourth of the total country 40,117,096. It is an area that reflects polarized life conditions, ranging from settlements of extreme poverty to high-income gated neighborhoods. The percentage of unemployment (8.2%) is higher than in the whole country (EPHC 2010[1]), and 75.2% live in their own house (INDEC 2001). The issue that preoccupied Argentineans the most seems to be insecurity.

The Use of the Well-Being Index in Argentina

In this section, we will describe the three surveys that were conducted capturing the quality of life in Argentina using the Well-Being Index.

The First Survey

The study of quality of life refers to the material environment (social welfare) and psychosocial environment (psychological welfare). It has been defined as a concept that involves both objective and subjective indicators in seven life domains (Cummins 1997). The use of domains in the quality of life surveys allows a more precise measurement of quality of life than global questions related to life as a whole. The addition of satisfaction across various life domains should reflect the totality of life satisfaction, which in turn is considered a valid measure of quality of life. The point at issue here is the possibility that the domains can be considered varying cross-culturally.

Our study objective was to capture potentialities rather than deficiencies (Max Neef 1986)[2] in a sociopolitical context. Doing so, we tried to capture the material environment in conjunction with the social one, taking into account the "individual," traditionally called "object," as "subject" and protagonist of his actions. The result better reflects he social and political reality.

The pilot test of the Well-Being Index (IWBG 2001) was conducted in Argentina in 2002 right after the national crisis.[3] The index has two scales: the Personal Wellbeing Index (PWI) and the National Wellbeing Index (NWI). The PWI is based on the Comprehensive Quality of Life Scale (ComQol) developed by Cummins and his colleagues (Cummins et al. 1994). The ComQol comprise both an objective and subjective measure of life quality, and its domains were initially identified through a review of domain names used in the literature. This was subsequently followed by a three-phase process (Cummins et al. 1994) and empirical validation to generate the seven broad domains that comprised the scale (Cummins 1997). The PWI scale contains eight items of satisfaction, each one corresponding to a quality of life domain as standard of living, health, achieving in life, relationships, safety, community connectedness, future security, and spirituality/religion. These eight domains are theoretically embedded, as representing the first level deconstruction of the global question: "How satisfied are you with your life as a whole?" (PWI-A Manual 2006). The national well-being index reflects nearly the same domains but couched in a national context.

The first survey involved 500 respondents between the ages 18 and 67 (46.2% were between the ages 18 and 27), living in different parts of the country. Two difficulties were encountered in the conduct of the survey: language/meaning and the use of the telephone.

---

[1] EPHC. Encuesta Permanente de Hogares Continua, produced each 3 months by the National Institute of Statistic and Census (INDEC), Argentina.

[2] Manfred Max Neef is a Chilean economist who proposed to explain the crisis of Latin America countries not only in an economic way. He produced a human scale approach to international development based in the idea that the development is about people not about objects. He considers that "needs" should be understood as finite and universal, and "satisfiers" are infinite and culturally determined. In Max Neef (1986).

[3] Graciela Tonon developed the first application of the index in Argentina. She is a primary researcher of the International Well-Being Group organized by Dr. Robert Cummins in the Australian Center on Quality of Life, Deakin University Australia.

As the survey instrument was originally developed in different context, it was necessary to modify it to the Argentinean context.[4] The index was originally developed in English which was then translated to Spanish, especially Argentinean dialect of Spanish.

The major difficulty was the translation of the item "feeling part of your community." To shed light on this difficulty, we must first provide the reader with a little history. When democracy returned to the country in 1983, Argentineans began to feel that they can "work in the community" because "work in the community" was outlawed by the military government. To "feel part of the community" was understood as making decisions collectively and in a participatory manner, working together to resolve social problems affecting Argentineans at large. But an economic crisis developed in the beginning of the 1990s; a new president came to power and a new era unfolded. Political and social reforms were initiated in 1990s. A plan of privatization developed by the government mandated a new course of action contrary to tradition, forging a new relationship between public and private sectors of the economy (Svampa 2002, p. 94). The model of a "distributor State" began to change to an "absent State." This resulted in the appearance of new actors in public policy. Svampa (2002, p. 59) asserted that citizenship was based on the notion of the "owner and consumer citizen" rather than the "political citizen." This shift generated more interest and participation by the public because they are more inherently interested in improving their economic situation more so than the political situation at the national level. Argentineans began coalesce by creating local organizations to defend their rights and "feel part of the community." They began to develop social networks to help one another in the absence of support from the government. Thus, the definition of the concept "community" had changed accordingly.[5] Our research team in the Psychology Doctoral Program of Universidad de Palermo (Argentina) is now involved in a community quality of life research project with the objective of developing new indicators that are more sensitive in capturing the concept of "positive community."

The other difficulty that we encountered in the conduct of this survey was the use of the telephone. To deal with this problem, we intercepted and interviewed people in public places (supermarkets, streets, schools, etc.).

As we expected (scale from 0 to 10 points), respondents expressed anger (dissatisfaction) toward the national government (1.1). Also, they expressed dissatisfaction with the economic situation (1.9), national security (1.6), and with social conditions (2.2). In contrast, the survey also revealed that the average level of satisfaction with personal life has risen while satisfaction with living conditions has decreased. Most importantly, the results indicate that there is a significant difference between the personal index of well-being (6.5) and the national index (2.07). High satisfaction ratings were evidenced in relation to friends (7.9), personal relations (7.6), and family (7.7). Another interesting finding are satisfaction with health (7.6), spirituality/religiosity (7.1), and with being part of the community (6.3). These findings remind us of Marks (2004, p. 13) who pointed out the negative relationship between GDP and life satisfaction in Latin American countries (i.e., that low GDP is associated with high life satisfaction).

The Second Survey

The second study was launched in 2003[6] after the change of government. In that context, we used the same index with 192 respondents, ages varying between 18 and 67 with both males and females participating. As expected, the change of government produced more positive feelings toward the national scene, but nevertheless, it was still mostly negative. People expressed less dissatisfaction with the national government (3.6), the economic situation (3.5), social conditions (2.9), and the possibility of initiating and managing their own business (3.8) than a year ago. Satisfaction with public safety was still very low (1.7). In this vein, the overall findings showed that life was better for Argentineans after the new elected government took power.

---

[4] The first translation of the WBI was produced by Tonon, G. and Aguirre, V. in 2002.

[5] Tonon, G. (comp.) (2009b).

[6] Calidad de vida de jóvenes de la zona sur del Conurbano Bonaerense. **Director Dra. Graciela Tonon. Programa de Investigación en Calidad de Vida. Facultad de Ciencias Sociales. Universidad Nacional de Lomas de Zamora. 2004.**

Satisfaction with health (7.9), spirituality/religiosity (7.4), and community (6.8) were moderately high. Compared to the pilot study, the average level of satisfaction with personal life was higher than the level of satisfaction with living conditions in the country. Satisfaction with friends was 8.6, with personal relations was 8.05, and with family 8.04. Again, a significant difference was observed between the personal index (7.6) and the national index (5.4), albeit this difference was smaller compared to the pilot study.

The Third Survey

In 2005,[7] we used the well-being index for the third time in the Departments of Great Buenos Aires with 289 respondents (ages 16–19), male and female. The level of satisfaction with life as a whole was 7.2 and with quality of life in the country was 5.2. Similar to the two preceding surveys, the highest satisfaction ratings were with friends (8.6), satisfaction with personal relations (8.01), and with family (7.5). Increases in satisfaction were noted in relation to government (4.4), the possibility of initiating and managing one's own business (4.5), the economic situation (3.8), social conditions (3.8), public safety (3.6), and health (8.03). Even though satisfaction ratings were low, it seems that changes in the political climate may have increased the quality of life for Argentineans overall. Another interesting finding is the decrease in satisfaction with spirituality/religiosity (5.9) and community (6.04), compared to the 2003 ratings.

Quality of Life, Social Inequalities, and Economic Opportunities

In 2007–2008, we developed a research project to measure human capabilities and quality of life of the population.[8] We used a sample of 976 people varying in gender (male and female), age (18–65 years old), and geographic location (different cities of the country). The measure was developed by Paul Anand (Open University, UK) and translated and adapted by Tonon et al. (2007).[9] The survey instrument was organized by different dimensions in the following order: satisfaction with life as a whole, family, work, health, house, leisure, religiosity, social support, personal security, neighborhood security, discrimination, self-perception, and freedom of expression of political and religious ideas. The particular indicators about the national situation were economic opportunities, access to health, satisfaction with health public and the private sector, access to education, access to job, type of job, government social programs, and attitude toward the voting process (Tonon 2008). The more important dimensions related to quality of life are satisfaction with life as a whole, health, and public safety.

In regard to satisfaction with quality of life, respondents scored moderate to low (2.8 on a scale of 7 points). However, only 21.5% expressed the fact that they frequently evaluate their lives and only 26.3% mentioned that they have clear lifetime goals.

It is important to note that life satisfaction represents a self-report about how people evaluate their life overall (Diener 2006, p. 3). Survey questions must be asked related to certain life domains to obtain more specific evaluations of their situation. Questions about life satisfaction in general may lead people to report their feelings related to what is going on with them at the moment.

With respect to feelings about public safety (whether they feel safe in a personal way and in the neighborhood they live in), questions were asked about perceptions people have in regard to walking alone in their neighborhood during the day, at night, and the possibility of being a victim of a violent attack in the future. Only 62.4% expressed feeling safe to walk in their neighborhood during the day and 33.8% at night. Specifically, 45.5% of the respondents indicated that they feel insecure to walk in their neighborhood at night. The perception of the likelihood of being a victim of a violent attack in the future registered at 49.7%.

---

[7] *Calidad de vida de jóvenes de la zona sur del Conurbano Bonaerense: participación pública y acceso a la salud.* Director Dra. Graciela Tonon. Programa de investigación en calidad de vida. Facultad de Ciencias Sociales. Universidad Nacional de Lomas de Zamora. 2005–2006.

[8] *Oportunidades reales y capabilidades de la población argentina: su impacto en las políticas públicas* Departamento de Derecho y Ciencia Política. Universidad Nacional de La Matanza. Directora Dra. Graciela Tonon. (2007–2008).

[9] Dr. Paul Anand is the director of *Capabilities Measurement Project*, Open University. Gran Bretaña.

In regard to health, 10.7% of the survey population expressed that their health limited them in their daily life, and 37% of this segment mentioned that they did not have private health insurance.[10] In regard to the survey population at large, 62.1% indicated that they have private health insurance, but only 30.1% of this total uses public hospitals. An important finding is that the level of satisfaction with health-care services is higher in relation to public hospitals (5.7 on a scale of 7 points) than private hospitals (3.7). Furthermore, 42.3% indicated that they earn around 266[11] dollars/month and 26% earn around 533 dollars/month. In other words, employment may represent a limitation to health care. Another limitation to health care may be related to education. The survey indicates that 67.9% of respondents felt those limitations were not well educated (18.4% did not complete primary school, whereas 48.9% did).

The survey results also revealed that 61.7% of the respondents owned their home where they lived, but only the 3% indicated that they can obtain a loan. The rest of the population either rent or live in housing provided by family/friends. Considering the number of people without their own house, 55% mentioned that they could not buy because they did not have enough money and that they could not obtain a loan.

The ESCVP Scale (Satisfaction with Quality of Life in the Country)

In 2010, we began to use the ESCV Scale (Tonon 2009) that measures the level of satisfaction with quality of life in the country – a scale with 5 points with 1 corresponding to "totally dissatisfied" and 5 to "totally satisfied." The scale was developed with the national situation in mind. We surveyed 401 people living in the Departments of Great Buenos Aires, varying in gender (male and female) and age (18–70 years old).

The survey instrument (see questionnaire in Appendix) contained different items related to satisfaction with the quality of life in the country, street safety, the preservation of the environment, the State health system, the State educational system, job opportunities, the possibility of home ownership, the national economic situation, social security, government policies in relation to citizen needs, the transparency of government decisions, government social welfare programs, government assistance in emergency situations, tax system, political freedom, care of public places, respect of cultural diversity, and respect of religious diversity.

The results show that the level of satisfaction with the quality of life in the country was 2.75. The highest satisfaction ratings were in relation to political freedoms (3.5) and for respect of religious diversity (3.2). The lowest ratings were in relation to satisfaction with social security (1.8) and the possibility of home ownership (1.9). The remaining satisfaction items varied between 2 and 2.8.

Conclusion

The results of the various studies reported in this chapter indicate that the average level of satisfaction with personal life is greater than satisfaction with the life in Argentina. Moreover, across all the studies, high satisfaction ratings were obtained in relation to "friends," which indicates the importance people give to friendship that may be reflective of a cultural characteristic in Argentina.

Since the change of political regime in 2003, Argentineans' satisfaction with quality of life in the country increased significantly but never reached moderate levels. Satisfaction with government increased too. Satisfaction ratings that were consistently low are related to public security.

Our research also indicates that the concept "community" evolved over time, from the *consumption citizen* of the 1990s to a *political citizen*. Related to this finding is the additional finding (from ESCVP survey of 2010) that reflects growing satisfaction with political freedom.

Finally, it is important to note that integrating qualitative and quantitative research in the study of quality of life can offer better and more complete information about the quality of life in the country, which in turn should guide future public policy.

Acknowledgment I would like to acknowledge Joe Sirgy for his assistance and guidance in preparing the final version of this chapter. I also would like to express my gratitude to Bob Cummins, Paul Anand, and members of my team, particularly Lía Rodriguez de la Vega.

---

[10] In Argentina, there is a free basic Health System for all, even though the employed have their own private health insurance.

[11] In this period, 1 dollar was 3.5 pesos.

Dr. Political Science. Postdoctoral studies CIMESS-Universitá degli studi di Firenze. Magister in Political Sciences. Social worker. Director UNI-COM and *Research Program on Quality of Life*. Faculty of Social Sciences. Universidad Nacional de Lomas de Zamora, Argentina. Member ISQOLS since 2001. Board of Directors ISQOLS since 2005. Vice president of Professional Affairs ISQOLS 2007–2008. Chair Latin-America ad hoc Committee ISQOLS 2009–2010. Vice president of Membership and Publicity ISQOLS 2011-2012. Professor Psychology Doctoral Program. Course "Research in Quality of life", Universidad de Palermo, Argentina. Professor Faculty of Social Sciences, Universidad Nacional de Lomas de Zamora. Professor Department of Law and Political Sciences, Universidad Nacional de La Matanza. Member Editorial Review Board *Applied Research in Quality of Life*. Member Human Development and Capability Association. Member Capabilities Measurement Project, Open University, UK. Permanent invited researcher Latin American Network Childwatch International. Primary Researcher International Well being Group. Author of ten books in Spanish language.

Appendix

Scale of Satisfaction with Quality of Life in the Country (ESCVP, Tonon 2009)

All questions refer to the general situation in the country at large. The scale varies from 1 to 5 in which:

1	2	3	4	5
Totally dissatisfied	Dissatisfied	Neither satisfied nor dissatisfied	Satisfied	Totally satisfied

1. How satisfied are you with the quality of life in the country?

1	2	3	4	5

2. How satisfied are you with street safety in daily life?

1	2	3	4	5

3. How satisfied are you with the preservation of the environment?

1	2	3	4	5

4. How satisfied are you with the State health system?

1	2	3	4	5

5. How satisfied are you with access to the State health system?

1	2	3	4	5

6. How satisfied are you with the State educational system?

1	2	3	4	5

7. How satisfied are you with access to State educational system?

1	2	3	4	5

8. How satisfied are you with job opportunities in your area?

1	2	3	4	5

9. How satisfied are you with the possibility that people have in owning a house?

1	2	3	4	5

10. How satisfied are you with the general economic situation in the country?

1	2	3	4	5

11. How satisfied are you with the social security system in the country?

1	2	3	4	5

12. How satisfied are you with government policies in relation with citizen needs?

1	2	3	4	5

13. How satisfied are you with the transparency of government decisions?

1	2	3	4	5

14. How satisfied are you with government social welfare program?

1	2	3	4	5

15. How satisfied are you with government assistance provided to people in emergency situations?

1	2	3	4	5

16. How satisfied are you with the tax system?

| 1 | 2 | 3 | 4 | 5 |

17. How satisfied are you with political freedom that people enjoy in the country?

| 1 | 2 | 3 | 4 | 5 |

18. How satisfied are you with how people maintain and care of public places?

| 1 | 2 | 3 | 4 | 5 |

19. How satisfied are you with how people respect cultural diversity?

| 1 | 2 | 3 | 4 | 5 |

20. How satisfied are you with how people respect religious diversity?

| 1 | 2 | 3 | 4 | 5 |

References

Anand, P., & Hunter, G. (2004). *Capabilities and wellbeing: evidence based on the Sen-Nussbaum approach to welfare.* The Open University. UK.

Cummins, R, McCabe, M. Romeo, Y., & Gullone, E. (1994). The comprenhensive quality of life scale: instrument development and psychometric evaluation on tertiary staff and students. *Educational and Psychological measurement, 54,* 372–382.

Cummins, R. (1997). *Comprehensive quality of life scale- Adult manual.* Fifth Edition. Melbourne. School of Psychology. Deakin University.

Diener, E. (2006). Guidelines for national indicators of subjective well-being and ill-being. *Applied Research in Quality of Life, 1,* 151–157.

Encuesta Permanente de Hogares continua. Tercer Trimestre. (2010). Instituto Nacional de Estadística y Censo. Ministerio de Economía. Argentina

INDEC. (2001). Censo Nacional de población, hogares y viviendas. http://www.indec.mecon.ar/webcenso/index.asp. (14-2-2011).

INDEC. (2003). *Qué es el Gran Buenos Aires?* Retrieved February 16, 2011, from http://www.indec.gov.ar/nuevaweb/cuadros/4/folleto%20gba.pdf

INDEC. (2007). tasa de delincuencia. Ministerio de Justicia, Seguridad y Derechos Humanos. Subsecretaría de Política Criminal. Dirección Nacional de Política Criminal. Retrieved February 17, 2011, from http://www.indec.mecon.ar/principal.asp?id_tema=358

INDEC. (2011). *CENSO 2010.* Ministerio de Economia. Argentina http://www.censo2010.indec.gov.ar/archivos/novedades/gacetilla (3-10-2011).

Lechner, N. (1996). Las transformaciones de la política. *Revista Mexicana de Sociología, 58*(1), 3–16.

Marks, N. (2004). *The power of well-being. 2.* Nef. London

Max Neef, M. (1986). *Desarrollo a escala humana.* Sweden: CEPAUR.

PNUD Argentina Informe de desarrollo humano. (2010). Retrieved February 8, 2011, from http://www.undp.org.ar/desarrollohumano/docsIDH2010/PNUD_INDH_2010_Nov_2010.pdf

Svampa, M. (2002). *Las nuevas urbanizaciones privadas. Sociabilidad y socialización: la integración social "hacia arriba".* En Beccaria, L y otros.Sociedad y sociabilidad en la Argentina de los 90. Biblos Editorial. Buenos Aires.

The Internatonal Well-being Group (2001) *WBI.* Australian Centre on Quality of Life. Deakin University Australia.

The International Well-Being Group. *Personal well-being-adult (PWI-A)* Manual 2006.

Tonon, G. (2003). *Calidad de vida y desgaste profesional.* Espacio Editorial. Bs. As.

Tonon, G. (comp.) (2006). *Juventud y protagonismo ciudadano.* Espacio Editorial. Bs. As.

Tonon, G. (comp.) (2008). *Desigualdades sociales y oportunidades ciudadanas.* Espacio Editorial. Bs. As.

Tonon, G. (2009a). Escala de satisfacción con la vida en el país (ESCVP).

Tonon, G. (comp.) (2009b). *Comunidad, participación y socialización política.* Espacio Editorial. Bs. As.

Tonon, G., & Aguirre, V. (2009–2002). Traducción del well-being index. Internacional Well-being Group. Australian Center of Quality of Life. Deakin University. Australia. Retrieved Febraury 9, 2011, from http://www.deakin.edu.au/research/acqol/auwbi/index-translations/wbi-spanish-argentina.pdf

"Failed" and "Failing" States: Is Quality of Life Possible?

26

Richard J. Estes

Introduction

Nation-states (hereafter "nations," "countries," or "states") are internationally autonomous political entities that are bound together by a system of laws, a defined (but not necessarily contiguous) geographic space, and a commitment to the pursuit of the collective well-being of their inhabitants.[1] Though quite diverse in geographic size, population characteristics, type of polity, and economic system, nations share a variety of features common with one another (Britannica Online 2011a; Moran et al. 2006; Weingast and Wittman

2006). Rank ordered more or less in terms of their importance, they include (1) recognition of their political sovereignty by other nations; (2) a coherent set of principles that guide their interactions with other sovereign states; (3) secure physical borders; (4) the administration of justice within a system of laws to which, optimally, the governed have assented (e.g., via a written constitution and an independent judiciary); (5) the provision of a range of "public goods" designed to meet the collective needs of their populations (e.g., the creation of monetary and banking systems, road-building and other transportation networks, the development of communications infrastructure, and the provision of at least limited health, education, and related human services)[2]; (6) special initiatives designed to meet the income security and related needs of their most vulnerable inhabitants (e.g., children, the elderly, persons with chronic illnesses or disabilities, unemployed persons, etc.); and (7) a commitment to promotion of the general well-being of the society-as-a-whole (Kim et al. 2010; Plato 2000; Sachs 2005; Schyns and Koop 2010). In democratic societies, states also carry responsibility for the conduct of fair and open elections and for the promotion of a broad range of civil liberties and political freedoms – all of which are considered necessary elements in the functioning of pluralistic, participatory, societies (Freedom House 2010; Human Rights Watch 2010; Tsai 2006).

---

[1] The concept of the "nation-state(s)" embraces two distinct components: the "state" or "states" refer to discrete political and geopolitical territories over which the state, acting as a "government," claims sovereignty; "nation" or "nations" refer to the cultural or ethnic characteristics of the people who reside in the state (Britannica Online 2011a). The term "nation-state" implies that the two concepts coincide with one another (i.e., that the people of a given geographic territory share more or less the same cultural, religious, and ethnic characteristics), albeit the vast majority of modern nation-states are characterized by substantial cultural diversity even though their geopolitical borders are fully recognized and accepted by the international community (CIA, 2011). Since the European Treaty of Westphalia in 1648, sovereign nation-states defer to one another as co-equal and autonomous powers with full authority over the territories and people they govern (Britannica Online 2011b). The concept of sovereign nation-states constitutes the basis for membership and voting privileges in the United Nations as well as in most major nongovernmental and non-state actor organizations, i.e., one nation, one vote.

R.J. Estes (✉)
School of Social Policy & Practice (SP2), University of Pennsylvania, 3701 Locust Walk, Philadelphia, PA 19104-6214, USA
e-mail: restes@sp2.upenn.edu

---

[2] Individual political systems determine the precise role of the state in each of these sectors, i.e., either as facilitators or providers of such functions (Moran et al. 2006; Weingast and Wittman 2006). Overall, the role of the state is to ensure that such functions are performed whether by the private or public sector or through cooperative arrangements with both.

K.C. Land et al. (eds.), *Handbook of Social Indicators and Quality of Life Research*,
DOI 10.1007/978-94-007-2421-1_26, © Springer Science+Business Media B.V. 2012

From ancient to modern times, nations also have sought to advance the collective well-being of their citizens through the removal of, or at least reductions in, the obstacles that interfere with the pursuit of progressively higher levels of collective development (Annas 1993; Michalos 2011; UNDP 2010; World Bank 2011). So successful has been the concept of the nation-states in the modern era that their numbers increased from 55 prior to the collapse of the Austro-Hungarian (1867 to October 31, 1918), Ottoman (July 27, 1299, to October 29, 1923), and Russian (1682–1917; 1917–1991) empires to 192 member states of the United Nations in 2010 (United Nations 2011). And the expectation is that more territories will gain political sovereignty over the near term, e.g., the Palestinian territories (from Israel), the Western Sahara (from Spain and Morocco), and, possibly, the Falkland Islands (from the United Kingdom), among others. South Sudan, which voted for separation from the Republic of the Sudan in January 2011, is expected to join the United Nations as a sovereign state in July 2011.

But not all countries are created equal (Bates 2008; Ghani and Lockhart 2008; Tsai et al. 2010), nor are all able to carry out their core functions to the same extent (Chomsky 2006; Estes 2010, 2011a; Kim et al. 2010; Mallaby 2004; Schyns and Koop 2010; Tsai 2007; UNDP 2010; World Bank 2011). Many lack the minimum resources needed to facilitate their development (e.g., Chad, Sierra Leone, the Sudan) while others, even when in possession of critical fiscal and human resources, are trapped in decades-long economic quagmires, civil wars, and unstable political regimes (e.g., the Democratic Republic of the Congo, Kampuchea, Tajikistan). As a consequence, per capita income levels in most "failed" and "failing" states (hereafter referred to collectively as either "FSs" or "the FSs") tend to be low by world standards (e.g., Burundi, Laos, Rwanda), and often, they are governed by oppressive and corrupt political regimes (e.g., Haiti, Myanmar, Yemen, Zimbabwe). Intraregional warfare is common among the FSs (e.g., Sierra Leone and Somalia) as is the brutal treatment of their minority populations (e.g., Burundi, Cote d'Ivoire, Iran, and Nigeria).

Indeed, a substantial number of the world's autonomous nations ($N=37$) were classified as either "collapsed," "failed," or "failing" states in 2010 and were placed in an "alert" category by the Fund for Peace and *Foreign Policy* magazine on the basis of the intensity of their collective instability (Fund for Peace 2011a, b, c). These FSs have a combined population of approximately 1,300 million persons, or 18% of the world's total in 2010 (UNPOP 2010). Another 92 countries, including three of the world's most populous nations – China, India, and Indonesia – were grouped by the Fund for Peace in their "warning" category on the basis of (1) dramatically uneven patterns of development (especially in the political sectors [Human Rights Watch 2011]), (2) high levels of public corruption (Transparency International 2010), and (3) troublesome patterns of recurrent diversity-related social conflict (Amnesty International 2010; Freedom House 2010). Countries at the top of the "warning" states list were judged to be at considerable risk of becoming FSs should their current negative socio-political trajectories remain unchanged, e.g., Tajikistan, Mauritania, Laos, and Rwanda (Fund for Peace 2011a).

This chapter examines the relationship that exists between quality of life, political instability, and the capacity of the FSs to satisfy the basic security and material needs of their populations. Particular attention is given to understanding the development outcomes, or their absence, achieved by the FSs in advancing broad-based development goals under conditions of extreme social instability. More specifically, the chapter (1) identifies the world's most socially vulnerable countries using the *Failed States Index* developed jointly by the Fund for Peace and *Foreign Policy* magazine (Fund for Peace 2011a), (2) identifies the extent to which these countries are able to advance their collective development objectives, (3) identifies the major factors that inhibit the pursuit of quality of life in countries experiencing high levels of social turmoil, and (4) suggests alternative approaches that can be taken by the FSs in rebuilding their societies consistent with international norms (Ghani and Lockhart 2008; Rotberg 2004). The chapter also explores the special obligations that are incumbent on more socially advanced countries in helping the FSs strengthen their performance capacities (Europa 2011; Sachs 2008; United Nations 2010a, b, c, d; World Bank 2011).

Methodology

The present study is the thirteenth in a series of analyses of global and regional social development trends. The purpose of all 13 studies has been to (1) identify significant changes in "adequacy of social provision"[3] of nations throughout the world and (2) assess national and international progress in providing more adequately for the basic social and material needs of the world's growing population. Thus, this chapter reports a time-series analysis of the development performances of 36 "collapsed," "failed," or "failing" states over the 20-year period from 1990 to 2010. Throughout the chapter, data are reported at four levels of analysis: (1) development trends occurring within the FSs vis-à-vis those of other geopolitical groupings of countries, (2) social patterns for the FSs-as-a-group, (3) FSs subgroup socio-political variations, and (4) socio-political trends occurring in each of the 36 FSs.

Study Instruments

Two indexes are used throughout the analysis: (1) the "Failed States Index" (FSI) and (2) the author's extensively pretested "Index of Social Progress" (Estes 2010).

Created in 2005 jointly by the Fund for Peace and *Foreign Policy* magazine, the FSI uses 12 social, economic, and political indicators to assess the capacity of 177 countries to provide for the basic security, political, and material needs of their populations (Table 26.1). Ratings for each indicator are placed on a scale of 0–10, with 0 being the lowest *intensity* (i.e., the most stable) and 10 being the highest intensity (i.e., the least stable). The total FSI score is the sum of the 12 indicator scores with a range in values from 0 (most favorable) to 120 (least favorable). In 2010, FSI scores ranged from 18.7 and 19.3 for Norway and Finland (both politically stable and socially advanced countries) to 114.3 and 113.3 for Somalia and Chad (both deeply impoverished countries characterized by unstable political regimes and high levels of diversity-related social conflict). FSI scores are used to rank order the Fund's 177 countries into four broad categories that reflect the intensity of their level of socio-political instability: (1) "alert" ($N=37$), (2) "warning" ($N=92$), (3) "moderate" ($N=35$), or (4) "sustainable" ($N=13$).

Table 26.1 The failed states index (FSI)

Social indicators	
1	Mounting demographic pressures
2	Massive movement of refugees or internally displaced persons creating complex humanitarian emergencies
3	Legacy of vengeance-seeking group grievance or group paranoia
4	Chronic and sustained human flight
Economic indicators	
5	Uneven economic development along group lines
6	Sharp and/or severe economic decline
Political indicators	
7	Criminalization and/or delegitimization of the state
8	Progressive deterioration of public services
9	Suspension or arbitrary application of the rule of law and widespread violation of human rights
10	Security apparatus operates as a "state within a state"
11	Rise of factionalized elites
12	Intervention of other states or external political actors

Source: Fund for Peace (2011a)

Excluding only the recently independent Timor-Leste (2002), the current study's group of 36 "failed" and "failing" nation-states fall within the FSI's "alert" category of conflict-ridden nations, i.e., countries that because of their highly unstable and deteriorating social conditions are unable to participate fully in the community of nations (Chomsky 2006; Rotberg 2003; Van de Walle 2004; Zartman 1995). Twenty-two of these countries are located in Sub-Saharan Africa, 13 in Central and Western Asia, and one, Haiti, in Latin America.

In its present form, the ISP, and its statistically weighted version, the WISP,[4] consist of 41 social indicators subdivided into 10 subindexes (Table 26.1): *Education* ($N=4$), *Health Status* ($N=7$), *Women Status* ($N=5$), *Defense Effort* ($N=1$), *Economic* ($N=5$), *Demographic* ($N=3$), *Environmental* ($N=3$), *Social Chaos* ($N=5$), *Cultural Diversity* ($N=3$), and *Welfare Effort* ($N=5$). Composite index and subindex scores

---

[3] "Adequacy of social provision" refers to the changing capacity of governments to provide for the basic social, material, and other needs of the people living within their borders, e.g., for food, clothing, shelter, and access to at least basic health, education, and social services, etc. (Estes 1988).

[4] The WISP's statistical weights were derived through a two-stage principal components and varimax factor analysis in which indicator and subindex scores were analyzed separately for their contribution in explaining the variance associated with changes in social progress over time. Standardized indicator scores were multiplied by their respective factor loadings, averaged within their subindex, and the average subindex scores, in turn, were subjected to a second statistical weighting. Scores on the WISP range from a high of 72 to a low of 17 for 2010 (Estes 2010).

Table 26.2 Indicators on the weighted index of social progress (WISP) by subindex, 2010 (41 indicators and 10 subindexes)

Subindex indicators

Education subindex (N=4)

Public expenditure on education as percentage of GDP, 2008–2009 (+)

Primary school completion rate, 2008–2009 (+)

Secondary school net enrolment rate, 2008–2009 (+)

Adult literacy rate, 2008 (+)

Health status subindex (N=6)

Life expectation at birth, 2008 (+)

Infant mortality rate, 2008–2009 (−)

Under-five child mortality rate, 2008 (−)

Physicians per 100,000 population, 2005–2008 (+)

Percent of undernourished population, 2006–2008 (−)

Public expenditure on health as percentage of Gross Domestic Product, 2008–2009 (+)

Women status subindex (N=5)

Female adult literacy as percentage of male literacy, 2009 (+)

Prevalence of contraceptive use among married women, 2008 (+)

Lifetime risk of maternal death, 2005 (+)

Female secondary school enrollment as percentage of male enrolment, 2008 (+)

Seats in parliament held by women as percentage of total, 2010 (+)

Defense effort subindex (N=1)

Military expenditures as percentage of GDP, 2009 (−)

Economic subindex (N=5)

Per capita Gross Domestic Product (as measured by PPP), 2009 (+)

Percent growth in Gross Domestic Product (GDP), 2009 (+)

Unemployment rate, 2006–08 (−)

Total external debt as percentage of GNI, 2009 (−)

Gini index score, most recent year 2005–09 (−)

Demography subindex (N=3)

Average annual rate of population growth, 2009 (−)

Percent of population aged <15 years, 2009 (−)

Percent of population aged >64 years, 2009 (+)

Environmental subindex (N=3)

Percentage of nationally protected area, 2004–2008 (+)

Average annual number of disaster-related deaths, 2000–2009 (−)

Per capita metric tons of carbon dioxide emissions, 2007 (−)

Social Chaos subindex (N=6)

Strength of political rights, 2010 (−)

Strength of civil liberties, 2010 (−)

Number of internally displaced persons per 100,000 population, 2009 (−)

Number of externally displaced persons per 100,000 population, 2009 (−)

Estimated number of deaths from armed conflicts (low estimate), 2006–2007 (−)

Perceived corruption index, 2009 (+)

Cultural diversity subindex (N=3)

Largest percentage of population sharing the same or similar racial/ethnic origins, 2009 (+)

Largest percentage of population sharing the same or similar religious beliefs, 2009 (+)

Largest share of population sharing the same mother tongue, 2009 (+)

Welfare effort subindex (N=5)

Age First National Law – Old Age, Invalidity and Death, 2010 (+)

Age First National Law – Sickness and Maternity, 2010 (+)

Age First National Law – Work Injury, 2010 (+)

Age First National Law – Unemployment, 2010 (+)

Age First National Law – Family Allowance, 2010 (+)

Source: Estes (2010)

on the ISP and WISP are used to assess the extent of state failure vis-à-vis the satisfaction of basic human needs (Table 26.2).

Thus, for purposes of this study, the FSI is treated as a taxonomy that is used to classify countries by their level of socio-political instability whereas the WISP is used to assess the depth of that instability using a wide range of social indicators. Owing to the volume of data gathered for this analysis, only statistically weighted Index of Social Progress (WISP) scores and scores on the WISP's ten subindexes (world average = 10.0, $SD = 1.0$) are reported in this chapter.

Data Sources

The majority of the data used in this analysis were obtained from the annual reports of specialized agencies of the United Nations, the United Nations Development Programme, the World Bank, the Organization for Economic Cooperation and Development, and the International Social Security Association. Data for the *Environmental* subindex were obtained from the World Resources Institute, the United Nations Commission on Sustainable Development, and the World Bank. Data for the *Social Chaos* subindex were obtained from Amnesty International, Freedom House, Human Rights Watch, the International Federation of Red Cross and Red Crescent Societies, the Stockholm International Peace and Research Institute, and Transparency International.

Data for the *Cultural Diversity* subindex were gathered from the *CIA World Factbook*, the *Encyclopedia Britannica*, and the work of independent scholars in the fields of comparative linguistics, religion, and ethnology. The formal social welfare programs data were obtained from policy reports prepared by the International Social Security Association and the U.S. Social Security Administration.

Data for the FSI were prepared jointly by the U.S. think tank, the Fund for Peace, and *Foreign Policy* magazine (formerly a publication of the Carnegie Endowment for Peace). Data for the FSI were collected by means of CAST software which electronically searches tens of thousands national and international publications monthly for changes occurring in national social, political, and economic conditions. The data obtained from these searches are used to assign destabilization "intensity" scores for the FSI's 12 component indicators (Fund for Peace 2011b, c).

Time Periods

FSI data are reported for 2010 only and, then, for the purpose of identifying nation-states that fall within the "failed" and "failing" states categories. WISP index and subindex findings, on the other hand, are reported separately for three discrete time periods, i.e., 1990, 2000, and 2010. In addition to the WISP data, supplemental social indicator data for the study's 36 countries are summarized in Tables 26.4–26.8. Figures 26.1–26.6 provide world and group WISP indicator data ranked by 2010 polity failure level for all 36 countries.

Findings

The study's findings are reported in four parts. Part 1 discusses the nature of state failure and identifies the 36 "failed" states included in this analysis. The geographic location of these states is identified in Table 26.3 as are several critical factors that contribute to the inability of the FSs to reverse their current negative development trends, e.g., being land-locked ($N=11$), being poor countries that are heavily in debt to the international community ($N=17$), being classified by the United Nations as "Least Developing Countries" ($N=22$), or

all three ($N=7$). Part 1 also reports 2010 WISP index and WISP rank data (Fig. 26.1) for the 36 countries-as-a-group and, in turn, for the FSs by major continental and subcontinental grouping (Figs. 26.2 and 26.3). Figure 26.4 reports WISP subindex scores separately for "failed" ($N=15$) and "failing" states ($N=21$) for the year 2010, i.e., the same base year for which scores on the *Failed States Index* are reported.

Part 2 identifies the major elements of state failure and reports selected population (Table 26.4), economic (Table 26.5), and political (Table 26.6) indicators for all 36 countries using selected social indicators drawn from the Weighted Index of Social Progress (Table 26.2). Patterns of central government expenditures are summarized in the data reported in Table 26.7. Table 26.8 reports WISP scores values and change in WISP rank positions for 1990, 2000, and 2010.

Part 3 contrasts development trends occurring in the 36 FSs with those of other major aggregations of countries (Figs. 26.5 and 26.6) for the years 1990, 2000, and 2010, i.e., for *Developed Market Economies* (DME, $N=34$), the *Commonwealth of Independent States* (CIS, $N=19$), "*Developing Countries*" (DC, $N=54$), and socially "*Least Developing*," but not necessarily failed or failing, countries (LDCs, $N=19$).[5] In earlier studies using the WISP, the FSs were grouped with the DCs ($N=12$) and LDCs ($N=22$) with the exception of Georgia and Uzbekistan which were classified with the Commonwealth of Independent States (CIS). The average WISP scores reported in Figs. 26.5 and 26.6 adjust for the re-designation of the 36 FSs into their own category. The impact of this reclassification resulted in

---

[5] The four primary groupings used in the more comprehensive analysis of world social development trends are (1) *Developed Market Economies* (DMEs) consisting primarily of economically advanced countries (plus selected middle-income countries added to the Organizations of Economic Cooperation and Development [OECD] on the basis of their current rapid pace of economic development, e.g., the Czech Republic, Mexico, South Korea, Turkey); (2) the *Commonwealth of Independent States* (CIS) consisting entirely of successor states to the former Soviet Union (FSU); (3) *Developing Countries* (DCs) consisting primarily of low- and middle-income countries located in developing Africa, Asia, and Latin America; and (4) *Least Developed Countries* (LDCs) which, for a variety of historical and socio-political reasons, experience net negative patterns of socio-economic development from one time period to another (UN-OHRLLS 2009a, b, c, d).

Table 26.3 Selected characteristics of failed or failing states organized by major geographic region and subregion, 2010 ($N=36$)

Continent / Subregion	Country	LDC[a]	Land locked	HIPC[b]	Total	Type of state
AFRICA ($N=22$)						
East ($N=7$)	Burundi	X	X	0	2	Failing
	Eritrea	X	0	0	1	Failing
	Ethiopia	X	X	X	3	Failing
	Kenya	0	0	0	0	Failed
	Malawi	X	X	X	3	Failing
	Somalia	X	0	0	1	Failed
	Uganda	X	X	X	3	Failing
Middle ($N=5$)	Cameroon	0	0	X	1	Failing
	Central African Rep	X	0	X	2	Failed
	Chad	X	X	X	3	Failed
	Congo, Demo Rep	X	0	X	2	Failed
	Congo, Rep	0	0	X	1	Failing
North ($N=1$)	Sudan	X	0	0	1	Failed
South ($N=1$)	Zimbabwe	0	X	0	1	Failed
West ($N=8$)	Burkina Faso	X	X	X	3	Failing
	Cote D'Ivoire	0	0	X	1	Failed
	Guinea	X	0	X	2	Failed
	Guinea-Bissau	X	0	X	2	Failing
	Liberia	X	0	X	2	Failing
	Niger	X	X	X	3	Failing
	Nigeria	0	0	0	0	Failed
	Sierra Leone	X	0	X	2	Failing
ASIA ($N=13$)						
Central ($N=7$)	Afghanistan	X	X	X	3	Failed
	Bangladesh	X	0	0	1	Failing
	Iran	0	0	0	0	Failing
	Nepal	X	X	0	2	Failing
	Pakistan	0	0	0	0	Failed
	Sri Lanka	0	0	0	0	Failing
	Uzbekistan	0	X	0	1	Failing
West ($N=4$)	Iraq	0	0	0	0	Failed
	Georgia	0	0	0	0	Failing
	Lebanon	0	0	0	0	Failing
	Yemen	X	0	0	1	Failed
South East ($N=1$)	Myanmar (Burma)	X	0	0	1	Failing
East ($N=1$)	Korea, North	0	0	0	0	Failing
LATIN AMERICA ($N=1$)						
Caribbean ($N=1$)	Haiti	X	0	X	2	Failed
Total		22	11	17	50	Failed & Failing

Sources: UN-OHRLS (2009a, b, c); IMP (2010)

[a]*LDC* Least Developing Country

[b]*HIPC* Heavily Indebted Poor Country

slight increases in average WISP scores for the CIS (from a group average WISP score of 54.1 with the FSs to a group average of 54.4 *without* the FSs), DCs (from a group average WISP score of 47.4 with the FSs to a group average of 49.2 *without* the FSs), and the LDCs not classified as FSs (from a group WISP score average of 35.4 with the FSs to a group average of 38.6 *without* the FSs).

Part 4 suggests a range of proactive steps that can be taken by the FSs themselves *and* the international community in helping FSs reverse their current pattern of negative social development. The proposed actions are intended to promote a more positive outcome for the future of the FSs, i.e., outcomes not unlike those achieved by South Africa following the end of apartheid or the countries of Central and Eastern Europe once they were free of Soviet domination.

Part 1: The Nature of State Failure

The word "failure" refers to "the nonperformance of something due, required, or expected" (Dictionary.com). The concept can be applied to any unit of analysis (e.g., individuals, groups, organizations, or to larger aggregations such as countries or civilizations). For our purposes, the concept will be applied to the failure of individual countries in satisfying the most basic security and material needs of their populations.

When applied to countries, "failure" is used to describe the lack of state performance in meeting essential obligations toward their inhabitants and, in turn, toward the larger community of nations (Bates 2008; Clapham 2004). Among others, state failures include (1) the loss of recognition of state sovereignty by the international community (Carment 2004; Chomsky 2006); (2) the inability to maintain secure geographic borders (Ghani and Lockhart 2008); (3) the persistence of internal, intraregional, and international warfare (Huntington 1996); (4) the inability to operate stable monetary or other essential economic institutions (IMF 2010a, b); (5) the absence of transparent legal and justice systems (Klare 2004; Rose-Ackerman 2004); (6) high levels of public corruption (Transparency International 2010); (7) the inability to exploit available natural and human resources (UNIFEM 2010; WRI 2008); (8) the inability to control, or at least reduce, internal diversity-related social conflict (SIPRI 2009); (9) lack of respect on the part of the state for individual freedoms and liberties (Freedom House 2010; Human Rights Watch 2011); (10) the failure to create political space in which people can participate actively in the making of the laws and policies by which they agree to be governed (Kasfir 2004; Lyons 2004); (11) the absence of a viable civil society sector (Anheier et al. 2010); (12) chronic dependency on foreign aid and other external support sources to meet basic needs (Glennie 2008; Mallaby 2004; Moyo 2009); and (13) the state's inability, perhaps unwillingness, to provide for the special needs of their most vulnerable populations, e.g., children, the aged, persons with severe illnesses and disabilities, etc. (Save the Children 2010; UNICEF 2010a, b).

Thus, countries fail "…when they are consumed by internal violence and cease delivering positive goods to their inhabitants" (Rotberg 2004:1). These failures can be quite profound (as with Afghanistan, Iraq, North Korea, and Zimbabwe) but, more typically, occur in a just a few critical sectors, e.g., Burundi, Iran, Sierra Leone.

State failures can be conceptualized as existing along a continuum of success and failure on which weaker states are located at one end of the spectrum and are described as "collapsed," "failed," or "failing," and stronger states are located at the other end of the spectrum and are conceptualized as being either "moderate" or "sustainable" vis-à-vis their capacity to perform expected state functions. This more relativistic view of state failure is that taken by Bates (2008), Chomsky (2006), Clapham (2004), Rotberg (2004), van de Walle (2004), and also by the Fund for Peace (2011a).

However, this perspective differs sharply from that expressed by Huntington (1996) and others, including the Club of Rome (2011), concerning their often dire predictions of the prognosis of the failure of entire civilizations in response to cultural and other assaults against the integrity of the nation-state.[6]

"Failed" and "Failing" States

Table 26.3 identifies the study's 36 "failed" and "failing" states (FSs) by their major continental and subcontinental groupings, i.e., Africa = 22, Asia = 13, Latin America = 1. The majority of African FSs are located

---

[6] In his 1996 book *The Clash of Civilizations and the Remaking of World Order*, Huntington identified clashes among the following civilizations that could be expected to dominate political affairs in much of the twenty-first century: (1) Western, (2) Latin America, (3) Islamic, (4) Sinic (Chinese), (5) Hindu, (6) Orthodox, (7) Japanese, and (8) African. The clashes are expected to take many forms ranging from cultural disintegration to military confrontations, but in the end, each would profoundly alter the character of the nations engaged in the conflicts and, in the process, change the course of future world history.

in the continent's Eastern ($N=7$) and Western ($N=8$) subregions whereas the majority of Asian FSs are located in Asia's Central ($N=7$) and Western ($N=4$) subregions. Twenty of the 22 African FSs are located in the continent's Sub-Saharan region, long regarded as the poorest and most socially vulnerable region in the world (UNDP 2010).

Table 26.3 also identifies several additional factors associated with country status as a failed or failing state, i.e., 22 of the 36 FSs are officially classified by the United Nations as "Least Developing Countries" (LDCs), 11 are land-locked states (of which 9 are also LDCs), and 17 are "heavily indebted poor countries" of which 14 are LDCs, 7 are both land-locked and LDCs, i.e., Ethiopia, Malawi, Uganda, Chad, Burkina Faso, Niger, Afghanistan (UN-OHRLLS 2009a, b, c, d). Thus, a majority of the study's FSs are trapped in geographic spaces with limited natural resources and transportation networks that seriously impede their capacity for more autonomous development. The presence of high debt levels among so many of the FSs reflects decades of public borrowing (mostly from the World Bank and the International Monetary Fund) to fund large-scale projects whose benefits have yet to be realized, i.e., major dams and hydroelectric projects, road-building projects, the introduction of market reforms, among others (International Monetary Fund 2010b). High levels of public indebtedness often are associated with these projects as is public corruption including the outright theft by high-ranking officials of a large portion of the borrowed funds (Transparency International 2010).

Cash poor and geographically trapped, many of the FSs develop authoritarian regimes for the purpose of limiting public criticisms of their incompetence, e.g., Democratic Republic of the Congo, Iran, North Korea, Yemen. The situation is worse in countries still struggling with post-colonial legacies (i.e., Guinea-Bissau, Georgia, Libya, Uzbekistan, Zimbabwe) and in those characterized by decades-long diversity-related social conflicts (e.g., Chad, Iraq, Myanmar, Sudan). In none of these situations is overt public dissent tolerated; rather, political oppression is more the norm, e.g., Afghanistan, Central African Republic, Cote d'Ivoire (Human Rights Watch 2010). In the end, though, the populations of these nations suffer dramatically while, at the same time, scarce national resources are allocated to officially promulgated persecution campaigns, e.g., Burundi, Eritrea, Haiti, Iraq, Iran, Pakistan,

Uganda (African Development Bank 2010; Asian Development Bank 2010; Leonard and Straus 2003; Obioma 2001; Widner 2004).

Failed States and Scores on the Weighted Index of Social Progress (WISP)

Figure 26.1 summarizes WISP scores (which in 2010 ranged from 17 [least favorable] to 73 [most favorable]) and ranks for the 36 FSs on both the WISP and *Failed States Indexes* (for which higher scores indicate higher levels of intensity of state failure).

Figure 26.1 shows a pattern of general consistency between the two scores, albeit the comparative ranks for particular countries vary from one scale to another, e.g., Afghanistan and Chad are among the lowest ranked countries on both metrics, but the WISP assigns somewhat higher rankings for the Sudan, Zimbabwe, and the Democratic Republic of the Congo than does the FSI. However, both scales place these countries in the "failed states" category. As expected, the Pearson correlation coefficient for both metrics is quite high ($r=-.60$, $P<.01$).

Also of interest in Fig. 26.1 is the highly erratic pattern of WISP score rankings for the 36 FSs. This pattern is unusual among clusters of related nations and reflects the asymmetrical nature of development within the FSs, i.e., situations in which even minor progress in some areas are offset by major losses in others. Nearly all of the WISP ranks reported place the 36 FSs in the bottom sixth and seventh percentiles of WISP ranks; however, Lebanon, Uzbekistan, and Georgia attained WISP ranks higher than 68, i.e., ranks that placed them in the third or fourth WISP percentile of 161 countries. And these also are countries that the Fund for Peace identifies as existing along the margins of the FSI, i.e., between "failed" and "moderately" performing states.

WISP Score Averages for Africa by Subregion

Figure 26.2 summarizes WISP score data for each of Africa's five major subregions for the years 2000 and 2010, i.e., Eastern ($N=7$), Middle ($N=5$), Northern ($N=1$), Southern ($N=1$), and Western ($N=8$) subregions. Data also are reported for all FSs located in Africa ($N=22$).

26 "Failed" and "Failing" States: Is Quality of Life Possible?

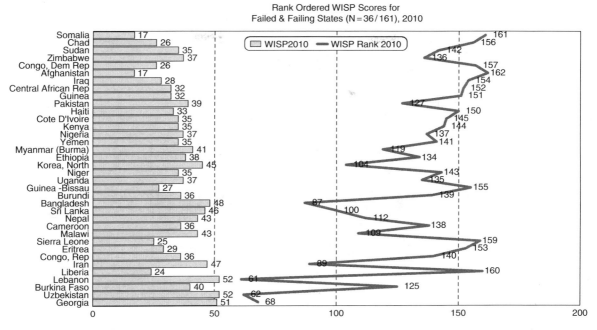

Fig. 26.1 Rank ordered WISP scores for failed and failing states (*N* = 36/161), 2010

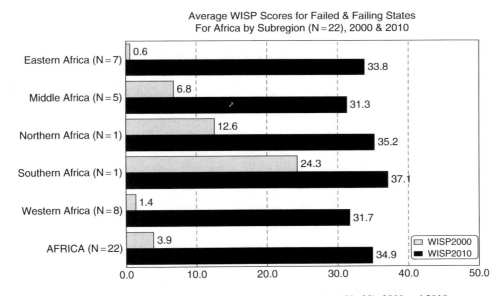

Fig. 26.2 Average WISP scores for failed and failing states for Africa by subregion (*N* = 22), 2000 and 2010

In every instance, WISP scores are considerably higher for Africa and its subregions for 2010 than in 2000. The pattern of these scores tells three stories: (1) Africa continues to be the world's socially least developed continent, however, even with her higher WISP score averages in 2010; (2) following decades of chronic social decline, African development is now moving forward…and doing so at a comparatively rapid pace; and (3) recent improvements in African development are associated with reforms undertaken by African nations with the assistance of major bilateral aid-granting initiatives originating in Europe, Japan, and the United States

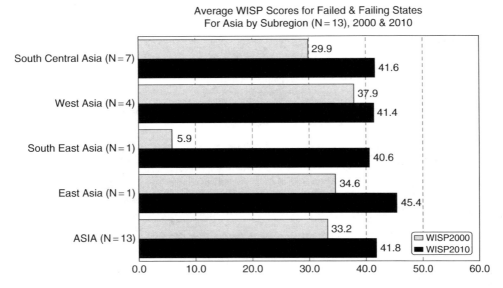

Fig. 26.3 Average WISP scores for failed and failing states for Asia by subregion (*N* = 13), 2000 and 2010

as well as through multilateral development assistance provided by the United Nations Millennium Development Campaign (MDC). The countries with the most extensive natural and human resources – located primarily in Northern and Southern Africa – contain the fewest "failed" states (*N* = 1 each), whereas those with the lowest concentrations of resources contain the largest number of FSs – Eastern (*N* = 7), Middle (*N* = 5), and Western (*N* = 8) Africa. But for the continent-as-a-whole, comparative success with social development is finally taking root in Africa-as-a-continent (Estes 2011a), albeit many of her vulnerable countries located in her Middle and Central subregions remain classified as "failed" or "failing" states, e.g., Burkina Faso, Burundi, Cote d'Ivoire, Central African Republic, Chad, Democratic Republic of the Congo, Sierra Leone, Somalia, and Uganda.

The generally negative situation that exists for Africa's most fractious states and subregions could change for the better should the continent-as-a-whole continue to integrate more fully the net social gains reflected in Fig. 26.2.

WISP Score Averages for Asia by Subregion

The majority of the world's population resides in Asia, i.e., somewhat more than 60% of the world's total in 2010 (UNPOP 2010). Not surprisingly, Asia is the location of three of the world's four most populous nations – China, India, and Indonesia – as well as many of the planet's most religiously, ethnically, and culturally diverse societies. Despite its geographic size and complex cultural mix, only 13 of the continent's 54 nations are classified as "failed" or "failing" states by the Fund for Peace (2011a). As reported in Table 26.3, the majority of Asian FSs are located in its newly independent South Central (*N* = 7) and war-ridden Western (*N* = 4) subregions; only two are located in the continent's Eastern (North Korea) and South Eastern (Myanmar) subregions.

The WISP data reported in Fig. 26.3 for Asia indicate a substantially higher level of social development for Asia (2010 group average = 41.8) than for Africa (2010 group average = 34.9). And Asia's subregions, on average, have enjoyed higher levels of social development for a longer time period than have Africa's due, in part, to (1) their longer years of political independence; (2) varied and rich natural and human resources; (3) extensive intranational and global transportation networks; (4) in recent years at least, comparatively fewer contemporary civil wars and insurgency movements; (5) a greater commitment to individual freedoms and civil liberties; and (6) Asia's recently emerging role as the world's manufacturing center (Estes 2007, 2011b).

As is the situation among African FSs (Estes 1995), Asia's FSs are characterized by comparatively low levels of political participation. The region's FSs also

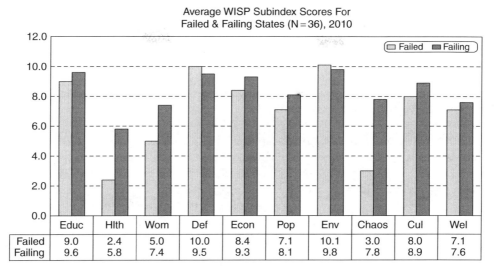

Fig. 26.4 Average WISP subindex scores for failed and failing states (*N*=36), 2010

experience sharp fluctuations in the stability of their export-oriented economies, a situation compounded by their nearly equal dependency on the importation of large quantities of raw materials needed to sustain their export economies (e.g., of energy sources, steel, and raw materials).

Unfortunately for Asia, among their major exports are large numbers of well-educated young people who leave their countries of origin in search of improved economic opportunities elsewhere (UNHCR 2009a, b). The region also is home to a disproportionate number of the world's internally displaced persons – many who were forced to abandon their homelands due to civil strife or ethnic conflicts (UNHCR 2009a). Of significance, too, is the high level of official development assistance on which many of the Asian FSs depend to meet their basic security and material needs (World Bank 2009).

Political corruption, widespread thefts of public resources, and weak economic infrastructures combine with the absence of rational legal systems and functioning commercial environments to dissuade many international corporations from engaging in commercial exchanges with Asian FSs. The situation is especially problematic in the FSs of South Central Asia which only recently emerged from domination by the former Soviet Union and those of West Asia which hold onto religious fundamentalism and the vestiges of ethnic discrimination as guideposts for the development of their nations.

Despite their development challenges, the prognosis for Asia's "failed" states is generally favorable given the strength of their 2010 development performances on the WISP. East, South Central, and West Asia are expected to advance more quickly than the Southeastern subregion, but Asia's Southeastern subregion already has attained a remarkably high level of development progress since 1990 (ADB 2010; Estes 2010).

Failed States Average Subindex Scores on the WISP

Figure 26.4 reports the sectoral social development performances for both "failed" and "failing" states. With the exception of scores on the *Defense Effort* and *Environmental* subindexes group performances on the WISPs, eight other subindexes are more favorable for the "failing" states than for already "failed" states. Virtually all of the subindex scores for both groups of nations, however, are well below the world average of 10.0 set for each subindex and, in the case of "failed" states, are substantially below the world averages, e.g., 2.4, 3.0, and 5.0 on the *Health, Social Chaos,* and *Women Status* subindexes, respectively. In general, there is no "good news" in any of the subindex scores reported here for either group of FSs, albeit the scores for both groups were universally higher in 2010 than in 2000. Even with the present 10-year advances in

WISP index and subindex performances, none of the composite scores were sufficiently high as to bring about a reclassification of any nation from the FSs category.

Part 2: Selected Demographic, Economic, Political, and Central Government Expenditure Patterns of "Failed" and "Failing" States

Demographic Characteristics

The 36 "failed" and "failing" states included in this analysis have a combined population of more than 1,300 million people – 18% of the world's total in 2010 (UNPOP 2010). As reported in Table 26.4, the average size of "failed" states is larger (41.8 million) than that of "failing" states (28.6 million), but both clusters of nations include countries with populations approaching or exceeding 150 million persons, e.g., Pakistan ($N = 176$ million), Bangladesh ($N = 156$ million), and Nigeria ($N = 149$ million).

"Failed" and "failing" states also are characterized by comparatively youthful populations. Forty-two percent of the populations of "failed" states are younger than 15 years of age, and 36% of the populations of "failing" states are younger, on average, than 15 years of age. Niger, Chad, Democratic Republic of the Congo, Uganda, Afghanistan, Somalia, Nigeria, the Cameroons, and Burkina Faso are among the world's most youthful (and least educated) nations due, in no small measure, to decades-long warfare in these countries which resulted in the premature deaths of young men and women in their 20s, 30s, and 40s. Both sets of countries contain very small percentages of persons aged 65 years of age and older, i.e., 3.3% of the "failed" states and 4.5% of the "failing" states. These data contrast sharply with those for the world-as-a-whole ($N = 161$) which has a youth population averaging 29% and an aged population averaging 8%.

Thus, shorter life expectation combined with high mortality rates is a dominant feature of life in the FSs. This pattern is reinforced by higher rates of infant and child mortality, higher incidences of infectious and communicable diseases, and lower levels of adult literacy (Table 26.4). Along all of these dimensions, the study's FSs perform more poorly than the world on average and certainly well below comparable patterns reported for the world's most socially advanced countries (Estes 2010).

Economic Characteristics

The overwhelmingly negative situation of the FSs vis-à-vis the world-as-a-whole is further compounded by the highly negative economic data reported for the FSs in Table 26.5. In comparison with world economic performances, "failed" and "failing" states performed at lower levels in terms of the size of their national economies, rates of economic growth, their extraordinarily high levels of external public indebtedness, high unemployment rates (with many exceeding 30 or more percent), and inequitable patterns of wealth distribution.

The situation is only somewhat better in the "failing" states than in those that already have collapsed, e.g., higher per capita income levels and Gini coefficients in a small number of "failing" states, e.g., Lebanon ($13,000) and Iran ($12,000), and more favorable Gini coefficients for Ethiopia (.30), Bangladesh (.33), North Korea (.37), Myanmar (.39), and Malawi (.39). The majority of "failed" and "failing" states were unable to compete with the economic development performances of the world-as-a-whole, a reality that keeps most of these nations trapped in a quagmire of social and economic poverty (Rotberg 2003; Sachs 2005; Sen 1999; United Nations 2010b; UNDP 2010; WRI 2008). Even so, and on virtually every economic indicator, average economic scores are more favorable for "failing" than "failed" states.

Political Characteristics

Responsibility for the highly negative social and economic profiles of the FSs is explained by the political data summarized in Table 26.6. Along virtually every indicator reported in the table, both "failed" and "failing" states performed at substantially lower levels than the world-as-a-whole. Scores on the *Political Freedom* and *Civil Liberties* indexes (Freedom House 2010), for example, are among the worst reported in the author's more comprehensive analysis of worldwide social development trends (Estes 2010), as are scores on the *Global Corruption Perceptions Index* and the *Global Corruption Barometer* (Transparency International 2010). The percentage of seats held by women in the parliaments of

26 "Failed" and "Failing" States: Is Quality of Life Possible?

Table 26.4 Selected population-related indicators for failed and failing states rank ordered by failed state index scores, 2010 ($N=36$)

Countries	Population (Millions) 2009	Population growth rate 2009	Age dependent population		Life expectation at birth 2008	Infant mortality 2008–2009	Adult literacy rate 2008
			<15 years 2009	>65 years 2009			
Failed states (N = 15)							
Somalia	9.8	3.2	45.0	2.7	49.8	108.5	38.0
Chad	10.3	3.3	46.0	2.8	48.7	124.0	32.7
Sudan	41.1	2.0	39.0	3.6	58.1	69.3	69.3
Zimbabwe	11.4	0.6	39.0	4.1	44.2	56.3	91.4
Congo, Dem Rep	68.7	2.8	46.0	2.6	47.6	125.8	66.6
Afghanistan	33.6	4.5	46.0	2.2	43.9	133.7	28.0
Iraq	28.9	2.7	41.0	3.3	67.9	35.4	77.6
Central African Rep	4.5	1.3	40.0	3.9	47.0	112.0	54.6
Guinea	1.5	1.9	43.0	3.3	57.8	87.8	38.0
Pakistan	176.2	2.4	37.0	4.0	66.5	70.5	53.7
Haiti	9.0	1.4	36.0	4.4	61.2	63.7	53.0
Cote D'Ivoire	20.6	1.6	40.0	3.9	57.4	83.1	54.6
Kenya	39.0	2.3	43.0	2.6	54.2	54.8	86.5
Nigeria	149.2	2.5	42.0	3.1	47.9	85.8	60.1
Afghanistan	23.8	3.1	43.0	2.4	62.9	50.8	60.9
Subgroup averages	*41.8*	*2.4*	*41.7*	*3.3*	*54.3*	*84.1*	*57.7*
Failing states (N = 21)							
Myanmar (Burma)	48.1	1.1	27.0	5.5	61.6	53.8	91.9
Ethiopia	85.2	2.0	43.0	3.2	55.2	67.1	35.9
Korea, North	22.7	0.5	21.0	9.6	67.2	26.4	100.0
Niger	15.3	3.4	50.0	2.0	51.4	75.7	29.0
Uganda	32.4	3.4	49.0	2.5	52.7	79.4	74.6
Guinea -Bissau	10.1	3.0	43.0	3.5	47.8	115.2	51.0
Burundi	9.0	3.1	38.0	2.8	50.4	101.3	65.9
Bangladesh	156.1	1.9	31.0	3.9	66.1	41.2	55.0
Sri Lanka	21.3	0.4	24.0	7.5	74.1	12.7	90.6
Nepal	28.6	2.1	36.0	4.0	66.7	38.6	57.9
Cameroon	18.9	1.9	41.0	3.6	51.1	94.6	75.9
Malawi	14.3	2.2	46.0	3.1	53.1	68.8	72.8
Sierra Leone	6.4	3.7	43.0	1.8	47.6	122.8	39.8
Eritrea	5.6	4.1	42.0	2.5	59.5	39.1	65.3
Congo, Rep	4.0	3.0	40.0	3.8	53.6	80.5	85.0
Iran	66.4	1.4	24.0	4.9	71.4	25.9	82.0
Liberia	3.4	1.6	42.0	3.1	58.3	79.9	58.1
Lebanon	4.0	1.2	25.0	7.3	72.0	11.1	87.0
Burkina Faso	15.7	3.1	46.0	2.0	53.0	90.8	24.0
Uzbekistan	27.6	1.2	29.0	4.5	67.8	31.8	99.2
Georgia	4.6	−1.0	17.0	14.3	71.5	26.0	99.7
Subgroup averages	*28.6*	*2.1*	*36.0*	*4.5*	*59.6*	*61.1*	*68.6*
Total (N = 36)	*1,227.3*						
Group averages (N = 36)	*34.1*	*2.2*	*38.4*	*4.0*	*57.4*	*70.7*	*64.0*
SD (N = 36)	*43.5*	*1.1*	*8.3*	*2.4*	*8.8*	*33.9*	*22.0*
World averages (N = 161)	*6,800.0*	*1.4*	*28.9*	*7.6*	*67.9*	*34.3*	*82.7*

Data Sources: United Nations Development Programme (2010); World Bank (2010)

Table 26.5 Selected economic indicators for failed and failing states rank ordered by failed states index, 2010 ($N = 36$)

Countries	PC GDP (PPP) 2009[a]	% growth GDP 2009[a]	External debt as % GDP 2009[a]	Unemployment rate 2011[b]	GINI coefficient (varied)
Failed states ($N = 15$)					
Somalia	$600	2.6	14.7	47.4	42.7
Chad	$1,347	1.6	27.0	10.0	47.0
Sudan	$2,201	4.0	105.1	4.0	36.4
Zimbabwe	$200	−2.4	282.6	6.0	50.1
Congo, Dem Rep	$320	2.7	100.0	10.0	47.0
Afghanistan	$700	2.3	23.0	3.8	35.2
Iraq	$3,553	4.2	76.0	30.0	36.0
Central African Rep	$759	2.4	68.0	8.0	61.3
Guinea-Bissau	$1,100	4.7	70.0	46.5	38.6
Pakistan	$2,625	3.7	31.0	5.1	30.6
Haiti	$1,153	2.9	7.0	60.0	59.2
Cote D'Ivoire	$1,707	3.8	54.0	11.4	44.6
Kenya	$1,572	2.2	24.0	40.0	42.5
Nigeria	$2,150	2.9	6.0	2.9	43.7
Yemen	$2,473	3.8	25.0	11.5	33.4
Subgroup average	*$1,497*	*2.8*	*60.9*	*19.8*	*43.2*
Failing states ($N = 21$)					
Myanmar (Burma)	$1,200	6.6	27.0	5.0	38.7
Ethiopia	$936	8.7	13.0	5.0	30.0
Korea, North	$1,800	3.7	6.1	4.4	36.8
Niger	$676	1.0	79.0	2.8	50.5
Uganda	$1,219	7.1	13.0	3.2	45.7
Guinea	$600	3.3	203.0	46.5	47.0
Burundi	$393	3.5	202.0	14.0	42.4
Bangladesh	$1,420	5.9	25.0	4.3	33.4
Sri Lanka	$4,779	3.5	85.8	5.2	40.2
Nepal	$1,156	4.7	36.0	1.8	47.2
Cameroon	$2,228	2.4	13.0	7.5	44.6
Malawi	$859	7.7	24.0	1.1	39.0
Sierra Leone	$809	4.0	163.0	50.0	62.9
Eritrea	$700	2.0	44.0	25.0	42.7
Congo, Rep	$4,248	7.6	155.0	25.5	47.0
Iran	$11,575	1.8	6.0	10.5	43.0
Liberia	$397	4.6	606.0	85.0	52.6
Lebanon	$12,962	8.0	154.8	12.5	36.0
Burkina Faso	$1,189	3.5	23.0	8.1	39.5
Uzbekistan	$2,879	8.1	11.0	0.7	36.8
Georgia	$4,778	−4.0	31.0	13.3	40.4
Subgroup average	*$2,705*	*4.5*	*91.5*	*15.8*	*42.7*
Group average ($N = 36$)	*$2,202*	*3.8*	*78.7*	*17.4*	*42.9*
SD ($N = 36$)	*$2,755*	*2.7*	*112.7*	*20.2*	*7.8*
World average ($N = 161$)	*$13,529*	*0.7*	*99.7*	*11.9*	*40.9*

Data source

[a]World Bank (2010)

[b]CIA World Factbook (2011)

26 "Failed" and "Failing" States: Is Quality of Life Possible?

Table 26.6 Selected political indicators for failed and failing states rank ordered by failed state index scores, 2010 ($N=36$)

Countries	Year of independence	Type of polity 2010[a]	Head of state 2010[a]	Political freedom Index (−) 2010[b]	Civil liberties index (−) 2010[c]	Corruption perceptions index (+) 2009[d]	Global corruption barometer (−) 2010[e]	Failed state index (−) 2010[f]	Parliamentary seats held by women (+) 2010
Failed states (N = 15)									
Somalia	1960	Republic	Executive	7.0	7.0	1.1	.	114.3	6.1
Chad	1960	Republic	Executive	7.0	6.0	1.6	.	113.3	5.2
Sudan	1956	Republic	Executive	7.0	7.0	1.5	.	111.8	18.1
Zimbabwe	1980	Republic	Executive	6.0	6.0	2.2	.	110.2	15.2
Congo, Dem Rep	1960	Republic	Executive	6.0	6.0	1.9	.	109.9	8.4
Afghanistan	1919	Republic	Executive	6.0	6.0	1.3	61	109.3	27.7
Iraq	1932	Republic	Ceremonial	5.0	6.0	1.5	56	107.3	25.5
Central African Rep	1960	Republic	Executive	5.0	5.0	2.0	.	106.4	10.5
Guinea	1958	Republic	Executive	7.0	6.0	1.8	.	105.0	19.3
Pakistan	1947	Republic	Executive	4.0	5.0	2.4	49	102.5	22.5
Haiti	1804	Republic	Executive	4.0	5.0	1.8	.	101.6	4.1
Cote D'Ivoire	1960	Republic	Executive	6.0	5.0	2.1	.	101.2	8.9
Kenya	1963	Republic	Executive	4.0	4.0	2.2	45	100.7	9.8
Nigeria	1960	Republic	Executive	5.0	4.0	2.5	63	100.2	7.0
Yemen	1967	Republic	Executive	6.0	5.0	2.1	.	100.0	0.3
Subgroup Average	*1946*	*–*	*–*	*5.7*	*5.5*	*1.9*	*54.8*	*106.2*	*12.6*
Subgroup median	*1960*	*–*	*–*	*6.0*	*6.0*	*1.9*	*56.0*	*106.4*	*9.8*
Failing states (N=21)									
Myanmar (Burma)	*1948*	*Republic*	*Executive*	*7.0*	*7.0*	*1.4*	*.*	*99.4*	*15.3*
Ethiopia	*–*	*Republic*	*Ceremonial*	*5.0*	*5.0*	*2.7*	*.*	*98.8*	*21.9*
Korea, North	*1948*	*Republic*	*Executive*	*7.0*	*7.0*	*3.5*	*.*	*97.8*	*15.6*
Niger	*1960*	*Republic*	*Executive*	*5.0*	*4.0*	*2.9*	*.*	*97.8*	*12.4*
Uganda	*1962*	*Republic*	*Executive*	*5.0*	*4.0*	*2.5*	*86*	*97.5*	*30.7*
Guinea-Bissau	*1973*	*Republic*	*Executive*	*4.0*	*4.0*	*1.9*	*.*	*97.2*	*10.0*
Burundi	*1962*	*Republic*	*Executive*	*4.0*	*5.0*	*1.8*	*.*	*96.7*	*30.5*
Bangladesh	*1971*	*Republic*	*Ceremonial*	*3.0*	*4.0*	*2.4*	*.*	*96.1*	*18.6*
Sri Lanka	1948	Republic	Executive	4.0	4.0	3.1	.	95.7	5.8
Nepal	1768	Republic	Ceremonial	4.0	4.0	2.3	.	95.4	33.2
Cameroon	1960	Republic	Executive	6.0	6.0	2.2	54	95.4	13.9
Malawi	1964	Republic	Executive	3.0	4.0	3.3	.	93.6	20.8
Sierra Leone	1961	Republic	Executive	3.0	3.0	2.2	71	93.6	13.2
Eritrea	1993	Republic	Executive	7.0	7.0	2.6	.	93.3	22.0
Congo, Rep	1960	Republic	Executive	6.0	5.0	1.9	.	92.5	7.3
Iran	1979	Republic	Executive	6.0	6.0	1.8	.	92.2	2.8
Liberia	1847	Republic	Executive	3.0	4.0	3.1	89	91.7	12.5
Lebanon	1943	Republic	Ceremonial	5.0	3.0	2.5	34	90.9	3.1
Burkina Faso	1960	Republic	Executive	5.0	3.0	3.6	.	90.7	15.3
Uzbekistan	1991	Republic	Executive	7.0	7.0	1.7	.	90.5	17.5
Georgia	1991	Republic	Executive	4.0	4.0	4.1	3	90.4	5.1
Subgroup average	*1949*	*–*		*4.9*	*4.8*	*2.5*	*56.2*	*94.6*	*15.6*

(continued)

Table 26.6 (continued)

Countries	Year of independence	Type of polity 2010[a]	Head of state 2010[a]	Political freedom Index (−) 2010[b]	Civil liberties index (−) 2010[c]	Corruption perceptions index (+) 2009[d]	Global corruption barometer (−) 2010[e]	Failed state index (−) 2010[f]	Parliamentary seats held by women (+) 2010
Subgroup median	*1961*	–	–	*5.0*	*4.0*	*2.5*	*62.5*	*95.4*	*15.3*
Group average (N=36)	*1948*	–	–	*5.2*	*5.1*	*2.3*	*55.5*	*99.5*	*14.3*
Group median (N=36)	*1960*	–	–	*5.0*	*5.0*	*2.2*	*56.0*	*97.8*	*13.6*
SD (N=36)	*328*	–	–	*1.3*	*1.3*	*0.7*	*28.9*	*7.0*	*8.6*
World average (N=161)	–	–	–	*3.6*	*3.5*	*7.5*	*25.0*	*35.3*	*16.8*

Sources

[a]Central Intelligence Agency (2010); Encyclopedia Britannica (2010)

[b]Freedom House (2010). Scores range for 1–7 with 1 representing the most free

[c]Freedom House (2010). Scores range for 1–7 with 1 representing the most free

[d]Transparency International (2009). The degree to which public sector corruption is perceived to exist in 178 countries worldwide

[e]Transparency International (2010). Percent users reporting they paid a bribe to receive attention from at least 1 of 9 different service providers

[f]United Nations Development Programme (2010)

"failed" states also are much lower than the world on average, albeit those of selected countries are more favorable, e.g., Nepal (33%), Uganda (31%), Burundi (31%), Afghanistan (28%), Iraq (26%), Pakistan (23%), and Ethiopia (22%).

The type of polity (e.g., Republic) and type of head of state (e.g., ceremonial vs. executive) of the FSs matter less to their development profile than does the commitment of the governments of the FSs to the promotion of individual freedoms and liberties. Countries can, for example, be organized as Republics, even engage in popular elections, and still maintain highly oppressive political systems that deny their citizens personal freedoms (e.g., Iran, Zimbabwe). The vast majority of "failed" states and many "failing" states fall precisely within the latter category.

Once again, the study's FSs, on average, performed more weakly on the political indicators than did the world-as-a-whole using the same set of indicators. The study's 36 FSs performed less favorably on all nine of the political indicators reported here than did the world-as-a-whole.

Central Government Expenditure Patterns

Central government expenditures (CGEs) represent public investments in sectors of perceived importance to the growth and development of societies; they also reflect the relative importance of each sector to one another. Thus, high public investments in the health and education sectors represent a society's commitment to human-capacity building or human-resource development whereas higher levels of expenditures for defense and military purposes typically occur in countries that are experiencing serious internal or external turmoil. Further, under free-market conditions, the proportion of the economy under the direct control of the central government will be lower compared with that accounted for by the private sector expenditures.

Table 26.7 summarizes patterns of CGE for "failed" and "failing" states (N=36); comparable data also are reported for the world-as-a-whole (N = 161). As reflected in the table, no significant differences were found between general government consumption levels as a percentage of GDP for 2008–2009 for the FSs relative to those observed for the larger community of nations, i.e., 34.3% for the FSs vs. 35.9% for the world-as-a-whole. The governments of "failed" states, however, accounted for a smaller share on average of total national economic expenditures (31.5%), albeit a small number of "failed" states were responsible for 35% or more of all national economic transactions, e.g., Iraq (87%), Yemen (51%), and Zimbabwe (44%). By comparison, the CGEs of six "failing" states accounted for more than one-third of the total expenditures of their

26 "Failed" and "Failing" States: Is Quality of Life Possible?

Table 26.7 Selected central government expenditure priorities of failed and failing states, 2010 ($N=36$)

Countries	General Gov't consumption as % GDP 2008–2009[a]	Public expenditures as % GDP			Military expenditures as % GDP 2008–2009[a]
		Education 2008–2009[b]	Health 2008–2009[b]	Debt-to-GDP 2008–2009	
Failed states (N = 15)					
Somalia	.	,	1.2	14.7	2.9
Chad	19.9	1.9	2.7	27.0	6.5
Sudan	.	6.0	1.3	105.1	4.2
Zimbabwe	43.7	4.6	4.1	282.6	2.3
Congo, Dem Rep	22.9	,	1.2	100.0	1.1
Afghanistan	9.2	,	1.8	23.0	1.9
Iraq	87.3	,	1.9	76.0	6.3
Central African Rep	.	1.4	1.4	68.0	1.8
Guinea	21.0	1.6	0.6	70.0	2.0
Pakistan	28.0	2.6	0.8	31.0	3.1
Haiti	16.4	1.4	1.2	7.0	0.0
Cote D'Ivoire	21.4	4.6	1.0	54.0	1.6
Kenya	33.6	6.9	2.0	24.0	1.9
Nigeria	24.1	0.9	1.7	6.0	0.9
Yemen	50.9	9.6	1.5	25.0	4.4
Subgroup average	*31.5*	*3.8*	*1.6*	*60.9*	*2.7*
Failing states (N = 21)					
Myanmar (Burma)	.	1.2	0.2	27.0	1.7
Ethiopia	.	6.0	2.2	13.0	1.4
Korea, North	.	,	3.0	6.1	29.0
Niger	.	3.4	2.8	79.0	1.2
Uganda	27.6	5.2	1.6	13.0	2.0
Guinea -Bissau	.	5.2	1.6	203.0	3.0
Burundi	39.1	5.1	5.2	202.0	3.8
Bangladesh	12.8	2.7	1.1	25.0	1.1
Sri Lanka	29.5	,	2.0	85.8	3.5
Nepal	26.3	3.4	2.0	36.0	1.6
Cameroon	19.1	3.3	1.3	13.0	1.6
Malawi	48.2	5.8	5.9	24.0	1.2
Sierra Leone	.	3.8	1.4	163.0	2.3
Eritrea	34.1	2.4	1.5	44.0	6.3
Congo, Rep	39.2	1.9	1.7	155.0	1.3
Iran	31.0	5.1	3.0	6.0	2.8
Liberia	.	,	2.8	606.0	1.0
Lebanon	43.7	2.7	3.9	154.8	4.1
Burkina Faso	27.7	4.2	3.4	23.0	1.3
Uzbekistan	85.6	9.4	2.3	11.0	0.5
Georgia	50.4	3.1	1.5	31.0	5.6
Subgroup average	*36.7*	*4.1*	*2.4*	*91.5*	*3.6*
Group average (N = 36)	*34.3*	*4.0*	*2.1*	*78.7*	*3.3*
SD (N = 36)	*22.1*	*2.5*	*1.2*	*111.2*	*4.7*
World average (N = 161)	*35.9*	*4.5*	*3.6*	*99.7*	*2.4*

Data sources
[a]Central Intelligence Agency (2010); World Resources Institute (2010)
[b]World Bank (2010)

national economies, e.g., Uzbekistan (86%), Georgia (50%), Malawi (48%), Lebanon (44%), the Republic of the Congo (39%), and Burundi (39%).

Country debt-to-GDP levels are less dramatic for the FSs than for the world-as-a-whole, i.e., 78.7% vs. 99.9%. This may be due to the lack of credit worthiness of the FSs which depend more on multilateral foreign assistance to finance essential services. In some cases, the FSs debt-to-GDP levels well exceeded 100% of their total annual economic productivity, e.g., Liberia (606%), Zimbabwe (283%), Guinea-Bissau (203%), Burundi (202%), etc. These situations are especially problematic for already deeply impoverished nations.

CGEs for the health, education, and military sectors varied considerably by country. Overall, expenditures for the health sector (average = 2.1%) tended to be lower than expenditures for the education sector (average = 4.0%) whereas expenditures for the military sector (average = 3.3%) fell between those for the education and health sectors. Expenditures on all three sectors by the FSs were less favorable than those reported for the world-as-a-whole, i.e., health (average = 3.6%), education (average = 4.5%), and the military (average = 2.4%). Percent expenditures by sector varied for individual countries, of course, but the general pattern tends to remain more or less the same, i.e., higher investments in the education and health sectors and lower expenditures for the military (except in situations where the countries are engaged in active conflicts, e.g., Eritrea, Georgia, Iraq, North Korea).

Part 3: Failed States in Comparative Perspective

Failed states do not exist in a vacuum; instead, they are full members of the community of nations and, as such, enjoy all the rights and privileges that are extended to other sovereign states, including membership in the United Nations and other important world bodies. "Failed" and "failing" states help to establish the policy agenda for the world community and, frequently, despite their relative poverty, contribute resources to carrying out various types of global initiatives, e.g., through participation in regional peace-keeping efforts, disaster relief efforts, and serving as places of initial settlement for refugees from neighboring states. Owing to their overall structural weaknesses, however, the FSs more typically are the beneficiaries of world generosity and, as

with the United Nations *Millennium Development Campaign*, receive substantial amounts of international aid on a preferential basis (United Nations 2010a, b, c, d). In extending international largesse in this way, the larger community of nations seeks to help the FSs overcome at least some of the most important obstacles to their development. Aid-giving nations, however, tend to avoid becoming mired down by the intricacies of the local politics of recipient countries although appreciable investments are made by aid-giving countries in helping the FSs: (1) improve their levels of political transparency, (2) create political space for the development of a viable civil society, and (3) develop more participatory political systems (MDC 2011; Transparency International 2010). Indeed, many of the world's largest aid-giving bodies condition their grant-making activities on the basis of such criteria, e.g., the *Millennium Development Account* approach to international development promulgated by President George W. Bush of the United States (MDC 2011), the Development and Cooperation programs of the European Union (Europa 2011), as well as the United Nations' *Millennium Development Campaign* (United Nations 2005, 2010a, b, c, d). Thus, aid-receiving FSs experience considerable pressure in realigning their political systems in a manner more consistent with world norms.

Figures 26.5 and 26.6 summarize social development trends measured on the WISP for the FSs for the years 1990, 2000, and 2010 vis-à-vis those of four other development groupings, i.e., Development Market Economies (DMEs, $N=34$), the Commonwealth of Independent States (CIS, $N=19$), Developing Countries (DCs, $N=54$), and Least Developing Countries (LDCs, $N=19$).

As a group, the FSs fared less well on the WISP than other groupings of nations, in most cases substantially so, including of the group of 19 non-FSs classified by the United Nations as "Least Developing" countries. Though the scores of the last two groups do more closely approximate one another, in reality, the group of FSs are far more fragile than are the LDCs, especially for the period 1990–2000.

The good news for the FSs is that their aggregate WISP scores increased by an average of 140% between 2000 and 2010 – one of the highest rates of increase ever reported for a group of related nations on the WISP. The impressive strength of the changes in these aggregate scores suggests that, between 2000 and 2010, many of the FSs were beginning to introduce greater political stability and higher levels of public performance into their

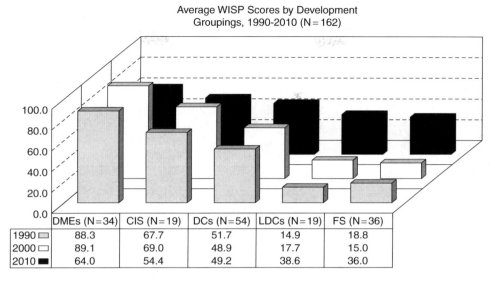

Fig. 26.5 Average WISP scores by development groupings, 1990–2010 (*N* = 162)

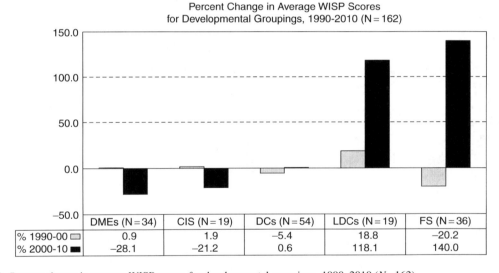

Fig. 26.6 Percent change in average WISP scores for developmental groupings, 1990–2010 (*N* = 162)

development profiles (Colletta et al. 2004; Helman and Ratner 1992/1993; Meierhenrich 2004).

The FSs that made the most substantial gains on the WISP between 2000 and 2010 included Malawi (+36 ranks); Ethiopia (+ 27 ranks); Bangladesh (+ 27 ranks); Niger (+12 ranks); Uganda (+12 ranks); Nepal (+11 ranks); Burundi (+11 ranks); Eritrea (+9 ranks); Yemen (+5 ranks); Korea, North (+5 ranks); and Afghanistan (+1 rank). Three additional FSs retained their WISP rank positions for both 2000 and 2010, i.e., Central African Republic, Guinea-Bissau, and Sierra Leone (Table 26.8).

Eighteen of the FSs lost significant social ground on the WISP between 1990 and 2000 and, again, between 2000 and 2010 (Table 26.8). The WISP rank losses experienced by both FSs groups over the two time intervals were especially severe for the group of "failed states" (an average of −38.4 WISP rank position losses between 1990 and 2000 and an additional average loss of −7.4 WISP rank positions between

Table 26.8 WISP scores and WISP rank positions for failed states rank ordered by 2010 failed states index (FSI), 1990, 2000 and 2010 ($N=36$)

Countries	WISP 1990 (base = 124)	WISP 2000 (base = 163)	WISP 2010 (base = 163)	WISP90 rank (base = 124)	WISP00 rank (base = 163)	WISP10 rank (base = 163)	Change in WISP rank positions 1990 > 2000	Change in WISP rank positions 2000 > 2010
Failing states (N = 15)								
Somalia	1	1	17	119	153	161	−34	−8
Chad	−2	−4	26	121	155	156	−34	−1
Sudan	13	13	35	105	137	142	−32	−5
Zimbabwe	37	24	37	76	120	136	−44	−16
Congo, Dem Rep	14	−2	26	103	154	157	−51	−3
Afghanistan	3	−19	17	116	163	162	−47	1
Iraq	35	28	28	80	116	154	−36	−38
Central African Rep	9	2	32	111	152	152	−41	0
Guinea	−1	5	32	120	148	151	−28	−3
Pakistan	24	23	39	88	121	127	−33	−6
Haiti	28	23	33	83	121	150	−38	−29
Cote D'Ivoire	16	12	35	99	141	145	−42	−4
Kenya	24	12	35	90	141	144	−51	−3
Nigeria	11	14	37	110	134	137	−24	−3
Yemen	.	8	35	.	146	141	.	5
Subgroup Averages	*15.2*	*9.4*	*30.9*	*101.5*	*140.3*	*147.7*	*−38.4*	*−7.4*
Failing states (N = 21)								
Myanmar (Burma)	36	35	41	78	109	119	−31	−10
Ethiopia	−10	−12	38	124	161	134	−37	27
Korea, North	47	35	45	66	109	104	−43	5
Niger	3	−4	35	117	155	143	−38	12
Uganda	12	7	37	107	147	135	−40	12
Guinea -Bissau	.	−4	27	.	155	155	.	0
Burundi	18	3	36	95	150	139	−55	11
Bangladesh	19	32	48	94	114	87	−20	27
Sri Lanka	57	53	46	49	74	100	−25	−26
Nepal	17	22	43	97	123	112	−26	11
Cameroon	21	15	36	92	133	138	−41	−5
Malawi	13	9	43	104	145	109	−41	36
Sierra Leone	2	−10	25	118	159	159	−41	0
Eritrea	.	−15	29	.	162	153	.	9
Congo, Rep	27	22	36	86	123	140	−37	−17
Iran	45	46	47	69	90	89	−21	1
Liberia	12	−6	24	109	158	160	−49	−2
Lebanon	45	52	52	68	78	61	−10	17
Burkina Faso	8	3	40	113	150	125	−37	25
Uzbekistan	.	52	52	.	78	62	.	16
Georgia	.	63	51	.	54	68	.	−14
Subgroup averages	*21.9*	*19.0*	*39.6*	*93.3*	*125.2*	*118.7*	*−33.7*	*6.1*
Group averages (N=36)	*18.8*	*15.0*	*36.0*	*97.0*	*131.5*	*130.8*	*−36.5*	*0.8*
SD (N=36)	*16.3*	*20.9*	*8.8*	*19.2*	*28.3*	*28.6*	*10.0*	*15.7*
World averages (N=161)	*48.1*	*48.5*	*48.7*	*62.0*	*80.5*	*80.5*	*0.0*	*0.0*

Source: Estes (2010)

2000 and 2010). WISP rank losses for the group of 21 "failing states" were only slightly lower.

Obviously, both subgroups of countries are in considerable turmoil concerning their political futures with the exception of the 11 countries for which substantial improvements in their WISP rank positions were reported. The situation for the three states for which no changes in either direction occurred (Central African Republic, Guinea-Bissau, and Sierra Leone) could move in either direction, but as of now, they are succeeding in not losing the precious social gains achieved during earlier development decades.

Part 4: Working Toward a More Positive Future for Collapsed, "Failed," and "Failing" States: A Global Agenda for Action

State failure is not inevitable, even for the poorest and most resource-deprived countries. But state failures do occur, and the challenges involved in bringing them back from collapse are complex and will not easily yield to ready-made solutions. As illustrated in the discussion throughout this chapter, each nation must find its own approach to rebuilding itself – one that builds on its history and, at the same time, propels the nation forward. Fortunately, there exists a range of tools for helping collapsed, failed, and failing states regain their capacity to perform as functioning polities in providing for the security and material needs of their inhabitants (Ghani and Lockhart 2008; Lyons 2004; Meierhenrich 2004; Posner 2004; Rose-Ackerman 2004; Snodgrass 2004; Widner 2004).

General Considerations

A general approach to rebuilding "failed" and "failing" states has a number of components.

1. Nations first must recognize that they have arrived at a crisis point where, without concerted effort, only further deterioration is likely.
   (a) Recognition of being on the brink of social implosion is not easily achieved, especially if the society's elites continue to benefit from the existing social order even as the quality of life of most of the nation's inhabitants declines (e.g., Burundi, Chad, Haiti, Tajikistan).
   (b) Recent revolutionary events in the Middle East and Africa – e.g., Egypt, Iraq, Libya, Tunisia, Yemen (CNN 2011), as well as the past failures of the Austro-Hungarian, Ottoman, and Russian empires, are illustrative of the conflict associated with the denial of state failure by authoritarian regimes.
   (c) Typically, a major national, often regional, crisis prompts the country's leaders to recognize its crisis situation, e.g., the collapse of major markets, unsustainable levels of unemployment, widespread strikes, street protests or riots, criticism of the country leadership by its own citizens and by major international NGOs, or condemnatory resolutions taken by the United Nations Security Council.
   (d) Each of these actions forces the country's leaders to recognize that the status quo is no longer working and that new approaches to state performance must be found.
2. Once the reality of state failure has been recognized, then, leaders within the failed or failing states must attempt to understand the underlying causes of the failure.
   (a) Always difficult to discern, such causes may include the geographic makeup of the nation, problems with accessing locally available natural and human resources, public corruption, high levels of public indebtedness, intolerable levels of diversity-related social conflict, and, typically, years of incompetent public leadership.
   (b) Such an assessment must be systematic and, to the fullest extent possible, involve all sectors of society in the assessment process, including representatives of the people and peoples' organizations.
3. Typically, new national leadership will be identified or will emerge as part of the assessment process. The new leadership may come from all areas of public life but, ideally, will include a mix of persons with significant political, economic, and related experience.
4. Having identified the mix of factors that undermine the current and future integrity of the state, the nation's new leaders must identify *a range of options* that are available to them in responding to the crisis.
   (a) Such options take the form of "scenario" development, i.e., the framing of alternative futures that the nation may wish to achieve for itself.

(b) National scenario development can be an exceedingly complex process and, in every case, is time and resource consuming and requires the involvement of a large number of societal stakeholders.

(c) Almost always, the process of scenario development involves the utilization of internal and external resources, some of which are people-centered, but others draw from the nation's natural resource reserves.

5. Central to the process of national scenario development is the engagement of the most experienced and best educated members of society in a series of carefully thought through efforts directed at reversing the country's downward spiral.

(a) Such people are found in virtually every society, but engaging them productively in the rebuilding process will require the country's elites to enlarge their power base to include such persons.

(b) Important stakeholders in a country's reconstruction process also may be available from outside of country, especially among those who have played important roles in the country's past social and economic development, including trading partners.

(c) These persons also may include senior members of major international nongovernmental organizations who are intimately familiar with the history of the country and its current development priorities.

6. National scenario development also will require the identification of monetary and other assets that draw on the nation's internal resource base, e.g., its geographic location, natural and human capital resources, network of relationships with neighboring states and international trading partners, and other types of physical, fiscal, social, and cultural capital.

7. Failed and failing states also must draw on the resources of the international community in their rebuilding efforts. These resources include:

(a) Technical assistance from multilateral development assistance organizations, sustained foreign aid over at least the near term, and the adoption of approaches to development that have demonstrated their effectiveness in other more or less comparable situations

(b) The development experiences of other countries that have undergone similar types of transitions in the recent past

8. Failed and failing states also must enter into mutually beneficial partnerships with other nations. These partnerships are important for two reasons:

(a) To strengthen the internal capacity of the failed and failing states

(b) To avail failed and failing states of the positive experiences of their partner states

9. And, finally, the ideal situation is for such national rebuilding partnerships to be formed between the FSs and other nations of the South (vs. former colonizing powers whose motives for engagement may be suspect). The reasons for these types of relationships also are twofold:

(a) The past experiences at nation-building of the world's already socially advanced countries may not be reflective of the development needs of failed or failing states.

(b) The promotion of effective South-South relationships is a worthwhile goal in and of itself.

At a minimum, monetary assistance is needed from economically and socially advanced nations to finance the South-South partnerships which, by their nature, are fraught with economic challenges. Such assistance may take the form of grants-in-aid, favorable trading practices, reduced import tariffs, and the like. They also may take the form of bi- or multilateral technical assistance programs that draw on the expertise of people with a broad range of practical and theoretical skills, i.e., from experienced farmers and skilled craftspersons to former and current statespersons.

This general approach to reestablishing the nation-building capacity of failed and failing states reflects a "strengths approach" to social and economic development. The approach draws substantially on both the internal resource base of the FSs themselves and, at the same time, is premised on active engagement of FSs in strong working partnerships with international nongovernmental organizations and other countries of the South. The approach also recognizes that respect for the social histories, traditions, and values of the failing states is part of the rebuilding formula … as is a full understanding of the contemporary social, political, and economic challenges that confront them.

Conclusions

This chapter began by questioning the extent to which advances in quality of life were possible under conditions of extreme political and economic collapse.

"Failed" and "failing" states (FSs) identified by the Fund for Peace were used as the basis for exploring this question. Data from the Fund's *Failed States Index* (FSI) were supplemented with time-series data obtained from the author's own statistically weighted *Index of Social Progress* (WISP). The latter index used social indicator data covering the 20-year period 1990–2010. Where appropriate, additional literature and statistical resources were added to the information database in order to arrive at the clearest possible picture of the dynamics of socio-political development under the most adverse conditions confronting humanity. A number of critical findings emerged from this analysis.

1. For the majority of "failed" and "failing" states, the process of entropy is so strong that nothing may be possible to halt their eventual social implosion. The pursuit of quality of life in such situations, in a Shakespearean sense (Wells 1986), is illusionary at best and, when it does occur, is possible only for individuals who are able to isolate themselves from the crises by which they are surrounded, i.e., self-contained communities that do not depend on the larger society for their collective well-being.

   (a) This was the model that insulated European religious communities from the turmoil of the Reformation during the sixteenth and seventeenth centuries, i.e., beginning in 1517 with the publication of Martin Luther's *The Ninety-Five Theses* that established Protestantism in what, until then, was exclusively Catholic Europe to the Treaty of Westphalia in 1648 which gave the West its current system of sovereign nation-states (devoid of papal control) that ended the continent's centuries-long religious wars.

   (b) This also is the model adopted by medieval Japan (1635–1868) and contemporary China (1949–1978) when they voluntarily closed themselves off from the outside world in order to consolidate their social identities.

2. The attainment of increased levels of quality of life under conditions of profound social deterioration also may occur for individuals in possession of sufficient material resources that make it possible for them to remove themselves from the immediate consequences of national social collapse, e.g., those who can retreat to "country estates" or immigrate to other countries.

3. Most inhabitants of "failed" and "failing" states, however, cannot and do not participate in either of the above situations and, therefore, experience considerable emotional and, often, physical dislocations as states unravel and cease to perform their core functions.

4. Personal and collective social deterioration are especially problematic when people are forced to live well below subsistence levels or in situations in which they are forced to participate in barbarous acts of aggression toward their neighbors, or both.

Thus, social development requires peace, or at least minimum levels of positive social, political, and economic stability. War, conflict, and other serious threats to individual and collective security make it impossible for the vast majority of the inhabitants of a country to pursue the fullest possible realization of their potential. On this issue, Plato (428–348 BCE) was correct in stating in *The Republic* that "justice" (and, in turn, "happiness" [and "pleasure"]) is not only desirable for its own sake but also maximized among those who pursue it (Plato 2000). Both Plato and his student, Aristotle (384–322 BCE), emphasized the critical role of the state in removing the "barriers" to the pursuit of happiness, but both argued that the state itself could not guarantee or be held accountable for the happiness of individuals. Confucius (551–479 BCE), writing more than a century earlier, proposed that "harmony" (and, by inference, "collective happiness") was the end goal of society and could be attained only through well-ordered social hierarchies. He carefully identified the structure of these hierarchies and delineated the societal problems that would occur if the prescribed norms were not followed. Unlike Plato and Aristotle, Confucius dismissed the pursuit of individual happiness as a central concern of societies (or even of individuals) and focused, instead, on the role of the state in providing for the needs of larger collectivities. Confucian approaches to collective harmony and structured social relationships continue to inform the social contracts that exist between citizens and their governments throughout much of Northeast Asia today (Van Norden 2001).

As evidenced by the data reported in this chapter, the attainment of personal or collective happiness is not possible for the vast majority of inhabitants of collapsed or collapsing societies. Such states simply do not possess the minimum conditions required for positive social development over time. And, not only do failed and failing states severely impede the personal and collective quality of life of their own inhabitants, they also threaten that of their neighboring states. Viewed from an even larger perspective, the collapse of failed and failing states also threatens the quality of life of the larger world community which, increasingly, is called upon to intervene in the myriad crises created by state failures.

Acknowledgement Zhou Huiquan (Mary) of the Chinese University of Hong Kong is acknowledged for her research assistance in updating the statistics contained in this chapter.

References

African Development Bank. (2010). *African economic outlook, 2010*. From http://www.afdb.org/en/knowledge/publications/african-economic-outlook/. Retrieved October 17, 2010.

Amnesty International. (2010). *The state of the world's human rights, 2010*. From http://thereport.amnesty.org/. Retrieved October 10, 2010.

Anheier, H., Toepler, S., & List, R. (Eds.). (2010). *International encyclopedia of civil society*. New York: Springer.

Annas, J. (1993). *The morality of happiness*. Oxford: Oxford University Press.

Asian Development Bank (ADB). (2010). *Asian development outlook, 2010: Macroeconomic management beyond the crisis*. From http://www.adb.org/documents/books/ado/2010/. Retrieved October 25, 2010.

Bates, R. H. (2008). *When things fell apart: State failure in late-century Africa*. New York: Cambridge University Press.

Britannica Online. (2011a). *Supranational political powers*. From http://proxy.library.upenn.edu:7116/EBchecked/topic/467746/political-system/36702/National-political-systems?anchor=ref416908. Retrieved February 20, 2011.

Britannica Online (2011b). *Peace of Westphalia*. From http://www.britannica.com/EBchecked/topic/641170/Peace-of-Westphalia. Retrieved February 20, 2011.

Carment, D. (2004). Preventing state failure. In R. I. Rotberg (Ed.), *When states fail: Causes and consequences* (pp. 135–150). Princeton: Princeton University Press.

Central Intelligence Agency. (2010). *World factbook*. From http://www.odci.gov/cia/publications/factbook/. Retrieved February 11, 2011.

Central Intelligence Agency (CIA). (2011). *World Factbook, 2011*. From http://search.yahoo.com/search?fr=mcafee&p=cia+world+factbook+2011. Retrieved August 30, 2011.

Chomsky, N. (2006). *"Failed" states: The abuse of power and the assault on democracy*. New York: Holt.

Clapham, C. (2004). The global-local politics of state decay. In R. I. Rotberg (Ed.), *When states fail: Causes and consequences* (pp. 77–93). Princeton: Princeton University Press.

Club of Rome. (2011). *Publications*. From http://www.clubofrome.org/eng/featured_publications_bank/. Retrieved February 20, 2011.

CNN (2011). *Unrest in the middle east and Africa: Country by country. February 26*. From http://edition.cnn.com/2011/WORLD/meast/02/25/mideast.africa.unrest/index.html?iref=allsearch. Retrieved March 1, 2011.

Colletta, N. J., Kostner, M., & Wiederhofer, I. (2004). Disarmament, demobilization, and reintegration: Lessons and liabilities in reconstruction. In R. I. Rotberg (Ed.), *When states fail: Causes and consequences* (pp. 170–181). Princeton: Princeton University Press.

Encyclopedia Britannica. (2010). Britannica On-line. From http://www.britannica.com/. Retrieved February 20, 2011.

Estes, R. J. (1988). *Trends in world social development*. Westport: Praeger Publishers.

Estes, R. J. (1995). Social development trends in Africa: The need for a new development paradigm. *Social Development Issues, 17*(1), 18–47.

Estes, R. J. (2007). Asia and the new century: Challenges and opportunities. *Social Indicators Research, 82*(3), 375–410.

Estes, R. J. (2010). The world social situation: Development challenges at the outset of a new century. *Social Indicators Research, 98*(3), 363–402.

Estes, R. J. (2011a). Development trends among the world's socially least developed countries: Reasons for guarded optimism. *Globalization and Its Challenges*, In Spooner, B. (Ed.), Philadelphia: University of Pennsylvania Press), in press.

Estes, R. J. (2011b). Economies in transition. In A. Michalos & K. Land (Eds.), *Handbook of quality of life research*. Dordrecht: Springer, in press.

Europa. (2011). *Development and cooperation*. From http://europa.eu/pol/dev/index_en.htm. Retrieved February 17, 2011.

Freedom House. (2010). *Freedom in the world, 2010*. From http://www.freedomhouse.org/. Retrieved February 11, 2011.

Fund for Peace. (2011a). *The "failed" states index: Postcards from hell*. The sixth annual collaboration between *Foreign Policy* magazine and *The Fund for Peace*. From http://www.foreignpolicy.com/articles/2010/06/21/2010_failed_states_index_interactive_map_and_rankings. Retrieved February 12, 2011.

Fund for Peace. (2011b). *"Failed" states index scores*. Foreign Policy & the Fund for Peace. From http://www.fundforpeace.org/web/index.php?option=com_content&task=view&id=229&Itemid=366. Retrieved February 13, 2011.

Fund for Peace. (2011c). *Methodology behind CAST*. From http://www.fundforpeace.org/web/index.php?option=com_content&task=view&id=107&Itemid=145. Retrieved February 13, 2011.

Ghani, A., & Lockhart, C. (2008). *Fixing "failed" states: A framework for rebuilding a fractured world*. New York and London: Oxford University Press.

Glennie, J. (2008). *The trouble with aid: Why less could mean more for Africa*. London: Zed Books.

Helman, G. B. & Ratner, S. R. (1992/1993). *Saving "failed" states. Foreign Policy, 89*. From http://www.foreignpolicy.com/articles/2010/06/21/saving_failed_states. Retrieved February 12, 2011.

Human Rights Watch. (2010). *Defending Human Rights Worldwide*. Retrieved March 17, 2011 from http://www.hrw.org/

Human Rights Watch. (2011). *World report, 2011*. From http://www.hrw.org/en/world-report-2011. Retrieved February 20, 2011.

Huntington, S. P. (1996). *The clash of civilizations and the remaking of world order*. New York: Simon & Shuster.

International Monetary Fund (IMF). (2010). *World Economic Recovery*. Retrieved April 15, 2011 from http://www.imf.org/external/pubs/ft/weo/2010/02/index.htm

International Monetary Fund (IMF). (2010a). *World economic outlook, 2010*. Washington: International Monetary Fund.

International Monetary Fund (IMF). (2010b). *Debt relief under the heavily indebted poor countries (HIPC) Initiative*. From http://www.imf.org/external/np/exr/facts/hipc.htm. Retrieved February 16, 2011.

Kasfir, N. (2004). Domestic anarchy, security dilemmas, and violent predation: Causes of failure. In R. I. Rotberg (Ed.), *When states fail: Causes and consequences* (pp. 53–76). Princeton: Princeton University Press.

Kim, K. S., Lee, Y. W., & Lee, Y. J. (2010). A multilevel analysis of factors related to poverty in welfare states. *Social Indicators Research, 99*(3), 391–404.

Klare, M. T. (2004). The deadly connection: Paramilitary bands, small arms diffusion, and state failure. In R. I. Rotberg (Ed.), *When states fail: Causes and consequences* (pp. 116–134). Princeton: Princeton University Press.

Leonard, D., & Straus, S. (2003). *Africa's stalled development*. Boulder: Lynne Rienner.

Lyons, T. (2004). Transforming the institutions of war: Post-conflict elections and the reconstruction of "failed" states. In R. I. Rotberg (Ed.), *When states fail: Causes and consequences* (pp. 269–301). Princeton: Princeton University Press.

Mallaby, S. (2004). *The world's banker: A story of "failed" states, financial crises, and the wealth and poverty of nations*. New York: Penguin.

Meierhenrich, J. (2004). Forming states after failure. In R. I. Rotberg (Ed.), *When states fail: Causes and consequences* (pp. 153–169). Princeton: Princeton University Press.

Michalos, A. C. (2011). The good life: Eighth century to the third century BCE. Chapter 1 in the current Handbook.

Millennium Development Corporation (MDC). (2011). *The millennium challenge campaign*. From http://www.mcc.gov/. Retrieved February 17, 2011.

Moran, M., Rein, M., & Goodin, R. (Eds.). (2006). *The Oxford handbook of public policy*. New York and Oxford: Oxford University Press.

Moyo, D. (2009). *Dead aid: Why aid is not working and how there is a better way for Africa*. New York: Farrar, Straus, & Giroux.

Obioma, I. (2001). *Contending issues in African development: Advances, challenges, and the future*. London: Greenwood Press.

Plato (2000). The republic. In Ferrari, G. (Ed.), Translated by Griffith, T. Cambridge: Cambridge University Press.

Posner, D. N. (2004). Civil society and the reconstruction of "failed" states. In R. I. Rotberg (Ed.), *When states fail: Causes and consequences* (pp. 237–255). Princeton: Princeton University Press.

Rose-Ackerman, R. (2004). Establishing the rule of law. In R. I. Rotberg (Ed.), *When states fail: Causes and consequences* (pp. 182–221). Princeton: Princeton University Press.

Rotberg, R. I. (2003). *State failure and state weakness in a time of terror*. Cambridge: World Peace Foundation.

Rotberg, R. I. (2004). The failure and collapse of nation-states: Breakdown, prevention, and repair. In R. I. Rotberg (Ed.), *When states fail: Causes and consequences* (pp. 1–50). Princeton: Princeton University Press.

Sach, J. (2008). *Common Wealth: Economics for a Crowded Planet*. New York: Penguin Press.

Sachs, J. D. (2005). *The end of poverty*. New York: Penguin Press.

Save the World's Children. (2010). *The state of the world's mothers, 2010*. From http://www.savethechildren.net/alli-ance/what_we_do/every_one/news.html. Retrieved February 14, 2011.

Schyns, P., & Koop, C. (2010). Political distrust and social capital in Europe and the USA. *Social Indicators Research, 96*(1), 145–167.

Sen, A. (1999). *Development as freedom*. New York: Knopf.

Snodgrass, D. R. (2004). Restoring economic functioning in "failed" states. In R. I. Rotberg (Ed.), *When states fail: Causes and consequences* (pp. 256–268). Princeton: Princeton University Press.

Stockholm International Peace and Research Institute. (2009). *SIPRI yearbook, 2009: Armaments, disarmament and international security*. Stockholm: SIPRI.

Transparency International (TI) (2009). *CPI Survey and Indices*. Retrieved February 1, 2011 from http://www.transparency.org/policy_research/surveys_indices/cpi/2009

Transparency International. (2010). *Global corruption report, 2010*. From http://www.transparency.org/publications/gcr. Retrieved February 11, 2011.

Tsai, M. C. (2006). Macro-structural determinants of political freedom in developing countries: A cross-national analysis. *Social Indicators Research, 76*(2), 317–340.

Tsai, M. C. (2007). Does globalization affect human well-being? *Social Indicators Research, 81*(1), 103–126.

Tsai, C. L., Hung, M. C., & Harriott, K. (2010). Human capital composition and economic growth. *Social Indicators Research, 99*(1), 41–59.

United Nations. (2005). World Summit, 2005. Retrieved April 1, 2011 from http://www.globalissues.org/article/559/united-nations-world-summit-2005

United Nations. (2010a). *The millennium development goals report, 2010*. From http://www.un.org/millenniumgoals/pdf/MDG%20Report%202010%20En%20r15%20-low%20res%2020100615%20-.pdf. Retrieved January 31, 2011.

United Nations. (2010b). *Millennium development goals: 2010 progress chart*. From http://unstats.un.org/unsd/mdg/Resources/Static/Products/Progress2010/MDG_Report_2010_Progress_Chart_En.pdf. Retrieved January 31, 2011.

United Nations. (2010c). *Summit on the millennium development goals: Reports*. From http://www.un.org/millenniumgoals/reports.shtml. Retrieved January 31, 2011.

United Nations. (2010d). *Keeping the promise: United to achieve the millennium development goals: Outcome document*. From http://www.un.org/en/mdg/summit2010/pdf/mdg%20outcome%20document.pdf. Retrieved January 31, 2011.

United Nations (2011). *Member states of the United Nations*. From http://www.un.org/en/members/index.shtml. Retrieved February 14, 2011.

United Nations Children's Fund (UNICEF) (2010a). *The state of the world's children, 2010*. http://www.unicef.org/rightsite/sowc/pdfs/SOWC_Spec%20Ed_CRC_Main%20Report_EN_090409.pdf. Retrieved January 31, 2011.

United Nations Children's Fund (UNICEF). (2010b). *Progress for children: Achieving the MDGs with equity (No. 9)*. From http://www.unicef.org/publications/index_55740.html. Retrieved February 12, 2011.

United Nations Development Fund for Women (UNIFEM). (2010). *Progress of the world's women, 2010/2011*. From http://acelebrationofwomen.org/?p=24595. Retrieved January 28, 2011.

United Nations Development Programme (UNDP). (2010). *Human development report, 2010: The real wealth of nations: Pathways to human development*. From http://hdr.undp.org/en/reports/global/hdr2010/. Retrieved February 2, 2011.

United Nations High Commissioner for Refugees (UNHCR). (2009a). *UNHCR statistical yearbook*. From http://www.unhcr.org/pages/4a02afce6.html. Retrieved October 10, 2010.

United Nations High Commissioner for Refugees (UNHCR). (2009b). *MDGs and refugees*. From http://www.unhcr.org/pages/49e5a9e56.html. Retrieved October 10, 2010.

United Nations Office of the High Representative for Least Developed Countries, Landlocked Developing Countries, and Small Island Developing Countries (UN-OHRLLS) (2009a). The criteria for LDCs. From http://www.un.org/special-rep/ohrlls/ldc/ldc%20criteria.htm. Retrieved 13 Oct 2010.

United Nations Office of the High Representative for Least Developed Countries, Landlocked Developing Countries, and Small Island Developing Countries (UN-OHRLLS) (2009b). List of LDCs. From http://www.unohrlls.org/en/ldc/related/62/. Retrieved 13 Oct 2010.

United Nations Office of the High Representative for Least Developed Countries, Landlocked Developing Countries, and Small Island Developing Countries (UN-OHRLLS) (2009c). LDC facts and figures. From http://www.unohrlls.org/en/ldc/related/63/. Retrieved 13 Oct 2010.

United Nations Office of the High Representative for Least Developed Countries, Landlocked Developing Countries, and Small Island Developing Countries (UN-OHRLLS) (2009d). Resolutions. From http://www.un.org/special-rep/ohrlls/ldc/resolutions.htm. Retrieved 13 Oct 2010.

United Nations Population Division (UNPOP) (2010). World population prospects: 2008 Revisions. From http://www.un.org/esa/population/publications/wpp2008/wpp2008_highlights.pdf. Retrieved 13 Oct 2010.

Van de Walle, N. (2004). The economic correlates of state failure: Taxes, foreign aid, and policies. In R. I. Rotberg (Ed.), *When states fail: Causes and consequences* (pp. 94–115). Princeton: Princeton University Press.

Van Norden, B. W. (Ed.). (2001). *Confucius and the analects: New essays*. New York: Oxford University Press.

Weingast, B. R., & Wittman, D. A. (Eds.). (2006). *The Oxford handbook of political economy*. New York and Oxford: Oxford University Press.

Wells, R. H. (1986). *Shakespeare, politics, and the state*. London: Macmillan and Company.

Widner, J. A. (2004). Building effective trust in the aftermath of severe conflict. In R. I. Rotberg (Ed.), *When states fail: Causes and consequences* (pp. 222–236). Princeton: Princeton University Press.

World Bank (2009). The enhanced heavily indebted poor countries initiative. From http://web.worldbank.org/WBSITE/EXTERNAL/TOPICS/EXTDEBTDEPT/0,,contentMDK:20260411~menuPK:528655~pagePK:64166689~piPK:64166646~theSitePK:469043,00.html. Retrieved 10 Jan 2011.

World Bank. (2010). *World Bank Development Indicators, 2010*. From data.worldbank.org/.../world-development-indicators/wdi-2010.

World Bank. (2011). *World development report, 2011: Overcoming conflict and fragility*. New York: Oxford University Press.

World Resources Institute (WRI). (2008). *World resources: Roots of resilience*. Washington: World Resources Institute.

World Resources Institute (WRI). (2010). *World Resources Report, 2009*: Environmental Report. From http://pdf.wri.org/environmentalindicators_bw.pdf. Retrieved August 15, 2011.

Yunus, M., & Weber, K. (2008). *Creating a world without poverty: Social business and the future of capitalism*. New York: Public Affairs.

Zartman, I. W. (Ed.). (1995). *Collapsed states: The disintegration and restoration of legitimate authority*. Boulder: Lynne Rienner Publishers.

Index

A

Aboriginal Australians, 460
Absolute Utility Theory, 516
Academy of Marketing Science, 9
Accuracy of Time Diaries, 165–166
Achieving in life, 191, 267, 268, 285, 288, 416, 417, 426, 460, 464, 548
Achilles, 27
Acquisition/Possession Satisfaction Model, 333, 335–336
Acquisition satisfaction, 336, 337
Activities, 3, 26, 74, 100, 138, 159, 181, 210, 246, 274, 297, 314, 336, 359, 374, 381, 402, 470, 478, 535, 572
Activities and Affect in the General Social Survey (GSS), 174
Activity coding, 163
Additive approach, 218, 223, 225
Administration of justice, 555
Adults, 12, 87, 101, 127, 155, 167, 192, 243, 266, 314, 355, 373–379, 384, 402, 435, 459, 475, 507, 542, 558
Affect, 6, 26, 66, 79, 101, 113, 139, 173, 184, 201, 241, 266, 297, 319, 331, 357, 376, 385, 399, 464, 473, 510, 532
Affect Balance Scale (ABS), 6, 373, 388, 391–392, 396, 468
Affect-Balance Values for Selected Countries, 392
Affectometer, 6
Afghanistan, 70, 439, 441, 503, 504, 507, 511, 514, 517, 560–562, 566–571, 573, 574
Africa, 10, 13, 126–128, 186, 381, 399, 401, 404, 410, 411, 413, 420, 425, 437, 439–441, 453, 499, 503, 505, 506, 512, 516, 519, 557, 559–564, 575
African slave trade, 532
Age, 7, 27, 72, 90, 103, 119, 150, 161, 182, 207, 250, 269, 305, 316, 345, 355, 373, 404, 436, 459, 473, 502, 535, 547, 558
Age structure, 503, 521
Aggregating indicators, 203, 216–217, 223–225, 227, 228
Aggregating observed units, 217–218
Agreeableness, 92
Airports, 148, 149, 506, 508
AKRASIA, 39, 40
Albania, 387, 437, 444–450, 504, 507, 510, 511, 514, 517
Algeria, 499–526
Algerian Wellbeing, 522
Allocation, 113, 211, 265, 400, 401, 444
Allocative efficiency, 278
Al-Qaeda, 519
Alternative Work Arrangements, 14, 302–303
American Chamber of Commerce in Hong Kong, 475
American Consumer Satisfaction Index (ACSI), 332

American Demographics' Index of Well-Being (AD-IWB), 189, 191, 194
American Demographics magazine, 194
American Journal of Public Health, 14
American Planning Association, 13
American Time-Use Survey (ATUS), 159, 163, 166–169, 176
America's Children: Key National Indicators of Well-being, 15
Amnesty International, 436, 452, 556, 558
Analytic approaches, 203, 204, 209, 211, 215, 218, 227
Analytic Hierarchy Processes (AHP), 223
Analytic tools and strategies, 201, 203–205, 215
Anaxagoras of Clazomenae, 31
Anaximander, 28, 54
Anaximenes, 28
The Annals, 4
ANOMIA, 47, 48
Anonymous Iamblichi, 47–48
Antigua, 529–531
Antiphon, 26, 33–34, 39, 56, 59
Antiphon of Rhamnous, 33–34, 59
Apology, 26, 28, 37, 38
APONIA, 54, 57
Arab Human Development Report, 506, 509, 515
Arab world, 506, 516
ARETE, 27, 37, 51, 53
Argentina, 413, 529–532, 535, 536, 540, 547–554
Aristotle, 12, 26, 27, 29, 31, 33, 35, 37, 48–54, 56, 57, 59, 60, 64, 106, 109, 110, 138, 374, 501, 577
Aristotle of Stageira, 48–53
Asia, 13, 125, 127, 128, 171, 185, 381, 401, 403, 404, 410, 412, 420, 433, 437–441, 453, 454, 473–495, 499, 505, 512, 557, 559–562, 564–565, 577
AsiaBarometer, 13
Assessing discriminant capacity, 226
Assessing robustness, 225, 228
Assessment of Spirituality and Religious Sentiments (ASPIRES), 318
ATARAXIA, 54, 57
Attitude, 7, 9, 13, 58, 101, 144, 152, 174, 195, 240, 245, 273, 280, 286–288, 297, 316, 318, 320, 360, 367, 403, 408, 414, 486, 499, 500, 550
Australian Centre on Quality of Life, 376, 461
Australian Life Quality, 459–460
Australian Quality of Life measure, 375
Australian Social Trends, 15
Australian subjective wellbeing, 460

582   Index

The Australian Unity Well-Being Index (AUWBI), 12, 79, 80, 86, 196, 376–378, 460–461
Australia-United States Free Trade Agreement, 463
Authentic happiness, 242, 501
Autonomous nations, 452, 556
AUWBI. *See* The Australian Unity Well-Being Index (AUWBI)
Availability, 68, 76, 114, 166, 174, 176, 212–214, 221, 243, 337–339, 348, 352, 367, 381, 404, 436, 480, 542
Aymara, 529
Azerbaijan, 437, 445–450, 499, 507, 509, 511, 513, 514, 517

B

Bahamas, 529–531, 535
Bahrain, 504–507, 510, 511, 513, 514, 516, 517, 525, 526
Baltic States, 397, 433, 436, 437, 440–443, 451, 454
Bangladesh, 7, 399–402, 405–407, 409, 410, 413, 415, 417–419, 426, 503, 504, 507, 511–514, 517, 560, 566–569, 571, 573, 574
Barbados, 529–531, 535
Barbuda, 529–531
Barometers of Quality of Life around the Globe, 11
Bayesian networks approach, 231–232
Being part of the community, 549
Belize, 529, 530
Benchmarking, 204, 219–220
Benin, 503, 504, 507, 511, 513, 514, 517, 518
Biological measures of positive and negative states, 144
Bolivarian Republic of Venezuela, 529
Bolivia, 529–532, 534–536, 540
Book 5 of the *Laws*, 47
Book X of Diogenes Laertius's text, 54
Bottom-up, 52, 153–156, 207, 229, 247–248, 298, 357, 409, 412
Bottom-up spillover, 331, 345, 347, 353
Bottom-up Spillover Model, 335, 345–350, 353
Bradburn's Negative Affect (NA) and Positive Affect (PA) scales, 6
Brazil, 124, 125, 127, 170, 433, 439, 440, 530–532, 534, 539, 540, 542, 5229
Brief Multidimensional Student's Life Satisfaction Scale, 357
British Medical Journal, 14
Broaden-and-Build Theory, 104–106
Broad versus narrow measures, 141
Brunei, 504–507, 510, 511, 514, 517
Bureau of Justice Statistic's annual National Crime Victimization Survey, 4
Burkina Faso, 503–507, 509–511, 514, 517, 518, 560, 562, 564, 566–569, 571, 574
Burundi, 556, 560–562, 564, 567–575
"Butterfly" trajectory of the Lorenz system, 105

C

Cameroons, 504, 511, 513, 514, 517, 518, 560, 566–569, 571, 574
Canadian Chamber of Commerce in Hong Kong, 475
Canadian University of Victoria's Centre on Ageing, 375
Capability, 63, 64, 71, 101, 189, 232, 422, 535, 552
Capacity for enjoyment, 74, 75
Cardiovascular disease, 102, 139, 243
Caribbean, 439, 529–543, 560
Caring of the elderly, 503

Carnegie Endowment for Peace, 559
Cascading structural amplification, 277
"CASIO" Model of Life Satisfaction, 242, 244
CAST software, 559
Census and Statistics Department, 474, 481, 487
Center for Coordination of Research on Social Indicators, 4, 8
Central African Republic, 503, 562, 564, 573, 575
Central government expenditures, 449, 559, 566–572
Chad, 503–507, 509, 511, 512, 514, 517, 556, 557, 560, 562, 564, 566–569, 571, 574, 575
Change of the presidency, 547
Character strengths, 100, 106–110, 319, 324
Charter for Peace and National Reconciliation, 519
Child and Youth Well-Being Index (CWI), 191, 196, 355
Childcare Programs, 303, 306
Children, 10, 28, 73, 87, 108, 149, 159, 183, 212, 243, 265, 303, 341, 355–368, 373, 405, 434, 466, 473, 501, 534, 555
Child welfare, 282, 289
Child Well-being Index, 11, 355
Chile, 439, 440, 529–532, 534–536, 540
China, 127, 128, 133, 304, 352, 365, 403, 407, 410, 413, 425, 433, 434, 437, 440, 444–450, 453, 454, 463, 478, 486, 492–495, 508, 556, 564, 577
Chinese University of Hong Kong, 477, 479, 486, 487
Chronic and acute life events, 363–364
CIA World Factbook, 436, 447, 503, 506, 508, 520, 521, 559, 568
City University of Hong Kong, 475
Civil Liberties, 435, 448, 475, 513, 555, 558, 564, 566, 569, 570
Cleinias, 37, 38
Cluster Analysis, 218, 222, 226
Cochrane Collaboration, 14
Cold indicators, 221
Collective socialization, 280
Collectivism, 69, 403, 414
Colombia, 395, 439, 440, 529–532, 534, 536, 541, 542
Combining indicators, 203–205, 215, 218–229
Commission on Youth, 474, 490
Common Wealth of Independent States (CIS), 433, 436, 437, 440–442, 452, 454, 505, 559, 560, 572
Community, 5, 23, 100, 138, 185, 215, 243, 267, 303, 314, 331, 357, 375, 382, 405, 453, 460, 473, 500, 537, 548, 555
Community-connectedness, 196, 267, 416, 417, 426, 460, 464, 523, 524, 548
Community Indicators Consortium, 13
Community indicators projects, 13
Community Model, 333, 335, 340
Community QOL indicators, 13
Comparability, 11, 69, 130, 145–146, 213, 221, 223, 224, 385, 480
Compensation effect, 9
Complexity, 101, 201–202, 204, 216, 219, 221, 223, 226, 227, 231, 233, 272, 289, 367, 469, 470, 488
Components of happiness, 66, 241
Components of subjective well-being, 138, 140
Composite index construction, 181–199
Composite indicators, 183, 189, 204, 219–221, 226–228, 493
Composite International Diagnostic Interview Short Form (CIDI-SF), 101
Composite QOL index, 181, 183–188, 196, 198, 485
Compositional approach, 218
Comprehensive quality of life scale (ComQol), 5, 267, 357, 358, 416, 548

Index

Compressed Work Week, 303, 304, 307
Compression of morbidity, 277
Computing well-being, 154–155
Conceptions of well-being, 138–139
The Condition of Education, 15
Conjoint analysis, 223
Connectedness, 314, 318, 319, 378, 404
Conscientiousness, 73, 92, 153, 286, 318
Consultations with the Poor, 400, 406, 407
Consumer Complaint Model, 333, 334, 352
Consumer Confidence Index (CCI), 182, 195, 352, 475
Consumer Expectations Index (CEI), 195, 352
Consumer life cycle model, 333, 335–340
Consumer life domain, 331, 335, 338
Consumer Price Index (CPI), 181–184, 197, 198, 331, 333, 352, 468, 486
Consumer Price Index-Urban (CPI-U), 182, 183
Consumer Reports, 331, 334, 352
Consumer Union, 331, 334
Consumer well-being (CWB), 14, 331–353
Consumption citizen, 551
Consumption Equity Model, 333, 352
Consumption levels, 114–121, 570
Consumption satisfaction, 336–338
Consumption Satisfaction Model, 335
Contact networks, 469–470
Contact with other people, 468–469
Contamination by Current Mood, 151
Contentment, 66, 69, 92, 110, 149, 153–155, 241, 246, 248, 249, 302, 422
Convention on the Reduction of Statelessness (1961), 513
Convention relating to the Status of Stateless Persons (1954), 513
Convergence with Other Measures, 144
Core meaning, 64–66
Correlation analysis, 219, 221, 228
Costa Rica, 395, 529–532, 535–537
Cost of Living Model, 333, 352
Cote d'Ivoire, 504, 507, 509–511, 514, 517, 556, 560, 562, 564, 567–569, 571, 574
Countries, 5, 69, 80, 113, 145, 159, 181, 213, 266, 305, 323, 333, 365, 376, 381, 399–424, 433, 459, 473, 499, 529, 547, 555
Courage, 27, 37, 39, 43, 45, 49, 107, 108, 138, 501
Course of life-events, 71, 73–74
Creating synthetic indicators, 216–217
Crime, 4, 15, 17, 26, 113, 128, 147, 148, 192, 193, 212, 243, 274, 282, 283, 342, 344, 385, 386, 459, 460, 481–483, 486, 487, 533, 540–543
Crime rate, 137, 189, 193–195, 484, 486–489, 542, 548
Criticisms of composite indicators, 226
Cuba, 529–531, 535
CUHK Hong Kong Quality of Life Index, 474, 483–489, 495
Cultural differences, 153–154, 366, 367, 403, 413
Cultural Diversity, 194, 411, 435, 436, 451–453, 551, 554, 555, 557–559
Cultural Diversity Sub-index, 387
Cultural response bias, 82, 152
Current Population Survey, 160, 163, 272, 303
Cynics, 24
Cyrenaics, 24

D

DAIMONES, 32, 34, 37
Danish Quality of Life Survey, 374
Darfur region of western Sudan, 512
Dashboards, 204, 218–219, 233
Data envelopment analysis (DEA), 184, 185, 223, 228
Datenreport, 4, 15
Decentralized Organizational Structures, 298, 299
Defense Effort, 193, 387, 435, 437, 451–453, 557, 558, 565
Defining and Measuring Quality of Life, 24, 374–376, 382, 391
Defining macro-units, 215
Definition of happiness, 66
Delphic/Homeric religion, 26
Democratic Republic of the Congo, 556, 562, 564, 566
Democritean ethics, 34, 36
Democritus, 26, 27, 34–36, 39, 42, 54, 55, 59
Democritus of Abdera, 34–36
Demographic, 2, 83, 95, 103, 125–127, 163, 167–169, 174, 189, 191, 193, 194, 196, 230, 303, 308, 366, 412, 413, 435, 437, 465, 468, 502, 503, 522, 523, 557, 566
Demographic Sub-index, 387
Department of Health, 2, 15, 474
Departments of Great Buenos Aires, 547, 548, 550, 551
Depression, 76, 87, 92–96, 100, 102, 103, 109, 137, 139, 145, 155, 183, 241, 244–248, 274, 306, 314, 319–321, 357, 360, 361, 409, 444
Depression, Anxiety and Stress Scale, 93
Deprivational approach, 220
Desirability-bias, 69
Desirability of subjective well-being, 139–140
Developed Market Economies (DMEs), 559, 572
Developed World, 16, 127, 381, 382, 390, 396–397
Developing and managing indicators, 202–205, 212
Developing a system of indicators, 205, 209
Developing countries, 116, 117, 132, 192, 272, 399–424, 441, 507, 508, 516, 523, 559, 562, 572
Development, 1–18, 24, 64, 81, 99, 113, 147, 169, 181, 208, 240, 266, 297, 322, 331, 355, 373, 381, 399, 433, 459, 474, 499, 532, 548, 555
Development Market Economies, 572
Development Strategy, 534–535, 539, 543
Diabetes, 103, 239, 348, 414
Diary, 159–163, 165–168, 171–174, 176, 177
Diary-estimate comparisons, 166–167
Differential Weighting, 222, 223
DIKAIOSUNE, 45
Dimensional analysis, 221–222, 227, 232
Diogenes Laertius, 32, 35–37, 53, 54, 56, 57
Disability adjusted life years (DALYs), 374, 375, 409, 542
Discrimination against indigenous groups, 540
Disposal satisfaction, 338
Djibouti, 504, 505, 507, 511, 514, 517
Domain satisfaction, 5, 65, 247, 267, 400, 409, 423, 524, 537
Domestic violence, 482, 542
Dominica, 529–531
Dominican Republic, 401, 529–532, 536
Donnes Sociales, 4
Dow-Jones Industrial Average (DJIA), 181–184
Dramatists, 24, 25
Drug-related violence, 542–543

E

East Asia, 13, 127, 401, 403, 404, 412, 420, 473–495, 499
Easterlin "paradox," 410, 537
Ecological Efficiency, 395–396
Economic, 1, 31, 71, 81, 113–134, 137, 160, 181, 206, 240, 266, 297, 335, 355, 373, 381, 399, 433, 459, 473, 500, 530, 547, 555
Economic and Social Research and Training Center for Islamic Countries Report, 506
Economic characteristics, 566
Economic growth, 10, 113–134, 137, 138, 148, 149, 199, 375, 376, 381, 410, 444, 447, 452, 454, 491, 492, 502–509, 519, 531, 532, 534, 535, 539, 542, 566
Economic indicators, 14, 137, 138, 146–149, 152, 153, 155, 232, 388, 447, 481, 503, 516, 522, 529, 530, 535, 537, 557, 566, 568
Economic opportunities, 275, 520, 533, 534, 547, 550–551, 565
Economic poverty, 533–534, 538, 543, 566
Economic situation, 416, 467, 478, 480, 520, 521, 523, 524, 530–533, 537, 539, 549–551, 553
Economic sub-index, 387, 435, 481–484, 486–489, 558
Economic wellbeing, 190, 192, 196, 206, 220, 297, 465–466
Economies in transition, 433–454
Economist Intelligence Unit (EIU), 186, 188, 189, 191, 195
Economist Intelligence Unit's Quality of Life Index (EIU-QOLI), 195
Ecuador, 529–532, 536, 540, 542
Education, 2, 31, 68, 99, 119, 138, 163, 185, 205, 240, 265–289, 303, 333, 363, 377, 384, 405, 434, 459, 473, 502, 533, 547, 555
Educational indicators, 15, 268
Education Bureau (EDB), 474
Education Index, 384, 507–509
Efficacy Index, 8
Efficiency analysis in economics and management science, 185
Egypt, 7, 504–509, 511, 514, 517, 526, 575
Elder Care Programs, 303, 306
Elderly Commission, 474
El Salvador, 529–532, 536, 540–542
Emotional well-being, 5, 101, 110, 267, 274–276, 285, 319, 357
Empedocles, 26, 31–32, 59
Empedocles of Acragas, 31–32
Employee assistance programs (EAPs), 306, 307
Employment, 6, 73, 145, 152, 169, 195, 265, 266, 269, 270, 273, 275, 276, 281, 282, 286, 287, 303–306, 378, 407, 410, 419, 425, 465, 468, 475, 478, 480, 503, 525, 526, 537, 539, 542, 551
Employment and Economic Development, 266
Employment benefits, 303, 305
Encyclopedia Britannica, 436, 448, 559, 570
Engagement and interest, 140
English, 37, 48, 50, 54, 120, 152, 240, 286, 319, 326, 358, 374, 418, 419, 421, 459–461, 529, 549
Environment, 2, 3, 7, 12, 17, 35, 36, 63, 64, 71–73, 75, 85, 86, 95, 101, 113, 119, 141, 148, 155, 192, 195, 196, 211, 213, 219, 245, 246, 269, 282, 283, 298–300, 307, 337, 341, 344, 346, 350, 355, 357, 359, 362, 365, 375, 399, 405–407, 412, 416, 426, 442, 460, 475, 481, 513, 515, 523, 524, 533, 534, 539, 547, 548, 551

Environmental, 13, 16, 17, 63, 64, 101, 116, 117, 155, 192, 212, 221, 225, 231, 233, 247, 282, 283, 289, 301, 324, 338, 356, 358, 360, 361, 366, 367, 374, 375, 381–383, 395, 401, 402, 415, 434, 435, 437, 451–453, 469, 479, 481–484, 487, 491, 493, 502, 536, 542, 557
Environmental Protection Department, 474, 486
Environmental subindex, 387, 435, 451, 483, 485–489, 558, 565
Epicurus, 26, 27, 34, 35, 44, 60
Epicurus of Samos, 53–59
EPISTEME, 40, 47
Equal weighting, 185, 187–190, 198, 222
Eritrea, 503, 560, 562, 567–569, 571–574
ESCVP, 547, 551
Estes' Index of Social Progress (ISP), 11, 187, 189, 193–194
Ethical Corporate Mission and Culture, 298–300, 307
Ethical Supervisory Behavior, 298, 301
Ethiopia, 400, 407, 413, 417, 419, 421, 503, 560, 562, 566–571, 573, 574
Ethnic differences, 364–365
Eudaimonia, 26, 37, 47–51, 54, 56, 59, 110, 138, 374
Eudaimonic Happiness, 518
Eudaimonic measures of SWB, 402
Eudemian Ethics, 48, 51, 52
EUNOMIA, 47, 48, 56
Eurobarometer, 11
Eurobarometer Survey, 11, 67, 275
European Community Household Panel Study (ECHP), 11
European Quality of Life Survey (EQLS), 11
European Social Survey, 11
European Union, 12, 133, 385, 388, 390, 437, 439, 443, 450, 451, 454, 510, 572
European Values Study (EVS) survey, 11
Euthydemus, 37
Exosystem, 360, 364
Expenditure on health from GDP, 510
Experience-sampling (on-line) measures, 144, 154
Experience sampling methodology (ESM), 359
Experimental Sampling Method (ESM), 160
External buffers, 86–90, 95, 405
Extraordinary happiness, 26
Extraversion, 73, 92, 318, 361
Extrinsics, 317

F

Factor Analysis, 101, 194, 208, 222, 227, 387, 422, 423, 435, 493, 523, 557
Factorial k-means analysis, 218, 222
Failed States Index, 556, 557, 559, 562, 568, 574, 577
Falkland Islands, 530, 556
Family, 5, 24, 71, 93, 102, 113, 143, 161, 182, 212, 243, 267, 297, 331, 355, 373, 403, 436, 466, 473, 515, 533, 549, 558
Family Council, 474
Family structures, 355, 362, 373, 469, 470, 525
Federal Interagency Forum on Child and Family Statistics, 15
Fertility rate, 120, 121, 125, 281, 503
Fitness Programs, 303, 306–307, 348
Flextime, 303
Flourishing, 100–106, 110
Flow of experience, 71, 74

Index

Flow of life-experiences, 71
Food and Health Bureau, 474
Fool's Hell, 23
Fool's Paradise, 23–26, 34, 36, 42, 53, 58, 59
Fordham Index of Social Health, 11, 189
Fordham Institute for Innovation in Social Policy, 194
Forecast trends in social conditions, 15
Foreign Policy magazine, 556, 557, 559
Forgiveness, 108, 319–321
Forgiveness and gratitude, 319, 321
Formative criterion, 216, 217
Forms of observation, 220–221
Foundation for Child Development Child and Youth
    Well-Being Index Project, 196
Four theories of pleasure, 44
Fragmentation, 234, 533, 539, 541, 543
Framingham Heart Longitudinal Study, 93
Freedom House, 195, 433, 434, 436, 440, 448, 513, 555, 556,
    558, 561, 566, 570
French, 408, 460, 519, 529, 530
Friends, 5, 7, 27, 28, 33, 49, 52, 54, 56, 60, 73, 74, 79, 85, 90,
    102, 144, 150, 174, 185, 186, 243, 248, 253, 321, 325,
    338, 339, 341, 344, 346, 349, 355, 357, 359, 360, 376,
    377, 400, 423, 468–470, 478, 479, 493, 515, 537,
    549–551
Frisch Essential Symptom Scale (FESS), 250
Frisch's QOL Theory, 240, 249
Front de Libération Nationale, 519
Functional Ability, 239, 240, 242, 246–249
Function of hedonic experience, 74
Fund for Peace, 556, 557, 559, 561, 562, 564, 577
Future security, 191, 196, 267, 282–283, 285, 289, 416, 417,
    426, 460, 464, 523, 524, 548

G

Gabon, 503, 504, 507, 511, 514, 515, 517
Gambia, 503, 504, 507, 511, 514, 517
GDP per capita, 12, 113–122, 124–134, 225, 381, 384, 397, 401,
    404, 459, 479, 482, 490, 503–505, 511, 512, 531, 532
GDP per capita growth, 531
Gender, 128, 163, 168, 169, 172, 174, 186, 195, 196, 270, 284,
    288, 358, 362, 364, 366, 373–379, 383, 386, 404, 408,
    410, 413, 415, 462, 465, 468, 469, 499, 513, 524, 525,
    537, 550, 551
Gender and QOL, 378
General Health Questionnaire, 475
General life satisfaction index, 484, 486, 488, 489
General Medicine, 239–254
General satisfaction index, 487
General social survey (GSS), 4, 12, 130, 166, 167, 172, 174,
    175, 275, 278, 412, 460, 468, 470
Genuine Progress Indicator (GPI), 11, 189, 190, 192
Geographic change, 124
Geographic distribution, 118–119
Georgia, 303, 437, 445–450, 530, 559, 560, 562, 567–569, 571,
    572, 574
German Socio-Economic Panel Study, 6, 92
German Socio-Economic Panel Survey, 130
Gini coefficient, 192, 194, 447, 491, 532, 566, 568
Gini Index, 435, 459, 460, 465, 558

Glaucon, 38
Global Assessment of Functioning (GAF) approach in the
    DSM-III-R, 101
Global Assessment of Functioning (GAF) Scale, 248
Global corruption barometer, 448, 566, 569, 570
Global Corruption Perceptions Index, 448, 566
Global Freedom of the World Survey, 513
Global interconnectedness, 509
Globalization (globalisation), 12, 352, 381–397, 401, 433, 492,
    534, 539
Globalization model, 333, 335, 352
Global multi-item measures, 413–414
Global single item measures, 408–409, 411
Gorgias, 32, 40, 41
Government, 2, 47, 100, 127, 137, 159, 183, 240, 266, 303,
    332, 376, 400, 434, 459, 474, 510, 534, 547, 557
Government of Hong Kong Special Administrative Region, 474
Government performance index, 484, 486–489
Gratitude, 54, 108, 109, 319–321
Grenada, 529–531
Grenadines, 529–531
Gross National Product, 138, 147
Group incentive programs, 302
Guaraní, 529
Guatemala, 12, 529–532, 534–536, 540–542
Guinea, 504, 507, 509, 511, 514, 517, 560, 567–569, 571, 574
Guinea-Bissau, 504, 505, 507, 510, 511, 514, 517, 560, 562,
    568, 572, 573, 575
Guyana, 503, 504, 507, 511, 513, 514, 517, 529–531, 535

H

Haiti, 529–532, 534–536, 556, 557, 560, 562, 567–569, 571,
    574, 575
Half way House, 516
Handbook of Psychiatric Measures, 242
Happiness, 6, 24, 63–76, 83, 99, 113, 138, 174, 183, 239, 267,
    297, 313, 332, 374, 382, 401, 501, 531, 577
Happiness Economics, 410–411
Happiness Ingredients, 246–247
Happy Life Expectancy, 187, 190, 194
Happy Life Expectancy (HLE) for Developed, 394
HARMONIA, 29
Hawthorne studies, 3
HDI. *See* The Human Development Index (HDI)
Health, 1, 33, 63, 99, 113, 138, 173, 184, 205, 239–254, 267,
    303, 313, 333, 355, 373, 383, 400, 434, 459, 473, 501,
    533, 547, 555
Health and population, 5, 502
Health and Quality of Life Outcomes, 14
Healthcare costs, 503
Health-Related Indicators, 535–536
Health-related QoL, 3, 8, 13, 14, 16, 248
Health-related QoL assessment, 16
Health Status, 3, 16, 103, 193, 274–276, 284, 287, 320, 374,
    375, 379, 387, 408, 435, 478, 557, 558
Health USA, 15, 17
Health Utility Index, 375
Hector, 27
Hedonic and eudaimonic well-being, 100
Hedonic level of affect, 66

586   Index

Hell, 23, 53, 500
Heraclitus, 25, 26, 30–32, 54, 59
Heraclitus of Ephesus, 30–31
Hesiod, 25, 27, 28, 59
Hesiod of Ascra, 28
High income nations, 131
High-involvement Programs, 298, 300
Hippias, 32
Historical development, 1
History of Islam, 500
History of the Quality of Life (QOL) Concept, 240
Home, 13, 25, 93, 118, 141, 161, 183, 240, 269, 303, 333, 364, 377, 407, 459, 474, 510, 548, 565
Home Affairs Bureau, 474
Homeostasis, 79–96, 399, 461, 467
Homeostatically Protected Mood, 91, 93, 95, 96
Homeostatic Theory, 93, 378
Home ownership, 339, 340, 343, 466, 548, 551
Homer, 25–27, 40, 49, 59
Homer's Odyssey Bk XI, 26
Homophily, 279
Honduras, 12, 529–532, 534, 536
Hong Kong Council of Social Service, 475, 480, 481, 483
Hong Kong Federation of Youth Groups, 475
Hong Kong Polytechnic University, 477, 479
Hong Kong Sustainable Development Index, 475
Hospitalization/medical/disability insurance, 305
Hot indicators, 221
Household and gender equity, 386
Household composition, 88, 469
Household, Income and Labour Dynamics in Australia (HILDA) Survey, 460
Housing, 9, 14, 15, 38, 119, 123, 143, 149, 168, 169, 185, 186, 189, 190, 192–195, 198, 212, 239, 245, 275, 282, 333, 335, 338–340, 342, 344, 352, 406, 407, 426, 434, 465, 466, 468, 470, 473, 478–484, 486–489, 491, 503, 505, 521, 522, 551
HPMood, 91–93, 95, 96, 464, 467
Human capabilities, 509, 547, 550
Human Development Index (HDI), 11, 114, 185, 187, 189, 190, 268, 382–388, 399, 404, 409, 459, 476, 489, 492, 506–508, 522, 535
Human Development Report, 383, 384, 459, 476, 489, 492, 505, 506, 508, 509, 512, 515, 516, 518
Humanity, 107, 108, 318, 513, 526, 577
Human Poverty Index, 385, 409, 506–508
Human Relations Movement, 3
Human Well-Being Index (HWI), 382, 385–387
Human Well-being Index (HWI) for Developed, 386
HWI. *See* Human Well-being Index (HWI)

I

Ibn Masquawayh, 501
Iliad, 27
Illiteracy, 435, 505, 509, 522, 535
Image of Muslims and Islam, 500
Impending Disaster Scenario, 516
Income and happiness, 12, 302
Income Distribution, 410, 459, 530, 532–535, 539, 542, 543
Income security, 277, 555

INDEC. *See* Statistic National Institute (INDEC)
Independent Commission against Corruption, 474
Index of current economic conditions, 484, 486–489
Index of Economic Well-Being (IEWB), 190, 192
Index of Social Health (ISH), 11, 187–190, 194, 268
Index of Social Progress, 11, 187, 189, 190, 193, 194, 268, 382, 387, 434–437, 557–559, 562, 577
India, 70, 124–128, 345, 403, 413, 420, 433, 434, 440, 556, 564
Indicator, 1, 29, 72, 95, 99, 113, 137, 159–177, 181, 201, 239, 267, 297, 313, 333, 355, 375, 382, 399, 434, 460, 474, 500, 529, 547, 557
Indicator of press criticism, 487
Indicators in a system, 12, 202, 212–214
Indicators of Social Development, 435, 474
Indicators of Social Development Project, 474, 477–480, 483, 490–495
Indigenous languages, 529
Individualism, 377, 402, 403, 413, 414
Indonesia, 433, 440, 503, 504, 506–508, 511, 513–515, 517, 556, 564
Inequality in Sweden, 4
Infant mortality, 137, 194, 196, 435, 436, 482, 535, 558, 567
Informant reports, 144, 155
Inner manufacturing of feeling, 74–75
Inner process of evaluation, 75
Innovative Benefits, 307
Instant satisfaction, 65
Instrumental materialism, 352
Insurance Benefits, 305
Interest rates, 140, 153, 340, 343, 465, 467, 468
Intergenerational effects, 268–269
Internal buffers, 90–91, 95
International Federation of Red Cross, 436, 558
International Federation of Red Cross and Red Crescent Societies, 436, 558
International Living Index, 268
International quality-of-life (IQOL) orientation, 350
International Social Security Association, 436, 558, 559
International Society for Quality of Life Research, 14, 375
International Society for Quality of Life Research [ISOQOL], 14, 375
International Society for Quality of life Studies[ISQOLS], 10, 13, 254, 375
Internet, 14, 115, 118, 119, 151, 163, 164, 169–171, 177, 197, 213, 334, 345–347, 382, 388, 469, 494, 508, 516, 526
Internet well-being, 345
Interpretative and evaluative models, 205, 209, 211–212
Intimate Relationships, 110, 281–285, 289
Intrinsic and Extrinsic religious orientations, 316
Intrinsic-Extrinsic Religiousness, 316–317
Intrinsics, 4, 15, 287, 300, 316–318, 321, 509
Iran, 504–508, 511, 514, 516, 517, 526, 556, 560–562, 566–571, 574
Iraq, 439, 504, 507, 508, 510, 511, 514, 517, 560–562, 567–572, 574, 575
Islamicity, 499
Islamic Perspective, 500–502
Islamic salvation Front, 519
Item-Order Effects, 150–151, 155
Item Response Theory, 145, 151, 222, 358, 422
Izdihar, 516

J

Jamaica, 529–531, 541
Job Characteristics Model, 300
Job Enrichment Programs, 298, 300–301
Job satisfaction, 9, 17, 65, 76, 147, 186, 189, 194, 242, 297–302, 307, 318, 479
Job Sharing, 303, 304, 307
Johnston's (1988) QoL Index, 268
Joint representation of indicators, 218–219
Jordan, 504, 507, 511, 514, 515, 517
Journal of Clinical Epidemiology, 14
Journal of Macromarketing, 10
Journal of the American Medical Association, 14
Justice, 4, 10, 15, 27, 28, 30, 34, 38, 39, 45–49, 57, 59, 72, 107, 108, 301, 409, 525, 526, 555, 561, 577

K

KALLIPOLIS, 38
KALON, 53
Kampuchea, 556
Kazakhstan, 437, 445–450, 499, 503, 504, 507, 509–511, 514, 517
KCI. *See* Kids count index (KCI)
Kids Count Index (KCI), 191, 196
Knowledge, 8, 15, 16, 24, 32, 35, 36, 39, 40, 42–44, 51, 54, 55, 58, 107, 108, 121, 127, 129, 148, 168, 181, 183, 186, 189, 192, 213, 231–234, 265–266, 278, 279, 282, 283, 285–289, 300, 325, 339, 340, 343–345, 348, 349, 383, 384, 386, 501, 509, 513, 538
Koran, 501
Korea barometer surveys, 12
Korea, North, 560–562, 564, 566–569, 571–574
KOSMOS, 29
Kuwait, 504–507, 511, 513, 514, 517, 518
Kyrgyzstan, 445–450, 504, 507, 509–511, 514, 517

L

Laboratory of Educational Processes and Social Context, 522
Lack of physical exercise, 103, 361
Lancet, 14
Languishing, 101–104, 106, 108, 109
Laos, 437, 440, 444, 450, 453, 456
Lasting satisfaction with one's life-as-a-whole, 66
Latin America, 12, 125, 128, 401, 403, 410, 412, 437, 439, 440, 529–543, 548, 552, 557, 559–561
Latinobarometro, 12, 531, 532, 537
Laws, 30, 33, 36, 47, 59, 72, 374, 385, 464, 478, 481, 483, 490, 503, 525, 526, 542, 552, 557
Lazarsfeld's model, 205
LCI. *See* Netherlands' Living Conditions Index (LCI)
Learned effectiveness, 276, 278, 283, 286, 288
Least developing, 437, 441, 446–449, 453, 559
Least developing countries, 559, 560, 562, 572
Lebanon, 503, 504, 507, 510, 511, 514, 515, 517, 560, 562, 566–569, 571, 572, 574
Legitimacy blackmail, 515
Legitimation of knowledge and status, 266
Le plan de développement 2010-2014, 521
Le Programme de Soutien à la Croissance Economique, 521

Le programme de soutien à la croissance économique, 521
Letter to Herodotus, 54, 55
Letter to Menoeceus, 54, 55
Letter to Monoeceus, 56
Letter to Pythocles, 54
Levels of communication, 221
Lewinian Lifespace Model, 83
Liberia, 560, 567–569, 571, 572, 574
Libya, 504, 505, 507, 511, 514, 516, 517, 526, 562, 575
Life-ability of the individual, 73
Life-ability of the person, 63–64
Life-chances, 24, 63, 64, 71–74, 265, 266, 268
Life-course perspective, 231
Life expectancy, 1, 99, 113, 119–121, 125–127, 129, 159, 184, 185, 187, 189, 190, 192, 194, 195, 225, 267, 277, 376, 377, 383, 384, 394, 395, 476, 484, 486–489, 503, 506, 510–512, 535
Life insurance, 305
Life satisfaction, 5, 52, 64, 82, 101, 113, 137, 174, 196, 233, 239, 267, 297, 314, 332, 355, 375, 388, 399, 476, 503, 536, 547
Life satisfaction approach, 241–242, 246
Life satisfaction approach to happiness, 241–242, 246
Lifespan effect, 377–378
Limits of economic measures, 146–147
Literacy, 126, 127, 189, 192, 194, 267, 268, 280, 285, 307, 378, 384, 435, 446, 505–509, 513, 522, 535, 558, 566, 567
Livability of the environment, 72
Lived Poverty Index (LPI), 13
Living conditions, 12, 23, 63, 75, 76, 82, 123, 195, 204, 230, 231, 239, 245, 249, 251, 268, 382, 391, 411, 414, 422, 426, 473, 521, 549, 550
LOGOS, 30
LPI. *See* Lived poverty index (LPI)
Lyceum, 48, 54

M

MacArthur foundation's midlife in the united states survey (MIDUS), 101, 103, 104
Macrosystem, 360, 364, 367
Magna moralia, 48
Maintenance satisfaction, 336–338, 342
Major depression, 100, 103, 244
MAKARIOS, 54
Malawi, 560, 562, 566–569, 571–574
Malaysia, 440, 504, 506–508, 511, 514, 517, 518
Maldives, 504, 507, 509, 511, 514, 515, 517
Mali, 503, 504, 506, 507, 509–511, 513, 514, 517–519
Management, 3–4, 8–9, 14, 16, 17, 82–85, 105, 185, 202, 210, 211, 213, 225, 273, 276, 278, 282, 283, 297–301, 303, 304, 307, 475
Managing their own business, 549
Marginalization of ethnic groups, 540
Maritime transportation, 506
Marketer's orientation model, 350
Marketing, 9–10, 14–17, 213, 331, 350, 353
Marriage, 5, 9, 65, 72, 75, 76, 104, 106, 138, 141, 142, 169, 174, 186, 247, 281, 289, 377, 406, 410, 412, 413, 426, 452, 478, 482, 501, 523, 537
Marriage dissolution, 281

Materialism model, 333, 351–352
Material well-being, 5, 10, 134, 186, 191, 195, 196, 233, 240, 267, 269–274, 285, 288, 357, 407, 473
Mauritania, 503, 504, 507, 511, 514, 517, 519, 556
MBP. *See* Money magazine's "best places" (MBP)
MDS. *See* Multidimensional scaling (MDS)
Meaning and purpose in life, 101, 314, 316, 319, 402, 518
Meaning of a happy life, 538–539
Measurement artifacts, 144, 150–152, 155
Measurement of overall quality of life, 181–199
Measuring educational attainment, 284–285
Measuring subjective QoL in developing countries, 408
Medical care, 14, 24, 164, 333, 335, 459
Medical outcomes study, 103
Medicare Australia, 459
Memory, 49, 53, 54, 68, 91, 141, 144, 151, 155, 160, 162, 198, 415
Mental calculus, 75
Mental health, 35, 64, 100, 113, 139, 239, 313, 348, 361, 374, 473, 536
Merging indicators, 219–221
Mesosystem, 330, 364
Mexico, 7, 404, 409–411, 422, 425, 433, 439, 440, 529–532, 534, 536–538, 540–543, 559
Michalos' (1980-82) North American Social Report, 268
Microsystem, 360–363, 367
Middle-East, 25, 412–413, 499, 506, 516, 575
Middle performing countries, 434, 441, 443, 453
Millennium development account, 572
Millennium development campaign, 439, 440, 464, 572
Miringoff's index of social health, 268
Models with formative indicators, 207–209
Mode of administration, 151, 418
Modern economic growth, 113–134
Money Magazine's "Best Places" (MBP), 193
Monitor changes over time, 14
Morbidity, 139, 212, 240, 248, 267, 276, 277, 375–378
Morocco, 504, 505, 507, 511, 514, 517, 522, 556
Mozambique, 503, 504, 506, 507, 510, 511, 514, 517
Muhammad, 500
Multi-attribute compositional model, 223
Multi-attribute decision making, 223
Multidimensional measurement
      of religiousness/spirituality, 315
Multidimensional scaling (MDS), 170, 218, 222, 290
Multidimensional students' life satisfaction scale, 357
Multi-level approach, 229–231
Multinational time budget study, 160
Multiple discrepancies theory (MDT), 6, 7, 92
Muslim identity, 499
Myanmar, 512, 556, 560, 562, 564, 566–569, 571, 574
Mystery religion, 26

N

Nàhuatl, 529
National Accounts Of Well-being, 137–156
National government, 8, 155, 185, 186, 198, 549
National Health Interview Survey, 276
National Income and Product Accounts, 2
National Longitudinal Survey of Youth (NLSY), 271

National Planning Council Association, 13
National Quality Research Center, 332
National Well-being Accounts (NWBA), 137–138, 187, 193
National Well-Being Index (NWI), 12, 196, 376, 378, 392, 416, 460, 461, 522–525, 548
Nations, 6, 10, 12, 15, 16, 72, 103, 113, 133, 149, 229, 267, 366, 388, 393, 420, 454, 460, 526, 555, 566, 575
Nation-states, 193, 452, 555–557, 559
`Native' scales, 404, 420, 422–423
Need Satisfaction Model, 333, 335, 343–345
Neighborhood characteristics, 280, 363
Nepal, 410, 413, 560, 567–571, 573, 574
Netherlands' Living Conditions Index (LCI), 195, 198, 268
Neuroticism, 92, 247, 379
Nevis, 529–531
New Economics Foundation, 476
New England Journal of Medicine, 14
Nicaragua, 529–532, 534–536, 542
Nicomachean Ethics, 48, 50–52, 374
Nicomachean Ethics, 48, 50–52, 374
Nicomachus, 48
Niger, 503–507, 509, 511, 514, 517, 519, 560, 562, 566–569, 571, 573, 574
Nigeria, 401, 409, 503–505, 511, 513, 514, 517, 556, 560, 566–569, 571, 574
NOMOI, 33, 34, 47
NOMOS, 33
North Korea, 561, 562, 564, 566, 572
Number-Use and Other Scaling Effects, 151
NWBA. *See* National Well-Being Accounts (NWBA)
NWI. *See* National Well-being Index (NWI)

O

Objective Characteristics and Living Conditions, 245
Objective indicators, 4, 5, 113–117, 119, 128, 134, 189, 194, 195, 232, 267, 382, 396, 460, 474, 502, 536, 537
Objective Measurement of Quality of Life, 382–383
OBJECTIVE TIME, 159, 160
Objective Time, 159, 160
Objective Versus Subjective Measures, 152
Occupation, 168, 169, 276, 282, 286
OCSC. *See* Overall Consumer Satisfaction-Composite (OCSC)
Odysseus, 26, 27
Odyssey, 26, 27
OECD. *See* Organization for Economic Cooperation and Development (OECD)
Oedipus at Colonus, 25
OIC. *See* Organization of Islamic Conference (OIC)
Older Sophists, 32
Olympian gods, 28
Oman, 504, 507, 511, 514, 516, 517, 525, 526
On-Line Versus Recall Measures, 141
Ontogenic, 360, 366
Open-ended questions and interviews, 144
Openness, 92, 105, 121, 318, 324, 400, 518, 521
Optimal weights for a QOL index, 189
Orators, 24, 25
Organization for Economic Cooperation and Development (OECD), 4, 233, 266, 268–270, 285, 289, 399, 436, 443, 450, 451, 454, 459, 513, 558, 559

Index

Organization of Islamic Conference (OIC), 499, 500, 503, 505, 506, 508, 512, 513
Orphic/Bacchic, 26
Orphism, 25–27
OSA. *See* Secret Armed Organization (OSA)
OSL. *See* Overall Satisfaction with Life (OSL)
Output, 83, 101, 113, 159, 169, 173, 175, 177, 185, 194, 195, 202, 212, 267, 365, 375, 385
Outputs from time inputs, 173, 175–176
Overall Consumer Satisfaction-Composite (OCSC), 335
Overall satisfaction, 65, 242, 245–247, 332, 335, 336, 348, 388, 389, 391, 475
Overall Satisfaction with Life (OSL) for Developed Countries, 388–389
Own business, 549, 550

P

Pakistan, 365, 503–505, 507, 508, 511, 514, 515, 517, 560, 562, 566–571, 574
Palestine Refugees, 512
Palestinian territories, 504, 507, 556
Panama, 529–532, 536
Paradise, 23, 69
Paraguay, 529–532, 534, 536
Parallel structures, 298, 299, 307
Parent attachment, 361, 362
Parent-child relations, 362
Parenthood, 169, 251, 281–282, 289
Participation in decision-making, 298, 300
Participatory research, 400, 406, 408
Part-time work arrangements, 303, 304
Paternalism, 152–153, 513
Paved runways, 506, 508
Pay and incentive plans, 298, 302
PCA. *See* Principal component analysis (PCA)
PCI. *See* Perceived corruption index (PCI)
Peer attachment, 361, 362
Per Capita GDP, 225, 479, 482, 503–505, 530
Per capita income, 114, 120, 132, 134, 137, 267, 399, 409, 447, 530–533, 535, 537, 556, 566
Perceived corruption index (PCI), 435, 513, 558
Perceived quality of life in Europe and US, 390, 391
Perceived quality of peer support, 362
Perceived Value Model, 333, 335, 345
Performance analysis, 222
Performance feedback, 298, 301
Pericle, 31, 32
Personal and national well-being (PWI/NWI), 12, 93–95, 149, 267, 357, 378, 388, 392–393, 396, 404, 405, 415–417, 420, 422, 426, 460–464, 466, 468, 522–525, 548
Personal computers, 171, 332, 508
Personality, 73, 74, 83, 91, 92, 141, 147, 151, 155, 156, 247, 286, 314, 316–319, 322–324, 351, 357, 360, 361, 364, 366, 374, 379, 398, 409
Personal life, 196, 478, 479, 549–551
Personal relations, 12, 79, 101, 196, 275, 277, 314, 366, 416, 417, 422, 423, 426, 460, 473, 523, 524, 541, 549, 550
Personal safety, 30, 48, 249, 267, 282–283, 285, 289, 416, 417, 426, 473, 481, 482, 523, 524
Personal transportation, 14, 338, 339, 344, 345

Personal well-being, 113, 319, 378, 379, 392, 393, 522, 531
Personal Well-being Index (PWI), 12, 357, 388, 391–393
Personal Wellbeing Index and National Wellbeing Index, 12, 196, 393, 461, 548
Personal Well-being Index-School Children-3rd Ed, 357
Peru, 400, 407, 413, 417, 423, 426, 439, 440, 529–532, 536, 540–542
Phaedo, 31, 38
Philebus, 41, 42
Physical and Spiritual Model, 83
Physical well-being, 473
PHYSIS, 33, 34, 47
Plato, 5, 25–27, 31–33, 35–48, 50, 52–54, 56, 57, 59, 106, 501, 577
Plato of Athens, 35–48
Pleasant and unpleasant events, 74
Poems of Hesiod, 28
Poets, 24, 25, 27, 38
Policymaking, 8, 138, 140, 153–154
Policy Uses of National Accounts of Well-being, 146
Political characteristics, 566–570
Political citizen, 549, 551
Political democracy, 121, 127–130
Political Freedom, 71, 195, 196, 440, 447, 448, 551, 554–556, 569, 570
Political freedom, 71, 195, 196, 440, 447, 448, 551, 554–556, 569, 570
Political impact, 221
Political indicators, 121–122, 128, 129, 448, 557, 569, 570
Political Life and Freedom, 510–516
Political sovereignty, 555, 556
Politics, 8, 10, 25–27, 33, 48, 52, 56, 185, 186, 199, 397, 412, 500, 572
Pollution, 63, 115, 119, 128, 129, 134, 138, 149, 192, 199, 212, 243, 412, 434, 474, 475, 478, 479, 486, 540, 541
Popular morality, 24
Population growth, 435, 444, 446, 503, 519, 525, 548, 567
Portuguese, 364, 365, 529, 532
Positive and negative affect, 6, 76, 193, 241, 244, 298, 339, 345, 350, 403, 423
Positive emotions, 99, 100, 104–106, 110, 139, 140, 142
Positive psychology, 93, 99, 100, 107, 110, 239, 242, 246, 249, 252–254, 319, 321
Possession of material things, 335
Possession satisfaction, 336, 337
Possession satisfaction model, 333, 335–336
Poverty, 2, 24, 84, 99, 145, 192, 225, 266, 282, 355, 366, 379, 382, 385, 387, 400, 433, 476, 502, 530, 547, 566
Prayer fulfillment, 318
Prediction of Outcomes, 144
2003-present Bureau of Labor Statistic's ATUS, 168
President Bouteflika, 519–522
`Presocratic' philosophers, 25, 31
Press criticism index, 484, 486, 488, 489, 491
Press freedom index, 484, 486–489
Priam, 27
Principal component analysis (PCA), 208, 221–223, 227, 228
Process of measurement, 201–202
Prodicus, 32
Productive efficiency, 278
Productive well-being, 473

Profit-sharing plans, 302
Promotion from within, 301–302
Protagoras, 12, 26, 27, 32–33, 37, 39–41, 59
Protagoras of Abdera, 32–33
Psychiatry, 241, 247, 248, 252
Public enlightenment through social reporting, 15
Public goods, 555
Public Opinion Program of University of Hong Kong, 483, 490
Public Policy and Social Issues Division of the American Marketing Association (AMA), 9
Public safety, 352, 412, 481, 482, 549, 550
Public transportation, 333, 352, 548
PWI/NWI. *See* Personal and national well-being (PWI/NWI)
Pythagoras, 26, 28–30, 42, 54, 59, 501
Pythagoras of Samos, 28–30

Q
QALYs. *See* Quality Adjusted Life Years (QALYs)
Qatar, 503–507, 510, 511, 513, 514, 517, 518
Quality Adjusted Life Years (QALYs), 8, 374, 375
Quality Circles, 298, 299
Quality model, 333, 334, 352
Quality of life (QoL)
    and its components, 383, 492
    in the country, 547, 550, 551, 553
    and health, 2, 8, 13
    definition of health, 2
    measurement, 183, 223, 359, 399–401, 408, 409
    QOL index, 11, 181, 189, 193, 195–199, 267, 268, 411, 483, 485–487, 490, 491, 493, 494
    in South Africa, 10
Quality of Life Research, 2–17, 29, 52, 60, 99, 100, 267, 308, 333, 367, 374, 375, 396, 399–402, 405, 407, 408, 415, 423, 474, 475, 494, 495, 502, 549
Quality of Life Research Centre in Copenhagen, 374
Quality of society, 63, 72–73
Quality of work life (QWL) programs, 3, 4, 8, 9, 14, 16, 17, 297–308
Quechua, 529
QWL movement, 297
QWL programs. *See* Quality of work life (QWL) programs
QWL Programs Related to the Work Environment, 298–300

R
Race, 31, 32, 105, 168, 169, 191, 196, 271, 284, 288, 320, 344, 364, 366, 374
Rate of time preference, 277, 287
Reaction time, 144
Real Hell, 23
Real Paradise, 23, 26, 33, 34, 36, 42, 53, 58
Recent Social Trends, 2
Red Crescent Societies, 436, 558
Reducing data structure, 203, 215–216, 229
Redundancy, 194, 221, 421
Reflected appraisal, 76
Reflective criterion, 216, 217
Relationships, 3, 39, 73, 79, 99, 113, 137, 175, 185, 202, 243, 266, 298, 314, 336, 355, 375, 382, 402, 453, 473, 506, 531, 548, 556

Relationship satisfaction, 470
Relationship status, 465, 466
Relative Utility Theory, 516
Relay Assembly Test Room experiment, 3
Religiosity, 313–326, 522–524, 549, 550
Religious Commitment Inventory-10, 315
Religious coping, 317–318, 323
Religious Orientation Scale (ROS), 316, 317
Religious Problem Solving Scale (RPSS), 317
Report to the Nation on Crime and Justice, 15
Republic, 5, 12, 15, 38, 44–47
Republic of the Congo, 556, 562, 564, 566, 572
Resource problems, 541
Respect of religious diversity, 551
Response-styles, 69, 462, 524
Retirement benefits, 303, 305
Review Panel of the Pilot Project on Child Fatality Review, 474
Rhetoric, 28, 32, 33, 48, 49, 411
Role clarity, 17, 298, 301
ROS. *See* Religious Orientation Scale (ROS)
RPSS. *See* Religious Problem Solving Scale (RPSS)
Rule of Law, 72, 478, 481, 483, 490, 525, 557
Russell Sage Foundation, 4
Russian Federation, 433, 437, 441, 442, 444, 451, 452, 454
Russian Longitudinal Monitoring Survey, 12
Rwanda, 556

S
Safety, 2, 5, 30, 47, 48, 71, 123, 138, 191, 196, 249, 267, 282–283, 285, 289, 315, 334, 339, 341, 344, 345, 350, 352, 357, 379, 411, 412, 416, 417, 426, 439, 459, 460, 462, 464, 473, 474, 481, 482, 523, 524, 542, 548–551
Saint Kitts, 529–531
Saint Lucia, 529–531
Saint Vincent, 529–531
Satisfaction in domains of life, 537
Satisfaction in non-work life, 302
Satisfaction in work life, 298–299
Satisfaction of basic needs, 333, 352, 407, 411
Satisfaction with health, 549, 550
Satisfaction with life as a whole, 1, 10, 35, 65, 66, 75, 79, 382, 408, 409, 412, 413, 423, 461, 464, 532, 550
Satisfaction with life in developed, 390
Satisfaction with Life Scale (SWLS), 67, 95, 152, 357, 358, 404, 408, 413–414, 416, 423
Satisfaction with possessions, 331
Satisfaction with quality of life, 339, 547, 550, 551
Satisfaction with shopping, 331
Satisfaction with the quality of life in the country, 551
Satisfaction with wealth, 466–467
Saudi Arabia, 504, 507, 508, 511, 514, 517, 518
School-aged children, 373
School perceptions and engagement, 363
School performance, 242, 269, 362–363
Science indicators, 15
SDI. *See* Social development index (SDI)
Secret Armed Organization (OSA), 519
Segmentation effect, 9
Selecting indicators, 221–222
Selection, 76, 139, 210, 212, 213, 221, 223, 226, 227, 232, 266, 267, 281, 284, 289, 340, 350, 436, 464

Index

Selection bias, 284, 288
Senegal, 504, 507, 509, 511, 513, 514, 517
Serra Leone, 510
SES. *See* Socioeconomis status (SES)
Severance pay, 306
SF-36. *See* Short-form 36-item health survey (SF-36)
Shopping satisfaction model, 333, 335
Short-Form 36-item Health Survey (SF-36), 13, 374, 375, 400, 402, 404, 414, 417, 418, 420, 428
Sick leave, 305, 306
Sierra Leone, 384, 386, 503, 504, 506, 508–511, 514, 517, 518, 556, 560, 561, 564, 567–569, 571, 573–575
Simonides, 27
Simultaneous aggregation of indicators and units, 218
SINET: Social Indicators Network News, 15
Skeptics, 24, 144
SLs. *See* Social Leaders (SLs)
Smiling and behavior, 144
Smoking cigarettes, 103
Social and Cultural Report, 15
Social capital, 28, 47, 48, 56, 59, 160, 161, 269, 278–280, 284, 289, 463, 470, 491
Social change, 1, 2, 15, 125–127, 211, 525, 526
Social Chaos, 387, 435–437, 442, 451–453, 557, 558, 565
Social Chaos Sub-index, 387, 435, 436, 558
Social conditions, 11, 15, 16, 35, 155, 196, 375, 382, 416, 460, 476, 523, 524, 547, 549, 550, 557
Social desirability, 68, 69, 151, 167, 176, 272, 322, 359
Social development index (SDI), 474, 475, 479–484, 489–495
Social health, 11, 16, 187–190, 194, 268, 423
Social indicators, 4, 13, 16, 159–177, 184, 434, 436, 441, 477, 481, 559, 577
Social indicators movement, 4, 10, 11, 14, 15, 52, 240, 245, 408
Social indicators research, 4–7, 10, 11, 40, 48, 157
Social Indicators Research Book Series, 10, 157
Social Indicator Surveys, 477
Social inequalities, 177, 265, 547, 550–551
Socialization, 265, 273, 286, 315, 335
Social Leaders (SLs), 387, 434, 441, 443–445, 447, 450, 454
Socially least developing countries, 441
Social programs and events, 303, 306, 307
Social resources, 104, 106, 279, 283, 289, 302, 410
Social Science Research Council Center for Coordination of Research on Social Indicators, 4
Social security, 13, 72, 150, 305, 436, 459, 535, 551, 553
Social trends, 2, 15
Social Weather Stations, 11
Social well-being, 2, 36, 101, 249, 375, 382, 406, 477, 502
Socioeconomis status (SES), 207, 269, 274, 280, 282, 284, 364
Socrates, 25, 26, 28, 31, 33, 35, 37–47, 57, 64, 106
Socrates' trial, Apology, 26
Somalia, 187, 441, 504, 508, 511, 514, 517, 556, 557, 560, 564, 566–569, 571, 574
Sophists, 25, 31–33, 37
Sophist tradition, 502
Sophocles, 25
South Africa, 10, 186, 399, 401, 410, 411, 413, 425, 561
South African QoL Trends project, 411
Southern Africa, 411, 441, 564
Southern Regions of the United States, 2
South-South relationships, 576
South Sudan, 556

Soviet Union, 433, 452, 453, 499, 505, 509, 510, 559, 565
Spanish, 358, 364, 417, 529, 532, 549, 552
Speusippus, 37, 48
Spillover, 9, 298–299, 302, 347
Spillover between job satisfaction and life satisfaction, 298
Spillover effect, 9
Spirituality, 137, 267, 313, 414, 473, 518, 523, 548
Spirituality/religion, 267, 548
Spirituality/religiosity, 549, 550
Spiritual transcendence, 318–319
Spiritual transcendence scale (STS), 318, 319
Stability Over Time and Responsiveness to Major Life Events, 145
Standard of living, 9, 17, 121, 154, 191, 196, 239, 240, 243, 249, 253, 267, 269–274, 285, 302, 335, 351, 364, 374, 375, 383, 384, 416, 417, 426, 460, 464, 466–468, 506, 517, 518, 523, 524, 531, 537–538, 543, 548
Standards of fulfillment, 245–246, 249, 251
States of Central and Eastern Europe, 436, 437, 441, 450–451, 454
Statistical Commission of the United Nations, 4
Statistic National Institute (INDEC), 547
Statistics Canada's National Survey of Giving, Volunteering, and Participation, 278
Status indicators, 220
Stockholm International Peace and Research Institute, 436, 558
Stockholm International Peace and Research Institute and Transparency International, 558
Stoics, 24, 54
Stress index, 484, 486–489
Structural models approach, 229
Structure of Well-Being Concepts, 142
Students' Life Satisfaction Scale, 357–359
Subjective enjoyment of life, 64–65, 76
Subjective indicators, 5, 13, 113, 130, 134, 159, 189, 196, 204, 212, 229, 232, 355, 375, 378, 388, 396, 400, 412, 474, 516–518, 548
Subjective indicators of quality of life, 375, 516–518
Subjective Measurement of Quality of Life, 388
Subjective quality of life, 174, 313, 335, 382, 399, 400, 408, 420, 423, 476, 478–481, 490–495, 525
Subjective time, 159, 173–176
Subjective time measures, 173–176
Subjective well-being (SWB), 1, 63, 100, 137, 196, 230, 239, 297, 365, 375, 382, 401, 478, 516, 529
Subjective well-being indicators, 529, 536–537
Sub-Saharan African states, 509
Substance Abuse and Mental Health Services Administration, 104
Successful aging, 99, 240, 241, 275
Sudan, 441, 505, 508, 512, 514, 517, 519, 556, 560, 562, 567–569, 571, 574
Sum of pleasures and pains, 66, 75
Sunni Al-Ghazali, 502
Supplemental pay benefits, 303, 305–306
Suriname, 503, 505, 506, 508, 512, 513, 515, 518, 529–531, 534
Survey of Income and Program Participation, 4, 272
Survey of Living Conditions in the Arctic (SLiCA), 12
Survey: Political Rights, 513, 515
1990s U.S. Time-Diary Collections, 168
SWB. *See* Subjective well-being (SWB)
Swedish ULF system, 268
SWLS. *See* Satisfaction with Life Scale (SWLS)
Syria, 505, 506, 508, 512, 515, 518

T

Tajikistan, 437, 444–450, 499, 505, 508–510, 512, 513, 515, 518, 556, 575
Tandem analysis, 218, 222
TCEI. *See* Total Consumption Expenditure Index (TCEI)
Teamwork, 104, 108, 298, 299, 301, 307
TECHNE, 40, 53
Techniques for aggregating indicators, 223–229
Telephone lines, 508
TELOS, 33, 37, 40
Temperament, 7, 75, 145, 153, 154, 357, 366
Temperance, 39, 107, 108
Terminal materialism, 352
Thales, 28, 54
Theognis, 25, 26, 31
Theogony, 28
Theories X and Y, 4
The Quality of Life in Korea, 12
The Republic, 5, 38, 44–47
"Third" Variables, 244, 272, 283–284
Time Crunch Scale, 175
Time-Diary Methodology, 160–164
Time-diary studies, 161
Time orientation, 277, 283
Time pressure, 173–175, 307
Time series, 1, 4, 11, 15, 18, 105, 113–134, 168, 187–189, 194–196, 202, 221, 384, 392, 557, 577
Time use, 159–177, 190, 193, 411
Tobago, 529–531
Togo, 70, 505, 508, 509, 512, 515, 518
Top-Down, 65, 76, 153–156, 184, 207, 229, 247–248, 298, 357, 409, 411
Top-experience, 65
Total Consumption Expenditure Index (TCEI), 334
Total expenditure on health, 510–512
Total Quality Management (TQM), 298, 301
Toward a Social Report, 2
TQM. *See* Total quality management (TQM)
Traditional approach, 203, 215–218
Tragedy, 25–27, 316, 525
Trait negative affect, 275
Transcendence, 107, 108, 134, 319
Translation Across Languages, 151–152
Transparency International, 515, 558
Transparent International Corruption Perceptions Index, 492
Travel and tourism services, 347, 349
Trend indicators, 221
Trends and Patterns in Time Use, 168–169
Trinidad, 529–531
True pleasures theory, 43, 59
Trust in others, 142, 144, 153, 412
Tunisia, 505, 508, 509, 512, 515, 516, 518, 526, 575
Turkey, 171, 352, 433, 436, 437, 441, 443, 445–450, 452, 499, 505, 506, 508, 512, 518, 559
Turkmenistan, 13, 437, 444–450, 499, 505, 508–510, 512, 515, 518
Two-Dimensional Conceptual Model, 83

U

UAE, 503, 505, 506, 510, 513, 518
Uganda, 503, 505, 508, 510, 512, 515, 518, 560, 562, 564, 566–571, 573, 574

Uncertainty and sensitivity analysis, 225–226, 228
Unemployment, 1, 134, 145, 147, 149, 153, 183, 192, 194, 195, 225, 267–270, 273, 282, 283, 304, 305, 376, 385, 435, 436, 447, 459, 460, 465, 475, 479, 483, 484, 486–489, 491, 509, 519–521, 531, 537, 547, 548, 558, 566, 568, 575
UNESCO. *See* United Nations Educational, Scientific, and Cultural Organization (UNESCO)
UN Global Compact, 508
United Arab Emirates, 503, 505, 508, 512, 518
United Nations, 4, 121, 125, 233, 383, 384, 436, 437, 440, 445–449, 453, 512, 520, 533, 535, 555, 556, 558, 559, 562, 564, 572, 575
United Nations Commission on Sustainable Development, 436, 558
United Nations Development Programme, 233, 331, 333, 476, 481, 558
United Nations' Economic Commission for Latin American and the Caribbean, 533
United Nations Educational, Scientific, and Cultural Organization (UNESCO), 4, 213
United Nations General Assembly to the United Nations Relief and Works Agency, 512
United Nations Millennium Development Campaign, 440, 564, 572
United Nations Security Council, 757
United States, 123–127, 129, 131, 133, 167, 169, 171, 181, 189, 195, 240, 267, 384, 386, 387, 389, 392, 394, 395, 401, 439, 441, 443, 445–449, 453, 462, 463, 503, 506, 530, 531, 537, 542, 543, 563
Universality, 318, 367, 539
University of Hong Kong, 475, 477, 479, 483, 486, 487, 490
Urbanization, 12, 72, 119, 122, 124, 540–541
Uruguay, 529–532, 534, 536, 540
USA General Social Survey (USA GSS), 12, 130, 275, 412
USA GSS. *See* USA General Social Survey (USA GSS)
US National Cancer Institute, 16
US Social Security Administration, 436, 559
1965 U.S. Time-Use Study, 167
1975 U.S. Time-Use Survey, 167
1985 U.S. Time-Use Survey, 167
US Trends in Time Use, 172
Utilitarianism, 7, 57
Utilitarians, 7, 40, 64, 66, 71, 75, 139, 316
Utility of life, 64
Uzbekistan, 437, 440, 444–450, 499, 505, 508–510, 512, 515, 518, 559, 560, 562, 567–569, 571, 572, 574

V

Validity of self-report measures of well-being, 142–143
Value-Based Index of National Quality-of-Life, 189
Values in Action (VIA) Project, 107–110
Veenhoven's Happy Life-Expectancy Scale (HLE), 194, 394
Venezuela, 529–532, 540
VIA Project. *See* Values in Action (VIA) Project
Victorian Quality of Life Panel, 460
Virtues, 6, 31, 39, 45, 49, 51, 53, 57, 100, 106–110, 319, 324, 501

Index

W

Warm indicators, 221

Wealth, 17, 27, 31, 33, 38, 39, 43, 47, 49, 50, 52, 56, 59, 72, 81–83, 85–87, 123, 137, 138, 149, 154, 233, 234, 240, 245, 269, 275, 284, 287, 376, 381, 385, 386, 396, 405, 410, 411, 414, 459, 465–468, 470, 501, 515, 533, 537, 541, 543, 566

Wealth and happiness, 405

Weighing area satisfaction by importance, 246

Weighted Index for Social Progress (WISP), 194, 382, 387, 388, 396, 434–454, 457, 557–560, 562–566, 572–575, 577

Weighted Index of Social Progress (WISP) for Developed, 434

Weighting criteria, 205, 221–223, 227, 228

Weighting satisfaction by importance, 247

Welfare Effort, 194, 387, 435, 436, 451–453, 557, 558

Welfare Effort Sub-index, 387

Wellbeing in Developing Countries Research Group (WeD) in Bangladesh, Ethiopia, Peru, and Thailand, 400

Well-Being Index, 355, 386, 547–550

Wellness, 2, 267

Western Sahara, 499, 556

What is "happiness"?, 63

WHO. *See* World health organization (WHO)

WHOQOL. *See* World Health Organization Quality of Life (WHOQOL)

WHOQOL-100. *See* World health organisation quality of life-100 (WHOQOL-100)

WHOQOL-BREF, 374, 400, 414–415

Wisdom and knowledge, 107, 108

Women Status, 193, 387, 435, 451, 453, 457, 458, 465

Work at Home, 170, 303, 307, 334

Worker's compensation, 305

Work-Life Balance, 374, 376–377

Works and Days, 28

World Bank, 213, 233, 436, 476, 481, 506, 558, 562

World Database of Happiness, 69, 70, 72, 73, 388, 401, 408

World Development Indicators, 476

World health organisation quality of life-100 (WHOQOL-100), 13, 373, 375, 400, 402, 404, 408, 414–415, 418, 420

World Health Organization (WHO), 2, 13, 16, 36, 100, 249, 374, 375, 408, 420, 423, 481, 502, 505, 510, 536, 541

World Health Organization Quality of Life (WHOQOL), 13, 408, 414–415

World Resources Institute (WRI), 436, 558

World Values Survey (WVS), 185–189, 278, 393, 409, 499, 513

WRI. *See* World resources institute (WRI)

WVS. *See* World Values Survey (WVS)

Y

Yemen, 503, 505, 508, 512, 515, 516, 518, 526, 556, 560, 562, 568–571, 573–575

Youth, 10, 108, 110, 155, 164, 191, 194, 196, 280, 319, 355–368, 405, 474, 479, 480, 483, 490, 503, 518, 519, 521, 522, 526, 566

Youth indicators, 15

Z

Zimbabwe, 70, 556, 560–562, 567–572, 574